BRADSHAW'S DESCRIPTIVE RAILWAY HAND-BOOK

Published by Collins
An imprint of HarperCollins Publishers
Westerhill Road
Bishopbriggs
Glasgow G64 2QT
www.harpercollins.co.uk

1st edition 2014
Reprinted 2015

Originally published in 1861 as Bradshaw's descriptive railway hand-book of Great Britain and Ireland

A catalogue record for this book is available from the British Library

ISBN 978-0-00-759189-3
ISBN 978-0-00-794958-8

10 9 8 7 6 5 4 3 2

Printed in China

This facsimile edition is sourced from the National Library of Scotland's original copy of Bradshaw's descriptive railway hand-book of Great Britain and Ireland.
London: W.j.Adams, 1861
NLS shelfmark: R.268.h
www.nls.uk

BRADSHAW'S DESCRIPTIVE RAILWAY HAND-BOOK

OF

GREAT BRITAIN AND IRELAND.

SECTION I.

BRADSHAW'S TOURS

THROUGH THE COUNTIES OF

KENT, SUSSEX, HANTS, DORSET, DEVON, THE CHANNEL ISLANDS, AND THE ISLE OF WIGHT.

CONTENTS TO SECTION I.

PAGE.

HAMPSTEAD JUNCTION 17

ISLE OF WIGHT—

First Route—Ryde to Newchurch 87

Second Route—Ryde to the Needles ... 90

Third Route—Culver Cliff, through the centre of the Island 92

LONDON—Historical Sketch of 5

Guide through London 6

Places of Amusement, &c. 11

Places of Worship 1

LONDON AND BLACKWALL—

Fenchurch Street to Blackwall 16

London Bridge to Hampton Court 13

London Bridge to Herne Bay....................... 14

LONDON, BRIGHTON, & SOUTH COAST—

Brighton to Worthing, Chichester and Portsmouth.................................. 58

Croydon to Epsom 52

Croydon to Wimbledon 52

Hayward's Heath to Lewes and Newhaven 54

Lewes to Hailsham, Eastbourne and Hastings 54

Lewes to Uckfield 54

London to Brighton .... 49 to 58

Three Bridges to Horsham & Petworth 53

Three Bridges to East Grinstead 53

LONDON, CHATHAM, AND DOVER—

London and Beckenham to Canterbury and Dover.. 27

LONDON AND SOUTH WESTERN—

Barnes to Hounslow and Feltham 65

Basingstoke to Salisbury and Exeter ... 76

Bishopstoke to Gosport and Portsmouth 80

Bishopstoke to Salisbury..................... 78

Brockenhurst to Lymington.................. 93

Godalming to Portsmouth 75

Guildford to Farnham and Alton 74

Kingston to Hampton Court 72

PAGE

LONDON AND SOUTH WESTERN—*continued*—

London to Richmond, Staines, and Windsor 64

London to Southampton and the Channel Islands........ ....64 to 87

Portsmouth to the Isle of Wight ...87 to 93

Southampton to the Channel Islands ... 83

Southampton to Dorchester and Weymouth 93

Staines to Wokingham and Reading ... 70

Weybridge to Chertsey 73

Wimbledon to Croydon 71

Wimbledon to Epsom and Leatherhead 71

Wimborne to Blandford 94

Woking to Godalming........................ 74

LONDON, TILBURY, AND SOUTHEND—

Bishopgate and Fenchurch Street to Tilbury and Southend 18

MID-KENT—Lewisham to Beckenham 22

NORTH LONDON—

Bow to Hampstead Road 16

SITTINGBOURNE AND SHEERNESS 27

SOUTH EASTERN—

Ashford to Canterbury 40

Ashford to Hastings.......................... 45

Canterbury to Deal, Ramsgate, and Margate 42

Caterham Junction to Caterham 52

Canterbury to Whitstable 41

Lewisham to Beckenham 22

London Bridge to Folkestone & Dover 28 to 49

London Bridge to Greenwich............... 20

London to Woolwich, Gravesend, and Rochester 21

Paddock Wood to Maidstone 37

Reigate to Reading 29

Strood to Maidstone 28

Tunbridge Junction to Hastings 34

ILLUSTRATIONS

MAPS:— PAGE.

Island of Alderney 84
Guernsey 84
Isle of Man 84
Isle of Wight 86
Jersey 84
London .... Back of Title
London, Environs of 1
Island of Sark 84

VIEWS:—

CATHEDRALS:—

Durham 6
Hereford 6
Ely 6
Lichfield 6
Lincoln 6
Ripon 6
Salisbury 6
St. Asaph 6
St. Paul's 6
Wells 6
Westminster 6
Worcester 6
York 6

CASTLES:—

Belvoir 68
Carnarvon 68
Chepstow 68
Conway 68
Dudley 68

VIEWS:— PAGE.

Castles, continued—

Farnham 68
Goodrich 68
Kenilworth 68
Naworth 68
Raglan 68
Stirling 68
Warwick 68
Windsor 68

Crystal Palace, Sydenham 50

ISLE OF WIGHT:—

Blackgang Chine 88
Bonchurch Church 88
Brading 88
Carisbrooke Castle 88
Ryde 88
St. Catherine's Church 88
St. Lawrence Church 88
Shanklin Chine 88
West Cowes 88

LONDON:—

Buckingham Palace 50
Houses of Parliament 50
London Monument 50
London, View of 50
Mansion House 50
Nelson's Monument 50
Royal Exchange 50
The Tower 50

INDEX.

Abbey Wood, 23
Abinger, 30
Abinger Hall, 30
Acton, 17
Addington Place, 37
Addiscombe, 52
Addlestone, 73
Adgeton, 88, 90
Adisham Down, 41
Afton Down, 92, 93
Albury, 30
Albany Barracks, 91
Albany Park, 30
Alderney, 86
Aldershott, 31
Aldingbourne, 61, 62
Aldwick, 61
Allen, 88
Allington, 28
Allhallows, 27
Almondington Green, 62
Alton, 75
Alum Bay, 92
Alvington, 91
Amesbury, 80
Anchor Farm, 32
Andover, 76
Anerley, 28
Anglesea, 81
Angmering, 60
Angmering Park, 60
Anstie Bury, 30
Apley, 88
Appledore, 45
Applesham, 62
Appuldercombe, 88, 89, 90
Arreton, 90, 91
Arreton Down, 92, 93,
Arreton Street, 90
Artington, 31
Arundel, 60, 61
Arundel Castle, 60
Ascot, 71
Ascot Heath, 71
Ascot Race Course, 71
Ash, 74
Ashburnham, 35
Ashburnham Park, 35
Ash Common, 31
Ashey Mark, 92
Ashford, 39
Ashington, 60
Ashstead, 30, 71
Ashurst, 33
Aston Down, 22, 93
Atherfield, 92
Atherington, 60
Axminster, 77

Badlesmere, 40
Badworth Park, 60
Bagshot Green, 31
Bairborough, 26
Balcombe, 53
Balham, 51, 71
Balls St. and Bodkin, 41
Barcombe, 54
Barking, 8
Barking Road, 18
Barming, 37
Barn Elms, 65
Barnsley, 88
Barnes, 13, 65
Barton, 91
Barton Point, 91
Basingstoke, 76
Baskets, 91
Bate Bridge, 66
Battersea, 51
Battersea Park, 13
Battle, 35
Battle Abbey, 35
Battle Powder Mills, 35
Bay Hill, 30
Beachy Head, 56
Beaufort, 35
Beaver Green, 40
Beechborough Park, 40
Beddington, 52, 71
Bellancle, 27
Belle Vue, 33
Belvedere, ...
Bench, 30
Benkesbourne, 41
Bennendon, 39
Benfleet, 18
Bentley, 75
Berwick, 54
Betchworth, 30
Beverley Park, 41
Bexhill, 55
Bickley, 27
Billinghurst, 60
Bingham Town, 81
Binnel Point, 88, 89
Binstead, 60, 88
Birchmore, 91
Birdham, 62
Birling, 37
Bishopstoke, 78
Bishop's Waltham, 78
Bisley, 32
Blackgang, 89
Black Gang Chine, 89, 90
Blackgrove, 32
Blackheath, 21
Blackland, 91
Blackwall, 15, 17, 40
Blackwater, 32
Blandford, 94
Blean Church, 41
Blendley Heath, 32
Bletchingley, 32
Blue Bell Down, 38
Bognor, 60, 61, 62
Bohemy House, 35
Bonchurch, 88 89,
Boniface Down, 88, 89
Bookham, 30
Borden, 27
Bosham, 62
Bostall, 41
Botanic Gardens, Royal, Kew, 12
Botley, 80
Bournemouth, 95
Bow, 16
Bowling Green, 37
Boxgrove, 62
Boxhill, 30
Bracknell, 71
Bradburn Park, 37
Bradfield, 32
Brading, 88, 90
Brading Down, 92
Bramber, 60
Brazil Mill, 66
Brede, 35
Brenchley, 37
Brenston, 88
Brentford, 66
Brettleford, 91
Brickham Common, 30
Brickland, 29
Bridge, 41
Bridge Wood, 26
Brighton, 56
Brixton Down, 92
Broad Clyst, 77
Broad Ditch, 26
Broad Moor, 30
Broad Oak Common, 41
Broad Street, 26, 41
Broadwater, 37, 60
Brockenhurst, 93
Bromley 18, 27
Bromley Green, 40
Brooke, 40
Brook House 33
Broom Park, 41
Brusted, 33
Brusted Place, 33
Buckhurst Park, 33
Buckland, 29
Burford Grove, 30
Burgess Hill, 56
Burham, 27, 28
Burlavington, 60
Burnham, 60
Bury, 60
Burying Place, 30
Butcher's Grove, 66
Byes, 32
Byrling, 28

Cable Hook, 40
Calbourne, 91, 92
Calley Farm, 29
Calworth, 60
Camden Road, 17
Cannon Heath, 37
Canterbury, 40, 41
Capel, 37
Capet, 30
Carisbrooke, 91, 92
Carisbrooke Castle, 91
Carisbrooke Church, 91
Carisbrooke Priory, Ruins of, 91
Carshalton, 52
Cary's Stone, 92
Castle Cornet, 83
Castle Hill, 61
Castelnau, 65
Caterham, 52
Caterham Junction, 52
Catford Bridge, 21
Catherine's Hill, 31
Catsfield, 35
Chale, 89
Chale Bay, 90
Challock, 40
Chalmead Farm, 19
Chandler's Ford, 78

Chardhurst, 30
Chard Road, 77
Charman Dean, 60
Charlton, 22, 49
Chart Hill, 39
Chart Sutton, 39
Chartwell, 33
Chatham 26
Cheeseman's Green, 40
Chelsea, 51
Chelsea Church, 13
Chelsea Horticultural Gardens, 11, 13
Chelsea Hospital, 11, 13
Chertsey, 73
Chestfield, 41
Chevening Park, 33
Chichester, 61
Chiddenden Wood, 39
Chiddingstone, 33
Chidham, 62
Chitney Marsh, 27
Chilham, 41
Chillerton, 91
Chilworth, 31
Chipstead, 52
Chiswick, 13
Chiswick Horticultural Gardens, 13
Chiverton, 88, 90
Chobham, 32
Chobham Hall, 32
Chobham Park, 32
Christchurch, 93
Christchurch Road, 93
Church Street, 41
Cisbury Hall, 60
Clandon Park, 30, 31
Clanmore, 92
Clapham, 60, 71
Clare House, 37
Claremont, 73
Clarendon, 80
Cliffe, 25, 26
Cobham, 26
Cobham Wood, 25
Cokeham, 60
Cold Harbour, 30
Cold Kitchen, 30
Coldwatham, 60
Cole Harbour, 26
Coleckmore Farm, 30
Coleward, 41
College Farm, 31
Collickmoor, 30
Colyton, 77
Comb Bank, 33
Comb Lodge, 60
Comfort's Place, 32
Compton, 31, 92
Coning's Brooke, 40
Cook's Bridge, 44
Cook's Castle, 88
Cooper's Hill, 70
Coophurst Farm, 30
Cophill Farm, 29
Copping Bridge, 88
Corfe Castle, 95
Cotterel, 30
Cotte's House, 30
Couler's Hole, 29
Court Week, 60
Cowden, 33
Cowes, 91
Cowling, 25, 26
Cowling Street, 27
Cranbrook, 38, 39
Cranford Bridge, 66
Crauley, 30
Crawley, 53
Crewkerne, 77
Cripple Path, The, 89
Crondall, 31
Cross Stock, 32
Cross Ways, 32
Crowhurst Park, 35
Crowpect, 26
Croydon, 51, 71
Crystal Palace, 28, 50
Cubham Wood, 33
Cuckfield, 55
Culver Cliff, 88, 93
Cupson, 26
Curlew, 92
Custon, 27
Cuxton, 26

Dale Park, 60
Dartford, 23
Darvel House, 35
Datchet, 68
Deal, 43
Dean, 79
Dean Court, 40
Dean's Farm, 29
Deepdene, 30
Delee Lower, 27
Delee Upper, 27
Dell Quay, 62
Denbigh House, 30
Dene Park, 41
Denhies, 30
Delton Place, 37
Deptford, 15, 19
Deptford Dockyard, 11
Devil's Dyke, 56, 58
Dingle Dale, 39
Dinton, 77
Dilton, 30
Ditchling Beacon, 56
Ditton, 73
Dog Kennel, 32
Dollingden Farm, 39
Donnington, 62
Dorking, 30
Doubleton, 33
Dorchester, 95
Dover, 47
Dover Castle, 84
Dover House, 60
Drayton, 61
Dudsall Court, 32
Dulwich Gallery, 11
Dunbridge, 79
Dunnose, 88

Eartham 61
East Ashling, 62
Eastbourne, 54
East Cowes, 91
East Cowes Castle, 91
East Dean, 61
Eastergate, 61
East Farleigh, 37
East Grinstead, 53
East Ham, 18
East Hamstead, 92
East Horsley, 30
East Malling Wood, 37
East Moulsey, 72
East Sheen, 65
East Sutton, 39
Eastwell Park, 39
Edenbridge, 33
Edgware Road, 18
Effingham, 30
Egham, 70
Egypt, 91
Elderton, 39
Elensden, 41
Eling, 93
Emsworth, 62
Enfield Well Place, 33
Epsom, 51, 71
Eridge Castle, 35
Erith, 23
Esher, 73
Etchingham, 35
Eton College, 69, 70
Ewell, 71
Ewhurst, 30
Ewood Mill, 29

Fairlight Downs, 36
Fairy Hill, 88
Falmer Hill, 58
Falvers, 31
Fareham, 81
Farley Green, 31
Farnborough, 76
Farnham, 31, 74
Farningham, 27
Faversham, 27, 41
Fay gate, 53
Fearlee, 88
Felbridge Park, 32
Feltham, 61, 66, 67
Feniton, 77
Finchley Road, 18
Fishbourne, 62
Fishburn Rock, 88
Fleetpond, 76
Flower House, 32
Folly, 30
Folkestone, 46
Fonthill Abbey, 80
Ford, 60
Forest Hill, 50
Fort Regent, 85
Foundling House, 33
Four Elms, 33
Foxearthwood,
Fox Hills, 31
Frant, 35
Freeshurst, 30
Freshwater, 92
Freshwater Gate, 92
Frintington, 62
Frittenden, 39
Frog Grove Green, 31

Gadbrook Common, 29
Gad's Hill, 25, 26
Gallybury Down, 92
Gang Hill, 31
Galton Park, 29
Gasson's House, 32
Gatcombe, 91
Gatcombe House, 90
Gillingham, 27, 77
Gillingham Fort, 26
Gipsey Hill, 51
Glynde, 54
Godalming, 31, 71, 75
Goddard's Green, 39
Godmersham, 40
Godshill, 88
Godstone, 32
Godstone Green, 32
Gomshall, 31
Gomshall and Sheire, 30
Goodwood, 61, 62
Goose Green, 30
Goring, 60
Gorsley Wood, 41
Gosden, 31
Gosden Green, 62
Gosport, 81
Goulds, 32
Grateley, 77
Gravesend, 5, 24
Gray's Pier, 23
Grays Thurrocks, 18
Greenhithe, 15, 23
Greenwich, 20
Greenwich Hospital, 11, 20
Great Brainden, 37
Great Dunbury, 39
Great Kennedy, 88
Great Kennerley, 90
Great Leonard Street, 37
Grève-de-Lecq, 86
Grove Ferry, 42
Grove Heath, 32
Guernsey 83
Guildford, 30, 61, 74
Guildford Castle, 31
Gurnet Farm, 91

Hackney, 16
Hailsham, 54
Hale End, 32
Halfpenny House, 31
Hall Farm 3

Halnaker, 61
Halnaker House, 61
Halnaker Park, 62
Halton, 66
Hammersmith, 65
Hampstead Heath, 18
Hampton, 66
Hampton Court, 72
Hampton Court Palace, 11, 13
Hampstead Road, 17
Ham Street, 45
Hangley Wood, 39
Hamon's Copse, 29
Hanworth, 66
Hanworth Farm, 66
Harbledown, 41
Hardham, 60
Hartfield, 33
Hartley, 39
Hartswood, 29
Haslar Hospital, 81
Haslemere, 75
Hassock's Gate, 56
Hastings, 35, 46
Hastings Castle, 36
Hastingleigh, 40
Hatch and Hatchland Place, 31
Hatch Farm, 29
Haughton, 60
Havant, 62, 75
Haven Street, 88
Hawkhurst, 39
Hayward's Heath, 53
Hazel Hall, 31
Headcorn, 39
Headley, 29
Head Wane, 61
Heath Farm, 41
Hedge Court, 32
Heene, 60
Hempstead Park, 39
Henfold Farm, 29
Henley Park, 31
Hermitage The, 32
Herne Bay, 15, 41, 42
Herne Common, 41
Hersfield Place, 39
Hersham, 73
Heston, 66
Heston House, 66
Hever Castle, 33
Heytesbury, 80
Hide Farm, 32
Higham, 25
Higham Upper, 26
Highdown Hill, 60
Highgate, 39
Highgate Cemetery, 11
High Halston, 27
Highley, 62
Hill Farm, 32
Hill House, 29
Hill Park, 33
Hinxhill, 40
Hobbs, 32
Hobby Hall, 33
Hockenbury Green, 39
Hoe Bridge, 32
Hole Farm, 33
Holloway, 30
Hollington Lodge, 35
Holmbury, 31
Holmbury Hill, 30
Holmwood Common 30
Holt's Green, 62
Homebush Green, 37
Homerton, 16
Honiton, 77
Hoo, 26
Hooe, 58
Hook, 32
Hook Hill, 32
Hooness Fort, 26
Horley, 53
Horne, 32
Horse Lodge, 88
Horsham, 53, 60
Horshill, 32
Horsmondean, 37
Horsted, 27
Hospital Bridge, 66
Houghton, 61
Hound House, 31
Hounslow, 66
Hounslow Barracks, 66
Hounslow Powder Mills, 66
Hoy's Back, 31
Hunston, 62
Hunter's Hole, 31
Hurbwood Common, 31
Hurst Castle, 92
Hurstmonceux Castle, 55
Hythe, 46

Ickham, 41
Isfield, 54
Isle of Dogs, 15
Isle of Portland, 96
Isle of Thanet, 42
Isleworth, 65
Islington, 16
Ivy House, 32, 33

Jenkin's Land, 32
Jersey, 85

Kemp Town, 57
Kenardington, 40
Kenley, 53
Kennington, 40
Kentish Town, 17
Kew, 13, 17, 65
Kew Gardens, 13
Kew Street, 27
Kilburn, 17
Kilsom, 39
Kingsford Street, 40
King's Forest, 91
Kingsgate, 44
Kingsham, 62
King's Key, 91
Kingsland, 16
Kingsnorth, 40
Kingston, 41
Kingston (Isle of Wight), 91
Kingston-on-Railway, 72
Kingston-on-Sea, 59
Kingston-on-Thames, 72
Kingswood, 31
Kingswood Garden, 29
Kinnersley House, 29
Kite Hill, 91
Kit's Coty House, 28
Knapp Hill, 32
Kneighton Park, 61
Knellar Hall, 66
Knighton, 88
Knowle Park, 33

Ladywell, 21
La Hogue Bie, 85
Lamberhurst, 37
Lampton Field, 66
Lancing, 59, 60
Langland, 88
Larkfield, 37
Lawbrook, 31
Leatherhead, 29, 30, 71
Ledgen, 26
Lee, 31
Lee Park, 41
Lee Place, 32
Leeds Castle, 39
Legham, 32
Leigh, 18, 29, 34
Leigh Park, 33
Leith Hill, 30
Leominster Station, 60
Lepring, 62
Lewes, 54
Lewisham, 21
Lidsey, 61
Limehouse, 15, 17
Limmer Pond, 61
Limpsfield, 32, 33
Lindfield, 55
Lingfield, 32
Lingwood, 92
Linhurst, 33
Liphook, 75
Liss, 75
Little Bognor, 61
Littlebourne, 41
Littlehampton, 60
Littleton, 31
Littleton Farm, 29
Live House, 32
Livesome Bridge, 30
Lockhurst Hatch, 31
London, 1
- Admiralty, 7
- All Soul's Church, 9
- Ancient Masters, Gallery of, 11

London—*continued.*
- Antiquarian Society, 7, 11
- Apsley House, 9
- Bank of England, 10
- Battersea Park, 13
- Bond Street, 9
- Billingsgate, 14
- Blind School, St. George's Fields, 11
- *Bridges*:—
  - Blackfriars, 12
  - Chelsea Suspension, 13
  - Hammersmith, 13
  - Hungerford Suspension, 6, 12
  - London, 10
  - Putney, 13
  - Southwark, 12
  - Vauxhall, 13
  - Waterloo, 6, 12
  - Westminster, 7, 12
- British Institution, 11
- British Museum, 11
- Buckingham Palace, 11
- Burford's Panorama, 11
- Burlington Arcade, 10, 11
- Carlton Gardens, 9
- Chancery Lane, 6
- Chapel Royal, 7
- Christ's Hospital, 11
- Club Houses, 9
- College of Surgeons Museum, 11
- Commercial Docks, 11, 15
- Cornhill, 10
- Courts of Law, 7
- Covent Garden Market, 10
- Crosby Hall, 11
- Custom House, 11, 14
- Deaf and Dumb Asylum, 11
- Dulwich Gallery, 11
- East India House, 10, 11
- Egyptian Hall, 10
- General Post Office, 10
- Geological Museum, 11
- Guildhall, 10, 11
- Guy's Hospital, 11
- Henry VII., Chapel of, 8
- Horse Guards, 7
- Houses of Parliament, 7
- Hyde Park, 9
- Hyde Park Corner, 9
- Institution of Civil Engineers, 11
- Kensington Gardens, 10
- Kew (Surrey) Botanical Gardens, 12
- Kew Palace Gardens, 12
- King's College, 6, 11
- Lambeth Palace, 7

London—*continued.*
Leicester Square, 10
Linnæan Society, 11
London and Tower Hamlets Cemetery, 11
London Docks, 11, 14
London Missionaries' Museum, 11
Lowther Bazaar, 11
Mansion House 10, 11
Marlborough House, Exhibition of Turner's Paintings, &c. 11
Mint, The, 11
Monument, The, 10, 11
Museum of the Asiatic Society, 11
National Gallery, 6, 11
New Palace Yard, 7
Northumberland House, 6
Oxford Street, 9
Pall Mall, 9
Pantechnicon, 11
Pantheon, 12
Piccadilly, 9
Picture Galleries, Private, 12
Poets' Corner, 8
Polytechnic Institution, 12
Portland Place, 9
Royal Academy, 12
Royal Exchange, 10, 12
Royal Institution Museum, 12
Royal Panopticon, 10
Regent Street, 9
St. Bartholomew's Hospital, 12
Saull's Museum, 12
St. Clements Danes, Church of, 6
St. George's Hospital, 12
St. James's Park, 9
St. Katharine's Docks, 14
St. Mary's Church, 6
St. Mary-le-Bow, Church of, 10
St. Martin's-in-the-Fields, Church of, 6
St. Paul's Cathedral, 6, 12
St. Stephen's Church, 10
School of Design, 11
Society of Arts, 12
Soane's Museum, 12
Soho Bazaar, 12
Somerset House, 6, 12
Statues, Monuments, &c.:—
Achilles, 9
Canning George, 7

London—*continued.*
Charles I., 7
Duke of Wellington, 10
Duke of York 9, 11
Monument, The, 10
Napier, General Sir Charles, 6
Nelson, 6
Peel, Sir Robert, 10
Strand, The, 6
Surrey Zoological Gardens, 12
Temple Gardens, 6
Thames Tunnel, 12, 14
Theatres, The, 12
Tower, The, 10, 12
Treasury, The, 7
Tussaud's Wax Exhibition, 12
Westminster Abbey, 8, 12
Westminster Hall, 7
Westminster Palace, 8
West India Docks, 15
Whitehall Gardens, 7
Zoological Gardens, 9, 12
London Necropolis, 32
Long Down, 90
Loseley House, 31
Love House, 39
Low Bell, 27
Lower Sydenham, 21
Lower Halling, 26, 27
Luccombe Chine, 89
Luddesdown, 26
Luton, 26
Lyding Chapel, 27
Lymington, 92, 93
Lyndhurst, 83
Lyons, 60

Madehurst, 60
Maidstone, 28, 37
Malden, 71
Mantham, 60
Mapledon, 33
Marcliff, 91
Marden, 38
Marden North, 62
Margate, 44
Marsh Green, 33
Mason Bridge East, 29
Matfield Green, 37
Maumbury Ring, 95
Mayford, 32
Mayor House, 31
Mayton, 41
Mead House, 29
Mereworth Castle, 37
Meroe, 31
Merridone, 30
Merrow's Race Course, 31
Merstham, 53
Merstham Hatch, 46
Merton, 71
Mickleham, 30
Mid Lavant, 62
Milbourne Port, 77
Milford, 75
Milk House Street, 39
Mill Cove, 88
Milton, 27
Minster, 42
Mirables, 18
Mitcham, 52, 71
Mitchel Grove, 60
Mitchet Farm, 31
Mitener, 62
Moat Farm, 32
Mont Orgueil Castle, 86
Montreal Park, 34
Moor Street, 26
Morden, 52, 71
Mortimer Farra, 23
Mortlake, 13, 66
Mote, 27
Mote, The 41
Mottesdon Down, 92, 93
Mount Morris, 46
Mount Norris, 40
Mulling Wood, 26
Mustham, 28

Nackington, 41
Nag's Hall, 32
Nashes, 32
Needles, The, 88
Needles Down, 93
Needles Light, 92
Neshanter Cave, 92
Netley Abbey, 31, 82
Nettlecomb, 88, 89
Nettleston Point, 88
Newark Abbey, 31
Newark Abbey Ruins, 32
Newchurch, 90
New Cross, 50
Newdigate, 29
Newenden, 35
Newhaven, 54
New House, 35
New Hythe, 26
Newland's Corner, 30
Newport, 89, 90, 91, 92
New Street, 40
Newtown Harbour, 92
New Wandsworth, 51
New Warren, 31
Night Timber, 61
Niton, 89
Niton House, 89
Nobright, 32
Node Hill, 91
Noder, 91
Norbury Park, 30
Nork House, 29
Normandy, 31
Norrel's Green, 3
Norris Castle, 91
North Bersted, 61
Northbrook Place, 31
North Field, 61
Northfleet, 23
North Foreland Light House, 44
North Hall, 60
North Heath, 60
Northlands, 62
North Park, 32
North Stoke, 60
North Street, 27
North Wood, 60
Northwood House (Isle of Wight), 91
Northwood (Isle of Wight), 91
Norton, 61, 92
Norwood, 51, 66, 71
Norwood Cemetery, 12
Norwood Place, 29
Norwood Upper, 51
Nudhurst and Petworth, 61
Nunhead Cemetery, 12

Oakhams, 33
Oakley, 76
Oatlands, 73
Ockley, 30
Offington, 60
Oftham, 60
Oftham Green, 37
Old Brook, 62
Old Castle, The 89
Old Park, 62
Old Roar, 36
Ore Place, 35
Osborne, 91
Osborne House, 90
Osterley Park, 66
Ottershaw, 32
Overton, 76
Oxenheath, 37
Oxted, 32

Paddock Wood Junction, 37
Park Crescent, 60
Park Cross, 91
Park Fall Place, 29
Park Farm, 30, 32
Park House 29, 31
Parkhurst Reformatory, 91
Parkpale, 30
Park Woods, 26
Peace Bridge, 65
Peartree, 32
Peaslake Bottom, 31
Pegwell Bay, 44
Penhurst, 33, 34, 35
Penhurst Park, 34
Pepper Arrow, 31
Peppering, 60

Perbright, 31
Perry Hill, 27
Perry's Farm, 32
Petersfield, 75
Petworth, 60
Pevensey, 55
Pexham, 30
Pigfish, 37
Pirford, 32
Pitbrook Bridge, 30
Pitland Land Slip, 89 90
Pitsea, 18
Pitt House, 31
Plaistow, 18
Pluckley, 39
Plumbton, 40
Polegate, 54
Polesden, 30
Ponds and Pursers, 31
Poole, 94
Poole Junction, 94
Porchester, 81
Porchester Castle, 63
Portland Bill, 97
Portland, Isle of 96
Porton, 77
Portsdown Hill, 63
Portsea, 62
Portsmouth, 62, 75, 88
Portsmouth Dockyard 63
Postergate, 32
Postern Plain, 39
Poyle Park, 31
Preston Viaduct, 58
Priory, The 88
Priory House, 32
Puckester Cove, 88, 89
Pulpit Rock, 88
Purfleet, 15, 18
Putney, 65
Puttenham, 31

Quarr Abbey, 88
Quarry House, 32
Queenborough, 27
Queen s Bower, 90

Racton, 62
Rainham, 18, 27
Rainham Park, 26
Ranscombe, 26
Ramsgate, 43
Reading, 32
Reculver, 45
Red Hill, 29, 53
Red Hill Farm, 29
Red Leaf, 34
Red Wood, 26 27
Reigate Junction, 29, 53
Reigate Mills, 29
Reigate Park, 29
Reigate Town, 29
Riabel Wood, 41
Rice Bridge, 29
Richborough, 45
Richmond, 13, 66
Richmond Park, 65
Richmond WesleyanCollege, 67
Ridge Bridge, 31
Ridland, 30
Ridland Farm, 31
Rind, 88
Ringwood, 94
Ripley Park, 32
River, 49
River Hill, 34
Robertsbridge, 35
Rochdale, 15, 25
Rochampton, 65
Romping Downs, 31
Romsey, 78, 83
Rookery, 30
Rookley, 90
Rook's Nest, 32
Rosherville, 24
Rosherville Gardens, 24
Rowfant, 53
Rowland's Castle, 75
Royal Naval School, 21
Royal Observatory, 21
Rozel, 86
Rucking, 41
Rumbold's Wyke, 62
Runnymede, 66, 70
Ryde, 87, 88, 90
Ryde House, 88
Ryde Park, 88
Ryde Pier, 87, 88
Rye, 45
Ryeham, 41

Salisbury, 77, 79
Salisbury Plain, 80
Salmonds, 34
Salt Hill, 62, 71
Salvington, 60
Sandford, 81
Sandgate, 47
Sandhurst College, 32
Sandhurst Green, 39
Sandown, 88
Sandown and Sandford, 90
Sandown Castle, 43
Sandowne Cottage, 88
Sandowne Lake, 88
Sand Rock, 89
Sand Rock Spring, 89
Sandwich, 43
Sappers' Museum (Woolwich), 12
Sark, 86
Scammels, 30
Scone Point, 92
Scratchell's Cave, 92
Seal, 31
Sea Salter, 41
Sea View, 89
Sedlescombe, 35
Selling, 27
Semley, 77
Sevenoaks, 33, 34
Sevington, 40
Shackleford, 32
Shadoenden Lodge, 40
Shadoxhurst, 40
Shakspeare's Cliff, 48
Shalcombe Down, 92
Shalford, 31
Shalford House, 31
Shanklin, 88, 89
Shanklin Beacon, 88
Shanklin Chine, 88
Sheepcombe, 60
Sheerness, 15, 27
Sheldwick, 40
Sherborne, 77
Shitle Bridge, 90
Shopwick, 62
Shoreham, New 59
Shoreham, Old 59
Shortlands, 27
Shottington, 40
Shripland 61
Shripudy, 61
Shrub Hill, 30
Sidelsham, 62
Singleton, 62
Singlewell, 25
Sion House, 66
Sitlingbourne, 27
Smeeth, 40
Sneeken Hall, 65
Snell Hatch, 40
Snodland, 26, 28
Snoll Hatch, 37
Snout's Farm, 32
Sompting, 60
Southampton, 81
South Bersted, 61
South Brook, 31
Southend, 19
South Park, 33
South Park Hill, 34
Southsea, 62
South Street, 41
Spicer's Hall, 90
Spottisbury, 94
Spring Grove, 66
Squerries The, 33
Stafford's Wood Common, 32
Staines, 67
Standing Street, 39
Stanford-le-Hope, 18
Stanford's End, 33
Stanstead House, 62
Staplehurst, 38
Staple Street, 41
Starborough Castle, 32
St. Aubin, 86
St. Aubin's Bay, 86
St. Brelade's Bay, 86 [90
St. Catherine's Down, 89,
St. Catherine's Pillar, 90
St. Catherine's Point, 89
St. Catherine's Tower, 89
St. Clare, 88
St. Dunstan's, 41
St. Helens, 85
St John's, 88
St. Lawrence, 88, 89
St. Leonards, 35, 55
St. Margaret's, 49
St. Mary's Cray, 27
St. Peter's, Port, 83
St. Stephen's, 41
Steephill, 88
Steephill Cove, 88
Stepney, 16
Steyning, 60
Stile, 32
Stockwood, 32
Stoke, 31
Stoke House, 62
Stoke Pogis, 70
Stokes Bay, 88
Stone, 90
Stonebury Hill, 31
Stone Cross Green, 40
Stonehenge, 80
Stone House, 41
Store Bridge, 30
Stoughton, 62
Stratford, 18
Strattle, 88, 90
Stratton House, 32
Streatham 51, 71
Strood, 25
Stubbs, 30
Studhill, 41
Stumblehole, 30
Stuppington Farm, 41
Sturminster, 94
Sturry, 42
Succombe, 88
Succombe Chine, 88
Summer Hill, 37
Sunbridge, 33
Sunbury, 63
Suttenden Farm, 27
Sutton, 66, 77
Sutton Park, 31, 32
Sutton Place, 31
Sutton Valence, 39
Swalecliffe, 41
Swallenden Farm, 39
Swithland, 39
Sydenham, 50
Sylam, 27

Tandridge, 32
Tandridge Park, 32
Tangmere, 60, 62
Tanhurst, near Leigh Hill, 30
Tankerton Castle 41
Tapnel, 92
Templecombe, 77
Tenderden, 12
Teynham, 27
Thakeham, 60
Thames Ditton, 72

Thannington, 41
Thompson's Farm, 41
Thorndean Wood 41
Thorness, 91
Thorney Island, 62
Three Bridges, 53
Ticehurst, 35
Ticehurst Road, 35
Tilberstow Hill, 32
Tilbury, 18
Tirwick, 62
Tisbury, 77
Tongham, 31, 74
Totton, 93
Tower Hill, 31
Troublefield, 88
Tudeley, 37
Tunbridge Junction, 34
Tunbridge Wells, 34
Tweedale, 26, 27
Twickenham, 13, 67
Twickenham Green, 66
Twickenham Station, 66
Twyford, 78
Tyler's Green, 32

Uckfield, 54
Udimore, 35
Undercliff, 89
Under River, 34
Upton Church, 71
Upper Galton, 29
Upper Laylands, 30
Upper Waltham, 61

Vauxhall, 64
Ventnor, 88, 89
Ventnor Cove, 89
Vineyard, 89
Virginia Water, 70

Wadhurst, 35
Walmer, 43
Walmer Castle, 43
Waltham, 60
Walton, 29, 62, 73
Walton Park, 29
Wandsworth, 64
Wanthurst, 39
Wareham, 95
Warehorne, 40
Warlingham, 52
Warminghurst, 60
Warning Camp, 60
Warren Hill, 31
Washington, 60
Watch Gate, 35
Wateringbury, 37
Waverley Abbey, 31
Way Street, 41
Week, 31
Wepham, 60
Wescott, 30
Wescott Parsonage, 30
Westbourne, 62
Westbrook Place, 31
West Brook Villas, 60
West Burton, 60
West Chiltington, 41
West Cowes, 88, 91
West Cowes House, 91
West Dean, 62
Wested, 37
Westenhanger, 46
Westergate, 61
Westerham, 33
Westerton, 62
West Farleigh, 37
West Ferring, 60
Westfield, 32, 35
West Grinstead Park, 60
West Hampnett, 62
West Hauk, 40
West India Docks, 17
West Itchenor, 62
West Lavant, 62
West Malling, 28, 37
West Mount, 88
West Peckham, 37
West Stoke, 62
West Tarring, 60
Westwell, 40
Westwood, 31
Weybridge, 73
Weyburn House, 31
Weyhill, 76
Weyhill Fair, 76
Weymouth, 96
Whatlington, 35
Whimple, 77
Whippingham, 88
Whitchurch, 76
White Mark, 88
Whitstable, 27, 41
Whitton, 66
Whitton Warren, 66
Whitwell, 89
Wild Bank Common, 60
Wickhall Camp, 77
Wilderness, 33
Willingdon, 54
Wilton, 77
Wimbledon, 65, 71
Wimbledon Park, 71
Wimborne, 94
Winchelsea, 46
Winchester, 77
Winchfield, 31, 76
Windsor, 68
Windsor Castle, 12, 69
Wingham, 41
Winham, 88, 90
Winsley Green, 39
Wishing Well, 89
Witley, 75
Woking, 74
Wokingham, 32, 58
Woldingham, 32
Wolton, 65
Wolverton, 89
Wonersh, 31
Wonham, 32
Woodchurch, 40
Woodfall, 37
Woodgate, 60
Woodhouse, 31
Woodlands, 62
Woolwich, 22
Woolwich Arsenal, 12, 22
Woolwich Dockyard, 22
Wooton, 31
Wootton and Bridge,
Worplesdon, 31
Worthing, 59
Wotten, 30
Wraysbury, 68
Wroncate, 88, 89
Wye, 40

Yacht Club House, 91
Yalding, 37
Yalding Down, 37
Yapton, 60
Yarborough Pillar, 91
Yarmouth, 92
Yousel, 40

BRADSHAW'S DESCRIPTIVE RAILWAY HAND-BOOK

OF

GREAT BRITAIN AND IRELAND.

SECTION I.

NOTE.—Shunts, or Marks thus ⌒ *, or thus* ⌒ *, introduced into the following pages are intended to show the point at which a Branch deviates from the Main Line. Its position to the right or left hand of the Column indicates the right or left hand of the railway on which the deviation takes place. The termination of the Branch is known by the Shunt being reversed.*

MIDDLESEX

Is a very important inland county, containing, with the British Capital, much of the wealth and political influence of the inhabitants of these realms.

Middlesex, from its gently waving surface, is particularly suited for agriculture. For the most part, the ground rises from the banks of the Thames towards the north; and within a few miles from London, a range of gently swelling eminences, of which Hampstead, Highgate, and Muswell Hill, are the chief, protects the metropolis from the northern blasts. These heights afford many pleasing and extensive prospects; and some equally extended views may be obtained from Harrow Hill, which from rising in a sort of insulated manner, forms a prominent object for many miles around. Middlesex is a well cultivated county; the vast quantities of manure from the metropolis have been of great service in improving the land; and on this account the produce is some weeks earlier within a few miles contiguous to London, than at a more considerable distance. No important metallic strata have been discovered in any part of the county; and appearances indicate that they lie at a depth much too great to be made subject to the operations of the miner.

LONDON.

HOTELS, BOARDING AND PRIVATE HOUSES.—For these, see the Advertising pages of *Bradshaw's Railway and Steam Navigation Guide*, under the heading of HOTELS, &c., London.

LIST OF PARISH CHURCHES,

ALPHABETICALLY ARRANGED.

WITHIN THE CITY.

Allhallows, Thames-street
Allhallows Staining, Mark-lane
Allhallows Barking, Tower-street
Allhallows, Bread-street
Allhallows, London Wall
Allhallows, Lombard-street
Bridewell Precinct
Christ Church, Newgate-street
St. Alban, Wood-street
St. Alphage, Sion College
St. Andrew, Holborn
St. Andrew Undershaft, St. Mary Axe
St. Andrew Wardrobe, Doctors' Commons
St. Ann, Aldersgate
St. Antholin's, Watling-street
St. Austin's, St. Paul's
St. Bartholomew, Cripplegate
St. Bartholomew the Great
St. Bartholomew the Less
St. Benedict, Gracechurch-street
St. Benedict, Paul's Wharf
St. Botolph, Aldersgate
St. Botolph, Aldgate
St. Botolph, Bishopsgate
St. Bride, Fleet-street
St. Catherine Coleman
St. Catherine Cree, Leadenhall-st.
St. Clement, Eastcheap
St. Dionis Backchurch, Fenchurch-street
St. Dunstan-in-the-East, St. Dunstan's-hill
St. Dunstan-in-the-West, Fleet-street
St. Edmund the King, Lombard-street
St. Ethelburga, Bishopsgate
St. George, Botolph-lane
St. George, Queen-square

St. Giles, Cripplegate
St. Helen, Bishopsgate
St. James, Garlick-hithe
St. Lawrence, Jewry
St. Magnus, London-bridge
St. Margaret, Lothbury
St. Margaret Patn., Rood-lane
St. Mary Woolnoth, Lombard-st.
St. Mary Aldermary, Bow-lane
St. Mary, Aldermanbury
St. Mary-at-Hill, Eastcheap
St. Mary, Abchurch
St. Mary, Old Fish-street
St. Mary-le-bow, Cheapside
St. Mary Somerset, Thames-street
St Martin, Ludgate
St. Martin Outwich, Threadneedle-street
St. Matthew, Friday-street
St. Michael Basishaw, Basinghall-street
St. Michael, Cornhill
St. Michael, Wood-stret
St. Michael, Queenhithe
St. Michael, College-hill
St. Mildred, Bread-street
St. Mildred, Poultry
St. Nicholas Coleabby, Old Fish-street
St. Olave, Hart-street
St. Olave, Jewry
St. Peter, Cornhill
St. Peter-le-Poer, Bread-street
St. Sepulchre, Snow-hill
St. Stephen, Wallbrook
St. Stephen, Coleman-street
St. Swithin, London Stone
St. Thomas, Chancery-lane
St. Vedast, Foster-lane

WESTMINSTER, &C.

Battersea
Christ Church
St. George
St. John Pruge
Bermondsey
St. James
Christ Church
St. Paul's
Bethnal Green
St. John
Bethnal Green, Jews' Chapel
St. Peter
St. Andrew
St. Phillip
St. Bartholomew
St. James the Great
St. James the Less
St. Matthias
St. Jude
Bethnal Green, St. Simon
St. Thomas
Bishopsgate, All Saints
Bloomsbury, St. George
Bedford Chapel
Christ Church
Brompton
Camberwell
St. George
Christ Church, Old Kent-road
St. Mary
Emmanuel Church
Camden Church
St. Paul
Peckham Church
East Dulwich Church
Licensed Victuallers' Asylum
Chelsea
(Upper)
Christ Church
St. Saviour
Parish Church
St. Jude
St. John
Christ Church, Surrey
City-road, St. Matthew
Clerkenwell, St. James
St. John
St. Mark
St. Philip
St. James, Pentonville Chapel
Duke's-place, St. James
Dulwich College Chapel
East Ham
Edgeware
Finchley
St. John, Whetstone
Trinity Church
Fulham
St. John
St. Mary
Gough Square, Trinity Church
Hackney
(West)
(South)
St. Thomas, Upper Clapton
St. Philip, Dalston
St. James, Clapton
St. Barnabas, Homerton
Ram's Chapel
St. Peter, West Hackney
Highgate
Holborn, Trinity Church
St. Peter, Saffron-hill
St. John's Chapel, Bedford-row
St. Etheldreda, Ely-place
Hornsey
St James, Muswell-hill
Ilford, Little
Islington, St. Mary
Chapel of Ease, Holloway
St. John, Upper Holloway
St. Paul, Ball's Pond
Trinity, Cloudesley-square
St. Peter
St. James, Holloway
All Saints
St. Stephen
Christ Church, Highbury
St. Matthew
St. Andrew
St. Mark
St. Jude
St. Michael
St. Philip
St. Luke
St. Barnabas
St. Silas
St. Matthias
Kensington, St. Mary
Christ Church Chapel
St. Paul's Chapel
St. Barnabas
St. John
St. James
Trinity, Broughton
St. Mary, West Brompton
Brompton Chapel
All Saints
St. Peter, Notting Hill
St. Philip
King's College Chapel, Strand
Lambeth Chapel
St. Matthew, Dunnark-hill
St. Mark
St, Michael, Stockwell
St. Luke
St. John, near Brixton
Trinity Chapel
South Lambert Chapel
Stockwell Chapel
St. James, Kennington
Holland Chapel
Verulam Chapel
All Saints
St. Mary, Prince's-road
St. John, Waterloo
St. Thomas
St. Andrew
Christ Church, N. Brixton
St. Barnabas, Kensington
St. Matthew, Brixton
St. John, N. Brixton
Trinity, Tulse Hill
Lambeth, St. Mary
Limehouse
St. James
St. John
St. Paul
Luke (St.) Old-street
St. Barnabas, King-square
St. Paul Old-street-road
St. Mark
Marylebone (St.)
St. Mary
All Souls
Trinity
Christ Church
St. John's Wood
Parochial Chapel
St. Peter's Chapel
St. Paul's Chapel
St. Paul, Lisson-grove
St. James's Chapel
Portman Chapel
Christ Chapel
Brunswick Chapel
Quebec Chapel

All Saints, (S. & W.)
St. Thomas
St. Mary
St. Andrew
All Saints
St. Mark
St. Stephen
St. Luke
Paddington
St. John
St. Mary
Bayswater Chapel
Holy Trinity
St. Stephens
All Saints
Christ Church
St. Saviour
Pancras (St.) Middlesex
Parish Chapel
Kentish Town
Camden Town
St. Paul
Regent's-square
Somers Town
Christ Church
All Saints
St. John
Fitzroy Chapel
Gray's Inn-lane Chapel
St. Mary Magdalene
St. Mark
St. Anne, Highgate
St. Bartholomew
Percy Chapel
Trinity
St. Luke
St. Thomas, Agar-terrace
St. Jude
St. Matthew
Woburn Chapel
St. James, Hampstead
Free Chapel, Burton-street
Foundling Hospital Chapel
St. Andrew
Queen-square, St. George
Rotherhithe, (St. Paul)
Christ Church
Trinity
All Saints
Shadwell, (St. Paul)
Shoreditch, St. Leonard
Christ Church
St. James
St. John
St. Mary
Southwark, St. George
St. John, Horsleydown
St. Olave
St. Saviour
St. Thomas
St. Peter
St. Stephen
St. Jude
St. Mary Magdalen
St. John's Chapel
St. George's Chapel
St. Michael's Chapel
St. Mark
Spitalfields, Christ Church
Spital-square, St. Mary
St. George-in-the-East
Christ Church
St. Mary
St. Giles
Trinity Church
St. Matthew
West-street Chapel
St. Thomas, Charter House
Tottenham, and St. Michael
Wood Green
Holy Trinity
St. Paul
Tower, St. Peter ad Vinculo
Wapping
Westminster, St. Anne
St. Clement Danes
St. George, Hanover-square
Grosvenor Chapel
Hanover Chapel
St. Mark, North Audley-street
St. Peter, Pimlico
St. Paul, Knightsbridge
St. Michael, Chester, 59
St. George, Albemarle-street
St. Mary, Park-street
Charlotte Chapel
Trinity Chapel
Berkeley Chapel
Belgrave Chapel
Curzon Chapel, May Fair
Eaton Chapel, Eaton
St. Mary
St. Gabriel, Pimlico
St. Matthew, Great Peter-street
Holy Trinity
St. Andrew
All Saints, Knightbridge
St. John, Broad-court
St. Mark
St. James
St. Philip, Regent-street
St. Luke, Berwick-street
Archbishop Tenison's Chape
York-street
St. James's Chapel
St. John
St. Mary, Tothill-fields
St. Margeret
Broadway
Christ Church
St. Stephen
St. Martin-in-the-Fields
St. Michael
Spring-gardens Chapel
St. Mary-le-Strand
St. Paul, Covent-garden
Savoy Precinct
Whitechapel, St. Mary
St. Mark
St. Jude

INDEPENDENT CHAPELS.

Aldersgate-street (Welsh)
Artillery Chapel, Spitalfields
Barbican
Barnet
Battle-bridge
Bayswater (Craven-hill)
Bedford Chapel Charrington-road, St. Pancras
Bermondsey, Jamaica-row
Bermondsey, Neckinger-road
Bethnal-green-road
Bethnal-green, Gibraltar Chapel
Bethnal-green, Zion Chapel
Bethnal-green, Park Chapel
Bethnal-green, Sidney-st. Chapel
Bethnal-green, Virginia Chapel, Bishopsgate-street
Blackheath, Congregational Ch.
Brentford, Albany
Brentford, Boston-road
Brixton-hill, Trinity
Brixton-hill, Union
Broad-street, New
Camberwell-green
Camberwell, New-road
Camberwell, Albany-road
Camberwell, Mansion-house
Camden Town, Ebenezer
Camden Town, Park Chapel
Carey-street, New-court
Chelsea, King's-road
City-road
Caledonian-road Chapel
Caledonian-road, Offord-road
Clapham
Clapham, Park-road
Clapham-road, Clayland's Chapel
Clapton, Upper
Clapton, Lower, Pembury
Commercial-road, Wycliffe Chapel
Commercial-road, Bloomsbury
Craven Chapel, Golden-square
Dalston
Deptford
Deptford (Welsh)
Drury-lane, Whitfield Chapel
Ealing
Edgware
Edgeware-road, Trinity Chapel
Enfield, Baker-street
Enfield, Chase-side

Enfield, Highway
Enfield, Countess of Huntingdon
Falcon-square
Fetter-lane
Fetter-lane (Welsh)
Finchley
Finsbury Chapel
Grafton-street
Greenwich, Maize-hill
Greenwich-road
Hackney, Hampden
Hackney, Old Gravel-pit
Hackney-road, Adelphi Chapel
Hackney, St. Thomas'-square
Hammersmith, Broadway
Hammersmith, Ebenezer Church
Hanwell
Haverstock-hill
Hendon
Highgate
Islington, Barnsbury
Islington, Upper-street
Islington, Lower-street
Islington, Union-street
Islington, Canonbury
Jewry-street
Kennington-lane, Esher-street
Kensington, Hornton-street
Kentish Town
Kingsland
Kingsland, Maberley Chapel
Lambeth, York-road
Mile End, Brunswick-street
Mile End, Bedford-square
Mile End, Congregational Chapel
Mile End, New Town
Millwall
New North-road, Pavement Chapl
New North-road, Salem Chapel
New-road, Tonbridge Chapel
Old Kent-road, Arthur-street
Old Kent-road, Marlbro' Chapel
Orange-street
Paddington Chapel
Peckham, Hanover Chapel
Peckham Rye Chapel
Pentonville, Claremont Chapel
Pimlico, Buckingham
Pimlico, Eccleston Chapel
Poultry
Ratcliffe, Queen-street
Regent's Park, Albany Chapel
Robert-street, Grosvenor-square
St. John's Wood
St. John's Wood, Portland Chapel
Shadwell, Ebenezer Chapel
Sloane-street, Union Chapel
Soho, Wardour Chapel
Southgate-road, De Beauvoir Twn
Southgate, 1, Chase-side
Southwark, Guildford-st. (Welsh)
Southwark (temporary), 39, Bridge House-place, Newington Causeway
Southwark, Cole-street
Spa Fields
Stockwell Green
Stoke Newington, Abney Chapel
Surrey Church, Blackfriars-road
Tabernacle, Moorfields
Tabernacle, New, Old-street
Tottenham Court-road
Tooting
Totteridge
Walworth, Lock's Fields
Walworth, Sutherland
Wapping, Gravel-lane
Weigh House, Fish-street-hill
Westminster, James-street
Whitechapel, Sion Chapel
Winchmore Hill

BAPTIST CHAPELS.

Aldersgate-street
Alie-street, Little, Whitechapel
Alie-street, Great, Zoar
Artillery-lane
Bayswater, Westbourne-grove
Blandford-street
Bloomsbury-street
Brick-lane, St. Luke's
Bunhill-row, Blue Anchor-alley
Brentford, New
Brentford, Old
Bethnal-green, Heart's-lane
Bethnal-green, Peel-grove
Bethnal-green, Squirries-street
Bethnal-green, Twig Folly
Battersea
Borough, High-street
Borough-road
Borough Surrey Tabernacle
Borough Trinity-street
Borough, Crosby-row
Blackfriars-road, Church-street
Bedford Chapel, Charrington-st., St. Pancras
Butterland-street, City-road
Bermondsey, Jamaica-row
Bermondsey, New Church-street
Bermondsey-road
Chelsea, Cooks-green, King's-road
Clapham, Cranmer-court
Clapham Common
Clapham, Courland-grove
Clapham, New Park-road
Clapham, Wirtemberg-place
Camberwell, Cottage-green
Camberwell, Denmark-place
Chadwell-street, Pentonville
Chelsea, College-street
Chelsea, Paradise-walk
Chelsea, King's-road
Commercial-street, Whitechapel
Commercial-road, East, Wellesley-street
Commercial-rd., Devonshire-place
City-road, Nelson-place
Dean-street, Soho, Meard's-court
Devonshire-square
Dalston, Queen's-road
Dorset-square, Edward-street
Dorset-square, Hill-street
Eldon-street, Finsbury
Edgware-road, New Church-street
Edgware-road, Shouldham-street
Euston-square, Gower-street
Gray's-inn-road, Henry-street
Gower-street
Homerton-row
Hackney, Mare-street
Hackney-road, West-street
Henrietta-street, Brunswick-sq.
Hendon
Highgate
Hoxton, Buttesland-street
Hoxton, High-street
Islington, Cross-street
Islington Green
John-street, Gray's-inn-road
Keppel-street
Kent-road, Alfred-place
Kennington, Charles-street
Kennington, Ebenezer
Kentish Town, Hawley-road
Kingston
Kingsgate-street, Holborn
Kensall Green
Lincoln's Inn Fields, Little Wild-street
Lee, High-road
Lambeth, Waterloo-road
Lambeth, Regent-street
Lambeth, Kennington-road
London-road, Earl-street
London-road, Garden-row
Lisson-grove, St. John's-place
Mile End, Darling-place
Macclesfield-place, St. Luke's
Maze Pond
Moorfields (Little), White-street
New Park-street
New Cross, Mason-street
New North-road, Wilton-square
Old Ford-lane
Old Pancras-road
Praed-street, Edgware-road
Pimlico, Prince's-row
Pimlico, Westbourne-street
Regent-street, Riding House-lane
Regent's-park
Rotherhithe, Lucas-street
Stockwell, Chapel-street
Store-street
Somers Town, Chapel-street

Shoreditch, Austin-street
Shoreditch, Mason's-court
Shoreditch, Cumberland-street
Shadwell, Devonport-street
Shadwell, Victoria-street
Stratford Grove
St. Luke's, Bunhill-row
St. Luke's, Brick-lane
St. Luke's, Ratcliffe-grove
Salter's Hall, Cannon-street
Shepherd's Bush (Baptist Independents)
Shouldham-street, Bryanston-sq.
Soho Chapel, Oxford-street
Spencer-place, Goswell-road
Tooley-street, Unicorn-yard
Tottenham Church-road
Vernon-square, Pentonville
Westminster, Princess-place
Westminster, Romney-street
Wilderness-row, Goswell-street
Walworth, Arthur-street
Walworth, East-street
Walworth, Lion-street
Winchmore Hill

WESLEYAN CHAPELS.

First London Circuit.—City-road; St. John's-square; Hackney-road; Jewin-street, City, Welsh Service; New North-road; Angel-Alley, Bishopsgate-street-without; Wilson-street; Radnor-street; Chequer-alley.

Second London Circuit.—Great Queen-street; Lincoln's Inn Fields; King's Cross, Liverpool-street; Camden-town, King-street; Kentish-town; Gloucester-place; Harp-alley, Farringdon-street; Palace-yard, Palace-row, Newroad; Finchley; Barnet; Whetstone.

Third London Circuit.—Spitalfields, Brick-lane; St. George's, Back-road; East India-road, Poplar; Brunswick, Limehouse; Globe-road; Stratford, Chapel-street; Old Gravel-lane; Mill-Wall.

Thames Mission.—Seaman's, Commercial-road.

Fourth London Circuit.—Long-lane, Southwark; Albion-street, Rotherhite; Silver-street, Rotherhithe; Stafford-street, Peckham; The Grove, Guildford-street; Union-street, Friar-street; Salisbury-terrace, Lock's-fields.

Fifth London Circuit.—China-terrace, Lambeth; Walworth; Waterloo-road; Southville, Clifton-street; Brixton-hill; Vauxhall, Lower Norwood; Lordship-lane, Dulwich; South Lambeth, Dorset-street; Upper Sydenham.

Sixth London Circuit.—Hinde-street, Manchester-square; Stanhope-street, Hampstead-road; Brunswick, Milton-street; Dorset-square; Bayswater, Wellington-terrace; Victoria-terrace, Portland Town; Kensal Town; Norland-road; Harlesden Green.

Seventh London Circuit.—Chelsea, Sloane-terrace; Westminster, Romney-terrace; Justice-walk; Ranelagh-road; Battersea.

London is the capital of Great Britain, and indeed, if its commercial and political influence be considered, of the civilised world. The British metropolis, if we include its suburban districts, contains the largest mass of human life, arts, science, wealth, power, and architectural splendour that exists, or, in almost all these particulars, that ever has existed in the known annals of mankind. In making this assertion, it should be borne in mind that the power of some ancient cities — even of Rome herself — was relatively, but not positively greater; and that the only well authenticated superiority is that which may be traced to the architecture of a few early cities. The site of our gigantic metropolis is the very best that could have been selected for commercial purposes, as it is enabled, by means of the Thames, to carry on a water communication with every part of the globe. The architectural growth of London, however, may with reason be an object of pride and gratification to its inhabitants. The position of other great cities may indeed exhibit more striking features, but the situation of our metropolis happily combines all which may contribute to its wealth and convenience. Seated on a gentle slope, descending to the margin of a noble river, its plain is bounded on the north and south by two beautiful ranges of hills

The growth of London to its present size is most remarkable. In 1560, Finsbury and Holborn, St. Giles' and St. Martin's, were scattered villages. Westminster was not only a distinct but a distant city. A long dreary road led from Ludgate to the village of Charing—and beyond this all was open field and garden.

We should far exceed our limits were we even briefly to trace the progress by which the City of London extended itself in all directions, and rapidly increased in importance and magnitude to its present position, which is solely attributable to the commercial enterprise of its inhabitants. The annual value of the exports and imports, from and into the port of London, is computed to amount to between sixty and seventy millions sterling; and articles of domestic or foreign merchandize, including cattle and provisions—sent for the consumption of the inhabitants—amount to the value of £50,000,000, making, with the imports and exports, the sum of £120,000,000 worth of property annually moving to and from London.

The portion of this immense metropolis which is distinguished by the name of "The City" stands on the north bank of the Thames, from the Tower to the Temple, occupying only that space formerly encompassed by the wall, which in circumference measures about three miles.

When the great fire of 1666 destroyed almost the whole city within the walls, London possessed an architect worthy of raising the fallen capital from her ashes. But the citizens rejected the beautiful plan of Sir Christopher Wren, who proposed to make St. Paul's the centre of the metropolis, and to carry spacious streets radiating in direct lines to the principal parts of the suburbs. A terrace was to adorn the banks of the river. The citizens opposed and frustrated this design, and hence the metropolis retains so many of the defects which subject London to the just criticisms of a stranger, on account of all its public buildings being huddled together in nooks and corners.

The first impressions of a visitor to London are generally of an unfavourable character, particularly if he enter it by one of the railway termini, situated in the more thickly populated parts. The dense atmosphere, the squalid appearance of the people, exclude all feelings of pride or admiration from our thoughts. But if he enter London by one of the Great Western roads, from Knightsbridge for instance, he is immediately struck with its surpassing grandeur. On the left there is a view of Kensington Gardens and its beautiful foliage; of Hyde Park, open, elevated, and lined on one side by private houses, some of which appear like palaces. On the right, Belgrave Square, with its magnificence, is invisible, it is true, but the entrance to Hyde Park by three arches, the Duke of Wellington's splendid mansion, and the opening range of buildings of which it is the first, but scarcely the grandest, on one side; on the other the bold and imposing arched gate, surmounted with the colossal statue of the Great Duke; the Green Park, sloping, open, and ornamented by noble buildings, including the towering structures of Westminster Abbey, Westminster Hall, the Houses of Parliament, and in the distance the Surrey Hills, is sufficient to give an idea of great architectural magnificence, and to excite in the spectator's imagination, some slight idea of the grandeur of London, spreading its great dimensions interminably before and around him.

The stranger who enters London by this road will orm a different opinion of it from the one who arrives through a road leading to the city. In either case, however, it must be seen in detail, to be adequately appreciated.

When we regard the extension of the communications between the metropolis and the most distant parts of the country, and the immense number of strangers who visit London in the course of a year, we believe a short description of what there is to be seen, and how to see it, will not be the least interesting feature of this work.

VISITORS' GUIDE THROUGH LONDON.

If the reader be a stranger in London, visiting the great metropolis simply on pleasure, he will most probably wish to walk through the principal streets or thoroughfares first, to make himself acquainted with their peculiar characteristics, as a general basis upon which he may subsequently extend his rambles in different directions, according to the particular objects that attract him most, or the time he intends to remain. Selecting St. Paul's as the starting point, the visitor can proceed eastward or westward according to his own predilections. The man of business will probably prefer a visit to the centre of our commercial emporium, the heart of London, and proceeding down Cheapside visit the Exchange and the other public buildings in the city, a description of which he will fi.d in *Bradshaw's Guide to London.*

The majority of visitors will no doubt prefer going westward first, and therefore we cannot do better than proceed with them in that direction, commencing our inspection of the sights of London by taking an exterior view of St. Paul's. For this purpose the visitor should walk entirely round it to observe all the architectural details, and enjoy the feelings of veneration and delight which the striking and impressive view of the cathedral is sure to produce. The extreme beauty and colossal proportions of this mighty temple are worthy of the highest admiration. The front view in particular at Ludgate Hill is very grand. The façade, consisting of a pediment, sustained by a double colonnade, and flanked by two towers, which though not particularly beautiful in themselves, harmonise well with the rest of the edifice, and give effect to the grandeur of the vast dome which, rising from the centre of the cross, is seen emerging from the two inferior towers, and swelling nobly and grandly high into mid-heaven.

In front of the cathedral formerly stood that famous Paul's Cross, where sermons were preached to the people in the open air, and where politics and religion were mixed up in a manner to which the present times is a stranger. The site is now occupied by a fine statue of Queen Anne. Passing on to the left we enter the cathedral by the door of the northern portico to view the interior, or ascend to the top of the dome and look down on the scene below, at what may be considered the most stupendous and magnificent sight it is possible to imagine. The building is in the from of a cross, having, in its greatest length, a principal nave, divided from two side aisles by rows of massive pillars. Eight immense piers, each of them forty feet at the base, support the great dome of the central area. Over the intersection of the nave and transept swells the noble dome, so much admired from without. It is painted in fresco, with subjects taken from the life of the patron saint, and artists have recently been engaged in restoring those noble paintings, a work of considerable difficulty, when the dizzy height at which their labours must be carried on is taken into consideration.

Around about the aisles and angles of the vast pile are the monuments erected to the memory of the illustrious dead. They are not very fine specimens of art, but we forbear to criticise in the presence of the tombs of Nelson and Wellington, placed in the centre of the mighty temple, with the dome overhead, and all that is grand and imposing around. We can only offer the tribute of our homage of mind and heart to these heroes, whose names loom out from the pages of our history like the giants of a past race, before whom modern heroes dwindle into insignificance.

Pausing for a moment in thought, and recalling to mind the simplicity of character, the pure patriotism, genius, and deeds of the heroes whose tombs we contemplate, we could not but associate with their names, that of the great architect, so worthy of being placed on the same tablet with theirs, and then turning to admire the noble simplicity of that inscription over the entrance to the choir, in honour of "Sir Christopher Wren, builder of this church and city, who lived more than ninety years, not for his

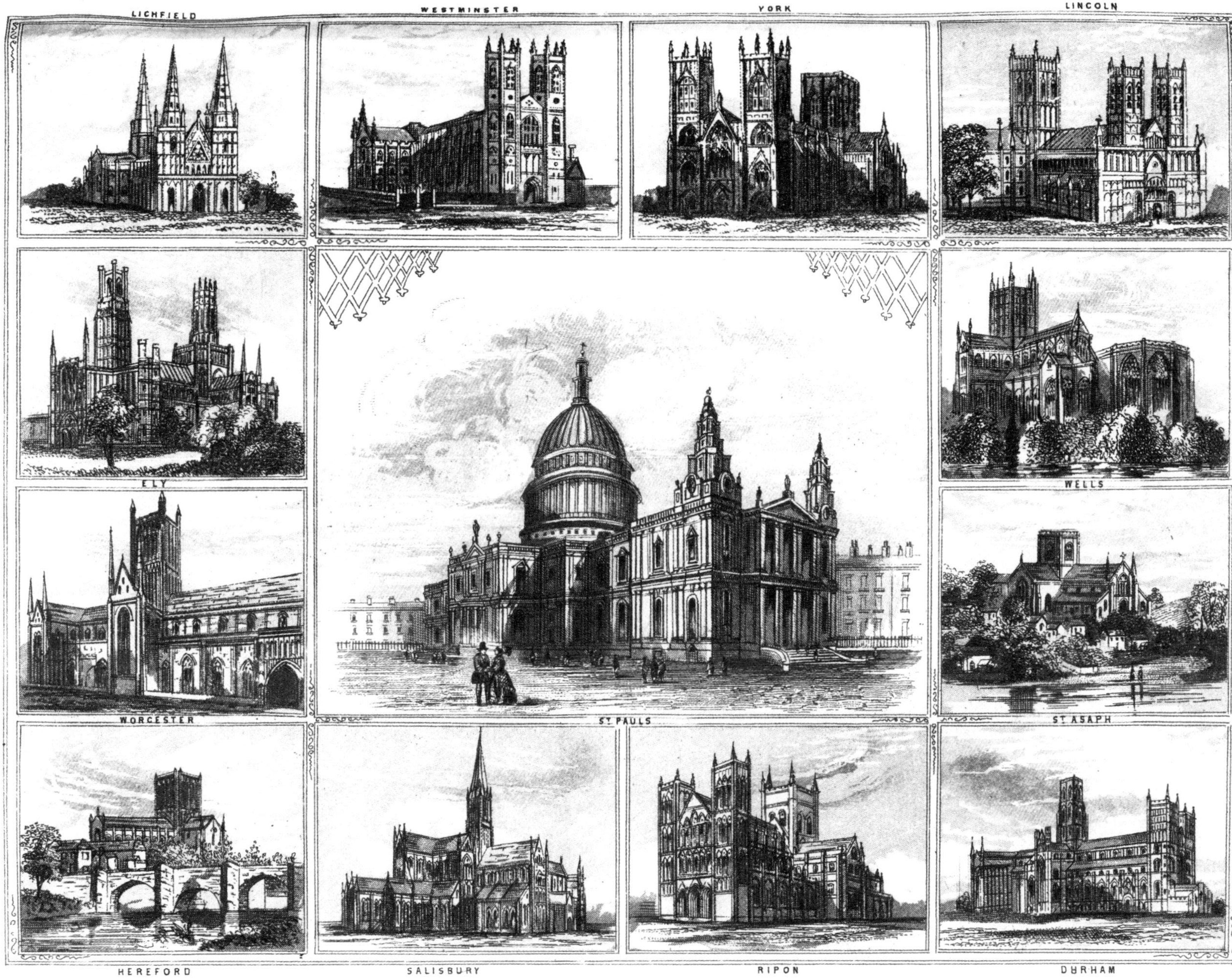

CATHEDRALS OF ENGLAND.

own but the public good. Reader if you seek his monument look around you," and visit Sir J. Soane's museum, in Lincoln's-Inn-Fields, where his watch and other relics may be seen. On ascending to the whispering gallery the visitor can view the concave of the dome and its storied frescoes, then ascend upwards towards the summit, and in so doing admire the construction of the dome, which is really extraordinary. It consists of three separate shells, sprung from a common base, but separating and becoming distinct at the top. The inner one, which forms the dome as seen from within, is of the hemispheric form. it is built of brick. A short distance from its base, is a second dome, likewise of brick, which springs from the first, and ascending with a curve of a much greater circle, goes far above the inner shell, terminating in the key-stone and lantern which support the ball. Still encompassing the second shell is a third, which constitutes the dome as seen from without, and whose curve is thought to be singularly beautiful. It is formed of wood and iron most ingeniously combined, and protected from the weather by a sheeting of lead. It is ribbed and subdivided, not unlike an orange after the first peel is removed.

A light gallery encircles the top of the dome, to reach which upwards of 500 stone steps must be ascended, and this is the station from which the most extensive and complete view of London is commanded, affording a glimpse of the most extensive mass of buildings in the world. On all sides, as far as the eye can reach, the solid mass extends itself, along the great avenues, into vast suburbs. The frequent occurrence of reserved squares and patches of green lawns, is the most pleasing feature in the scene. The most conspicuous object, however, is the river, winding its way like a huge artery, beautiful and picturesque bridges spanning the stream, while steamers, wherries, and sailing vessels pass up and down the river. Then the traffic in the streets, the movement along the great thoroughfares of equipages and vehicles, the myriads of human beings hurrying to and fro, is a sight which is quite bewildering and overpowering; so that after extending one's gaze over to the Surrey Hills, and admiring the outline of the Crystal Palace, one is glad to descend and leave the noble temple under the influence of feelings, strangely mingled, of admiration at its grandeur, veneration for the mind which had conceived the idea, the power which had executed this great work, and respect for that religion which could inspire the hearts of men to so stupendous an undertaking. Proceeding on, we descend Ludgate Hill, and in so doing admire the handsome shops and elegant articles exhibited for sale. At the bottom of the hill we pass the crossing, in Bridge Street, the obelisk of which is erected to the memory of Alderman Waithman, of reform celebrity; the street to the left leads to Blackfriars' Bridge, and Farringdon Street on the right hand, to Holborn and Oxford Street.

Ascending Fleet Street, the great arterial thoroughfare of London towards the west, we pass on the left the office of the inimitable *Punch*, and a few doors beyond, that of *Bradshaw's Guide*, nearly opposite to which is Johnson's Tavern, where the great and learned doctor met his contemporaries, Goldsmith and others.

A short distance further on, we reach Chancery Lane, the well known thoroughfare, of legal repute, to the right. On the left are numerous avenues leading to the Temple, formerly the residences of the "Knights Templars," and now leased by the common law students. There is in the tranquil retirement of these buildings, and garden facing the river, an appearance of delicious quietness, when contrasted with the noisy region of Fleet Street. Leaving this most interesting neighbourhood, we proceed through Temple Bar, the western boundary of the city, where the heads of criminals were formerly exhibited. Proceeding on the left side, we pass Essex Street, leading to the river, and the church of *St. Clement's Danes*, facing which is the office of the *Illustrated London News*, and a few doors beyond is a magnificent building, constituting the establishment of Messrs. Smith and Son, the newspaper and railway advertising agents. Further on we reach the church of *St. Mary's*, Strand, a beautiful edifice, possessing architectural features of great merit. We then observe a noble gateway on the left, which is the entrance archway to Somerset House, a magnificent pile of buildings, in the form of a quadrangle, with wings. Entering the court yard we observe Bacon's allegorical sculpture of Father Thames, and the statue of George III. The edifice is now devoted to the business of Government, and consists of the offices for the collection of the Inland Revenue, the Audit, the Duchy of Cornwall, the Admiralty, the General Registrars' &c. Under the open arches, at the principal entrance, are (on the left) the apartments of the Royal Society, and Society of Antiquaries, and on the right, those of the London University, and the Government School of Design. King's College adjoins. The Venetian front of Somerset House, towards the river, is of striking magnificence, and its balustraded terrace affords a fine view of the river.

We will now survey Waterloo Bridge, which crosses the Thames in this neighbourhood. It is without exception the noblest work of the kind in Europe. It is a beautiful object, the arches being all of the same height, and the road quite level, which produces a fine effect. From the centre of the bridge there is a finer view of that part of London which lies on the banks of the Thames than from any other. Looking down the river, and immediately joining the bridge on the left, rises the noble front of Somerset House—the finest object of the kind in London, not excepting the new Houses of Parliament, which appear too low. A little further on, looking like a green *oasis* in the midst of a dark wilderness of warehouses and wharfs lay the pleasant gardens of the Temple. Behind these rise numerous spires, towers, &c. Lower down is Blackfriars, Bridge, rising behind which in unrivalled grandeur and beauty is the dome and towers of St. Paul's Cathedral, and below this the Monument, the spires of other city churches, &c., receding till they are lost in the mist which always hangs over the city.

Looking up the river there is not much worthy of notice except the view of the Hungerford Bridge, a beautiful suspension bridge, and beyond, Westminster with the two Houses of Parliament, too far to be seen to advantage. We will therefore continue our ramble along the Strand to Charing Cross. The Strand is a fine street running parallel with the river. This part of the town was formerly the favourite abode of our ancient nobility. Their mansions looked towards the Strand, while the space between them and the river was formed into gardens, terraces and steps conducting to the level of the stream, which was at that time the great highway.

At Charing Cross, a great many streets unite and pour their crowd of pedestrians in all directions. Northumberland House, the only noble residence that remains in this *locale*, surmounted by the proud lion which guards the arms of that family, is a conspicuous object at the end of the Strand. The next is the much admired equestrian statue in bronze, of Charles I. In front to the right is Trafalgar Square, in the centre of which is the appropriate column and statue erected in honour of Nelson, and a recently erected statue of the late General Sir Chas. Napier. Behind this is that singularly dull, heavy-looking building, the *National Gallery*, by the side of which, standing out in beautiful outline, is the celebrated church of *St. Martin's-in-the-Fields*, built by Gibbs.

The National Gallery extends along the whole of the north side of the square. Although this gallery of paintings is inferior to the great continental galleries, still it is a highly valuable collection, and has been enriched by gifts and bequests of works of art of great value. Independent of the late Mr. Vernon's munificent presentation of 162 pictures of the modern school, there are 215 works of the ancient masters, with some of the finest specimens of our own. If, however, our National Gallery is not so rich in pictures as many of the museums of small cities abroad, it must not be concluded that the people of this country do not value and appreciate the fine arts. It is only by accidental visits to the residences of noblemen and gentlemen who possess the greatest treasures of that we obtain an idea of the almost boundless wealth of the country in this respect. We think it not hazarding too much to say that there are a greater number of fine pictures in England than in all the other countries of Europe together; and we doubt not that the National Gallery will, as it is in contemplation to remove it from its present site, and to make extensive purchases of valuable works of art, in process of time, through gifts and bequests, exhibit the most splendid collection of pictures that has ever been accumulated in one establishment

Instead of proceeding westward through Trafalgar Square, we will turn to the left, through the celebrated avenue of Government Offices, situated on both sides of *Whitehall*.

The first range of buildings of importance on the right is the *Admiralty;* and further on the *Horse Guards*, a fine stone building, surmounted by a small tower and clock. It is easily recognised by the mounted sentinels in the small recesses on the sides. The building opposite, built as a banquetting hall by Inigo Jones as a portion of the then proposed Royal Palace, is now the *Chapel Royal*, fronting which Charles 1st was executed.

Beyond, on the right is the *Treasury*, with its fine massive exterior, reaching from the Horse Guards to Downing Street. Facing this on the left is Whitehall Gardens, in one of which mansions resided the late Sir Robert Peel, up to the period of his untimely and lamented death.

Proceeding on through Parliament Street, we come to the street leading to *Westminster Bridge*, and beyond to the open space, known as New Palace Yard, opposite *Westminster Hall*, the *New Houses of Parliament*, and *Westminster Abbey*. The view here is exceedingly grand and imposing. The statue of Canning seems to personify the best attributes of a constitutional minister of a great country.

Westminster Hall.—The external appearance of this celebrated edifice is far less noble than is generally anticipated. Nothing, however, can be simpler or grander than the effect of the hall when seen from within. You find yourself in a vast edifice, near three hundred feet in length, having on every side only plain walls of stone, and no column or obstruction of any sort to intercept the view and break the character of simplicity and vastness. High over head rises a bold and hardy roof, supported by no column, but propped up with inconceivable lightness and grace on a series of wooden groinings, springing from stone mullions on the side walls. This roof is built entirely of chesnut wood, carved all over, put together with the greatest ingenuity, and richly ornamented with the heraldic emblems of Richard II., by whom it was built. It is almost entirely the same as it was when constructed towards the commencement of the fifteenth century, and yet without any impress of decay. In the various specimens of Gothic architecture which are to be seen throughout the Continent, there is nothing which bears any resemblance whatever to this, for its eccentricity, beauty, and lightness, which no one can observe without astonishment and admiration.

The New Houses of Parliament, or the **New Palace of Westminster,** as it is called, is the largest Gothic edifice in the world. It comprises the *Houses of Parliament*, the *Courts of Law*, and *Westminster Hall*, in one edifice. If we proceed to the centre of Westminster Bridge, we shall obtain a fine view of the river frontage, which is divided into five principal compartments, pannelled with tracery, and decorated with rows of statues and shields. The terrace is appropriated to the exclusive use of the Speaker and the members of both Houses. When old Westminster Bridge is replaced by the new iron bridge now in course of construction, the view of the Houses of Parliament will be much finer, as the old bridge is too lofty, and seems to crush the delicate Gothic style of the beautiful building. At present it is seen to the best advantage from the opposite bank of the Thames, along the walk in front of Lambeth Palace, the residence of the Archbishop of Canterbury. The small towers give a picturesque effect to the river front, but the three principal ones, the Victoria, Central, and Clock, do not add to the beauty of the building.

Retracing our steps to New Palace Yard, we enter the Palace through Victoria Tower, a truly royal entrance.

The rebuilding of the Houses of Parliament is the most important architectural work which has been undertaken in this country since the re-edification of St. Paul's Cathedral; and it may be added, that in arrangement, detail, warming, and ventilation combined, so perfect a structure was never before planned. The exterior of the House of Lords presents no enriched architectural features, but the interior is, without doubt, the finest specimen of Gothic civil architecture in Europe, its proportions, arrangement, and decorations being perfect, and worthy of the great nation at whose cost it has been erected.

Entering the house from the Peers' Lobby, the effect is magnificent in the extreme. The length and loftiness of the apartment, its finely proportioned windows, with the gilded and canopied niches between them, the Royal throne, glowing with gold and colours, the richly-carved panelling which lines the walls, with its gilded emblazoned cove, and the balcony of brass, of light and elegant design, rising from the canopy; the roof, most elaborately painted; its massy beams and sculptured ornaments, and pendants richly gilded; all unite in forming a scene of royal magnificence, as brilliant as it is unequalled.

The House of Commons is in a direct line with the House of Lords, at the north end of the structure. The aspect of the house altogether, is that of plain and business-like serenity, adapted to the deliberation of legislators. The Speaker's chair is placed in such a position that, supposing all the doors open between them, the Chancellor on the woolsack and the Speaker in the chair would exactly face each other. Yet although this palace of the parliament cannot for centuries rival in its associations the humble structure of St. Stephen's Chapel, let us hope that the future representatives of Great Britain will not prove inferior to their predecessors in genius and patriotism.

Westminster Abbey.—This noble pile, in magnificence of extent, grandeur of proportions, and elaborate beauty of construction, can most favourably be compared with the noblest specimens of Gothic architecture in Europe. It possesses a symmetrical and homogeneous character throughout. There appears one defect in the external appearance which is sufficiently obvious, and that is, the too great length compared with the height, though this, within, adds vastly to the character of grandeur and continuity, as you glance along the naves from extremity to extremity. If, however, there are any impressions on the mind at variance with unqualified admiration in contemplating this grand structure without, those impressions vanish as the visitor enters the cloister, and, passing the noble portal, stands in the midst of columns, arches, and swelling naves, surrounded by the mighty dead of England, treasured remains, sculptured effigies, and recorded epitaphs of those who have emblazoned our history with the brightness of their deeds, immortalised our language, and shed undying glory on our race. No one can wander through these precincts, the aisles of the Abbey, examine the monuments and read the inscriptions, without a feeling of awe and admiration, and offering the homage of his mind at the throne of departed genius.

In the chapel of Henry VII. the mind is awed by the gorgeous character of the architecture, and the splendour of the monuments which entomb the buried majesty of England's Kings; while above are seen the swords, helmets, and waving banners of the Knights of some of the noblest orders of Christendom, to complete the impression of the scene, and fill the imagination with images of magnificence and pomp.

It is in the Poets' Corner, however, that the pilgrim's footsteps most fondly linger. It is there that his eyes trace and retrace names, and study lineaments, connected with his sublimest and tenderest associations. No place in the world is so capable of recalling to "memory's light" so many associations connected with whatever is most god-like in human genius. Supposing each country to have—but alas it has not!—a like hallowed receptacle for the remains of its most honoured children, which is there of modern times that can boast such a name as Shakspeare? Where shall we look for the counterpart of the divine Milton? Where else for the genius which characterised Newton?

The monuments of the Poets' Corner are blackened by time, but the memory of those to whom they are sacred is still, and will ever be, green in the hearts of their countrymen and their descendants, and in every region of the world inhabited by those who speak the language in which they wrote.

> "That venerable shrine where repose the ashes of
> our patriots, poets, and sages."

Upon leaving the Abbey, we will proceed through St. James's Park, which we can glance at in passing, to the Duke of York's Monument, at the bottom of Regent Street, and conclude our walk by a view of Carlton Gardens, Pall Mall, &c. The view from the statue over the park is exceedingly fine, embracing the towers of the Abbey and the new Houses of Parliament. On the other hand, the wide and noble avenue of Regent Street, the princely edifices of the nobility, many of them built in a grand and chaste style of architecture, and the magnificent Club Houses, render this one of the finest quarters in London.

Starting from this point the ensuing day, the visitor should wend his way up Regent Street, the first point of interest in which is where it opens into a circus, at the intersection of Piccadilly, leading to Hyde Park, Chelsea, Hammersmith, &c.—one of the greatest thoroughfares in London, or perhaps in the world. Continuing his walk up this fine street, the visitor cannot fail to admire it. The rows of symmetrical and ornamented edifices produce a fine effect—on each side are a collection of brilliant shops, filled with most costly articles, attesting at once the wealth, luxury, refinement of the land, and the *acmé* of excellence to which the manufactures of this country have attained.

Proceeding on, we reach the intersection of Oxford Street, where Regent street again opens out and forms a circus. This is another thoroughfare between the east and the west, the left leading to Oxford Street, Hyde Park, &c.—the right to Holborn and the City. Continuing our walk along Oxford Street we find the shops assume a still more elegant and fashionable appearance—their extent, neatness, and elegance of arrangement are admirable. Oxford Street consists of a straight line of shops, not less than two miles in length, with a broad footpath on each side, and a carriage-road in the centre. This street is perpetually thronged with splendid equipages, on account of its being the grand avenue in which run most of the side streets leading to the squares, &c., where the nobility and people of fashion reside. This is called the neighbourhood of the squares, and is deservedly the boast of London. In the whole of that part of the town, north of Oxford Street, there are scarcely any shops, most of the houses being occupied by persons of distinction. This is considered by far the finest part of London.

From Regent Circus, Oxford Street, the visitor may proceed Northwards, passing *All Soul's Church*, with its quaint steeple, and up that street of palaces, Portland Place, to Regent's Park, and the Zoological Gardens.

The Zoological Gardens in Regent's Park, in the season, is perhaps the most fashionable resort of the metropolis. This is an institution which had its origin in that spirit of association which has achieved so much for England. The payment of a trifling subscription, by many people, has led to the creation of a beautiful garden, of a tasteful and pleasing arrangement. Specimens of rare, curious, and beautiful animals have been collected from every corner of the globe; and the study of the structure, character, and habits of what is most interesting in the works of the Creator is thus rendered easy and entertaining to the young. The arrangement of the species is made with great care and order, and many of the animals are lodged in rustic cottages, in the style of the country from which they come. Here, too, are strange exotic plants—so that a walk through this garden is in a measure like a rapid journey over the world.

Returning from Regent's Park to the end of Oxford Street, the visitor can then enter Hyde Park, and walk through it to Kensington Gardens, which is also a beautiful place. Thence retracing his steps towards Hyde Park Corner, his attention will be attracted to the statue of Achilles in the Park, and the colossal equestrian statue upon the top of the Triumphal Arch on Constitution Hill; both erected in honour of the late Duke of Wellington. Apsley House, the residence of the late and present Duke, at the corner of Hyde Park, is also an object of general interest.

Proceeding up Piccadilly the visitor should not omit to walk up Bond Street, to take a view of this the most fashionable promenade of London, where the young men of family and *ton* take their walks, and exhibit the latest fashions of the day. The shops here are not so ostentatious as those in the more general thoroughfares, but they are extremely elegant, and their articles most *recherché*, and here the ladies of aristocracy and wealth may be seen alighting from their carriages and splendid equipages to make some purchase, or examine the latest *modes* from Paris.

Retracing his steps to Piccadilly, the visitor should not omit to visit the Burlington Arcade, the prettiest gallery in London. It is a fac-simile of a portion of the Palais Royal, but the tradesmen who occupy these shops are of a less wealthy class, and the place is considered as the fashionable gentleman's lounge.

From Piccadilly the visitor should return towards the city through Leicester Square and Covent Garden Market. In the former, on the south side, is the Royal Panopticon, and in the centre Mr. Wyld's Great Globe. Covent Garden Market is celebrated for being the mart for the most delicate and choicest fruit grown or imported into England.

From Covent Garden the visitor should take one of the streets leading to the Strand, whence he can easily regain his hotel; and the next day, starting again from St. Paul's, go eastward, and extend his visit to the City, and entering Cheapside from St. Paul's Churchyard, the first objects which attract our attention are the statue of Sir Robert Peel, and the *General Post Office*, in St. Martin's-le-Grand. On the right, at no great distance, stands the celebrated Church of *St. Mary-le-Bow*, which is esteemed to be situated in the heart of the City of London, and all persons born within the sound of its bells are vulgarly designated "Cocknies." The crowd of persons in Cheapside from morning till night is always very great, and prevents any one loitering to indulge in observation or remark. At the end of King Street, which runs northward from Cheapside, is *Guildhall*, the Civic Palace, where the principal business of the corporation is conducted and the magnificent civic banquets given. The hall contains some fine monuments, the two colossal figures of Gog and Magog; and a noble statue to the Great Duke, just completed. Returning to Cheapside, the next building worthy of notice is the *Mansion House*, the official residence of the Lord Mayor. The *Egyptian Hall* is a lofty room of considerable splendour. Near it is seen the Church of *St. Stephen's*, Walbrook, said to be the master piece of Sir Christopher Wren. The *Bank of England* is nearly opposite, the statue of the Duke of Wellington in front, and behind this the *New Royal Exchange*. The building of the Bank of England offers no feature worthy of notice, but the interior can only be visited by an order of one of the Governors. It is well worth a visit. The statue of the Great Duke is by Chantrey, and is indeed a noble ornament to the city. The Royal Exchange is a splendid piece of architecture, and should be examined in detail, to see how admirably it has been adapted to the purpose for which it is designed.

Cornhill on the right is as glittering as ever with jewellers' shops, beyond which is Leadenhall Street, where the fine massive, but heavy, building of the *East India House* appears on the right. Beyond this there is nothing of interest to the visitor, who is recommended to retrace his steps to the side of the Wellington statue, and proceeding thence down King William Street, glance at the statue of the Sailor King, to the left of which is the Monument and then walk on to London Bridge, the traffic over which, and the view of the river below, will afford him subjects of interesting contemplation respecting this metropolis of a country which, though inconsiderable in extent, with a climate healthful indeed, yet unsuited to rich productions, and on the whole unpropitious, its coasts destitute of natural harbours, and exposed to the inconvenience of frightful storms, has yet risen by commerce to an eminence of wealth, power, and consideration, of which the world has hitherto known no example.

Returning towards King William's statue, the visitor should cross over and proceed down Little East Cheap, and Great Tower Street, in which are the offices of the wealthy city of London Wine Brokers, which will lead him by a short route to that most interesting spot called Tower Hill, and in sight of the Tower of London, which he will undoubtedly visit.

The Tower of London, erected by William the Conqueror, connects itself with every succeeding event in the history of our race. In more barbarous times than those in which we live, it has been the prison-house, and the place of execution of illustrious victims of tyranny. Perhaps there is no single spot in Europe, or in the world, so calculated to awaken impressive and profitable recollections, and so pregnant with interest to Englishmen, as this place. Within these venerable vaults, human nature has been exhibited in all its extremes. The pomp of royalty, wretchedness of solitude, horrors of murder and martyrdom, all stand associated with the eventful history of the building. The Yeomen of the Guard, better known as beefeaters, in the picturesque costume of the days of Elizabeth, conduct the visitors over it. Within the court-yard, a number of objects are pointed out that are rich in historical interest, of the most romantic and mournful character. There stands the Bloody Tower in which the unfortunate young prince, Edward V. and his brother, are said to have been smothered by order of Richard III. The Beauchamp Tower is also shown, as the prison in which the ill-fated Anne Boleyn, and the highly gifted and unfortunate Lady Jane Grey were confined, and the small room in which the gifted Sir Walter Raleigh wrote his "History of the World," and which he occupied fifteen years. The Armoury is one of the most extensive in the world. There is one immense room containing, it is said, two hundred thousand muskets, tastefully and beautifully arranged. On all sides are trophies of victories by land and sea, and in a noble gallery called the Horse Armoury, are arranged in complete panoply, mounted, with lance in hand, the effigies of many of England's greatest monarch warriors, clad in the very armour which they had worn; and among the weapons possessing historical interest, which are here preserved, is the identical axe which severed the head of Anne Boleyn. The regalia of England is preserved in a very massive strong tower, without windows, and quite dark from without, being lit by a powerful lamp, which exhibits the brilliancy and value of the precious stones. Everything is admirably arranged for exhibition; the imperial crown, and other most precious articles are turned round, so as to be seen, on all sides, by means of ingenious machinery, touched by the ancient dame who exhibits them.

On quitting the Tower, the visitor can proceed to inspect some of the magnificent docks and warehouses further down the river—which are surpassing importance to the Port of London, and the great commercial interests of the Kingdom, all of which cannot fail to prove of interest to the observant and inquiring traveller.

Terms and Times of Admission to the following Buildings, Institutions, &c., in London and its suburbs.

Ancient Masters, 49, Pall Mall, 10 to 5, 1s.
Antiquarian Society, Somerset House. Admission by an order from any of the members.
Blind School, St. George's Fields, free.
British Institution, 52, Pall Mall, 1s. February, March, and April, 10 to 5, Exhibition of British Artists; June, July, and August, 10 to 6, Ancient Masters.
British Museum, Great Russell Street, Bloomsbury, Monday, Wednesday, and Friday, May 8th to August 31st, 10 to 7; September 1st to May 7th, 10 to 4, free. Closed on the first 7 days of January, May, and September, Ash Wednesday, Good Friday, and Christmas Day. The magnificent new reading room cannot be seen without a letter of recommendation from a person of known respectability.
Buckingham Palace, Royal Stables, Picture Gallery, &c., order granted by application by letter to the Lord Chamberlain, when Her Majesty is out of town.
Burford's Panorama, Leicester Square, 10 to dusk, 1s. each view.
Burlington Arcade, Piccadilly, free.
Chelsea Hospital, Chelsea Royal Military Asylum; admission upon application. Botanic Gardens, by order, to be obtained at Apothecaries' Hall.
Chiswick Horticultural Gardens. Admission by card, obtained only from subscribers, from 9 to 6.
Christ's Hospital, Newgate Street; a fine collection of Paintings, and its Dining Hall: tickets by application to any of the Governors.
College of Surgeon's Museum, Lincoln's Inn Fields, Monday, Tuesday, Wednesday, and Thursday, 12 to 4, surgeon's order.
Commercial Docks, Shipping, free.
Crosby Hall, Bishopsgate Street, free.
Crystal Palace, Sydenham.
Custom House, Lower Thames Street, 9 to 3, free celebrated for its long room, of nearly 200 feet.
Deaf and Dumb Asylum, Old Kent Road, free.
Deptford Dock Yard, Deptford, 10 to 3, free.
Duke of York's Column, St. James's Park, 12 to 3, 6d.
Dulwich Gallery, Dulwich College, every day except Friday; April to November, from 10 to 5; November to April, from 11 to 3.

East India Museum, East India House, Leadenhall Street, Saturday from 11 to 3, or at any time by special order, free.

Geological Museum, Jermyn Street, free, 10 to 4.

Greenwich Hospital, 10 to dusk; Painted Hall, 3d.; Chapel, 2d. Mondays and Fridays, free, 10 to 4.

Guildhall, King Street, Cheapside, 10 to 3; good collection of Paintings, free.

Guy's Hospital, St. Thomas's Street, Borough, Medical Museum, on introduction by any of the students.

Hampton Court Palace, every day except Friday, free. Cardinal Wolsey's Hall, the noble Shrubberies, Parks, and Gardens, and the Gallery of Paintings. A fee of 1d. to the Vinery.

Highgate Cemetery, Highgate, free.

Institution of Civil Engineers, 25, Great George Street, Westminster, member's order.

Kensal Green Cemetery, Kilburn, free.

Kensington Museum (with which is now blended the Government School of Design), is open daily from 10 till 4, and from 7 till 10 on Monday and Thursday evenings; free on Mondays, Tuesdays, and Saturdays; on the other days, 6d. each person. A choice collection of pictures, and a large display of objects in relation to education, architecture, trade, &c. Students are admitted on payment of a small fee.

Kew, Surrey, Botanical Gardens, open from 1 to 6, every day, free. Palace Gardens, Thursday and Saturday, free.

King's College, Somerset House, Anatomy and Curiosities, introduction by member or student.

Linnæan Society, 22, Soho Square, Library open on Monday, Tuesday, and Thursday; and the Museum on Wednesday and Friday, from 12 to 4. Order from member.

London Docks, East Smithfield, free. The Wine Vaults only by orders, which can be obtained from the wine brokers or merchants in the city.

London Missionaries' Museum, Bloomfield Street, Finsbury; Tuesday, Thursday and Saturday, 10 to dusk, free.

London and Tower Hamlets Cemetery, free.

Lowther Bazaar, 35, Strand; Lounge, free.

Mansion House, connecting Cornhill with Poultry, 11 to 3, trifle to attendant, when the Lord Mayor is out of town.

Marlborough House, Exhibition of Turner's collection of Paintings, Vernon Gallery, &c. Same days and hours as National Gallery. Free.

Mint, Tower Hill, 11 to 3, free; a letter of recommendation from a member of parliament or one of the city aldermen to the Deputy Masters necessary.

Monument, Fish Street Hill, 9 to dusk, 6d.

Museum of Asiatic Society, Grafton Street, Tuesday, Wednesday, and Thursday; order from any of its members.

National Gallery, Trafalgar Square; Mondays, Tuesdays, Wednesdays, Thursdays, May 1st to September 1st, 10 to 6; November 1st to April 30th, 10 to 5; closed six weeks from middle of September, free.

Norwood Cemetery, Norwood, free.

Nunhead Cemetery, Peckham, free.

Palace Gardens, Thursday and Saturday, free.

Pantechnicon, Pimlico, a Bazaar, free.

Pantheon, Oxford Street, Conservatory, Aviary, Bazaar, free. A very amusing Lounge.

Polytechnic Institution, 309, Regent Street, 12 to 5, and 7 to 10, closed on Saturday evenings, 1s.

Private Picture Galleries, only accessible by special introduction. Those of the Marquis of Westminster, Upper Grosvenor Street; Earl of Ellesmere, Belgrave Square; Duke of Sutherland, St. James's; Lord Ashburton, Piccadilly; Sir Robert Peel, Whitehall Gardens; Duke of Devonshire, Piccadilly; Joseph Neild, Esq., 6, Grosvenor Square; Mr. Hope's Collection, are worth visiting; letters for tickets must be addressed to the noble owners.

Royal Academy, Trafalgar Square; 8 to 7, 1s. May, June and July. Exhibition of Modern Paintings.

Royal Exchange, Cornhill, open till 4 p.m.

Royal Institution Museum, Albemarle Street, 10 to 4, by member's order. Minerals.

Royal Society, Somerset House, General Museum, member's order and trifling fee to the attendant.

St. Bartholomew's Hospital, West Smithfield, Picture Gallery and Medical Museum.

St. George's Hospital, Hyde Park Corner, medical student's order.

St. Paul's Cathedral, Ludgate Hill, open daily, from 10 till dusk, to see the whole of which costs 3s. 2d.

Sapper's Museum, Woolwich, Curiosities, admission upon application.

Saull's Museum, 15, Aldersgate Street, Geological admission on Thursdays, at 11 a.m. free.

School of Design, Kensington Museum.

Soane's Museum, 13, Lincoln's Inn Fields, every Tuesday, Thursday and Friday in April, May, and June from 10 to 4, free, by previous application at the door, or by letter for tickets.

Society of Arts, John Street, Adelphi, daily, except Wednesday, 10 to 3, member's order.

Soho Bazaar, Soho Square, free.

Somerset House, Naval Models, free.

Surrey Royal Gardens, Penton Place, Walworth, admission 1s.

Thames Tunnel, Rotherhithe and Wapping, 1d., accessible by the river steamers.

Tower of London, Tower Hill, 10 to 4; Armouries, 6d.; Jewel Office, 6d.

Tussaud's Wax Exhibition, Baker Street, Bazaar, Portman Square, summer, 11 to 10, in winter, 11 to dusk, and 7 to 10, 1s. principal room, 6d. each Napoleon, &c.

Theatres.—Adelphi; Astley's; City of London; Covent Garden (Italian Opera); Drury Lane; Haymarket; Italian Opera, Haymarket; Lyceum, (Italian Opera), Wellington Street, Strand; Marylebone, Church Street, Paddington; Olympic, Wych Street; Pavilion, Whitechapel Road; Princess', Oxford Street; Queen's, Tottenham Court Road; Sadler's Wells, Islington; St. James's, King St.; Standard, Shoreditch; Strand; Surrey, Blackfriars Road; Victoria, New Cut, Lambeth.

United Service Institution Museum, January to September from 11 to 5, rest of the year from 11 to 4; admission by member's ticket.

Water Colours, Old Society of Painters in—Exhibition of Water Colour Drawings, 5, Pall Mall East, 9 to dusk, 1s., May, June, and July.
Water Colours, Exhibition of the New Society of Painters in, 53, Pall Mall, 9 to dusk, 1s., May, June, and July.
Westminster Abbey, 9 to dusk, 6d.
Woolwich Arsenal, 9 to 11½, and 1 to 4, free. All foreigners must apply through their ambassador to the Secretary at War for an order.

Windsor Castle, by command of Her Majesty the Queen, the State Apartments at Windsor Castle, will in future be open for inspection of visitors without any fee. Tickets of admission to be obtained gratis from the Lord Chamberlain's office at the Castle, after 1 p.m. The days of admission are Mondays, Tuesdays, Thursdays, and Fridays, April to October, 1 to 3; November to March, 12 to 2.
Zoological Gardens, Regent's Park, 1s.; Mondays 6d. 10 to dusk.

From London Bridge to Hampton Court, by Steamer.

THE BRIDGES.—Beyond the dates of their erection and completion, but little interest can be attached to these convenient communications from shore to shore, which our limited space will only allow us to detail, we therefore present at once the most important facts necessary to be known concerning them. *Southwark Bridge*, constructed of cast-iron, was commenced in 1814, and finished in 1818, at a cost of £800,000, under the direction and from the designs of Rennie. Passengers are charged one penny toll; *Blackfriars Bridge* was begun in 1760, and opened in 1769, after an expenditure of £260,000. There are nine arches. In 1841 it underwent a complete renovation. *Waterloo Bridge* was also completed under the superintendence of Thomas ,Telford, and having occupied six years in construction was opened on the Waterloo anniversary in 1817. It is 2,546 feet long, and 46 feet wide. The toll is one halfpenny; *Hungerford* (or Charing Cross) *Suspension Bridge* was erected by Brunel, at a cost of £106,000, and opened 1st May, 1845. Toll one halfpenny, but free access is given to steamboat passengers for embarking and disembarking; *Westminster Bridge* commenced in 1738, and completed in 1750. It has of late undergone considerable repairs, and is now being pulled down, a new one being in course of erection in lieu thereof. *Vauxhall Bridge*, begun in 1813, finished in 1816, is another cast iron bridge, 860 feet long. There is a toll of one penny for passengers.

CHELSEA.—Approaching Chelsea, the *Botanical Gardens* will be seen on the right of the river, adjoining the Hospital, and containing two of the finest Lebanon Cedars in England, presented by Sir Joseph Bankes. The river frontage of *Chelsea Hospital* is next seen, founded by Charles II., at the instigation of Nell Gwynne. Old *Chelsea Church* is a prominent object, and forms a picturesque termination to the long grove called Cheyne walk. There are monuments to the memory of Sir Hans Sloane and Sir Thomas More, in the churchyard. Battersea on the opposite side of the river is chiefly noticeable for its market gardens and an old church. Battersea Bridge is a very clumsy wooden structure; but a new suspension bridge has been recently opened at Chelsea. It is a large and elegant iron structure, and at the point where it crosses the river the Thames is 735 feet in width. This bridge, whether as regards its constructive properties or its architectural beauty, may safely be classed among the most succesful efforts of the kind that have been produced in modern times. It was designed and carried out by Mr. Page, the government engineer. Its importance is enhanced from the circumstance of a line of railway having been constructed from this point, *viâ* Wandsworth Common, thereby connecting the west end of London with the Crystal Palace. Battersea Park, at the Surrey end of the bridge, is rapidly progressing towards completion.

PUTNEY.—Passing over Putney Bridge, another dangerous old wooden communication, there is a toll of one penny for passengers Putney, the birthplace of Gibbon the historian, and Fulham, the residence of the Bishop of London, will be seen respectively on the left and right banks of the river.

HAMMERSMITH. — An elegant iron suspension bridge, 688 feet long, and 20 feet wide, is here thrown over the Thames. It was erected at a cost of £80,000, and the toll is one halfpenny. Hammersmith is four miles from Hyde Park Corner.

CHISWICK.—Old *Chiswick Church* is a picturesque relic of antiquity. The churchyard contains several interesting monuments to celebrated artists, among which are those to the memory of Hogarth and De Loutherbourg. The Horticultural Society have their gardens here, where the celebrated Floricultural Fêtes are held; and the Duke of Devonshire's mansion adjacent is memorable, as having been the place where Fox died in 1806, and Canning in 1827. Mortlake and Barnes present a pretty appearance on the opposite side of the river: At Mortlake the famous Dr. Dee lived, and Partridge, another astrologer was buried there.

KEW.—Near Kew Bridge, which replaced an old wooden one in 1789, is Strand-on-the-Green, where Joe Miller, of facetious memory, is reputed to have lived and died. *Kew Church* was built in 1714, and enlarged by George III., and has some interesting tombs to the memory of three celebrated artists, Gainsborough, Zoffany, and Meyer. Sir Peter Lely had a house close by. *Kew Gardens*, containing the finest collection of exotics in the kingdom. are much frequented. There is a *Chinese Pagoda* 165 feet high, and some picturesque mosques and temples about the grounds, which are open free to the public every day (except Sundays) from 12 till dusk. The mansion of the King of Hanover is on the site of the old palace built here by George III. The palace gardens are open for inspection. See page 65.

RICHMOND.—Passing by *Sion House*, which contains one of the largest greenhouses in the kingdom, the seat of the Duke of Northumberland, and leaving Brentford and Isleworth to the right, we arrive at *Richmond Bridge*, a handsome edifice of stone, the view from which has always been a source of admiration. Henry VII. altered its name from Sheen, and gave it his own appellation of Richmond, when he rebuilt the palace on the green, which had been destroyed by fire in 1498. Queen Elizabeth died here in

1603. *Richmond Park* contains 2,000 acres, and was first enclosed by order of Charles I. It is nearly ten miles in circumference. *Richmond Hill*, the praises of which have been long sung in book and ballad, commands a magnificent view over the country, and even Windsor Castle may be distinguished in the distant prospect. At the parish church, half ancient and half modern, lie buried James Thomson the poet, who resided here at *Rosedale House*, Dr. Moore, author of several valuable works, and father of Sir John Moore, Viscount Fitzwilliam, Gibson the painter, Edmund Kean, the tragedian, and others. There are some excellent inns and hotels here; the Star and Garter being frequented by all the élite of the country. Steamboats ply twice a day during the summer months; omnibuses run at certain times of the day, and it is but just to add that they are the fastest and best appointed out of the metropolis, and trains run constantly from the London and Richmond branch of the South Western Railway.

Twickenham, (10 miles from Hyde Park Corner, three miles south-west of Brentford, and one mile west of Richmond), is a favourite resort for picnic and pleasure parties. Here was Pope's villa, now demolished, and Strawberry Hill, the mansion of Horace Walpole, whose valuable collection of curiosities was some eight years back disposed of by auction. The Dowager Lady Waldegrave (the daughter of the celebrated singer Braham) is now endeavouring to restore it to its former celebrity, and re-collecting that scattered valuable collection. The remains of many distinguished persons are buried in the church. Here may be seen a tablet to the memory of Pope by Bishop Warburton, as also one to Pope's favourite nurse, who attended him for 38 years, erected by Pope himself in 1725. A new church built on the green, and some handsome alms-houses belonging to the city of London Carpenter's Company deserve especial notice. There are numerous villas and estates belonging to the nobility and gentry scattered over the beautiful surrounding country. The Hampton Court omnibuses pass through Twickenham to and from London several times daily.

Hampton Court Palace, open free to the public every day in the week except Fridays, from 10 till dusk; on Sundays from two till dusk. This magnificent palace, originally a manor of the Knight's Hospitallers, was built by Cardinal Wolsey in the early part of the reign of Henry VIII., and was subsequently enlarged and enriched by succeeding monarchs. The last sovereigns who resided here were George II. and his queen, since which period various persons have occupied the apartments, the crown reserving the right of resuming possession. The *Lion Gate*, fronting the entrance to Bushy Park—an appanage of the late esteemed and amiable Queen Dowager Adelaide — is the chief avenue, leaving the Maze to the right, and continuing through the Wilderness by a path overshadowed with lofty trees, the chief wing of the Palace is seen, in front of which extends a long walk ornamented on each side with parterres, and an exotic shrubbery with a spacious fountain in the centre. This building was completed in 1604, from designs by Sir Christopher Wren, and comprises the whole of the state apartments. The Grand Staircase and the Guard Chamber lead to the Picture Galleries, where the Cartoons of Raphael (seven in number) and the unequalled collection of the finest works of the ancient masters furnish an inexhaustable attraction. Returning to the middle court will be observed under the archway the flight of steps leading to Wolsey's Hall, 106 feet long, 40 feet wide and brilliantly illuminated by 13 windows each 15 feet from the ground. At the raised end is the bay window, on one of the panes in which the Earl of Surrey wrote his lines to the fair Geraldine. The walls are hung with tapestry of exquisite workmanship and costly material, the subject is the life of Abraham; the figures are of collossal size and the draperies are worked in gold and silver and set off with a variety of rich ornaments. These tapestries, supposed to have been designed by Raphael, are said to have formed a portion of the gifts interchanged between Henry VIII. and Francis at the celebrated "Field of the Cloth of Gold." The doorway in the centre of the dais leads to the withdrawing room. The curious clock over the gateway of the second court should not escape observation. The beautiful gardens in front of the palace have been the wonder and admiration of all visitors. They were laid out in their present Dutch style with the canal and watercourses by William III. The private gardens extend from the sides of the palace to the banks of the river, and contain some remarkably fine orange trees, most of them in full bearing. The famous vine, 110 feet long, and at three feet from the root 27 inches in circumference, usually bears from 2,000 to 3,000 bunches of grapes in a season. In this portion of the grounds is *The Maze*, so constructed that all the paths apparently leading to the centre turn off to a more distant part and involve the adventurer in constant perplexity. *The secret of success is after the first turning to the left to keep the right hand towards the fence the whole of the remaining way.* The principal taverns are the *Red Lion*, the *King's Arms*, and the *Toy Hotel*, all much frequented for their eels, which are fine, and the *cuisine* excellent.

From London Bridge to Herne Bay.

For the sake of variety, we shall proceed to describe the journey by water, which, on a fine day, is not only the most agreeable, but, as furnishing an excellent opportunity of seeing the scenery of the Thames, is perhaps most desirable to strangers.

Leaving London Bridge, a perfect forest of masts, belonging to ships of all sizes and all nations, looms out in the Pool.

BILLINGSGATE, situated chiefly at the back of that cluster of buildings by the Custom House, has been since the days of William III. the most famous fish-market in Europe.

LONDON BRIDGE.—The present bridge was erected from the designs of Rennie, nearly on the site of the old bridge demolished in 1825, and opened by William IV. on the 1st of August, 1831. The length is 950 ft. and the width between the parapets 84 ft., there are five arches, the centre of which has a span of 150 ft., rising 23 ft. above high water.

THE CUSTOM HOUSE, begun in 1813 from designs by Smirke, and finished four years afterwards, at a cost of nearly half-a-million, by Mr. Peto (uncle of the present Sir S. M. Peto, Bart.), contains about 200 distinct apartments, each having a range of communication with the long room, which is 197 ft. long and 50 feet high. From ten till three a visitor will obtain free ingress, and the principal business of "clearing" being here conducted, 100 clerks are constantly engaged in this apartment alone. Billingsgate, which for the last two centuries has been the finest fish-market in England, is seen a little to the left.

THE TOWER.—Supposed to have been built by Julius Cæsar, and afterwards re-constructed by William the Conqueror. The last state prisoners confined here were Thistlewood and his associates, imprisoned for the Cato-street conspiracy in 1820. There is free access to the public from ten till four, one shilling being charged to view the Regalia, &c. The entrance is through four successive gates at the southern extremity of an open space of ground called Tower Hill. Within the outer wall the buildings occupy an area of 12 acres. The building on the site of the old armoury, burned down in 1841, is restored and now used as barracks.

ST. KATHARINE'S DOCKS.—On the same side of the river at a short distance from the Tower are seen the warehouses belonging to St. Katharine's Docks, which cost nearly one million in construction, and were opened in 1828. The docks and basin, 24 acres in extent, annually receive about 1,500 vessels. The principal entrance is through a gateway at the north-west angle of the warehouses.

LONDON DOCKS.—The entrance is through a basin opposite Wapping Old Stairs. The docks, which are capable of containing 200 vessels, were opened in 1805, the principal enclosure comprising an area of 20 acres. Enormous warehouses and vaults surround these. Some idea of their magnitude may be formed from the fact that the tobacco warehouse alone covers a space of five acres, and that one of the vaults for retaining wine in bond has an area of seven acres. Upwards of 60,000 pipes of wine are usually kept here.

THE TUNNEL, affording a subaqueous communication from Wapping to Rotherhithe, was commenced in 1825 and opened in 1843 by the projector and engineer, Sir I. K. Brunel. It is about 1,30 ft. in length and 25 ft. in height, with a double archway brilliantly lighted with gas, and open day and night at a toll of one penny for each passenger. The entrance is down a spacious staircase of about 60 steps on each side.

LIMEHOUSE.—Here begins the Regent's Canal, which after several windings and tunnels through the northern parts of London joins the Paddington Canal and forms an important part of our inland navigation. The pier affords an easy communication with Poplar. What is called the Pool, where all the coal vesselsi ie, terminates at Limehouse reach. The Commercial Docks are on the opposite side of the river, after passing which is seen

DEPTFORD, where the dockyard and its bustling animation gives a lively appearance to the shore, reminds one of Peter the Great, who, in 1698, came to Sayes Court and studied the craft of ship-building at the once picturesque retreat of Evelyn, the autobiographist and author of "Sylvia." But, alas for the glories of Sayes Court—its glittering hollies, long avenues, and trim hedges! That portion of the victualling yard where oxen are slaughtered and hogs salted for the use of the navy occupies the enchanting grounds wherein Evelyn was wont to delight, and on the site of the mansion itself is the common workhouse of the parish. Approaching Greenwich Reach, where large quantities of whitebait are caught in the season, the opening of the river discloses a pretty view of a distant country beyond, and, with a few more revolutions of the paddle-wheel, we are brought to our destination.

WEST INDIA DOCKS.—Nearly opposite Greenwich, in the Isle of Dogs, thus named from having once been the repository for the royal hounds, will be seen the West India Docks, began in 1800, and finished in 1802. They communicate with the Thames at Limehouse, and terminate at Blackwall, covering an area of 204 acres, and capable of receiving about 600 vessels of from 200 to 300 tons burthen. The expense of their formation was £1,380,000.

GREENWICH.—See page 20.

Blackwall.—There is a fine pier here, whence packets run to and from Gravesend, in conjunction with the trains of the Blackwall railway. Fine views of the shipping in the river, Greenwich, Isle of Dogs, and the country round. Opposite is seen Shooter's Hill with its commemorative castle of Severndroog, built in 1784 by Sir William Jones, the celebrated Orientalist, to celebrate the conquest of a castle thus named on the coast of Malabar. White-bait dinners form the chief attraction to the taverns adjacent; and here Her Majesty's ministers for the time being regale themselves annually on that fish; the season is from May to the latter end of July, when parliament generally closes for the season. See page 17.

WOOLWICH.—See page 22.

ERITH—See page 23.

Purfleet (on the Essex coast, 16 miles from London, nine miles south-east from Romford, and four miles west of Grays), has a romantic aspect from its high chalky cliffs and chasms. The government powder magazine is kept here, having been in 1762 removed hence from Greenwich. There are generally about 3,000,000 pounds of gunpowder preserved in the building. A pier affords convenient access, and the Gravesend steamers regularly call on their passages going and returning.

GREENHITHE.—See page 24

GRAVESEND.—See page 24.

ROCHESTER.—See page 25.

Sheerness (two miles from Queenborough), a busy shipping town on the north-western point of the Isle of Sheppy. A steamboat on the Medway plies frequently between Sheerness and Chatham. The junction of the Thames and Medway with the Channel is called the Nore; the Nore boat carries a beacon at night to guard mariners from a treacherous shoal which exists in this vicinity.

It was planned and fortified by Charles II. to guard the Thames and Medway, but was reduced by the Dutch Admiral De Ruyter within twelve months after. The dockyard is on a very extensive scale, covering about 60 acres, and has cost, since 1815, three millions in improvements. In consequence of the nature of the ground, nearly 100,000 piles had to be driven before a sufficiently stable foundation could be obtained. The dockyard contains residences for the commander-in-chief, the lieutenant-governor, and the usual staff of superintendents, masters, master shipwrights, &c. The ordnance department has also an office here, and the batteries mount 100 guns. The vessels of the royal navy are here laid up in ordinary, and there are sometimes as many as seventy of those "floating castles" moored at Blackstakes, a little above Sheerness. In 1798, the fleet stationed at the Nore mutinied, a circumstance happily unprecedented in the annals of our gallant navy.

Herne Bay (15 miles from Margate, four from Reculvers and Whitstable, and nine from Canterbury), is much frequented as a bathing place in the season, and accessible by steamers. daily, in the season, and by railway, *via* Sturry, on the London and South Eastern Line. The pier, opened in 1833, is 3,640 feet long. Libraries, Hotels, an Assembly Room, and other adjuncts to the town have been erected on a large scale.

LONDON AND BLACKWALL RAILWAY.

The growing importance of the London and Blackwall Railway, the immense number of passengers passing through its London terminus, the increase anticipated from the working arrangements of the company with the Eastern Counties and the Tilbury and Southend Railways, rendered an enlargement of the Fenchurch Street station necessary in 1853 The new terminus is a fine-looking building, and comprises booking offices and waiting rooms, from which you ascend by a flight of stairs on each side to the platform accommodation above for the following lines:—London and Blackwall, the North London, the Eastern Counties, and the Tilbury and Southend. These platforms are all covered with one roof, 100 feet span, and upwards of 300 feet long. The approach to the north side of the line has been much widened to admit of another line of carriages, as the traffic has so much increased, and the amount of goods conveyed to and from the eastern and western parts of the Metropolis for transmission on the various other lines of railway has become very great.

The line originally proceeded for a considerable distance under a covered way, lit by sash windows. This was considered necessary at the time of the construction of the Blackwall Railway, to prevent accidents by horses taking fright from the noise and smoke of the engines, as they dart over the bridges crossing the streets of London. The first bridge crossing the Minories is a specimen of these enclosed viaducts. Through the windows we have a glimpse of the Tower of London; but soon emerge from the covered way, amid roofs of houses and chimnies. We then pass the sugar-baking establishments of Goodman's-Fields, which was a dairy farm in olden times. At the old theatre, now burnt down, Garrick the tragedian and Braham the singer made their *debût*, The London Docks, Wapping (what Englishman can forget the inimitable Incledon's "Wapping Old Stairs?") St. George's-in-the-East, a neighbourhood densely crowded with a busy, dingy, working, or sea-going population. On the left we pass *Shadwell Church*, and also *St. Mary's Church* and *Schools*. We then continue our course nearly parallel to the Commercial Road, crossing by a stone bridge the north side of the Regent's Canal Dock, the terminus of the Regent's Canal. We next arrive at Stepney Station, and begin to breathe more freely, after having left behind the regions of smoke and gigantic chimnies.

STEPNEY.

Telegraph station at London Bridge Station, 2 miles.

OMNIBUSES to and from all parts of London every quarter of an hour.

MONEY ORDER OFFICE, No. 10, High Street.

Dean Colet lived here.

At this point is a short link connecting various systems of railway communication viz: North London, Eastern Counties, and Tilbury, and along which we now direct our course. On the left, but at some distance from the railway, is seen the square tower of *Stepney Church*, the mother church of most of the parishes in the eastern part of London. Immediately beneath us on the left is the Commercial Road, leading from Whitechapel to Blackwall, a distance of nearly 4 miles. Near the junction of the Camden Town and Blackwall Railways, is the Commercial Road, 80 feet in width, and which is crossed by an iron viaduct, called Bow Spring Bridge, designed by L. Clase, Esq., and made by Messrs. Fox and Henderson, of Birmingham. Notwithstanding the great length of the viaduct, and the material of which it is constructed, it has a light and picturesque appearance. Having traversed the Commercial Road by Bow Spring Bridge, we soon leave the city and Pool of London behind us, and pass through fields to Bow Common, where to the right we have an extensive but distant view of the East India Docks, and, beyond them, a view of the Surrey and Kentish hills; on the left, the city of London, and Tower Hamlets Cemetery, occupying nearly thirty acres of ground, beautifully disposed, ornamented with cypress, cedar, and other trees, and most of the graves decorated with flowers and shrubs. Beyond the cemetery is seen the extensive buildings of the city of London Union Workhouse, which from its extent and architecture has a palatial appearance. We next descend into a deep cutting, and, passing under the Bow Road, arrive at the junction station on the main line of the

NORTH LONDON RAILWAY.

Camden to Bow, and East and West India Docks.

THE prodigious extent of buildings in the immediate vicinity of London has rendered a corresponding increase of the means of conveyance from one district to another indispensable. A few years since, Chelsea, Brompton, Kensington, and Bayswater, forming the beautiful western suburbs of the metropolis, were comparatively unknown to most of the inhabitants of Eastern London. Many of the parishioners of Shadwell, Limehouse, and Poplar might have heard of the Regent's Park and Primrose Hill, but had never visited either, for want of some direct communication brought as it were, to their very doors. Such a facility was provided for them by the opening, in 1851, of the Camden Town, or North London Railway, which traverses the eastern and northern suburbs of the metropolis, and enables the Londoner to make the journey from Fenchurch Street, City, to Primrose Hill and the Regent's Park (the latter attractive at all seasons, on account of its "Zoological Gardens"), at a very trifling expenditure of time and money.

BOW.

Telegraph station at Fenchurch Street, 3 miles.
MONEY ORDER OFFICE, No. 28, Southside.

At Bow the train receives and puts down passengers; and soon after starting from which we find ourselves in an open country; on the right is VICTORIA PARK, on the left we have an extensive view over the Hackney marshes, terminating with a considerable portion of the well-wooded scenery of Essex. Passing onward, through the verdant fields, we come to the retired village of *Homerton*, the church and parsonage house of which are pleasing specimens of architecture. We now arrive at

HACKNEY.

Distance from station, ½ mile.
Telegraph station at London, Fenchurch Street, 5½ miles.
OMNIBUSES every 5 minutes to and from the city and Oxford-street, London.
MONEY ORDER OFFICE, Church Street.

On the right, from the midst of roofs of houses, thickly planted trees in the churchyard and adjacent gardens, rises the picturesque tower of the old church, and the pyramidal tower of the new church. In the old Church General Fairfax was married; De Foe lived here, and Dr. South, the wit, was a native. The square building on the right side is the Hackney Railway station. After a short stoppage the train moves on towards Kingsland, which is in a deep cutting, passing under the Kingsland Road.

KINGSLAND.

OMNIBUSES to and from London (both city and west end), every quarter of an hour.
MONEY ORDER OFFICE at 9, Orchard Place.

After taking up passengers at the Kingsland station, we proceed through a cutting towards Islington, and passing under the Great North Road we arrive at the Islington and Highbury station, at the point where the road branches to Holloway and Highbury. Through the high level of Islington the railway is in cutting. We quit this near the Caledonian Road, and cross the same by a bridge.

NEWINGTON ROAD station.

ISLINGTON.

Distance from station, ½ mile.
HOTEL.–Angel.
OMNIBUSES to and from London (both city and west end), every 5 minutes.

MONEY ORDER OFFICE, No. 86, Upper Street.

We next pass over the Great Northern Railway, which presents one of the most singular views through which the railroad passes. From this bridge, looking down the gorge of a deep valley, we observe the lines of the Great Northern Railway gently curving to the entrance of the tunnel. In the centre of the Great Northern Railway, a short distance from the tunnel, are two immense piers, upwards of 60 feet in height, which support the viaduct of the Camden Town Railway. Beyond this viaduct lie Copenhagen fields, the site of the new *Smithfield Market.* The large building with the lofty tower is the *New Prison*, erected at the expense of the Corporation of London in 1842, and will contain 1,000 prisoners. After passing several beautiful villas we reach Camden Town, where the railway is constructed upon a brick viaduct of good proportions. The main roads are crossed by wrought-iron boiler-plate bridges upon the same principle as that of the celebrated tubular bridge over the Menai Straits. Some of these bridges are of considerable span, and the details of their construction are well worthy the close examination of those who can appreciate works of this kind. We soon enter upon ground intersected with the rails of the London and North Western Railway, until we reach the end of our journey at the terminus of the Camden Town Railway, in the Hampstead Road.

CAMDEN ROAD,

Telegraph station at Highbury.
HOTEL.—Brecknock Arms.
OMNIBUSES every five minutes to all parts of town.

MONEY ORDER OFFICE at 89, High Street.

The internal economy of a railway, and the activity, regularity, and order with which these great undertakings are conducted, may be gathered from a visit to the Camden Town Goods Station of the London and North Western Railway. The Camden Station is exclusively devoted to goods and cattle traffic, and the reception of locomotives. In ten years after it had been laid ont for these purposes, so vast were the requirements of the augmented traffic, that it was necessary to pull down the original buildings and to remodel the station entirely. The merchandise received from up and for down trains averages between 800 and 900 tons daily. During the six months ending August, 1848, 73,732 railway wagon loads of goods entered and departed from Camden Station. A change of carriages here takes place from the North London to those of the

HAMPSTEAD JUNCTION,

Along which we now bend our course. After passing KENTISH TOWN we come to

HAMPSTEAD HEATH.

Situated in the midst of a fine open country, which, from its elevated character, presents many beautiful views of the city and country to the south, including even Windsor Castle, in Berkshire. The air is remarkably salubrious. Soon after passing the stations of FINCHLEY and EDGEWARE ROADS, at the distance of about two miles we cross the main line of the London and North Western, and thus pass on to the lines of the

NORTH & SOUTH WESTERN JUNCTION.

Willesden Junction to Kew.

About one mile beyond this Junction we cross the Great Western, and another mile brings us to the town of

ACTON.

POPULATION, about 2,750.

Here Sir Mathew Hale, Bishop Lloyd, and Baxter lived. The old Catholic church is worth a visit.

HAMMERSMITH BRANCH.

A short branch, 1¼ mile, turns off to the left here, by which the tourist is enabled to visit

HAMMERSMITH.

POPULATION, about 16,500.

The most remarkable object here is the Suspension Bridge, a light and elegant structure completed by Tierney Clarke in 1827, at a cost of about £80,000.

Retracing our route to Acton, and pursuing our course onward about amile and a half, we are brought to our destination at

Kew, particulars of which will be found at pages 13 and 65.

London and Blackwall continued.

Having returned to Stepney the stations of LIMEHOUSE, WEST INDIA DOCKS (particulars of which will be found on page 15), and POPLAR, are respectively passed, and the train stops at

BLACKWALL.

Distance from station, ¼ mile.

Telegraph station.

HOTEL.—Brunswick.

STEAM BOATS to and from Gravesend, daily.

MONEY ORDER OFFICE at No. 53, Three Colt Street, Limehouse, 3 miles.

See page 15.

LONDON, TILBURY, AND SOUTHEND.

Stepney and Ilford to Tilbury.

This line commences by a junction with the Blackwall at Stepney, and also with the Eastern Counties at Ilford. Passengers may book at either Bishopsgate or Fenchurch Street; but the latter affords greater facilities as to the number of departures. A few minutes only are occupied in passing the stations of BROMLEY, PLAISTOW, and EAST HAM, before arriving at the town of

BARKING.

POPULATION, 4,930.

Telegraph station at Stratford, 3½ miles.

HOTELS.—The Ship; Bull.

BARKING is a market town in the county of Essex, so called from a creek on which it is situated. The town is of considerable extent, and chiefly inhabited by fishermen, by whom the fish markets of London are frequently supplied. The parish is divided into four wards of Barking, Great Ilford, Chadwell, and Rippleward, abounding with fertile lands and beautiful prospects. A fair is held here annually, round a famous oak denominated Fairlop. This oak sustained its dignity in the forest for many years, and though it has suffered from the rough treatment of visitors, it still maintains a majestic appearance peculiar to itself. The Westmoreland's seat at East Ham belonged to Anne Boleyn.

The route from Bishopsgate, *via* Ilford, unites here, when the trains proceed together, *via* RAINHAM, to

PURFLEET.—Here are immense powder magazines belonging to Government; also *Belvedere*, seat of R. Webb, Esq.

GRAY'S THURROCKS.

POPULATION, 1,713.

Telegraph station at Tilbury, 2½ miles.

MARKET DAY.—Thursday.

FAIR.—May 23rd.

TILBURY.

A telegraph station.

HOTEL.—World's End.

STEAM BOATS to and from Gravesend, Southend, Sheerness, Margate, and Ramsgate, daily.

MONEY ORDER OFFICE at Gray's, 7 miles

The districts known by the names of East and West Tilbury are situated in the county of Essex, and the former is celebrated for its fort, which effectually protects the metropolis from the attack of any hostile fleet.

Tilbury Fort was built by Henry VIII. to rescue the towns on the river from such chances of invasion as were then probable, and Charles II. considerably enlarged and strengthened it when the Dutch fleet sailed up the Medway in 1667, and burned three men of war opposite Chatham. Some traces of the camp formed here to oppose the threatened descent of the Spanish Armada are yet visible at West Tilbury, where Queen Elizabeth by a spirited harangue inspired her army with dauntless courage, not however fated to be put to a very severe test. The fury of the elements conspiring with the brave attacks of our navy proved a final blow to their hopes of conquest, and the remnant of the "Invincible Armada" was miserably stranded on the Orkneys. Of the whole fleet, originally consisting of one hundred and thirty vessels, with twenty thousand land forces on board, only fifty-three ships returned to Spain, and they were in a wretchedly shattered condition.

Such recollections as these connected with the old fortress before us invest it with greater interest than its architectural aspect would seem of itself to claim.

The esplanade is of vast dimensions, and the bastions the largest of any in England. On the side near the river is a strong curtain, in the centre of which is the water gate.

This is the station for passengers to or from Gravesend. The platform between the station and the pier is covered with oval plates forming a half tube, to afford shelter in bad weather; and steamers ply between this station and the pier at Gravesend at the departure and arrival of every train. Here an Emigrants' Home has been constructed.

STANFORD-LE-HOPE.

Telegraph station at Tilbury, 5½ miles.

MONEY ORDER OFFICE at Horndon-on-the-Hill, 1 mile.

The bend which the river makes here is called "The Hope."

PITSEA and BENFLEET stations.

LEIGH.

Telegraph station at Southend, 4 miles.

HOTEL.—The Bell.

MONEY ORDER OFFICE at Southend, 4 miles.

The line of railway from Leigh to Southend—the continuation of the Tilbury line—is about 2½ miles in length. It has, owing to the situation of the two towns, been carried up a steep gradient the greater portion of the distance. This will be better understood when we state that the Leigh Station is very nearly level with the Thames, and the Southend terminus stands on the summit of the hill, at the west end of the town, near to the Royal Hotel. This station is commodiously built, well-lighted, and situate in a good position for the town, being neither so close as to prove a source of annoyance, nor so far as to place it beyond the reach of the worst of walkers. The trains proceed with great caution down the incline, shutting off steam shortly after leaving the platform at Southend. *Hadleigh Castle*, in the vicinity, is a picturesque ruin, majestic even in its decay, which will furnish a pleasing addition to the sketch-book of the artistic rambler.

SOUTHEND.

A telegraph station.

HOTELS.—Ship, Chas. Woosnam, family and commercial hotel, a very comfortable house, and deservedly recommended; Royal Hotel, near the railway station.

A picturesque village in the county of Essex, situated at the mouth of the Thames, nearly opposite Sheerness. It has lately become known as a watering-place. Several handsome rows of houses have been erected, and bathing machines established. The company that assemble here in the season will be found more select than at Margate, but it suffers severely in its climate when an easterly wind prevails. There are assembly rooms, theatre, library, a wooden terrace pier, 1,500 feet long, with a causeway 4,000 feet by 14 feet, which enables passengers to land at low water, and forms besides a pleasant promenade for those who love to enjoy the salubrity of the sea-breeze, and several places of worship. The view of the Thames from Southend is very pleasant, and the town is gradually rising in importance. It is situated on a wooded hill; and the beautiful terrace, commonly called New Southend, being built on a considerable eminence, gives the town an elegant appearance. The houses from this position command a delightful and extensive view of the sea, Nore, Medway, Sheerness, and the panoramic views of the shipping and steamers which are constantly passing up or down the river. The air generally is considered very dry and salubrious.

The vicinity presents several temptations to the pedestrian, and though the surrounding scenery is not characterised by many striking landscapes, the prospects are varied and interesting. Southend is forty-two miles from London, and five from Rochford, having a communication with the metropolis by coach as well as by a steam-boat, which leaves London Bridge every Tuesday, Thursday, and Saturday.

SOUTH EASTERN RAILWAY.

THE South Eastern Railway is virtually in possession of the whole line of communication through the county of Kent, and the importance of the Company may be estimated by the present and prospective traffic of that fertile county, the produce of which will necessarily be increased and developed by the facilities this means of conveyance affords for reaching distant markets. Additional lines will no doubt be extended into every district as the spirit of enterprise spreads over the county.

By means of the South Eastern Railway all the watering places on the coast of Kent, viz., Gravesend, Herne Bay, Margate, Broadstairs, Ramsgate, Deal, Dover, and Folkestone, can be reached in a few hours; and the inhabitants of the metropolis are thus enabled to enjoy the advantages of a visit to the sea-side at their favourite towns, the climate, temperature, and atmosphere of which many prefer and find more beneficial than that of the watering places on the South Coast.

THE LONDON TERMINUS of the South Eastern Railway is situated on the Surrey or Southwark side of London Bridge. Its exterior view is not remarkable for architectural beauty or grandeur, although it is both large and convenient. From a comparatively insignificant terminus of the Greenwich line, it has been enlarged, and adapted to meet the requirements of the traffic of the various lines of which it is now the conjoint *termini.* The South Eastern Railway conveys to and from this terminus the passenger and goods traffic of a great portion of the county of Kent, and, *via* Dover and Calais, Folkestone and Boulogne, or Dover and Ostend, the passenger and goods traffic to and from France and the North of Europe.

The London, Brighton, and South Coast Railway conveys the traffic of the counties of Surrey and Sussex, and also that with France, *via* Newhaven and Dieppe; and lastly, the passengers of the Sydenham Railway to and from the Crystal Palace

The main or central building of the London Terminus belongs to, and is appropriated as the booking offices of, the South Eastern and North Kent Railways, the offices of the London and Greenwich being on the left towards Tooley Street. The right or south-western portion belongs to, and is appropriated as the booking offices of, the London and Brighton and Sydenham Railways. On the left of the entrance there is an arcade, similar in some respects to the Lowther Arcade in the Strand, with shops, and a large refreshment room in the centre.

The interior of the station or terminus is admirably adapted for the traffic of all these lines. The platforms are spacious and extensive; the wooden roofs over them are light and airy; and the plates of glass with which they are covered admit and diffuse sufficient light to every part of the vast area.

The arrangements appear so excellent that the trains receive or discharge their passengers from the respective lines simultaneously, without the least confusion being observed in any part of the united termini. Still one thing is wanting to render these complete, viz., the establishment of a Luggage Room, upon the Parisian plan, into which all baggage should be taken from the vans on the arrival of the trains, deposited on a counter, and delivered up only to the owner, upon his producing the respective duplicate ticket, and entrance to this room should alone be allowed to those persons who can produce that voucher. This would at once obviate the annoyance, delay, inconvenience, and risk which all travellers have to encounter, as regards that most necessary yet troublesome appendage, at all the stations in the kingdom, and prevent the possibility of any members of the "swell mob," who attend every station, from profiting by the disorder, confusion, and scrambling, which take place when the traveller's luggage is unceremoniously flung down upon the platform at the stations for the owner himself to pick up.

The approach to this terminus from King William Street, over London Bridge, with its moving throng and exciting panoramic view—the ships and steamers on the river, the magnificent dome of St. Paul's on the one hand, and the Monument on the other, with all the noble buildings encircling them, form one of the finest and most imposing views in London, or probably in the world—this extraordinary thoroughfare being a peculiar characteristic of the metropolis of England.

We commence our description of the Railway Routes in the county of Kent with the most northern, viz.:—

GREENWICH BRANCH,

From the London Bridge Terminus.

Although this line has numerous competitors in the almost innumerable Thames steamers that ply between London and Greenwich, and the trips on board of which seem to be so much enjoyed by the pleasure-seeking crowds of London, the population of the great city is so immense that it pours forth its tributary streams in all possible directions over the bosom of the Thames whithersoever the steamers convey them, and into every corner of the country to which the railways from London will transport them. Hence, notwithstanding the competition of the steamers to and from Greenwich, there are as many as sixty trains daily by this railway to and from London. The line runs over viaducts the whole distance through the populous districts of Bermondsey and Rotherhithe, affording occasional glimpses of the shipping on the river, until the train reaches

DEPTFORD.

A telegraph station.

HOTELS.—Fountain, White Hart.

OMNIBUSES to London, New Cross, and Greenwich, every half hour, daily.

POST HORSES, FLYS, &c., at the station and hotels.

DEPTFORD is a town in the county of Kent, built on the banks of the Thames. The principal object of attraction at Deptford is its dockyard, which has three building slips; but it is chiefly used as a victualling yard, the river being crowded with transports. Evelyn, the author of *Sylvia*, had a seat here, which Peter the Great occupied when studying ship building Sir F. Drake, after his famous voyage, entertained Queen Elizabeth on board the Pelican. There are also several private yards for the building of sailing vessels.

The General Steam Navigation Company's Engine and Boiler Manufactory and Dockyard, for their large fleet of steamers is at the entrance of Deptford Creek, and is one of the most important and interesting establishments on the banks of the Thames.

On quitting Deptford the train crosses the river Ravensbourne, and in a few moments reaches

GREENWICH.

POPULATION, 105,784.

A telegraph station.

HOTELS.—Trafalgar, Charles Hart; the Ship Tavern, Thos. Quartermaine.

OMNIBUSES to and from London, Deptford, and New Cross, daily, every half hour.

STEAMERS to and from London, calling at all the piers on the river, every five minutes, daily.

MONEY ORDER OFFICE, 12, Nelson Street.

BANKERS.—London and County Bank.

Greenwich Pier is five miles from London Bridge.

GREENWICH presents a striking appearance from the river, its Hospital forming one of the most prominent attractions of the place. Here was the palace erected by Humphrey Duke of Gloucester, and by him called Placentia; and here were born Henry VIII. and his two daughters, Queens Mary and Elizabeth. Charles II. began the present magnificent edifice, and William III. appropriated it to its present patriotic purpose, since which time successive sovereigns have contributed to enrich it with various additions. As the first generally seen, we shall begin our description with an account of its interior. The Chapel and Picture Gallery are open gratis on Mondays and Fridays; on other days threepence each is charged for admission. It is as well to remind the reader that the Hospital consists of four distinct piles of building, distinguished by the appellations of King Charles's, King William's, Queen Mary's, and Queen Anne's. King Charles's and Queen Anne's are those next the river, and between them is the grand square, 270 feet wide, and the terrace, by the river front, 865 feet in length. Beyond the square are seen the Hall and Chapel, with their noble domes, and the two colonnades, which are backed by the eminence whereon the Observatory stands throned amid a grove of trees. In the centre of the great square is Rysbrach's statue of George II., carved out of white marble, from a block taken from the French by Sir George Rooke, and which weighed eleven tons. On the west side is King Charles's building, erected chiefly of Portland stone, in the year 1684. The whole contains about 300 beds, distributed in thirteen wards. Queen Anne's building, on the east side of the square, corresponding with that on the opposite side, was begun in 1693, and completed in 1726. There are here 24 wards with 437 beds, and several of the officers' apartments. To the south-west is King William's building, comprising the great hall, vestibule, and dome, erected between 1698 and 1703, by Sir Christopher Wren. It contains eleven wards and 554 beds. Queen Mary's building was, with the chapel, not completed till 1752. It contains 13 wards and 1,100 beds. The **Painted Hall,** a noble structure opposite the chapel, is divided into three rooms, exhibiting, as you enter, statues of Nelson and Duncan, with 28 pictures of various sizes; the chief are Turner's large picture of "The Battle of Trafalgar," the "Relief of Gibraltar," and the "Defeat of the French Fleet under Compte de Grasse." On the opposite side is Loutherbourg's picture of Lord Howe's victory on the memorable 1st of June, 1794, whilst above are suspended the flags taken in battle. The other pictures up the steps are chronologically arranged, the most prominent being the "Death of Captain Cook," the "Battle of Camperdown," "Nelson leaping into the San Josef," and the "Bombardment of Algiers." It may not be generally known that every mariner, either in the Royal Navy or merchant service, pays sixpence a month towards the support of this noble institution, which has, of course, besides, a handsome revenue (£130,000) derived from other sources. The pensioners, who are of every rank, from the admiral to the humblest sailor, are qualified for admission by being either maimed or disabled by age. Foreigners who have served two consecutive years in the British service are equally entitled to the privileges, and the widows of seamen are exclusively appointed nurses. The Hospital was first opened in January, 1705, and now the pensioners provided with food, clothes, lodging, and a small stipend for pocket money, number nearly 2,500. The number of out-pensioners is about 3,000. The "Royal Naval School," for training the sons of seamen to the naval service, is a most interesting institution, administering the best instruction to now about 450 boys.

The "Royal Observatory," occupying the most elevated spot in Greenwich Park, was built on the site of the old castle, the foundation stone being laid on the 10th of August, 1675. The first superintendent of this establishment was Flamstead, and he commenced his observations in the following year. It stands about 300 feet above the level of the river. For the guidance of the shipping the round globe at its summit drops precisely at 1 p.m., to give the exact Greenwich time. The noble park is chiefly planted with elms and chesnut trees, and contains 188 acres. It was walled round with brick in the reign of James I. The views from the summit are very fine, embracing perhaps the finest prospects of London and the Thames, the forests of Hainault and Epping, the heights of Hampstead, and a survey of Kent, Surrey, and Essex, as far as the eye can reach. The flitting of the fawns through the distant glades, the venerable aspect of the trees themselves—many of them saplings in the time of Elizabeth—and the appearance of the veteran pensioners, some without a leg or arm, others hobbling on from the infirmity of wounds or age, and all clad in the old-fashioned blue coats and breeches, with cocked hats, give beauty and animation to a scene which no other country in the world can boast.

A small doorway in the south-western extremity of the park brings us out with a udden contrast on to Blackheath, where Wat Tyler assembled the Kentish rebels in the reign of Richard II., and where Jack Cade and his fellow insurgents are said to have held their midnight meetings in a cavern which still remains, though so choked up as to be considered nearly inaccessible.

On proceeding from the Park towards Blackheath may be seen a group of emancipated youths eager and impatient to mount the donkey-steeds they have just hired, to take possession of and elicit the stubborn and wilful propensities of the race, or to display such feats of horsemanship as shall charm an admiring fair one in the surrounding groups, or more frequently to excite roars of laughter, witticisms, and jokes, when the luckless rider is thrown, and exhibits that peculiar indescribable foolish appearance all persons, simple or gentle, manifest under similar circumstances.

Further on the visitor is certain to observe a dark eyed daughter of Bohemia examining the hand of some fair maid who has escaped from East Cheap or Cheapside on a visit to far-famed Greenwich, to have her fortune told by one of the Gipsies of the heath. Ever and anon one of the ruder sex, facetiously sceptical, but evidently credulous in the occult art of the prophetess, wishes to look into futurity through the Gipsey Sybil, and then return to his avocations to wait the future fate she has predicted.

These are the principal objects of attraction and amusement in Greenwich and its beautiful Park, which have diverted for centuries generation after generation of the good folks of London; and we cannot but hope that the Park and the Heath may be preserved for ages to come, as an oasis in the desert, when the mighty city has spread its suburbs far beyond it, into the hills and dales of the surrounding country.

NORTH KENT LINE.

The North Kent line commences at New Cross.

LEWISHAM (Junction).

A telegraph station.

FAIRS.—Horses, cattle, and pigs, May 12th and October 13th.

LEWISHAM is a small village, in a beautiful situation on the high road to Seven Oaks and Tunbridge, and near the river Ravensbourne.

MID KENT.

Lewisham to Beckenham.

The stations are LADYWELL, CATFORD BRIDGE, and LOWER SYDENHAM, none of which call for much remark. Arriving at

BECKENHAM.

MONEY ORDER OFFICE at Bromley.

The church is ancient, with some brasses and monuments worth notice. In the churchyard is a *Lich* gate, for the reception of the corpse on arrival, an erection peculiar to this county, carried down from the Saxon era.

Langley Park and Kilsey Park are near. The thriving town of Bromley, on the Ravensbourne, is 1½ mile distant. The Bishops of Rochester have palace here, with some pretty grounds, where there is a chalybeate spring, called St. Blaze's well. The church has a Norman font, a monument to Dr. Hawksworth, and the tomb of Dr. Johnson's wife. Bishop Warner's college for clergymen's widows is in this town.

North Kent continued.

BLACKHEATH.

Distance from the station, ¼ mile.

A telegraph station. Office open from 7½ a.m. to 10 p.m.; Sundays, 8 to 10 a.m., 1 to 3, and 6 to 9 p.m.

HOTEL.—Green Man.

This heath is celebrated for many remarkable events that have been witnessed on it in former periods of our history. The Danes encamped here while their fleet lay in the Thames a little above Woolwich. Wat Tyler and Jack Cade also encamped here with their followers, and since then the exploits of highwaymen and others have rendered the heath equally notorious. But it is now a favourite resort of the inhabitants of London, who come in crowds during the holidays and summer season—donkey riding being a favourite amusement. The heath is exceedingly picturesque, and commands several very fine views.

Lee and its church to the right.

From this station we pass through a tunnel 1,680 yards long, and arrive at

CHARLTON.

CHARLTON is a small village, most pleasantly situated, and remarkable for the numerous picturesque villas and residences it contains. From its being in the vicinity of Woolwich, and its charming neighbourhood, it is much frequented whenever a review or other military spectacle attracts visitors from town.

Pursuing our course we pass through two more tunnels, respectively 100 and 120 yards long, and arrive at

WOOLWICH DOCK Station, a short distance from which is

WOOLWICH ARSENAL Station.

WOOLWICH.

A telegraph station. Office open from 7½ a.m. to 10½ p.m.; Sundays, 8 to 10 a.m., 1 to 3 and 6 to 8 p.m.

HOTEL.—Royal Pavilion.

STEAM BOATS from the pier to London every ¼ of an hour, calling at the different piers on the river.

MARKET DAY.—Friday.

BANKERS.—London and County.

Of course nearly all the interest connected with Woolwich is concentrated in the government establishments, which are acknowledged to be the finest in the world. These, consisting of the Dockyard, Arsenal, and Royal Military Repository, we shall describe in the rotation generally adopted when seeing them. Coming from Shooter's Hill and crossing Woolwich Common, the extensive range of buildings forming the barracks of the Royal Artillery first attracts attention. The principal front extends above 1,200 feet. In the eastern wing is the chapel, containing 1,000 sittings, and the other principal parts of the building are the library and reading-room, plentifully supplied with newspapers and periodicals. The whole establishment affords excellent accommodation for upwards of 4,000 men. The troops, when on parade, present a very animated appearance. The "Royal Arsenal" will be observed but a short distance off, composed of several buildings, wherein the manufacture of implements of warfare is carried on upon the most extensive scale.

On entering the gateway the visitor will see the "Foundry" before him, provided with everything necessary for casting the largest pieces of ordnance, for which, as in the other branches of manufacture, steam power has been lately applied. Connected with the "Pattern Room," adjoining, will be noticed several of the illuminations and devices used in St. James's Park to commemorate the peace of 1814. The "Laboratory" exhibits a busy scene, for here are made the cartridges, rockets, fireworks, and other chemical contrivances for warfare, which, though full of "sound and fury," are far from being considered amongst the enemy as "signifying nothing." To the north are the storehouses, where are deposited outfittings for 15,000 cavalry horses, and accoutrements for service. The area of the Arsenal contains no less than 24,000 pieces of ordnance, and 3,000,000 cannon balls piled up in huge pyramids. The "Repository" and "Rotunda" are on the margin of the Common, to the south of the town, and contain models of the most celebrated fortifications in Europe, with curiosities innumerable. To the south-east of the Repository is the "Royal Military Academy," for the education of the cadets in all the branches of artillery and engineering. The present building, partly in the Elizabethan style, was erected in 1805, and though 300 could be accommodated, the number of cadets at present does not exceed 160. In going from the Arsenal to the Garrison there will be noticed, on the right of the road, an extensive building, forming the head quarters of the Royal Sappers and Miners. On the same side of the way is the "Field

Artillery Depôt," where the guns are mounted and kept in readiness for instant action. The Hospital is to the left of the Garrison entrance, fitted up with 700 beds, and under the superintendence of the most skilful medical officers. From the Arsenal we proceed to the Dockyard, which, commencing at the village of New Charlton on the west, extends a mile along the banks of the river to the east. There are two large dry docks for the repair of vessels, and a spacious basin for receiving vessels of the largest size. The granite docks, and the Foundry and Boiler-maker department, recently added, have been great improvements. Timber-sheds, mast-houses, storehouses, and ranges of massive anchors, give a very busy aspect to the place, which was first formed in the reign of Henry VIII., and considerably enlarged by Charles I. The new "Royal Marine Barracks," designed by Mr. Crew, and just finished, cost £100,000. An excellent feature is the kitchen, appropriated to every forty men, so that the meals may be taken apart from the bedroom. There is also a school attached for two hundred boys and girls. The following form the arrangements of admission to the above important buildings:—To the Arsenal, the Royal Repository, and the Dockyard, *free;* the hours being from 9 till 11 a.m., and 1 till 4 p m. Visitors are required to leave their names at the gates. The other buildings require the escort of one of the principal officers.

Though within the last four years nearly 2,000 additional houses have been built, the town presents few inducements for a prolonged visit, and has no feature of interest in itself whatever. The old church looks better at a distance than close, and there are a few monuments in the churchyard bearing names familiar to the eye and ear. Perhaps, after his visit to the Arsenal, the visitor will feel most interest in that to Schalch, a Swiss, who died in 1776, at the advanced age of ninety years, sixty of which he passed as superintendent of the foundry there. Indeed, it was to him chiefly that the establishment owed its origin, for he was the cause of its removal from Moorfields, and the improvements made in conducting the operations.

From Woolwich we have the choice of four speedy modes of transit to town:—1st, by steamer direct to London Bridge and Westminster; 2nd, by steam ferry across to Blackwall, and so on by railway to Fenchurch-street; 3rd, by a similar conveyance to the new station of the Eastern Counties Railway, on the Essex bank of the river, which brings us to Shoreditch; and 4th, by the North Kent line. The excursionist may consult his own convenience for preference of choice. A delightful walk may be found over *Shooter's Hill* to *Elsham*, then by *Danson's Park* and *Welling.*

PLUMSTEAD Station.

Resuming our seat in the train, we proceed, skirting *Plumstead* marshes, the ordnance trial ground, to

ABBEY WOOD.

Distance from station, 1 mile.

A telegraph station.

OMNIBUSES to and from Bexley Heath.

MONEY ORDER OFFICE at Woolwich.

BELVEDERE station.

ERITH.

Distance from station, 1 mile. A telegraph station

OMNIBUSES to and from the trains; also to North Cray, Bexley, and Crayford.

FAIR.—Whit Monday.

MONEY ORDER OFFICE at Dartford.

ERITH presents its picturesque church and wooded uplands to the right, and is a tempting village to loiter in when opportunity serves. A fine pier, at which the boats of the "Diamond" Company call, has been constructed for the accommodation of those who embark or disembark here, and an "Arboretum," with extensive pleasure grounds, has been recently opened to attract visitors. Erith Church is a charming study for either artist or antiquary. The ivy which clings about the structure, and the masses of foliage that rise beyond, give it a very striking aspect. The structure consists of a nave and chancel, with a low tower and spire, and evidently has a venerable length of years, for besides the date of some of its monuments going back as far as the year 1420, it has been identified as the spot where King John and the Barons drew up their treaty of peace. In the south chapel is an alabaster tomb, much mutilated, to the memory of Elizabeth, Countess of Shrewsbury, and her daughter Anne, Countess of Pembroke, who both died in the reign of Elizabeth. Adjacent are some fine brasses in good preservation, though the inscriptions attached to them have been quite obliterated. They all belong to the Waldens, members of the same family. *Belvidere*, the seat of Lord Saye and Sele, is an elegant mansion, in a very romantic situation, commanding extensive views over the country round. It was rebuilt towards the close of the last century, and contains some fine apartments of true aristocratic splendour. From Northumberland Heath, a spacious tract of fertile ground in this parish, the metropolitan markets are largely supplied with Kentish cherries, and in the neighbourhood some handsome houses and villas have been lately erected.

DARTFORD.

POPULATION, 5,763.

Distance from station, 1 mile.

A telegraph station.

HOTEL.—Bull.

OMNIBUSES to and from the trains; also to Fremingham, *via* Sutton, twice daily.

FAIR.—August 2nd.

MONEY ORDER OFFICE.

BANKERS.—Hills, Mc.Rea, and Co.

DARTFORD, built in a valley between two hills, derives its name from its situation on a ford of the River Darent. The insurrection of Wat Tyler originated in this town, and it has also been the scene of many other important events, the record of which would excite but little interest in the passing railway traveller. The trade is, however, considerable. It exports agricultural produce, and there are important gunpowder mills, corn and paper mills, establishments for calico and silk printing, and iron foundries in the neighbourhood. It has a large market, held on Saturdays. A large embattled gateway, and a stone wall enclosing 12 acres, are be seen, the sole remains of its great nunnery, founded by Edward III. in 1371.

GREENHITHE.

Distance from station, 1 mile.

A telegraph station.

MONEY ORDER OFFICE at Gravesend.

Greenhithe Pier, 20 miles from London. *Ingress Abbey*, in the Gothic style, built with the stones of old London Bridge. The chalk-pits behind are pleasing.

Gray's Pier, where Fidler's Reach and Northfleet Hope unite.

NORTHFLEET.

Distance from station, ¼ mile.

A telegraph station.

INN.—The Leather Bottle

On the London side of Northfleet, on the left or our line may be seen the beautiful asylum for decayed gentlemen, founded by the philanthropic brewer, Mr. Huggins.

NORTHFLEET has an ancient church, one of the largest in Kent, containing several monuments of interesting antiquity, among which will be found one to Dr. Brown, physician to Charles II., and some curious brasses of the fourteenth century. The extensive ex avations about here, forming a sort of miniature Switzerland, not only give the scenery a wild and romantic aspect, but furnish valuable materials for the potteries.

Rosherville.—Hotel: the Rosherville Hotel, first class, family and commercial. Rosherville, though a suburb of Gravesend, belongs to the parish of Northfleet, and its neat pier is soon seen to the right, forming an elegant communication with that extensive range of buildings erected a few years since on the estate of the late Jeremiah Rosher. The Rosherville Gardens are open daily to the public, at the moderate admission fee of sixpence, and present a combination of attractions, produced by the united agency of nature and art, that leave them almost without a rival. It is absolutely astonishing to see what a fairy-land has been here created out of a chalk-pit. There are gala nights throughout the summer, when fireworks, music, and illuminations are added to the other enchantments of the spot. The Clifton Baths, on what is called "The Parade," are commodiously fitted up for cold, shower, warm, and vapour bathing, and seem to have been built in grotesque mimicry of the Pavilion at Brighton.

GRAVESEND.

POPULATION, 16,633.

Telegraph station, No. 45, The Terrace.

HOTELS.—The New Inn; the Terrace Hotel; the Clarendon.

OMNIBUSES at the station; also to Ightham (*via* Wrotham), Fairseat, and Meopham, once daliy.

STEAM PACKETS to London, several times a day; to Sheerness and Southend, daily, during the summer; to Tilbury, daily, every hour.

MARKET DAYS.—Wednesday and Saturday.

FAIRS.—May 4th and October 24th.

BANKERS.—London and County Bank.

GRAVESEND is one of the most pleasantly situated, and most easily attained, of all the places thronged upon the margin of the Thames. It is, moreover, a capital starting point for a series of excursions through the finest parts of Kent, and has, besides, in its own immediate neighbourhood, some tempting allurements to the summer excursionist in the way of attractive scenery and venerable buildings. The Terrace Gardens, on each side the entrance to the pier, are really very creditably and tastefully laid out, and as a day-admission-ticket can be had for twopence, expense is no obstacle to the public frequenting them. Directly you traverse the streets of Gravesend you see at a glance for what the town is famous. Shrimps and water-cresses tempt the visitor in every possible variety of supply, and places where both are obtainable, with "Tea at 9d. a-head," are in wonderful numerical strength. Taverns and tea gardens are abundant, and most of them have mazes, archery grounds, and "gipsy tents" attached. There is an excellent market, held every Wednesday and Saturday; a Town Hall, built in 1836; a Literary Institution, with a Library, Billiard-rooms and Assembly Rooms inclusive, built in 1842; churches and chapels in abundance; numerous libraries and bazaars; water-works on the summit of Windmill Hill; baths by the river, and a commodious Custom House near the Terrace Gardens. WindmillHill is, however, the magnet of the multitude, and is crowned by an excellent tavern, called "The Belle Vue," to the proprietor of which belongs the old windmill—the first erected in England, and as old in its foundation as the days of Edward III. Here refreshments are provided on the most liberal scale, and an admirable Camera, together with some pleasure-grounds, and a labyrinth of ingenious construction, offer the best and most captivating allurements to visitors. The moderate outlay of one penny entitles the visitor to a telescopic view from the gallery, where the horizon forms the only limit to the vision. There is, on a fine day, a magnificent prospect of the river Thames, as it winds towards the Nore, a distinct survey of the counties of Kent and Essex, and even glimpses of the more distant ones of Surrey and Sussex, including the most noted eminences in each. The shipping at the Nore can be clearly distinguished, although thirty miles distant; Southend in Essex, Hadleigh Castle, the village church of Leigh, a place renowned for its shrimp and oyster fisheries, the isles of Sheppey, Grain, and Calvey are all visible to the east; north and north-west are the Laindon Hills on the opposite shore, farther westward Highgate and Hampstead Hills, with a portion of Epping Forest; south-west, Shooter's Hill, with its commemorative castle of Severndroog, appears rising from a woody undulation; Knockholt Beeches, verging on the very borders of Sussex; and nearer to the hill the sequestered villages of Swanscombe—where Sweyn, the Danish king, encamped, and the "Men of Kent" ably resisted William the Conqueror—Springhead, of water-cress celebrity, Southfleet, and Northfleet. Looking in a more southerly direction, and beyond the fertile parishes of Wrotham, Ifield, Singlewell, and Meopham, the extensive plantations and sylvan glades of Cobham Park rise on the left, surrounding the ancient hall of the old Lords of Cobham, and now the property of the Earl of Darnley; whilst immediately beneath the eye of the spectator ranges over the unbroken line of picturesque buildings that comprise Rosherville, Gravesend, and Milton, with (on the opposite coast) Tilbury Fort and its extensive moat, the Ferry-house, the villages of the East and West Tilbury, Stanford-le-Hope, Horndon, Shadwell, East and West Thurrock, and a castellated mansion called Belmont. The fertile valley, seen from this height, looks like a Brobdignag estate on a Lilliputian scale; the smoke seems to stand still in the air, the reapers in the field look like Dutch-clock automata, whilst the cattle that here and there dot the plain appear as if some holiday Miss had emptied out the contents of Noah's Ark. The hedges shrink to rows of boxwood, and the gigantic oaks dwindle to diminutive shrubs. But of all the places round, none should neglect an excursion to COBHAM, four miles distant, where, in the old wood and hall, a day's enjoyment can be most fully insured. There are several vehicles always ready to be hired, that will take the visitor at a reasonable rate by the road; but as those who can appreciate a delightful walk will not find the distance too fatiguing, we shall proceed to indicate the route for the pedestrian. The Hall and Picture Gallery are open to the public every Friday; admission is by tickets, price one shilling each, supplied at Caddel's Library, and the proceeds thus resulting are applied to the school and other free institutions of the neighbourhood.

Taking the footpath at the back of Windmill Hill, the pedestrian will find it traversing a picturesque country, now crossing the sweeping undulation of a corn field, and anon skirting a shaded copse, with bluebells and primroses starting up in prodigal luxuriance through the tangled underwood. We next pass through a hop plantation, and in summer, when the bine has sprung up to the top of the poles, and the shoots have thrust themselves off to the next, and so joined in a leafy communion of luxuriant vegetation, the scene becomes truly Arcadian, and an excellent substitute for the vineyards of the south. Leaving the little village of Singlewell to the right, we have a finger-post to guide us, and a few minutes after reach the outskirts of this sequestered village. The first object to which the visitor will naturally direct his attention is the old church, occupying rising ground in nearly the centre of the parish, and having on the southern side an extensive view. The antiquarian may here enjoy a great treat in inspecting the ancient monuments to be found in the interior, as there are several brasses of the Cobham family, successive generations of which, from the year 1354, have lived and died in the parish. On an altar-monument, in the middle of the chancel, are two full length effigies, with several children around them in a kneeling position. This was erected to the memory of George Lord Cobham, who had been the governor of Calais in the reign of Elizabeth, and who died in 1558. On the tomb of Maud de Cobham is a curious sculptured figure of a dog, and one similar will be found in the chancel on the tomb of Joan, wife of Reginald Braybroke. They are worthy notice, as exemplifying the attachment felt towards two faithful canine adherents to the fortunes of the family. Outside, on the southern wall, there are some elegant tablets, too, of the Darnley family. In 1714, the Hall and estate came by marriage into the possession of an Irish family of the name of Bligh, one of whom, in 1725, was created Earl of Darnley, and the seat of the Earls of Darnley it has continued to be ever since. The Hall is a massive and stately structure, consisting of two wings and a noble centre, the work of Inigo Jones. The oldest portions are those at the two extremities, flanked with octagonal towers. The Picture Gallery, having a choice collection of paintings by the old masters, and the unique gilt hall, form the most prominent features of attraction in the interior, but the apartments besides are elegantly furnished, and the quadrangle and old brick passages of the outbuildings wear about them an aspect of unmistakeable antiquity. On the south side, leading up to the principal entrance, is a noble lime tree avenue, extending upwards of 3,000 feet in length. In the park, which is nearly seven miles round, there are some noble oak and chesnut trees, many of them measuring twenty feet and upwards in circumference. It has also the reputation of producing venison of superior flavour, derived from the peculiar excellence of the herbage, and it was on this fare probably that both Queen Elizabeth and Charles II. were regaled when they visited Cobham; for the former, according to Styrpe, was welcomed with a "delectable banquet and great cheer." In a romantic spot, towards the south-east end of the park, on an eminence called "William's Hill," there is a spacious mausoleum, erected in 1783, by the present Lord Darnley's grandfather. It is built of Portland stone, in an octagonal form, after the Doric order, and cost £9,000, but never having been consecrated, it has not been devoted to the purpose for which it was intended.

Cobham Wood is a glorious region for the rambler, and the footpath to Rochester, through the very heart of its sylvan solitudes, a delightful track to follow. The pedestrian can also return, through the wood, Upper Shorne, and Gad's Hill where Prince Hal and his eleven men in buckram robbed Jack Falstaff, to Gravesend by way of Chalk. Either way a day's enjoyment is complete.

The first station from Gravesend is

HIGHAM.

Gad's Hill, (1 mile); *Cliffe*, (3 miles); *Cowling*, with its castle, (3¼ mile)—an embattled gateway forming a picturesque object.

From Higham we pass through a tunnel, 1¼ mile long, under Higham Down, a chalky ridge. Emerging from which we arrive at

STROOD.

A telegraph station.
HOTEL.—Old George.
STEAM BOATS to Sheerness daily.

A bridge over the Medway, replacing the old bridge built in the reign of Rufus, recently demolished, joins this town with

ROCHESTER.

Distance from station, ½ mile.

Telegraph station at Strood, ½ mile.

HOTELS.—Victoria and Bull Inns; Crown.

STEAM BOATS to and from Sheerness, twice daily.

SAILING VESSELS (hoys) to and from London, twice weekly.

MARKET DAYS.—Friday and Saturday; 4th Tuesday in each month for cattle; every Tuesday for corn.

FAIRS.—May 15th, 19th; September, each three days. August 26th, 27th, and 28th.

MONEY ORDER OFFICE.

BANKERS.—Branch of London and County; Day and Nicholson.

At Rochester, which has a population of 14,938, and returns two members, some projecting gable houses are to be seen in the High Street, with an old town-hall, built 1687; Sir C. Shovel's clock-house; Watt's alms-house for poor travellers, "not being rogues or proctors;" Henry VIII.'s grammar school; and St. Nicholas Church, built 1421.

It is an ancient borough town in the county of Kent, having been a British town before the Roman invasion, and stands in a rich vale on the banks of the Medway, on an angle of land formed by that river. On the east it is connected by a continued range of buildings with the town of Chatham, and on the west by the village of Strood. The three places form almost a continuous line of houses, and are often collectively called the "Three Towns."

The **Cathedral** has a half-ruinous look outside, but contains some excellent Norman work, especially the west door and the nave, lately restored by Cottingham; the pinnacled tower, 186 feet high, is of later date. Total length, 306 feet, with a double transept—one 122 feet, the other 90 feet long. With the exception of the west front and the great tower, the exterior of the cathedral is destitute of ornament; its plain massive walls presenting a remarkable contrast to the highly decorated and varied appearance of its great rival at Canterbury. There are effigies of bishops, including Gundulph, and the founder of Merton College, Oxford; service at 10½ a.m. and 3¼ p.m. on week days. Close at hand are remains of a chapter-house, cloister, &c.

The **Castle of Rochester,** of more remote origin than the cathedral itself, attracts the notice of the traveller by its venerable and majestic appearance—magnificent even in ruins. It stands on a rock over the river, and is 70 feet square and 102 feet high, in four stories, with turrets at the corners, like the Tower of London, of which Bishop Gundulph was also the founder. Much civility is shown to visitors. A gallery runs all round the keep, and seats are placed at intervals here and there in the different stories, to afford views of the splendid prospects that keep breaking upon the sight in all directions with increased extent and grandeur as you wind round and round to the top, whence the whole panorama is exposed to view without interruption; admission, daily (Sundays excepted), 3d. each. The Medway, at high water, here appears a fine broad stream between green sloping banks.

An amphitheatre of hills encircles the beautiful landscape. The Medway below serpentines round the castle, and then the cathedral and the bridge, all combining to render the whole a complete picturesque panorama.

Rochester now consists principally of one long street, called High Street, which crosses it from east to west, terminating on the river a little below the new iron bridge.

In the vicinity are *Upnor Castle*, a fort built by Queen Elizabeth to guard the town (1½ mile); *Cobham Park and Hall*, (3 miles); *Gad's Hill*, (2½ miles); and *Blue Bell Down* on the Maidstone road, a walk over which, crossing over Aylesford Bridge, and back by the banks of the river, will be found interesting and alluring, for its varied prospects.

DISTANCES OF PLACES FROM THE CITY.

	Miles.		Miles.
Bairborough	3	Hooness Fort	4
Bridge Wood	2	Lower Halling	4
Broad Ditch	3	Luddesdown	4
Broad Street	3	Luton	3
Cliffe	5	Moor Street	6
Cobham	4	Mortimer Farra	3
Cole Harbour	5	Mulling Wood	5
Cowling	4	New Hythe	6
Crowpect	4	Park Woods	5
Cuxton	2	Rainham Park	4
Cupson	4	Ranscombe	1
Gillingham Fort	2	Red Wood	4
Higham Upper	3	Snodland	5
Hoo	3	Tweedale	4

CHATHAM.

Distance from station, 2 miles.

A telegraph station.

HOTELS.—The Sun; the Mitre.

STEAM BOATS to and from Sheerness, twice daily.

MARKET DAY.—Saturday.

FAIRS.—May 15th, Sept. 19th (each for 3 days).

MONEY ORDER OFFICE.

BANKERS.—London and Cou ty Bank; Day and Nicholson.

A parliamentary borough, returning one member, but best known for its naval dockyard, on a bend of the Medway, 19 miles from the Nore, and about 2 miles from the Strood terminus of the North Kent Railway. Omnibuses run through Rochester to meet every train, and the Sheerness steamer touches here. Population, 28,424, including 7,000 or 8,000 dockyard-men and soldiers. Depôts of the marines, of several regiments of the line, and East India service, are stationed at Chatham. It was a fishing village in Saxon times. In the disgraceful reign of Charles II., the Dutch Admiral De Ruyter came up so far as to burn the ships and carry off the Royal Charles.

After passing through a tunnel of 1¼ mile, under Higham Down, a chalk ridge is seen stretching out into the river opposite Chatham. Rochester and Chatham form one straggling dirty town, hemmed in by chalk downs, which, on the Chatham side, rise up rather steeply to a very considerable height. There are the "Lines," which are strengthened by Fort Pitt, Fort Clarence, and other military works. They should be ascended for the extensive view of the towns, the Medway and Thames, they offer, &c. Chatham is here seen stuck like a wedge in a gap of the downs.

The *Dockyard* (to be seen by application at the gate) was commenced by Queen Elizabeth, following the wise policy of her father, and is about a mile long. It contains six building slips, wet and dry docks, *Rope House*, 1,140 feet long, blacksmiths' shops, steam saw-mills, oar and *block machinery* by Brunel, a duplicate of that at Portsmouth, copper sheathing and paint mills, pattern room, arsenal, &c. Several ships in ordinary are moored in the river. A ship-gun battery and school are attached to the

Marine Barracks.—There are barracks also for the Royal Engineers and Sappers and Miners, with a school for young officers and recruits, where practical lectures are given upon every thing relating to the art of war. Good libraries for both services, and naval and military hospitals. Here Drake and Hawkins founded the *Chatham Chest*, or fund for the benefit of seamen. In the parish church (which replaces one mentioned in Domesday Book), is the monument to *Stephen Burroughs*, the first Englishman who, with Willoughby, sailed by the north-east passage to Russia.

Sheerness, at the Medway's mouth, is another naval dockyard, in a dull, flat part of the Isle of Sheppey, near the Nore. Fossils are abundant in this island. Sailors say that "at Plymouth it always rains, at Portsmouth it always blows, but at *Sheerness* it always rains and blows," which may give an idea of the delightful climate prevailing here.

POPULATION, 8,549.

DISTANCES OF PLACES FROM THE TOWN.

	Miles.		Miles.
Allhallows	7½	Lidgen	4
Bellancle	4	Low Bell	4½
Borden	8	Lower Halling	4
Burham	4½	Lyding Chapel	4
Chitney Marsh	7½	Mote	7½
Cowling Street	4½	North Street	4
Delee Upper	1½	Perry Hill	4
Delee Lower	1½	Rainham	4
Gillingham	2	Red Wood	4½
High Halston	4½	Suttenden Farm	2½
Horsted	2	Sylam	2½
Key Street	7½	Tweedale	2½

LONDON, CHATHAM, AND DOVER.

Beckenham to Chatham and Dover.

The trains of this company run from Victoria, the West End terminus of the London and Brighton Railway, passing along the Crystal Palace line, to Beckenham. The first station arrived at is SHORTLANDS, and three quarters of a mile further

BROMLEY.

POPULATION, 4,500.

Principally composed of one long street; market house, supported on pillars. Dr. Johnson's wife and Hawkesworth, the author of the "Adventurer," lie buried here.

BICKLEY and ST. MARY'S CRAY stations.

FARNINGHAM.—Lullingstone and Egnesford Castles in the neighbourhood.

MEOPHAM and SOLE STREET are then passed; and at a distance of six miles beyond, the arrival of the train is announced at STROOD (the North Kent junction), which, together with ROCHESTER and CHATHAM, have just before been described.

NEW BROMPTON station.

RAINHAM,

One of the villages on the Old Roman road, Watling Street, passing which we arrive at the station at

SITTINGBOURNE,

Near to which is the old town of *Milton*, situated on a creek or arm of the Swale, in which the celebrated "Milton Natives" are dredged. The town was a demesne of the Saxon kings. In their struggle with king Alfred, the Danes had a camp here, the remains of which, popularly called "Castle Rough," yet exist. In the centre of the town there is an ancient court house. The church is large and handsome, with an embattled tower, chiefly in the decorated English style.

MARKET DAY.—Saturday.

Much corn is shipped here.

SITTINGBOURNE & SHEERNESS.

A branch 7 miles long turns off to the left at this place, running direct across the western extremity of the Isle of Sheppy, passing through QUEENBOROUGH, to

SHEERNESS, described above, and at page 15.

Chatham and Dover continued.

Continuing our route we pass the station of

TEYNHAM,

In the vicinity of which are *Rodmersham Lodge* (2 miles); *Teynham Lodge* (2½ miles); *Norton Court* (2 miles); and arrive at

FAVERSHAM.

MARKET DAYS.—Wednesday and Friday.

FAIRS.—October 11, 12, 13.

This town is situated on a small stream running into the East Swale, which is navigable for vessels of 150 tons. It was a place of much note before the time of Stephen, who, however, built and endowed an abbey here for Cluniac monks, and in which himself, his queen, and his son Eustace were buried. At the dissolution, Stephen's remains were thrown into the river, for the sake of the leaden coffin in which they were contained. Some portions of the outer walls still exist. The church is cruciform, and built of flint, in the decorated style; the tower and spire (a copy of that of St. Dunstan's in the East, at London), are of modern date. The Market House was erected in 1594. There is a well-endowed Grammar School. Here James II. was held prisoner on his attempt to escape from England. There are some inports and a considerable coasting trade, which necessitates the establishment of a Custom House. Gunpowder is a branch of manufacture.

Near the town is *Davington*, where there was a nunnery founded by *Fulke de Newnham*, in 1153, the sister's house and the church still remaining. Near *Ospringe* (1 mile) is Judd's Hill, the Roman *Durolevum*, close to which is *Tindal House*; *Ospringe House* (1 mile); *Monte Video House* (1 mile); *Lees Court* (3 miles) the seat of Lord Sondes; *Belmont* (3 miles), Lord Harris; *Chilham Castle* (4 miles); *Nash Court* (3¼ miles); and *Norton Court* (2 miles).

Our progress along the main line is again interrupted by a short branch to WHITSTABLE, see page 41.

Resuming our journey along the main line, a distance of 6½ miles beyond the station of SELLING brings us to the present terminus of the line at

CANTERBURY.—For description see page 40. The remaining portion of this route to Dover, still in progress, is travelled by omnibus, which runs in connection with most of the trains to and from London.

South Eastern continued.

MAIDSTONE BRANCH.

Strood to Maidstone.

On leaving Strood, the line, skirting the banks of the swift Medway, soon brings us to

CUXTON, or CUCKSTONE.

This place contains a population of 384, who are engaged in the hop trade, beautiful crops of which are yearly obtained from this neighbourhood. The old church is an antique edifice, and contains some pews as old as the time of the Reformation. In the vicinity are the villages of Luddesdown, the church of which contains a tomb to the old lords of the manor, the Montacutes; Meopham, with its ancient church, rebuilt in 1333 by Archbishop Meopham, a native; and *Meopham Bank*, the pretty seat of W. N. Smith, Esq., and *Wouldham.* Proceeding through a magnificent hop country we arrive at

SNODLAND.

In the vicinity are *Burham* and *Byrling*, in the church of which are buried many of the Sayes and Nevilles, to whom there are brasses. The farm called Cornfort and Birling Place, with its gate and ruins, were their seats. On the banks of the Medway near, are the Episcopal ruins of *Halling.*

Soon after leaving Snodland the train crosses the Medway, and we arrive at

AYLESFORD.

The ancient *Aegelesford*, has a population of 1,487, employed in the hop gardens. Here the Saxons under Hengist and Horsa were defeated by the Britons under Vortimer, A.D. 455, but Catigern, his brother was killed, and to whose memory is said to have been erected the remarkable cromlech, popularly called *Kit's Coty House*, still to be seen one mile N.E. from the village. In the year 1016 the Danes were pursued hither by Edmund Ironside. There is an excellent Free Grammar School. The Church, beautifully situated on an eminence, is an ancient foundation, and contains brasses of the Colepeppers, Rycants, and Sedleys (the Poet of Charles the Second was of this family, and resided here). Close to the Medway to the west are the remains of the Carmelite Friary, founded by Lord Grey of Codnor, A.D. 1240, made habitable by restorations and additions at various times, and now the seat of the Earl of Aylesford. The celebrated traveller, Rycant, was born here, 1628. In the vicinity are *Boxley Abbey* (1¾ miles) Lady Finch, and *West Malling* (3 miles) with the remains of its Benedictine Nunnery, a beautiful specimen of Norman architecture. At St. Leonard's, a tower 71 feet high, the remains of its ancient chapel. *Bradbourne House* (2 miles). *Allington* (2 miles), with its old castle, which was the seat of Sir Thomas Wyatt, the scholar of Henry Eighth's day, and his son, who suffered for treason against Queen Mary. *Preston Hall* (1 mile).

MAIDSTONE, see page 37.

SOUTH EASTERN MAIN LINE.

This has been called the "Pleasure Line;" and certainly the beauty and extent of the country traversed by its trains justly entitle it to that distinguishing appellation. It is not only the great medium of daily communication between London and Paris, or England and the Continent, but its iron roads and branches intersect the beautiful county of Kent in all directions, affording the inhabitants of the great metropolis facilities of visiting the numerous watering places on its coast, and enabling them to become acquainted with its picturesque scenery, cities, and baronial halls, and the astonishing fertility of its soil.

London to Reigate.

No sooner is the train in motion than we escape from the confinement of the station and emerge into purer air—although the first mile we pass over no less than a dozen streets, thronged with a restless, busy population, who inhabit the dense neighbourhood of Horsleydown and Bermondsey.

The Greenwich Railway diverges to the east, and to the west is the branch to the Bricklayers' Arms, built upon arches, and extending by the side of the Surrey Canal over a long tract of market-garden ground.

With a distant glimpse of the wood-crowned heights of Greenwich, and a near view of a large red brick building—the Royal Naval school—we arrive at the great locomotive station of the Brighton and Dover Companies; the Nunhead Cemetery, about a mile to the right. A range of undulating eminences beyond Peckham and Dulwich rapidly pass in view, and a few miles further on, almost before the eye can take in the range of picturesque suburban scenery, we reach New Cross—see page 50.

From New Cross the train diverges from the North Kent line, and proceeds through a deep cutting that conceals all view of the country, to the Dartmouth Arms Station at Forest Hill, an exceedingly pretty spot, which is becoming a favourite residence of an increasing number of families from the metropolis. A mile beyond this is the Sydenham Station, *in the midst of very lovely scenery*, and in view of the fairy-like scene of the *Crystal Palace*, with its marvellous transepts, and wings, and galleries, situated in the most exquisite and park-like grounds—ornamented with a noble terrace, commanding one of the finest views in England, and embellished with waterfalls, cascades, and splendid fountains—all on such a vast and magnificent scale as to suggest the idea of its being the Palace of the Celestial Empire of China, rather than that of the people of England—by whom it ought to be liberally supported. For further description of the Crystal Palace, see London and Brighton route, page 50. At a short distance beyond Sydenham the line leaves the border of Kent and diverges more into the county of Surrey. The Anerley Station, although in a pretty situation, deserves no particular mention, in comparison with the celebrated one of Norwood—see page 5.

A short distance beyond Caterham Junction the railway enters the celebrated Merstham Tunnel, which is said to have cost £112,000.

Emerging thence the train reaches the village of

MERSTHAM.

Distance from station, ¼ mile.

A telegraph station.

Mails.—One arrival and departure, daily, between London and Merstham.

Money Order Office at Reigate.

Merstham is situated to the right of the line—formerly famous for its apple orchards. There are valuable stone quarries in the vicinity. The old church on the hill contains some curious monuments and tombs. The seat of Sir W. G. H. Joliffe, Bart., M.P., is a noble looking mansion.

After this the line enters the Great Junction Station at

REIGATE (Red Hill.)

A telegraph station.

Hotel.—Railway Hotel.

Money Order Office at Reigate.

This is one of the most important junctions of the Kent and Sussex Railways.

The *London and Brighton Railway* diverges from this station southward, through Sussex, see page 53.

The Reigate and Reading Branch goes to the west, through the vale of Dorking to Guildford and Reading, communicating thence to any part of the kingdom—see below.

On alighting at this station the traveller will find himself in the midst of the celebrated valley of Holmesdale, surrounded on all sides by elevated hills. To the north appears the great chalk range, bearing a rugged and abrupt front, broken into precipitous cliffs, or crowned with undulating heights. To the south is seen the sand-stone ridge, with the celebrated mount of coloured stone, known as the "Red Hill."

REIGATE TOWN.

Population, 4,927.

Distance from station, ½ mile.

A telegraph station.

Hotels.—White Hart, and Swan.

Post Horses, Flys, &c., at the station and hotels

Market Days.—Tuesdays.

Fairs.—Whit-Monday and December 9th.

Money Order Office

Bankers—London and County Joint Stock Banking Company.

Reigate, situated near the River Mole, in the valley of Holmesdale, at the foot of the ridge of chalk hills which traverse the country from east to west, consists of a main street of well-built houses, crossed at the eastern end by the Old Brighton Road, which, for upwards of a mile out of town, is adorned by the detached residences of the gentry. The houses of the lower classes present models of architecture, and are beautifully decorated with imbricated tiles of various patterns, a style of cottage ornament characteristic of this part of the country. The church stands on a gentle eminence east of the town, and is a spacious structure of almost every period of Gothic architecture, some parts of which are extremely beautiful. From the summit of Park Hill an extensive view is obtained of the wealds of Surrey and Sussex; and that of Reigate, with the priory and its park, is of singular beauty. On the north side of the town, in the principal street, was situated the castle, some few traces of which are yet visible. It was one of the principal seats of the powerful Earls of Warwick and Surrey; and here the insurgent barons are reported to have held frequent meetings, preceding the celebrated Congress of Runnymede. There is a long passage under the castle mound leading into a vaulted room, called the Baron's Cave, which is said to have been used by the barons as a hiding-place for arms. The church has a few curious and ancient tombs.

Distances of Places from the Station.

	Miles.		Miles.
Brickland	2	Leatherhead	6
Buckland	1¾	Leigh	3
Calley Farm	0¾	Littleton Farm	1
Chalmead Farm	2	Mason Bridge East	3
Cophill Farm	4	Mead House	1
Couler's Hole	1	Newdigate	7
Dean's Farm	7	Nork House	5
Ewood Mill	5	Norwood Place	4
Gadbrook Common	3	Parkfall Place	4
Galton Park	1	Park House	4¾
Hamon's Copse	5	Red Hill Farm	1
Hartswood	1½	Reigate Mills	1
Hatch Farm	1	Reigate Park	0¾
Headley	4	Rice Bridge	2
Henfold Farm	4	Upper Galton	2
Hill House	4	Walton	3½
Kingswood Garden	3¾	Walton Park	2
Kinnersley House	3		

READING, GUILDFORD, AND REIGATE BRANCH.

Reigate to Reading.

This line connects the county towns of Berkshire and Surrey (Reading and Guildford), and extends from the latter across the garden of Surrey to Reigate; at the same time communicating with four trunk lines—the Great Western, the South Western, the Brighton, and the South Eastern Railway. To the pleasure tourist we scarcely know any presenting so many picturesque attractions. Its route lies from Reading along the South Eastern line, across Berkshire, by Wokingham and Sandhurst, entering Surrey by Tinley; then crossing the South Western line, onward with a branch to Farnham; at the base of Hog's Back to Guildford; next by a branch to Godalming, and continuing at the foot of the celebrated range of chalk hills past Dorking and Reigate to Red Hill. We have alluded to the picturesqueness of the Surrey portion, which will be new ground to many a tourist; though it is perhaps, the most beautiful scenery of its class in England. Its landscapes present a rich succession of "morceaux" for the painter in its picturesque uplands, woodland, dells, verdant vallies, rocky hills and undulating parks and heaths, all lying within the eye of the traveller along this line. Betchworth Park is among the most beautiful specimens of this scenery between Reigate and Dorking, although the part of the chalk hills seen from that point is greatly exceeded by the bolder sublimity of Box Hill, the venerable giant of the chain, with its luxuriant clothing of patronymic evergreen.

As a pleasure line, this portion is very popular, passing as it does through an exceedingly fine country, with the scenery of which excursion trains have already made thousands of visitors familiar.

BETCHWORTH.

Within a short distance, situated most beautifully in a romantic park washed by the "Sullen Mole," are the ruins of *Betchworth Castle.*

They are most picturesque, and the grey walls, contrasting with the rich green of the ivy creeping over a great part of them, stand out finely against the deep blue sky.

Proceeding on our way, with the lofty down on our right, we pass over the Mole by a viaduct 50 feet high, and then through Box Tunnel to the station at

BOX HILL.

Tourists alight at this station for the hill with its celebrated prospects. It took its name from the Box trees planted thereon in the reign of Charles I. and is now a resort for pic-nic parties.

This is the nearest station likewise for *Mickleham*, a charming village, 2¼ miles distant.

Hotels.—Running Horse, Fox and Hounds.

Norbury Park (2½ miles), H. P. Spirling, Esq. A beautiful seat surrounded by fine plantations. One mile beyond this is the town of *Leatherhead*, see page 71.

DORKING,

Situated on the north-western side of the town.

Population, 3,490.

Distance from the station, ½ mile.

A telegraph station.

Hotels.—Red Lion, and White Horse.

Omnibuses to and from the station; to Epsom station several times daily; to Brighton and London thrice weekly.

Market Day.—Thursday.

Fair.—The day before Holy Thursday.

Money Order Office.

Bankers. — London and County Joint Stock Banking Company.

Dorking is situated in a valley near the river Mole, nearly surrounded with hills, and commands some of the finest views in the kingdom. This town is of considerable antiquity, and so conveniently situated that it carries on a large trade in flour and corn, and employs several mills on the Mole. The church is a fine old edifice and contains several handsome monuments. It is celebrated for its poultry, particularly for a five-toed breed, called Dorkings, supposed to have been introduced by the Romans. It is a favourite summer resort of invalids and lovers of rural scenery, and it would be difficult to name any place better calculated for both classes, as the salubrity of the air and the beauty of the surrounding country cannot be surpassed or equalled within so short a distance of the metropolis. There are several very beautiful country-seats, villas, and mansions around the town, too numerous, however, to be enumerated in our pages.

Distances of Places from the Station.

	Miles.		Miles.
Abinger Hall	3	Livesome Bridge	2½
Anstie Bury	4½	Merridone	1½
Ashstead	8	Mickleham	3
Bay Hill	1½	Norbury Park	3
Bench	2	Ockley	7
Bookham	2	Park Farm	1½
Boxhill	2	Parkpale	2½
Brickham Common	2½	Pexham	1½
Broadmoor	2	Pitbrook Bridge	1¼
Burford Grove	2	Polesden	3
Capet	7	Ridland	1½
Chardhurst	2	Rookery	1½
Cold Harbour	4½	Scammels	2½
Collickmoor	2	Shrub Hill	2
Combe	1¾	Store Bridge	2
Deepdene	3	Stubbs	2
Denhies	2	Stumble Hole	2
Effingham	4	Tanhurst near Leith Hill	5
Folly	1½	Upper Laylands	2½
Freeshurst	2	Wescott	2½
Holloway	1½	Wescott Parsonage	1½
Holmbury Hill	1½	Wotten	2
Holmwood Common	2½		
Leith Hill	5		

The line, still skirting the Downs, soon brings us to the station of

GOMSHALL and SHEIRE.

A telegraph station.

Sheire was the residence of Bray, the antiquarian, who edited Evelyn's Memoirs. In the immediate vicinity is *Abinger Hall* (2 miles), the seat of Lord Abinger. *Netley Place* (1½ mile). *Albury Park* (1½ mile), H. Drummond Esq., M.P. Near which is *Newland's Corner*, from which a most extensive prospect may be obtained.

East Horsley (3 miles).

Ewhurst (5 miles).

Distances of Places from the Station.

	Miles.		Miles.
Abinger	2¼	Coleckmore Farm	4¼
Albany Park	0½	Coophurst Farm	4¼
Albury	1	Cotte's House	2
Burying Place	3	Cotterell	2
Clandon Park	3	Crauley	5¼
Cold Harbour	5	Denbigh House	5
Cold Kitchen	2	Dilton	3

Distances Continued.

	Miles.		Miles.
Dorking	6	Lockhurst Hatch	3
Effingham	5	Mayor House	2½
Falvers	3	Meroe	3
Farley Green	5	Netley Abbey	1½
Forest Green	5	Norrel's Green	4¼
Gomshall	0½	Park House	5
Goose Green	5	Peaslake Bottom	3
Giludford	6	Pitt House	2¾
Hatch and Hatchland Place	3	Ponds and Pursers	3
Hazel Hall	3	Ridge Bridge	4¼
Holmbury	2½	Ridland Farm	5
Hound House	3	South Brook	2
Hurbwood Common	5	Stonebury Hill	3
Kingswood	1	Sutton Place	2
Lawbrook	2	Tower Hill	0¾
Lee	2	Wood House	2¾
		Wooton	3

CHILWORTH.

Distance from station, 1 mile.

A telegraph station.

MAILS.—One arrival and departure, daily, between London and Chilworth.

MONEY ORDER OFFICE at Guildford.

On an eminence in the vicinity, and towards the south, is St. Martha's ancient chapel. *Chilworth Manor* is the property of Godwin Austin, Esq.

About two miles further is

SHALFORD.

Distance from station, ½ mile.

A telegraph station.

MAILS.—One arrival and departure, daily, between London and Shalford.

MONEY ORDER OFFICE at Guildford.

Half a mile from the station is the village, near which is Shalford House, the demesne of Sir Henry Austin, whose mansion is embellished with some fine specimens of carved wood, and a collection of good paintings by the old masters.

GUILDFORD.

POPULATION, 9,500.

A telegraph station.

HOTELS.—White Lion and White Hart.

OMNIBUSES to and from the station.

POST HORSES, FLYS, &c., at the station and hotels.

CARRIERS to London (twice weekly); also to Ash, Albury, Alford, Loxwood, Rudgwick, Bookham, Effingham, Bisley, Knaphill, Bramley, Chichester, Midhurst, Haslemere, Chiddingfold, Cranley, Dunsfold, Ewhurst, Frimley, Godalming, Huscomb, Horshell, Woking, Kidford, Chobham, Liphook, Petersfield, Petworth, Pulborough, Ripley, Send, Sheire, Wisborough Green, Wonersh, Worplesdon, Pirbright.

MARKET DAYS.—Saturday, Tuesday, & Wednesday.

FAIRS.—May 4th and November 22nd.

MONEY ORDER OFFICE.

BANKERS.—Messrs. Haydon, Mangles Brothers.

The situation of this town on the banks of the Wye, and spreading over the steep hill as it rises from the side of the river, is particularly picturesque. It consists of a principal street, nearly a mile long from the bridge on the west to Stoke on the east, whence several smaller streets extend into the suburbs.

Guildford Castle is supposed to have been built as early as the time of the Anglo-Saxon kings. The principal part now remaining is the keep, of a quadrangular form, rising to the height of 70 feet, and built on an artificial mound of earth. Admission may be had free on application to the proprietor of a school adjoining the castle grounds.

Two miles to the eastward of the town is a fine circular race-course. The roads in the neighbourhood are extremely picturesque—that from Guildford to Farnham in particular, running along a ridge of high chalk hills, and thus commanding an extensive prospect. The trade of the town is considerable, from its central situation and convenient distance from the metropolis. The guild or town-hall and the corn market are handsome buildings.

DISTANCES OF PLACES FROM THE STATION.

	Miles.		Miles
Artington	1¾	Newark Abbey	5
Catherine's Hill	0¾	New Warren	1½
Compton	2½	Northbrook Place	3¼
Clandon Park	2¾	Pepper Harrow	6
Gang Hill	1½	Puttenham	4½
Gosden	3	Shalford House	2
Halfpenny House	1½	Stoke	1
Hog's Back	3¼	Sutton Park	2¾
Littleton	1½	Westbrook Place	3
Losely House	2	Wonersh	3
Merrow Race Course	2½	Worplesdon	3
Henley Park	3¾		

ASH.

Distance from the station, ¼ Mile.

A telegraph station.

OMNIBUSES to and from the station; also to the Farnham station.

MONEY ORDER OFFICE at Farnham.

DISTANCES OF PLACES FROM THE STATION.

	Miles.		Miles.
Aldershott	3	Mitchet Farm	2
Ash Common	1¼	Normandy	2
Bagshot Green	2¾	Perbright	5
College Farm	0¾	Poyle Park	1½
Compton	4	Puttenham	2¾
Crondall	7	Romping Downs	2
Farnham	5	Seal	2
Fox Hills	1½	Warren Hill	4
Frog Grove Green	2½	Waverley Abbey	4
Godalming	5¾	Week	1
Henley Park	3	Westwood	1¼
Hunter's Hole	2	Weyburn House	3
Tongham	1	Winchfield Station	9

The line now diverges or turns more towards the north, to ALDERSHOTT station (North Camp), and thence to FARNBOROUGH, the junction station with the South Western Railway, see page 76.

The line then proceeds through the valley of the Blackwater to

BLACKWATER,

A short distance from *Heron Court*, the seat of the Earl of Malmesbury.

A telegraph station.

HOTEL.—White Hart.

A mile further is SANDHURST Royal Military College, situated to the right of the line, in the centre of a fine park. Peculiar interest attaches to this establishment, from the fact of its being the school where some of our ablest military men have acquired that rudimentary education which they have afterwards turned to such good practical account in the field.

The railway then takes almost a direct line for several miles to

WOKINGHAM.

POPULATION, 2,272.

Distance from the station, 1 mile.

A telegraph station.

HOTEL.—Bush.

POST HORSES, FLYS, &c., at the station and hotels.

FAIR.—Whit Tuesday.

MONEY ORDER OFFICE at Wokingham.

Wokingham is situated on the River Wey, on the borders of Windsor Forest. The town consists only of three streets, with an old town-hall and a market-place in the centre. Its trade has received a considerable impetus, and, from the facilities of railway communication it now possesses, will, no doubt, continue to improve and prosper.

DISTANCES OF PLACES FROM THE STATION.

	Miles.		Miles.
Bisley	3	Horshill	1
Chobham	2½	Knapp Hill	3
Chobham Hall	3½	London Necropolis	2½
Chobham Park	3	Mayford	3
Cross Stock	2	Newark Abbey Ruins	2
Dudsall Court	3¾	Ottershaw	3¼
Grove Heath	3	Pirford	2
Hale End	3	Ripley Park	3
Hermitage, The	2	Shackleford	3
Hide Farm	2¾	Sutton Park	3
Hoe Bridge	1	Westfield	2½
Hook Hill	1½	Wokingham	1

From this station the railway passes over a level but highly cultivated country, interspersed with villages and country-seats, until it reach the terminus at

Reading, for the description of which, and other information, see Section II., page 4.

South Eastern Main Line continued.

Reigate to Tunbridge.

On leaving Reigate, the railway turns off towards the south-east, past the village of Nutfield, a short distance beyond which is Bletchingly, both situated on a range of hills. Bletchingley church is a handsome building containing several fine monuments—and there are the remains of a castle in the neighbourhood.

A little further on, the line passes through Bletchingley Tunnel, and shortly after the train reaches

GODSTONE.

Distance from station, 3 miles.

A telegraph station.

HOTEL.—White Hart.

CONVEYANCES.—Omnibuses to and from London, through Limpfield, daily.

FAIR.—July 22.

MONEY ORDER OFFICE at Godstone.

The name of the village adjacent is derived from a corruption of "good stone," significant of the excellence of the quarries there worked. There was formerly a mineral spring of some repute a short distance from Godstone. The parks and mansions in this neighbourhood are much admired, and from some of the hills there are beautiful views of the surrounding country of Surrey and Kent. Tandridge and Limpsfield are pretty villages, about two miles distant.

DISTANCES OF PLACES FROM THE STATION.

	Miles.		Miles.
Anchor Farm	2½	Lingfield	4
Blackgrove	3½	Moat Farm	3¾
Bletchingley	2½	Nagshall	2½
Blendley Heath	2½	Nashes	3½
Bradfield	3½	Nobright	3½
Byes	3	North Park	4
Comforts Place	3½	Oxted	3
Cross Ways	0¼	Park Farm	3
Dog Kennel	3	Postergate	4
Felbridge Park	5	Peartree	4½
Flower House	2¼	Perry's Farm	2½
Gassons House	2¼	Perry's	3
Godstone	3	Priory House	4
Godstone Green	4	Quarry House	4
Goulds	3	Rook's Nest	2½
Hedge Court	7	Snout's Farm	2
Hill Farm	1½	Starborough Castle	8
Hobbs	3	Stile	3
Hook	3	Stockwood	3
Horne	4	Stratton House	2¼
Ivy House	2¼	Tandridge Park	2
Jenkins' Land	2½	Tilberstow Hill	2½
Live House	0¾	Tyler's Green	2¼
Lee Place	2¼	Woldingham	4½
Legham	2	Wonham	3

Passing over Stafford's Wood Common, the line now traverses a fine and open country, entering the county of Kent at a spot bearing the diminutive cognomen of "Little Browns." The intervening miles are rapidly left behind, and we again pause for a few brief minutes at Edenbridge, the first station in the county of

KENT.

This county forms the south-eastern extremity of the island of Great Britain, bounded on the north by the Thames; on the east and south-east by the German Ocean and the Straits of Dover; on the south-west by the English Channel and county of Sussex; and on the west by that of Surrey.

From the diversity of its surface, the noble rivers by which it is watered, the richness and variety of its inland scenery, and the more sublime beauties of its sea coast, this county may be said to rank among the most interesting portions of our island; while the numerous remains of antiquity, the splendid cathedrals, venerable castles, and mouldering monastic edifices, are connected with some of the most remarkable events in English history.

Two chains of hills, called the Upper and Lower, run through the middle of the county from east to west, generally about eight miles asunder; the northern range is part of the extensive ridge which runs through Hampshire and Surrey to Dover, where it terminates in the well known white cliffs. Beyond the southern or lower range is what is called the Weald of Kent, a large tract of rich and fertile land. Kent is essentially and almost solely an agricultural county. The Isle of Thanet is remarkably fertile, but in the Isle of Sheppey only one-fifth of the land is arable; the rest consists of marsh and pasture land, and is used for breeding and fattening sheep and cattle.

The Thames, the Medway, the Stour, the Rother, and the Darent are the principal rivers; while numerous small streams diffuse fertility in every direction.

EDENBRIDGE.

A telegraph station.

HOTEL.—Albion (at the station).

OMNIBUSES at the station; also to Westerham.

FAIR.—May 6th.

MONEY ORDER OFFICE at East Grinstead.

The village of Edenbridge, situated 1 mile from the station, derives its name from the little river Eden, one of the tributary streams of the Medway. There are several chalybeate springs in the neighbourhood. The church of Edenbridge is a fine ancient edifice, containing several handsome tombs; also a curious monument of the Earl of Wiltshire. A few miles distant is the village of Westerham; and a short distance south of the line is

Hever Castle, once the residence of the unfortunate Queen Anne Boleyn. The castle was erected in the reign of Edward III. by William de Hean. It subsequently fell into the hands of the Cobhams, who disposed of it to Sir Geoffrey Boleyn, a rich mercer of London, and great grandfather of the unfortnnate Queen Anne Boleyn. It is still an imposing building, and many of the rooms present the same appearance as during the happy visits of Henry VIII. Various shields, with the arms and alliances of the Boleyn family, are displayed on the windows. The castle is still inhabited; it is surrounded by a moat, the entrance embattled and defended by a drawbridge and portcullis. Anne of Cleves died here in 1557.

The village of Chiddingstone, near Hever, is one of the prettiest in the county, and the whole district is remarkable for most beautiful scenery.

The neighbourhood here begins to get thronged with objects of attraction sufficient to draw the tourist from his main route.

DISTANCES OF PLACES FROM THE STATION.

	Miles.		Miles.
Brook House	1½	Hartfield	7½
Brusted	5	Hever Castle (Ralph Waldo, Esq.), in ruins	4
Brusted Place	4½	Ivy House	3¼
Buckhurst Park	7½	Limpsfield	5
Chiddingstone	3½	Linhurst	1
Chartwell	3½	Mapledon	2
Comb Bank	6	Marsh Green	1¾
Cowden	4½	Oakhams	2½
Cubham Wood	7	Seven Oaks	7½
Foundling House	3	Squerries, The	3½
Four Elms	1¾	Stanfords End	1¾
Hall Farm	4	Sunbridge	8
Hole Farm	1¾	Westerham	5
Hill Park	5		

From Edenbridge station to the next, there are a succession of agreeable prospects, diversified by a few impediments to a good view in the form of an intervening cutting.

PENSHURST.

Distance from station, 2 miles.

A telegraph station.

HOTEL.—Leicester Arms.

POST HORSES, FLYS, &c. at the station and hotel.

FAIR.—Monday after June 24th.

MONEY ORDER OFFICE at Tunbridge.

This is a small but exceedingly pretty village, celebrated for its fine old castle, the property of the Sidney family. This noble structure stands in a magnificent park, and covers a large area with its court, halls, and quadrangles. It also contains a valuable collection of paintings, which visitors, by the kindness of the noble owner, are permitted to view.

South Park, the seat and property of the late Lord Hardinge, is two miles distant towards the south, and a few miles in the opposite direction in the north is the beautiful village of *Seven Oaks*, containing *Knowle Park*, the seat of the Sackvilles—a most picturesque place. The mansion is built in the old English style of architecture, castellated and with square towers. Knowle Mansion and Park form one of the most splendid seats in the kingdom. The collection of paintings is also very fine, and particularly rich in works of the great Italian masters.

Wilderness, the seat of the Marquis of Camden, about two miles beyond Seven Oaks, is a more modern mansion, but most beautifully situated.

DISTANCES OF PLACES FROM THE STATION:—

	Miles.		Miles
Ashurst	4½	Doubleton	1
Belle Vue (Col. Austen's)	3	Enfield Well Place	2
Chevening Park (Lord Stanhope's)	7	Groombridge	5½
Chiddingstone	2	Hobby Hall	3¾
		Knowle Park (Lord Amherst's)	4

Distances Continued.

	Miles.		Miles.
Leigh	2	River Hill (John Rogers, Esq.)	4
Leigh Park	2½	Salmonds	2
Montreal Park (Lord Holmesdale)	5½	Seven Oaks	4
Penshurst	2	South Park Hill	3½
Penshurst Park (Lord de l'Isle Dudley)	1¾	Under River (F. Woodgate, Esq.)	4½
Red Leaf (William Wells, Esq.)	0¾		

A few miles more, in the course of which we thrice cross the winding Medway, brings us to

TUNBRIDGE JUNCTION.

POPULATION, 4,539.

A telegraph station.

MARKET DAY.—Alternate Tuesdays.

FAIR.—October 11th.

This, besides being the branch station for passengers to Tunbridge Wells, has a convenient refreshment-room appended.

TUNBRIDGE WELLS AND HASTINGS BRANCH.

Tunbridge Junction to Hastings.

The railway commences through a series of deep cuttings, and then proceeds through a tunnel of considerable length. The strata on each side of the line is composed of ironstone and sand-stone, diversified with clay, in a manner quite peculiar to the county.

TUNBRIDGE WELLS.

POPULATION, about 15,500.

A telegraph station.

HOTELS.—The Calverley; Kentish Royal; Royal Sussex.

OMNIBUSES to and from the station, also to Paddock Wood.

POST HORSES, FLYS, &c., at the station and hotels

COACHES to Brighton, *via* Maresfield, Uckfield, and Lewes, daily.

MARKET DAYS.—Daily.

MONEY ORDER OFFICE.

BANKERS.—Beeching and Co.; Molyneux and Co.; ranch of London and County.

TUNBRIDGE WELLS is situated on the Tun and four branches of the Medway, all crossed by bridges. It is noted for its excellent Grammar School with sixteen exhibitions. The castle, of which a fine noble gateway flanked by round towers still remains, was built by Richard Fitz Gilbert, Earl of Clare and Hertford, who likewise founded a priory here for Augustine Canons, the refectory of which may be seen. Open on Saturdays from 10 till 4, by permission of the proprietor. This town is, with the exception of Bath, the most ancient of the inland watering places. Nature has eminently favoured it by the salubrity of its air, the potency of its mineral springs, and the adjacent appendages of romantic and agreeable scenery. Dudley Lord North, a young nobleman of the Court of James I., whilst on a visit to Eridge House, happened to taste the waters, and these renovating a constitution impaired by too much indulgence, caused him to bring the place into fashionable repute. From that time visitors gradually increased, streets were laid out, lodging-houses built, and now, though the caprice of fashion has somewhat depreciated the fame of our own spas, Tunbridge Wells may still boast a large share of patronage in the season, which extends from May till November. The town is built upon a sandy soil, and is divided into four districts, called respectively Mount Ephraim, Mount Pleasant, Mount Sion, and the Wells. The houses are chiefly detached villas, with lawns in front, and large gardens in the rear. Those that are situated on the mounts have extensive views, that combine hill and dale, forests and fields, commons, meadows, and corn lands, with a large tract of hop-grounds. The drinking spring rises at the end of the Parade, which has a row of trees on one side, and a colonnade with shops on the other. The water is a strong chalybeate, and possesses great tonic power. The climate is congenial, and the air upon the downs has a fine bracing and exhilarating property. There is almost perfect immunity from fog, and being sheltered from the north-east winds by the north downs, the temperature throughout the winter is pleasant and equable. Crowborough Common, at the Beacon, seven miles from the Wells, stands at an elevation of 800 feet above the level of the sea. The inns and boarding-houses are generally of a superior description. About a mile and a half south-west of the town are some rocks of considerable height, surrounded with wood, which are much admired by visitors. The manufacture of wooden toys and articles of domestic use, long celebrated as "Tunbridge Ware," is still carried on here to a considerable extent, and was formerly the principal produce of the place. Tunbridge Wells is forty-six miles from London by railway. Excursions may be made to Penshurst, five miles distant; Bridge Castle, two miles distant; Hever, seven miles distant; *Southborough Bounds* three miles, *Summerhill* two miles, a fine Elizabethan building, once the residence of the Earl of Leicester and General Lambert; *Oxenheath*, four miles; and Bayham Abbey, the seat of the Marquis of Camden, six miles distant, the ruins being exceedingly picturesque. The modern mansion is in the Gothic style. There are other fine seats and handsome villas in the vicinity, and the environs of Tunbridge abound in beautiful walks and drives.

From Tunbridge Wells the railway proceeds southward, and enters the county of Sussex, passing through a short tunnel at starting, and then proceeds through a deep cutting

FRANT.

Distance from station, 1 mile.

A telegraph station.

HOTELS.—Spread Eagle, and Abergavenny Arms.

MONEY ORDER OFFICE at Tunbridge Wells.

A short distance from this station is *Eridge Castle*, the demesne of the Earl of Abergavenny, situated in a noble park, well stocked with deer. There are several handsome villas in the neighbourhood, the scenery of which is exceedingly varied, and some of the views of the country around are both extensive and beautiful.

Between Frant and Robertsbridge the scenery becomes less picturesque, though the country is highly cultivated, and the hop-grounds are particularly fine. Near the Wadhurst station there is rather a long tunnel, and the church of Wadhurst is worthy a visit.

WADHURST.

Distance from station, 1 mile.

A telegraph station.

MARKET DAY.—Saturday.

FAIRS.—April 29th and November 1st.

MONEY ORDER OFFICE at Wadhurst.

TICEHURST ROAD.

Distance from station, 1 mile.

A telegraph station.

MARKET DAY.—Sat. FAIRS.—May 4, and Oct. 7.

MONEY ORDER OFFICE at Ticehurst.

Ticehurst is rather a large town, situated on high ground, about three miles and a half to the east of the station, in the midst of a splendid agricultural country.

ETCHINGHAM.

Distance from station, 1 mile.

A telegraph station.

MONEY ORDER OFFICE at Wadhurst.

The church at Etchingham is a fine old edifice, reputed to be one of the best specimens of Norman architecture in the country.

The stations at Frant, Etchingham, and Battle are built in the Gothic character; those at Wadhurst, Ticehurst Road, and Robertsbridge are in the Italian style, of red and white brick and Caen stone.

ROBERTSBRIDGE.

Distance from station, ¼ mile.

A telegraph station.

HOTEL.—Old George.

MARKET DAY.—Thursday.

MONEY ORDER OFFICE at Robertsbridge.

The village is situated on the banks of the river Rother, and only remarkable for the houses being constructed of red brick, which gives the place a peculiar appearance.

BATTLE.

Distance from station, 1 mile.

A telegraph station.

HOTEL.—George.

OMNIBUSES to and from the station.

POST HORSES, FLYS, &c., at the hotel.

MARKET DAY.—The second Monday in each month. FAIRS.—Whit Monday and November 22nd.

MONEY ORDER OFFICE.

BANKERS.—The London and County Bank, Branch; Smith, Hilder, and Co.

This town was formerly called Epiton, and received its present name from being the spot on which the Saxons, under Harold, were defeated by William, the Duke of Normandy, in 1066. After the contest the Conqueror founded a magnificent abbey to commemorate his victory, and the high altar in the church is said to have stood on the very spot where the body of the heroic Saxon prince was found. The noble gateway of the abbey has a fine effect when seen from the town. In the abbey was formerly preserved the celebrated Battle Abbey Roll, which formed a list of those families which came over from Normandy with the Duke.

The mingled scene of hill and dale, wood and village, presents one of those fair spots in nature which refresh the traveller, who, hurrying through tunnel and cutting, to annihilate time and space, too often disregards the beauty of the country through which he passes.

DISTANCES OF PLACES FROM THE STATION.

	Miles.		Miles.
Ashburnham	5	Darvel House	3
Ashburnham Park	4	Hollington Lodge	3
Battle	1	Newenden	9
Battle Abbey (Lady Webster's)	1	New House	5
Battle Powder Mills	2½	Ore Place	4
Beaufort	2	Penshurst	4
Bohemy House	3	Sedlescombe	2¾
Brede	4	Udimore	6½
Catsfield	3	Watch Gate	1½
Crowhurst Park	2	Westfield	3½
		Whatlington	3

Four miles further is

ST. LEONARDS STATION,

for description of which see page 55.

HASTINGS.

Distance from station, ¼ mile.

A telegraph station.

HOTELS.—The Marine, on the Parade; Albion; Castle.

OMNIBUSES to and from the station to meet every train.

Post Horses, Flys, &c., at the hotels and station, to meet every train.

Market Days.—Saturdays (corn); daily (poultry).

Fairs.—Whit Tuesday, July 26 and 29, and November 27.

Money Order Office at Hastings.

Bankers.—Branch of London and County.

The recognised salubrity and mildness of the air, together with the openness of the coast and the smoothness of the beach, have long made Hastings a favourite and a recommended resort. The shore is not abrupt, and the water almost always limpid, and of that beautiful sea-green hue so inviting to bathers. The constant surging of the waves, first breaking against the reefs, and next dashing over the sloping shingle, is not unwelcome music at midnight to the ears of all who *sleep* in the vicinity of the shore. Dr. James Clark states, that in winter Hastings is most desirable as a place of residence during January and February. "During the spring also it has the advantage of being more effectually sheltered from north and north-east winds than any other place frequented by invalids on the coast of Sussex. It is also comparatively little subject to fogs in the spring, and the fall of rain may be said at that time to be less than on other portions of the coast. As might be expected from the low and sheltered situation of Hastings, it will be found a favourable residence generally to invalids suffering under diseases of the chest. Delicate persons, who desire to avoid exposure to the north-east winds, may pass the cold season here with advantage. Owing to the close manner in which this place is hemmed in on the sea by steep and high cliffs, it has an atmosphere more completely marine than almost any other part of this coast, with the exception, of course, of St. Leonards, which possesses the same dry and absorbent soil." The breadth and extent of its esplanade, also, and the protection afforded by the colonnades for walking exercise, are circumstances of considerable importance to the invalid, and render a conjoined residence at Hastings and St. Leonards a very efficient substitute for a trip to Madeira.

The Castle of Hastings, for a time the favourite residence of the Conqueror, has remained a mass of magnificent ruins; its towers, bastions, and ancient walls forming an object truly picturesque, as seen from any point of view, but looking even grand in their sombre desolation, as meeting the eye of the pedestrian when ascending the eminence leading to Fairlight Downs.

A few years back the visitors to the castle were shown *two* coffins, a small one and a larger one, which they were assured contained the ashes of a mother and infant. These have been lately removed, and the space of ground enclosed by the walls which used to shelter such vestiges of a more barbarous age is now employed by a market gardener to administer to the culinary wants of the townsfolk of Hastings and St. Leonards.

The approach to Hastings Castle is from the further extremity of Wellington Square, and, with the perpendicular cliff that fronts the sea for its base, the outer walls appear originally to have had the form of a triangle with rounded angles. For some time past the interior has been laid out as a flower garden and shrubbery, and the person who has charge of the lodge accommodates, for a small fee, visitors with seats and refreshments. The view, though not equal to that from Fairlight Downs, is varied and extensive, and commands towards the south an ample marine expanse, whilst Beachy Head, Eastbourne, and Bexhill may be seen towards the west.

Whilst in the neighbourhood, it should not be forgotten that a delightful excursion may be made to Battle Abbey, not more than six miles distant. The grounds are now in possession of the Webster family, who have liberally thrown them open to public inspection every Friday, at $1\frac{1}{2}$ p.m. It is here that the "Battel Roll," a sort of primitive "Court Guide," is carefully preserved, and furnishes a list valuable to the antiquary and historian of those families who came over with William the Conqueror.

A glance into the booksellers' windows, where engraved vignettes of some neighbouring attraction allure the eye in every direction, will at once reveal to the visitor the tempting beauty of the environs. A week may be delightfully spent in exploring the fairy-like nooks about Fairlight alone. Situated in a sweet umbrageous spot, down which, by narrow winding steps, hewn out of the solid rock, one only can descend at a time, is the weeping rock. The view of this constantly-dripping well, as the spectator looks up to the jutting rock from the beautiful cottage of Covehurst below, is well calculated to inspire the mind with that feeling under which credence would be given to any legend that accounted for this freak of nature, by ascribing it to the influence of supernatural agency. The stone weeps, as it were, from myriads of pores, and, although the water falls in continuous drops, no trace of it is left in the reservoir; passing through the rock, its appearance is as mysterious as its disappearance is magical. It is explained by the soil beneath being loose and sandy, over a heavy beach stone foundation, and, acting as a subterraneous drain, the water is conducted beneath the surface, appearing as a truculent stream about a hundred yards from the rock, and then again disappearing down a declivity. The beautiful appearance the rock presents in winter, when the drip is frozen and the icicles hang from the sloping crags in clusters of crystals, will not be easily forgotten by those who have had the good fortune to witness, at this period, such a mimic stalactite cavern.

Then, in the vicinity of the well are the fish-ponds with romantic walks around it, and a comfortable farm-house adjacent, where refreshments can be had at a small cost, and where the ale is—but we forbear our eloquence. The picturesque waterfall of Old Roar should not be overlooked, nor the Lover's Seat, so charmingly enthroned amid shrubs and evergreens, nor the other favoured localities, which are enough to make a Pennsylvanian lawyer turn poetical. Let the pedestrian, however, make his way to the signal house belonging to the coast-guard station at that point, and he will have a panoramic view around him which it would be worth his while walking from Cornhill to Grand Cairo only to behold and then walk back again.

The whole forms a complete circle; the sweep of inland scenery extending to the hills in the neighbourhood of London, and the sea view reaching from Beachy Head to Dover Cliffs, between seventy and eighty miles apart, and stretching out to the heights of Boulogne. The entire area of the prospect, both by land and water, cannot be less than three hundred miles. Among many minor objects visible may be enumerated ten towns, sixty-six churches, seventy martello towers, five ancient castles, three bays, and forty windmills. The best time for seeing it is the afternoon, when the setting sun lights up the old town of Hastings in the foreground, and brings into strong shadow the opposite coast of France. Upon favourable atmospheric influences it is, indeed, a view never to be forgotten.

South Eastern Main Line continued.

Tunbridge to Paddock Wood.

On leaving Tunbridge, the line passes through the beautiful park of *Summerhill*, the property of Baron de Goldschmidt, and thence, on past the villages of Tudely and Capel to the

PADDOCK WOOD JUNCTION.

A telegraph station.

Money Order Office at Tunbridge.

Distances of Places from the Station.

	Miles.		Miles.
Bowling Green	$1\frac{3}{4}$	Mereworth Castle (Lady Despencer's)	5
Brenchley	3	Pigfish	$2\frac{1}{2}$
Great Brainden	3	Snoll Hatch	$1\frac{3}{4}$
Homebush Green	2	Wested	1
Horsemondean	$4\frac{1}{2}$	Woodfall	$1\frac{3}{4}$
Lamberhurst	$5\frac{1}{2}$	Yalding	$3\frac{1}{2}$
Matfield Green	$4\frac{1}{2}$		

MAIDSTONE BRANCH.

Paddock Wood to Maidstone.

The branch to Maidstone from Paddock Wood follows the course of the Medway throughout, and enables the traveller to snatch some rapid glimpses of a woody country, presenting the true characteristics of a Kentish landscape. On each side of us we find the land studded with substantial homesteads and wealthy looking farms, rising in the midst of corn fields or orchards, or surrounded by the British vineyards, the Kentish hop-grounds.

YALDING.

Distance from station, $1\frac{1}{2}$ mile.

A telegraph station.

Fair.—October 15th.

Money Order Office at Maidstone.

The village of Yalding is not remarkable for anything of interest to the traveller. A short distance from it are Yalding Downs and Barnes Hill; and to the left of the station there are several country seats and mansions, in most beautiful parks.

WATERINGBURY.

Distance from station, $\frac{1}{2}$ mile.

A telegraph station.

Hotel.—Duke's Head.

Money Order Office at Maidstone.

This is a large and handsome village, retaining its rural character, combined with an unusual degree of charming neatness and taste. The cottage gardens are sweetly pretty. The church is rather handsome, and contains several tombs of the Style family. Wateringbury Place in the vicinity is a fine mansion, situated in very beautiful grounds.

Distances of Places from the Station.

	Miles.		Miles
Addington Place (Hon. Wingfield Stratford)	$4\frac{1}{2}$	East Malling Wood	2
Barming	2	Great Leonard Street (Lunatic Asylum)	2
Birling (Hon. & Rev. J. Neville)	5	Larkfield	3
Bradburn Park (Capt. Twisden's)	$3\frac{1}{4}$	Mereworth Castle	3
Broadwater	2	Offham Green	$4\frac{1}{4}$
Cannon Heath	$1\frac{1}{2}$	Oxenbeath	$3\frac{1}{4}$
Clare House (J. A. Wigan, Esq.)	3	West Farleigh	1
Delton Place (Jno. Golding, Esq.)	3	West Malling	4
		West Peckham	4
		Yalding Down	1

A mile beyond, above the line, is the neat village of Teston, the scenery around which, with the bridge across the Medway, is quite picturesque. *Barham Court*, the mansion and park of the Earl of Gainsborough, is in the vicinity. There are several unusually pretty villages and villas on the right side of the river and railway. East and West Farleigh, on the banks of the Medway, though consisting only of scattered houses, are exceedingly pleasing. The church in the latter place is a very ancient one covered with ivy, and, with the hop-grounds and orchards, has quite a sylvan appearance.

EAST FARLEIGH

Is close to the bridge over the Medway.

A telegraph station.

Money Order Office at Maidstone.

Two miles beyond this the train enters the present terminus of this line at Maidstone. It is a very neat and commodious structure, within a few minutes' walk of the High-street.

MAIDSTONE.

Population, 20,801.

Distance from station $\frac{1}{4}$ mile. A telegraph station.

HOTELS.—The Mitre; The Royal Star and Bell.

OMNIBUSES to and from station, also to London direct, and to Faversham *via* Debtling, Stockbury Valleys, Key Street, Sittingbourne, Milton, Rochester, Chatham, Strood, and Canterbury.

POST HORSES, FLYS, &c., at the hotels.

MARKET DAYS.—Thursdays and Saturdays.

FAIRS.—2nd Tuesday in every month (cattle), Feb. 13th, May 12th, June 20th, Oct. 17th (Hops).

MONEY ORDER OFFICE at Maidstone.

BANKERS.—The London and County Joint Stock Bank. Mercer, Randall, and Co.

MAIDSTONE is a parliamentary borough, and the capital of Kent, on the Medway, in a tract of land of great fertility, among orchards, hop grounds, and woodlands. The distance from London has been recently reduced 13 miles by the opening of the North Kent line from Strood, the information for which will be found on page 27. It is not only a shorter route, but commands a splendid view of the valley of the Medway and the adjacent hills.

The town is on the slopes of the hills, so that, rising from the banks of the river, at the north entrances are the cavalry barracks (of wood!), and the county jail, the latter being a most complete and extensive pile, nearly two-thirds of a mile round its quadrangular wall, and covering 14 acres. It includes the assize courts, and was built in 1829, of the ragstone which is so abundant in the neighbourhood. The county asylum occupies a site of 37 acres. In High-street stands the old brick Town Hall, over the corn market, the butter market being in an adjoining street.

Round the church are grouped some interesting remains. The church itself is an embattled straggling building of great length, nearly 230 ft.; and was made collegiate by Archbishop Courtenay, who is buried here in the middle of the chancel. His arms are over the old stalls and stone seats on the south side. It was here that the royalists were surrounded by Fairfax, when he took the town, after a hard fight, in 1648.

The Primates had a palace here from King John's time, of which a part, still inhabited, hangs over the river on one side of the churchyard. Another old looking house is styled the castle; behind, are the ruins of Courtenay's College, of which Grocyn, the Greek scholar, and friend of Erasmus, was for a while master; after teaching at Oxford he was buried here. Here also are fragments of a priory, and the Grammar School. There is a great air of quiet antiquity about this part of Maidstone. In West-Borough (over the bridge) is the ancient chapel of a hospital founded in the 13th century by Archbishop Boniface, while another chapel (now a school) was occupied by the Walloons, or Dutch Protestants, expelled by the Spanish butcher Alva, in Elizabeth's time. The flax spun here for thread is still called Dutch work, in remembrance of these persecuted emigrants. William Hazlitt was a native of Maidstone, born 1778.

In the ragstone quarried here Dr. Mantell found his fossil *iguanodon*, which he thinks must have been nearly 70 ft. long. A restoration of this river-monster is at the Crystal Palace.

Besides hops, cherries, filberts, &c., paper is a staple production, especially at the Turkey and Pole mills, on the Len; and the Toril mills, near the old pest house, up the Medway. Coppices for hop-poles, props, &c. are dispersed about. The hop was first cultivated in Kent in the time of Henry VI., about the middle of the 15th century.

The walk along the Rochester road to **Blue Bell Down** (four miles) affords a charming panorama of orchards, copses and hills; and the views from the Down itself amply repay the long ascent to it.

South Eastern Main Line continued.

Paddock Wood to Ashford.

From Paddock the main line proceeds rapidly in the direction of the coast, and although the country presents very charming alternations of waste and woodland scenery, yet it does not offer objects of sufficient interest to describe in detail. Views of hop fields are shut in by excavations which, like the change of slides in dissolving views, transform the landscape every moment.

MARDEN.

Distance from station, ¼ mile.

A telegraph station.

FAIR.—October 11.

MONEY ORDER OFFICE at Staplehurst.

The only object worthy of notice is Marden church. *Boughton Place* in the neighbourhood is a very fine estate, from some points of which may be obtained several extensive views over the Weald of Kent.

Two miles more and the train reaches the station at

STAPLEHURST.

A telegraph station.

HOTELS.—South Eastern, King's Head.

FAIRS.—Monday after July 20th, Wednesday after September 20th.

MONEY ORDER OFFICE.

The village of the same name is near the station; its fine old church and quaint antique houses are much admired.

The village of Cranbrook, in the heart of the Weald of Kent is remarkable for its handsome church, considered one of the most interesting edifices in the county. The remains of Sissinghurst Castle, four miles, are also well worthy a visit.

DISTANCES OF PLACES FROM THE STATION.

	Miles.		Miles.
Bennendon	7	Hempstead Park	6
Chart Hill	3	Hersfield Place	2¼
Chart Sutton	3	Highgate	8¼
Chiddenden Wood	5½	Hockenbury Green	1
Cranbrook	6	Kilsom	1
Dingle Dale	8	Love House	1½
Dollingden Farm	6¾	Milk House Street	4
East Sutton	3¾	Postern Plain	2¼
Elderton	1¾	Sandhurst Green	9¾
Foxearthwood	5	Standing Street	8¼
Frittenden	4	Sutton Valence	3¼
Goddard's Green	6½	Swallenden Farm	7½
Great Dunbury	1¼	Swithland	2½
Hangley Wood	5¼	Wanthurst	1¼
Hartley	6½	Winsley Green	4½
Hawkhurst	8¼		

HEADCORN.

Distance from station, ½ mile.

A telegraph station.

HOTELS.—The George, King's Arms.

MARKET DAY.—Wednesday. FAIR.—June 12th.

MONEY ORDER OFFICE at Staplehurst.

This village possesses no feature of particular or general interest, beyond the splendid old oak tree in the churchyard. The churches of Chart Sutton, Sutton Valence, and Sutton Castle, are worth visiting.

From Headcorn the railway passes the villages of Smarden and Bedenham on the right side, and then reaches

PLUCKLEY.

Distance from station, 1¼ mile.

A telegraph station.

FAIRS.—Whit Mondays (Toys and Pedlery), Feast of St. Nicholas (cattle).

MONEY ORDER OFFICE at Ashford.

In the neighbourhood of Pluckley there are several villages and country seats. *Bethersden* the seat of the Lovelaces, a family now extinct, two and a half miles. Great Chart, once a large market town, and many others.

Leeds Castle, however, in general absorbs the attention of the traveller. Of Norman architecture, situated in a beautiful park, and being still in good preservation, it is one of the most imposing and interesting castles in the county of Kent.

ASHFORD.

POPULATION, 5,009.

Distance from station, ½ mile. A telegraph station.

HOTELS.—The Victoria, near the railway station; Saracen's Head; Royal Oak.

MARKET DAYS.—Every Tuesday (corn), 1st, 3rd and 5th Tuesday in every month (cattle).

FAIRS.—May 17th, Sept. 12tn, and Oct. 24th for horses, cattle, and pedlery.

MONEY ORDER OFFICE at Ashford.

BANKERS.—London and County Joint Stock Bank. Jemmett and Co.

This was a quiet agricultural town in East Kent till the South Eastern Railway Company made it the chief station for their works, since which the population has greatly increased. It is on the Stour, at the junction of the branches to Canterbury, Margate, and Hastings, with the main line to Dover, from which it is 21 miles. Among the buildings erected by the Company are a carriage house 645 ft. long; a repairing shop, 395 ft. by 45; an engine room 210 ft. by 63; besides factories for wheels, boilers, &c. Such is the wear and tear a wheel undergoes that it requires to be fresh turned after every 2,000 miles of travelling. A church has also been built for their workmen, by the Company. The parish church is a large and handsome edifice, in the Gothic style, containing several brass and stone monuments of the families of the neighbourhood—as the Smythes of Westenhanger, the Fogges of Repton, &c.

Three miles N.E. is **Eastwell Park,** the seat of the Earl of Winchelsea, standing on a ridge which commands a view of the Thames on one side and the British Channel on the other. There is an extensive lake in the park, with a pretty model ship of war floating on it, fully rigged. The church contains many tombs of the Finches and Moyles; but the most remarkable monument is that to Richard Plantagenet, the last descendant of that royal house, who died here in obscurity as a bricklayer to the Moyles, 22nd Dec., 1550. His name is inserted in the register book under that date. The story concerning him is that he never knew who his father was till the battle of Bosworth Field, when he was taken into Leicestershire, and carried to Richard III.'s tent. The king embraced him and told him he was his son. "But child (says he), to-morrow I must fight for my crown, and if I lose that I will lose my life too. If I should be so unfortunate, shift as well as you can, and take care to let nobody know that I am your father, for no mercy will be shown any one so near to me." When the battle was lost he sold his horse and fine clothes, and, to hide all suspicion of his descent, put himself apprentice to a bricklayer. In this situation he was discovered reading a Latin book by his employer Sir T. Moyle, to whom he told his secret as it has come down to us. Not long ago there was a brick house in the park built by Richard. His singular fate is the subject of a very charming book called the "Last of the Plantagenets."

Within two or three miles of Ashford are the following seats:—*Merstham Hatch*, Sir Norton Knatchbull, Bart.; *Hothfield*, Sir R. Tufton, Bart., for ages the seat of the Thanet (or Tufton family), and near Ripley, where Sheriff Iden seized and killed Jack Cade, who was hiding here. *Surrenden*, Sir E. Dering, Bart., M.P., another ancient family descended from the Sir Edward whose sufferings in the civil war are eloquently described by Southey in the "Book of the Churches." *Godington*, N. Toke, Esq., was the seat of Sheriff Toke, a hearty, vigorous old man, who died 1680, when 93 years old, having walked to London a little before to court his sixth wife. He and his four predecessors at Godington counted 430 years among them.

All this east end of the Weald of Kent is thick with woodlands, like the rest of that fertile tract, but the roads are damp and heavy.

DISTANCES OF PLACES FROM THE STATION.

	Miles.		Miles.
Badlesmere	8	Mount Norris, (Lord Rokeby)	5
Beaver Green	1¼	New Street	2½
Beechborough Park	1	Plumbton	2
Blackwall	2	Sevington	2
Bromley Green	3¼	Shaddenden Lodge	3½
Brooke	4	Shadoxhurst	4½
Cable Hook	3¼	Sheldwick	9¼
Challock	5	Shottington	3¼
Cheeseman's Green	2	Smeeth	5
Coleman Green	4	Snell Hatch	2
Conings Brooke	2	Stone Cross Green	3¼
Dean Court	4½	Tenterden	12
Godmersham	5¼	Warehorne	6
Hastingleigh	8	West Hauk	1½
Hinxhill	3	Westwell	3¼
Kenardington	7	Woodchurch	7
Kennington	2	Yousel	2½
Kingsford Street	1½		
Kingsnorth	3		

ASHFORD AND CANTERBURY BRANCH.

Ashford to Canterbury, Ramsgate, &c.

Here the line branches off to Canterbury, Whitstable, Sandwich, Deal, Ramsgate, and Margate, and, from the accommodation it affords to the towns through which it passes, and the exquisite beauty of the scenery along its route, will not suffer in comparison with any line of similar length in the kingdom. It follows throughout the meanderings of the river Stour, and traversing the most fertile districts in the country, has one uninterrupted panorama of luxuriant fertility during its whole length.

On leaving Ashford, the little villages of Brook and Wye are passed in succession to the right, imbedded in a valley sheltered by rising hills, and thickly studded with lofty and umbrageous patches of woodland.

WYE.

Distance from station, ½ mile.

A telegraph station.

OMNIBUSES to and from Faversham, daily.

FAIRS.—May 29 and October 11.

MONEY ORDER OFFICE at Wye.

The town of Wye is close to the river Stour, and consists of two main streets. It has a handsome church, and was once a royal manor, granted by William the Conqueror to the Abbey of Battle. Here was a monastic college, the remains of which are still to be seen.

Emerging from a tolerably deep cutting, we next trace to the left a most charming and picturesque village, and shortly reach

CHILHAM.

Distance from station, ¾ mile.

Telegraph station at Wye, 4 miles.

OMNIBUSES to and from the station; also to Godmersham and Canterbury.

FAIR.—November 8th.

MONEY ORDER OFFICE at Canterbury.

Chilham House or Manor is a noble building, situated in beautiful grounds, which command extensive views over the entire Vale of Ashford and the Stour.

Thence the windings of the Stour, spanned ever and anon by some rustic bridge of wood or stone, enhances the romantic beauty of the landscape, and we seem to be for many miles treading the sylvan labyrinth of a miniature Rhine-land.

Shortly afterwards, the towers of Canterbury Cathedral rise into sight, followed by the lofty buildings of the city itself, and whilst watching the course of the railway to Whitstable, which branches off to the north, the accustomed warning sound of the whistle rings in our ears, and we glide beneath the commodious structure of the station at

CANTERBURY,

In the western suburb. A telegraph station.

POPULATION, 18,398.

HOTELS.—Royal Fountain; Rose; Flenr-de-lis.

OMNIBUSES to the station; also to Barham, Dover, Ellam, Elmstead, Faversham, Goodnestone, Wye, Sittingbourne, and Eastry.

MARKET DAYS.—Wednesdays and Saturdays.

FAIRS.—May 4th and October 11th.

MONEY ORDER OFFICE.

BANKERS.—The London and County Bank. Hammond and Co.

The appearance of Canterbury, from whatever part approached, is exquisitely beautiful, and as we enter, symbols of its antiquity stare us in the face everywhere; narrow passages, crazy tenements, with over-hanging windows, peaked gables, and wooden balustrades, jut out on every side. Here and there some formless sculpture of a fractured cherub or grotesque image, peer out from a creaking doorway. Crypts and vaults seem natural to every house, and yet withal, an air of liveliness pervades the town, that renders the contrast truly pleasing and striking. The city lies in a fertile vale, sheltered by gently rising hills, from which streams of excellent water are derived.

When Becket was murdered here, 1170, in the great contest between the civil and ecclesiastical powers, Canterbury became the centre of pilgrimages from all quarters of Christendom to his shrine. Many old timbered houses, and small ancient rough-cast churches are seen here; but the noble

Cathedral is the first object of notice, as it rises above the town. It is a double cross 574 feet long inside, with an east transept of 159 feet, and a west one of 128 feet. The oldest part is the half Norman choir, begun 1174; the nave and west transept finished 1420; the great tower is 235 feet high; the west tower is 130 feet. The west front of the great window is of Richard II.'s time. On one side is a beautiful porch, built as late as 1517. The north-west transept, called the Martyrdom, because Becket was killed there, has a beautifully stained window; the opposite one contains the monuments of Cardinal Langton, and the Duke of Clarence. A decorated screen leads into the choir, with the monuments of Archbishops Kemp, Stratford, Sudbury, &c.; those of Chicheley, Bourchier, and other primates, with Henry IV. and Queen Joan, the Black Prince, and Archbishop Canterbury, &c., are near Trinity Chapel, in the north-east transept. Here stood Becket's shrine, or the gold chest containing his bones, which Erasmus saw; it shone and sparkled, he says, "with rare and precious jewels, the chief of them gifts of kings." During the jubilee of 1420, in an ignorant and superstitious age, as many as 100,000 worshippers crowded to the shrine, expecting to obtain heaven *per Thomæ sanguinem*, "by the blood of St. Thomas," whose chief merit was rebellion to his sovereign. The hollows worn by the knees of devotees may be observed in the pavement. In one year their offerings amounted to £954 6s. 3d., while at the Virgin Mary's altar in the crypt there were only £4 1s. 8d., and at the high (or Christ's) altar, *nothing*. The bones were burnt at the Reformation. At the east end of the cathedral is Becket's crown, a chapel so called, where are monuments of Cardinal Chatillon, &c., and the ancient chair of the primates. Below is a very curious Norman crypt, where the Walloons aud the Protestant refugees used to meet for worship.

Near this splendid pile are the cloisters, with 811 coats of arms placed round; the later English chapter house, in which Henry II. did penance in sackcloth, two years after Becket's death; the Archbishop's deserted palace; baptistry and treasury; the beautiful gate of the Abbey, under which Augustine was buried; and the new missionary college, founded by H. Hope, Esq., built in the Gothic style, 1849. St. George, St. Paul, Holy Cross, and St. Martin's churches are among the most ancient—especially the last, which stands outside the town, on the site of the first one built by Augustine, having an ivy-covered tower, and the font in which Etheldred was baptized. It has been restored lately with great care. Riding Gate is in Watling Street, on the old road from London, which Chaucer's pilgrims travelled from the Tabard in Southwark, and put up at Chaucer's Inn, in Mercery Lane here, of which few traces are left. Close to this gate is the Donjon or Dane John Terrace, a pleasant spot, laid out as a public walk, and which presents a most gay and lively scene when the élite of the neighbourhood assemble here, once weekly, to enjoy their favourite opera airs, skilfully played by the band of the regiment that may be quartered at the barracks. Westgate is near this; and some other portions of the city walls remain.

Canterbury has a Guildhall, sessions house, cavalry and other barracks, with several schools and hospitals. St. Nicholas's hospital, at Harbledown, was founded by Archbishop Lanfranc in the 11th century. That part of the neighbourhood near the Dover road, is dotted all over with fine seats.

DISTANCES OF PLACES FROM THE STATION.

	Miles.		Miles.
Adisham Down	5	Lee Park	4½
Benkesbourne	3	Littlebourne	4
Beverley Park	1½	Mayton	2½
Blean Church	2	Mote, The	2
Bridge	3	Nackington	4
Broad Oak Common	2	Riabel Wood	2
Broom Park	7	South Street	4½
Dene Park	6	St. Dunstan	1½
Elensden	4½	St. Stephens	1½
Gorsley Wood	4½	Staple Street	4½
Harbledown	0¾	Stone House	1½
Heath Farm	1½	Stuppington Farm	2½
Herne Common	5	Thannington	1½
Ickham	5	Way Street	5
Kingston	5	Wingham	6

CANTERBURY AND WHITSTABLE BRANCH.

Canterbury to Whitstable.

WHITSTABLE.

Distance from station, ¼ mile.

A telegraph station.

HOTELS.—Two Brewers; Bear and Key.

OMNIBUSES to and from the station; also to Faversham.

FAIR.—Thursday before Whit-Sunday.

MONEY ORDER OFFICE at Whitstable.

WHITSTABLE is the harbour of Canterbury, and is celebrated for its oyster fishery, the produce of which, under the name of natives, is highly esteemed in the London and other markets. The town, though rather mean in appearance, and irregularly built, has a bustling and thriving appearance, from its fishing and coal trade.

DISTANCES OF PLACES FROM THE STATION.

	Miles.		Miles.
Balls Street & Bodkin	2	Herne Bay	5
Bostall	1	Rucking	3
Broad Street	1½	Ryeham	1½
Canterbury	6	Sea Salter	3
Chestfield	2	Studhill	2¾
Church Street	0½	Swalecliffe	2
Coleward	2	Tankerton Castle	0½
Elensden	2¾	Thompson's Farm	2¾
Faversham	7	Thorndean Wood	2¾

Ashford, Canterbury, and Ramsgate Branch continued.

Canterbury to Deal, Ramsgate and Margate.

Quitting the Canterbury station, the line proceeds through a similar fertile tract to that which accompanied its progress thither. Cattle grazing knee-deep in luxuriant pastures, farm-houses, cottages, and orchards on one side, and sunny fields, rich in corn and clover, sloping down on the other; these are the chief characteristics of the route for the next eleven miles.

STURRY.

A telegraph station.

HOTEL.—The Swan.

OMNIBUSES to and from the station; also to Herne Bay, thrice daily, Canterbury, &c.

FAIR.—Whit-Monday.

MONEY ORDER OFFICE at Canterbury.

HERNE BAY.

Distance from Sturry station, 6 miles.

Telegraph station at Sturry, 6 miles.

HOTELS.—Pier, and Dolphin.

OMNIBUSES to and from Sturry station, thrice daily

STEAMERS to and from London, twice daily, in summer. (See *Bradshaw's Railway Guide.*)

MARKET DAY—Saturday. FAIR—Easter Monday.

HERNE BAY, so named from the old village of Herne, about a mile and a half distant, which was thus called from the number of herons frequenting the coast at this point, was not twenty years ago more than a scanty collection of houses, irregularly built along the beach. It has now become a fashionable and somewhat populous watering-place, with long lines of streets, many of them still unfinished, stretching out in every direction. In 1831, a pier from one of Telford's designs was commenced, and now presents an elegant and substantial structure, extending 3,640 feet over the sands and sea. At the extremity are commodious flights of steps for the convenience of small vessels and passengers landing at low water, and a fine parade sixty feet in width and upwards of a mile in length has been formed on the adjoining shore. The air is very bleak but invigorating, and the sea purer, it is considered, than at Margate. A considerable portion of the adjacent land, and the very site of the town itself, was anciently covered by the waves, constituting the estuary which admitted the passage of the largest vessels, and divided the Isle of Thanet from the mainland. Mrs. Thwaites, the widow of a wealthy London merchant, has proved a munificent benefactress to the town, for, in addition to having built and endowed two large charity schools, she has caused to be constructed also a clock tower, which serves the purpose of a lighthouse as well. A new church has been built in the centre of the town, with a chapel of ease and a dissenting chapel, and there is also an infirmary for boys from the Duke of York's military school at Chelsea. On the Parade is a large bathing establishment, with an elegant assembly-room adjoining, to which apartments for billiards, reading, &c., are attached. Libraries and bazaars have also been recently introduced in the usual number and variety. The old village church, with its embattled roof and square tower, is a spacious edifice, comprising a nave, two aisles, and three chancels.

GROVE FERRY.

A telegraph station.

MONEY ORDER OFFICE at Canterbury.

From Sturry the main line proceeds in an east-north-east direction, through a highly cultivated country, and enters the Isle of Thanet, near Grove Ferry, where the railway crosses the Wausum, and, proceeding five miles further, reaches the Minster Junction Station, whence a branch line diverges to the ancient towns of Sandwich, and Deal, which we will describe first, and the other, the main line, proceeds to Ramsgate and Margate.

MINSTER JUNCTION.

Distance from station, ¼ mile.

A telegraph station.

OMNIBUSES to and from the station; also to Canterbury, *via* Monkton.

FAIR.—Palm Monday.

MONEY ORDER OFFICE at Ramsgate or Sandwich.

Many of our readers may not be aware that this spot, and the whole neighbourhood, is the classic ground of England, and replete with historical associations of surpassing interest. From the Downs to the north of the village of Minster there is a prospect of great extent and singular beauty. Not only may the Isle of Thanet, with all its churches save one, be seen at a glance, but in the distance are perceptible the towers of Reculver, the Isle of Sheppy, the Downs and town of Deal, the bay and town of Sandwich, the champaign districts of East Kent, the spires of Woodnesborough and Ash, the ruins of Richborough, the green levels of Minster and Saltpans, watered by the Stour, and far on the land horizon at the head of the valley the stately towers of Canterbury Cathedral, the picture finishing with a sweep of hills which spread north and south to the extent of one hundred miles.

Minster is a delightful looking village, and exceedingly interesting. The fine old church is said to be the oldest Christian church in England. The interior has been recently restored, and is very beautiful.

DEAL BRANCH.

After leaving Minster, the line crosses the Stour by a double swing bridge built on a new and ingenious principle. Each line has its bridge; one turns to the right on a pivot on the side of the Minster branch, and the other to the left, from a pivot on the side of Ash, which is the next parish. By this arrangement greater stability is obtained, with a nicer power of adjustment. This bridge is considered a curiosity by engineers, and it will well repay examination. It far surpasses the celebrated bridge at Norwich.

The line then proceeds over Sandwich flats past the hamlet of Saltpans. At this spot the memorable ruins of Richborough come fully into sight; and shortly after the train sweeps round the sandy hill on which they stand. This was a celebrated Roman station, which guarded the southern entrance of the great Roman haven, the area of which is now in the hands of agriculturists, and "*Corn now waves where Cæsars once bore sway.*" The remains of a Roman amphitheatre are still very apparent. In the centre of the great quadrangle is the celebrated prostrate cross, built to commemorate the introduction of Christianity into England. It is placed on the top of an immense heathen altar, and marks the spot on which Augustin preached the gospel. No monument in the kingdom equals this simple cross in interest, yet few have been treated with greater neglect. We commend it to the care of the clergy of Canterbury, the successors of Augustin and his eighty monks.

A short distance further, or four miles and a half from Minster, is the station of

SANDWICH.

Population, 12,710.

A telegraph station.

Hotel.—The Bell.

Market Days. — Wednesdays (corn); alternate Mondays (cattle). Fair.—December 4th.

Money Order Office at Sandwich.

Bankers.—The London and County Bank. Sub-Branch of National Provincial Bank of England.

The traveller, on entering this place, beholds himself in a sort of Kentish Herculaneum, a town of the martial dead. He gazes around him, and looks upon the streets and edifices of a bye-gone age. He stares up at the beetling stories of the old pent-up buildings as he walks, and peers curiously through latticed windows into the vast low-roofed, heavy-beamed, oak-panelled rooms of days he has read of in old plays.

Sandwich is a town of very remote antiquity, and contains more old buildings than almost any other in England. It is rich in ancient hospitals, chantries, hermitages, and venerable churches, many of which, with their towers and buttresses, will take the imagination of the gazer back to the old monkish times, when Sandwich was the theatre of more stirring and important historical events than perhaps any town or port of our island.

Seven miles beyond Sandwich, the train reaches the terminus at

DEAL.

Population, 7,067.

Distance from station, ½ mile.

A telegraph station.

Hotel.—Royal.

Market Day.—Saturday,

Fair.—April 5th and October 10th.

Money Order Office at Deal.

Bankers.—Branch of the National Provincial Bank of England.

This town stands close to the sea shore, which is a bold and open beach, being defended from the violence of the waves by an extensive wall of stones and pebbles which the sea has thrown up. The sea opposite the town, between the shore and the Goodwin Sands is termed the Downs. This channel is about eight miles long and six broad, and is a safe anchorage; and in particular quarters of the wind, as many as 400 ships can ride at anchor here at one time. Deal was formerly a rough-looking, irregular, sailor-like place, full of narrow streets, with shops of multifarious articles termed slops or marine stores. It is however being much improved, and is now resorted to for sea bathing, especially on account of its good repute for moderate charges. The bathing establishment at Deal is well conducted, and there are good libraries.

It is a great pilot station for the licensed or branch pilots of the Cinque Ports; the Deal boatmen are as fine, noble, and intrepid a race of seamen as any in the world, and as honest as they are brave. *Deal Castle* is at the south end of the town. The village of

Walmer is a detached suburb of Deal, towards the south on the Dover Road. Since Her Majesty resided here, Walmer has been much improved and extended. It now contains several handsome villas, inhabited by a large body of gentry. The air is very salubrious, and the surrounding country pleasant and agreeable.

Walmer Castle, one of the fortresses built by Henry in 1539, is the official residence of the Lord Warden of the Cinque Ports. It is surrounded by a moat and drawbridge. The apartments are small but convenient, and command a splendid view of the sea; but they will always have a peculiar interest for Englishmen, as having been the residence of the Duke of Wellington, and at which he died in 1852.

Sandown Castle is about a mile to the north of Deal; it consists of a large central round tower, and four round bastions with port holes, and on the sea-side it is strengthened with an additional battery.

From Minster to Ramsgate the line is on a tolerably steep incline.

Kent and the Kentish coast have long been celebrated for their delicious climate and exquisite pastoral scenery, and the railway passes through a fine panorama of marine and picturesque views, until it reach

RAMSGATE.

Population, 11,838.

A telegraph station.

Hotel.—Royal; Royal Albion; Royal Oak.

MARKET DAYS.—Wednesday and Saturday.

FAIR.—August 10th, at St. Lawrence.

MONEY ORDER OFFICE at Ramsgate.

BANKERS.—Branch of the National Provincial Bank of England. Burgess and Son.

RAMSGATE was little better than a mere fishing village before the close of the last century, and all the noble streets and terraces stretching seaward are the growth of the present. Its prosperity has been literally built on a sandy foundation, more permanent than the adage would teach us to believe, for the sands, which are really unequalled for extent, were long the prominent attraction of visitors. In 1759 was commenced the pier, built chiefly of stone from the Purbeck and Portland quarries, involving an expenditure of nearly £600,000. This stupendous structure affords an excellent marine promenade of nearly three thousand feet in length. The form is that of a polygon, with the two extremities about two hundred feet apart. The harbour comprises an area of nearly fifty acres, and can receive vessels of five hundred tons at any state of the tide. The first object that arrests attention at the entrance to the eastern branch of the pier is the obelisk, fifty feet in height, which commemorates the embarkation of George IV. from here on his Hanoverian excursion in 1821. The next is a tablet, at the octagonal head, setting forth the name of the engineer and the dates of the erection. Opposite is the lighthouse, casting at night a brilliant reflection over the dark waste of waters, and forming a striking feature in the scenery of the coast. Far away, like a phosphoric gleam upon the channel, is the floating beacon called "the Gull," which, with two smaller ones near Deal, becomes visible after dusk from the pier. Eight seamen and a captain, who has only occasionally a month's leave of absence, are entrusted with the management of the beacon, and in this desolate and dangerous region they are doomed to battle with the elements at all seasons, cheered alone by the reflection that through their vigilance thousands are perhaps annually preserved from the perils of shipwreck. The Goodwin sands, traditionally said to have been the estate of earl Godwin, father of King Harold, form the roadstead called the Downs, and extend from the North Foreland to Deal, but as they are continually shifting under the influence of the winds and waves, their exact locality can never be ensured.

Nowhere is the accommodation for bathers more perfect than at Ramsgate, whether the green bosom of the Channel be selected for a plunge, or a private bath chosen instead. Most of these establishments, where baths can be had at all hours, are elegantly fitted up with hot air stoves, luxuriant ottomans, and refectories and reading-rooms adjacent. A communication with the upper portions of the town, built upon the high range of cliffs, is formed by two convenient flights of stone steps, called Augusta Stairs and Jacob's Ladder. The lawny esplanade that has been formed before the crescents facing the sea enables a promenader to obtain an ample sea view, and the Downs being continually studded with shipping, the picture is generally extremely varied and animated. Some elegant churches in the florid Gothic style, and numerous places of dissenting worship, are to be met with in convenient situations about the town, and in Harbour-street is the new Town Hall, erected in 1839, with a capacious market underneath, teeming with every kind of comestible of various degrees of excellence.

Boarding-houses, hotels, and dining-rooms are in the usual watering-place abundance, and the limits of expenditure may be adjusted to the depth of every purse. The bazaars and libraries provide evening amusement in abundance, through the agency of music and raffles; and though the books partake of the elder Minerva press school of composition, and the raffling is generally for articles of indifferent worth, the excitement attendant upon both is quite sufficient for sea-side denizens.

No one of course would think of stopping a week at Ramsgate without going to Pegwell Bay, where the savoury shrimps and country-made brown bread and butter are supposed to have been brought to the very highest degree of perfection. And for a quiet stroll in another direction there is Broadstairs, two miles to the north-east, very genteel and very dull; the aspect of this "exceedingly select" place of residence being so imposingly quiet as to make one involuntarily walk about on tip-toe for fear of violating the solemn sanctity of the place. It is, however, a very agreeable excursion for a day, and an excellent plan is to go by the path across the cliffs, past the elegant mansion of Sir Moses Montefiore, and return by the sands at low water. The old arch of York gate, built by the Culmer family in the reign of Henry VIII., is the sole vestige of the once extensive fortifications that bristled up at the back of the old quay. There was a pier, too, swept away by the terrific storm in 1808, which destroyed that of Margate, but the rough wooden substitute is not the less picturesque, and there is a fine wholesome odour of sea-weed about the old rugged rafters, enough to make one willing to forego the fashionable for the fragrant. A mile beyond is Kingsgate, where Charles II. landed, and furnished a pretext for endowing it with a regal title. Another mile, and the North Foreland lighthouse, 63 feet in height, may be reached, and entered too, if the curious visitor will disburse a small gratuity to the keeper. It is well worthy of inspection.

Four miles distant from Ramsgate, the traveller reaches the terminus at

MARGATE.

POPULATION, 9,107.

Distance from station, ½ mile. A telegraph station.

HOTELS.—Gardner's Royal; White Hart.

STEAMERS to London daily in summer, thrice weekly in winter.

MARKET DAYS.—Wednesday and Saturday.

MONEY ORDER OFFICE at Margate.

BANKERS.—Cobb and Co.

There is not, in the whole range of our sea-side physiology, a more lively, bustling place than this said Margate: albeit, by those who are fettered down to cold formalities, and regard laughter as a positive breach of good-breeding, it is pronounced to be essentially and irredeemably vulgar. The streets are always a scene of continued excitement, and troops of roguish, ruddy-cheeked urchins, escorted by their mammas or their nursery-maids, traverse every thoroughfare about the town from morning until night. There is a theatre also, and a kind of minor Vauxhall, called the *Tivoli*, where those who care little for out-of-door enjoyments can spend a passable hour in such dramatic and musical gratifications as the artists and the place can best afford. Bazaars and marine libraries afford too, in "the season," the latest metropolitan vocal novelties; and the same raffling and rattling of dice-boxes, to test fortune's favouritism, is carried on as at Ramsgate, but with a greater spirit of freedom and earnestness. In short, for those who do not go to the coast for retirement, and who like to have an atmosphere of London life surrounding them at the sea-side, there is no place where their desires can be so easily and comprehensively gratified as here.

The increasing extent and importance of the town makes one regard the traditions told of its early origin as being nearly akin to the fabulous, yet a few centuries back, known to the local chroniclers as coeval with the period of "once-upon-a-time," Margate was a small fishing village, with a few rude huts thrown up along the beach, and having a *mere* or stream flowing at that point into the sea, whence it derived its present appellation. When London folks, however, grew wiser, and found that short trips had a wonderful power in preventing long doctors' bills, the place grew rapidly into repute, and the old Margate hoy—immortalised by Peter Pindar—disgorged its hundreds of buff-slippered passengers annually. Since then steam has done wonders, and Margate visitors have to be numbered by hundreds of thousands in the same space of time. The only drawback to its salubrity as a place of residence is that a cold cutting north-easterly wind is frequently encountered, and not being sheltered by a range of hills, the effect on an invalid of delicate constitution is of rather an injurious tendency than otherwise. But this apart, the air is keen, fresh, and invigorating, and, with persons in good health, will have a material influence in keeping them so. It is generally a few degrees cooler in July and August than Ramsgate. The sixth day of April, 1810, saw the commencement of the present pier, and five years afterwards it was finished from a design by Rennie, and at a cost of £100,000. It is nine hundred feet in length, sixty feet wide, and twenty-six feet high. A day ticket, for one penny will not only give admission to the promenade, but afford an opportunity besides of hearing a band perform for a few hours in the evening. There is a lighthouse at the extremity, which is an elegant ornamental Doric column as well, and was erected in 1829. At an expenditure of £8,000 the well-known Jarvis's Jetty was constructed in 1824, out of the finest old English oak that could be procured. It extends 1,120 feet from the shore, and forms a pleasant cool promenade when the tide is out, although a scurrilous wag has compared it to walking along an excessively attenuated cold gridiron. The Clifton Baths, by the Fort, cut out of the chalk cliffs, are unquestionably the most commodious, and have some interesting appendages in the shape of a library, winding passages, curious vaults, daily newspapers, and an organ. The other bathing-houses, though well conducted, are of a more ordinary character.

Margate being situated partly on the acclivities of two hills, and partly in the valley below, the streets partake of that tortuous and undulating character which is so much pleasanter to look at than to climb. On the Fort, in front of East-crescent, the handsome structure of Trinity Church is conspicuously situated, and to the south-east the old parish church of St. John occupies a similarly elevated position. In this latter there are some curious old tombs and monumental brasses that should not be forgotten. A literary and scientific institution is supported by the annual subscriptions of the inhabitants, and has a library, lecture-room, and museum, that may vie with any out of London.

Extending about a mile along the shore there is a stout barricade of stone, erected as a defence to the incursions of the sea, at an outlay of £20,000. The sum of £4,000 more rebuilt the Town Hall and Market Place in 1821; and from this it will be seen the townsfolk have not been chary of their coin in contributing to the security and embellishment of their native place. Inns and hotels of every grade are scattered in and about the town with prodigal luxuriance, and lodging-houses are everywhere. The staple manufacture of the landladies here may be set down as—beds.

The visitor should not neglect to make a pilgrimage to the old Roman station of Reculver and Richborough, the ruins of the old castle of the latter being still in a state of tolerable preservation.

Races are held on the downs, by Dandelion, in the middle of September, and generally attract a large concourse of spectators.

HASTINGS BRANCH.

Ashford to Hastings.

HAM STREET and APPLEDORE stations.

RYE.

POPULATION, 4,071.

A telegraph station.

HOTEL.—George.

OMNIBUSES to Peasmarsh, Beckley, Northiam, Newenden, Rolvenden, and Benenden.

MARKET DAYS.—Wednesday (Corn), Saturday (Meal), and every Wednesday fortnight (Stock).

FAIRS.—Whit-Monday and August 10th.

MONEY ORDER OFFICE.

BANKERS.—Curteis, Pomfret, Pix, Billingham, and Pix. Branch of London and County Bank.

RYE, a borough town in the county of Sussex. It stands on an eminence near the mouth of the river Rother. In the reign of Edward III., Rye sent nine armed vessels to the royal fleet when that monarch invaded France. In the next reign it was burnt and plundered by the French. From this and other unfavourable circumstances, the town remained for many years in a state of great decay, but its prosperity has in a great measure been restored.

WINCHELSEA.

Distance from station, 1½ mile.

A telegraph station.

HOTEL.—New Inn.

PASSENGER VANS to Hastings.

MARKET DAY.—Sat. FAIR.—May 14th (Cattle).

MONEY ORDER OFFICE at Rye.

The original sea port, which bore its name, was swallowed up by the sea on the eve of St. Agatha, 1287, and although the buildings were then erected further inland, the sea, unappeased by the former sacrifice, broke in anew, and finally, in the time of Queen Elizabeth, altogether choked up the harbour. The ruins of the castle of Ounber, built by Henry VIII., are still standing, and so are three out of the four town gates, but they are in a ruinous condition.

HASTINGS.

Descriptive particulars of this place will be found on page 35.

South Eastern Main Line continued.

Ashford to Folkestone and Dover.

The main line on leaving Ashford makes a gradual approach towards the coast, swerving slightly to the south-east, and having on each side a delighful champaign country. At one part of the route the vestiges of a celebrated fortress suddenly burst upon the vision through the trees to the right, forming all that remains of *Westenhanger Castle*.

The second object worthy of notice is

Merstham Hatch, the property of the Knatchbull family since the reign of Henry VII. The mansion is a modern building, of considerable architectural beauty, situated in a very fine park, and the interior is most elegantly fitted up.

Mount Morris, the seat of Lord Rokeby, is in a splendid park, the heights of which command extensive views of the South Downs, the Channel, and the coast of France.

From this point the line passes almost immediately to the north of the extensive level of Romney Marsh, which may occasionally be seen from the carriages.

WESTENHANGER.

Distance from station, ½ mile.

A telegraph station.

MONEY ORDER OFFICES at Folkestone and Ashford.

Two and a half miles from here are the ruins of *Westenhanger Castle*, once the abode of the ill-fated Fair Rosamond, which are well worthy a visit from any person staying in the neighbourhood.

HYTHE.

HOTEL.—White Hart.

Telegraph station at Westenhanger.

HYTHE lies 3½ miles to the south of Westenhanger Station, easily accessible by omnibuses that meet the trains.

The town of Hythe is small, but clean and healthy, and prettily situated at the foot of a hill extending down to the sea. It is beginning to be resorted to by visitors, for whom accommodation is provided on reasonable terms. The church on the hill has a light tower, ornamented by four turrets. It is one of the Cinque ports. Near Hythe commences Romney Marsh, extending along the coast for twenty miles, and including about 60,000 acres, which within the last few years have been successfully drained and cultivated.

The deep chalk cutting that succeeds our departure from Westerhanger introduces us to Saltwood Tunnel, and, emerging from this, we immediately catch on the right the first transient glimpse of the sea—that sight which involuntarily quickens our pulse, and sends a pleasurable emotion tingling through our veins. A lofty amphitheatre of hills, stretching away in the blue distance, varies the view in the opposite direction. Then comes an embankment, and, borne across a viaduct 90 feet above the valley below, we come almost magically within a fine view of Folkestone and its harbour, immediately afterwards reaching the station at

FOLKESTONE.

POPULATION, 6,726.

A telegraph station.

HOTELS.—Pavilion; Royal George; Clarendon.

OMNIBUSES to and from the station; also to Sandgate, Ashford, Canterbury, &c.

POST HORSES, FLYS, &c., at the hotels.

STEAMERS.—To Boulogne, twice daily in the summer, in two hours, and once in the winter.

MARKET DAY.—Thursday.

FAIRS.—June 28th, and Thursday in Easter Week.

MONEY ORDER OFFICE.

BANKERS.—Branch of the National Provincial Bank of England.

FOLKESTONE is rapidly becoming a much frequented watering place, as well as a favourite point of embarkation to France; the distance to Boulogne is only twenty-seven miles, and the voyage generally accomplished in two hours and a half. The opening of the South Eastern Railway, and the establishment of a line of packets between this port and Boulogne, has been the means of rescuing Folkestone from its previous obscurity, and bringing it to its present position. It is situated on the side of a range of hills on very uneven ground, the streets are narrow, steep, and irregular, and the sea-worn chasms about the shore seem still to perpetuate in appearance that reputation for contraband traffic which once was its distinguishing feature. The air is very salubrious, and has been thought of much efficacy in nervous debility, whilst the country round is highly picturesque, and abounds in varied and beautiful landscapes. Visitors here may enjoy all the benefits of sea bathing and sea air, with more retirement than at Dover or Ramsgate.

Folkestone Hill is 575 feet high, and commands is beautiful prospect of the town and adjacent country through which the railway is seen winding its devious course. To those who do not mind a little pedestrianism, and who delight in formidable ascents and footpaths trembling on the brink of ocean, we can conscientiously recommend a walk across the cliffs to Dover, which besides presenting a succession of romantic scenery will be found to afford some advantageous opportunities for inspecting the shafts connected with the ventilation of the railway tunnels running underneath.

Sandgate, a small watering place two miles from Folkestone, has been much frequented within the last twenty years by invalids, who wish for quiet and retirement. It has several detached villas, and the roads between Folkestone and Sandgate, either along the shore or over the cliff, are exceedingly picturesque and romantic. *Sandgate Castle* is of great antiquity. The country around is highly interesting, and abounds in beautiful views and landscapes, ruined castles, and other remains of olden times.

After leaving Folkestone, the traveller will encounter the most wonderful portion of the line. The rapidity of our progress is such as to allow but little time, however, for examination of the extraordinary engineering works and achievements. Prepared by a shrill shriek of the whistle, we plunge into the Martello tunnel, and then, scarcely with a breathing interval, enter the second or Abbot's Cliff tunnel. Emerging from this, the line continues along a terrace supported by a sea wall for nearly a mile, and presenting a delicious scenic contrast with the marine expanse that opens to the right. This brings us to the Shakspeare Cliff tunnel, double arched for greater security, on escaping from which, an embankment raised from the shingle again receives us, and darting through the smaller excavation of Arch-cliff Fort, we are brought, with varied sensations of dreamy wonder and delight, beneath the elegant terminus at Dover.

The viaduct on the Dover side is also considered a fine work; it is about half a mile long, and formed of heavy beams of timber securely framed and bolted together, but left open so as to offer less resistance to the waves in bad weather.

DOVER.

POPULATION, 22,244.

A telegraph station.

HOTELS.—The Ship; The Lord Warden; The Gun.

POST HORSES, FLYS, &c., at the hotels.

BOATS to mail packets when outside harbour, fare, 2s. each person.

PORTERAGE of luggage to packets and station, 1s. to 1s. 6d. each person.

COACH to Walmer and Deal, four times daily.

STEAMERS to Calais, Boulogne, and Ostend, daily, except on Sundays.

MARKET DAYS.—Wednesday and Saturday.

FAIRS.—November 23rd, lasting over three market days, and Charlton Fair in July.

MONEY ORDER OFFICE at Dover.

BANKERS.—National Provincial Bank of England.

This much frequented point of continental embarkation has of late years occupied a prominent position among the watering-places of our island. The line of continuous terraces of noble-looking mansions spreading along the margin of its coast, the pureness of its atmosphere, the bold and rocky headlands that distinguish its marine scenery, all contribute to give it an important position among the recently created destinations of our sea-loving citizens. The associations, too, that cling to the white cliffs of Albion—not, as of yore, frowning defiance to our Gallic neighbours, but with a better spirit illuminating their weather-beaten features with sunny smiles of welcome—all tend to draw every year crowds of fleeting visitors to a spot so renowned in song and story. It has been well said, that scarcely any great man, from King Arthur to Prince Albert, has failed, at some period or other, to visit Dover, and all history confirms the assertion.

Divided from the French coast by a passage of only twenty miles across the British Channel, Dover is advantageously situated on the margin of a picturesque bay, sheltered by the promontory of the South Foreland, and screened by its lofty cliffs from the piercing northerly winds.

At the entrance to the town from the London-road was the Hospital of St. Mary, commonly called the *Maison Dieu*, and now the guildhall and gaol. It was erected in the reign of King John, by Hubert de Burgh (afterwards Earl of Kent), and intended for the accommodation of pilgrims passing through Dover on their way to or from the Continent. After many changes and alterations, as well as being fortified during the civil war, it was purchased from Government by the corporation in 1834, and converted the following year into a guildhall, sessions chamber, and gaol. The old priory gate, half monastery, half farm, is still remaining, at the beginning of the carriage road towards Folkestone.

Over the butter market in the London-road was the old Town Hall, erected in the reign of James I., on the site of an ancient cross. It is now the Dover Museum, and may be inspected daily from ten till five by the public. The collection comprises various specimens of birds, reptiles, fishes, insects, minerals, fossils, weapons, dresses, coins, and other articles illustrative of the manners and customs of different nations.

Under the museum, the butter market presents, on a Saturday, a busy and lively scene, and the commodities that then pour in from every part of the surrounding country are both plentiful and excellent.

Ancient as Dover is as a town and port, it is, as we have said, comparatively modern as a watering-place. In 1817, houses were commenced on the Marine Parade, and, about the same period, Liverpool Terrace, and the contiguous lawns, Guildford and Clarence, were projected, followed, in 1838, by the noble mansions of Waterloo Crescent and the Esplanade. These form, in conjunction with others, a continuous range of imposing buildings that extend nearly from the Castle cliff to the north pier. Close to the sea is the Promenade, which, during the summer season, presents a complete galaxy of beauty and fashion, not unfrequently enlivened by the performance of military music. The facilities afforded to bathers merit great commendation, and the clear transparency of the water is not the least of the advantages here derived.

If not the most elegant thoroughfare in Dover, Snargate Street is decidedly the most picturesque. With the towering white cliffs on one side, and a row of excellent shops on the other, it presents a contrast that seems to link agreeably the permanent majesty of the past with the fleeting characteristics of the present. Here is situated the Post Office, nearly opposite to Rigden's library, the theatre, the Apollonian Hall, in which concerts are frequently given, and a bazaar, which affords a pleasant lounge for those who like to court the smiles of fortune in a raffle. Adjoining the Wesleyan Chapel, also in the same street, is the entrance to the grand military shaft leading to the heights and barracks above. The communication is by an arched passage and a vertical excavation, having three spiral flights of 140 steps each. The barracks are sufficiently capacious to contain many thousand troops; and beyond, following the military road, we come to the grand redoubt, occupying the site of an ancient Pharos, the ruins of which are called Bredenstone, or the "Devil's Drop." Nowhere will the tourist find more extensive and beautiful views than a promenade at sunset on these heights will afford. Westward is the town of Boulogne, with its lofty column to commemorate an invasion which never took place; eastward, rising as it were from the ocean, is the white tower of the Hotel de Ville, and the revolving phare of the town of Calais. Turn which way we will there is something to admire. On one side is the magnificent Castle, still rearing its stately battlements in majestic grandeur, after braving the blasts of a thousand winters, and bringing back to the eye of the imaginative beholder the by-past glories of the days of chivalry; on the other, the noble cliff, an object sufficiently striking from its own native sublimity, but rendered doubly attractive and interesting to every spectator by its association with the greatest work of our greatest bard. Perhaps in the whole circuit of the kingdom there is not another spot so calculated to awaken in the bosom of an Englishman feelings of pride and exultation, as the objects around call up in succession reminiscences of those martial and intellectual achievements by which the inviolate island of the sage and free has attained her present unquestioned supremacy amongst the nations of the world. An evening stroll on these picturesque heights will amply repay the trouble of the ascent.

Shakspeare's Cliff is about one mile west of the pier, and is exactly 313 feet above high-water mark, being somewhat less than it was in the days of our great dramatist. The descriptive passage that has stood sponsor to it has been so often quoted that we may be well spared its repetition here. A steady foot and a cool head will enable a visitor himself to learn from experience "how fearful and dizzy 'tis to cast one's eyes so low."

But the Castle is, after all, the great lion of Dover, and as the first object that strikes conspicuously upon the eye of the traveller as he emerges from the railway terminus, it is sure to woo his footsteps thither as the cynosure of attraction. Starting on his pilgrimage, early enough, if possible, to behold the artistic effect of the grey sombre ruins, magnified by contrast with a skiey background from which the shades of departing night have not altogether fled, we can promise the pedestrian a rare treat. A sunrise scene from the cliffs round the Castle will honestly challenge comparison with a sunset from the Alps. Well aware that this savours of a bold assertion not altogether orthodox, we merely recommend such as would doubt its veracity to ask Boots to call them at two o'clock in the morning, and try it. Rising northward of the town, from a bold and abrupt ascent of more than 300 feet, and poised upon a commanding eminence, which seems to defy alike the ravages of time and war, Dover Castle answers more to our expectations of what a fortress ought to be than any other defensive building in the kingdom. Its early origin is involved in the mystery of tradition, though there can be little doubt that a British fortification was the nucleus of its future architectural strength. Julius Cæsar has had the honour of erecting the present fortress ascribed to him, but recent antiquaries have come to the conclusion that it was raised between the years A.D. 43 and 49, during the reign of Claudius. The three leading characteristics of the ground plans and buildings are Roman, Saxon, and Norman. All that can now be traced of the fortifications of the former is encircled by a deep ditch. The Saxon portion of the structure is presumed to have been commenced by Alfred the Great, and the foundation of the present keep to have originated with the ingenious Gundulph, Bishop of Rochester, about the year 1153. In its present state the Castle occupies about thirty-six acres.

On approaching the entrance to the Castle from the old Deal road the stranger's notice is first attracted by the faint tinkle of a small bell, moved by a string from the tower of Fulbert de Dover, now used as a debtor's prison. A grated window fronts the road, at which a prisoner stations himself to solicit alms, aided by a further appeal on a board, which bears the following inscription:—

"Oh! ye whose hours exempt from sorrow flow,
Behold the seat of pain, and want, and woe!
Think while your hands the entreated alms extend,
That what to us ye give to God ye lend."

It is seldom that an application of so mournful a nature can be neglectfully regarded. With a glance at the curious piece of brass ordnance, cast at Utrecht in 1544, and twenty-four feet in length, known as "Queen Elizabeth's pocket pistol," we ascend the road leading to the keep, and pass through the gateway from Peverell's Tower, so denominated from an illegitimate son of the Conqueror, who had the command of this post. The keep, situated in the centre of the quadrangle, is a large square edifice rising to an altitude of 100 feet from the ground, and 370 feet above the level of the sea, presenting from its summit a view of almost unequalled grandeur. The famous well, 400 feet deep, was once an important feature of the tower, but it is now arched over for the better security of the public. The old Roman church, and the pharos, or lighthouse, adjoining, are the next objects of interest; its form is that of a cross, with a square tower. On the western side of the church is Cocklecrow or Colton's Gate. Some curious excavations have been made in more modern times for the reception of soldiers, about 2,000 of whom can be here conveniently accommodated; light and air are conveyed into the different apartments by circular apertures cut in the chalk, and by other openings carried through to the face of the cliffs. These remarkable subterranean barracks can be seen on Tuesdays and Fridays by an order from the commanding royal engineer, which can be easily obtained on those days between the hours of ten and twelve at the Ordnance Office, Archcliff Fort. Subterranean communications exist in every direction. Blanchard, the celebrated French æronaut, ascended, in 1785, from the quadrangle of the Castle keep, and, after a voyage of two hours and a half, descended in safety on the continent, at the distance of six miles from Calais. Our modern steam-boat communication with that port has long since outrivalled the ærial voyager in speed.

By the Castle jetty below there have been lately built some neat houses, under the most precipitous part of the cliffs. The situation is pleasant enough, but the tenants must have strong faith in the durability of chalk. For ourselves, not having nerves of iron, all we can say is, that we should decline a lease of 99 years, even upon the most advantageous terms.

Dover harbour suffers much from the accumulation of shingle, and all expedients to remove it, however ingenious, have been ultimately found futile. The simplest, as usual, has proved the best; by means of flood-gates, which are closed at high-tide, the water which flows into the basin and pent is retained; at low water these sluices are opened, and the shingle driven back again by the force of the current.

The Custom House is a spacious building conveniently contiguous to the quay. All passengers' baggage coming from the Continent must be conveyed here for examination. The office hours are from ten till four.

Hotels and taverns, varying in price and accommodation, are unusually numerous; and even cheap coffee-houses, conducted on what is somewhat indefinitely styled "the London system," are now to be met with.

The pretty villages of Charlton and River, and St. Margaret's, with its fine view of the South Foreland, are all within a pleasant three miles' walk or drive from Dover. There is St. Radegund's Abbey, too, an ivied ruin of the twelfth century, which will well repay a visit. Vehicles of every kind can be obtained at a reasonable rate, and for those who delight in water excursions, steam-boats will be found in daily communication with Margate, Ramsgate, and most of the watering-places of the southern coast.

SUSSEX,

One of the Southern Counties, is varied by the inequalities of the Downs and by intervening vallies, to which the wooded scenery and pasture land give a rural and a rich diversity of appearance. It belongs to the chalk formation, and has some high ranges of downs and hills. The north is occupied by *Wealden* formation, covering 420,000 acres, and the south by the chalk formation. On the east are marshes and alluvial lands, and on the west coast it is much indented by, at others it runs out into, bold cliffs.

This county is celebrated for its breed of sheep, which are fed on the South Downs, the name by which they are distinguished. This, and the adjoining counties of Hants and Surrey, were by the Romans denominated Belgæ, from the circumstance of their being inhabited by a people called Belgians, who supplanted the British Celts.

The railway communication of the county of Sussex is supplied by the London, Brighton, and South Coast Railway Company. The London and Brighton main line, commencing at the London Bridge Terminus, proceeds past Sydenham and Croydon to Reigate, thence enters the county of Sussex at Crawley, and passes due South to Brighton, having branch lines extending along the coast to Lewes and Hastings, and Newhaven to the north, and to Shoreham, Worthing, Arundel, Chichester, Havant, and Portsmouth on the south.

The London and Brighton Railway is 50½ miles in length, and traverses a considerable portion of the counties of Surrey and Sussex.

The Brighton Company was the first to commence running excursion trains, which are now provided by most of the other companies throughout the United Kingdom, as affording a profitable source of revenue to the companies, and being the means of "popu larising" the towns, localities, and scenery in connection with the respective lines.

Railways may now be considered as accelerators of pleasure as well as of business, bringing as they do the most favourite watering places along the coast within the compass of a brief and agreeable journey. Of these mediums of transit, we know of few more inviting to the tourist than the one we are about to describe, passing as it does, through a succession of the most varied and diversified scenery, fraught with a host of welcome associations, and terminating at a sea-side town, which fashion in pursuit of pleasure has justly selected for a marine residence.

LONDON, BRIGHTON, AND SOUTH COAST.

London to Croydon.

The London terminus of the Brighton Railway, though approached by the same line as the South Eastern Railway, is a distinct building, occupying a considerable place to the south, at the righ hand or furthest corner of the fabric, and embraces in its arrangements every thing calculated to promote the convenience of the passengers, and all that can contribute to their security.

So entangled is the mighty maze of London with its suburbs, that on emerging from the station it is some time before we entirely lose sight of its multifarious characteristics; we seem, Asmodeus-like, to be fleeting over the habitations of a dense and crowded district. The first part of the line to New Cross is carried over arches, and continues so for some time, passing by a viaduct over market gardens, as far as the Greenwich Junction, and then turns off towards New Cross, where the Company has a large depôt for repairing locomotives. Immediately the line emerges from the streets and houses that obstruct the view, and the Crystal Palace at Sydenham, sparkling in the distance, appears in sight.

NEW CROSS.

From this station the line passes through cuttings that exclude all view of the country; the passengers, however, cannot fail to admire the ingenuity with which the declivities on each side have been converted into flower and kitchen gardens. Emerging from this cutting a wide and extensive prospect of undulating ground is opened on both sides. To the east appears a succession of gardens; to the west, a glimpse of the cemetery at Nunhead is obtained. Sydenham and Norwood appear next in succession, studded with white villas, and on every side a range of wooded and picturesque scenery is unfolded to the view.

FOREST HILL.

Telegraph station at Croydon, 5 miles.

To the right we see Dulwich, famous for the picture gallery, in "Dulwich, or God's Gift, College, founded by Edward Alleyne, the Player, the 'Proteus, for shape, and the Roscius, for tongue.'" Built in 1619, supported by an income of £8,637 arising from landed property and bequests, and which is open for view to the public by ticket. (See *Bradshaw's Guide to London.)* To the left lies the village of Sydenham, celebrated for its beauty and salubrity, and shortly after we reach the station at

SYDENHAM.

Telegraph station at the Crystal Palace.

HOTEL.—Royal.

OMNIBUSES from Norwood to all parts of London every quarter of an hour.

POST OFFICE at the Crystal Palace.

MONEY ORDER OFFICE at Upper Norwood.

This station is situated in the midst of most beautiful scenery and in view of the Crystal Palace. A small branch railway conveys passengers from the station to the palace, from which a continuation of the same railway will convey them on to Croydon to rejoin the main line, if their destination be onwards. Whether the reader be going on a visit to the palace or merely passing it *en route* to a more distant station, the view of the gleaming dome and marvellous structure, which crowns the breezy heights of Sydenham, will always excite his wonder and admiration.

CRYSTAL PALACE.

Situated about half way between Sydenham and Anerley station, on the right side of the railway from London to Croydon, the site of the Crystal Palace on the summit of Penge Park, is one of the most beautiful in the world. Standing on the brow of the hill, some two hundred feet above the valley through which the railway passes, the building is visible for many miles in every direction. But when the train approaches the spot where the brilliant and fairy fabric, in the midst of the most enchanting scenery, is revealed suddenly to the eye, the impression produced elicits our warmest admiration. The models of the diluvian and antediluvian extinct animals, the Irish elk with its magnificently branching antlers, the two Iguanodons, the Megalosaurus, &c., &c., in the foreground among the Geological Islands and Lakes; the cascades and terraces, the luxuriant foliage, flower-beds and fountains, ascending up to the splendid and unrivalled fabric of glass which rears its radiant and glittering bulk upon the Surrey hill, form a *coup d'œil* of wonderful beauty, magnificence, and grandeur, the view of which we may envy the Brighton Railway traveller who enjoys the sight daily, in virtue of his season ticket.

Any one who appreciates the beautiful will always feel gratified even with a passing view; but every person who can spare the time should visit it on a fete day.

Excursion trains to and from London Bridge afford every facility. The building, the grounds or park, the salubrity of the air, the waterworks, the garden inside and out, the fine art courts and collections, form a combination of attractions unsurpassed in any country.

The visitor from London is conveyed to the station of the Crystal Palace in twenty minutes. On emerging from the train he ascends the flight of stairs in the south wing and reaches the centre nave or great transept in a few moments, and immediately beholds that unrivalled view which we all admire with feelings of pride and satisfaction as the most wonderful work human hands and mind have yet achieved.

The whole of the sides of the nave and the divisions on either side are lined with plants and trees from every clime, interspersed with statues and works of art, and embellished with beautiful fountains in the centre. The great transept, with its trees and flowers and fountains divides the nave into two equal parts—the northern division dedicated to art, and the southern to commerce, or to the industrial display of the manufactures of the United Kingdom, which, by the way, under injudicious management is becoming not only less attractive than formerly, but quite contemptible. The transept has the appearance of an immense conservatory, embellished with the finest and rarest models and *chefs d'œuvres* of ancient and modern statuary. This series of courts represents and illustrates the architecture of ancient art.

The **Pompeian Court** is the exact fac-simile of the interior of a building discovered in the ruins of Pompeii. Mosaic pavements and walls, divided into compartments, in which mythological subjects are beautifully painted.

THE TOWER
BUCKINGHAM PALACE
LONDON
NELSON MONUMENT
CRYSTAL PALACE SYDENHAM
LONDON MONUMENT
ROYAL EXCHANGE
HOUSES OF PARLIAMENT
MANSION HOUSE

The **Egyptian Court** is highly suggestive of the grand and massive character of Egyptian architecture and its lion-faced Sphinxes, its solemn heads of colossal women, its gigantic figures, and its walls covered with hieroglyphics.

The **Greek Court,** containing copies of unrivalled works of sculpture, groups of great beauty, and specimens of perfect architecture.

The **Roman Court,** richly stored with Roman sculpture, models, and curious gems.

The **Alhambra Court,** representing several courts of the *famous palace* of the Moorish Kings of Granada, the Court of Lions, and Hall of Justice.

The **Assyrian and Nineveh Court,** displaying the wonders of Nineveh, with its colossal divinities, Rhea, and the gigantic Sphinxes, its eagle-winged and human-headed bulls, and its cuneiform hieroglyphics. And then on the opposite side are the several courts, in which are given illustrations of the Byzantine, Mediæval, and Renaissance styles of architecture, including models of the French, English, German, and Italian schools, each court being complete in itself, and entered by a characteristic doorway.

Modern Picture Gallery.—In this extensive space will be found one of the best lighted and most spacious galleries of modern pictures to be found in England. These works of art have been contributed by proprietors, and also by artists, and many of them are deposited here for sale. Thus this portion of the building combines the attractions of private collections and public exhibitions, with the additional advantage, that only the best works of art are accepted for exhibition.

On leaving the central transept the visitor descends a flight of granite steps leading to the Upper Terrace, which extends within the two dvancing wings of the palace, and commands a splendid view of the gardens, and of the whole country beyond the railway, to the summit of the Surrey hills.

The Terrace Garden is adorned with a central circular basin, throwing out a *Jet d'Eau*, besides others of an elliptical shape. At the extremity of each wing there is a tower in the form of a Greek Cross, which have each on their summit a tank, containing 924 tons of water, to be distributed for any purposes throughout the building. The high towers, of which there are two. one at each end of the building, have been erected for the purpose of carrying the tanks that supply the fountains in the lower basin, and are, with the exception of the tank and stays, constructed of cast-iron.

Flights of steps lead to the Italian and Flower Garden and Terrace below, and to a series of basins and caves, receiving fountains, and waterfalls, containing six times the amount of water thrown up by the Grand Eaux at Versailles.

Along the great walk the water of the upper basin flows down in a series of cascades, until it falls into an open colonnade, and then rushes into falls on each side of the walk, half a mile in length, which supply numerous other fountains.

On ordinary occasions the basins and fountains give life and freshness to the garden, but on fete days the vast waters are unloosed, and rushing upwards in a thousand streams, or dashing over the colonnades, make the whole garden ring with their tumultuous murmurings, producing a magnificent effect, a splendid brilliancy in the sunbeam, joined to the fragrance and freshness of the flowers, of which few can form a conception who have not witnessed it. One of the most curious features of the Palace is the Geological Islands, and the specimens of the extinct animals, life-like gigantic models of which are distributed over the islands and lakes.

There is a splendid Refreshment Room for the first class visitors, where parties can have hot dinners served in first-rate style, at not unreasonable prices.

For the convenience of the inhabitants of Belgravia and the west end of London, a line has been formed to run from Victoria Station, Chelsea, *via* BATTERSEA, NEW WANDSWORTH, BALHAM, STREATHAM, at which there is a tunnel, LOWER NORWOOD, and GIPSEY HILL to the Crystal Palace. The scenery along the line is remarkable for its fertility and beauty. It joins the main line from London Bridge at Norwood Junction, a little below the Palace.

Resuming our seats in the train we arrive at ANERLEY Station.

NORWOOD, UPPER.

Distance from station, 1½ mile.

Telegraph station at the Crystal Palace, 1½ mile.

HOTELS.—Beulah Spa, Royal Albert, Royal Crystal Palace.

MONEY ORDER OFFICE.

NORWOOD is situated on the sides and summit of a considerable eminence, in a most salubrious spot, surrounded with beautiful views of hill and dale, and woodland scenery and of all the most picturesque sites in the two counties of Kent and Surrey. The view, from Upper Norwood, of the west-end of London presents a superb panorama. When the Beulah Spa of Norwood was in its zenith of fame and celebrity, the gipsies were greatly petted by the visitors, but they disappeared with the decline of the Spa, and now rarely visit the neighbourhood. Norwood lies near the Croydon Railway, of which there is a station in the vicinity. The train passes through a lovely and picturesque country.

CROYDON.

POPULATION, 28,000.

Distance from station, 1 mile.

A telegraph station.

HOTELS.—Greyhound, Crown.

MARKET DAYS.—Thursday and Saturday.

FAIRS.—July 6th and October 2nd.

MONEY ORDER OFFICE.

BANKERS.—London and County Bank ; Chasemor and Robinson.

The town of Croydon derives its name from *croie*, chalk, and *dune*, or hill, from which latter term we obtain our English word " downs " as signifying an extensive range of hills. It is situated in the midst of a beautiful country, and is a place of considerable antiquity. It consists of one principal street, more than a mile in length, and a number of smaller ones. The church is a noble building, and has a lofty square tower adorned with pinnacles. The Archbishops of Canterbury, for several centuries, made the old manor house, near the church, their accasional residence. A mile and a half from the town is Addiscombe, at which there is a college for the education of cadets for the service of the East India Company.

At this point there are four distinct lines of rails, an arrangement which insures the safety of travellers at the station, the main line being left free for the passage of any express or special train, and the current train turned off into what are technically termed the "sidings."

The line now passes through a fine open country, and shortly reaches the junction of the Epsom Branch of the Croydon Railway.

EPSOM BRANCH.—Croydon to Epsom.

CARSHALTON.

Distance from station, ¾ mile.
Telegraph station at Crystal Palace.
HOTELS.—Greyhound, King's Arms.
FAIRS.—July 1st and 2nd.
MONEY ORDER OFFICE at Carshalton.
SUTTON, CHEAM, and EWELL Stations.

EPSOM.

POPULATION, 3,390. A telegraph station.
HOTEL.—Spread Eagle.
MARKET DAY.—Wednesday. FAIR.—July 25th.
RACES in April, September, and week before Whitsuntide.

This place is interesting in many points of view, but more especially for its celebrated race-course. It is on the west side of Banstead Downs. During the race week Epsom has the appearance of a busy crowded city; and if the weather be fine, there are seldom less than 60,000 persons assembled here on the great day when the Derby Stakes are contested. The distance was done by Surplice, in 1848, in two minutes forty-eight seconds. Epsom is famous for its mineral spring, from which Epsom salts (sulphate of magnesia) is prepared.

Returning to Croydon we will now pass over the

CROYDON AND WIMBLEDON BRANCH.

Croydon to Wimbledon.

The first stations being BEDDINGTON and MITCHAM, both on the river Wandle. The church of the latter is worth a visit. We then approach the station of MORDEN, near which is *Merton*, possessing much historical interest. Here are the remains of a rich abbey founded for St. Augustine Canons; and here Ethelred I. was defeated by the Danes, 871, and eceived his death wound. Here were enacted "the provisions of Merton," in the reign of Henry III.; and here the glorious Nelson lived. The church is partly of Norman, and partly of the early English styles. *Morden Park*, ½ mile.

WIMBLEDON.—See page 71.

London and Brighton Main Line continued.

Croydon to Three Bridges.

After leaving Croydon we pass through a short cutting, and emerge upon an embankment upwards of two miles long, which affords delightful views of the surrounding scenery; and at the distance of about 4½ miles from Croydon, arrive at the station of

CATERHAM JUNCTION.

This place commands a fine view of several mansions and seats in the surrounding parks. That of *Selsdon Park*, the property of G. R. Smith, Esq.; of *Purley House*, the property of E. B. Kemble, Esq, once the residence of John Horne Tooke; and *Sandershead Place*, the habitation of George Clise, Esq.

CATERHAM BRANCH.—South Eastern.

This branch, the length of which is 4⅝ miles, turns off to the left from Caterham Junction, and passes the stations of KENLEY and WARLINGHAM. The line runs through the valley of Caterham, the country about which is hilly, and beautifully diversified.

CATERHAM.

A telegraph station.
HOTEL—Railway.

The village itself does not possess anything worthy of notice; but there are extensive stone quarries about 1½ mile distant, the quality of which material being well adapted for building, will in all probability cause many villas and residences to be erected here.

London and Brighton Main Line continued.

Proceeding on our way to the south the train passes close to the village of

Chipstead, the church of which, dedicated to St. Margaret, is of Norman style, and of considerable antiquity. Sir Edward Banks, the well-known contractor and builder of the London, Southwark, and Waterloo Bridges, is buried in this quiet and rural churchyard, near the scenes of his early career, where he commenced life in the neighbourhood as a labourer. *The Oaks* (2 miles), Lord Derby.

Proceeding on, some high grounds now intercept our view, until the line enters the Merstham tunnel, rather more than a mile long, and in some parts nearly 190 feet below the surface. The transition from the gloomy darkness of the tunnel to the daylight we had temporarily forsaken is certainly agreeable, and we are rewarded on emerging by a pretty view of the little village of Merstham, and the adjacent country.

After passing Merstham station, which is a minor one, we obtain a fine view of *Gatton* and its picturesque park, the property of the Dowager Countess of Warwick, and famous before the Reform Bill as having returned two members to parliament, with a population of a hundred persons, living in scarcely two dozen houses. Half a mile further on, an embankment 20 feet high brings us to

REIGATE or RED HILL

See page 29.

This station is reciprocally used by both the Brighton and Dover trains, the latter diverging to the east, and we at once enter the valley of Holmesdale. The hills to the north seclude both the villages of Nutfield and Bletchingly. Leaving Reigate to the right, we proceed across the embankment formed by Earl's Wood, from which a succession of beautiful varied scenery lures the eye. Leith Hill, Box Hill, and the eminences round Dorking may be clearly discerned.

HORLEY.

Distance from station, ¾ mile.
A telegraph station.
HOTEL.—King's Head.

Horley was once famous for its iron works. It has traces of an old castle. The church is a fine edifice, and contains some handsome monuments.

From the Horley station the line begins for some time rising, and the view on every side continues, as before, uninterrupted.

Four miles beyond, the railway passes over the boundary line into the county of Sussex, and arrives at

THREE BRIDGES.

A telegraph station.
This station is the junction point of the

HORSHAM BRANCH.

Three Bridges to Horsham and Petworth.

This branch is 8½ miles in length. The line proceeds nearly in a west-south-west direction to the station at

CRAWLEY,

a neat, clean town, of some note in the coaching times.

The line passes through a rural district, presenting no feature of importance, to

FAY GATE,

in the vicinity of Lord St. Leonard's estate.
MONEY ORDER OFFICE at Horsham.
Telegraph station at Horsham, 3½ miles.

HORSHAM.

POPULATION, 5,947.
A telegraph station.
HOTELS.—King's Head, and Anchor.
MARKET DAYS.—Saturdays (corn), Mondays (poultry).
FAIRS.—April 5th and 18th, July 17th, November 27th, and Monday before Whitsuntide.

This town stands on the River Adur, and is considered, in a commercial point of view, one of the most important in the county.

BILLINGSHURST and PULBOROUGH Stations.

PETWORTH.

HOTELS.—The Swan; Half Moon.

This town has a population of 2,427, and occupies a very healthy situation near the river Rother. The principal attraction is *Petworth House*, close by, the superb residence of General Wyndham, formerly that of the Earls of Northumberland. Here are a fine collection of paintings, many by Vandyke, old tapestry and various works of art, together with the sword used by Hotspur at the battle of Shrewsbury The park, in which the museum stands, is 12 miles in circumference. In the church may be seen many of the tombs of the Percys and Wyndhams.

EAST GRINSTEAD BRANCH.

Three Bridges to East Grinstead.

This branch is about 6½ miles long, passing through the small village of ROWFANT, four miles beyond which brings us to the town of

EAST GRINSTEAD.

MARKET Day.—Thursday.
FAIRS.—Last Thursday in every month; also April 21st, June 25th, November 8th, and December 11th.

This was one of the places disfranchised by the Reform Act of 1832. It contains a population of 3,820, and a good sized church with a monument, the inscription on which purports the church to have been founded by R. Lewkner, Esq., the wife of whom had been connected with the courts of Edward IV. and Henry VII.

London and Brighton Main Line continued.

Three Bridges to Hayward's Heath.

The line now passes over an embankment of considerable length, and the railway thence commences a descent. Passing through a series of cuttings, we enter the Balcombe tunnel, the second of the great tunnels along the line, soon after emerging from which we arrive at the Balcombe station.

The line proceeds southward, and enters the Weald of Sussex through Tilgate Forest, and to the Balcombe tunnel.

BALCOMBE.

Distance from station, 1 mile.
Telegraph station at Hayward's Heath, 4 miles.
MONEY ORDER OFFICE at Cuckfield.

To the left, on the hills, is *Wakehurst Place*, the estate of Sir A. Cockburn, St. Leonard's Forest on the right. The rivers Adur, Arun, and Ouse have their source in this forest, within a circle of three or four miles in diameter.

A short distance further on the line crosses the Ouse by the viaduct of that name, one of the finest works in the kingdom, which is only excelled by the viaduct over the Dee on the Chester and Shrewsbury Railway. It consists of 37 arches, and its summit commands extensive views of the surrounding country.

As we are whirled along it, the prospect presents us with an unbounded scene of beauty, the country round being steeped in the most luxuriant verdure, and hill and dale, woodland and pasture land, succeed each other in infinite variety to the very verge of the horizon.

HAYWARD'S HEATH (Junction).

Distance from station, 1¼ mile.
A telegraph station.
MARKET DAY.—Friday, at Cuckfield.
FAIRS.—April 23rd and Nov. 18th, on the heath; Sept. 16th and Thursday in Whit-week, at Cuckfield.
MONEY ORDER OFFICE at Cuckfield.

NEWHAVEN BRANCH.
Hayward's Heath to Lewes and Newhaven.

The line passes through an undulating, and in some places a hilly, country, to

COOK'S BRIDGE.—Three miles further the train reaches

LEWES.

POPULATION, 9,533.
Distance from station, ½ mile. A telegraph station.
HOTELS.—White Hart, family; Crown, commercial.
MARKET DAY.—Tuesday. FAIRS—Whit Tuesday, May 6th, July 26th, and Sept. 21st.

LEWES is a borough town in the county of Sussex, and one of the largest and most important in the whole county. It stands on the banks of the River Ouse, about seven miles from the sea-coast. Lewes is a place of great antiquity, and the vestiges of walls and entrenchments still remaining prove how strong the fortifications must have been. It is well built, and contains several excellent streets, with uniform and elegant buildings. There are also two large suburbs, one on the west side of the town called Southover, and the other on the east side of the river, on a chalk cliff, and hence called Cliff. It contains seven churches, and the ruins of an old castle, and will be memorable in future ages as having been the abode of the Russian prisoners captured by the Allied Powers of England and France in the fierce contests of 1854-55.

UCKFIELD BRANCH.
Lewes to Uckfield.

From hence this line, 7 miles long, passes through the villages of BARCOMBE and ISFIELD to

UCKFIELD.

HOTELS.—Maidenhead; Bell.
Besides its two chalybeate springs in the neighbourhood it has no particular attractions.

NEWHAVEN.

A telegraph station.
HOTEL.—Bridge Inn.
STEAM PACKETS to Dieppe daily in summer, to Jersey, twice weekly.
FAIR.—October 16th.

NEWHAVEN, formerly a very obscure port or fishing town at the mouth of the river Ouse, is now a rising place, and become of some importance, as the port of communication between London, Dieppe, and Paris. Louis Philippe landed here in 1848, after his flight from France.

Branch Line continued.
Lewes to Hailsham, Eastbourne, & Hastings.

The line from Lewes turns eastward, round the foot of Mount Caburn, and after passing through a valley in the South Downs, reaches the station at

GLYNDE.

Distance from station, ½ mile.
Telegraph station at Lewes, 3 miles.
MONEY ORDER OFFICE at Lewes.

The station is near the village of Glyndebourne, in the vicinity of which is *Glynde Place*, the seat of Sir J. Langham, and *Firle Place*, the property of Viscount Gage. The South Downs, at Firle Beacon, rise to the height of 820 feet.

The line then passes the villages of Selmeston and Alceston to the station at

BERWICK,

a little to the north of the village of the same name.
Telegraph station at Lewes, 7½ miles.
HOTEL.—Fuller's Arms.
MONEY ORDER OFFICE at Eastbourne.
Four miles beyond, the line reaches the station at

POLEGATE (Willingdon).

Distance from station, 1 mile.
A telegraph station.
MONEY ORDER OFFICE at Eastbourne.
Short lines branch off here in opposite directions to Hailsham and Eastbourne.

HAILSHAM (Branch).

A telegraph station.
HOTELS.—Turmunus, George, and Crown.
MARKET DAY.—Wednesday (cattle).
FAIRS.—April 6th and June 3rd.
MONEY ORDER OFFICE at Hailsham.

HAILSHAM, three miles from the junction, is a quiet little market town, situated on a gentle declivity. It has the remains of a priory, and the pinnacled church of Edward III.'s time is rather handsome.

EASTBOURNE (Branch).

Distance from station, 1 mile.
Telegraph station at Lewes, 16 miles.
HOTEL.—Lamb.
MARKET DAY.—Saturday.
FAIRS.—March 12th and October 10th.
MONEY ORDER OFFICE at Eastbourne.

EASTBOURNE has, within a very few years, become fashionable as a watering-place. The bathing is very good, and a number of machines are employed

It has also the advantage of mineral springs, the waters of which are said to resemble those of Clifton A theatre, a ball-room, a library, and reading-rooms are the principal attractions of the town, and there are good walks and rides. It lies about three miles west of Beachy Head, is much recommended for its bracing air, and offers the somewhat rare attractions of the beauty of country scenery and stately trees, almost close to the sea. Eastbourne town lies about a mile and a half from the beach or sea-houses, the actual watering place. The sea-houses comprise hotels, lodging houses, baths, &c. Beachy Head on the right is a favourite excursion point. To the leftis the esplanade, and further inward the large circular fort of redoubts; and in the distance several martello towers. Eastbourne has one of the finest chruches iu the country—Norman and early English.

Hastings Branch Line continued.

Immediately on leaving Polegate, eastward, commences the Pevensey level, the scene of the Norman Conquest; and the coast from hence to Hastings is rich in association with this grand chapter of our civilisation.

PEVENSEY,

near the town of that name.

Telegraph station at St. Leonards, 9¼ miles.

HOTEL.—Royal Oak.

MARKET DAY.—Thursday (Southdown Sheep).

FAIRS.—July 5th and Sept. 15th.

MONEY ORDER OFFICES at Eastbourne and Hailsham.

Though formerly a place of so much importance as to give name to the hundred, it has now dwindled to an inconsiderable village; and the sea, which formerly laved the castle walls, has now receded to a distance of two miles. A number of martello towers, erected at the time of the last war—we hope the phrase will be just as applicable for a hundred generations yet to come—remain as memorials of the means resorted to for the defence of the coast. The history of Pevensey might be easily expanded by a skilful topographist into a volume, but a brief enumeration of the leading features will suffice to acquaint the visitor with its bygone glories. It first appears in our chronicles in A.D. 792, when honourable mention is made of it as having been generously given by Bervald, a general of Offa, to the Abbey of St. Denis at Paris. In the reign of Edward the Confessor it was dignified by twenty-four burgesses, and was ravaged by Earl Godwin, falling shortly after the reign of Henry III. into hopeless decay. The castle was attacked by Simon de Montfort in 1265, and, in 1339, by the partisans of Richard II., when it was bravely defended by the Lady Jane Pelham. The outer walls of the castle enclose an area of seven acres, and are about twenty feet in height. Within is a smaller fortification, moated on the north and west, and of a quadrangular form, with round towers. The entrance was formerly by a drawbridge. The eastern wall of both is the same, and stands upon a shelving eminence. The circumference of the inner wall is about 25 rods, and of the outer walls 250. When entire it must have been of great strength. Antiquaries differ about its first builders, but if not of Roman origin it is at any rate constructed of Roman materiais, and, though the adjective savours somewhat of a pun, it may be added that its present aspect is decidedly romantic. The church is but an ordinary looking structure, with a square tower at the west end. It is dedicated to St. Nicholas. The rich pastures of Pevensey level afford fine grazing for cattle, and have contributed much to the profit and renown of the graziers surrounding.

The Castle of Hurstmonceaux, on an eminence five miles distant, at the end of a long valley, looks a noble and imposing structure, and, although a ruin, is in very good preservation.

The railway proceeds along the coast to the station at

BEXHILL,

The village of which name is situated on a rising ground not far from the sea. It is a quiet, retired place, having some good iron springs, and is situated in a beautiful country.

Telegraph station at St. Leonards, 3 miles.

HOTEL.—Bell.

FAIRS.—June 28th, and 1st Monday in July.

Many persons prefer the retirement of Bexhill, with its fine bracing air, to the excitement and bustle of the neighbouring towns.

ST. LEONARDS.

A telegraph station.

HOTEL.—Royal Victoria; Royal Saxon.

MARKETS.—Daily.

MAILS.—Two arrivals and departures, daily, between London and St. Leonards.

BANKERS.—Charles Henry Southall, on account of Messrs. Smith, Hilder, and Co., of Hastings.

ST. LEONARDS, the recognised "west-end" of Hastings, with which is now connected, a fine noble archway marking the boundary of the two townships, was planned and executed by the well-known architect, Mr. Decimus Burton, who only commenced his bold project in 1828. Hotels of eastern magnificence, public gardens, looking like realisations of the Arabian Nights' descriptions, libraries where the most fascinating novel gains an additional charm from the luxurious sea-fronting ottomans, on which their perusal may be indulged, together with an esplanade peerless in its promenading conveniences—these are but a few of the manifold attractions which St. Leonards holds forth to tempt the errant visitor into becoming a stationary resident.

On the hill, by the railway station, as you approach Bulverhithe, may be seen the ruins of the Conqueror's Chapel, supposed to mark the spot where he landed. Recent antiquaries have laboured to prove that it must have been nearer Pevensey.

HASTINGS TERMINUS,

And description of town, see page 35.

London and Brighton Main Line continued.

Hayward's Heath to Brighton.

Two miles to the right of Hayward's Heath is Cuckfield, a pleasantly situated market town, which has a handsome church in a picturesque spot. The neighbourhood of Lindfield on the other side is also very beautiful.

A cutting of nearly two miles leads us to an embankment over St. John's Common.

Four miles further is the station at

BURGESS HILL.

Telegraph station at Hassock's Gate, 2 miles.

MONEY ORDER OFFICE at Hurst.

The line passes through a beautiful, cultivated, and fertile country to

HASSOCK'S GATE

A telegraph station.

MONEY ORDER OFFICE at Hurst.

From the Hassock's Gate station, a graceful piece of Gothic architecture marks the entrance to the Clayton tunnel, which is cut through blocks of chalk. These enormous chalk hills are composed of lime, in chemical combination with carbonic gas, the same which sparkles in a bottle of soda water; and if nature had not combined these substances, the first shower of rain would raise the lime to a great heat. and these stalwart cliffs would crumble into atoms

On the left is Ditchling Beacon, 864 feet high, on the South Downs, where about a half a million of prime sheep are fed. The train thence passes Clayton and Patcham tunnels. On the right is Devil's Dyke, noted for its extensive view over the woodland in the Weald. As the train approaches the village of Preston, and the platform of the Brighton terminus, the guards collect the tickets, and the passenger has an opportunity of noting the two branch lines that diverge from Preston, one across the Preston viaduct to Lewes, and the other through a deep cutting towards Shoreham, Worthing, Chichester, and Portsmouth.

BRIGHTON.

POPULATION, 69,673.

A telegraph station.

HOTELS.—The Bedford Hotel; Royal York; Bristol; Old Ship; Pier; the Clarence, &c.

OMNIBUSES to and from the station and Hove every train, and Shoreham, daily.

MARKET DAYS.—Tuesday (corn), and Saturday.

FAIRS.—Holy Thursday, and September 4th.

BANKERS.—The Brighton Union Bank; Hall, West and Co; London and County Bank

The BRIGHTON TERMINUS is an elegant structure, fitted up in the most convenient manner. There is a portico in the Roman architectural style, which projects on pillars into the street, and is surmounted by an illuminated clock.

This once famous resort of royalty and fashion may now, through the literal as well as metaphorical levelling of the railroad, be fairly entitled to the appellation of the Marine Metropolis. Merchants who formerly made Dulwich or Dalston the boundaries of their suburban residences, now have got their mansions on the south coast, and still get in less time, by a less expensive conveyance, to their counting-houses in the city. Excursions are now made with greater facility, and possibly more enjoyment, to Brighton, than would have, a few years back, sufficed for the common-place pilgrimage to Hampton Court; and a constant succession of trains, conveying a host of pleasure-seekers and business men to and fro, now traverse with marvellous frequency and precision the line that has sprung, by the magical enterprise of man, from tracts of waving corn-fields and boundless breadths of pasture.

About two miles from Brighton, Hollingbury Hill—no mean eminence of itself—stretches northward towards Lewes, and occupies a conspicuous position in the landscape. Before you is a majestic range of buildings—such as perhaps no other town in the kingdom can boast—sweeping down the sides of the cliff in every direction, and sheltering the three miles of architectural magnificence which forms the sea frontage, whilst beyond spreads the swelling sea, an object of such grandeur as in its ever-changeful expanse to outvie the lavish richness with which art has fringed its cliffs and shingled shores.

As will be at once apparent on descending the street leading from the station, the town is seated on an eminence that declines gradually towards the south-east, with a sloping undulation towards the Steyne, and then again ascends to the eastward. The twang of saltness that greets the lip, and the freshening, invigorating tone of the breeze, are agreeable proofs, on your first entrance, of the bracing bleak atmosphere that characterises the climate, though in various portions of the town, more sheltered, the air will be found adapted to the exigencies of the most delicate invalid. The panoramic view that first bursts upon the eye is so striking of itself, that it may be worth while glancing at it in detail, for the benefit of the visitor's future peregrinations.

To the left are seen two noble turfed enclosures, both thickly planted with shrubs, and laid out in the style of our metropolitan squares. The further section, intersected by a road, is the old Steyne, in the northern enclosure of which is Chantrey's bronze statue of His Majesty the fourth George, erected in 1828, at a cost of £3,000, collected among the visitors and inhabitants. This memorial crowns the square, and, as it were, points out the actual founder of the magnificence and prosperity of the place. The building which rises with domes and minarets, and is fretted with greater variety than taste, is—we cannot say how long it will remain—the Marine

Pavilion of her Majesty, erected for George the Fourth, after a fanciful oriental model, which, despite its supposed resemblance to the Moscow Kremlin, has had no precedent before or since. Adjoining are the royal stables, the main architecture of which is a vast glazed dome, lighting a circle of about 250 feet. It will be seen that the chief streets are not only wide and handsome. but well paved and brilliantly lighted, whilst the shops are of absolute metropolitan magnificence, with goods equalling in quality, and, on the average, not much excelling in price, the wares destined for a London sale. The profusion of squares, terraces, crescents, and steynes, with the bold beauty of the esplanade itself, produces a pleasing impression of variety, enhanced by the amphitheatre of hills that enclose the town beneath, and loom out in startling relief against the summer sky. The groups of animated nature identified at the corner of every thoroughfare, and the busy stragglers of the streets, are all of the marked watering-place description —pleasure seekers, out for the day, and eager to be ubiquitous, hurrying to and fro, through the market, to the spa, the race-course, the windmill, the beach, the shops, and the chain-pier, in as rapid succession as the most ingenious locomotion could devise. Then appear invalids, trundled out in bath chairs on to the Parade, to catch the earliest sunbeams; scores of laughing, chubby, thoughtless children, skilled manifestly in the art of ingeniously tormenting maids, tutors, governesses, and mammas; prawn-sellers and shell-fish hawkers a few, and flymen a multitude, all idly vociferating, whilst, intent upon their customary constitutional walk, the morning *habitués* of the promenade swing lustily past. Let us mingle with the throng, aud obtain a closer intimacy with the principal features of the place.

Kemp Town—the most magnificent range of private dwellings in the kingdom—is on the estate of Thomas Read Kemp, Esq., of Black Rock, at the eastern extremity of Brighton, and is fronted by an esplanade, which is a delectable spot whereon to cultivate the intellectual. On a clear day the eye may reach from Beachy Head to the Isle of Wight, catching between the points many a bold outline of cliff and crag. The cliff here is 150 feet high, and the tunnel under the road, cut through the rock from the centre of the crescent lawn, is a very ingenious mode of shortening the distance to the lower esplanade. From Kemp Town a brisk walk over odoriferous downs brings us to Rottingdean, a village rather peculiar than either pretty or picturesque. It is famous chiefly for its wells, which are empty at high water, and full to overflowing at ebb tide. There is, however, an excellent inn for the accommodation of company, unexceptionable in the quality of its fare.

Returning past the old Steyne, we arrive opposite Mahomed's baths, in the busiest part of Brighton. Here we find fishermen mending their nets, boats laid up for repair, the fish-market and vendors engaged in every characteristic employment to be met with in a maritime town. Here also are pleasure-boats and sailing-vessels to be hired, where, if a party club together, a few hours' sail may be compassed for a dozen shillings. From here the Market Hall is but a short distance; it stands on the site of the old Town Hall, and was built in 1830. It answers every purpose in being spacious, unconfined, and well supplied daily with fresh and fine comestibles. The new Town Hall – a vast pile of building, with three double porticoes—cost £30,000, and has a handsome assembly-room on the upper story, rendered available for divers purposes of provincial legislation and amusement.

A few, very few, years back, the battery was on the western verge of the town, and beyond it the several houses seemed to be fairly in the country. A quiet hotel or two, and a bathing establishment, reminded us that we were still in Brighton, and a solitary villa, belonging to the Countess St. Antonio—a kind of Italianized cottage, with two wings, then the scene of many a gay rout, notwithstanding its humility—just kept the fashion of the place in mind as, many a time and oft, we lingered on the rough and barren road to Shoreham, strewn with the flowers of hoar antiquity.

The line of extension has now become almost interminable, and most conspicuous in the elongation of the western esplanade is Brunswick-terrace, built from the designs of Mr. Busby, a son of Dr Busby, of musical memory. The terrace consists of forty-two splendid houses, and has a very majestic aspect. Between the two great divisions of the frontal line lies Brunswick-square, open to the sea towards the south, and the whole is fronted by an artificial esplanade, which extends a mile in length. Along this delightful walk the votaries of fashion are wont to exercise their "recreant limbs," and recruit their wasted energies with the invigorating sea-breeze.

The chain-pier, which has been for years entitled to the first consideration of the Brighton visitor is well worthy of being still considered its greatest lion.

Hazlitt has said, "there is something in being near the sea like the confines of eternity. It is a new element, a pure abstraction." The mind loves to hover on that which is endless and ever the same, and the wide expanse which is here visible gratifies this feeling to the uttermost. The approaches to the pier are handsome and spacious, and the reading-room at the north end, with its camera above, is a delightful lounge for the promenader, who, having inhaled health by instalments of breathing, may therein plunge into the world of fiction, and enjoy a perusal of the last new novel with the zest of a marine atmosphere.

Churches, chapels, and meeting-houses, of all ages and for all denominations, are plentifully strewn over the town. The most modern is the handsome church of St. Peter's, erected about twenty years ago, in the best pointed style, by Sir C. Barry, the well-known architect of the new Houses of Parliament. But the oldest, and perhaps the most interesting, is the ancient parish church of St. Nicholas, standing on the summit of a hill at the north-west extremity of the town. It is an excellent sea and land-mark, and is said to be as old as the reign of Henry VII. From this pleasant locality the esplanade and parade are seen to much advantage. Gay loiterers of pleasure, and donkey parties, regiments of schools, and old bathing women, literary loungers, who read out of doors, and stumble against lamp-posts in interesting passages—these, and a host of other peripatetic humanities, make the beach populous between Hove and Kemp Town.

With regard to inns, taverns, hotels, lodging and boarding-houses, nowhere are they more numerous than here, their excellence of accommodation of course varying with price. Bathing establishments, too, are almost as numerous, whilst, for amusements, there is no provincial town in the kingdom that can offer such a variety of assembly and concert-rooms, libraries, bazaars, and other expedients for slaughtering our common enemy—Time. In the New-road is the theatre—one of the prettiest out of London—and close adjoining is the Post-office, concerning which, in these economical days of epistolary communication, it may be as well to know the precise hours of dispatch and delivery. The London letters are delivered at 7 30 a.m. and 1 p.m.; the box for London closes at 10 45 a.m. and 9 30 p.m. The number of extra receiving houses about the town materially increases the accommodation.

The race-course is about a mile and a half northward of the town, on the summit of one of the loftiest and most commanding downs in the neighbourhood. The races generally take place early in August.

As the Brighton excursionist will go to the Devil's Dyke, as a matter of course, we do not stay to tell him how he shall behold therefrom the Isle of Wight, spread beneath him like a map, or Beechy Head, looming like a snow-peak to the east, and the Downs far away, mingling with the horizon. But be it gently whispered, that on the margin of this demoniacal defile there standeth a small hostel, the glories of whose bread and cheese and ale have been sung by many an aristocratic voice. Everybody that ever was there assures you that for baking and brewing it stands unrivalled, although we shrewdly suspect that the preparatory course of Southdown oxygen hath a wonderful agency in eliciting this appreciation of a fare so humble.

BRIGHTON AND LEWES BRANCH.

The Preston viaduct of this short line is a magnificent structure, consisting of an elliptic arch 50 feet span, and 73 feet high, flanked on one side by 18, and on the other by 9 semicircular arches, 30 feet span; the former are built on a curve of three-quarters of a mile radius, and the latter on a 10 chain radius. The length of the viaduct is 400 yards, and ten millions of bricks were used in the construction. In consequence of its being on the curve, one side is above 40 feet longer than the other; all the arcades radiate towards the centre of the curve, and the piers are one foot eight inches thicker at one end than the other, in order to render the openings parallel. The viaduct is universally admired for its beautiful proportions. The view from its summit is exceedingly fine. On the elevated ground to the right is the extensive terminus of the Brighton Railway, and in front lies the town of Brighton and its fine expanse of sea.

After crossing the above viaduct, the line passes through a short tunnel (sixty yards) beneath the Ditchling Road, and the deep chalk cuttings on either side. Just beyond the cutting a bridge crosses the road, forming the northern boundary of the parish of Brighton. After passing through another cutting of considerable length and depth, the line extends along the side of the hill at the back of the Cavalry Barracks, and consists of embankment and cutting combined. Another cutting brings us to Moulscombe, a neat villa, the grounds of which are bisected by the railway, and again connected by a bridge. A deep cutting leads us to Hodshrove, where the Lewes turnpike road is crossed by a skew-bridge of three arches, which are of noble proportions and of massive strength. From this point, the line which had hitherto run on the western side of the Lewes road, lies entirely on the eastern side. A high embankment and deep cutting follow; and we then pass another long one skirting the front of the Earl of Chichester's Park at Stanmer. This is the most beautiful domain on the line; the estate comprehends the whole parish and village of Stanmer, including the church. The park occupies a valley formed by one of those bold ranges of hills which adorn the coasts of this county; and its undulating surface, varied by thick masses of foliage, forms a rich contrast to the open downs by which it is environed. The Stanmer elevation brings us to the foot of

FALMER.

Telegraph station at Lewes, 4¾ miles.

HOTEL.—Swan.

MONEY ORDER OFFICES at Lewes and Brighton.

A deep cutting commences here, which is succeeded by a tunnel, followed by another deep cutting; then a shorter one, and we obtain a sight of Lewes, St. Anne's Church and the Castle being the most prominent objects. Nothing remarkable occurs after this till we reach the foot of Water Shoot Hill, where the railway crosses the Winterbourne, and taking a course to the right by a short tunnel enters Southover, passing under the road which leads from Lewes to Newhaven. It then crosses the priory grounds, and thus arrives at the station at

Lewes, which is in High Street, at the foot of School Hill. For description, see page 54.

PORTSMOUTH BRANCH.

Brighton to Worthing, Chichester, and Portsmouth.

On leaving the terminus the line turns off abruptly towards the east, and passing through the New England tunnel, cut in the chalk cliff beneath Henfield Road, reaches the station at

HOVE.

This village is now a suburb, or continuation of Brighton. The old church of Hove is a fine edifice, and there is a new cross-shaped one, with a tall spire.

There are fine walks here over the Downs. The summit of a high cliff in the neighbourhood, called the Devil's Dyke, is much visited for the fine views it affords of the surrounding country.

PORTSLADE and SOUTHWICK stations.

KINGSTON-ON-SEA.

A telegraph station.

HOTEL.—Kingston Inn.

MONEY ORDER OFFICE at Shoreham.

This village is situated on the right of the line; it has a harbour and wharf, and is said to be prosperous and thriving.

The line proceeds along the shore, presenting no feature worth remarking, and reaches

NEW SHOREHAM.

A telegraph station.

HOTELS.—Surrey Arms, Buckingham Arms, and Swiss Cottage.

MARKET DAY.—Every alternate Monday (corn)

FAIR.—July 25th.

OLD SHOREHAM, on the right of the line, has a fine old Saxon church, which has been recently restored, and is much admired as a beautiful specimen of Saxon architecture.

NEW SHOREHAM is a borough town and a port, situated at the mouth of the River Adur, over which there is a suspension bridge. The harbour is about a mile to the eastward of the town.

The SWISS GARDENS, a kind of Vauxhall, are beautiful. The grounds are admirably laid out, and a constant succession of amusements provided in exchange for the shilling that entitles you to the admission. The cottage is called the "Swiss Cottage"—not that the peasants are so lodged in Switzerland, but that in novels and noblemen's parks structures of one story high are thus denominated. The material must have cost less than the workmanship, for the doors, windows, and less substantial parts of the fabric are composed of little pieces of stick with the bark on—not expensive by any means, but so picturesque, as a young lady will be sure to remark within your hearing. Inside this Helvetian habitation there is a *salon â manger*, on a great scale, besides several little saloons for refreshment and flirtation, being, in fact, refectories for two inside—the most compact and comfortable places you can imagine. Added to this, there is a little theatre, a concert, music, swings, and oracles of divination, for all who choose to consult the mystic temple of the Sybil. Of the whole place it may be said, with justice, that there is not in England another so well designed, or preserved in such excellent order.

Few districts in England exhibit more interesting relics of the early history of the island than this part of Sussex. Shoreham was certainly a place of importance previous to the Conquest. Subsequently its geographical position must have added still more to its consequence. From the Downs to Portsmouth the coast is, even in our day, most difficult of access—ten centuries ago it was without a landing-place for vessels of burden, or for craft of any sort, with strong winds from three points of the compass, except Newhaven and Shoreham. As easterly winds are—happily for folks of rheumatic tendency—more rare than any others for nine months in the year, these two places probably monopolised all the intercourse between Great Britain and her French territories. For this reason splendid and unique specimens of Norman architecture abound in Sussex. Of these, not one of the least remarkable is the parish church of New Shoreham. It was originally formed as a crucifix, and covered a great deal of ground. The embellishments are still of rare richness and variety, and are full of interest as marks of the state of the arts in those remote days.

LANCING STATION

Is close to the pretty "sea-side" village of that name, known as Lancing-by-Sea, which is in some repute as a quiet, retired bathing-place, but it is excessively dull and *ennuyant*.

Telegraph station at Worthing, 2½ miles.

HOTELS.—The Farmer's, and Sussex Pad.

MONEY ORDER OFFICE at Shoreham.

A few miles beyond this we reach the more important station and town of

WORTHING.

POPULATION, 5,370.

A telegraph station.

HOTELS.—Sea House and Steyne.

OMNIBUSES to and from the station and Storrington.

MARKET DAYS.—Wednesday (corn), and Saturday.

FAIR.—July 20th.

MONEY ORDER OFFICE.

BANKERS.—London and County Bank; Henty, Upperton & Co.

This market town has lately become very fashionable as a watering-place. Its rise from an insignificant hamlet to its present rank has been rapid almost beyond precedent, even in the annals of this coast. It is said to owe this distinction to the superior mildness of its temperature, arising from the shelter afforded by the Downs, which, at the distance of scarcely a mile, environ it, and exclude the chilling blasts of the northern and eastern winds, rendering bathing practicable even in the depth of winter. The climate is perhaps somewhat relaxing. The sands, extending nearly ten miles in length, are level, hard, and compact, and afford a beautiful ride or walk. Like Brighton, the town follows the line of the sea, the esplanade extending for three-quarters of a mile along the shore. Towards the close of a summer or autumnal evening no more delightful promenade can be imagined than this beach, as it echoes to the hollow murmuring of the waves, rippled with the sea breeze, whilst afar off can be seen the gas-lights of the town of Brighton, forming a continuous chain of beads of light.

DISTANCES OF PLACES FROM THE STATION.

	Miles.		Miles.
Ashington	7½	Muntham	7
Bramber	7	North Hall	6½
Broadwater	0½	Offington	1¾
Charman Dean	3	Park Crescent	0¾
Cisbury Hall	2½	Salvington	1½
Clapham	6	Sheep Combe	4
Cokeham	2	Sompting	2½
Finding	4¾	Steyning	6½
Goring	3¾	Thakeham	9
Heene	1	Warminghurst	5½
Highdown Hill (Miller's Tomb)	4	Washington	5½
Horsham	17	West Brook Villas	0¾
Lancing	2	West Chiltington	10
Lyons	0½	West Ferring	5
Michel Grove	3½	West Grinstead Park	12
		West Tarring	1

The line proceeds three miles further on, and reaches the station at

GORING

Telegraph station at Worthing, 2½ miles.

MONEY ORDER OFFICE at Worthing.

After which an additional four miles bring us to the station at

ANGMERING.

Telegraph station at Arundel, 2¼ miles.

MONEY ORDER OFFICE at Arundel.

The line passes through a fine and highly cultivated country, and reaches the station at

LITTLEHAMPTON,

A short distance from a small hamlet on the coast, which has some admirers as a retired watering place.

Telegraph station at Arundel, 3 miles.

HOTELS.—Norfolk, George, and New.

MAILS.—Two arrivals and departures, daily, between London and Littlehampton.

MONEY ORDER OFFICE.

ARUNDEL.

A telegraph station.

Distance from station, 2 miles.

HOTEL.—Norfolk.

OMNIBUSES to and from Storrington, thrice weekly.

MARKET DAYS.—Monday and Saturday.

FAIRS.—May 14th, August 21st, Sept. 25th, and Dec. 17th.

MONEY ORDER OFFICE.

BANKERS. — London and County Bank; Henty, pperton and Co.

ARUNDEL is situated on the declivity of a steep hill, which commands a fine prospect. At the foot of this eminence runs the river Arun, over which is built a handsome stone bridge. From the Worthing Road the appearance of the town, with its stately castle, extensive park, and winding river, is singularly beautiful. On the north-east part of the town stands the

CASTLE, which has the remarkable privilege of entitling its owner to the dignity of an earl without creation. It is in the possession of the Howard family. The late Duke of Norfolk restored it to its former magnificence, and it is now one of the most elegant Gothic residences in England. The situation of the castle is one of great beauty. It stands on an eminence, embosomed in a luxuriant grove, and commands a fine and extensive view of the surrounding country, the sea, and the Isle of Wight.

DISTANCES OF PLACES FROM THE STATION.

	Miles.		Miles.
Angmering Park	4½	Houghton	4½
Atherington	2½	Leominster Station	2
Badworth Park	1½	Madehurst	4
Billinghurst	16	Michel Grove	6
Binsted	1½	North Heath	10½
Bognor	6½	North Stoke	4½
Burlavington	7½	North Wood	5½
Burnham	4	Offham	3½
Bury	5	Peppering	4
Coldwatham	8	Petworth	11
Comb Lodge	5¼	Waltham	6
Court Week	2	Warning Camp	3
Dale Park	3	West Burton	6
Dover House	3	Wepham	4
Hardham	7½	Wild Bank Common	6
Horsham Station	22	Yapton	1½

FORD.

Telegraph station at Arundel, 1¾ miles.

MONEY ORDER OFFICE at Arundel.

YAPTON.

Telegraph station at Arundel, 3 miles.

Distance from the station, 1 mile.

MONEY ORDER OFFICE at Arundel.

The line passes on a level, with the open sea on one side and the South Downs on the other, and reaches the station at

WOODGATE.

Telegraph station at Chichester, 5 miles.

Distance from station, ¾ mile.

HOTELS.—Claremont, Norfolk.

MAILS.—One arrival and departure, daily, between London and Woodgate.

MONEY ORDER OFFICE at Arundel.

DISTANCES OF PLACES FROM THE STATION.

	Miles.		Miles.
Aldingbourne	1	Kneighton Park	1¾
Aldwick	5	Lidsey	2
Arundel	5¼	Limner Pond	2
Bognor	4	Little Bognor	2½
Calworth	2	Night Timber	5
Castle Hill	1½	North Bersted	2
Eartham	3	North Field	1½
East Dean	6	Norton	1¾
Eastergate	0¾	Nudhurst & Petworth	12
Feltham	2½	Poor House	1¼
Goodwood	4	Shripland	2
Guildford	34	Shripudy	2
Halnaker	3	South Bersted	2
Halnaker House	3½	Tangmere	2½
Head Wane	2½	Upper Waltham	6
Houghton	6	Westergate	1¼

The station of Woodgate communicates with Bognor, a pleasant bathing place, towards the south.

BOGNOR.

POPULATION, 1,913.

Telegraph station at Chichester, 5 miles.

HOTELS.—York, and Norfolk.

MONEY ORDER OFFICE.

BOGNOR is a pleasant bathing place, with good beach, crescent, &c., and much frequented, the air being very pure, and the situation delightful. It was made a market town in 1822, and owes its rise to Sir Richard Hotham, in 1785.

DRAYTON.

Telegraph station at Chichester, 2 miles.

Distance from station, ½ mile.

MONEY ORDER OFFICE at Chichester.

CHICHESTER.

POPULATION, 8,662.

A telegraph station.

HOTEL.—Dolphin.

COACHES.—To and from Godalming, daily; Petworth, and Midhurst, thrice weekly.

MARKET DAYS.—Wednesdays and Saturdays.

FAIRS.—St. George's Day, Whit Monday, St. James's Day, Michaelmas Day, and ten days after.

MONEY ORDER OFFICE.

BANKERS.—London and County Bank; Cooper and Co.

Like Chester, Chichester is an old town on the square Roman plan, but the marks of antiquity are less decided. The Romans called it *Regni*, but Cista, the king of the south Saxons christened it *Cisaceaster*, from which the modern name is corrupted. It is a clean neatly built cathedral city and parliamentary borough (returns two members), in *Sussex*, on the South Coast Railway, 16 miles from Portsmouth. Four principal streets within the site of the ancient walls intersect at the middle, where stands Bishop Story's decorated English *Market Cross.* This prelate also founded the *Grammar School*, 1497, in which Archbishop Juxom, the learned Selden, and Collins and Hardis, the poets, were educated. The *Guildhall* was once the chapel to a friary. The last of the four gates was removed when the gaol was built, 1783. there are eight churches, some of which suffered in the civil war, two being actually dismantled by the royalists, 1642, to strengthen the walls.

The CATHEDRAL is a cross building of the 12th century, 314 feet long, or 377 feet with the Lady chapel, and 133 feet through the transept. Norman and early English work prevails in the nave and the north transept. The Lady chapel, over the Richmond vault, was built about 1300, and contains the library of old books. Several new stained windows have been added lately. In the north aisle is Flaxman's monument to *Collins* (who was born here 1720) reading the best of books, as Johnson describes him in his last days. Another monument to *Huskisson* the statesman. Bernardi's paintings in the style of Holbein, and a series of so-called portraits of kings and bishops since the Conquest may be noticed. In the cloisters called "Paradise," 200 feet long, is the monument of *Chillingworth* the great "propugnator invictissimus" (*i. e.*, invincible *bruiser* of the Protestants) who died here, 1643. He was a man of little stature, but a great controversialist, so that Anthony à Wood said, "If the great Turk or the devil could be converted, he was able to do it." At the north-west corner is the bell tower, 120 feet high, standing by itself. The fine eight-sided spire is 300 feet high. At the Bishop's *Palace* is a chapel partly as old as Henry III., and an old timber-roofed hall and kitchen. It was first built by Bishop Sherborne about 1530. Selsey (8 miles) near Selsey Bill, in the English Channel, was the seat of the bishopric, till it was moved to Chichester by the Normans, 1075. There is an old church. The sea now covers the site of some monastic buildings.

Goodwood (three miles), seat of the Duke of Richmond, stands in a large park under the South Downs. Here the July races are held, and which are always attended by the *haut ton* and the leading members of the Turf. It is about six miles round, and well wooded, and contains two cork trees, and about 1,000 cedars, planted 1762. From the grotto on Cairney seat (built out of a ruined church), is a fine view of the coast, Isle of Wight, the Downs, &c. The house was built by Sir W. Chambers, and enlarged by Wyattville, with centre and wings. It is 378 feet long, the wings falling back at angles of 45 feet. Stone and flint are used. In the hall is a standard and other trophies from Waterloo (which the late Duke attended as an amateur). The drawing room is 58 feet long. One portrait is that of a beautiful Duchess of Richmond of Charles II.'s time—the original, it is said, of Britannia on the copper coinage. Large stables and dog kennels (the latter cost 6,000*l.*), with a tennis-court, are behind.

DISTANCES OF PLACES FROM THE STATION.

	Miles.		Miles.
Aldingbourne	5	Northlands	3
Almondington Green	6	Old Brook	2
Applesham	1½	Old Park	2½
Birdham	4	Racton	4
Bognor	7	Rumbolds Wyke	2
Bosham	3	Salt Hill	2
Boxgrove	3½	Shopwick	2
Chidham	5	Sidelsham	5
Dell Quay	2	Singleton	6
Donnington	1½	Stanstead House	9
East Ashling	3	Stoke House	3
Emsworth	7	Stoughton	5
Fishbourne	2	Tangmere	3½
Frintington	5	Thorney Island	8
Goodwood	3	Tirwick	15
Gosden Green	6	Walton	2
Halnaker Park	3½	Westbourne	7
Highley	3¾	West Dean	5
Holt's Green	3	West Hampnett	3
Hunston	2	West Itchenor	6
Kingsham	1	West Lavant	2½
Lepring	4	Westerton	3
Marden North	8	West Stoke	3
Mid Lavant	3	Woodlands (Captain James Lyon)	8½
Mitener	6		

BOSHAM and EMSWORTH stations.

HAVANT,

A telegraph station.

HOTEL.—Bear.

OMNIBUSES to Hayling.

MARKET DAY.—Saturday.

FAIRS.—June 22nd and October 17th.

MONEY ORDER OFFICE.

The junction of the South Coast and South Western Lines is at Portcreek, between Havant and Cosham, but it is necessary to go to Portsmouth to pass from one line to the other.

PORTSMOUTH.

POPULATION, 72,096.

A telegraph station.

HOTELS.—The Fountain; the York, and Pier.

OMNIBUSES to and from the station; also to Waterloo and Petersfield.

STEAM BRIDGE to Gosport every half hour.

MARKET DAYS.—Thursday and Saturday

MONEY ORDER OFFICE.

BANKERS.—Branch of the Bank of England; Grant, Gillham and Long; National Provincial Bank of England.

PORTSMOUTH, the first naval port in the British Islands, and a parliamentary boough, &c., 94 miles from London by the South Western Line (9 only, *via* Gosport, or 95 by way of the Brighton and South Coast Line). A direct line to this important town is now in progress, which will reduce this distance 15 or 20 miles.

Portsmouth, Portsea, Southsea, &c., are seated on a low island, about 4 miles long, between Portsmouth and Langstone Harbours, and inside the Spithead anchorage, and the Isle of Wight, whose beautiful hills are seen about 5 miles over the water. The Dockyard is at Portsea; and on the Gosport side of the harbour are the Victualling Office, Haslar Hospital, and other establishments. Portsdown Hill is to the north.

Portsmouth is the principal rendezvous of the British navy. It is situated on the western side of the island of Portsea, at the mouth of the bay termed Portsmouth Harbour, and consists of the old town of Portsmouth, included within its fortified walls, and the new towns of Portsea and Southsea. Portsmouth Harbour ranks among the first in Great Britain, for its capaciousness, depth, aud security. At its entrance it is very narrow, but soon expands to a great width. The anchorage is good in all parts, the depth sufficient for ships of any draught, the shelter complete, and the extent capable of accommodating the entire navy of England. One thousand sail can ride at anchor in the celebrated roadstead of Spithead, between Portsmouth and the Isle of Wight.

The power of the English navy consists in the vast collection of materials, the number of ships, the skill and experience of the officers, and the excellence of the seamen nurtured in a commercial marine which traverses every sea. Add to this the vast wealth, accumulated capital, and untold treasures of the United Kingdom, the production of previous and still sustained industry, all of which give life and energy to the other resources of the empire, and then we possess the real causes of the naval superiority of Great Britain.

Portsmouth has very little to offer in its buildings, or in the country in its neighbourhood, which is flat and uninteresting. There is no beautiful or striking scenery to please the eye; but its chief attractions consist in the fortifications, the dockyard, the men-of-war, the sailors and soldiers, and other features of a Government town—all of which are full of interest to a mere civilian, especially if fresh from the interior. The fortified lines, in particular, should be noticed, as Portsmouth (including Portsea) is a specimen rare in these islands, but common enough abroad, of a perfect English fortress, being inclosed in ramparts, bastions, ravelins, wet ditches, glacis, &c., constructed on scientific principles, and defended by batteries commanding all the most accessible points landward and seaward. The only entrances are by the four or five drawbridges and gates in the ramparts. Beyond these are the populous and increasing suburbs of Landport, Kingston, Southsea, &c. Southsea, in front of Spithead, is rising into a fashionable bathing-place; many good houses and villas, and a new church have been built; and though it stands low, the situation is open and healthy. Hollingworth's Subscription Rooms are on the beach; bathing and boats at all times, and an excellent promenade, laid out by the late Lord Fitzclarence, when Lieutenant-Governor, but disfigured by two ridiculous statues of Nelson and Wellington. It was at this spot that Nelson, accompanied by Hardy, embarked for the last time on the 14th of September, 1805, to hoist his flag on board the Victory; he was attended by the tears and blessings of the crowd—the scene was wonderfully affecting. "I had their hurrahs before," said the poor shattered hero, "now I have their hearts!" About three months later the Victory, which now lies in the harbour, came back again with his remains on board. About ½ mile along the beach is Southsea Castle, which, like Cumberland Fort, 3 miles further, is regularly fortified. The latter has room for four regiments.

St. Thomas's *Church*, in High-street, with a gilt ship over the cupola for its vane, is a venerable old cross, built in 1220, but altered and re-edified since that date. One monument is to Charles II.'s favourite, the Duke of Buckingham, who was stabbed by Felton in an old-fashioned house at the top of the street, now marked No. 10. The Registry contains the entry of Charles II.'s marriage, 22nd May, 1662, with Catherine of Portugal, who brought him Bombay for her dowry On the parade, which every one should attend for the daily *guard-mounting* at 11 a.m., is the church of an old religious house; here the garrison musters, and many officers in both services are interred. There is a fine prospect of Spithead from the ramparts here.

In St. Mary's-street lived *John Pounds*, a poor crippled cobbler, who may claim to be the founder of Ragged Schools. Working all day long at his trade he enticed the indigent children from the streets, and before his death, in 1839, had taught hundreds of them on a plan of his own.

At the bottom of High Street is a rather picturesque brick bridge, to Point, designed by Inigo Jones. Trading vessels lie up in the Camber, near this. From the lower end of Point, the floating bridge runs to Gosport. Here a boat may be taken for the Victory; she lies a little above the Neptune flag-ship. A brass plate marks the spot on which Nelson fell, shot through the shoulder. The uniform he wore is now at Greenwich; and the shot itself was in the possession of his physician, the late Sir W. Beattie.

The DOCKYARD covers 117 acres, with a water front of 4-5ths of a mile; it was begun by Henry VII. and his son Henry VIII., who here built the *Harry Grace a Dieu*, a large unwieldly hulk, the largest ship of her day. Apply at the gate for permission to go through the yard; you write your name down, and as soon as a party of about half a dozen is made up, a policeman takes you round. If you are a foreigner, you should apply to the Admiralty, through your Ambassador, for an order, or should you resemble one in appearance, it is advisable to provide yourself with an Admiralty order. Among other things you will see the *Rope House*, 1,100 feet long, where hempen cables of 2,400 yarns and two feet round are twisted; anchors of all sizes up to five tons, and the forges where they are made, with Nasmyth's wonderful steam hammer at work; Brunel's block machinery, which will, with ease, make 140,000 blocks yearly, (1,400 are required for a 74 gun ship); the building slips and sheds, from which ships of 130 guns are launched; new factories, and basins for steamers, and the screws, storehouses of every description; a statue of William III. and models, at the Naval College. Vast quantities of timber are left to season in the Ponds and on Common Hard, as a preservative from dry-rot. There is an armoury at the gun wharf, which is a branch of the Woolwich Arsenal.

Several ships in "ordinary," *i. e.*, laid by for future occasion, are moored up and down the harbour; but when ready for service, their place is Spithead roadstead, outside, so called from the Spit sand which lies to the west. There Sir Charles Napier's fleet, including the great screw-ship, the Duke of Wellington, of 131 guns, was reviewed by the Queen, in her beautiful yacht, the Victoria and Albert.

To this anchorage, Hawke, Howe, St. Vincent, Exmouth, &c., brought their prizes after their various triumphs. One buoy marks where the "Royal George," with Admiral Kempenfeldt and 300 seamen, besides women and landsmen, sunk at her anchors, 1782: only a few escaped, one of whom was the late Sir P. Durham. Her hull, after lying whole at the bottom of the sea, was at length blown up by electricity, in 1839; articles are still sold at Portsmouth as made from her well-seasoned timbers. The Royal William, or old Billy, flag-ship, used to lie here; when broken up she was above 100 years old. Osborne House, the seat of Her Majesty, Ryde, and other beautiful parts of the Isle of Wight, are here easily discerned; also vessels lying at the Motherbank, close to the Island; and Stokes Bay, at which place it is contemplated to erect a floating steam bridge, so as to connect the Isle of Wight with the intended line from hence to the Gosport station, where the rate of steamers is tried.

Within a short distance from Portsmouth, excursions may be made to the *Isle of Wight* (see page 87) and the following places:—*Porchester Castle*, at the top of Portsmouth harbour, can be reached by boat (the pleasantest way, passing all the men of war), or by railway. It is the *Portus Magnus* of the Romans, and stands under Portsdown Hill. To the genuine walls, 8 to 12 feet thick, of the original founders, a great square keep, and other additions, some as late as Queen Elizabeth's reign, have been added. In one corner of the space they enclose (about 620 feet square) is an ancient church. A pretty walk, through the village, leads up to the Nelson Obelisk on the Portsdown Hill. This chalk ridge is 400 to 500 feet high, and has several good points of view, embracing the port and sea to the south, and a richly wooded tract to the north, most of which belongs to the Thistlethwaytes of Southwick, where are some remains of a priory in which Henry VI. was married to Margaret of Anjou. Near Purbrook is *Merchistoun*, the seat of Admiral Sir Charles Napier, not far off the mansion of his cousin, the late General Sir C. Napier, the conqueror of Scinde. *Leigh Park*, near Havant, the seat of Sir G. Staunton, Bart. From Havant, at the east end of Portsdown, looking down on Chichester Cathedral, there is a bridge to Hayling Island, a flat pasture tract like its neighbour, and separated from it by Langstone harbour. A quiet bathing place has been established at Hayling. Portsdown Fair begins July 26th.

Conveyances by railway to Southampton, Winchester, London, Dorchester, Chichester, Brighton, Hastings, Dover, &c. By steamers to Ryde, Cowes, Southampton, several times a day, from the Albert and Victoria piers; to Plymouth and Liverpool once a week.

LONDON AND SOUTH WESTERN.

The main branches of this railway communicate with the suburbs of London, and are mostly celebrated for their picturesque beauty, viz.:—Richmond, Windsor, Kew, and the valley of the Thames, Hampton Court, Kingston, Claremont, Guildford, &c.; also with Portsmouth, Winchester, Southampton, Salisbury, Isle of Wight, and Weymouth, *via* Dorchester.

Of all the many alluring rambles held forth to the tourist who wishes to avail himself of the speedy communication by rail with some of the most picturesque scenery in England, there is no line that possesses more intrinsic advantages, or which intersects in its various routes so many places of glorious memory as the South Western, from the metropolis to the south-western coast of Hampshire and Devonshire.

The METROPOLITAN TERMINUS of the South Western is at Waterloo Road. Omnibuses convey passengers to and from all parts of town. The terminus is a spacious building, admirably adapted for the different railway offices and the various departments connected with the Company. The gentle pace at which the trains first move afford time for observing the extensive engine houses and workshops at Nine Elms. The line passes over viaducts or arches through a part of the densely populated parish of Lambeth, over the tops of houses, past the grounds of Lambeth Palace, in a line with which is Lambeth Church, and across the river may be seen the splendid towers of the new Houses of Parliament.

SURREY.

THIS is one of the most interesting, if not the most fertile, of the English counties. Almost the whole surface of the county is undulating, and consists of hill and dale, intersecting each other in every variety of form. In some parts extensive heaths give an air of wildness to the prospect which is strikingly contrasted by the innumerable beauties scattered over the surface of the county by the hand of art, while the hills, which frequently approach the height of mountains, decline into richly wooded dales and plains, covered with luxuriant harvests. In many parts the landscapes are diversified with picturesque uplands, romantic heights, woodland dells, verdant valleys, and plains covered with waving corn. The most striking feature of the county, however, is its extensive chalky downs, lying nearly in the centre. The railway communications of the county are numerous, and intersect it in all directions.

MAIN LINE.—London to Clapham.

VAUXHALL.

Telegraph station at London, 1¼ mile.

STEAM VESSELS to London Bridge, and Chelsea, Pimlico, Fulham, Battersea, Wandsworth, Putney, Richmond, Kew, and Hammersmith Bridge (calling at all the piers on the banks of the river), every five minutes.

MONEY ORDER OFFICE, No. 4, Wandsworth Road.

Thence we pass on through Vauxhall, and entering upon an embankment bounded on each side by spacious market gardens, the line passes Battersea New Town and park on the one hand, and Battersea Rise and Clapham on the other, at which point the Richmond, Staines, and Windsor line diverges to the right, while the main line turns off towards the left to Wimbledon.

As the Richmond and Windsor railway is the first branch of the South Western, we will commence our description with that.

WINDSOR AND RICHMOND BRANCH.

Wandsworth to Barnes.

The Richmond line properly branches off about the point where the road to the village of Battersea leaves the Wandsworth road, and at a short distance from Battersea. It then pursues a pretty course through the villas, orchards, and nursery gardens which stud that locality, till it reaches Wandsworth. The river Wandle and the valley are crossed by a splendid viaduct.

WANDSWORTH.

Telegraph station at London, 4¾ miles.

This station is situated within a short distance of the parish that gives it the name of Wandsworth, which with the other suburban districts we have passed through, contains a number of elegant villas, belonging to the opulent class of city merchants. On leaving Wandsworth we have for a moment a picturesque peep at the Thames, and the line pursues a southerly direction through a deep cutting of some extent, until we reach

PUTNEY.

Telegraph station at Barnes.

OMNIBUSES to London, *via* Fulham, Chelsea, and Brompton, every quarter of an hour.

STEAM BOATS.—To London every hour, calling at the different Piers on the river side, and to Richmond, Hammersmith, and Kew, daily, in summer.

On emerging from the cutting and passing this station, we proceed over a level country to Barnes Common, which the line crosses.

BARNES.

Distance from station, ½ mile.

A telegraph station.

MONEY ORDER OFFICE at Hammersmith.

BARNES is memorable, among other associations, as being the place where Sir Francis Walsingham entertained Queen Elizabeth and her retinue, at an enormous expense, though the next year he died at his house in Seething Lane so poor, that his friends were obliged to bury him privately at night. The church, about a quarter of a mile from the river, is one of the most ancient in the neighbourhood of the metropolis, having been erected in the reign of Richard I. (1189). Here lived Jacob Tonson, the bookseller, the founder and secretary of the Kit-Cat Club.

LOOP LINE.

Barnes to Hounslow and Feltham.

It diverges from the Richmond line at Barnes station, and is carried across the river Thames, in front of Barnes-terrace, by means of a light and elegant bridge, consisting of three arches. From this the line proceeds through the property of the Duke of Devonshire; and the first station, CHISWICK, is placed at the southernmost corner of his Grace's park. This station, besides accommodating the residents, is within a very short distance of the Horticultural Society's Gardens, and is one of the principal means of approach on *fete* and other days. The railway then passes on to Kew Bridge, where it crosses the turnpike road.

KEW.

POPULATION, 1,009.

Distance from station, ½ mile.

Telegraph station at Barnes.

HOTELS.—Coach and Horses; Rose and Crown; Star and Garter.

OMNIBUSES to and from the station; also every five minutes to and from London.

STEAM BOATS to London, frequently during the day in summer.

MONEY ORDER OFFICE at Brentford, 1½ mile.

KEW, a picturesque village on the banks of the Thames, about seven miles from London, and one mile from Richmond. The palace contains a few pictures, but the gardens are the principal objects of attraction. They are not very large, nor is their situation advantageous, as it is low and commands no prospects; but they contain the finest collection of plants in this country, and are decorated with various ornamental buildings. The first which appears is the orangery, or green-house. Near it, in a grove, is the temple of the Sun, of the Corinthian order. There is also a medico-botanical garden, and contiguous to it, the flower garden, of which the principal entrance forms one end. The two sides are enclosed with high trees, and the other end is occupied by an aviary of vast depth. From the flower garden, a short winding walk leads to the menagerie, the centre of which is occupied by a large basin of water, originally stocked with curious water-fowl, and enclosed by a range of cages of exotic birds. The gardens also contain the temples of Bellona, the God Pan, Æolus, Solitude, and Victory, the House of Confucius and the great Pagoda, from the top of which is an extensive view of a rich and variegated country. The Palm House is one of the finest in Europe; it cost upwards of £30,000.

The royal pleasure grounds are open to the public on Thursdays and Sundays, from Midsummer until Michaelmas. The Botanic Gardens are also open every day from one till six.

> "So sits enthroned in vegetable pride
> Imperial Kew, by Thames's glistening side,
> Obedient sails from realms unfurrow'd bring
> For her the unnamed progeny of spring."

From this point the line passes principally through market gardens to Boston Lane, where the Brentford station is conveniently placed.

BRENTFORD.

POPULATION, 8,879.

Distance from station ½ mile.

Telegraph station at Barnes.

HOTELS.—Red Lion; George IV.

OMNIBUSES to and from London, Inglefield Green, Egham, and Isleworth.

MARKET DAY.—Tuesday. FAIRS.—May 17th, 18th, and 19th; Sept. 12th, 13th, and 14th.

BANKERS.—Branch of London and County Bank.

BRENTFORD has a weekly market and two annual fairs. It is the county town, where members of Parliament are elected. Here the Brent falls into the Thames. The town is a long straggling street.

ISLEWORTH.

Distance from station, ¾ mile.

Telegraph station at Barnes.

FAIR.—First Monday in July.

MONEY ORDER OFFICE at Hounslow.

ISLEWORTH, with its picturesque ivy-mantled church tower, was noted for affording excellent sport to anglers. The salmon caught in this part of the Thames was formerly of a peculiarly fine quality, but the gas works and steam navigation have driven them higher up the stream.

This place, however, is still frequented by anglers, who consider there is not finer fishing any where than in the Thames from Kew to Richmond.

Sion House, the magnificent edifice of the Duke of Somerset, where Lady Jane Grey resided, now belonging to the Duke of Northumberland, was built here, on the site of a suppressed nunnery. The grounds form a fine lawn, extending from Brentford to Isleworth.

HOUNSLOW.

POPULATION, 3,514.

Distance from station, 1 mile.

Telegraph station at Barnes.

HOTEL.—George.

OMNIBUSES to and from Harlington and London, daily.

FAIRS.—Trinity Monday and Monday after Michaelmas Day.

DISTANCES OF PLACES FROM THE STATION.

	Miles.		Miles.
Barracks	1¾	Isleworth	1
Bate Bridge	1½	Knellar Hall	0½
Brazil Mill	1¾	Lampton Field	1
Brentford Station	2¾	Mortlake	3½
Butcher's Grove	2	Norwood	2½
Granford Bridge	2½	Osterley Park	1¾
Feltham	2	Powder Mills	1½
Halton	2	Spring Grove	2
Hampton	2	Sunbury	3
Hanworth	2	Sutton	1¼
Hanworth Farm	1¾	Twickenham Green	1¼
Heston	1¾	Twickenham Sta.	1
Heston House	1¾	Whitton	0½
Hospital Bridge	1½	Whitton Warren	1¼
Hounslow	1	Wolton	0¼

Richmond Branch continued.

Barnes to Windsor.

A great portion of the line is but a few feet above the natural surface of the country, and many of the roads are crossed on a level. The country through which it passes does not present many picturesque views, the property almost throughout being circumscribed by orchards and market gardens. The want, however, of the beautiful along the line is amply compensated by the lovely views in the neighbourhood of Richmond; and from Richmond to Datchet there is a succession of splendid scenery.

The first station at which we arrive is

MORTLAKE.

Telegraph station at Twickenham.

INN.—Kings Arms.

MONEY ORDER OFFICE at Richmond.

The remainder of the course is through fields and gardens, passing a little to the south of the grounds of Kew, or to the terminus in the Kew Road at Richmond.

RICHMOND.

POPULATION, 9,065.

Distance from station, ½ mile.

A Telegraph station.

HOTELS.—Star and Garter; Roebuck; Castle.

OMNIBUSES to and from the station; also to London, *via* Kew, Hammersmith, and Kensington; conveyances also to Hampton, Kingston, and Twickenham. These are the fastest and best appointed vehicles out of London.

STEAM VESSELS from London, calling at Putney Hammersmith Bridge, and Kew, daily in summer.

RICHMOND is a delightful town in Surrey, on the South Western Railway and the river Thames, 10 miles from London, in the midst of scenery which, though often praised and admired, never grows old or wearisome. It may be also reached by the omnibus from St. Paul's, every hour and half hour, or by the Hampton Court steamer from London and Hungerford Bridges. The last way is the best for enjoying the scenery of the river above Richmond; but the shoals and the long bends or reaches make it rather tedious, especially at low tides. The town stands on an eminence on the south bank of the Thames—it extends about a mile up the hill—and is skirted and intermingled with agreeable gardens.

Richmond had a royal palace from the time of Edward I., called *Sheen, i.e.* Shining, till Henry VII. gave it the title which he bore as Earl of Richmond. borrowed from his castle of that name in Yorkshire, and revived by Charles I. for the ancestor of the Lennox family. Both places are seated on a high point, "Riche-mont," overlooking a vast range of country. A brick gate and some old walls on one side of the Green are the sole remnants of the *palace*, which Henry VIII. gave to Wolsey in exchange for Hampton Court, but as it soon returned to the crown it became the residence of Elizabeth, who died here in 1603, and of Henrietta Maria, the queen of Charles I. On the green in front tournaments were held before Henry VII. and Henry VIII. This place is also noted for having had the earliest calico print works established in it (1696) by a Frenchman—these have since thriven in a more congenial spot. The old park was behind the palace, and now makes part of Kew Gardens; the great park, on the top of the hill, was not enclosed till Charles I.'s time. In ascending to it you pass the brick church in which Thomson the poet, Mrs. Yates, and Kean the actors, Dr. Moore the author of "Zeluco" and father of Sir John Moore, are buried; it contains also Flaxman's monument of Mrs. Lowther. Thomson died at *Rosedale House*, now the Dowager Countess of Shaftesbury's seat, and here his desk, garden seat, &c. are to be seen. The sight of the church put Collins in mind of writing his pretty lines on him, beginning, "In yonder shade a Druid lies." At the top of the hill, half a mile from the town, where Sir J. Reynolds's house stands, you catch the splendid prospect so often celebrated:—

> "Thy hill, delightful *Shene!* Here let us sweep
> The boundless landscape. Now the raptured eye
> Exulting, swift to huge Augusta* send,
> Now to the sister hills† that skirt her plain,
> To lofty Harrow bow, and now to where
> Majestic Windsor lifts his princely brow.
> * * * *
> Slow let us trace the matchless vale of Thames;
> Fair winding-up to where the muses haunt
> In Twit'ham's bowers— * *
> * * to Royal Hampton's pile,
> To Claremont's terraced heights and Esher's groves."
>
> THOMSON.

It would be worth while to read the noble lines which follow this quotation in the poet's "Summer,"

* London. † Hampstead and Highgate.

sitting under elms on this spot; there is a glow and dignity in them equal to the magnificence of the prospect spread out before one's eyes. The great lodge which was Sir R. Walpole's seat, *Pembroke Lodge*, the seat of Lord John Russell, and *the New Terrace*, offer some of the best points of view in the park. The Marquis of Lansdowne, the mansion now occupied by the Duchess of Gloucester, formerly the seat of Lord Sidmouth, called the *Ranger's Lodge*, and many more, have houses on or round the hill.

The Wesleyan body have a COLLEGE here for their theological students—a handsome Tudor range, 250 feet long, in which is a good statue of their founder. Close to the bridge (built in 1747, and still taxed) are three small aits or wooded islands. The railway viaduct strides across on three wide arches below.

Within a few miles are Kew Gardens and its pagoda; Twickenham, the favourite retreat of Pope; East Sheen, where Sir W. Temple lived. Ham, the ancient seat of the Dysart family, in which the famous John, Duke of Argyle was born (Scott, in his "Heart of Mid Lothian," brings him to Richmond Park, to introduce Jeanie Deans to Queen Caroline), and Hampton Court, with its half Tudor, half French palace, pictures, cartoons, Lely beauties, gardens, and other attractions.

The line crosses the Thames over the railway bridge at Richmond—a very handsome structure of three arches.

TWICKENHAM.

A Telegraph station.

HOTELS.—King's Head, and Royal.

OMNIBUSES to and from London, Hampton, and Hampton Court, daily.

MONEY ORDER OFFICE at Richmond.

TWICKENHAM is a most picturesque village on the Thames. Between Richmond bridge and this village is a rural walk, on the border of the river; and probably no promenade of a similar extent, in any part of England, presents a display of scenery so soft and so highly cultivated. The margin of the Thames is lined with stately dwellings, whose ornamental grounds descend to the water's edge; among which was the residence of Pope. Here he translated a part of the Iliad, and wrote the Dunciad, the Essay on Man, &c., and hence are dated a great number of his letters; here also he died. Twickenham church contains the medallion monument erected to Pope by Bishop Warburton. Twickenham Ait, on which stands the Eel-pie House, is a little below the deep.

FELTHAM and ASHFORD Stations.

STAINES.

POPULATION, 2,430.

Distance from station, ¾ mile.
Telegraph station at Twickenham.

HOTEL.—Angel and Crown.
MARKET DAY.—Saturday.
FAIRS.—May 11th and September 19th.
BANKERS.—Ashby and Co.

STAINES is a pleasant market town, in the county of Middlesex, standing on the north bank of the Thames, over which is thrown a bridge, which connects the counties of Middlesex and Surrey. In the old records it is called Stana, a Saxon word for a stone, and Camden supposes that the name was derived from a stone which was fixed on the banks of the river, to mark the extent of the authority of the city of London over the Thames, westward. This town contains a handsome church, besides which there are other places of public worship for dissenters. Nearly all the houses extend along the sides of the high road, but there are a considerable number built in other directions.

A little northward of Staines Bridge is the City Boundary Stone, on which is inscribed, "God preserve the City of London, A.D. 1280." This marks the limit of the Lord Mayor's jurisdiction over the Thames. When the civic authorities make their tour of inspection, they disembark here, and wine is placed for them on the said stone; and such Sheriffs and Aldermen as are not "Free of the Water," are *bumped* at the stone.

WINDSOR BRANCH.

The first Station from the Junction at Staines, is WRAYSBURY, near the confluence of the Colne with the Thames; *Cooper's Hill* and *Runnymede*.
DATCHET STATION.

WINDSOR.

A telegraph station.

HOTELS.—Castle, and White Hart.

MARKET DAYS.—Wednesday and Saturday.
FAIRS.—Easter Tuesday, July 5th, and Oct 25th.
BANKERS.—The London and County Bank, Neville, Reid, and Co.; draw on Williams and Co. Branch of Berks Union Banking Co.; draw on London and Westminster Bank.

This is a parliamentary borough (two members), with a population of 9,596, and a few public buildings, such as the Town Hall, built 1686, containing several royal portraits, and the modern church, in which are some of G. Gibbon's carvings; but the chief attractions are the *Castle* and Park, the seat of her majesty *the Queen*, and of her ancestors from the period of the Conquest.

Eton College also is within a short distance. Windsor is accessible by railway, *via* the South Western (25 miles), or the Great Western (21 miles)—the former by way of Datchet in front of the Castle—the latter by Slough and Eton.

WINDSOR is built on the banks of the Thames, and has long been celebrated for its royal Castle and Park. It is situated on a hill which commands a delightful prospect over the adjacent country. It was first built by William the Conqueror, soon after his being seated on the throne of this kingdom. Edward III. was born here, and had such an affection for the spot that he caused the old building to be pulled down, and a magnificent palace to be erected on its site, under the direction of the celebrated William of Wykeham; and re-established the princely order of the Garter.

No Briton can view unmoved the stately towers of "Windsor's castled keep." The mind is irresistibly carried back to the time when the Norman conqueror so far bent the stubborn necks of our Saxon ancestors, as to compel them to extinguish their fires on the sound of the innovating curfew. Rival houses have in turn held regal sway within its storied walls. Its history is the history of our country, and some of its "brightest and blackest" pages are inseparably linked with the towers that arrest the eye of the traveller as he approaches the station. Its annals take us back to times when the rebellious Barons compelled King John, in its immediate neighbourhood, to sign the first great charter of our country's rights. York and Lancaster have each struggled for its possession. It has witnessed the extinction of royal houses, and sheltered within its walls the representative of England's short-lived Commonwealth. Within its precincts the Tudors have signed decrees to light the fires of Smithfield, and Cromwell has declared to Continental despotism, that no man shall be persecuted on account of his protestantism. Great names, too, are associated with its annals, and he who has read the history of his country can pass in review, before his mind's eye, a long list of warriors, statesmen, churchmen, poets, and others, celebrated for their virtues or their talents, while he is also forcibly reminded that many names are mixed up with its history which he would willingly consign to oblivion.

The castle is divided into two courts, the upper and the lower, separated from each other by the Round Tower. On the north side of the upper court are situated the state apartments, and on the south the various apartments belonging to the officers of state. The lower court is chiefly remarkable as containing that beautiful structure St. George's Chapel.

The Castle.—The **State Apartments** are open on Mondays, Tuesdays, Thursdays, and Fridays, from 11 until 6. Tickets gratis, at Moon's, New Oxford Street; Colnaghi's, 14, Pall Mall East; Mitchell's, 33, Old Bond Street; Ackermann's, 96, Strand. Guide books may be had, from 1d. to 1s. These tickets are available for a week from the day of issue, but not transferable; and no payment is to be made to the servants at the Castle. The private apartments are always closed, but a good panorama of their contents may be seen at Taylor's Illustrated Gallery, High-street, Windsor; admittance, 1s. Guide Books, 2d. each. Choral service at St. George's Chapel at 10½ and 4.

There is an ascent by the postern steps to the Castle for visitors arriving by the South Western rail; or you may go round to Henry VIII.'s gate, which leads into the town. It stands on a site of 12 acres, on the summit of a hill, commanding a magnificent view from the terrace, which is 1,870 feet, or ⅓ of a mile long. The great circular keep (open daily) from which the standard waves when the Queen is here, divides the upper and lower ward; it is about 150 feet above the quadrangle, or 300 feet above the park, and machicolated round the top, like most of the towers here. Twelve counties are visible in clear weather from the keep. Here state prisoners were confined. Since 1824 the restoration of the Castle, carried on by Sir Jeffry Wyattville has cost about £900,000. The state rooms, private apartments, &c. are in the upper ward; St. George's church, the deanery, apartments of the knights, baronets, &c. in the lower, as you enter from Henry VIII.'s gate.

The state apartments should be visited in the following order:—They are on the north side of the quadrangle.

Audience Chamber.—Ceiling by Verrio. Coronation of Esther, and the triumph of Mordecai, in Gobelin tapestry; portraits of Mary, Queen of Scots, the "daughter, consort, and mother of kings," as she is styled.

Presence Chamber.—Charles II.'s queen, Katherine, on the ceiling. Subjects from Esther, in tapestry. Myten's portrait of George I.'s mother. Gibbon's carved work. Bacon's mantel-piece. This room is generally used as the ball room.

Guard Chamber.—Old armour, including that of John of France (taken at Poitiers), and David of Scotland (captured at Neville's cross), both of whom were prisoners here in the reign of Edward III., who was born in the Castle, 1312. Also Henry, Prince of Wales, (son of James I.), Prince Rupert's, &c. Chantrey's bust of Nelson, on a stand made out of the Victory's mast. Busts of Marlborough and Wellington (the latter by Chantrey), with the yearly banners presented to the Queen, on 2nd August and 18th June, for Blenheim and Waterloo. Henry VIII.'s shield, by B. Cellini, the famous goldsmith.

St. George's Banqueting Hall—200 feet long, 34 feet broad; Gothic ceiling, full of escutcheons of the Knights of the Garter since 1350. Portraits of sovereigns from James I., by Vandyke, Lely, Kneller, &c. Throne, chair of state, &c. in oak. Knights of the Garter are here knighted.

Ball Room—90 feet long, by 34 broad; one fine Gothic window; furniture of the time of Louis XIV. ("Louis Quatorze" style); Emperor of Russia's malachite vase; Jason and the Golden Fleece, in tapestry.

Throne Room.—Carvings by Gibbons; ornaments of the Order of the Garter, in the ceiling and carpet; with portraits by Lawrence, &c.

Waterloo or **Grand Dining Room** is 98 feet long, and 45 high to the lantern ceiling, In the Elizabethan style. Full of portraits, &c. of Waterloo men, sovereigns, and statesmen of that age; carvings by Gibbons; oak furniture; most of the portraits by Lawrence; among them are Picton, Anglesey, Wellington, Hill, Blucher, Castlereagh, Metternich, Pope Pius VI,, Cardinal Gonsalvi (one of the best), Emperor Alexander, Platoff, Canning, and Humboldt.

Grand Vestibule, 47 ft. long, 45 high, armour, banners, &c.

Grand Staircase.—Chantrey's statue of George IV.

CASTLES OF ENGLAND

State Ante-room.—Verrio's Banquet of the Gods, in the ceiling; tapestry, Gibbons' carvings; Reynolds' George III.

Small Vestibule, near the Waterloo Room. Large paintings by West, of the events in Edward III.'s reign. Carvings by Gibbons.

Rubens' Room.—All paintings by Rubens' mostly life size, including his portrait by himself, his wife, Battle of Nordlingen, &c. Fine view from the Oriel; and chair made of wood from old Alloway Kirk.

Council Chamber of Charles II.'s time Kneller's Duke of Marlborough, Lely's Charles II. and Prince Rupert. Pictures by Flemish masters, &c.

King's Closet, adorned with marine emblems. Quentin Matsys' misers, and other pictures, Flemish, Italian, &c.

Queen's Closet.—A small room with "Adelaide Regina, 1853," in the roof. Charles II. and William III.'s silver tables. George IV.'s state bed. Portraits by Holbein, pictures by C. Lorraine, Teniers, &c.

Queen's Drawing Room.—Large pictures by Quccarelle.

Vandyck Room.—Portraits by Vandyck of Charles I, his Queen, and family, Sir K. Digby, Duchess of Richmond, &c.

On the south and east sides of the quadrangle are the Queen's private apartments. In the middle is a bronze statue of Charles II. with bas-reliefs by Gibbons.

St. George's Collegiate Church, in the Lower Ward, was first built by Edward III, and rebuilt by George III, It is a long straggling cross in the decorated Gothic style, with battlements, buttresses, &c., and a highly ornamented roof. The stalls and banners for the Knights of the Garter are in the choir. The windows are painted with subjects from West and Williment; that in the east window is the Resurrection by the former. There are various chapels and monuments; one of the oldest being that by Canon Ovenbridge, in 1522, near the cenotaph to the Princess Charlotte. In a vault near the fourth stall, Henry VI. and Henry VIII. are buried. (Henry VI. was born in the Castle.) Edward IV. is also buried here under a curious tomb of iron work by Matsys; and George III. and most of his family lie in the Tomb House or Mausoleum at the east end. George III.'s affectionate tablet to Mary Gaskoine, servant to his daughter Amelia, is in the cloisters.

There is a descent by the hundred steps to the town near the apartments for the Naval Knights. The Military Knights are lodged in the Lower Ward, they were established by Henry VIII. and paid 1s. per day. The Dean and Chapter were also allowed 1s. per day out of the same fund; but while the emoluments of this body have been made to increase with the relative value of money, that of the Knights has remained the same.

The York and Lancaster gate, or main entrance to the Castle, fronts the Long Avenue. The Little Park is about four miles round. It contains Adelaide Lodge, at the bottom of the pretty slopes, the Royal Gardens; and Frogmore, the seat of the Duchess of Kent; but Herne's Oak with "great ragged horns," to which the Merry Wives of Windsor inveigled Falstaff, disguised like Herne, with huge horns on his head, was cut down many years ago, though another tree has taken its name in Queen Elizabeth's walk.

From the Castle gate a noble avenue of tall spreading elms, three miles long, and nearly 300 ft. broad, leading to the great Park, to Snow Hill, a low eminence surmounted by Westmacott's massive statue of George III, 66 ft. high, including the pedestal. Cooper's Hill, Runnymede, and the Thames, Harrow Hill, &c. are visible. Here the scenery becomes wild and forest like. The original Windsor Forest extended over 15 or 20 miles, almost to Reading. Near this is Cranbourne Lodge in the neighbourhood of the *Conqueror's Oak*, an ancient tree, nine or ten centuries old, 26 ft. in girth and quite hollow. Queen Anne's, Queen Caroline's, Queen Charlotte's, Queen Adelaide's and Queen Victoria's trees are also seen, the last being bare for 50 ft. from the root.

From the statue it is two miles further to *Virginia Water*, for description of which, see page 67.

Eton College, on the Bucks side of the Thames, was founded 1440 by Henry VI., upon the plan of Winchester; its object being to supply King's College at Cambridge, as William of Wykeham's supplies New College at Oxford. Two brick quadrangles, in one of which is the founder's bronze statue, the chapel and upper school, built by Wren; and in the other the ancient Commons' Hall; the new buildings are in the Tudor style, The chapel is Gothic, 175 ft. long, with turrets at each corner. Bacon's statue (marble) of Henry VI. is under the west window. A brass of Lord Gray (1521), deserves notice; the oldest is 1424. Sir H. Wotton and John Hales are buried here. Busts of Gray, Fox, Canning, &c., in the upper school, and other Etonians. Peel, the late Duke of Wellington, Chatham, Porson, are on the list. Album, with autographs of the Queen, Prince Albert, Louis Philippe, &c. in the library, which contains many books, MSS., curious maps, &c. A collection of portraits at the Provost's apartments.

At **Salt Hill** the *Eton Montem* used to be held every Whitsuntide, till 1847, when it was discontinued. Regatta on the 4th June; boat races on the last Saturday in July, at Brocus Meadows, when the seniors are elected to Kings. Further up the river is Monkey Island, and a fishing temple built by the Duke of Marlborough.

Upton Church is a complete specimen of the Norman style, and contains the grave of Sir W. Herschel the astronomer, whose observations were carried on at Slough; but the great telescope, 40 ft. long, is removed. At *Stoke Pogis* Church, an ancient building covered with ivy, *Gray* is buried;

it was the scene of his beautiful Elegy in a Country Churchyard. In *Stoke Park*, the seat of the Penns, (descended from the founder of Pennsylvania), are some remains of an old house which belonged to Coke the great lawyer; portraits, &c., in the present mansion.

Down the river you come to Old Windsor or *Windlesford*, where the Saxon and early Norman kings fixed their seats at first; and *Ankerwyke*, the Harcourt's seat, where there is a famous oak, 33 ft. girth, as old as the Conquest. Runnymede, which comes from the Saxon *Rune-mede*, or Council-field, is near Charter Island, and is the spot on which the barons (fighting, however, for their own hand as the Scotch say), extorted the Great Charter from King John in 1215. *Ditton Park* is Lord Montague's seat.

STAINES, WOKINGHAM, AND READING.

Staines to Wokingham and Reading.

On leaving Staines we soon arrive at

EGHAM.

Telegraph station at Windsor, 5 miles.

HOTELS. — Crown, Victoria Arms, Coach and Horses.

RACES (at Runnymede) in August.

The church contains tombs of Abbot John, of Chertsey, and Sir J. Denham, father of the poet.

In the vicinity are *Egham Lodge*, seat of J. Dobinson, Esq.: *Kingswood Lodge*, Mrs. Read. Runnymede (½ mile), memorable as the Council Meadow, where the English Barons compelled King John to sign the Magna Charta on Trinity Monday, 15th June, 1215. *Runnymede House*, seat of N. Reid, Esq.; *Cooper's Hill*, so beautifully described by the poet Denham. We then pass along two miles of beautiful scenery and reach

VIRGINIA WATER.

Telegraph station at Windsor, 5 miles.

HOTEL.—Wheatsheaf.

This beautiful lake, situated in Windsor Forest, was planned by the Duke of Cumberland, above 100 years ago. Open daily to the public. It is the largest piece of artificial water in the kingdom, if that can be called artificial where man has only collected the streams of the district into a natural basin. The surrounding scenery is exceedingly pleasing and picturesque. After passing through a woody dell, we come to some serpentine walks, which lead in different directions; those to the right conducting us to a somewhat steep hill, on the summit of which stands a handsome Gothic battlemented building, called *Belvidere*; and those to the left leading to the margin of the lake. At the head of the lake is a cascade, descending some twenty feet, over massive fragments of stone, into a dark glen or ravine. Near it is an obelisk standing on a small mount, and bearing the following inscription, added by William IV.:—"This obelisk was raised by the command of George II., after the battle of Culloden, in commemoration of the services of his son William, Duke of Cumberland, the success of his arms, and the gratitude of his father." There is a road hence to the banks of the lake, where we can reach a rustic bridge, and get a fine view of the waterfall and its cavern adjacent, formed of stones brought from Bagshot Heath, where they indicated the ruins of a Saxon cromlech. At the point where the lake is widest, a fishing temple was erected by George IV.

A bold arch carries the public road to Blacknest, over a portion of the grounds, and adjoining is an ornamental ruin, called the "Temple of the Gods," manufactured from some really antique fragments of Greek columns and pediments, that used to lie in the court-yard of the British Museum. The effect is striking, and much more so if the spectator will for a moment let fancy delude him into the belief that he is gazing on a real temple of ancient Athens. The tall trees, clustering round in one part, and in another opening on to glades of truly sylvan aspect, impart a romantic beauty to the landscape from this point, which utterly defies description. It is worth while to cross the little bridge above alluded to, and, passing one of the streams that feed the lake, pursue its windings among the underwood, or strike into the path which leads to Bishopsgate, a beautiful village, environed by all the charms of wood and water diversity. Here resided for some time Shelley, who has consecrated the allurements of this spot by some of his finest poems, written in the vicinity. There are several ways of approaching Virginia Water, each so attractive that it is difficult to decide upon the best; but, by whichever route the excursionist comes, we would suggest the adoption of another road for the return. About two miles beyond the town of Egham is a neat wayside inn, called the "Wheatsheaf," from the garden of which there is direct access to the lake. From Egham Hill a road diverges through Windsor Park to Reading, nineteen miles distant. A few hundred yards above the inn is a branch road to the right, leading to Blacknest, where there is also an entrance through the keeper's lodge. Besides this, there is a delightful drive of five miles to Virginia Water from Chertsey.

Stoke Pogis, two miles from Slough, is hallowed ground, from containing the churchyard which suggested Gray's well-known "Elegy," as well as the remains of the pensive poet himself. Gray died on the 30th of July 1771, in the 55th year of his age, and was buried, according to his own affectionate wish, by the side of his mother; thus adding another poetical association to this beautiful and classic region. Burnham is a small but most picturesque village, four miles from Slough, with a marvellous miniature forest, called "Burnham Beeches"—the finest spot in the world for a pic-nic, and absolutely unrivalled for the romantic character of its sylvan scenery. There are the ruins of an Augustine nunnery close by, which, though now partly fashioned into a farm-house, had the honour of having been built by an expatriated king of the Romans, in 1228.

SUNNINGDALE station.

ASCOT.

Telegraph station at Windsor, 4 miles.
HOTEL.—Swan.
RACES in June. This place is celebrated for its race course on the Heath (nearly 2 miles in circuit), with a Royal Grand Stand, two stables, large coach house, commodious weighing houses, &c., all constructed by the Duke of Cumberland. The sport at these races is first-rate. They are generally attended by the Royal Family in state, and the élite of the court, nobility, and fashion of England.

On the west side of the park, five miles from the town is *Ascot Heath* and its *Race Course.* There is a Grand Stand and a separate one for the Queen. Further on, Bingfield and its beechwoods, all beautiful. Indeed the whole of Berkshire, from end to end, abounds in endless attractions to the lover of country scenery Twenty years ago Ascot Heath was as wild a district as any in Great Britain, with hardly a house visible from it but the Royal Kennels, and an apology for a race stand. Now the buildings appropriated to the turf form a little city of Olympian palaces, the most complete range of racing Chateaux extant. The sport, too, is indeed worthy of being set before a Sovereign. On most occasions there are upwards of thirty races, some of them bringing together the best horses in the land, and the whole generally go off with considerable éclat.

We shortly after reach BRACKNELL station, containing a population of 108. It has a pretty modern church, built by Coe.

WOKINGHAM.—The particulars of this place will be found at page 32.
Reading, see page 4, Sec. II.

South Western Main Line continued from page 64.

Clapham to Kingston.

Soon after rejoining the Main Line at Clapham Common, a branch to the left leads to the Crystal Palace, *via* Balham, Streatham, and Norwood. See page 51.

CLAPHAM.

POPULATION, 914.
Distance from station, 1 mile.
Telegraph station at London, 4¼ miles.
MONEY ORDER OFFICE, No. 2, Holland Place, Clapham.

Wimbledon Park, the seat of the Earl Spencer, is seen to the right; thence crossing the old Surrey Railway, we at the same time pass over Garratt Lane, the little village adjoining, which was formerly the scene of a mock election, rendered popular by Foote's grotesque farce of the "Mayor of Garratt."

The adjacent country now begins to assume a very pleasant and diversified appearance, and the patches of woodland scenery that break forth in bold relief against the distant horizon furnish an agreeable foretaste of the picturesque views yet to come. Passing beneath a few arches which connect the roads leading from various adjacent villages, we reach the station at

WIMBLEDON.

Distance from station, ¼ mile.
Telegraph station at Kingston, 4¾ miles.
HOTEL.—Rose and Crown.
MONEY ORDER OFFICE at Putney.

WIMBLEDON was formerly celebrated in the annals of duelling, a practice which has now become synonymous with our notions of "*such killing being murder,*" and therefore, like many other customs and habits of uncivilised beings, it has been discountenanced and condemned by that general spirit of good feeling and sense which now happily pervades all classes of the community.

MERTON.

Distance from the Wimbledon station ¾ mile.
Telegraph station at Kingston, 4 miles.
HOTEL.—White Hart.
MONEY ORDER OFFICE at Tooting.

The pretty village of Merton, where Lord Nelson lived, is a favourite resort of excursionists.

CROYDON BRANCH.

Wimbledon to Croydon.

This is a short line connecting the South Eastern and Southern with the Western Counties; the stations being MORDEN, MITCHAM, BEDDINGTON, CROYDON, see page 51.

LEATHERHEAD BRANCH.

Wimbledon to Epsom and Leatherhead.

This branch is intended subsequently to unite with the London and Portsmouth Direct, at Godalming, *via* Epsom.—At present it is opened to Leatherhead, about half-way. The stations *en route* from Wimbledon are OLD MALDEN,
EWELL, the church of which has some curious monuments,
EPSOM, noticed page 52,
ASHTEAD.—Ashtead Park, the seat of Colonel Howard.

LEATHERHEAD.

HOTELS.—Swan, Duke's Head.
FAIR.—Oct. 10th, for horses and pigs.
This place is situated on the river Mole.—The church was built about the year 1346, in the form of a cross, but has since been restored. Close by is an old timbered house, thought to be the "woning" of "Elynor Rumming," the famous ale wife, whose "tunning" is celebrated by Skelton, the poet-laureate of Henry VII.

South Western Main Line continued.

Emerging from the excavation, we proceed onwards over an embankment, which affords one continued series of delightful views across a country which art has contributed in the highest degree to adorn, at the extremity of which a cursory glimpse of the old square tower of Kingston church is obtained.

Malden.—The line now passes beneath two bridges, and we reach the station at

KINGSTON.

Distance from station, 1 mile.

A telegraph station.

HOTELS.—Sun, Griffin, and Southampton Hotel, (Railway Station).

MARKET DAY.—Saturday. FAIRS.—Whit-Thursday, Friday, and Saturday, August 2nd and 3rd, November 13th, and seven following days.

MONEY ORDER OFFICE at Old Kingston.

KINGSTON-ON-RAILWAY, situated in a charming verdant cutting, is a new place which has sprung up in the course of a few years, from its vicinity to the railway station. It has a good street, and contains some elegant houses. The neighbouring Common is the spot on which took place the last struggle of the Royalists, in favour of Charles I., then a prisoner in Carisbrooke Castle.

Kingston-on-Thames, a mile beyond, is a market town of 15,000 inhabitants, built on the site of a Roman station, and for a time the favourite seat of the Wessex Kings, several of whom were crowned here. The very *stone* on which they were inaugurated is to be seen railed in, opposite the Town Hall, near Queen Anne's statue. It is a block of Bath stone, three feet and a half long. From Kingston the line proceeds on an embankment for about five miles, affording some choice views of the richly wooded country by which this county is surrounded. About a mile from Kingston the line branches off to Thames Ditton and Hampton Court.

HAMPTON COURT BRANCH.

Kingston to Hampton Court.

THAMES DITTON.

Telegraph station at Kingston, 2 miles.
HOTEL.—Swan.
COACHES (from Kingston) to and from London, once daily; to and from Brighton, thrice weekly.
MONEY ORDER OFFICE at Kingston.

THAMES DITTON is well-known among anglers; fine barbel, roach, perch, dace, and chub, with sometimes jack and trout, may be caught.

HAMPTON COURT.—East Moulsey.

Telegraph station at Kingston, 3 miles.

HOTELS.—King's Arms, first-class, for families, private and commercial gentlemen. Greyhound, family and commercial.

RACES.—Hampton, on Moulsey Hurst, in June.

MONEY ORDER OFFICE at Walton-on-Thames.

The situation of Hampton Court, which stands on the north bank of the Thames, about twelve miles from London, is so happily described by Pope, that we cannot resist quoting the favourite passage:—

"Close by those meads for ever crowned with flowers,
Where Thames with pride surveys his rising towers,
There stands a structure of majestic frame,
Which from the neighbouring Hampton takes its name
Here Britain's statesmen oft the fall foredoom
Of foreign tyrants and of nymphs at home;
Here thou great Anna, whom three realms obey,
Dost sometimes counsel take, and sometimes—tea."

In summing up the points of its early history, we may briefly state, that in the thirteenth century the manor of Hampden was vested in the Knights of St. John of Jerusalem. Cardinal Wolsey, its illustrious founder, was the last of the enlightend churchmen of old, whose munificence patronised that style of building, which, originating with the ecclesiastics, seemed to end in his fall. He is supposed to have furnished the designs, and having been commenced in 1515, the building, when finished, was in so magnificent a style that it created great envy at court. The banquets and masques, so prevalent in the age of Henry VIII., were nowhere more magnificently ordered than here; and however vast the establishment of the Cardinal, it could not have been more than sufficient for the accommodation of his train or guests. Numerous sovereigns since that time have made it their temporary abode; and the last who resided here were George II. and his Queen, since which period various members of the court have occupied the apartments, the Crown reserving the right of resuming possession. At present, about 700 decayed gentlemen and gentlewomen, with their servants, occupy offices connected with the establishment, to which they are recommended by the Lord Chamberlain. The Lion Gate, which fronts the entrance to Bushy Park, an appurtenance granted to Queen Adelaide, is the chief avenue; and, continuing through the Wilderness, by a path overshadowed with lofty trees, we find ourselves by the side of the palace, in front of which extends a long walk, ornamented with parterres, an exotic shrubbery, and a spacious fountain in the centre. The grand east front extends 330 feet, and the grand south front 328 feet, from the designs of Sir Christopher Wren. The grand staircase and the guard chamber lead to the picture galleries, to which so many cheap catalognes furnish descriptive guides that our enumeration of their magnificent contents is unnecessary. Suffice it to say, the paintings are about 1,000 in number. Retracing our steps to the middle court, we may observe, under the archway, the flight of steps leading to Wolsey's Hall. It is 106 feet long, forty feet wide, and illuminated by thirteen windows, each fifteen feet from the ground. On one of the panes of the bay window at the end, extending nearly to the floor, the young Earl of Surrey wrote his lines to the fair Geraldine. On each side the walls are hung with tapestry of the most costly material and rarest workmanship, said to have formed a portion of the gifts interchanged between Henry and Francis, at the celebrated "Field of the Cloth of Gold." In the centre of the dais there is a doorway leading to the withdrawal room. The beautiful gardens in front of the palace have been repeatedly the admiration of all visitors. They were laid out by William III., in the Dutch style, with canal and watercourses, and the compass and shears were industriously employed in making birds, beasts, and reptiles, out of yew, holly, and privet. The private gardens extend from the sides of the palace to the banks of the river, and contain, besides some remarkably fine orange trees, many of them in full bearing, a fine oak nearly forty feet in circumference, and an ancient elm called "King Charles's swing." The large space of ground on the opposite side of the palace is called "The Wilderness," and was planted with shrubs by order of William and Mary. Most of the walks are completely overshadowed, and on a hot summer day a stroll through these umbrageous paths is exceedingly inviting. In this portion of the grounds is situated the Maze, so constructed that all the paths apparently leading to the centre turn off to a more distant part, and involve the inquisitive adventurer in constant perplexity. Though we are not quite sure that the revelation does not spoil the chief sport, the secret of success in threading this miniature labyrinth is, that after the first turning to the left the right hand should be kept towards the fence the whole of the remaining way. The greatest curiosity, however, is perhaps the famous Vine, which, sheltered and nurtured in a hot-house, is 110 feet long, and, at three feet from the root, is twenty-seven inches in circumference. It bears from two to three thousand bunches of the black Hamburg grape in the season. We may now mention the arrangements made for the reception of visitors.

The State Apartments, Public Gardens, and Picture Galleries are open daily (Friday excepted) throughout the year, from ten till dusk; and on Sundays after two, P.M. The Public Gardens have generally a military band in attendance, and a small fee is expected by the gardener for exhibiting the orangery and the vine.

The Chesnut Avenue of Bushy is world-famous "Look across the road," says a pleasant companion to the spot, "upon those dark masses of a single tree with thousands of spiral flowers, each flower a study, powdering over the rich green, from the lowest branch to the topmost twig. Now you shall have a real reward for your three hours' toil under a lustrous sun. Look up and down this wondrous avenue. It's mile length seems a span; but from one gate to the other there is a double line of unbroken green with flowers rich as the richest of the tropics contending for the mastery of colour. Saw you ever such a gorgeous sight? Fashionable London even comes to see it; but in Whitsun week, and during the some twenty days of the glories of the chesnut thousands come here to rejoice in the exceeding beauty of this marvel of nature, which the art of the Dutch gardeners, whom William of Nassau brought to teach us, have left as a proud relic of their taste."

South Western Main Line continued.
Kingston to Weybridge.

ESHER.

This is the nearest station for Esher and Claremont; the former, once a place of some importance, is now little better than an inconsiderable village. Esher Place is remarkable as having been the residence of Wolsey, when Bishop of Winchester; and a small castled turret, near the River Mole, is exhibited as the place of his temporary imprisonment.

Claremont, which is adjoining, has a melancholy interest, from the death of the lamented Princess Charlotte, which took place in 1817. The palace has since belonged to her husband, the King of the Belgians, who subsequently appropriated it to the use of the exiled Orleans family, when Louis Philippe left France in 1848, and who have resided in it since his death, in comparative seclusion.

From the Ditton station we cross Walton Heath and reach the station at

WALTON & HERSHAM.

Distance from station, 1 mile to either place.

HOTELS.—(Walton) Duke's Head; Castle Inn.

FAIRS.—Wednesday and Thursday in Easter Week.

The Walton station is a short distance from Hersham, one mile to the left, and the same distance from Walton to the right. In the old church of St. Mary's, which may be seen rising amongst the trees, will be found various interesting monuments of considerable antiquity. A "scold bridle" is shown.

Apps Court, near Walton, was another of the many residences once belonging to Wolsey; and *Ashley Park*, the seat of the Fletcher family, is memorable for having been the temporary abode of Cromwell, prior to his assuming the Protectorate.

Proceeding along the line we obtain a view of

Oatlands, the seat of the late Duke of York, and recently that of the late Lord Ellesmere. The mansion is a spacious and elegant structure, surrounded by grounds of the most enchanting description, possessing all the beauties, natural and artificial, which unlimited expenditure and refined taste could combine.

Emerging from the Walton cutting we gain a somewhat lofty embankment, affording some picturesque views, through which the translucent Wey meanders like a glistening thread.

WEYBRIDGE.

Distance from station, ¾ mile.

A Telegraph station.

HOTELS.—Hand and Spear, Ship.

Here is a commodious hotel adjoining the station, with some extensive grounds. The scenery in this neighbourhood is beautiful, and St. George's Hill commands a delightful view of Windsor, Richmond, and Chertsey.

A little distance beyond Weybridge station a short line branches off to Addlestone and Chertsey.

CHERTSEY BRANCH.
Weybridge to Chertsey.

ADDLESTONE station.

CHERTSEY.

Distance from station, ½ mile.

HOTEL.—Swan.

MARKET DAY.—Wednesday.

FAIRS.—First Monday in Lent, May 14th, August 6th, and September 25th.

CHERTSEY is as old as the days of the ancient Britons, and probably was one of their principal places. Soon after the conversion of the Saxons from Paganism, in 666, a Benedictine monastery was founded here by Frithwald, a petty prince of Surrey, and by him richly endowed. In the original charter it is written, "I beseech those whose names are annexed to subscribe themselves witnesses that I, Frithwald, who am the giver, together with the Abbot Erkenwald, on account of my ignorance of letters, have expressed with the sign of the Holy Cross." It is from this pretty evident that princes in those days had somewhat of Jack Cade's antipathy to those who could "read, write, and cast accompt," and therefore they also "made their mark, like a simple, plain-dealing, honest man." The Danes, who were the general "snappers-up of unconsidered trifles," pillaged the abbey in 1009, killed the abbot and monks, and laid the whole building desolate; but being afterwards rebuilt by Egbert, King of Kent, it became more magnificently embellished than ever, and was one of the most important monasteries in the kingdom. Henry VI. was buried here, under a sumptuous mausoleum, but the body was exhumed in 1504, by Henry VII., and conveyed with great pomp, first to Windsor, and afterwards to Westminster Abbey. It is useless to look now for any vestige of its former grandeur; all that remains is a part of its wall, forming the boundary of an orchard, and part of an archway is still visible on the north side of the town. In the centre of the town is the church, rebuilt in 1808, but having a portion of the old chancel and tower remaining. Even so late as the year 1814, and occasionally since, the curfew has been tolled here, from Michaelmas to Lady-day, the day of the month being indicated during the time of ringing. A handsome stone bridge of seven arches was erected, in 1786, across the Thames, connecting the counties of Surrey and Middlesex. At a house in Guildford Street, formerly distinguished as the Porch House, lived Abraham Cowley, the poet, who has perpetuated, in prose and verse, his love for this seclusion in a hundred quaint prettinesses. Beneath the window of the room in which he died (July 28th, 1667) is a tablet thus appealing to the sympathies of the passers-by, "Here the last accents flowed from Cowley's tongue." A pretty summer house that he built, and a seat under a sycamore tree, both mentioned in his poems, were existing till the middle of the last century. After the excursionist has refreshed his physical energies at one of the many excellent inns that here abound, by all means let him ascend St. Anne's Hill, about a mile out of the town, and he shall find himself, at the summit, elevated some 250 feet above the ocean level, with a glorious panorama round about him of the finest parts of the river between Richmond and Windsor. There is a spring at the top, that summer's heat and winter's cold alike prove unable to dry up or freeze. The mansion on the southern slope of the hill was once the residence of Charles James Fox, the statesman, to whom a cenotaph has been erected in the church.

South Western Main Line continued.

From the hill before Weybridge to Woking, a distance of six miles, there is a gradual descent. After crossing the bridge which spans the Basingstoke Canal, here intersected by the canal from Guildford, and passing several villages, we pass over the Woking embankment, whence a succession of picturesque views will delight the traveller. Ottershaw Park affords a pleasing specimen of English forest scenery. The fine effect of these majestic trees, with nothing behind them but the sunny splendour of a summer morning, or the rich glow of an evening sky, realises all that Claude has embodied in his pictures.

WOKING.

Distance from station, 1 mile—A telegraph station.

HOTELS.—White Hart, Railway.

FAIR.—Whit Tuesday.

On both sides of the line Woking Common is seen to extend for miles, only broken by the windings of the Basingstoke Canal, and terminated by a long range of woodland scenery, which stands out in picturesque relief against the horizon.

Three-quarters of a mile beyond Woking a line branches off to the left to Guildford and Godalming, direct to Portsmouth, from which another branch diverges at Guildford, and extends to Ash, Farnham, and Alton.

Guildford.—Particulars of this will be found on page 31.

ALTON BRANCH.
Guildford to Alton.

ASH.

Distance from station, 1 mile.

A Telegraph station.

MONEY ORDER OFFICE at Farnham.

TONGHAM, station for Aldershott.

FARNHAM.

POPULATION, 3,515,
Distance from station, ½ mile.
Telegraph station at Ash.
HOTEL.—Bush.
MARKET DAYS.—Thursdays.
FAIRS.—Holy Thursday, June 24th, November 13th, October 10th.
BANKERS.—John and James Knight.

FARNHAM contains much to interest the tourist. Putting its celebrity for hops out of the question, there is the old castle, which has been the seat of the bishops of Winchester since the time of King

Stephen, and the neighbourhood abounds with vestiges of former monastic splendour. The exquisitely beautiful ruins of Waverley Abbey, about a mile from the town, are alone a reward for any pilgrimage that may be made from the station. It has the earliest Cistercian foundation in England. *Moore Park* was the seat of Temple, whose heart was buried in a silver box under the sun-dial. Swift was his secretary at the time, and here wrote his correspondence with Stella.

BENTLEY.

Distance from station, 1 mile.

MARKET DAY.—Saturday. FAIRS.—January 25th, June 22nd, Saturday in Easter Week, October 25th.

MONEY ORDER OFFICE at Alton.

ALTON.

POPULATION, 2,828.

HOTEL.—Swan.

MARKET DAY.—Saturday. FAIRS.—Last Saturday in April, July 5th, and September 29th.

Returning to Guildford the line takes a southerly direction, and at the distance of 3¾ miles brings us to the important town of

GODALMING.

POPULATION, 2,218.

Distance from station, ¼ mile.

Telegraph station at Guildford, 3¾ miles.

HOTEL.—King's Arms.

MARKET DAY.—Wednesday.

FAIRS.—February 13th, and July 10th.

BANKERS.—Mellersh and Keen.

This town is situated on the banks of the Wye, at a point where that river divides into several streams; it is a considerable trading and manufacturing town. The manufactures are stocking weaving of all kinds, fleecy hosiery, blankets, worsteds, cotton cloths, &c. It consists of a principal street, running east and west, and several smaller ones; the church is much admired, and has a handsome spire.

LONDON AND PORTSMOUTH DIRECT.

Godalming to Portsmouth.

This route is a continuation of the line *via* Guildford and Godalming to Portsmouth, bringing the latter place about 21 miles nearer London than by the old route, *via* Bishopstoke.—The stations are, MILFORD, WITLEY the station for *Petworth*, HASLEMERE, LIPHOOK, LISS.

PETERSFIELD, a neat little town of great antiquity. It has a population of 5,550, and returns one member to parliament. Near the chapel there is an equestrian statue of William III, built by the Joliffes of Merstham,

ROWLAND'S CASTLE and HAVANT.

Portsmouth, described page 62.

South Western Main Line continued. Woking to Basingstoke.

From Woking the line shortly crosses the road by a viaduct of one arch, and then enters the Goldworthy Hill excavation, on emerging from which it proceeds over the Frimley embankment, about four miles in length, whence an almost unbounded view of the surrounding country bursts upon the sight. The eye ranges over one vast landscape of hills and valleys thickly wooded, and presenting a *coup d'œil* of surpassing beauty, above which may be seen the Surrey hills stretching away for miles, and bounding one of nature's panoramas which defy description. Crossing a small streamlet, called Blackwater Brook, we leave the county of Surrey for Hampshire, and passing beneath a road, we reach FARNBOROUGH Station.

HAMPSHIRE,

ONE of the southern counties of England, bounded on the east by Surrey and Sussex; on the south by the English Channel; and on the west by Wiltshire and Dorsetshire. It extends in length, from north to south, about fifty-five miles; in breadth, from east to west, about forty. The surface of Hampshire is beautifully varied with gently rising hills, fruitful valleys, and extensive woodlands. The chief part of the county is enclosed, though large tracts of open heath and uncultivated lands remain, especially in that part which borders Dorsetshire. The manufactures of Hampshire are not considerable; the principal are those of woollen goods. Great quantities of excellent malt are made at Andover; malt and leather at Basingstoke, also silk, straw hats, and paper; vast quantities of common salt, and of Epsom and Glauber salts, at Lymington; and in the neighbourhood of Redbridge there are valuable salt marshes. The minerals of Hampshire are scarcely deserving of notice, though the chalk strata and the rocks along the coast present very interesting objects to the geologist. Hampshire is much resorted to for the purpose of sea-bathing, and also as a fashionable summer residence, and bathing houses have, in consequence, been erected all along the coast. The scenery of the New Forest is particularly admired, and the whole county abounds with villas and country seats.

The railway communication of the county is supplied principally by the South Western Railway Company, from Farnborough Station to Winchester, Southampton, Portsmouth, Salisbury, &c., &c., and the Great Western have a branch line between Reading and Basingstoke.

FARNBOROUGH.

A telegraph Station.

MONEY ORDER OFFICE.

At this station the Farnborough cutting ends, and we proceed along an embankmeut which again reveals some pleasing rural scenery, but the country between here and Winchfield does not demand any lengthened description. This is the nearest station for the Camp at Aldershott.

Passing FLEETPOND, we soon arrive at

WINCHFIELD.

Telegraph station at Farnborough, 6 miles.

HOTEL.—Beauclerk Arms.

OMNIBUSES to Odiham, North Warnborough, Hartley, Hartley Row, Hartford Bridge, Wintney and Phœnix, five times daily, and to Bromhill, Hickfield, Strathfieldsaye, and Wokingham.

MONEY ORDER OFFICE.

Leaving the station we enter a deep excavation, and soon after a short tunnel; a lofty embankment follows, which presents us with a series of delightful prospects, amongst which the Odiham hills and their singular clump of trees on the summit figure conspicuously on the left. Prior to entering on the Hook Common excavation we pass beneath Odiham bridge, which leads to the seat of the late and present Duke of Wellington, Strathfieldsaye, situated about six miles off to the right.

The Heriot hills, crested by lofty firs, soon burst into view, and not long after we pass the interesting ruins of Old Basing, which was, in the Saxon era, a place of considerable note, and the scene of contests during the civil wars. The viaduct the line now passes over affords a good view of the old town, and a short distance beyond we reach

BASINGSTOKE.

A telegraph station.

HOTELS.—Angel; Red Lion; Wheat Sheaf.

MARKET DAYS.—Wednesday and Saturday.

FAIRS.—Easter Tuesday, Wednesday in Whitsun Week, September 23rd and October 10th.

BASINGSTOKE is a straggling, ill-built town, situated on the left in the valley. It is, nevertheless, a place of great antiquity, and appears in Domesday Book as a "market town." It enjoyed the privilege of sending members to parliament, and exercised that right as early as the reigns of Edwards I. and II. Charles the First conferred upon it its first charter of incorporation, and it is still a municipal borough, possessing an annual revenue of nearly 2,000*l.* Formerly it carried on a rather considerable business in druggets, which has since fallen off, and the inhabitants now mainly depend on the corn and malt trades. It possesses several charities, one of which was established by a bequest from Sir J. Lancaster, the navigator, who was a native.

A beautiful ruin, on the brow of the hill to the right, stands out in bold relief against the horizon, and cannot fail to attract notice. It is the dilapidated remains of the Holy Ghost Chapel, destroyed by the Puritans under Cromwell. A day passed at Basingstoke will be well bestowed in visiting the neighbourhood so rich in historical associations.

Basingstoke to Salisbury, Yeovil, and Exeter.

After leaving Basingstoke the line proceeds through a chalky range, from which various parks may be seen extending on every side—blended with scattered villages Passing the stations of OAKLEY, OVERTON, and WHITCHURCH, we arrive at the important station of

ANDOVER.

Distance from station, 1 mile.

A telegraph station.

HOTEL.—Star and Garter.

MARKET DAY.—Saturday.

FAIRS.—Mid-Lent Saturday, May 12th, Nov. 16th.

A bustling agricultural town and borough in West Hants, with a population of 5,395, represented by two members in the House of Commons. The Roman way from Winchester to Cirencester passed in this direction, and here the Romans fixed a station, which they called Andaseron; but when Ethelred the Saxon was present at the baptism of Olaus of Norway, it was called Andofera, whence we get the present name. One of the villages in the neighbourhood is yet named Winchester Street (stratum)—a proof of how little things have altered in the country parts of England for ages downwards.

The town stretches two-thirds of a mile along this highway, on the little river Anton. It has a modern town-hall on arches, a new church built in 1849, many malt-houses, and a factory for silk shag. The Old Church dates back to the conquest. There is a large trade in agricultural produce, especially about the time of *Weyhill Fair.* This takes place between the 10th and 15th of October, at Weyhill, 3 miles north-west of the town, when immense quantities of sheep, horses, hops, cheese, leather, &c., change hands. As many as 300,000 sheep are brought to market; and the country people take the opportunity of hiring themselves to new masters —their common practice being to change their situations annually.

This town obtained an unenviable notoriety some few years ago, in consequence of mal-practices alleged to exist in the Union, and which formed at the time the subject of official inquiry. The facts elicited during this inquiry created a deep sensation throughout the country, and produced a feeling both in and out of Parliament, the expression of which has drawn attention to the working of the poor-law system, which has resulted in an amelioration of the condition of those whom necessity has driven to take up their abode in our workhouses.

James II. slept here November 1688, where his son-in-law, Prince George of Denmark, deserted him to join the Prince of Orange, who was advancing from the West of England. "What!" said James, "*Est-il-possible* — gone?" This was the prince's nickname, from his constant habit of using that phrase.

Several Roman and Saxon camps may be found in this quarter by the persevering antiquary. Within a short distance are *Amport House*, seat of the Marquis of Winchester, and *Hurstbourne Priors*, which belongs to the Earl of Portsmouth (a lunatic). The old seat of the Winchester family, was that Basing House defended so gallantly for two years against the Puritan party, until Cromwell came in person and carried it by storm, when the plate, jewels, &c., were seized, and the noble pile burnt to the ground. Some few traces of it are yet visible at Old Basing near Basingstoke; a descendant of his was the Duke of Bolton, who married Polly Peachum.

GRATELEY AND PORTON stations are next passed, and in a very few minutes the train arrives at

Salisbury, for description of which see page 79.

DINTON.—*Dinton House*, seat of W. Wyndham, Esq., is on the river Nadder, and was the birth-place of the great Lord Clarendon, 1608. Wickhall Camp, an ancient encampment, is near.

The next stations in succession are TISBURY, SEMLEY, GILLINGHAM, TEMPLECOMBE, and MILBOURNE PORT.

SHERBORNE.

This town has a population of 3,878, and is prettily situated on the slope of a hill in the vale of Blackmore. It was once the seat of a bishopric, but was removed to Old Sarum in 1075. The abbey was a long time after in existence, but was burnt in the reign of Henry VI. The abbey church was afterwards made parochial, and is one of the finest ecclesiastical structures in the west of England. There are likewise some remains of a castle. Near it is the mansion of the Earl of Digby, which was partly built by Sir Walter Raleigh, surrounded by picturesque scenery and sheltering groves, one of which was planted by this unfortunate but great man.

Yeovil.—See page 23, sec. II.

SUTTON, CREWKERNE, and CHARD ROAD stations.

AXMINSTER.

Population, 2,769; situated on the river Axe. Some of the best and finest description of carpets are made here.

COLYTON station.

HONITON.

Population, 3,427. Returns two members to parliament, and produces lace of a very costly description.

FENITON, WHIMPLE, and BROAD CLYST stations.

Exeter.—See page 25, sec. II.

South Western Main Line continued.

Basingstoke to Bishopstoke.

MITCHELDEVER station. — The line now passes through a country bearing the true Hampshire characteristics of forest scenery, until we reach

WINCHESTER.

A telegraph station.

HOTELS.—The George; Black Swan.

MARKET DAYS.—Wednesdays and Saturdays.

FAIRS.—First Monday in Lent, and October 24th.

RACES in June

This old capital of the British *Belgœ*, county town of *Hampshire*, a bishop's see, and parliamentary borough (two members); stands among round chalk hills, sloping down to the Itchen, on the South Western Railway, 63½ miles from London, and 12¼ from Southampton. The ancient Britons styled it *Gwent*, a white; which the Romans, who made it one of their head quarters, altered to *Venta Belgarium*; and the West Saxons, after them, to *Wintancestre.* Many of the later Saxon kings and their successors down to Henry VIII., occasionally made Winchester a place of residence. The *Winchester* bushel, the standard of dry-measure, and Henry I.'s standard yard, are to be seen at the Town Hall in High-street, a modern building. The *County Hall* is close to the gate of a *castle* built by William the Conqueror, and was itself once the castle chapel. The hall is 110 feet long, and contains a curious relic, called Arthur's Round Table, 18 feet in diameter, on which are portraits of this king of romance and his peerless knights. King Arthur, if he ever existed, was a British, and not Saxon sovereign. At *Caer Gwent*, now Caerlea, in Monmouthshire, there is an amphitheatre called after him; but from the likeness of names, his memory has taken root here; so much so that Henry VII.'s eldest son received his name, Arthur, from Winchester being the place of his birth, 1486. The table just mentioned, though restored, is as ancient as the time of King Stephen. Egbert of Wessex was here crowned by the Wittenagemote, Bretwalda, or King of all Angle-land, or England, as it was thenceforth called. Canute made Winchester the capital of England. The body of Rufus was brought hither by a charcoal-burner, after his death from Tyrrel's arrow in the New Forest. Richard I. was crowned here on his return from Austria. Even as late as the 17th century it was a favourite resort of Charles II., who began a palace of red brick, now used as a barracks, on the Castle Hill, near the County Hall.

Winchester is nearly square, like all Roman towns, and has a main street—High-street, intersected by several narrower streets. In the middle of High-street is the Butter Cross, a beautiful piece of open arches and pinnacled work, in three stories, 45 feet high, of the time of Henry VI. Great inconvenience having been experienced by the citizens in having to purchase their necessaries at different localities, a splendid new Market House, affording accommodation for the sale and purchase of all domestic essentials, was opened in October, 1857. The *Corn Exchange* was built in 1839, a plain substantial structure. A little way from this is the *Cathedral*. more remarkable for its antiquity and length (518 feet) than for its appearance. The west front, however, and the front view of the entrance are imposing. The old parts (except the Saxon crypt), are Bishop Walkelin's Norman transepts and tower—a low, solid pile 140 feet in height. Domesday Book was kept in the north aisle till a place was found for it at Westminster. In the Lady Chapel, at the east end, Queen Mary was married to Philip of Spain, in 1554. The Gothic nave was built by Bishop Edindon and the famous William of Wykeham, whose statue is placed over the great window. Edindon refused the see of Canterbury, saying, "that though Canterbury was the higher *rack*, Winchester was the better *manger*.' It is still the richest benefice, after London, being worth £10,500. The beautiful screen carved roof, and the choir, is the work of Bishop Fox, the founder of the Corpus Christi College, Oxford. The bones of a dozen Saxon kings were collected by him and placed in this part of the church; but, in the troubles of the civil war, they were dispersed, though several boxes were labelled with their names. There are some monumental chapels and effigies—such as William of Wykeham, Cardinal Beaufort, Bishop Fox, William Rufus, Bishop Hoadley, Izaak Walton, James Wharton, the poet, &c. One of the first organs made in England was placed here by Bishop Elfey, in the year 951; it was a ponderous thing containing 400 pipes, blown by 24 pair of bellows. In the close are remains of the cloisters of St. Swithin's priory, and of Wolvesley Castle, which was a seat of the bishops, built by King Stephen's brother, de Blois. The palace was built by Wren.

William of Wykeham's *College*, was founded in 1339, and is an ancient Gothic pile, with additions made in the last century. The chapel, hall, and cloisters are beautiful. The scholars here are regularly transferred to New College, Oxford, which was also founded by this munificent prelate. More than forty bishops have been educated here.

There is a model prison near the Cemetery. St. John the Baptist's Hospital is a very ancient foundation, a part of which is now used as an assembly room. The church of St. John is very old. St. Swithin's is over King's Gate postern. There are eleven altogether, formerly they were *ninety*, of which twenty were burnt in the war of succession between King Stephen and the Empress Maud. and more were destroyed when Cromwell took the city in 1645. West Gate is the only gate remaining in the old walls. The late Dr. Lingard, the Roman Catholic historian, was born here, 1769. *Hong Kong* is the Chinese seat of Mr. Andrews, the great carriage builder at Southampton, and here Kossuth the Hungarian leader was fêted in 1851.

On the road to this town, about three quarters of a mile from Winchester, is the ancient church of *St. Cross*, begun by Bishop Blois in the Norman style, and finished by Wykeham and Cardinal Beaufort, the latter especially, who rebuilt most part of the hospital which is attached. The mastership held by Lord North has gradually dropped into a lucrative sinecure, to the injury of the foundation, but this abuse is now under inquiry. A piece of dry bread and a (dirty) cup of (thin) beer are still given to any wayfarer who asks for refreshments in terms of the founder's desire. It is a striking instance of the tenacity with which the form of old customs is kept up in England, though the spirit of simple hospitality which the founder inculcated has entirely disappeared.

On St. Catherine's Hill are traces of a camp; most of the highways from the city are in the direction of the old Roman roads. Among the seats around are the following:—*Twyford*, down the Itchen, belongs to J. Dampier, Esq. Here was a Roman Catholic School, in which Pope was educated. At *Compton* is an old church. *Hursley*, the seat of Sir W. Heathcote, Bart., belonged to Richard Cromwell, who succeeded his father as Protector. When the old house was pulled down in 1746, the great seal of the Commonwealth was found. *Worthy Park*, up the Itchen, the seat of Mr. Turner, near Headbourne Worthy. The learned Bingham was rector here. *Avington* was a seat of the Duke of Buckingham. *Old Alresford House*, Lord Rodney. The late primate Howley was born at Alresford. *Swarraton Grange*, Lord Ashburton. *Tichbourne*, Sir E. Doughty, Bart., descended from the Titchbournes who were seated here from the time of Henry II. *Bishop's Waltham* (9 miles), in Waltham Chase, was an ancient seat of the Winchester prelates, and their are traces left of their palace, in which William of Wykeham died. He was born (1324) at Wyckham or Wickham a few miles south. The Chase is now reclaimed or enclosed. In the last century it was overrun by a gang of poachers, or Waltham Blacks.

After leaving the station at Winchester the line proceeds through the Barracks Hill excavation, above which are the Barracks, erected on the site of an old palace, where Henry III was born.

The village of *Twyford*, where Pope was educated at the school of the Rev. Mr. Wyeham, is in the vicinity; thence passing Otterbourne, another straggling village to the right, we reach the station of

BISHOPSTOKE.

A telegraph station.

The little village that gives name to the station is most pleasantly situated, but contains no object worthy of remark. This station is the junction point with the branch line to Salisbury, and also the point of union between the Gosport and Southampton trains, the line to the former diverging slightly to the left.

SALISBURY BRANCH.

Bishopstoke to Salisbury.

CHANDLER'S FORD station.

ROMSEY.

A telegraph station.

HOTEL.—White Horse.

MARKET DAY—Thursday. FAIRS—Easter Monday, August 16th, Nov. 18th, and every Tuesday fortnight, from July 31st to Dec. 25th.

Like many other places of great antiquity, Romsey owes its foundation to a monastic establishment. Edward here founded a Benedictine abbey on a very extensive scale, and appointed his daughter abbess. It was enlarged by Edgar, whose son's remains were interred in its church. Romsey suffered considerably during the incursions of the Danes, who sacked the town and plundered the abbey in the 10th century. Although mentioned in Domesday Book, its first charter of incorporation only dates as far back as the reign of James I. It possesses a very ancient-looking church which belonged to the abbey, cruciform in shape, with a low tower. This church has been frequently altered and rebuilt. The Archæological Society has lately restored this interesting edifice, which, although mostly in the early English, yet retains traces of the Norman style. For nearly two hundred years an apple tree grew on the roof of this ancient structure, but it has recently been removed for fear of its injuring the building. The church contains a screen, several old frescoes, sculptures, tombs, &c. Remains of the abbey are still to be seen, and Roman coins, &c., have been found in the neighbourhood. The town has a population of 5,347, employed in general agricultural trade, paper mills, and sacking making.

DUNBRIDGE.

Telegraph station at Romsey, 2½ miles.

MONEY ORDER OFFICE at Romsey.

DEAN station.

SALISBURY.

Distance from station, ¼ mile. A telegraph station.

HOTELS.—White Hart; Red Lion; Three Swans.

OMNIBUSES AND COACHES to Stapleford, Deptford, Craford, Heytesbury, Boreham, Shaftesbury, Wilton, Barford, Fovant, Donhead, Ludwell, Gillingham, Milborne Port, Sherborne, Wincanton, Mere, Hindon, Knoyle, Bodenham, Charlton, Downton, Breamore, Fordingbridge, Devizes, Boscomb, Park House, Tidworth, Woodyates, Thickthorn, Blandford, Weymouth, Shrewton, Lavington, Wardour, and Bournemouth.

MARKET DAYS.—Tuesday and Saturday; second Tuesday in every month for cheese.

FAIRS.—Tuesdays after January 6th, and 25th March, second Tuesday in September, second Tuesday after October 10th; for sheep, July 15th and October 30th.

BANKERS.—Wilts and Dorset Banking Company; Everett & Co.; National Provincial Bank of England.

Salisbury is a parliamentary borough (two members) and a bishop's see, in Wiltshire, at the terminus of a branch of the South Western line, 96 miles from London, on the rich green pastures of the Avon. Population 11,657. It is not an old town, compared with other sees, the real original Old Sarum being on the hill to the north of Salisbury, where the walls and ditches of the Roman *Sorbiodunum*, out of which it sprung, are easily traced, as well as roads branching from it. Here a Cathedral was planted after the Conquest (for which that of Sherborne was deserted), but in 1220 another migration took place, and the present magnificent edifice was begun by Bishop Poore. It was for the most part finished in the course of 32 years, so that it has the great advantage of being not only uniform in design but offers a complete specimen of the style of that age, namely, early English. The shape is a double cross, from end to end 442 feet long; through the greater transept the width is 203 feet, and 147 through the less. The west front (which with the spire is of later date than the body) is 130 feet wide and 200 high, and ornamented with niches, turrets, tracery, &c., and a large painted window; the lower eastern window is a very handsome new one, placed as a memorial to the late dean; the upper eastern window is a very splendid one—subject, the "Brazen Serpent," by Mortimer—the gift of a former Earl of Radnor. Above all rises a most beautiful *steeple*, consisting of a slender crocketted spire, 190 feet long, resting on a tower, which makes its total height from the ground above 400 feet. It is reported to be 22 inches out of the perpendicular; but whether or not it is a most imposing object from all points. There are said to be as many windows in the cathedral as days in the year. Several effigies and monuments are here—some as far back as the 11th century, transferred of course from the old cathedral. Among them are a boy bishop, and William de Long êpée (or Long-sword) son of Richard I., alsoBishop Jewell, author of the Apology for the English church, and Harris, the author of Hermes, and ancestor of the Malmesbury family. The last is a work of Bacon's; there are two by Flaxman. The cloisters are 190 feet square; they were restored by the late Bishop Denison. In the octagonal chapter house, besides the stained windows and carvings, there is a good library, the Salisbury Missal or Roman form of prayer, which was the model for all the rest, a carved table, &c., and an original copy of Magna Charta. At the large old palace is a series of portraits, beginning with Bishop Duppa of Charles I.'s time. Both the cathedral and city were fully examined by the members of the archæological visit in 1844. Most of the streets, except the main one from Fisherton Street to Milford Hill, are laid out straight and regular, with rills 4 to 5 feet broad running through them from the Avon, Nadder, and Wiley; but unfortunately the city lies low, and, though its water meadows are pleasaut to look at, the courts in which the poor live are in a filthy state. The *Council Chamber* was built 1795 by Sir R. Taylor; portraits of James I., Queen Anne, &c. St. Thomas's church is Gothic; it contains a carved monument of wood. Large county gaol at Fisherton, built 1822, St. Edmund's Church, at the north-east corner of the city, was once collegiate. South of Milford Hill is St. Martin's, and in the centre of the city stands St. Thomas's. The churches are all about the same age. From the close behind the palace, an ancient bridge of the 13th century crosses the Avon to Harnham. There are two grammar schools; in that belonging to the city *Addison* was educated, at the Cathedral Grammar School in the close. He was born at Millston, higher up the river. There are also several hospitals and charities; one being a college for the widows of clergymen, founded by Bishop Seth Ward,—another, a set of alms-houses by Bishop Poore,—and a third, a hospital by Longsword's wife, Ella.

Two or three ancient wooden houses remain, which are curious specimens of ancient domestic architecture. In the Market Place, which was the scene of the execution of Buckingham, by order of Richard III., in 1483, is an ancient hexagonal Cross on pillars, called the *Poultry Cross*, built in Richard II.'s reign. Chubb, the deistical writer, was a tallow chandler here. Shoes and excellent cutlery figure among the manufactures. There are many objects of interest in the neighbourhood. At Stratford, near the ancient city, the Pitts had a seat; and in this way *Old Sarum* had the honour to be represented by the great Earl of Chatham.

Trafalgar (4 miles), on the Avon, is the seat of Earl Nelson, bought for the family by Parliament, on the death of Nelson in 1805. At *Clarendon* (3 miles), once a royal forest, the "Constitutions of Clarendon" subjecting the clergy to the civil power, were enacted 1163; this led to Becket's rebellion. *Clarendon Park*, Sir F. Bathurst, Bart. Near this, an ancient boundary called *Grime's Ditch*, may be traced along the hills into Dorset and Hants. *Cranborne Chase*, now enclosed, was to the south of it. There is an old church in the town; and at Tollard Royal is King John's hunting seat. *Longford Castle*, the seat of the Earl of Radnor, was at first built (1591) in the shape of a *triangle*, in honour of the Trinity. Besides many interesting portraits, it contains a curious *steel* chair, covered with bas reliefs, illustrative of Roman history. *Wardour Castle* is Lord Arundel of Wardour's seat, —a modern Grecian house in a large park, which contains the remains of a castle, famous in the civil war for the defence made in it by Lady Blanche and a few men against the forces of Hungerford. There are several religious pieces and relics (the family being Roman Catholic), portraits, &c., and a handsome chapel. *Fonthill Abbey*, the largest park in the county, belongs to Alfred Morrison, Esq., but formerly the seat of Beckford, the author of that most original eastern story, "Caliph Vathek," who here lived in the most selfish retirement, not seeing or being noticed by any one. *Heytesbury* (16 miles) on the Wiley, the seat of Lord Heytesbury, is a little decayed borough, with a collegiate church, and many barrows, &c. in the neighbourhood. Here these remains of antiquity begin to multiply, especially on Salisbury plain. Many were investigated by Mr. Cunningham, a draper, of Heytesbury, to whom Sir R. C. Hoare dedicated his "Ancient Wiltshire," in which will be found the fullest account of these memorials. They are of various kinds and shapes,—round, oval, square, &c. For warfare or burial (the barrows are usually graves), and have evidently been occupied by Britons, Romans, Saxons, &c., in succession, who attended them to suit their convenience. About 70 principal camps and stations may be counted, many of them ending in *bury*. *Salisbury Plain* is a turfy naked tract, 20 miles long east and west, almost as level as the sea, covered with sheep tracks, among which it is easy to lose oneself. The old coach road to the west of England crosses it; and the mail has been more than once dug out of the drift snow. In the winter of January 1854, a miller's wagon was thus overwhelmed; the poor driver got out to look for the road and perished; had he been content to stay where he was, he would have been saved by next morning. It is 500 or 600 feet above the sea. In the flattest and most solitary part are the celebrated Druid circles of *Stonehenge*; two ovals inside two circles, can be pretty well traced, with the avenues leading to them. There are, or were, about 140 stones. The people say that it is impossible to count the same number twice over, and that it would be unlucky to count them right—which must be a little discouraging to the schoolmaster. It has ever been considered the greatest wonder in the west of England, and many hundreds of strangers visit it annually. They are of a similar kind to those found on the Downs, where they lie about like sheep, under the name of Grey Wethers. Stonehenge is apt to disappoint the stranger at the first sight; and to some it is a trifle indeed. An American was once brought here by his friends, and made to shut his eyes as he drew near. Being placed under one of the Trilithons (one stone across the top of two others), he was told to look up, but instead of expressing astonishment, he wondered that they should think anything of it. To him who had gone in large ships in full sail under a vast natural archway of rock, it was nothing; but a little while after, the sight of Salisbury Cathedral, that glorious triumph of man's skill, sent him into raptures. Vespasian's camp and the circus (a round camp) are close to *Amesbury*, where there is an old church, and the seat of Sir E. Antrobus Bart. Avon hamlet lies two miles north-west of Salisbury. *Wilbury Park*, formerly Sir W. Cubitt's seat, now Sir A. Malet's, Bart. *Millston* was the birth-place of Addison, born in 1672; his father being the rector.

HAMPSHIRE.

GOSPORT AND PORTSMOUTH BRANCHES.

Bishopstoke to Gosport & Portsmouth,

By Botley and Fareham to Gosport, and Fareham and Cosham to Portsmouth, or from Gosport by ferry across to Portsmouth, or *vice versa.*

From Bishopstoke the line diverges to the south east, in order to preserve a connecting link between two towns which must ever be the focus of our military and maritime interest.

BOTLEY station.

FAREHAM.

POPULATION, 3,451.
A telegraph station.
HOTEL.—Red Lion.
MARKET DAY.—Tuesday. FAIR.-June 29th.

MONEY ORDER OFFICE at Fareham.

BANKERS.—Branch Hampshire Banking Company.

The trade of this place consists of coal, corn, canvas, and ropes. Much resorted to in the sea-bathing season.

GOSPORT.

POPULATION, 7,414.

A telegraph station.

HOTEL.—Crown.

OMNIBUSES to Anglesea and Alverstoke, daily.

STEAM BOATS to Ryde, Cowes, and Southampton.

MARKET DAY.—Thursday.

FAIRS.—May 4th and October 10th.

MAILS.—Two arrivals and three departures, daily. between London and Gosport.

MONEY ORDER OFFICE at Gosport.

BANKERS.—South Hampshire Banking Company.

GOSPORT, in the reign of Henry VIII., was merely a miserable village, inhabited by poor fishermen, and its present importance may justly be ascribed to its convenient situation on the western side of Portsmouth harbour, and its contiguity to the Royal Naval Arsenal. The stores, fortifications, and long range of forts, all formed about the commencement of the present century, give a very forcible idea of the value attached to its commanding position; but the streets, narrow and dirty, have anything but a prepossessing appearance to a stranger. The ferry across the harbour, which is here nearly a mile broad, is contrived by means of the steam floating bridge, sufficiently capacious to convey vehicles as well as foot passengers across to Portsmouth, in a journey that rarely occupies more than eight minutes. The toll is one penny for each time of passing. About one mile north of Gosport, near Forton Lake, is the new Military Hospital, and at the extremity of that point of land which forms the western extremity of Portsmouth Harbour is Haslar Hospital, founded at the suggestion of Earl Sandwich, and completed in 1762. It is capable of affording accommodation to about 2,000 invalids. The average expenses of this establishment, intended exclusively for the reception of sick and wounded seamen, is about £5,000 per annum. The portico of the centre part of the building is surmounted by the royal arms, flanked by two figures personifying Commerce and Navigation. A new suburb, called *Bingham Town*, contains some genteel modern residences; and *Anglesea*, a little village on the coast, about two miles from Gosport, near Stokes's Bay, affords a miniature watering-place for those among the residents who are not disposed to go further from home.

PORCHESTER.

Telegraph station at Fareham.

MONEY ORDER OFFICE at Fareham.

This place has an ancient castle, which serves for prisoners of war and ordnance stores.

COSHAM station.

Portsmouth, described page 62.

South Western Main Line continued.

Bishopstoke to Southampton.

The line traverses a country skirted in each direction by thick woody undulations. On approaching the town, however, the scenery becomes somewhat less interesting.

SOUTHAMPTON.

POPULATION, 36,510.

A telegraph station.

HOTELS.—Radley's; The Dolphin.

OMNIBUSES to Shirley, Millbrook, Totton, and Bitterne.

STEAMERS to and from the Isle of Wight.

MARKET DAYS.—Tuesday, Thursday, Friday, and Saturday.

FAIRS.—May 6th, Trinity Fair in Trinity week.

BANKERS.—National Provincial Bank of England. Atherley and Fall; Hampshire Banking Co.; Maddison and Pearce.

The station, which is close to the quay, and has a commanding position on the banks of the Southampton Water, is admirably adapted for the convenience of passengers. On his way to the High-street, the traveller will obtain a favourable view of the picturesque bay. Bounded on one side by the sheltering glades of The New Forest, and opening on the other to the Channel and the Isle of Wight, a series of beautiful views meet the eye, which cannot fail to charm by their exquisite contrast and variety. On leaving the terminus by the down line gate, we pass the platform, the old castle, lately the goal, and a little further is the new Corn Market, on the site of the old Custom House, and turning to the right we enter one of the finest streets that ever ornamented a provincial town—this being High-street —a prominent object in which is the Old Bar Gate, which formed the principal entrance into the town.

Southampton is the chief mail-packet station in the kingdom, and a parliamentary borough in Hampshire (two members), seventy-nine miles from London by the South Western Railway, on a point at the head of a fine inlet called Southampton Water, into which the Test and Itchen run.

Southampton was the scene of Canute's reproof of his flatterers, when he bid them place his chair on the edge of the water and commanded the waves to retire—a scene often described by the historian and painter. Another hero of romance was Sir Bevis of Hamptune (as the town was formerly called—and the county Hamptune-shire), who figures in company with the Giant Ascupart, it is said, on the ancient *Bar Gate*, between two towers, stretching across High-street, and supporting the Town Hall, fifty-two feet long. In the suburbs is an earthwork called Bevis Mount. There are also, near the sea, remains of part of the town walls, with two gates and two or three towers, one of which was a debtors' prison. *Domus Dei Hospital* was founded in the reign of Henry III., but has been modernized. A chapel occupies the site of the old castle.

St. Michael's Church, marked by a lofty spire, is the oldest in Southampton. That of *Holyrood* is also ancient; within is a half-pious half-poetical epitaph, by Thomson, on Miss Stanley, usually given in his works. *All Saints* is a careful Grecian building, by Revely the architect; its roof is admired. At the Grammar School, the excellent Dr. Watts, a native of this town (born 1674), was educated. His father kept a boarding-school here. Pococke, the eastern traveller, and C. Dibdin, the song-writer, were born here. The *Baths* are three quarters of a mile from the platform, on the other side of the town, where they show a gun named after Henry VIII. Andrews' *Coach Factory*, in the High-street, has a large and important business. Mr. Andrews, five times mayor of Southampton, received Kossuth on his landing here in 1851.

Among the other public buildings and institutions of Southampton we may mention the *Custom House*, a plain neat building, situate on the Quay, near the Royal Pier; the *Free Grammar School*, in Bugle Street, founded by Edward VI.; a commodious Literary and Scientific Institution, and numerous charitable foundations, all admirably conducted. Concerts and Balls are held in the *Royal Victoria Assembly Rooms*, situated in Portland Terrace, close to the High Street, and the *Long Rooms*, built in 1761, by the baths. The *Theatre*, a very neat and commodious structure, is in French Street, and stands upon the site of the ancient Hospital of St John.

Southampton has a considerable foreign and coasting trade in wine, fruit, timber, &c. When the mud banks are covered at high tide, its inlet is a fine sheet of water seven miles long, and one to two broad, and exactly the spot for a sail, with groves along the shores, especially the west, in which the nightingales are heard all night long. It is eleven or twelve miles to Cowes, opposite which is *Osborne House*, the seat of Queen Victoria.

A pleasant promenade is the Royal Victoria Pier, built in 1832. It is an elegant wooden structure, extending 246 feet into the water, having a carriage way in the centre twenty feet wide, and a footway, on each side of eight feet. A toll of twopence is requred from each passenger, and the bustle that prevails on the arrival and departure of steamers auses the scene to become one of very lively interest. The Southampton Water is here three miles wide, and in the centre about forty feet in depth, so as to admit ships of any burthen. Sheltered by lofty woods, and free from all rocky obstructions, this beautiful bay presents a very convenient harbour. Bathing machines, swimming baths, and other means of salutary ablution, adapted both to the invalid and the robust, are provided for those who choose to avail themselves of the accommodation afforded. There is a regatta in July, and some well regulated races, which take place on a beautiful spot of ground on Southampton Common.

Since Southampton, owing to the advantageous effects of the railway, has become one of our leading commercial ports, some new docks have been formed, on a scale of great magnitude, and ample accommodation afforded for housing and bonding goods, as well as for the reception of shipping and the convenience of passengers passing in and out of the port. Situated at the confluence of the river Itchen with the Southampton Water, the dock basin presents a surface of sixteen acres of water, eighteen feet deep from low water mark, enclosed by massive walls of masonry, and with a noble entrance 150 feet between the pier heads, without lock or gate. The *Post Office* is in Hanover Buildings. Letters are delivered three times daily; at 7 a. m., 3 p. m., and 6 30 p. m. There is thus constant epistolary communication.

The direct road to Portsmouth leads across the river Itchen, where a floating bridge conveys the passenger over to the opposite shore for a toll of one penny, and in a passage occupying about four minutes in duration. It is a large flat-bottomed vessel, plied by steam, between two vast chains stretched parallel from one bank to the other. Near the ferry is the Cross House, a building traditionally said to be about three centuries old, and to have been erected at the expense of a lady who, waiting shelterless for a boat to take her across the ferry, caught a fatal cold, which led to her bequeathing a sum of money for the erection, and a legacy for keeping it in repair. On the right hand of the road is a finger-post to Netley Abbey, of which place, as one of the great attractions to Southampton visitors, we now propose giving a few details.

Netley Abbey lies three miles along the eastern shore, over the floating-bridge at Itchen Ferry; near to it is a military college in course of erection. It was founded 1240, by Roger de Clare. Remains of the church, chapter-house, refectory, &c., exist, all picturesquely wound with ivy or overshadowed with ash and other trees. Sir Horace Walpole gives the following graphic description:—"The ruins are vast, and contain fragments of beautiful fretted roofs, pendant in the air, with all variety of Gothic patterns of windows, topped round and round with ivy. Many trees have sprouted up among the walls, and only want to be increased by cypresses. A hill rises above the abbey, enriched with wood. The fort, in which we would build a tower for habitation, remains, with two small platforms. This little castle is buried from the abbey in wood, in the very centre, on the edge of a hill. On each side breaks in a view of the Southampton sea, deep blue, glistening with silver and vessels; on one side terminated by Southampton, on the other by

Calshot Castle; and the Isle of Wight rises above the opposite hills. In short, they are not the ruins of Netley, but of Paradise. Oh, the purpled abbots! What a spot they had chosen to slumber in! The scene is so beautifully tranquil, yet so lively, that they seem only to have retired into the world."

Those disposed to enjoy a more extensive pedestrian excursion may, after leaving the Abbey, return to Southampton by a circuit through the country, by Hound and Hamble, which will reveal for them some very pretty features of pure pastoral scenery.

There are other seats and pretty spots in the neighbourhood, such as *Bittern Grove*, the site of *Clausentum*, a Roman station, and belonging to D. Urquhart, Esq., the political writer; Bannister Grove, Postswood (near the remains of *St. Dennis's Priory*, Townhill Park, &c, ; and *Stoneham Park*, J. Fleming, Esq., near the church in which Lord Hawke is buried. Across the Hamble's mouth is Hook, a pretty place near some low cliffs. Up the Test, which is lined with water meadows, are Upton, *Broadlands*, the seat of Viscount Palmerston, and Romsey, with its old abbey church, lately restored. On or near the western side of Southampton Water, are *Marchwood*, *Cadlands*, Lady M. Drummond; *Eaglehurst*, near *Calshot Castle*, which stands on a long bank of pebbles, and was built by Henry VIII. *Lyndhurst*, in the heart of the *New Forest*, the best trip of all. The scenery here is as richly woodland and as secluded as the most solitary could desire. Fonleage, Bolderwood, and other seats are at hand. At *Stony Cross* stood the Canterton Oak (till 1745), from which Tyrrel's arrow glanced and killed William Rufus, 2nd August, 1100. He was carried home by a charcoal-burner, Purkis, whose direct descendants, all charcoal-burners, are still, or were lately, alive. The spot is marked by an inscription. Hampshire bacon is perfection here—reared on acorns.

A fine excursion may be taken from Southampton to the

CHANNEL ISLANDS,

A distance of 104 miles; and, as the communication is frequent, and the passage to Guernsey averages about eight hours only, we would here introduce a brief sketch of the leading features of these islands, before proceeding to the Isle of Wight. The fares run about 18s. and 12s.

GUERNSEY

Lies thirteen miles west of Jersey, seven west of Sark, and fifteen south-west of Alderney. The chains of rocks lying east and west between these islands and the coast of Normandy appear to be the remnants of an ancient connection with the mainland. It is of a triangular form, about nine miles long and six in its greatest breadth, its circumference, following the sinuosities of the coast, being about thirty-nine English miles. The southern shore of the island, and a small part of the eastern, is a bold and continuous cliff, rising from the sea perpendicularly to the height of 270 feet. The land slopes gradually to the north, till it subsides in a low flat, not much above the level of the sea; this is the most fertile part of the island. Half a dozen brooks, the greatest of which has not a course of more than three miles, descend into the bays. The island is wholly of granite formation, and the soil which lies between its clustered rocks is an accumulation of decomposed syenite.

Nearly in the centre of the east side of the island is a long curve or irregular bay, in which lies the town of St. Peter's Port. As St. Helier's, in Jersey, has its rock in the harbour with Elizabeth Castle, so St. Peter's Port has its rock with Castle Cornet. Both formerly were the residences of the respective governors of the islands. Like Mont Orgueil, Castle Cornet is a very ancient fortification, and many are the stories of its memorable sieges recounted in the local histories. The castle is at present in a tolerable state of repair, mounts some cannon, and is garrisoned by a regiment of soldiers; but though there are some good houses and strong works within, it is not, in the modern acceptation of the word, a formidable fortification. Nothing can be more charmingly picturesque than the town of St. Peter's, seen from the water. It is built on the slope of an eminence, with the houses overtopping each other; and on approaching after sunset, the various lights from the windows give it a brilliant appearance of illumination. Of late years the town has been considerably extended, and now may be said to include a circumference of about three miles. In the older part the streets are narrow, steep, and crooked, flanked by substantial but antiquated dusky mansions, but the environs abound in pretty villas, and as far transcend the expectation of the tourist as the town may seem to fall below it. The new town occupies such an elevated position that from the level of the market-place the side of the ravine is ascended by a flight of 145 steps, to the top of what is called Mount Gibel. About a quarter of a mile from this spot are the public walks, or "new ground." This plot of land, comprising about eight English acres, was purchased by the parish about 70 years ago, and is laid out partly in groves and partly as a grand military parade. One of the principal "lions" of the town is its Fish Market, one of the most striking edifices of the kind ever erected. It is 198 feet in length, 22 feet wide, and 28 feet high, the whole being entirely covered over and well lighted by seven octagonal sky-lights, beneath which there are Venetian blinds for the purposes of ventilation. The double row of slabs, that extend the whole length of the building, are chiefly of variegated marble, and are supplied with abundance of fresh water. The total cost of Fountain-street and the Fish Market amounted to nearly £58,000. Turbot, cod, and mullet are in abundance, and of excellent quality, as well as amazing cheapness. The Butchers' Market-place, adjoining, was erected in 1822, and under the Assembly Rooms is the Vegetable Market, both commodious and suitable to the purpose. The prices are slightly lower than in London. The poultry consumed in Guernsey is chiefly French, very little country produce being brought to market. A glance at the average prices will not be uninteresting:—Turkeys sell at from 3s. to 4s.; fowls, 2s. 6d. per couple; geese, 2s. 6d. each; Guernsey eggs, 8d. to 1s. per dozen, and French eggs, from 5d. to 6d. There is a neat theatre in New-street, and some assembly rooms, built by subscription, in the spacious ball-room of which the public meetings are generally held. At the top of Smith-street stands Government House, a neat building, the residence of the Lieutenant Governor. From the roads and harbour, the church of St. James, the new college, and Castle Cary, which stand in the highest part of the town, form very striking and commanding objects. Castle Cary was erected in 1829, at a cost of £4,000, and is two stories in height, exclusive of the basement and centre tower or turret, but from the little ground attached to it the whimsical appellation of Castle Lackland has been appropriately bestowed.

Doyle's Column, erected in honour of Sir John Doyle, stands on the heights between the bays of Fermain and Moulin-street. It is about 150 feet nigh from the base to the top, and 250 feet above the level of the sea. A winding staircase inside affords access to the gallery, which is surrounded by an iron balustrade, and commands a varied and extensive view.

St. Peter's church is of a more elaborate architecture than any in the island; it consists of a nave, two aisles, and a chancel, with a tower in the centre, surmounted by a low spire. The porch on the northern side is very handsome; granite pillars support the arched roof, and on the walls are some exquisitely beautiful marble monuments. The garrison service and the evening service are performed in the English language. There are also numerous other places of religious worship, appropriate to the tenets of every other denomination. Elizabeth College—a fine building, standing on an elevation behind the town, with a spacious area around it beautifully laid out—was founded and endowed by Queen Elizabeth, in the year 1563, who assigned eighty quarters of wheat rent for its support. For nearly three centuries this institution existed in little more than its name, but means were successfully adopted, in 1824, to place this admirable institution on the footing of a college. The course ncludes Hebrew, Greek, Latin, divinity, geography, history, mathematics, arithmethic, and French and English literature, for £12 per annum, to which, for a small additional sum, may be added the Spanish, Italian, and German languages, music, drawing, fencing, and drilling. Another excellent institution in the town is the hospital or workhouse, which is admirably managed, and has been, since its erection in 1743, for the destitute a refuge, and for the young a seminary for instruction.

The harbour is formed artificially by a long pier, and there is a good roadstead near the village of St. Martin, where a great number of vessels take shelter during gales. In his excursions through the environs, the visitor will be struck with the superior neatness of the cottages of Guernsey, as compared with Jersey, and remark with interest the universal passion that prevails for flowers. On the front of most of the cottages may be seen, trailed up, splendid geraniums, and amongst the other flowers cultivated, we must not forget the far-famed Guernsey lily, the pride of the island, and the favourite of every gardener and cottager who has a bit of garden ground. The Guernsey lily is a native of Japan, and was said to have been originally introduced into the island by accident. A vessel having some roots on board was wrecked off the coast here, and these being washed on shore, germinated, grew upon the beach, and were soon after universally cultivated and admired.

Of the salubrity of the Guernsey climate there can be no doubt, as well from the restorative effect produced upon invalid visitors as from the general health and longevity enjoyed by its inhabitants. It is considerably warmer than the southern coast of Devonshire in all seasons, without, however, being more humid, a character which it has rather undeservedly acquired. The heat of summer is tempered by a gentle sea-breeze, and, like all other maritime situations, the cold of winter is mitigated by the caloric imparted to the atmosphere from the surrounding ocean. Frosts are neither severe nor durable; indeed, whole winters often pass away without a single fall of snow. The luxuriance of the various exotics, which flourish at this season unguarded, afford unequivocal evidence of the mildness of the climate. The white double rose camelia blooms abundantly in the month of November, and orange-trees endure the winter with only a slight covering of matting occasionally thrown around them.

The island is easily examined. The northern extremity is narrow, bare, and ugly, a large portion of it having only been reclaimed from the sea a few years ago. The most attractive natural scenery is to be found on the southern and south-western sides; and though it is neither so productive nor so luxuriantly wooded as Jersey, the island is far from being destitute of beautiful localities. Fermain Bay, Petit Bo, and Moulin-Huet, are all three worth a visit, but will certainly not compare with the bays in Jersey. Some interesting Druidical monuments were discovered in the year 1812, having been till that time covered by heaps of sand. Some antique vessels and remains of human bones were found within, and there is also an obelisk of Celtic origin, but without inscription. The best way to see the island to advantage is to make a pedestrian journey round it, doubling the headlands, and skirting the cliffs in every direction.

The bulk of the people of Guernsey may be divided into two classes—the middle and the labouring, or rather the tradespeople in the town, and the country people, who are very hard-working and abstemious. The jury is unknown in Guernsey: all judicial power is veste din the bailiffs and the jurats, but there is a right of appeal from the Royal Court to the Privy Council. The rate of living is very reasonable, and the hotels are, with the boarding-houses—which are generally preferred by visitors who stop more than a few days—exceedingly liberal in their entertainment and reasonable in their charges.

Not one of the least advantages of the Channel Islands, and of Guernsey in particular, as a place of residence, is the prevailing custom, which exempts from local taxation strangers not possessed of real property in the island, and not carrying on any trade or profession. With the exception of a small duty on spirits, there is an utter absence of all imposts on imported goods, and the visitor is neither plagued with passports nor delayed by the annoyances of a Custom-house scrutiny. The population of the island is about 30,000, and the annual mortality, as appears from the latest registration in 1847, was only one in about eighty-five. In 1846, the effective strength of the militia was estimated to be about 2,600 men, from sixteen to forty-five years of age, and these are divided into four regiments and an artillery battalion.

JERSEY,

Which many prefer to the island already described, is in form an irregular parallelogram, about ten miles long, and five broad. Its greatest length from south-east to north-west is about twelve miles, whilst it embraces a circumference, inclusive of its many curves and winding sinuosities, of about fifty miles, and a superficies of some 50,000 acres. Sloping from north to south, in contradistinction to Guernsey, the whole of the northern coast, with the eastern and western projections, will be found composed of rugged and precipitous rocks, while the southern shore, though fringed with crags and undulating cliffs, lies low, and has a considerable portion of that fine sandy beach so inviting to those who come chiefly to bathe and promenade by the sea shore. The town of St. Helier's, where the steam-boat passengers from Southampton disembark, lies on the eastern side of the beautiful bay of St. Aubin's; and if the visitor be fortunate enough to arrive at high water, the first appearance of the island, with its noble bay, sloping shores, and thickly wooded heights, profusely studded with villas and cottages, will be found happily to unite the attributes of the beautiful and the picturesque. The town itself is very Swiss-like in its aspect, and backed by its lofty stronghold, Fort Regent, which is seen overtopping the houses in all directions, it at once impresses the visitor with a conviction that the elements of novelty are everywhere around him. Though little more than what a thriving, bustling sea-port town may be expected to be, with its boarding-houses and hotels, a court-house and a market, an old parish church and a modern district one—built in what is called the Gothic style—two or three dissenting chapels, a theatre, and shops of quiet respectability—the hand of improvement has been lately much more manifest, and it has now assumed all the elegance and attractiveness of a fashionable watering-place. The extensive fortification, Fort Regent, which is generally the first object that strikes the eye of the traveller, was begun in 1806, and before its completion cost no less than £800,000. The magazines and barracks are in the bastions and under the ramparts, and are bomb-proof. The powder magazine is capable of containing 5,000 barrels, and the whole fortress, which has certainly been constructed on the best principles of defence, is abundantly supplied with excellent water from a well 234 feet deep, and 10 feet in diameter, bored through the solid rock. This has completely thrown into the shade the more ancient and picturesque fort called Elizabeth Castle, built on a huge sea-girt rock, passed in approaching the town from England; but an excursion to it—which can only be made on foot, by a pebble causeway, at low water—should be certainly undertaken, for the sake of the charming views it affords. Having inspected the town and its environs, paid a visit to Elizabeth Castle, and the rock adjoining, where, according to the legend, the hermit St. Helier lived, who bestowed his name on the town, it is not a bad plan to obtain a distinct bird's-eye view of the island previous to examining it on a series of excursions, *La Hogue Bie*, or Prince's Tower, a singular structure, erected on a high artificial mound about three miles from St. Helier's, affords the opportunity of enjoying this to advantage. From the summit the eye embraces the whole island. Climbing the heights at the back of the town and passing St. Saviour's Church, from the churchyard of which there is an excellent view over the town, the adjoining country, and St. Aubin's Bay, we arrive at this famous tower, which has of course a very romantic, but not at all authentic, legend to account for its origin. From this eminence, to quote one of Mr. Inglis's most graphic descriptions of the spot, "Jersey appears like an extensive pleasure-ground—one immense park, thickly studded with trees, beautifully undulating, and dotted with cottages, Fertility is on every side seen meeting the sea; the fine curves of several of the bays may be distinctly traced, with their martello towers and other more imposing defences; several of the larger valleys may be distinguished by the shadow which is thrown upon one side, while all around the horizon is bounded by the blue sea, excepting towards the east, where the French coast is seen, stretching in a wide curve towards the north and south, and which, in one direction, approaches so near to Jersey, that the white sea-beach is distinctly seen, and in clear weather even the towns that lie near to the coast." This view instantly makes you anxious to range over the island, to penetrate into the valleys and ravines, to wander through the orchards, fields, pastures, and gardens, and to descend to the bays and creeks, which one naturally and justly pictures full of beauty and repose. The new roads, that intersect the island in many directions, are excellent and commodious, but the old roads, though dreadfully perplexing and intricate, should be assuredly explored by those who desire to arrive at a fair estimate of the scenic attractions of the island. One object in the construction of the old roads in former days was to puzzle pirates or bewilder an enemy, and thus effectually retard and obstruct their attempts to subdue the islanders. During the heat of summer it is delightfully refreshing to turn aside into one of those bye-paths, that scarcely admit even a straggling ray of the noon-tide sun; but later in autumn, the decomposition of decaying vegetable matter going on in their shady depths render it advisable to prefer the new.

Those whose stay in the island is limited will, of course, be glad to make the most of its duration, and to that end we shall suggest how these excursions may be briefly made. The first day should be spent about St. Helier and its environs, with a visit to La Hogue Bie, and then passing on eastward to Mont Orgueil Castle, with its magnificent prospects, and the little village adjoining of Gorey, the seat of the Jersey oyster fishery. The village is built partly close to the sea and harbour, and partly on the height which rises towards the entrance to the castle. Upwards of 250 boats are engaged in the oyster fishery here, which it is computed returns about £29,000 to the island from its annual produce. Besides being itself striking and picturesque, Mont Orgueil has some most interesting recollections in connection with it. It stands upon the summit of a rocky headland jutting out into the sea, and though its origin and architect are alike unknown, it is recognised as having been a fortress of some importance in the reign of King John. In a few places the walls are entire, but it can hardly be regarded as other than an imposing ruin, from the summit of which a view is gained sufficiently charming to repay for the toilsome ascent. Here, for a short time, lived Charles II. in the early days of his wanderings, and here also was imprisoned for three years William Prynne, who, the victim himself of bigoted prejudices, ought to have more zealously curbed his own. He was liberated in November, 1640, not before he had turned his imprisonment to some account by penning several moral disquisitions on the castle and his condition, in one of which we find the following quaint appeal in the preface:—"If thou reap any information, consolation, reformation, or edification by any of these publications, let the author enjoy thy prayers and best respect, and his stationer thy custom." The garrison at Mont Orgueil now consists only of a serjeant and two privates, whose duty is simply confined to hoisting a flag on holidays. From the summit, the Cathedral of Constance, in Normandy, can on clear days be distinguished.

On the second day the tourist can explore, in the opposite direction, westward, and cross from St. Helier's to St. Aubin, either by a boat across the bay, or by taking a more circuitous land route over the fine firm sand at low water. Once the chief town in Jersey, and now even in its decadence eminently adapted for those who desire a quiet retreat, St. Aubin is beautifully situated. There is one steep straggling street, which drops abruptly down from an eminence towards the sea, but it is remarkably clean, and, though irregularly built, contains many excellent houses. The bay has also the benefit of a good pier, and the high cliffs around afford a shelter from the breezes, which are very prevalent in Jersey. "A perfectly calm day," says a resident, peculiarly qualified to give his opinion on the subject, "is very rare, even in summer, and generally speaking even the finest weather may be called blowy weather." Between St. Aubin's and St. Brelade's many interesting points of view will be disclosed, and the bay of St. Brelade's is considered by Inglis to be the most attractive of all the island bays. He says—"Boulay Bay is grander; St. Aubin's nobler; Rozel and Grève-de-Lecq more secluded; but in none of them do we find, so much as in St. Brelade's, the union of the barren, the wild, and the picturesque; and in none of them do the works of men harmonise so well with the natural scenery that surrounds them." On the western side of the bay stands the old parish church quite at the water's edge, and only elevated a little above it, for the sea at high tide sweeps over the crumbling monuments in the churchyard. The church itself is exceedingly small, and has neither spire nor tower, but over the nave it is roofed like a house. There is certainly a round turret, which rises from the ground, but it is built in a nook, and ascends only to a small belfry. In the churchyard stands one of the old chapels of the island, built long before the churches, and this is the only one in tolerable preservation. It was called the Fisherman's Chapel. If the day be now not too far spent, the excursion may be extended to the north western extremity of the island, and the tourist can thus visit Plement Point and Cape Grosnez. The caves adjoining are marine excavations in the lower part of a rocky hill, and are celebrated, like those in the Grève-de-Lecq, as great attractions to strangers. The northern coast of Jersey may well have one or two days exclusively appropriated to it. There is from Grève-de-Lecq to Boulay Bay a distance of between six and seven miles, and along this circuit objects of interest will be found rife in every direction. The bold scenery in Boulay Bay has been very much admired, and in fact the stupendous barriers of the northern coast contrast finely with the interior of the island, so luxuriantly wooded and so proverbially fertile. A favourite resort of pic-nic parties, and one of the sweetest of the island bays, is Rozel, situated a short distance from Boulay Bay, at the north-east corner of the island. Hemmed in by high cliffs and banks, with a few fishermen's huts scattered along the beach, and deep wooded glens branching into the interior, it is just the place where a cold veal pie would taste most deliciously, or a sentimental ballad produce the most impressive effect.

The climate of Jersey is exceedingly mild, in consequence of the southern situation and aspect of the island, and the temperature being equalised by the vicinity of the sea. Frost never continues any length of time. Snow falls but seldom, and melts immediately, and even with Guernsey, there is a sensible difference of climate. Melons there are raised in hot-beds, but they grow profusely in the common garden-ground of Jersey. The inhabitants are social in disposition, and few places equally limited in extent enjoy a greater variety of amusement. In autumn and winter there is a continual round of assemblies, and in spring and summer the military reviews impart a lively aspect to the town. English habits are thoroughly engrafted on the island, the English language has become familiar to all classes, and throughout the whole of Jersey the barbarous Norman French may be pronounced on the decline.

ALDERNEY, SARK, &c.

Those who have an opportunity afforded them to visit the little islands of Alderney and Sark will not regret availing themselves of the offer, should there be fair weather attendant on the excursion. Sark—also called Serk or Sercq—is six miles to the east of Guernsey, and is rather more than three miles in length. Its average breadth is not quite a mile, and in one part it is actually not many yards wide, but the island is still a thriving and fertile spot, and maintains in independent comfort a population of nearly 600 healthy and hardy islanders. The cliffs by which it is bounded are from 100 to 200 feet high. The Coupée Rock, its chief wonder, is a narrow neck of land, about five feet broad, with a precipitous descent on each side of about 350 feet down to the sea. It is a favourite spot with "pic-nics," but in windy weather is not to be ventured upon without caution. This remarkable island is a little kingdom in itself, being governed by a parliament of forty resident copyhold tenants, which meets three times a-year, under the command of the Lord of Sark. This assembly appoints the police force of the island, which consists of two individuals, and that this formidable couple are found sufficient may be presumed, from the fact, that though there is a gaol erected, no individual has ever been lodged in it since it was built. Midway between Sark and Guernsey are Herm and Jethou, two insignificant islets, the one containing a population of 200 and the other of 20. About twenty miles from Guernsey, north-east by north, and forty from Jersey, is the little island of Alderney, so famous for its celebrated cows. The island is about four miles long, a mile and a-half broad, and eight miles in circumference. The south-east coast is composed of some striking lofty cliffs, ranging from 150 to 200 feet in height. The inhabitants, chiefly fishermen, consist of about 1,000 individuals Six miles to the west of Alderney are "The Caskets," a dangerous cluster of rocks, included in the compass of a mile. They have three lighthouses, so placed as to form a triangle, and be a protection to shipping, It was on these rocks that Prince William, only son of Henry I., perished by shipwreck, in the year 1119; and where, in 1744, the *Victory* was lost, with 1,100 men. From this it will be seen, that even when the attractions of Guernsey and Jersey are on the wane, there are some resources left in these excursions, which will give the tourist, who has no misgivings of the sea and the stalwart Channel boatmen, the opportunity of enjoying an additional round of novelties.

ISLE OF WIGHT.

THIS beautiful island is divided into two parts by the river Medina, or Cowes, which rises in the south, and enters the sea at the town of Cowes, opposite the mouth of Southampton Bay. The south-east coast is edged with very steep cliffs of chalk and freestone, hollowed into caverns in various parts, and vast fragments of rock are scattered along the shore. The south-west side is fenced with lofty ridges of rock, and tbe western extremity of them is called the Needles. Among the products are a pure white pipe clay, and a fine white crystalline sand; of the latter, great quantities are exported for the use of the glass works in various parts.

The island is accessible by way of Portsmouth, Southampton, or Lymington, from which places there are steamers to Ryde, Cowes, and Yarmouth respectively; the first two are more convenient for Ventnor and the back of the Island; the last for Freshwater and the Needles. Supposing Ryde to be the starting point, two routes will take in almost everything in the island, which a hasty visitor would care to see. Those who desire to make a real acquaintance with all its attractions may spend many pleasant weeks in it, finding new walks every day.

FIRST ROUTE.

	Miles.		Miles.
Ryde to Brading	4	Ventnor to St. Lawrence	2
Sandown ...	2	Niton........	3
Shanklin ...	3	Blackgang..	2
Succombe ...	2	Gatcombe...	4
Bonchurch...	1	Ryde........	8
Ventnor......	2		

N.B.—Black Gang to Freshwater 14½

SECOND ROUTE.

Ryde to Wooton	3	Calbourne to Freshwater......	
Newport......	4	Alum Bay	2
Carisbrooke..	1	Needles ...	0½
Calbourne ...			

The best part of the first or eastern route may be done by means of the Ryde and Cowes coaches in one day, for 9s. or 10s.; or fly to hold four may be had for a guinea a day. No coach travels the western route. which is much to be lamented, as there is no question that a drive over the Downs on this side of the Island (supposing a good road to be made), would be one of the most splendid imaginable.

FIRST ROUTE.

Ryde to Newchurch.

RYDE.

POPULATION, 7,147.

Distance from station at Portsmouth, 8 miles.

A telegraph station.

HOTELS.—Barnes' Royal Pier; Sivier's Hotel.

COACHES to the Eastern Route, daily.

STEAMERS to and from Cowes, Portsmouth, and Southampton several times daily, from 7 a.m. to 6 p.m.

EXCURSION STEAMERS round the Island in the summer, on Mondays and Thursdays, at 12 noon, fare 3s.

MARKET DAYS.—Tuesday and Friday.

FAIR.—July 5th. REGATTA in August.

MONEY ORDER OFFICE at Ryde.

BANKERS.—National Provincial Bank of England. Branch Hampshire Banking Co.

RYDE is a beautiful bathing place, sloping to the sea, 25 minutes (by steam) from Portsmouth, across Spithead. Long timber pier of 2,000 ft. (or two-fifths of a mile), commanding a fine prospect and a healthy blow; for which the charge is 2d. per head, and 1d. per package! New Victoria Yacht Club House, built 1847. Chantrey's bust of Mr. Sanderson, in the Market Place. Holy Trinity Church, modern Gothic, with a spire 146 ft. high. Baths, hotels, lodgings (with gardens), are numerous, as are the walks and points of view around.

DISTANCES OF PLACES FROM RYDE.

	Miles.		Miles.
Apley	0¾	Priory, The	0¾
Barnsley	1½	Quarr Abbey	2
Binstead	0¾	Ryde House	1½
Copping Bridge	5½	Ryde Park	1½
Fairy Hill	1¼	St. Clare	1½
Fearlee	5	St. John's	1
Fishburn Rock	2¾	*Stokes Bay	4
Haven Street	2½	Troublefield	0¾
Needles, The	18	West Cowes	8
Nettleston Point	2	West Mount	1½
Pier, The	0¼	Whippingham	3½
Place Street	0½	White Mark	2½
Portsmouth	8		

St. John's, the seat of Sir R. Simeon, Bart.

BRADING.

Distance from station at Portsmouth, 12 miles.
Telegraph station at Ryde.
HOTELS.—Bugle; Wheat Sheaf.
COACHES to and from Newport, daily.
MARKET DAY.—Saturday.
FAIRS.—May 1st and Sept. 21st.
MONEY ORDER OFFICE at Ryde.

BRADING, a decayed place, with an old Town Hall near the church, in which are the monuments of the Oglanders of Nunwell. In the churchyard is the grave of little Jane, the subject of one of Legh Richmond's well known stories. He was Vicar of Brading, and her cottage is pointed out under Brading Down. The harbour is like a shallow lagoon between Bembridge Point and St. Helen's old chapel. Yaverland and its curious little church, Culver Cliff, 400 ft. high, with the Yarborough pillar on the top, and Whitecliff Bay below, are to the left.

SANDOWN.

Distance from station at Portsmouth, 14 miles.
Telegraph station at Ventnor.
HOTELS.—Star and Garter (Hale's).
COACHES to and from Ryde and Newport, daily.
MONEY ORDER OFFICE at Shanklin.

SANDOWN, a bathing place, with a fine sweep of sandy beach, and an old fort.

DISTANCES OF PLACES FROM SANDOWN.

	Miles.		Miles.
Adgeton	1	Ryde	6
Brading	2	†Sandown Cottage	1
Culver Cliff	2	Sandown Lake	1
Knighton	3		

* From here the Floating Bridge is proposed being worked, so as to connect Ryde with the Terminus about to be built at this place.

† Was the seat of Wilkes. The pillar there was set up by him to his friend Churchill.

SHANKLIN.

Distance from station at Portsmouth, 16 miles.

Telegraph station at Ventnor.

HOTELS.—Daish's and Williams'.

COACHES to and from Ryde and Newport, daily.

MONEY ORDER OFFICE.

This beautiful retreat is hid away among trees and corn-fields in summer, and is close to a chine or gash in the cliff, filled in with shrubs and trees, with a good beach for bathing and walking on below. Cook's Castle, a ruined tower, 2 miles to the right. The road winds over the bold headland of Dunnose, with Shankiin Down on one side, 780 ft. high, Luccombe Chine on the other. Notice the views of Sandown Bay and the country behind you. Upon descending, the first glimpse of Undercliff appears on the right, looking something like the entrance to Matlock, while the broad blue stretches away to the left.

DISTANCES OF PLACES FROM SHANKLIN.

	Miles.		Miles.
Allen	2	Horse Ledge	0½
Beacon (Shanklin)	1	Langard	1
Bonchurch	3	Luccombe Chine	1
Boniface Down	0¼	Shanklin Chine	0¼
Brenston	2	Steephill Cove	2
Chiverton	1½	Strattle	3½
Cook's Castle	2	Winham	1½
Dunnose	1¼	Wroncate	2
Great Kennedy	4		

BONCHURCH.

Distance from station at Portsmouth, 20 miles.

Telegraph station at Ventnor, 2 miles.

HOTEL.—Bonchurch.

COACHES to and from Ryde and Newport, daily.

MONEY ORDER OFFICE at Shanklin.

BONCHURCH, so called because the church is dedicated to St. Boniface. An exemplary young clergyman, the author of "Shadows of the Cross," and John Stirling, whose Life, written by Carlyle, has excited considerable interest, are buried in it. The road is overshadowed with trees, and passes a lake and the Pulpit Rock. There is a charming path from Shanklin to Bonchurch, through the Sandslip. Boniface Down, near Ventnor, rises steeply up 700 or 800 ft. above the sea.

DISTANCES OF PLACES FROM BONCHURCH.

	Miles.		Miles.
Appuldercombe	2	Pulpit Rock	1½
Beacon The	1¼	Rind	3½
Binnel Point	1	Sandford	2½
Boniface Downs	1½	Steephill	0¾
Dunnose	0¾	Steephill Cove	0½
Godshill	3	St. Lawrence	2
Lake, The	2½	Succombe	1
Mill Cove	0½	Ventnor	2
Nettlecomb	2	Wroncate	0¾
Puckester Cove	3½		

VIEWS IN THE ISLE OF WIGHT.

VENTNOR.

Distance from station at Portsmouth, 22 miles.

A telegraph station.

HOTELS.—Royal—first-class hotel and boarding establishment, of a superior description; Marine—first-class family and commercial house. Esplanade Hotel and Boarding House, situated on the beach near the sea, and close to the Baths.

COACHES to and from Ryde, Cowes, and Newport, daily.

MARKET DAY.—Saturday.

BANKERS.—National Provincial Bank of England.

VENTNOR, the capital of Undercliff, had no existence 40 years ago, but is now a respectable town, with a population of 2,569. This is owing to its delightful situation in front of the sea, and being protected by the cliffs behind. Trees have not grown so fast as houses, which being of stone have a white glare in the summer sunshine; but it is in winter that its peculiar advantages are felt by the invalid, who then enjoys a climate not to be had in any other part of England except Torquay. Lodgings are abundant and moderate. Myrtles, fuchsias, and other plants grow to a large size. The Downs behind, affording endless rambles, are covered with heath and thyme. Houses occupy every accessible spot up and down the cliffs, with the Channel and the shipping perpetually in view. There is a new church, with assembly rooms, baths, &c. A fine, pebbly beach below, and attractive walks of all kinds. In the season provisions are scarce, and therefore dear, a drawback felt at Shanklin and other places on this side of the Island. Four or five coaches by way of Brading or Newport run to and fro between this and Ryde daily. Occasionally a steamer touches for Cowes or Ryde; but this is rare, and the landing is by boat. Excellent lobsters, crabs, and prawns. Some curious caves have been formed in the cliffs by the sea along the beach.

About three miles inland is **Appuldercombe,** the seat of the Earl of Yarborough, a building of the last century, in a large park on the slope of a down, at the corner of which is the Worsley pillar. Sir R. Worsley here made a collection of marbles and paintings. Many of the family are buried in Godshill church, which is one of the best in the island, and about four miles further.

From Ventnor to Black Gang the road winds along through *Undercliff*, among rocks, gardens, fields, seats, farm-houses, &c., dispersed most picturesquely about in a rocky ledge or strand formed by successive landslips from the neighbouring cliff, which rises up like a wall on your right, 100 to 150 feet high, the road itself being nearly as much above the sea, to your left. It is worth while to *walk* along the edge of this cliff for the sake of the panorama to be obtained of the scene below. Do not take this path at Ventnor, as it may be reached by leaving the road near St. Lawrence's Well, and walking up the steps cut in the face of the cliff. A footpath also winds close to the sea out of sight of the road.

DISTANCES OF PLACES FROM VENTNOR.

	Miles.		Miles.
Blackgang	7	Steephill	0½
Luccombe Chine*	0½	St. Boniface Downs‡	0½
Mirables	3½	Undercliff	2
Sand Rock†	4	Ventnor Cove	0½
Shanklin	2	Wishing Well	0¾

ST. LAWRENCE.

Distance from station at Portsmouth, 24 miles.

Telegraph station at Ventnor.

HOTEL.—St. Lawrence.

COACHES to and from Ryde and Newport, daily.

MONEY ORDER OFFICE at Ventnor.

There is a spring of deliciously cool water on the road side, under an alcove. The church is a pretty little rustic building, with the grave-yard planted with flowers. Since it was lengthened it is 40 feet long, and will hold 40—a small number, but quite large enough for the population of the parish.

DISTANCES OF PLACES FROM ST. LAWRENCE.

	Miles.		Miles.
Appuldercombe	1¾	Sea View	0½
Binnel Point	0½	Spring The	0¼
Bonchurch	2	‖Vineyard	3
§Church The	0¼	Wolverton	2
Nettlecomb	2	Wroncate	2¾
Newport	11		

NITON.

Distance from station at Portsmouth, 27 miles.

Telegraph station at Ventnor, 6 miles.

HOTEL.—Royal Sand Rock.

COACHES to and from Ryde, Cowes, and Newport, daily.

MONEY ORDER OFFICE at Ventnor.

NITON has an old church, a little inland from the road, to the right. The seat of Sir J. W. Gordon, Bart, is passed before you come to this turning. The *Cripple Path*, a crooked way up the cliff. A milkwoman was once blown over this cliff, and, though she fell 60 or 70 feet, was picked up unhurt, having been buoyed up by her clothes. To the left are Puckester Cove, Sandrock, St. Catherine's Light, Pitland Landslip, only to be seen by following another path nearer the shore.

DISTANCES OF PLACES FROM NITON.

	Miles.		Miles.
Black Gang Chine	2	¶Puckester Cove	1
Chale	2	Sandrock Spring	1½
Cripple Path, The	0¼	St. Catharine's Down	1
Nettlecomb	1½	St. Catharine's Point	1½
Niton House	0½	St. Catharine's Tower	1¼
Old Castle, The	1	Whitwell	1
Pitland Land Slip	1½	Woolverton	1

* Visited by the Queen and Prince Albert. † Here is a capital Hotel. ‡ 600 feet high. § The smallest in Great Britain. ‖ Inigo Jones' Gate from Hampton Court. ¶ Where Charles the Second landed in a Storm in 1675.

CHALE.

Distance from station at Portsmouth, 29 miles.

Telegraph station at Ventnor, 7 miles.

HOTEL.—Chine.

COACHES to and from Ryde and Newport, daily.

MONEY ORDER OFFICE at Ventnor.

Black Gang Chine is a gap in the cliff, which hangs over the beach in Chale Bay. It is bare and somewhat dark-looking, with an iron spring trickling through it. The highest point is 600 or 700 feet, making it a tiresome job to ascend or descend the steps cut in the side on a summer's day. But it is worth while to go down to the beach to watch the great waves as they roll in, especially if it is at all windy. Here the poor "Clarendon" came ashore. Behind it is *St. Catherine's Down*, about 800 feet high, or 100 higher than Black Gang. There are the remains of a beacon on the top, which was used for the lighthouse till that was shifted to its present place; also a chapel or hermitage. Behind this stands a pillar, erected to commemorate the visit of a Russian Prince to this country. Though the highest point in the island, the view is by no means so good as many from the downs in the middle of it. In Chale Churchyard are the graves of several wrecked persons, especially of the crew of the "Clarendon," East Indiaman. Hence to Freshwater is a succession of little bays and chines, none of much interest; a pathway follows the edge of the cliff. The high road passes through Thorwell (in a gap of the downs), Brixton or Bryston, and Brotlestone, all pretty places, under the downs to the right hand, which command an excellent prospect.

From Chale back to Ryde across the Island is through a pleasant but much less striking country than in the first part of the route. The road passes over Arreton Down.

Godshill church, in which the Worsleys are buried, has a good pinnacled tower. *Appuldercombe*, their delightful seat, is to the right. It can be visited on Tuesdays and Fridays, from 11 to 4, by ticket only; to be had of T. Sewel, Esq., Newport. It contains a good collection of paintings, sculptures, and drawings. Before you get to Newchurch, a turning to the left, you pass the cottage of the Dairyman's Daughter, Arreton church, in which she is buried, and the Hare and Hounds, a neat tidy little country inn, close to which is a point from which the view corresponds to one described by Legh Richmond in his interesting work.

DISTANCES OF PLACES FROM CHALE.

	Miles.		Miles.
Chale Bay*	0¾	Pitland Land Slip‡	1
Churchyard†	0¼	St. Catharine's Pillar§	0¾

NEWCHURCH.

Distance from station at Portsmouth, 15 miles.

Telegraph station at Newport, 5 miles.

COACHES to and from Newport and Ryde, daily.

MONEY ORDER OFFICE at Newport.

NEWCHURCH, with its white spire, stands at the end of a short village, near the stream which runs into Brading harbour. The parish is the largest in the island, with a population of 11,539, stretching across it so as to take in both Ryde and Ventnor. Fine views on both sides of the Down, which is 6 miles from Ryde.

DISTANCES OF PLACES FROM NEWCHURCH.

	Miles.		Miles.
Adgeton	2	Rookley	3½
Arreton	1½	Ryde	6
Arreton Street	1	Sandown and Sandford	3
Brading	3	Shitle Bridge	3¼
Chiverton	1½	Spicer's Hall	1
Gatcombe House	4	Stone	1¼
Great Kennerley	2½	Strattle	2
Long Down	3	Winham	2
Queen's Bower	1¼		

SECOND ROUTE.

RYDE TO THE NEEDLES.

Coach to Newport, 1s. You leave on the right, Binstead and its old church, near the coast. Beyond it are some slight remains of *Quarr Abbey* at a farm house; and an old stone quarry. Further on, towards Cowes are Whippingham church, and *Osborne House*, the seat of her Majesty the Queen. It has been entirely rebuilt, and stands on a ridge commanding a view of Spithead, the Solent, the Hampshire Coast, &c. When the Queen is there, the royal standard floats over the great tower. The Medina soon appears in its whole length down to Cowes, especially from some points near

NEWPORT.

Distance from station at Portsmouth, 15 miles.

A telegraph station.

HOTEL.—Bugle; Star; Green Dragon.

COACHES to and from Cowes, Ryde, Yarmouth, and the places on the Eastern Route of the Island.

BOAT between Wootton Bridge and Portsmouth, daily.

MARKET DAY.—Saturday (Corn), and every other Saturday (Cattle).

FAIRS.—Whitsuntide and Michaelmas.

MONEY ORDER OFFICE.

BANKERS.—National Provincial Bank of England; Branch Hampshire Banking Co.

NEWPORT, the capital of the Island, a clean, well built country town, in a hollow, on the river Medina, which divides the Island nearly in halves. Cracknell biscuits are manufactured here; but Cowes is the real place where they were first made. Population 8,047.

*Where the Clarendon was lost. †Graves of the crew of the Clarendon. ‡Took place in 1799. §In honour of the visit of a Russian Prince to the Island.

It sends two members to parliament. Town Hall. built 1816, by Nash. Old church, in which Charles I.'s daughter Elizabeth is buried. Large House of Industry for the Island, on the Cowes road; not far from the Albany barracks, whither recruits are sent for exercise, and the Parkhurst Reformatory for boys.

DISTANCES OF PLACES FROM NEWPORT.

	Miles.		Miles.
Albany Barracks	0½	†Church, Old	0¼
Alvington	2	King's Forest	0½
Arreton	2½	Kite Hill	5
Barton Point	4	Marcliff	4½
Birchmore	2½	‡Node Hill	2
Blackland	2½	Norris Castle	0½
Brettleford	2½	Park Cross	4
Carisbrooke	1	Parkhurst Reformatory Institution	0½
*Carisbrooke Castle	1½	Thorness	4
Carisbrooke Church	1¼	West Cowes	5
Carisbrook Priory, Ruins of	1¼	Wootton and Bridge	3½

WEST COWES.

POPULATION, 4,785.

Distance from station at Southampton, 11 miles.

A telegraph station.

HOTEL.—Fountain.

COACHES to and from Ryde and Newport, daily.

VESSELS.—The rendezvous of ships of all nations, for orders.

STEAM VESSELS to Portsmouth, Ryde, and Southampton, six times a day; to Yarmouth, once daily.

REGATTA in August.

MONEY ORDER OFFICE.

BANKERS.—National Provincial Bank of England.

COWES, five miles from Newport. An immense quantity of shipping call off here annually, from all parts of the globe, for orders from their owners or consignees, as to the destination of their cargoes; and in the winter months fleets of merchantmen of all nations rendezvous here weatherbound. It lies at the mouth of the Medina and is a stirring port, noted for its shipbuilding (especially at White's yard), and yachting. There is deep water here; the Royal Yacht Club hold their *regatta* in August. Handsome Club-house, Old castle, built by Henry VIII., from which Cowes derives its name. Dr. Arnold was a native of Cowes. There is a ferry to East Cowes, across the Medina, beyond which *Norris Castle* and *Osborne House* are visible. Sailing boats 2s. per hour.

On the beach are bathing machines, and it is much visited by fashionable company.

* Built before the Conquest. † Tomb of Charles First's daughter, Princess Elizabeth. ‡ Monument to Tyerman the Missionary, and lines by Montgomery.

DISTANCES OF PLACES FROM COWES.

	Miles.		Miles.
Barton	2	Kingston	1¼
Baskets	1¾	Noder	1½
East Cowes	0¾	Northwood	1½
*East Cowes Castle	1½	†Northwood House	0½
Egypt	1	Osborne	1¼
Gurnet Farm	1	West Cowes House	0¼
King's Key	3	Yacht Club House	0½

CARISBROOKE.

Distance from station at Portsmouth, 16 miles.

A telegraph station at Newport, 1 mile.

HOTEL.—The Castle.

COACHES to and from Newport, Cowes, and Ryde, daily.

MONEY ORDER OFFICE at Newport.

CARISBROOKE, the former capital, where the Governor used to reside. Old Church, close to some slight traces of a priory, founded after the Conquest, by William Fitz-Osborne, a Norman Knight, who built the *Castle*. This stands on a hill beyond the village and, including the wards, occupies a site of two acres within the walls. The fine gateway is machicolated, *i. e.*, provided with slits for shooting arrows, &c., down on any one below. The keep commands a good view. There are some remains of the outer walls and towers; and they show (but this is doubtful) the window through which the unfortunate Charles I. tried to make his escape when imprisoned here 1648, in Colonel Hamond's charge. A modern-built chapel and the barracks are disused. There is a well 200 feet deep of pure cold water, which is raised by a patient ass. A candle is let down to show the depth to the visitors. The views from it are pleasing, but not remarkable Parkhurst Forest is seen, but scantily wooded. Roads turn off to Gatcombe Park, and to Shorwell, under the Downs; but the views are much inferior to those obtained from their summit, along which, however, there is no regular road.

At *Swainstone*, the seat of J. Simeon, Esq., a road turns off to *Newtown*, on a low creek of the Solent. It was a parliamentary borough till the reform bill disfranchised it; the town hall remains. The church was rebuilt 1837. All this coast is low and the least interesting of any in the Island.

DISTANCES OF PLACES FROM CARISBROOKE.

	Miles.		Miles.
Atherfield	6	Church, Old	0¼
Calbourne	4	Gatcombe	2
Castle, The	0½	Newport	1
Chillerton	3	Well, The	6½

CALBOURNE.

Distance from station at Portsmouth, 20 miles.

Telegraph station at Newport, 5 miles.

HOTEL.—Albion.

COACHES to and from Newport, Ryde, and Cowes, daily.

MONEY ORDER OFFICE at Newport.

* Earl of Shannon. † Now a School

CALBOURNE has an old church and is near to Westover Park. To the right, about two miles, is Shalfleet church, which contains a Norman porch, and the escutcheon of William de Montacute, to whom Wight was granted by Richard II.

The road skirts the north base of the Downs, with a prospect over the partly cultivated tract to the north, the Solent, and Hampshire. At length we reach *Freshwater Village*, at the head of Yarmouth Creek, Freshwater Gate being to the left. Dr. Hook the philosopher was born at the parsonage.

At the entrance of this creek is

YARMOUTH.

Distance from station at Southampton, 19 miles.
Telegraph station at Cowes, 12 miles.
HOTEL.—George.
CARRIERS to and from Cowes, Newport, and all parts of the Island, daily.
STEAMERS to Lymington and Cowes, daily. Fares, to Lymington, 1s. 6d. and 1s.; Day Tickets, 3s. To Cowes, 2s. 6d. and 1s. 6d.; Day Tickets, 4s. and 2s. 6d.
MARKET DAY.—Friday.
FAIR.—July 25th.
MONEY ORDER OFFICE.
BANKERS.—National Provincial Bank of England.

YARMOUTH, another decayed borough, originally founded by the Rivers family. There is a town hall, one of Henry VIII.'s forts, and a church, in which is a monument of Sir Robert Holmes, Captain of the Island, at the visit of Charles II. in 1671. He resided at what is now the King's Head Inn. A steamer to Lymington. Hurst Castle is opposite.

DISTANCES OF PLACES FROM YARMOUTH.

	Miles.		Miles.
Aston Down	2½	Freshwater Gate	3
Calbourne	4½	Hurst Castle	2½
*Church, The	0¼	Lingwood	2
Clanmore	1	Lymington	5
Compton	3	Newtown Harbour	4
Curlew	4½	Norton	0¾
East Hamstead	3	Scone Point	1
Forts, The	1	Tapnel	2½
Freshwater	2		

FRESHWATER.

Distance from station at Portsmouth, 24 miles.

Telegraph station at Newport, 9 miles.

HOTELS.—Lambert's Hotel; Royal Albion.

COACHES to and from Ryde, Cowes, and Newport, daily.

MONEY ORDER OFFICE at Yarmouth.

FRESHWATER GATE, where the baths and lodging houses are stationed, is half a mile from the village, on the south side of the Downs, in a gap of the cliffs, which rise up 500 and 600 feet above the sea, white and dazzling, producing a grand effect. They are streaked with parallel lines of flint. Lobsters, &c., are good. Between this and the Needles are several remarkable objects, most of which can be visited only in a boat (10s. or 20s. the trip), when there is little sea. Even with fine weather the long swell is apt to be disagreeable. In Freshwater Bay, fronting the baths are Deer Island; Neshanter cave, 120 feet deep, 35 wide; the Arch Rock, 600 feet out from the shore; Watcombe bay and its caves; Neptune's cave, 200 feet long; Beak cave, 90 feet; High Down Cliff, 217 feet high, swarming with puffins, razor-birds, &c.; Frenchman's Hole, 90 feet; Holmes's Parlour and Kitchen; Roe's Hall, 600 feet long, close to the *Wedge Rock*, so called because of a great block jammed in a gap, into which it has fallen; Old Pepper Rock; Main Bench Cliff, full of birds; Scratchell's Bay and Scratchell's Cave, 200 feet high, with an overhanging roof; Needles Cave, 300 feet long; the *Needles Rocks*, four or five blunt peaks, with deep water round them, at the west end of the Island. There was a sharp rock 120 feet high, but it fell down in 1776. On the cliffs above, 469 feet high, is the lighthouse, seen 27 miles. Round this point, (or 1½ mile across the downs, from Freshwater) is

ALUM BAY.

HOTELS.—Needles Hotel and boarding house.

STEAMERS to Lymington, thence per rail to Brockenhurst.

The cliffs on one side are white, and on the other are curiously variegated with strata of ochre, fuller's earth, grey and white sand, &c. Here large prawns are found. The cliffs gradually fall to Cary's Sconce, where a strong fort is being constructed. Copperas stones, lignite, or wood coal, alum, pipe clay, shells, and fossils are discovered in this quarter of the Island.

DISTANCES OF PLACES FROM FRESHWATER GATE.

	Miles.		Miles.
*Alum Bay	2¾	Neshanter Cave	3½
†Cary's Stone	2	‖Parsonage, The	2
‡Light House	2½	Scratchell's Cave	2
§Neptune's Cave	3¼		

THIRD ROUTE.

This route, seldom taken by visitors, but a most attractive one for walkers, is towards Head-on-Hill (where fine white sand is dug for the glass-makers), and along the *Downs*, through the middle of Wight. The distances from Culver Cliff are:—

	Miles.		Miles.
To Afton Down	19	To Hare & Hounds on Arreton Down	6¾
,, Ashey Mark	4	,, Motteston Down	16½
,, Brading Down	3	,, Needles Light	23½
,, Brixton Down	15	,, Newport	9
,, Carisbrook	10½	,, Shalcombe Down	18
,, Freshwater Gate	20½	,, Yarborough Pillar	1
,, Gallyberry Down	13		

Culver Cliff, 400 feet high. View over White Cliff Bay, Spithead, &c. Yarborough Pillar, on Bembridge Down, overlooks the harbour. It was built up in 1849, in honour of the late earl; and serves as a landmark.

* Sir Richard Holmes' Monument—Governor of the Island in 1671, when visited by Charles II.

Arched Rock (600 feet). † A Fort is being erected here. ‡ 715 feet above the level of the sea. § 200 feet. ‖ Birth place of Dr. Hook, the philosopher.

Brading Down. A noble view here, from the ring; Portsmouth, Spithead, Chichester Cathedral, Osborne, Sandown Bay, Shanklin Down, and one-third of the Island, all seen on a sunshiny day. Brading church, *Nunwell*, the seat of Sir H. Oglander, Bart., are immediately below.

Ashey Down. Fine views from the sea marks, but you must shift about to take them in. Newchurch, &c., visible.

Arreton Down. View of the cultivated tract to Undercliff and Shorwell. The road follows Long Lane into Newport, but a short cut may be found to Carisbrook or Gatcombe, shortening the distance to the Western Downs, by a mile or two. After Carisbrook you ascend to Bowcomb and Roughborough Downs, and thence to Galebery or Galleyberry Downs by a rough path, which now and then leads through a turnip field as it approaches the heath, and then brings you into a solitary hollow, smooth and green round its sides, and patched with furze bushes. You may walk for miles without meeting a soul, except a shepherd, or a farmer on horseback. At Galleyberry there is a splendid view of this half of the Island, with the ridge of Down before you, to the Needles, up and down like the back of a camel, To get refreshment, you must descend the slope, to Shorwell, Brixton, Calbourn, &c., at the bottom. Another fine view from *Brixton Down*. Brixton is a pretty place (though not more beautiful than most others in the Island), with a chine down to the shore.

Motteston Down 700 feet high, near the Druid stone. Sir John Cheke, King Edward's tutor, was born at this village. Shalcombe Down; then

Afton Down, 500 feet high. Tumuli on the top.

Needles Down, 500 feet. A road up to the light, with Alum Bay on one side, and Scratchell's Bay on the other. The Hampshire and Dorsetshire coast to the right, and Portland Bill (perhaps), may be seen in the distant horizon.

South Western Main Line continued.

Southampton to Dorchester and Weymouth.

This line of railway passes through a country of picturesque character and antiquarian interest. It branches off from the South Western Railway at the upper end of the town of Southampton, and passes through a tunnel under the old road to London. The tunnel is nearly 531 yards in length, and is cut through a soil of gravel and clay. The railway then passes on *viâ* the stations of Redbridge, Totton (for Eling), and Lyndhurst Road, (none of which require special notice), to

BROCKENHURST.

Distance from station, 1 mile.

A telegraph station.

Money Order Office at Lymington.

This station is most exquisitely situated amidst the charming scenery of the New Forest. In the churchyard are some very large yew and oak trees. The Rev. William Gilpin, the author of "Forest Scenery," &c., &c., founded two schools here, and endowed them with the profits arising out of the sale of a part of his writings, &c. Some of these realised as much as £1,200, in the year 1802, and subsequently, after his death, another lot fetched as much as £1,500. He lies buried in Boldre churchyard.

LYMINGTON BRANCH.

Turning to the left from this station, a run of about twenty minutes brings us to the parliamentary borough of

LYMINGTON.

A town prettily situated on the right bank of the river Lymington. Its maritime operations are chiefly confined to the Isle of Wight, with which it has frequent communication. Salt is extensively manufactured in the neighbourhood. The parish church, dedicated to Thomas à Becket, has many striking monuments.

South Western Main Line continued.

CHRISTCHURCH ROAD.

Telegraph station at Brokenhurst, 5 miles.

Hotel.—King's Arms.

Market Day.—Monday.

Fairs.—Trinity Thursday, and Oct. 17th.

Bankers.—Wilts and Dorset Banking Co.

Christchurch (at the confluence of the Avon and Stour) is a town containing some beautiful relics of the past in the ruins of its ancient collegiate church and priory, which are well worthy of notice. The church, which has been restored, is 310 feet long. It has a trade in knit and silk stockings, &c.

RINGWOOD.

A telegraph station. On the borders of the New Forest.

Hotel.—White Hart.

Market Day.—Wednesday.

Fairs.—July 10th and December 11th.

Money Order Office.

Bankers.—Redgard & Sons.

The line now passes from the county of Hampshire into

DORSETSHIRE,

Which is bounded on the north by Wiltshire, on the east by Hampshire, on the west by Devon and part of Somerset, and on the south by the British Channel. Its form is everywhere irregular; its long northern side has a considerable angular projection in the middle; the sea shore on the south runs out into numerous points and headlands, till it stretches to the Isle of Portland; thence westward the coast is not so deeply indented, but inclines obliquely towards Devonshire.

Great numbers of sheep and oxen are fed in the vale of Blackmore; which is distinguished by its rich pasture. Many of the other vales on the south western side are likewise uncommonly luxuriant. The inhabitants of Dorsetshire have paid great attention to the rearing of sheep, and it has been estimated this county alone produces more than 800,000 of these animals.

Dorsetshire, from the mildness of its climate and the beauty of its situation has been termed the garden of England. The soils vary in different parts. About Bridport the lower lands are mostly deep rich loams; on the higher hills, throughout the western district, the soil is sandy loam, intermixed with a common kind of flint. There are nearly forty rivers in this county, the principal of which are the Stour and Frome.

The chalk hills, which run through every county from the south-east part of the kingdom thus far, terminates at the further extremity of this; but on the coast chalk cliffs extend beyond it into Devonshire. Dorsetshire is distinguished for its woollen manufactures, and its fine ale and beer. The products are corn, wool, hemp, fire-stone, and some marble; and there is plenty of poultry of all sorts. The principal minerals are two kinds of freestone. Potters' clay is very abundant.

WIMBORNE.

POPULATION, 2,295.

Distance from station, 1 mile.

A telegraph station.

HOTELS.—Crown, King's Arms.

COACHES to Blandford daily.

MARKET DAY.—Friday. FAIRS.—Friday before Good Friday, and September 14th.

MONEY ORDER OFFICE.

BANKERS.—National Provincial Bank of England.

The town is about half a mile from the station. The Minster, or Collegiate Church, 180 feet long, is a most interesting relic of antiquity, said to have been erected between the years 705 and 723. The whole building has a cathedral-like appearance, and consists of a nave, choir, and transepts. Amongst the illustrious dead whose ashes repose within its walls, are those of king Ethelred, whose remains are said to have been interred here.

The station of Wimborne is at the base of an embankment; it is built, like most of the others on this line, of red brick, with dressings of yellow brick, in the Tudor style of architecture.

Wimborne to Blandford.

STURMINSTER and SPOTTISBURY Stations.

BLANDFORD.

POPULATION, 2,504, engaged principally in the manufacture of buttons, and agriculture. At various periods in its earlier history it has sustained much damage by fire, which had the effect of almost annihilating the place, although now a town of considerable importance. The date of the last fire may be seen on the side of a pump. In the church are monuments to the Pitts.

The line proceeds from Wimborne over the wooden viaduct across the river Stour, and the next station we reach is Poole Junction, to which town a *branch rail* of two miles runs.

POOLE JUNCTION station.

POOLE.

Distance from station, 2 miles.

A telegraph station.

HOTEL.—Antelope.

OMNIBUSES to and from Parkstone, and Bournemouth.

MARKET DAYS.—Monday and Thursday.

FAIRS.—May 1st, and November 2nd.

MONEY ORDER OFFICE.

BANKERS.—National Provincial Bank of England.

A Dorsetshire borough and port, on the South-Western Railway, 122 miles from London, by a small branch out of the main line. The neighbourhood is a dreary plain of sand and furze. Population 9,225, who return two members. Having been founded since the Conquest, it is a comparatively modern town, but has always preserved a respectable position as a third or fourth class port. The harbour, though six or seven miles long, and nearly as broad (when the tide is up) is choked with sand, but there is a good deep-water channel inside the bar. Salt fish and American timber are imported; and one of the chief exports is potters' clay from Purbeck, of so good a quality that it is proposed to establish potteries on a great scale here—especially as the transit for coal is now easy and direct. There are two miles of quay room. Here Charles X. landed 1830, after his flight from Paris.

The town is pretty well built, on a point of land between the harbour and Holes Bay, (the entrance to which is crossed by a bridge at the bottom of High Street), but offers nothing remarkable in its public structures, except an old disused town hall, built 1572, and the large modern church, in which is an altar-piece of carved work. One piece of antiquity is an old gate built in the reign of Richard III. In the middle of the harbour (or *pool*, which gives name to the town), is Brownsea Island, the seat of Sir S. Foster, Bart. Near the mouth of the harbour is an oyster bank, from which vast quantities are carried to the creeks of Essex and the Thames.

North of Poole, towards Wimborne Minster are *Upton*, the seat of Sir E. Doughty, Bart. *Candford Lodge*, occupied by the late Dowager Queen Adelaide, in 1844, now belongs to Lady Guest, the great iron proprietress; for a few years it was a convent (when in possession of Lord de Mauley), and is near an ancient house called John of Gaunt's.

Kitchen Heath, with patches of woodland about here. *Lytchett Minster*, Sir S. Scott, Bart. *Bloxworth* is near a camp—there is another at *Henburgh* (G. Harris, Esq.) *Charborough*, among woods, the seat of J. Drax, Esq., M.P., deserves notice for a small building in the grounds, with an inscription stating that "under this roof, in the year 1686, a set of patriotic gentlemen of this place, concocted the plan of the *Glorious Revolution*, &c." At *Wimborne Minister*, an old Saxon town, is a large and handsome minister church, lately restored, cross-shaped, 180 feet long, and Roman in the oldest part. One of its effigies is supposed to represent king Alfred's brother. There are also monuments to two of De Foe's daughters, and some lines by Prior on that of Ettriche the antiquary. The tithes are worth nearly £3,000 a year. *Kingston Lacy* is the seat of W. Bankes, Esq., a descendant of Bankes, the traveller, where there is a good picture gallery, and an Egyptian *obelisk* from Philoë, on the Nile, of the base of which the late Duke of Wellington laid the first stone in 1827.

About seven miles east of Poole, in *Hampshire*, is *Bournemouth*, a quiet bathing place in the chine of the low cliffs, among much woodland. About ten miles south-east, the Needles, rocks, and cliffs at the west end of the Isle of Wight are visible, especially in the bright gleam of a setting sun. *Heron Court*, Karl of Malmesbury's seat.

WAREHAM.

Population, 7,218.

Distance from station 1 mile.

A telegraph station.

Hotel.—Red Lion.

Omnibuses to and from Swanage, and Corfe Castle.

Market Days.—Tuesday and Saturday.

Fairs.—April 6th, July 5th, and September 11th.

Money Order Office.

Bankers.—National Provincial Bank of England.

The town, situated on a rising ground, at the top of Poole harbour was once a Roman station and a port, now a borough (returns one member), in the neighbourhood of which much potters' and fire-stone clay is found. There was a Norman castle here; and the church of St. Mary is half Norman. The corner of Dorsetshire between this and the sea is called the Isle of Purbeck. though only a peninsula about 11 miles long. A chalk ridge runs through it, 640 to 650 feet high, to Swanage and Studland bays; beyond which are the beds of Kimmaridge clay (in which alum and lignite coal have been worked) and Purbeck stone—the latter much variegated, rich in shells, and Saurian fossils, and of a smooth marble quality. The West India Docks, and many old churches, have been built of it. In a gap of the downs, about five miles to the south, is

Corfe Castle, originally Saxon, of which the keep, chapel, king's and queen's towers, the drawbridge, &c., remain. Here Edward, "king and martyr" as he is styled in the calendar, was assassinated by his mother-in-law, Elfrida, in 978. It was the scene of other melancholy events; and during the civil war became famous for the gallant defence made by the wife of Chief Justice Bankes, in behalf of the king, Lady Bankes being assisted by her daughters, maids, and five soldiers only. After investing it for ten weeks the Roundheads were obliged to raise the siege. The church is Norman. *Studland*, the seat of the Right Honourable G. Bankes. The coast, from this round Durlestone and St. Alban's Head, and further, is all cliff, without the least shelter. On the summit of *St. Alban's Head*, 440 feet high, is an ancient square vaulted chapel, resting on a single pillar, with no windows, but a Norman door. *Encombe House*, near this, Lord Eldon's seat. Further along the coast, towards Weymouth, is *Lulworth Cove*, a beautiful sheltered inlet overlooked by swelling downs, the cliffs of which swarm with sea birds. *Lulworth Castle*, the Welds' seat, was built 1609, in the shape of an exact cube, 80 feet each way, out of the materials of an abbey. Here Charles X. resided for a while in 1830.

Wool (near which are the ruins of Bindon Abbey), and Moreton stations.

DORCHESTER.

A telegraph station.

Hotels.—King's Arms, Antelope.

Market Days.—Wednesday and Saturday.

Fairs.—February 14th, Trinity Monday, July 6th, August 6th, and September 29th.

Bankers.—R. and H. Williams; Wilts and Dorset; Eliot and Pearce.

The station is about a quarter of a mile from the town, well situated, and neat in its arrangements, the arrival and departure platforms and coverings being complete, and well ordered in every respect.

Dorchester is a small parliamentary borough, and the capital of Dorsetshire, in a pretty part of the South Downs, at the termination of the South Western railway, 141 miles from London. It returns two members; population, 6,394. A trade in sheep, grain and other agricultural produce. It is pleasantly situated on an ascent above the river Frome. The town forms an irregular square, and consists principally of three spacious streets, which join each other about the middle; these, with the subordinate ones, are well paved, and, in general, adorned with handsome buildings of brick and stone. In early times it was a Roman town called *Durnovaria*, after a burn or water *Dwr* which runs through it,—the Frome, crossed by three small bridges. Parts of the ancient *walls* remain, about 6 ft. thick, the stones or tiles being laid herring-bone fashion, which usually marks Roman work. Another undoubted relic of their rule is *Maumbury Ring*, an amphitheatre cut in the chalk, 30 ft. deep, and about 340 ft. diameter. It is to the south of the town, close to the Roman way. Remains of seats are visible; and when Mary Channing was burned here in 1705, for poisoning her husband, it held 10,000 spectators. It is calculated to hold 12,960. Poundbury, Maiden Castle, and other camps raised by the Britons or Saxons are within view. Many coins called Dorn pennies were found on the site of the large County Gaol.

Dorchester has three churches, one rather old, and St. Peter's, with a tower; County Hall and Town Hall, a cloth factory and barracks. The walks in the neighbourhood are pleasant. About 700,000 South Down sheep are fed on the hills, and early house lamb is sent to market; while the pastures to the north, on the Stour &c. yield excellent Dorset butter (which being washed is often sold for fresh), and Double Dorset streaked skim cheese. Black Down, one of the highest points, is 817 feet above the sea.

WEYMOUTH.

A telegraph station.

HOTELS. — Luce's Royal; Drew's Victoria; Jeffries.

MARKET DAYS.—Tuesday and Friday.

RACES.—In September.

BANKERS.—Eliot and Pearce.

Nothing can be more striking and picturesque than the situation of this delightful watering-place. The town is built on the western shore of one of the finest bays in the English Channel, and being separated into two parts by the river, which forms a commodious harbour, it is most conveniently situated for trade. A long and handsome bridge of two arches, constructed of stone, with a swivel in the centre, was erected in 1820, and thus the divided townships enjoy a communication. The town, especially on the Melcombe side of the harbour, is regularly built, and consists chiefly of two principal streets, parallel with each other, intersected with others at right angles; it is well paved and lighted, and is tolerably supplied with fresh water. Since the town has become a place of fashionable resort for sea-bathing, various handsome ranges of buildings, and a theatre, assembly rooms, and other places of public entertainment, have been erected, and these are now rapidly extending and increasing in every direction. The principal of these are Belvidere, the Crescent, Gloucester Row, Royal Terrace, Chesterfield Place, York Buildings, Charlotte Row, Augusta Place; and Clarence, Pulteney, and Devonshire Buildings, are conspicuous; to which may perhaps be added Brunswick Buildings, a handsome range of houses at the entrance of the town. From the windows of these buildings, which front the sea, a most extensive and delightful view is obtained, comprehending on the left a noble range of hills and cliffs, extending for many miles in a direction from west to east, and of the sea in front, with the numerous vessels, yachts, and pleasure boats, which are continually entering and leaving the harbour.

To the west of the harbour are the barracks, a very neat and commodious range of buildings. The Esplanade is one of the finest marine promenades in the kingdom. It is a beautiful terrace, thirty feet broad, rising from the sands, and secured by a strong wall, extending in a circular direction parallel with the bay for nearly a mile, and commanding a most beautiful panorama of the sea, cliffs, and the mountainous range of rocks by which the bay is enclosed.

On the Esplanade is the Royal Lodge where George III. and the Royal family resided, and here also will be found the principal public libraries, echoing with the dulcet strains of some experimental musician.

The Theatre is a neat and well arranged edifice, in Augusta Place, but it is seldom inconveniently crowded. Races are held early in September, and during their continuance a splendid regatta is celebrated in the bay, which has a fine circular sweep of two miles; and being sheltered by a continuous range of hills from the north and north-east winds, the water is generally very calm and transparent. The sands are smooth, firm, and level, and so gradual is the descent towards the sea, that, at the distance of 100 yards, the water is not more than two feet deep. Bathing-machines of the usual number and variety are in constant attendance, and on the South Parade is an establishment of hot salt-water baths, furnished with dressing-rooms and every requisite accommodation. At the south entrance of the harbour are the higher and lower jetties, the latter of which is a little to the east of the former. The sea has been for a long series of years retiring from the eastern side of the harbour, and part of the ground over which it formerly flowed is now covered with buildings, other parts being enclosed with iron railings, which form a prominent feature on the Esplanade. On the Weymouth side are the Look Out and the Nothe, affording extensive and interesting prospects; on the latter is a battery, formerly mounted with six pieces of ordnance, which, on the fort being dismantled, were removed into Portland Castle. Within the walls a signal post has been established, which communicates with several other stations, and apartments have been built for the accommodation of a lieutenant and a party of men. The bay affords ample facilities for aquatic excursions at any time, its tranquil surface being never disturbed except by violent storms from the south or south-west. Yachts and pleasure boats are always in readiness, and the fares kept strictly under municipal supervision.

No place can be more salubrious than Weymouth. The air is so pure and mild, that the town is not only frequented during the summer, but has been selected by many opulent families as a permanent residence; and the advantages which it possesses in the excellence of its bay, the beauty of its scenery, and the healthfulness of its climate, have contributed to raise it from the low state into which it had fallen from the depression of its commerce, to one of the most flourishing towns in the kingdom.

About a mile to the south-west are the remains of Weymouth or Sandsfoot Castle, erected by Henry VIII. in the year 1539, and described by Leyland as "a right goodly and warlyke castle, having one open barbicane." The burning cliff at Weymouth—a kind of miniature volcano—has long attracted the notice of uaturalists, and will well repay a visit. At Nottington, about two miles and a-half distant, on the Dorchester road, is a mineral spring, the water of which is considered efficacious in cases of scrofula.

About four miles south from Weymouth, is the island of Portland, which, though thus called, is in

SLACKS' ELECTRO PLATE

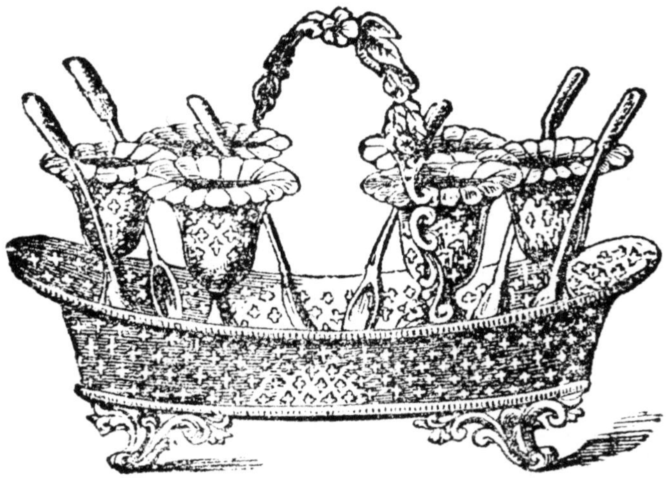

Is a strong coating of pure Silver over Nickel (by Elkington & Co.'s patent process).

MANUFACTURED SOLELY BY

R. & J. SLACK.

The fact of twenty years' wear is ample proof of its durability, and in the hardest use can never show the brassy under surface so much complained of by purchasers of Electro-plate.

EVERY ARTICLE FOR THE TABLE AS IN SILVER.

Old Goods Replated equal to New.

EGG FRAMES,

38s. 6d. to 70s.;

CORNER DISHES,

£6 15s.

The set of Four, forming Eight Dishes;

TEA AND COFFEE SETS,

from £5.

	Electro-plated Fiddle Pattern.			Strong Plated Fiddle Pattern.			Thread Pattern.			King's & Thread with Shell.		
	£	s.	d.	£	s.	d.	£	s.	d.	£	s.	d.
12 Table Forks	1	10	0	1	18	0	2	8	0	3	0	0
12 Dessert Forks	1	0	0	1	10	0	1	15	0	2	2	0
12 Table Spoons	1	10	0	1	18	0	2	8	0	3	0	0
12 Dessert Spoons	1	0	0	1	10	0	1	15	0	2	2	0
12 Tea Spoons	0	12	0	0	18	0	1	3	6	1	10	0

SLACKS' FENDER AND FIRE-IRON WAREHOUSE

CONTAINS THE GREATEST VARIETY OF NEW PATTERNS,

Iron Fenders, 3s. 6d. to 6s.; Bronzed Fenders, 9s. 6d. to 40s.; Steel Fenders, with Ormolu Mountings, 65s.; Fire Irons, 3s. 6d. to 30s.

SLACKS' DISH COVERS are the cheapest (for quality) in London, in Electro-plate, Britannia Metal, and Best Block Tin, from 18s., set of six.

SLACKS' DOMESTIC BATHS are made of the Best Material and Strongest Make.

Hip Baths, from 15s.; Sponging Baths, 10s.; Open Baths, 17s.; Children's Baths, 9s. 6d. A large assortment always on view.

SLACKS' CATALOGUE, with 350 Drawings and Prices, may be had gratis or post free. No person should furnish without one. Orders above £2 carriage free.

RICHARD & JOHN SLACK,

336, STRAND, OPPOSITE SOMERSET HOUSE.

reality, a peninsula, connected with the mainland by an extremely narrow isthmus, called Chesil Bank, a line of shingles thrown up by the sea, and extending for more than eight miles, from Portland to Abbotsbury. It is not more than two miles broad and four long; and though the shores are steep and rugged, the surface of the soil at the summit is smooth, and yields wheat, oats, and barley of average quality. At the southern extremity, called Portland Bill, are the higher and lower lighthouses, and a signal station, called the "Lowes;" near the former is a remarkable cavern, from which the water rises as from a fountain. On the eastern side are Rufus and Pennsylvania Castles, and on the northern side are Portland Castle, and another signal station.

A trip to the island is one of the most favourite excursions generally offered, among other temptations, to travellers, and will furnish materials for an interesting day's enjoyment. Indeed, this picturesque coast is unrivalled. The sea view is agreeably diversified with grand and striking objects, to break the monotony that usually pervades a marine prospect. The coast of this part of Dorsetshire itself presents also grand and striking points. St. Alban's Head and Tulworth Cove, with their bold and soaring cliffs, are sublime and astonishing features in the vast picture that we look upon from hence. The surrounding country is full of castellated remains and interesting historical associations. In the neighbouring isle of Purbeck are the ruins of Corfe Castle, memorable for the assassination of King Edward the Martyr. Milton Abbey is even yet beautiful, under the decaying winters of many ages; and at Sherborne Castle there are many architectural fragments that still attest the genius of the ill-fated but high-minded Raleigh, and a garden, too, whose shades, planted by his hand, now overlook and wave above those walls which once afforded them shelter, honour, and protection. The rides about Smallmouth Sands, Upway, and beyond the source of the river Wey, are replete with picturesque and ever-changing objects, and the beauty of the town itself is not a little enhanced by the remaining ruins of Weymouth Castle, a scanty relic of the troublous times of old.

The latitude of Weymouth is one degree farther south than London, and many plants which require protection from the cold in other parts of the country here flourish through the winter in the open air. The geranium grows luxuriantly, and requires little care, and the large and small-leaved myrtle are out-of-door plants. Indeed, so salubrious is the climate, that Dr. Arbuthnot, who came in his early days to settle at Weymouth, observed that no physician could either live or die there. This, however, savours more of flattery than fact, as present observation will fully testify.

As a place for sea-bathing Weymouth is perfect, and the accommodation of about twenty or thirty machines, always ready, near the centre of the Esplanade, greatly facilitates that operation. The sands over which the bathers have to walk are well known as of the finest description; the declivity of the shore is almost imperceptible, and totally free from those obstructions which are noticed on many parts of the southern coast, so that the most timid can indulge in the luxury of open sea-bathing, with the additional comfort of perfect security, and of sea-water, pure, clean, and transparent. Neat and commodious warm salt-water baths will also be found on the South Parade, opposite the harbour.

Abbotsbury, near the west end of the fleet or lake inside the Chesil bank, is the seat of the Earl of Ilchester, and has a decoy and swannery. Further along the coast is

BRIDPORT. — For particulars see Section II., page 16.

Patent Despatch Box and Writing Desk.

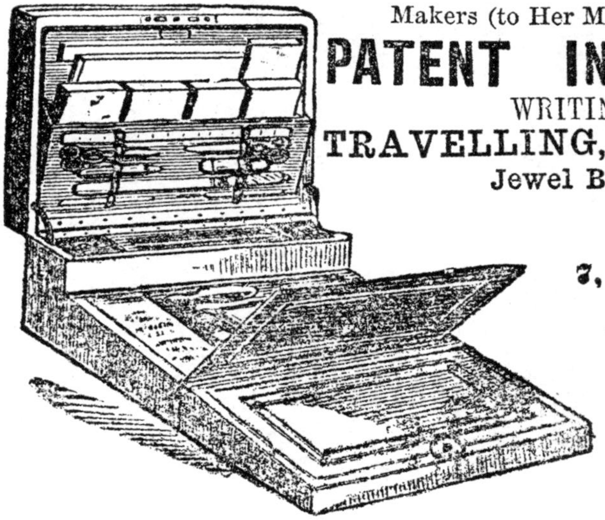

TOULMIN & GALE,

Makers (to Her Majesty's Government, Bank of England, &c.) of

PATENT INDIAN DESPATCH BOXES,

WRITING DESKS, DRESSING CASES,

TRAVELLING, TOILETTE, & CARRIAGE BAGS,

Jewel Boxes, Cases for Presentation, &c.

SISE LANE, CITY,

AND

7, NEW BOND STREET, LONDON,

(OPPOSITE THE CLARENDON).

Orders received through

SMITH, TAYLOR, & Co., Bombay,
J. HIGGINBOTHAM, Madras,
THACKER, SPINKS, & Co., Calcutta,
GEORGE HOLMES, Hong Kong.

Illustrated Catalogues, Post Free.

Established 125 Years.

Morocco Leather, second quality, £5. 5s.
Russia Leather, finest quality, £9. 9s. With Dressing Case, £14 14s. [27-Lo

J. H. BOOBBYER, late STURCH and BOOBBYER,

(Established nearly 200 years, for the supply of Goods of the best Manufacture at the lowest prices).

A PRIZE MEDAL for Superior Locks was awarded to **J. H. BOOBBYER**, at the Great Exhibition of 1851, and first-class Prize Medal for superiority of Goods exhibited by him at the Paris Universal Exhibition of 1855, from the Universal Society for Encouragement of Art and Industry.

Wholesale and Retail Ironmongery, Brass Foundry, Nail and Tool Warehouse.

Iron, Copper, and Zinc Nails; Patent Locks of all descriptions, Lever and Machine made. China, Glass, and Wood Furniture of all kinds, with Patent Shifting Spindles. Dr. Arnott's Ventilator, 4s.; and the new Registered Venetian Ventilator, so much admired, &c., 6s. 6d. each.

AGRICULTURAL DIGGING FORKS,

PATENT SPADES, DAISY RAKES, and

ALL KINDS OF GARDEN AND OTHER TOOLS.

Patent Spindled China Mortise Furniture, White, 1s. 2d. per set; Black, 1s. 4d.; White and Gold, 2s. per set; White China Finger Plate, 4s. per Dozen.

J. H. Boobbyer's Superior Four-Lever Drawer and Cut Cupboard Locks, 2s. each, the best make; also Mortise Locks for Room Doors. Locks of every sort made to Order, to go on place of Old Locks, at any price required, if not found on stock.

14, Stanhope Street, Newcastle Street, Strand, London, W.C.

[17-Lo.

FREE AND SAFE BY POST.

EVERY WATCH IN THE LATEST STYLE, AND MOST CAREFULLY FINISHED.

GOLD CASES AND JEWELLED.	QUALITY.		
GENTLEMEN'S.	A Gs.	B Gs.	C Gs.
Horizontal Construction, enamel dial......	10	8	6
Ditto, gold dial and strong case..............	12	10	7
Bennett's superior London-made patent Lever, jewelled..................................	17	14	12
LADIES'.			
Horizontal Construction, Gold Dial.........	10	8	6
Patent Lever (Geneva)..............................	12	10	8
Ditto (English) highly finished	16	14	12

SILVER CASES AND JEWELLED.	QUALITY.		
GENTLEMEN'S.	A Gs	B Gs	C. Gs.
Horizontal construction	5	4	3
Superior Lever (Geneva) 10 jewels	7	6	5
Bennett's London-made Lever	8	6	5
LADIES'.			
Horizontal Construction, neat and flat ...	5	4	3
Superior Geneva Lever	6	5	4
Small London-made Lever	7	6	5

POST OFFICE ORDERS PAYABLE TO

JOHN BENNETT, 65 & 64, CHEAPSIDE, LONDON,

AND AT THE CITY OBSERVATORY, 62, CORNHILL.

SECTION II.

BRADSHAW'S TOURS

THROUGH THE COUNTIES OF

BERKS, BUCKINGHAM, WILTS, DORSET, DEVON, CORNWALL, SOMERSET, GLOUCESTER, THE SOUTH WALES DISTRICTS, OXFORD, WARWICK, SALOP, CHESTER, FLINT, CARNARVON, ANGLESEA, AND THROUGH IRELAND.

CHINA AND GLASS ROOMS,

Nos. 49 and 50, OXFORD STREET, LONDON.

PARIAN CHINA ORNAMENTS IN STATUARY, GROUPS, AND FIGURES.

AMAZON.

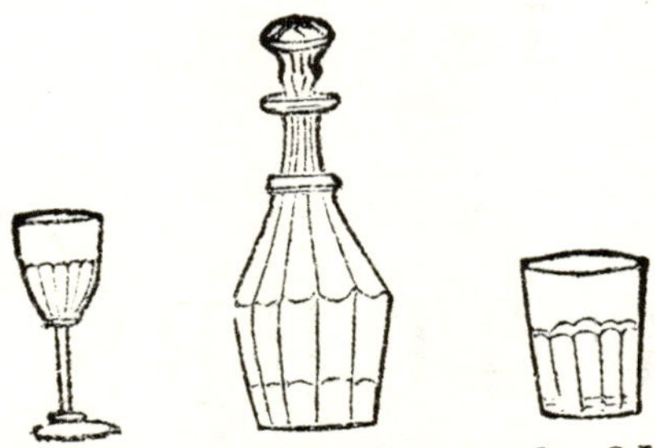

5s. 6d. Dozen.	12s. 6d. Pair.	4s. 6d. Dozen.

Small Breakfast Set (White China, Gold edge)—6 cups and saucers, 2 plates, 1 slop, 1 sugar, and 1 milk jug, 12s 6d.

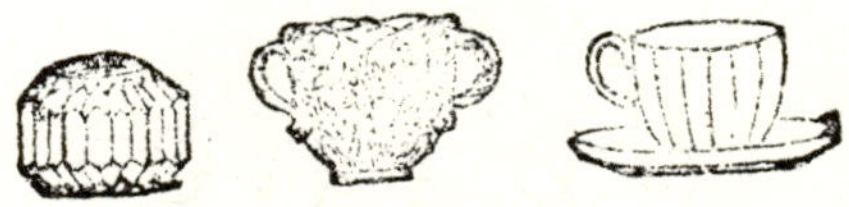

2s. Pair.	Parian Violet Vase, 1s. 6d.	White & Gold China, 4s. 6d. Half-dozen.

JOHN W. SHARPUS

Begs respectfully to call the attention of the Public to his IMMENSE STOCK, which is now replete with all the most MODERN AND CLASSIC DESIGNS IN

CHINA, GLASS, EARTHENWARE,

PARIAN STATUARY, AND BOHEMIAN GLASS.

DINNER SERVICES.

	£	s.	d.
Dinner Services, to dine 12 persons ....from	2	2	0
Ditto, richly gilt ....from	3	13	6
Handsome painted and gilt ....from	5	15	6
Rich coloured Bands, handsomely gilt ....from	7	7	0
Porcelain Services, rich coloured bands, handsomely gilt..........from 25 guineas.			

A variety of patterns, expressly for India and the Colonies, at the same moderate prices.

DESSERT SERVICES.

	£	s.	d.
For twelve persons, in neat coloured borders ..from	1	1	0
Ditto, antique borders and coloured wreaths ..from	1	8	0
A variety, coloured borders, with gold and flowers, on the finest Porcelain..........from	3	15	0
Ditto, ditto, from 5 to 10 guineas and upwards.			
China Breakfast Set, gold edge, viz., 6 breakfast cups and saucers, 2 plates, 1 slop, 1 sugar basin, 1 milk jug ....from	0	12	6

A LARGE ASSORTMENT OF PATTERNS AT THE SAME MODERATE PRICES.

TEA SERVICES.

	£	s.	d.
White china, gold edge ....from	0	17	0
Neat painted band and flowers..........from	1	8	0
Elegant pattern, handsomely painted and gilt from	2	2	0
Splendid Services, of the most elaborate workmanship and design, rich painted and gilt, £8 8s. to	14	14	0

GLASS DEPARTMENT.

	£	s.	d.	
Particularly neat cut Wine Glasses	0	5	6	per dozen.
Handsome cut ditto ....from 12s. 6d. to	1	1	0	per dozen.
Neat good strong Tumblers	0	4	6	per dozen.
A large variety of patterns ...10s. 6d. to	1	4	0	per dozen.
Pale Ale Tumblers, for India..12s. 6d. to	2	2	0	per dozen.
Modern shape Decanters..........	0	8	6	per pair.
Cut glass and engraved ....21s. to	2	2	2	per pair.
Custard and Jelly Glasses......4s. 6d. to	0	10	6	per dozen.
Cut glass Water Jugs ....5s. to	1	1	0	each.
Best glass Salts (modern shaped) ..9d. to	0	2	9	each.

A Price Catalogue may be had on application, containing full description of Kitchen Requisites, Toilet Ware, Papier Trays, Cutlery, Plated Cruet Frames, Hot Water Plates and Dishes, and every requisite required for furnishing, at extremely reduced Cash Prices.

A China Dinner Service, to Dine 12 persons, Torquoise and Gold, 15 Guineas.

All orders from the Country must be accompanied with a reference or remittance. [29-Lo.

CONTENTS TO SECTION II.

PAGE

BIRKENHEAD—
Chester to Birkenhead and Liverpool...... 70
Chester to Manchester 70
BRISTOL AND EXETER—
Bristol to Exeter.............................. 21
Durston to Yeovil 23
Highbridge to Burnham 22
Tiverton Branch.............................. 25
Weston Super Mare Branch................. 22
Yatton to Clevedon 21
CHESTER AND HOLYHEAD— 71
Bangor to Carnarvon......................... 79
Chester to Conway, Bangor, & Holyhead 72
Chester to Mold 72
COLEFORD, MONMOUTH, USK, AND PONTYPOOL.............................. 41
CORNWALL—Plymouth to Truro 33
GREAT WESTERN—
Chippenham to Dorchester and Weymouth 15
Didcot to Oxford, Birmingham, Wolverhampton, & Shrewsbury...6 to 11, & 53 to 64
London to Reading, Bath, and Bristol...1 to 21
Maidenhead to Wycombe 3
Maiden Newton to Bridport................. 17
Melksham to Devizes........................ 15
Reading to Basingstoke...................... 5
Reading to Hungerford....................... 5
Slough to Windsor............................ 3
Swindon to Gloucester and Cheltenham... 12
Twyford to Henley............................ 4
Westbury to Salisbury 16
West Drayton to Uxbridge 2
HEREFORD, ROSS, AND GLOUCESTER—
Gloucester to Ross and Hereford........... 37
KNIGHTON—Craven Arms to Knighton 45
LLANELLY—
Llanelly to Llandilo and Llandovery...... 49
LLANIDLOES AND NEWTOWN.............. 66
MANCHESTER, SOUTH JUNCTION, AND ALTRINCHAM—
Bowdon and Altrincham to Manchester... 71

PAGE

NORTH DEVON—
Exeter to Barnstaple and Bideford......... 28
OSWESTRY AND NEWTOWN.................. 66
ST. GEORGE'S HARBOUR—Conway to Llandudno.. 76
SHREWSBURY AND CHESTER—
Brymbo Minera Branch........................ 69
Gobowen to Oswestry and Welshtown... 66
Shrewsbury to Wrexham and Chester ... 65
SHREWSBURY AND HEREFORD—
Hereford to Shrewsbury 43
Kington to Leominster 44
SHREWSBURY AND WELSHPOOL 64
SOMERSET CENTRAL—
Highbridge to Glastonbury and Wells ... 22
SOUTH DEVON—
Exeter to Torquay and Plymouth 28
Newton Junc. to Torquay and Brixham.. 30
SOUTH STAFFORDSHIRE—
Dudley to Walsall, Burton, and Derby... 61
SOUTH WALES—
Glo'ster, to Newport, Swansea, Carmarthen, and Milford Haven........... 37 to 53
TAFF VALE—
Cardiff to Aberdare and Merthyr Tydvil 46
TAFF VALE EXTENSION 41
VALE OF CLWYD—
Rhyl to Denbigh 74
VALE OF NEATH—
Neath to Merthyr Tydvil 47
WARRINGTON AND STOCKPORT—
Warrington to Timperley 71
WEST CORNWALL—
Truro to Redruth and Penzance 34
WEST MIDLAND—
Newport to Abergavenny and Hereford... 41
Leominster to Kington 44
Oxford to Worcester and Wolverhampton 55
Honeybourne to Stratford-on-Avon 55
Shipton to Chipping Norton................. 55
WORCESTER AND HEREFORD 58

IRELAND.

BELFAST & NORTHERN COUNTIES— PAGE
Belfast to Ballymena and Portrush 105
Cookstown Junction to Cookstown 106
BELFAST AND COUNTY DOWN 104
CORK AND BANDON 90
DUBLIN AND BELFAST JUNCTION—
Drogheda to Dundalk and Newry 100
DUBLIN AND DROGHEDA—
Drogheda to Kells 100
Dublin to Howth................................ 99
Dublin to Malahide and Drogheda...99 to 100
DUBLIN AND WICKLOW 98
DUNDALK, ENNISKILLEN, & LONDONDERRY 109
GREAT SOUTHERN AND WESTERN—
Dublin to Cork and Killarney .... 83 to 95
Kildare to Carlow, Kilkenny and Waterford ....83 to 85

PAGE

Great Southern and Western—Continued.
Limerick Junction to Limerick 87
Portarlington to Tullamore 85
KILLARNEY LAKES, Excursion to the 91
,, ,, Prince of Wales' Tour at the 109
KINGSTOWN TO DUBLIN...................... 81
LIMERICK AND FOYNES 87
LONDONDERRY AND COLERAINE......... 108
MIDLAND GREAT WESTERN—
Dublin to Mullingar, Athlone, & Galway 95
Mullingar to Cavan and Sligo 95
NEWRY, WARRENPOINT, AND ROSTREVOR 101
PORTADOWN, DUNGANNON, & OMAGH.. 102
ULSTER—
Monaghan to Armagh and Belfast 101

ILLUSTRATIONS.

PAGE.

MAPS:—

Ireland ....End of Book

North Wales 78

PLANS:—

Bristol 20

Dublin 82

Oxford 8

VIEWS, Etc.:—

Abergele, Bee Hotel 78

Bangor, British Hotel 78

,, George Hotel, Bangor Ferry...... 78

Penrhyn Arms Hotel 78

Britannia Tubular Bridge 80

Capel Curig Hotel 78

Carnarvon, Royal Sportsman Hotel 78

PAGE.

VIEWS, Etc.:—

Coalbrookdale Church 62

,, Iron Bridge 62

Coalbrookdale Literary and Scientific Institute 62

Conway Suspension Bridge 80

Dee Viaduct, Llangollen 80

Garron Point, Giant's Causeway 108

Giant's Causeway 108

Holyhead, Royal Hotel 78

Llanberis Lake 80

,, Royal Victoria Hotel 78

Llanrwst, Victoria Hotel 78

Powerscourt Waterfall, Wicklow 108

Ross Island, Killarney 108

Round Tower, Wicklow 108

Snowdon 80

INDEX.

Abbey of Bonamargy, 107
Abbey of Innisfallen, 92
Aber, 76
Aberafon, 48
Aberbeeg, 41
Abercarne, 41
Abercastle, 51
Aberdare, 46
Aberdylais, 47
Aberedw, 40
Aberffraw, 80
Abergavenny, 43
Abergele, 74
Abermanse, 51
Abernant, 48
Abersychan, 41
Abertillery, 41
Aberystwith, 44, 66
Abingdon, 6
Achill, 98
Acton, 2
Acton Burnell, 64
Acton Hall, 69
Acton House, 101
Acton Lodge, 101
Adare, 88
Addlestrop, 55
Addlestrop House, 55
Admaston, 62
Adra Hills, 88
Agbrook, 26
Aghadoe, 93
Aird's Snoot, 107
Albrighton, 32, 62
Aldermaston, 5
Aldermaston Park, 5
Alfoxton, 23
Alfred Mine, 36
Allua Lake, 90
Alrewas, 61
Alscot Park, 57
Altrincham, 71
Alveston, 57
Amlwch, 80
Anglebay, 52
Anglesea, 79
Angnew Mountain, 107
Annaghmore, 102
Antrim, 105, 106
Antrim Castle, 105
Appleford, 6
Arbutus Island, 92
Ardagh House, 100
Arddleen, 66
Arklow, 98
Arley Hall, 72
Armagh, 101
Arran Mowddwy Mountains, 68
Arthur's Round Table, 79
Ascot, 55
Ashcott, 22
Ashford, 28
Ashton Hill, 21
Askeaton, 88
Astley, 71
Aston Hall, 71
Aston Park, 66
Athcarne, 100
Athelney, 23
Athenry, 97
Athlone, 96
Athy, 84
Attingham, 64
Aughaanarc, 98
Aughrim, 84, 97, 98
Aurabella, 89
Avoca, 98
Aylesborough, 57
Aynho, 10, 53

Badbury Camp, 16
Badworth Park, 14
Bagillt, 73
Bagillt Hall, 73
Bagnalstown, 84
Bailey Hill, 72
Bala Lake, 68
Balbriggan, 100
Baldoyle, 99
Ballinadoon, 96
Ballinahinch, 104
Ballinamallard. 109
Ballinasloe, 97
Ballinhassig, 90
Ballintry, 107
Ballybay, 109
Ballybeg, 100
Ballybunian, 88
Ballycastle, 107
Ballygally Head, 107
Ballygowan, 104
Ballyhale, 85
Ballyleidy, 104
Ballylurch, 85
Ballymena, 106
Ballymoney, 106
Ballynakill Harbour, 98
Ballynure, 105
Ballyclare, 105
Ballygowan, 105
Ballyspellan Spa, 85
Ballyworkan, 101
Balmoral, 1 3
Banbury, 53
Bandon, 90
Bangor, 76
Bangor (Ireland), 104
Bangor Iscoed, 68
Bannow Bay, 86
Bantry Bay, 90, 95
Banwell, 22
Barmouth, 67
Barnsley Park, 12
Barnstaple, 28
Barnwood, 14
Baron's Court, 108
Barrington, 55
Barton, 10
Barton, 61
Baschurch, 24, 65
Basildon, 6
Basingwerk, 73
Basingwerk Abbey, 73
Basley Wood, 7
Bason Bridge, 22
Bassaleg Junction, 41
Bath, 18
Bathampton, 15, 18
Batheaston, 18
Batheaston Church, 19
Bathford, 18
Batsford, 55
Battefield, 65
Battlesbury 16
Bay of Dublin, 81
Bayton Hall, 16
Beacon Hill, 11, 38
Beaminster, 17
Bear Wood, 5
Bearley, 53
Beaulieu Road, 38
Beaumaris, 78
Beaumaris Castle, 76
Beauparc, 100
Beauparc House, 100
Beaver Valley, 77
Bebbington, 70
Beddgelert, 77, 78
Bedminster, 20
Beer Ferris, 32
Beggar's Down, 12
Belfast, 103
Bellaghy, 106
Bellaghy Castle, 106
Bellaghy House, 106
Bellarena, 108
Bellisle, 89
Belvoir, 104
Bendon, 27
Benglog Falls, 77
Bengore Head, 107, 108
Benmore Head, 107, 108
Bennett's Bridge, 85
Bentley Hill, 61
Benton Castle, 51
Berkshire, 3
Berrington, 44
Berrington Park, 44
Berwick Hall, 65
Berwick Park, 65
Berwyn Mountains, 68
Bettws-y-Coed, 77
Bevere, 59
Bicton, 26, 64
Bideford, 29
Bidstone Light House, 70
Bigswear, 38
Billingbear, 5
Bilston, 54, 62
Birkenhead, 70
Birmingham, 54
Black Head, 37
Blackdown Hills, 24
Blackrock, 81
Blackrock Castle, 90
Blackrock Light House, 70
Blaen Hafran, 66
Blaenavon, 41
Blaina, 41
Blanchardstown, 95
Blandford Park, 55
Blarney, 89
Blarney Castle, 89
Blenheim, 10
Bletchington, 11
Blockley, 57
Bodelwyddan, 74
Bodington Manor, 14
Bodmin Road, 34
Bodorgan, 80
Bodryddon, 74
Bolney Court, 4
Bont Newydd, 78
Booterstown, 81
Bordesley, 54
Boreaton Park, 65
Boringdon, 32
Borristown, 87

Boscawen-Oon, 36
Bosheston, 52
Bosheston Meer, 52
Boskenna, 36
Botallick Mine, 36
Boughrood, 42
Boughton, 59
Boulston, 53
Bourton 21,
Bow, 26
Bowdon, 71
Bownham House, 12, 13
Bowood, 15
Box, 17
Boyne Hill, 100
Bradenstoke Priory, 15
Bradford, 15
Bradford Abbas, 17
Bradwick, 25
Bransford Road, 58
Bratton, 16
Bray, 84, 98
Bray Head, 98
Brecon, 43
Brecknock, 41, 47
Bremhill, 15
Brent, 31
Brettle Lane, 60
Bridge Trafford, 70
Bridgend, 47
Bridgewater 23
Bridport, 17
Brimscomb, 13
Brinny House, 90
Bristol, 19
Britannia Bridge, 76, 79
Briton Ferry, 47
Brixham, 31
Broadhaven Creek, 52
Broadheath, 71
Bromborough, 70
Bromfield, 45
Brompton Bryan, 44
Bromyard, 44
Brookworth, 14
Broom, 45
Broughton, 72
Brown Island, 92
Browne Hill, 84
Brownslade, 52
Bruce's Castle, 107
Bruton, 17
Brymon House, 23
Brympton House, 23
Brynkinaill, 66
Buckinghamshire, 2
Buckland Abbey, 32
Bucknell, 45
Buckstone, 42
Bude, 26
Budwick Mine, 35
Buildwas Abbey Ruins, 36, 64
Builth, 41
Bullo Piel, 38
Bull's Scaughter Bay, 52
Burford, 55
Burnham, 22
Burnham Village, 3
Burton-on-Trent, 61
Bury Lane 71
Buttevant, 89
Buttevant Castle, 89
Buttington, 66
Bwrdd Arthur, 78
Bynea, 49

Cabra Castle, 102
Cadbury Castle, 17
Cader Berwyn, 68
Cader Iris, 66
Caergwrle, 72
Cairn Lough, 107
Cairncastle, 107
Cairnlea Mountain, 107
Calclase, 37
Caldy Island, 49, 52
Callington, 32
Calne, 15
Camborne, 35
Camla Vale, 102
Campden, 57
Cape Clear, 90
Capel Curig, 68, 77, 78
Carclew, 35
Cardiff, 45
Cardigan, 51
Carew, 53
Carew Castle, 51
Carmarthenshire, 49
Carlow, 84
Carmarthen, 49
Carnarvon, 78
Carnedd Dafydd, 77
Carnedd Llewelyn, 77
Carntown Castle, 100
Carrantual, 93, 94, 95, 96
Carrick-a-rede Rock, 107
Carrickfergus, 105, 107
Carrickfergus Junc. 105
Carrickmines, 98
Carrick-on-Suir, 86
Carrigans, 108
Carton, 83, 85, 96
Cashel, 88
Castle Cary, 17
Castle Carey, 107
Castle Combe, 15
Castle Comer, 85
Castle Connell, 88
Castle Dawson, 106
Castle Dillon, 102
Castle Dinas Bran, 67
Castle Howard, 98
Castle Martin, 52
Castle Meragn, 108
Castle Shane, 102
Castle Upton, 106
Castlebar, 97
Castlebear Hill, 2
Castlebellingham House, 100
Castlebellingham, 100
Castleblaney, 109
Castleblaney House, 109
Castlecary, 16
Castlemartyr Castle, 90
Castell Dolforwyn, 67
Cavan, 96
Cave Hill, 104
Caversham, 5
Caynham Court, 44
Cefn Bryn, 48
Ceunant Mawr Fall, 78
Chacewater, 35
Chadleigh, 26
Chalfont St. Giles, 2
Chapel Bridge, 41
Charlbury, 55
Charlcombe, 19
Charlecote, 57
Charlestown, 34
Charleville, 89
Charleville Castle, 89
Cheek Point, 85
Chees, 22
Cheltenham, 14
Chepstow, 39, 42
Cherrington Grove, 12
Cherry Island, 91
Chester, 69
Chiltern Hills, 4
Chimney Tops, 107
Chippenham, 15
Chipping Norton, 55
Chirk, 67
Chirk Castle, 67
Churcham, 37
Churchdown, 14
Churchill, 60
Church Stretton, 45
Cirencester, 12
Cirencester Abbey, 12
Claines, 59
Clarbeston Road, 50
Clare Castle, 88
Claverdon, 53
Clawdd Côch, 78
Clearwell Park, 42
Clearwell Castle, 39
Clevedon, 21
Clew Bay, 98
Clifden, 98
Clifford Castle, 41
Clifton Hot Wells, 20, 21
Clogh-i-Stookan Rock, 107
Clogwyn-Dû-r-Arddu, 78
Clonakilty, 90
Clondalkin, 83
Clones, 109
Clonmacnois, 88
Clonmel, 86
Clonsilla, 95
Clonsilla House, 95
Clopton House, 57
Cloughreen, 92, 94, 95
Cloyne, 90
Clwydian, Hills, 72
Clytha, 42
Coalbrookdale, 62
Codford, 16
Codsall, 62
Coleraine, 106
Coles Hill, 73
Collumpton, 25
Colwyn, 75
Comber, 104
Comme Dhur, 93, 94
Condover, 64
Connemara, 97
Conway, 75
Conway Castle, 75
Cookham, 3
Cookstown, 106
Cootehill, 109
Copplestone, 28
Cork, 89
Cornbrook, 71
Cornbury, 10
Cornewell, 55
Cornwall, 33, 34
Corsham, 17
Corsham House, 15, 17
Corville, 87
Corwen, 68
Cortarvin, 101
Cothele, 32
Cotley, 16
Cound, 64
Court Martinrath, 107
Courtfield, 38
Courtown Castle, 85
Coutham Head, 108
Cowbridge, 47
Craig Ddrwg, 67
Craig Eglwyseg, 67
Craig-y-linn, 47
Cramiglann, 92
Cranmore, 17
Craufordsburn, 104
Craven Arms, 45
Crediton, 26, 28
Creed Place, 13
Crinnis Mine, 34
Crib-y-Distul, 78
Crickhowel, 43
Crieve Roe, 102
Croaghpatrick, 98
Croaghu Kinshela, 98
Croft Castle, 44
Croome Park, 59
Cropredy, 53
Cross Inn, 49
Cross Keys, 41
Crow Rock, 52
Crumlin, 41
Culham, 6, 7
Culham Court, 4
Culloville, 109
Cumnor Place, 10
Curragh Race Course, 84
Curraghmore, 86
Cushendall, 107
Cushendern Bay, 107

Cushendern House, 107
Cwm, 41
Cwm Avon, 41
Cwm Dyli, 78
Cwmbran, 41
Cwn Brwnog, 78
Cymner Abbey Ruins, 67

Daisy Bank, 62
Dalesford House, 55
Dalkey, 81
Dancing Marston, 57
Daresbury, 71
Dargle Glen, 98
Dartmoor, 25, 31,
Dartmoor Forest, 25
Dartmouth, 31
Datchet Mead, 3
Dawlish 29, 26
Dee Viaduct, 68
Deganwy, 76
Delgany, 98
Delphi, 98
Delwyddellan Castle, 77
Denbigh, 74
Denbighshire, 75
Denham, 2
Denham House, 45
Denis Island, 92, 94
Denmore. 44
Deptford Inn, 16
Derby, 61
Derricunihy, 94
Derwydd Road, 49
Devil's Bridge, 44, 66
Devil's Glen, 98
Devil's Kitchen, 77
Devil's Punch Bowl, 91, 93, 94, 95
Devizes, 15
Devonport, 34
Devonshire, 25
Dexton Church, 42
Didcot Junction, 6
Dimbody Abbey, 86
Dingestow, 41
Dinham House, 44,
Dinmore, 43
Dinorwic Slate Quarries, 78
Ditchley 10, 55
Djouce Mountain, 98
Dobbins Valley, 102
Dock, 49
Doddleston, 70
Dolbadarn, 78
Dolgelly, 67
Dolwen, 66
Donabate, 99
Donore, 96
Doon Mountains, 88
Dorchester, 17
Dorrington, 45
Doublebois, 34
Dowlands, 27
Down, 104
Down Hill, 106
Down House, 12
Downpatrick, 104
Downton, 45
Downton Hall, 44
Drakelon House, 62
Drayton Green, 2
Drogheda, 100
Drogheda House, 100
Droitwich, 59
Dromore, 89
Dromore House, 108
Dromore Road, 108
Drumbanagher Castle, 101
Drumgoff Inn, 98
Drumnasole, 107
Drumnaul Castle, 107, 108
Dublin, 81
Duck Island, 92
Dudley, 60
Dudley Castle, 60
Dudley Port, 61
Duleek, 100
Dunadry, 105
Dundalk, 101
Dundonald, 104
Dundoun House, 106
Dundrum, 87, 98
Dundrum House, 87
Dundry Beacon, 21
Dungannon 86
Dungarvan, 86
Dunham Hill, 70
Dunham Massey Park, 71
Dunleary, 81
Dunleer, 100
Dunloe, Gap of 92, 93, 94
Dunluce Castle, 108
Dunmore, 85
Dunmore, 109
Dunmore Park, 85, 86
Dunmurry 103
Dunmurry House, 103
Dunraven Castle, 47, 49
Dunscomb, 28
Dunseverick, 107
Dunseverick Castle, 107
Dunster, 23, 24
Durston, 23
Duyorth, 37
Dysart Hills, 85
Dyserth Castle, 74

Eagle Island, 92
Ealing, 2
Easington, 13
East Anthony, 32
East Castle, 17
East Hall, 72
Eastham, 70
Eastnor Castle, 59
Eatington, 57
Eaton Hall, 70
Ebbw Vale, 41
Eccles, 71
Eccleston, 69
Ecclesville, 108
Eddystone Lighthouse, 33
Edgeworth, 12
Edington, 22
Eggesford, 26
Egginton Heath, 61
Egremont, 70
Eliseg Cross, 67
Ellesmere Old Castle, 65
Elmore Court, 14
Elsfield, 10
Ely, 47
Ely Lodge, 109
Enfield, 96
Englefield, 5
Enmore Castle, 23
Enniskerry, 98
Enniskillen, 109
Ensham, 10
Enys, 35
Erddig Hall, 68
Erle Stoke, 16
Eton, 3
Evershot, 17
Evesham, 57
Exeter, 25
Exmouth, 26
Exminster, 29
Eywood Park, 44

Fair Head, 107
Fairfach, 49
Falmouth, 35
Farlagh, 75
Farley Castle, 15
Faringdon Road, 11
Farranfore, 95
Fawley, 42
Fearnall Heath, 59
Fenny Compton, 53
Fermanagh, 109
Fern's Lock, 96
Ferryside, 49
Festiniog, 77
Fethard, 86
Fettes, 65
Fin M'Coul, 107
Fintona, 108
Fir Grove, 90
Fisherton de la Mére, 16
Fladbury, 57
Flaherties' Castle, 98
Flaxley Abbey, 14
Flimstone Chapel Ruins, 52
Flint, 73
Flint Castle, 73
Fonthill Abbey, 16
Ford Bridge, 43
Forden, 66
Florence Court, 109
Forest of Dean, 14, 42
Forton, 14
Foss Cross, 12
Foryd, 74
Foumon Castle, 47
Four Crosses, 66
Four Sisters, 108
Foxley, 39
Foynes, 88
Fremington, 28
Freshford, 15
Freshwater Bay, 52
Frodmore, 13
Frodsham, 70
Frome, 17

Gaerwen, 79
Galway, 87
Gannock Castle, 75
Gap of Dunloe, 92, 93, 95
Gardden Lodge, 68
Garnant, 49
Garnish, 95
Garnons, 39
Garson Point, 107
Garth Point, 76
Garvn, 66
Gatcombe, 39
Geashill, 86
Geraghmene, 93, 94
Geversyllt Hall, 69
Giant's Ball Alley, 108
Giant's Causeway, 107
Giant's Granary, 108
Gill Hall Castle, 108
Giltar Head, 52
Glamorganshire, 45
Glasbury, 41
Glastonbury, 21
Glastonbury Tor, 22
Glanrhyd, 49
Glena Bay, 91, 95
Glenariff, 107
Glenarm, 107
Glendalough, 98
Glengariff, 91, 95
Glen of the Downs, 98
Glencoe Valley, 107
Gloucester, 13
Gloucestershire, 11
Glyder Bach, 77
Glyder Fawr, 77
Glympton, 10, 55
Glyn Farrell, 47
Glyn Neath, 47
Glynn Park, 105
Gobbins, The 107
Gobowen Junction, 65
Godolphin, 37
Golden Barrow, 16
Gongane Barra, 90
Goodrich Court, 14, 37
Goold's Cross, 78
Goonhills Downs, 36
Goragh Wood, 101
Gormanston, 100
Gormanston Castle. 100
Gower Road, 49
Gowran, 84
Grampound, 34
Grange Court, 37

Gray Man's Path, 107
Great Bridge, 61
Great Orme's Head,
Great Tew Park, 55
Greencastle 105
Greig Hill, 42
Gresford, 69
Gresford Lodge, 69
Griffith's Crossing, 78
Grimstone, 17
Groes Lon, 78
Gronant, 73
Grosmont Castle, 42
Groveley Castle, 16
Groveley Wood, 16
Gronant, 74
Gunnersbury Park,
Guskus Mine, 35
Gupton, 52
Gumperton, 53
Guilsfield Church, 66
Gwespyr, 73
Gwrych Castle, 74
Gwysaney, 72
Gwynear, 35
Gwyrnefed, 42

Haddon Castle, 70
Hafod, 44
Hagley, 60
Halkin Mountain, 73
Halsewell, 23
Halston, 65
Halton Castle, 71
Haldon Downs, 26
Hamilton's Baun, 102
Hamilton's Seat, 107
Hampton Cliffs, 19
Hampton Court, 38
Hampton Hill, 100
Hamshill, 16
Hanbury Hall, 59
Handborough, 55
Handsworth, 54
Hanging Langford, 16
Hanwell, 2
Hanwood, 64
Hardwicke Grange, 64
Harefield, 2
Haresfield, 13
Harlech, 67
Harpsden Court, 4
Hartlebury 60
Hartlebury Castle, 59, 60
Hartsheath, 72
Hatfield Court, 14
Hatherleigh, 26
Hatton, 22, 53
Hatton Park, 59
Haughmond Priory, 64
Haulbowline Island, 91
Haverfordwest, 51
Hawarden, 72
Hawarden Castle, 72
Hawkstone, 64
Hawkstone Park, 64
Hay, 41
Hay Park, 44
Hayle, 35, 36
Headford, 91
Headington, 10
Heatley, 71
Heavitree, 26
Hefeste Waterfalls, 47
Hele, 25
Helegan, 37
Helsby, 70
Helsby Hill Camp, 71
Helston, 37
Hen and Chickens, The, 108
Hengstown Down, 32
Henley, 4
Henlip, 59
Hensbarrow, 37
Hensol, 46
Henwick, 58
Hereford, 38, 43
Heron Island, 92
Heyford, 53
Heytesbury, 16
Heytesbury House, 16
Heythrop, 10
Heythorpe, 55
Heywood House, 15
Hick's House, 13
Highworth, 11
Highbridge, 22
High Grove, 14
Highnam Court, 13
Highnam Park, 14
High Wycombe, 3
Hilbree Island, 73
Hill House, 12, 13
Hill of Down, 96
Hill Priory, 52
Hindon, 16
Hirwain, 48
Hockley, 54
Hollyhill, 108
Holme Lacey, 38
Holt, 68
Holsworthy, 26
Holyhead, 80
Holyhead Harbour, 80
Holywell, 73
Holywood, 105
Honeybourn, 57
Hook Point & Light, 86
Hooton, 70
Hope, 72
Hopton Heath, 45
Horns, The, 13
Horse's Back, 107
Horse Shoe Harbour, 108
Horton, 31
Howth, 83, 84, 99
Hoylake, 73
Hungerford, 5, 6
Hungry Hill, 90, 95
Hunt's Moor Park, 2
Hyde Court, 13
Hyde Hark, 96

Ilfracombe, 28
Ince, 70
Ingon House, 57
Inniscarra Castle, 90
Innisfallen Island, 92
Inniskeen, 109
Innistroge Castle, 85
Innoshannon, 90
Instow, 28
Ireland, 81
Irvingstown, 108
Island of Anglesea, 81
Island of Ross, 92
Iver, 2
Ivy Bridge, 31

Johnstown, 85
Johnstown Hall, 51
Jonesborough, 101
Joyce's Country, 98

Kanturk, 91
Keeper Mountain, 88
Kells, 101
Kelston, 19
Kemble, 12
Kenbane Head, 108
Kenbaan Castle, 107
Kenmare, 95
Kenmure, 99
Kenyon Junction, 71
Kerrien, 36
Kerrier, 36
Kewstoke, 22
Keynsham, 19
Kidderminster, 60
Kiddington, 10, 55
Kidweily, 49
Kidwelly Castle, 49
Kilcock, 96
Kilcoleman Castle, 89
Kildare, 83
Kilhuddery, 98
Kilkenny, 84
Killaloe, 88
Killarney, 91
Killeries, 97
Killester Abbey, 99
Killymcon, 106
Killucan 96
Kilmacow, 85
Kilmallock, 88, 90
Kilmeaden Castle, 86
Kilruddery, 84
Kilrush, 88
Kimble, 12
Kincora, 88
King and his Nobles, 107
King O'Nial's Castle, 108
King's Bridge, 32
King's Bridge Road, 31
King's County, 87
Kingskerswell, 30
Kingsland, 44, 62
King's Stanley, 18
Kingsweston, 20
Kingswood, 20, 53
Kingstown, 81
Kington, 44
Kinlet Hall, 44
Kinmel, 75
Kinsale, 90
Kintbury, 6
Kirklington, 11
Kirtlington, 53
Knighton, 45
Knight Island, 92
Knock, 104
Knock Castle, 16
Knockin, 65
Knocklong, 88
Knockninoss, 90
Knollbury Banks, 55
Knott Mill, 71
Knowle, 53
Kylemore Pass, 91
Kymin Hill, 42
Kynance Cove, 37

Lache Hayes, 69
Lake Badarn, 78
Lakes of Killarney, 92
Lamb Island, 91, 92
Lamorna Cave, 36
Lampeter Road, 49
Lamphey Court, 53
Landogo, 42
Land's End, 36
Landulph, 32
Langford, 16, 28
Langley, 2
Langley Park, 2
Langport, 23
Lanovor, 41
Lansdowne Hill, 19
Laragh Bridge, 98
Larne, 107
Latchford, 71
Laurenny Hall, 53
Laycock Abbey, 15
Layde Church, 107
Laytown, 100
Leadbrook, 73
Leamington, 53
Leasowe, 70
Leaton, 65
Ledbury, 14, 38, 59
Lee, The 90
Leebotwood, 45
Leenane, 98
Leeswood, 72
Leigh Court, 20
Leigh Down, 21
Leixlip, 84, 95
Leixlip House, 95
Leominster, 38, 43
Leslie Hall, 106
Liddington Castle, 11
Lidstep Point, 52
Limerick, 87

Limerick Junction, 87
Limpley, 15
Linney Head, 52
Lion's Head, 91
Lisbellaw, 109
Lisburn, 103
Lisburn House, 103
Liskeard, 34
Lisnaskea, 109
Lissan, 106
Little Mill Junction, 41
Littlemore, 7
Liverpool, 71
Lizard, 37
Llagay, 77
Llanberis, 77
Llancaich, 41
Llandaff, 46
Llanddwyn, 80
Llandebie, 49
Llandegai, 77
Llandenny, 41
Llandilo, 49
Llandinam, 66
Llandore, 48
Llandovery, 40, 49
Llandrilio, 75
Llandrindod Spa, 40, 43
Llandulas, 74
Llandudno, 76
Llanelian, 75
Llanelly, 49
Llanfair, 79
Llanfawr, 66
Llanfihangel, 43
Llanfyllin, 66
Llangadock, 49
Llangadwaladr, 80
Llangennech, 49
Llangibby Castle, 41
Llangollen 68
Llangoed Castle, 41
Llangurid, 40
Llangwffen, 80
Llangynog, 66
Llanhilleth, 42
Llanidloes, 66
Llanrwst, 75
Llansamlet, 48
Llan St. Sior, 74
Llantarnam, 41
Llanthony Abbey, 43
Llantillis Crossenny, 42
Llantillis House, 42
Llantrissant, 47
Llantydwr, 43
Llanty silioHall, 68
Llanwern, 41
Llanwyrted Wells, 40
Llanymynech, 66
Llan-yr-Afange, 66
Llechwedd-y-Rŷ, 78
Llong, 72
Lloydsborough, 87
Llwydcoed, 48
Llynclys 66
Llyn Coron, 80
Llyn Cwellyn, 78
Llyn Gwynant, 77
Llyn Idwal, 77
Llyn Llydiaw, 78
Llyn Ogwen, 77
Llyn Peris, 78
Llyn-y-Cwm, 77
Locking, 22
Loftus, 86
Lombardstown, 91
Londonderry, 106, 108
Long, 71
Long Ashton, 21
Longford, 14, 96
Longhope, 37
Longleat Park, 17
Longnor, 64
Lostwithiel, 34
Loudwater, 3
Lough Allen, 88
Lough Bray, 98
Loughcooter Castle, 97
Lough Corrib, 98
Lough Dan, 98
Lough Derg, 88
Lough Garnear Bruff, 88
Lough Larne, 107
Lough Neagh, 105
Loughor, 49
Lough Tay, 98
Louth, 100
Lowtherstown, 108
Lucan, 83, 84, 95
Lucan Abbey, 95
Lucan House, 95
Ludford, 44
Ludgvan, 36
Ludlow, 44
Ludlow Castle, 44
Luggelaw, 98
Lugnaquilla, 98
Lurgan, 103
Lurg Eidem, 107
Lyncombe, 19
Lydiard, 14
Lydney, 39
Lyme Regis, 27
Lymm, 71
Lympstone, 26
Lynmouth, 28
Lynn Gwynn, 40
Lynn Llydiaw, 78
Lynton, 28
Lypiatt Park, 12, 13

Maam Turc Inn, 98
Mac Carthy's Island, 92
Machynlleth, 66
Mac Gillycuddy's Reeks 91, 94, 95
Macroom Castle, 90
Madresfield, 59
Madron, 36
Maeslwch Castle, 41
Mageny, 84
Magherafelt, 105
Magilligan, 108
Magor, 41
Maguire's Bridge, 109
Maiden Early, 5
Maidenhead, 3
Maiden Newton, 17
Maiden Rocks, 107
Mainhead, 26
Maizmore, 14
Malahide, 83, 99
Malahide Court, 99
Malbay, 88
Mallow, 89, 91
Malmesbury, 12
Malvern, 58
Malvern Hills, 14
Malvern Link, 58
Malvern Wells, 58
Manacle Rocks, 37
Manchester, 71
Mangerton, 91, 93, 94, 95
Manor Bay, 52
Manorbeer Castle, 52
Mannorbulloch, 87
Marazion Road, 36
Margan Abbey, 49
Margan Park, 47
Marlborough, 5
Marlow Road, 3
Marsh Brook, 45
Marshfield, 45
Marston, 10
Marston, 17
Marston Biggot, 17
Martock, 23
Maryborough, 86
Maviston Abbey, 88
May Hill, 38
Maynooth, 83, 95
Meadfoot, 30
Meath, 99
Medley, 10
Medmenham Abbey, 4
Megavissey, 37
Meini Herion, 75
Melbury House, 17
Melidan, 73
Melksham, 15
Mellown, 108
Mells Park, 17
Menai Bridge, 79
Meneage, 37
Menheniot, 34
Menlo Castle, 97
Merlyn Court, 47
Merrion, 81
Merquis, 72
Merry Maidens, The 36
Merthyr, 41, 46, 48
Mickle Trafford, 70
Middlebury, 16
Middleton Park, 11
Milford, 51, 84
Milford Road, 51
Millstreet, 91
Miltown, 108
Milverton, 24
Minchinhampton, 13
Minehead, 23, 24
Minera, 69
Minety, 11
Minsterley, 64
Misserden Park, 12, 13
Mitcheldean Road, 37
Moat Lane, 66
Moccas, 38,
Modbury, 32
Moel Fammau, 77
Moel Ferna, 68
Moel Siabod, 77
Moel-y-Wyddfa, 78
Moher, 88
Moira, 103
Moira Castle, 103
Mold, 72
Mollington, 70
Monaghan, 109
Monaghan Road, 109
Mona Marble Quarries, 78
Monasterevan, 86
Moneymore, 106
Monkstown Castle, 90
Monmouth, 42
Monmouthshire, 41
Montgomery, 66
Moor Park, 44
Morchard Road, 28
Moreton 43,
Moreton-in-the-Marsh, 55
Mornington, 96
Mortimer, 5
Mortimer's Cross, 44
Moss Valley, 69
Mostyn, 73
Mostyn Hall, 73
Mountain Ash, 46
Mount Aelian, 78
Mount Alyn, 69
Mount Branden, 85
Mount Cafellente, 47
Mount Callan, 88
Mount Coote, 89
Mount Edgecumbe, 32
Mountjoy, 108
Mountpleasant, 101
Mountrath, 87
Mounts Bay, 36
Mourn Abbey, 90
Mouse Island, 92
Moydrum Castle, 97
Moy Valley, 96
Muckross Abbey, 92,94,96
Mullinavatt, 85
Mullingar, 96
Mulrea, 98
Multyfarnham, 96
Murlough Bay, 107
Murrough, 97
Muzzle Hill, 10
Mymbyr Lake, 77

Nachore Mountain, 107
Nailsea, 21
Nanerth Cliffs, 44
Nannau Park, 67
Nant Francon, 77
Nantlle, 78
Nantyderry, 41
Nant-y-fridd, 69
Nant-y-Gwrydinn, 77
Narberth Road, 50
Narrow Water Ferry, 101
Narrow Water Castle, 101
Navan, 100
Navanrath, 102
Neath, 47
Needwood Forest, 61
Nether Stowey, 23
Netherton, 60
Newbliss, 109
Newbridge, 41, 46, 47
New Brighton, 70
Newbury, 5
New Milford, 51
Newnham, 38
Newnham Park, 32
Newport, 41, 98
Newridge, 99
New Ross, 86
Newry, 101
Newton Bridge, 71
Newton Junction (Newton Abbots), 30
Newton St. Cyres, 28
Newtown, 66
Newtownards, 104
Newtownbutler, 109
Newtownstewart, 108
New Weir, 42
Nial's Grave, 102
Nimpsfield, 13
Ninehead, 24
Northland, 109
Northleach, 12
Norton, 71
Nuneham Courtney, 10
Nunney, 17
Nursing Child, 107

Oakengates, 62
Oak Island, 92
Oakle Street, 37
Oakley Park, 44
Oak Park, 84
O'Brien's Bridge, 88
O'Donoghue's Horse, 92
O'Donoghue's Prison, 91 92
Offa's Dyke, 42, 67
Ogmore Castle, 49
O'Hara Brook, 106
Oldbridge, 100
Oldcastle Head, 52
Old Connaught House, 98
Old Court, 98
Old Trafford, 71
Omagh, 108
Ombersley Park, 59
Onibury, 45
Oran Castle, 97
Oranmore Castle Ruins, 97
Ordsal, 71
Orielton, 53
Ormean, 104
Osterley Park, 2
Oswestry, 65
Oughterard, 98
Oxford, 7
All Souls College, 8
Baliol College, 8
Brazenose College, 8
Christ Church, 8
Corpus Christi, 8
Exeter College, 9
Jesus College, 9
Lincoln College, 9
Magdalene College, 9
Merton College,
New College,
Oriel College,
Pembroke College, 9
Queen's College, 9
St. John's College, 9
Trinity College,
University Buildings 8
University College, 9
Wadham, 9
Worcester College, 9
Oxfordshire, 7
Oystermouth, 48

Paddington Station, 1
Padeswood, 72
Paignton, 31
Painswick 13
Pandy, 43
Pangbourne,
Pantyffynon, 49
Par, 34
Parkgate, 70
Park Hall, 65
Park Place, 4
Park Wells, 43
Passage, 86, 91
Patricroft, 71
Pass of St. Kew, 22
Pater, 52
Patrick's Well, 88
Pelsall, 61
Pembrey, 49
Pembridge, 44
Pembroke Castle,
Pembrokeshire, 50
Penally, 53
Penbury Park, 12, 13
Pencarlenich, 35
Pencoed, 47
Pengwern, 74
Penhros Park, 80
Pen Hale, 35
Penlan Castle, 51
Penllergâr, 48
Penmaen Mawr, 76
Penmon Priory, 78
Penpergwm, 41
Penrhyn Castle, 76, 77
Penrhyn Slate Quarries, 77
Penrice, 37
Pentewan, 34
Pentilie, 32
Pentre, 71
Pentyrch, 46
Penwith, 35
Peterston, 47
Pen-y-groes, 78
Penzance, 35
Perdeswell, 59
Perran Porth, 35
Perran St. George, 35
Perranzabulae, 35
Pershore, 57
Peterston, 47
Picranround, 35
Picton, 53
Picton Castle, 51
Pinhay, 27, 28
Pipers, Th6 3e
Piping Pebworth, 57
Pistyll Rhaiadyr, 68
Pitchford, 64
Plâs Newydd, 72, 77
Plas Pen Myndd, 79
Plas Power, 69
Plâs-y-Pentre, 67
Plealey Road, 64
Plinlimmon, 44, 67
Pluten, 91
Plymouth, 32
Plymouth Breakwater, 32
Plymouth Sound, 33
Plympton, 32
Polgooth Mine, 34
Polwhele, 34
Pontardulais, 48
Pont-ar-Ithon, 41
Pont ar Tynach, 66
Pontesbury, 64
Pont-neath-Vaughan,
Pontnewydd, 41
Pontnewynnydd, 41
Pontrhydyrun, 41
Pontrilas, 43
Pont-y-Cysylltau, 67
Pont-y-Prid, 47
Pontypool, 41
Pontypool Park, 41
Pontypool Road, 41
Pool, 35
Pool Quay, 66
Poorstock, 17
Porkington, 65
Portadown, 101, 102
Portarlington, 86
Port Coon Cave, 108
Port Dinorwic, 78
Port Eliot, 32
Port Fad. 108
Port Gannixy, 107
Porth, 46
Porthall, 108
Portlaw, 86
Portmarnock, 99
Port Moon, 108
Port-na-baw, 107
Port-na-Collian, 107
Port-na-Shania, 107
Port-na-Pleaskin, 107
Port Noffer, 107
Port Reostax, 107
Port-rea-Tobber, 107
Portrush, 106
Portskewet, 41
Portsmouth Arms, 28
Portstewart, 106
Port Talbot, 47
Poul-a-Phonca Fall, 98
Powderham Castle, 26
Powerscourt, 98
Powick, 59
Powis Castle, 66
Poyntz Castle, 51
Poyntzpass, 101
Pradhoe, 64
Pradoe, 65
Prestatyn, 73
Presteign, 44
Priest and his Flock, 107
Priestfield, 54, 62
Priest Leap Pass, 90
Priest's Hole Cave, 108
Prince's End, 62
Puffin Island, 78
Pulpit, The, 108
Purple Mountain, 91, 93, 94, 95
Purthin Waterfalls, 47
Purton, 11
Pwll Dwu, 41
Pwllheli Road, 78
Pyle, 47
Pyrland, 24

Quaker's Yard, 41, 46, 47
Quedgeley House, 13 14
Queen's County, 87
Queen's Ferry, 73
Queenstown, 90
Quinta, 67

Rabbit Island, 91, 92
Radnor, 44
Raglan Road, 41
Raglan Castle, 41, 43
Raheny, 99
Raheny House, 99
Raheny Park, 99
Randalstown, 106
Rathdrum, 98
Rathkeale, 88
Rathlin Island, 107
Rat Island, 52
Reading, 4
Red Bay Castle, 107
Redesdale, 98

Redlynch. 17
Rednal, 65
Redruth, 35
Rendcomb Park, 12
Renshaw, 10
Rendon Park, 12
Resolven, 47
Rhaiadr Mawr, 76
Rhayadr-y-Wennol, 77
Rhayader, 44
Rhayader-Gwy, 40
Rhinog Faur, 67
Rhosili Bay, 48
Rhuddlan, 74
Rhuddlan Castle, 74
Rhug, 68
Rhyl, 74
Richhill, 102
Ringfadroch, 107
Risca, 41
Roch Castle, 51
Rodborough, 13
Rock Ferry, 70
Rock Lane, 70
Rollrich Stones, 55
Ronan Island, 92
Roscom Round Tower, 97
Roscrea, 87
Ross, 14, 37, 59
Ross Bay, 92
Rossbarkie, 92
Ross Castle, 92
Rossett, 69
Ross (Ireland), 85
Ross Island, 92
Rostherne, 71
Rostrevor, 101
Rostrevor Lodge, 101
Rough Island, 92
Round Gurnet Head, 36
Round Oak, 60
Rowed Asted, 14
Rowsedown, 28
Ruabon, 68
Rudford, 14
Rudge, 13
Ruel, 72
Runcorn, 71
Runcorn Gap, 71
Rundlestone, 36
Rush and Lusk, 99
Rush Hall, 61
Rush House, 99
Ruthin, 68, 79
Ruthmore, 90
Ruyton, 65

Saintfield, 104
Sale, 71
Salisbury, 17
Salisbury Hill, 19
Salisbury Plain, 16
Sally Gap, 98
Salruc Pass, 98
Salt Ash, 34
Saltford, 19
Salthill, 81
Saltney, 69, 72
Salt Pans, 107
Saltram, 32
Sandtord, 7
Sandhill, 24
Sandhurst, 14
Sandycroft, 72
Sapperton Park, 12
Scilly Islands, 36
Scorrier Gate, 35
Scratchbury, 16
Seagull Island, 107
Seagull Rock, 107
Seacombe, 70
Sedgemoor, 22
Seisincote, 55
Selattyn, 67
Selmont, 39
Sennen Cove, 36
Shahy Mountains, 90
Shane's Castle, 106
Shangolden, 88
Shankhill, 98
Shannon, The 88
Shapwick, 22
Sheep Island, 52, 107
Sheldon Abbey, 98
Shepton Mallett, 17
Shiffnal, 62
Shinnagh, 91
Shiplake, 4
Shipton, 55
Shobdon Court, 44
Shotover Hill, 10
Shottesbrooke Church, 4
Shottery, 57
Shrewsbury, 63
Shrivenham, 11
Sidmouth, 26, 27
Silchester, 5
Sion Mills, 108
Skelby Park, 48
Skenfrith Castle, 42
Skerries, 99
Skerries Light, 80
Skibbereen, 90
Skower and Skokam Islands, 51
Skyrrid Vawr, 43
Slebech, 53
Slemish Mountain, 107
Sligo, 96
Sloperton, 15
Slough, 2
Snowdon, 67, 68
Soho, 54
Solihull, 54
Soloa Valley, 51
Somerset, 17
Somerton, 53
Somerville, 100
Sonning, 5
Southall, 2
Southam, 14
Southam Road, 53
South Court Mill, 10
South Leigh, 10
South Molton Road, 28
South Newton, 16
Spa of Ballyspellan 75
Sparkford, 17
Spetchley Park, 59
Spike Island, 91
Spital, 70
Springfield, 61
St. Agnes, 34
St. Agnes Beacon, 35
St. Asaph, 74
St. Austell, 34
St. Bride's Bay, 51, 52
St. Brival's, 42
St. Budeaux, 32
St. Burgan's Church, 36
St. Clears, 50
St. Cyres, 28
St. David's, 51
St. Devereux, 43
St Fagan's, 47
St. Germans, 34
St. Gwan's Head, 52
St. Ives Road, 35
St. Johnston, 108
St. Just, 37
St. Keverne, 37
St. Kevin's Bed, 98
St. Kitt's Hill, 32
St. Lawrence, 22
St. Leven, 36
St. Martin's, 67
St. Michael's Mount, 35
St. Thomas, 29
St. Vincent's Rocks, 20
Stackpole Head, 52
Stackpole Park, 52
Stack Rock, 108
Stag Island, 92
Stancomb Cross, 13
Standish House, 13
Stanlow Point, 70
Stapleford, 16
Stapleton, 21
Star Cross, 26, 29
Steeple Langford, 16
Steventon, 11
Stillorgan, 98
Stillorgan House, 98
Stillorgan Park, 98
Stoadley Chapel, 10
Stockton House, 16
Stoke, 15
Stoke Edith Park, 39
Stoke Park, 3
Stone House, 13
Stonesfield, 10
Stoocans, 107
Stow-on-the-Wold, 55
Strabane, 108
Strabane Glen, 108
Stradkelly, 107
Stratton, 26
Stratford-upon-Avon, 55
Stretford, 71
Stroud, 11, 12, 13
Studgrive, 14
Sufton Court, 39
Sugar Loaf, 43, 83, 98
Sugwas, 39
Sullivan's Cascade, 92
Summer Hill, 69
Sundorne Castle, 64
Sutton, 70
Swakeley's, 2
Swanslake Bay, 52
Swansea, 48
Swan Village, 54
Swords, 83
Swindon Junction, 11
Sydenham (Ireland), 105
Symond's Yat, 42

Taff's Well, 46
Talacre, 73
Talargoch Lead Mines, 74
Talley Road, 49
Tanat, Vale of, 66
Tanderagee, 101
Tanderagee Castle, 101
Taplow, 3
Tarbert, 88
Tatton Park, 71
Taunton 24
Tedsmore Hall, 65
Teignmouth, 26, 29
Templemore, 87
Tenbury, 44
Tenby, 49, 50
Tetbury, 12
Thancks, 32
Theale, 5
Thelwall, 71
Thomastown, 85
Thornfield, 105
Thorn Island, 52
Thurles, 87
Tillysburn, 105
Timperley, 71
Tinnahinch, 98
Tintern Abbey, 39, 42
Tintern Abbey (Ireland) 86
Tipperary, 87
Tipton, 62
Titley, 44
Tiverton, 19, 25
Tiverton Junction, 25
Tol Peden Penwith, 36
Tomies, 91, 93, 94
Toome, 106
Topsham, 26
Tor Abbey, Ruins of, 30
Tor Point, 107
Torc, 91, 93, 94, 96
Torquay, 26, 30
Torr 30
Totness, 31
Towednach, 36
Towyn, 66

Trafford Hall, 70
Trafford Park, 71
Tralee, 88, 95
Tram Inn, 43
Tramore, 85
Treaman, 46
Treborth, 78
Tredegar, 41
Trefnant, 75
Trelech Cross, 42
Treeren Dinas, 36
Treforest, 46
Trefusis, 35
Treganna Castle, 35
Trelissich, 35
Trellowyn, 53
Trengwainton, 36
Treowen, 42
Trereiffe, 36
Trevalyn Hall, 69
Trevena Mine, 36
Trew, 102
Trewarthenich, 35
Trifaen, 77
Trillick, 108
Troedyrhiew, 46
Trooper's Lane, 105
Trosten Mountain, 107
Trowbridge, 15
Troy House, 42
Truro, 34
Tuam, 97
Tuffley Court, 13
Tullamore, 86
Tullaroan, 85
Tully Castle, 109
Tunnel Rock, 107
Turrey, 99
Tutbury Castle, 61, 62
Twins, The, 108
Twll Dû, 77
Twyford, 4
Twyford Abbey,
Ty Croes, 80
Tydee, 41
Tyrawley, 98
Tyrone, 108

Uffington Castle, 5, 11
Umberleigh, 28
Upton 14, 59
Upton (Ireland), 91
Upton Castle, 53
Upton Magna, 62
Ush Hill Tower, 89
Usk, 41
Uxbridge, 2

Vaenol, 77
Vale of Avoca, 98
Vale of the White Horse, 11
Vale of Clwyd, 74
Vale of Llangollen, 67
Vale of Mawddach, 67
Valle Crucis, 67
Valley, 80
Vicar's Cairn, 102
Victoria, 41
Victoria Bridge, 108

Wacnoer, 77
Walcot, 62
Walford, 65
Wallingford, 6
Wallingford Road, 6
Wallowarren, 37
Wallscourt, 88
Walsall, 61
Walton Junction, 71
Walwin Castle, 51
Wanstrow, 17
Wantage, 5, 11
Wapley, 44
Wargrave, 4
Warminster, 16
Warrenpoint, 101
Warrington, 71, 72
Warwick, 53
Watchet, 23, 24
Water Eaton, 10
Waterfall, 90
Waterford, 85
Watt's Dyke, 65,
Wednesbury, 54, 61
Weir's Snoot, 107
Welcombe, 57
Wellington, 24, 62
Wells 23
Welshpool, 66
Wenvoe Castle, 46
Westbury, 15, 21
Westbury - upon - Severn 37
West Bromwich, 54
West Gwans, 52
West Drayton, 2
West Hall, 72
West Malvern, 51
Weston Downs, 19
Weston Park, 95
Weston Point, 71
Weston Super Mare, 22
Westport, 98
Westwood Park, 59
Whaddon, 14
Wheal Alfred, 35
Wheal Darlington Mine, 36
Wheal Kitty, 35
Wheal Leisure, 35
Wheal Towan, 35
Wheal Vor, 36
Wheatsheaf, 69
Whitcomb Park, 13
Whitchurch, 6
Whiddy, 95
White Abbey, 105
White Castle, 42
White Horse Hill, 5
White Rocks, 108
Whitland, 50
Whitlands, 27, 28
Whitsand Bay, 36
Whittington, 65
Whittington Castle Ruins, 65
Wichnor Park, 61
Wick, 22
Wicklow, 98
Wicklow Castle, 98
Wicklow Gap, 98
Wigmore, 45
Wiley, 16
Willington, 62
Wilmcote, 53
Wilton, 16
Wilton Woodford, 16
Wiltshire, 11
Wincanton, 17
Windmill Hill, 52
Windsor, 3
Wishford, 16
Witham, 17
Witham Park, 17
Withycombe, 27
Witney, 10
Woburn Green, 3
Wokey Cavern, 22
Wokingham, 5
Wolf Rock, 35
Wolverhampton, 54, 62
Wonastow, 42
Woodbury Road, 26
Woodchester, 13
Wood Eaton, 10
Wooden Bridge, 98
Woodhouse, 65
Woodlands, 84, 95
Woodspring Priory, Ruins of 22
Woodstock, 10
Woodstock Park, 10
Woodstock Road, 53
Wooferton, 44
Woolaston, 40
Woolcombe House, 17
Woolhampton, 5
Woolhampton House, 5
Wooten, 14
Wootton Basset, 14
Worcester, 57
Worle, 22
Worle Hill, 22
Worms Head, 48, 50, 52
Wraxhall House, 17
Wrekin, 64
Wrexham, 68
Wychand Forest, 10
Wychwood Forest, 5
Wycombe, 3
Wye, The 40, 42, 44
Wyndcliffe, 39, 42
Wynnstay, 68, 69
Wytham, 10
Wythenshawe Hall, 71

Yarnbury Castle, 16
Yatton, 21
Yatton Court, 44
Yealmpton, 32
Yeovil, 17, 23
Yetminster, 17
Y-Lliwed, 78
Youghal, 90
Ystrad, 46

Zennor, 36

BRADSHAW'S DESCRIPTIVE RAILWAY HAND-BOOK

OF

GREAT BRITAIN AND IRELAND.

SECTION II.

NOTE.—Shunts, or Marks thus , or thus , introduced into the following pages are intended to show the point at which a Branch deviates from the Main Line. Its position to the right or left hand of the Column indicates the right or left hand of the railway on which the deviation takes place. The termination of the Branch is known by the Shunt being reversed.

GREAT WESTERN RAILWAY.

London to Slough.

THE *Metropolitan Terminus* of the Great Western Railway is situated on the western side of the Paddington Canal, in a line with Praed-street, Paddington, at the north-west extremity of London, and at a short distance from the northern avenues to Hyde Park, thus affording an easy access to and from all parts of town. Omnibuses leave the City one hour before the departure of each train, and call at all the booking-offices on their way, which, in addition to the cabs, leave the passenger at no loss for a prompt conveyance to this Terminus—one of the largest and most commodious stations in London. Its external appearance is not very remarkable,—but the booking-offices are convenient, the waiting-rooms comfortable, the platforms, for the arrival and departure trains, spacious enough to accommodate the largest number of excursionists ever accumulated,—and the vast area embraced by the immense roofs by which the station is covered, impart to the mind of the traveller the impression that he is about to start by the railway of a first-rate company.

It is the joint work of Messrs. Brunel and M. D. Wyatt, the former having arranged the general plan, engineering, and business portion; the latter the architectural details in every department. The principle adopted by them, was to avoid any recurrence to existing styles and to make the experiment of designing everything in accordance with the structural purpose or nature of the materials employed—iron and cement. The office buildings are 580 feet long, varying from thirty to forty in width. The departments for directing and managing the affairs of the Company are carried on in the upper portion of the building, and those in connection with the traffic to and from the station in the lower part.

The space occupied by the platforms and lines of railway under the curved roofing is 700 feet long, and 240 feet six inches wide, and contains four platforms and ten lines of railway. The two platforms on the departure side of the station are respectively twenty-seven feet and twenty-four feet six inches wide; and the other two, on the arrival side, are twenty-one feet and forty-seven inches. The latter is of stone. The roofing over the above space is divided into three longtitudinal openings, with two transepts, each fifty feet wide at one-third and two-thirds of the length, the length of which are each 700 feet, and their respective widths seventy feet, 102 feet six inches, and sixty-eight feet. The central half of the curved roofs is glazed, and the other portion is covered with corrugated galvanized iron. The work was done by Messrs. Fox, Henderson, and Co.

On the departure of the train, it threads the sinuosities of the station at an easy rate, and we have time to notice the metamorphosis that has taken place in the environs of the line; walls have become green embankments, embankments diminished into hedges, and hedges grown into avenues of trees, waving a leafy adieu as we are carried past. The increasing velocity of the train now conveys us rapidly into the suburbs of the metropolis—past Kensa

Green Cemetery on the right, Wormwood Scrubbs on the left, and a transient glimpse is obtained of the London and North-Western Railway winding its course towards the midland counties.

The route at first lies through the Thames Valley, then, after passing the elevated plains to the north of Marborough Downs, it gradually descends down into the fertile and picturesque valley of the Avon. Emerging from a slight excavation, we come to an embankment crossing Old Oak Common so named from its having been the site of a thick forest of oaks. The village of Acton, which lies to the left is linked to the metropolis by one almost uninterrupted line of ouses, through which the North-Western Junction Railway passes, connecting the North-Western Railway with those of the South-Western.

EALING STATION. — *Gunnersbury Park*, Baron Rothschild; *Castlebear Hill*, and *Twyford Abbey*, close by. Thence passing the pretty hamlet of *Drayton Green*, we stop at

HANWELL.

Distance from station, ¼ mile.

A telegraph station.

MONEY ORDER OFFICE at Southall.

From this station the line passes in a gentle curve over the Wharncliffe Viaduct, a massive and elegant structure, which commands extensive views on both sides. The Uxbridge road is seen winding beneath, and afar off may be discerned, outlined in the blue distance, the undulating range of Surrey hills, with the rich, leafy, loftiness of Richmond Hill and Park occasionally intervening. In the foreground will be noticed *Osterley Park*, the seat of the Earl of Jersey; and the most interesting object in the landscape is Hanwell Asylum, generously devoted to the reception of the indigent insane.

SOUTHALL.

A telegraph station.

HOTEL.—Red Lion.

MARKET DAY.—Wednesday.

At this station a short branch, 3¾ miles, turns off to the left, by which a connection with the South Western is formed at

Brentford, see page 65, Sec. I.

Crossing the Paddington and Grand Junction Canal, we pass alternately through excavation and embankment on to

WEST DRAYTON.

Distance from station, ¼ mile.

A telegraph station.

HOTELS.—Crown; King's Head; De Burgh Arms.

MONEY ORDER OFFICE at Uxbridge.

Here, in the early mornings of summer and golden evenings of autumn, descends many a brother of the rod and line, who, in the confluence of the Colne and Crane, finds a prolific source of pleasure from his favourite pastime.

We now cross the western boundary of Middlesex, and then pass over a small corner of Buckinghamshire, between West Drayton and Maidenhead, into the county of Berks.

UXBRIDGE (Branch).

POPULATION, 3,236.

Telegraph station at West Drayton, 2 miles.

HOTELS.—Chequers; King's Arms.

MARKET DAY.—Thursday (Corn).

FAIRS.—25th March, 31st July, 29th September, 11th October.

BANKERS.—Hull, Smith & Co.; Branch of London and County Joint Stock.

The inhabitants are principally engaged in the corn trade, some in agricultural tool making, and others in making windows, chairs, bricks, &c. Is interesting historically as the place where King Charles I. tried to negotiate with Parliament in 1645. It was also occupied by Oliver Cromwell, in 1647—the Crown Inn replacing the old one where he held his head quarters.

In the vicinity are *Swakeley's* (1½ mile), and a short walk beyond is *Harefield*, frequently visited by Milton; and crossing the Colne to *Chalfont St. Giles*, may be seen the house where the blind bard wrote his "Paradise Regained," —returning by *Denham*, so well described by Davy, in his "Salmonia."

Soon after leaving West Drayton we cross the river Colne and its branches, with *Hunt's Moor Park*, and the beautifully sequestered village of Iver (which, alike to artist or antiquary, will be found replete with objects of interest and attraction), on the right, and enter

BUCKINGHAMSHIRE,

Arriving at the station at

LANGLEY.

To the right, at a short distance, is *Langley Park*. A few minutes more brings us to

SLOUGH.

A telegraph station.

HOTEL.—Crown.

MARKET DAY.—Thursday.

After the bustle incident to the arrival of fresh passengers, and the departure of others, has in some degree subsided, it will be found that the arrangements for the comfort and convenience of those alighting at this station are equal, if not superior, to those of any other line.

A magnificent hotel, for aristocratic visitors, here

so frequently found, is within a few minutes' walk, and numerous taverns, less ornamental, and, consequently, less expensive, are in the immediate neighbourhood.

Slough is now chiefly noticeable as the station or medium of communication, by the branch railway, to Eton and Windsor. It is two and a half miles in length, and passes Eton College, near the Thames.

WINDSOR BRANCH.

Slough to Windsor.

ETON.

ETON is celebrated for its college, founded in 1440, by Henry VI., to which resort annually about 400 students, chiefly the sons of noble and opulent families. The triennial celebration of *Eton Montem* on Salt Hill, but now discontinued, the "salt," or money, given to the captain of the school, for his support at the University, frequently realising nearly a thousand pounds. Passing over a neat bridge, which connects Eton with Windsor, the visitor will enter the town, associated with historical and literary reminiscences of the highest interest. We give a description of Windsor Castle in Section I., page 68.

The scenery around Windsor is remarkable for its sylvan beauty; and the weary citizen, who desires to enjoy a summer holiday, cannot do better than procure an admission ticket to Windsor Castle from the printsellers, Messrs. Colnaghi, of Pall Mall, and then make his way to the Great Western Railway, in time for an early train. Within the next three hours he may see all the regal splendours of the palatial halls of Windsor; and then, having refreshed the inward man at any of the "hostelries" which abound in that town, he may stroll forth into the country, and contrast the quiet and enduring charms of nature with the more glittering productions of art, with which wealth and power surround themselves. He may walk in the shades of the forest, sung by Pope; he may saunter over Datchet Mead, immortalised by Shakspeare, in his story of Jack Falstaff and the buck-basket; or he may prolong his stroll to the quiet village of Horton, where Milton lived, and sang its rural charms in the immortal rhymes of "L'Allegro" and "Il Penseroso."

Great Western Main Line continued.

Slough to Maidenhead.

Between the lofty and luxuriant foliage of Stoke Park, about two miles to the right of Slough, may be descried, modestly peering through the surrounding trees, the spire of Stoke Pogis Church, the scene of Gray's "Elegy," and his final resting place. As the train proceeds, the broad and verdant fields spread out on each side of us in all the pride of luxuriant vegetation.

Burnham Village is close by, situate in the midst of picturesque woodland scenery, popularised by the adventures of Albert Smith's Mr. Ledbury.

MAIDENHEAD.

POPULATION, 3,607.

Distance from station, 1½ mile.

A telegraph station.

HOTELS.—White Hart; Bear.

MARKET DAY.—Wednesday.

FAIRS.—Whit Wednesday, September 29th, and November 30th.

MONEY ORDER OFFICE.

BANKERS.—Stephens, Blandy, & Co.

WYCOMBE BRANCH.

Maidenhead to Wycombe.

From Maidenhead we pass TAPLOW, COOKHAM, MARLOW ROAD, WOBURN GREEN, and LOUDWATER, stations of no great importance, and arrive at

HIGH WYCOMBE.

Telegraph station at Maidenhead, 11¾ miles.

HOTEL.—Red Lion.

MARKET DAY.—Friday.

FAIRS.—Monday before New Michaelmas.

BANKERS.—London and County Banking Co.

WYCOMBE is a borough in Buckinghamshire on the Wyck. In the vicinity are many corn and paper mills.

BERKSHIRE.

THIS county is bounded by the counties of Oxford and Buckingham on the north, on the east by Surrey, on the south by Hampshire, and on the west by Wiltshire. A range of chalk hills, entering this county from Oxfordshire, crosses it in a westerly direction, and forms the southern boundary of the Vale of the White Horse. Independent of this range of hills, the county is characterised by gentle eminences and vallies, having much fertile land, and abounding with picturesque and beautiful scenery.

Reading is the county town of Berkshire, and Windsor Castle its greatest ornament.

Great Western Main Line continued.

Maidenhead to Reading.

Upon leaving the station the railway soon spans, by a bridge of ten arches, the river Thames, which here glides through a flat, but most charming country. Having crossed the Windsor road, and diverged gradually to the southward we suddenly dip into an excavation of considerable depth; the characteristic chalky sides of which are replete with geological interest. This cutting, which continues for upwards of five miles, completely shuts out the surrounding country; but coming suddenly upon the Ruscombe embankment, we are amply repaid by a magnificent expanse of landscape. Hill and dale, dotted with elegant villas and noble mansions, woodland and water scenery, together with wide far-stretching meadow and corn-land, follow each other in varied succession to the very verge of the horizon. We have scarcely had time, however, to feast our vision with this delightful prospect, before we are again buried in a cutting, though of shorter duration, and through this we reach the station at

TWYFORD (Junction).

A telegraph station.

HOTELS.—Station Hotel; King's Arms.

In the neighbourhood are *Stanlake* (1 mile). *Shottesbrooke Church* ($2\frac{1}{2}$ miles), a beautiful miniature cross, with a tall tower and spire, formerly attached to an ancient college here. A short line hence branches off to Henley-upon-Thames, passing by *Wargrave*.

HENLEY BRANCH.

SHIPLAKE station.

HENLEY.

MARKET DAY.—Thursday.

It is delightfully situated on a sloping bank of the Thames, (over which there is a handsome stone bridge of five arches, by Sir R. Taylor, connecting the counties of Oxford and Berks) amid extensive beech woods. The church has a fine tower, and some interesting decorated work. There is a handsome town hall, on pillars, forming a market piazza. The musical divine, Dean Aldrich, was rector here, and bequeathed his library for the use of the inhabitants paying church rates. Close by are *Park Place*, *Bolney Court*, *Harpsden Court*, and *Culham Court* (two miles), near which are the remains of *Medmenham Abbey*, surrounded by sheltering groves, a fit place for the abode of sleek friars, who might have plenty of fish for Lenten days. This place, however, was made famous in the last century for the whim of Lord le Despenser, who fitted the old ruin up after its original style, and created much scandal in mocking religion, and in the repetitions of debaucheries to which that of the monks of old were pious orgies.

The *Chiltern Hills* behind rise to 820 feet at Nettlebed, and 760 at Nuffield; they give name to a nominal office in the Chancellor of the Exchequer's gift, by which a member of parliament is enabled in a formal manner to vacate his seat.

Great Western Main Line continued.

Within a few minutes after quitting the station, we emerge from the excavation, and cross, on an embankment, the river Loddon. From this we enter into another cutting of great depth conducting us to an embankment which affords a pleasing view of the county bordering on the woody lands of Oxfordshire. Crossing, on a level embankment, the river Kennet, we soon after reach the station at

READING.

A telegraph station.

HOTEL.—George.

MARKET DAYS.—Wednesday and Saturday.

FAIRS.—Feb. 2nd, May 1st, July 25th, & Sept. 21st.

BANKERS.—Branch of London and County Bank. Stephens and Co.; J. and C. Simonds and Co.

READING is situated on two small eminences, whose gentle declivities fall into a pleasant vale, through which the branches of the Kennet flow till they unite with the Thames at the extremity of the town. The surrounding country is agreeably diversified with an intermixture of hill and dale, wood and water, enlivened with a number of elegant seats. The prospect from the Forbury, a beautiful outwork on the north-east side of the town is very extensive, commanding a fine view over a considerable portion of Oxfordshire.

This old town is in a fertile and well-watered part of Berkshire, at the junction of the Thames and Kennet. It returns two members to parliament, and has a population of 21,456. The manor belongs to the corporation. A large and important mitred abbey, founded by Henry I. in 1125, to atone for putting out his brother Robert Curthose's eyes frequently attracted the court here down to 1540, when that vigorous defender of the faith, Henry VIII., hung the last abbot for refusing to account for his stewardship. Henry I. was buried in it. A Norman gate and part of the outer flint walls (8 feet thick) are left. The latter took in a circuit of half a mile. Reading was inhabited by the Saxons many years before the invasion of the Danes; and it appears that it had two castles, one of which probably stood on the spot where the abbey was founded. In 1263 Henry III. held a parliament here, and another was adjourned hither in 1453. The *County Gaol* occupies the best part of the abbey site. Some old gable buildings and ancient looking streets are yet seen at Reading; but a handsome new town has sprung up round Eldon Road and Square, Queen's Road, &c., on the south east side of the Kennet. St. Lawrence's church, near the Forbury, has a chequered flint tower, and remnants of antiquity, with a monument to Dr. Valpy. St. Mary's, in St. Mary's Butts, was first built in the 12th century, but rebuilt in 1550 with materials from the abbey. Bishop Lloyd was vicar here; as was also the present Dean Milman. There was a nunnery attached to it. St. Giles's, in Bridge Street, has been lately restored. It suffered in the long siege of 1642, when Colonel Ashton held the town against Essex.

The *Town Hall* was built 1785, and contains various portraits, among which are those of Queen Elizabeth, Sir T. White, a native, and the founder of St. John's College, Oxford, and that strange compound of intellectual vigour, superstition, and bigoted meanness, Archbishop *Laud*, born at Reading, 1573. He, in common with Merrick, the poet, Addington, the premier, and Lord Chancellor Phipps, all Reading men, was educated in the Grammar School, formerly held beneath the Town Hall, originally founded 1486. Laud bequeathed property worth about £500 a year to his native town. Henry VII 's charter, with his illuminated portrait, is kept in the Town Hall. A portrait of the late Mr. Justice Talfourd has recently been presented by his widow.

A new cattle market has been built close to the railway station. The principal manufactures of this place are canvas, ribbons, and pins; and great quantities of malt, flour, and timber are sent hence to London. An ancient factory was built by Kendrick, a clothier, when Reading was an important clothing town.

Numerous excursions may be made from this town, as there is scarcely a corner of Berkshire which does not deserve a visit; it is full of beech woods, and beautiful country lanes and alleys. The Kennet, Thames, &c., are bordered by luxuriant pasture, and the healthy downs on the west offer a panorama of delightful prospects. To the west of Reading are the Chiltern Hills, which, like the others, are covered with sheep walks. *Maiden Early* (2 miles) was the seat of Lord Stowell. *Sonning* was once the seat of a bishoprick. *Bear Wood*, J. Walter, Esq., M.P., the proprietor of the *Times* newspaper. *Billingbear* is the seat of Lord Braybrooke, editor of "Pepys' Memoirs." *Wokingham* (6 miles) on the Roman road to Silchester, has an old church, and is within the bounds of Windsor Forest. Towards Windsor is Binfield and its beech woods, in which Pope used to ramble. Grundy cheese (like Stilton) is made here. At *Silchester*, just over the Hampshire side, are pieces of the walls of a Roman city, the *Calleva Attrebatum*. *Englefeld*, the Saxon *Englafelda*, where the Danes were once defeated, has one of those large parks, so common in Berkshire, and an epitaph by Dryden on the defender of Basing House. *Newbury*, a great corn town on the Kennet, once noted for its cloth manufactures, especially when Jack of Newbury (not a fish, as the sign might lead one to think) led his company of stout tailors—all proper men—to the famous battle of Flodden Field. Newbury was a new town, founded upon the decay of *Spinœ*, a Roman station in the neighbourhood. Further up the river is *Hungerford*, giving name to a celebrated family. Hence a visit may be paid to *Marlborough*, on the Wiltshire Downs, where a Collegiate School is planted; and near which (at Tisbury), *Jay*, of Bath, was born, 1769. He was placed in the academy of the excellent Cornelius Winter (whom Bishop Jebb styles a "celestial creature") at Marlboro', and went out before he was sixteen to preach to the poor despised rustics. "Our prudent tutor taught us not to rail or abuse, but simply to preach the gospel, and to avoid the offence of *folly*, when we could not avoid that of the cross." Three years after he commenced his long career at Bath. From Hungerford you may follow the Berkshire Downs round to Reading, past Lambourn, Ashdown (where Alfred beat the Danes), Uffington Castle, Wayland Smith's Stone, (which Scott introduces in Kenilworth), the White Horse Hill (893 feet high, with the figure of a galloping horse, 370 feet long, cut in the chalk). *Wantage*, where the great Alfred was born in 849, and his jubilee kept in 1849, along Ickleton Street (a Roman way on the ridge) to East Ilsley (noted for its great sheep fairs), and so to Reading, a strip of about 40 or 45 miles, never to be forgotten by a light-heeled pedestrian. On the Oxfordshire side of the Thames are *Caversham*, W. Crawshay, Esq., which has been rebuilt two or three times since it was visited by Elizabeth and Charles I.

BASINGSTOKE BRANCH.

Reading to Basingstoke.

This line passes through a very pretty level country, surrounded by numerous parks, and handsome seats and mansions.

MORTIMER (Stratfield).

Telegraph station at Reading, $7\frac{1}{4}$ miles.
MONEY ORDER OFFICE at Reading.

BASINGSTOKE,

(For further particulars see Section I., page 76)
is delightfully situated in a well wooded part of Hampshire, and derives considerable advantage from the junction of several roads which meet together at this town. It has a handsome market-house and sessions court. On an eminence at the northern extremity of the town are the ruins of an elegant chapel, which possessed great architectural beauty, but which has been suffered to fall into ruins.

HUNGERFORD BRANCH.

Reading to Newbury and Hungerford.

THEALE.

Distance from station, $\frac{1}{2}$ mile.
Telegraph station at Reading, $5\frac{1}{4}$ miles.

ALDERMASTON.

Distance from station, 2 miles.
Telegraph station at Reading, $8\frac{3}{4}$ miles.
MONEY ORDER OFFICE at Theale.
Aldermaston Park, D. H. D. Burr, Esq., situated $1\frac{1}{2}$ mile from here.

WOOLHAMPTON.

Telegraph station at Reading, $10\frac{3}{4}$ miles.
MONEY ORDER OFFICE at Theale.
Woolhampton House, Viscount Falmouth.
On passing THATCHAM, we arrive at

NEWBURY.

POPULATION, 6,574.
Telegraph station at Reading, 17 miles.
HOTELS.—White Hart, Jack of Newbury.
MARKET DAY.—Thursday.
FAIRS.—Holy Thursday, July 5th, September 4th, and November 6th.
MAILS. — Two arrivals and departures, daily, between London and Newbury.

BANKERS.—Branch of the London and County Bank; Bunny and Slocock.

This town is situated in a fertile plain in the county of Berks, watered by the Kennet, which crosses the town near the centre. The principal streets in it are disposed nearly in the shape of the Roman Y, the angles branching off from the market place, and the foot of the latter being formed by the village of Speenhamland; they are spacious and well paved. The church is a plain Gothic stone edifice, which, with the tower, was built at the expense of John Winchcombe, generally called "Jack of Newbury." This town was formerly celebrated for its extensive manufactories of woollen cloth, when the above Winchcombe was reputed the greatest clothier in England; but at present scarcely anything but serge is made. It has a considerable traffic in malt by the Kennet and Avon Canal.

The station of KINTBURY is soon reached, and we pass on to

HUNGERFORD.

Telegraph station at Reading, 25¾ miles.

HOTEL.—Black Bear.

OMNIBUSES to Lavington, *via* Great Bedwin, Burbage, Pewsey, &c., fare, 3s.; to Marlborough, 4s. and 2s. 6d.; to Devizes, 10s. and 6s.

MARKET DAY.—Wednesday. FAIRS.—Last Wednesday in April and Sept., and first Wednesday in Oct.

BANKERS.—Branch of the London and County Bank; W. Tanner and Co.

HUNGERFORD is a market town, which stands partly in the county of Berks, and partly in that of Wilts. The Kennet flows past this town, which opens a communication with the river Thames on the east, and the Avon and Bristol Channel on the west. The town principally consists of one long main street, with a few smaller ones branching from it. In the centre stands the market house, over which there is a large room for public business, and here is still preserved the Hungerford Horn, presented to the corporate body by John of Gaunt. It is made of brass, and is blown every Horn Tuesday to assemble the inhabitants for the election of the town constable.

Great Western Main Line continued. Reading to Didcot.

Passing slowly from the station at a pace that affords us a pleasing bird's eye view of the town, we are carried forward on the same level embankment, and crossing the valley of the Thames soon reach the Roebuck excavation. An embankment, followed by a brief though deep cutting, through the grounds of Purley Park, gives us some charming prospects on the Oxfordshire side, with a mass of woodland scenery scattered over the undulating ground, and cresting even the high summits of the Mapledurham hills beyond.

PANGBOURNE.

A telegraph station.

This place is a very ancient one. Roman remains have been discovered. It is connected with *Whitchurch* on the opposite side of the Thames by a wooden bridge.

Soon after leaving the station the railway takes a north-westerly direction, and at the village of *Basildon*, crossing a viaduct over the Thames, leaves behind it the county of Berks, and enters that of Oxford. Pursuing this northerly direction for a short distance, on the borders of the two counties, we pass a deep cutting, whence, crossing on an embankment the river Thames for the last time, we reach the station of

GORING.—Here are still visible the remains of a Nunnery for Augustines, founded in the reign of Henry II.

WALLINGFORD ROAD station.

WALLINGFORD.

POPULATION, 8,064.

Distance from station, 3 miles.

A telegraph station.

HOTEL.—Lamb.

MARKET DAYS.—Tuesday and Friday.

FAIRS.—Tuesday before Easter, June 24th, September 29th, and December 17th.

BANKERS.—The London and County Bank.

WALLINGFORD, to which the station affords easy access, is an ancient and somewhat picturesque town, agreeably situated on the banks of the venerable Thames, and includes among its "lions" the remains of a formidable castle. The churches of St. Leonard's and St. Mary are of great antiquity. St. Peter's, a modern edifice, has a tower of very peculiar construction. A massive stone bridge, with nineteen arches, spans the river. It has a considerable trade in corn and malt.

On leaving the station the railway returns into the county of Berks, and the country assumes a more agricultural and less romantic aspect than that which we had previously traversed. Alternately dipping into excavation, and flitting over embankment, we are carried across Hagbourne Marsh, and passing over the Wantage and Wallingford road, we arrive at

DIDCOT (Junction).

A telegraph station.

MONEY ORDER OFFICE at Wallingford.

OXFORD BRANCH.—Didcot to Oxford.

After passing a small and uninteresting village called Appleford, we come to a lofty embankment, from which some expansive and diversified views of the surrounding country are obtained. One mile further is the station of

CULHAM (Junction).

Distance from station, 2 miles.

A telegraph station.

MONEY ORDER OFFICE at Abingdon.

ABINGDON (Branch).

HOTELS.—Crown and Thistle; Queen's Arms.

MARKET DAYS.—Monday and Friday.

FAIRS.—First Monday in Lent, May 6th, June 20th, August 5th, September 19th, Monday before Old Michaelmas Day, Monday after October 12th, and December 11th, for cattle and horses.

RACES in September.

A small parliamentary town in *Berks*, with about 6,000 inhabitants, returning one member. It is situated at the junction of the Wiltshire and Berkshire canal on the Thames, and the mouth of the river Ock, occupying a very favourable situation on the borders of Berkshire. The town consists of several wide streets, converging in a spacious area, where the markets are held every Monday and Friday. It takes its present name from a rich mitred abbey which was founded by the Saxon kings. Before that, it was called *Seukestram* or *Shovesham.* Some traces of the abbey are seen at a brewery. Leland, who travelled the country as historiographer to Henry VIII., states that it was then a magnificent building. Geoffrey, of Monmouth, died abbot here, 1417. Henry I., called Beauclerc, for his learning, was sent to this abbey by his father the Conqueror, to be educated.

The few buildings worth notice are St. Nicholas's old church, a market house and county hall, of ashlar stone, the county bridewell, a grammar school founded in the 16th century, and Christ's hospital, an old cloistered building of the same date, founded by Sir John Mason, a native, and statesman of James I.'s age. Malting and sack-making are the chief employments. In Leland's time it "stondeth by clothing," like many other agricultural towns, from which this important branch of manufacture has fled to the north, where machinery, coal, and other conveniences are more abundant.

OXFORDSHIRE.

THIS rich midland county takes its name from the city of Oxford, and contains 481,280 acres, divided into 14 hundreds, and 219 parishes, and possesses one city, and twelve market towns. It is an inland county, bounded on the east by Buckinghamshire, on the west by Gloucestershire. On the south-south-west and south-east its limits unite with those of Berkshire. The south-east part is hilly and woody, having a continuation of the Chiltern hills running through it; the north-west is also elevated and stony; and the middle is, in general, a rich country, watered by numerous streams, running from north to south, and terminating in the Thames. Of these the most considerable are, the Windrush, Evenlode, Cherwell, and Thame. The produce of this county is chiefly like that of most midland farming counties: much butter and cheese are made, and numerous calves are reared and fed for the London markets.

About three miles beyond Culham, we come in sight of Bagley Wood, seen to the left of the line, and soon after the little church of Sandford is observed peering through the trees to the right, and the Pauper Lunatic Asylum, a considerable pile of buildings, at Littlemore. A brief view of hills, a rapid glimpse of vallies, veined with pleasant streams, and studded with picturesque masses of woodland, a prolonged whistle from the engine, and a sudden whirl under a lofty, elegant portico, and we are at

OXFORD,

POPULATION, 27,843.

Distance from station, 1 mile.

A telegraph station.

HOTELS.—The Roe Buck, Corn Market Street; the Star, and Angel.

FAIRS.—May 2nd, Monday after St. Giles, Sept. 1st, and Thursday before New Michaelmas.

MAILS.—Two arrivals and departures, daily, between London and Oxford.

BANKERS.—Branch of the London and County Bank; Thompson and Parsons, (Old Bank); W. W. and J. Undershell; Bucks and Oxon, Union Bank.

MONEY ORDER OFFICE.

OXFORD is the capital of the rich midland county of the same name, and one of the most ancient cities of England. It has for ages been celebrated for its university, which, in extent, number of its colleges, wealth of endowments, and architectural beauty, stands unrivalled by any similar institution in Europe; in fact, the period of its existence as a seminary for learning is supposed to date anterior to the time of Alfred. It is situated on a gentle eminence in a rich valley between the rivers Cherwell and Isis, and is surrounded by highly cultivated scenery—the prospect being bounded by an amphitheatre of hills. From the neighbouring heights the city presents a very imposing appearance, from the number and variety of its spires, domes, and public edifices; while these structures, from their magnitude and splendid architecture, give it on a near approach an air of great magnificence. The rivers are crossed by bridges. This city was distinguished by its attachment to the unfortunate Charles I., who here held his court during the whole civil war.

The High street extends east and west, under different names, the whole length of the city. From Carfax Church it is crossed, at right angles, by St. Giles, the other principal street; and from these two branch off nearly every other street in the city. The High street of Oxford is justly considered the finest in England, from its length and breadth, the number and elegance of its public buildings, and its remarkable curvature, which, from continually presenting new combinations of magnificent objects to the eye, produces an uncommonly striking effect. There are also several other handsome streets of recent creation. Oxford has long been famous for good sausages and brawn. The "Crown" is a small inn, entered from the Corn Market by a gateway

This inn was kept by the mother of Davenant, and was the resort of Shakspeare in his journies from London to Stratford-on-Avon.

"Ye fretted pinnacles, ye fanes sublime,
Ye towers that wear the mossy vest of time ;
Ye massy piles of old munificence,
At once the pride of learning and defence ;
Ye cloisters pale, that, lengthening to the sight,
To contemplation, step by step, invite ;
* * * *
Ye temples dim, where pious duty pays
Her holy hymns of everlasting praise—
* * * *
Hail ! Oxford, hail !"
—*T. Warton's Triumph of Isis.*

This venerable seat of learning has an advantage over Cambridge, in being placed among more attractive scenery, and combining in itself a greater variety of splendid architecture. It stands at the junction of the Cherwell and Thames, 63 miles from London by the Great Western railway, which is continued hence, on the broad or mixed gauge, to Banbury, Birmingham, Worcester, &c. The railway and the meadows round the city were all under water in the floods of 1853. Population, 27,850, who return two members to Parliament, while the University is represented by two more.

Distant prospects of the city may be obtained from the Shotover and Hinksey hills. It is called Oxeneford in Domesday Book, or the ford of oxen; and this homely interpretation is duly supported by the city arms. King Alfred, it is asserted, founded the University; but this appears to be doubtful, as his biographer, Asser, mentions nothing of it. Its pre-eminence is, however, admitted as a settled point by legal authorities. There was a nunnery (St. Frideswide's) here from the year 730; and the monks attached to it, or to the monasteries founded after the Conquest, had the training of Henry I., who here acquired his surname of *Beauclerc*, from his literary parts.

Two main streets, each about two-fifths of a mile long, cross at a market place, called Carfax, a corruption of *quatre vōces* or four ways, where was a conduit, now at Nuneham Courtney, and contain in or near them some of the best buildings. High Street runs east and west, and St. Giles' Street north and south. At one end (the east) of the former thoroughfare is Magdalene Bridge, by which the city should be approached, as from that spot a view may be obtained which is stated to exceed that of most other towns, by experienced travellers; it is curved, and the size, grandeur, and variety of the buildings, as you turn through it, offer a most striking display. Another fine prospect may be had of the broad part of St. Giles' Street, north of Carfax.

City Buildings.—The best of these are—the *Town Hall* (built 1752), 135 feet long. The *Council Chamber* contains portraits of James II., the Duke of Marlborough, and others; the *Music Room*, built 1748, by an amateur architect, Dr. Camplin; the *Infirmary*, founded by Dr. Radcliffe; and the *County Gaol*, on the west side of the town. The last occupies the site of a castle founded after the Conquest, by Robert d'Oyley, and razed by Parliament, in the civil war, with the exception of the tower of St. George.

Churches.—*St. Aldates*, or *Old's*, as it is called, is an old edifice near Christ Church, in the south quarter of Oxford. *St. Cross* or Holywell, an ancient Gothic church, near the Cherwell; *All Saints*, in the middle of High Street, in the classic style, built by Dean Aldrich. *St. Giles'*, at the top of that street, is an early Gothic edifice; *St. Michael's*, near the bottom, and *St. Martin's*, at the bottom, near Carfax, are two others. That of *St. Mary Magdalene* is also a very ancient foundation, to which a new aisle was added in 1841, in honour of the martyrs Cranmer, Ridley, and Latimer, who were burnt (the last two in 1535, and Cranmer the year following) in Canditch, near Baliol College. Close to this church is the beautiful *Martyrs' Cross*, a three-storied Gothic pile, 73 feet high, by Scott. Statues of these celebrated Protestant confessors, by Weekes, are placed in the niches, and the whole lodged here in 1841, exactly three centuries after the publication of Cranmer's Bible. The famous Bocardo prison, in which they were confined, was in a gate of the old wall at the top of St. Giles' Street. *St. Mary's*, in High Street, is marked by a fine Gothic spire, 180 feet high; it is the University Church. *St. Peter's*, near Magdalene Bridge, is a restored Norman and pointed edifice. The *Cathedral*, part of Christ Church College, in Aldates Street. It was originally the Church of St. Frideswide's Priory, and was made the seat of a bishop in 1542 by Henry VIII. The oldest portion is the Norman door; the fine early Gothic cloisters are 54 feet long—spire 144 feet high. Some quaint effigies are seen; one of Schmidt's old organs; a quaint and a curious wooden shrine of the saint.

University Buildings.—There are nineteen colleges and five halls in Oxford, having about 6,000 members, and a total revenue of nearly £480,000.

All Soul's College, in High Street, was founded 1437, by Archbishop Chichley; a Gothic front, 194 feet long, and two courts, with a chapel and library behind. A leather screen in the chapel; the library was built by the Codrington family. Archbishop Sheldon, Jeremy Taylor, Herrick the poet, and Blackstone the lawyer, were of this college.

Baliol College, in Broad Street, was founded in 1282, by the Baliol family; old court and new chapel. Wickliffe was master of this college before he became professor of divinity, and John Evelyn was a member. Ridley, Latimer, and Cranmer were burnt at the stake in front of Baliol.

Brazenose College, is on the site of Little University Hall, and had an immense brass knocker, or "nose," on its Tudor gate; founded 1509. John Fox, the martyrologist, Spelman, and several other antiquaries, were among its members.

Corpus Christi, in Merton Lane, founded 1527, by Bishop Fox, who projected the union of the Roses. His crozier, portrait, and statue are in the library. In the president's gallery are portraits of the famous seven bishops, Kew, Trelawney, &c., Hooker and Bishop Jewel were members.

CHRIST CHURCH, which includes the cathedral, in Aldates Street. It was founded 1525 by Wolsey, who built the largest of its three courts, about 260 feet square. In the tower over the front (380 feet long) is the "Mighty Tom," which weighs 12,000lbs. Every night at ten minutes past nine it strikes 101 strokes, that is as many as there are students on the foundation. Wolsey's Hall is full of portraits, and the library, of busts, &c.; while, for members it reckons Sir T. More, Bishop Atterbury, Dr. South, Lord Mansfield, Robert Boyle, Sir P. Sidney, Locke, Camden, Ben Jonson, Canning, Peel, Gladstone.

EXETER COLLEGE, founded 1315, by the bishops of Exeter; the front, which has been modernized, is 220 feet long, many of the members are from the diocese of Exeter. One was Noy, who proposed the levy of ship-money to Charles I.

JESUS COLLEGE is chiefly used by the countrymen of the founder, Hugh Price, a Welshman; two courts. Portraits of Charles I. (by Vandyke) and Elizabeth in the hall. Archbishop Usher and Beau Nash were members.

LINCOLN COLLEGE, founded 1427, by the bishops of that diocese; two small courts. Archbishop Potter and John Wesley were members.

MAGDALENE, or as it is generally called *Maudlin* COLLEGE, is in High Street, and was founded 1448, by William of Waynflete. Two old courts and a third modern one, behind a front, 1,300 feet long; in which are an old and a new gate, and a beautiful pinnacled tower of the 15th century, 150 feet high. The president entertains the Sovereign at public visits. Queen Victoria and Prince Albert were here in 1841. In 1687, James II. made his celebrated attempt to force the Romish divine, Farmer, into the presidency instead of Hough. Dr. Renth, the late president, died in his 99th year, in 1856. Addison's walk is here, in the large and beautiful grounds, by the Cherwell. Among other members were Wolsey, Latimer, John Hampden, Hammond, Collins, the poet, and Gibbon. A new *Grammar School*, built 1851, on the site of *New Inn*; and another in 1822, on the site of Hertford College, of which Fox was a member.

MERTON COLLEGE, in John Street, is the oldest, being founded in 1264, by Walter de Merton (in Surrey). Three courts; the most ancient part is Bishop Rede's library, built 1376. The chapel is nearly as old; and contains a new painted ceiling and some good brasses. William of Waynflete, Bishop Hooper, and Massinger, Sir R. Steele, and Duns Scotus, were members, as well as Bodley, founder of the library. *St. Alban's Hall* adjoins this college.

NEW COLLEGE, is approached from Broad Street, and was founded by William of Wykeham, in 1379, for draughting his scholars from Winchester; good quadrangle, cloisters, and Gothic chapel, in which the founder's crozier is kept. Good gardens, City Wall.

Reynolds painted the window, or rather gave the design for it; which Warton refers to in a complimentary couplet. Philpot the martyr, Bishop Ker, Sir H. Wotton, &c., were of this college.

ORIEL COLLEGE is in Merton Lane, founded in 1324, by Edward II., whose golden cup is here. Raleigh, Sandys, Butler, poets, Dr. Arnold, and Archbishop Whateley, were members of this college. *St. Mary's Hall*, founded in 1383, is attached.

PEMBROKE COLLEGE, in Aldates Street, is a modern foundation, not older than 1724. It contains a quadrangle, oriel gate, and new hall, built 1849, in the Gothic style. Carew, the poet, John Pym, the orator of the Long Parliament, Archbishop Newcomb, Dr. Johnson, Blackstone the lawyer, and Whitfield, were members.

QUEEN'S COLLEGE is in High Street, founded in 1340, in honour of Edward III.'s Queen, Philippa; two courts. Archbishop Potter, Henry V., Cardinal Beaufort, Wycherley, the poet, Bernard Gilpin, the "apostle of the north," and Jeremy Bentham, were members. *Edmund Hall* formerly belonged to Osney priory.

ST. JOHN'S COLLEGE, in St. Giles' Street, was founded 1555, by Lord Mayor White, and receives many scholars from Merchant Tailors' School. The chapel was part of a Cistercian college, founded by Archbishop Chichley; Laud's MSS. in the library. Fine gardens. Archbishop Laud, and Bishop Juxon, were of this college.

TRINITY COLLEGE, in Broad Street, founded 1555, by Sir T. Pope, a native of Deddington; two courts, one by Wren. In the chapel, very fine carvings, by Gibbons, and a picture of the Resurrection (after West) in needlework, portraits of Sir T. Pope and T. Warton, the poet, in the hall, where the fellows dine

> ——— "untaxed, untroubled, under
> The portrait of their pious founder,"

and Warton's *Progress of Discontent.* Archbishop Sheldon, Chillingworth, Selden, Lord Somers, Lord Chatham, Warton, and others, were members of Trinity. Chillingworth was born at Oxford.

UNIVERSITY COLLEGE, in High Street. It was founded as far back as 1280, by William of Durham (though by some attributed to King Alfred); front 260 feet long, with two gates, carvings by Gibbons in the chapel. Of this college Archbishop Abbot, Bishop Ridley, Dr. Radcliffe, and Sir W. Jones, were members.

WADHAM was founded in 1613, by Nicholas Wadham; court, Gothic chapel, timbered hall. Blake, Bishop Wilkins, Dr. Kennicott, Sir C. Wren, and Dr. Bentley were members. Bishop Wilkins was Warden when the Royal Society was founded—the first meeting was held at his house.

WORCESTER COLLEGE, in Beaumont-street, founded in 1714, on the site of Gloucester Hall.

What are called the University Buildings, as distinct from the different colleges, are those grouped together in Broad Street, in a handsome square, round the Radcliffe Library. Here are the schools (where lectures on divinity, medicine, &c., are read), partly in the Gothic style. The *Bodleian Library*, founded in 1602, by Sir T. Bodley, contains nearly a quarter of a million of books, old, new, and rare MSS. Over this is the Picture Gallery, in which are portraits, busts, the Arundel marbles specimens of natural history, &c. Convocation Room, and the *Theatre*, for public meetings, built by Archbishop Sheldon in 1669, from Wren's designs, though only 80 feet by 70, will hold 4,000 persons. The *Clarendon Printing Office* was built by Vanburgh. A new printing office is behind it, near the observatory, a large quadrangular pile, 250 feet by 290, built 1829. The *Radcliffe Library*—

"Yon proud dome, fair learning's amplest shrine"—

is a handsome building of 16 sides, 100 feet diameter, built 1749, by Gibbs, at the cost of Radcliffe, the physician: busts, marbles, books, and drawings are here. Its dome, thus alluded to by Warton, is one of the most conspicuous objects in the views of Oxford. In the *Ashmolean Museum*, which is nothing better than a large curiosity shop, are the head and feet of the famous *Dodo*, whose portrait is in the British Museum. The rest of him was destroyed as rubbish, by order, in 1755. One of the most complete accounts of this solitary specimen of a race which has become extinct in the present age of man, may be found under "Dodo," in the *Penny Cyclopœdia.*

In St. Giles' Street stands the *Taylor Institute*, a handsome modern building, in the Italian style, built by Cockerell. The centre is 150 feet long, and the wings 70. It is designed to be a complete gallery of art and science. It is also a college for modern languages. Various drawings, paintings, busts, &c., are collected here. The *Botanic Garden* is fronted by one of Inigo Jones's gates.

Beaumont Street, near the castle, is so called after a palace built here by Henry I. Here Henry II. lived, and his two sons, Richard of the Lion's Heart, and John Lackland, were born. Another native was Anthony à Wood, the antiquarian, and the well known author of the History of Oxford, and of its eminent members.

North of the town, a little up the Thames, is Osrey Mill, on the site of an abbey formerly of great note. Not far from this stood Godstow nunnery, where Rosamond Clifford was wooed by Henry II. Fair Rosamond was a nun here, and was buried under the chapter house; her bones were scattered at the Reformation. The well known story of the bower in which she was concealed by Henry from his jealous queen, Eleanor, and the dagger and the cup of poison, is denied by critical historians.

Distances of Places from the Station.

	Miles		Miles.
Barton	3	South Court Mill	3
Blenheim	6½	South Leigh	6
Elsfield	3	Stoadley Chapel	6½
Ensham	4	Water Eaton	3
Headington	3	Wytham	1½
Marston	2	Wood Eaton	3
Medley	1½	Witney	9
Muzzle Hill	10	Woodstock	6½

And all places near Wolvercot.

Objects of Notice near Oxford.

Blenheim, the Duke of Marlborough's seat, is the great attraction. It was part of the Manor of Woodstock, and was given to the great Marlborough, by Queen Anne, to commemorate the important victory over the French, of 2nd August, 1702, on which day, every year, the holder of the seat presents a stand of colours to the queen. The house was built by Vanburgh, and is an excellent example of his heavy, but picturesque style; it is nearly 390 feet long; the way the chimnies are disposed is much admired. The interior is adorned in the style of that day, with rich tapestries, painted ceilings, &c. A piece of ornamental water in the parks, by "Capability" Brown; also a pillar, 130 feet high, celebrating Marlborough's victories, the inscription being written by Lord Bolingbroke; and Rosamond's Well, which is all that remains of the White Castle, a bower, &c., the chief scene of Scott's Woodstock.

Warton's inscription on a spring here is pretty—

"Here quench your thirst, and mark in me
An emblem of true charity,
Who while my bounty I bestow
Am neither heard nor seen to flow."

Woodstock Park was a favourite seat of King Alfred, and succeeding monarchs. Edward Third's son, the Black Prince, was born here, in 1330; near the park gate stood a house in which Chaucer the poet resided. Good leather gloves are made at Woodstock. *Ensham* the seat of Lord Parke, and *Cornbury* that of Lord F. Churchill, are both near *Wychand Forest*, a well wooded tract of oak, beech, and other timber, which is to be reclaimed and cultivated. Warton (who is poet of Oxford and the localities around) wrote some of his best lines, "The Hamlet," here. Some rare fossils are found in the rock below, which is a soft shelly oolite. Stonesfield in particular, on the old Roman way or Wheman Street, has furnished valuable specimens, and a Roman pavement was discovered there in the last century. *Witney* (10 miles) is still a flourishing seat of the blanket manufacture. *Cumnor Place* (in Berkshire), which belonged to the abbots of Abingdon, was the scene, according to Scott's Kenilworth, of poor Amy Robsart's murder, by Verney, at the command of her husband, the Earl of Leicester. In the church, a marble effigy of Anthony Foster, who was implicated in the tragedy; but he is there described as a gentleman and scholar. The "Black Bear" still figures at the village inn. *Nuneham Courtney*, on the Thames, is the seat of the Harcourts, at which are to be seen curious county maps, worked in tapestry, and a picture gallery.

Ditchley, Lord Dillon's seat, was the birthplace of the celebrated Lord Rochester, as notorious for his profligacy as for his sincere repentance. Near this is *Kiddington* (4 miles), with an old church, of which Warton was rector; it is described in his Ode on the First of April. *Renshaw* is the old seat of the Dormers. *Heythrop*, belongs to the Earl of Shrewsbury. *Glympton, i. e.*, the Glyme town, from the river which runs through it, is the seat of E. Way, Esq. At *Aynho*, the Cartwright's seat, near Deddington, in Northamptonshire, is a picture gallery. From *Shotover Hill* (4 miles), 600 feet high, there is a good prospect of Oxford and its spires.

Middleton Park, the seat of Earl Jersey, is near an old church. *Kirtlington*, Sir G. Dashwood, Bart., was an old Saxon village, called *Kyntingtun*. *Bletchington*, A. Annesley, Esq. *Ambrosden*, the seat of Sir G. Turner, Bart., was formerly the vicarage of Bishop Kennet, who published an account of the village in his "Parochial Antiquities."

For continuation of this route to Birmingham, Shrewsbury, &c., see page 53.

Great Western Main Line continued. Didcot to Swindon Junction.

Leaving Didcot on a rise of seven feet in a mile, we now enter an excavation of about half-a-mile, and emerging thence, bend gradually to the west on an embankment, when again plunging into a short cutting, we are carried past Milton, a small village to the left, and in a few minutes afterwards stop at

STEVENTON.

A telegraph station.

Money Order Office at Abingdon.

Here commences the "Vale of the White Horse," deriving its singular denomination from the gigantic carving of that useful quadruped, on a high chalky hill beyond—but the cuttings that soon after succeed, "not long, but deep," effectually screen a very pretty country from the eyes of the traveller, save at occasional intervals, when an elevated embankment offers some transient glimpses.

Borne over the Wiltshire and Berks Canal, we soon after reach

Wantage Road Station for

WANTAGE.

Distance from station, 3½ miles.

Telegraph station at Faringdon Road, 3¾ miles.

Hotel.—Bear.

Market Day.—Saturday. Fairs.—First Saturday in March and May, July 18th, and October 17th.

Bankers.—The London and County Bank.

This ancient market town is memorable as the birth-place of our *great* Alfred; and during the time of the Saxons it was a royal residence. The famous Wayland Smith's Cave, on Childry Downs, is not far from the town. In the romance of "Kenilworth," Wayland Smith plays a prominent part, and his character—though founded on a slight foundation—has been drawn by the author of Waverley with amazing power and freshness, forming another of those poetical creations which his wizard pen has left to solace sickness, console sorrow, inspire genius, and defy imitation.

FARINGDON ROAD.

Distance from station, 5 miles.

A telegraph station.

Hotels.—Bell, Crown.

Market Day.—Tuesday.

Fairs.—February 13th, Whit Tuesday, Tuesdays before and after Michaelmas, and October 29th.

Bankers.—Barnes & Co.

The town is *five* miles to the right; its church is a very ancient structure, erected on the hill, and contains within several noble monuments; whilst the exterior displays evidence of the havoc committed upon it during the civil wars, the spire having been destroyed by the artillery of the Parliamentary forces. Edward the Elder, one of the Saxon kings, died in a palace here in 925.

To those who duly estimate the worth of a fine prospect, we recommend a visit up the hill to Farringdon High Trees, which, in its extensive survey, includes the major portion of three counties—Oxfordshire, Wiltshire, and Gloucestershire. By sunrise or sunset, a view from this spot is amongst the finest panoramas from nature's exhaustless pencil.

Leaving the station, and progressing on an ascent of about seven feet in a mile, we are carried on an embankment past the village of Baulking, about two miles distant from which is Kingston Lisle, with its celebrated "Blowing Stone," in which there are several apertures, and by blowing into any one of these a sound is produced that can be heard for miles distant. Uffington Castle is close by, and a little further on is seen the celebrated *White Horse*, which was carved by order of Alfred, in memory of the triumphant victory which, in 873, he gained over the Danes, at Ashbury.

SHRIVENHAM.

Distance from station, 1 mile.

A telegraph station.

Mails.—Two arrivals and departures, daily, between London and Shrivenham.

On leaving this station we pass through an excavation, and thence on to an embankment, which commands a fine view of *Highworth* on the right, and *Beacon Hill* and *Liddington Castle* on the summit to the left.

WILTSHIRE,

An inland and fertile county, divided into South and North. The aspect of the former displays considerable beauty, as the principal valleys in this division of Wiltshire lie along the banks of the rivers, the most remarkable of which diverge, like irregular radii, from the country around Salisbury and Wilton; these display rich meadows and corn land, interspersed with towns, private residences, and extensive plantations of wood.

North Wiltshire differs completely from the southern division of the county. Instead of the gentle undulations of the south, it appears a complete level, and is so thickly wooded, that at a short distance it resembles one vast plantation of trees. When examined in detail, however, it is found to contain many fertile and richly cultivated spots. The chief commodities are sheep, wool, wood, and stone, and the principal manufactures are in the different branches of the clothing trade.

SWINDON JUNCTION.

Distance from station, 1 mile.

A telegraph station.

Refreshment rooms at the station.

MARKET DAY.—Monday.

FAIRS.—Monday before April 5th, second Mondays after May 12th and September 11th, second Mondays before October 10th and December 12th.

MAILS.—Two arrivals and departures, daily, between London and Swindon.

MONEY ORDER OFFICE.

BANKERS.—County of Gloucester Banking Co.; North Wilts Banking Co.

SWINDON, on the Great Western, like Wolverton, on the North Western, and Crewe, on the Grand Junction, is one of the extraordinary products of the railway enterprise of the present age. It is a colony of engineers and handicraft men. The company manufacture their own engines at the factory, where cleaning and everything connected with constructive repair is carried on.

The refreshment room at this station is admirably conducted, and abundantly supplied with every article of fare to tempt the best as well as the most delicate appetites, and the prices are moderate, considering the extortions to which travellers are occasionally exposed.

The valley of **Stroud** through which the railway passes from Swindon to Gloucester, is well known to travellers and tourists as presenting a continuous series of lovely landscapes. The valley is almost in the character of a mountain gorge, with a branching stream in the bottom, which partially furnishes the motive power for the numerous cloth and fulling mills of the district, the quality of the water, too, being peculiarly adapted for dyeing purposes.

CHELTENHAM BRANCH.

Swindon to Cirencester, Stroud, Gloucester and Cheltenham.

PURTON.

Distance from station, 1 mile.

A telegraph station.

MAILS.—One arrival and departure, daily, between London and Purton.

The next station is MINETY, soon after leaving which, we enter

GLOUCESTERSHIRE,

ONE of the western counties, which presents three beautiful varieties of landscape scenery, viz.: the hill, vale, and forest. The hill district, including those of Cotswold and Stroudwater, may be considered as a continuation of the central chain proceeding south from Derbyshire, and passing through this county into Wiltshire, there expanding into the Salisbury downs, and afterwards running in a western direction towards the Land's End in Cornwall. The downs, which formerly lay open, producing little else than furze, are now converted into arable enclosed fields, and communications have been opened between towns, where formerly the roads were impassable.

That part of the county called the vale district, is bounded on the east by the Cotswold hills, and the river Severn on the west; it is usually subdivided into the vales of Evesham, Gloucester, and Berkeley. The characteristic features of the entire district are nearly the same; though if a difference be admitted, it will probably be in favour of that of Berkeley.

The vale of Evesham follows the Avon eastward to Stratford, and in respect to climate, produce, &c., resembles that of Gloucestershire, which in its outline is somewhat semicircular, the river Severn being the chord, and the surrounding hills the arch; the towns of Gloucester, Tewkesbury, and Cheltenham, forming a triangle within its area.

The vale of Berkeley, called the Lower, is of a more irregular surface than the upper one. The scenery is in general very beautiful. The forest district is separated from the rest of the county by the river Severn; and principally contains the Forest of Dean, which was celebrated for its fine oaks. Lead and iron ores exist in abundance. Coal is also very plentiful.

At a distance of 6¼ miles beyond Minety, the train stops at

TETBURY ROAD (Tetbury).

Population of the township, 2,615; the station itself is near to the little village of Kemble.

Distance from station, 6½ miles.

HOTELS.—Talbot; White Hart.

MARKET DAY.—Wednesday.

FAIRS.—Ash Wednesday, Wednesday before and after April 5th, July 22nd.

BANKERS.—County of Gloucester Bank.

CIRENCESTER—(Branch).

Distance from station, ¼ mile.

A telegraph station.

HOTELS.—King's Head; Ram.

MARKET DAYS.—Monday and Friday.

FAIRS.—Easter Tuesday, July 18th; Monday before and after Oct. 11th; Nov. 8th.

BANKERS.—County of Glo'ster Banking Co.; Branch of Glo'stershire Banking Co.

DISTANCES OF PLACES FROM THE STATION.

	Miles.		Miles.
Barnsley Park	5	Lypiatt Park	8
Beggar's Down	6	Malmesbury	8
Bownham House	8	Misserden Park	7
Cherrington Grove	7	Northleach	10
Cirencester Abbey	0½	Penbury Park	4
Down House	3¾	Rendcomb Park	5
Edgeworth	5½	Rendon Park	5
Foss Cross	6	Sapperton Park	3
Hill House	4	Stroud	2

CIRENCESTER is one of the greatest marts in England for wool. The magnificence of the church in this place entitles it to rank amongst the first in the kingdom. Here three Roman roads meet, and from the variety of Roman coins, tessellated pavement, and other antiquities found in the neighbourhood, it seems to have covered a much wider area than at present.

Cirencester was formerly fortified, and the ruins of the walls and streets may still be seen in the adjacent meadows.

Cheltenham Branch continued.
BRIMSCOMB.

A telegraph station.
HOTEL. — Railway.
MONEY ORDER OFFICE at Stroud.

STROUD.

POPULATION, 78,60.

A telegraph station.

HOTELS.—George; Lamb.

MAILS.—Two arrivals and departures, daily, between London and Stroud.

MARKET DAY.—Friday.

FAIRS.—May 12th and August 21st.

STROUD is a market town, situated near the confluence of the river Frome and the Slade Water. Woollen cloth forms the staple manufacture of the town and its environs. Returns two members to Parliament.

DISTANCES OF PLACES FROM THE STATION.

	Miles.		Miles.
Bownham House	2	Misserden Park	5
Creed Place	6¼	Nimpsfield	4
Easington	4½	Painswick	3
Frodmore	2	Penbury Park	6
Haresfield	4½	Quedgley House	6
Hill House	5	Rodborough	1
Hock's House	6	Rudge	2¾
Horns, The	1	Stancomb Cross	3
Hyde Court	3	Standish House	4½
King's Stanley	3	Tuffley Court	5
*Lypiatt Park	2	Whitcomb Park	6
Minchinhampton	3	Woodchester	2

STONEHOUSE.

Distance from station, ½ mile.
A telegraph station.
HOTELS.—Crown and Anchor; Plough.
At this point the line joins the Bristol and Birmingham rail, which proceeds on the left to Bristol, and on the right to Gloucester and Cheltenham.

GLOUCESTER.

POPULATION, 17,572.

A telegraph station.

HOTEL. — Fowler's first class commercial and private family Boarding House and Temperance Hotel is highly recommended.

MARKET DAYS.—Wednesday and Saturday.

FAIRS.—April 5th, July 5th, Sept. 28th, and Nov. 28th.

BANKERS.—County of Glo'ster Banking Co.; Glo'stershire Banking Co.; National Provincial Bank of England; Thomas Turner.

* Here Guy Fawkes met the Plotters.

A cathedral city, capital of the county, and parliamentary borough (2 members), on the Severn, and the Bristol and Birmingham Railway, 114 miles from London, in a flat spot, which was under water in the floods of 1853. At Kingsholme, to the north, on the site of a Roman station, called *Glevum*, the later Saxon kings had a seat, which, Canute attempting to take, was defeated, in the battle of Alney Island, close by. Laxington and other pleasant hills overlook the vale of Gloucester, a rich loamy tract of 60,000 acres, where considerable corn, fruit, beans, turnips, and hay are raised, though much of the butter and double Gloucester cheese, for which the county is noted, comes from the Wiltshire meadows. The corn market is held every third Monday, from July to November.

This town is situated on an eminence, in that division of Gloucester called the vale, near the banks of the Severn, and when viewed from that river it presents a very imposing appearance. The city possesses many elegant public buildings, and a magnificent cathedral, which is particularly celebrated for its architectural beauty. The *Cathedral* is a cross, 426 feet long; the oldest parts are the Norman crypt and nave, built in 1089. The later English choir is the work of Abbot Wigmore (about 1330), and a "whispering" passage, 75 feet long, near the fine east window, which is 79 feet long by 35 broad, or one of the largest in England. The west front was built in 1437; the tower, which is 225 feet high, was begun a little later, but not finished till 1518; the Lady Chapel, 92 feet long, is the most modern part. There is a very old tomb of Edward II. (who was murdered at Berkeley Castle), also monuments of Robert Curthose the Conquerer's brother, and *Dr. Jenner*, the discoverer of vaccination. Some of the Lacy family are buried in the Chapter House. The beautiful cloisters were built between 1351 and 1392. Of the 12 churches, those of St. Catherine and St. Mary de Lode are Norman in part, and St. Nicholas is early English. At St. John's is a tablet to the Rev. T. Stock, who with *Raikes* established the "four original *Sunday Schools* in this parish and St. Catherine's, in 1780." From this small beginning sprung that gratuitous system of Christian instruction which has covered the face of England and Wales with schools. Gloucester boasts another evangelist in *Whitfield*, who was born at the Bell Inn, while Bishop Hooper, whom it enlisted in the noble army of martyrs, was burnt in St. Mary's Square. Close to the rail and the ship canal basin is the County Gaol (on the castle site), where the separate system was first tried, 1790. Shipping come up to this basin by a cut from the Severn, near Berkeley; there is a good import trade. In this part also are the *Spa Gardens* and pump room, over a mineral spring of some value. The Shire Hall was built by Smirke; the Infirmary covers a space of 7½ acres. In Commercial Street is a *Museum*, the gift of the Guises of Elmore Court. Pins are made here.

In the environs are the gate of Lanthoney Abbey, *Highnam Court*, seat of T. G. Parry, Esq., in the rennaissance style; Church Down, a solitary hill, having the Cots Wolds to the right, from 800 to 1,100 feet high; Cheltenham and its mineral waters;

Hempstead, Hardwicke, Painswick, and other seats; Newent old priory; *Flaxley Abbey*, seat of Sir M. Boevey, Bart.; the Forest of Dean, an interesting hilly wooded tract, stretching to the Wye, and producing iron, coal, stone, &c.; Ross, and its spire, built by Kyrle, the "man of Ross," overlooking the Wye, the beautiful scenery of which may be visited from here, as well as the Malvern hills, with the Hydropathic establishments of Drs. Wilson and Gully. Ledbury, which has a fine old Norman church; and *Goodrich Court*, seat of the Meyricks, near Ross, which has a remarkable collection of armour, &c., and is near a fine old Norman castle of the Pentroches.

DISTANCES OF PLACES FROM THE STATION.

	Miles.		Miles.
Badgworth	3	Longford	$1\frac{1}{2}$
Barnwood	$0\frac{1}{2}$	Maizmore	3
Brookworth	3	Quedgeley	3
Churchdown	$2\frac{1}{2}$	Rudford	1
Elmore Court	5	Sandhurst	3
Forton	3	Studgrive	2
Hatfield Court	5	Upton	3
High Grove	3	Whaddon	3
Highnam Park	4	Wooten	1

CHELTENHAM.

POPULATION, 35,051.

A telegraph station.

HOTELS.—The Plough, first-class, for families and private gentlemen; the Queen's, first-class, for families and gentlemen. Commercial houses, the Fleece and the Lamb.

MARKET DAY.—Thursday.

FAIRS.—Second Thursday in April, 2nd Thursday in Sept., Holy Thursday, Dec. 11th and 18th.

BANKERS.—Branch of Glo'stershire Banking Co.; National Provincial Bank of England; County of Glo'ster Bank.

CHELTENHAM takes its name from the river Chelt, and is celebrated for its medicinal waters. It has been for the last sixty years one of the most elegant and fashionable watering places in England. The town is built on a flat marshy soil, on the borders of a rich and fertile valley, and the surrounding Leckhampton hills protect it from the cold winds. The season for drinking the waters is from May to October. The climate in winter is generally mild, though in July and August the heat is felt to be oppressive. Its surface is elevated about 165 feet above Gloucester, and the funnel shape of the valley, with a large river in its centre (the Chelt, which runs through to the Severn), elicits currents of air, which ventilate the atmosphere, and contribute much to the purity and salubrity of the town.

It is a parliamentary borough (one member), situated in a charming spot under the Cotswold hills, in Gloucestershire, 7 miles from Gloucester, on the Bristol and Birmingham Railway. Most of it is modern and well-built. The assembly rooms are in High Street, $\frac{3}{4}$ mile long. A little on one side of this is *Pitville* Spa and Pump Room (built in 1824), with its Grecian portico and dome, in the midst of pleasing grounds. On the other, the promenade leads to the *Montpellier* Spa and *Rotunda* pump-room, and Lansdowne Crescent. A pump-room, built in 1803, stands at the *Old Wells*, first used in 1716, and approached by an avenue of elms, an object of deserved attraction, from its extent and symmetry. There is also the Chalybeate Spa. Both contain aperient salts of soda and magnesia, with a little iodine and iron; and are of great benefit in cases of weak stomachs, liver complaints, and plethora. Two are chiefly chalybeate. The parks and gardens about the town have much picturesque beauty, and are open throughout the year for a trifling fee, besides being the scene at intervals of numerous fetes and floricultural shows.

A *Proprietary College*, in the Tudor style, was built in 1843, 240 feet long. The parish church of St. Mary is in part as old as the 11th century. Christ church and St. Peter's, among the modern ones, deserve notice—the latter being in the Norman style, with a round tower, &c.

In 1831, Mr. Gurney tried his locomotive carriages along the high road to Gloucester, running the distance in 55 minutes, several times a day.

In the neighbourhood are many good walks and points of view, viz., Battledown, Leckhampton Court, and Cleck Cloud, 1,134 feet high. Behind Leckhampton are the *Seven Springs*, one of the principal heads of the river Thames. *Southam* is the Tudor seat of Lord Ellenborough. *Boddington Manor*, J. Neale, Esq. Charlton Park, &c.. &c.

Great Western Main Line continued.

Swindon to Chippenham.

About a mile to the left is the market town which gives its name to the station, and which is now rapidly rising into importance. The old town is pleasantly situated on the summit of a considerable eminence, commanding extensive views of Berkshire and Gloucestershire.

The line here continues on a rapid descent of about seven feet in a mile, and by embankment crosses several roads, leading from the neighbouring towns and villages. About a mile to the right, is Lydiard, near which can be recognised the lofty trees of the park, the ancient seat of the Bolingbroke family. Sweeping in rather a serpentine course over a richly-cultivated country, we next pass in succession a cluster of small hamlets to our left; and looking forward, scenery of that quiet pastoral description so characteristic of English rural life is continued to the very verge of the horizon.

WOOTTON BASSET.

Distance from station, $\frac{1}{4}$ mile.
A telegraph station.
HOTEL.—Old Royal Oak.
MARKET DAY.—Thursday.

FAIRS—May 4th, Nov. 13th, and Dec 19th.

We now proceed on an embankment, having a rapid descent in our favour of about fifty feet in a mile. This elevation affords a comprehensive view of the adjoining valley of "Bath's clear Avon," through which the companionable canal is still seen gleaming amid the line of pollards that fringe its edge. Passing through a short excavation we again emerge on a level, whence to the left can be discerned afar off, the stately structure of Bradenstoke Priory. Thence by alternate cutting and embankment we reach

CHIPPENHAM.

POPULATION, 6,283.
Distance from station, ¾ mile.
A telegraph station.
HOTELS.—Angel, George.
MARKET DAY.—Thursday.
FAIRS.—May 17th, June 22nd, Oct. 29th, and Dec. 11th.
BANKERS.—North Wilts Banking Co.; Branch of Wilts and Dorset Banking Co.

This is a parliamentary borough, on the Great Western Railway, in North Wiltshire, on the river Avon, but not otherwise remarkable, except as being a great seat of the cheese trade. Population, 6,283, who send two members to parliament. A little cloth and silk are made. It has two tanneries, a foundry, four banks, a new Town Hall and Market House, built for £12,000, at the cost of J. Neeld, Esq., M.P., of Grittleton, and a long bridge on 23 arches. The old church large and handsome. In the time of Alfred it was a city of strength, and was taken by the Danes in 880. It is delightfully situated in a valley on the south bank of the river Avon, by which it is almost surrounded.

In the neighbourhood are *Lacock Abbey*, seat of – Talbot, Esq., the inventor of Photography; *Bowood*, the seat of the Marquis of Lansdowne; *Sloperton*, formerly the seat of Moore, who died in 1852, and is buried at Bromham, near Spye Park, the Starkies' seat. At Bremhill, the poet Bowles died, being the vicar, in 1850.

Calne, a parliamentary borough returning one member, has a large old church. It was here that St. Dunstan, then primate, held a synod in 977, to settle a dispute between the clergy and monks, and contrived by making the floor give way, to bring a pretended judgment on his opponents.

Corsham House, Lord Methuen, is a Tudor building, with a gallery of Dutch and other masters. *Castle Combe*, in a sheltered hollow, on a branch of the Avon, is the seat of G. P. Scrope, Esq., who has written the history of this ancient barony.

POPULATION, 5,195.

WILTS, SOMERSET, AND WEYMOUTH.

Chippenham to Frome, Yeovil, Dorchester, and Weymouth.

MELKSHAM.

Distance from station, ¾ mile.
A telegraph station.
HOTEL.—Bear, King's Arms.
MARKET DAY.—Monday.
FAIRS—July 27th, and 2nd Monday in every month.
MONEY ORDER OFFICE.
BANKERS.—The North Wilts Banking Co.

This village has a population of 2,931; consists of one long street, the buildings of which are mostly of freestone. Celebrated for its mineral springs.

DEVIZES BRANCH.

Melksham to Devizes.

From this point a small portion of the line subsequently intended to run direct between Hungerford and Melksham, turns off, and is now open to Devizes, a distance of about 7 miles.

DEVIZES

Is an ancient borough, in the centre of Wiltshire, with a population of 6,554. Its stapletrade is woollen. St. John's Church is some what remarkable, from the variety of architectural designs it displays. It returns two members to parliament.

Wilts and Somerset Main Line continued.

TROWBRIDGE.

Distance from station, ¼ mile.
A telegraph station.
HOTEL.—George.
MARKET DAY.—Saturday. FAIR.—August 5th.

This town is the largest in the county, with the exception of Salisbury. It has a population of 10,157, and is situated on the river Ware. The church is large and highly decorated. It is one of the largest clothing towns in the west of England. Leland says of it, in his time even, "it flourisheth by drapery." Crabbe, the poet, was rector here. George Keat, the poet, was a native. Ruins of *Farley Castle* (3½ miles) are very picturesque. A short branch here turns off to

BRADFORD (Branch),

A town that "stondeth by clooth making," said Leland, three centuries ago, and the same may be said of it now. The Avon is crossed by two bridges, one a very ancient one, with a chapel over one of the piers. This line continues its course, *via* FRESHFORD, LIMPLEY STOKE, and BATHAMPTON to

Bath (see page 18), a distance of 12½ miles from Trowbridge.

Wilts and Somerset Main Line continued.

From Trowbridge we continue by the Valley of the Avon, with the grounds of *Rowed Ashton* and *Heywood House* on the left, and arrive at

WESTBURY.

HOTEL.—Lopez Arms.

This is an ancient borough, with a malting and broad cloth trade. Bryan Edwards, the historian, was a native. About two miles north-east is an ancient encampment, on the edge of the chalk downs near *Bratton;* on the escarpment below it is the figure of a white horse, the origin of which is doubtful and obscure. Four miles beyond is *Erle Stoke Park*, the seat of Lord Broughton.

We now bear to the left, leaving the Weymouth line, on the

SALISBURY BRANCH.

Westbury to Salisbury.

Our first station is that at

WARMINSTER.

HOTELS.—Bath Arms; Lamb.

This is a neat and respectable town, close to the western border of Salisbury Plain, on which, in the neighbourhood, are many remains of the old Britons. There is likewise a huge rampart and ditch called "*Old Ditch*," which may be attributed to the Saxons. The church is spacious and handsome. The tower is of the reign of Edward III.

Proceeding on our way with *Battlesbury*, *Middlebury*, *Scratchbury*, *Cotley*, and *Golden Barrow*, close by on our left (all ancient encampments), we arrive at

HEYTESBURY.

HOTELS.—Bath Arms; Lamb.

This town is situated in a pleasant valley on the river Wiley, with a population of 1,210, chiefly employed in the woollen manufacture. Here Queen Maude lived. In the ancient church (rebuilt in 1404) Cunningham, the antiquary, is buried. Close by is *Heytesbury House*, the seat of Lord Heytesbury. In the vicinity are more remains of our rude forefathers, in the shape of barrows, camps, entrenchments, and other earthworks, evidently occupied by Britons, Romans, Saxons, and Danes in succession. *Knock Castle*, 3 miles east, a more remarkable one than all.

Proceeding by the banks of the Wiley, we arrive at

CODFORD.

In the vicinity are a Druidical circle on Codford Hill, *Bayton Hall*, A. B. Lambert, Esq.; *Bayton Church*, built in 1301, with an ancient font, and *Stockton House*. *Codford St. Mary's* Norman church is deserving a visit.

WILEY.

In the neighbourhood are *Deptford Inn* (½ mile), *Fisherton de la Mére* (1 mile). *Yarmbury Castle* (2 miles), a most interesting earthen work or fortification, occupying an elevated situation above the plain. *Badbury Camp* (1 mile), supposed to be the *Mons Badonicus* of the Romans. and the *Baddiebrig* of the Saxons. Here Arthur defeated Cedric, in 520. The decayed town of *Hindon*, 6 miles west, near which is *Fonthill Abbey*, Alfred Morrison, Esq., but formerly the seat of Beckford, the author of that most original Eastern story, "Caliph Vathek," and who lived here in the most selfish retirement. It has the appearance of a vast monastic edifice, crowned by a lofty tower, visible at the distance of 40 miles, and commands views over beautifully picturesque and abundantly diversified scenery. He died and was buried at Bath.

LANGFORD.—In this vicinity are Steeple Langford, Hanging Langford, Stapleford, Groveley Wood (here the Wiltshire hounds meet), and at East Castle, are earthworks 214 yards round. Groveley Castle contains 14 acres, is single ditched, with ramparts, and commands a beautiful view; and Hamshill, with its ditches: all of these are thought to have been British towns, occupied by the Romans. The train then proceeds on to

WISHFORD.

Here is an excellent Free Grammar School, and a handsome church. In the vicinity are South Newton and Wilton Woodford, at which the ancient Bishops of Sarum had a palace. Soon after we arrive at

WILTON.

HOTELS.—Bell, Pembroke Arms.

WILTON is a place of great antiquity, and its importance is indicated by the circumstance of its having given name to the county. It was the scene of one of Alfred's victories over the Danes in 871; and the occasional residence of the West Saxon Kings. A Benedictine abbey, for nuns, existed here at an early period, of which Alfred, and his successors, were great benefactors. The church was the abbey church. The new church is an elaborate imitation of the Lombard style, on which the Norman is founded. There is a county cross. It has much declined of late years: the population are partly engaged in the cloth and carpet factories. At that of Messrs. Blackmore, the Axminster carpet, shewn at the Great Exhibition, from Gruner's designs, was manufactured. It is rather curious that this branch of manufacture was first introduced into England by a Frenchman of the name of Duffoly under the protection of the Herberts, in Elizabeth's time. Wilton Castle is built upon the site of the abbey; it was rebuilt by Wyatt. Here Sidney's sister, Pembroke's mother, lived, and Sir Philip wrote part of his *Arcadia*. The old castle was altered by Holbein and Inigo Jones, and visited by Charles I. Here may be seen the old rusty arms of Sir William Herbert ap Thomas, which he wore when in France with Henry V. There is a fine collection of marbles, and portraits by Vandyke; Titian, by himself; Richard II., supposed to be the oldest oil painting extant; pictures by Rubens, &c. The park is beautifully timbered, having many very aged trees. John of Wilton, of the thirteenth century; John of Wilton, in the time of Edward III.; Thomas of Wilton, in the time of Edward IV.; and Massinger, the dramatist, were natives.

Salisbury—See Section I., page 79.

Wilts and Somerset Main Line continued.
Westbury to Dorchester and Weymouth.

Crossing the borders of the county from Westbury we soon arrive at

FROME.

HOTELS.—George, Crown.

Is agreeably situated on the north-east declivity of several hills contiguous to Selwood Forest. It has considerable manufactures of woollen cloth, and an excellent grammar school, founded by Edward VI. At *Nunney* (3 miles) are the ruins of a castle. *Marston Biggot* (2 miles) Earl of Cork and Orrery. *Mells Park* (4 miles). *Longleat Park* (3½ miles) the extensive domain of the Marquis of Bath.

WITHAM JUNCTION, near which is *Witham Park.*

EAST SOMERSET.

This line runs, *via* the stations of WANSTROW and CRANMORE, to

SHEPTON MALLET.

Population, 3,885, engaged in the manufacture of crape and silk to some extent. The market cross is worth notice. It was built in the year 1500, in the form of a sexagon, with a spire and ornamental sculpture.

The distance from here to Wells is performed by omnibus at present.

Wells, see page 23.

Wilts and Somerset Main Line continued.

BRUTON, situated on the banks of the Brue; has a fine old English perpendicular church, an endowed hospital founded by Saxey, auditor to Queen Elizabeth, and a free grammar school by Edward VI.

CASTLE CARY

Has the remains of a castle founded by William de Percheval, in the reign of Stephen. The town of *Wincanton*, five miles east, on the river Cale, and beautifully sheltered by shady woods. Here the first blood was shed in the revolution of 1688, between the Prince of Orange and James' adherents.

SPARKFORD.

Near it on the left, is *Cadbury Castle,* one of the most stupendous fortifications in the kingdom, belonging to the days gone by, whose everyday life is but legendary and mythical. A part of the ruins is called King Arthur's palace.

Passing MARSTON station, we cross the river Yeo and stop at the station at

Yeovil, see page 23.

From Yeovil a branch line to the right, of nearly 20 miles in length, joins the Bristol and Exeter line, which see, page 23. We proceed southward, and passing the ancient village of *Bradford Abbas* and the stations of YETMINSTER and EVERSHOT (near which are *Woolcombe House* and *Melbury House*, at Redlynch, the seat of the Earl of Ilchester, from the grounds of which a view may be had of an immeasurable tract of country), we arrive at MAIDEN NEWTON, from which a branch to the right takes us to Bridport.

MAIDEN NEWTON AND BRIDPORT BRANCH.

POWERSTOCK.—The old town of *Beaminster* may be visited from this station. Its church has a tower 100 feet high, most elaborately ornamented with sculptures of various kings, and others illustrative of the woollen trade, for which this town was famous.

BRIDPORT.

HOTEL.—Bull.

A small port on the river Brit, noted from the earliest period for its hempen manufactures. Its staple productions are twine, fishing nets, and canvas, and much hemp for the purpose is grown. "He was stabbed with a Bridport dagger" was an old saying for a man that was hung.

Wilts & Somerset Main Line continued.

Leaving Maiden Newton and passing along the Valley of the Frome, by the station of GRIMSTONE, we arrive at

Dorchester, see Section I., page 95.

Weymouth, see Section I., page 96.

Great Western Main Line continued.
Chippenham to Yatton.

Leaving the Chippenham station we continue for some time on an embankment, and then dipping into an excavation we arrive at

CORSHAM.

Distance from station, ¾ mile.

A telegraph station.

HOTEL.—Methuen Arms.

King Ethelred had a palace here, and it was once the favourite residence of the Earls of Cornwall. *Corsham House*, the seat of Lord Methuen, has a very fine collection of paintings.

Sir Richard Blackmore, the poet, was a native.

Shortly after leaving this station we enter the Box Tunnel which is upwards of one mile and three quarters in length, through the solid heart and immense mass of Box Hill. At intervals a gleam of light appears down the shafts that have been cut through the rock to the surface above. Emerging once more into daylight we proceed over a wide-ranging pasture land, spotted and diversified with herds and flocks.

Passing Box Station (near which is *Wraxhall House*), we soon after enter a small tunnel, which is cut through Middle Hill, adjoining a once-noted spa, so called, but now quite forsaken. Emerging from this we pass on an embankment two miles in length that carries the line onward over the Avon into the county of

SOMERSET.

FEW of the English counties present so great a variety of scenery and soil as Somerset. It possesses every gradation, from the lofty mountain and barren moor to the rich and cultivated vale, and then descends to the unimprovable marsh and fens. From Taunton to the coast extends a range of hills which slope towards Bridgewater, and on the other side they descend into a cultivated vale. Westward of this, and only terminating in the wild district of Exmoor Forest, the county is entirely mountainous and hilly. Between these there are many steep vallies, which form, when richly wooded, some of the most striking features of the beautiful scenery for which this coast is so deservedly celebrated.

Somerset, from its favourable climate and soil, stands very high in reputation for agricultural and rural produce.

The hamlets of Bathford, Bathampton, and Batheaston are now passed in rapid succession, and swerving slightly to the south, the outskirts of the "Stone-built city" itself rise in all their magnificence before us, as if evoked by a magician from the fertile pastures we have so recently quitted. A loud and prolonged whistle is borne upon the air as herald of our arrival, and we enter the elegant and commodious station at

BATH.

POPULATION, 54,240. A telegraph station.

HOTELS.—The York House; White Lion; White Hart; The Castle; The Greyhound; Amery's; George's Royal.

OMNIBUSES to and from the station.

MARKET DAYS.—Wednesday and Saturday.

BANKERS. — Stuckey's Banking Co.; George Moger and Son; Tugwell and Co.; Branch of West of England and South Wales District Bank; National Provincial Bank of England.

The view from the station is one calculated to impress a stranger very favourably with the importance of the city, so renowned in the world of fashionable invalids. He sees on one side of him the river Avon, gliding placidly beneath Pulteney Bridge, and on the other a range of lofty hills, studded with terraces and isolated villas, whilst before expand the white edifices of the city. The modern city of Bath is of great beauty, and delightfully situated, in a valley, divided by the river Avon. The surrounding country is well wooded, and, from the inequality of the ground, presents a great variety of beautiful scenery, whilst, from its sheltered position, the temperature of the vale is mild. Lansdown Hill, nearly three miles in extent, was the scene of a desperate battle, fought there between the royalists and parliamentary forces, terminating in the defeat of the latter. This magnificent elevation is now the most picturesque part of the city, having groves and terraces throned above each other almost to the summit, commanding a prospect of great extent and diversified beauty. Mansions of aristocratic appearance are scattered in all directions; spacious streets, groves, and crescents, lined with stately stone edifices, and intersected by squares and gardens, complete a view of city grandeur scarcely surpassed by any other in the kingdom. The gaieties of Bath are celebrated all over Europe; but it must be conceded that, since the reign of Beau Nash, they have terribly degenerated.

Bath is not only renowned for its antiquity and waters, but is one of the best built cities in the United Kingdom, standing in a spot remarkable for its attractive scenery, on the Avon and the Great Western Railway, 107 miles from London, at the centre of a fine circle of hills, 500 to 700 feet high. These hills furnish the blue lias, or oolite, and Bath stone, so much in use by architects, and of which the city has been erected. It is the seat of a bishop, whose diocese extends over Somersetshire, and its population of 54,240 send two members to parliament.

The peculiar virtue of its hot-springs were soon discovered by the Romans, who built a tower here, called *Aquæ Solis* (waters of the sun), a name which, under the form of Aix, Ax, Aigs, &c., still distinguishes many watering-places on the continent. The Saxons who resorted here significantly styled one of the main roads which led to it, Akeman Strutt, *i.e.*, the road for *aching men.*

Besides the private baths in Stall Street, there are four public ones leased from the corporation. King's Bath, the largest, a space 65 feet by 40, with a temperature of 114°; in the middle of it a statue to "Bladud, son of Lord Hudibras, eighth king of the Britons from Bute, &c., &c., the first discoverer of these baths, 863 years B.C.," and so forth. King's Bath is in Stall Street, on one side of the colonnade and the pump-room, where the band plays. It was rebuilt in 1796, on the site of that in which Beau Nash, with a white hat for his crown, despotically ruled as master of the ceremonies in the last century. His statue is seen here, by Hoare. Over the front is a Greek tee-total motto, signifying "Water is the thing." Queen's Bath, close to the other, and so called when James I.'s queen, Anne of Denmark, came here to take the waters. Hot Bath, which has a temperature of 117° (the highest), and is supplied by a spring which gives out 128 gallons per minute. Cross Bath, temperature 109°, yielding only 12 gallons a minute. This is the one recorded by Pepys in his diary, 1668. "Up at four o'clock, being by appointment called to the *Cross Bath.* By and bye much company came; very fine ladies, and the manners pretty enough, only methinks it cannot be clean to go so many bodies together in the same water. Strange to see how hot the water is;" and he wonders that those who stay the season are not all parboiled. Another bath is the property of Lord Manvers. The water is nearly transparent; about 180,000 gallons daily are given out to these baths, and this has been going on for centuries! Sulphate of lime is by far the chief ingredient; then muriate and sulphate of soda, and a little carbonic acid rising up in bubbles. They are remarkably beneficial in rheumatism, paralysis, skin complaints, scrofula, gout, indigestion, and chronic diseases of the liver, &c. House painters, among others, come here to be cured of the injury done to their hands by white lead.

Bath is a city of terraces and crescents—viz:—the Circus, the North and South Parades, the Royal and Lansdowne Crescents, and others, either in the town or on the hills around. Some of the best buildings are by Wood, author of "Description of Bath." Among the 20 churches is the Abbey Church, or Cathedral, which replaces a monastery, founded in 970, by King Edgar; it is a cross, 240 feet long, built in the 16th century, and has 52 windows inside, with a rich one in the fine east front, and some good tracery in Prior Bird's Chapel. There are monuments to Waller, the parliament general (effigy, with a broken nose), to Bishop Montague, who restored the church, 1606, to Nash (lines by Dr. Harrington); Quin, the actor (lines by Garrick); Mary Frampton (lines by Dryden); Col. Champion, by Nollekens; and Anstey, author of the coarse witty "New Bath Guide."

St. James's is a modern Grecian church with a high tower, in Stall Street. Another church, with a fine early English spire, stands in Broad Street. St. Saviour's, at the eastern extremity of the city, and St. Stephen's, on Lansdowne, are modern Gothic churches; and several others of note. Milsom Street and Bond Street contain the best shops. Near are the Circus, and the Assembly Room, a handsome pile, built in 1771 by Wood, with a ball-room 106 feet long, and an octagon full of portraits. Another of Wood's works, the Royal Crescent, is worth notice; Smollett called it "an antique amphitheatre turned inside out." The Guildhall, a noble building in the Grecian style, is in High Street. Near at hand is a well-stocked market. Its supply of fish is very good.

Within a short distance is the General Hospital, founded chiefly through Beau Nash's exertions, for the benefit of poor people, from all parts, using the Bath waters. Bellot's Hospital, an old building, founded in 1609. The Casualty and United Hospitals are among the various munificent institutions here. Partis's College was founded for ladies of decayed fortune. St. John's Hospital, founded in the 12th century, and rebuilt by Wood, near Cross Bath, has an income of £9,000.

There is a full and interesting museum of Roman antiquities and fossil remains at the Literary Institution, near the Baths and Parade. A club-house in York Buildings, and several public libraries.

A large Grammar School, rebuilt in 1752, stands in Broad Street; here Sir Sidney Smith was educated. Beau Nash died in St. John's Court, 1761, old and neglected. A well-built theatre is in Beaufort Square. The Sydney or Vauxhall Gardens at Great Pulteney Street (so called after the Pulteney who became first Earl of Bath). Victoria Park, with a drive, pillar, botanic garden, &c., occupies the Town Common. There are also obelisks to the Prince of Orange and the Prince of Wales, father of George III. The new savings bank, in the Italian style, was built in 1842.

Of nine bridges over the Avon three are suspension bridges, two are viaducts for the railway, and the best looking is that on the North Parade, a single arch of 188 feet span.

All the hills command fine views, of more or less extent, and are marked by buildings, &c. On Odd Down (south), is the Union Workhouse. A vast quarry of Bath stone is opened in Coomb Down (south west), on which are the Abbey Church Cemetery, and Prior Park College—a handsome building. In Pope's time it was the property of his friend, Ralph Allen (the Allworthy of Fielding's *Tom Jones*), and Warburton. Allen built Sham Castle, on Claverton Down. The beautiful vale of Lyncombe is near this. Lansdowne Hill, 813 feet high, on the north, has a cemetery, two large colleges, one belonging to the Wesleyans; pillar to the memory of Sir B. Granville, who fell here, in 1645, and a striking campanile tower, built by Beckford, of Fonthill, who died here in 1844, and is buried in the cemetery. He wrote "Caliph Vathek," a most original story, which created quite a "*furore*" in those days. His daughter, the beautiful Sally Beckford, is Dowager Duchess of Hamilton.

Other points are Batheaston Church and Salisbury Hill, 600 feet high, near the old Roman road, on the east; Hampton Cliffs, at Bathford, on the west; Charlcombe and Weston Downs; Kelston (or Kelweston) Round. At Twerton a factory for the cloth or Bath coating for which the town was once noted. Paper is made here. Further off are the ruins of Hinton Priory, and Farleigh Castle.

The "ever-memorable" John Hales, and Miss Edgeworth's father (whose entertaining memoirs are well worth perusal), were born at Bath.

From the Bath station the railway is carried on a viaduct, continued by alternate excavation and embankment, over the Old Bath Road. We soon after pass into an excavation, and then through a tunnel. Amid a succession of very varied and beautiful scenery along the line, we reach the station of

TWERTON, and soon after, that of

SALTFORD.

Telegraph station at Bath, 4½ miles.

HOTEL.—Railway.

A very deep excavation here follows, and through a Gothic gateway conducts us to the Saltford Tunnel. An embankment succeeds across the valley of the Avon, and passing over a viaduct we arrive at

KEYNSHAM.

Distance from station, ¼ mile

A telegraph station.

HOTEL.—White Hart.

MARKET DAY.—Thursday. FAIRS.—March 24th and 26th, April 27th, and August 15th.

Proceeding over a lofty embankment, which affords a commanding prospect on every side, and enables us to trace the windings of the silvery Avon, along its verdant shores, edged with towering poplars and branching elms. Nature here seems to have put on her loveliest robe, but Art, as if envious of her beauty, jealously encloses us in a ponderous cutting at the very moment we are most enthusiastically enjoying the prospect.

The train then passes through several tunnels, and flitting over a three-arched bridge that spans the Avon, we again reach an embankment, during our passage over which our speed is gradually slackened, and we pass beneath that splendid archway, the entrance to

BRISTOL.

POPULATION, 137,328.

Distance from station, 1 mile. A telegraph station.

HOTELS.—The Queen's Hotel; Clifton.

OMNIBUSES to and from the station.

MARKET DAYS.—Wednesday, Friday, and Saturday. FAIRS.—March 1st and September 1st

BANKERS.—Branch of the Bank of England; Baillie, Ames, and Co.; Miles and Co.; Stuckey's Banking Co.; National Provincial Bank of England; West of England and South Wales District Banking Co.

The terminus of the railway is situated on an eminence rising from Temple Meads, where the two lines diverge respectively to London and Plymouth.

BRISTOL is a cathedral city, sea-port, and parliamentary borough in Gloucestershire, 118 miles from London, on the Great Western Railway, and the *Via Julia*, or Roman road, made by Julius Agricola, which crossed into Wales at Aust Ferry. The beautiful watering place of *Clifton* is on the west side. *Bedminster*, within the borough bounds, belongs to Somersetshire. Its port is artificially made by excavating floating docks, 3 miles long, out of the old bed of the Avon (for which a new course was made), about 8 miles from King's Road in the Bristol Channel, the tide rising 40 to 50 feet. Since the tolls were reduced in 1848, the registered tonnage has risen to 71,000, and the foreign trade doubled. Much West India and Irish produce finds way into the country through this port. The chief manufactures are engines, glass, hats, pottery, soap, brushes, &c., besides various smaller branches, and a trade in sugar, rum, &c. This place has, from the earliest times, been an important seaport, from whence old navigators used to start. One of the foremost was Sebastian Cabot, a native, who sailed hence in 1497 to discover Labrador. Kidrapping, also, for the American plantations used to be practised here, and it shared with Liverpool in the iniquities of the slave trade. In the present day it is noted for having sent the first steamer across the Atlantic, the *Great Western* (Capt. Hosken), which sailed on the 2nd May, 1838, and reached New York in 15 days. Two members. Coal and oolite are quarried.

The oldest part of the town is in Temple, Peter, and other streets, where picturesque timber houses are seen. There are many buildings worth notice. At College Green (where a new High Cross has been erected) is the *Cathedral*, a plain, shapeless, early English church, built in 1142-60, and about 174 feet long internally; it has a tower 133 feet high, with some effigies of the Berkeleys, &c., and various interesting monuments and inscriptions. The latest is that of Southey, a native. Near is a Norman chapter-house 43 feet long, the cloisters, gate, &c., of a priory founded by the Berkeley family; also a part of the Bishop's Palace, set fire to in the riots of 1831, when Wetherell was appointed Recorder. The bishop now resides at Stapleton. A more interesting church is that of *St. Mary Redcliffe*, a truly beautiful early and later English cross, 247 feet long, rebuilt in the 15th century by the famous William Canynges, and now partly restored. St. John's, St. Peter's, St. Stephen's, St. James's, the Temple, and St. Mark's are all ancient edifices. At All Saints, E. Colston, a great benefactor to his native place, is buried. The *Guildhall*, in Broad Street, has been rebuilt in the Elizabethan style, and among other curiosities it contains an ancient chapel. Henry VII' sword (he visited it in 1487, taking care to entail a sumptuary fine on the citizens because their wives dressed too gaudily), a series of grants from 1164, seals from Edward I., Lord Mayor Wallis's pearl scabbard sword (given in 1431), and Alderman Kitchen's silver salver (as old as 1594), which, being stolen in the riots of 1831, was cut into 167 pieces, *recovered, and put together again!* Other buildings are, the Council House, with a statue of Justice, by *Baily* (who is a native); new Custom-house (rebuilt since the riots, in Queen Square, near William of Orange's statue; Exchange, in Corn Street, built by Wood, of Bath, in 1743; Merchant Tailors' Old Hall, in Broad Street; Stuckey's Bank, which was sent ready made from Holland; Philosophical Institution, with Baily's exquisite *Eve at the Fountain* in its museum. Bishop's College and the Blind Asylum are in the Park, near the Horticultural Rooms; Proprietary and Baptist Colleges; Queen Elizabeth's Hospital on Brandon Hill, which is 250 feet high.

St. Vincent's Rocks are 300 feet high; at the Observatory a suspension bridge over the Avon to Leigh Wood is begun, but not finished. Another beautiful spot is at the Zoological Gardens, near Cook's Folly, on Durdham Down. The *Clifton Hot Wells*, or sulphur springs, near here, are excellent in cases of scrofula and chronic diseases. The following most feeling lines were written at this place by the second Lord Palmerston, in the last century:—

"Whoe'er, like me, with trembling anguish brings
His dearest earthly treasure to these springs,
Whoe'er, like me, to soothe distress and pain,
Shall court these salutary springs in vain;
Condemn'd, like me, to hear the faint reply,
To mark the fading cheek, the sinking eye;
From the chill brow to wipe the damps of death,
And watch in dumb despair the shortening breath,
If chance should bring him to this humble line
Let the sad mourner know this pang was mine,
Ordained to love the partner of my breast,
Whose virtue warmed me, and whose beauty blessed;
Framed every tie that binds the heart to prove,
Her duty friendship, and her friendship love;
But yet remembering that the parting sigh
Appoints the just to slumber, not to die,
The starting tear I checked—I kissed the rod,
And not to earth resigned her—but to God."

Lansdowne Square, Windsor and York Crescents, and the Victoria Rooms (a pretty Grecian temple), are here. On the Down above, there is a Roman camp. Here many plants, and quartz or Bristol stones are found. Mr. Pepys records his approval of another native production, "Bristol milk," or old sherry. At Temple Mead are various metal works, sugar refineries, &c. One of Wesley's first chapels was built in 1739 in the Horse Fair; and there is a Wesleyan College at Kingswood (4 miles off) where Whitfield and he often preached the Gospel to the poor outcast colliers, till the "tears made white gutters down their black cheeks."

Admiral Penn, Sir Thomas Lawrence (born at the White Lion), and Chatterton, are among the long list of natives of Bristol.

Twelve or more bridges cross the Avon and the line of Docks—the cutting forming a sort of loop line to the river. Of about 120 places of worship, 42 are churches

Within a short distance are *Leigh Court* and its picture gallery, the seat of P. Miles, Esq., M.P. *King's Weston*, the Clifford's old seat, belongs to the same gentleman. *Stapleton* is the seat of the Bishop of Gloucester and Bristol, near the new diocesan college; Hannah More was born here in 1744, but her chief residence was at Barley Wood, under the Mendip Hill. At *Westbury*, "in some of the finest ground of that truly beautiful part of England," Southey was living about 1796 or 1797, writing *Madoc* and *Thalaba*, and cultivating his acquaintance with Davy, the chemist, "a miraculous young man." This was one of the "happiest portions" of his useful and contented literary life. The rail should be followed to Clevedon and Weston-super-Mare, to enjoy the fine coast scenery of the Bristol Channel.

CLIFTON, a beautiful suburb of Bristol, from which it is about a mile distant, is chiefly built on the southern acclivity of a steep hill or cliff, which has given rise to its appellation. The highly romantic and picturesque country, in the midst of which it is situated, provides on every side the most varied and extensive prospects. On the opposite shore of the Avon, the richly cultivated lands of Somersetshire present themselves, rising gradually from the verge of the river to the summit of Dundry Hill. In some places the rocks, venerably majestic, rise perpendicularly, or overhanging precipices, craggy and bare, and in others they are crowned with verdure of the most luxuriant description. The walks and rides are varied and interesting, the air is dry and bracing, and the vicinity of two such animated places as Bristol and Bath, give the resident at any time the opportunity of rapidly exchanging his solitude for society. The "Hot Wells," where "pale-eyed suppliants drink, and soon flies pain," are beautifully situated beneath the rocks looking on the river, along the banks of which a fine carriage-road leads from the well round the rocks to Clifton Down, but a readier and more picturesque mode of access is furnished by an easy serpentine path winding up among the cliffs behind the Hot Wells. Pieces of the rock, when broken, have much the appearance of a dark red marble, and when struck by a substance of corresponding hardness, emit a strong sulphurous smell. In the fissures of these rocks are found those fine crystals, usually called Bristol diamonds, which are so hard as to cut glass and sustain the action of fire. The spring has been known for many centuries, but it was not till 1690 that it was enclosed by the corporation of Bristol. There is now a neat pump-room with hot and cold baths. The temperature of the spring, which yields forty gallons a minute, is 76° Fahrenheit. As at Bath and Buxton, the predominating constituents are the salts of lime. When drawn into a glass the water emits a few bubbles of carbonic acid gas, and for various conditions of deranged health it is found to be a potent restorative. The range of buildings called York Crescent, affords an agreeable southern aspect, but the elevated situation leaves the houses much exposed to high winds. The Mall, the Parade, and Cornwallis Crescent furnish excellent accommodation to visitors, and, according to their respective differences of position, yield a sheltered winter or an open airy summer residence. The most prevalent winds are those from the west and south-east. Rain frequently falls, but from the absorbent nature of the soil, the ground quickly dries. The Giant's Cave is contained within the upper beds of the limestone in St. Vincent's Rocks. The cavern opens on the precipitous escarpment of the rock, at the height of about 250 feet above the river, and sixty feet below or to the west of the Observatory. A rude and broken ledge extends from the north-eastern summit of the rock downwards to within twenty feet of the opening, across which space none but an expert cragsman would venture to pass. The environs of Clifton are replete with scenery of the most enchanting description.

BRISTOL AND EXETER.

Bristol to Highbridge.

On leaving the station at Bristol, the lofty roof and portly walls glide away almost insensibly from our vision, and leave us in exchange the free air and undulating grounds of a wide and open country, through which the continuous iron line is seen wending onward. The embankment on which we are carried reveals to us passing glimpses of luxuriant lands, and tower-crested eminences, fertile to the summit, the chief charms and characteristics of all Somerset. About two miles from Bristol we pass under the old turnpike road to Wells and Bridgewater, and in another mile come upon an elevation which unfolds a bold and romantic view of the surrounding country. Ashton Hill, and Leigh Down, with the pretty picturesque village of Long Ashton, form a very attractive picture to the right; and opposite, soaring above the level of the sea to 700 feet, rises the majestic eminence of Dundry Beacon, the turreted summit of which becomes a prominent object for many miles. A cutting here intercepts the view and we pass the stations of

BOURTON, NAILSEA and YATTON, places of no importance, except the latter as being the junction of the

CLEVEDON BRANCH.

Continuing our journey to the right, we reach, in about four miles further, by alternate embankment and excavation,

CLEVEDON.

A telegraph station.

HOTELS.—Bristol, Royal.

This is a charmingly situated and rapidly improving watering place, much frequented by the citizens of Bristol during the summer season. Situated on the margin of the Bristol Channel, with rugged and precipitous rocks rising boldly up from the

"Deep waters of the dark blue sea,"

Clevedon presents a very attractive place of resort to both the occasional tourist and valetudinarian, who seeks a quiet retreat for health's sake. Myrtles and other delicate shrubs flourish in the gardens at all seasons, so temperate is the air.

Bristol and Exeter Main Line continued.

After leaving Yatton we catch a very pleasing view of the Channel, with its dimpled surface spotted with white sails, and its range of ruddy headlands stretching far away in the distance. Green hills, diversified by open downs and richly cultivated corn lands, constitute a delightful contrast in the opposite direction; and thus, amid a varied succession of prospects, we reach the station at

BANWELL.

Distance from station, 2¼ miles.

This little village has become of some notoriety from the discovery of two caverns in its vicinity, one called the Stalactite, and the other the Bone Cave, which attract a great number of visitors. Locking and Hatton adjacent, with their antiquated churches —the cavern of Wokey, and the Chees—celebrated cliffs of Cheddar, are all worth visiting.

Leaving the Banwell station, we pass the villages of Wick, St. Lawrence, Kewstoke, and further on, Worle Hill, which commands a series of extensive maritime and inland views, and variegated landscapes.

WESTON-SUPER-MARE Junction.

WESTON - SUPER - MARE.—(Branch).

Distance from station, 2 miles.
HOTEL.—Bath.

WESTON-SUPER-MARE has the advantage of being very accessible from Bristol, Bath, Exeter, and other towns on the line of the Great Western Railway. It has none of the picturesqueness arising from old streets and buildings, but, situated on the margin of Uphill Bay, near the Bristol Channel, it possesses the usual attractions of a neat watering place, having within the last ten years become considerably enlarged and frequented. The receding of the tide leaves a disfiguring bank of mud along the beach, which is a great drawback to the enjoyment of bathing; but a good market, numerous shops, and a delightful neighbourhood for rambling, present some counterbalancing advantages. Worle Hill is one of the pleasantest spots that a tourist could desire to meet with. In traversing the northern or sea side of the hill, the path lies, most of the way, through a copse of young fir trees, presenting occasional openings of the Channel and the rocky coast beyond. Towards the eastern end of the hill beautiful prospects are unfolded over a large and richly cultivated plain, extending to Woodspring Priory and Clevedon, with two or three churches standing up amid the elms and ashes. The nearest of these is Kewstoke Church, situated on the slope of Worle Hill itself. It derives its name from St. Kew, who once formed his cell on the bleak hill top. From the church a craggy track, called the Pass of St. Kew, consisting of a hundred natural and artificial steps, leads over the hill to the village of Milton on the opposite side, and these are said to have been worn by the feet of the pious recluse, as he daily went to perform his devotions at the church, which then occupied the same spot as it does at present. The ruins of the Priory at Woodspring are of considerable extent, and very picturesque, situated in a very solitary position at the farther end of a wide marshy but cultivated flat; they are divided from the sea by a narrow ridge of rocks, called Swallow Cliffs, quite out of the way of any frequented road. Crossing the broad mossy top of Worle Hill we can descend upon the village of Worle, which is prettily situated on the southern slope of the hill, and commands a delightful view over the richly cultivated flat to the range of the Mendip Hills. In short, the inducements to prolong a visit to Weston will be found principally to arise from the charming localities by which it is surrounded. The climate is bracing, and the air is very salubrious. The postal arrangements are—Letters delivered at 10 a.m.; box for London closing at 4 p.m.

Bristol and Exeter Main Line continued.

HIGHBRIDGE.

Distance from station, ½ mile.
A telegraph station.
HOTEL.—Railway.
MONEY ORDER OFFICE at Burnham.

The scenery around here becomes exquisitely pastoral, and almost immediately after quitting the station, the majestic hill known as Glastonbury Tor is seen in the distance, and can be distinctly discerned, with its ruined temple on the summit, though 13 miles off. The neighbourhood abounds with religious monuments.

BURNHAM (Branch).

This place from its invigorating atmosphere and affording, as it does, the usual requisites of a sea-side retreat, has become valuable to the tourist in the summer season. Steamers run regularly, plying between this place and Cardiff.

☞ SOMERSET CENTRAL.

Highbridge to Glastonbury and Wells.

The line proceeds through a country equally characterised by its luxuriant verdure as that about Highbridge, and crossing the river Brue, we pass through a short cutting which shuts out the prospect; but on emerging from this, and entering on an embankment, we again have a panoramic view of Arcadian villages, waving woods, and winding hedge-rows.

The Stations on this line are those of BASON BRIDGE, EDINGTON (a nice trip hence over the Panlet Ridge to Sedgemoor), SHAPWICK, ASHCOTT, stations of no particular note, and

GLASTONBURY.

A telegraph station.

HOTELS.—George or Pilgrims; White Hart.

MARKET DAY.—Tuesday. FAIR.—Sept. 19th.

This town, containing a population of 3,125, is situated near a high hill called the Tor, on which is a tower that serves for a sea mark. Here are considerable ruins of a famous abbey, which occupied an area of 60 acres. The Grange Inn was formerly an hospital for the accommodation of pilgrims who visited the abbey, and to see the holy thorn, said to have been planted by Joseph of Arimathea, and to blossom on Christmas eve. The last abbot of this place was hanged on the top of the Tor, by order of Henry VIII., for not acknowledging his supremacy.

WELLS.

HOTELS.—Mitre; Somerset; Star.

This ancient city is prettily situated in a valley at the foot of the Mendip hills, and has a population of 4,736. Conjointly with Bath it forms the see of a bishop, and returns two members to Parliament. Its cathedral ranks amongst the most important, and presents one of the most splendid specimens of Gothic architecture in England.

Bristol and Exeter Main Line continued.

Highbridge to Durston Junction.

BRIDGEWATER.

Distance from station, ¼ mile.
A telegraph station.
HOTELS.—Royal Clarence, Globe, White Hart.
MARKET DAYS.—Tuesday, Thursday, and Saturday.
FAIRS.—Second Thursday in Lent, June 24th, Oct. 2nd.

A port and borough in Somersetshire, on the Great Western Railway, 29 miles from Bristol, a bay, and the mouth of the Parret. Common red bricks of an excellent quality, and the white scouring "Bath Brick" as it is called, though peculiar to Bridgewater, is only made here by two or three firms. They are manufactured from the slime deposited on the banks of the Parret, where untouched by the salt water (which spoils it), and burnt at the top of the kiln, above the red bricks.

It returns two members, and has a population of 10,317. About 8,500 tons of shipping belong to the port; small vessels of 200 tons come up to the quay. Admiral Blake was born here in 1599, the son of a merchant. He sat for his native town in parliament. "He was the first man (says Clarendon) who brought ships to contemn castles on shore, which ......were discovered by him to make a noise only; and......who infused that proportion of courage into the seamen, by making them see what mighty things they could do if they were resolved." There was a fortress on Castle Hill, built after the Conquest, by Walter de Douai, from whom, or from the bridge which he began, the town takes its name, Bridge-Walter.

At this spot the Duke of Monmouth was proclaimed, before his defeat at *Sedgemoor*, 1685. It is a level marshy tract, four miles south east, intersected by the Cary, but much altered since that event. Many of the wretched prisoners were brought here to be butchered by Jefferies and his satellite, Kirke.

The large Gothic parish church has a good porch, and a fine spire, 174 feet high, with the "Descent from the Cross," after Guido. Other buildings are the Town Hall, with a great cistern over it, for supplying the town with water, a Market House, surmounted by a dome, &c., but none very remarkable.

In the neighbourhood are *Brymore House*, seat of Hon. P. Bouverie, where Pyne, "King Pyne," of the Long Parliament, lived. *Enmore Castle*, Earl Egmont, *Halsewell*, Colonel Tynte; gallery of Vandykes, &c. All these are to the west of the town, in view of the Quantock Hills; and the road may be followed to Watchet, Dunster, Minehead, and other rocky parts of the coast. At *Nether Stowey*, Coleridge lived, in 1796-8, after his marriage, in company with his friend Charles Lloyd, the poet; and here he wrote his "Ancient Mariner," and the tragedy of "Remorse." Wordsworth at the same time was his neighbour, at Alfoxton or Allfoxden, where he composed his "Lyrical Ballads," the subject of many interminable discussions with the friends, as they walked over the hills together.

DURSTON JUNCTION.

POPULATION, 258.
Distance from station, 1 mile.
A telegraph station.
MONEY ORDER OFFICE at Taunton.
Has a priory and preceptory at Buckland Sororum.

YEOVIL BRANCH.—Durston to Yeovil.

The route from Durston takes in the stations of ATHELNEY, LANGPORT and MARTOCK. They require no special comment.

YEOVIL.

Distance from station, ½ mile. A telegraph station.
HOTELS.—Mermaid, Three Choughs.
MARKET DAY.—Friday.
FAIRS.—June 28th and Nov. 17th.
BANKERS.—Stuckey's Banking Co.; Branch of Wilts and Dorset Banking Co.

An ancient town, the seat of a considerable glove trade. It has a fine Gothic church, and a large market house, well calculated for its large market, which occurs on Fridays. In the vicinity is *Brympton House*, the old seat of the Fane family.

Bristol and Exeter Main Line continued.

Durston to Tiverton and Exeter.

On leaving the Bridgewater station the line is continued by embankment across the river Parret, and soon after we enter the fertile valley of the Tone. The river, which gives name to this luxuriant district rises in the Quantock hills, near the town of Wiveliscombe, and, flowing for some miles, passes Taunton, to which town it gives name. Taunton Dean is famed for its fruitful ground, which is proverbially alleged to produce three crops a year. After gliding along several scenes of wild fertility and romantic beauty, we pass a hill which quite shuts out the prospect, and entering a brief but deep cutting, we reach the neat and commodious station at

TAUNTON.

A telegraph station.

HOTELS.—Castle; London Inn.

MARKET DAYS.—Wednesday and Saturday.

FAIRS.—June 17th and July 7th.

BANKERS.—Badock & Co.; Stuckey's Banking Co.; Branch of West of England and South Wales District Bank.

The town, as seen from the station, has a most pleasing appearance. It is situated in the central part of the luxuriant and beautiful vale of Taunton Dean.

TAUNTON is an ancient borough town, population 14,176 (two members), in a rich and beautiful part of Somersetshire, on the Bristol and Exeter railway, 163 miles from London. The wide and cultivated dean, or shallow strath, in which it stands is watered by the Tone (wherefore the Saxons called it *Tantun*), and overlooked by the tower of its Gothic church, which is of Henry Seventh's age. The tower is 153 feet high, of light and elegant proportions, covered over with heads of lions, &c., and set off with pinnacles, battlements and niches, in the elaborate style of that day, of which, indeed, Somersetshire furnishes many excellent specimens. There is some good carved work inside, about the pulpit and niches, and a fine organ. Quaint epitaph to Sheriff Grey, founder of a hospital, who left this place a poor boy:—

"Taunton bore him—London bred him,
Piety trained him, virtue led him,
Earth enriched him, Heaven caressed him,
Taunton blest him, London blest him;
This thankful town, that mindful city,
Shared his piety and his pity;
What he gave and how he gave it
Ask the poor, and you shall have it,
Gentle reader, may Heaven strike
Thy tender heart to do the like;
And now thy eyes have read this story,
Give him the praise, and Heaven the glory."

And another on a tailor, who invented ruffs. The *Assize Court* is an ancient building, 120 feet long, erected in 1577, close to the gate of the Castle, which was founded here by Ina, King of Wessex, and rebuilt after the Conquest by the Bishops of Winchester. It was successfully defended by Blake against the Royalists in the civil war, but dismantled by Charles II. Here the ill-fated Monmouth proclaimed himself king in 1685. Forty young ladies presented him with a banner, worked at the cost of the town, for which they were specially excepted in King James' proclamation of amnesty, issued some months afterwards. After his defeat at Sedgemoor, near Bridgewater, King James's Chief Justice, Jefferies, the worthy tool of such a monster, held his bloody assize at Taunton, when *hundreds* of poor wretches were condemned to death, after being persuaded to throw themselves on the king's mercy. His executioner, Kirke, hanged one man three times on the White Hart sign post, and cried out he would do it again if he could. The joy of the town, therefore, when the Prince of Orange appeared, was proportionately great. The Town Hall and Assembly Room, built in 1723, are over the market place, which stands in an open spot at the junction of the principal streets, called the Parade. A new room at the Taunton Institution was established in 1823. There is now being built a new Shire Hall, to be used instead of the old assize courts. The streets are in general airy and well built, which adds considerably to the pleasant aspect of the town. The outskirts are furnished with large spreading gardens and orchards. One of the best and most conspicuous buildings is the *Wesleyan Collegiate Institution*, a Tudor range, 250 feet long (built 1847); it contains room for 100 students. This, among others, was the result of the centenary celebration.

A little outside Taunton, across the Tone, is Price's Farm, the site of a friary; and in this direction you come on a very ancient bridge, of one arch, called Ram's Horn, and which is said to be a Roman structure.

Within a short distance of Taunton are also *Pyrland*, the seat of R. King, Esq. *Sandhill*, that of Sir T. Lethbridge, Bart., is near Combe Florey, the rectory formerly of Sydney Smith. *Milverton*, in a pretty spot, was the birth place of the philosopher, the late Dr. Thomas Young. *Ninehead* is the seat of E. Sandford, Esq. More distant excursions may be made to Watchet, Dunster, Minehead, &c., on the coast of the Bristol Channel; and the sources of the Ex, in Exmoor Forest, a wild and interesting tract, where the red deer is sometimes seen.

Leaving the Taunton station we are subjected for a short time to the confinement of a cutting, on passing which we perceive the Bridgewater and Taunton canal on our left, while the eminences to our right are crowned with picturesque villages. Proceeding on an embankment, the little hamlet of Bishop's Hall is passed, and we soon after cross several streams tributary to the Tone, that gleam and sparkle between the patches of meadow land and forest scenery by which they are skirted in their progress. After crossing a viaduct over the Tone, the arch of Shaw bridge, and passing an excavation, we are carried forward by a sinuous embankment to

WELLINGTON.

POPULATION, 3,926.

A telegraph station.

Distance from station, ½ mile.

HOTEL.—Squirrel.

MARKET DAY.—Thursday.

FAIRS.—Thursday before Whit Sunday, Easter and Holy Thursday.

MONEY ORDER OFFICE.

BANKERS.—Fox Brothers; Stuckey's Banking Co.

Here is a Gothic church of which W. S. Salkeld was rector in James I.'s time. The Duke of Wellington, who derives his title from this place, is lord of the manor. A pillar, in honour of the Hero of Waterloo, was erected on Black Down Hill. This range of hills is on the Devonshire borders, and produces stone used by scythe grinders, &c.

Quitting the station, and again crossing the Tone, we enter an excavation which conducts us to the White Ball Tunnel, a fine piece of arched brick work, nearly one mile in length. About the centre we attain the highest elevation between Bristol and Exeter, and on emerging from its obscuration we find ourselves in the magnificent county of Devon, with the Wellington memorial cresting the summit of a distant hill on our left, and the long range of precipices, known as the Blackdown Hills, far away before us, apparently extending to the very verge of the sea.

DEVONSHIRE.

This county is one of the most beautiful in England, and in point of size is only exceeded by that of York. It is about 280 miles in circuit. Its external appearance is varied and irregular; and the heights in many parts, particularly in the vicinity of Dartmouth, swell into mountains.

Dartmoor, and the waste called Dartmoor Forest, occupy the greater portion of the western district, which extends from the vale of Exeter to the banks of the river Tamar.

The cultivated lands of West Devon are nearly all inclosures, being in general large in proportion to the size of the farms. North Devon comprehends the country round Bideford.

Amidst a succession of scenery almost purely pastoral we are again startled by the premonitory whistle of the engine, and find ourselves opposite

TIVERTON JUNCTION (Uffculme).

Distance of town from station, 5 miles

Hotel.—Railway.

TIVERTON BRANCH.

TIVERTON.

A telegraph station.

Hotel.—Angel.

Market Day.—Tuesday. Fairs.—Tuesday fortnight after Whitsunday, and September 29th.

Bankers.—National Provincial Bank of England; Dunsford and Barne.

Tiverton has a population of 11,144, returning two members to parliament. It is a place of considerable antiquity, being a small village in the time of Alfred the Great, and described in the Doomsday Survey as belonging to the king. The manorial rights originally, by virtue of a gift from Henry I., belonged to Richard Rivers, afterwards Earl of Devon, who built a castle, and, residing here, greatly added to the prosperity of the place.

Bristol and Exeter Main Line continued.

Leaving the Tiverton junction, the line is continued for some time on an embankment, but the beauty of Devonshire scenery is more to be found in the village lanes and unfrequented byeways, than near the somewhat monotonous levels which a railway of necessity maintains. Thus the six miles' walk across the hills from Tiverton to Collumpton is a marvellous treat to the pedestrian, whereas the railway tourist sees nothing but a rather dreary succession of green flats, this particular part being devoid of those striking characteristics in the landscape we have hitherto described, and the view of which renders the journey so interesting.

COLLUMPTON.

Distance from station, ¼ mile.

A telegraph station.

Hotel.—White Hart.

Market Day.—Saturday.

Fairs.—May 12th and October 28th.

Bankers.—Branch of Devon Banking Co.

This little town, though containing a population of only 2,765, is one of great antiquity, having been in the possession of Alfred the Great, and afterwards belonging to Buckland Abbey. It has some manufactories for woollen and paper.

HELE.

A telegraph station.

Money Order Office at Collumpton.

Again borne onwards by our never-tiring iron steed, at a speed outstripping the breeze of summer, we become conscious of a moving panorama, which has regained most of the alluring features that we have been recently regretting.

We traverse the valley of the Culme—past Bradninch, through cutting and over embankment—and the winding Exe and Cowley Bridge, and then, after a few minutes of woodland scenery, our speed slackens, the well-known whistle of the engine follows, and we are hurried beneath the portico of a commodious building, which forms the station at

EXETER.

A telegraph station.

Hotels.—Half Moon, High Street.

Fly Fares.—To and from any part of the City, 1s.; to and from Heavitree, 1s. 6d.; to and from Mount Radford, 1s. 6d; beyond the boundaries of the City, 1s. per mile. A fraction of a mile considered as a mile.

Market Days.—Tuesday and Friday.

Fairs.—Ash Wednesday, Whit-Monday, August 1st, and Dec. 6th.

Bankers.—Milford and Co.; Sanders and Co.; Branch of West of England and South Wales District Bank; Branch of Devon and Cornwall Banking Co.; National Provincial Bank of England.

Exeter is pleasantly situated on an eminence rising from the eastern bank of the river Exe, which encompasses its south-west side, and over which it has a handsome stone bridge.

Exeter is the capital of Devon and the West of England, a Bishop's see, city, and parliamentary borough, on the Great Western (Bristol and Exeter) Railway, 194 miles from London. It is also a port, eight miles from the Channel, up the Exe, from which it derives the Saxon name, Excester, or the fortress on the Exe, so called because of the Roman station planted here. Population, 40,688; two members. Exeter stretches for nearly two miles over a hill above the river, and is, therefore, not only pleasantly seated, but well drained, except in some parts of the suburbs. At the top, north of the town, are the picturesque ruined walls and gate of *Rougemont* (Red Hill) *Castle*, first built by the Conqueror, and rased by Parliament, when Fairfax took it in 1646, after a siege. This is one of the best points of view, and is the spot where Colonel Penruddock was beheaded by Cromwell, for his premature rising for the king. The Sessions House stands within the bounds; close to it is the fine elm walk of Northernbay. Friar's Walk, Pennsylvania Hill, and Mount Radford also command good views. "There be divers fair streets in Exeter (says Leland, in Henry VIII.'s time), but the High Street that goeth from the west to the east gate is the fairest." The gates he saw are gone, but parts of the strong walls remain, from whence there are good prospects. Where the street falls suddenly, two or three dry bridges have been built (the iron bridge in North Street, for instance), to save the descent. Another of stone, in line with High and Fore Streets, crosses the river, which runs rather swiftly here. In High Street is the venerable-looking *Guildhall*, containing portraits of Charles I., Queen Henrietta Maria and her daughter, the Duchess of Orleans, General Monk (by Lely), George II., &c. Lemprière was master of the *Grammar School* at St. John's Hospital. The *Theatre* is on the site of old Bedford House, where the Duchess of Orleans was born in the civil war.

On the east, near High Street, stands the fine *Cathedral*, which, as usual, is a cross 375 feet long, internally. It is mostly early English, but the Norman towers, 145 feet high, belong to an older edifice erected by Bishop Warlewast, and half ruined in the siege of 1137, when King Stephen took the town. The nave, choir, &c., were rebuilt as we see them now, between 1281 and 1420. Bishop Grandison's west front is perhaps the most striking part. It has been lately restored, and is full of statues of kings, bishops, and scripture characters in niches. The window is also stained with a profusion of figures and coats of arms. The vault of the nave deserves notice. In the north tower is the great Peter bell, weighing 5½ tons; ascend this tower for the view. A lady chapel, 56 feet by 30, is of the 14th century. The bishop's throne is of beautiful carved oak, 52 feet high, and as old as 1470. Among the monuments are Humphrey Bohun, Bishop Bronescombe (1280), Bishop Stafford, the Courtenays, &c., and a fine one to Northcote, the painter, by Chantrey. The *Chapter House* is Gothic, 50 feet by 30, with a carved timber roof, and contains a library of 8,000 vols. A ship canal brings vessels up to the quay, where there is a very considerable trade carried on. Some of the best cider is made in the environs.

Excursions may be made from this point to Crediton, the original seat of the bishopric; Heavitree where Richard Hooker was born; Topsham, Powderham Castle (Earl of Devon), and Exmouth, down the Exe; over the Haldon Downs to Chudleigh and Ugbrook (Lord Clifford); Exmouth, Sidmouth, Dawlish, Teignmouth, and Torquay, and other beautiful spots along the coast; *Bicton*, seat of Lady Rolle, near Hayes Farm, where *Raleigh* was born. The entire coast of Devonshire is, perhaps, the most attractive in England.

Bude—a small port and picturesque village in the north-eastern extremity of Cornwall—has, within the last half-dozen years, risen to the dignity of a fashionable marine resort, to which distinction the excellent facilities it affords to bathers, and the picturesque scenery of its environs, have in a great measure contributed. The bed of the harbour, which is dry at low water, is composed of a fine bright yellow sand, chiefly consisting of small shells. The sea view is of a striking, bold, and sublime description—the rocks rising on every side to lofty broken elevations; and those who desire a sequestered and romantic retreat will find in Bude the very object of their wish. The Bude Canal was commenced in 1819, and completed in 1826, at a cost of £128,000. It terminates within three miles of Launceston, forming an internal communication through Devon and Cornwall of nearly forty miles. Bude is fifty-two miles from Exeter.

The Exeter and Exmouth railway is now open, and runs *viâ* the stations of TOPSHAM, WOODBURY ROAD, and LYMPSTONE. The route here described, however, is by the old coach road, which, by the lover of the picturesque and the still lingering fascinations connected with the old mode of travelling, may have its superior attractions.

Passing through Topsham the road is studded with those charming old-fashioned villages that still linger in all their primitive simplicity along the western coast. From a hill called Beacon Hill, encountered in the progress, the eye is presented with a line of coast extending from Exeter to the southern boundary of Torbay, Berry Head, a distance of about twenty miles. This line is broken by several hills that ascend gradually from the opposite side of the river, clad with verdure to the summit, and sheltering the little village of Starcross in a wooded enclosure beneath. Mamhead and Powderham Castle, the seat of the Earl of Devon, heighten the beauty of the prospect, which is additionally embellished by the noble buildings connected with those estates.

Exmouth has, within the last few years, made rapid strides in the march of improvement. The Beacon Hill is covered with buildings, and the Parade is stretching away right and left, with no visible signs, hitherto, of limitation.

Situated on the eastern side of the river Exe, two projecting sand banks form a partial enclosure, leaving an opening of about one-third the width of the harbour. The Exe is here about a mile and a half across, and though the entrance is somewhat difficult, the harbour is very convenient, and will admit the passage of ships of more than 300 tons burden.

There are two good inns, numerous boarding-houses and apartments, and a good subscription library and reading-room, but the visitor must create his own amusement, chiefly in the rides or pedestrian excursions, which the beauty of the surrounding country will so well afford the opportunity of enjoying. The proper time for bathing here is at high water, but there are hot and cold baths that can be taken at any hour, conveniently situated under the Beacon Terrace. Like many other maritime towns in Devonshire, Exmouth has in its immediate neighbourhood a valley sheltered on all sides from the winds, and capable of affording a genial retreat to those affected with complaints in the lungs. This will be found at Salterton, four miles to the east, and here the romantic caverns of the secluded bay, the rough but richly-pebbled beach, and the continuous marine prospect, will form irresistible temptations to explore the way thither. Dr. Clarke says, in speaking of the climate—"Exmouth is decidedly a healthy place, and notwithstanding the whole of this coast is rather humid, agues are almost unknown." Invalids often experience the greatest benefit from a residence here, more particularly on the Beacon Hill, the most elevated and finest situation in the neighbourhood, and which, as some compensation for the south-west gales, commands one of the most magnificent views in Devonshire. Along the southern base of this hill there is also a road of considerable extent, protected from the north and north-east winds, and well suited for exercise when they prevail; and here it may be remarked, that between the summer climate of North and South Devon there is as marked a difference as between the cast of their scenery, the air of the former being keen and bracing, and its features romantic and picturesque, while in the latter the rich softness of the landscape harmonizes with the soft and soothing qualities of the climate. An omnibus runs twice a-week from Exmouth to Sidmouth. The postal arrangements are:—Letters delivered 7 45 a.m.; box closes 5 45 p.m.

About a mile from Exmouth is the secluded and picturesque village of Withycombe, and two miles further a fine old ruin, known as the Church of St. John in the Wilderness, will attract attention. It was built probably in the reign of Henry VII., but the old tower, one of the aisles, and part of the pulpit, now alone remain.

Sidmouth, eleven miles from Exmouth, is one of the most agreeably-situated little watering-places that can be imagined. It lies nestled in the bottom of a valley, opening to the sea between two lofty hills, 500 feet high, whence a most extensive and varied prospect of a beautiful part of the country is afforded on one side, and on the other a view of the open sea, bounded by a line of coast which stretches from Portland Isle, on the east, to Torbay, on the west. The summit of Peak Hill, on the west, is a lofty ridge, extending from north to south; that of Salcombe Hill, on the east, is much broader, and affords room for a race-course: both are highest towards the sea, where they terminate abruptly, forming a precipice of great depth, on the very verge of which the labourer may be seen guiding the plough several hundred feet perpendicular above the sea.

Although Sidmouth is irregularly built, its appearance is generally neat, occasionally highly picturesque, and in some parts positively handsome. The magnificent villas and cottages on the slopes are, almost without exception, surrounded with gardens; they command pleasing prospects, and are delightfully accessible by shady lanes, which wind up the hills, and intersect each other in all directions. Old local topographers speak of Sidmouth as a considerable fishing town, and as carrying on some trade with Newfoundland, but its harbour is now totally choked up with rocks, which at low water are seen covered with sea-weed, stretching away to a considerable distance from the shore. Its history may be very briefly recounted. The manor of Sidmouth was presented by William the Conqueror to the Abbey of St. Michel in Normandy, and was afterwards taken possession of by the Crown, during the wars with France, as the property of an alien foundation. It was afterwards granted to the monastery of Sion, with which it remained until the dissolution.

Hotels, boarding and lodging-houses are scattered over every part of Sidmouth and its vicinity, and the local arrangements are throughout excellent. The public buildings are soon enumerated, for they only consist of a church, near the centre of the town, a very ordinary edifice of the fifteenth century, enlarged from time to time, a neat little chapel of ease, and a new market-house, built in 1840. Around here, and in the Fore-street, are some excellent shops, and the town is well supplied with gas and water. The sea-wall was completed in 1838. There was formerly an extensive bank of sand and gravel, thrown up by the sea, a considerable distance from the front of the town, but this being washed away in a tremendous storm, this defence was resorted to as a more permanent protection from the encroachment of the waves. It now forms an agreeable promenade, upwards of 1,700 feet long.

Sidmouth is sheltered by its hills from every quarter, except the south, where it is open to the sea, and has an atmosphere strongly impregnated with saline particles. Snow is very rarely witnessed, and in extremely severe seasons, when the surrounding hills are deeply covered, not a vestige, not a flake, will remain in this warm and secluded vale. The average mean winter temperature is from four to five degrees warmer than London, and eight degrees warmer than the northern watering-places.

"In Sidmouth and its neighbourhood" (says the author of the "Route Book of Devon"), "will be found an inexhaustible mine for the study and amusement of the botanist, geologist, or conchologist. A very curious relic of antiquity was found on the beach here about five years since—a Roman bronze standard or centaur, representing the centaur Chiron, with his pupil Achilles behind his back. The bronze is cast hollow, and is about nine inches in height. The left fore leg of the centaur is broken, and the right hind leg mutilated. The under part or pedestal formed a socket, by which the standard was screwed on a pole or staff."

The present great features of interest in the neighbourhood are the landslips, ten miles distant, which, extending along the coast from Sidmouth to Lyme Regis, are most interesting to the geologist and the lover of nature.

This range of cliffs, extending from Haven to Pinhay, has been the theatre of two convulsions, or landslips, one commencing on Christmas-day, 1839, at Bendon and Dowlands, whereby forty-five acres of arable land were lost to cultivation—the other about five weeks after, on the 3rd of February, 1840, at Whitlands, little more than a mile to the eastward of the former, but much smaller in magnitude than the previous one.

There are one or two situations, says an excellent local authority, overlooking the more western or great landslip, which seem to be admired as peculiarly striking—the view of the great chasm, looking eastward, and the view from Dowlands, looking westward, upon the undercliff and new beach. The best prospect, perhaps, for seeing the extraordinary nature of the whole district, combined with scenery, is from Pinhay and Whitlands, and looking inland you see the precipitous yet wooded summit of the main land, and the castellated crags of the ivy-clad rocks, on the terraces immediately below, and the deep dingle which separates you from it. By turning a little to the north-east Pinhay presents its chalky pinnacles and descending terraces; whilst to the west the double range and high perpendicular cliffs of Rowsedown offer themselves. By turning towards the sea is embraced the whole range of the great bay of Dorset and Devon, extending from Portland on the east to Start Point on the west, bounded on either side by scenery of the finest coast character.

NORTH DEVON RAILWAY.

Exeter to Crediton, Barnstaple, & Bideford.

ST. CYRES (Newton St. Cyres).

Distance from station, ½ mile.
Telegraph station at Crediton, 2½ miles.
HOTEL.—Railway.
MONEY ORDER OFFICE at Crediton.

Four miles from St. Cyres is *Dunscomb*, the seat of Sir T. Bodley, the founder of the Bodleian Library, Oxford.

CREDITON.

POPULATION, 3,934.
Distance from station, ½ mile.
A telegraph station.
HOTEL.—Ship.
MARKET DAY.—Saturday.
FAIRS.—May 11th, Aug. 21st, and Sept. 21st.

In the time of the Saxons, this was a place of great importance, and a bishopric until the year 1409, at which time the see was transferred to Exeter.

We next pass through the stations of COPPLESTONE, MORCHARD ROAD, LAPFORD, EGGESFORD, SOUTH-MOLTON ROAD, PORTSMOUTH ARMS, and UMBERLEIGH, having no particular attraction, and arrive at

BARNSTAPLE.

HOTELS.—Fortescue Arms; Golden Lion.

MARKET DAY.—Friday. FAIR.—Sept. 19th.

BANKERS.—Drake, Gribble, and Co.; Branch of West of England and South Wales District Bank; National Provincial Bank of England.

This sea port town is situated on the river Taw, which is crossed by a bridge of sixteen arches. It first became a chartered town in the reign of Edward I., and was formerly surrounded by walls, and defended by a castle. It had also the privilege of a city and a harbour. The streets are well paved, and the houses built of stone. The principal manufactures are baise and woollens, chiefly for the Plymouth market. It has also a trade in bobbin net, paper, pottery, tanning, malt, and shipbuilding. Its population is 8,667.

ILFRACOMBE.

Telegraph station at Barnstaple.

HOTELS.—The Clarence, situated at the higher end—and the Britannia and Packet Hotels, at the lower end of the town. There is a boarding house on the quay, and excellent private lodgings in every part of the town.

MARKET DAYS.—Saturday, for meat, poultry, eggs, and vegetables.

FAIRS.—One in April, the other in August.

BANKERS.—Branch of the National Provincial Bank, and also of the Devon and Exeter Savings Bank.

ILFRACOMBE is a considerable sea port town, and now a fashionable watering place, on the north coast of Devon, near the mouth of the Bristol Channel. The harbour is considered the safest and most convenient along the whole coast. It is formed like a natural basin, and is almost surrounded by craggy heights that are overspread with foliage. The town is built partly at the bottom of a steep declivity, and partly up the side of it. New buildings and streets have been built, to afford accommodation to visitors. The terraces and public rooms, forming the centre of Coronation Terrace, have been constructed—the hot and cold baths at Crewkhorne have been formed, and a number of new houses erected on the eastern side, commanding an extensive prospect over the town and Bristol Channel to the Welsh coast.

BATHS.—The direct way to Crewkhorne is by North-field to the baths, and through the tunnel.

WALKS AND RIDES.—The walks in this neighbourhood are very beautiful, and afford delightful excursions and views.

Lynton and **Lynmouth.**—The scenery in the neighbourhood of these two places is "wild and beautiful—magnificent and lovely" to use the words of a handbook of Devon—the writer of which observes that it is quite beyond his powers to attempt a description of the scenery abounding in this fascinating neighbourhood. The accommodations for visitors are pretty nearly equal in each.

LYNTON HOTELS.—The Valley of the Rocks Hotel; the Castle Hotel; and Crown Inn.

LYNMOUTH.—An excellent inn called the Lyndale Hotel.

There are in both places lodging houses innumerable. The tourist should proceed to the far-famed Valley of the Rocks on foot, along the Cliff Walk, whence the scenery is very fine. The view in the valley is exceedingly grand. The East and West Lyn Valleys are very beautiful also; but the tourist should employ a guide to accompany him on his first visit to these and other principal points of attraction in this picturesque neighbourhood.

FREMINGTON and INSTOW stations.

BIDEFORD.

A telegraph station.

HOTEL.—Commercial.

MARKET DAYS.—Tuesday and Saturday (corn).

FAIRS.—Feb. 14th, July 18th, Nov. 13th.

BANKERS.—National Provincial Bank of England; Harding and Co.

This is a small municipal borough, containing a population of 5,775, chiefly employed in shipbuilding, the manufacture of sail-cloth, cordage, pottery, and bone lace. It has a free grammar school, at which Z. Mudge, a native, was the master; and Shebbear, also a native, and author of *Chrysal*, &c., was educated. Hervey wrote part of his *Meditations* whilst curate at the church here. Strange, the philanthropist, who died of the plague in 1646, is buried here.

SOUTH DEVON RAILWAY.

Exeter to Torquay and Plymouth.

This part of the line is invested with additional interest, from the magnificent scenery which opens on each side as we proceed. There is scarcely a mile traversed which does not unfold some peculiar picturesque charm or new feature of its own to make the eye "dazzled and drunk with beauty."

Once at Exeter, we have all the romantic allurements of the watering places of the west within our reach, where the possessor of robust health may find a fund of illimitable enjoyment in the rich bouquet that nature has spread before him on the freshening shores of Devon, and the invalid, those desired qualifications most conducive to a speedy and permanent convalescence.

On leaving Exeter we pass in rapid succession the stations of ST. THOMAS, EXMINSTER, and STAR CROSS, and in a very few minutes arrive at

DAWLISH.

POPULATION, 2,671.

Telegraph station at Teignmouth, 3 miles.

HOTELS.—London; Royal.

DAWLISH, one of the stations of the South Devon Railway, is one of the prettiest places along the coast to pass a quiet summer month. Within the last century, rising from a mere fishing village to the dignity of a fashionable watering-place, it has become extended from the valley in which it lies to a considerable distance east and west; and though the incursion of the railroad has materially affected the fine expanse of the esplanade, it still possesses an excellent beach, bounded on the east by the Langstone Cliffs, and on the west by the rocks familiarly known by the appellation of the Parson and Clerk. The bathing is exceedingly good, and the facilities afforded for its enjoyment admirably arranged. The houses, built in handsome terraces along the sides of the hill and strand, and fronted by lawns and gardens, are very handsome and picturesque, the majority of them commanding an ample sea view. The parish church is at the upper end of the town, and was partly rebuilt in 1824, being rendered sufficiently commodious to accommodate a congregation of nearly two thousand people. There is a good organ, and a handsome window of stained glass in the interior. The walks and drives in the vicinity of the town are remarkably pretty and interesting, the shady lanes at the back, winding through the declivity of the hills, affording an endless variety of inland and marine scenery. The climate is considered more genial even than that of Torquay; but so nearly do these places approximate that, for all general purposes, the remarks made upon the atmospherical characteristics of Torquay will be found equally applicable to those of Dawlish. Of late years, considerable improvement has been effected in the watching and lighting arrangements of the town, and some new buildings have added much to its external beauty. Circulating libraries and hotels, with the other usual accessories to a fashionable marine resort, are numerous and well provided, and the excursionist may here crown the enjoyments of the day with such a stroll on the beach by moonlight as can be obtained at few other places.

TEIGNMOUTH.

POPULATION, 5,013.

A telegraph station.

HOTELS.—Royal; Devon.

BANKERS.—Sub Branch of National Provincial Bank of England; Watts, Kelson, and Co.

TEIGNMOUTH, three miles from Dawlish, is recognised as the largest watering-place on the Devonian coast; but, from the irregularity of the streets, it is only in the esplanade that it can rival the others before named. A large export trade is carried on here, which gives a life and animation to the streets, and the bustle that occasionally prevails is often felt as an agreeable change to the monotony of a country residence. The climate is mild, and similar in character to that of Torquay, the prevailing winds being those from the west and south-west. In respect both to the excellence and accommodation of houses and apartments, there are few places more convenient for either a temporary or permanent residence than Teignmouth. An excellent supply of gas and water is enjoyed by the town, and all the comforts, with most of the luxuries, of life are easily and economically obtainable. There are two churches, situated respectively in East and West Teignmouth, the former being the more modern, and the latter—particularly as regards the interior—being the more interesting. The Assembly Rooms, with Subscription, Reading, Billiard, and News Rooms attached, furnish an agreeable source of amusement, and libraries are, with hotels, plentifully scattered through the town.

The river Teign, which here flows into the Channel, yields an abundant supply of fish, and the pleasure of a sail up the river to the interior is to be numbered among the allurements of a sojourn. A bridge, considered the longest in England, has been thrown across the Teign at this point, erected in 1827, at a cost of nearly £20,000. It is 1,672 feet in length, and consists of thirty-four arches, with a drawbridge over the deepest part of the channel, to allow free passage for vessels.

Near the mouth of the river is a lighthouse exhibiting a red light. The noble esplanade—or Teignmouth *Den*, as it is curiously styled—is a deservedly favourite promenade with all visitors, and the bold and towering cliffs that overhang the sea impart a most romantic aspect to the surrounding scenery. Excursions either on sea or land may be made from Teignmouth with the greatest facility of conveyance, and the environs are so extremely rich in natural and artificial attractions that they are almost inexhaustible. Three fairs are held in the months of January, February, and September, and an annual regatta takes place in August. The post-office is in Bank Street.

NEWTON JUNCTION.

(Newton Abbots).

Telegraph station at Teignmouth, 5 miles.

HOTEL.—Globe.

MARKET DAY.—Wednesday.

FAIRS.—Last Wednesday in Feb., June 24th, first Wednesday in Sept., and Nov. 6th.

Here is a stone where William of Orange first read his declaration.

TORQUAY AND DARTMOUTH BRANCH.

Leaving Newton we pass the stations of KINGSKERSWELL and TORR, and arrive at

TORQUAY.

POPULATION, 14,000.

Distance from station, 1¼ mile.

A telegraph station.

HOTELS.—Royal; Apsley House.

TORQUAY has been somewhat characteristically described as the Montpelier of England, and truly it is deserving of the appellation. Situated in a small bay at the north-eastern corner of Torbay, the larger one, it is sheltered by a ridge of hills clothed by verdant woodland to the summit, and has thus an immunity from the cold northern and easterly winds, which few other spots so completely enjoy. From being a small village with a few scattered houses, chiefly occupied by officers' wives, during the period of the last French war, when the Channel fleet were at anchor opposite, it has rapidly risen to a thriving populous town, wlth about eight thousand permanent residents within its limits. To borrow the description of "The Route Book of Devon," "the town, beginning with the lower tier, is built round the three sides of the strand or quay formed by the pier, and is composed chiefly of shops of the tradesmen, having a row of trees in front, planted between the flag pavement and the carriage way. The next tier, which is approached by a winding road at each end, and steps at other places, is comprised of handsome terraces; and the third, or highest, having a range of beautiful villas. The views from either of these levels are most enchanting, taking in the whole of the fine expansive roadstead of Torbay, within whose circumference numerous fleets can ride in safety, and where is always to be seen the trim yacht and pleasure-boat, the dusky sail of the Brixham trawler, or coasting merchantman, and frequently the more proud and 'spirit-stirring leviathan of the deep—' one of Britain's best bulwarks—a man-of-war.' To this also must be added, the beautiful country surrounding, commencing by Berry Head to the south, until your eye rests upon the opposite extremity, encircling within its scope the town of Brixham, the richly cultivated neighbourhood of Godrington and Paignton, with the picturesque church of the latter, and the sands rounding from it to the fine woods of Tor Abbey, and the town and pier immediately below. But it is not within the circle of the town of Torquay, such as we have described, that residences for strangers and invalids are exclusively to be found; the sides and summits of the beautiful valleys which open from it are dotted over with cottages, pavilions, and detached villas, to the extent of two or three miles, in every direction, to whicb the different roads diverge. About half a mile from Torquay, in the once secluded cove of Meadfoot, which is now being converted into a second town, terraces surpassing those in Torquay are already rising, and the forest of villas has connected the two towns. The sea views from these heights are magnificent, and the situation most attractive." This, though it must be admitted a very alluring picture, falls far short of the reality, as it bursts upon the eye of the stranger who visits it for the first time. The groupings of the various villas, and the picturesque vistas which every turning in the road discloses, are enough to throw a painter into ecstacies, and render his portfolio plethoric with sketches. As before stated, the whole of the build ings are of modern origin. The pier, which forms a most agreeable promenade, was begun in 1804, and with the eastern pier, about forty feet wide, encloses a basin of some 300 feet long by 500 broad. This is the favourite lounge. Another on the Torwood-road is "The Public Gardens," skilfully laid out, under the direction of the lord of the manor, who has placed about four acres of his estate at the disposal of the public. Passing up the new road, made under Walton Hill, to the Paignton Sands, we come to the remains of Tor Abbey, once more richly endowed than any in England, and now forming a portion of the delightful seat belonging to Mrs. Cary, a munificent patroness of the town. Between Torquay and Babbicombe is Kent's Cavern, or Hole, consisting of a large natural excavation capable of being explored to the extent of 600 feet from the entrance. Dr. Buckland here discovered numerous bones of bears, hyenas, elephants, and other expatriated animals, now no longer happily found in this country. Amusements of evey kind are easily attainable. A theatre, concerts—held at Webb's Royal Hotel—assemblies, libraries, news and billiard rooms, cater for every imaginable taste, and the Torquay Museum, belonging to the Natural History Society there established, has a most valuable collection, An excellent market, inns proportionate to the depths of every purse, and apartments to be obtained at reasonable rates, form not the least of the advantages to be derived from a protracted sojourn in this delightful region; but there is one greater attraction yet—its climate.

If those English invalids who, in search of a more congenial temperature, hastily enter on a long journey to some foreign country, and wilfully encounter all the inconveniences attending a residence there, were but to make themselves acquainted with the bland and beautiful climates which lie within an easy jaunt, and offer their own accustomed comforts in addition, how many a fruitless regret and unavailing repentance might hereafter be spared. To all suffering under pulmonary complaints, Torquay offers the greatest inducement for a trial of its efficacy as a place of winter residence. Dr. James Clark, in his excellent work on climate, says, "the general character of the climate of this coast is soft and humid. Torquay is certainly drier than the other places, and almost entirely free from fogs. This drier state of the atmosphere probably arises in part from the limestone rocks, which are confined to the neighbourhood of this place, and partly from its position between the two streams, the Dart and the Teign, by which the rain is in some degree attracted. Torquay is also remarkably protected from the north-east winds, the great evil of our spring climate; it is likewise well sheltered from the north-west. This protection from winds extends over a very considerable tract of beautiful country, abounding in every variety of landscape, so that there is scarcely a wind that blows from which the invalid will not be able to find a shelter for exercise either on foot or horseback. In this respect Torquay is most superior to any other place we have noticed. It possesses all the advantages of the south-western climate in the highest degree, and, with the exception of its exposure to the south-west gales, partakes less of the disadvantages of it than any other place having accommodation for invalids. The selection will, I believe, lie among the following places as winter and spring residences—Torquay, Undercliff, Hastings, and Clifton; and perhaps, in the generality of cases, will deserve the preference in the order stated." So high an eulogium from so impartial and eminent an authority has seldom been bestowed. That it is well deserved, however, may be further seen from the meteorological observations registered, which give the mean winter temperature as about 46 degrees, being five degrees warmer than even Exeter. In summer, from the cooling influence of the sea breeze, the temperature, during the last five years, has never at the highest exceeded 80 degrees. So equable a temperature is, we believe, not to be met with elsewhere in Great Britain.

A delightful sandy beach, within ten minutes' walk of the town, presents facilities for sea-bathing that render a plunge into the clear and sparkling bosom of the bay perfectly irresistible to all who have the taste for its enjoyment. Bathing-machines and baths of every description may be had between Torquay and its suburb Paignton, and as a brisk walk after so refreshing a submersion is the orthodox sequel, it may be some satisfaction for the pedestrian to know that the environs abound in those landscape-looking vistas seen through green lanes and over-arching woodland which form the true characteristic of Devonian scenery.

Paignton Station.—The situation of this place is really beautiful, commanding a central aspect of Torbay. Its picturesque church and the sands rounding from it to the fine woods of Tor Abbey, and the town and pier below it, form a pleasing *coup d'œil.*

Brixham Road station.

BRIXHAM,

Close at hand, is chiefly noted for its extensive fisheries, employing more than two hundred vessels and fifteen hundred seamen. The weekly average amount received for fish is no less than £600. It was here that the Prince of Orange landed, and to commemorate the event a monument has been fixed in the centre of the fish-market, with a portion of the identical stone he first stepped upon inserted, and inscribed thus:—"On this stone, and near this spot, William Prince of Orange first set foot, on his landing in England, 4th of November, 1688."

The railway being yet incomplete, omnibuses run in connection with the trains from Brixham Road to

DARTMOUTH.

Hotels.—Commercial; Castle.

This sea-port town is situated at the mouth of the river Dart, navigable about ten miles inland. Its harbour is very capacious, affording safe anchorage for five hundred large vessels at the same time. The coast scenery here is exceedingly romantic, and the excursion hence made to the source of the Dart is one of the great attractions with visitors.

South Devon Main Line continued.

TOTNESS.

Population, 4,419.—A telegraph station.

Hotel.—The Seven Stars.

Market Day.—Saturday.

Fairs.—First Tuesday in every month, Easter Tuesday, May 12th, July 25th, and October 1st.

Totness is situated on the river Dart. The ancient Roman fosseway forms a prominent feature in this town. There is a good deal of woollen cloth manufactured here, but the chief employment of the inhabitants is in the fishery. Its principal attractions are a Guildhall, assembly room and theatre, banks, libraries, &c.

After a very brief stoppage at Brent and Kingsbridge Road stations, we arrive at

IVY BRIDGE.

A charming spot in the valley of the *Erme*, much frequented in summer. The hills (1,100 feet high at one point) here begin to ascend towards *Dartmoor*, which lies to the north-west. It is a desolate tract of granite moorland, 20 miles long by 12 broad, once a forest, but now covered with peat. Copper and tin are worked. Some of its rugged peaks, here called tors, are 1,200 to 2,000 feet high; and under one is the Dartmoor *Convict Prison*. The Dart rises at Cranmere; on account of its striking scenery and fishing, it should be descended all the way to the fine port of Dartmouth.

CORNWOOD and PLYMPTON stations.

PLYMOUTH.

A telegraph station.

HOTELS.—Royal Hotel; Chubbs' Commercial.

FLY CHARGES.—For two persons, any distance, not exceeding one mile, 8d.; every additional half-mile, 4d. For three or four persons per mile, or raction of a mile, 1s.; every additional half-mile, 6d. No fare, however, to be less than 1s.

BANKERS.—Branch of the Bank of England; Harris & Co.; Devon and Cornwall Banking Co.

A borough, first class fortress, and naval dock-yard in *Devonshire*, at the mouth of the Channel, 246 miles from London by the Great Western Railway. The dockyard and harbour are at Devonport, the victualling office is at Stonehouse, and there are other establishments in the neighbourhood, but Plymouth is the common name for all. Two members. Population 52,221. The view from the Hoe, or cliffy height on which the *Citadel* is planted, commands a magnificent prospect of the sound or outer anchorage, Mounts Batten and Edgecumbe hedging it in on both sides, and the breakwater which protects the main entrance. Two rivers run into the sound, the Plym on the east side, and the Tamar on the west, or Devonport. The mouth of the first, on which Plymouth stands, widens into a deep inlet called the Catwater. Close to the town is Sutton Pool, a tide-harbour in which vessels of various tonnage lie. About 35,000 tons of shipping are registered at this port, and the total amount of customs may be stated at £10,000. It is a convenient starting place for emigrants, for whom a depôt has been established.

There is a tower, and some other remains of a castle, on the Hoe, which was first regularly fortified in 1670. Here are the new botanic gardens. The climate of this part of Devonshire is somewhat moist, but it keeps up a perpetual verdure to make amends.

Some of the best buildings are designed by Foulston, who died in 1842. This architect built the Public Library, in 1812; the Exchange, in 1813; and the Athenæum, in 1819. But his first and largest works were the Assembly Rooms, Royal Hotel, and Theatre, in one immense block, in the Ionic style, 270 feet by 220; built 1811, for the corporation. Foulston also restored the old *Parish Church* of St. Andrew, in which is a monument to C. Matthews, the comedian. Its bell tolls the curfew *couvrez feu*, or, "put out fire," every night, striking according to the days of the month. At the *Guildhall* is a portrait of Sir F. Drake, its most eminent native, who was at the cost of cutting a stream, 24 miles long, from Dartmoor, to supply the Town Reservoir. Christ Church is a modern Gothic church, by Wightwick, who also designed the new *Post Office*, in the Grecian style.

At the western extremity of the town is Mill Bay, where Docks have been formed for the Great Western Packet Station. On the side of Stonehouse (which, though one town with Plymouth, is part of Devonport borough) are the Naval and Military *Hospital*, the Marine *Barracks*, and the *Victualling Office*, the last a solid granite quadrangle, which cost one and a-half million sterling. It occupies a site of 15 acres, and includes biscuit baking machinery, cooperage, and immense provision stores. Line-of-battle ships can come alongside the quay.

EXCURSIONS FROM PLYMOUTH.—These are almost endless in variety, and equally beautiful. The visitor will be soon made acquainted with clotted cream, junket, white pot, squab pie, and other west country mysteries, and the unbounded hospitality of the people. Within a few miles are the following:—*Mount-Edgecumbe* (on the Cornwall side of the Sound), the seat of Earl Mount-Edgecumbe, in a beautiful park, overlooking Plymouth, the breakwater, sea, &c. A fort in the Sound was first built when the Armada invaded these shores; and it was from this port that Howard of Effingham, Drake, and Hawkins, sailed out to attack it. *Deus afflavit, et dissipantur;* and where is Spain now! Maker Church, 300 or 400 feet high, is the best point for enjoying the prospect. Below is the Ram Head of the ancient geographers, and still called Rame, and Whitesand Bay, a rare spot for seaweed and shells. Fine creeks and bays hence to the Land's End. On the Cornish side, also, are—*East Anthony*, the old seat of the Carews; *Thancks*, Dowager Lady Graves, and St. German's Norman Church, near *Port Eliot*, the seat of Earl St. Germans. It contains part of a priory founded by King Athelstane. On the Devonshire side of Plymouth are —*Saltram*, Earl Morley's seat; good pictures by Reynolds, &c. *Boringdon* was their old seat, higher up the Catwater. *Newnham Park*, G. Strode, Esq. *Plympton* (5 miles), a decayed borough, the birthplace of Sir J. Reynolds, whose portrait, by himself, is in the Guildhall. Traces of a castle. *Yealmpton*, *Modbury*, *Kingsbridge*, &c., are on the various creeks of South Devon, which increase in beauty towards Dartmouth and Torquay; most of the streams come from Dartmoor. Fruit, &c., are abundant in this mild and fertile region.

Up the Tamar.—This beautiful stream divides the two counties for some miles. Past *St. Budeaux* (on the right, or Devonshire side), a fine spot, opposite Saltash. Then *Landulph* (on the left) where Theodore Palæolipus, the survivor of the last Emperor of Constantinople, is buried. The tomb was opened about 1830. One of his daughters married an Arundell, of *Clifton*, an old seat here. Lead mines here, and at *Beer Ferris* (Devon side), which is charmingly placed on the corner where the Tavy turns off, overlooking both rivers. The Tavy runs past *Buckland Abbey* (fragments of a priory), the seat of Sir T. T. Drake, Bart., a descendant of the great navigator, who was born at Tavistock. This is the centre of an important mining district, with some remains of an abbey, belonging to the Bedford family. Following the Tamar, you come to *Pentilie* (J. Coryton, Esq.), and *Cotehele*, both on the Cornwall side. The latter seat, for centuries in the Edgecumbe family, is one of the most interesting in England, for its architecture, furniture, and ornaments, all genuine relics of a mediæval age. *Callington*, to the left, near *St. Kitt's Hill*, the granite peak of *Hengstown Down*, 1,067 feet high, from the summit of which there is a famous prospect. The river winds hence to Launceston.

CORNWALL.

CORNWALL, from its soil, appearance, and climate, is one of the least inviting of the English counties. A ridge of bare and rugged hills, intermixed with bleak moors, runs through the midst of its whole length, and exhibits the appearance of a dreary waste. The most important objects in the history of this county are its numerous mines, which for centuries have furnished employment to thousands of its inhabitants; and, the trade to which they give birth, when considered in a national point of view is of the greatest relative consequence. In a narrow slip of land, where the purposes of agriculture would not employ above a few thousand inhabitants, the mines alone support a population estimated at more than 80,000 labourers, exclusive of artizans. The principal produce of the Cornish mines is tin, copper, and lead. The strata in which these metals are found, extend from the Land's End, in a direction from west to east, entirely along the country into Devonshire. Nearly all the metals are found in veins or fissures, the direction of which is generally east and west. The annual value of the copper mines has been estimated at £350,000. Logan stones deserve to be mentioned amongst the curiosities of this county. They are of great weight, and poised on the top of immense piles of rocks.

CORNWALL RAILWAY.

Plymouth to Truro.

Almost before we get clear of Plymouth our arrival is announced at

DEVONPORT,

A place of great importance, partly overlooking the Sound (where it is defended by Mount Wise battery), and the anchorage at the Tamar's mouth, called *Hamaoze*. Here is the royal *Dockyard*, on a space of 71 acres, inclusive of 5 more at the Gun Wharf (built by Sir J. Vanburgh). The Dockyard includes various docks and building slips, storehouses, a rope house 200 fathoms long, blacksmiths' shop, &c. Above this is a floating bridge to Torpoint and the splendid *Steam Docks* and factory at Keyham, which occupy another 75 acres. There are two basins, 600 to 700 feet long, besides docks, all faced with solid stone, and built at a total cost of one and a half million, along with foundries, smithery, &c. One wrought-iron caisson is 82 feet long, and 13 feet thick. Devonport has a population of 50,159, and returns two members. A pillar opposite the Town Hall was placed there in 1824, when the name was altered from Plymouth Dock. There are various barracks near Mount Wise, where the Governor of the district and the Port Admiral reside.

Plymouth Sound, and its three harbours, would hold, it is calculated, 2,000 vessels, such is its extent. One of the most striking scenes it has witnessed in modern times was the appearance of Napoleon here, in 1815, on board the Bellerophon, after his attempted escape to America. Across the mouth (having entrances on each side), 3 miles from the town, is the famous *Breakwater*, first begun in 1812, by Rennie. It is a vast stone dyke, gradually made by sinking 2½ million tons of stone, from the neighbouring cliffs; about 10 or 12 yards wide at the top, and spreading to 70 or 80 yards at the bottom—the side next the Atlantic being the most sloping. Its entire length is 1,700 yards, nearly a mile; but it is not straight, as the two ends bend inwards from the middle part, which is 1,000 yards long. A lighthouse stands at the west corner, 63 feet high. Several tremendous storms have tested its solidity and usefulness; once inside this artificial bulwark, the smallest craft is as safe as if it were on the slips of the Dockyard.

The Eddystone Lighthouse is ten miles from it, on a granite rock in the open channel. It was erected by Mr. Smeaton, and is a striking instance of human ingenuity, which has hitherto baffled all the fury of the elements. The first stone was laid on the 1st of June, 1757. Mr. Smeaton conceived the idea of his edifice from the waist or bole of a large spreading oak. Considering the figure of the tree as connected with its roots, which lie hid below ground, Mr. S. observed that it rose from the surface with a large swelling base, which at the height of one diameter, is generally reduced by an elegant concave curve to a diameter less by at least one-third, and sometimes to half its original base. Hence he deducted what the shape of a column of the greatest stability ought to be to resist the action of external violence, when the *quantity of matter* of which it is to be composed is given. To expedite the erection of the building, the stones were hewn and fitted to each other on shore, and after every precaution to ensure security had been taken, the work was completed in October, 1759. It has proved highly beneficial to all nations, which fact was strikingly exemplified by Louis XIV. France being at war with England while the lighthouse was being proceeded with, a French privateer took the men at work on the Eddystone rocks, together with their tools, and carried them to France, the captain expecting a reward for the achievement. While the captives lay in prison the transaction came to the knowlege of the French monarch, who immediately ordered the prisoners to be released and the captors to be confined in their stead, declaring that though he was at war with England he was not so with mankind. He therefore directed the men to be sent back to their work with presents.

The form of the present lighthouse is octagonal, and the framework is composed of cast iron and copper. The outside and basement of the edifice are formed of granite, that kind of stone being more competent than any other to resist the action of the sea. Round the upper store-room, upon the course of granite under the ceiling, is the following inscription:—

"Except the Lord build the house,
They labour in vain that build it."

Over the east side of the lantern are the words—

"24th August, 1759.
Laus Deo."

The number of keepers resident at the lighthouse

was at first only two, but an incident of a very extraordinary and distressing nature which occurred showed the necessity of an additional hand. One of the two keepers took ill and died. The dilemma in which this occurrence left the survivor was singularly painful: apprehensive that if he tumbled the dead body into the sea, which was the only way in his power to dispose of it, he might be charged with murder, he was induced for some time to let the corpse lie, in hopes that the attending-boat might be able to land, and relieve him from the distress he was in. By degrees the body became so putrid that it was not in his power to get quit of it without help, for it was near a month before the boat could effect a landing.

Since the above occurrence three men have been stationed at Eddystone, each of whom has, in the summer, a month's leave to visit his friends, and are provided with food and all other necessaries by a boat appointed for that purpose; but they are alway stocked with salt provisions, to guard against the possibility of want, as in winter it sometimes happens that the boat cannot approach the rock for many weeks together.

The range of the enjoyments of the keepers is confined within very narrow limits. In high winds so briny an atmosphere surrounds this gloomy solitude, from the dashing of the waves, that a person exposed to it could hardly draw his breath. At these dreadful intervals the forlorn inhabitants keep close quarters, and are obliged to live in darkness, listening to the howling storm, excluded in every emergency from the hope of human assistance, and without any earthly comfort but that which results from their confidence in the strength of the building in which they are immured. In fine weather they just scramble about the edge of the rock when the tide ebbs, and amuse themselves with fishing; and this is the only employment they have, except that of trimming their nightly fires. Singular as it may appear, there are yet facts which lead us to believe it possible for these men to become so weaned from society as to become enamoured of their situation. Smeaton, in speaking of one of these light-keepers, says, "In the fourteen years that he had been here he was grown so attached to the place. that for the two summers preceding he had given up his turn on shore to his companions, and declared his intention of doing the same the third, but was over-persuaded to go on shore and take his month's turn. He had always in this service proved himself a decent, sober, well-behaved man; but he had no sooner got on shore than he went to an alehouse and got intoxicated. This he continued the whole of his stay, which being noticed, he was carried, in this intoxicated state, on board the Eddystone boat, and delivered in the lighthouse, where he was expected to grow sober; but after lingering two or three days, he could by no means be recovered." In another place, he says, "I was applied to by a philosopher kind of a man to be one of the light-keepers, observing, that being a man of study and retirement, he could very well bear the confinement that must attend it. I asked him if he knew the salary? He replied no; but doubted not it must be something very handsome. When I told him it was £25 a-year, he replied he had quite mistaken the business; he did not mean to sell his liberty for so low a price; he could not have supposed it less than three times as much." Another man, a shoemaker, who was engaged to be the light-keeper, when in the boat which conveyed him thither, the skipper addressing him, said, "How happens it, friend Jacob, that you should choose to go and be cooped up here as a light-keeper, when you can on shore, as I am told, earn half-a-crown and three shillings a-day in making leathern hose (leathern pipes so called), whereas the light-keeper's salary is but £25 a-year, which is scarce ten shillings a-week?" "Every one to his taste," replied Jacob promptly; "I go to be a light-keeper because I don't like *confinement*." After this answer had produced its share of merriment, Jacob explained himself by saying that he did not like to be *confined to work*.

From Devonport we resume our journey, passing the stations of Saltash, St. Germans, Menheniot, Liskeard, Doublebois, and Bodmin Road.

LOSTWITHIEL,

The only features of attraction here are the parish church and the ruins of a building called the palace. The former was built in the 14th century, has a fine spire and a curious font. The latter is said to have been the residence of the Dukes of Cornwall.

Par station.

ST. AUSTELL, or St. Austle,

a large mining town in West Cornwall, near the sea, with several important mines round it in the granite, producing tin, copper, nickel, with clay, and china stone, for the Staffordshire potteries. Good building stone is also quarried. Graw or stratum is the most valuable product, found in round masses, and smelted in the neighbourhood. The chief mines are Polgooth, Crinnis, Pentewan, &c.; there are only one or two of copper. Tram rails have been made to the little harbour of Pentewan, and Charlestown, in the bay, to ship the ores. Among the buildings are several chapels, a stannary (or tin) hall, and an ancient stone church with a good tower, on which, and over the south porch of the church, are various carvings. Population, 3,565.

The tin mines which were worked in Cornwall by the roving Phœnicians long before Christ, yield here, and at St. Agnes, &c., about 5,000 tons, worth £70 a ton, yearly. Copper, now the staple article of the county, used to be thrown aside by the tinners, till the beginning of the last century. Polgooth, a tin mine, two miles south-west, in a barren spot, is now almost worked out; formerly it was worth £20,000 a year. It is 120 fathoms deep. Crinnis, which was worth between £80,000 or £90,000, is still very productive in copper. At Carclaze the tin is worked in the light granite of the downs, by lateral shafts, open to the day.

Grampound Road.—About two miles from this station is the rotten borough of Grampound, one of the many existing in Cornwall (which, being a crown duchy, the court influence was the paramount), but disfranchised for gross corruption, in 1841.

TRURO.

Distance from station, 1 mile.

A telegraph station.
HOTEL.—Red Lion.

MARKET DAYS.—Wednesday and Saturday.

FAIRS. — Wednesday after Mid-Lent, Wednesday in Whitsun week, November 19th, December 8th.

TRURO, the mining capital of Cornwall, and a parliamentary borough (two members), on the Corn wall Railway, which at present begins here and terminates at Penzance, leaving a break between Truro and Plymouth, which is being rapidly filled up. Its population is 10,733 within the borough bounds, which enclose a space of 1,200 acres, at the head of a creek of the Fal (where the rivers Kenwyn and Allen fall in), covered by foundries, blast houses, pottery and tin works, &c. When the tide is up the creek looks like a fine lake, two miles long. Like most Cornish towns, Truro originated in a castle built by the Earls of Cornwall, on Castle Hill. It is now the principal coinage town in the Duchy, where the metal is stamped, previous to being exported. Bar tin is sent to the Mediterranean, &c., and ingots to the East Indies, while much of the copper ore is taken across to Swansea.

The principal streets diverge from the market place, near which is St. Mary's Church, a handsome later Gothic edifice, with a tower. It contains various monuments to old Truro families. There are two other churches, besides one at Kenwyn, north of the town, near the county infirmary. The *Coinage Hall* is an old building, formerly used as a stannary parliament, *i.e.*, a parliament of tinners (*stannum*, tin). Town Hall, built in 1615. Theatre and Assembly Room, at High Cross. A good museum at the Royal Institute of Cornwall. Attempts have been made to establish a mining college, chiefly by the liberal exertions of Sir C. Lemon, after whom Lemon Street, on the Falmouth Road, takes its name. At the top of it is a *pillar* to the African travellers, Richard and J. Lander, natives of Truro, the latter of whom perished on his third trip to that insalubrious coast.

Within a short distance are the following places, mostly seated on the Fal or its branches. *Polwhele* was the seat of Polwhele the antiquary, a member of an ancient Cornish family. "By Tre, Pol, and Pen, you may know the Cornishmen," is a well known rhyme. *Pencarlenich*, seat of J. Vivian, Esq.,—another old name. *Tregothnan*, the seat of the Earl of Falmouth, a beautiful spot. Here Admiral Boscawen was born, in 1711. *Trewarthenich*, another fine seat, near Tregony, *Trelissich*, on the west side of the Fal. *Carclew*, near Penryn, the seat of Sir C. Lemon, Bart. *Enys*, of J. Enys Esq. *Trefusis*, beautifully placed opposite Falmouth, is the seat of Lord Clinton.

Falmouth was formerly an important mail packet station. Below it are Pendennis Castle and St. Anthony's Light, on the opposite sides of the entrance. The former, built by Henry VIII., was famous in the civil war for its resistance to parliament, against whose forces it held out till 1646. The richest mines are in the granite moorlands to the north, near St. Agnes, &c., or in the neighbourhood of the rail to Penzance. At *Perranzabulae*, 5 miles from Truro, an ancient British church was uncovered, 25 feet in 1835, by shifting sands (which in former times overwhelmed everything on this side of the coast), and gave occasion to Mr. Trelawney's work, the "Lost Church Found," in which he shows what the primitive English church was before corrupted by Popery. This and other parishes were named from the famous St. Tiran, the patron of tinners, who, like many other eminent preachers of that age, came from Ireland. The story is that he sailed over on a mill stone, but perhaps this was the name of the ship. Near St. Agnes Beacon is a camp called Picran Round, Chacewater, Wheal Towan, Wheal Leisure, Pen Hale, Perran St. George (all near Perran Porth, the last 100 fathoms deep); and Buduick mine may be visited, Polperro, Wheal Kitty, Wheal Alfred and others, most of them indicative of the arbitary names conferred on mines by the lively fancy of the Cornishmen. Population, 4,953.

WEST CORNWALL RAILWAY.

Truro to Hayle, Penzance, &c.

CHACEWATER and SCORRIER GATE stations.

REDRUTH.

POPULATION, 7,095.

A telegraph station.

HOTELS.—London; King's Arms.

MARKET DAY.—Friday. FAIRS.—May 2nd, July 9th, Sept. 5th, and Oct. 12th

REDRUTH, is a market town, in the county of Cornwall. It consists of one long street, from which branch several smaller ones. This town derives nearly all its importance from its central situation with respect to the neighbouring mines, the working of which has increased the population to treble its original number, as nearly all the commercial transactions of the miners are carried on here.

On leaving Redruth, and passing the unimportant stations of POOL, CAMBORNE, GWINEAR ROAD, and HAYLE, we arrive at

ST. IVES ROAD.

The town of St. Ives has a population of 9,872, chiefly depending on the coasting trade and pilchard fishery. *Treganna Castle*, the seat of Mr. Stephens, occupies a lofty situation outside the town, and commands an extensive prospect.

MARAZION ROAD station.

PENZANCE.

A telegraph station.

HOTELS.—Union; Star.

MARKET DAYS.—Thursday and Saturday.

FAIRS.—Thursday before Advent, Thursday after Trinity Sunday, and Corpus Christi day.

BANKERS. — Bolithos, Sons, and Co.; Batten, Carne, and Co.

This flourishing port is at the farther end of Cornwall, on the west side of Mount's Bay, at the terminus of the West Cornwall Railway. It is a municipal, but not a parliamentary borough, with a population of 9,214. Tin, copper, china, clay, granite, and pilchards, are the principal articles of trade here. The harbour, enclosed by a pier, 600 feet long, is shallow, but it is easy to reach and get out of. All the best shops are in the Market Place, where the four principal streets centre. The stannary court for the hundred of Penwith is abolished. An excellent Geological Society was founded in 1813; and is enriched by a full collection of specimens obtained by Dr. Boase, from every corner of the county, and carefully arranged. The churches and houses are of stone. Madron is the mother church. Sir Humphrey Davy, the great chemist, was born at Penzance, 1778; after serving his apprenticeship to a chemist here, he went to assist Dr. Beddoes at the Pneumatic Institution. Penzance is a cheap and healthy place for a resident. The soil in the neighbourhood is light and rich, from the granite dust at the bottom, and produces uncommonly heavy crops of *potatoes*, the returns being 300 to 600 bushels an acre. Sand, shells, and pilchards, are used to manure it.

Mount's Bay, which is spread out before the town, is 18 miles wide at the mouth, from the Lizard Point on the east, to the Rundlestone on the west side. The shore is low and uninteresting; but what geologists call raised beaches are seen. *St. Michael's Mount*, the most striking object in it, and to which it owes its name, is a conspicuous granite rock, four miles east of Penzance, about a quarter of a mile from the shore, off the town of Marazion. It is reached (at low water only) by a causeway, and stands 250 feet high. A few fishermen's cottages are round the base, and at the top are remains of a priory, founded before the Conquest, and for ages resorted to by pilgrims, whose rock is at the end of the causeway. Here the wife of the Pretender, Perkin Warbeck, found refuge in 1497. There are traces of a great variety of minerals; and it commands by far the best prospect of the bay. In olden times it was called *Ictes*, and was a tin depôt. The flow of pilgrims to this point was the making of Marazion, which formerly possessed a good trade, but is now an insignificant town. *Marghasion* is its Cornish name, indicative probably of its position, and its being once held by Sion Abbey. Sometimes it is called Market-Jew, which is a corruption of another Cornish name, *Marghasjewe.*

Penzance is between the two districts which hem in the opposite sides of the bay, and form the tail end, as it were, of Cornwall, Kerrien towards the Lizard, and Penwith to the Land's End. Both possess a coast not very lofty, but broken and dangerous. They differ in their geological character —the Lizard district being mostly slaty or "killas," and serpentine; and that of the Penwith, round the Land's End, granite, here called moorstone. Penwith signifies, in the expressive old British language, the "point to the left," as it looks like a tract almost cut off fr m the main land. It is much the richest in minerals; though at one time Kerrien was remarkable for its produce in this respect. The surface of both is a heathy moorland, with little pleasant hollows here and there. In Penwith, eight or ten miles from Penzance, are the following places:—The Guskus Mine, near St. Hilary; Wheal Darlington Mine, near Penzance; and the Alfred Mine, near Hayle. Wheal (or Huel) is the common name for a mine, and synonymous with; he English *Wheel*, into which, being worked on the joint stock or "cost book" system, every shareholder puts a *spoke*, all directed to one centre. *Trereiffe* is the seat of the Le Grices; *Trengwainton*, of Mr. Davy. Near *Ludgvan*, (which was the rectory of Borlase, the county historian), is a large camp, 145 yards across. In the neighbourhood of Madron, or Maddern, are a pillar stone or two, and *Lanyon Cromlech*, which consists of a top stone or "quoet," nearly 50 feet girth, resting on four other stones. *St. Buryan Church* is a granite building, on a point of the moorland, 47 feet high; it was once collegiate, and first founded by King Athelstane. Here, too, are various curiosities, as the Merry Maidens, Boscawen-Oon, the Pipers, &c., generally styled "Druid," but in many cases the result of natural causes. A Cromlech at Boskenna, near the Camp and Lamorna Cave. Boscawen-Oon is a circle of 19 stones, near the church, and gives name to the family of the Earl of Falmouth, one of whose members was the famous admiral. *St. Levan* is close to a wild part of the coast. A little distance to the east is Treeren-Dinas, a camp in which stands the best *Logan Stone* (rocking stone) in Cornwall; it weighs 90 tons, but it is moved with a touch. One day in 1824 it was overturned by Lieut. Goldsmith and his crew, in consequence of a bet; but the people round were so highly indignant that he was compelled to replace it, which he did in a very ingenious manner, having, at the instance of Davies Gilbert, Esq., the President of the Royal Society, obtained help from the Plymouth Dockyard. *Tol Peden Penwith*, as the extreme south point of the hundred is called, has a vast hole in the granite cliffs, through which the sea dashes up with a tremendous roar. A dangerous rock called the Rundlestone lies about one mile off it, marked by a buoy; and the dark Wolf-rock further out. The effects of the Atlantic and the weather upon the hardest rocks (as granite is supposed to be) are visible all along this broken and disintegrated coast—a wild desolate region to the eye, but extremely healthful and inspiriting. Rare hells, sea weeds, and plants, should be looked for. The *Land's End*, the ancient *Antivestaeum*, is in St. Sennen, the most westerly parish in England—being, in fact, in a line with Dublin and the Western Islands of Scotland. On one side of the village sign-post is inscribed, "The first Inn in England" (if you come from the west), and the other, "The last Inn in England." Sweetbriar grows here wild. Sennen Cove is a little creek in Whitsand Bay. Longships Reefs, half a mile long, has a lighthouse on it, 83 feet high. Some miles out are the Seven Stones light vessels. About 25 miles south-west are the *Scilly Islands*, a group of 50 or 60 granite islands and reefs, with an industrious population of 2,594. They belong to the Godolphin family. St. Mary's is the largest. Here Sir Cloudesley Shovel, and four ships with 2,000 men were wrecked in a dreadful storm in 1707. A lighthouse has been fixed on St.

Agnes since this fearful event. Formerly there were fewer islands than at present, and it is said that a vast tract between them and the mainland was overwhelmed many centuries ago. That there is some truth in these traditions is evident, from what we see going on at the present time.

St. Just (pronounced *St. Juest*, to distinguish it from another near Truro, which is sounded *St. Jeast*, near Cape Cornwall), is rich in minerals, Druid circles, and other objects of interest. Here are the Levant and Botallic mines, both prosperous concerns, and finding tin and copper. *Botallick Mine* is worked in the very face of the cliffs, and runs out 100 fathoms under the sea. It was descended by the Duc de Nemours, Prince de Joinville, and their party, in 1852. The Mayne or Maen stone is pointed out as that on which the Saxon King, Ethelbert, and six other kings, dined, in the year 600. Round Gurnet's Head and Zennor are various Druid stones. Towednack belongs to the Gilberts, of Tredrea, and is part of the borough of *St. Ives*—a fishing port, on a wide, sandy bay. At the top of it is *Hayle* and its foundries.

In the district of **Kerrier,** which offers much to interest the naturalist, in particular, are the following—Trevena Mine is near; *Godolphin*, also, the old seat of that ancient family (now represented by the Duke of Leeds), is on a hill, in the same parish, with a valuable mine at Wheal Vor.

Helston, taking its name from the marshy tract between it and the sea, is a parliamentary borough, but not otherwise remarkable. *Meneage* was the old name for the corner of Cornwall (down to the Lizard). it has good pasture, and a breed of small moorland horses. The Goonhills Downs run through the middle. *Wallowarren*, the seat of Sir R. Vyvyan, Bart., is near to Marogan's old church. The metal Titanium was first discovered at Manaccan on Helford Creek. *St. Keverne* was the birth-place of *Incledon*, the singer. Off the coast are the Manacle Rocks. The cliffs here are serpentine, soapstone, &c., covered with a profusion of heath, and extend past Black Head to the *Lizard*. This headland, which homeward bound ships from the westward always try to get sight of, is 18 miles from Penzance, and low, but pointed, whence the ancient name, *Ocrinum*, a corruption of *Acritum*. A little northwest of it is *Kynance Cove*, a place frequently visited by parties, on account of its high serpentine and soapstone cliffs, which exhibit the most beautiful colours, and contains little veins of minerals and spars. Vases and other ornaments are made from this stone. Population, 3,355.

Hensbarrow, six miles north, is one of the loftiest of the Cornish Downs, 1,029 feet high. Near Charlestown on the bay, is *Duyorth*, a seat belonging to the Rashleighs, of Menabilley. It is well planted. *Penrice* is another seat, in a sheltered spot, favourable for cultivation. Further down the coast is *Megavissy*, an important fishing town in the pilchard season, but so filthy, that it is a very hot-bed of disease when the cholera is abroad. In 1849, its ravages were so great that the population were turned out to camp it under tents, while their houses were being cleaned and sweetened. Till lately pilchards paid tithe to the vicar. They are caught by the seine or net. *Heligan*, near this, belongs to the Tremaynes.

SOUTH WALES RAILWAY.

Gloucester to Newport.

This line of railway affords great facilities to tourists and lovers of the picturesque for visiting the beautiful scenery of Wales.

Gloucester is now the central point of communication between the north and the south, the east and the west of the kingdom. From Plymouth there is an uninterrupted run through Bristol and Gloucester into the farthest points of the north where the iron road has yet pierced its way.

Upon starting, the line proceeds over an embankment and viaduct over the low meadows near the Severn, and then passes over the two bridges, and continues along the west bank of the Severn. The beautiful spire of Higham new church appears in view, and is quickly left behind, and in a few minutes the train reaches the first station on the line, which is called "OAKLE STREET," a rural spot, convenient for Churcham.

GRANGE COURT JUNCTION. — Westbury-upon-Severn, 1 mile distant. The trains of the Hereford, Ross, and Gloucester Railway turn off at this station to the right.

HEREFORD, ROSS, AND GLOUCESTER.

Gloucester to Ross and Hereford.

LONGHOPE (late Hopebrook).

Distance from station, 1 mile.
Telegraph station at Gloucester, 11½ miles.
HOTEL.—Railway.
MONEY ORDER OFFICE at Newent.

MITCHELDEAN ROAD station.

ROSS.

Telegraph station at Hereford, 12¼ miles.

HOTELS.—Royal; King's Head.

MARKET DAY. — Thursday. FAIRS. — Thursday after March 10th, Ascension Day, June 21st, July 20th, Thursday after October 10th, December 11th.

BANKERS. — J. W. R. Hall; Morgan and Co.; Pritchards and Allaway.

Ross has a population of 2,500; is situated on a rocky elevation on the east bank of the Wye. In the church are several monuments of the Rudhall family, one of whom opposed Cromwell in his siege of Hereford. There is also one of Mr. J. Kyrle, the celebrated "Man of Ross," who was interred here. From the churchyard are some very beautiful views. Ross has great attractions during the summer months. *Goodrich Court*, the seat of Sir S. R. Meyrick, in the neighbourhood, is visited for its armoury. It may be seen on application.

FAWLEY station.

HOLME LACEY.

MONEY ORDER OFFICE at Hereford.

This is the ancient seat of the Scudamore family, now in the possession of Sir E. F. Scudamore Stanhope, Bart. The mansion and grounds excite much interest, having a good picture gallery, and a giant pear tree, covering a quarter of an acre. Here Pope wrote the "Man of Ross."

HEREFORD.

A telegraph station.

HOTELS.—City Arms, Green Dragon.

MARKET DAYS.—Wednesday and Saturday.

FAIRS.—Tuesday after Candlemas, Easter Wednesday, May 19th and 28th, July 1st, and October 20th.

BANKERS.—National Provincial Bank of England; Hereford Banking Co.; Matthews and Co.; Hoskins and Morgan.

HEREFORD, the capital of Herefordshire, and a parliamentary borough, on the Shrewsbury and Hereford, Newport, Abergavenny, and Hereford, and Hereford, Ross, and Gloucester lines. By rail, *viâ* Gloucester, the distance from London is 144¼ miles, but the direct distance by road is only 134, or 33 beyond Gloucester. Population, 12,113.

Hereford, as its old Saxon name explains it to be, stands at a *military Ford* on the Wye, which King Harold protected by a castle, the site of which, at Castle Green, is now occupied by the Nelson Column, where an old bridge of the fifteenth century crosses the river a little higher. To this castle the barons brought Edward II.'s favourite, De Spenser, and executed him, in 1322; and four years later the unfortunate king himself was here deprived of his crown. Parts of the town are low and old fashioned. Some remains of the old town walls are still visible. The soil without is a rich tract of meadow, orchard, and timber; and the internal trade is chiefly in agricultural produce, good cider and perry (which require a little brandy to qualify them), wool, hops, and prime cattle—the last being a splendid breed, white-faced, with soft reddish brown coats. A few gloves and other leather goods are made. Salmon are caught.

The present *Cathedral*, lately restored, standing near the river, and dedicated to St. Mary, is the third on this site, the first one having been founded in the ninth century by King Offa, to atone for the murder of Ethelbert. It is a handsome cross, 325 feet long, begun by Bishop Herbert de Lozinga in 1079, when the Norman style prevailed, and finished by Bishop Borth in 1535, who built the beautiful north porch. The west front was spoiled by Wyatt, in restoring it after the fall of the tower above in 1786. There are two other Norman towers, and a great tower, which firmly support a tall spire. Some of the Gothic side chapels, and the monuments of Bishop Cantilupe, Bishop de Bethune, &c., deserve notice. A curious Saxon map of the world is in the library. The college of the Vicars-Choral, and the grammar school are in the cloisters; the latter was founded in 1385.

The triennial music festivals are held in the *Shire Hall*, a handsome building, by Smirke, built in 1817. Near this is an ancient *Town Hall*, constructed of carved timber, 84 feet long, by 34 broad, in the time of James I., and resting on an open arcade, where the market is held; John Able was the builder. The county gaol, on the road to Aylstone Hill, is on the site of a priory, founded by the De Lacys; the infirmary, near the Castle Green. At the opposite end of the town, past Above Eign, is the *White Cross*, built in 1347, to serve as a market for the country people when the town was ravaged by the plague. Near the bridge and the old palace, is the preaching cross of the Black Friary. All Saints Church and St. Peter's are both Norman, though altered by late restorations. The tower of All Saints leans seven feet from the perpendicular. St. Martin's is a new Gothic church, in place of one ruined in the civil wars, when Hereford was occupied by the royalist party. Poor *Nell Gwynne* was born here.

In the neighbourhood are various points of interest. Up the Wye are—Belmont; Sugwas, once a country seat of the bishops; *Garnons*, Sir G. Cotterell, Bart., in a fine spot, under Bishopstone Hill; *Moccas*, Sir V. Cornewall, Bart., in an immense park. *Sufton Court* (near a camp) is the seat of the Herefords, an ancient family. *Hampton Court*, the old seat of the Coningsbys, belongs to — Arkwright, Esq., a descendant of the great cotton spinner. *Foxley*, Sir R. Price, Bart., was planned by Price, who wrote the "Essay on the Picturesque," according to the principles laid down in that work. *Stoke Edith Park*, E. Foley, Esq. On Aconbury Hill, south of the town, are a Roman camp and traces of a priory. Leominster, a parliamentary borough, has many old timbered houses, especially one built by the architect of the Hereford Town Hall. At Ledbury is a fine Norman church.

South Wales Main Line continued.

Grange Court to Newport.

The forest hills are soon approached, and then we obtain a glimpse of the Severn, and passing on through Broadoak, we reach the station at

NEWNHAM,

Situate in a cutting.

Telegraph station at Gloucester, 10½ miles,

HOTEL.—Bear,

MARKET DAY.—Friday.

FAIR DAYS.—June 11th and October 18th.

NEWNHAM stands on an eminence rising from the western bank of the Severn, which is here nearly a mile across at high water. In the Norman times, it appears to have been a fortified town, designed to repress the incursions of the Welsh. The houses are principally ranged in one long street, and the church stands on a cliff, near the river.

Immediately after leaving this station a short tunnel passes underneath the East Dean Road, and, emerging thence, a fine reach of the Severn, called Bullo Pill, is presented to view.

The line passes along the margin of the river for several miles, and in some places the water is so near, that at high tides it approaches close to the railway.

GATCOMBE station (Purton).

LYDNEY.—At the distance of 5½ miles from this station is *Clearwell Castle*, the seat of the Dowager Countess of Dunraven.

The railway here crosses the rivers Severn and Wye.

WOOLASTON.

Distance from station, 4 miles.

Telegraph station at Chepstow, 5¼ miles.

MONEY ORDER OFFICE at Chepstow.

We here leave the county of Gloucester, and enter that of

MONMOUTH,

A small English county, bordering on the principality of Wales, which, in point of fertility, picturesque scenery, and historic remains, is the most interesting district, in proportion to its size, of any in the kingdom. The general aspect of this county is inviting, both from its diversity and fertility. A continual recurrence of hill and dale, wood and water, corn fields and meadows; the sublimity of wildly magnificent, and the beauty of mild and cultivated, scenery, combine to delight the eye of the beholder at every turn he takes in this district. Nor is the air less congenial to health than the face of the country is interesting to view. The river Wye, which runs through this county, is celebrated for its picturesque scenery. The peculiar characteristic of this beautiful river are its sinuous course, the uniformity of its breadth, and the variegated scenery on its banks. So considerable is its serpentine course, that the distance from Ross to Chepstow, which is not seventeen miles in a direct line, is by water forty-three. The effects of this sinuosity are numerous, diversified, and striking; and they principally arise from two circumstances, the mazy course of the river, and the loftiness of its banks. In consequence of this, the views it exhibits are of the most beautiful kind of perspective. From the constant shifting of the foreground and side screens, the same objects are seen from a variety of sides, and in different points of view.

CHEPSTOW.

POPULATION, 4,295.

Distance from station, ¼ mile. A telegraph station.

HOTEL.—Beaufort Arms.

FLYS &c.—Fare to Tintern Abbey and back, time not exceeding eight hours, carriage and pair for seven persons, 16s.; driver and gates 6s.; for ten persons, 20s. and 6s. Fly for two persons, 8s. and 3s. 6d.; ditto for four persons, 10s., and 3s. 6d. gates. Posting, 1s. 6d. per mile. Single horse, 1s.

MARKET DAYS.—Wednesday and Saturday, and last Monday in each month.

FAIRS.—Monday before March 1st, Whit Friday, June 22nd, August 1st, Friday on or before Oct. 29th.

MONEY ORDER OFFICE.

BANKERS.—Bromage, Snead & Co.

CHEPSTOW is a market town, in the county of Monmouth, situated near the mouth of the river Wye. The town is large and has within the last few years been much improved. It was formerly surrounded by walls, and defended by a castle.

Excursionists visit Tintern Abbey, Wyndcliffe, and Chepstow Castle, which are thus described in Mr. Cliffe's Guide Book of South Wales:—

Tintern Abbey.—The graceful Wye, filled up to its banks, and brimming over with the tide from the Severn Sea, glides tranquilly past the orchards and fat glebe of "Holy Tynterne." On every side stands an amphitheatre of rocks, nodding with hazel, ash, birch, and yew, and thrusting out from the tangled underwood high pointed crags, as it were, for ages the silent witness of that ancient Abbey and its fortunes; but removed just such a distance as to leave a fair plain in the bend of the river, for one of the most rare and magnificent structures in the whole range of ecclesiastical architecture. As you descend the road from Chepstow, the building suddenly bursts upon you, like a gigantic stone skeleton; its huge gables standing out against the sky with a mournful air of dilapidation. There is a stain upon the walls, which bespeaks a weather-beaten antiquity; and the ivy comes creeping out of the bare, sightless windows; the wild flowers and mosses cluster upon the mullions and dripstones, as if they were seeking to fill up the unglazed void with nature's own colours. * * *

The door is opened—how beautiful the long and pillared nave—what a sweep of graceful arches, how noble the proportions, the breadth, the length, and the height.

The Castle is a noble and massive relic of feudalism; the boldness of its site, on a rock overhanging the river, the vastness of its proportions, render it a peculiarly impressive ruin. The entrance is a fine specimen of Norman military architecture: the chapel is one of the most elegant structures ever built within a house of defence. It was originally founded almost immediately after the Conquest.

The **Wyndcliffe** rises in the back ground of the view, from the road out of Chepstow to Monmouth. Having ascended the crag, the eye ranges over portions of nine counties, yet there seems to be no confusion in the prospect; the proportions of the landscape, which unfolds itself in regular, yet not in monotonous succession, are perfect; there is nothing to offend the most exact critic in picturesque scenery. The "German Prince," who published a tour in England in 1826, and who has written the best description of the extraordinary view which Wyndcliffe commands—a view superior to that from Ehrenbreitstein on the Rhine—well remarks that a vast group of views of distinct and opposite character here seem to blend and unite in one!

The stupendous iron Railway Bridge by which the line is carried over the river Wye, is one of the most remarkable in the country. Bridges of this size are so rare that we think it right to direct the attention of the reader to this one. Mr. Stephenson's magnificent Britannia bridge displays one method of crossing wide spans. The Chepstow bridge of Mr.

Brunel is another mode, and shows, as might have been expected, his peculiarly original and bold conception, accompanied by extraordinary economy, by arranging his materials in the form of a large suspended truss, and attaching the roadway to suspended chains kept in a state of rigidity by vertical trusses or struts, inserted between the chains and a circular wrought iron tube, spanning the river, 309 feet in length. The railway having to cross a rapid and navigable river without interruption to vessels, the Admiralty very properly required that the span over the mid channel should not be less than 300 feet; and that a clear headway of 50 feet above the highest known tide should be given. The bridge is 600 feet long; there are three spans over the land of 100 feet each, which are supported upon cast iron cylinders, six feet in diameter, and one and a quarter inch thick. These were sunk to an average depth of 48 feet through numerous beds of clay, quicksand, marl, &c., to the solid limestone rock, which was found to dip at an angle of 45 degrees; it had therefore to be carefully levelled horizontally, and the cylinders bedded level. These were then sunk by excavating them within, and pressing them down with heavy weights, in doing which very great difficulties were overcome—immense volumes of fresh water were tapped, requiring a 30-horse engine to pump them out. They were, when finally filled with concrete, composed of Portland Cement, sand, and gravel, which set in a few days, as hard as a rock. The concrete is filled up to the level of the roadway, so that, should the cylinder decay, it might be taken out and replaced in sections in safety.

There are six cylinders at the west end of the main span; upon those a standard, or tower of cast iron plates, fifty feet high, is erected. A similar tower of masonry is built at the east end, on the rocky precipice of the Wye.

On the west standard is a cross girder of wrought iron, and upon which the tubes rest. The tubes serve to keep apart and steady the towers; and to their ends are attached the suspending chains. Now, in an ordinary suspension bridge, the chains hang in a festoon, and are free to move according to the limited weights passing under them; but this flexibility would be inadmissible in a railway bridge, and the continuity of the bridge would be destroyed if a very small deflection took place when passed over by a heavy locomotive. With a view to give the necessary rigidity, Mr. Brunel introduced at every third part a stiff wrought iron girder, connecting firmly the tube to the roadway girders; and, with the aid of other adjusting screws, the suspension chains are pulled or stretched as nearly straight as possible. Other diagonal chains connect these points, so that at whatever part of the bridge an engine may be passing, its weight is distributed all over the tube and chains by these arrangements. The tube is strengthened within by the introduction of diaphragms or discs at every 30 feet, which render it both light and stiff. The bridge cost £65,420; and required 1,231 tons of wrought, and 1,003 tons of cast iron. The bridge has been visited by a great number of engineers from all countries; indeed, it is only by a personal inspection that the numerous ingenious contrivances and arrangements can be understood. The whole seems to be very simple, yet engineers fully enter into the complexity of the design, and the minute and carefully proportioned scantlings given to every part. We would especially call their attention to the cast iron ring or circle attached to the ends of the tube to prevent collapse; to the wedges introduced under the vertical trusses to adjust the exact tension upon the chain; to the curve given to the tubes themselves, increasing their strength; and to the rolling-boxes under the vertical trusses, by which means the road girders are maintained in a position to expand or contract, independently of the movements of the main tubes.

Scenery of the Wye.—The Wye rises in the Plinlimmon Mountains, in the heart of South Wales, and winds along the borders of several counties, past Builth, Hay, Hereford, Ross, Monmouth, to the Bristol Channel, below Chepstow; a course of 130 miles, through scenes of great beauty and celebrity. The *Upper Wye* reaches down to Hay, on the borders of Herefordshire; after which, that portion which crosses the county is rather tame; but at Ross the *Lower Wye* begins, and ends at Chepstow. "The former (says Mr. Cliffe, in his *Book of South Wales*) has not been estimated as it deserves, because it is off the beaten track; but the opening of the railroads to Hereford (in 1853) has brought the charming scenery of the *Upper Wye* within easy reach." It is a rapid stream, occasionally swollen by deep floods, running between high rocky banks all the way.

From *Llangurig*, which is 10 miles from its source, the river rushes through deep glens and ravines, past the junction of the Dernol, and the Nanerth cliffs (three miles long) to *Rhayader-Gwy*, *i.e.*, the Falls of the Gwy (the Welsh name of this river), so called from a cascade made by the river, close to the bridge. It stands among mountains, and has some fragments of a castle. Within a few miles is Llyn Gwyn, in which croaking trout are caught. Hence to Builth is 14 miles. The Elan, Clarwen, and Ithon join before you reach Builth, the last at Pont-ar-Ithon, a fine spot. The Ithon may be ascended to *Llandrindod Spa*, where there are excellent saline, sulphur, and iron springs, in a healthy, though unattractive spot, with a pump-house.

Builth, in a fine part of the river, has remains of a castle, and a long bridge. Trout and salmon fishing; fine scenery. Just above it, the *Irvon* joins; it should be ascended for its charming scenery to *Llanwyrted Wells* (14 miles) and Llandovery (23 miles). When Llewellyn was hemmed in by the English under Mortimer, in Edward I.'s reign, he tried to get assistance to disguise his movements from the Welsh garrison of Builth Castle. It was in winter, and he had his horse's shoes reversed; this, however, was revealed to the English by the blacksmith. The garrison refused to help him, and as he was retreating up the Ithon, he was surprised and killed. *Bradwyr Buallt* is the designation applied to Builth to this day. The Welsh prince was killed at Cwm-Llewellyn, near the Park Wells; and the body buried at Cefn-y-bedd, a mile or two further on the Llandovery road. There are two roads down the Wye from Builth, the high road being on the west side; but the east road is the most interesting, especially about Aberedw, which lies in a beautiful defile, where the

Ebw falls in, opposite Erwood. The castle was Llewellyn's hunting seat. Near it is the church on a cliff, a hole in which is Llewellyn's cave. Further on the Machwy (Little Wye) joins; it should be followed a little way to the Pwll Dwu or Black Rock, and its waterfall, 40 feet down. Then comes *Llangoed Castle* (J. Macmamara, Esq.), on the Brecknock side, and *Boughrood* (an old castle), on the Radnor side, which commanded the old ford here. Brecknock is eight miles from this, and from that place the fine scenery of the Usk may be descended. The Hatterel, or Cradle mountains, to the right are 2,545 feet high.

Glasbury, 15 miles from Builth. Three Cocks, a good inn. *Gwyrnefed* is Colonel Wood's seat. W. Wilkins took the name of De Winton nearly twenty years ago, and *Maeslwch Castle* is the property of Captain De Winton.

Hay, four miles from here, is an old Norman town, founded by Bernard Newmarch; part of the castle remains, which was destroyed by Owen Glyndwr. It is exactly on the borders of three counties. Here the Upper Wye scenery ends. Barges are able to reach this point. *Clifford Castle*, three miles from Hay, was the birthplace of Fair Rosamond Clifford. It was built by the Conqueror's kinsman, Fitz-Osborne.

PORTSKEWET, MAGOR, and LLANWERN stations.

NEWPORT.

A telegraph station.

HOTEL.—King's Head; West Gate.

MARKET DAYS.—Wednesday and Saturday.

FAIRS.—14 days before Holy Thursday, August 15th, Nov. 6th, Holy Thursday.

BANKERS.—West of England; Bailey and Co.

This is a sea port town of some importance, having a population of 19,323. It has a constant steam packet communication with Bristol and various parts of South Wales; and by means of its ready access by railway with the many iron districts in the neighbourhood, its traffic in that mineral, as well as coal, of late years has greatly increased. With the exception of the church, which presents various styles of architecture, the town itself has no prepossessing attractions. The scenery from the church-yard is very imposing, taking in, as it does, a wide expanse of country, as well as an extensive view of the Severn. Outside the town a stone bridge of five arches crosses the river Usk. It was erected at a cost of something over 10,000*l.*

MONMOUTHSHIRE LINE.

The Eastern and Western Valleys Lines turn off at this point to the right, passing through districts rich in mineral products, but not of essential importance to the general tourist. The stations on the Western Line are BASSALLEG JUNCTION, TYDEE, RISCA, CROSS KEYS, CHAPEL BRIDGE, ABERCARNE, NEW BRIDGE, CRUMLIN, LLANHILLETH, ABERBEEG, CWM, VICTORIA, EBBW VALE, ABERTILLERY, and BLAINA. Those on the Eastern Branch, LLANTARNAM, CWMBRAN, PONTNEWYDD, PONTRHYDYRUN, PONTYPOOL, PONTNEWYNNYDD, ABERSYCHAN, CWM AVON, and BLAENAVON.

Returning to Newport we now proceed by the

WEST MIDLAND.

Newport to Abergavenny and Hereford.

In ten minutes after leaving Newport we reach PONTNEWYDD, and in ten minutes more, the station of

PONTYPOOL ROAD.

Distance from the town of the same name, 1½ mile.

Near is *Pontypool Park*, Hanbury Leigh, Esq. This forms the junction with the

TAFF VALE EXTENSION.

A short line, 16 miles long, running into the Taff Vale Line at Quaker's Yard. The stations on the line are PONTYPOOL, CRUMLIN, TREDEGAR, RHYMNEY JUNCTION, LLANCAICH, and QUAKER'S YARD.

Merthyr Tydvil, see page 46.

LITTLE MILL JUNCTION.

Here the line crosses, and forms a connection with the

COLEFORD, MONMOUTH, USK, AND PONTYPOOL.

Little Mill Junction to Monmouth.

USK

Is a place of great antiquity, on the river of that name. Considerable remains of a castle, where Richard III. and Edward IV. are reputed to have been born, are to be seen; likewise part of a priory. Fine salmon fishing.

Llangibby Castle (3 miles).

Passing LLANDENNY Station, we arrive at

RAGLAN ROAD,

which is available for foot-passengers only.

Here are the fine remains of the castle built by Sir W. Thomas in the 14th century. The Marquis of Worcester defended it for four years against the Parliament: it is now a most picturesque ruin. It gives title of Baron Raglan to a descendant—the late Lord Fitzroy Somerset, Commander-in-Chief in the late war in the Crimea. He was military secretary to Wellington, and lost an arm at Waterloo. What it was in the 16th century we may learn from the poet Churchyard; he speaks of it as—

> "A castle fine
> That Raglan hight—stands moted almost round,
> Made of freestone, upright, straight as line,
> Whose workmanship in beauty doth abound."

DINGESTOW,

or Dynystow. In a barn, among beautiful orchards, may be seen the remains of Grace Dieu Abbey.

MONMOUTH.

Telegraph station at Abergavenny, 14 miles.

HOTELS.—Beaufort Arms; King's Head.

BANKERS.—Bromage, Snead & Co.; Bailey and Co.

MONMOUTH, the capital of Monmouthshire, is

on a delightful part of the Wye, at the junction of the Monnow, a parliamentary borough, returning one member, conjointly with Newport and Usk, with an agricultural population of 5,710, which is rather on the decrease; but this will no doubt be augmented by the recent opening of the railway from Pontypool. It was the ancient *Blestium*, from which a Roman road, in the direction of the present one, went to Usk. There was a castle here, even in Saxon times, which afterwards became the residence of Henry IV., and here, in 1387, his famous son, Henry V. was born—"Harry of Monmouth"—the immortal Prince Hal of Shakspeare.

The few remains of this castle (which belongs to the Duke of Beaufort), stand among houses on a ridge over the Monnow, to the west near the gaol, the walls being 6 to 10 feet thick. Here is shown the room in which Henry was born, and the great hall by the side of it. There is a statue of him in the Market Place.

Within a short distance of the town are the following objects of notice:—The *Wye*, so celebrated for its uniform breadth, lofty cliffs, winding course, and picturesque scenery, which is perpetually changing its character. Elegant and commodious boats are kept here for the use of tourists. "The stranger cannot do better than hire Samuel Dew, whom he will find by Monmouth Bridge. Sam is one of the steadiest aud cleverest of Wye watermen, knows the river well, and is quite used to guiding those who are in search of the beautiful."—*The Land we Live in.*

Near the junction of the Trothey, about a mile from Monmouth, is *Troy House*, an old seat of the Duke of Beaufort, with old portraits and gardens, where the Marquis of Worcester gave Charles I. a dish of fruit "from Troy." "Truly, my lord," said the king, "I have heard that corn grows where Troy stood, but I never thought that there had grown any apricots there before." Here is Henry's cradle (so called), and the armour he wore at Agincourt. About 6 miles down the Wye is Beacon Hill, 1,000 feet high, near Trelech Cross (three Druid stones), and below that Landogo Bigswear, Tintern Abbey, Wyndcliffe, Chepstow (17 miles by water); *Wonastow*, seat of Sir W. Pilkington, baronet, is a very old seat, which belonged to the Herberts. *Treowen*, near it, is another, but now turned into a farm house. Up the Trothey is *Llantillio House.*

A pretty road leads to Beaulieu Grove on the top, near the handsome spire church of Llantillio Crossenny, and the ruins of *White Castle*, a fortress built by the early Norman possessors of this county. In ascending the beautiful valley of the Monnow, there are two other castles, worth notice— Skenfrith and Grosmont—the latter being under Greig Hill, near a small cross church. Most of these structures were formerly part of the Duchy of Lancaster, through John of Gaunt, but now belong, with large possessions, to the Beaufort family. From Monmouth, up the Wye, you pass Dixton Church, a pretty rustic building; then the New Weir, Symond's Yat, Courtfield (where Henry V. was nursed), &c., till you come to Ross. But the best plan is to descend from that place (see the *Wye)*. An excursion may be made to the *Forest of Dean*, and its interesting scenery. You pass (taking the Coleford Road) the *Buckstone*, an immense Logan stone, on a hill, 56 feet round at the top, and tapering off to 3 at the bottom. Coleford Church is modern, the old one having been destroyed in the civil wars, when Lord Herbert routed some of the parliament people here. About 3 miles north-east is the Speech House, where the miners hold their meetings. To the south, in the direction of Offa's Dyke, which may be still traced, is *Clearwell Park*, the seat of the dowager Countess of Dunraven, where a great heap of Roman money was found in 1847, and St. Briaval's, with its *May Pole* and hundred court, part of a Norman castle. There are many deserted mines. The wood is cut for hoops, poles, and other purposes.

A good stone bridge crosses the Wye, and one the Monnow — an ancient stone building, called the Welsh Gate, with a Norman chapel (St. Thomas's) at the foot. Many of the houses are white-washed, and, as they are dispersed among gardens and orchards, the view of the town in summer is picturesque. The parish church of *St. Mary* has a tapering spire 200 feet. It was attached to a priory, of which there are remains in a private house adjoining. The handsome oriel window is called the "study" of Geoffrey of Monmouth; but he was born in the 11th century, long before such a style was invented. He was a Welsh monk (Geoffry ap Arthur), who turned the British Chronicles, fables and all, into rugged Latin. To him, however, we are indebted for Shakspeare's King Lear, and the Sabrina of Milton's *Comus.*

Monmouth was once famous for its woollen caps, "the most ancient, general, warm, and profitable covering for men's heads on this island," according to Fuller. The manufacture was afterwards transferred to Bewdley. There is, or was, a Capper's chapel in the church, "better carved and gilded than any other part of it." Fletcher takes care to remember this.

The well-endowed *Free School* was founded by W. Jones, who, from a poor shop-boy at this place, became a rich London merchant. Newland was his birth-place; and there, after quitting London, he showed himself under the disguise of poverty, but being told to try for relief in Monmouth, where he had been at service, he repaired hither, was kindly received, and then revealed who he was.

One of the best walks is at Chippenham Meadow, near the junction of the Monnow and Wye, under a grove of elms. Anchor and May Hills are good points of view. Past May Hill (across the Wye) is *Kymin Hill*, the east half of which is in Gloucestershire.

West Midland Main Line continued.

Little Mill to Abergavenny.

Passing the station of NANTYDERRY, or Goitre, we arrive at PENPERGWM, near which is *Llanover*, the seat of Lord Llanover, and three miles to the right is *Clytha.* Proceeding along the valley of the Usk, we soon arrive at

ABERGAVENNY.

A telegraph station.
HOTEL.—Angel.
MARKET DAY.—Tuesday.
FAIRS.—Third Tuesday in March, May 14th, June 24th (wool), Tuesday before July 20th, September 25th, and November 19th. RACES in April.

This interesting old place, of 4,797 inhabitants, stands among the Monmouthshire Hills, near the Sugar Loaf, Blorenge, and other peaks, in a fine part of the Usk, where the Gavenny joins it, and gives name to the town, which the Romans who had a station here, called *Gobannium*. It was formerly noted for its old castle and springs, founded by Hammeline de Balun at the Conquest, the former for the purpose of guarding the pass into Wales. This feudal structure afterwards came to the Nevilles, who still take their title from it. A Tudor gate, from which there is a fine prospect, is the chief remain. Later still Abergavenny became celebrated for its Welsh wigs, made of goats' hair, some of which sold at 40 guineas each. Physicians also used to send patients here to drink goats' whey. But its present prosperity arises from its flannel weaving, and the valuable coal and iron works at Clydach, Blaenavon, &c., in its neighbourhood—a state of things likely to be much increased by the Newport, Abergavenny, and Hereford Railway, part of that important chain which unites South Wales to Liverpool and the north of England.

The old bridge of 15 arches crosses the Usk. The church has some ancient tombs of the Beauchamps, and other possessors of the lordship. Traces of the priory exist near it. There is also an old grammar school, and a modern Cymreidiggion Society's Hall for Welsh bardic meetings—Monmouth being essentially Welsh, though separated from the principality since Henry VIII.'s time. Antiquaries say that, until feudal tenures were abolished by Charles II., Abergavenny castle used to give its holders their title by mere possession—like Arundel Castle, in Sussex, instead of by writ or by patent.

The views from the Sugar Loaf, which is 1,856 feet high, are magnificent. It takes three hours to ascend it. A still more beautiful prospect is enjoyed from St. Michael's old Chapel on Skyrrid Vawr. The White Castle is near this mountain. *Raglan Castle*, which the famous Marquis of Worcester held out so stoutly against Cromwell, is also near (8 miles), on the Monmouth road. Its machicolated gate, hall, chapel, the yellow tower, &c., are in excellent preservation, through the care of its owner, the Duke of Beaufort. *Llanthony Abbey* stands in a wild part of the Hhondu. The scenery of the Usk, from Abergavenny up to Brecon, is very romantic, as it winds round the black mountains, in one of the highest peaks of which it rises above Trecastle. Excellent trout fishing.

BRECON.

Telegraph station at Abergavenny, 21 miles.
HOTELS.—The Castle; Swan.
MARKET DAYS.—Wednesdays and Saturdays.
FAIRS.—First Wednesday in March, July 5, Sept. 9, Nov. 16; also in March, and November 16, for hiring. RACES in September.

This place is situated in the midst of very beautiful mountain scenery, has a population of 5,673, returning one member to parliament. It is 20 miles from Abergavenny, and communicable by coach every day. The principal buildings consist of three churches, County Hall, and Market House, very handsome new Assize Courts, built in 1843, Barracks, Theatre, Infirmary, a bridge of seven arches over the Usk, from which is a fine view; there are also an Independent Training College and Grammar School, at which Jones, the county historian, was educated. Here are the remains of an old castle, consisting of the "Ely Tower," so called from Dr. Mortan, Bishop of Ely, who was a prisoner at the instance of Richard III., and as the scene of the conference between the Bishop and the Duke of Buckingham. Newmarch, a Norman baron, was the founder of this castle. Hugh Price, the founder of Jesus College, at Oxford, was born here; and Shakspeare's Fluellen, or Sir David Gow lived in the neighbourhood. He was knighted at Agincourt by Henry V., when at the point of death, having sacrificed his own life to save the king's. Another native of Brecknock was Mrs. Siddons. The "Shoulder of Mutton" Inn is pointed out as the place of her nativity. It stands in a romantic part of the Usk, by the banks of which beautiful walks are laid out. To the north of it (22 miles by the lower and 17 by the upper road) is Builth, where Llewellyn was given up to the English. There are good sulphur springs in this quarter, viz:—Park Wells, Llanwrtyd Wells, Llandrindod Wells, &c. Making the descent of the Usk you come to Crickhowell, where there is good angling; and (what is rare in the county) a spire church.

LLANFIHANGEL and PANDY stations.

PONTRILAS.

Telegraph station at Hereford, $10\frac{3}{4}$ miles.
MONEY ORDER OFFICE at Hereford.
ST. DEVEREUX and TRAM INN stations being passed, we shortly arrive at

Hereford, particulars of which will be found at page 38.

SHREWSBURY AND HEREFORD.

Hereford to Shrewsbury.

MORETON.

POPULATION, 1,512.
Telegraph station at Hereford, $3\frac{1}{2}$ miles.
HOTELS.—White Hart; Railway.
DINMORE (Hope-under-Dinmore) and FORD BRIDGE stations.

LEOMINSTER.

Distance from station, $2\frac{3}{4}$ miles.
A telegraph station.
HOTELS.—Lion; Royal Oak.
MARKET DAY.—Friday.
FAIRS.—Feb. 13th, Tuesday after Mid-Lent, May 2nd, July 10th, Sept. 4th, Nov. 8th, Friday after Dec. 11th. RACES are held in August.
BANKERS.—National Provincial Bank of England; Branch of Hereford Banking Company.

This place has a population of 5,214, principally engaged in the manufacture of hats, leather gloves, and coarse cloth; it has also a considerable trade in wheat, wool, hops, and cyder. It has several free and national schools, meeting houses, and charitable institutions. Many of the buildings, which are of timber and plaster, grotesquely ornamented, present indications of the antiquity of the town. The buildings of greatest note are the church, rebuilt in the early part of the seventeenth century; the Butter Cross, erected about 1633, of timber and plaster, Market House, and House of Industry. This last formed part of a priory.

Nearest station to *Bromyard* 9 miles to the right. We here branch off to the left on the

KINGTON & LEOMINSTER BRANCH.

Leominster to Kington.

The first station is KINGSLAND, 2 miles from which is *Mortimer's Cross*, the scene of the last severe conflict, which settled Edward IV. on the throne of England. *Yatton Court* near.

PEMBRIDGE STATION

1½ mile to the right. *Shobdon Court*, the seat of the Hanbury family.

Proceeding by the river Arrow, we pass TITLEY Station (near which is *Eywood Park*, and a fine entrenchment, of an oval form, at *Wapley*), and arrive at

KINGTON.

HOTELS.—King's Head; Oxford Arms.

Pleasantly situated under the Bradnor Mountain. It has a little clothing trade, and a church, with a detached tower, its spire resembling three hollow cones, placed one above the other. Five miles north is the old border town of *Presteign*.

The tourist may now, if he please, avail himself of conveyances by which he may reach the sources of the Wye, Plinlimmon, and Aberystwith. The route, laying through *Radnor*, with its old border castle of the Mortimers; by the glens and cascades of Radnor Forest; *Rhayader*, and its crags, and pools (full of fish), and old castles. He should, from this point, ascend the Wye, if he would see scenery that is really full of the poetry of nature; and he will not feel this more than when he views the Nanerth Cliffs, and the junction with the Dernol.

The road then proceeds along the valley of the Ystwith, by *Hafod* (the grandly-situated seat of Mr. Hoghton), and the *Devil's Bridge*, whence he may go along the valley of the Rheidol, and see the cascades, to Aberystwith.

Pursuing our way from Leominster, we soon pass the station of BERRINGTON and EYE; near which is *Berrington Park* (Lord Rodney).

WOOFERTON STATION

then succeeds. This is the nearest station for *Tenbury*, with its old butter cross and market place.

Leaving Wooferton, and passing along, with the river Teme on our right, we arrive at

LUDLOW.

A telegraph station.

HOTEL.—Angel.

MARKET DAY.—Monday.

FAIRS.—Monday before February 13th, Tuesday before Easter, May 1st, Whit Wednesday, August 21st, September 28th, and December 6th.

BANKERS.—Ludlow Bank; Rocke, Eyton and Co.; Ludlow and Tenbury.

LUDLOW is a parliamentary borough, with 5,376 inhabitants, returning two members, and standing on a beautiful bend of the Teme, in Shropshire, but close to the borders of Herefordshire, from which the river divides it. Several country seats are planted on the hills around, ot which there are very pleasing prospects from the walls of the old *Castle*. This fine ruin was originally built by Roger Montgomery, one of the Conqueror's favourite knights, to whom the defence of the Welsh borders was entrusted. The only remains are the keep, 110 feet high, with some other towers, under various names, a chapel in the Norman style, and a great hall. In this hall Milton's *Comus* (which he wrote at Horton in Buckinghamshire) was performed before Lord President Brackley, the story being founded on an incident which befel two members of his family. Here Henry VII. a Tudor, and Welshman by descent, kept his court, and married his son Arthur to Katherine of Arragon, an important event in its consequences; for being afterwards married to Arthur's brother Henry, and divorced by him, the great Reformation of religion followed. In Elizabeth's time the wise and sagacious Sir Henry Sidney, father of Sir Phillip, was Lord President of Wales; and after the restoration, was succeeded by Lord Carbery, the patron of Butler, who found a home, and wrote the first three cantos of Hudibras here.

Ludlow is well built. Two bridges cross the Teme which, north of the town, is joined by the Corve. One of these leads over to Ludford, in Herefordshire, which belongs to the Charltons of Ludford House; the other is close to the only remaining town gate. St. Lawrence's, near the Market Place, is a large cross-shaped church of Henry VII.'s time, 230 feet long, the tower, porch, and oak roof of which deserve notice. Edward the Sixth's Grammar School, and the Guildhall, where the sessions are held, are in Mill Street. A little paper is made here, but the trade is almost entirely agricultural.

Within a short distance are the following seats:—*Dinham House*, belonging to the Earl of Powis, formerly occcupied by Prince Lucien Bonaparte; *Hay Park* and *Moor Park* are the Salweys' seats; *Oakley Park*, the seat of the Honourable R. W. Clive; *Croft Castle*, William Kevil Davies, Esq.; *Caynham Court*, Sir William Curtis; *Downton Hall*, Sir Charles Rouse Boughton. *Kinlet Hall*, near Cleoberry Mortimer, is a seat of the Childes. *Tenbury*, on the Teme, is a pretty place, among hop grounds and orchards. *Wigmore*, (7 miles), is in a rocky picturesque spot, with a ruined castle on a hill above it, built by the Norman kings to command the Welsh marches, for the Mortimers, who took their title of Earl of March from this circumstance. One of them was the opponent of Henry IV.

"Revolted Mortimer!
* * * * *
When on the gentle Severn's sedgy bank
In single opposition, hand to hand,
He did confound the best part of an hour
In changing hardiment with great Glendower.
Three times they breathed, and three times did they drink
Upon agreement of sweet Severn's flow—
Who then, affrighted with their bloody looks
Ran fearfully among the trembling reeds."

Richard's Castle took its name from another border fortress. *Downton* was the seat of Knight, author of an "Analytical Inquiry into the Principles of Taste," who built it, to exemplify those principles, with "Gothic towers and battlements without, and Grecian ceilings, columns, and entablatures within;" his design being not to copy the style of any particular age or country, but to produce a picturesque dwelling compounded from all, and adapted to the character of the scenery, which is equally irregular. *Brampton Bryan*, seat of the Earl of Oxford, descended from Lord Chancellor Hailey, whose MSS. are in the British Museum.

Bromfield and Onibury are stations of no great importance.

Craven Arms.—This forms the junction of the

KNIGHTON RAILWAY.

Craven Arms to Knighton.

This line is only twelve miles long, but it is intended subsequently to extend it in connection with the Central Wales and Llanelly Railways to South Wales Line, thereby bringing Milford Haven and the South Wales Districts in direct communication with the more important manufacturing districts of the North West. The line runs *viâ* Broom and Hopton Heath to

BUCKNELL.

Population about 600.—Church is a mixture of the Norman and Early English.

KNIGHTON.

Population, about 1,700, partially engaged in the manufacture of woollens. Situated on the River Teme. There are races held here annually, in June; the course is a little more than a mile round.

Marsh Brook station.

CHURCH STRETTON.

A telegraph station.
Hotel.—Crown.
Market Day.—Thursday. Fairs.—March 10th, May 14th, July 3rd, and September 25th.
Leebotwood and Dorrington stations.

CONDOVER.

Telegraph station at Shrewsbury, 4½ miles.
Shrewsbury, see page 63.

South Wales continued.

Newport to Cardiff.

From Newport, we pass through a short tunnel and cross the river Ebw, soon after arriving at

Marshfield Station, situated in a dreary extent of country, called the Westloeg Level. Crossing the river Rumney, we enter

GLAMORGANSHIRE,

One of the most southern counties in Wales, by far the largest and most beautiful in the principality, and generally considered the garden of Wales.

The mountains are not so high as those in many of the surrounding counties, but their extreme abruptness imparts an air of wildness and elevation which greatly exceeds the reality. But what principally distinguishes this county is the profusion of coal, iron, and lime-stone, with which it everywhere abounds. These mineral riches have raised Glamorganshire to great importance during the last half century. Immense establishments have been erected in the wildest part of the country; canals and roads have been formed, at great expense, to connect them with the coast; and these circumstances, reacting over the whole district, and even far beyond it, have spread the influence of improvement throughout—the facilities of intercourse creating new sources of industry.

CARDIFF.

Population, 18,357.
A telegraph station.
Hotels.—Cardiff Arms, Angel.
Market Day.—Saturday.
Fairs.—Second Wednesday in March, April, and May, June 29th, September 19th, and November 30th.
Bankers.—National Provincial Bank of England. Wilkins and Co. Branch of West of England and South Wales Banking Company.

Cardiff, a borough town, and capital of Glamorganshire, is built on the east bank of the river Taff or Tay, near its entrance into the mouth of the Severn. The inhabitants carry on a considerable trade with Bristol, and export a great quantity of wrought iron and coal to foreign parts.

The new Bute Docks, made on a tract of waste land, by the Marquis of Bute, who is lord of the manor, are about one mile below the town, deep enough for ships, with a basin of one and a half acres, and an entrance 45 feet wide. A ship canal 1,400 yards long, 67 yards wide, runs up to the town. The coal and iron of Merthyr Tydvil and the neighbourhood are the chief exports, and the quantity almost doubles itself every two or three years.

There are remains of the town walls, with the

Norman keep, 75 feet high, of the *Castle*, in which Robert Curthose (*i. e.*, short legs), died in 1133, he having been imprisoned there for life by his brother, Henry I. The parish church is very old, and has a good tower. The new *Town Hall*, just built by H. Jones, is a handsome Italian pile, 175 feet long, including a police court, merchants' hall, corporation room (71 feet by 36), crown court, judges' and other rooms, and a nisi prius court. There is also a large county gaol.

Within a short distance are—*Hensol*, which belonged to Lord Chancellor Talbot; and *Wenvoe Castle*, the seat of R. Jenner, Esq., with a front of 374 feet.

TAFF VALE.

Cardiff to Aberdare and Merthyr.

LLANDAFF.

POPULATION, 1,821.

Telegraph station at Cardiff, 3¼ miles.

HOTEL.—Railway.

MONEY ORDER OFFICE at Cardiff.

LLANDAFF, a small decayed village, but the seat of a diocese, founded in the 5th century, having a half ruined *Cathedral*, 270 feet long, chiefly in the early English style. The south door is Norman. Some old monuments are seen—one being ascribed to Dubritias, the first bishop.

From Llandaff, in the course of about half an hour, we are hurried past the stations of PENTYRCH, TAFF'S WELL, TREFOREST, and NEWBRIDGE, the junction of the Rhondda Valley line, *via* PORTH to YSTRAD.

ABERDARE BRANCH.

MOUNTAIN ASH and TREAMAN stations.

ABERDARE.

POPULATION, 14,999.

A telegraph station.

HOTELS.—Boot and Railway.

MARKET DAY.—Saturday.

FAIRS.—April 1st and 16th, November 13th.

The scenery of the vale of Cynon here is charming. A little beyond there is a junction with the Vale of Neath Railway to Merthyr (see page 47).

Taff Vale Main Line continued.

QUAKER'S YARD and TROEDYRHIEW stations.

MERTHYR.

POPULATION, 63,080.

A telegraph station.

HOTELS.—Castle, Bush.

MARKET DAYS.—Wednesday and Saturday.

BANKERS.—Wilkins and Co.; Branch of West of England and South Wales District Banking Company.

MERTHYR TYDVIL is a parliamentary borough, and great mining town, in South Wales, 21 miles from Cardiff, with which there is railway communication by a branch out of the South Wales line. It stands up the Taff, among the rugged and barren-looking hills in the north-east corner of Glamorganshire, the richest county in Wales for mineral wealth. About a century ago the first iron works were established here, since which the extension has been amazingly rapid. Blast furnaces, forges, and rolling mills are scattered on all sides. Each iron furnace is about 55 feet high, containing 5,000 cubic feet; and capable of smelting 100 tons of pig-iron weekly, and as there are upwards of 50, the annual quantity of metal may be tolerably estimated; but great as that supply may seem, it is scarcely equal to the demand created for it by railways. The largest works are those belonging to Lady Guest and Messrs. Crawshay, where 3,000 to 5,000 hands are employed At Guest's Dowlais works there are 18 or 20 blast furnaces, besides many furnaces for puddling, balling, and refining; and 1,000 tons of coal a day are consumed.

Visitors should see the furnaces by night, when the red glare of the flames produces an uncommonly striking effect. Indeed, the town is best visited at that time, for by day it will be found dirty, and irregularly built, without order or management, decent roads or footpaths, no supply of water, and no public building of the least note, except Barracks, and a vast *Poor-House*, lately finished, in the shape of a cross, on heaps of the rubbish accumulated from the pits and works. Cholera and fever are, of course, at home here, in scenes which would shock even the most "eminent defender of the filth," and which imperatively demand that their Lady owner should become one of "the Nightingale sisterhood" for a brief space of time. Out of 695 couples married in 1845, 1,016 persons signed with marks, one great secret of which social drawback is the unexampled rapidity with which the town has sprung up; but we do hope that proper measures will be taken henceforth by those who draw enormous wealth from working these works, to improve the condition of the people. Coal and iron are found together in this part of Wales, the coal being worked mostly by levels, in beds 2 to 3 feet thick. Besides the large and small works in and about Merthyr, there are those at Aberdare (a growing rival to Merthyr), Herwain, Pentwain, Blaenavon, Brynmawr, Nantyglo, Ebbw (*w* as *oo*) Vale, Beaufort, Tredegar, Rhimney, Sirhony, &c., nearly all seated at the head of valleys, and many of them being in the neighbouring county of Monmouth, which, though reckoned part of England, is essentially Welsh in its minerals, scenery, and people. Railways and canals now traverse these valleys to the sea.

Merthyr Tydvil, as well as its church, derives its name, signifying the Martyr Tydvil, from St. Tudfyl, the daughter of Brychan (a Welsh chief) who was put to death for her religion in the early ages of the British church. Many such confessors are commemorated in the designation bestowed on parishes in Wales.

In the neighbourhood are the following objects of notice. The Taff may be descended to Quaker's Yard and *Newbridge*, where there are large metal works, and a bridge, called *Pont-y-prid* in Welsh, remarkable as the production of a self-taught local architect, named Edwards, who built it, in 1751. It is a single arch, with a rise of one-fourth the span, which is 140 feet, yet it is only 2½ feet thick in the crown. Once and twice it fell when completed, but the third time the builder was successful, experience having taught him to diminish the strain from its own weight, by boring three large holes on each side near the piers. Following the Neath rail, you come to Pont-neath-Vaughan, at the head of the one Vale of Neath, within a few miles of which are some of the best *Waterfalls* in South Wales,—those of the Hefeste, Purthin, and its branches, which are 40 to 70 or 80 feet down. One on the *Mellte* is particularly worth notice, as it flows for half-a-mile through a limestone cave, and then re-appears just before it sweeps down a fall of 40 feet, with so clean a curve that people have actually taken shelter from the rain under it, on a narrow ledge in the face of the rock. The smaller spouts are called Scwbs (*w* as *oo*). These are all in Brecknockshire; but there is one of 90 feet at Merlin Court, half-way down the Vale of Neath; and to the right of this an ancient Roman way, called the Sarn Helen, or *via* Julia Montana, may yet be traced, It went from Neath over the mountains to Brecknock, which was an important Roman station. The direct road from Merthyr to Brecknock is about 18 miles, through a lofty mountain pass, called Glyn Tarrell, having the Brecknockshire Beacons, 2,862 feet high on one side, and Mount Cafellente, 2,394 feet high, on the other.

South Wales continued.

Cardiff to Neath.

Our onward progress from Cardiff brings us through Ely, St. Fagans, and Peterston, to

LLANTRISSANT.

Population, 1,007.

Distance from station, 1½ mile.

Telegraph station at Bridgend, 9 miles.

At a distance of 8½ miles is the market town of *Cowbridge* and its ancient well-endowed grammar school; and 5 miles beyond is situated *Foumon Castle*, the seat of Oliver Jones, Esq.: it belonged to the St. Johns of Bletsoe, and Colonel Jones, the regicide, and contains a beautiful portrait of Cromwell.

Pencoed station.

BRIDGEND.

A telegraph station.

Hotels.—Wyndham Arms; Railway.

Market Day.—Saturday.

Bankers.—Sub Branch of National Provincial Bank of England.

Five miles from this improving town, at which the county elections are held, lies situated, on the coast, *Dunraven Castle* (anciently called Dindryfan, and the residence of Caractacus), the beautiful and romantic seat of the Dowager Countess of Dunraven, the heiress of the late Thomas Wyndham, Esq., who represented the county of Glamorgan in parliament for upwards of 40 years.

Pyle station.

PORT TALBOT.

A telegraph station.

Hotels.—Talbot Arms, and Railway.

Money Order Office at Neath.

Three miles distant is *Margam Park*, the seat of C. R. M. Talbot, Esq., M.P., the descendant of the Mansells. Here is an orangery, 327 feet by 81, which contains the produce of a cargo from Holland, intended for Queen Mary, but wrecked here in 1694. A bay tree, 60 feet high, and 45 in diameter, spread, and a magnificent forest of oak trees, for which the Government in 1800 offered £40,000.

Briton Ferry station.

NEATH.

Population, 5,841.

A telegraph station.

Hotel.—Castle.

Market Day.—Wednesday.

Fairs.—Last Wednesday in March, Trinity Thursday, July 31st, September 12th, and last Wednesday in October.

Neath, is a coal and mining port, with an ancient castle, and some abbey ruins. Here the fine Vale of Neath may be ascended to the beautiful waterfalls at its summit (see Merthyr Tydvil, page 46).

VALE OF NEATH RAILWAY.

Neath to Merthyr.

From Neath we again turn out of our course, and pass the stations of Aberdylais, Resolven, and Glyn Neath. From this point, *Craig-y-linn*, the highest mountain in Glamorganshire, with its lakes and ravines, and which here makes a bold horse-shoe sweep, raising its huge bulk against the sky, may be reached.

HIRWAIN, junction of line to Aberdare, LLYDCOED, and ABERNANT stations follow, arriving at

Merthyr Tydvil, see page 46.

South Wales continued.

Neath to Llanelly.

LLANSAMLET station.

LANDORE (Swansea Junction).

Here passengers change carriages for Swansea, two miles distant. The view they obtain here of the valley down to Swansea is very striking. If at night, the lurid glare from countless coke ovens—if by day, the dense clouds proceeding from hundreds of chimney stalks overhanging the valley, and at all times, the arsenical sulphurous vapour filling the air, and which you may both smell and taste, give the scene a character scarcely to be seen elsewhere.

SWANSEA.

A telegraph station.

HOTELS.—Mackworth Arms, and Castle.

RACES in September. Regatta in July.

MARKET DAYS.—Wednesday and Saturday.

FAIRS.—Second Saturday in May, August 15th, October 8th, July 2nd, second Saturday after October 8th.

BANKERS.—Branch Bank of England; Branch of Glamorgan Banking Co.; and West of England.

This important seat of the *copper trade*, is also a parliamentary borough (one member), jointly with Neath, &c., and stands at the head of a fine bay, on the west side of *Glamorganshire*, 216 miles from London, by the Great Western and South Wales Railways, population, 31,461. No copper ore is found in this part of Wales, but coal being abundant, it is brought hither from Cornwall and foreign countries to be fluxed. For this purpose, six-sided calcines, 17 to 19 feet long, and oval furnaces, 11 feet long, are used in the copper works, of which eight are here, on the river Pauley, or by the sea-side; one employing 500 to 600 men. The earliest was established about 1720, after the Cornish tinners began to take notice of copper, which hitherto they had thrown away. The ore or shiff goes through various processes, such as calcining and melting, calcining the coarse metal, which leaves about one-third copper; then melting this to fine metal, leaving three-fifths or more than half copper; calcining the fine metal; melting the same to pigs of coarse copper, which gives nine-tenths pure metal; and lastly, roasting for blistered copper and refining it into cakes for use, which are 18 inches by 12. In this way a yearly average of 20,000 tons of copper are smelted here, from the ore brought not only from Cornwall, but from America and Australia, valued at about one and a half million sterling.

Swansea being at the mouth of the Tawe or Towey, is called Abertawe or *Abertowy* by the Welsh. By running out two piers into the bay, one being 1,800 feet long, a good harbour has been enclosed, but it is dry at low water; and floating docks are constructed. About 18,000 tons of shipping belong to this port. A castle was built here by the Normans, of which a massive quadrangular tower remains, and presents an object of some beauty Beneath it is the Post Office, a building in the mediæval style, recently erected. A large Market House, built in 1830, is 320 feet long. There are three churches, but the only one deserving notice is the parish church of St. Mary, which was rebuilt in the last century. Some of the numerous chapels are well built. The public Assembly Rooms and Infirmary are handsome edifices. The *Royal Institution of South Wales* was established in 1835, and contains an important library of works relating to Welsh history, with a museum of coal fossils, antiquities, &c. This was the head quarters of the British Association at their visit in 1854. Besides works for copper smelting, there are others for tin, zinc, pottery, &c.; all fostered by the abundance of coal and lime raised in the neighbourhood. Anthracite coal, chiefly for steamers, abounds here, and was used by the whole of the British steam fleet reviewed in the Solent bv Her Majesty Queen Victoria, on April 23rd, 1856. Gower, the poet, and Beau Nash were born at Swansea. The river Towey runs up the vale to the Black Mountains at its head, parallel to the canal. *Skelly Park* is the seat of Sir J. Morris, Bart. *Penllergâr*, J. Llewellyn, Esq. Several other seats overlook the west side of the bay, and the fine sandy beach, two or three miles long, terminating at Oystermouth, a pretty little bathing place, with an old Norman castle, near the Light or Mumbles Head. Hence the county runs out in a peninsula, much resembling in size, shape, and character, that in the south west of Milford Haven. *Gower* is the name, or *Gwyr* in Welsh, signifying crooked; it is a mass of rugged limestone, traversed by a red sandstone ridge, which is 584 feet high, at *Cefn Bryn*, where there is a cromlech called Arthur's Stone. At the Conquest it was settled by various Norman knights, and the Flemings and Somersetshire men in their train. Round the castles they built at Swansea, Penrice, Ruich, Rhosili, and Loughor, their descendants are distinct from the aborigines to this day. There are similar colonies in the county of Wexford. The poet Gower's family were natives of this part. Druid stones, old castles, and encampments, frequently occur in this country. The cliffs and caves along the coast deserve attention; while the Worm's Head, at the west extremity, near Rhosili Bay, is a scene of awful grandeur in bad weather. It is so called from the shape of the cliffs which run out three quarters of a mile long, dipping and rising like a great sea serpent (or worm). Under the very extremity, which is 200 or 300 feet high, there is a vast funnel cave. The scenery of Swansea Bay is so beautiful that it is universally styled by both natives and tourists, "The Bay of Naples in miniature." Aberaton or Port Talbot, a bustling mining town, near which is *Margam Abbey*, the seat of C. R. M. Talbot, Esq., M.P., beautifully wooded, and remarkable for its orangery and gardens. There are remains of an abbey of the 12th century. Further on are Ogmore and Dunraven Castles, &c.

GOWER ROAD (Mumbles) and LOUGHOR stations.

Leaving the Loughor Station, we cross by a low bridge the Loughor river, and enter

CARMARTHENSHIRE,

Which is mountainous and woody. The air is mild and salubrious, and the whole county is remarkably healthy and fertile. Coal and limestone are found in great abundance.

LLANELLY.

POPULATION, 8,415.

Distance from station, ½ mile. A telegraph station.

HOTELS.—Falcon; Ship and Castle; and Thomas Arms.

MARKET DAY.—Saturday. FAIRS.—Holy Thursday, July 29th, September 30th, and November 10th.

LLANELLY RAILWAY AND DOCKS.

Llanelly to Llandilo and Llandovery.

Again turning to the right from Llanelly, we pass through DOCK, BYNEA, LLANGENNECH, PONTARDULAIS, and PANTYFFYNON.

CROSS INN and GARNANT stations, OR a short branch to the right.

LLANDEBIE, DERWYDD ROAD, and FAIRFACH Stations.

LLANDILO.

Telegraph station at Llanelly, 20¼ miles.

HOTEL.—Cawdor Arms.

MARKET DAY.—Saturday.

FAIRS.—Feb. 20th, May 6th, every Tuesday, from May 14th to June 21st, Monday before Easter, August 23rd, Sept. 28th, Nov. 12th and 22nd, and Monday before Dec. 25th.

TALLEY ROAD and GLANRHYD stations.

LLANGADOCK.

MARKET DAY.—Thursday.

FAIRS.—January 16th; March 12th; May, last Thursday; June 9th; September 1st; Thursday after the 11th; December 11th.

POPULATION.—2,820; many engaged in the production of limestone and coal, which prevail in this district.

LAMPETER ROAD station.

LLANDOVERY.

MARKET DAYS.—Wednesday and Saturday.

FAIRS.—January 1st, Wednesday after the 17th; March 19th; Whit-Tuesday; July 13th; October, Wednesday after the 10th; November 26th.

This straggling little town is surrounded by hills, which to the northward begin to assume a very wild and barren aspect. Here are the remains of a castle, destroyed by Cromwell.

South Wales Main Line continued.

Llanelly to Milford Haven.

PEMBREY.

Telegraph station at Llanelly, 4 miles.

MARKET DAY.—Saturday.

KIDWELLY.

HOTEL.—Pelican.

MARKET DAY.—Saturday.

FAIRS.—May 24th, August 1st, and Oct. 29th.

This is a small decayed borough, having a population of about 1,560, engaged principally as tin-workers—it has also a very limited export trade *Kidwelly Castle* is here situated: it is reported to have been erected by William de Landres, a Norman adventurer, who conquered Glamorganshire about the year 1094. It now belongs to the Earl of Cawdor. The gateway is good, and altogether presents a noble relic of ancient magnificence. Here King John took refuge whilst at war with the barons.

FERRYSIDE Station.

CARMARTHEN.

A telegraph station.

HOTELS.—Ivy Bush, and Boar's Head.

MARKET DAYS.—Wednesday and Saturday.

FAIRS.—April 15th, June 3rd, July 10th, August 12th, Sept. 9th, Oct. 9th, and Nov. 14th.

CARMARTHEN is the capital of *Carmarthenshire*, on the South Wales Railway, and the river Towey with a population of 10,524, who, jointly with Llanelly, return one member. It is one of the most healthy towns, and commands a view of one of the finest vales in the principality. It has a good foreign and coasting trade; and boasts of a handsome town hall and market house, a Presbyterian college, free grammar school, &c., &c. A column to the memory of Sir T. Picton, who represented the borough in parliament, stands on the west of the town, near the old Guildhall; also the Assembly Rooms, with a beautiful front built of freestone, in which are Reading Rooms, supported by public subscriptions. General Nott (to the memory of whom a handsome monument in bronze has been erected in Nott Square), together with Lewis Bailey, Bishop of Bangor, and author of the "Practice of Piety," were natives. The shire prison is on the castle site. A large *diocesan training school* for South Wales occupies 10 acres, and has a Gothic front of 200 feet long. In the old church is a monument to *Sir R. Steele*, who married Miss Scurlock, of

Ty Gwyn, and died at the Ivy Bush, in King Street, to whom the Inn is reported to have belonged; the effigy of Rhys ap Thomas; with a good copy of the Transfiguration. Shipping of a small class come up to the quay; the harbour is 3 miles lower down, near the bay, which makes a fine semicircular sweep, 17 miles across. On the east side are the wild limestone cliffs of Worm's Head, 300 feet high, singularly shaped, and on the other Tenby, a beautiful watering place, near the lighthouse on Caldy Island.

ST. CLEARS.

Telegraph station at Carmarthen, 8¼ miles.

HOTELS.—Railway, and Swan.

MARKET DAY.—Saturday. FAIRS.—May 4th, June 1st, Oct. 12th.

This is a mere nominal borough and market town, with a population of 1,240, engaged in the coasting and provision trade. There are the remains of a Norman castle and priory, given to All Soul's College, Oxford.

The line now leaves Carmarthen, and enters

PEMBROKESHIRE.

THE surface of this county is, generally speaking, composed of easy slopes, but not mountainous, except a ridge of hills which runs from the coast to the border of Carmarthenshire. Pembroke cannot boast of being either a trading or a manufacturing county, though it possesses many facilities for commerce. The South Wales mineral basin terminates here, and becomes shallower as it approaches the extremity. The strata are raised near the surface, and then the quality is impaired.

WHITLAND.

Telegraph station at Carmarthen, 13¾ miles.

MONEY ORDER OFFICE at St. Clears.

NARBERTH ROAD (For Tenby).

Distance of town from station, 3¾ miles.

Telegraph station at Haverfordwest, 11¾ miles.

HOTEL.—De Rutzen Arms.

MARKET DAY —Saturday.

FAIRS.—March 21st, May 13th, June 2nd and 29th, August 10th, September 22nd, October 27th, and December 11th.

NARBERTH is a small neat town in the county of Carmarthen, with a population of 2,822. It has the privilege of being represented in parliament in connection with the borough of Haverfordwest, Fishguard, and St. Davids. It has no particular object of attraction, beyond being the best and nearest way by coach from Narberth Road station to the town of

TENBY.

POPULATION, 2,982.

Telegraph station at New Milford, 13 miles.

HOTELS.—White Lion, and Coburg.

MARKET DAYS.—Wednesday and Saturday.

FAIRS.—May 4th Whi Tuesday, July 4th, Oct. 2nd, and Dec. 4th

RACES in August or September.

TENBY, on the coast of Pembrokeshire, and eleven miles from Pembroke itself, was at a very remote period occupied by the ancient Britons as a fishing town, and is most romantically situated on the eastern and southern sides of a rocky peninsula, stretching out into the Bristol Channel, and rising to the elevation of 100 feet above the level of high water. The houses are well built, and command fine views of the sea; and the beautiful situation of the town, the fine beach, and firm and smooth sands, the transparency of the sea water, and the pleasant walks and extensive drives in the vicinity, have raised it from the decline into which it had for many years previously fallen to a high rank among the most favourite watering-places on the coast. Under the Castle-hill baths, provided with every convenience, are supplied by a capacious reservoir, filled from the sea at every tide. This establishment comprises two spacious pleasure-baths, one for ladies and one for gentlemen, four smaller cold-baths, and also a range of warm sea-water and vapour-baths, with apparatus for heating them to any degree of temperature required. The surrounding scenery is extremely beautiful and picturesque. The majestic masses of rock, of various forms and hues, which line the coast; the numerous bays and distant promontories that stretch out into the sea; the receding coast of Carmarthenshire, with the projecting headland of Gower enclosing the great bay of Carmarthen, on the western boundary of which the town is situated; the small islands of Caldey and Lundy, with the distant shores of Somersetshire and Devonshire, combine to impart a high degree of interest and variety to one of the finest marine expanses in the kingdom. On one side of the town there is a drive of eleven miles to the ancient town of Pembroke, through a fine campaign country, studded with churches, villages, and gentlemen's seats, surrounded with plantations and pleasure-grounds, and on the other the country is agreeably diversified with swelling eminences, clothed with verdure, and small valleys richly wooded. The remains of the ancient castle are considerable, though in a very dilapidated condition. A portion of the keep still remains, and the principal gateway, with a square tower and a bastion, are also in a tolerable state of preservation. The ancient walls, which surrounded the town, are still in many places entire. The sands afford delightful promenades, and abound also with shells of varied descriptions, not less than one-half of the British collection of 600 varieties having been found on this coast, among which have been several of value commonly esteemed foreign. The church is a venerable and spacious structure, dating as far back as the year 1250. There is constant steam communication with Bristol. Post-office arrangements:—Letters delivered at 8 30 a.m.; box closes 10 p.m.

CLARBESTON ROAD.

POPULATION, 178.

Distance from station, 3 miles.

Telegraph station at Haverfordwest, $5\frac{1}{4}$ miles.

MARKET DAY.—Saturday.

MONEY ORDER OFFICE at Narberth.

HAVERFORDWEST.

A telegraph station.

HOTEL.—Castle.

MARKET DAYS.—Tuesday and Saturday.

FAIRS.—March 20th, April 14th, May 12th, June 12th, July 18th, August 9th, September 4th and 23rd, October 18th, and December 10th.

BANKERS.—Wilkins and Co.; J. and W. Walters.

HAVERFORDWEST is a borough town in Pembrokeshire, South Wales. It stands on a western branch of the river Claddau, which at spring tides is navigable for vessels of a hundred tons burden, and for whose accommodation a number of convenient quays have been erected. The town is built on the steep declivity of a hill, and presents a very picturesque appearance, as the houses rise in terraces one above the other, the whole being crowned by the ruins of the castle. The interior of the town, however, is in many respects inconvenient and disagreeable, as many of the streets are so narrow and steep as almost to prevent horses and carriages from ascending them. But, on the other hand, the spirit of modern improvement has prevailed to a considerable extent, and many new streets and public buildings have been erected. There are three churches, a handsome guild hall, the gaol, and the keep of an ancient castle.

DISTANCES OF PLACES FROM THE STATION.

	Miles.		Miles.
Abercastle	$17\frac{3}{4}$	Milford	$7\frac{1}{2}$
Abermause	17	Pembroke Castle	$11\frac{1}{2}$
Benton Castle	9	Penlan Castle	17
Bishop's Palace at St. Davids	$17\frac{1}{4}$	Picton Castle	$4\frac{3}{4}$
Cardigan	26	Poyntz Castle	7
Carew Castle	15	Roch Castle	6
Cathedral (St. Davids)	$16\frac{1}{2}$	Skower and Skokam Islands	12
Cromlech (2 miles) from Nevern Church	18	Soloa Valley	8
Devil's Punch Bowl	20	St. Bride's Bay	5
Huntsman's Leap	21	St. Davids	16
		Walwin Castle	4

MILFORD ROAD.

Telegraph station at Haverfordwest, $4\frac{3}{4}$ miles.

MONEY ORDER OFFICE at Haverfordwest, 5 miles.

Johnston Hall, in the vicinity, is the seat of Lord Kensington. Anthracite, or smokeless coal, abounds in this district, and it is only wanting to be better known, in order to be generally used in the steamers belonging to the naval and merchant services. It was used by Her Majesty's steam fleet at the review on the 23rd of April, 1856.

It has been proposed to construct a railway, $3\frac{1}{2}$ miles long, from this station to the town of Milford; other modes of conveyance are at present in use.

MILFORD.

HOTELS.—Royal; Victoria.

MARKET DAYS.—Tuesday and Saturday.

The town of Milford has a population of 2,377 partially engaged in ship-building. It is pleasantly situated; but since the removal of the royal dockyard and Irish packet station from here, about 1815, to Pater and Pembroke, on the opposite side of the Haven, its importance in a commercial point of view has much declined.

Milford is prettily situated on a sloping point of land, about six miles from the entrance of the Haven, to which it gives its name. Milford Haven ought to be viewed from the water. The lower and broadest portion of the Haven runs in an easterly direction for about twelve miles, and then turns abruptly to the north, forming several reaches towards Haverfordwest. The scenery around Milford is very picturesque. On a fork of land, formed by the confluence of the two rivers Cleddy and Cleddau, stands Rose Castle, an ancient seat of the Owens, and higher up on the estuary is Picton Castle.

NEW MILFORD.

This has become a station of much importance, being the one used for the interchange of traffic to and from the South of Ireland. First class steamers sail every week day between this and Waterford and Cork to suit certain trains.—*See* "*Bradshaw*" for the month.

PEMBROKE.

The capital of the county, and Pater or Pembroke Dock, the seat of a royal dockyard, at the head of that magnificent inlet called Milford Haven, opposite to Neyland station (from which it is distant $1\frac{1}{2}$ mile). The terminus of the South Wales line, opened in April, 1856. A branch is in progress to unite it with the main line and the beautiful watering place of Tenby; in conjunction with which, and two or three other little boroughs, it returns one member to parliament. Population, 10,107. Both the town and shire take name from the Welsh words, *Pen fro*, signifying the head of the peninsula, as the town lies on a long point, marked on both sides by a creek of Milford Haven. In this commanding spot, Arnulph de Montgomery began a Norman *Castle* in 1092, which a few years after was strengthened by the famous Richard de Clare, or Strongbow, before he sailed for the conquest of Ireland. Its ruins still exist on a hill over the town; the round keep is 75 feet high. There is a large cave under the hall; and in one of the town-gates the Earl of Richmond (whose mother was of the Welsh family of Tudlor or Tudor, descended from Edward I.) afterwards Henry VII. was born. He landed on this part of Wales after his escape from confinement in Brittany; and supported by Rhys ap Thomas, and other Welsh adherents, marched towards Bosworth Field, where his defeat of Richard III., and subsequent marriage with Elizabeth of York, terminated for evert of the roses.

There is nothing else worth notice in the town, except the old church of St. Michael. Two short bridges cross to Monckton (where there was a priory), and to the suburbs on the north side, from whence roads, about 2 miles long, lead to Pembroke ferry and to the dockyard at *Pater*, which covers a site of 88 acres, 15 or 16 of which are occupied by iron building slips. The sea front is nearly half a mile long; one new slip has an open glass and metal roof. Important docks are in progress, which will cost £100,000. The whole is defended by strong forts at Hobb's Point Jetty, formerly the station for the Waterford Mail Packets, now discontinued, near the large hotel. Until 1814 the dockyard was at Milford, 5 miles to the left, on the north side of the Haven, which has declined since its removal. The establishment of a packet station for New York and the south of Ireland, which is one of the chief objects contemplated by the South Wales Railway Company, may contribute to revive it. It possesses a little coasting trade. *Pill Priory* is near.

On Thorn Island, on the southern side of the entrance into Milford Haven, there are newly-erected fortifications, which are now strongly garrisoned. The noble Haven which it overlooks is in fact the mouth of the Cleddau or Cleddy, and is 12 miles long, by two miles broad, with 15 bays or creeks in it. As there is plenty of deep water, it would easily hold the entire British navy. At the entrance is St. Anne's light. Imogen (one of the sweetest of Shakspeare's heroines), says, in "Cymbeline," when she receives her husband's letter:—

"Oh for a horse with wings! Hear'st thou, Pisanio?
He is at *Milford Haven*. Read and tell me
How far 'tis thither. If one of mean affairs
May plod it in a week, why may not I
Glide thither in a day? * *
* * * And, by the way,
Tell me how Wales is made so happy as
To inherit such a haven!"

Here, in "a mountainous country, with a cave," disguised as a boy, the poor betrayed lady afterwards meets with her royal brothers Guiderus and Arviragus, supposed to be sons of the old shepherd Belarius.

'*Bel.* This youth, howe'er distressed he appears, hath had
Good ancestors.
Arv. How angel like he sings.
Gui. But his neat cookery! He cut our roots in characters;
And sauc'd our broths, as Juno had been sick,
And he her dieter."

In the course of the plot, Lucius, the Roman General, lands here:—

"——— the legions garrisoned in Gallia,
After your will have coursed the sea; attending
You here at *Milford Haven*, with your ships."

During the troubles of Henry IV.'s reign, a force of 12,000 French actually landed here to support the rising of Owen Glyndwr.

The peninsula between Milford Haven and the Bristol Channel is bounded by a remarkable broken mestone coast, along which is a succession of the most striking views. When traversed from end to nd, it is a walk, from Anglebay, at the Haven's mouth to Tenby, in Carmarthen bay, of 20 or 25 miles. Cars may be hired, but, as inns are very rare, it is advisable to take provisions, or you must trust to the chance of shelter at some hospitable farm house. Of these, however, there are but few.

Starting from the old fort near Angle or Nangle Bay, you pass round the east side of the entrance to the Haven, with St. Anne's Head and Light on the opposite side, and the island closing up St. Bride's Bay, a most enchanting spot, in the distance behind. Rat and Sheep Islands are seen below, the latter near a Danish camp. The broad swell of the Atlantic dashes on the cliffs. At Gupton (seven miles from Angle fort) a little stream comes down to Freshwater Bay, from Castle Martin, an old place, noted for its breed of black hill cattle, and for a cromlech. It had a castle formerly. *Brownslade*, near it, is the seat of J. Mirehouse, Esq. At Linney Head (three miles from Gupton) the finest part of this coast trip commences. "A greater extent of carboniferous limestone is exposed to view along these shores than in any part of Britain."—Cliffe's *Book of South Wales*. Keep at the edge of the downs to enjoy it thoroughly. Out in the sea is the Crow rock, a dangerous one, covered at high water. The Castles are two rocks separated from the main land. Then Flimstone chapel (a ruin); near Bull's Scaughter Bay, another group of stacks or castle rocks, swarming with razorbills, guillemots, kittiwakes, and other sea birds, in a very wild part; another camp near a dark chasm, called the Devil's Cauldron; and then *St. Gwan's Head* (seven miles from Linney Head), so called, it is said, after King Arthur's nephew, Sir Gawaine, or Gwain, of old romances. Here the cliffs are 160 or 170 feet high, and the strata in vast horizontal blocks In a gap, looking down to the sea, is a ruined hermitage, to which you descend by about 53 broken steps; it is only 20 feet long. The saint's hiding place in the east wall, and his well are shown, with remnants of past superstition. *Bosheston Meer*, a little further, is a cave, which runs up the land more than quarter of a mile. The roaring of the waves and the wind along this natural tunnel is at times terrific. Before reaching it you pass a remarkable crack in the cliffs, called the Huntsman's Leap. Across Broadhaven Creek (which runs up to Bosheston) to Stackpole Head; then *Stackpole Park*, the modern seat of the Earl of Cawdor, the chief owner of the soil in this quarter. There was a Norman castle of the 11th century here, built by a baron, whose effigy is in Cheriton church, Fine view from Windmill Hill. Round East Freshwater Bay and Swanslake Bay to *Manorbeer Castle* (8 miles from West Gwan's) close to the shore. It is a fine existing specimen of what a feudal dwelling was in early times. It was built by William de Barri, and was the birth place of Giraldus de Barri (or Cambrensis, *i.e.*, the Welshman); Lord Milford is the present owner. Hence, round Oldcastle Head and Lidstep Point, to Giltar Head (15 miles from Manor Bay), turning into Carnarvon Bay. Caldy Island and its lighthouse, about 2 miles off. About 20 miles to the E.S.E., if the weather is favourable, you may catch sight of the Worm's Head, on the other side of the bay, a most striking object. Caldy has a chapel and remains of a priory upon it, incorporated with the seat of a gentleman who is lord of the island. At *Penally*, a pretty chapel and old cross; shells and seaweeds on the shore. Old castle at Trellowyn, and mineral springs at Gumperton. Then Tenby (2 or 3 miles from Giltar Point), a most delightful bathing place to stop at.

Up the *Cleddy* are *Lawrenny Hall*, seat of L. Phillipps, Esq., on a bold point where two creeks branch off, one to Carew, Landshipping Quay, near which the two Cleddys unite. The west Cleddy may be followed to *Boulston*, an old seat of the Wogans; and Haverfordwest. The east Cleddy, to *Picton*, Lord Milford's seat—a well wooded park, with an old Norman castle; and *Slebech*, the seat of Baron de Rutzen. Here is an old church of the Knights Templars.

In the neighbourhood of Pembroke are the following:—*Upton Castle*, seat of Rev. W. Evans. *Lamphey Court* (2 miles), belongs to C. Mathias, Esq., and is close to the fine ruins of a deserted palace of the bishops of St. Davids, in a rich Gothic style; the great hall is 76 feet long. There is another by the same builder (Bishop Gower), at the city of St. Davids, the see of which, now much despoiled, had at one time six different residences for its prelates. Its cathedral, which is cruciform, 200 feet by 120 feet, with fine tower, 127 feet, is being restored, and contains the shrine visited by Henry I. and Edward I., the road to which (16 miles from Haverfordwest) is the most execrable in the United Kingdom, but replete with scenery magnificently grand. *Carew* (4 miles), is another of those old baronial seats so abundant in South Wales; it was built in Henry I.'s reign, by the ancestor of the Fitzgeralds. There are two great halls 100 feet and 80 feet long. Effigies in the church; and an old roadside cross, 14 feet high. *Orielton* (6 miles) belongs to the Owens.

There has been a Steam Packet communication opened out between this place and Ireland, of which the traveller, if he think fit, might avail himself. The Irish tour will be found at the end of this Section, at page 80.

GREAT WESTERN.

Oxford to Birmingham and Wolverhampton.

WOODSTOCK ROAD.

Distance from station, 3 miles.

A telegraph station.

HOTEL.—Bear.

MARKET DAY.—Tuesday.

FAIRS.—April 5th, Whit Tuesday, August 2nd, Oct. 2nd, Tuesday after Nov. 1st, and Dec. 17th.

The town of Woodstock has a population of 7,983, and returns one representative to parliament. Its principal trade consists in the manufacture of doeskin gloves and other leather productions. Great historical interest attaches to this place, as having been occasionally the residence of Henrys I. and II. It was here that Henry II. constructed the "bower" for fair Rosamond Clifford.

KIRTLINGTON, HEYFORD, SOMERTON, and AYNHO stations.

BANBURY.

POPULATION, 8,715.

Distance from station, ¾ mile.

A telegraph station.

HOTELS.—Red Lion, White Lion.

MARKET DAY.—Thursday.

FAIRS.—Thursday after Jan. 17th, first Thursday in Lent, second Thursday before Easter, Ascension Day, Thursday in Trinity Week, Old Lammas Day.

BANKERS.—London and County Bank; Gillett and Tawney; T. R. and E. Cobb.

BANBURY is situated on the river Cherwell; the navigable canal from Coventry to Oxford passes by this town—and at a distance of five miles it is conveyed through a hill by a tunnel three quarters of a mile in length. In the grounds adjoining the Ram Inn is a well of sulphurated water; and at a short distance from the town is another spring of chalybeate water. The pyrites aureas, or golden fire-stone is often found here in digging wells. A great number of the inhabitants are employed in the manufactory of plush and shag cloth. Banbury is famous for its cakes, cheese, and ale—the former being still sold in the metropolis. Here was the scene of the defeat of the Yorkists at Danesmere, in 1469, when the Earl of Pembroke, with several others, were beheaded.

CROPREDY.

Distance from station, ½ mile.

A telegraph station.

MONEY ORDER OFFICE at Banbury.

FENNY COMPTON.

Distance from station, ½ mile.

A telegraph station.

MAILS.—One arrival and departure, daily, between London and Fenny Compton.

MONEY ORDER OFFICE at Southam.

SOUTHAM ROAD & HARBURY.

Distance from station, 1 mile.

A telegraph station.

MONEY ORDER OFFICE at Southam.

LEAMINGTON AND WARWICK.

Particulars of these places will be found in Section III., pages 15, 16.

HATTON.—A short line, 8¼ miles long, here turns off to the left, running viâ CLAVERDON, BEARLEY, and WILMCOTE, to

Stratford-on-Avon, page 55.

KINGSWOOD and KNOWLE stations.

SOLIHULL.

A telegraph station.

HOTEL.—George.

CARRIERS to and from London, and all parts of Warwickshire.

MAILS.—One arrival and departure, daily, between London and Solihull.

MONEY ORDER OFFICE.

ACOCK'S GREEN and BORDESLEY stations.

Birmingham.—See Section III., page 19.

HOCKLEY station.

SOHO (junction of the Stour Valley Line).

A telegraph station.

MONEY ORDER OFFICE at Birmingham.

HANDSWORTH.

POPULATION, 787.

A telegraph station.

MONEY ORDER OFFICE at Birmingham.

WEST BROMWICH and SWAN VILLAGE stations.

WEDNESBURY.

A telegraph station.
HOTEL.—Turk's Head.
MARKET DAY.—Friday.
FAIRS.—May 6, and August 3.

This is a very old market town, having a population of 14,281, almost entirely engaged in the iron trade—every description of cast-iron work being done here. Its products of coal and iron are of a very valuable description, the coal beds varying in thickness from three to fourteen feet. It is of a very superior quality. There are some traces of an old fort of Saxon origin. The interior of the church, a neat Gothic structure of the eighth century, has some beautiful carving, with several monuments of the predecessors of the families of Lords Dudley and Harcourt.

BILSTON.

Distance from station, 1 mile.

A telegraph station.

HOTEL.—King's Arms.
MARKET DAYS.—Monday and Saturday.

FAIRS. — Whit Monday, and Monday before Christmas.

MONEY ORDER OFFICE.

BANKERS.—Jones and Company.

This place forms a great centre of the iron trade, and has become one of growing importance. The people are engaged in the manufacture of almost everything useful in iron and steel wares, and the districts around are rich in the products of iron, coal, quarry-stone, &c., &c.

PRIESTFIELD.

Telegraph station at Wolverhampton, 1½ mile.

MONEY ORDER OFFICE at Bilston.

WOLVERHAMPTON.

A telegraph station.

HOTELS.—The Swan; Star and Garter.

OMNIBUSES to and from Bridgnorth (Crown Hotel), daily.

MARKET DAY.—Wednesday.

FAIR.—July 10th, lasting three days.

BANKERS. — Wolverhampton and Staffordshire Bank, Old Church Yard; Bilston District Bank, Cock Street; Messrs. Holyoake and Co.'s Bank, Cock Street; Messrs. Fryer's Bank, Lichfield Street.

This ancient town, which in Saxon times was noted for its college, founded by Wulfruna, sister of King Egbert, and thence called *Wulfrunes-hampton*, from which it derives the modern name, is now a parliamentary borough (two members), and the capital of the *iron trade*. By the North Western, or narrow-gauge line, it is 126 miles from London (or 13 miles from Birmingham); by the broad gauge, *viâ* Oxford and Worcester, 142 miles. The branch covers about 30 square miles of barren soil, beneath which are rich crops of coal, iron, and stone. Population 119,748. All kinds of articles in iron, brass, tin-plate, japan work, &c., are made here, as locks and keys, hinges, fenders, coffee mills, tea trays, bolts, files, screws, and other tools, besides engines, &c. Smelting-houses and foundries abound on all sides (see *Bradshaw's Hand-Book to the Manufacturing Districts).* The making of tin-plate, that is, of iron tinned over, is a staple business. That of japanning was first introduced by Baskerville, the Birmingham printer, whose portrait may be seen in the counting-house of Messrs. Longman, in Paternoster Row.

Wolverhampton stands on high ground, and has never suffered from the plague, but it did not escape the cholera in 1849, though the deaths were few compared with those at Bilston and Willenhall. The houses are of brick, and there are not any remarkable edifices. The *Grammar School*, founded in 1513 by a native, who became lord mayor of London, is well endowed, and replaces a hospital built by the Leveson or "Luson" (ancestors of the Gower) family. There is a literary institute with a public library.

Of its eight churches, St. Peter's is the most ancient and striking. It is a later English cross, having a tall tower and carved stone pulpit, with monuments of the Levesons, and of Colonel Lane, who, with his sister, were the means of effecting the escape of Charles II., after the battle of Worcester, 1651. It was that officer who was hid away with the king in the Royal Oak. A pillar cross in the churchyard is 20 feet high. Until lately, the manor belonged to the dean and chapter of Windsor, to whom it was granted by Edward IV.

For continuation to Shrewsbury, see page 62.

Before proceeding further North, we will retrace our journey to Oxford, and introduce our traveller to some of the scenes of Shakspeare.

WEST MIDLAND (Oxford Section).

Oxford to Chipping Norton Junction.

HANDBOROUGH (Junction).

BLENHEIM PARK to the right. A government grant of half a million of money was expended in the erection of a magnificent palace at this place for the Duke of Marlborough in the reign of Queen Anne. Besides a beautiful chapel, it contains a library of more than 17,000 volumes. It also contained a most costly collection of paintings, until recently (1861), the most valuable portion of them having been accidentally destroyed by fire. It is a calamity the nation will deeply deplore. The grounds are laid out with great taste; and the park, which is richly wooded, is about 2,700 acres in extent.

Thence crossing the Evenlode several times in our course, and skirting the park rails of the Duke of Beaufort's princely domain, *Blandford Park*, we arrive at

CHARLBURY.

HOTEL.—The Bell.

Ditchley (2 miles), Lord Dillon, was the birthplace of the notorious Lord Rochester. Near it is *Kiddington*, with an old church, of which Wharton was rector: 6 miles distant is *Heythorpe*, another seat of the Duke of Beaufort. *Glympton*, on the river Gline, E. Way, Esq. From this station *Wychwood Forest*, (a fine wooded track of much sylvan beauty) soon to be reclaimed, may be visited. Wharton the poet has immortalised the scenery about here. Still passing along the valley of the Evenlode, we pass ASCOTT station, arriving at

SHIPTON.

4 miles south is the old town of *Burford*, full of quaint houses, with paneled gables and tracery work. The church is cruciform, with several large chapels attached, all partaking of the Norman or early perpendicular character. A battle took place here in 752 between the rival Kings of Wessex and Mercia. Three miles on the Northleach road is Lord Dynevor's elegant mansion at *Barrington*.

Three miles beyond Shipton we arrive at the junction of the

CHIPPING NORTON BRANCH,

And at a distance of four miles further, at the ancient town of

CHIPPING NORTON.

HOTEL.—White Hart.

An old Market town situated on the rise of a hill. There is a Free Grammar School, and a venerable church with an embattled tower, and an ancient rood loft. In the vicinity are *Knollbury banks*, an old encampment, and there is the site of an old castle, beyond is *Cornewell* (2½ miles), —— Pennystones, Esq.; *Heythorpe* (2 miles); and *Great Tew Park* (4 miles); and an interesting Druidical remain called the *Rollrich stones* (3 miles).

Returning to the junction of the Main line, we pursue our journey onwards to

ADDLESTROP AND STOW ROAD.

HOTEL.—Unicorn.

Dalesford House, the seat of the celebrated Warren Hastings, and *Addlestrop House*, of the Leigh family, are close by. Stow-on-the-Wold, is a small market town on the summit of a hill, 883 feet high. The church, with its embattled tower 81 feet high, is consequently a prominent object through a circumference of many miles. It has many points and some curious monuments deserving attention.

Again proceeding on our way, we soon arrive at

MORETON-IN-THE-MARSH.

HOTELS.—Unicorn, White Hart.

A small town on the old Foss Way; an old building once the Market House stands in the centre In the vicinity are *Batsford* (3 miles), Lord Redesdale. *Seisincote* (2 miles), the four mile-stone (2 miles), where Oxfordshire, Glo'ster, Worcester, and Warwickshires unite, and where Canute was defeated by Edmund Ironside.

BLOCKLEY, CAMPDEN, and HONEYBOURNE stations, the last of which is the junction of the branch to the classic town of Stratford.

STRATFORD-ON-AVON BRANCH.

The Stations *en route* are LONG MARSTON, and MILCOTE.

STRATFORD-UPON-AVON.

POPULATION, 3,372.

Telegraph station at Hatton, 8¼ miles.

HOTELS.—Shakspeare, Ann Hitcham, Family and Commercial—comfortable house; White Lion, John Warden; Red Horse, John Gardner.

BANKERS.—Branch of Warwick and Leamington Banking Co.; Branch of Stourbridge and Kidderminster Banking Co.

This interesting part of Warwickshire is directly accessible by a branch of the Oxford, Worcester, and Wolverhampton line, by which means it is within about 100 miles journey by rail from London. A Roman road, called the Fossway, crossed the river at this point, and hence the name. It is a municipal borough, but derives its chief importance from being the *birthplace of Shakspeare,* who was born here 23rd April (St. George's day), 1564, in an old-fashioned timbered house, opposite the Falcon, in Henley Street, which, after some changes, and the risk even of being transferred as it stood to America, by a calculating speculator, was at last purchased by the Shakspeare Club, and adopted by Government as a tribute to his memory.

Stratford-upon-Avon,

"Where his first infant lays sweet Shakspeare sung,
Where the last accents faltered on his tongue,"

And to which the genius of one man has given immortality, is situated on a gentle ascent from the river Avon, in the county of Warwick. If the visitor ascends the uplands on the high road to Warwick, he will behold a panorama of remarkable richness and variety. Hill and dale in graceful undulations—luxuriant wooded parks—the winding Avon tracked by the fringe of willows on its banks—the peaceful town and its venerable church—and, afar off, the gradually towering outline of the Malvern hills form, altogether, a landscape essentially English, and such as is rarely to be found in any other country than our own. But rich and pleasant as the prospect is, it takes its crowning glory from the immortal poet, the mighty genius whose dust reposes at our feet. It is his genial spirit which pervades and sanctifies the scene; and every spot on which the eye can rest claims some association with his life. We tread the very ground that he has trod a thousand times, and feel as he has felt.

Four rooms in this house remain probably as they were in the poet's days; and in one of them he was born. The whitewashed walls are covered with names of visitors, who also enter them in a book, or rather a work, which now extends to several volumes. It was inhabited by the descendants of his sister Jane till 1806, and used as butcher's shop and a public house. Many of the houses wear still an air of picturesque antiquity, especially a carved one in High Street. Here also are the Town Hall and Market House, both modern buildings. But the Guildhall, which belonged to an early *religious foundation*, is an ancient pile of the 15th century, used as a Free Grammar School, having an oak roof, &c. Here Shakspeare received his education—his father being a glover. The Town Hall is embellished with Shakspeare's statue (the gift of Garrick), and contains Wilson's portrait of him, and Gainsborough's of Garrick, who presided at the Shakspeare Jubilee, in 1769 (the year after the hall was rebuilt). It was celebrated on the 6th and 7th September, with great rejoicing. Dr. Arne performed his oratorio of *Judith* at the church, and the dedication ode was recited by Garrick; after which another actor (King), in the character of a macaroni or dandy, attacked Shakspeare as "an ill-bred fellow, who made people laugh and cry as he thought proper." On this occasion, the corporation presented Garrick with a medallion of the Poet, cut out of his *mulberry tree*—the famous tree under which Garrick and Macklin were entertained in 1742, by Sir Hugh Clopton, at New Place, where Shakspeare died, on his birth-day in 1616, exactly 53 years old.

From the old bridge, built in the reign of Henry VIII. by Lord Mayor Clopton, there is a full view of the venerable old *church*, and the placid scenery by which it is surrounded. It stands close to the river by itself, on the south side of the town, at the end of an avenue of limes; and is an early Gothic edifice, lately restored by the Shakspeare Club (which meets here every 23rd of April), with a lofty octagonal spire. Entering the carved porch and oak door, you come upon a view of the spacious interior, with its stained windows, Clopton banners and escutcheons, carved stalls (for its college principals), and the great Poet's Monument on the west side of the chancel. It is a half figure of him, sitting as if about to write (the pen has been stolen), under a Grecian (not Gothic) niche in the wall. The bust was originally flesh-coloured, but, horrid to relate, it was *painted white* in 1793, at the suggestion of his deluded commentator, Malone. Some lines in English (there are also two in Latin) beginning, "Stay, passenger, why goest thou so fast?" contain (perhaps have been borrowed), the germ of Milton's noble lines. The ashes of Shakspeare lie under the slab immediately below, inscribed with the well-known verse, "Good friend, for Jesvs' sake, forbeare," &c. His wife, Anne Hathaway, died in 1623; his favourite daughter, Susannah Hall, and his old friend, John à-Combe, lie near—the latter under an effigy by G. Johnson, the author of the poet's bust. "There are other monuments around, but the mind refuses to dwell on anything that is not connected with Shakspeare. His idea pervades the place; the whole pile seems but as his mausoleum. * * Its spire is the beacon, towering amidst the gentle landscape, to guide the literary pilgrim of every nation to his tomb."—W. Irving's *Sketch Book*.

STRATFORD CHURCH, AND THE RIVER AVON.—Even divested of the abounding interest which association with the name of Shakspeare gives to them, there is something eminently striking and picturesque in the appearance of the church and river from the neighbouring meadows. The Avon, which, from its source at Naseby, winds like a silver thread through fertile vallies and rich groves in peacefulness and beauty, at this point takes a broader sweep, and proudly swells, as conscious of the tutelary genius of the spot. The church, too, here encircled by its lofty elms, and standing on the river's brink, has a grand and venerable aspect.

THE TOMB OF SHAKSPEARE.—From the town, the approach to the church is through an avenue of lime trees, arched overhead; this terminates at the north entrance into the nave, which consists of a handsome porch, buttressed and embattled, and apparently of a later date than the adjoining aisle. The first impression upon entering through the porch is one of grateful wonder at the elegance and amplitude of the interior. At a glance we can scan the lofty roof, the transepts, chancel, nave, and aisles. We catch the delicate tracery of the windows, and their dim religious light; we see the noble monuments and stately effigies, but the mind refuses yet to ponder on these things,

"A touch more rare
Subdues all other thoughts—"

and noiselessly we hasten forward till we reach the spot "where sleeps the Monarch of the Mind."

The far-famed mural monument and bust are on the left of the chancel, immediately above the line of graves containing the remains of the Poet, his daughter Susanna, her husband, Dr. Hall, and in all probability, many others of the family. The bust is of the size of life, and stands fixed under an arch between two Corinthian columns of black marble. There are several inscriptions upon the tablets.

Below the monument, upon the stone covering the Poet's grave, are the following extraordinary lines:—

"Good friend for Jesvs' sake, forbeare,
To dig the dust enclosed here,
Blest be ye man yt spares these stones,
And cyrst be he that moves my bones."

It has been conjectured that Shakspeare's anxiety for the repose of his bones might have arisen from there being a door immediately below his bust, which formerly gave access to the charnel house.

But, whatever may have been his motive, we owe to this inscription the preservation of these sacred relics for upwards of two hundred years; and we trust the simple, but impressive denunciation, will cause them to remain undisturbed.

STRATFORD-UPON-AVON.

"Thou cradle of the Bard! What glories grace thee!
Thee, deathless Avon, and thy willowed stream,
Where many a pilgrim comes and loves to trace
The scenes that nurtured Shakspeare's godlike dreams.
The humblest sod whereon a daisy grows
Is hallow'd ground.
There stands the cottage where the Muse watch'd o'er
Her favourite child, and yon is Lucy's lawn
Often thereon the Poet loved to pore
Over visions which began to dawn
And beamed of immortality—yon fane
Enshrines his ashes, and the lowliest hind
Holds his breath as though 'twould stain
The slab where sleeps the Monarch of the Mind."

The country round Stratford is peculiarly English —gardens, orchards, green meadows, a park here and there, and gently swelling hills,—but nothing striking. At *Shottery*, a little on the Alcester road, is the rustic cottage in which Ann Hathaway lived, and which was inhabited by her family down to 1838; it is built in the usual way, of stone and timber, and thatched. One mile north, are *Clopton House* (three centuries old), and *Welcombe*, the seat of C. Warde, Esq., under the hills, from which there are some good prospects of the town and county. *Ingon House* was Shakspeare's at his death, having been bought by him in 1597, though built originally by the Cloptons, into whose hands it returned, by purchase from the poet's descendants after the Restoration. In 1752 it was sold to Mr. Gathell, a Lichfield clergyman, who, on account of a dispute about the rating, pulled it down. He had already cut down the poet's tree, to save himself the trouble of showing it to visitors. Fortunately, a cutting was planted by Garrick over the grave of Shakspeare's favourite grand-child, Lady Barnard, in Abington churchyard (near Northampton), and another is said to be at East Cliffe, (Hastings); while the remains of the desecrated tree were sold in the shape of boxes, cups, &c., by Mr. T. Sharp, of Stratford. Immediately behind was a little farm which belonged to Shakspeare's mother. *Alveston*, T. Townshend, Esq., on the Avon, is near *Charlecote* (or Chalcot as it is called), the seat of G. Lucy, Esq., a truly old English pile, of the Elizabethan age, built of brick in 1558, by Sir Thomas Lucy, the poet's Justice Shallow. The "Three Luces" or pikes swimming among cross crosslets, are here conspicuous; and they are seen again in the church, which has been lately rebuilt. *Alscot Park*, on the Stour, belongs to J. West, Esq.; further up the stream is *Eatington*, the old seat of E. Shirley, Esq. To the west are *Piping Pebworth*, and *Dancing Marston*, as they are universally called, in some lines attributed, of course, to Shakspeare.

West Midland Main Line Continued.

Honeybourne to Worcester and Wolverhampton.

Again on the Main Line, we next pay a visit to the small town of

EVESHAM.

Distance from station, ¼ mile

A telegraph station.

HOTEL.—Crown.

MARKET DAY.—Monday.

FAIRS.—Feb. 2nd, Monday after Easter, Whit-Monday, Sept. 21st.

BANKERS.—Gloucester Banking Co.; Branch of Herefordshire Banking Company.

This place has a population of 4,605, engaged chiefly in agriculture, with a little stocking and ribbon manufacture. It was remarkable for its mitred Abbey, founded by St. Egwin in 709. The tower and gateway still remain.

FLADBURY station.

PERSHORE.

Distance from station, 2 miles.

Telegraph station at Evesham, 5½ miles.

HOTEL.—Angel.

MARKET DAY.—Tuesday.

FAIRS.—Easter Tuesday, June 26th, Thursday before All Saints, and November 1st

BANKERS.—Gloucester Banking Co.

The staple manufacture here is stockings. At this place the ruins of the Abbey House, the only relics of a large monastic establishment may be seen. The situation of the town is very beautiful, and the surrounding scenery is picturesque, particularly Aylesborough, about a mile from the town.

WORCESTER.

A telegraph station.

HOTELS.—Star and Garter; the Hop Pole; the Bell; the Unicorn; the Crown.

MARKET DAYS.—Wednesday and Saturday.

FAIRS.—Saturday before Palm Sunday, Saturday before Easter, August 15th, September 19th, and 1st Monday in December.

RACES in July and November.

BANKERS.—Berwick and Co.; National Provincial Bank of England; City and County Banking Co.

WORCESTER, the capital of Worcestershire, in a fine part of the Severn, is a parliamentary borough (two members), and seat of a diocese, with a population of 27,528.

One distinct branch of manufacture is glove making, to the amount of half-a-million pairs of leather and kid gloves annually, employing between one thousand and two thousand persons. Another is boots and shoes; and the third is fine porcelain china, which was established here about a century ago by Dr. Wall (the same who made the Malvern Waters known). Chamberlain and Grainger's are the two oldest.

The main streets, High Street, Foregate, and Broad Street, are well-built, broad, and clean; and most of the houses of brick. Stone is abundant. A fine view from Froster.

Worcester, which the Saxons called *Weorgauceaster*, and similar names, being near the Welsh border, was provided with a fortress by the Conqueror. It was built by Urso d'Abitot, on Castle Hill; the county gaol occupies the site, built in 1819. No traces are left, nor of the city wall, which was erected at the same period.

The *Cathedral*, dedicated to St. Peter, was formerly the church of a priory, founded by the Saxon kings. It stands on the south side of the city, between the river and the Birmingham canal. The oldest part dates from 1218, when it was rebuilt after a fire. The style, therefore, is early English, of a simple and unadorned character; the crypt, however, is Norman. It is shaped like a double cross, 384 feet long, and has a handsome tower, 170 feet high, set off by pinnacles and statues in niches, especially that of St. Wulstan. There is a well-carved bishop's throne, and an excellent organ. Music festivals are held here for the benefit of widows and orphans of clergymen, every third year, in turn with Gloucester and Hereford. That in 1788 was attended by George III., and the west window put in to commemorate his visit. The east window was finished in 1792. Another has been stained in memory of the late Queen Adelaide. Many interesting monuments are seen; among which, the oldest is King John's, whose body was shown to crowds of people in 1797, and replaced. Another ancient tomb is Lyttleton's, the lawyer *(Coke on Lyttleton)*, who died in 1481; a Beauchamp, and two Crusaders, in effigy; Arthur, son of Henry VII. (whose widow, Katherine, was married to Henry VIII.); the excellent Bishop Hough; the bas-reliefs, twelve in number, being some of the best works of the sculptor, Roubiliac; Bishops Gauden and Stillingfleet, the former the author of *Eickon Basilike, or the Image of a King*, which so much strengthened the sympathy for Charles I. after his death, and several older prelates. In the Cathedral Precincts are the cloisters, 120 feet square, a Gothic chapter house, of ten sides, a copy of Rubens' *Descent from the Cross*, a King's College or School, founded by Henry VIII.; and an old palace, from which there are good prospects. Portraits of George III. and Queen Charlotte are here. There is another of the king in the Guildhall, in the market-place, a brick building, erected in 1723. It contains regal portraits of Charles I. and II. (with their statues), Queen Anne, and other personages, in the large hall, which is 110 feet long. The new Corn Exchange is here; Hop Market in Foregate. A theatre was built in 1780, and is 66 feet high. Handsome bridge across the Severn, built in 1781, on five arches. It has a fine view of the Malvern, Welsh, and Lickey Hills, and the beautiful fruit and hop country in the neighbourhood. In the Grammar School, founded by Queen Elizabeth, Lord Somers was educated: he was born here in 1650. Another student was S. Butler, the poet, a native of Strensham, near Pershore.

Of the twelve city churches, several deserve notice. *St. Andrew's*, near the cathedral, is an early Gothic church, with a beautiful spire, built in the last century by a common mason; it is 155 feet high, and only 20 feet diameter at the bottom, where it rests on a tower 90 feet high. *St. Peter's*, in Diglis Meadow, was originally built in the thirteenth century. Near this is the little harbour made by the junction of the canal with the river. Close to it are *St. Alban's* and *St. Helen's*, both very old churches. Across the bridge is *St. Clement's*, a Norman copy of a former church. *St. John's*, Bedwardine, is also half Norman.

There are several charitable institutions here, amply endowed, such as *Queen Hospital*, for twenty-nine women; *St. Oswald's*, for twenty-eight women; *Judge Berkeley's*, for twelve persons; and the *General Infirmary* (near the Gaol and the Race Course), on Pitchcroft Meadow, founded in 1770. The various charities possess an income of £4,500 a-year. A large *House of Industry* stands not far from the Gas Works. Near Sidbury Gate there stood not long ago part of a very old hospital. where the second Duke of Hamilton died of the wounds which he received in the famous *Battle of Worcester*, which was fought on the 3rd September, 1651, in Perry Wood, on Red Hill. Charles II., who was crowned here a little while before, occupied an old house (which is still standing) in *New Street*, from which he escaped by the back door, as the enemy pushed in at the front; and, accompanied by Lord Rochester and Father Hubblestone, his confessor, fled to White Ladies' Nunnery, at Boscabel. Cromwell styled this decisive battle his "crowning mercy," and named a ship, which was launched from Woolwich yard, the "Worcester," in consequence.

WORCESTER AND HEREFORD.

Leaving Worcester in a south westerly direction, a run of twenty-five minutes brings us, *via* the stations of Henwick, Bransford Road, and Malvern Link, to the important town of

GREAT MALVERN.

Population, 3,771.

Hotels.—The Foley Arms; the Abbey, family; Belle Vue; Beauchamp.

Malvern Wells, 2 miles from Great Malvern. *Hotels*—Essington's; Admiral Benbow; St. Ann's, and Holywell.

There are also many excellent boarding and lodging houses in both places.

West Malvern, situated on the opposite side of the hills to that of Great Malvern, and distant from it about 3 miles by the turnpike road, but not more than 1½ mile across the hill. *Hotel*—The Westminster Arms.

A healthy, fashionable, and agreeable watering place, consisting of Great and Little Malvern, about four miles apart. Both lie on the slope of the *Malvern Hills*, a long blue smooth ridge, on the borders of Worcestershire and Herefordshire, dividing the valleys of the Severn and Wye. The Worcestershire Beacon, near Great Malvern, is 1,300 feet high; while the Herefordshire Beacon, near Little Malvern, is 1,440 feet. Limestone and sandstone, with sienite, granite, &c., are the chief ingredients in this range, which is green to the summit, and produces excellent mutton. Though now rather bare, it was formerly well-wooded, and still offers much attractive scenery. But the chief recommendation, next to the mineral springs, is the pure and invigorating air, an advantage which renders it well adapted for the fashionable hydropathic, or *Water-Cure*, system here carried out with much success at the establishments of Drs. Gully and Wilson. Its merits, and the scenery of the neighbourhood have been described by Lane and Bulwer. Sheridan Knowles and his wife (*née* Miss Elphinstone), were patients. Hotels and boarding-houses are numerous, and the walks and drives of great beauty.

St. Anne's and Holywell, springs much resorted to, are slightly tepid and sulphurated, and useful, especially in glandular and skin complaints. Pump-rooms are attached to each, and a church has been lately built at the Holywell, which is nearest Little Malvern. Great Malvern Church is a handsome later Gothic cross, built by the Sir Reginald Bray, who designed Henry VII.'s beautiful chapel at Westminster. It contains some ancient effigies which were in the former church, and a modern tomb, by Hollins, to Mrs. Thompson, of *Malvern Priory*. This seat adjoins the gate and other remains of a religious house, founded at the Conquest, of which the author of the *Visions of Piers Plowmen* was a member. The parish church of Little Malvern also deserves notice for its antiquity, stained windows, &c., though it is partly dilapidated. The seat of Lady Clare, an old timbered house, and the Roman Catholic chapel, are picturesquely situated. Great Malvern church also possesses some good painted glass.

The prospect from the hills embraces part of eight or nine counties, including the vales of the Severn and Evesham, or the Avon, the cathedrals of Worcester, Gloucester, and Hereford, Tewkesbury Minster, the Welsh Hills, &c., and is the finest in the kingdom. The beacons above-mentioned were fortresses which commanded the passes through the hills. In one part are seen the remains of a trench which marked the boundary of the chase as divided between the Bishop of Hereford and the Duke of Gloucester.

On the Herefordshire side is *Eastnor Castle*, the seat of Earl Somers, a descendant of the great lawyer of William III.'s time, the view from the summit of which is magnificent. At *Ledbury*, near this, is a large old church, with a beautiful window and spire, well worth a visit. The sexton is a rare oddity, full of wit and anecdote. There is an ancient market house. Hop fields and orchards are seen here, reminding one of Kent.

In the neighbourhood of Worcester are many other interesting spots:—*Bevere* (2 miles), supposed to have been a beaver colony, is a handsome seat on an island in the Severn, from which the Malvern hills are visible. Hither the citizens retreated during the plague of 1637, and it is frequented for bathing. *Perdiswell* is the seat of Sir O. Wakeman, Bart. *Claines* is near the remains of White Ladies' or Whitestone Nunnery, in which are preserved the bed and cup of Queen Elizabeth, who visited it in 1585. (This is distinct from White Ladies above mentioned). *Henlip* or *Hindlip*, the seat of Viscount Southwell, stands on the site of an old building in which Thomas Abingdon lived when he hid away some of the Powder Plotters in the secret passages which abounded in it. It was the wife of this Thomas who wrote the anonymous letter to her brother, Lord Monteagle, which led James I. to discover the plot. *Westwood Park*, near Droitwich, the fine old Elizabethan seat of Sir J. Pakington, Bart., fourth in descent (by the mother's side), from Sir Herbert Pakington, the "Sir Roger de Coverley" of Addison. *Ombersley Park* belongs to Lord Sandys, a descendant of Sandys, the poet, and Archbishop Sandys; it contains many old portraits. *Hartlebury Castle*, near Stourport, the seat of the Bishops of Worcester for many centuries past; but most of it was rebuilt after the Restoration. *Hanbury Hall*, B. Vernon, Esq., an old seat. *Spetchley Park*, another old seat of the Berkeleys, now of R. Berkeley, Esq., their monuments are in the church. *Croome Park*, one of the largest in the county, is the seat of Earl Coventry, formerly of Urso d'Abitot, first earl of Worcester. The parish is called Croome d'Abitot. *Madresfield*, Earl Beauchamp's old seat, is full of fine ancient portraits, &c. Their old seat was at *Powick*, called Beauchamp's Court. *Boughton*, on the Teme, (which joins the Severn a little below the city), is the seat of J. W. Isaac, Esq. At *Hatton Park* there is a useful mineral spring, the property of J. Mann, Esq.

At *Upton* (9 miles), the celebrated Dr. Dee, the astrologer, was born. Near Malvern, in the direction of Upton, is a small but exquisitely built and decorated Roman Catholic chapel, and priest's residence. *Ross* can be visited from this place, *via* Ledbury and Hereford, and is a most interesting excursion.

Hereford—Described at page 38. A coach runs between Malvern and Hereford once each week day, to meet the train to and from Worcester.

FEARNALL HEATH station.

DROITWICH JUNCTION.

POPULATION, 7,096.

A telegraph station.

HOTEL.—The Royal.

MARKET DAY.—Friday.

FAIRS.—Friday in Easter week, June 18th, September 24th, and December 18th.

DROITWICH is built on the banks of the river Salwarpe. It possesses a canal six miles in length, and capable of admitting vessels of 600 tons burden, and communicates with the river Severn. Its principal manufacture is that of fine salt, which is obtained by evaporating the water of brine springs, which are more than 100 feet below the surface of the earth.

HARTLEBURY.

Distance from station, 1 mile.

Telegraph station at Kidderminster, 3¾ miles.

MONEY ORDER OFFICE at Stourport, 2½ miles.

Here is situated Hartlebury Castle, for many centuries the residence of the Bishops of Worcester, which was reduced in the time of the Commonwealth, and rebuilt by Bishop Hough. The library of Bishop Hurd, together with some of Pope and Warburton's books, are at the castle.

KIDDERMINSTER.

Distance from station, 1 mile.

A telegraph station.

HOTELS.—Lion, Black Horse
MARKET DAY.—Thursday.
FAIRS. — Palm Monday, Holy Thursday, June 20th, and September 4th.
BANKERS.—Stourbridge and Kidderminster Banking Co.

KIDDERMINSTER stands on both banks of the river Stour, which divides it into two unequal parts, and the buildings extend in a continued range from north to south-east, nearly a mile in length, and taken as a whole it forms a very regular and compact town, consisting principally of two good streets, one parallel to the canal, and the other forming part of the road to Birmingham. It returns one member. Population, 18,462. The church stands at the end of a street leading from the market-place, in a commanding situation, on the brow of a hill. It is a handsome Gothic building—the windows have very rich tracery, and the view of the town is uncommonly fine. There is a well-conducted and amply-endowed grammar school, founded by Charles the First. Kidderminster has long been celebrated for its manufactures, which are now on a very extensive scale, especially that of carpets, which has become very extensive, and has most essentially promoted the trade, wealth, and population of the town.

CHURCHILL and HAGLEY stations; the latter the seat of Lord Lyttleton.

STOURBRIDGE.

Distance from station, 1 mile.

A telegraph station.

HOTEL.—Talbot.
MARKET DAY.—Friday.
FAIRS.—March 29th and September 28th.
BANKERS.—Stourbridge Banking Co.; Birmingham and Midland Banking Co.

A handsome town, noted for its glass manufacture. Population 7,847. The surrounding districts abound in iron, coal. &c.

BRETTEL LANE, BRIERLEY HILL, ROUND OAK, and NETHERTON stations.

DUDLEY.

POPULATION, 37,962.
Distance from station, ¼ mile.
A telegraph station.
HOTELS.—Dudley Arms, Bush.
MARKET DAY.—Saturday.
FAIRS.—First Monday in March, May, August, and October.

BANKERS.—Dudley and West Bromwich Banking Co.; Birmingham Banking Co.

DUDLEY is a borough town in the county of Worcester. It received its name from a celebrated Saxon chieftain, who, as early as the year 700, built the Castle which commands the town.

The night view from Dudley Castle of the coal and iron districts of South Staffordshire reminds the spectator of the Smithy of Vulcan, described by Homer. The lurid flames that issue from the summits of the huge columnar chimnies light up the horizon for miles around, and impart to every object a gloomy aspect. On whichever side the view is taken in open day, the evidences of mining industry present themselves, in the vast number of smoking, fiery, and ever active works, which teem in this part of South Staffordshire. Taking Dudley Castle as a centre, we have to the north, Tipton, Gornal, Sedgley, Bilston, Wolverhampton, Willenhall, and Wednesfield. More easterly we find Great Bridge, Toll End, Darlaston, Wednesbury, West Bromwich, and Swan Village, which is a similar group to the former, and marked with precisely the same features—mining perforations, red brick houses, and black smoke. Turning towards the south, we find the iron towns fewer and wider apart, and lying, as it were, confusedly in four counties—Birmingham, for instance in Warwickshire; Smethwick, Dudley Port, Rowley Regis, Wordsley, and Kingswinford in Staffordshire; Oldbury, Hales Owen, Dudley, and Stourbridge, in Worcestershire. So singular, indeed, is the intersection of these four counties that in going from Birmingham to Dudley Castle, by way of Oldbury—a distance of about eight miles by coach-road—we pass out of Warwick into Staffordshire, thence into Worcester, and a third time into Staffordshire, for although Dudley town is in Worcestershire, Dudley Castle and grounds are in Staffordshire. These several towns belong to the mining and manufacturing district, known by the name of the South Staffordshire *coal field* district, because it has a layer of coal running, so far as is known, beneath its surface.

Dudley Castle belongs to Lord Ward, who is also proprietor of a considerable portion of Dudley and its mines. It is situated in a large and highly picturesque park; and, with its warders' watch and octagon towers, triple gate, keep, vault and dungeon, dining, and justice halls, and chapel, though in a state of dilapidation, must be considered as a fine old ruin. The view from the summit of the keep is wide-spreading and singularly interesting; to the north-east you have Lichfield cathedral; to the east, the busy hive of Birmingham; whilst to the south-west, nature has formed the Malvern Hills. These objects are all visible, and form an interesting background to the environs of Dudley.

As the eye sweeps the horizon from the summit of the keep, to discern the precise character of each object and locality, the mind is struck with one particular fact, that almost every town, village, house, man, woman, child, every occupation and station, are more or less dependent on, and are at the mercy of, lumps of coal and iron, and that the human race will mainly owe their moral regeneration to these two materials. The miner digs, the roaster calcines, the smelter reduces, the founder casts, the blacksmith forges, and the whitesmith files; these are but parts of the vast hive, whose busy hum of industry is heard far and wide, and whose skilful handiworks find a ready reception in every quarter of the globe. Leave Birmingham to itself, and direct your eye to West Bromwich—which has sprung up as it were but yesterday—and there you will perceive the best *puddlers* at work—the converters of pig-iron into its barred state—by far the most important of all the processes in the manufacture of that metal. Wolverhampton, Wednesbury, Bilston, and Dudley, have each their respective industries, and carry the division of labour to the minutest degree. Bloxwich, is almost exclusively employed in making awl-blades and bridle-bits; Wednesfield keeps to its locks, keys, and traps; Darlaston its gun-locks, hinges, and stirrups; Walsall its buckles, spurs, and bits; Wednesbury its gas-pipes, coach springs, axles, screws, hinges, and bolts; Bilston its japan-work and tin-plating; Sedgley and its neighbourhood, its nails; Willenhall its locks, keys, latches, curry-combs, bolts, and grid-irons; Dudley its vices, fire-irons, nails, and chains; Tipton its heavy iron-work; while Wolverhampton includes nearly all these employments in metal work. Looking further south, there may be descried Oldbury, Smethwick, Rowley Regis, Hales Owen, and Stourbridge—all of which are engaged in some form or another, in the manufacture of iron. We have not space to enlarge upon these facts, which are only a few in the vast multitude that are comprised in the area over which the view from the Castle extends, and therefore must content ourselves with laying a single one before the reader. The quantity of cast-iron produced throughout England and Scotland in 1851, amounted to nearly three millions of tons, and the share in that production by this district may be estimated at about one-third of that quantity, or five millions in value. Assuredly this limited area presents the most remarkable concentration of industry of which the world can boast.

SOUTH STAFFORDSHIRE.

Dudley to Walsall, Derby, and Burton.

On leaving Dudley, we pass the stations of Dudley Port, Great Bridge, and Wednesbury, and arrive at

WALSALL.

A telegraph station.
Hotel.—George.
Market Day.—Tuesday.
Fairs.—February 24th, Whit-Tuesday, Tuesday before Michaelmas.
Races.—Tuesday before Michaelmas.

This is a borough town, population 25,680, who return one member. The principal buildings are the church (rebuilt in 1821 on the site of an old one), old Town Hall, Queen Mary's grammar school (in which Lord Chancellor Saunders and Bishop Hough were educated), Harper's almshouses, and the manufactories of sadlers' ironmongery, which constitutes the principal trade of the place. In the vicinity are *Springfield*, R. Jesson, Esq., and *Bentley Hall*, E. Anson, Esq.

Passing Rushall station, we then reach

PELSALL.

Telegraph station at Walsall, 3¼ miles.
Money Order Office at Walsall, 3¼ miles.

This is a celebrated mining place, with a population of 1,1[illegible].

Passing Brownhills, and Hammerwich stations, we come to

Lichfield, for particulars of which see Section III., page 23.

TRENT VALLEY JUNCTION.

At this point an important connection takes place with the main line of the London and North Western, enabling parties to go to almost any part, north or south, of England.

ALREWAS.

Population, 1,144.
Distance from station, ¾ mile,
Telegraph station at Lichfield, 5 miles.
Hotels.—Crown, White Hart.
Money Order Office at Lichfield, 5 miles.

In the vicinity is *Needwood Forest*, belonging to the Duchy of Lancaster through King Henry IV. The principal portion is oak timber: (here is the Swilcar Oak, a very ancient tree, 21 feet in girth); *Egginton Heath*, on which Sir J. Gill defeated the royalists in 1644. Near at hand is the *Hall*, the old seat of the Leighs, but now held by Sir H. Every, and quite modernised; and *Tutbury Castle*, on the river Dove, which overflows its banks, but verifies the old adage,

"In April Dove's flood
Is worth a king's good."

WICHNOR.

Telegraph station at Burton.
Distance from station, 1 mile.
Money Order Office at Lichfield.

In the vicinity is *Catton Hall*, seat of Lady Wilmot Orton. *Wichnor Manor*, seat of J. Levett, Esq., was held by Sir R. de Somerville, under the Earl of Lancaster, with the understanding that he should be bound to present a flitch of bacon to every married couple who, after being married a year and a day, should make oath that they had never quarrelled or wished themselves unmarried. Very few claimants are recorded by the most searching historians.

Barton station.

BURTON-ON-TRENT.

Population, 6,374 A telegraph station.

HOTELS.—Queen's, George.

MARKET DAY.—Thursday.

FAIRS.—February 5th, April 5th, Holy Thursday, July 16th, October 29th.

BANKERS.—Burton Union Banking Co.

This great seat of Sir John Barleycorn is on the Staffordshire side of the Trent. A very ancient bridge crosses the river to the Derbyshire side, straggling through 1,545 feet, on thirty-seven arches. There was a chapel at one end, built in 1322, by Edward II., to commemorate the defeat of Lancaster; and there is still an old mill, on the site of that mentioned in Domesday Book, founded in 1004. In that record the town is called *Byrtune*, and it had been an Abbey, some fragments of which may be traced on the river near the modern church. The Marquis of Anglesea is Lord of the Manor. Bass, Allsopp, Worthington (besides nine or ten others), are the chief ale kings here, and acres covered with barrels and casks may be seen: Vast quantities of pale ale are exported to tropical climates, and drunk by thirsty souls at home as a tonic. Contrary to common usage, the brewers, in preparing it, employ hard instead of soft water. Cotton and hardware are also manufactured here. *Drakelow House*, Sir T. Gresley, Bart., is near. To the north-west, five miles by rail, is the gate and other remains of *Tutbury Castle*, overhanging the Dove, in which the military chest of Lancaster was fished up in 1831, supposed to have been dropped by him when flying from his sovereign. He was caught at Pomfret and beheaded. Here John of Gaunt kept his court, appointing a king of the minstrels, whose successors retain office in the present day, and Mary Queen of Scots was a prisoner for some years. Isaac Hawkins Browne, the poet, was born here in 1760. The front of the old Norman church deserves notice.

WILLINGTON station.

Derby, see Sec. IV., page 9.

West Midland Main Line continued.

We again retrace our route to Dudley, and, in resuming our journey north-west, pass the stations of TIPTON, PRINCE'S END, DAISY BANK, BILSTON, and PRIESTFIELD (in a distance of five miles only), arriving at

WOLVERHAMPTON,

particulars of which will be found at page 54.

Great Western Main Line continued.

CODSALL and ALBRIGHTON stations.

SHIFFNAL.

A telegraph station.
HOTEL.—Jerningham Arms.
MARKET DAY.—Tuesday.
BANKERS.—Shropshire Banking Co.

In the church at this place is a monument erected to the memory of W. Wakeley, who lived to the advanced age of 124.

OAKENGATES station.

WELLINGTON.

POPULATION, 4,601.

HOTEL.—Bull's Head.

MARKET DAY—Thursday.

FAIRS.—March 29th, June 22nd, Sept. 29th, and Nov. 19th.

Coalbrookdale is situate in the north-west angle of the parish of Madeley, about 14 miles from Shrewsbury, 5 from Wellington, and 6 from Shiffnal. It is easily accessible from the railway stations at these towns, but the Wellington and Severn Junction Railway, which will probably be extended into the valley, now terminates at Lightmoor, about a mile distant.

The Dale itself is a narrow wooded glen, opening at its widest and deepest part from the gorge through which the Severn flows in a south-easterly direction, and running for about 2½ miles into the table land out of which the Wrekin rises. Few places possess greater natural attractions or are situate among more romantic scenery, of which, from various points on the hill sides, fine and extensive views, "ever charming, ever new" are obtained of the fertile vale of the Severn, of Benthall and Wenlock Edge, of the Wrekin, Clee, Stretton and Breidden hills, of the distant Malvern hills, or the more distant Welsh mountains. The admirers of beautiful scenery, therefore, will derive great enjoyment from a visit to it; whilst the archæologist will be interested in the almost perfect ruins of Buildwas abbey, or in the picturesque though less extensive remains of the once stately priory of Wenlock; the geologist, in the field for research which the developments of the silurian and carboniferous systems here afford; or the visitor, in the well known iron works in the Dale and its neighbourhood. It is fortunate for the beauty of the place that it is situate on the edge only of the coal field which bears its name, and that the workings on the outcrop of the seams which appear in the Dale have long since been superseded by pits to the deeper measures. The coal field is one of the smallest in England, having an area of about 32 square miles, but is very productive, from the number of seams of coal and ironstone found in it. About 325,000 tons of ironstone, and 750,000 tons of coal are now annually raised from it. Its fossils are numerous, and include remains of marine, lacustrine, and land plants and creatures. It is remarkable from the greater part of it lying upon the upper members of the silurian system, which is largely developed in Benthall and Wenlock Edge, and extends over the adjacent parts of Shropshire and Herefordshire, and into central Wales; and in which the distinctive fossils are very abundant.

The position of the Dale, with its stream of water, commended it in early times to the monks of Wenlock for a preserve of fish and game; but this use of it gave way, as its advantages were known, for an industry of a more important kind, and iron works have existed here from time immemorial. Records exist of a "Smethe," or "Smeth-house," in the reigns of Henry VIII. and Edward VI., and

COALBROOKDALE CHURCH

THE IRON-BRIDGE COALBROOKDALE.

THE LITERARY & SCIENTIFIC INSTITUTION,
COALBROOKDALE.

occasionally notices of them occur through the times of Charles I., Cromwell, and Charles II., down to 1711, when the family of Darby, which acquired, and through successive members has transmitted the proprietorship of the works, settled here.

With the growth of the iron trade the works have been much extended, but their relative importance has altered since the larger coalfields have been opened. Several important processes in the manufacture, or valuable applications of iron have originated here. About 1718, the use of mineral fuel in the blast furnace superseded the use of charcoal. About 1768, iron rails were laid down on the tramways, and soon afterwards a method of puddling was adopted and patented. In 1779 the first iron bridge was made and erected. This still stands in substantial repair, at a point where it crosses the Severn with a single arch, having a span of 100 feet 6 inches.

Many of the castings for the early engines of Boulton and Watt were made here, and about 1788, inclines for the varying levels of canals were first arranged here by Telford, at the suggestion of William Reynolds.

Since the introduction of the method of rolling bars of iron, the forges, and subsequently the furnaces, the lights and smoke from which formerly produced in the valley those appearances which suggested to strangers ideas of unearthly regions, have been removed to Horsehay, and other positions in the coalfield.

At the Coalbrookdale Co's works at Horsehay about 17,000 tons of bar iron, of various qualities and descriptions, are annually made; but the large foundries still carry on in the Dale their busy and extensive manufacture. Perhaps at no other place is there made so great a variety, not only of articles but of patterns of the same article. Every casting for agricultural, mechanical, architectural, sanitary, or domestic purposes can be produced here. Not only are articles of its manufacture sent to all parts of the United Kingdom, but they find their way to America, and to countries as distant as Chili and China. Besides the bridge at Ironbridge, the bridges over the Severn at Buildwas, over the Perratt at Bridgewater, over the Cut at Bristol, over the Trent near Rugeley, and over the Severn at Preston, Boats were cast here, with many of less note. In castings of a finer description, and of superior artistic design and excellence, such as stoves, fenders, gates, and palisading, the foundries maintain a high reputation, its productions having gained a Council Medal at the Exhibition of 1851, and two Silver Medals at the Paris Exhibition of 1855. Many articles are now bronzed by a patent electro-type process, which deposits upon them a coating of brass. This method received the award of a medal at Paris. A method of protecting iron from atmospheric influences will probably be soon rendered available.

The population of the Dale is about 2,000. It is collected into an ecclesiastical district, for which a beautiful church has been lately erected. A commodious building having a large lecture room, a well supplied reading room, a library of 3,000 vols., and a room for the local school of art has been recently completed for the use of the Literary and Scientific Institution.

There are also a chapel for Wesleyans, and a meeting house for members of the Society of Friends.

ADMASTON, WALCOT, and UPTON MAGNA stations.

SHREWSBURY.

HOTELS.—The Lion, an old-established Family and Commecial House, which may with confidence be recommended; George Curtis, Proprietor. The Raven—This establishment is now by no means a commonplace Hotel, the spirited proprietor having been even lavish in his disposition to make its arrangements such as will satisfactorily meet the most fastidious taste; and being under the able management of the late proprietor of the Lion, the house may be considered to rank in the position it formerly occupied as the Head Hotel. The George, an excellent Family and Commercial Hotel, highly and deservedly recommended. Mr. G. Fox, Proprietor.

MARKET DAYS.—Wednesdays and Saturdays.

FAIRS. — For the sale of horses, cattle, and sheep, every second Tuesday; for butter and cheese, monthly, on the Wednesday after the first cattle fair.

BANKERS.—Beck, Downward, Scarth, and Bowen (Shrewsbury and Welshpool Bank); Burton, Lloyd, Salt, and How (Salop Bank); Rocke, Eyton, Campbell, and Bayley (Shrewsbury Old Bank); and National Provincial Bank of England.

This fine old capital of Shropshire, and parliamentary town, is 42 miles beyond Birmingham, 161¾ miles from London by the North Western (or 171 *via* Birmingham), and 171 by the Great Western. The new line between Gloucester and Hereford affords another route by way of Leominster, Ludlow, &c., and is 195¼ miles. The station is a splendid Tudor building, which, together with the site, cost £100,000. Two members. Population, 19,681. No particular manufacture, but celebrated for its cakes and brawn. It is beautifully placed on a peninsula of the Severn; one main street entering it from Abbey Foregate, by English Bridge and Wyle Cop, and leaving it on the opposite side by Mardol and Welsh Bridge over to Frankwell, whilst another from Drayton comes in at the neck of the isthmus from Castle Foregate. On this favourite site the Britons began a town which the Mercian Saxons, after driving them out, called Scrobbesbyrig, signifying a wooded hill. From this its modern name and that of the county are derived. Henceforth it became an important frontier position; and here Roger de Montgomery, one of the Conqueror's firmest adherents, built his Norman castle, planting it at the neck of the isthmus, in the most commanding spot that could be selected. The great keep and walls still remain, partly restored. Close to it is the County Gaol, built by Telford in 1793, on the plan of Howard, whose bust by Bacon is placed over the gateway.

Shrewsbury, which the Welsh style Amwythig, or delight, is a good specimen of an old town, with its narrow irregular streets and ancient buildings,—all, however, somewhat highly picturesque to the eye.

Many of the houses are timbered. The Market House, in High-street, is an Elizabethan edifice, dating from 1595, beneath which is the Corn Market, and a statue of Richard, Duke of York, father of Edward IV. who was ably supported by this town in his contest with the Yorkists, and two of his sons were born at the Black Priory, and his portrait (not painted till 1695) is in the Drapers' Hall, another ancient building. There was a still older structure here, the Booth Hall of Edward II.'s time, but this has been replaced by the handsome County and Town Hall built by Smirke, containing several portraits of kings, and the famous Admiral Benbow, who was a native of this place. The Council House, with its gate and old hall, 50 ft. long, still remains; adjacent to it is St. Nicholas Chapel, now a stable. The theatre, 100 ft. long, formerly the site of the Charlton's seat. Next to the old Post Office Inn is the Clothworkers' Hall, deserving notice. The Grammar School, founded (1550) by Edward VI. and possessing an income of about £3,500, takes a very high rank as a place of instruction, and is now under the charge of Dr. Kennedy, one of the first scholars in England. There is a chapel and a museum, in which are several Roman antiquities from Wroxeter. Bishop Butler, author of the well known Geography, was formerly head master; and it boasts of Sir P. Sidney, Wycherley, the poet, Waring, the mathematician, and others, as pupils. G. Bagley, the linguist, was for sometime master of Allatt's school; he published a curious and important work, the "Grammar of Eleven Languages," all of which he had acquired by his own exertions.

Of nine churches the oldest is Holy Cross, a Norman structure, near English Bridge. It was the church of an abbey founded by Roger Montgomery, portions of the monastic buildings being incorporated into modern houses. There is one relic, a beautiful stone pulpit, in the decorated Gothic style, covered with ivy. Further on the London-road, past Lord Hill's Column (136 ft. high), is the little old church of St. Giles, lately restored. White Hall is north of the road, an Elizabethan house, built by Prince, a lawyer. Another ancient church, St. Mary's in Castle-street, cross-shaped, with a spire 220 feet high. Many years ago a hare-brained fellow undertook to slide down a rope laid from the top of this spire to the other side of the river, but he was killed in the attempt. St. Alkmond's, near this, has a spire 184 ft. high; the church is modern. St. Chad's, on Claremont Hill, is also modern, having a round Grecian body, set off with Rubens' "Descent from the Cross" in the great window. From it runs the sheltered avenue of the Quarry Promenade, down to the river, planted with limes in 1719. This is a very agreeable spot. On the opposite side of the Severn, at Kingsland, is the House of Industry. From hence the well known author of Sandford and Merton chose a foundling, and educated her with the intention of making her his wife, but the scheme did not succeed. Miss Edgeworth's "Belinda" is in part founded on this circumstance. At Kingsland is celebrated the show on the second Monday after Trinity Sunday, when the different trades, with music and banners, assemble here—a remnant of the Romish festival of Corpus Christi.

The Severn winds about in a remarkable manner both above and below Shrewsbury, but its banks are most uninteresting. A little above the town is *Berwick Hall*, the seat of the Hon. H. W. Powys. Near Bicton is the famous *Shelton Oak*, 44 feet in girth, which they say Owen Glendower ascended to watch the issue of the battle of 1403. This battle, in which Henry IV. defeated the combination of great men under Hotspur, was fought in 1403, at *Battefield*, three miles north of the town, where a half-ruined church marks the site of the victory. Which of the town clocks measured that long hour's fight between the defunct Harry Percy and Falstaff it is impossible to say, as we have it solely on that fat rogue's authority.

"*Fal.* There is Percy: if your father will do me any honour, so; if not, let him kill the next Percy himself. I live to be either earl or duke, I assure you.

"*Prince Henry.* Why, Percy I killed myself, and saw thee dead.

"*Fal.* Didst thou? Lord, Lord, how this world is given to lying! I grant you I was down, and out of breath, and so was he; but we rose both at an instant, and fought a long hour by Shrewsbury clock. If I may be believed, so; if not, let them that should reward valour bear the sin upon their own heads."

Sundorne Castle is the seat of D. Corbet Esq., not far from the remains of *Haughmond Priory*, a mixture of the Norman and pointed styles. Further north are *Hardwicke Grange* and *Hawkstone*, both the seats of Viscount Hill, nephew of the first peer, the Hero of Almarez, &c. *Hawkstone Park* contains several curiosities, grottoes, &c., and points of view,—one of the best being Sir Rowland Hill's Column, 112 feet high. *Longnor* belongs to Lieut.-Col. Corbet, and was the birth-place of Dr. Lee, the self-taught Oriental scholar. *Condover*, the seat of E. W. S. Owen, Esq., an ancient Elizabethan house, with many pictures, &c. *Cound*, Rev. Henry Thursby Pelham. *Pitchford* has an old church, and is the seat of John Cotes, Esq. *Acton Burnell*, Sir C. F. Smythe, Bart.; here are remains of an old castle and grange, in which Edward I. held a parliament or great council in 1282. *Attingham* belongs to Lord Berwick, a charming spot on the Severn, where the Tern joins it. Lower down are the ruins of *Buildwas Abbey*, and the busy mineral district round Coalbrookdale, Wenlock, &c. In the distance is the noble peak of the *Wrekin*, 1,320 feet high above the plain, which commands an immense prospect.

SHREWSBURY AND WELSHPOOL.

Ten and a half miles of this line is now open to the public. It passes through Hanwood, Plealey Road, and Pontesbury, to **Minsterley,** a small chapelry, containing 988 inhabitants.

SHREWSBURY AND CHESTER.

To the tourist, this line of railway holds out peculiar attractions. The Vale of Gresford, the grounds of Wynnstay, the valley of the Dee, and the vale of Llangollen, offer some of the most beautiful views, unsurpassed for grandeur and picturesque effect. Here Cambria discloses herself between the mountains of Trevor and Berwyn, and by her own sacred Dee, the happy valley, which leads to scenes of the richest beauty, where amidst her mountains and lakes she revels in all her native splendour of rocks, woods, and streams. Throughout the rest of the line, as it crosses the valley of the Ceiriog, and passes along the borders of Wales to St. Oswald's town of Shrewsbury, the scenery is most lovely and park like; and the adjoining Welsh mountains form a noble and varied background to many a delightful view. It is both a business and pleasure line. It curves so as to either nearly touch or pass through the borders of Wales; it intersects a very important iron and coal district in Denbighshire, and passes either close to, or as near as possible the chief towns on its route—Oswestry, Llangollen, and Wrexham.

Proceeding on our way, with the "fair Sabrina" on our left hand, we pass *Berwick Park*, the seat of Lord Berwick, and arrive at

LEATON.—In the immediate vicinity is the little village *Fettes* or *Fitz*, a charming place situated on a gentle but commanding eminence, embracing a diversity of scenery, presenting the finest view the county can boast of.

Shortly after leaving this station we pass the village of Walford, and the seat of R. A. Slaney, Esq., M.P. for Shrewsbury.

BASCHURCH.

HOTEL.—Borreston Arms.

The village of Baschurch is of great antiquity, and its salubrity and general cleanliness render it a desirable place of residence. It has an old British fortress, with a fine prospect from Ness Cliff.

The British prince, Cynddylan, was buried here.

One mile distant to the left of the line is *Boreaton Park*, and in the same direction the pretty little village of Ruyton, formerly one of the "Eleven Towns," with some remains of an old castle. In the same direction (4 miles) is the site of the old castle of the l'Estranges at *Knockin*.

We now traverse a swampy, flat, and uninteresting part of the country, viz., Bagley Moors, and Whyke Moss, and then crosses the river Perry.

On the left are seen a long range of high mountains called the Welsh or Breedden hills, about five miles distant; on the summit of one of them is a pillar erected in honour of Rodney's victory over the French; and *Tedsmore Hall*, the fine seat of T. Owen, Esq.

The next place we arrive at is

REDNAL.

This station is situated in the parish of West Felton, the church of which is a fine old edifice. *Pradoe* (1 mile), Hon. T. Kenyon.

Thence passing the elegant mansion in a picturesque park of *Woodhouse*, W. M. Owen, Esq., and soon after *Aston Park*, we arrive at

WHITTINGTON.

This station is looked upon as the prettiest on this line. The village of Whittington is in a picturesque situation, and so situated that the roads from Shrewsbury to Llangollen, and from Ellesmere to Oswestry pass through it. About half a mile from the station are the ruins of Whittington Castle, which are strikingly picturesque and beautiful; and having been the birth-place and residence of Fulk Fitz-Gwarin, one of the barons who extorted from King John the Magna Charta, as well as the scene of his surprising adventures, and belonging to the Peverells, it is regarded with much interest by all visitors.

In the vicinity are (1 mile) *Halston*, the ancient house of the Myttons, in which the famous General of that name was born, and (5 miles) *Ellesmere Old Castle*, from the site of which nine counties may be seen. In the church are a pinnacled tower, beautiful window, and tombs of the Kynaston's. Ellesmere town is clean and neat, and its appearance is much enlivened by a beautiful lake close to which it stands.

Two miles further and we arrive at

GOBOWEN JUNCTION.

At this place we cross *Watt's Dyke* one of the huge ramparts erected or raised by the Mercian Saxons as a defence against the Britons. The

OSWESTRY BRANCH.

Gobowen to Oswestry and Welshpool.

This is a short line about two miles long, presenting few objects worthy of notice or description. *Park Hall*, the property of R. H. Kinchant, Esq., is a singular and interesting mansion, built in the Tudor style. *Porkington*, the seat of W. Ormsby Gore, Esq., is beautifully situated, and commands some of the finest and most extensive views in the country. Farther on to the right is "Old Oswestry," an ancient military post, situated on an eminence, a very picturesque looking object from the railway.

OSWESTRY.

POPULATION, 4,817.

A telegraph station.

HOTEL. — Wynnstay Arms. We unhesitatingly mention this establishment as being one in which the traveller may anticipate every comfort and attention without that disagreeable drawback — excessive charges.—Mr. D. Lloyd, Proprietor.

MARKET DAYS.—Wednesday and Saturday.

FAIRS.—Third Wednesday in January, March 15th, May 12th, Wednesday before June 24th, August 15th, Friday before September 29th, December 10th.

This is a very ancient town, famous as being the site of the conflict between Penda and Oswald in 642, when the latter lost his life. It took its name from this circumstance. Its early importance may be gathered from a description given of it by a Welsh poet of the 15th century, who describes it as "the London of Powis"—and Churchyard apostrophizes it as "a prettie towne, full fine." There are but few fragments of the castle left, but these are interesting from the fact that here the Duke of Hereford (Henry IV.) and the Duke of Norfolk met to settle the dispute between them. The church is a large and handsome building. It is of great antiquity.

Oswestry stands upon higher ground than any other town in Shropshire. The country for several miles round is delightfully varied with hills, vales, wood, and water, and abounds in rich scenery.

Any tourist making one of the inns in this town his head quarters for several days in fine weather, would find much worth his notice in the neighbourhood.

Although a continuous line from Oswestry, the title of the company here takes that of the OSWESTRY and NEWTOWN, running through the stations of LLYNCLYS, LLANYMYNECH, FOUR CROSSES, ARDDLEEN, POOL QUAY, and BUTTINGTON, to WELSHPOOL; but, should time permit, we recommend the tourist to leave the road at Oswestry, and pass by the vale of *Tanat* for its beautiful scenery, *Llangynog*, and old cell of St. Melangel, near it, to *Llanfyllin*, celebrated for its ponies; thence by *Guilsfield* Church (at *Garvn*, closeby a Roman camp and road) to

WELSHPOOL,

A place of considerable trade, in flannels, and in malt. The Severn here becomes navigable. About 1 mile from the town is *Powis Castle*, the ancient seat of the Clive family, occupying a commanding situation, it overlooks a vast tract of country, and is a large and magnificent seat.

Eight miles north-west is *Llanfawr*. On the hill above is the site of the old Roman station *Castell Caer Einion*. The River *Vyruwy*, here is a good angling stream, indeed the whole of the streams, and the Linns (of which there are several) abound with fish, and on every hill there are the remains of camps or entrenchments.

FORDEN station.

MONTGOMERY.

At this place are the remains of two castles, and an immense camp with four ditches to be seen. The church is cruciform, and contains some interesting monuments.

Making for the banks of the Severn, here distant about two miles, we come to *Castell Dolforwyn*, an old ruin on a hill—but surrounded by beautiful scenery. About four miles beyond is the busy little town of

NEWTOWN.

There is an old church here, some of the ornaments of which were spoil from the Abbey Cwmhir, in Radnorshire. A spacious flannel hall has been erected.

LLANIDLOES AND NEWTOWN.

A short distance beyond Newtown is a romantic glen and waterfall; we then come to *Llan-yr-Afange* (the Beaver's pool) and four remarkable camps.

MOAT LANE, LLANDINAM, and DOLWEN stations.

LLANIDLOES,

Situated at the confluence of the rivers Clywedog and Severn, returns one member to parliament, and has a population of 3,045, principally engaged in the manufacture of woollen and coarse flannels. The church contains some interesting remains.

From this we may visit the source of the Rheidol, and *Blaen Hafran*, the source of the Severn on the edge of Plinlimmon. The road hence to *Machynlleth* is full of grand scenery (a distance of 18 miles), and we may add, the wildest road in the kingdom.

MACHYNLLETH, is supposed to be the Roman *Maglona*. Here Owen Glyndwr assembled his parliament on being chosen Prince of Wales. The neighbourhood is full of objects of antiquity.

ABERYSTWITH, on the coast of Cardiganshire, situated on a bold eminence, overhanging the sea, at the junction of the Ystwith and the Rhydol. The castle—its chief lion—was built by Gilbert de Strongbow, in the reign of Henry I., and now a mere ruin, is throned upon a projection of slate rock, protecting the town on the sea side, while on the other it commands the entire estuary of the two rivers, meeting at their point of confluence. Northward of the castle is a level beach, some hundred yards in length, to which succeeds a long range of slate rocks, worn into caverns and recesses by the dashing of the waves. Among the ruins is the favourite promenade, which, from its elevation, commands a magnificent view of the whole line of coast that forms Cardigan Bay. Nearly in the middle of this bay Aberystwith is seated, whence may be seen to the north a long irregular line, formed at first by the projecting coast of Merioneth, and then continued out to sea by the long mountainous promontory of Carnarvon, terminated by the Isle of Bardsey. There is no station southward of Carnarvonshire from which the Welsh Alps may be so advantageously seen as from Aberystwith Castle, or some of the surrounding cliffs. The lofty hills which bound the estuary of the Dovey, and raise their broad backs far above the Cardigan rocks, are surmounted by Cader Idris and its subject cliffs. These are overtopped by the giant mountains of Carnarvonshire, among which, in clear weather, the sharp peak of Snowdon itself may be discerned pre-eminent above the neighbouring crags. This wide expanse of water, diversified by numerous steamers and vessels in every direction—some steering out for different ports in the bay, some further out at sea, and slowly shaping their course for Liverpool, Bristol, or Irish havens, while others, almost stationary, are busily employed in fishing—affords a varied and pleasant panorama of marine scenery. Pont ar Fynach, or the Devil's Bridge, is not more than twelve miles distant.

TOWYN (12 miles beyond), a thoroughly Welsh town, and a most rural watering place. St. Cadfan's Church will delight an antiquarian. Hence follow the mountain road, by the majestic *Cader Idris*, whose Cyclopean precipices are upheaved in our very path, to

DOLGELLY, where it will be found necessary to have a guide for its exploration, unless you have an ordnance map. Nearly 3,000 feet high, its summit commands a most extensive panoramic view, with Snowdon on one side, Wrekin on another, Plinlimmon to the South, and the Brecknockshire Beacons beyond. Dolgelly itself is a lovely place, and may be made the centre of many an interesting excursion.

The beautiful ruins of *Cymner Abbey; Nannau Park*, the scene of the deadly feud between Howel Sele and Glyndwr; the *Waterfalls;* the *Vale of Mawddach;* the Precipice walk around Moel-Cynwch; the Torrent Walk, the property of the Caerynwych family, and the Abergwynant Walks, the property of Sir Henry Bunbury; and the watering place, *Barmouth*, may be visited from this. Ten miles up the coast from Barmouth is *Harlech*, with its historical old ruined castle, from which *Craig Ddrwg* and the *Rhinog Faur* (upwards of 2,000 feet high) may be climbed, with every yard full of Druidical and British remains.

On the completion of the lines of railway from Llanidloes to Llandovery and the south, the whole of central Wales, abounding in rugged defiles, in secluded glens, darksome rivers (but full of fish), the sources of the Severn and the Wye, and many a relic of our stalwart ancestors, will be opened up to the tourist.

Great Western continued.

Proceeding onwards from Gobowen, with *St. Martin's* one mile on the right, and *Selattyn* one mile to the left, we soon come to the Chirk Viaduct, which carries us across the lovely vale of Ceiriog, and into the Welsh county of Denbigh, and stop at

CHIRK.

HOTEL.—Castle Arms.

Pleasantly situated on the brow of a hill, surrounded by fertile meadows and wooded banks. The neighbourhood affords various rural entertainments for tourists and visitors. Chirk Viaduct is considered a beautiful engineering gem, and viewed from a hill on the south-west side of the valley, near Pont Feun, is seen to great advantage, and discloses through its arches the lovely vale of Ceiriog.

Parallel with the Chirk viaduct is the aqueduct, built by Telford, which conveys the Ellesmere canal over the vale of Ceiriog.

In 1164, here took place the most sanguinary battle ever fought between the English and Welsh. Many of the English slain were buried in Offa's dyke near, which still goes by the name of the Pass of Graves.

Overlooking the village is the remarkably interesting and ancient mansion called *Chirk Castle*, the seat of R. Myddelton Biddulph, Esq. This noble looking edifice has been preserved from ruin, and may be regarded as a perfect model of the "time-honoured castles of the ancient lords of the soil." From its summit the prospect is not only extensive, but grand, overlooking seventeen counties.

A short distance further on to the left is *Brynkinallt*, the residence of Lord Dungannon, of the Trevor family. The Iron Duke's mother belonged to this family, and here the illustrious warrior passed a great portion of his boyhood; and beyond, in the same direction is the *Quinta*, the seat of Thos. Barnes, Esq.

Proceeding onwards, with the Chester and Ellesmere canal running for some distance parallel with us, we arrive at the station at

LLANGOLLEN ROAD.

A telegraph station.

HOTELS.—Llangollen; The Hand; Royal.

This station is most admirably situated for parties desirous of visiting the finest scenery in North Wales, as coaches are generally in attendance to meet each train, to convey passengers to the principal places in the vicinity. The drive on the great Holyhead road from this station cannot be surpassed for beauty in the kingdom. It traverses the whole length of the Vale of Llangollen and the valley of the Dee up to Corwen—every turn of the road presenting the most beautiful scenery.

The Vale of Llangollen is said to equal any of the beauties of the Rhine, and it no doubt surpasses them in works of art, the aqueduct and viaduct being splendid ornaments to this lovely work of nature.

Llangollen lies in the hollow of the Dee, called in Welsh, *Glyndwrdwy*, i. e., valley of the Dyfyrdwy; and being the first glimpse of peculiar mountain scenery which the visitor comes upon, it is indebted to this as much as to its own character for the celebrity it enjoys. The population of the town is 1,600 or 1,700, including some engaged in the flannel and woollen manufacture. *Plâsnewydd*, or New Hall, where the Maid of Llangollen, Lady E. Butler, and her friend (so graphically delineated by the late Charles Matthews), Miss Ponsonby, lived in happy retirement, remains in the same state as when occupied by them. The two former residents are buried in the old Gothic church, which is dedicated to Saint Collen, whose full name is *Collen ap Gwynnawg ap Clyddwg ap Cowrda ap Caradoc Freichfas ap Lleyr Merion ap Einion Yrth ap Cunedda Wledig.* What an affliction to have to invoke the saint by his full name, or to be christened after him! A *Gothic Bridge* in four arches is as old as the 14th century. The Vale is best seen in the evening light; but the "Vale of the Cross at its upper end—which is generally confounded with it—and that of Llandysilio, on the Holyhead road, opposite the former, are both superior to Llangollen."—(Cliffe's *North Wales).* It lies between hills in which limestone and coal, and in other parts excellent slate, are quarried. What the latter article will bear may be seen from the slabs laid down opposite St. Mildred's, in the Poultry, London; the grain is so firm, that though millions of feet have passed over that pavement, it is as smooth and sound as ever.

Opposite the bridge the hills rise upwards of 900 feet high, and are surmounted by the remains of an old British fortress, which commanded the pass, called *Castle Dinas Bran (dinas* means a fort). A winding path leads to it from the Tower farm.. Going down the Dee, you come to Plâs-y-Pentre, a seat between the river and the canal, below which is the Pont-y-Cysylltan, or *aqueduct* which carries the Ellesmere canal over the valley. It is constructed on 19 arches of 45 feet span, and is 1,007 feet long, and 126 feet high in the middle, and took Telford ten years to finish.

A little above Llangollen is *Valle Crucis*, or the Valley of the Cross, which may be ascended to view the striking remains of an abbey, founded in the 13th century, beyond which is the more ancient Cross called *Eliseg*, which gives name to the pass. The road leads hence over Craig Eglwyseg, and other peaks 1,500 to 1,800 feet high, to the head of the *Vale of Clwydd*, and to Ruthin and Denbigh *Castles*.

Down the Dee, below the Cysylltan aqueduct is *Wynnstay*, the hospitable and extensive mansion of Sir W. W. Wynne, Bart., in a beautiful park of 9 miles circuit. Watt's dyke intersects the grounds, in which are an obelisk 101 feet high, a cenotaph to the memory of those soldiers who fell in the Irish rebellion of '98, and a tower to commemorate the victory of Waterloo. Since writing the above, the mansion has been totally destroyed, with its very valuable contents, by fire.

Still higher up the Dee are, *Llantysilio Hall*, seat of A. Reid, Esq., near the canal reservoir; and (at the 7th mile stone) Glyndwr's Mount, marking the site of Sycharth, or Sychuant, the seat of the famous Owen Glyndwr ,or Glendower, whose county this was. A mile or two further is Corwen Church, a half Normun building. A cross in the church yard is called Owen Glyndwr's sword; a dagger which belonged to that chief is at Col. Vaughan's seat, *Rhug*. The great Holyhead road here strikes off through the mountains to Capel Curig (26 miles), Snowdon, and Bangor; while another follows the Dee to Bala Lake (13 miles), and takes its source in the Arran Mowddwy mountains. These range 2,950 feet high at the most, and fall as a continuation of the Berwyn mountains, which appear nearer Llangollen, and at Moel Ferna (*Moel* means *bald*), within a few miles of it, are 2,100 feet high, and at Cader Berwyn, about 2,560 feet high. Under this last point (12 miles south-west) is the famous *waterfall* of *Pistyll Rhaiadyr*. Here in a dark well-wooded hollow one of the head springs of the Tanat runs down 140 feet at once, thence through a rock, and down another fall of 70 feet. There are several paths to it over the hills. It gives name to Llanrhaiadyr church, in the valley below.

Soon after leaving Llangollen Road Station, we come to

The Great Dee Viaduct. — Crossing the Dee at one of the loveliest spots in the principality of Wales, where nature has grouped the various elements of beauty in the richest profusion, and art has recorded its triumphs by first-class works, the view from the top of the viaduct, for extent and beauty, is unequalled. Beneath winds the Dee, from which rise the Eglwyseg Rocks with serrated outline on the left bank, while the mountains forming the continuation of the Berwyn range abut on the right bank; their lower slopes are richly cultivated, and on successive terraces are dotted the white cottages of the Welsh peasantry, whilst masses of dark wood crown the projecting heights. The aqueduct of Pont Cysylltan, is seen as you cross about a mile distant from the viaduct, and forms a striking feature in the prospect.

Castle Dinas Bran, Barber's Hill, and the Eglwyseg Rocks, form a background unrivalled for picturesque effect, and enclose the vale in an amphitheatre of loveliness. Railways, canals, lime quarries, and the distant iron works, mark the progress of commercial enterprise.

This stupendous viaduct consists of 19 semicircular arches of 60 feet span; and the height from the bed of the river to the top of the parapet at the centre pier is 148 feet. Its length is 1,532 feet. The viaduct is founded on the solid rock, and is built of stone, with the exception of the interior arching, which is of hard fire bricks. The grain of the stone is beautiful, and the work is so built as to convey to the mind the idea of great strength and solidity. Passing Cefn we see on our right *Wynnstay* and its pretty park, and to the left the works of the British Iron Company, stopping at

RUABON.

HOTEL —Wynnstay Arms.

The village of Ruabon is most pleasantly situated, and there are mansions, iron and coal works in the neighbourhood. Ruabon Church is well worthy of a visit. It contains several fine monuments, particularly one to the memory of Sir Watkin Wm. Wynne, Bart., which is much admired.

The railway here runs parallel with Watt's and Offa's Dykes for a long distance. The mountainous district to the right from Wrexham to Ruabon is a valuable mining country, extremely prolific in coal and iron, and shortly before reaching Wrexham the traveller will perceive *Erddig Hall*, the seat of Simon York, Esq., delightfully situated on a hill, with a beautiful little river flowing at its foot. The view of this mansion from the railway is exceedingly picturesque.

WREXHAM.

A telegraph station.

HOTEL.—Wynnstay Arms.

POST HORSES, FLYS, &c., at the station and hotels. Tariff—1s. 6d. per mile, post boy 3d. per mile.

MARKET DAYS.—Thursday and Saturday.

WREXHAM is a populous town in the county of Denbigh. Population 6,714, who return one member. It stands in a fertile plain adjoining the Royal Vale of Cheshire. It is well built, the church is a very handsome edifice, built in the 15th century, and is equal in point of beauty to many of our Cathedrals. It is 178 feet long, 72 feet wide, and has a tower 185 feet in height, which portion is considered a masterpiece of architectural display; it also contains a chaste monument by Roubiliac to Mary Middleton, with some fine monuments of the neighbouring gentry. In addition to this edifice there are several other places of worship. The town being situated in the centre of an extensive mining and manufacturing district is considered the metropolis of North Wales. The town-hall is a large edifice at the top of High Street.

In the vicinity is *Gardden Lodge*, the seat of G. Walmsley, Esq., on a hill to the right, built on the site of an old fortress and encampment, in the vicinity of which a battle was fought between the English and the Welsh in 1161-2.

At *Holt* (6 miles) there are an interesting stone bridge, of ten arches, over the Dee, erected in the 14th century; some remains of an extensive castle and Roman earthworks. At *Bangor Iscoed* are the vestiges of a British college, which was founded by King Lucius in 180, and contained 2,400 monks, 1,200 of whom were slain, unarmed, on a battle field, near Chester, by Ethelfrith.

The train now traverses for a considerable distance what is called "free" or neutral ground, where at one time trade and commerce could only be transacted between the ancient Britons, the Danes, and afterwards the Saxons.

Recrossing Watt's Dyke, we arrive at the junction of the

Brymbo, Minera, &c., Branch.

This mineral branch diverges to the right, and passes across the coal field to the lime rocks of Minera. It is 6¼ miles in length. There are several smaller branches made for the accommodation of the works at Frood, Brynmally, Westminster, South Sea, Brymbo, and Vron, to the extent of about six miles in addition.

At a place called Wheatsheaf the locomotive portion of the branch terminates, and the lower self-acting inclined plane commences, by which the loaded wagons descend, and draw up the empty ones to Summerhill level.

At Summerhill the branch pierces through the crest of a hill by a tunnel, and enters the Moss Valley, which is here a narrow ravine, beautifully wooded, having its sides studded with cottages and gardens, which are chiefly small freeholds, the property of the workmen.

From Moss Valley the main branch rises by a steep inclined plane to Peutre, at an inclination of 1 in 4 At the top it pierces through the summit of the Peutre by a tunnel, on emerging from which is Brymbo Valley and iron works. From the tun el the railway winds its course for about four miles to Minera, celebrated for its lead mines and limestone rocks. As the railway winds along the slope of the hills a most magnificent panoramic view is obtained, extending from the Mersey, dotted with white sails, across the Vale Royal, over Cheshire and Shropshire to the Severn, flanked on the left by the Hope Mountains, and on the right by the Berwyn range to which succeed the Brydden, the Wrekin, Caer Caradoc, and the distant Cheshire hills; and while the eye is charmed with the beauty of the landscape, the mineral treasures and the varied mechanical contrivances by which their value is brought out, commands the attention and admiration of the geologist and scientific visitor.

Great Western Main Line continued.

Passing a fine ancient mansion, called *Geversyllt Hall*, the property of Sir Watkin W. Wynne. Bart., and then, by some deep cuttings and long embankments, we reach

GRESFORD.

The station is built in the English villa style, and its picturesque simplicity harmonises exceedingly well with the beautiful and romantic scenery around. The church is seated on the brow of a lofty eminence, commanding a very fine view of the Vale Royal of Cheshire; it is seen at a great distance off, and is famed as one of the seven wonders of Wales, for its beautiful Gothic architecture. *Gresford Lodge*, R. Ormsby Gore, Esq. Passing along the beautiful and highly picturesque Vale of Gresford, *Mount Alyn*, the residence of the late Col. M Goodwin, on the left, and through a cutting, interspersed with streaks of coal, we cross the river Alyn, to the right of which is seen *Trevalyn Hall*, the seat of Sir John Trevor. A short distance from the line is a high hill, called the Rofts, formerly a British encampment, and arrive at

ROSSETT.

The beautiful ravine, *Nant-y-fridd*, and the ruins of *Caergwrle Castle*, originally a British post, which defended the neighbourhood, may be visited from this.

Soon after passing this the line proceeds over a flat, fertile country called the Lache Hayes, to the left of which, as far as the eye can see, is the long range of Clwydian Hills, the centre one being distinguished by the name of Moel Fammau, or the mother of hills. There is a monument on the summit of this mountain, erected to commemorate the fiftieth anniversary of the reign of George III. The view from this elevation is very extensive. The hills nearest the line are those of Hope Mountains, containing minerals of every description in profusion. The iron and coal works are seen burning at night for a considerable distance. We likewise perceive the village of *Doddleston* on the left. The church contains a monument to the memory of Chancellor Egerton, Lord Ellesmere. The next station is

SALTNEY.

This place is becoming of considerable importance in connection with the coasting trade, from its being the nearest shipping port to the whole of North Wales, Shropshire, and the mining districts in Staffordshire. To the right is the beautiful little village of *Eccleston*, a favourite resort of pleasure parties from Chester.

Leaving Saltney, we soon after cross the river Dee by the largest cast-iron girder bridge in the kingdom, and a viaduct of 47 arches; then, passing through the west angle of the city walls, over the Ellesmere and Chester Canal, and through the tunnel beneath Northgate, we arrive at the Station at

CHESTER.

A telegraph station.

HOTEL.—Albion, J. Chambers, first-class Family and Commercial Hotel. We can recommend this with confidence as an excellent, comfortable house.

MARKET DAYS.—Wednesday and Saturday.

FAIRS.—Last Thursday in February, July 5th, and October 10th. RACES in May and October.

BANKERS.—Dixons and Wardell; Williams and Co.; North and South Wales Bank.

CHESTER is a genuine Roman city, built four-square, within walls, which remain to this day. It is also a cathedral town and borough, with 27,766 population, returning two members, a peer, the Prince of Wales, who bears the title of Earl of Chester, and the capital of Cheshire, on the river Dee, thirteen miles from Liverpool, where four lines meet. The joint station, which cost nearly a quarter of a million, is 1,010 feet long. Chester, so called by the Saxons because of the camp, or *castram* here. was named *Deva* by the Romans, who joined it by a road right across the country to Colchester, called the *Via Deva*. Two main streets were cut by them into the rock, terminating in the four city gates; above these on both sides are lines of shops and covered ways, called the *Rows*, to which you ascend by a few steps. Several old timber buildings with gable fronts are seen. *St. John's* is the oldest of its eleven or twelve churches, having solid Norman pillars, &c. The *Cathedral*, built of the red sandstone so common here; the west front, not older than the 16th century, is the best part of it. A beautiful early English *Chapter House* is close by. The bishop's throne was the shrine of St. Werburgh, founder of the abbey here. The present primate was translated from Chester. Falaner, a scholar, Dr. Cowper, Sir J. Vanburgh, the mathematician, Molyneux and Brerewood, Bradshaw, the poet, Higden, the author, Dean Whittingham, translator of the Geneva Bible, and Kynaston and Downham, divines, were natives. The *Cheese Market* is in the Old Linen Hall. The cheeses weigh from 60 to 160 lbs. and are highly coloured; to make them keep, the whey is entirely pressed out. The famous Cheshire pastures were at one time almost worn out, when they were renovated with bone dust, and made five times as valuable as before. The *Shire Hall* and *Assize Court* is an imposing Grecian pile, by Harrison, with a portico copied from the Acropolis at Athens. Here is the old *Castle*, built by the Conqueror's nephew, Hugh Lupus; it includes an armoury, barracks, chapel, and Julius Cæsar's tower. The ancient *Walls*, now hemmed in by houses, form a walk, 4 to 6 feet broad, and nearly 2 miles long round the town, and are curious from their antiquity. They were patched up or rebuilt by Alfred's daughter In some parts they are only a few feet high; but where the cliff overhangs the river you look down 50 or 60 feet. The sharp edges of the Welsh hills are seen here and there; from the Phœnix Tower, Charles I. witnessed the defeat of his troops at Rowton Moor, in 1645. One old bridge of 7 arches dates back to the 11th century. The *Grosvenor Bridge*, designed by Harrison, and built by Trubshaw, is a fine arch of 200 feet span, with a rise of only 40 feet. The *Roodee*, or race course, is outside the walls, near the railway. In Crook Street chapel is *Matthew Henry's* pulpit, where he used to preach; his monument is in Trinity church. Chester has a middling shipping trade, by means of a cut to the sea from Saltney. The Welsh border is within a walk of 2 miles.

Eaton Hall (3 miles), seat of the Marquis of Westminster, is visited from here, and stands in a large straggling park. Tickets may be had at the booksellers, or at the Royal Hotel. Parties of three—to the *house*, 5s.; to the *garden*, 3s.; the proceeds being handed over to the Chester hospitals. The Hall is a very picturesque modern Gothic pile, about 450 feet long, with several pinnacles and turrets, and rebuilt in 1803 on the site of the old seat. In the long gallery are family portraits, with West's "Cromwell Dissolving the Long Parliament," and various foreign masters. A pretty iron bridge, 150 feet span across the river.

Haddon (or Hawarden) *Castle*, seat of Sir S. Glynne, Bart., near an old keep, is in Denbighshire, 7 miles off.

For continuation of route to Holyhead, see page 72.

BIRKENHEAD.

Chester to Birkenhead and Liverpool.

Leaving Chester, the first stations we pass are MOLLINGTON, SUTTON, and HOOTON, from the latter of which *Parkgate* is accessible by omnibus; the next place arrived at is

BROMBOROUGH, near to which is Eastham Ferry, the landing place for the Mersey steamers. It is a charming spot, and a place of great resort in the summer by pic-nic parties from Liverpool. Bromborough Mill, situated in a delightful dell.

SPITAL station.

BEBBINGTON.—Here is an old spire church, and just beyond are Upper Bebbington and the Stamton Stone Quarries, in which ripple marks have been found.

ROCK LANE, the station for Rock Ferry, between which and Liverpool steamers are constantly plying.

BIRKENHEAD.

A telegraph station.

HOTELS.—The Woodside, Adelphi, and Castle.

This place contains a population of 24,285, chiefly engaged in shipbuilding; large docks of 150 acres, made by Rendall, and opened in August, 1847; 4 chapels, court house, St. Aidan's college, founded in 1849; gas and water works, Abattoir pier Market place, 430 feet long; St. Mary's church which overlooks the river was part of a restored abbey, ruins of a priory founded in 1150 by Hamon de Massey, 2 churches, fine park and great square. In the vicinity are Seacombe, Egremont, Leasowe Castle, and New Brighton, with the Blackrock Lighthouse and Bidstone Light, all of which are bathing places on the Mersey.

LIVERPOOL, see Section III., pages 42, 51.

Chester to Manchester,

(*Via* Warrington and Newton Junction).

The first station on our route is DUNHAM HILL, close to which are Wimbold's, Trafford Hall, Mickle Trafford, and Bridge Trafford, near which is Helsby Hill Camp, the marshy shores of the Mersey, the old church and manor house of Ince, seat of I. Ince, Esq., and Stanlow Point, where there was a ferry, and the Abbots of St Werburgh had a retreat.

HELSBY station.

FRODSHAM.

POPULATION 2,099. Telegraph station at Warrington.

HOTEL.—Bear's Paw.

MARKET DAY.—Saturday.

FAIRS.—May 15th and August 21st.

This place is situated in a pretty spot under Overton Hill. It has a fine old Norman church (from which there is a good view), grammar school, graving dock, an old castle given by Edward I. to Llewellyn's brother David, for the betrayal of which he was executed. It was burnt in 1642. It has a population of 3,000, employed in the salt works. Here died T. Hough, aged 141 years; and its inhabitants are celebrated for their longevity.

Next in succession is RUNCORN ROAD, three miles to the left of which is Runcorn, where markets are held on Fridays, near Weston Point, under the cliffs, and opposite the Mersey, called Runcorn Gap. It has a population of 8,050, employed in the salt and coal trade. *Halton Castle* commands fine views; it was built by Fitz Nigel, and a little beyond is *Aston Hall*, the seat of Sir A. Aston, for many years Ambassador at the Court of Spain. The canal suddenly falls here by ten locks.

NORTON and DARESBURY stations.

Warrington.—See Section III., page 33.

The arrival of the train at Newton Bridge, the junction of the line with the London and North Western, is soon announced; and passing the stations of KENYON, BURY LANE, ASTLEY, PATRICROFT, ECCLES, and ORDSAL, we arrive at

Manchester, See Section III., page 37.

WARRINGTON AND STOCKPORT.

Warrington to Timperley.

LATCHFORD.—Here the river Mersey twists into a series of curious knots.

THELWALL station.

LYMM.

POPULATION, 3,156.

Telegraph station at Warrington, 4 miles.

HOTEL.—Plough.

Both the church, with a pointed cross, and hall, with old bay windows, the residence of James Barratt, Esq., are very ancient.

Passing the stations of HEATLEY, DUNHAM MASSEY, and BROADHEATH, we arrive at

TIMPERLEY.—Three miles from this place is *Wythenshawe Hall*, seat of T. W. Tatton, Esq. It is also the point of connection with the

MANCHESTER, SOUTH JUNCTION, AND ALTRINCHAM.

Bowdon to Manchester.

A walk of a mile from this station brings us to Altrincham, and a quarter of a mile further, to Bowdon, and here the traveller would do well to spend a few hours.

ALTRINCHAM AND BOWDON.

POPULATION, 4,488.

A telegraph station.

HOTELS.—Stamford Arms; Unicorn.

MARKET DAY.—Tuesday.

FAIRS.—April 22nd, August 5th, and Nov. 22nd.

Dunham Massey Park, the seat of the Earl of Stamford and Warrington, is in the neighbourhood. It is peculiarly celebrated for its salubrious atmosphere, and much frequented by the citizens of Manchester on account of its beautiful orchards and fruit gardens. At Bowdon is *St. Nicholas's* ancient church, containing the tomb of Booth, first Lord Delamere, who was defeated by Lambert in 1659, owing to his espousing Charles I.'s cause too early. The view from the church tower is superb. *Rostherne* church 4 miles south, once the sphere of labour of Adam Martindale, contains the monuments of the families of Egerton, of Tatton; Brooke, of Mere; Leigh, of West Hall, and the ancient families of Massey and Daniel. *Tatton Park*, the seat of Lord Egerton, is near the village.

We now retrace our steps to TIMPERLEY on our way to Manchester, passing SALE and STRETFORD to OLD TRAFFORD, in the vicinity of which is *Trafford Park*, seat of Sir Humphrey De Trafford, Bart., descended from one of the most ancient of all the old families in this county. The park is extensive, but rather bare; the house of plain brick.

CORNBROOK and KNOTT MILL stations.

Manchester, see Section III., page 37.

CHESTER AND HOLYHEAD.

To tourists the Chester and Holyhead line offers an admirable means of reaching easily the most interesting spots in North Wales. Conway, with its glorious old castle and bridges, and Carnarvon, are within easy distance, as is also Snowdon's huge peak, with the Clwydian Vale, and many other vallies of great beauty and celebrity, with an infinity of picturesque hills, waterfalls, and ruins. The Menai Bridge should not be forgotten by the traveller along this line of railway, nor its still more wondrous neighbours the Conway and Britannia Tubular Bridges. The latter, in particular, is a mighty construction, its proportions being gigantic in the extreme, and impressing the beholder with admiration at its surpassing grandeur and design.

Upon the opening of this railway Holyhead resumed its importance as a packet station for steamers plying to Dublin. The Chester and Holyhead Railway affords increased facilities of communication between London and Dublin, which were previously usurped by Liverpool. The Chester and Holyhead Railway shortened the time occupied in the journey from London to Dublin about five hours, the journey from London to Holyhead occupying eight hours, and the voyage by fast steam packets from thence to Dublin four hours. Thus the line is a very important one, in shortening the distance between the chief city in the British Isles and the important capital of Ireland, and adds another noble power to government in the facilities of communication.

That very noble pile of buildings, in the Italian style, the Chester station, is the longest of all the railway termini in England, and is the joint station for the following railways:—The London and North Western, the Chester and Holyhead, the Chester and Shrewsbury, and the Birkenhead companies. Each of these have a separate terminus there.

The station consists of a façade facing the city of Chester, 1,050 feet long, built of dark coloured bricks, relieved with stone facings and dressings. The centre, which is two stories in height, contains on the ground-floor the usual offices, waiting and refreshment rooms; and on the upper, the offices of the Chester and Holyhead, and Shrewsbury and Chester Companies, in which the business connected with the whole of their lines is conducted.

The wings formed by projecting arcades, with iron roofs, are appropriated to private and public vehicles waiting the arrival of trains.

On the inner side of the office buildings, a large platform extends, which is chiefly used for departing trains, and is 700 feet long by 20 feet wide; this, and three lines of rails, are all covered in with an iron roof, 60 feet span, which is one of the most elegant yet constructed.

In consequence of one of the public roads of the city crossing the rails close to the station, it was necessary to erect a bridge across the line.

Before pursuing his journey on the Main Line the tourist cannot do better than take a rapid survey of the line to Mold, for which purpose we here introduce a short sketch.

CHESTER TO MOLD.

From Chester we pass Broughton, to the right of which is *Hawarden*, a small market town in Flintshire, with Sir S. Glynne's seat, *Hawarden Castle*, which was built in 1752, on the site of the old fortress. It contains old portraits, antiquities, and the ruins of the keep of the old seat which was destroyed in 1678, by Sergeant Glynne, and was a place of great celebrity during the Welsh Wars. We then reach Broughton Hall, and soon after, the station at

HOPE,

Situated on Watts' Dyke and the Alyn, over which there is an old bridge, has the ruins of a castle where Queen Eleanor (Edward I.'s wife) remained on her way to Carnarvon. Hope church contains the Trevor's tombs.

Fairs are held here on Shrove Tuesday, May 10th, August 12th, and October 27th.

In the vicinity are the borough of Caergwrle, with a population of 720, who return one member; Plas Tey, seat of C. Trevor, Esq., and Bryn Yorkyn, E. Yonge, Esq.

PADESWOOD,

Near which are *Leeswood*, seat of J. W. Egton, Esq., and *Plâs Newydd*, the Marquis of Anglesea's; thence we soon reach Llong, near which is a tower, the old three-storied and machicolated seat of the Wynnes, where the Mayor of Chester was murdered by the Welsh Prince Reinallt in 1475.

Llong station.

MOLD.

Hotel.—Black Lion.

Market Days.—Wednesday and Saturday.

This town contains a population of 3,482,—who return one member—employed in the cotton factories and mines, three bridges, county hall for assizes, by Jones; school, mills, new market, St. Mary's church, a fine edifice of the time of Henry VII., with a new font, by Archdeacon Clough; and tombs of Bishop Wharton, Davies of Llannerch, Wynn, the painter, and several tumuli. In the vicinity are Large earthwork, Bailey Hill, from which an extensive view may be obtained; *Ruel*, seat of Colonel Phillips; *Merquis*, Miss Griffiths; *Hartsheath*, Peutre, and Gwysaney.

Again we return to Chester, and continue our journey from

Chester to Rhyl.—Main Line.

From Chester the line of railway skirts along the side of the river Dee; afterwards its course, till near Conway, is close by the sea shore, and again it winds its way by the sea side to Beaumaris Bay, near Penmaen Mawr. The line of the railway being along the sea, much of the beautiful scenery of North Wales is lost; but by this route the undertaking was rendered easier of construction than it otherwise would have been. Yet there are many beautiful landscapes on the line, glimpses of the huge piles of mountains towering high above the vallies whence they rise; and ruins also to be noticed by the way-side, telling of ages past, adding historical interest to the charms of nature.

Upon leaving Chester the whistle of the engine announces our approach to the tunnel under North Gate Street and the adjacent gardens, and we immediately pass through this and merge through deep cuttings of red rock. The train then proceeds over the girder bridge, crossing the Ellesmere and Chester Canal, passing thence through the west angle of the city walls, on to the high and long embankment across the Tower Fields. The line is carried over a viaduct of 47 arches, and passes, on the left, the well known plains of Roodee, where the Chester races take place in the spring and autumn of the year.

Proceeding onwards, we cross the river Dee on the largest cast iron girder bridge in the kingdom, immediately after passing which the line traverses some deep cuttings in Brewer's Hall Hill, from the summit of which Oliver Cromwell bombarded the city. We then reach the Saltney station, where the Shrewsbury line diverges to the left, and our train proceeding over Saltney pasture lands, runs parallel for seven miles with the river Dee. The plain on the right beyond the river is called *Sealand*, from its having been enclosed from the sea by the River Dee Company. After passing a small bridge over a brook, we enter the

PRINCIPALITY OF WALES.

We are now approaching the Welsh Mountains; the *Clwydian Hills* are seen in the distance; the one in the centre called *Moel Fammau*, or the Mother of Hills, is the loftiest, on the top of which is a jubilee column, erected to commemorate the fiftieth anniversary of the reign of George III. The view from this elevation is most varied and extensive, comprising the Derbyshire Hills, the Wrekin in Shropshire, Snowdon, and Cader Idris in Wales, as well as the Cumberland Hills, and in clear weather even the Isle of Man.

Continuing our route, we pass, on the left, the branch railway to Mold, and shortly after reach *Sandycroft*, where there is a large foundry. Two miles to the left of this are seen the town and castle of *Hawarden*. There are several coal mines in the neighbourhood, and in the vicinity of Buckley are earthenware manufactories of considerable repute.

Proceeding onwards, we soon reach QUEEN'S FERRY station (Flintshire). On leaving this station the line passes through deep cuttings and a short tunnel, and immediately afterwards we have a fine view of the estuary of the Dee, which at high tide assumes the appearance of an arm of the sea, covered at times with innumerable vessels.

About a mile to the left is the mansion of Edward Bates, Esq., which commands a particularly fine view of the estuary and the Cheshire shore.

A little further on is *Leadbrook*, so named from the profusion of lead ore obtained in the neighbourhood and the adjacent hills, particularly in the *Halkin Mountain*, the metallic productions of which have been immense; one spot alone having yielded, in the space of a few years, upwards of a million sterling in value. The porcelain clay at Halkin is also considered very fine.

FLINT.

Telegraph station at Chester, 12½ miles.

HOTEL.—The Oak.

FAIRS.—1st Monday in February, July & Nov. 3rd.

This station is situated in the centre of the town, which is a sea port and market town, with a population of 3,296, who return one member, as well as the county itself. There are extensive collieries, the coals from which are shipped from here to Liverpool, Ireland, and various parts of Wales. The ruins of *Flint Castle* are seen on the right, at no very great distance from the railway, situated on a rock which juts out towards the sea. It is a memento of other ages, and is peculiarly rich in historical associations, one of the most celebrated events connected with it being the deposition of Richard II. The castle is but a mere shell, there being left only the grey ruined walls, and the two outside concentric walls with the gallery, to attest its former strength and grandeur.

On leaving the station the line proceeds over Flint Marsh, to the left of which is *Coles Hill*, where a battle was fought, between Owen Gwyndwr and Henry II., in which the latter was defeated.

The next station we come to is

BAGILLT.

Telegraph station at Chester, 14½ miles.

During the last twenty years this town has become of some importance, in consequence of several very extensive collieries and lead works which have been established here. A large portion of the lead ore produced in different parts of the kingdom is brought here for smelting. On the hill to the left are seen the ruins of *Basingwerk Abbey*, built by the Earls of Chester, beautifully situated just above the road, and commanding extensive views of the river Dee, Hilbree Island, &c. Close at hand is *Bagillt Hall*, the fine old seat of the Griffiths.

HOLYWELL.

Telegraph station at Rhyl, 15¼ miles.

HOTEL.—White Horse.

MARKET DAY.—Friday,

FAIRS.—June 22nd and November 3rd.

RACES in Autumn.

The station is very handsome, and of good design.

The important town of Holywell is situated about a mile from the station. Population 1,130, and built on the declivity of a hill, which gradually extends to Greenfield, the surrounding hill forming a kind of amphitheatre. It is one of the first towns in North Wales, in a commercial point of view. The far-famed Holy Well of St. Winifrede is worthy of a pilgrimage, its architecture is so rich, and well repays a halt at the station to go and visit it. The town owes its origin to this well, its stream having been made available to turn the machinery of extensive mills and manufactories; some of which are closed, but the Holy Well is as strong as ever in all its purity, ever gushing and throwing up 85 hogsheads of water per minute, as brilliantly clear as possible. It is visited by numbers of persons, who test its efficacy by the enjoyment of restored health. As a cold bath, perhaps, it is unequalled. Small cabins are built for the convenience of persons wishing to bathe. There are several paper mills in the vicinity.

A short distance further on, concealed in a wood, is the seat of Lord Fielding, the views from which are exceedingly fine, particularly that towards the sea. The next object that attracts attention is *Christ Church*, situated on a delightful rural eminence above the estuary of the Dee.

MOSTYN QUAY and STATION.

Telegraph station at Rhyl, 10 miles.

This place has become of considerable importance from the collieries in the neighbourhood, producing about 70,000 tons annually, and which are considered the most extensive works in all the coal fields of Flintshire, and extend from east to west about twenty miles.

About half a mile on the left is *Mostyn Hall*, at which is the window through which Henry VII. escaped from Richard III., and the family pedigree, 42 feet in length, traced from Adam, the mansion of the late Hon. E. M. L. Mostyn, one of the oldest families in North Wales.

Leaving this station the train passes over Gwespyr Marsh, which was enclosed from the sea in 1811, On the right, and nearly in the centre of the estuary of the Dee, is situated *Hilbree Island*, and in the same direction *Hoylake*, the extreme point of the peninsula of Wirral, in Cheshire.

The village of Gwespyr, celebrated for its quarries of freestone, is situated on the hill to the left. The Custom House of Liverpool is built of the stone from these quarries.

Talacre, the beautiful seat of Sir Pyers Mostyn, Bart., is situated on a gentle eminence. It is a very splendid mansion with two fronts, and commands magnificent views of the sea. The village on the hill is *Gronant;* above which is the Observatory. On the right, close to the shore, is the life boat house.

PRESTATYN.

Telegraph station at Rhyl, 3¾ miles.

Here the country is flat, but extremely fertile in corn, especially wheat, and continues so as far as Rhuddlan, and thence along the coast to Abergele.

Proceeding onward we pass the village of *Melidan*, with its rural Church, on the left; close to which, under a rock, are situated the Talargoch Lead Mines, celebrated as having produced more lead ore than any other mine in the country during the last century, the quantity raised averaging 3,000 tons annually. The ruins of *Dyserth Castle*, built in Henry II.'s time, are in the vicinity; and a mile beyond which is *Bodryddon*, the ancient seat of the Conways, situated in a fine forest.

RHYL.

Population, 1,563. A telegraph station.

Hotels.—The Mostyn Arms; the Royal; Belvoir; George; Queen's.

Market Day.—Tuesday. Supplied profusely every day in the season.

Rhyl is a fashionable watering place for the North Wallians and Liverpool people; it is reputed one of the best bathing places in Wales. The beauty of the scenery, salubrity of the air, and firmness of the sand, render it a place of considerable attraction to visitors from all parts of the kingdom. It is situated at the entrance of the celebrated vale of Clwyd, which extends twenty miles in length, and about ten miles in breadth, flanked on both sides with elevated hills. Snowdon can be seen.

In addition to the Hotels and Inns there are hundreds of elegant and respectable Lodging Houses, capable of affording excellent accommodation for visitors, at very moderate charges. There are bathing establishments and machines in abundance.

On the left of Rhyl are the celebrated range of British Posts, on the Clwydian Hills; established as a bulwark against an invading enemy.

VALE OF CLWYD.—Rhyl to Denbigh.

The district through which this line runs is remarkable for its picturesque beauty, and forms the threshold to some of the richest scenery in North Wales. Passing quickly the little station of Foryd, the arrival of the train is soon announced at the ancient town of

RHUDDLAN.

Fairs.—First Tuesday in February and May, and last Tuesday in July and October, and the Tuesday before the 25th December.

The town is situated on the eastern bank of the river Clwyd. Below it is *Rhuddlan Castle*, the ruins of which have a noble and imposing appearance from every point of view. The historical reminiscences connected with this fortress are of great interest, but too voluminous and ancient for our general readers. It was built by Llewellyn in 1015, and dismantled in 1646. In the church are tombs of Dean Shipley and the Conways. A mile from the castle is *Pengwern*, the seat of Lord Mostyn, most delightfully situated in the vale of Clwyd.

ST. ASAPH.

The city of St. Asaph is situated on a delightful eminence between the streams, near the confluence of the rivers Elwy and Clwyd. The principal attraction of this city is the *Cathedral*, which was first built of wood in 596, by St. Asaph, and rebuilt in 1770. The plan of the church is like most others, cruciform, with a square embattled tower rising from the intersection of the nave and transepts. The visitor on entering the sacred edifice will be struck with the solemnity which pervades the building; the chastened light, entering from the richly painted windows, evidently copied from those of Tintern Abbey, throws a softened tint over the Gothic stalls and chequered pavement of the choir, which to the eye capable of appreciating the beauty of the scene is highly pleasing and interesting. It contains tombs of Bishops ap Owen in 1512, and Barrow, the uncle of the celebrated Boac Barrow. The most eminent prelates of this see were Parry, Morgan (who translated the Bible into Welsh), Tanner, Beveridge, and Horsley.

The *Episcopal Palace* is an ancient one, rebuilt by the late bishop. The neighbourhood of St. Asaph is studded with a variety of gentlemen's seats, among which are *Pengwern*, Lord Mostyn; *Kinmel*, Lord Dinorben; and *Bodelwyddan*, Sir J. Williams, Bart

DENBIGHSHIRE.

Trefnant Station.

DENBIGH.

Hotels.—Bull; Crown.

The situation of this town from a distance is very imposing, lying as it does on the side of a rocky eminence, the top of which is crowned with the ruins of a castle founded in the reign of Edward I. It was blown up with gunpowder after the restoration of Charles II. The prospect from its ruins is of a magnificent character.

Chester & Holyhead Main Line continued.

Rhyl to Conway.

Upon leaving the Rhyl station the line proceeds on an embankment and drawbridge over the river Foryd. The extensive tract of land on the left is the celebrated spot where the battle of Rhuddlan Marsh took place in 785; this marsh was secured from the encroachments of the sea in 1799, enclosing about 27,000 acres of sandy loam land.

The village on the hill is called *St. George, or Llan St. Sior.*

ABERGELE.

Population, 2,858.

Telegraph station at Rhyl, 4¼ miles.

Hotel.—The Bee.

Market Day.—Saturday.

Fairs.—Feb. 12th, April 2nd, day before Holy Thursday, June 18th, October 9th. and Dec. 6th.

This station is close to the sea side, and at a little distance from the town. Its situation is very beautiful, the Clwydian range of hills forming a most picturesque and varied back ground to it; and *Gwrych Castle*, the elegant seat of Lloyd Bamford Hesketh, Esq., adding a peculiar charm to the whole.

It consists of only one wide street, but the salubrity of the air, and its sea shore, render it a favourite watering place for bathing. The scenery in the neighbourhood is magnificent, and is adorned with gentlemen's seats and thickly-wooded parks. In the vicinity are British and Roman camps, Cefn Oge cave, where Richard II. lay concealed until betrayed to Bolingbroke by Percy, and the Lysfaen telegraph 709 feet high, which communicates with Liverpool.

From Abergele the railway keeps close to the sea side for some distance, and then winds round to Conway. On proceeding onward from the Abergele station, we observe some huge rocks on the right, some miles before us, which are called the Great Orme's Head, a high promontory, projecting from the main land into the sea. We next pass the village of *Llandulas*, situated in a glen surrounded with lime-stone rocks. Nearly 100,000 tons of stone are extracted from the quarries here, and shipped annually to all parts of the country.

On emerging from the Penmaen Rhos tunnel, we see the village of *Colwyn* on the left; and further on up the valley, that of *Llanelian*, celebrated for its Cursing Well or Ffynnon Eilian.

Further on towards the shore, is the village of *Llandrilio*, formerly the residence of a British King.

Proceeding onwards on the left is seen the newly erected mansion of Sir Thomas Erskine, Bart. The line then passes through the small vale Mochdre, and winding round towards Conway we approach the river, where a most magnificent landscape presents itself. The fine old town of *Conway*, with its ancient castles, walls, and towers, appears in front, and the vast range of the Carnarvonshire mountains forming a back ground, has a beautiful effect. The line runs on an embankment several hundred yards parallel with the turnpike road, and then crosses the broad expanse of the river, through the tubular bridge, that wonder of modern engineering skill, and after a few seconds of darkness we emerge into daylight, beneath the lofty shattered walls of Conway Castle. Sweeping round the base of the castle on a circle, the railway glides on and enters the town of Conway, under a pointed arch constructed in the old walls of the town. This arch gives gre t picturesqueness of effect to the station, which adjoins it; and the castellated character of the wall is preserved by the battlements upon it. The station is an extremely handsome and well-designed building, in the Elizabethan style, with gabled wings, rising in steps, and projecting from the main portion.

CONWAY.

Population, 2,105. A telegraph station.

Hotel.—Castle.

Market Day.—Friday.

Fairs.—March 26th, April 30th, June 30th, August 10th, September 10th, and October 20th.

The ancient town of Conway is within the walls that were erected at the same time as the castle, and which are ornamented with circular towers. Although not a manufacturing town, it has always been a place of some importance.

The vale through which the river Conway flows, is remarkable for its beauty and fertility. Its luxuriant pastures, corn fields, and groves, are finely contrasted with the bleak appearance of the Snowdon mountain, which towers in frowning majesty above it.

Conway Cast'e, which belongs to the Marquis of Hertford, stands on a rock which rises considerably above the river. It was built in 1284, by King Edward I., to check the frequent revolts of the Welsh. The walls are of enormous thickness, and defended by eight massive round towers. The great hall of the castle measures 130 feet in length. The King's Chamber, as it is called, occupying one of the circular towers contiguous to the river, has a very pretty Got ic window, which seems to be the only part of the castle where any degree of ornament has been attempted. Richard II., when he fled from Ireland, in 1339, took refuge in this castle, where he agreed with the Earl of Northumberland and the Archbishop of Canterbury, to resign the crown to the Duke of Lancaster. From this circumstance arose the civil wars which desolated the country for so long a period. In *St. Mary's* church is a carved black font, screen, stained glass window, and tomb of Nicholas Hookes, whose father had 41 children, and his wife brought him 27.

The most favourable view of the castle and bridge is obtained a few hundred yards higher up the river, on the same side. Here it is seen boldly projecting in the foreground, with the beautiful new suspension bridge attached. Part of the town appears on the left, while the mouth of the river, open to the sea, forms the distance, which, with the vessels of various descriptions gliding on the surface, forms one of the most charming pictures that the ima ; nation can conceive. There are several very attractive places in the neighbourhood of Conway, and a traveller may spend several days very pleasantly here in making excursions to the various places in the vicinity, viz., to the ruins of *Gannock Cast'e*, the walks of Gloddaeth, the Vale of Llanrwst, &c., &c.

LLANRWST.

Hotel.—The Gwydir Arms.

Llanrwst, once noted for its Welsh harp makers, lies on the east bank of the river Conway, about 12 miles from Conway, and is situated in one of the prettiest spots of North Wales. It ought not to be overlooked.

The iron *Tubu'ar Bridge*, erected in 1848 by Stephenson, over the Conway, is one of the most unique examples of engineering skill ever imagined or carried into execution. Though inferior in length and weight to the Britannia Bridge, yet being built on precisely the same principles, and raised to its destined site by the same power, it may, from the circumstance of its h ving been the *first* erected, be deemed an *original* idea, beautifully carried out to its fullest extent in its mighty contemporary. The tubular viaduct over the Conway consists of two tubes, placed in juxta-position, one for the up, and the other for the down trains, each of them measuring 400 feet in length, and weighing 1300 tons. Its section is nearly rectangular, with a slight arch at the top to prevent the accumulation of rain. Its walls are formed of a series of iron plates, composed entirely of hard wrought iron, varying from half an inch to an inch in thickness; the greater strength being in the middle.

ST. GEORGE'S HARBOUR.

Conway to Llandudno.

The distant landscapes and marine views presented to the eye of the tourist as he passes along this little line, commanding as it does the full scope of the beautiful Bay of Beaumaris, are of a most varied and interesting character. In ten minutes after passing the junction the arrival of the train is announced at

LLANDUDNO.

This delightful place has now become one of great importance as a summer resort. It is situated $3\frac{1}{2}$ miles from Conway, on a promontory between the Bays of Conway and Llandudno. The water is very clear, and affords excellent bathing, and being protected on the north by the Great Orme's Head, the air is peculiarly salubrious. The old Church (dedicated to St. Tudno) stands on the mountain side. A new church was erected about 1839, but this is found much too small for the increasing requirements of the bathing season. There is also a fine market, well supplied with fish, vegetables, and in fact everything calculated to render the comforts of a temporary so ourn complete.

The scenery around is most picturesque, particularly so from the promenade which skirts the outer margi of the top of the mountain, at a height of 67 feet. The views from this point are of the most fascinating character. The town itself is in the very heart of the most attractive parts of North Wales. It can boast of some good water excursions, embracing some curious and picturesque caves both on the Great and Little Orme's Head.

Chester & Holyhead Main Line continued.

Conway to Bangor.

Upon leaving Conway station, the line proceeds through a tunnel under one of the towers, and thence through some deep cuttings to Conway Marsh. We then cross the Holyhead road, and pass old Conway race course on the right. Looking across the estuary the traveller will have a fine view of the ruins of Gannock Castle and Great Orme's Head. The railway then skirts the sea shore again, until it enters Penmaen Bach Tunnel, on emerging from which we perceive Penmaen Mawr, the terminating point of the Carnarvonshire range of mountains. On the summit of this hill are the ruins of an extensive fortress. It is surrounded by strong treble walls, within each of which are the foundation sites of more than 100 round towers, with ample room for 20,000 men.

PENMAEN MAWR station; the mountain is 1,540 feet high, and Penmaen Bach hill, 837 feet.

Proceeding onwards we pass in succession Penmaen Mawr tunnel, and Meini Herion, one of the most remarkable mountains in all Snowdon. On the right is *Puffin Island*, inhabited by vast numbers of birds called puffins. The railway continues for some time further along the sea shore.

The village of ABER, celebrated as being the last place where Llewellyn contended against Edward I., is a most delightful spot; having on the right the view of the Irish Channel, in front, Beaumaris and its wooded environs, and to the left the turrets of *Penrhyn Castle.* From this village, a deep and romantic glen, nearly 3 miles in length, forms the avenue to *Rhaiadr Mawr*, a celebrated cataract. The prospects in the neighbourhood afford views of most picturesque beauty, comprising the Snowdon mountains on the one hand, the Menai straits and the coast of Anglesea on the other, all together forming a rich panoramic view of splendid scenery.

The railway is then carried over the Ogwen river and valley by two extensive viaducts, commanding beautiful views of the surrounding scenery.

The train shortly enters the Bangor tunnel, through Bangor mountain, and, on emerging from it, arrives at

BANGOR.

A telegraph station.

HOTELS.—The George *(see view)*, Bangor Ferry, Miss Roberts, is a first-class house, delightfully situated between Bangor and Menai Bridge, and is deservedly celebrated for its excellent arrangements.

The British *(see view)*, W. Dew, a favorite establishment, highly spoken of for its arrangements and general management. It has one of the finest coffee-rooms in North Wales.

MARKET DAY.—Friday. FAIRS.—April 5th, June 25th, September 16th, and October 28th.

A cathedral town and bathing place in Carnarvonshire, North Wales, near Snowdon, and only $2\frac{1}{4}$ miles from the Britannia Bridge. You enter it by a tunnel 3,000 feet long. It is an excellent resting place, not only for the fine mountain scenery of this quarter, but for the *Britannia* and *Menai Bridges*, the *Penrhyn Slate Quarries*, *Beaumaris Castle*, and other excursions, by road, railway, and boat. More than 50,000 persons come here in the season, so that lodgings at such times are high and difficult to be had. About 40 years ago there were only 90 houses, now there are 920, to a population of 6,338.

The "city" is chiefly a long street, winding about under the rocks towards *Garth Point*, where there is the public promenade, besides a ferry over the Lavan Sands to Beaumaris, on the Anglesea side. The peaks round Snowdon, and the rocky headlands of Penmaen Mawr and Orme's Head are in view.

Among the buildings are the *Assembly Rooms*, *Shone's Library*, *County Dispensary*, *Glynne's Grammar School*, and a small plain *Cathedral*, 233 feet long, with a low tower, not older than the 15th century—the former one having been burnt by Owen Gwyndwr or Glendower. It was originally founded by St. Deiniol, as early as 550, whence Bangor claims to be the oldest diocese in Wales. The income is £4,000 per annum. This argument was used when there was a talk of suppressing it some years back. There are tombs of two Welsh princes, Gryfydd (or Griffith) ap Cynan and Owen Gwyndwr; and a new painted window placed here by Dean Cotton, through whose exertions the church has been restored. It is the parish church to the town, the service being in Welsh In the library is the missal and anthem book of Bishop Anian, who held the see in Edward I.'s time. Another bishop was Hoadley, appointed by George I.; he preached a sermon here from the text, "My kingdom is not of this world," so displeasing to the high church party, that it gave rise to a long dispute—the celebrated Bangorian Controversy.

A British camp and part of a castle may be seen on two points, near Friar's School. Further south is *Vaenol*, the seat of the late Assheton Smith, a mighty hunter in Hampshire, and owner of the Dinorwic Slate Quarries, under Snowdon. About 30,000 tons are annually sent down to Port Dinorwic by railway, and 1,000 hands employed. Opposite, on the Anglesea side, is *Plâs Newydd*, the seat of the Marquis of Anglesea, for many months the residence of the Duchess of Kent and Princess Victoria. It has the Anglesea pillar, fixed on Waterloo day in 1816, with a cairn, and an immense Druid cromlech. Anglesea was the last and most famous seat of Druid worship.

One mile east of Bangor, is *Penrhyn Castle*, the seat of Colonel Pennant, proprietor of the famous Penrhyn slate quarries, worth £70,000 a year: it is an extensive Norman pile, built by Wyatt, of Anglesea marble; and open on Fridays to the public. As may be supposed, many curious articles in slate are to be seen. The park fence, seven miles round, is all of that fabric.

The *Penrhyn Slate Quarries* are about five miles up the river Ogwen, under Snowdon, following the tramway, and well deserve a visit. You pass Llandegai Gothic Church, with the tomb of Lord Penrhyn, a great benefactor of this neighbourhood, who made the slate works what they are. He spent £170,000 on the shipping port alone. An inclined plane leads up to the edge of the vast mountain, on the sides of which above 2,000 hands are employed in hacking and splitting. The slates are trimmed and piled in thousands according to their size, under the names of duchesses, countesses, ladies, &c.; and are used for roofing, gravestones, schools, and other purposes. They have a fine smooth grain; many of the chapels and houses about here are wholly built of that material. The slates are brought down by rail, and shipped at Port Penrhyn (close by) to all parts of the world, to the extent of 70,000 tons yearly. The gross receipts may be calculated at £150,000 a year.

From the slate works the road ascends the wild pass of *Nant Francon* or Beaver valley, between the Glyder Fawr and *Carnedd Dafydd*, the latter a peak of the Snowdon range, 3,420 feet high. *Carnedd Llewelyn* to the north of it is 3,469 feet. The road crosses the Ogwen a the *Benglog Falls*, which are at the outlet of Llyn or *Lake Ogwen*, where a stream joins them from *Llyn Idwal* situate in a most gloomy hollow up the sides of *Glyder Fawr*, a peak to the south 3,300 feet high (you may wind over it past a gap called the *Twll Dû* or Devil's Kitchen and Llyn-y-Cwm to Llanberis). It is a difficult path, but offers fine prospects. From Ogwen lake the road descends to

Capel Curig a pretty spot on the *Llagay*, near the two *Mymbyr Lakes*, 14 miles from Bangor

HOTEL.—Capel Curig—(See view on plate.) This establishment is deservedly popular, and may with confidence be recommended. Mrs. J. Williams, Pro. From this Hotel the ascent of Snowdon is considered very easy, and offers the additional inducement for preferring this route, of perhaps the finest scenery in the whole of North Wales. Ladies commonly accomplish the ascent on ponies, the roads being good. The views of Snowdon are here truly magnificent. Hence down the pretty *Llagwy* past *Rhayadr-y-Wennol fall* to *Bettws-y-Coed* in a green sheltered nook of the Conway six miles further, a resort well known to anglers and artists.

From the Slate Works to the tops of *Carnedd Dafydd* and *Carnedd Llewelyn* is a fatiguing walk of four to six or seven miles; but there is a grand prospect from both. To *Delwyddellan Castle*, under *Moel Siabod*, 2,870 feet, and thence on to the vale of *Ffestiniog* requires a walk of 18 miles from *Capel Curig*.

The carriage road winds round the east base of Snowdon, passing *Trifaen* (so called from the three stones 15 feet high on the top) and the *Glyder Bach* or Little Glyder, 3,000 feet high, and joined to *Glyder Fawr*, or Great Glyder, by the *Waenoer*, a desolate plain half a mile wide, covered with weather beaten stones. *Moel Siabod* or Shabod is on the east side. At *Nant-y-Gwrydinn*, a road branches off to *Beddgelert*, 12 miles from Capel Curig, passing *Llyn Gwynant*, &c. Following the main road through Snowdon you come to the famous *Llanberis Pass*, a narrow and rugged defile, about three miles long, between the perpendicular cliffs of Glyder Fawr on the north and Snowdon on the south. It is united by the Sciont, which runs down to Carnarvon, and resembles the wild pass of Glencoe in Argyleshire, or the Gap of Dunloe near Killarney. Blocks of rock lie about on all sides. One immense heap called the *Cromlech* was turned into a sort of house by a herdwoman. It is near the Gorphwysfa or resting place at the top of the ascent from Capel Curig.

Two miles further, in a quiet glen, is

LLANBERIS.

HOTELS.—The Victoria; the Dolbadarn.

Here is a pretty later English church, enclosing the original timber structure dedicated to St Peris. It stands near *Llyn Peris*, in the very heart of the mountains, which appear here in all their native majesty. From Llanberis to the top of Snowdon is 3½ miles. Two miles further, between Lake Peris and Lake Badarn, there is an old ruined castle with which the Britons used to guard the pass, behind which the *Ceunant Mawr Fall* rolls down from Moel Aeliau. On the opposite side under the Glyder Fawr are the *Dinorwic Slate Quarries*, taking name from the Roman fort of Dinas Dinorwig lower down.

From *Dolbadarn* to the top of *Snowdon* is five to six miles, or a two hours' walk. Ponies and guides may be hired at Llanberis, but a stout pair of legs is the best help for those who choose to dispense with such assistants. Start early in the morning when the air is cool. For those who wish to see the sun rise a hut called the Snowdon Hotel, with two or three beds, is built on the top; but it is frequently obscured by clouds. Snowdon is composed of four great ridges of slate and porphyry, viz: *Moel Aeliau* on the west, 2,371 feet, *Clawdd-Côch* or the Red Dyke on the south, 2,473 feet, *Y-Lliwed* on the east and *Crib-y-Distul* or the Dripping Point on the north, 3,420 feet. These are separated by vast precipitous cwms (sounded *coombes*) or hollows, 1,000 feet deep in some parts; and they unite in one peak marked by an ordnance signal pole, called *Moel-y-Wyddfa*, the Conspicuous Head, 3,570 feet above the sea; the highest point in Wales or England. This is Snowdon proper. Snowdon is a fanciful English name for the whole ridge of the Carnarvonshire mountains. The Welsh call it Eryri or Eagle Top. It is 800 or 1,000 feet below the line of perpetual snow, which in reality lies here only from November to April.

The path from Dolbadarn is along the *Crib-y-Dystul* ridge, past *Cwm Brwynog*, and *Clogwyn-Dû'-r-Arddu* rock, over a lake and near the cliffs where the lamented Rev. Mr. Starr fell over in 1856. Then comes a steep part called *Llechwedd-y-Rŷ*, overlooking the Llanberis pass, and 1½ mile from the top. This is seven yards across, part of which is taken up by the Snowdon hotel; here coffee and a good fire may be obtained. If the weather is clear you may see the Wicklow mountains, the Isle of Man, the Yorkshire hills, &c., with above 20 lakes in North Wales, all spread out like a map.

Other starting points for Snowdon are from *Beddgelert*, over *Clawdd Coch*, six miles; *Llyn Cwellyn* on the Carnarvon Road, four miles; and from *Capel Curig*, by *Cwm Dyli* and *Llyn Llydiaw*, about 14 miles. The last, though the longest and most fatiguing, is said to be the finest route. Rare mountain plants are found on Snowdon.

BEAUMARIS.

Population, 2,599.

Hotel.—Bulkeley Arms.

Beaumaris, the capital of Anglesea, is beautifully situated at the entrance to the Menai Straits, about 4 miles from Bangor. It has remains of a castle, built in the thirteenth century by Edward I. The chapel and the great hall, 70 feet long, in which Queen Victoria (then princess) with the Duchess of Kent her mother, attended an Eisteddfod or Bardic meeting in 1832, are still in a state of preservation. *Baron Hall* is the fine seat of Sir R. B. W. Bulkeley, Bart.; in the grounds is the curious stone coffin of King John's daughter, Joan, named Llewellyn ap Jorworth, who founded a priory, of which there are remains at *Llanvaes*. Further on are *Penmon Priory* and the *Mona* (Mon is the Welsh name for Anglesea) *Marble Quarries*. Then *Puffin Island Light*, near which the *Rothesay Castle* steamer was wrecked in 1831, and 100 lives lost. Further on to the west there is a fine viev from a large camp called *Bwrdd Arthur* or Arthur's Round Table.

CARNARVON BRANCH.

Bangor to Carnarvon and Nantlle.

The stations on this branch are Treborth, Port Dinorwic (here are the slate quarries belonging to T. A. Smith, Esq., where 1,000 men are constantly employed), and Griffith's Crossing.

CARNARVON.

Population, 8,674.

A telegraph station.

Hotels.—Royal Sportsman; Uxbridge Arms.

Market Day.—Saturday.

It occupies the site of a Roman town called *Segontium*, of which there are various relics in the museum. The well-preserved castle, built between 1284 and 1320, is the most interesting object; it covers 2½ acres. There are remains of the gateway, the Queen's gates and the Eagle tower in which it is stated Edward II., the first Prince of Wales, was born. It should be mounted for the view. The outer walls are 10 feet thick and guarded by thirteen towers variously shaped. One of them is the town prison.

Hence the tourist may if he wish extend his railway journey *via* the stations of Bont Newydd, Pwllheli Road, Groes Lon, and Pen-y-groes, the station for Portmadoc, to Nantlle.

Bangor to Holyhead.

Upon quitting Bangor station we almost immediately enter the Egyptian arch of Belmont Tunnel, under the Carnarvon mountains, on emerging from which we have a beautiful view of the Menai Straits, with its accompaniments, Telford's Suspension Bridge and the Britannia Tubular Bridge. In viewing the massive towers and lengthened tubes of the

VIEWS OF NINE OF THE PRINCIPAL HOTELS IN NORTH WALES.

Royal Victoria Hotel Llanberris

Capel Curig Hotel

Victoria Hotel Llanrwst

Royal Hotel Holyhead

Penrhyn Arms Hotel Bangor

George Hotel Bangor Ferry

Royal Sportsman Hotel Caernarvon

Bee Hotel Abergelle

British Hotel Bangor

latter, its heavy and colossal proportions stand out in striking contrast with the slender and gossamer-like components of its older rival, the Menai Bridge, which is used for ordinary vehicles and foot passengers, both structures being situated within a mile of each other.

MENAI BRIDGE,

Two miles from Bangor, across the narrow channel which cuts off Anglesea, is best seen from the water below, above which it rises 100 feet, at high tide. It was built by Telford, between 1819 and 1826, to complete the coach route to Holyhead. From pier to pier (each 153 feet high) the main part of the bridge is 550 feet long, and 20 broad, including a carriage road of 12 feet. The first mail coach drove over this in a wintry storm. It is suspended from 16 chains, each having a total length of 1,715 feet, and fastened into 60 feet of solid rock on each side. The total weight of iron is 650 tons; it would bear about 1,300 tons. It is still the longest suspension bridge in this country, but is exceeded by those at Freibourg, in Switzerland (870 feet between the piers, and 167 high), across the Dordogne, near Bordeaux, and over the Danube, at Pesth.

THE BRITANNIA TUBULAR BRIDGE. This magnificent structure was made to carry the Chester and Holyhead Railway across the Menai Straits. Like the beautiful bridge at Conway, it is on the tubular principle, but on a much grander scale, and is one of the most ingenious, daring, and stupendous monuments of engineering skill which modern times have seen attempted. As this gigantic and amazing structure now spans the Menai, connecting the two opposite shores of Carnarvon and the Isle of Anglesea, we may justly express our admiration of it by calling it Mr. Stephenson's *chef d'œuvre*, but this would scarcely do justice to the remarkable bridge or its great architect, we therefore think it proper to add the following details:—

The idea of carrying a railway through a vast tube, originated with Mr. Robert Stephenson. It having been found extremely difficult to construct an arch of the immense span required; and as chain bridges were not sufficiently firm for the purpose of railway traffic, Mr. Stephenson suggested the application of iron tubes to pass from pier to pier. These tubes may be described as the double barrel of a gun on an immense scale, through which the trains pass and repass, at unslackened speed, as if it were a tunnel through solid rock on land, instead of being elevated a hundred and four feet above the sea. The suggestion of Mr. Stephenson was adopted, and the Britannia Bridge now forms an imperishable monument to his fame. The construction of the bridge, however, attracted crowds of engineers and others to watch the progress of the stupendous work, and to behold the means by which Mr. Stephenson triumphed over all the difficulties he had to encounter in a task of such magnitude. "They saw, day by day, with the liveliest satisfaction, the patient putting together of the tubes, the marvellous facility with which they were floated, and the wonderful machinery by which they were elevated to the destined altitude, until the whole was completed and the first trains run through it without its deflecting more than an inch, and there it still stands, scarcely bending to the heaviest trains, stretching itself as it basks in the warmth of the noonday sun, gathering itself back under the chill of night, bending towards every gleam of sunshine, or shrinking from every passing cloud."

The Britannia Bridge takes its name from a rock which rises about the middle of the stream, and which is bare at low water. Without this advantage the erection of the pier would have been impossible, in consequence of the strength of the current and the local difficulties. The Britannia pier is built on this rock, and even with this advantage from nature the span from each of the principal piers is 463 feet; the entire length of the bridge, 1,560 feet; and the headway at high water 100 feet, which leaves sufficient room for ships to pass under. We close our description with a brief summary of the leading statistics.

It is a wrought iron tube, made of plates riveted together; 104 feet above the water, 1,513 feet long, 14 feet wide (enough for two lines of railway), 26 feet high in the middle, and 19 feet at the sides, with a total weight of 11,400 tons. The total quantity of stone contained in the bridge is 1,400,000 cubic feet; the timber used in the various scaffoldings for the masonry platforms, for the erection of the tubes, &c., was 450,000 cubic feet. The centre pier is 230 feet high; through this it passes by an opening 45 feet long, which, with 460 feet on each side, makes the main part of the bridge 965 feet long. There are two other piers of less height. At each end are carved lions, 25 feet long. Summer heat lengthens the whole fabric about a *foot*. It was begun in 1846, and the first train went through on the 5th of March, 1850. The great tubes being first riveted together, were floated out on pontoons, and then raised by hydraulic presses into their place. These presses were shown at the Great Exhibition. A pillar, near Llanfair Church, is a memorial of the only accident which occurred in the prosecution of this remarkable work. From Bangor it is approached by the Belmont tunnel, 2,172 feet long.

Resuming our route from the Britannia Bridge the train enters thence into the Island of Anglesea, passing over an embankment, at the end of which is the Marquis of Anglesea's column, erected to commemorate the eminent military services of the late venerable Marquis of Anglesea. This island is 24 miles long and 17 broad, containing 4 market towns and 74 parishes; square miles, 402: population, 49,000, who jointly return one member. The soil is fertile; the chief products are grain and cattle.

The railway, after passing the station of LLANFAIR, now runs parallel for some miles with the Holyhead road, passing *Plas Pen Myndd*, the ancient seat of the ancestors of the Royal House of Tudor.

Further on the line gradually curves in a south-western direction, near which is Tre'r Dryu, or the habitation of the Arch Druid, abounding in rude memorials of the religious rites practised by our forefathers.

The line from GAERWEN crosses the river Cefni, on a noble viaduct of 19 arches, and shortly after enters the Trefdraeth Tunnel, cut through some very hard rock, on emerging from which a fine view of Carnarvon Bay presents itself, across which are seen the Carnarvonshire hills, called the Rivals.

The line now traverses the parish of Llangadwaladr, and arrives at

BODORGAN.

Telegraph station at Bangor, 13 miles.

On leaving this station the ancient town of Aberffraw may be seen on our left. In the neighbourhood of the town there is a splendid lake, two miles in circumference, called *Llyn Coron*, much frequented by anglers during the summer. Proceeding onwards through ordinary cuttings, over embankments and bridges in succession, we again come in sight of the Holyhead Road, and pass over the river Alaw, on the banks of which, in 1813, was found buried the sepulchral urn containing the remains of Broniventhe, the daughter of Llyr (King Lear), and aunt to the great Caractacus.

The line from Ty Croes runs parallel with the Stanley embankment, which crosses the sands and an arm of the sea. On the right is the mansion of the Hon. W. Owen Stanley, M.P., in *Penrhos Park*, and a quarter of a mile east of which is Penrhyn, a cliff projecting into the sea.

Beyond Valley station, to the right again, are some ancient forts and an obelisk monument, the latter erected to the memory of the late Captain Skinner, formerly master of one of the packets on this station, who lost his life in 1838. We shortly after arrive at

HOLYHEAD (Holyhead Island).

A telegraph station. Population, 5,622.

Hotels.—The Royal; the Castle.

Bankers.—North and South Wales; National Provincial; Williams and Co.

Market Day.—Saturday.

Holyhead, so called from a monastery founded by St. Gybi (sounded *Kubby*) in the sixth century, is the chief packet station for Ireland, and stands on Holy Island, on a bay between it and the west side of Anglesea, in North Wales, 64 miles from Dublin. The rail crosses the narrow strait or traeth dividing the island and main land, on an embankment, close to that which supports Telford's coach road, constructed in 1815, and reaches Bangor by way of Shrewsbury, Corwen, and Bettws-y-Coed. Holy Island is about 7 miles long, with a rugged coast, and mines of mona, or variegated marble, sometimes called verd-antique. *Rhoscolyn Church*, in the south, has a good view of its barren hills. The town, which contains 5,622 inhabitants, has little to show beyond its old church, in the midst of a Roman camp, and a triumphal arch, near the pier, commemorating the passing of George IV., on his visit to Ireland in 1821. Its port, however, deserves particular attention. The present tidal harbour lies within two piers, made by Rennie, the longest of which, opposite Salt Island, is 1,080 feet; from whence the packets start, and here 150 vessels may find shelter; but as it is small, and dries at low water, it is not of sufficient capacity. But the Great Harbour of Refuge, which Rendel commenced in 1849, and is now in course of construction, will enclose this harbour, as well as a great part of the bay, or about 320 acres, with deep water, not less than 6 fathoms' throughout, and room for 400 sail. The principal breakwater, that to the north, will be 5,000 feet long, 170 broad, and 30 above the bottom of the sea, in the deepest part. A smaller one, or pier, will be 2,100 feet long, and broad. These run out towards the Platter Rocks, having a width of three quarters of a mile, and are built of solid stone, from the Holyhead Hill to the west of the town, which is 710 feet high to the camp at top (Caer Gybi), and from which a tram rail brings down 25,000 tons of that material a week. The rock is schistus quartz, dislodged by galvanic explosions, and about 6,000,000 tons have been already sunk into the sea. The works were visited by the Queen and Prince Albert in 1853

All this coast is worth visiting; excursions may be made to the following:—On the west side of Holyhead Hill are the North and South Stack Rocks, hollowed into caves and swarming with wild birds. The Parliament Cave in the north stack is 70 feet high. On the south stack is a lighthouse 200 feet high, built in 1809, joined to the mainland by a small suspension bridge 110 feet long, towards which you descend the face of the cliff by the Stairs, 380 steps, altogether. The rock is frequently variegated, or greasy to the touch, like soapstone. The rail, on its way to Bangor, passes near the south coast of Anglesea, where you may inspect the curious little churches of *Llangwffen* and *Llanddwyn*, each on an island; also *Aberffraw* the decayed capital of the early North Wales princes, and *Bodorgan*, a seat of the Meyricks. From Holyhead, along the north coast, you pass *Skerries Light*, on a dreary rock: till 1835 it belonged to a private person, who sold it to the Trinity Board for £445,000! Such was the enormous revenue derived from passing ships. Then the three Mouse Rocks, off Cemmaes Bay, where the *Olinda* steamer was wrecked in 1854, in her passage outward from Liverpool. The rocks are high here. Next comes *Amlwch*, which has a harbour cut out of the slaty cliffs, for exporting copper from the famous *Pary's Mine*, first worked in March, 1768, and worth at one time £300,000 a year. It is in the side of a hill, two miles south of the town. Lead and silver are also found; and there are factories for alum and vitriol, from the sulphate of copper.

Holyhead Harbour of Refuge.—As the shortest and most direct route from London to Dublin, the passage *viâ* Holyhead has always engaged the attention of Government; so that before the introduction of railways, they had caused to be formed one of the finest mail-coach roads in the kingdom: this great work, executed by Telford, the renowned engineer, in the beginning of the present century, was considered his *chef d'œuvre*, with the graceful suspension bridge spanning the Menai Straits, and the road terminating in Holyhead, at what is now called the Old Harbour, from whence sailing packets, carrying the mails, took their departure direct for Kingstown (Dublin). The next road brought to bear upon this port, with the same object (that of shortening the distance as much as possible between the two capitals), was an iron one; and the Chester and Holyhead Railway Company, with a spirit and energy commensurate with the object to be obtained, overcame all difficulties; and, with Mr. Peto (now Sir

CONWAY SUSPENSION BRIDGE

DEE VIADUCT VALE OF LLANGOLLEN

THE BRITANNIA TUBULAR BRIDGE

B. BARRETT, BROS.
184 OXFORD STREET, 184
LONDON.

The most varied assortment of Railway and Continental

TRUNKS,

OVERLAND

AND

AIR-TIGHT CASES

FOR

INDIA.

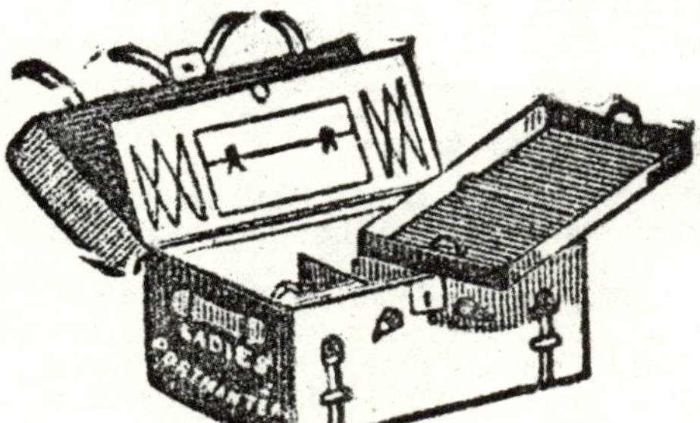

LADIES' PORTMANTEAUS.

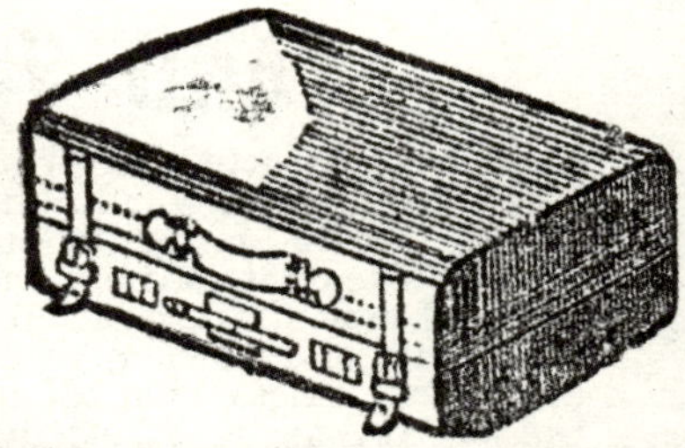

GENTLEMEN'S PORTMANTEAUS

A MOST NOTABLE PECULIARITY OF

BARRETT BROTHERS'

Overland Trunks

Is their extreme Lightness, an advantage entirely unattended by loss of Strength.

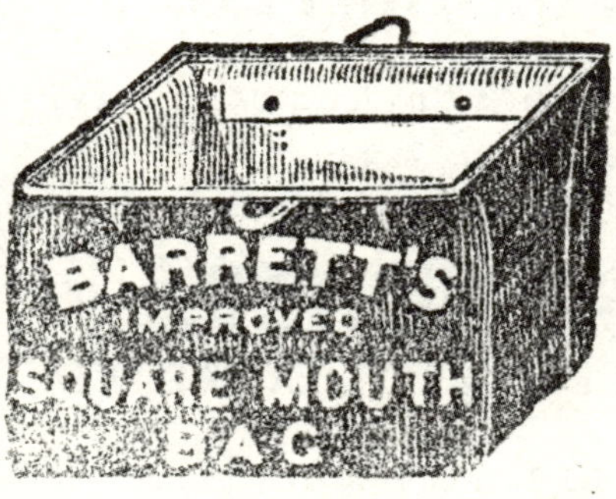

PLEASE NOTE

THE

ADDRESS,

184, OXFORD STREET, W.

Illustrated Catalogues forwarded on receipt of one Stamp.

[32-Lo.

S. M. Peto, Bart.) as their indefatigable chairman, and Mr. Stephenson as their engineer, they constructed the now world-known Britannia Tubular Bridge, through which the mails and passengers from London rapidly pass, at a level of 100 feet above the tide, then across the island of Anglesea to Holyhead Harbour, where the Company's and Mail Steam Packets are waiting to receive them, and a sea passage of four hours and a half (the 64 miles intervening) lands them in safety in Ireland.

The increasing importance of this station, together with its applicability, induced the Board of Admiralty to select this spot for the formation of one of the national Harbours of Refuge, and that work is now being carried out. The harbour is formed by a breakwater to the northward, about 5,000 feet in length, leaving the shore in the form of a bent arm. extending outwards from Soldier's Point and the Platter's Buoy; and another pier running out from the opposite shore, or Salt Island, eastward, a distance of 2,000 feet; these two arms enclosing an area 316 acres, three quarters of a mile long, and with a depth of six or seven fathoms, at low water, will, when completed, make one of the finest artificial refuge harbours and packet stations in the world.

The once small town of Holyhead, situated in a remote corner of Anglesea, will speedily become an important place. Already we have shown the continual attention given to it, as lying in the direct route from London to Dublin (which traffic and communication the London and North Western Company is year by year increasing and developing); and, when the new harbour is completed the town will still rise more into importance from having been selected as the point for carrying out a work of which England may well be proud—a harbour achieved on a most dangerous and unprotected coast, offering a free shelter to vessels of every nation, and a haven of refuge to the mariner of every flag.

Holyhead to Dublin.

THE passage across from Holyhead to Kingstown, a distance of 64 miles, is now generally performed in 4 to 6 hours, and the traveller has scarcely lost sight of the mountains of Carnarvon before those of Dublin and Wicklow become visible.

IRELAND.

THE entrance into the bay of Dublin unfolds one of the finest land and sea prospects ever beheld. On the right is the rugged hill of Howth, with its rocky bays, wanting only a volcano to render the surrounding scenery a fac-simile of the beautiful bay of Naples; whilst, nearer to the eye, at the extremity of a white line of masonry just fringing the sea, the light-house presents its alabaster front. On the left are the town of *Dalkey*, with its romantic rocks, mutilated castles, martello towers, elegant villas, and the picturesque town of *Dunleary*, whilst behind is seen a line of parks and plantations, above which the mountains of Wicklow ascend with the greatest majesty.

In the immediate neighbourhood of Kingstown, on the west side, are many excellent bathing-places. The sea here is singularly adapted for bathing. The sands are perfectly level; at least the eye cannot discern any declivity for a mile. When the tide is full, all these sands are covered to the depth of from two to three feet: when it is ebb-tide they are quite dry.

THE COUNTY OF DUBLIN, which returns two members, has its western limits formed by the Irish Sea, and the coast is rendered extremely picturesque in many parts by the bays and creeks into which it is broken. On the north and north-west it is bounded by the county of Meath. Part of the western border joins the county of Kildare, and, in the south, lie the mountainous tracts of Wicklow.

Except in the attractive varieties of its coasts, and the beauty of the mountainous district which borders the county of Wicklow, this county may be considered as possessing less diversity of natural scenery than many other parts of Ireland.

KINGSTOWN.

A telegraph station.

HOTEL.—Rathbone's.

Rates of Porterage.—1s. to 1s. 6d. for a quantity of luggage; 6d. for a portmanteau and hat-case.

MARKET DAY.—Saturday.

REGATTA.—In August.

Kingstown to Dublin.

After traversing the Dublin and Kingstown railway, and stopping at the stations of SALTHILL, BLACKROCK, BOOTERSTOWN, and MERRION, we arrive at

DUBLIN.

A Submarine and Electric Telegraph station.

HOTELS.—Bilton. 56, Upper Sackville Street, Lewis Heinkey; Reynolds', 12, Upper Sackville Street, F. Reynolds; Tuthill's, 51, Dawson Street, William Tuthill; Morrison's, 1, Dawson Street, John Baker; for Families.

Commercial Buildings, 11, College Green, Henry Baker; Commercial, 23, Suffolk Street, B. Saunders; Wynn's, 35 and 36 Abbey Street, Mrs. Pascoe; Commercial Hotels.

Shelborne. Stephen's Green, Martin Burke; Gresham, 21 and 22, Upper Sackville Street, John Radley; Imperial, 21 and 22, Lower Sackville Street, James O'Toole (manager); Prince of Wales, 31, Lower Sackville Street —; Macken's, 12, Dawson Street, John Ennis; Hibernian, 48, Dawson Street, George Nesbitt; Anderson's, 32 and 33, College Green, Spadaccini; Jury's, 7 and 8. College Green, William Jury; Family and Commercial Hotels.

BANKERS.—J. B. Ball and Co.; Boyle, Son, and Co.; Robt. Gray and Co.; J. B. Kennedy and Co.; D. Latouche and Co.; Hibernian Joint Stock Banking Co.; Bank of Ireland; National Bank of Ireland; Provincial Bank of Ireland; Royal Bank of Ireland.

RAILWAY STATIONS.—Galway, or Great Western, near the Queen's Inns and Broadstone Harbour; Drogheda and Belfast, near the Custom House and the Galway line; Great Southern and Western, or Cork line, King's Bridge, a fine granite front;

Kingstown, in Westland Row; Wicklow, in Harcourt Road. The Irish gauge is 5¼ feet.

MARKET DAYS.—Monday and Thursday, for cattle and sheep; Tuesday and Saturday for hay, &c.

DUBLIN, the capital of Ireland, and the second city of the British Islands, on the Liffey (*dew lin*, or "black stream" in Irish), near Dublin Bay, 60 miles from Holyhead, and 292 miles from London. Population, 254,850. Two members of parliament for the city, and two more for the university. It is about 3 miles in diameter and 11 miles in circuit. The appearance of Dublin is very much improved of late years. Streets have been widened, new squares skilfully laid out, and many public monuments freed from buildings which concealed their beauties. The police is also better attended to, and commercial activity seems to have revived. But the most beautiful spectacle that can be presented to the eye of a stranger is the vast panorama which suddenly opens itself on Carlisle Bridge. In front lies the magnificent Sackville Street, with its monument, splendid hotels, and the column erected in honour of Nelson; on the left the fine quays of granite, with their handsome balustrade, which bound for several miles the dark waters of the Liffey; on the right, and almost within the reach of the observer, thousands of masts rise between the banks of the river, between two ranges of lofty houses, and, at the foot of that admirable building which, with its majestic portico, elegant colonnade, pavement of marble, and dome of bronze, more resembles a noble Venetian palace than a prosaic Custom House. From the heights of the Phœnix Park one also enjoys a splendid prospect. In the midst of a vast lawn rises the palace of the Viceroy, surrounded by a treble fringe of shrubs and exotic plants. In turning the view towards the Liffey, the prospect embraces the heavy masses of the old city, with its steeples and towers, the Hospital of Invalids, and the high mountains in the distance which enclose, as with a girdle, the county of Dublin. Except Irish poplins and coaches (at Hutton's factory), the manufactures are of no consequence; but the shipping trade is important and increasing, the port having been so much improved that large ships can come up to the quays which line both sides of the river. The tonnage belonging to the port is about 45,000, and the total customs 1¼ million; wine being a staple article of import. Guinness's stout, and Kinahan's L.L. (or Lord Lieutenant's) whisky, are both noted. A long sea wall and pier of three miles runs to Poolbeg lighthouse, commanding a view of the beautiful bay, which is 6 miles across, with a sweep of 15 or 16 miles; but the best points for viewing it are from the Hill of Howth (500 feet high), and Killiney Hill (470 feet), at the north and south extremities, looking down on the city, on Dalkey Island, Kingstown harbour, Blackrock bathing-place, and Clontarf, where Brian Boru beat the Danes (1014). Another view from Dunsink observatory. Perhaps the best view of Dublin is that from Carlisle Bridge, which embraces Sackville Street, the Nelson Pillar, the Four Courts, Custom House, Post Office, the Bank, and University on College Green. It contains many large and splendid buildings, but our limits prevent us from giving more than a list of the most striking. The eastern half is the newest and best built.

PUBLIC BUILDINGS.—The *Bank* is the most perfect building in Dublin, built in 1739, for the Irish parliament, in the Ionic style, 147 feet long. The old House of Peers has the Battle of the Boyne worked in tapestry, and Bacon's statue of George III., and the House of Commons is a circular room 55 feet across. The *Four Courts*, or Courts of Law, near Richmond Bridge, built between 1776 and 1800, by Corley and Gandon, a noble range 450 feet by 170, with a fine portico, and a dome 64 feet span. The *Custom House*, near the Drogheda terminus, built in 1791, by Gandon, cost more than half a million, and being too large for the shipping business only, the Poor Law Board and other boards, are quartered here. River front 375 feet long, and dome 125 feet high, with a figure of Hope at the top. The *Post Office*, built in 1818, by Johnston, 223 feet long, with an Ionic portico. The *Inns of Court*, near the Midland Railway terminus, 110 feet long. The *Royal Exchange*, on Cork Hill near the Castle, built in 1779, by Corley, a beautiful Corinthian pile 100 feet square. The *National Educational Buildings* are at Old Tyrone House, with excellent training school attached, which the Queen has visited. *Kilmainham Hospital*, or Irish Chelsea Hospital, founded in 1680, and built by Wren, is on a small scale, with but 250 soldiers. An old brick pile, about 300 feet square, with part of preceptory of Knights Templars in the chapel. The Queen visited the old men in their dining hall, which has portraits. *Dublin Castle*, the Viceroy's seat since 1560, is in Dame Street, on Cork Hill, near College Green, and consists of two large courts, including government offices, St. Patrick's beautiful hall, armoury, chapel royal (the Viceroy attends every Sunday morning), in the modern Gothic style, and the great Birmingham Tower, where the records are kept. This is the oldest part, dating as far back as 1411. There are portraits of Viceroys in the council chamber.

The *Viceregal Lodge* is in Phœnix Park, on the west side of Dublin, with the chief secretary's house near it, and the depôt for the great Irish Ordnance Survey, which extends over more than 1,600 sheets. The park is 7 miles round, and contains barracks, Zoological Gardens, the Wellington Pillar, 205 feet high, and another to Lord Chesterfield, with a phœnix upon it, in allusion to the common name; but the proper name is *fionn uisge*, or fine water, after a spring which rises in it.

TRINITY COLLEGE, founded in 1591, by Queen Elizabeth, and rebuilt by Sir W. Chambers, is on College Green, with a Grecian front of 308 feet, and is composed of three quadrangles or squares—Parliament Square, 560 feet long, has the Chapel, Museum, &c. In Library Square is a fine room 210 feet long, with 150,000 volumes, the harp of Brian Boru, and Archbishop Usher's books, Wickliffe's MSS., and the *Book of Kells*, in which the Queen and Prince Albert have inscribed their names. The Provost's house is in Botany Bay Square. Portraits of Queen Elizabeth, Swift, Grattan, &c., are in the Theatre and Refectory; the gardens cover 20 acres. Usher, Berkeley, Swift, Goldsmith, Burke, O'Connell, Moore, &c., were of this college. The fellowships are not only well endowed, but the fellows are allowed to marry. Residence not being enforced, graduates come up only for examination.

City and County Buildings.—The Mansion House, in Dawson Street, where the Lord Mayor lives; portraits of viceroys and sovereigns. The Sessions House, built in 1797; County Gaol at Kilmainham; Newgate Prison, built in 1773, by Cooley; Richmond Bridewell, for women. Commercial Buildings, in Dame Street, which contain Stock Exchange, Chamber of Commerce, &c. Corn Exchange, on Burgh Quay, the defunct Conciliation Hall. City Police Barracks for 1,150 men, near an old (Marsh's) gate; Old Linen Hall, now used as stores, contains 575 rooms, and covers 3 acres. Markets at Smithfield, Spitalfields, Boot Lane, &c. Cemeteries at Harold's Cross and Glasnevin, one 27 acres, the other 20 acres; at the latte Curran and O'Connell are buried.

Societies, Hospitals, &c.—Royal Dublin Society at old Leinster House, 140 feet long, founded in 1731, Excellent museums of minerals, agricultural implements, busts, &c., and a Botanical Garden at Glasnevin, near the Cemetery. The King's Inn Library, Royal Irish Academy in Dawson Street, near the College, with a museum of Irish antiquities; College of Surgeons on Stephen's Green, with a Doric front, large museum, &c. Blue Coat Hospital at Oxmantown; a front of 300 feet. Sir Patrick Dun's Hospital, founded in 1781. County Hospital, on the site of a garden formerly belonging to Dean Swift. Military Hospital. Dr. Morse's Lying-in-Hospital, founded in 1745, near the Rotunda, in the Rutland Gardens, where public meetings are held. Claremont Deaf and Dumb and the Richmond Blind Schools. County Lunatic Asylum at Richmond. There are about 100 schools of all classes, attended by 16,000 children, and upwards of 20 benevolent societies.

Places of Amusement, Gardens, Statues, &c.—The Theatre Royal is in Hawkins Street; the Queen's Royal, Great Brunswick Street; the Music Hall, Lower Abbey Street. Portobello Gardens and the Phœnix Park Zoological Gardens. Archbishop Marsh's library contains 17,000 volumes; the Dublin Library is in D'Olier Street.—The *Statues* are—Nelson, on a column 120 feet high, in Sackville Street; George II. on St. Stephen's Green, which is nearly a mile round (United Service Club and Archbishop Whateley's house here); William III., a bronze, on College Green, opposite Trinity College; George I. in Dawson Street; George III. (by Bacon) in the Peers' Room at the Bank, another, by Van Nost, stands in the Exchange; George IV. in the Linen Hall; Sir M. O'Loghlen in the Four Courts. Merrion Square is the second in size.

Bridges.—Nine in all, 100 to 250 feet long. Beginning at the east side are—Carlisle, on three arches; Wellington, of iron; Essex, on five arches, 250 feet long; Richmond, near the Four Courts; Whitworth, on the site of Ormonde Bridge, which was rebuilt in 1428; Queen's, built in 1768; Barrack, on four arches (the oldest); King's, of iron; Sarah, in one arch.

Churches.—Nearly 60 churches and chapels belong to the Establishment; a modern cathedral, 9 churches, and 18 convents, &c., to the Roman Catholics; and about 25 other chapels. There are two cathedrals in the dirtiest part of the city, both much altered. *Christ Church*, the oldest (marked by a tower), is a mixture of Norman and Gothic of the 12th century, in the shape of a cross, 230 feet long. One effigy is that of Strongbow, the first conqueror of Ireland, dated 1170. *St. Patrick's* is an early English cross (with a spire), rebuilt in 1362, with buttresses, &c., and 300 feet long. It contains the Archbishop's throne, banners of the Knights of St. Patrick, a bust of Dean Swift, monuments of Stella and Duke of Schomberg, and brasses (the only ones in Ireland) of the Wallops, &c. *St. Andrew's* is a very fine modern Gothic church. *St. George's*, by the same architect (Johnston), is a Grecian church, with a spire 200 feet high. *St. Audeon's* is an old Gothic. *St. Anne's*, a modern Gothic, has the grave of Mrs. Hemans. *St. Michan's* and *St. Peter's* are large cross churches. Another *St. Michan's*, belonging to the Roman Catholics, is a Gothic chapel. The Roman Catholic Archbishop's, or the *Conception Church*, is a large Doric edifice, built in 1816. *St. Andrew's Chapel* is in the same style.

A list of the antiquities about Dublin may be seen in "Wakeman's Hand Book." Round Towers are left at Clondalkin and Swords. Howth and Malahide Castles are on the Drogheda line. Up the Liffey are the Strawberry Beds, near Woodlands; Lucan and Leixlip Castles, near the Salmon Leap; Maynooth College; and Carton (a portion of which was destroyed by fire in 1855), the Duke of Leinster's seat.

GREAT SOUTHERN AND WESTERN.

Dublin to Cork and Killarney.

After passing a few unimportant stations, we arrive at Kildare, the junction of the lines to Carlow and Kilkenny.

KILDARE,

A county in the province of Leinster. Nearly one-fifth part of this county is occupied by bog, including a considerable portion of the great chain of morasses termed the Bog of Allen. In other parts the county has a surface slightly undulated, but in no instance does it assume a mountainous character.

KILDARE JUNCTION (Kildare).

Distance from station, 1 mile.

A telegraph station.

Market Day.—Thursday.

Fairs.—February 12, April 5, May 12, June 29, and November 19.

Races.—Last week in April, 2nd Monday in June September, and October, on the Curragh.

Bankers.—Provincial Bank of Ireland,

The capital of a county of the same name, and a cathedral town, near the Barrow, with a population of only 2,666. It belongs to the Fitzgeralds, represented by the Duke of Leinster. Formerly it was noted for the monastery of St. Bridget, whose bright vestal lamp was kept constantly burning in her cell, o which there are some remains. She lived (as monkish writers say) contemporary with St. Patrick, and is buried with him at St. Columb, at Downpatrick. The cathedral, which is half a ruin, on the hill above the town, contains the Fitzgerald tombs. Close to it is a perfect *Round Tower*, 132 feet high. There are also remains of a castle, built by the English in the 14th century. The diocese is now incorporated with Dublin.

In the neighbourhood is the *Curragh Race Course* the "Newmarket" of Ireland, on a fine down 6 miles long; also an encampment on a large scale, rendered memorable by the temporary sojourn of the Prince of Wales in the summer of 1861. to acquire a more thorough knowledge of military discipline. About 15 miles east are the Wicklow Mountains. To the north is the great Bog of Allen, part of the vast tract of bog which fills the centre of Ireland.

> "Great Bog of Allen swallow down
> That odious heap called Philipstown,
> And if thy maw can swallow more,
> Pray take—and welcome!—Tullamore."

These two unhappy towns are planted in the very heart of this most desolate bog.

Kildare to Carlow, Kilkenny, & Waterford.

Passing *Athy*, on the Barrow, where there is an old castle, built by Lord Kildare in 1506, and has Markets on Tuesday and Saturday, and Fairs March 17th, April 25th, June 9th, July 10th, October 11th, and Dec., we then proceed to *Mageny*, and quickly enter

Carlow, a county in the province of Leinster, which returns two members, in the south-east part of Ireland. It is very fertile, both for tillage and pasture, and produces the best butter in the country. That portion which lies west of the river Barrow is mountainous, as is also that part which borders the county of Wicklow, but its general appearance is very picturesque and beautiful. It possesses inexhaustible quarries of limestone, beds of marls and different clays. In the mountains are found excellent iron ore, oxide of manganese, &c.

CARLOW.

Telegraph station.
HOTEL.—The Club House.
MARKET DAYS.—Mondays and Thursdays.
FAIRS.—May 4, June 22, August 26, and Nov. 8.

CARLOW, the capital town of the county, with a population of 9,940, who return one member, and are employed in the grain and butter trade, is built on the east bank of the river Barrow. The remains of a fine ruin overhang the river, and the ruins of St. Keran's abbey, a convent, and a Catholic college, founded in 1795, and a Roman Catholic cathedral, with a monument to Bishop Doyle; a church with a spire of 195 feet high. In the vicinity, *Oak Park*, Colonel Bruen, and *Browne Hill*, W. Browne, Esq., are the principal objects of interest. The castle is supposed to have been built by King John, to secure the passage of the Barrow. It was taken by The Fitzgerald in 1495, 1534, and the rebels in 1641, and it continued a fortress for several centuries. Here black fetid rain fell in 1849, which the cattle refused to drink.

Passing Milford, we soon reach Bagnalstown, close to which is the seat of J. Newtown, Esq., and then proceed to Gowran, where there are ruins of a castle built by the Ormondes, and burnt in 1650; and an early English church, with a font, and monuments of the Butlers: and Fairs are held March 8th, May 9th, August 10th, October 6th, and December 8th, after which we enter the county of

Kilkenny, the general aspect of which is hilly, but the elevations are seldom so precipitous or severe as to preclude the operations of the plough. The marble and coal of this county take rank as its most valuable productions. Mineral waters are found in several parts of the county; the most celebrated is termed the Spa of Ballyspellan, and situated in the parish of Farlagh. The banks of the Nore often present much pleasing scenery, particularly near the bridge of Ballylurch and the town of Ross. The lovely scenery on the banks of the Suir is truly worthy of the traveller's investigation. The county returns two members.

KILKENNY.

Telegraph station.
HOTEL.—Callanan's.
MARKET DAYS.—Wednesdays and Saturdays.
FAIRS.—March 28, Corpus Christi, cattle and wool.

KILKENNY.—This old capital of the "Pale," or limit of English authority, was founded by Strongbow 1172, and is now the chief town of Kilkenny county, a parliamentary borough, with one member, and seat of a diocese, on the river Nore, which is crossed by two bridges uniting it to Irishtown on the east side Population 24,100, who are engaged in the grain, provision, starch trade, &c. The Ormonde or Butler family have held possession of the town since 1400. Among the events which distinguish it, the principal one was the meeting of the Roman Catholic Supreme Council in 1642, after the great massacre in the preceding year, and during the distractions of the civil war in England. They met in an old building, now Huleatt's Commercial House

Good stone and dark marble are abundant in this locality; most of the houses are of this material. One of the best views of the town is from John's bridge, another from Green's bridge. *Kilkenny Castle*, the seat of the Marquis of Ormonde, is finely seated on a rock above the river; it has been restored in the baronial style, and contains much old tapestry, as well as a gallery of the Butler portraits, by Lely, and other artists of the 17th century, among which are portraits of Charles I. and II., James II., and other Stuarts. Those of the great Duke of Ormonde and his gallant son should be noticed. Many of the family are buried in the cathedral, which is a small cross of the 13th century, 226 feet long, with a good east window and a fine prospect from the summit. Here are monuments of the Graces, who had a castle where the Court House now stands. St. John's Church, once part of an abbey, also contains monuments of both families.

The Bishop's Palace, Chapter House, and a fine

round tower, 108 feet high, are near the cathedral. At the college on the river, founded by the Butlers, Bishop Berkeley, Swift, and Congreve were educated. There is also a Roman Catholic College in the Gothic style, in Cork Road, called St. Kyan's. One of their chapels is placed on the fine ruins of an abbey in Irishtown, founded in 1225, by the Pembrokes Butler's grammar school, where Swift, Congreve, Farquhar, Harris, the antiquary, and Bishop Berkeley were educated, Here Clynn wrote his "Annals." A pleasant promenade, called the Mall, is laid out on the Nore behind the town. Banim, the novelist, was a native.

The country becomes more hilly both up and down the Nore, towards its head, north and west of Kilkenny.

Dunmore Park and caves, belonging to the Ormondes; Tullaroan old church, near Courtown Castle, once the seat of the powerful Grace family, descended from Raymond le Gros. Ballyspellan Spa, near Johnstown, and the collieries in the Dysart Hills (the highest is 1,028 feet high), round Castle Comer. Here the Kilkenny or anthracite coal is quarried, in thin dirty seams; it burns without flame or smoke.

Passing Bennett's Bridge, where there are some large flour mills, and at which Fairs are held on February 24th, August 26th, September 19th, and December 21st, we proceed down the Nore, and come to Thomastown and Innistroge Castle, with Mount Brandon, a granite peak 1,696 feet high, to the left, overlooking the Barrow; beyond which are Blackstairs and Leinster mountains, the latter on the Wexford borders, 2,600 feet high. Then passing Ballyhale, we proceed to Mullinavatt, where Fairs are held March 29th, September 2nd, October 3rd, and 28th, December 9th, and soon after reach Kilmacow, and then enter the county of

Waterford.—This county is in the province of Munster, and returns two members. It is bounded on the north by the river Suir, on the west by the county of Cork, on the east by the harbour of Waterford, and on the south by the Atlantic Ocean. The eastern portion of the county is low and fertile.

WATERFORD.

Hotels.—Commin's, commercial and family, on the Quay; Dolbyn's, Commercial Buildings.

Telegraph station.

Market Days.—Monday, Wednesday, Thursday, and Saturday.

Fairs.—May 4, June 24, October 4.

The capital of Waterford county, and a parliamentary borough, port, &c., in the south of Ireland. The river Suir, upon which it stands, divides the county from Tipperary, and joins the Barrow a few miles below, making the distance to the open sea about 14 miles. Population, 29,300, who return two members, and are engaged chiefly in the provision trade. About 200 vessels, mostly of small tonnage, belong to the port; it has a thriving provision trade with Bristol, Liverpool, &c., and is provided with excellent quay-room, and water deep enough for ships of 1 000 tons.

The ancient Irish called it by several figurative names; but when the Danes settled here, in the 9th century, they styled it *Vater-fiord*, the "Father harbour," on account of its superiority. Here they built a round tower, called the *Ring*, or *Reginald's Tower*, which, as it still exists, must be one of the oldest in Ireland, after the Round Towers. Another event was the marriage of Richard de Clare, or Strongbow, to the King of Leinster's daughter, Eva, which has been painted by Maclise. Here, too, Henry II. landed, as "Lord of Ireland," in 1172. Thenceforth it was steadfastly loyal to the English crown, as in Perkin Warbeck's attempt to take it, and during the civil war, when Cromwell was repulsed. Among the latest events was the embarkation of James II. after the battle of the Boyne. It has returned two members to parliament almost ever since 1374.

The *Custom House* is a large building on the Quay. Further up the Suir, near Davis's brewery, is a curious *Wooden Bridge*, on 39 arches, 832 feet long; it was built in 1794, by Cox, of Boston, in America, and leads over to the ship yards at Ferrybank, and a hill called Mount Misery. Two or three bridges cross John's River, a small stream which flows through the town, named after King John, who resided here when Governor of Ireland, in a palace, of which there are some remains in a crypt at the Deanery, in the Mall. Close to this wide thoroughfare is the *Cathedral* of Waterford diocese (now merged into Cashel); it is a modern building, of no particular character, with a steeple, and various effigies preserved from the former church. Among them is a curious figure of one Rice, with worms, &c., crawling over him, and designed, it is said, from his body as it appeared a year after his death. *St. Olave's Church* is older than the present cathedral, though built only in 1734. There is a *Roman Catholic Cathedral*, and a *College*, with several professors attached.

The *Court House* was built by Gandon, the celebrated architect of some of the finest Dublin structures.

A large *House of Correction*, in Gaol Street, near Bally Bricken Green, where the gallows is set up. *Barracks* for the artillery in Morrison's Road. *Lunatic Asylum*, at John's Hill. The *County Hospital* is on the site of one founded by King John, and handsomely endowed. There is another ancient endowment called *Holy Ghost Hospital*, now an asylum for widows; it was founded in the 13th century; its chapel is a ruin. There are various scientific, literary, and benevolent societies, among which are the *Christian Brothers' School*, and *Bishop Gore's Hospital* for 10 clergymen's widows. The *Fever Hospital* was built in 1799, being the oldest for that object in Ireland. At present there is one in every county. *Fanning's Institution* for poor tradesmen, &c., was founded in 1843. Glass, starch, &c., are made here. In the vicinity are *Barron Court*, Sir H. W. Barron, Bart., M.P.; *New Park*, Rev. Sir J. Newport, Bart.; *Belmont*, R. Roberts, Esq.

Among the natives of Waterford were *Wadding*, the founder of the Irish Franciscan College at Rome, Archbishop Lumbard, and Hartrey the historian. The Earl of Shrewsbury takes the title of Earl of Waterford from this town, which was granted to his ancestor in 1447; and it gives that of Marquis to the Beresford family.

Proceeding down the Suir, you come to Cheek

Point, opposite *Dimbody Abbey* and the junction with the Barrow, and formerly a packet station for Bristol, &c. Passage is a part of Waterford borough, though 6 miles distant. There is a ferry to Dungannon on the Wexford side of the river, from which James II. took his farewell of Ireland. *Dunmore*, at the mouth, is a bathing place, with a deserted pier harbour, which originally cost £100,000, and was made for the Milford Mail Packets. Some Druid stones are near. All the coast from this point, westward, past Tramore, is exposed and dangerous; but at Dungarvan which returns one member, and has two good hotels (Eagle, Mary Power, and Devonshire Arms, Mrs. Magrath), there is a tolerable haven, with a ruined abbey, castle, &c. Opposite Dunmore is the *Hook Point* and *Light*, with an ancient tower, commanding a splendid view. It is a joke of the philologists. that when the conqueror of Ireland landed he said, "he would take it by *Hook* or by *Crook*, and that the brave inhabitants of Fethard *fought hard;*" hence, say they, these names are derived. Fethard is near *Loftus*, the Marquis of Ely's seat (where they show Strongbow's sword), *Tintern Abbey* (a ruin), and *Bannow Bay*, which, like all the Wexford shore, is choked with sand hills. There are an immense number of old forts built by the Norman invaders along this part of Ireland. Up the Suir, from Waterford, are, *Kilmeaden Castle*, which belongs to Lord Doneraile. Portlaw has a large cotton factory, established by the Malcomsons in 1818. *Curraghmore*, close to it, is the princely seat of the Marquis of Waterford; a large park and fine prospects. *Carrick-on-Suir*, a prosperous town, with a trade in corn, butter, &c., the land being rich and fertile. There is a Castle of the Butlers. Above this is *Clonmel*, where Sterne was born in 1713; and where the O'Brien *pronunciamento* was knocked on the head in 1848, the leader of which has returned to his native land, "a wiser and better man," having been pardoned by Her Majesty Queen Victoria. To the south are the fine rugged mountains of the Cummeragh, a name synonymous with the Cumraeg, or Cimbri, by whose descendants they are still peopled. *Manorbullach*, the highest point, is 2,598 feet above the sea. Fine black and red trout are seen in the lakes. The Knockmealdown and Galtee mountains, some of which are 1,200 to 1,600 feet high, further west, are continuations of this range. Up the Barrow. This fine stream takes name from burragh, a bar boundary, as it was long the boundary of the English dominion, or "Pale," in Ireland. *New Ross* was founded by Strongbow's daughter, Rose Macruine. It has a good trade in salmon and provisions. A wooden drawbridge crosses the river, which admits vessels of even 800 tons burden. Up the quay. It was the scene of much fighting in the rebellion of 1798, when Harvey and his followers were defeated by General Johnson. Here the first Temperance Society was established, in 1824. On the Wexford road is the Barn of *Scullabogue*, where 140 loyalists were burnt and shot by the rebels in 1798, under Father Murphy. Their General, Harvey, left on account of this massacre, but was captured in his hiding-place, on the Galtee Islands, and executed at Wexford, by sentence of court-martial.

Kildare to Cork.

We now return to Kildare, the point deviation to Carlow, &c., and soon reach *Monasterevan*, where are ruins of a monastery, built in the 7th century, rebuilt in the 8th, and refounded in the 12th, by the O'Dempseys. There is a Market here on Saturdays, and Fairs on March 28th, May 29th, July 31st, and December 8th. We now enter

King's County, which returns two members, and which, with the exception of Sheve-bloom Mountains, on its southern borders, is in general of a flat character, containing a great part of the ancient plain of Ireland. In 1801 nearly half the contents of the county w re bog, mountain, and waste, or not arable land. Great part of the Bog of Allen lies within the county limits; several tracts have been reclaimed, but not to a great extent. The continuous bogs and levels preclude all possibility of picturesque beauty.

PORTARLINGTON.

A telegraph station.

MARKET DAYS.—Wednesday and Saturday.

FAIRS.—January 5th, March 1st, Easter Monday May 22nd, July 4th, September 1st, October 12th and November 23rd.

PORTARLINGTON, which has a population of 3,107, who return one member, was formerly called Coltodry, and given by Charles II. to Lord Arlington, who sold it to Sir P. Kout, who forfeited it. William III. gave it to General Renvigny, who built the churches. In one of the schools at this place, the late "Iron Duke," and his brother, the Marquis of Wellesley, were educated.

TULLAMORE BRANCH.

GEASHILL.—Here is O'Dempsey's Castle; Fairs are held on May 1st, October 6th, and December 26th.

TULLAMORE.

A telegraph station.

MARKET DAYS.—Tuesday and Saturday.

FAIRS.—March 19, May 10, July 10, Sept. 13 Oct. 21, Dec. 13.

Here are the ruins of Sragh Castle, near those of Ballycowan. The town has a population of 6,343, employed in the linen trade.

Athlone, see page 96.

Gt. S. and Western Main Line continued.

Queen's County returns two members, in the eastern division of which the range of the Dysart Hills forms a prominent and picturesque object, rising in a detached group from the flat country by which they are surrounded. These hills command the view of a rich and beautiful country, adorned with extensive plantations and splendid demesnes. Considerable quantities of corn are produced in this county, and large tracts of land are profitably appropriated to pasturage.

MARYBOROUGH.

This place has a population of 3,673, engaged in the flax trade, and contains remains of an old castle, founded in 1560, ruins of an old church, and raths. Markets are held here on Thursdays; and Fairs January 1st, February 24th, March 25th, May 12th, July 5th, September 4th, October 26th, and December 12th.

We then proceed to MOUNTRATH, where Markets are held on Saturdays, and Fairs, February 17th, May 8th, June 20th, August 10th, September 19th, and November 6th.

Tipperary, a county in the province of Munster, which returns two members, and consists of twelve baronies. It contains some of the most productive districts in the country; the peasantry, however, are the most riotous, distressed, and poverty-stricken. Trade and manufactures are scarcely known out of the large towns. Water-power might be produced to any extent in this part of Ireland, and it is only necessary for the hand of industry to be rightly directed to ensure the most abundant return.

ROSCREA

Contains a population of 9,690, engaged in the coarse woollen factories, and has ruins of a castle built by King John in 1213. In the churchyard are the porch, &c., of an old abbey, St. Cronan's spire, and a round tower 80 feet high. A Roman Catholic Cathedral, with a tower of the Franciscan Friary, founded in 1490, and large infantry barracks (formerly the Damer's seat). Markets are held here on Thursday and Saturday, and Fairs on March 25th, May 27th, June 21st, August 8th, October 9th, and November 29th. Near at hand are *Borristown*, and *Corville*, the seat of the Hon. W. F. Pritie, and pass on to

TEMPLEMORE, which is situated on the river Suir, under the Devil Bit Mountains, and contains large infantry barracks, capable of holding 1,500 men. Close at hand are the *Priory*, the seat of the Cardens, ruins of the Knights Templar's Castle, and *Lloydsborough*, J. Lloyd, Esq., and we soon after reach

THURLES.

A telegraph station.

HOTEL.—O'Shee's.

MARKET DAYS.—Tuesday and Saturday.

FAIRS.—1st Tuesday in the month, Easter Monday, Aug. 21, and Dec.

Here the Danes and English were defeated in the 10th century, by O'Brien, who built the Castle, Carmelite Monastery, and Knights Templar's preceptory. It contains a population of 10,300, chiefly engaged in the corn trade. Close at hand are the ruins of a monastery, and two castles. Then, passing Goold's Cross, $4\frac{1}{2}$ miles from which is *Cashel*, the ancient seat of the Kings of Munster, whose palace stood on the Rock of Cashel, as also did a church built by St. Patrick, whose effigy is here, on the site of which are the ruins of Cormac's chapel, 53 feet long, built in 1134, by Cormac Macarthy, having frescoes, which being discovered by Archdeacon Cotton, he restored the pile. The old early English Cathedral, built by King Donald O'Brien, in 1169, 210 feet by 170, has a monument to Archbishop Macgragh, and was used until 1745; Archbishop Hedran's Vicars Choral Hall, built in 1421. The Episcopal Palace, Archbishop M'Guvill's Cistercian Abbey, built in 1260, with the tribute stone, and round tower of freestone, 90 feet high, and 56 in girth. Bore Abbey, founded by that Archbishop in 1272, lies to the west, and in the town there is an old friary. Here Henry II. was confirmed monarch of Ireland, by Pope Alexander, in 1172. The Earl of Kildare burnt the cathedral, because he thought the Archbishop was in it, and in 1147, Lord Inchiquin captured it for the Parliament. Markets are held on Wednesday and Saturday, and Fairs on the 26th March, 7th August, and 3rd Tuesday in every month. We continue the route to Dundrum, close to which lies *Dundrum House*, the noble seat of the Viscount Hawarden.

Limerick, the surface of which, although in many places diversified by hills, is not, generally speaking, mountainous, excepting on the south-east, where it is bounded by the Galtees, a ridge of lofty mountains which extend into Tipperary and the borders of Kerry, where the ground gradually rises, and forms a grand amphitheatre of steep mountains, in a wide area from Loghill to Drumcolloher. Returns two members to parliament.

LIMERICK JUNCTION.

LIMERICK AND FOYNES.

At LIMERICK JUNCTION the line branches off to the right to

LIMERICK.

A telegraph station.

HOTELS.—Moore's, J. W. Moore, Clare, Catherine O'Brien; Cruise's Royal, Edward Cruise.

MARKET DAYS.—Wednesday and Saturday.

FAIRS.—Easter Tuesday, July 4, August 4, and Dec. 4.

This old seat of the O'Briens, now the capital of Limerick county, a parliamentary borough and a thriving port, has a population of 67,000, who return two members, lies in a flat part of Munster, 50 miles from the mouth of the Shannon. Limerick is divided into Old Town and New Town. The latter, founded not more than 80 years ago, lies to the east, has some good streets and squares about Richmond Place and other quarters; while the Old (or Irish) Town, on King's Island to the north, is one mass of dilapidation and filth; the old crumbling houses being used by the poor wherever they can find something like a roof to cover them. King's Island, which lies between the Shannon and a loop of it called Salmon Weir River, is joined to the opposite shore by Thomond Bridge, rebuilt in 1839, and to the New Town by New and Ball's (or Baal's) Bridges. The Wellesley Bridge, opposite New Town, is a handsome level stone way, on 5 arches, with a swing in the middle for shipping to pass into the floating docks. By a weir below this bridge, and new embankments, sufficient water is obtained to bring vessels of 600 tons alongside the quay. The Irish Western Yacht Club make Limerick their head quarters. About 15,000 tons of shipping belong to the port; the customs are nearly a quarter of a million. Vast quantities of beef, pork, bacon, butter, for which it is particularly celebrated, and other "Irish provisions," are exported. The provision stores of Messrs. Russell should be visited; they cover 3 acres, and here 50,000 pigs and 2,000 head of cattle are salted annually. One feature of it is a "rat barrack" (or hole) where the rats are fed and periodically destroyed, and thus prevented from going to the stores.—*Hall's Ireland.* Excellent lace is made here by two or three firms; it is also noted for its fish-hooks, "every hook worth a salmon," made by O'Shaughnessey; and delicate gloves, sold at Bourke's, but the best "Limerick gloves" are now made at Cork.

The Cathedral of St. Mary is an ill-shaped common looking Gothic building, begun by the O'Briens of Thomond on the site of their palace, having a square tower of 120 feet high, which affords a beautiful view. Thomond means North Munster, of which the O'Briens were kings. The unfortunate, misguided, but highly respected Mr. O'Brien, whose attempted insurrection in 1848 ended so lamentably for himself, is their descendant. An older building is King John's Castle, at one end of Thomond Bridge, of which two heavy round stones and a gate are left. It was taken by Ireton (but through treachery) after a siege of six months, in 1641; and here he died of the plague the same year. At the other end of the Thomond Bridge (on the Clare side) is the famous Treaty Stone, shaped something like an arm-chair, upon which, it is stated, the treaty was signed on the 3rd of October, 1691, when James II.'s garrison of Irish and French surrendered to De Ginkell. One article stipulated that Roman Catholics should take the oath of allegiance, and should be preserved from any disturbance on account of their religion. This provision was adhered to by William III., but broken by Queen Anne: and hence the city of Limerick is called the "City of the Violated Treaty." Thus terminated the War of the Revolution in Ireland.

On the Roxborough road, near the *County Court* and *Gaol* (marked by a tower), is the large district *Lunatic Asylum*, 430 feet long. The *City Hall* was built in 1763. The *Chamber of Commerce* is at the Commercial Buildings.

Lord Chancellor Clare (Fitzgibbon) Speaker Pery, of the Irish Parliament, whose family are Earls of Limerick, and founders of the New Town, Archbishop Creagh, S. O'Halloran, W. Palmer, and Callopy, painters, were natives.

The scenery down the Shannon is not very tempting, but the rich correasses yield heavy crops of wheat and potatoes. At its mouth, on the south side, below Tarbert, is Ballybunian, a pretty watering-place, noted for its caves. Kilrush, on the opposite shore, is a place which suffered dreadfully in the late famine, in common with all this quarter of Ireland; in which whole villages were depopulated. From its mouth to its source under Quilca Mountain in Cavan, Shannon is 250 to 260 miles long; a steamer runs up as far as Athlone. Some of the best parts are—the Falls, near Castle Connell; O'Brien's Bridge; Killaloe, with its cathedral and old churches; the hills about Lough Derg, which has a round tower on Holy Island; Clonmacnois, above Shannon Bridge; and the mountain scenery of Lough Allen. Clonmacnoise, or Seven Churches, in particular, deserves notice as one of the seats of letters and religion in ancient Irish times (*i. e.*, before the Romish supremacy was known); there are ruins of a cathedral, two round towers, a palace, &c., and many graves.

From Limerick the following places may also be visited:—Adare (10 miles), at which are remains of an Austin Friary, O'Donovan's Castle, dismantled by Cromwell, and the Franciscan Abbey, and Adare Abbey, the beautiful seat of the Earl of Dunraven, the descendant of "Con of the Hundred Battles," who, like the late peer, is one of the best landlords in Ireland, lives on his estates, and attends to the amelioration of his tenants. A number of German Protestants, called Palatines, have been settled here for a century. Markets are held here on Saturdays, and Fairs monthly, except in June, July, and August. *Kincora*, the ancient seat of Brian Boru, near Killaloe, and the slate quarries in the Adra Hills; the Keeper and Doon Mountains, 2,265 feet high in one part; Lough Garnear Bruff, surrounded by a remarkable quantity of Druid stones and a castle of the Desmonds, the last of whom is said to be buried under the lake. Maviston Abbey is near *Shangolden*. In the middle of County Clare is Mount Callan, a fine peak 1,280 feet high, having a "cromlech" (or sun altar), and an "ogham stone" near the top. The cliffs on the coast to the west are wonderfully bold; those about Malbay and Moher drop sheer down to the sea for 600 to 1,000 feet. Here one of the Spanish Armada came ashore—at Spanish Point.

The line beyond Limerick turns westward, passing by PATRICK'S WELL and ADARE to

RATHKEALE.—This place contains three castles of the Desmonds. Here also some of the Germans from the Palatinate are settled.

ASKEATON.—Here is another of the Desmond's castles, with a priory founded by them, and a church which was built by the Knights Templars.

FOYNES.

From this place steamers sail down the Shannon to Tarbert and Kilrush, from the former of which a very agreeable tour, *via* Tralee, may be made to Killarney.

From Limerick the tourist may, if he be disposed, proceed onward by rail to Clare Castle, where are also the remains of a monastery built in 1290; also by another route to Castle Connel, at the southern extremity of Lough Derg.

Gt. S. and Western Main Line continued.

From Limerick Junction the line again turns off to the left for Clonmel and Waterford, a description of which latter town will be found on page 85.

Passing KNOCKLONG, which contains ruins of the O'Hurleys', the Lowes' and Clangibbon's Castles, and where fairs are held, May 23, and October 1, we proceed to

KILMALLOCK.

FAIRS are held here on Feb. 21, March 25, June 9, July 6, Nov. 8, and Dec. 4, close at hand are

Mount Coote, C. Coote, Esq.; *Ush Hill Tower*, E. Evans, Esq.

Here are the ruins of a Dominican Friary, founded in 1291, and dismantled by Cromwell. The church, partly in ruins, contains a bell tower, and tombs of the Fitzgeralds. The fortified town walls and gates, with the stone-built houses, &c., &c., all exist as in old times, though in ruins; some dismantled by Cromwell.

CHARLEVILLE, close to which is *Charleville Castle*, the seat of the Earl of Charleville. We now enter the county of

CORK.

WHICH greatly exceeds the other counties, both in population and extent, and returns two members. It reaches along the south coast of the island from Youghal Bay to the more westerly point of Beerhaven, a distance of 160 miles, and is remarkably mountainous. With the exception of a few spots of small extent, there is absolutely no level land; even the vallies, as they are called, are full of swells and ridges. The general appearance of the country is varied and beautiful, the principal defect being want of trees, which are seldom planted except by the great landowners. The richest part of this county is towards the north, and a great quantity of limestone is found in the fertile districts. The south coast has many excellent harbours, and abounds in rivers.

BUTTEVANT,

called by Spenser "gentle Mulla," where there are remains of a priory founded in 1290 by the Barrys, Earls of Barrymore, whose battle words were *Benter en avant*, Forward. Fairs are held here on March 27th, July 20th, October 14th, and November 22nd. Close at hand are *Buttevant Castle*, Sir J. C. Anderson, Bart., the ruins of the abbey, in which are the graves of those who fell in 1647 at Knockninoss, where Sir A. M'Donnell (William Colkille) was killed, and the remains of two old castles. To the east is *Kilcoleman Castle*, called by Spenser Kilnemullugh, and where he wrote his "*Faerie Queen*."

MALLOW (Junction).

A telegraph station.

HOTEL.—Imperial.

MARKET DAYS.—Tuesday and Friday.

FAIRS.—Feb. 10th, Monday before Shrove Tuesday, May 3rd and 12th, July 7th and 26th, Oct. 29th and 30th.

RACES in September.

BOATS 1s. 6d. per mile.

This place contains a population of 9,975, who return one member, and are engaged in the tan and salt works. The church, built in 1818, close to the ruins of the old edifice, which contains some old tombs. Here are warm springs, similar to those at Clifton in Somersetshire, first used in 1740, by consumptive patients. Close to Aurabella is a viaduct of 515 feet, on 10 arches, and the seat of R. Purcell, Esq., *Dromore*, A. Newman, Esq.; Murphy, the mathematician, was a native. Thence passing Blarney, where Fairs are held September 18th and November 11th, and Blarney Castle, built by The M'Carthy in 1446, and visiting, if time will permit, the Blarney Stone, which has the founder's name upon it, and to kiss which the traveller must be lowered 20 feet, so that, according to the village rhymers, "when having kissed it, nobody can refuse you anything;" and as a satire on which Millikin wrote the song, "The Groves of Blarney, they are so charming." A most beautiful prospect of the adjacent country can be obtained from the Stone.

CORK.

A telegraph station.

HOTELS.—Imperial, Royal, Victoria, Hibernian, George Street.

CARRIAGES and CARS at the station and hotels. Tariff of Car rates:—

	Within city limits, per mile.	Without, per mile.
For a drive of not over 20 miles...	0s. 9d.	1s. 0d.
,, over 20 and under 40 ...	1s. 3d.	1s. 6d.
,, ,, 40 ,, 60 ...	1s. 6d.	1s. 9d.
Every half-hour after first hour ...	0s. 9d.	1s. 0d.

For returning the same road as driven—if not kept waiting beyond half-an-hour—half the above rates; if detained beyond the half-hour, 1s. to be paid for a one-horse covered carriage; for a jaunting car, 6d. for each hour detained, and half fare back. If it is intended to hire the vehicle by time, intimation of such must be given to the driver prior to the engagement. After 12 at night the fares are doubled.

Tariff of Jaunting Cars:—Four-wheel carriage, 1s. 3d. per mile; two-wheel, 9d. per mile. To Blackrock Castle, 1s. 9d. to 2s. 3d.; to Blarney, 2s. 9d. to 3s. 3d.; to Glanmire, 2s. 3d. to 3s. 3d.; to Queenstown, 5s. 9d. to 7s. 3d.; to Passage, 2s. 9d. to 4s. 3d.; to Queen's College, 1s. to 1s. 6d., driver included. Tariff doubled after 12 at night.

MARKET DAYS.—Monday and Thursday, for cattle.

FAIRS.—Trinity Monday and October 1st.

BANKERS.—Provincial Bank of Ireland; Branch of Bank of Ireland; Branch of National Bank of Ireland.

A city, port, and capital of county Cork, and Munster province, on the river Lee. The rail reaches the town by a tunnel half a mile long. It has a population of 86,485, engaged in the glass, cutlery, and glove manufactories, and returns two members. Its splendid naval harbour is 11 miles lower down. Cork is not older than the year 600, when an abbey was founded on a low island in the Lee, where most of the city now stands. From the surrounding marshes it derives its name (*Coreagh*). A long street or walk, called the Mardyke, crosses the island, which is united to both banks of the stream by nine bridges, the best of which is the Anglesea iron bridge. The suburbs to the north and south stand higher; on the south bank is the new City Park of 240 acres, near the Bandon Railway. As might be expected, it suffers when the floods come down. The houses are built of stone, either thatched or slated, with many narrow, dirty streets, and but few remarkable public buildings. *St. Finbarr's Cathedral* is modern except the tower, which belonged to the old one. On the site of Gill Abbey is the new *Queen's College*, a handsome quadrangular Gothic pile, by Sir T. Deane, opened in 1849, when the Queen visited the town; her statue is here. There was a castle where the Court House stands. A large *Lunatic Asylum*, for the county, on Shannock Hill. The Botanic Garden is now a public *Cemetery*, established by Father Mathew, the Capuchin friar, who began his first temperance society here, in 1838. Besides savings banks and loan funds, there is a *Mont de pieté*, a pawnshop conducted on an economical principle for the benefit of the poor, imitated from those on the continent. There are large barracks on the hill above the town. A Museum at the Cork Institute, founded in 1807, and a good proportion of benevolent institutions for both creeds.

Cork is not a large seat of manufactures; a little glass, with some good cutlery and beer, are the chief products. Also Limerick gloves, so delicate as to be sold packed in a walnut shell. But there is a large export trade (to the value of £3,000,000) in grain, cattle, whisky, provisions, and especially country butter. About 400,000 firkins of the last went to market in 1850; it is duly classified and branded by a committee, and the prices fixed beforehand every market day.

The river is lined with granite quays, (inaccessible at low water), at which large vessels can unload; but the general place for unloading is at Passage, lower down, to which there is a railway of eight miles; but the descent should be made by boat to enjoy the beautiful views of the hills and country seats on both sides, and Blackrock and Monkstown Castles. The noble harbour, surrounded by hills on all sides, is five miles long, inclusive of the islands in it, having room and water enough for hundreds of vessels of any size. In war time 400 sail have left under convoy in one day. From this port Raleigh started on his last voyage (1617) to Guiana; and the Sirius, Captain Roberts, the second steamer to cross the Atlantic, left on the 1st June, 1838, reaching New York in 17 days. Queenstown (formerly Cove), is situated on a steep terrace, on Great Island, with its yacht club and pretty bathing rooms. It is a soft, sheltered spot for invalids. Here Wolfe, the author of "Not a drum was heard," died of consumption. There is a convict depôt on Spike Island; and an ordnance depôt at Haulbowline Island. Forts and old castles are perched on the highest points of ground. From the sea the appearance of the entrance, at first, is rather gloomy and disappointing.

All the scenery of this fine county is of a striking character, whether inland or along the coast. Cloyne (15 miles) with its Cathedral, Round Tower, and Druid Stone; Castlemartyr Castle, near Lord Shannon's seat; Youghal (28 miles), on the coast, where is shown Raleigh's house and his myrtles, and the fine remains of a Collegiate Church; Mourne Abbey (13 miles), under the Nagle Mountains.

CORK AND BANDON.

By the (single line) rail to Bandon, the coast about Clonakilty, Skibbereen, Cape Clear, and Bantry Bay, may be visited; and thence Glengariff and Hungry Hill, with their magnificent scenery. At the last is one of the most remarkable waterfalls in the kingdom, rivalling the Staubbach, in Switzerland. Cars may be hired, but a pedestrian trip is the true way to enjoy and make oneself acquainted with the country. The constant drizzle is the chief drawback, but this gives Ireland its emerald green. It is said there that it never leaves off but on the 30th of February.

Maclise and Barry the painters, Sheridan Knowles the dramatist, Dr. Maginn, one of the first editors of *Fraser's Magazine*, the Right Hon. J. W. Croker, of the *Quarterly*, Murphy, the Spanish traveller, General O'Leary, Miss Thomson (the Emperor Muly Mahomet's wife), Wood the antiquary, Milliken, Hogan, and Hastie, the Madagascar traveller, were natives.

The Lee, above Cork, may be ascended past Inniscarra and Macroom Castle, to the solitary lakes of Allua and Gongane Barra, and the Shahy Mountains, which are 1,796 feet high; thence over Priest Leap Pass to Glengariff, a distance of about 50 miles.

The line passes WATERFALL, BALLINHASSIG and Kinsale Road stations, four miles from which is

KINSALE,

with a population of 6,970, who return one member. It contains a church (in which no townspeople will be married), with tombs of the Southwells, the ruins of Castle-in-Park, founded in 1334. Fairs are held here on May 4th, September 4th, and November 21st, and Markets on Saturday and Wednesday. This place gives title to the De Courcys of Kinsale House, who are privileged to remain covered in the presence of the reigning sovereign. It was taken by the Spaniards in 1380, but recaptured from them in 1601. Sir E. Scott, in 1689, defended it for James II., who landed from Brest in the same year. Close at hand is *Ruthmore*, the seat of M. Cramer, Esq.

UPTON and BRINNY, in the vicinity of which are *Brinny House*, J. Nash, Esq.; *Upton*, the Rev. S. Payne.

INHOSHANNON ROAD, close to which are the ruins of Downdaniel and Shippool Castles. Here Fairs are held on May 29th and October 3rd; and in the vicinity are *Innoshannon Road*, seat of S. Adderley, Esq., and *Firgrove*, R. Quin, Esq., and then quickly proceed to

BANDON.

Telegraph station at Cork, 20 miles.

HOTEL.—French's.

MARKET DAY.—Saturday.

FAIRS.—May 6th and 25th, Holy Thursday, October 29th, November 8th, first Wednesday in every month, except May and November.

This place has a population of 9,303, employed in the camlet stuff, linens, leather, flour, beer, and whisky trades, who return one member, and contains a grammar school, founded by the great Earl of Cork. It is celebrated for its salmon fisheries. Sir R. Cox and Dr. Brady, the psalmist, were natives.

EXCURSION TO THE LAKES OF KILLARNEY.

See also Prince of Wales' Tour, page 109.

Scotland, Wales, and the most beautiful districts of England, whatever may be their attractions, do not offer much novelty to the majority of men who, in the excursion period of the year, rush from smoky London and the cares of business to feast their eyes upon the beauty, and allow their lungs to inhale the fresh air, of the fields, lakes, and mountains. To such persons we recommend a trip to Ireland, and the lovely Lakes of Killarney. The journey has been rendered comparatively moderate in cost, and convenient as regards time, by the arrangements of the London and North Western Railway Company. The directors issue excursion tickets for the entire journey there and back, giving the tourist fourteen days for the trip, and make all necessary arrangements with the Irish Southern and Western Railway Company for passing him on to his destination.

From Dublin to Killarney is a distance of 186 miles. From a railway train the traveller can, in general, get only partial and unsatisfactory glimpses of the country on either side of him; but such views as are obtained will impress the tourist on this route with the beauty of the scenery and the fertility of the soil. The course of the railway is through the counties of Dublin, Kildare, Queen's County, the "nether tip" of King's County, Tipperary, Limerick, Cork, and Kerry.

From MALLOW JUNCTION the line proceeds to LOMBARDSTOWN, thence to

KANTURK, which has an old castle belonging to the M'Carthys, erected on the river Blackwater, 120 feet by 80. Fairs are held here on March 17th, May 4th, July 4th, September 29th, November 31st, and December 11th, and Markets on Saturdays, (Yelverton, Lord Avonmore, was a native).

MILL STREET.—Markets are held here on Thursdays, and Fairs on January 6th, March 1st and 12th, June 1st, September 1st, and December 26th.

SHINNAGH and HEADFORD stations.

KILLARNEY.

A telegraph station.

HOTELS.—Finn's Royal Victoria Lake Hotel; Railway; Lake; Torc View; Kenmare Arms; Royal Hibernian.

TARIFF OF CARS.—Viz., one horse car, for two persons, 10d. per mile; for three or four, 1s. per mile. Carriage and pair horses, 1s. 6d. per mile. Ponies, 5s per day.

TWO-OARED BOAT, 7s. 6d. per day; four-oared, 15s.; and 6 oared, 21s. per day.

Car Drivers and Boatmen's hire *included in the above charges.* Guides are 3s. 6d. per day each, and Buglers, 5s.

BOATS on the lakes, 1s. 6d. per hour.

MARKET DAY.—Saturday.

FAIRS.—July 6th, August 10th, October 7th and 11th, November 28th, and December 28th.

BANKERS.—National Provincial Bank of Ireland.

The traveller who wishes to see the lakes, and be as near to them as possible, should not stay at the village, but take up his residence at one of the hotels near the Lake, not for the sake of avoiding the town, but for the convenience of being near the lakes, and within full view of the magnificent mountain scenery. For boating or car riding the situation is equally convenient, and as starting places for all the celebrated spots, whether of islands or mountains, must be considered as far superior to any station in the interior of the town. On looking from the windows of these hotels, the traveller will see at a glance that the beauty of the Killarney Lakes and Mountains has not been exaggerated.

The ROYAL VICTORIA HOTEL, Thomas Finn, proprietor, situated near the lakes, is only a mile from the terminus of the Killarney Junction Railway, and also commands magnificent views. The lake shines like molten gold in the light of a morning sun; its numerous green and romantic islands stud its breast with beauty, and the mountains rear their majestic crests across the waters, hemming them in with sublimity. Among the most conspicuous is Mangerton — the most round and lumpish of them all—celebrated for a lake about half way to its summit, called the Devil's Punch Bowl, the ascent to which is strongly recommended to all travellers. The Turk or Torc Mountain, the Purple Mountain, with its separate hills of Tomies and Glena; and the jagged, highly picturesque, and splendid range known as Mac Gillycuddy's Reeks, bound the view, and impress the visitor with a deep sense of their grandeur and beauty. We do not assert that the lake scenery of England and Scotland is inferior to Killarney; but we affirm that Lochs Lomond, Katrine, and Windermere—beautiful as they are—do not possess the various attractions of these comparatively small but most lovely lakes. There is but *one lake* that we have visited which seems to us to be more beautiful in some features, and more sublime in others, than the Lakes of Killarney, and that is Loch Awe, at the foot of the mighty Ben Cruachan—the queen of all lakes for beauty—the monarch of all mountains for sublimity. The Lakes of Killarney are considerably smaller than Loch Awe; and even Mac Gillicuddy's Reeks, in all their vastness, are pigmies to Ben Cruachan; but though on a smaller scale, both lakes and mountains are only second to those wonders of Argyleshire, in the effect they produce upon the mind of the cultivated enthusiastic lover of nature. One great source of the beauty of the Lakes of Killarney is the number of islands upon them. From the windows of the inn can be seen at one view the promontory or Island of Ross, and the ruins of *Ross Castle*, the seat of the renowned O'Donoghue—the "myth" of these parts—with whose name and fame almost every inch of ground is connected in some way or other, by history, tradition, legend, or song. In addition to this, covered with magnificent foliage, are Lamb, Heron, Cherry, Rabbit, Innisfallen Islands, O'Donoghue's Prison, and a score of others that become visible one after the other in rowing through the three lakes.

The *Lakes of Killarney* are three in number—the Upper, the Torc (or Middle), and the Lower; these, with their islands and other attractive objects, together with such matters of interest and importance as are to be met with in their immediate neighbourhood, we shall briefly describe.

The tourist, on approaching the Lakes, is at once struck by the peculiarity and the variety of the foliage of the woods that clothe the hills by which they are surrounded. The effect produced is novel and beautiful, and is caused chiefly by the abundant mixture of the shrub *Arbutus unedo* with the forest trees. The *arbutus* grows in rich profusion in nearly all parts of Ireland; but nowhere is it found of so large a size, or in such rich luxuriance, as at Killarney. On Denis Island there is one, the stem of which is 7 feet in circumference, and its height is in proportion, being equal to that of an ash tree of the same girth which stands near it. On Rough Island, opposite Sullivan's Cascade, is another fine specimen of *arbutus*, the circumference of which is 9½ feet. It strikes its roots apparently into the very rocks, thus filling up spaces that would otherwise be barren spots in the scenery. Its most remarkable peculiarity is, that the flower (not unlike the Lily-of-the-Valley) and the fruit—ripe and unripe—are ound at the same time, together on one tree.

Ross Castle is built on a point of land which advances into the Lower Lake; and in the rainy season is insulated by the waters collecting from the marsh. In summer, however, this peninsula (which the term Ross denotes) is connected with the island, as the castle is by a bridge and causeway. It is named Ross Island, and is the largest on the lakes. The castle is now in ruins, but a few years ago it had a military governor and a detachment of soldiers.

In Ross Bay is situated the boat-house. At the moment of embarkation the bugle is sometimes sounded, and an echo is heard as if proceeding from the castle, and more remotely from the slopes of Mangerton. This echo is the finest from the shores of the lakes, and is particularly beautiful if heard in the evening.

O'Donoghue's Prison is a steep rock, nearly 30 feet high, so called from a chieftain of gigantic stature, who is supposed to have consigned his enemies to this barren spot. His celebrated white charger has also a local record in another rock, resembling a horse, close to the Mucross shore, named O'Donoghue's Horse. To the north of O'Donoghue's Prison are Heron and Lamb Island; and further to the west is Rabbits, or Brown Island. Mouse Island, so called from its diminutive size, is a rock situated in the channel between Ross Island and Innisfallen.

Innisfallen is situated to the west of Ross Island, and is, as its name imports, a beautiful or healthy island. It has but two landing places, at one of which there is a mole where tourists disembark. This beautiful spot consists of 18 acres of delightful woodland, knoll, and lawn. Among the curiosities pointed out to the visitors are—a holly, 14 feet in circumference; a hawthorn growing through a tombstone near the abbey; a crab tree, with an aperture, through which the guide recommends ladies to pass; and the Bed of Honour, a projecting rock, shaded by an old yew, and so called from having been visited by the Duke o Rutland, when he was Governor of Ireland. The *Abbey of Innisfallen* was founded in the sixth century, by A. Finlan, but the ruins now visible are evidently of a much later date. At the south-east corner of the island is an ancient Chapel, with a Saxon doorway; it is called the Oratory. The pasturage on this island is celebrated for fattening cattle.

The Upper Lake consists of about 720 acres, and is completely surrounded by mountains, which give it a sublime and picturesque aspect. Its extreme length is about 1¾ mile, but its breadth varies greatly. The principal islands on its surface are—Ronan, where parties occasionally dine; Duck; Mac Carthy's; Arbutus; Rossbarkie, or Oak, from the shores of which there is a splendid prospect; Knight of Kerry's; Eagle; and Stag. A fine view of the whole lake may be had from the Cramiglann, which rises from the brink of the lake in majestic grandeur

Mucross Abbey adjoins the pretty village of Cloghreen, and is in the demesne of He ry A. Herbert, Esq., M.P., which includes the whole of the peninsula. The site was chosen with the usual judgment and taste of the "monks of old," who invariably selected the pleasantest of all places. The building consists of two principal parts—the *Convent* and *Church*. The steeple of the church, between the nave and the chancel, rests on four high and slender pointed arches. The principal entrance is by a handsome pointed doorway, luxuriantly overgrown with ivy, through which is seen the great eastern window. The intermediate space, as indeed every part of the ruined edifice, is filled with tombs, the greater number distinguished only by a slight elevation from the mould around them. A large modern tomb in the centre of the choir covers the vault wherein, in ancient times, were interred the Mac Carthys Mor, and, more recently, the O'Donoghues Mor of the Glens, whose descendants were buried here as late as 1833. The dormitories, kitchen, refectory, cellars, infirmary, and other chambers, are still in a state of comparative preservation. A recess is pointed out as the bed of John Drake, a pilgrim, who, about a century ago, took up his abode in the Abbey for several years. As will be supposed, his singular choice of residence has given rise to abundant stories, and the mention of his name to any of the guides or boatmen, will at once produce a volume of the marvellous. The cloisters, which consist of 22 arches, 10 of them semicircular, and 12 of them pointed, is the best preserved portion of the Abbey. In the centre grows a magnificent yew tree, which covers as a roof the whole area. It is more than probable that this tree is coëval with the Abbey, and was planted by the hands of the monks, who built the sacred edifice centuries ago. By visiting the "Gap of Dunloe," and returning in a boat through the lakes, much of the sylvan beauty and the wild grandeur of Killarney may be seen in one day, should the traveller be pressed for time. But, whether his stay be long or short, the first excursion he should make is to this far-famed "Gap." The attentive host and hostess of the Lake and Victoria Hotels will make all arrangements for his comfort. The usual mode of proceeding is to hire a car or pony, and ride half way through the pass; and thence proceed on foot over a shoulder of the Purple Mountain, to the head of the Upper Lake at Geraghmene, where a boat will be stationed to row him through the three lakes. By this journey he will be enabled to see all the most celebrated and remarkable portions of the scenery; hear the finest and most renowned echoes; and learn from the civil, well-informed, and garrulous guides and boatmen, the legends, traditions, and histories of each spot he passes. The distance from the Victoria Hotel to the entrance of the Gap is from 4 to 5 miles, and the car proceeds about 4 miles through it, until it becomes too rugged or impracticable for vehicles or ponies. The traveller—who, if he be wise, will take a stout staff in his hand—must walk the remainder of the way to Geraghmene, at the head of the lake, a distance of about 4 miles more. We will not, by any general description of the scenery, anticipate the recital of the beauties that will enchant, or the sublimities that will enrapture him, during this excursion, but name each loveliness in its place, and dwell upon each sublimity in the due succession of its scenery.

The first point of interest on the road is the ruined Church and Round Tower of Aghadoe. These ruins stand upon a gentle eminence, from whence a very good view of the lake is obtained. From this position the eye may wander over those delicious lakes and islands, and a mountain chain of 40 miles in length, stretching far beyond Mill Street, towards Cahirciveen and Valentia.

From Aghadoe to the entrance of the Gap of Dunloe, there is nothing to arrest attention. The Gap (for those who admire the wild, desolate, and sublime), is the most attractive portion of the scenery of Killarney. The entrance to it is abrupt and grand. The cleft between the mountains is supposed by the peasantry to have been caused by one blow from the weapon of one of the giants of the olden time, and is certainly magnificent enough to exercise a powerful influence over the minds of a much less imaginative people than the Irish. On the right of the winding road, Carrantual, and the kindred mountains, appear to look down upon the traveller from a height of more than 3,000 feet, affording no home but to the eagles; while, on the left, the scarcely less lofty peaks of the Purple Mountain and Tomies, raise their craggy heads above the clouds. That brawling river, the Loe, which gives name to the Gap, runs through it, expanding twice into gloomy lakes in the middle of the pass.

The Torc Cascade.

The Torc Cascade, supplied from the "Devil's Punch Bowl," in the mountain of Mangerton, is conveyed through a narrow channel called the Devil's Stream. It is a chasm between the mountains of Torc and Mangerton; the fall is between 60 and 70 feet. The path that leads to it, by the side of the rushing current which conducts it to the lake, has been judiciously curved, so as to conceal the full view until the visitor is immediately under it; but the opposite hill has been beautifully planted, art having been blended with nature and the tall young trees are intertwined with the evergreen *arbutus*, holly, and a vast variety of shrubs. As we advance, the rush of waters gradually breaks upon the ear, and at a sudden turning the cataract is beheld in all its glory.

The liberality of English tourists has accustomed almost all the poor people of the country to expect pennies and sixpences; and every now and then, in the traveller's progress through the gap, a little urchin, plump and good humoured, though shamefully ragged, will pop up at the road side, and ask for "a penny to buy a book!" or offer a tastefully made bouquet of heather and wild flowers to ensure the loose coppers or small coin of the Sassenagh. A little spring, a short distance from the gap, presents a scene of a different kind. A decent and comely-looking matron presides over the well, holding in one hand a wooden jug of goat's milk, and in the other a whisky bottle, and asks the traveller if he will not partake of her mixture. She strongly recommends it as the best of all preliminaries for a successful day among the mountains, and is usually surrounded by two or three nymphs of the same class as herself, all offering goat's milk and whisky, or, to those who prefer it, a draught of the clear cold water of the well, dashed with a due portion of the mountain dew, or national beverage. This matron, it appears, claims to be a Kate Kearney, the grand-daughter of the famous and veritable Kate Kearney,

"Who dwelt by the Lakes of Killarney,"

and whose name is well known to all the lovers of Irish melody.

The echoes in the gap are very fine and distinct, and the guides being generally provided with a bugle, produce notes which are echoed back again by the Carrantual on one side, and the Purple mountains on the other; the latter passing them on to all the nameless hills in the vicinity, till the sounds die away in the dim distance—the effect is exceedingly beautiful. On firing a small cannon the mountains are immediately alive with sounds, hill thunders to hill—mountain peak to mountain peak—gorge to gorge—and rock to rock—until it seems as if contending armies were battling in the clouds.

At the end of the gap, a beautiful view presents itself, the Comme Dhur, or Black Valley, with its wall of mountains, and fair river meandering lazily through the flat meadows. The walk over the hill brings the traveller to Geraghmene, a beautiful cottage at the head of the Upper Lake. Here the boat despatched from the Lake or Victoria hotels is generally in waiting to receive the traveller, and convey him on his homeward journey through the Upper, Middle, and Lower Lakes.

The Upper Lake is, perhaps, the most beautiful of the three; although the charms of each are so varied, that it is difficult to accord the palm of superiority over her lovely sisters to any of these watery graces.

After the fatigues of the Gap of Dunloe the tourist appreciates the luxury of rest, and enjoys, sitting at ease, the delicious progress of the boat through the placid waters. The hills are clothed with verdure—the islands reflect their shadows in the lake—a heron occasionally wings its graceful flight over head—and the soft notes of the bugle die away amid the woody recesses of the hills. Every change of landscape is but a variety of loveliness. The first halting place is at the base of a magnificent hill, wooded to the very top, and called the "Eagle's Nest." At this spot the lake narrows to a river, and is in fact a stream connecting the Upper with the Middle or Torc Lake. The echo here is the most famous of all those of the lakes; and any traveller who, being in too great a hurry to get to the end of his journey, might refuse to linger here for a while, would be set down in the estimation of boatmen and guides as utterly deficient in respect for Killarney.

A mile beyond the Eagle's Nest is the old Wier Bridge, of two arches, one only of which is practicable for boats, neither is the passage at all times safe or pleasant. The current by which the Upper Lake discharges its surplus waters into the Torc Lake is exceedingly rapid, and it is customary for the tourist to disembark here, while the boatmen shoot the rapids. When the travellers re-embark the boat proceeds to the beautiful island of Denis, where persons who bring their luncheons or dinner with them from the hotel, can be accommodated, at a snug cottage on the shore, with chairs and table, and a cook, who will dress salmon and potatoes, and supply hot water for whisky punch, for a small gratuity.

From this point to Glena Bay is a delightful sail to another beautiful cottage, erected for the same purpose. The travellers are then in the large or Lower Lake, and within an hour's sail from the Victoria, and half an hour's sail from the Lake hotel.

The Ascent of the Mangerton.

The ascent of this mountain is usually made first, because its summit commands a very extensive prospect; and secondly, because, at a short distance from the top, a crater-like hollow on its side receives the waters of the hill, and collects them into a receptacle, famous all over the country for its odd name of the "Devil's Punch Bowl." The ascent commences at Cloughreen, a village about four miles from the Victoria Hotel. The inn at Cloughreen, called Noche's, or the Mucross Hotel, from its close proximity to that beautiful domain, is a beautifully situated and well conducted house, of which all travellers speak highly. Ladies and those travellers who do not like the fatigue of climbing on foot, may ride nearly the whole of the way up to the Devil's Punch Bowl.

The longer the tourist remains at Killarney the more lovely its mountains, vallies, placid lakes, and rushing waterfalls, appear. The weather, too, is often highly favourable for viewing the scenery under all its aspects. One day, in a clear and cloudless atmosphere, the outlines of the hills stand sharply out against the deep blue sky, and the lakes lie silently and bright as sheets of burnished gold. On the day following, it may be wind and rain; then the high peaks of Carrantual and his sublime brothers of the "Reeks," shroud themselves in the driving mists; the wind curls the broad bosom of the lake into foam-crested waves; and the clouds, from which, for one half-hour, rain in torrents may pour down, open in the next, and admit the sunshine into the magnificent landscape; the rainbow spans Carrantual and the Purple Mountains, then melting away into the heavy clouds upon which it was reflected, allows the whole of the glorious panorama to glitter in the full blaze of a midsummer sun. The effects on such a day are constantly changing and ever beautiful. The alternations of colouring, from the deepest dun, in which the lakes and mountains are enwrapped at one moment, to the grey, brown, purple, green, and gold, which girt them about with beauty in the next, are especially delightful to behold, study, and admire. Not only the grandeur, but the smaller features of the scenery are beautiful at Killarney. Under the splendid yew trees, hollies, and arbutuses of lovely Innisfallen, or amid the still more umbrageous foilage of Mucross, it is impossible to walk a step without discovering a new beauty in the landscape. Innisfallen alone offers almost every variety that can charm the eye and fill the imagination of the lover of nature. Those who delight in the shade of thick woods and countless wild flowers, may indulge here at sweet leisure. The lover of the pastoral glade, or the smooth-shaven lawn, sloping down to the water, may at a short distance find the scenery he admires; while he who delights most in rocks, mountains, and torrents, can, from the same little island, gaze undisturbed upon many of the grandeurs, and some of the sublimities of nature.

Tour from Killarney to Glengariff and Bantry Bay.

From Killarney to Glengariff, a distance of forty miles by car, the road passes through scenery unsurpassed for beauty in any portion of the kingdom. For one third of the distance the lakes and mountains of Killarney continue in sight, and the tourist is enabled to acquire a still more intimate knowledge of them, in all their wondrous and lovely variations, than he can obtain even by sailing or roving about the lakes, or by coming down upon them from the heights of Dunloe or Mangerton. After passing Cloughreen, Mucross, and the splendid Torc Cascade (the music of whose rushing waters swells audibly upon the ear above the din of the car), the road winds round the shore of the Middle or Torc Lake, having the lake on the right hand, and on the left the Torc Mountain, clothed with the richest vegetation, and lifting his steep sides to a height of 1,760 feet. It then passes the connecting link of river between the Upper and the Middle Lakes, affording a fine view of the "Eagle's Nest," the "Purple Mountain," and high above them all, "Macgillycuddy's Reeks," and "Carrantual." The road is a continual ascent all the way from Cloughreen, and, after passing the beautiful waterfall of Derricunihy (beautiful, though inferior to the Torc Cascade), reaches a point at which all travellers should halt for awhile to survey the landscape around, above, and beneath them. This is the Police Barracks or Constabulary station. Standing here, or at any other point higher up the hill, a most magnificent view is obtained, including the whole of the lakes, the Gap of Dunloe, and Macgillycuddy's Reeks. Beyond this point, although Carrantual remains in sight the most conspicuous object in the landscape, there is little more to be seen of the lakes of Killarney. Let the traveller take his last look, and then prepare himself for a new panorama, as well worthy of his admiration as anything that he leaves behind him.

A ride of ten miles will bring him to the beautifully situated and picturesque town of Kenmare. The road descends gradually from the heights to the sea-level. Kenmare is built at the head of an arm of the sea. The Suspension Bridge across the "Sound," is one of the greatest ornaments, as well as conveniences, of the town.

From Kenmare to Glengariff is a distance of seventeen miles. Were it thrice seventeen the tourist who loves the wild, the rugged, and the majestic scenery of the mountains, would think it short. The road attains a height from Kenmare of 1,000 feet above the level of the sea, with a gradual ascent of 150 feet in a mile. It passes through two tunnels—a rather unusual circumstance on any road, except railroads. One of them is 200 yards in length; and passing through it in the open car, the tourist will obtain, at either end, a view of the hilly country which will make him wish that tunnels on common roads were somewhat more frequent. After passing the largest tunnel, which stands on the confines of Kerry, the road enters the county of Cork, and winds amid the rugged mountains of Glengariff to the sea, at the head of Bantry Bay. The characteristics of Glengariff are wildness and sublimity. The name, which signifies the rough or rugged glen, has been well bestowed, and aptly describes it. Hitherto this unrivalled scene has been comparatively little known. A good hotel, or at all events, an inn of some kind was necessary to attract tourists, and this great want has been supplied. Let no tourist who loves nature in all her moods, the wildest as well as the softest, be deterred from visiting Glengariff by any doubt as to his creature comforts on the way. They will all be well and cheaply attended to; and if, leaving for awhile the better known districts of Scotland, Wales, and England, and the great continental highways of the sight-seers, he will be fully rewarded for his pains and selection. The mere repetition of the only possible epithets which admiration can apply to scenery fails to convey a proper idea to the minds of those who are not passionate lovers of it. All that the tongue or pen can do, is to affirm that it is "magnificently beautiful." No words can describe the beauty of some scenes. We can feel, but we cannot exactly explain our sensations. We can say no more of Glengariff than that it is both sublime and beautiful, and that it seems to us far better worth the time and cost of a pilgrimage than hundreds of other scenes of greater celebrity. The valley is three miles long, a quarter broad, and is shut out from the busy world by stupendous precipices. Through its entire centre flows in summer a peaceful stream, which in winter takes to itself the voice of many waters, and rushes a foaming torrent into the sea. The vegetation upon its banks is profuse and lovely, but it requires a residence of some days at Glengariff to become thoroughly acquainted with the beauties of this little river, and all the loveliness and grandeur that surround it. From the inn at Glengariff—which stands upon the shore of the Bay of Bantry—a different, but equally magnificent, prospect is obtained. The Bay stretches its broad, deep waters, studded with islands, towards the Atlantic Ocean. He who would see its beauties of island and of mountain in their full extent, should take a boat, on a fine summer evening, and be rowed across to Bantry, The distance is but nine miles, and the scenery is most superb. The picturesque island of Garnish, crowned with a fort and martello tower, erected shortly after the French made their appearance in the bay sixty years ago, is at first the most conspicuous object after leaving the inn; but as the boat proceeds on its course, the island and the fort dwindle into insignificance against the dark background of the lofty Glengariff mountains. As these seem to recede, the low island of Whiddy appears in front, with its solitary ruin of the ancient castle of the O'Sullivans; and the eye may range across the noble bay quite spell-bound with the beauty of the scene from the towering summit of Dade, or "Hungry Hill," 2,100 feet high, to the thickly-wooded cove that leads to, and conceals, the town of Bantry.

Having now explored the beauties of Killarney, the tourist may continue his railway course northward, *viá* FARRANFORE, to the town of TRALEE. This forms part of a favourite route from Dublin to Killarney, *viá* Limerick, Foynes, the Shannon, Tarbert and Tralee, for the accomplishment of which great facilities by way of return tickets are offered in the summer months.

MIDLAND GREAT WESTERN.

Dublin to Mullingar, Athlone, and Galway.

Leaving Dublin, we pass BLANCHARDSTOWN, and CLONSILLA, close to the latter of which are *Clonsilla House*, the seat of R. French, Esq., and *Woodlands* (Col. T. White), and arrive at

Lucan, situated on the Liffey, in a beautiful spot. It is a watering place of some note, and has a boiling spring and mineral spa. In the vicinity are *Lucan Abbey*, J. Gandon, Esq., the seat of Gandon, the architect; *Lucan House*, C. Colthurst, Esq.: *Weston Park*, J. Reed, Esq., near the Salmon Leap. Here races are held in February, March, June, and October. We then proceed to

Leixlip, situated close to the Salmon Leap. The Royal Canal is here crossed by an aqueduct 100 feet high. *The Castle*, the seat of Hon. G. Cavendish, was built by Adam Fitz-Hereford, and here King John lived when Earl of Montaigne. *Leixlip House*, seat of J. Nesbitt, Esq., is close at hand. Markets are held on Saturday; and Fairs May 4 and October 9.

MAYNOOTH.

Telegraph station at Dublin, 15 miles.

MARKET DAY.—Saturday.

FAIRS.—May 4th, September 19th, & October 9th.

Here are the ruins of the Geraldines' Castle, built in 1430. St. Patrick's Roman Catholic College, a quadrangular edifice, containing chapel, rooms, and noble library of 18,000 volumes, covering 54 acres.

It was founded in 1795, and supported, until 1845, by a parliamentary grant of £8,900, since increased to £26,360 per annum. Close by is the princely mansion and domain of Ireland's *only* Duke (his Grace of Leinster), *Carton*, beautifully built, in Rye Water, erected by Cassels. It consists of a large centre, with wings. The dining-room is 52 feet by 24, and 24 high. Here is a splendid picture gallery, containing some of the *chef d'œuvres* of Holbein, Claude, Poussin, and several Dutch masters. The grounds, park, &c., cover 1,000 acres. Queen Victoria visited here in 1849; and in 1855 one of the wings was partly destroyed by fire, when the Duchess narrowly escaped an untimely fate.

Passing KILCOCK, where markets are held on Wednesday; and fairs March 25, May 11, August 11, and September 29, we reach FERN'S LOCK, ENFIELD, MOY VALLEY, HILL OF DOWN, and KILLUCAN, which has ruins of Hugh de Lacy's castle, and where fairs are held on March 27, May 25, September 29, and November 28, close to which is *Hyde Park*, seat of G. d'Arcy, Esq., we reach

MULLINGAR.

A telegraph station.

MARKET DAY.—Thursday.

FAIRS.—April 6th, July 4th, August 29th, and November 11th.

This place has a population of 9,906, employed in the wool and butter trade, and contains the ruins of two castles, and large infantry barracks for 1,000 men.

This station forms the junction of the line to Longford, which turns off to the right, and passing

Mullingar to Cavan and Sligo.

Multyfarnham, beautifully situated near Lake Deraveragh, has the ruins of an abbey, with a steeple 90 feet high, built in 1236, and which contains tombs of the Nugents. Here the Observantines held a chapter in 1529, and the Roman Catholics assembled in 1641. Fairs are held on March 4th, May 13th, September 1st, December 2nd. Close at hand are the beautiful seats of *Ballinadoon*, C. P. Murphy, Esq. *Donore*, Sir P. Nugent, Bart., M.P. *Mornington*, E. Daly, Esq.

From hence the line continues its course to CAVAN, a place of some importance, near to Lake Oughter.

We again proceed from Multyfarnham, in the direction of LONGFORD, and very soon enter the county of that name.

Longford, is only a small county, and returns two members. The general aspect of it is flat; but towards its northern extremity, where it projects into the counties of Leitrim and Cavan, its character varies, and the surface becomes rugged and uneven, partly consisting of good tillage ground, and partly of mosses and fens. A considerable quantity of linen is made in this county, and it is improving and extending in all directions.

LONGFORD.

A telegraph station.

HOTEL.—Sutcliffe's.

FAIRS.—March 25th, June 10th, August 19th, and October 22nd. MARKET DAY.—Saturday.

This is a small, though the principal, town of the county. It stands on the banks of the river Longford. It obtained considerable celebrity in an early age of history, on account of an Abbey, of which St. John, one of the disciples of St. Patrick was abbot. The castle of Longford has been the theatre of many interesting historical events, and belongs to the Pakenhams, Lord Longfords, to one of whom the "Iron Duke" was married.

SLIGO.

A considerable town, situated at the eastern extremity of Sligo Bay; its population is about 15,000; trade—linen, flour, &c.; its harbour capacious, and will admit vessels of heavy tonnage. There are some interesting remains of an ancient monastery destroyed by fire in the year 1414, but subsequently repaired.

Midland Great Western Main Line continued.

ATHLONE.

A telegraph station.

HOTEL.—Rourke's.

MARKET DAYS.—Tuesday and Saturday.

FAIRS.—1st Monday after January 6th, 21st March, Wednesday before Ascension, 1st Monday in September.

A borough town, returning one member The greater part is on the Westmeath side of the Shannon, which issues out of Lough Rea, a short distance north, but a portion is in Roscommon, on the opposite bank. The river flows over several rapids here, to clear which, a canal a mile long has been cut from the town to the lake. The houses are poor and dirty. Felt hats and woollen friezes are manufactured; and it enjoys a good carrying trade by steam and canal, as well as by rail; but its chief importance depends on its being a strong military post, commanding the ford over the Shannon, and the roads to the West of Ireland. To this end a castle was built here by Henry II., part of which remains, with later additions of great strength; it stood a long siege in the civil wars, and again in 1691, when General De Ginkell took it from the partisans of James II., for which he was created Earl of Athlone. James's commander, Col. Grace, was an old veteran, with whom the king had been very intimate. When summoned by De Ginkell to surrender, he fired his pistol in the air:—"These are my terms," he said, "and when my provisions are gone, I will eat my boots." He fell in the action, which was an easy one for the English, as Saint Ruth, the Irish leader, who was in the neighbourhood, neglected his duty to the besieged. He was killed a fortnight later, at the battle of Aughrim, 20 miles from this place (at Killcommadan Hill), where King James's supporters were finally routed. The castle includes barracks for 1,500 men, with an armoury, magazines, &c., altogether covering 14 acres. The ancient narrow bridge to the Leinster side, opposite it, is replaced by a new one of stone, built in 1844. On the old one was an inscription stating that it was erected by Lord Deputy Sidney (father of Sir Phillip), in Queen Elizabeth's time. *St. Peter's* church stands on the site of an abbey, founded when the castle was first raised. From the battery of the latter is a view of the flat, boggy shores of Lough Rea, and *Moydrum Castle*, the seat of Viscount Castlemaine, is three miles off.

The Great Northern and Western railway now turns off to the right. It will intersect the counties of Roscommon and Mayo to Castlebar, a distance of about 50 miles, 34¾ of which are now open, and the remainder expected towards the close of 1862.

We then reach BALLINASLOE, which is on the borders of the counties of Roscommon and Galway, and noted for its cattle fairs, which are held on the 5th October, May 7th, 4th and 6th July. The castle is an old, moated fort, of Elizabeth's time, and is the seat of J. T. Maher, Esq. There are markets on Saturday for corn. We reach

ATHENRY, where are the ruins of a castle and Dominican friary, built in 1261, by the De Birminghams. Markets are held here on Fridays, and fairs May 5th, July 2nd, October 20th, and Oranmore, where fairs are held on May 22nd and October 20th.

ORANMORE. — Here are the ruins of *Oranmore Castle*, built by the Earls of Clanricarde, on the site of which is *Oran Castle*, the seat of W. Blake, Esq., near the shallow and rocky bay of Oranmore. *Wallscourt*, Lord Wallscourt, and the round tower of *Murrough*, about 40 feet high, are close at hand.

Galway, a county in the province of Connaught, which returns two members, is bounded on the east by the river Shannon, the north-east by Roscommon, the west by the Atlantic, the north by Mayo, and on the south by Galway Bay. The general appearance of this county is remarkably beautiful, especially from the banks of the Shannon to the town of Galway. The soil is very fruitful; but agriculture. is generally speaking, in a backward state. This county possesses both rivers and lakes in great abundance. Lough Corrib alone extends more than 20 miles in length, and eleven in breadth.

GALWAY.

A telegraph station.

HOTELS.—Midland Great Western Station, and Clanricarde Arms.

MARKET DAYS.—Wednesday and Saturday.

FAIRS.—May 31st, September 21st, and October 31st. RACES in August.

BANKERS.—National Bank of Ireland; Provincial Bank of Ireland; Bank of Ireland.

The capital of County Galway, a parliamentary borough, has a population of 23,195, who return two members, and is a port in the west of Ireland, at the head of a fine bay. A small stream, three or four miles long, serving as the outlet to Lough Corrib, runs through the town into the harbour, which contains a floating dock of five acres, and has good anchorage outside. This is proposed to be the starting point for America, the run to which would be lessened about 350 miles.

Galway was founded in the 11th and 12th centuries by the Twelve Tribes, as they were called, consisting of the Burke, Blake, Joyce, D'Arcy, Lynch, Skerrett, and other families, several of whom still flourish—the Blakes for instance, represented by the Marquis of Clanricarde, so named after *Richard de Burgh*, who built the town wall, 1235, of which a gate or two remains. The great statesman and orator was a branch of this family. Beautiful black Connemara marble, one of the chief products, is sawn and polished at Franklin's mills. Fish, provisions, and a little paper also exported. Formerly there was a good trade in wine with Spain, which produced an infusion of foreign blood on this side of Ireland, where the round olive face and Spanish complexion may be frequently noticed. Many houses in Old Town, which belonged to merchants, yet retain, outside, their armorial bearings and moorish carvings, and are built in the Spanish style within. Lynch's house in Lombard Street, or Deadman's Lane, is an example; the crest is a *lynx*. The ancient cross-shaped *church*, with its spire, was built in the 14th century; in former times the living was a wardenship, independent of the bishop, which the tribes elected. On Clare River is the new *Queen's College*, a handsome Elizabethan quadrangle, by Sir J. Deane, opened in 1849; it is 275 feet by 215, and has a tower 110 feet high. The *Claddagh*, is a suburb, where the fishermen and their families live, exclusively, to the number of 5,000 or 6,000; their market being close to an old tower and gate. They are peaceable and clean, but superstitious, never going out to fish, nor allowing others to go out, except on lucky days, and are governed by their own laws and customs, under a "king" or admiral, chosen annually.

The noble bay, which is seven miles across, opposite the town, widens to 23 miles at the mouth, where the Arran Islands form a natural breakwater, and abounds with excellent harbours. On the Great Arran is a revolving light, 500 feet high; and from here, they tell you, Hy Brysail, the old Irish paradise, can be seen "on a clear day." At all events, America, a more sober and useful paradise, is not far off.

In the neighhourbood of Galway are, *Menlo Castle*, seat of Sir V. Blake, Bart.; *Roscom Round Tower*; *Loughcooter Castle*, Viscount Gough's seat, near the Slieve Boughty Mountains, 1,260 feet high: *Aughrim*, where De Ginkell defeated the forces of James II., 1691; *Tuam*, and its modern Roman Catholic cathedral; but the most interesting excursion is that to

CONNEMARA and the Killeries.

A trip of 35 or 40 miles; or, 90 miles, if extended through Mayo to Westport; through a grand country of lakes and mountains, with noble coast scenery, washed by the Atlantic. It was called the "kingdom" of Connemara, a word which means, "bays of the great sea," and till lately belonged to one or two proprietors, the first of whom was Colonel Martin of Ballynahinch. "He once boasted to the Prince of Wales, to put him out of conceit with Windsor Park, that the avenue to his hall door was thirty miles long." The fact being that it was the only road in the county, and ended at Ballynahinch.—Hall's *Ireland*. The women dress in homespun scarlet cloaks, and spin all day long. It is now settled by various new proprietors, and is in course of being reclaimed and cultivated. Here is the chief scene of the evangelical reformation, under the blessing of God in progress, of the devoted Bishop of Tuam and his Irish preaching clergy. From Galway the road goes along Lough Corrib to Oughterard, 16 miles, past *Aughaanarc*, an old seat of the Flaherties, and a vast collection of Druid stones spreading two miles; whence, by Maam Turc Inn, through Joyce's country, to Leenane, in the Killeries, is 19 more. The Maam Inn, under a mountain 2,000 feet high, commands a fine view of the lake, with another of the *Flaherties' Castle* in the distance. From Oughterard, by Ballynahinch to Clifden, is 14 miles. *Clifden*, is a beautiful mountain town, on an inlet, founded by the D'Arcys, about 30 years ago, and is the centre of the new reformation. Its late proprietor sold all his estates, and is now one of the most active of the working clergy here. In the neighbourhood are the Twelve Pins, or Peaks, the highest of which is 2,930 feet. Following the coast road to Leenane, 30 miles, you come to Ballynakill Harbour, Kylemore Pass, a grand thing to see; and Salruc Pass, is grand, in the Killeries, which is a narrow, but splendid, sea inlet, between high and picturesque mountains, like a Norwegian fiord (Inglis). Then to *Leenane*, near *Delphi*, the beautiful seat of the Marquis of Sligo. This round may be extended by following the equally bold and wild county of Mayo, to Newport, Westport, and Achill, another Protestant settlement, where some of the *cliffs* are 1,500 to 2,000 feet, sheer down to the sea, or to the mountains round Clew Bay, 2,600 feet high, and more, at Croaghpatrick and Mulrea; and in Tyrawley

DUBLIN AND WICKLOW.

Wicklow.—The greater part of this county, which returns two members, is mountainous. Towards the interior this Alpine region is boggy, uncultivated, and rendered additionally cheerless by the want of wood; but throughout a long extent of its borders, and particularly on the sea coast, it assumes a splendour and variety of scenery not to be surpassed in any part of the island. The mountains and rocky elevations are here magnificently bold, and the country is plentifully clothed with ornamental wood. Agriculture is still in a backward state, though considerable improvements have been recently introduced.

Passing DUNDRUM (has remains of an old castle), STILLORGAN, (has Darley's extensive brewery, and close at hand *Stillorgan Park*, H. Verschoyle, Esq., *Stillorgan House*, R. Guinness, Esq.; *Redesdale*, Archbishop of Dublin), CARRICKMINES (has ruins of an old castle) and SHANKILL (the hill is 912 feet high), we reach

BRAY.

A telegraph station.

HOTELS.—Quin's and Queen's,

MARKET DAYS.—Tuesday and Saturday.

FAIRS.—January 12th, March 1st, May 1st and 4th July 15th, August 5th and 20th, September 14th (for friezes), December 4, (for cattle).

This town, which is most beautifully situated, has remains of a castle (now used as barracks), and a race course. Here is a pretty lake, and a river abounding with trout. Close at hand are *Kilhuddery*, near the Sugar Loaf, seat of the Earl of Meath *Bray Head*, which commands an extensive view, G. Putland, Esq.; *Old Court*, Major Edwards *Old Connaught House*, Lord Plunkett, near which are the ruins of a castle, and coins have been found

On arriving at *Bray* we pass *Kilruddery*, Earl of Meath's seat, up the famous Dargle Glen, to Powerscourt, the seat of Viscount Powerscourt, and *Tinnahinch*, which belonged to Grattan. Glen of the Downs, near Delgany, under the Sugar Loaf Peaks, the highest 1,650 feet. Devil's Glen, fall of 100 feet, near Ashford on the Vartry. Wicklow Castle (31 miles from Dublin), on to Arklow Castle, built on a basalt cliff at the Avoca's mouth. Up the Avoca, by *Sheldon Abbey* (Earl of Wicklow), to the Wooden Bridge and Avoca inns, at the Second Meeting of the Waters (viz., the Aughrim and Avoca), from which a path may be taken to the left, past Au im, under Croaghr Kinshela (a granite peak, 1,985 feet high) to Drumgoff inn, and Lugnaquilla, the highest point (3,039 feet) of the Wicklow Mountains, in a wild and rugged spot, at the Slaney's Head. But the usual course is from the Second Meeting, up the "Sweet Vale of Avoca," past the Copper Mines, to the First Meeting of the Waters (the one alluded to by the poet), at the junction of the Avon-beg and Avon-more, under Castle Howard. By the Avon-more (3 miles) on to Rathdrum (11 miles from Arklow) and Laragh Bridge, to Glendalough, or Glen of the Two Lakes, in a desolate hollow of the mountains (2,100 to 2,500 feet high), the seat of an early bishopric, with St. Kevin's Bed (a hole in the cliff), parts of cathedral, church, &c. (destroyed by the Norman invaders), and a round tower 110 feet high. Thence you may take the road over Wicklow Gap, or pass, 1,560 feet high, to the head of King's River, down to Poul-a-phonca Fall, on the Liffey round to Dublin. Or by the direct route from Glendalough, to Lough Dan and Tay, on the Annamoe, near *Luggelaw* (the Latouches' seat), under Djouce Mountain (2,384 feet) and other peaks, on to the two Loughs Bray at the top of Glencree, by Sally Gap pass and Enniskerry to Dublin. Since the Rebellion, the Wicklow Mountains are traversed by good military roads; the highest parts are bare, but the lower well fringed with wood, on which account Swift compared the district to a "frieze coat, edged with gold lace."

WICKLOW.

A telegraph station.

HOTEL.—Byrne's.

MARKET DAY.—Saturday.

FAIRS.—March 28th, May 24th, August 12th, and November 23rd. RACES in May.

BANKERS.—National Bank of Ireland.

This town, the capital of the county of the same name, has a population of 2,798, who are employed in the copper and lead ore trade. It contains a church, with round mound, three chapels, race stand on the Murrough, ruins of an Abbey founded by the O'Byrnes in Henry the Third's time, barracks, &c. It stands on the sea coast, at the mouth of the river Leitrim, which was once defended by a fortified rock called the *Black Castle*. It is now, however, a place of but little strength in a military point of view, and of slight commercial importance, as it has no manufactures. The bay is much exposed to south-easterly winds, which render the neighbouring coast very dangerous. Two lighthouses have been erected, 268 feet high, with fixed lights.

DUBLIN AND DROGHEDA.

The first station on this line is Raheny, in the neighbourhood of which are *Raheny House*, J. Sweetman, Esq.; *Raheny Park*, J. ham, Esq.; *Killested Abbey*, D. Nugent, Esq.

The next station is the JUNCTION of the

HOWTH BRANCH.

We are no sooner clear of this than the train is announced at

BALDOYLE, situated on an isthmus leading to the Hill of Howth. It is a pretty bathing-place, but its harbour is very shallow, suited only for small boats.

HOWTH.

A telegraph station.

HOTEL.—Royal.

BOATS to and from Ireland's Eye. Tariff—2s., including all charges.

HOWTH is the name of a peninsula on the coast of Ireland, which forms the northern boundary of the bay of Dublin. On the northern side of this peninsula stands the town of Howth, which has risen within a very few years to a considerable degree of importance by the construction of a magnificent harbour for the protection of vessels bound for the port of Dublin. It consists of two piers, erected by Rennie at a cost of £800,000, which project for a considerable distance into the sea; one is rather more than 2,493 feet from the shore, and the other 2,020 feet: the entrance is 300 feet wide, and the area enclosed within this vast mass of masonry exceeds fifty English acres. The fixed light, built in 1818, is 43 feet high, and can be seen 11 miles distant. On landing at the harbour of Howth, the first object that attracts the attention of the traveller is a ruined abbey, which directly fronts him. Placed on a precipitous bank, considerably elevated above the water's edge, and surrounded by a strong embattled wall, it may be considered half temple, half fortress. It contains a fine tomb of a knight and lady. In the castle, Lord Howth's seat, are the old Abbey Bells, Tristram's sword, a picture gallery in which is a portrait of Swift. On Baily Point there is an immense fixed light, erected in 1813, 114 feet high, and visible 15 miles at sea.

Dublin and Drogheda Main Line continued.

Passing PORTMARNOCK, where are ruins of Rob's Wall Castle, built by the De Birminghams, church at Carrickhill, and two martello towers, we arrive at

MALAHIDE.

A telegraph station.

HOTELS.—Royal, Railway.

This place is celebrated for its oyster fisheries, and has an old church, with ancient tombs of the Talbots, and in the churchyard some beautiful old chesnut trees. Close at hand is *Malahide Court*, the princely seat of Lord Talbot de Malahide, built as a square castle, with round corner towers, and contains a noble hall, with oak carvings, altar-piece by Durer, a gallery of portraits, and pictures by Dutch and Italian artists. The line traverses the harbour on a wooden viaduct of 11 spans, each 50 feet wide

DONABATE, a living which was held by Pilkington, the author of "*Dictionary of Painters*," who was born at the seat of C. Cobbe, Esq., *Newbridge*, in 1730, the collection of pictures at which was selected by him. Close at hand is *Turrey*, the old seat of the Barnewell family (Lord Trimlestown), whose tombs are in the old church.

RUSH and LUSK.—The former has a pier harbour, defended by a martello tower. *Rush House*, the seat of R. Palmer, Esq., contains a fine gallery of old masters, and many antiquities, especially vases from Pompeii; and the latter place contains the east end of the Abbey Church, with fonts, and effigies of Sir C. Barnewell, W. Dermot, J. Birmingham, square steeple, stone-roofed crypt, with round turrets at three corners, and a round uncapped tower on the fourth; close to which is *Kenmure*, the seat of Sir R. Palmer, Bart., with an old church, with camp and martello towers close at hand.

SKERRIES.

Telegraph station at Malahide, $8\frac{3}{4}$ miles.

MARKET DAY.—Saturday.

FAIRS —April 28, August 10.

MONEY ORDER OFFICE at Balbriggan, 4 miles.

It has a pier harbour and Holmpatrick Church, and is celebrated for the landing of Sir P. Sidney in 1575.

Meath.—A great part of this maritime county is occupied by valuable pasture grounds, divided by verdant banks; and the general aspect of the country may be described as that of an undulating, rich and highly cultivated plain. The farms are often very extensive, but the farm houses, except when they belong to large proprietors, are in general wretched huts; and the houses of the humbler classes are nothing but mud hovels. Yet the mansions of the nobility and gentry are numerous throughout every district, and in several instances are spacious and splendid. The ecclesiastical structures of past ages, venerable and picturesque in all the varied stages of decay, abound in nearly every part of the county; and in their vicinity are still remaining several ruinous crosses of elaborate workmanship.

BALBRIGGAN

Telegraph station at Malahide, 12¾ miles.

MARKET DAY.—Saturday, for corn

FAIRS.—April 29, September 29.

This place has a population of 2,959, who are chiefly employed in the stocking, linen, tanning, muslin, and embroidering trades. The harbour is inside a pier 600 feet long, with a fixed light 35 feet high, visible 10 miles distant. The Carjee Half Tide Rock lies one mile N.E.; and *Hampton Hill*, the seat of E. C. Hamilton, Esq., is close at hand.

Then passing GORMANSTON (near which lies *Gormanston Castle* Viscount Gormanston), and LAYTOWN, we arrive at

DROGHEDA.

A telegraph station.

HOTEL.—Imperial.

MARKET DAYS.—Fridays and Saturdays.

FAIRS.—March 10, April 11, May 12, June 22, August 26, October 29, November 21, December 19.

BANKERS.—Branch of Bank of Ireland, Provincial Bank of Ireland, Branch of Hibernian Joint Stock.

A parliamentary borough in the county of *Louth*, on the Boyne, one member, population 16,880 Cotten and linen yarn is spun. It enjoys a good trade in Irish produce, and bas remains of two old monasteries and St. Lawrence's town gate, a Tholsel or assize court, linen hall, and various other buildings, including the cathedral of the Romish diocese of Armagh, whose primate resides here. Small craft can come up to the quays from the sea, which is six miles below.

Two or three events serve to render the town memorable. Here Lord Deputy Poynings held a parliament in 1496, which enacted "Poyning's Law," establishing the supremacy of English rule. It was given up to storm by Cromwell in 1649, in revenge for the Irish massacre of 1641, when 100,000 Protestants were put to death. He breached the wall from Cromwell's Fort which commands the town. His career in Ireland is still remembered in the saying, "may the curse of Cromwell be on you." And on the 10th of July, 1690, the famous battle of the Boyne took place, when William III. utterly defeated the Jacobite party. It was fought at *Oldbridge*, three miles above the town, and a pillar on a rock 150 feet above the picturesque banks of the river marks where Schomberg (William's general) fell, in his 82nd year. William was in the thickest of the contest and narrowly escaped being shot. James II. stood at a safe distance from his gallant Irish on Donore Hill, commanding a view of the field; he slept at *Carntown Castle*, the night before, and William at *Ardagh House*. Two elms mark where Caillemote, the leader of the French Protestant auxiliaries, was buried. Sheephouse Farm was a point strongly contested by both parties. "Change leaders," said the beaten Irish, "and we will fight the battle over again," but their despicable sovereign made off as fast as he could to Dublin, where he met the Duchess of Tyrconnel. "Your countrymen run well, madam," he said. "Not quite so well as your majesty," said the lady, "for I see you have won the race." William of Drogheda, and Miles, were natives. Near at hand is the Grange, J. Maguire, Esq.

KELLS BRANCH.

Drogheda to Kells.

DULEEK has a fine stone cross and old church Fairs are held here on March 25th, May 3rd, June 24th, October 18th, and close at hand are *Drogheda House*, Marquis of Thomond; *Somerville*, Right Hon. Sir W. Somerville, Bart., M.P.; *Athcarne*, De Batte's seat, and *Platten*, J. D'Arcy's; and BEAUPARC, with *Beauparc House*, the seat of J. Lambert, Esq.

NAVAN.

HOTEL.—Moran's.

MARKET DAY.—Wednesday.

FAIRS —Easter and Trinity Mondays, Second Monday in September, 1st Monday in December.

This town, which was an important military station in Edward the Fourth's time, has a population of 6,898, who are engaged in the provision, flax, flour, and paper trades; has some fine cavalry barracks, a church with an old tower, Athlumney Castle, in ruins, and close at hand *Boyne Hill*, the seat of Lieut.-Col. J. Gerrard; then passing BALLYBEG, we arrive at

KELLS.

A telegraph station.

MARKET DAY.—Saturday.

FAIRS.—February 27, May 27, July 16, September 9, October 16, November 17.

The church contains tombs of the Marquis of Headfort's family, whose castle, with an old cross and round tower 99 feet high, are close at hand.

Louth.—One of the smallest counties in Ireland. returns two members. It abounds in those rude vestiges of antiquity which consist of earth-works, chiefly designed for sepulchral purposes, or acting as places of defensive habitation. Cromlechs, and other relics of anti-Christian ages, although much lessened in number within the last century, are still numerous, and in several instances extremely curious. There are also many remains of ecclesiastical and military structures.

DUBLIN AND BELFAST JUNCTION.

Drogheda to Dundalk and Newry.

DUNLEER: here fairs are held monthly.

CASTLEBELLINGHAM, has ruins of the old castle of the Bellinghams, destroyed at the battle of the Boyne, and *Castlebellingham House*, Sir A. E. Bellingham, Bart. Fairs, Easter Tuesday, and October 10th.

DUNDALK.

A telegraph station.
HOTEL.—Arthur's; Imperial.
MARKET DAY.—Monday.
FAIRS.—Third Wednesday in every month, except the 17th of May.
BANKERS —Branch of Bank of Ireland, Branch of National Bank of Ireland.

A borough and seaport town in the county of Louth, with a population of 13,300, who return one member. It is situated on the banks of a river of the same name, at the mouth of the Irish channel. It is a place of some traffic, from which considerable quantities of corn are annually exported. The manufacture of cambric, which forms part of the trading pursuit of the inhabitants, was first established here in 1737.

Passing MOUNTPLEASANT and JONESBOROUGH, at the latter of which places Fairs are held on June 4th, August 15th, October 21st, and December 4th, we arrive at

NEWRY.

Distance from station, 3 miles.
A telegraph station.
HOTEL.—Dransfield's.
STEAMERS to and from Liverpool twice a week. Fares 10s. and 3s. Return Tickets, available for 14 days, 15s.
MARKET DAYS.—Tuesday, Thursday & Saturday.
FAIRS.—April 3rd and October 29th.

This town has a population of 26,000, who return one member, and are employed in the iron and brass foundries, tanneries, linen, and glass manufactures. It is situated close to the Newry mountains, which rise 1,385 feet, and contains the ruins of a monastery, with a yew tree planted by St. Patrick, founded in 1237, by Maurice M'Loughlin; a castle built by Sir J. De Courcey, and destroyed by Bruce in 1318. It has a considerable coasting trade, but only small vessels can approach the Quay, all larger vessels being obliged to discharge their cargoes at Warrenpoint, six miles below it.

GORAH WOOD station.

POYNTZPASS, so called from Sir T. Poyntz having forced his band through the Pass, has ruins of a castle which commands its entrance. Fairs are held here 1st Saturday in every month. Acton church: close at hand are *Acton House*, R. Dobbs, Esq.; *Acton Lodge*, P. Quinn, Esq. (the descendant of Sir T. Poyntz); *Drumbanagher Castle*, Colonel Close; and TANDERAGEE (which has *Tanderagee Castle*, built on the site of *O'Hanteris Castle*), the Duke of Manchester. Markets on Wednesday, and Fairs 1st Wednesday in every month, July 5th, and November 5th.

NEWRY, WARRENPOINT, AND ROSTREVOR.

WARRENPOINT.

Telegraph station at Newry, 6 miles.
HOTEL.—Royal: new, clean, and comfortable; conducted on English principles.
FAIRS.—Last Friday in every month.

This is one of the most picturesque and romantically situated watering places in Ireland, and consequently much frequented. It occupies a very pretty site on Narrow Water, at the head of Carlingford Bay, and on the line of the Newry Navigation. It contains a church, built by R. Hall, Esq., of Narrow Water Castle, in 1825; a Roman Catholic Chapel, Presbyterian and Wesleyan Chapels, &c. &c.

ROSTREVOR.

Distance from station, 2½ miles.
Telegraph station at Newry, 8½ miles.
MARKET DAY.—Saturday.
FAIRS.—Shrove Tuesday, August 1st, September 19th, November 1st, and December 11th.

This is a pretty and fashionable watering place in Carlingford Bay. It contains remains of *Castle Rory*, built by the Dungannons; a granite obelisk to General Ross, some salt works, which employ the greater portion of the 690 inhabitants. Close by is *Rostrevor Lodge*, D. Ross, Esq.

Dublin and Belfast Junction Main Line continued.

PORTADOWN.

A telegraph station.
HOTEL.—Manchester Arms.
MARKET DAY.—Saturday.
FAIRS.—Third Saturday in the month, Easter and Whit-Monday.

This town has a population of 2,560, engaged in the linen trade. Here are ruins of a castle given by Charles I. to the Obyns, and which belongs to the Duke of Manchester, Close at hand is *Ballyworkan*, seat of G. Pepper, Esq.

Armagh, which returns two members, is beautifully diversified with gentle hills; the soil is rich and fertile, except in the district called the Fewes, which is exceedingly mountainous, but even a considerable part of this rough tract has been brought into cultivation. Throughout the county, however, the farms are in general small. The linen manufacture in all its branches flourishes here, and, indeed, forms the chief employment of the inhabitants.

ULSTER.

Monaghan to Armagh and Belfast.

MONAGHAN.

A telegraph station.
HOTELS.—Mc.Philips' and Campbell's.
MARKET DAYS.—Monday (for linen and pigs), Tuesday, Wednesday, and Saturday, (for grain.)
FAIRS.—1st Monday in every month.

Coaches to Smithbro', Clones, Belturbet, Cavan, &c., run to and from this station in connection with the trains joining the Dundalk and Enniskillen line at Clones, and the Midland Great Western, at Cavan. In the vicinity are *Cortarvin*, the seat of

Lord Rossmore; *Castle Shane*, Right Hon. E. Lucas; *Camla Vale*, Colonel Westenra.

This town was built by the Blaneys in 1611, and has a population of 3,484, who are principally shopkeepers. Large flour mills are in the vicinity. The Ulster canal passes the town. Its public buildings consist of a county court house and jail, cavalry barracks, fever hospital, and workhouse. Close at hand are the ruins of some forts. *Cortalvin*, Lord Rossmore; *Castle Shane*, Right Hon. E. Lucas; *Camla Vale*, Colonel Westenra.

GLASSLOUGH, TYNAN, and KILLYLEA stations.

ARMAGH.

A telegraph station.

HOTEL.—Wiltshire's.

MARKET DAYS.—Tuesday, Wednesday, and Sat.

FAIRS.—May 21st, June 10th, Aug. 12th, Tuesday efore Oct. 10th, and Nov. 20th.

BANKERS.—Branch of Bank of Ireland; Branch of Belfast Banking Co.; Branch of Northern Banking Co.; Branch of Ulster Banking Co.; Provincial Bank of Ireland.

This is the seat of the primacy of Ireland and a city, returning one member. It is well seated on *Druira Sailech*, i. e., Willow Hill, near the Callan, and originated, it is said, in a church and college founded by St. Patrick, in 435, which became a celebrated school of learning. Some writers, indeed, go back to a royal city called *Eamania*, and a palace of the Ulster kings, three or four centuries before Christ, but this is fabulous. After suffering from war and other contests, in which it was burnt about 17 times, it was reduced to a mere heap of cottages, when Dr. Robinson (Lord Rokeby) succeeded, in 1765, to the primacy, and began to renovate it. To this munificent prelate it is indebted for some of its best buildings and endowments, such as the *Palace*, a quiet looking pile, 90 feet long, with beautiful gardens, open to the public, a chapel, some abbey ruins, and a column of 157 feet, built as a memorial to the Archbishop's friend, the Duke of Northumberland; the *College*, or royal school, near the Mall; a public lending *Library*, close to the cathedral, with 14,000 vols., from which any one within 30 miles may borrow—besides a reading-room in the Tontine Buildings. A well-organised *Observatory* on a hill 110 feet high, north of the college, containing transit zenith-sector, mural circle, telescope, Electro-Meter, &c.; assembly rooms, the county *Infirmary*, besides barracks, shambles, and bridges. To these Primate Beresford added a Fever Hospital, and Primate Stewart the Market-house.

The *Mall* is a well kept walk, near the Deanery, about 1,500 feet long. At one end is the Court House, built in 1809, of the coarse marble quarried here, with a Grecian portico, &c. The *County Jail* is near it. A *Lunatic Asylum* was built in 1825, for £20,000, on the Ballynahone ruin, not far from the town. Armagh is now, through the liberality of various primates of the see, one of the prettiest towns in Ulster. Most of the houses are of stone, with slated roofs. There are linen halls for the sale of the staple produce of the district, with corn mills, tanneries, &c., and 5 banks, one of the latter being built on the site of a monastery, founded in 610, by St. Columb. A Wesleyan chapel stands where John Wesley often preached. *St. Mark's* church is modern.

On top of the hill, on the site of St. Patrick's wooden church is the *Cathedral*, which was rebuilt in 1675, in the shape of a cross. It is only 183½ feet long, or less than many English parish churches; but it is yet one of the largest in Ireland, which has few grand ecclesiastical buildings to show, except those that are picturesque ruins. Armagh *Cathedral* has been lately restored by Cottingham (the restorer of St. Alban's church), chiefly at the cost of the present primate, Lord J. Beresford, whose total subscriptions for this object have amounted to £30,000. There is a bust of the excellent Archbishop Robinson, by Bacon, and other monuments by Rysbrach, Roubiliac, and Chantrey. Brian Boru was brought here to be buried after the battle of Clontarf. Not far off is the Roman Catholic cathedral, a handsome building in course of erection; works in abeyance, (1859).

The ecclesiastical province of Armagh takes in one half of Ireland (the other half belonging to Dublin), including six dioceses. That of Tuam was an archbishopric before 1834, when it was suppressed; hence the Romish Dr. M'Hale's boast, that he is the *only* Archbishop of Tuam.

One of the most distinguished holders of the primacy was the learned and pious Usher or Usther, whose family name (like the Butlers, Grosvenors, and others), originated in an office held about court by its founder. Usher came to the primacy in 1624, and retained it through good and evil report till episcopacy was abolished, and Charles I. brought to the block. He had the anguish of witnessing his sovereign's execution from the leads of Wallingford House (now the Admiralty), at Charing Cross; and commemorated the day by fasting and prayer, till his death, which happened at his friend Lady Peterborough's, at Reigate. A love of books, a sweet temper, and a quiet firmness of principle, were the chief traits in this amiable prelate's character.

In the neighbourhood are various objects of notice, such as Navanrath, said to be the real site of *Eamania*; Crieve Roe—Nial's grave, where a King of Ulster was drowned in 846; Dobbin's Valley, a beautiful cultivated hollow; the Vicar's Cairn; *Castle Dillon*, seat of Sir T. Molyneux, Bart.; Hamilton's Baun, *i.e.* a fort, about 60 feet square, the scene of many cruelties in the massacre of 1641, and on which Swift wrote some lines. The county has a cultivated and prosperous appearance.

RICHHILL (where Fairs are held on Shrove Tuesday, July 26th, October 15th).
PORTADOWN Junction.

PORTADOWN, DUNGANNON, AND OMAGH JUNCTION.

Portadown to Dungannon.

ANNAGHMORE and TREW and MOY stations.

DUNGANNON.

A telegraph station.

MARKET DAYS.—Monday (grain), Thursday (linen, cattle, provisions.)

FAIRS.—1st Thursday in every month.

The spirit of improvement manifest here, by its being the place of residence of the Earl of Lurgan, speaks greatly in his favour.

Coaches run in connection with the trains between Dungannon and Omagh stations.

Ulster Main Line continued.

LURGAN, which had a castle burnt in 1641, and rebuilt in 1690, and where Markets are held on Fridays, and Fairs the 2nd Thursday in every month August 5th, and November 22nd.

MOIRA.

Here is *Moira Castle*, the seat of the Hastings family, and the birth place of the first Marquis, the gallant Earl Moira, grandfather of the lamented and amiable Lady Flora Hastings, whose melancholy demise has cast an indelible stain on the British Court of the 19th century. Fairs are held on the 1st Thursday in February, May, August, and November. Markets on Thursday. We then arrive at

LISBURN.

Telegraph station at Belfast, 8½ miles.
HOTEL.—Mrs. Lennon's.
MARKET DAY.—Tuesday.
FAIRS.—July 21st and October 5th.
BANKERS.—Branch of Northern Banking Co.

LISBURN, 8 miles from Belfast, up the Lagan, is a pretty thriving seat of the linen trade (population 6,384), which was first introduced by the French Huguenots (Protestants), driven out of France in 1685, by Louis XIV.'s revocation of the Edict of Nantes. The present court-house was their chapel. Near Two Sisters' Elms are traces of a castle, built by the Lord Conway, who founded the town in 1627. *Lisburn House*, seat of Earl of Lisburn, at whose seat, Golden Grove, in Wales, Jeremy Taylor found shelter in the civil wars, and wrote some of his best works. He died here in 1667, and is buried in Blaris church, as also is Lieutenant Dobbs, who was killed in action against Paul Jones in 1778, which is the parish church of Lisburn, and the cathedral of Down diocese; it is marked by an octagonal spire. Bishop E. Smith was a native. Here are large damask thread and flax-spinning factories.

Passing DUNMURRY, where are the remains of walls, and *Dunmurry House*, the seat of W. Hunter, Esq., we arrive at BALMORAL, and soon after at

BELFAST.

A telegraph station.

HOTELS.—Imperial, Royal, Commercial, Queen's, and Plough.

CARRIAGES and CARS at the station and hotels. Tariff—1s. per hour (driver included).

TARIFF OF CARS, HACKNEY COACHES, &c.

	By Distance. s.	d.	Time. s.	d.
For the hire of a 2 wheeled carriage (1 horse) per mile	0	6		
Ditto ditto per hour			1	0
For every additional half mile	0	3		
Ditto ditto half hour			0	4
If by the day	8	0	8	0
For the hire of a 4 wheeled carriage (1 horse) per mile	0	8		
Ditto ditto per hour			1	4
For every additional half mile	0	4		
Ditto ditto half hour			0	6
If by the day	10	8	10	8
For the hire of 2 horse carriages per mile	1	0		
Ditto ditto per hour			1	8
For every additional half mile	0	6		
Ditto ditto half hour			0	8
If by the day	13	6	13	6

Luggage not exceeding 112lbs. is carried free. The tolls must be paid by the hirer, but no gratuities are to be given to drivers.

OMNIBUS FARES between Commercial Buildings, Botanical Gardens, and Queen's College, once hourly, from 9 a.m. to 7 p.m., 2d.; Castle Place, York Street, and the Ballymena railway station, 2d.; Commercial Buildings, Great Victoria Street, and the Ulster railway station, 2d.; Commercial Buildings, Queen's Quay, and the Belfast and County Down railway station, 1½d.

STEAMERS.—See *Bradshaw's Guide*.
MARKET DAY.—Friday.
FAIRS.—August 12th and November 8th for horses.
BANKERS.—Ulster Banking Co.; Belfast Banking Co.; Provincial Bank of Ireland; Branch of Bank of Ireland.

This is the great seat of the Irish linen trade, and the capital of Ulster, in Antrim county, at the mouth of the Lagan, where it falls into Belfast Lough, on a flat situation, among hills, which at Divis, rise into a fine mountain peak, 1,513 feet high. Though ranking the second port in Ireland, it stands first for manufactures and trade, returning one member. The tall chimnies and factories for spinning linen and cotton yarn are the most conspicuous buildings; none of the churches are worth remark; in fact Belfast is a modern town, scarcely going back beyond the last century. In 1805, the customs' duties were only £3,700, but in 1846, upwards of £360,000, while the registered tonnage of the port amounted to £62,000. The first graving dock was constructed in 1795, but since 1839 very great improvements have been made in the harbour, a deep channel having been cut right up to the town, so that large vessels drawing 16 or 18 feet water, which used to stop at Garmoyle, are now able to discharge cargo at the new quays, which with splendid docks, &c., have cost the corporation half a million of money. The rates also are low, and the consequence is that the tonnage inwards and outwards has nearly doubled. The lighthouse stands on screw piles, worming down into the sand and rock. There are building slips for vessels of 1,000 tons, besides foundries, machine factories, 50 spinning mills, weaving factories, dye and bleach works, provision stores, &c.

The staple manufactures include damask, diapers, drills, cambrics, plain and printed linens, and handkerchiefs of all kinds; among cotton goods are velvets, fustians, jeans, gingham, quilting, muslin, embroidery, calico printing, &c. A society for encouraging flax-growing in Ireland was established here in 1841; and there is an excellent *School of Design.* Goods are sold at the white and brown (or unbleached) Linen Halls, which Queen Victoria inspected on her visit to the town in 1849. The *Commercial Buildings*, in the Ionic style, were built in 1822. At the Literary Society is a good museum; the Botanical Society possesses a garden on the river, where an island of 20 acres has been laid out with shrubberies.

Belfast is honourably distinguished for its literary exertions, and abounds in schools and societies for the promotion of education as well as of arts and letters. Here Dr. Edgar began the temperance movement as early as 1828. Besides the Academy, founded in 1786, and the Royal Academical Institution, founded in 1810, both of a collegiate character, there is the new *Queen's College*, established under Sir R. Peel's Act, a handsome Tudor pile, 300 feet long, built by Lanion, and opened in 1849. Benevolent societies of all kinds are numerous.

Out of 50 churches and chapels (the presbyterian being nearly one half), the visitor may notice *St. Ann's*, with a copper roof and wooden spire, and the Grecian portico of *St. George's*, which originally belonged to a palace, begun by Lord Bristol (a freethinking bishop of Derry), at Ballyscullion. The palace of the Bishop of Down is here. One of the four chapels is the Roman Catholic Cathedral of Down.

It was at Belfast, and not till 1704, that the first English Bible published in Ireland, was printed. A handsome bridge (Queen's Bridge), on five arches, built in 1841, crosses the Lagan (besides two others) to the suburb of Ballymacarrett, in county Down. Formerly there was a long straggling bridge, 2,560 feet, which many a weary traveller must have found to be a bridge of size indeed. The Bay or Lough in which Belfast stands is a fine roomy channel, 15 miles long, and 3 to 6 broad. An excellent view of it is obtained from Mac Art's Fort, on the top of Cave Hill, a basalt peak, 1,200 feet high, 3 miles northwest. The stone quarried here is carried down to the harbour by a tram rail. Near it is White House factory, where Mr. Grimshaw built the first cotton mill in Ireland, in 1784.

It was from this place that John M'Cormac, Esq. a native, sailed to the Western Coast of Africa, from whence he was the first to introduce the Teak timber, of which so many ships of war have been and are still constructed in the British Government Dock Yards.

Within a few miles are *Ormeau*, the seat of the Marquis of Donegal, chief landed proprietor here; *Belvoir*, Sir R. Bateson, Bart.; and a vast Druidical remain, called the Giant's Ring, in the centre of which is a cromlech, or Druid's altar. Divis Mountain had a small observatory fixed there by the Ordnance Survey, till a storm carried it away. When Drummond's light was first exhibited in 1826, on Slieve Snaght in Donegal, it was seen here, though 66 miles distant. Cave Hill commands a fine view.

BELFAST AND COUNTY DOWN.

Belfast to Newtownards & Downpatrick.

Down, a maritime county, bounded east and south by the Irish sea, returns two members. Its surface is extremely irregular; in some parts mountainous and hilly, in others level and flat. The highest mountain is Slieve Donard, which rises 2,800 ft. above the level of the sea. Woods and forests are found in various parts, and taken as a whole, the county may be considered both productive and beautiful. There are several mineral springs here, but the chalybeate ones are the most numerous. The principal employment of the inhabitants is in making of linen and muslin; the bleaching is carried on to a considerable extent on the banks of the river Bann.

Passing KNOCK, DUNDONALD, and COMBER the latter of which has an old castle, Druidical remains, and a church, built on the site of an old abbey, Fairs, January 14th, April 5th, June 28th, and October 19th, we arrive at

NEWTOWNARDS, a town of muslin weavers and embroiderers, belonging to the Londonderry family, at the head of Lough Strangford, which is a lagoon full of islands, with nothing notable about it except Grey Abbey. "Will Watch, the bold smuggler," flourished at Newtownards. The railway is now open to Donaghadee harbour, whence a submarine telegraph was laid down in 1853, across to the Scottish coast. In front of the harbour are the Copeland Islands, near which, before a lighthouse was built, the Enterprise sunk in 1801; she was loaded with dollars, a part of which was afterwards recovered by Bell in his diving apparatus.

At **Bangor,** 5 miles north of Newtownards, a pretty bathing place, in the mouth of Lough Belfast, is the castle of Lord Bangor. The name is derived from the Bean choir or white (*i.e.* stone) church, built here in the 12th century, when stone churches were more uncommon, instead of the wooden buildings attached to an ancient monastery here. *Ballyleidy* belongs to the Lord Dufferin; the Dowager Lady Dufferin is a grand-daughter of Sheridan, and the author of a beautiful poem. *Craufordsburn*, seat of Sharman Crauford, Esq., the great advocate of tenant-right; here there is a customary charge of £5 to £20 an acre, paid by the incoming tenant to his predecessor, for the good will as it were, on the ground of improvements. Most of the people in the lowlands of this county are of Scottish descent.

Retracing our steps to the junction at Comber, we pass on, *via* BALLYGOWAN and SAINTFIELD to BALLYNAHINCH and the city of

DOWNPATRICK.

MARKET DAY.—Saturday. FAIRS.—First Saturday in each month.

Situated on the river Quoile, in a valley, at the south-west corner of Strangford Lough, has a population of nearly 5,000, and returns one member to parliament. The Cathedral contains the tomb of Lord Kehany; the window at the east end is worth notice.

Belfast to Holywood.

Passing SYDENHAM and TILLYSBURN, we arrive at

HOLYWOOD.

A telegraph station.
HOTEL.—Power's.
MARKET DAY.—Saturday.
FAIRS.—Every three months.

HOLYWOOD, or Hollywood, is a pretty bathing place on the Lough, 5 miles from Belfast, where the Irish Presbyterians signed the Solemn League and Covenant, 1644. The church is on the site of a priory, from which the name of the place is derived.

Antrim.—A maritime county in the province of Ulster, returns two members. The principal towns are Belfast, Lisburn, Carrickfergus, Antrim, and Ballymoney. The chief employment of its inhabitants is the manufacture of linen, and the flax is extensively grown; and many of the farmers are weavers. Their farms seldom exceed a few acres in extent. The county is in some parts mountainous and barren; the richer and more fertile districts lay towards the south.

BELFAST AND NORTHERN COUNTIES.

From Belfast, we pass the stations of GREENCASTLE, WHITEABBEY, and JORDANSTOWN, and arrive at the Junction of the

CARRICKFERGUS BRANCH.

In the course of five or six minutues after passing the station at TROOPER'S LANE, the arrival of the train is announced at

CARRICKFERGUS.

Distance from station, 1 mile.
A telegraph station.
OMNIBUSES to and from the station.
MARKET DAY.—Saturday.
FAIRS.—May 12, November 1.

A seaport town in the county of Antrim, situated on a bay called Belfast Lough, or Carrickfergus Bay, Its name signifies the Rock of Fergus, from an Irish chieftain Fergus, who was drowned here. A castle built by the De Courceys, on the site of this fort, still exists, with its two towers, and walls nine feet thick; it commands the harbour below, in which King William landed in 1689, on his Irish campaign. Parts of the town walls are left.

The town was once the principal seaport of the north of Ireland, but its trade has been for the most part transferred to Belfast; the fishery in the bay employs a great portion of its inhabitants, and many others are occupied in spinning and weaving. It is a principal depôt for military purposes. Bishop Tennison was a native. Close at hand are *Thornfield*, P. Kirk, Esq.; *Glynn Park*, Captain Skinner.

Belfast and Northern Counties Main Line continued.

Passing BALLYNURE (here Fairs May 16th, September 5th, and October 25th), BALLYCLARE, and DUNADRY stations, we reach

ANTRIM.

A telegraph station.
HOTEL.—Mc.Matly's.
MARKET DAYS.—Tuesday and Thursday.

FAIRS.—January 1st, May 12th, August 1st, November 12th.

BANKERS.—Ulster Banking Co.

This small town, which gives name to *Antrim* county, stands at the mouth of Six Mile Water, as it falls into Lough Neagh, has a population of 6,000, whose trade consists of paper, linen, &c. All this part of Ireland once belonged to the O'Neils or O'Nials; and in the petty contests which took place between them and the settlers planted over their heads by James I., Antrim had a full share. The last historical event was the death of Lord O'Neill, who was mortally wounded, in an action with the rebels of 1798, though the latter were defeated. St. Patrick, the missionary and church-builder, founded a church here in 495, which the present structure replaces. There is nothing remarkable in it, but close at hand is a perfect *Round Tower*, 95 feet high, well worth examination. There are about 80 of these singular towers in Ireland, of which about one-third are perfect. "They are from 60 to 130 feet high and only 8 to 11 feet in diameter; being shaped in general like the Eddystone Lighthouse. Each story is lit by a single window; and the whole pile is surmounted by a cap or conical roof." From the absence of any authentic early history of Ireland, it is difficult to account for their origin. Whether they were built by the Irish, or the Danes, whether for Christian or pagan uses, is a keen subject of dispute with antiquarians—each of whom, like Smith O'Brien, Esq., would "die on the floor" for his favourite theory, and would probably perish of *ennui* if the question were satisfactorily settled. Those in existence are always found to be near a church or abbey; and human bones have been discovered at the bottom of some. Dr. Petrie, the best informed of Irish writers on this fertile theme, thinks they were built for belfries, and also as storehouses in cases of attack. The square keep of Norman castles, and the peel towers on the Scottish border were designed for a similar purpose, and are built on much the same plan.

Lough Neagh, the largest lake in the United Kingdom (nearly 100,000 acres, 60 miles in circuit), is a fine sheet of water, At one period it was surrounded by immense forests, the fallen timber of which in process of ages has been converted into coal and lignite, in which cornelian and other pebbles are found. This lignite, which is a common production in certain localities, gave rise to a story that "the waters of the lake were petrifying;" while the stumps of trees seen at the bottom have been magnified into the "round towers of other days" of Moore's song. There are three small islands, and the Bann is its only outlet. As it is not more than 102 feet in the deepest part, the time may come when this immense basin of useless water will be drained, like the lake of Haarlem. Two miles from Antrim, on the west side of the bay, towards Randalstown, is *Shane's Castle*, the seat of the O'Neill's, but now owned by the Rev. Mr. Chichester.

A small feeder of the lake, Maine Water, runs through the grounds, which are large and well planted. The castle itself was burnt in 1816, and is a picturesque ruin; a small house near it is now occupied by the family, The castle is supposed to be haunted by the Banshee, whose wail is heard whenever one of the O'Neills die. This is firmly believed. A bloody or red hand is the arms of Ulster, from the story that "the first O'Neill was one of a company, the leader of which promised that whoever touched the land first should have it. O'Neill, seeing another boat ahead of his, took a sword, cut off his left hand, flung it ashore, and so was first to touch it." This hand appears in the arms of all baronet's dignity, created by James I., at the plantation of Ulster. Within a short distance are *Antrim Castle*, the seat of Viscount Massareene; and *Castle Upton*, the ancient Elizabethan seat of Lord Templetown.

COOKSTOWN JUNCTION.

COOKSTOWN BRANCH.

RANDALSTOWN.

Telegraph station at Antrim, 5¼ miles.
HOTEL.—O'Neill's Arms.
MARKET DAY.—Saturday.
FAIRS.—July 16th, November 1st.

This place, which was burnt by the rebels in 1798, has a population of 1,300, employed in cotton spinning and weaving; Barracks, Market House, five Chapels, and Dispensary.

Passing the intermediate stations of STAFFORDSTOWN, TOOME, CASTLEDAWSON, MAGHERAFELT, and MONEYMORE, we arrive at the terminus of the branch at

COOKSTOWN.

HOTELS.—Commercial; Stewart's Arms.
MARKET DAYS.—Tuesday and Saturday.
FAIRS.—First Saturday in each month.

This town contains upwards of 6,000 inhabitants, who are chiefly employed in the linen trade. In the vicinity is *Killymoon*, now in the occupation of Mr. Cooper (Saxon style, designed by Nash, who built Derryloran church), owner of the town. *Lissan*, seat of Sir T. Staples, Bart. There are also some forts and other remains to be seen.

Belfast and Northern Counties Main Line continued.

BALLYMENA.

A telegraph station.
HOTEL.—Ainsworth's.
MARKET DAY.—Saturday, for linens.
FAIRS.—July 26th, August 21st.
BANKERS.—Provincial Bank of Ireland; draw on Spooner and Attwoods.

Here are the ruins of an old castle, founded by the Adairs, which the rebels held in 1798. The town has a population of 6,000, principally employed in the linen trade.

Londonderry.—The general appearance of this county, which returns two members, is mountainous and barren, but the soil in the vallies is very fertile. A range of mountains running from the northern coast, the whole length of the county, in a southern direction, forms the principal ridge n the county. This mountainous region consists of wild Alpine tracts, uplands covered with heath, and rough gravelly basaltic eminences. Londonderry is particularly rich in its minera products, which if properly worked would give employmen and opulence to its inhabitants.

BELLAGHY.—Monthly cattle fairs are held, and in the vicinity are *Bellaghy House*, J. Hill, Esq., and *Bellaghy Castle* H. Hunter, Esq.

BALLYMONEY.—Fairs are held on May 6th, July 10th, August 10th, and markets on Thursdays; it has a population of about 4,000, who are engaged in the linen and butter trade, Close at hand are *Leslie Hill*, J. Leslie, Esq., *O'Hara Brook*, C. O'Hara, Esq.

COLERAINE.

A telegraph station.

HOTEL.—Clothworkers' Arms.

STEAMERS.—See *Bradshaw's Railway Guide*.

MARKET DAYS.—Monday, Wednesday, Friday and Saturday, for grain.

FAIRS.—May 12th, July 5th, November 3rd.

BANKERS.—Provincial Bank of Ireland.

A borough town, with a population of 5,857, who return one member, and are employed in the salmon and eel fisheries, and manufactures of paper, soap, candles, and leather, situated on the banks of the river Bann, about three miles from the sea. The town is large and handsome, and contains a church built in 1614, with old tombs, which stands on the site of the priory and old abbey. Close at hand is mount Sandel, 200 feet high; *Down Hill*, Mrs. Maxwell; *Dundoun House*, J. Boyd, Esq. The port to this town is very difficult of access, occasioned by the extreme rapidity of the river, which repels the tide, and renders the approach up of vessels of large burthen very difficult. Archbishop Vesey was a native.

Passing PORTSTEWART (a small bathing place, of which Dr. Adam Clarke, the commentator, was a native) and to whom a monument has just been erected, (1859), we arrive at

PORTRUSH.

Telegraph station at Coleraine, 6½ miles.
HOTEL.—Coleman's.
MONEY ORDER OFFICE at Coleraine, 6 miles.

This small, yet pretty bathing place, which has Dr. Adam Clarke's School and monument, and where the *mirage* is often seen, is beautifully situated on a basalt peninsula, opposite the Skerries Rocks, and has an excellent view of the

GIANT'S CAUSEWAY.

The railway being now completed to Portrush, an easy access is opened to this remarkable place, which by no means ought to be lost sight of. To those who have time, a most picturesque tour along the coast from Carrickfergus, about 64½ miles, is recommended. The route is thus divided: Carrickfergus to Larne, 12 miles; Glenarm, 12; Cushendall, 13; to Ballycastle, 14½; to Giant's Causeway (near Bushmills), 13 miles; inclusive of walking round Benmore and Bengore Heads, where the grandest scenery presents itself. From Carrickfergus to Larne, you leave Glenoe valley on one side, and Larne Lough and Island Magee (belonging to the Donegal family) on the other. The cliffs and caves of the island are frequently basaltic, especially at the Gobbins. Larne has a castle; Edward Bruce landed here in 1315; much lime is sent from thence to Scotland. Angnew mountain, to the left, 1,560 feet high. The new road begins here; at a ledge, cut or blasted out of the cliff's side, a few feet above the sea, while the old road is 600 or 700 feet higher, and commands a view of the Scottish coast. Off Ballygally Head are the Maiden Rocks and Lights. Cairncastle, up the hills to the left, which are 1,000 to 1,200 feet high. *Glenarm*, the seat of the Earl of Antrim, head of the M'Donnels, on a beautiful bay at the mouth of a fine glen and a stream from Slemish Mountain (1,451 feet high), and which commands one of the most extensive views of open sea in the United Kingdom. Much lime and stone are sent to Scotland. Then come Stradkelly, Cairn Lough (Collin Top to the left, 1,420 feet), Ringfadrock. *Drumnasole*, (seat of A. Turnley, Esq., the owner,) is here. Nachore Mountain, 1,180 feet, Drumnaul Castle, on Garson Point, whence a noble sea view across to Scotland. Here the road turns to Glenariff, the finest of many picturesque glens opening into Red Bay, so called because of the colour of the sandstone cliffs. Past Clogh-i-Stookan Rock (curiously shaped), the Tunnel Rock and Caves, near Red Bay Castle, to Cushendall and its basalt pillars. Near this are Layde Church, where Ossian, they say, is buried, Court Martinrath, Lurg Eidem, and other haunts of Ossian's hero, Fin M'Coul, and Trosten Mountain, 1,800 feet high; then Castle Carey and Cushendern House and Bay. Here the road turns off to Ballycastle, leaving *Fair Head* or *Benmore Head* to the right, a visit to which must on no account be omitted, as the basalt pillars exceed in beauty those of the Causeway. Proceeding over the desolate hills by the coast you come to Tor Point, near Cairnlea Mountain, (1,250 feet) and Murlough Bay, where the strata of the Ballycastle coal-field may be noticed,—a mixture of coal, with clay, slate, shale, sandstone, lime, and green basalt or whinstone. Coal is worked here. Boats may be obtained by going round Fair Head, it weather permits; but it may be examined, though not so well, by land. The vast basaltic mass is seen resting on an irregular base 300 feet thick, composed of the coal strata, above which it rises 336 feet higher, straight and solid as a wall, though found when examined to consist of jointed pillars packed closely together, some 20 to 30 feet across, and are, as geologists tell us, the "work of internal fires." Enormous blocks are heaped up round the base of the cliffs. A narrow chasm, called Gray Man's Path, cuts right through, and makes a rough sloping walk from the landward side down to the beach, with a glimpse of the sea; a broken pillar, like the shaft of a ruined temple, lies across it. Opposite Fair Head, three or four miles distant, is Rathlin Island, with Bruce's Castle (where he found refuge), hanging over basaltic rocks resembling those on the main land. After Fair Head comes Salt Pans; then Ballycastle, an old seat of the M'Donnels, the Antrim family (the resemblance of the late lamented Earl to Charles the First was proverbially striking), whose burial-place is here, with the Abbey of Bonamargy, founded by them; and Kenbaan Castle, on a singular rock composed of *chalk* and basalt. The next thing is the famous *Carrick-a-rede* rock, which stands out 60 feet from the shore, to which it is joined only by a slender rope bridge across the chasm, 80 feet from the water. A fine view from the heights above it. Sheep Island, Ballintry, and Dunseverick Castle follow next, where the peculiar scenery round Bengore Head to Giant's Causeway begins; but the best plan is to go on to the Causeway Inn, at the other end of it, a few miles further on, where guides and boats may be hired. Guide, 2s. 6d. a day. It is usual to walk from here along the beach to Dunseverick, and then take the boat back, to obtain the full advantage of the effects. For four miles the coast is a series of little caves, rugged bays or ports, and picturesque rocks, most fancifully shaped, among which you walk, with a sort of undercliff on one side, several hundred feet high, composed of piles of basalt, mixed with other rocks. Beginning at Port-na-baw, you pass Weir's Snoot, and the Great and Little Stoocans, two heap-like rocks, and turn into Port Gannixy. Then follow Aird's Snoot, and the *Giant's Causeway*, properly so called,—consisting of a low promontory or rocky pier sloping into the sea for 800 or 900 feet, and made up of about 40,000 dark basalt pillars, tolerably upright and regular, mostly five or six sided, whilst some have only three, and others as many as nine sides. They are all jointed, and stand 30 feet above the beach in the highest part, with an uneven surface 300 feet wide. Here they show Lord Antrim's parlour, the giant's gate, parlour, loom, theatre, &c.; then Port Noffer and Sea Gull rock, with the organ in the face of the cliffs, exactly like the pipes of an organ, the Dyke in Port Reostax; the Chimney Tops (three or four solitary pillars over a corner of the cliff), leading into Port-na-Shania, where a ship of the Spanish Armada came ashore, and then another giant's organ in the cliffs. Then the Horse's Back and Port-na-Collian, which contains several strange rocks, as the Priest and his Flock, the Nursing Child, the King and his Nobles, &c Port-rea-Tobber and a second Sea-Gull island, then follow; the cliff above being called Lover's Leap. The next and grandest bay and fall is Port-na-Pleaskin, which should be seen from *Hamilton's Seat*, 400 feet above, so calle from Dr. Hamilton, whose interesting letters from the Northern Coast made the locality known to the world. The succession of pillars and stratifications of the rocks along this remarkable coast are now fully visible. Horse Shoe Harbour, Lion's Head (a red rock), Kenbane Head, the Twins, Giant's Ball Alley, and Pulpit, follow next; then *Bengore Head;* the Giant's Granary and Four Sisters, in Port Fad; Contham Head leading round to Port Moon, which has a waterfall and a cave inside, Stack Rock, the Hen and Chickens, and other rocks, and at length Dunseverick Castle, built in the 12th century.

Westward of the Causeway, you may visit Port Coon Cave (100 yards long, into which boats can be rowed), the White Rocks, Priests' Hole Cave, and the remains of Dunluce Castle (formerly the M'Donnel's seat, on a wild rock cut off from the main land).

LONDONDERRY AND COLERAINE.

This line skirts the east and south banks of Lough Foyle, an arm of the sea about 15 miles long and 10 broad, dividing the northern portion of Derry from that of the county of Donegal, and runs, *via* BELLARENA, MAGILLIGAN, &c., to

LONDONDERRY.

A telegraph station.

HOTEL.—Imperial.

STEAMERS.—See *Bradshaw's Railway Guide.*

MARKET DAYS.—Wednesday, Thursday (flax), a d Saturday.

FAIRS.—June 17th, September 4th, October 17th.

BANKERS.—Branch Bank of Ireland; Branch of Belfast Banking Company; Branch of Northern Banking Company; Branch of Ulster Banking Company; Provincial Bank of Ireland.

The capital town of the county, which contains a population of 35,529, who return one member. It stands on the western bank of the Foyle, and consists of four principal streets, which cross each other at right angles, and from which a number of smaller ones diverge. As the ground on which the town is built is very hilly, many of the streets are exceedingly inconvenient for carriages, but every exertion has been made to repair this local disadvantage by the attention which is paid to the paving and lighting of them. The Cathedral is a very handsome edifice, built in the Gothic style of architecture. It was erected in 1633, and has, within the last few years, undergone extensive repairs. It has tombs of Drs. Knox and Hamilton, and two flags captured from the besiegers in May, 1689. Farquhar, the poet, and Dr. Hamilton were natives. Londonderry carries on a considerable commercial intercourse with America and the West Indies, it being favourably situated for commerce, and possesses an excellent secure harbour, with a splendid line of quays. This place stood a siege of 105 days in 1688 against James II. The walls around the city are still in good preservation, forming a favourite promenade. Close to the city court house is a celebrated gun called "Roaring Meg." The bishop's palace, built in 1761 (the walls of which are 1,800 feet in circuit and 24 feet high) is a fine building.

DUNDALK, ENNISKILLEN, AND LONDONDERRY.

Londonderry to Enniskillen & Dundalk.

CARRIGANS, close to which is *Dunmore*, the seat of R. M. Clintock, Esq.

ST. JOHNSTON, where fairs are held April 7th, October 13th, and November 26th.

PORTHALL station.

STRABANE has a population of 6,000, principally employed in the linen trade. Markets are held here on Tuesdays, and fairs first Thursday in every month, May and November 12th. Close at hand are *Miltown*, Major Dumfries; *Hollyhill* and *Strabane Glen*, J. Sinclare, Esq.

SION MILLS and VICTORIA BRIDGE stations.

NEWTOWNSTEWART.—This place was burnt by James II. after the siege of Derry, but rebuilt in 1722: here is shown the house in which James II slept. Close at hand are King O'Nial's castle, in ruins; *Baron's Court*, Marquis of Abercorn; *Newtownstewart*, Hon. Major Crawford. Markets are held here on Mondays, and fairs monthly.

MOUNTJOY, close to which is the seat of C. J. Gardner, Esq.

Tyrone.—A county in the province of Ulster, which returns two members, is bounded on the north by Londonderry, the south by Monaghan, the east by Lough-Neagh, and on the west by Donegal and Fermanagh. It is divided into four baronies.

OMAGH.

A telegraph station.

HOTEL.—Harkness'.

MARKET DAY.—Saturday.

FAIRS.—Monthly.

BANKERS.—National Provincial Bank of Ireland; Ulster Banking Company.

Here are ruins of an Abbey founded in 792, Church, five Chapels, Market and Court House, Barracks. Reading Room, Hospital, &c.

FINTONA, where markets are held on Fridays, and Fairs the 22nd of every month, and close to which is *Ecclesville*, seat of C. Eccles, Esq.

DROMORE ROAD, close to which is the town of Dromore, "the Great Ridge," which has a population of 14,954 employed in the linen trade; four chapels, market house, schools, clergy widows' houses, dispensary, factories, two bridges, on one of which there is a tablet to Bishop Percy; cathedral, built by Bishop Jeremy Taylor, whose tomb, together with that of Bishop Percy is here; Danish fort, remains of an elk, 10¼ feet between the horns. Fairs are held here on 1st Saturday in March, May 12th, August 6th, October 10th, December 14th; and Markets on Saturday for linen. Close at hand are *Gill Hall Castle*, Earl Clanwilliam; *Dromore House*, J. H. Quinn, Esq.

TRILLICK.—Markets are held here for butter, on Tuesdays, and Fairs on the 14th of every month, and close by are the ruins of *Castle Meragn.*

IRVINGSTOWN ROAD, near to which is Lowtherstown, where Markets are held on Wednesdays, and Fairs the 8th of every month, and April 12th.

Giant's Causeway.

Fermanagh. — This county, which returns two members, is divided by Lough Erne, which, properly speaking, consists of two lakes, the upper lake being nine miles in length, and from two to five in breadth, and the lower ten miles in length, and from two to eight in width, being connected with the former by a wide channel about seven miles long. The banks of these celebrated waters abound in picturesque scenes, although the surface of this county is not, in general, either productive or beautiful. Toward the northern division the land is tolerably productive, and farms are of considerable size. In other parts husbandry is more imperfectly understood.

Ballinamallard station.

ENNISKILLEN.

A telegraph station.

Hotel.—Imperial.

Market Day.—Tuesday.

Fairs.—10th of every month (March excepted).

Bankers.—Branch of Belfast Banking Company; Branch of Ulster Banking Company; National Provincial Bank of Ireland.

This town, which is situated in a fine spot on an island between Loughs Erne, contains a population of 14,678, who are engaged in the corn and general trade, and returns one member. It has three chapels, court house, county prison, infirmary, town hall (in which are the banners taken at the battle of the Boyne), linen hall, school, cavalry and artillery barracks, two bridges, brewery, tanneries, cutlery factory, Charles I.'s school, with ten exhibitions (five of £50 and £30). It is celebrated for the successful defence which the inhabitants made in 1688 on behalf of William III., and gives name to a regiment of dragoons. Close at hand are the beautiful seat and grounds of Lord Belmore, open to the public; *Florence Court*, Earl of Enniskillen; *Ely Lodge*, Marquis of Ely; *Tully Castle* and *Bellisle*, J. Porter, Esq.

Lisbellaw, Maguire's Bridge, Lisnaskea, and Newtownbutler stations.

CLONES.

Market Day.—Thursday.

Fairs.—Last Thursday in each month.

This town contains a population of about 3,000, principally engaged in the linen manufacture. It has the remains of an abbey, founded by St. Tierney.

Monaghan, which returns two members, is situate in the province of Ulster. Although this county is much incumbered with mountains and bogs, great portions of it are highly cultivated and improved (especially the northern parts). Numerous small lakes are in the country. The occupations of the population are chiefly agricultural, and the flax and turnip crops have of late been extensively cultivated. Agricultural and cattle shows are annually held, under the patronage of the country gentry. Large quantities of butter and other farm produce are sent to the English market.

Newbliss and Monaghan Road stations.

Ballybay.—Here Markets are held on Saturday, and Fairs on 3rd Saturday in every month. It is also the junction of a line to Cavan, 9 miles of which, to Cootehill are now open.

CASTLEBLANEY.

Telegraph station at Dundalk, 17¾ miles.

Hotel.—Mc.Master's.

Market Day.—Wednesday.

Fairs.—1st Wednesday in every month.

Castleblaney House, formerly belonging to Lord Blayney, has recently been purchased by Mr. Hope, who has put the beautiful grounds, spacious lake, &c., into exquisite order, and most liberally thrown them open to the public.

Culloville station.

Inniskeen was one of the chief seats of the Danes, and has ruins of several forts. Close at hand are *Northland*, Dean Adams; *Cabra Castle*, J. Pratt, Esq., close to the ruins of an old castle.

We now enter the county of Louth, and shortly after the town of

Dundalk.—See page 101.

THE PRINCE OF WALES' TOUR AT THE LAKES OF KILLARNEY.

The following particulars of the Prince of Wales' tour will be interesting:—

His Royal Highness and party patronized the Victoria Lake Hotel.

Friday.—The carriage was in attendance, and took his royal highness and party through Lord Kenmare's demesne, and thence to Ross Island. Having viewed all the beauties of this enchanting spot, they drove rapidly on to Muckross. Here they visited the venerable Abbey, with the history of which the Prince appeared not unfamiliar. On entering the aisle, he at once expressed a wish to see "The O'Donoghue's Tomb." He then asked to be shown the tombs of The M'Carthy More, and The O'Sullivan. Having inspected those, he expressed a desire to see the "Famous Yew Tree." Having examined for some time the mediæval giant, he went through the entire Abbey. The prince then drove to Muckross House, every part of which he examined minutely. He then drove along the beautiful shore of the Middle Lake to Dinis, thence to Torc Cascade, whose effect was much enhanced by the rains of the previous week. Having taken a lingering farewell of this fairy solitude, his Royal Highness next visited Torc Cottage, where Mr. Ross had a splendid lunch prepared. His Royal Highness and party then stepped on board a fine eight-oared barge, pulled by a crew whose dress and general appointments were faultless. Having crossed Torc Lake, and shot through Brickeenbridge, the barge soon reached Glena, with the beauty and exquisite seclusion of which the prince seemed fascinated. How much more was he delighted when Spillane, the worthy successor of the old historic Spillane, awoke the echoes with the National Anthem, with his matchless cornopean. The effect was thrilling. Several small cannon were also discharged at this point, and it was difficult to say whether the prince was most pleased with the aerial choir which multiplied, twenty-fold the undying "God save the

Queen," or the martial roar which rang from every hill, as from a many-mouthed battery. The prince laughed merrily, as Spillane, who to his knowledge of lake and legend unites a delicate wit, which is never out of place, gracefully said:—"Such is the impression which the arrival of your Royal Highness has made on the very echoes, that they have combined to give you such a welcome as you will not soon forget." The delighted party then proceeded along the Lower Lake, near its mountain shore, visiting O'Sullivan's cascade, and the many points of interest which surround the "seven-crested Tomies." They then pulled away for Innisfallen, with which, it is scarcely necessary to say, the prince was charmed. The exquisite verdure of Innisfallen suggested to the prince that here would be the spot to procure the best specimen of the Shamrock. On arriving at the Bed of Honour, while his Royal Highness was listening to Spillane's legend of the spot, the sharp eye of the latter detected, in the centre of the rock-bound retreat, which none, in our judgment, but an anchorite would seek as a place of rest, a very fine Shamrock, which, "by Royal authority" was at once severed from the soil, and carefully placed in moss, by Spillane, together with a very fine specimen of what is now well known in the botanic world as the "Killarney Fern," both to be sent, with a supply of their native earth, to become denizens of the Saxon sod at Windsor. The prince plucked two leafy stems from the plant, one of which he enclosed to his august mother, and the other to one of his sisters. The prince lingered on the island till the sun was about to go down, when he left for the Victoria, Spillane playing the sweet air to which Moore has wedded the beautiful song—

"Sweet Innisfallen! fare thee well!
And long may light around thee smile,
As sweet as on that evening fell,
When first I saw thy fairy isle," &c., &c.

SATURDAY.—At an early hour the prince proceeded in a carriage, to the foot of Mangerton, where Spillane had ponies in attendance. The day was auspicious. While riding up the bridle path to the Punch Bowl, his Royal Highness occasionally paused to look back at the scene of enchantment, which, at every interval assumed a new phase. At length he arrived at the summit of the mountain, at the back of the Punch Bowl, and, standing at the little mound left by the ordnance surveyors, he gazed around him with wonder and delight, exclaiming from time to time, "this is glorious." The magnificent panorama visible from this spot is thus graphically described by Mr. and Mrs. Hall:—"The view from the mountain top defies any attempt at description; it was the most magnificent we ever witnessed, and one that greatly surpassed even the dream of imagination. In the far away distance is the broad Atlantic, with the river of Kenmare, the bay of Bantry, the bay of Dingle [with the chain of mountains beginning at Slievemis and the lordly Cahircouree, and terminating in the sea, at a distance of nearly forty miles], and the storm-beaten coast of Iveragh. Farther off still [at another point] are [Tralee Bay] the Shannon, Kilrush, and Tarbert. Midway are the mountains of all forms and altitudes, with their lakes and cataracts, and streams of white foam. At our feet lie the three Killarney lakes, with Glena and Torc, and even Tomies, looking like protecting walls guarding them round about. The islands in the upper lake have, some of them, dwindled into mere specks, while the larger seem fitted only for the occupation of fairies. The river Flesk winds prettily along the valley; and the Flesk bridge, with its twenty-one arches, resembles a child's toy." Such was the scene—unrivalled in that "empire upon which the sun never sets"—on which the prince now gazed with wonder and admiration. There was a peculiar element of beauty in this glorious panorama on the occasion of the prince's visit. Dark clouds enveloped the horizon where the Shannon ceased to be visible, while ever and anon streams of light swept along the bosom of the majestic river, as if to penetrate the dark barrier which would hide that grand area of waters upon which the navy of the world might float. The prince amused himself for some time by rolling large stones into the unfathomed depths of the Devil's Punch Bowl, the Satanic lake looking, ere thus disturbed, as dark and still as death. Spillane then conducted the prince to the Horse's Glen, with the weird and gloomy grandeur of which he was almost startled. Having taken farewell of Mangerton and its mountain wonders, the prince and party returned to Cloughreen, the interesting village at its base. Here a scene of animated enjoyment awaited the prince, Mr. Ross having placed a boat on the lakelet behind Roche's Muckross Hotel, known as Colonel Herbert's "Preserves." The prince and his party were thus enabled to enjoy some excellent fishing. Taking boat then at Muckross Quay, the prince and party were borne, as quickly as a swift boat and eight gallant oarsmen could waft them, to the Victoria Pier. In the course of the evening some very beautiful specimens of "Arbutus Work," were exhibited to his Royal Highness, by Mr. James Egan, and also by the fair representatives of Mr. Jeremiah O'Connor. As it was getting late, however, the prince contented himself with the purchase of a beautiful chessboard and some other small, but elegantly finished articles, from Mr. Egan.

SUNDAY.—To-day, the prince following the example of his mother in Scotland and elsewhere, walked with his party to the neat little parish church at Aghadoe. The Venerable Archdeacon Foster read prayers. The Rev. Mr. Hudson, his curate, read the lessons of the day, and preached from the 45th chapter of Isaiah, and the 21st and 22nd verses. There was a respectable, though not a crowded congregation, who as the minister read that portion of the litany where prayer is offered up for "Albert, Prince of Wales, and all the Royal Family," seemed to respond with marked fervour. On the prince and party leaving the church, some of the peasantry exhibited a desire to press forward. On its being intimated to them that this was not desirable, a venerable old man replied—"Sure it is not every day we see a king, God bless him"—a sentiment which was cordially echoed by the people around, who, though many of them followed him to the ruined church and round tower of Aghadoe, acted with the greatest decorum, and did not again attempt to press around the royal person. The day was peculiarly favourable for a visit to the height of Aghadoe, where crumble the Round Tower and the ruins of the old church. The day being clear, but not too bright, the eye could take in, with distinctness, every object in that noble panorama, commencing with the far off mountains of the county of Cork.

MONDAY.—This morning the prince and party drove quietly into town on an "Irish car" of Mr. Finn's, and visited the Arbutus factories of Mr. Jeremiah O'Connor, and of Mr. Cremin, in both of which he made some large and select purchases. This promised visit performed, his royal highness, followed by hearty cheers from a large number standing in the vicinity of the Kenmare Arms, returned to the Royal Victoria, whence he soon after started for the Gap of Dunloe. This, too, was a glorious day. The prince's visit being a hurried one, he would not avail himself of the invitation courteously tendered to them by Mr. Daniel Mahony, of Dunloe Castle, the lord of the Gap, to show them the famous cave and its Ogham inscriptions. Arrived at the Black Lake, Spillane was about to wake the echoes with his cornopean, when the prince, who is a great admirer of our melodies, said—"Something Irish, Spillane." Spillane accordingly played the very appropriate air of "On Lough Neagh's banks," with what effect no one can imagine who has not been in the Gap of Dunloe. And now the prince had arrived on the verge of Coom Dhuy, or the Black Valley. Seated on the Table Rock, he gazed on a view which pen or pencil is inadequate to paint. On the right are the lordly Reeks, the whole of Coom Dhuy, and the white waterfal that crowns it; at the other, a noble view of the Upper Lakes. While the prince looked out on this scene, so beautifully described in "The Collegians," by Gerald Griffin, Spillane epitomised the sad story for his Royal Highness, who expressed a desire to read the admirable novel of our lamented countryman. Arrived at the Eagle's Nest, the echoes—the most exquisite of all—were awoke by the magical cornopean of Spillane, who played at the request of the prince, in succession, "Believe me if all those endearing young charms," and "The meeting of the waters." Before leaving this entrancing spot, the prince who has a fine tenor voice (and who is a musician as well as a painter), joined with the gentlemen of his party, and Spillane (who to his other qualifications as a guide, adds that of being an excellent singer), in the National Anthem, which they executed in capital style, the mountain orchestra performing its part with a volume and accuracy which would have raised *Il fanatico* to the seventh heaven. Descending to the Old Weir, which was full of water, the prince was greeted wlth three hearty cheers from a number of Killarney gentlemen, who were standing on the time-honoured bridge. The great body of water gave a fine effect to the *facilis descensus* of the gallant barque, as oars erect, as it were, "dropping diamonds" from their blades, she deftly bore her precious freight into O'Sullivan's Punchbowl, Spillane playing Lover's sweet song of "M'Carthy's grave," of which this part of the lake was the sad scene, and the details of which the inexhaustible Stephen recounted to his Royal Highness. Steering through the back channel, to Glena, the crew pulled "with a will" for the Victoria, touching on their way at Innisfallen.

TUESDAY.—This morning the Prince and party left at eight o'clock on a well-appointed "Irish car," belonging to the Victoria, for Valencia. Having arrived at Rossbeigh—a scene as beautiful in its way as Killarney itself—while the horses were being changed at the Headley Arms, Spillane, with ready tact, conducted the Prince and party by Lady Headley's and the other cottages of Rossbeigh—with the neatness and comfort of which his Royal Highness expressed himself much pleased—up the mountain road, where a noble view presented itself—extending far inland on the one side, and taking in on the other the whole range of the Tralee and Dingle mountains, now seen in their full majesty and unbroken outlines, while the sandy isthmuses which separate lovely Cromane Bay from Dingle Bay—the noblest arm of the Atlantic at this side of America—are shining in the sun, as if they were so much gold. Having remounted the popular car at the stage, the prince and party proceeded till they arrived at Kells. Here the scene was so peculiarly grand that his Royal Highness called a halt. What, between the Dingle and Tralee mountains, and the whole scene just glanced at, Drung Hill, and the dark and rocky promontories which gird the Iveragh side of Dingle Bay, the scene was one, indeed, to command attention, if not to raise the feelings in humility to Him whose word called all those marvels of beauty and power into being, and whose "voice" "dwells in that mighty tone," which, rising from the great deep, now speaks to the ear of an earthly prince, a message of man's littleness, from the Eternal.

WEDNESDAY.—This evening the prince and party arrived from Valencia, at half-past seven, having accomplished their journey from the Ferry Point in the short space of four hours.

THURSDAY.—This morning, at an early hour, the indefatigable prince, with his party, and Spillane, put their pluck and bottom to the test by ascending Carran Tuel—the "Monarch" of Irish mountains—whence they descended by Coom Dhuy—a feat also of considerable difficulty—into the Gap, thence to Lord Brandon's cottage.

FRIDAY. — The prince and party started this morning for Cork, from the terminus of the Killarney Junction Railway, receiving a genuine Irish cheer at parting, which he gracefully acknowledged. The prince hoped to reach Buckingham Palace, anxious to be "at home" on Sunday, the birthday of one of his sisters.

SECTION III.

BRADSHAW'S TOURS

THROUGH THE COUNTIES OF

HERTFORD, BUCKINGHAM, NORTHAMPTON, WARWICK,
STAFFORD, CHESTER, LANCASTER, YORK,
CUMBERLAND, WESTMORELAND, NORTHUMBERLAND,
DUMFRIES, LANARK, AYR,
AND THE NORTHERN COUNTIES OF SCOTLAND.

CHINA AND GLASS ROOMS,

Nos. 49 and 50, OXFORD STREET, LONDON.

PARIAN CHINA ORNAMENTS

AMAZON.

IN STATUARY, GROUPS, AND FIGURES.

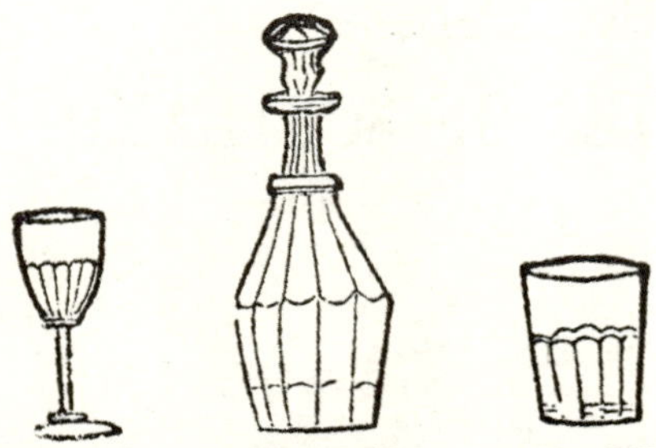

5s. 6d. Dozen. — **12s. 6d.** Pair. — **4s. 6d.** Dozen.

Small Breakfast Set (White China, Gold edge)—6 cups and saucers, 2 plates, 1 slop, 1 sugar, and 1 milk jug, 12s. 6d.

2s. Pair. — Parian Violet Vase, **1s. 6d.** — White & Gold China, **4s. 6d.** Half-dozen.

JOHN W. SHARPUS

Begs respectfully to call the attention of the Public to his IMMENSE STOCK, which is now replete with all the most MODERN AND CLASSIC DESIGNS IN

CHINA, GLASS, EARTHENWARE

PARIAN STATUARY, AND BOHEMIAN GLASS.

DINNER SERVICES.

	£	s.	d.
Dinner Services, to dine 12 persons ....from	2	2	0
Ditto, richly gilt ....from	3	13	6
Handsome painted and gilt ....from	5	15	6
Rich coloured Bands, handsomely gilt ....from	7	7	0
Porcelain Services, rich coloured bands, handsomely gilt..........................from 25 guineas.			

A variety of patterns, expressly for India and the Colonies, at the same moderate prices.

DESSERT SERVICES.

	£	s.	d.
For twelve persons, in neat coloured borders ..from	1	1	0
Ditto, antique borders and coloured wreaths ..from	1	8	0
A variety, colcured borders, with gold and flowers, on the finest Porcelain....................from	3	15	0
Ditto, ditto, from 5 to 10 guineas and upwards.			
China Breakfast Set, gold edge, viz., 6 breakfast cups and saucers, 2 plates, 1 slop, 1 sugar basin, 1 milk jug ....from	0	12	6

A LARGE ASSORTMENT OF PATTERNS AT THE SAME MODERATE PRICES.

TEA SERVICES.

	£	s.
White china, gold edge ....from	0	17
Neat painted band and flowers...............from	1	8
Elegant pattern, handsomely painted and gilt from	2	2
Splendid Services, of the most elaborate workmanship and design, rich painted and gilt, £8 8s. to	14	14

GLASS DEPARTMENT.

	£	s.	d.
Particularly neat cut Wine Glasses	0	5	6 per dozen.
Handsome cut ditto ....from 12s. 6d. to	1	1	0 per dozen.
Neat good strong Tumblers	0	4	6 per dozen.
A large variety of patterns....10s. 6d. to	1	4	0 per dozen.
Pale Ale Tumblers, for India..12s. 6d. to	2	2	0 per dozen.
Modern shape Decanters................	0	8	6 per pair.
Cut glass and engraved ....21s. to	2	2	2 per pair.
Custard and Jelly Glasses......4s. 6d. to	0	10	6 per dozen.
Cut glass Water Jugs ....5s. to	1	1	0 each.
Best glass Salts (modern shaped) ..9d. to	0	2	9 each.

A Price Catalogue may be had on application, containing full description of Kitchen Requisites, Toilet Ware, Paper Trays, Cutlery, Plated Cruet Frames, Hot Water Plates and Dishes, and every requisite required for furnishing, extremely reduced Cash Prices.

A China Dinner Service, to Dine 12 persons, Torquoise and Gold, 15 Guineas.

All orders from the Country must be accompanied with a reference or remittance.

CONTENTS TO SECTION III.

	PAGE
ALFORD VALLEY	97
BANFF, MACDUFF, AND TURRIFF JUNCTION	98
BANFF, PORTSOY, AND STRATHISLA	98
BORDER COUNTIES	65
CALEDONIAN—	
Carlisle to Edinburgh and Glasgow	72
Glasgow to Airdrie	83
Glasgow to Crofthead	82
Gartsherrie to Stirling	75
Hamilton Branch	78
Lanark Branch	75
CARLISLE & SILLOTH & PORT CARLISLE	64
CASTLE DOUGLAS AND DUMFRIES	67
CONISTON—Broughton to Coniston	53
DEESIDE—	
Aberdeen to Banchory and Aboyne	97
DUMBARTONSHIRE—	
Glasgow, Dumbarton, Helensburgh, and Loch Lomond	81
DUNBLANE, DOUNE, AND CALLANDER	88
DUNDEE, PERTH, AND ABERDEEN—	
Perth to Dundee and Arbroath	90
EDINBURGH AND GLASGOW—	
Bathgate Branch	84
Campsie to Lennoxtown	83
Glasgow to Falkirk and Edinburgh	83
Slamannan Branch	84
Stirling to Dunfermline	87
EDINBURGH, PERTH, AND DUNDEE—	
Edinburgh to Dundee and Perth	84
Leuchars to St. Andrews	86
Thornton to Dunfermline	85
Thornton Junc. to Leven and Kilconquhar	85
FIFE AND KINROSS	86
FORTH AND CLYDE JUNCTION	78
FURNESS—	
Furness to Ulverston and Carnforth	53
Piel to Furness Abbey and Broughton	52
GLASGOW AND AIRDRIE	83
GLASGOW, PAISLEY, AND GREENOCK	72
GLASGOW AND SOUTH WESTERN—	
Ardrossan, Troon, and Ayr	69
Ayr to Maybole and Dalmellington	71
Carlisle, Dumfries, and Glasgow	66
Muirkirk Branch	68
Newmilns Branch	68
GREAT NORTH OF SCOTLAND—	
Aberdeen to Huntly and Keith	97
INVERNESS AND ABERDEEN JUNCTION	98
Lossimouth Branch	99
ISLE OF MAN	44
KENDAL AND WINDERMERE	58
KINROSS-SHIRE	85
LANCASHIRE AND YORKSHIRE—	
Bolton to Clitheroe and Chatburn	49
Bolton to Kenyon	50
Bolton to Preston	52
Liverpool to Crosby and Southport	51
Manchester to Bolton, Wigan, and L'pool	49
Preston to Lytham, Blackpool, & Fl'twood	52
Wigan to Southport	50
LONDON AND NORTH WESTERN—	
Ashton to Stockport	47
Birmingham to Wolverhampton (*via* Bescot)	21
Birmingham to Wolverhampton (*via* Stour Valley) and Stafford	21
Bletchley to Bedford	7
Bletchley to Winslow and Oxford	9
Blisworth to Northampton and Peterbro'	11
Cheddington to Aylesbury	6
Coventry to Leamington	18
Coventry to Nuneaton	18
Crewe to Shrewsbury	32
Crewe to Stockport and Manchester	36
Crewe to Warrington and Preston	32
Leighton to Dunstable	7
London to Rugby	2
Macclesfield to Cheadle Junction	29
Manchester to Huddersfield and Leeds	47
Manchester to Liverpool	40
Northampton to Market Harborough	13
Preston to Carlisle	56
Rugby to Birmingham and Stafford	17
Rugby to Leamington and Warwick	15
Rugby to Stamford	15
Rugby to Stafford, *via* Trent Valley	22
Stafford to Crewe and Chester	30
Stafford to Shrewsbury	30
Watford to St. Albans	4
Winslow to Buckingham and Banbury	9
MARYPORT AND CARLISLE	56
Alston Branch	65
NEWCASTLE AND CARLISLE	64
NORTH STAFFORDSHIRE—	
Colwich to Stoke, Burton, and Derby	24
Kidsgrove to Crewe	27
North Road to Uttoxeter	28
Rocester to Ashbourne	28
Stoke to Macclesfield	26
PERTH, ALMOND VALLEY, AND METHVEN	90
PORTPATRICK	67
SCOTTISH CENTRAL—	
Blackford to Crieff	89
Greenhill Junction to Stirling & Perth	76 & 88
SCOTTISH NORTH EASTERN—	
Bridge of Dun to Brechin	94
Cupar to Blairgowrie	92
Dubton to Montrose	94
Kirriemuir Branch	93
Meigle Junction to Newtyle and Dundee	93
Perth to Forfar and Aberdeen	92
Stanley to Dunkeld	92
ST. HELENS—	
St. Helens to Warrington, Runcorn, and Liverpool	41
SYMINGTON, BIGGAR, & BROUGHTON	74
WHITEHAVEN & FURNESS JUNCTION—	
Foxfield to St. Bees and Whitehaven	53
WHITEHAVEN, CLEATOR, & EGREMONT	55
WHITEHAVEN JUNCTION—	
Cockermouth Branch	55
Whitehaven to Maryport	55

ILLUSTRATIONS.

PAGE

MAPS —

Channel Islands 46
Isle of Man 46
Lake District, England 60
„ Ditto, Scotland 100

PLANS:—

Birmingham 20
Glasgow 78
Liverpool 2
Manchester 40

VIEWS:—

Abbotsford 82
Balmoral 82
Birker Force 58
Great Langdale 58
Inverness 82

ISLE OF MAN:—

Castle Mona Hotel 46
Castletown 46
Douglas 46

VIEWS:—*Isle of Man*, continued. PAGE.

Fort Anne Hotel 46
Kirk Braddan Church 46
Peel 46
Ramsey 46
Tower of Refuge 46
Water Wheel, Laxey 46

Loch Lomond, Head of 82

MANCHESTER:—

Athenæum 88
Cathedral 38
Exchange 38
Exhibition, Art Treasures 38
Free Library 38
Free Trade Hall 38
Mechanics' Institution 38
Royal Institution 38
Watts' Warehouse 38

Perth 82
Ulleswater Lake 58
Windermere, Head of 58

INDEX.

Abbey, 63
Abbeyfield, 36
Abbot's Bromley, 23
Aberdeen, 95
Aberdeenshire, 95
Aberfoyle, 77, 78
Abergeldie Castle, 97
Abernethy, 87
Abington, 74
Aboyne, 97
Abruthven, 89
Acton, 33
Adam Hill, 70
Adlington, 29, 52
Adlington Hall, 29
Afton Bridgend Castle, 68
Aglionby, 64
Ailsa Craig, 70
Ainsdale, 52
Airdrie, 83, 84
Airdrie House, 83
Airey Force, 60, 61
Airley Castle, 94
Airthrie Wells, 77
Albion, 22
Alcot Park, 19
Alderley, 36
Alderley Park, 36
Alexandria, 82
Alford, 97
Allerton, 44
Allerton Hall, 41
Allesley Gate, 18
Alloa. 87
Alloa House, 88
Allonby, 63
Almond, 82
Almondbank, 90
Almond Valley, 91
Almondbury Castle, 48
Alsager, 27
Althorp Park, 12
Alston, 64
Alstonefield, 29
Alton, 28
Alves, 99
Alveston, 16
Ambleside, 54, 59, 61
Ampthill Park, 8
Ampthill, 8
Annan, 65
Anstey Hall, 22
Apley Castle, 31
Apperton, 2
Appleby, 62
Appleton, 41
Appley Bridge, 50
Aqualate Hall, 30
Aray, River and Falls of, 80
Arbory Hill, 74
Arbroath, 92
Arbuckle, 84
Arbury Hall, 18
Ardblair, 93
Ardet, 86
Ardler, 93
Ardoch, 68
Ardrishaigh, 80
Ardrossan, 69
Ardrossan Castle, 69
Arleedon, 54
Armitage, 24
Arroquhar, 82
Arthur's Round Table, 60
Ashbourne, 28
Ashbourne Hall, 28
Ashbourne Green Hall, 29
Ashbourne Grove, 29
Ashbridge Park, 5
Ashby St. Leger's, 14
Ashcombe Hall, 28
Ashness, 61
Ashorne, 16
Ashton, 10
Ashton-under-Lyne, 47
Ashton Hall, 56
Aspatria, 55
Asps, 16
Astley, 41
Astley Hall, 52
Aston, 19, 21
Aston Abbot's House, 7
Aston Hall, 21, 33, 35
Aston Cantlow, 16
Atherstone, 22
Atherstone Hall, 23
Atherton, 50
Auchengray, 74
Auchincruive, 71
Auchinleck, 68
Auchinleck House, 71
Auchinskeith, 68
Auchterarder, 89
Auchterhouse, 93
Auchterless, 98
Auchtermuchty, 86
Auchtertyre Camp, 93
Auldbar Road, 94
Auldgirth, 66
Avonbridge, 84
Axwell Park, 65
Aylesbury, 6
Ayre Point, 45
Ayrshire, 66
Ayr, 69

Bacton Castle, 47
Bagot's Park, 30
Balanakillie, 93
Balbeuchly, 91
Balbirnie, 86
Balcraig Castle, 93
Baldovan, 93
Baldragon, 93
Balfour, 86
Balgorice, 86
Ballaglass, 45
Ballasalla, 45, 46, 47
Ballater, 97
Ballathie, 92
Balloch, 80, 82
Balmachewan, 95
Balmoral, 97
Balmoral Castle, 97
Balvash Bay, 47
Balwearel Tower, 85
Bampton, 60
Banachra Castle, 82
Banbury, 9
Banchory Cottage, 97
Banchory Ternan, 97
Banff, 98
Bank Mill Bridge, 5
Bannockburn, 76, 78
Barford, 16
Barkskimmey Bridge, 71
Barlaston 25
Barnewell, 13
Barrasford, 65
Barr Beacon, 19
Barrhead, 82
Barrock Fell, 63
Barrow, 52
Barry, 91
Barton, 41
Barton Seagrave, 12
Basford, 31
Bassenthwaite Water, 60
Bathgate, 83, 84
Batley, 48
Baturres Castle, 67
Bay Horse, 56
Beacon Hill, 63
Bealmaha Pass, 82
Beaudesert, 30
Beaudesert Park, 24
Beattock, 74
Beaufront, 65
Bedford, 8
Bedworth, 18
Beechmont, 84
Beeston, 32, 48
Beeston Castle Hill, 32
Beith, 71
Bell Craig, 74
Bell Grange, 59
Bell Rock Lighthouse, 92
Belle Isle, 58
Bellingham, 65
Belmont, 82, 84, 93
Benaw, 82
Ben An, 77, 82
Ben Buck, 78
Ben Cleuch, 78
Ben Cruachan, 80, 82
Ben Lawers, 88
Ben Ledi, 77
Ben Lomond, 81, 82
Ben Macdhui, 97
Benmore, 88
Ben Nevis, 97
Benson Knot, 61
Ben Venue, 77, 82
Ben Voirlich, 90
Beresford Hall, 29
Berkhampstead, 5
Berkhampstead Castle, 7
Berkswell, 17, 18
Berkswell Hall, 18
Bescar, 50
Bescot, 21
Bescot Hall, 21
Betley, 31
Betley Court, 31

Bew Castle, 64
Bicester, 9
Biddulph, 27
Bidston Hill, 44
Biggar, 74
Billing Road, 13
Billinge Hill, 50
Bilisten Castle, 64
Bilton, 17
Birbeck Embankment and Viaduct, 61
Birdingbury, 15
Birkdale, 52
Birkenhead, 44
Birkland Cutting, 61
Birkly Fell, 54
Birmingham, 15, 19
Birnam (Dunkeld), 90
Birnam Wood, 90
Birstal, 48
Birthwaite, 59
Bishop Briggs, 83
Bishop's Court, 45, 46
Bishopton, 72
Bishton, 30
Bispham Hill, 50
Blackburn, 49
Black Combe Mountains, 53
Black Dub, 61
Blackford, 89
Black Lead Mines, 61
Blacklow Hill, 16
Blackpool, 52
Blackrod, 52
Blague Gate, 41
Blairadam, 85
Blairgowrie, 92
Blake Fell, 54
Blantyre, 77
Blantyre Priory, 78
Blaydon, 65
Bleasdale Tower, 56
Blea Tarn, 59
Blenkinsop Castle, 64
Blenkinsop Hall, 64
Bletchley, 8
Blisworth Junction, 10
Blithfield, 30
Bloomsbury, 21
Blyth Bridge, 25
Blowick, 60
Bogside, 88
Bold Hall, 34
Bolton, 49
Bolton-le-Sands, 57
Bonar Bridge, 99
Bonnington Fall, 75
Bo'ness, 84
Bootle, 44, 53
Bootle Fell, 53
Bootle Lane, 51
Bootle Village, 51
Borland, 68
Borough Hill, 33
Borren's Hill, 73
Borrow Bridge, 61
Borrowdale, 58, 59, 60, 61
Borrowdale Fells, 54, 59, 60
Bothwell Bridge, 78
Bothwell Castle, 88
Bourne End, 5
Bow Fell, 59, 60
Bowder Rock, 61
Bowhouse, 84
Bowling, 81
Bowness, 58, 59
Box Lane Viaduct, 5
Boxmoor, 4
Brackley, 9
Bradley, 48
Bradley Park, 48
Bradshaw, 49
Bradshaw Hall, 50
Bradshaw Leach, 50
Bradwell, 9, 10
Braehead, 74
Braemar, 97
Braemar Castle, 97
Braes of Ballochmyle, 70
Braidwood, 76
Brakenhill, 73
Bramhall, 29
Bramhall Hall, 9
Bramhall House, 29, 37
Brampton, 63, 64
Brathay Park, 58
Brathay, Vale of, 59
Brayton, 56
Brayton Hall, 56
Breadalbane, 82
Brechin, 94
Breeda Copper Mine, 47
Brereton Hall, 36
Brewood, 22
Bridge of Allan, 77, 88
Bridge of Dun, 94
Bridge of Earn, 87, 90
Bridge of Turk, 77, 81
Brigham, 55
Brixworth, 12
Broad Green, 41
Brock, 56
Brockhall Park, 14
Brodie, 99
Bromborough, 44
Bromley Cross, 49
Bromshall, 25
Broomhall, 85
Brother Water, 60
Brougham Hall, 60, 62
Broughton, 56, 59
Broughton, 74
Broughton Cross, 55
Broughton-in-Furness, 53
Broughton Tower, 53
Broughty Castle, 91
Broughty Ferry, 87, 91
Brown-hill, 70
Brownsover, 14
Brow Top, 60
Broxburn, 84
Broxmouth, 84
Brucefield, 88
Bruce's Howe, 97
Buberton, 75
Buchanstone, 98
Buckingham, 5, 9
Buckinghamshire, 5
Bull Gill, 55
Bulkington, 10
Bum-of-the-Vat, 97
Burgh, 63
Burneside, 58
Burntisland, 85
Burscough Bridge, 50
Burslem, 25, 27
Burton, 26
Burton-in-Kendal, 57
Bury Lane, 41
Bury Park, 3
Bury Wood, 22
Bushbury, 21, 22
Bushey, 3
Bushey Hall, 3
Butley Hall, 29
Buttermere, 54, 61
Butterton Hall, 26
Buxburn, 97

Caerlaverock, 66
Caldbeck Fells, 56
Calder Abbey, 54
Calder Castle, 54
Calder House, 75
Caldon Hill, 76
Caldron Lynn, 77
Caledonian Canal, 99
Calf Fell, 61
Calf of Man, 45, 47
Calgarth, 59
Callander, 77, 82, 83, 89
Calthwaite, 63
Calveley, 32
Cambus, 87
Cambuslang, 78
Cambusnethan, 76
Camden Road, 2
Camden Town Station, 2
Cameron Bridge, 85
Camerton, 55
Cam-na-Gaul Bay, 100
Camperdown, 91
Campsie, 83
Campsie Fall, 90
Cantley Sprout, 61
Cantray, 83
Cardenden, 85
Cardross, 81
Cargill, 92
Cark, 52, 59
Carlisle, 56, 63
Carl Lofts, 61
Carluke, 76
Carndonald, 72
Carnforth, 53, 57
Carnforth Lodge, 57
Carnoustie, 91
Carnwath, 74
Carnwath House, 74
Carron Bridge, 66
Carron Hall, 83
Carron Iron Works, 77
Carse of Gowrie, 90
Carslogie Castle, 86
Carstairs House, 75
Carstairs Junction, 75
Cartland Crags, 75
Cartmel, 58, 59
Cashiobury, 3
Cashiobury Park, 3, 4
Cassillis, 71
Cassilis Castle, 70
CastleAshby, 13
CastleBanks, 64
CastleCarrock, 64
Castlecary, 78, 83
Castledykes, 12
Castle Douglas, 67
Castle Finlay, 99
Castle Folds, 61
Castle Gilmour, 66
Castle Hill, 61, 74
Castle Hill Camp, 64
Castle Hill Tower, 75
Castle-hill Law, 97
Castle Menzies, 90
Castle Rigg, 59, 60, 61
Castlesteads, 64
Castleton of Braemar, 97
Castletown, 45, 46, 47
Castor, 13
Catrine Lea, 71
Catter Hill, 67
Cauldchapel, 73
Causewayend, 84
Causewayhead, 87
Cawdor, 99
Cawdor Castle, 99, 100
Cawsey Pike, 54
Chalk Farm, 2
Chapel Town, 49
Charlecote, 15, 20
Charlecote Park, 16
Chartley Castle, 30
Chatburn, 50
Chatelerault, 78
Chat Moss, 40, 41
Cheadle, 29, 36
Cheadle Heath, 36
Checkerbent, 50
Cheddington Hill, 5
Chelford, 36
Cheshire, 30
Chester, 32
Chesters, 65
Chetwynd Park, 30
Chidwall, 44
Chiltern Hills, 5
Chilvers Coton, 18
Chipchase Castle, 65
Chisnall Hall, 35
Chollerford, 65

Chollerton, 65
Chorley, 52
Churwell, 48
Clackmannan, 88
Clackmannan House, 88
Claughton Hall, 56
Claydon, 9
Claypott's Castle, 87
Clayton Bridge, 75
Cleator Moor, 55
Cleghorn, 75, 76
Clifford Hill, 12
Clifton, 28, 49, 62
Clifton Moor, 62
Clitheroe, 49
Clock Face, 41
Clocksbriggs, 94
Clopton House, 16
Closeburn, 66
Closeburn Hall, 66
Close House, 65
Cloud End, 27
Cloven Stones, 45
Coatbridge, 76
Cochrane, 72
Cockermouth, 54, 55, 59
Cockpool, 66
Cockshot, 61
Coilantogle Ford, 77
Coilsfield, 71
Coldbeck Fells, 61
Collessie, 87
Collins Green, 41
Colliston, 92
Colwich, 24
Colwith Force, 59
Colzean, 70
Comlongam Castle, 66
Compton Verner, 15, 16
Compton Wynyates, 15
Congleton, 27
Coniston, 58, 59
Coniston Priory, 54
Connell Ferry, 79
Coombe Abbey, 14, 15, 17
Coppull, 35
Corbridge, 66
Corby Castle, 63
Corington Mill, 74
Corkickle, 54
Corner Hall, 4
Cornhill, 98
Corra Linn Fall, 75
Corran Ferry, 100
Corsehill, 69
Corstorphine, 84
Coton Hall, 14
Cottesbrooke, 12
Coulter, 74
Counden Road, 17
Coupar Angus, 92
Courteen Hall, 12
Cove, 95
Coventry, 15, 17
Cowdenbeath, 85
Coylton Kirk, 70
Crackenthorpe, 62
Craigellachie, 98
Craigendarroch, 95
Craighall Putney, 93
Craigo, 95
Craigo House, 95
Craigievar, 98
Craiglascar Hill, 85
Craig Phadic, 100
Cranford Priory, 97
Crank, 41
Crathie, 97
Crewe, 27, 31
Crewe Hall, 31
Cresswell, 25
Crichup Linn, 66
Crick, 14
Crieff, 89
Crietown, 67
Crinan Canal, 80
CroftheAd, 82
Crofton Hall, 5
Crookstone, 72
Crosby, 51
Crosby Hall, 51
Cross Fell, 62
Crossgates, 85
Cross Keys Junction, 60
Crossmichael, 67
Crosthwaite Church, 60
Crow Park, 61
Croxteth Park, 44
Croy, 83
Crummock Lake, 54, 61
Crummock Water, 54
Cubbington, 16
Cuerden Hall, 35
Cuerden Park, 52
Culloden, 99
Culloden Cairn, 100
Culloden House, 99
Culloden Moor, 99
Culross, 88
Culross Abbey, 88
Culter, 97
Culter House, 97
Cults, 97
Culzean Castle, 70
Cumberland, 62
Cumberland Lakes, 61
Cummertrees, 65
Cupar, 86
Cupon Oak, 64
Currie Hill, 75
Curthwaite, 56

Dacre Castle, 60
Dairsie, 86
Daisy Field, 49
Dalmally, 79
Dallam Tower, 58
Dalbeattie, 67
Dalby Point, 46
Dalcross, 99
Dalemain Hall, 60
Dalmellington, 72
Dalmuir, 81
Dalreoch, 81, 82
Dalry, 69
Dalrymple, 72
Dalston, 56
Dalston Hall, 56
Dalton, 53
Danes Moor, 15
Darlaston, 21
Daubhill, 60
Daventry, 13
Dean Park, 13
Delapre Abbey, 12
Delph, 47
Dem House, 94
Denton, 47
Denton Hall, 47
Deepdale, 60
Deep Fields, 22
Derby, 26
Dereham, 55
Derwentwater, 60
Dest, 97
Dewsbury 48
Dhu Loch, 97
Diggle, 47
Dillicar Hills, 61
Dilston, 64
Dingwall, 99
Dinwoodie, 73
Dissington, 65
Ditchford, 13
Ditton, 41
Dixon Fold, 49
Dochfour, 100
Dochfour Loch, 100
Docker Gill Viaduct, 61
Donnington, 30
Dorford Hall, 32
Dornoch, 99
Dovedale, 29
Douglas, 45
Doune, 77, 89
Drayton Manor, 23
Drayton Parslon, 8
Drigg, 54
Droitwich, 20
Drone, 86
Dronley, 93
Droylsden, 47
Drum, 97
Drumburgh, 63
Drumcrieff, 74
Drummie, 91
Drumlithie, 95
Drumoak, 97
Drummond Castle, 89
Drumkilbo, 93
Dubbieside, 85
Dunblane, 87
Dubton Junction, 94
Dudley Castle, 20
Dudley Port, 22
Dumbarton, 81
Dumbartonshire, 81
Dumfries, 66
Dunairn, 84
Dunblane, 78, 88
Dundee, 86, 91
Dundyvan Iron Works, 81
Dunfermline, 85
Dungeon Gill, 59
Dunmail Raise, 60, 61
Dunnemarle, 88
Dunniker, 85
Dunning, 89
Dunkeld, 92
Dunkenny, 93
Dunolly Castle, 80
Dunshelt, 86
Dunstaffnage Castle, 80
Dunure Castle, 71
Dukinfield, 47
Dunsinane, 90
Dunstable, 7
Dupplin Castle, 90
Dyce, 97
Dyce House 97
Dysart, 85
Dysart House, 85

Eagley, 49
Easedale, 60
Eassie, 93
East Haven, 91
Eastgrange, 88
Eastham, 44
Easton Neston, 12
Eaton Hall, 27
Ecclefechan, 73
Eccles, 40, 41
Eccleshall, 31
Eden Hall, 63
Edensor, 25
Edgbaston, 21
Edgehill, 15, 24, 42
Edgware Road, 2
Edinburgh, 82
Edmond Castle, 64
Eggington, 26
Eggington Hall, 26
Egremont, 55, 59
Eilan-agash, 100
Elderslie, 72
Ellel Grange, 56
Ellenborough, 55
Elleray, 58
Elgin, 99
Elliock House, 66
Elterwater, 59
Elmdon Hall, 18
Elmdon Park, 18
Elmdon, 19
Elmhurst, 24
Elton, 13
Elvanfoot, 74
Emerdale, 59
Entwisle, 49
Euston Square Station, 1
Errol, 91
Errol House, 90
Esk Meals, 53

Eskdale, 58, 59
Esthwaite Water, 59
Ettingshall Road, 22
Etruria, 25, 26
Euxton, 35, 52
Euxton Hall, 35, 52
Ewanrigg Hall, 45

Fairfield, 58, 59
Fairy Hall, 21
Fairy Hole, 41
Falkirk, 78, 83
Falkland, 86
Falkland Road, 86
Falls of Corriemulzie, 97
Falls of Foyers, 100
Falls of Garrawalt, 97
Falls of the Clyde, 75
Farington, 35, 52
Farnell Road, 94
Farnworth, 41
Farthinghoe, 9
Fazakerley, 51
Fatlips Castle, 74
Fawsley, 12
Featherstone, 64
FeatherstonehaughCastle [64
Fell Fort, 59
Fenton, 25
Fenny Stratford, 8
Ferry House, 58, 59
Fiddler's Ferry, 41
Fifeshire, 84
Findhorn, 97
Finhaven Castle, 93
Fintry, 89
Fixby Hall, 48
Fleetwood, 52
Flimby, 55
Floriston, 73
Fochabers, 99
Foleshill, 17
Folly Summer-house, 64
Foot of Kirkstone, 60
Fordoun, 95
Forfar, 93
Forfarshire, 91
Forgandenny, 89
Formby, 51
Fort Augustus, 100
Fort George, 99
Fort William, 82, 100
Forteviot, 89
Forres Castle, 99, 100
Four Ashes, 22
Fourstones, 64
Foxfield, 53
Fox Howe, 59
Friar's Crag, 61
Freshfield, 52
Froghall, 28
Furness Abbey, 53
Furness Fells, 58
Fyvie, 98

Galgate, 56
Garelochead, 82
Galston, 68
Garley Bank, 86
Garnkirk, 83
Garstang, 56
Garston, 41
Gartcosh, 83
Gartley, 98
Gartley Place, 98
Gartsherrie, 83
Gathurst, 50
Gateside, 86
Gayhurst, 7
Gayton Wharf, 13
Gelt, Ravine of the, 64
Gerard's Bridge, 41
Gibscroft Camps, 88
Giller Coom, 61
Gill Foot, 54
Gillibrand Hall, 52
Gillie's Hill, 76
Gilsland Spa, 64
Glammis, 93
Glaramara, 54
Glasgow, 78
Glassel, 97
Gleaston Castle, 53
Glencoe, 82
Glencarse, 91
Glendarragh, 46
Glen Dochart, 90
Glen Fruin, 82
Glen Falloch, 82
Glen Moriston, 100
Glen Tilt, 90, 97
Glen Urquhart, 100
Glenelg, 100
Glenfinglas, 77
Glengarry, 100
Gleniffer, Braes of, 72
Glenluce, 67
Glenorchy, 82
Glenmoy, 46
Glenroy, 100
Gnosall, 30
Gogar, 84
Gogar House, 84
Gogar Bank, 84
Golborne, 34
Golcar, 48
Gorhambury, 3, 4
Gosforth, 54
Gowbarrow Park, 60, 61
Grandtully, 90
Grange, 53, 98
Grange Hall, 33
Granton, 84
Grasmere, 59, 61
Grayrigg Summit, 61
Gray, 91
Great Brickhill, 7
Great Gable, 54
Great Stanmore, 2
Greenfield, 47
Greenbank, 75
Greenhaigh Castle, 56
Greenhead, 57, 64
Greenhill, 76, 83
Greenloaning, 89
Greenock, 72, 80
Green Road, 53
Greens, 73
Greskin Hills, 73
Gretna, 73
Gretna Green, 65
Gretna Hall, 60, 73
Grey Mare's Tail, 66, 74
Grinan, 68
Grindon Hall, 22
Grisdale Pike, 54
Grotton, 47
Grove Park, 3, 4
Guard Bridge, 86
Guide Bridge, 47
Guild, 97
Guilsborough, 12
Gumerkeld, 62
Guthrie, 92, 94
Guthrie House, 92, 94
Guy's Cliff, 15, 16

Hadley, 30
Hadnall, 32
Hagley Park, 20
Hagley Hall, 21
Haigh Hall, 44
Halbeath, 85
Hale, 44
Hales Owen, 22
Halewood, 41
Halshaw Moor, 49
Halton Castle, 34
Haltwhistle, 64
Hamilton, 78
Hamilton Palace, 78
Hampstead, 2
Hampstead Valley, 21
Hampstead Hall, 21
Hampton, 18
Hampton Lucy, 15, 16
Handforth, 36
Hanley, 25
Hansbury Hill, 10
Hanslope, 7, 10
Harburn, 75
Harburn House, 75
Harecastle, 27
Hardendale, 62
Hard Knot, 54
Harpole Hills, 10
Harrington, 55
Harrow, 2
Harston Brook, 13
Hartfell, 66
Hartford, 33
Harthorpe, 60
Hartshead Pike, 47
Hartside, 74
Hartwell, 6, 12
Hatchend, 3
Hatfield, 3
Hatton, 93
Hatton Castle, 93, 95
Haughton, 30
Hawes Water, 60, 62
Hawkesbury Lane, 17
Hawkhead, 72
Hawkshead, 58
Haxters End Bridge, 5
Haydock Park, 41
Haydon Bridge, 64
Hayton, 41
Hayton Church, 64
Hazles, 44
Heaton Chapel, 37
Heaton Park, 40
Heaton Lodge, 48
Heaton Norris, 37, 47
Helensburgh, 81
Helvellyn, 59, 61
Hemel Hempstead, 4
Hermitage, The 64
Hertfordshire, 3
Hesket Newmarket, 56
Hest Bank, 57
Hexham, 65
Hexham Priory, 65
Higham Ferrers, 13
Highgate, 2
Highlandman, 89
Hightown, 51
High Peak, 56
High Wray, 59
Hindicar 54
Hindley, 50
Hindley Hall, 50
Hoddam Castle, 65, 73
Holborn Hill, 53
Holbrook Grange, 14
Hollingbury House, 26
Holker, 59
Hollybush, 72
Holme, 83
Holme Fell, 57
Holmes Chapel, 36
Holy Loch, 80
Holytown, 76
Holywood, 66
Honistar Crag, 54
Hooton Hall, 44
Horsehill, 72
Horton, 12
Houston, 84
Howbury, 9
How Mill, 64
Hoylake, 44
Huddersfield, 48
Hulton Park, 50
Hunsbury Hill, 12
Huntingtown, 90
Huntly, 98
Huntly Lodge, 96
Hurlford, 68
Hutton Hall, 63
Huyton Quarry, 41
Hyde Hall, 47

Icolmkill, 80

Ilam Hall, 29
Inch Cailliach, 82
Inch-Cape Rock, 92
Ince Hall, 34, 44, 51
Inchmarlo, 97
Inchture, 91
Ingestre, 24, 30
Inglisburn, 93
Inglismaldie, 95
Ingram's Crook, 76
Inguiere Hall, 61
Insch, 98
Inveramsay, 98
Inverarnan, 89
Inverary, 82
Inverary Castle, 82
Invercauld, 97
Invercauld Bridge, 97
Invergowrie, 91
Inverness, 99
Inverness-shire, 99
Inversnaid, 88, 93
Inverury, 97
Iona, 81
Ireby, 56
Ireleth, 53
Irthington Cross, 64
Irvine, 69
Island of Mull, 80, 81, 82
Isle of Man, 44
Islip, 9
Ivinghoe, 7

Johnstone, 71
Johnstone Castle, 82

Kaimes Hill, 84
Keel Hall, 26
Keith, 98
Keith Hall, 98
Kelty, 83
Kelmarsh, 12
Kemnay, 97
Kempston House, 9
Kendal, 58
Kenilworth, 15, 16, 18
Kenilworth Castle, 17, 20
Kennethmont, 98
Kennedy Castle, 67
Kensal Green Cemetery, 2
Kensal Green Tunnel, 2
Kenyon, 41, 50
Kersall Cell, 49
Kersall Moor, 49
Keswick, 54, 59, 60, 61
Kettering, 12
Kidsgrove Junction, 27
Kilbirnie, 71
Kilburn, 2
Kilconquhar, 85
Kilchurn, 82
Kilchurn Castle, 80
Kilfarnie, 93
Kilhavock Castle, 99
Killiecrankie, 90
Killin, 82
Kilmarnock, 68
Kilmarnock Cstl Ruins, 68
Kilmun, 79
Kilpatrick, 73, 81
Kilsyth, 78
Kilwinning, 69
Kilworth Beauchamp, 15
Killygovhan, 67
Kinaldie, 97
Kincardine, 88, 93
Kincardineshire, 92
Kinfauns, 91
Kinfauns Castle, 90, 91
King Edward, 98
King's Head Inn, 59
King's Kettle, 86
Kingsknowe, 75
King's Langley, 4
Kinloch, 93
Kinloss, 99
Kinnaird, 94
Kinnoul Hill, 90
Kinross, 85
Kintore, 97
Kippenross, 88
Kirby, 61
Kirkaldy, 84
Kirk Andreas, 45
Kirk Andrews, 63
Kirk Arbory, 46
Kirk Ballaugh, 45
Kirk Braddan, 46
Kirk Bride, 45, 63
Kirkburn, 78
Kirkby, 53
Kirkby Lonsdale, 57
Kirk Christ, 47
Kirk Clorist Lezavre, 45
Kirkconnel, 66
Kirkcudbright, 66
Kirk German, 46
Kirkgowan, 67
Kirkgunzeon, 67
Kirkham, 52
Kirkintilloch, 83
Kirk Jurby, 45
Kirkland Hall, 56
Kirklees Hall, 48
Kirk Lonan, 45
Kirk Malew, 46, 47
Kirk Manghold, 45
Kirk Marrown, 46
Kirkmarum, 45
Kirk Michael, 45, 46
Kirk Onchan, 45
Kirk Patrick, 46
Kirkpatrick, 73
Kirk Stanton, 45, 46
Kirkstone Fells, 59
Kirkstone Pass, 60
Kirkstone Top, 60
Kirktonhill, 95
Kirriemuir, 93
Kirtle Bridge, 73
Kitterland, 47
Kittybrewster, 97
Knebworth, 3
Knock, 28
Knockgeorgan Hill, 69
Knowsley, 44, 51
Knypersley, 27
Kyle, 100
Kyle Castle, 68
Kyles of Bute, 79

Ladybank, 86
Lady's Well, 98
Lake Skene, 66
Lambley, 64
Lamington House, 74
Lamington Old Tower, 74
Lamplugh, 54
Lamport, 12
Lanark, 75
Lancaster, 56, 59
Landon Castle, 67
Lang Bank, 72
Langdale, 54, 58, 61
Langdale Chapel, 59
Langdale Pikes, 58, 59
Langho, 49
Langley Bury, 4
Larbert, 76
Larbert House, 76
Largo, 83
Launton, 9
Laurencekirk, 95
Laxey, 45
Lea Green, 41
Leamington, 15, 18
Leamington Spa, 15
Leasowes, 20
Leasowe Castle, 44
Leathe's Water, 60
Leeds, 49
Leek, 28
Leegate, 56
Lees, 47
Lee House, 75
Legberthwaite, 60
Leigh, 25, 50
Leighton Buzzard, 6
Leighton Junction, 6
Lennox Castle, 82, 83
Lennoxtown, 83
Leslie, 86
Lethenty, 98
Leuchars, 86
Leuchars House, 86
Leven, 85
Levens Hall, 58
Levenshulme, 37
Leyland, 35, 52
Lhanbryde, 99
Lichfield, 23
Lidlington, 8
Lilbourne, 14, 15
Lillies, 6
Lilleshall Abbey, 30
Lilleshall House, 30
Lillington, 16
Lincluden Castle, 67
Lindal 53
Linethwaite, 54
Linford, 10
Linlithgow, 83
Linn A'an, 95
Linn of Dee, 97
Linn of Muich, 97
Linn of Quirch, 97
Linslade Hall, 7
Linslade Wood, 7
Liscombe House, 7
Liscombe Park, 7
Little Stanmore, 3
Liverpool, 42, 51
Livingston, 84
Lochaber, 100
Lochar, 100
Loch Achray, 77
Lochanhead, 37
Loch Ard, 88, 92
Loch Awe, 88
Loch Beauly, 100
Loch Crinan, 80
Loch Earn, 88
Loch Eck, 80
Loch Ericht, 88
Loch Etive, 91
Loch Fine, 91, 93
Lochgelly, 85
Lochiel, 100
Loch Katrine, 77, 88, 91
Loch Leven, 83
Loch Lomond, 77, 82, 89, 90, 91
Loch Lubnaig, 88
Lochmaben, 33
Lochnagar, 97
Loch of Muich, 95
Loch Ness, 100
Loch Rannoch, 88
Loch Tay, 82, 88, 89
Loch Vennachar, 77, 82
Loch Winnoch, 72
Lockerbie, 73
Lockerbie Hall, 74
Lodore Fell, 61
Logie, 77
Logierait, 90
Long Bridge, 16
Longford, 17
Longforgan, 91
Longsight, 37
Longton, 25
Longton Hall, 25
Longtown, 63
Longwood, 48
Lossiemouth, 99
Lostock, 50
Lostock Junction, 52
Lostock Lane, 52
Loughrigg Fell, 59
Loughton, 9
Loup's Fell Cutting, 61
Lower Darwen, 49
Lower Woodhouse, 57
Lowes Water, 54

Low Gelt Bridge, 64
Low Gill, 61
Low Row, 64
Lowther Castle, 60, 62
Lowther Park, 62
Lowton Hall, 27
Low Wood, 58
Lugar Water, 70
Lugar, 67
Lumphanan, 97
Luncarty, 92
Luncarty Bleach Works, 90
Lundin Links, 85
Luss, 81
Luton Hoo, 7
Lyme Hall, 29
Lytham, 52
Lytham Hall, 52
Lyulph's Tower, 60

Macclesfield, 28
Mackerfield, 35
Madeley, 31
Magus Muir, 87
Maiden Camp, 86
Maiden Castle, 86, 87
Maiden Castle Hill, 86
Mains, 91
Maltraeth, 31
Manchester, 37
Man Mountain, 53
Marchington, 26
Market Harborough, 15
Markinch, 86
Marr Lodge, 97
Marsden, 47
Marsh Lane, 51
Marston Gate, 6
Marston Green, 18
Marton, 15
Maryhill, 81
Marykirk, 95
Maryport, 54, 55
Mary's Holme, 64
Mauchline, 68
Mauchline Castle, 71
Mauchline Moor, 68
Mauldslee Castle, 76
Mawcarse, 86
Maxtoke Castle, 20
Maxtoke Park, 19
Maxwelltown, 67
Maybole, 72
Mayfield, 29
Meaford Hall, 25
Mealfourvonie, 100
Medbourne Bridge, 100
Meigle, 93
Melbreak Fell, 54
Mercote Hall, 18
Meresby Hall, 55
Merevale, 23
Methven, 90
Methven Castle, 90
Midcalder, 75
Middle Fell, 64
Middleton, 48
Miles Platting, 47
Milk Water, 72
Mill Beck, 59
Millbrook, 8
Miller's Bridge, 51
Milliken, 71
Milliken Park, 72
Mill Mannock, 71
Mill Mead, 10
Millom Park, 53
Mills of Drum, 97
Milltimber, 97
Milltown, 83
Milnathort, 86
Minathorpe, 57
Milton, 10, 64, 76
Miltown, 45
Minshull Vernon, 32
Mirfield, 48
Moffat, 74
Moffat Water, 66
Mole Hill, The, 74
Monaltric, 97
Monifieth, 91
Monkland Well, 83
Monkton, 68
Monteith, 77, 78
Mont Keen, 97
Montrose, 94
Monymusk, 97
Moore, 33
Moor Park, 8
Moot Hill, 63
Morayshire, 98
Moreton Hall, 27
Morley, 48
Morsedale Hall, 61
Moses Gate, 49
Moss Bank, 41
Mossgiel Farm, 71
Mossley, 47
Moss Side, 52
Motherwell 76
Mottram Park, 29
Mount, The, 86
Mow Cop, 27, 32
Muchalls, 95
Muirkirk, 68
Mulben, 98
Muncaster Hall, 54
Murthly 90, 92
Murtle, 97
Muthill, 89
Myterefield, 91
Myton, 16

Nairn, 99
Nantwich, 32
Naseby, 13
Nash Mills, 4
Natley, 58
Naworth Castle, 63, 64
Netherby, 63, 72
Nethercleugh, 73
Nether Hall, 55
Netherton, 54
Nevay, 93
Newbiggin Hall, 63
Newbold Pacey, 16
Newbold Revel, 22
Newbold-upon-Avon, 17
New Brighton, 44
Newburgh (Perth), 87
Newburgh, 50
Newby Bridge, 58, 59
Newcastle, 65
Newcastle-un-Lyme, 26
New Cumnock, 68
New Galloway, 67
New Lanark, 75
Newlands, 52, 61
New Lane, 50
New Milns, 68
Newnham Paddox, 14
Newnham Priory, Ruin, 9
Newport, 30
Newport Pagnell, 7
Newton, 78
Newton Bridge, 34, 41
Newton Hill, 95
Newton Road, 21
Newton Stewart, 67
Newtown, 87
Newtown House, 93
Newtyle, 93
Norbury, 28
Northampton, 10, 11
North Rode Junction, 28
Northwich, 32, 33
Norton Bridge, 24, 31
Norton-on-the-Moors, 25
Norton Park, 33
Nuneaton, 18, 22
Nunnery, 45
Nunwick, 64

Oakamoor, 28
Oakley, 88
Oakley House, 9
Oakshaw Head, 72
Oaks, The, 49
Oban, 80, 82
Ochils, 77
Ochiltree, 70
Offchurch Bury, 15, 16
Okeover Hall, 29
Oldbury, 21
Old Cumnock, 68
Oldfield Road, 48
Oldham, 47
Old Howley Hall, 48
Old Meldrum, 98
Olney, 7, 13
Ordsal Lane, 41
Orgem Hall, 3
Ormskirk, 41, 44
Orrel Lodge, 50
Orrell, 50
Orton, 98
Orton Scar, 61
Oscott College, 20
Oundle, 13
Over Darwen, 49
Overstone, 12
Overton, 13
Overtown, 76
Oxenholme 58
Oxford, 9
Oxley Hall, 3
Oyne, 98

Packington, 17
Packington Hall, 18
Packington Park, 20
Paisley, 72
Pannanich Springs, 95
Panmure Castle, 94
Panshanger, 3
Park, 47, 52, 97
Park Street, 4
Parton, 55, 67
Pass of Leny, 76
Pass of Awe, 79
Patna, 71
Patricroft, 41
Patterdale Inn, 60
Patterdale Hall, 60
Peasely Cross, 41
Peel, 45, 46
Peel Hall, 40
Pemberton, 50
Pendleton, 49
Penkridge, 22
Penrith, 60, 62
Penwortham Priory, 36
Peover Hall, 36
Perry Bar, 21
Perry Hall, 21
Perth, 87, 89
Perthshire, 88
Peterboro', 13, 15
Petterill Bank, 63
Piel, 52
Pillar, The, 54
Pimbo Lane, 50
Pinner, 2
Pinner Park, 2
Pitcaithley Spa, 87, 90
Pitcaple, 98
Pitcullo, 86
Pitfirran, 85
Pitlethie, 86
Pitsford, 12
Pittencrieff, 85, 86
Pittodric, 98
Plaidy, 98
Plumpton, 63
Pluscarden, 99
Point of Ayre, 45
Point Firkin, 81
Polesworth, 22
Pollockshaws, 82
Polmont Junction, 83
Ponsonby Hall, 54
Pooley Bridge, 60
Portlethen, 95
Port Carlisle, 63

Port Glasgow, 72
Portobello, 21
Portsoy, 98
Port le Murray, 45, 46
Port of Monteith, 78, 80
Pots and Pans, 48
Pottersbury, 12
Potteries, 26
Poulton-le-Fylde, 52
Poynton, 29
Poynton Hall, 29, 37
Prescott, 44
Prestbury, 29
Preston Brook, 33
Preston, 35, 52
Prestonfield, 84
Preston Juntion, 34
Preston Road, 51
Prestwick, 69
Prieshill, 68
Primrose Hill Tunnel, 2
Primrose Green, 4
Prince Charles's Monument, 100
Princethorpe Priory, 16
Priory, the, 64
Prudhoe, 64

Quair Castle, 75

Radford, 16
Radway Green, 27
Railston, 72
Rainford, 41, 50
Rainford Junction, 41
Rainhill, 41
Raise Gap, 59, 60
Rait Castle, 100
Raith, 85
Rake's Hall, 52
Ramsey, 45
Randolph's Field, 76
Ranton Abbey, 30
Rathobyres, 84
Ratho, 84
Ratho Hall, 84
Ratho House, 84
Ravenglass, 53, 54, 58
Ravenscraig Castle, 85
Rawlinson's Nab, 58
Rawyards, 84
Rayrigg, 58
Redditch, 20
Red House, 21
Red Pike, 54
Reddish, 47
Reedsmouth, 65
Reeford, 24
Regent's Park, 2
Renfrew, 72
Rennie, 54
Renton, 82
Restenet Priory, 93
Ribby Hall, 52
Ribchester, 49
Rickerby, 63
Ridgmont, 8
Riding Mill, 66
Ridley Hall, 64
Ringstead, 13
Roade, 10
Roby, 41
Rocester, 28
Rockcliffe, 72
Rock Ferry, 44
Rockingham, 15
Rode Hall, 27
Rookery, 41
Rongha Bridge, 60
Rose Castle, 56, 63
Rose Hill, 64
Rosemount, 92
Rothersthorpe, 12
Rothes, 98
Rothie, 98
Rothiemay, 98
Rowardennan, 82
Rowdown Common, 5
Rowel, 57
Rowley, 30
Rudyard, 28
Rueberry, 66
Rugby, 14, 15
Rugeley, 24
Runcorn, 41
Runcorn Gap, 41
Rushen, 47
Rushen Abbey, 46
Rutherglen, 78
Ruthrieston, 97
Ruthwell, 66
Rydal, 59
Rydal Head, 59, 60
Rydal Hall, 53, 59
Rydal Mount, 59
Rydal Water, 59
Ryton, 65
Ryton Hall, 65

Saddleback, 56, 60, 61, 62
Saddleworth 47
St. Alban's Abbey, 3
St. Andrews, 86
St. Bees, 54
St. Bees Head, 54
St. Constantine's Three Caves, 64
St. Fillans, 88
St. Helens, 41 44, 55
St. Marnoch, 68
St. John's Vale, 60
Salcey, 12
Salesbury Hall, 49
Salford, 49
Saltcoats, 69
Sandbach, 36
Sandhills, 51
Sandon, 24
Sandwell Park, 20
Sankey Bridges, 41
Sanquhar, 67
Sauchieburn, 78
Scafell, 54
Scafell Pikes, 61
Scale Force, 54
Scales Tarn, 61
Scarisbrick, 44
Scathwaite, 61
Schehallion, 88
Scone Palace, 90
Scorton, 56
Scotby, 64
Scotswood, 65
Scropton, 25
Sea Fell 59
Seaforth, 51
Seascale, 54
Seat Sandal, 60
Seaton, 15
Sedbergh, 61
Sedgwick, 58
Seighford, 30
Sellafield, 54
Seton, 53
Shaff Hill, 64
Shadwell Park and Hall, 21
Shap, 61
Shap Fells, 61
Shap Summit, 62
Shaw Hall, 52
Shaw Park, 88
Sheriff's Muir, 78
Shewston, 9
Shildon, 19
Shilton, 22
Shoolthwaite Moss, 60
Shrewsbury, 31
Shrigley Hall, 29
Shropshire, 30
Shortwoodshaw, 92
Shugborough, 30
Shugborough Hall, 24
Shugborough Park, 29
Silecroft, 53
Silverdale, 53
Simarburn, 65
Sinclairtown, 85
Sizerth Castle, 58
Skelgill, 59
Skelwith Force, 59
Skelwith Bridge, 58
Skiddaw, 56, 60, 61, 62
Skye, 100
Slaggyford, 64
Slaithwaite, 48
Slamannan, 84
Slateford, 75
Smeathwaite, 60
Smethwick, 21
Snafell, 45
Snitterfield, 16
Soho, 21
Somerford Hall, 22
Somerford Park, 27
Sorn Castle, 71
Sough, 49
Soulbury, 7
Sound of Sleat, 100
South Alloa, 88
South Barrule, 45
South Barrule Mines, 46
South Luffenham, 15
South Platt Cairns, 84
Southwaite, 63
Southwick, 67
Southport, 41, 44, 50, 52
Speke, 41
Spon Lane, 21
Spread Eagle, 22
Springfield, 86
Staffa, 80
Stafford, 22, 30
Stafford Castle, 30
Staffordshire, 21, 22, 31
Staleybridge, 47
Stamford, 15
Standish, 34
Standon Bridge, 31
Stanley, 92
Stanley Castle, 72
Staveley, 58
Stechford, 19
Steps Road, 83
Stevenston, 69
Stewarton, 68
Stewart's Raiss, 72
Stewkley, 7
Stickle Tarn, 59
Stirling, 76
Stirlingshire, 76
Stobhall, 92
Stockgill Force, 59
Stockport, 36, 47
Stocksfield, 65
Stoke, 25
Stoke Hammond, 7
Stoke Park, 10
Stone Junction, 24
Stonebyres, 75
Stoneclough, 47
Stonehaven, 95
Stoneleigh Abbey, 15, 16, 17
Stonyhurst College, 36
Stony Stratford, 7, 12
Storr's Hall, 58, 59
Stourton Quarry, 44
Stow Hill, 24
Stowe, 9
Strachur, 79
Stratford-upon-Avon 15, 16, 20
Strath-Earn, 90
Strath Glass, 100
Strath Spey, 100
Strathire, 76
Strathmiglo, 86
Strathmore, 88, 91
Stranraer, 67
Stretton, 15, 23
Stye Head, 61
Styford Park, 66
Styperson Park, 29

Sudbury, 2, 26
Sudbury Hall, 25
Sulby, 45
Sutton, 41
Swanbourne, 9
Swinnerton Park, 26
Swinfin, 24
Symington, 74

Tabley Hall, 36
Tain, 97
Tallentire Hall, 55
Tamworth Castle, 20
Tamworth, 22
Tarbolton, 71
Tarleton Knott, 57
Tarporley Hall, 32
Tattenhall, 32
Tatton Park, 36
Taymouth, 90
Tay Port, 87
Tebay, 61
Tebay Fell, 61
Teddesley Park, 22, 30
Terrenzean Castle, 68
Thainston, 97
Thankerton, 74
Thedingworth, 15
Thirle Mere, 60, 61
Thornton, 85
Thorpe, 13
Thrapstone, 13
Thirlwall, 64
Thornhill, 66
Thrimby, 62
Thurnham Hall, 56
Tillicoultry, 88
Tillifour, 98
Tillifowrie, 97
Tillynaught, 98
Tilstone Lodge, 32
Tindrum, 82
Tinto Hill, 73
Tinwald, 67
Tippermuir, 90
Tipton, 22
Tirebeggar Hill, 98
Tixall, 30
Tongue, 97
Torryburn, 88
Tirebeggar Hill,
Tixall, 30
Tongue, 97
Torphins, 97
Torryburn, 88
Torver, 53
Towcaster, 10
Tower of Repentance, 65
Trailtron, 73
Trench Crossing, 30
Trentham, 25
Triermain Castle 64
Tring, 5
Tring Park, 5
Troon, 69
Trossachs, 77, 82, 87
Troutbeck, 58
Tullibardine, 89
Tulheth Hall, 36
Turnberry Castle, 70
Tunstall 25
Turriff, 98
Tutbury, 26
Two Waters, 4, 5
Twyford Abbey, 2
Tynwald Hill, 45, 46

Uddingston, 78
Ufton, 16
Ulleswater, 59, 60, 61, 63
Ulverston, 53, 59
Unthank Hall, 64
Upholland, 50
Upper Pollock, 82
Uttoxeter, 25

Valley of Newlands, 54
Valley of the Nene, 13
Verulam, 3

Waddon Chace & Hall, 8
Wallace Hill, 68
Wallace's Cave, 75
Wall, 65
Wall End, 59
Walter Hill, 97
Walton House, 64
Wamphray, 73
Wandell Bower, 74
Wansfell Park, 59
Wansford, 13
Wardhouse, 98
Wardrew Castle, 64
Wark, 65
Wartle, 98
Warrington, 33, 41
Warrington Junc., 34, 41,
Warwick, 15, 16, 18
Warwick Castle, 15, 20
Warwick Hall, 64
Warwickshire, 14, 22
Wasperton, 16
Wast Water, 54, 59, 61
Watch Cross, 64
Watendlath, 61
Water Eaton, 8
Waterhead, 58, 59
Waterloo, 44, 51
Watermillock, 61
Waterside, 71
Watford, 3
Waverton, 32
Wavertree, 44
Weaste, 41
Wednesfield, 21
Wednesfield, Heath, 21
Weedon, 6, 12, 13
Welford, 15
Wellesbourne, 16
Wellingborough, 13
Wellington, 31
Wem, 32
Wemyss, 86
Westbrook Park, 5
Westburne, 78
Westhoughton, 50
Westmoreland, 57
Weston, 24
Westwood Hall, 28
Wetheral, 64
Wetheral Safeguards, 77
Whaddon, 7
Whalley, 49
Wheelock, 36
Whifflet, 76
Whiston, 13
Whitchester, 64
Whitchurch, 32
Whitehaven, 54
Whitehaven Castle, 54
Whitehill, 74
White Hill, 5
Whitehouse, 97
Whitley Abbey, 17
Whitley Castle, 17
Whitley Park, 17
Whitmore, 31
Whitmore Hall 31
Whitnash, 16
Whittlebury, 12
Wichnor, 24
Wick, 97
Widdicar, 54
Wigan, 34, 50
Wiggington Bridge, 5
Wigton, 56
Wigton Hall, 56
Willaston, 32
Willenhall, 21
Willesden, 2
Wilmston, 36
Winchburgh, 84
Windermere, 58
Windgate House, 74
Wing Park, 7
Winsford, 32
Winslow, 9
Winstanley Hall, 50
Winwick Hall, 34
Wishaw, 76
Wishaw Castle, 76
Woburn, 7, 8
Woburn Abbey, 8
Wolseley Park, 30
Wolverton, 10
Wolverhampton, 21, 23
Woodcote Hall, 30
Woodend, 74
Woodhall, 55
Woodland, 53
Woodside, 92, 97
Woodsome Lees, 42
Woolton Hall, 41
Wooton, 6, 10
Wooton Underwood, 6
Workington, 54. 55
Workington Bridge, 55
Workington Hall, 65
Worlaston, 32
Wormwood Scrubs, 2
Worsley, 40
Worsley Hall, 41
Wortley, 48
Wray Green, 52
Wreay, 63
Wrenbury, 32
Wrine Hall and Hill, 31
Writhington Hall, 35
Written Rocks, 64
Wroxhall Abbey, 15, 16
Wylam, 65
Wylam House, 65
Wythburn Chapel, 59
Wythburn Water, 60

Yardley Chase, 13, 19
Yarton, 32

BRADSHAW'S DESCRIPTIVE RAILWAY HAND-BOOK

OF

GREAT BRITAIN AND IRELAND.

SECTION III.

NOTE.—Shunts or Marks thus , or thus , introduced into the following pages are intended to show the point at which a Branch deviates from the Main Line. Its position to the right or left hand of the Column indicates the right or left hand of the railway on which the deviation takes place. The termination of the Branch is known by the Shunt being reversed.

LONDON AND NORTH WESTERN.

EUSTON SQUARE STATION.

PASSING under the magnificent Doric entrance, which forms so grand a feature of the metropolitan terminus of this line of railway, the huge pile of building at once arrests the eye. It was designed by Philip Hardwick, Esq., and erected by Messrs. William Cubitt and Co., at a cost of about £150,000.

The structure, of the interior, is of plain Roman style of architecture, and is 220 feet long by 168 feet in width. At the southern front there are five entrances. The outer doors lead into what is called the "outer vestibule," having a beautifully designed mosaic pavement, constructed of patent metallic lead, within a border of Craigleith stone. On the northern side of the "outer vestibule" are five other entrances, leading into the grand hall or vestibule; and this hall for size and grandeur is probably unique; in dimensions it is truly gigantic, being 125 feet in length, 61 feet in width, and 60 feet in height. At the northern end is a noble flight of steps, leading to a vestibule, in which are doors entering into the general meeting room, the board room, and the conference room, and the gallery which runs round the hall, thus giving facility of communication to an infinity of offices connected with the railway traffic. The style of architecture is Roman Ionic, and has been treated with great skill. The bas-reliefs which adorn the panels in the corners of the hall are eight in number, and typify the chief cities and boroughs with which the North Western Railway communicates. They are London, Liverpool, Manchester, Birmingham, Carlisle, Chester, Lancaster, and Northampton. London is typified by a female figure, crowned, bearing in her hands the sceptre of royalty, and the rudder, emblem of maritime power. Below her sits an old man with a long beard, symbolical of Father Thames, and by her knees a genius, his arm resting on a globe, and at his feet emblems of music, painting, and the drama, indicating the universality of the art of knowledge of the great metropolis of the world. The background is filled with St. Paul's and a group of shipping. Liverpool is a sitting female figure, resting on a rudder, with a genius by her side holding a quadrant. An aged man, having shells and corals in his hair, symbolises the Mersey: in his right hand he holds a trident, and his left rests upon a well filled cornucopia. A portion of the Exchange and a group of shipping fills up this characteristic group. Manchester is individualised by a laurel-crowned female, sitting and holding a distaff, her hand resting on a bale of cotton; a genius by her side holding the shuttle, indicative of the cotton-spinning notoriety of the important city. Mercury, emblem of commerce, sits in the foreground, busy drawing plans on a piece of paper, and the background is composed of piles of cotton goods, a huge factory, and the tower of the cathedral. Birmingham has the symbols of the iron trade—Vulcan, with his hammer and anvil being in the foreground; a beautiful vase, showing the variety and perfection of the iron works, and the portico of the new Town Hall, fill up the group. Chester with its far-famed dairy produce, its cheeses, its walls, and venerable cathedral is well characterised. Carlisle shows cattle market, manufacture, and maritime symbols, with its cathedral tower; Lancaster its furniture and other manufactures; and Northampton has its emblems, the shoemaker, as well as agricultural symbols, and a horse to typify its celebrated horse fair.

The large group in alto-relievo over the door leading to the general meeting room, is an extremely picturesque and effective composition—representing Britannia, supported by Science and Industry.

The statue of the late George Stephenson, who effected more than any other engineer has done towards the development of the railway system, is a very appropriate ornament to the great hall. The statue, which is of fine Carrara marble, is ten feet in height. The figure is habited in the costume of the times, and holds in the right hand a scroll, upon which is inscribed the elevation of an aqueduct.

Leading from the grand hall on the basement, on the eastern and western sides are several glass doors, connecting it with the booking offices and platforms.

London to Cheddington.

Upon starting from the Euston Square station the train proceeds somewhat leisurely as far as Camden Town station, passing under arches, and between brick walls, above which may be seen at intervals, elegant villas and rows of houses, the inhabitants of which must be great admirers of the locomotive, with its shrieking whistle, to choose their residence in the immediate vicinity of this terminus.

The train runs up an incline to

CAMDEN ROAD.

Telegraph station at Highbury.

MONEY ORDER OFFICE 89, High Street.

This station is the London depôt of the company, and from thence two lines diverge to the right and left, the former going to Islington, Bow, Stratford, or Fenchurch Street, and the latter to Kew, Richmond, Windsor, &c.

On quitting the Camden station, we leave Regent's Park and Hampstead on the left, and the beautiful grounds of Highgate on the right; thence we proceed past Chalk Farm, a spot once celebrated as the scene of repeated duels. Passing on, we enter the Primrose Hill tunnel—thence we are conveyed under the Edgeware Road, and beneath a number of bridges, chiefly used for connecting private property severed by the line. Beyond this is the pretty village of

KILBURN; and the open country, which now begins to appear on either hand, is sufficiently beautiful to interest the traveller. On the right is the spire of Hampstead church—to the left that of Notting Hill, and we have scarcely time to admire their architecture before we are enclosed in the banks of a deep cutting, through which we proceed a few seconds, and then enter another tunnel, called the Kensal Green Tunnel, the celebrated cemetery—the Pere la Chaise of London—being on the left side, which is worthy of a visit, from the number of eminent individuals who are entombed within its limits. The tombs of His Royal Highness the late Duke of Sussex, the Princess Sophia, Ducrow, and George Robins (the princes of horsemanship and auctioneering), are worth a visit. The cemetery approaches the railway, and extends over a part of the tunnel. The railway now enters a richly pastoral country, and as the beauties of nature have hitherto been veiled from us by a succession of tunnels and cuttings, we welcome the landscapes which are presented to our view, as we begin to experience the exciting effect of railway travelling.

Passing through an open country, by an express or fast train, where the eye can embrace an uninterrupted view—the steady, but swift motion of the train imparts a peculiarly pleasing sensation, which may be compared to the sense of enjoying the changing scenes of a constantly varying panorama, without being required to perform the least effort or labour to obtain it.

The scenery now rapidly improves; passing Wormwood Scrubs on the left, we may notice the junction line of the North and South-Western Companies, curving towards the south. To the right appears some of the prettiest scenery in Middlesex; on the left is the rich foliage of Twyford Abbey—and before us expands the valley of the Brent.

WILLESDEN.

Distance from station, 1 mile.

Telegraph station at Highbury.

MONEY ORDER OFFICE, 116, Edgeware Road.

The grave of the celebrated Jack Sheppard and his mother will be found in the churchyard at this place.

The line now proceeds through fertile meads, the river Brent winding gracefully through the vale, and crossing this by a viaduct, we pass Apperton and Sudbury, to the south or left, and reach the station at

SUDBURY.

Telegraph station at Highbury.

HOTEL.—Swan.

MAILS.—Two arrivals and departures, daily, between London and Sudbury.

MONEY ORDER OFFICE at Harrow.

Soon after leaving Sudbury we obtain a view of "Harrow-on-the-Hill" on the left, which, with its conspicuous church, becomes an interesting object in the landscape. The Harrow station is rather more than a mile from Harrow, lying in the vale below.

HARROW.

Distance from station, 1 mile.
A telegraph station.
HOTEL.—King's Head.

OMNIBUSES to and from the station.

POST HORSES, FLYS, &c., at the station and hotels. Tariff—1s. 6d. per mile.

COACHES to and from London, daily.

MAILS.—Three arrivals and departures, daily, between London and Harrow.

MONEY ORDER OFFICE.

On account of the delightful prospect which the churchyard and summit of Harrow Hill affords, and the associations connected with Harrow, it is a place of frequent resort.

Crossing the meadow from the station we reach the foot of the hill, and if we ascend the summit, the view will be found to deserve all the encomiums bestowed upon it. The hill, rising almost isolated from an extensive plain, with the church and school on one side, and the old churchyard sloping on the other, forms in itself a combination of objects inexpressibly attractive and picturesque; but when the eye ranges over the vast expanse, and the landscape is lit up with the gorgeous and glowing sunset of a summer's eve, the prospect becomes extremely fascinating. It commands a delightful view of the wide, rich valley through which the Thames stretches its sinuous course; on the west it embraces a view of the fertile portions of Buckinghamshire and Berkshire; on the east London, with the dome of St. Paul's; and to the south the towers of Windsor castle and the sweeping undulations of the Surrey hills. Harrow school was founded by John Lyon in the reign of Queen Elizabeth, and is still considered one of the first in the kingdom. The church contains a monument to Dr. Drury, by Westmacott, on the north side of the nave, representing the schoolmaster seated, with two of his pupils studying beside him—the likenesses identifying them with the late Sir Robert Peel and Lord Byron, whose names have contributed to the interest attached to the locality. The poet in one of his letters describes the regard he had for a particular spot in the churchyard, where he used to sit for hours looking towards Windsor—

> "As reclining at eve on yon tombstone he lay
> To catch the last gleam of the sun's setting ray."

Upon leaving Harrow station, we proceed over a slight ascent, passing Little Stanmore on the right—a small village, possessing an elegant little church erected by the Chandos family.

Great Stanmore is two miles distant, and is situated on an eminence, adorned with handsome seats and villas.

After passing through a short cutting, the little village of Hatchend, which closely adjoins the railway on the right, appears pleasantly situated on the gentle slope of a hill. The bridge beneath, which we are now carried over, connects Hatchend with the village of Pinner, which, with the trees scattered around it, and the rich foliage of Pinner Park, forms a landscape of very considerable beauty.

PINNER.

Distance from station, 1 mile.

Telegraph station at Watford, 4 miles.

MONEY ORDER OFFICE at Harrow.

MAILS.—One arrival and departure, daily, between London and Pinner.

At this point we pass from Middlesex into

HERTFORDSHIRE.

WE cross the Oxley ridge, which forms a part of a chain of hills, and constitutes the boundary of the two counties. From this elevated position we have an opportunity of admiring the appearance of Hertfordshire.

There is no county of its size so rich in associations, and in stately seats of noblemen and gentlemen as the small inland county of Hertfordshire.

York, Kent, and Surrey are only richer from their greater size. It is true that Herts has no cathedral; but she has St. Alban's Abbey, one of the oldest and most instructive of all our mediæval buildings; then she has Verulam, with its rich store of Roman remains; Gorhambury, sacred to the shade of the great Lord Bacon; Hatfield, rich in the wisdom of the Cecils; Panshanger, with its noble old oaks and picture gallery, second to none in Italian art in England; Cashiobury, with the pictures by Vandyke, Wilkie, Landseer, and Lely, and its woods and waters; the Grove, with that noble gallery of portraits formed by the great Lord Chancellor Clarendon; Moor Park, with its trees, not to be surpassed in England; Knebworth, with the Lytton associations and its Bulwer interest, &c; and in conclusion Herts, with its sweet sylvan scenes, and trout streams—the Colne and the Chep.

To see the west side of Hertfordshire easily, an excursion tourist should get out at the Watford station.

Proceeding onward we enter the valley of the Colne, which forms a pretty landscape, and shortly after reach the station at

BUSHEY.

Distance from station, ¾ mile.

Telegraph station at Watford, 1½ mile.

MAILS.—Two arrivals and departures, daily, between London and Bushey.

MONEY ORDER OFFICE at Watford.

Just beyond Bushey, a handsome viaduct conducts us over the river Colne, and shortly after, we arrive at the WATFORD station, which is about a mile from the town.

WATFORD.

POPULATION, 3,800.

HOTEL.—Essex Arms.

MARKET DAY.—Tuesday.

FAIRS.—March 31st, Aug. 29th and 30th, Sept. 9th.

MAILS.—Three arrivals and departures, daily, between London and Watford.

BANKERS.—London and County Bank.

DISTANCES OF PLACES FROM THE STATION.

	Miles.		Miles.
Bushey Hall	1	Grove Park	1
Bury Park	3	Orgem Hall	4¼
Cashiobury Park	0¾	Oxley Hall	2

WATFORD is a busy, thriving, and populous town, situated on the banks of the river Colne, and consists of only one street, with minor ones diverging from it. It is deficient in points of picturesque or antiquarian interest, but there are several places of attraction in the neighbourhood, viz.—*Cashiobury Park*, the seat of the Earl of Essex, at whose instigation the tunnel at this place, 1725 yards long, was suggested to the Railway Company; and *Grove Park*, the residence of the Earl of Clarendon.

ST. ALBANS BRANCH.

Watford to St. Albans.

A run of seven miles from Watford, leaving the little village of PARK STREET a little to the right, brings us to the town of

ST. ALBANS

POPULATION, 7,000.
A telegraph station.
HOTELS.—Peahen, George.
MARKET DAY.—Saturday.

FAIRS.—March 25th, 26th, October 10th and 11th.
MAILS.—Two arrivals and departures, daily, between London and St. Albans.
MONEY ORDER OFFICE.
BANKERS.—Branch of London and County Bank.

This ancient town of Herts, should be visited for its venerable abbey church, and that of St. Michael's, which contains an excellent full-length statue of Lord Bacon, as he used to sit, thinking, in court. Bacon had a country house at Gorhambury, close by, and this figure of the "greatest, wisest, meanest of mankind," whose career is sketched with so much truth and reverence by Macaulay, in one of his best essays, was erected in the church, by Sir T. Meantys, or Mewtis, his admirer, as he calls himself. The *Abbey Church*, lately restored, is a cross-shaped pile, 539 feet long, exceeding most cathedrals, and interesting for the variety of styles it exhibits, its beautiful screen, tracery, painted ceiling, old brasses, &c., and the pillar of St. Amphibalus, who converted St. Alban, to whom King Offa, in 793, dedicated the priory. He is reckoned one of the earliest English martyrs, having suffered in 293, on Holmhurst Hill, close to the church. St. Albans was the scene of two battles in the Wars of the Roses; the first in 1455, when Warwick, the king-maker, defeated Henry VI., and the other in 1461, when Margaret of Anjou routed Warwick. Many of those who fell were buried in the old church. It contains, also, the tombs of Good Duke Humphrey, and Matthew Paris, the historian. The body of Duke Humphrey (the same from whom dinner-hunters sometimes got an invitation), was found embalmed in *pickle* in 1703. Many Roman bricks or tiles, were used to rebuild this church, all collected from the spoils of *Verulamium*, one of the chief Roman cities in England; the sites of its walls, &c., are still traced, and relics frequently discovered. It was one of the places taken by Boadicea, in the time of Claudius, most of the inhabitants being put to the sword.

The gaol was the abbey gate-house. Much straw-plait is made here for the London market. Dame Juliana Berners, who wrote the "Book of St. Albans," the oldest work on hawking (1481), was abbess here; and there is a brass to her memory, the likeness on which, curiously enough, bears a great resemblance to a descendant of her family, in the present day, Lord Berners, of Didlington. At *Gorhambury*, now the seat of Earl Verulam, rebuilt in the last century. There are a few fragments of the old house which Lord Bacon's father erected.

L. & N. W. Main Line continued.

Upon leaving the station at Watford, the train passes beneath a bridge, and a short distance beyond we enter the Watford Tunnel, and, on emerging therefrom, we continue for some time through an excavation, and, on the prospect opening on the left, we see the village of Langley Bury, a short distance from which is *Grove Park*, the seat of the Earl of Clarendon; and beautifully situated on the distant rising ground is the ancient village of King's Langley, so much frequented by King John. The Grand Junction Canal here runs close to the line, on the south of the embankment, and while the traveller looks with a smile of compassion upon the rival route

"Which, like a wounded snake, drags its slow length along,"

we arrive at the station of

KING'S LANGLEY.

Telegraph station at Watford, 3½ miles.
MAILS.—Two arrivals and departures, daily, between London and King's Langley.
MONEY ORDER OFFICE.
HOTEL.—Rose and Crown.

The village of King's Langley on the right, is remarkable for the square tower and short spire of its ancient church: there are several paper mills in the neighbourhood, that of the Messrs. Dickinson and Longman, at Two Waters, deserves a visit; good fishing abounds. Several iron coffins were found here in 1840.

Proceeding onwards, the line crosses the King's Langley Viaduct, and thence by a bridge over the Grand Junction Canal, from which the prospect is extensive and beautiful. On the left is Moor Park, in the distance, and Primrose Green and King's Langley in the foreground. On the right, and near the line are Nash Mills, and a little further on a picturesque dingle, beyond which is *Gorhambury Park*, the seat of the Earl of Verulam. We thence pass through a short cutting, upon emerging from which, the village of Two Waters, and Corner Hall, surrounded with rich foliage, form a pleasing landscape. The line then enters a cutting nearly two miles long, on leaving which the train immediately arrives at the station at

BOXMOOR (Hemel Hempstead).

Telegraph station at Watford, 7 miles.
HOTEL.—King's Arms.
OMNIBUSES to and from Hemel Hempstead.
MARKET DAY.—Thursday, at Hemel Hempstead.
FAIRS.—Holy Thursday, Thursday after Trinity Sunday, and 3rd Monday in September.

Money Order Office at Hemel Hempstead.

Bankers.—Bucks and Oxon Union, and London and County.

Travellers would infer that this station derives ts name from a moor in the vicinity; but the moor is at some distance, and the scenery in the neighbourhood of the station is exceedingly pretty and fertile. On leaving the station the line passes over an embankment, and the country becomes very interesting. To the left is Rowdown Common, with the richly wooded hills behind it, and on the right the village of Two Waters. The country is also interspersed with pretty cottages, with the church of Hemel Hempstead among the distant hills. *Westbrook Park*, the Hon. Dudley Ryder's seat, is in the vicinity.

Crossing the Box Lane Viaduct, the line runs parallel for some distance by the side of the Grand Junction Canal, which forms another agreeable feature in the picturesque scenery of this beautiful valley. Upon crossing the canal it proceeds along an embankment, which affords a fine prospect. We pass various hamlets on each side, and then reach the village of Bourne End on the left, where the embankment terminates; thence we pass through a cutting, on emerging from which we pass under Haxter's End Bridge, where the right-hand bank of the cutting terminates. On reaching Bank Mill Bridge a landscape of very great beauty bursts upon our view, including a view of the tower of Berkhampstead Church, the town itself, and the ruins of its ancient castle. Thence the line proceeds through a cutting, along an embankment, and arrives at the station of

BERKHAMPSTEAD.

Population, 2,943.

Telegraph station at Tring, 3¾ miles.

Hotel.—King's Arms.

Market Day.—Saturday.

Fairs.—Shrove Tuesday, Whit Monday, Michaelmas Tuesday and Wednesday.

Mails.—Two arrivals and departures, daily, between London and Berhampstead.

Money Order Office.

Bankers.—London and County Bank.

The elevated position of this station commands a delightful view of the valley on the left, in the bosom of which lies the town of Great Berkhampstead, where the author of the 'Task," the poet Cowper, was born, in 1731, and whose father was rector of this town. The church is cruciform, and as old as the cross. The beauties of the vale excite general admiration, and one cannot avoid remarking how singularly happy "Nature" or the "Muses" are in selecting the birthplaces of her favourite minstrels. What lovelier spot could be chosen to prompt the first accents of poetry than the groves and meads of this lovely valley. What could be more inspiring to the great bard than the scenery around Stratford-on-Avon; or where could a spot be found more adapted to inspire the muse of the Scottish minstrel, Burns, than the banks of the Doon?

Berhampstead Castle, in ruins, was built soon after the Conquest, by Robert Montaigne.

After leaving this station we observe the houses of the town extend by the side of the line for some distance; whilst White Hill appears in the contrary direction. The line proceeds along the embankment, thence through a cutting into Northchurch Tunnel; on emerging from which we find ourselves again on an embankment, with a charming prospect on each side. *Ashbridge Park*, the seat of the Lady Alford, lies on the right. Passing alternately by embankment and cutting, we reach Wigginton Bridge, and obtain a view of the Chiltern Hills, the name of which is so familiar to us in connection with retiring members of parliament.

Tring Park is then seen to the left of the line, beautifully situated among hills, studded with trees, and containing a splendid mansion, built by Charles II., for the unfortunate Nell or Eleanor Gwynn, who caused that monarch to found Chelsea, and rebuild Greenwich Hospitals.

TRING.

Population, 3,218.

Distance from station, 1¾ mile.

A telegraph station.

Hotels.—King's Arms, Rose and Crown.

Market Day.—Friday.

Fairs.—Easter Monday and Old Michaelmas Day

Mails.—Two arrivals and departures, daily, between London and Tring.

Money Order Office.

Bankers.—Butcher and Co.

At this station the railway reaches its greatest elevation, being 420 feet above the level of the sea, and 300 above that of Camden Town depôt. This elevation is attained by a series of gradients never exceeding 1 in 300. The town of Tring has a handsome church containing some good monuments, and a curious enriched font.

On leaving Tring station the line enters a deep cutting through the Chiltern Hills. This range› hills, once covered with woods, is part of a chain of hills extending from Norfolk (south-eastward) into Dorsetshire. They form at this point the northern basin of the Colne, and separate it from that part of Buckingham which is designated the vale.

Upon issuing from this cutting a great extent of country becomes visible on both sides of the line, which now passes from the county of Hertford into

BUCKINGHAMSHIRE.

The face of this county is much varied; the fertile vale of Aylesbury spreads through the middle of the county, and furnishes a rich pasture to vast numbers of cattle. The natural fertility of this vale has been highly extolled, and is almost unrivalled. It lies between the Chiltern Hills and a parallel range of hills, running at a distance of only a few miles along the western side of Buckinghamshire.

Proceeding along the side of the canal, we have on our left Cheddington Hill, which conceals the village of Cheddington from our view.

CHEDDINGTON (Junction).

Distance from station, ½ mile.

Telegraph station at Wolverton, 16¾ miles.

MONEY ORDER OFFICE at Tring, 4½ miles.

From this station a branch rail, seven miles long, turns off on the left to Aylesbury, which we will describe, and then continue our progress with the main line.

AYLESBURY BRANCH.

MARSTON GATE station.

AYLESBURY.

POPULATION, 26,794.
Telegraph station at Tring, 11¼ miles.
HOTELS.—George, White Hart.
OMNIBUSES to and from Prince's Risboro', daily.
COACHES to Thame, daily.
MARKET DAY.—Saturday.
FAIRS.—Jan. 18th, May 8th, June 14th, Oct. 11th, on which occasion the farmers hire all their servants from year to year, Sept. 25th, and Saturday before Palm Sunday.
BANKERS.—Branch of London and County Bank; L. D. Hunt; Thos. Butcher and Son.

The town of Aylesbury, for the accommodation of which this line was formed, is nine miles west of the main line, delightfully situated in a fertile vale, which affords pasturage to an extraordinary number of sheep. It derives its importance chiefly from its being the mart for the produce of the rich vale in which it is situate.

It is an agricultural town and borough (returning two members), in Bucks. It stands on a low hill in the rich vale of Aylesbury, a loose tract of luxuriant grass land, in the centre of the county, worth £25 an acre. Chalk Hills bound it to the north and south. Drayton describes it as "Lusty, firm, and fat."

Aylesbury was a Saxon manor, which William the Conqueror granted to one of his followers, on the tenure of finding straw for his bed, three eels, and three green geese. For many generations it belonged to the Packingtons, who had such hold on the town, that Dame Packington, in Elizabeth's time, by letter appointed "my trusty and well-beloved so-and-so to be my burgessors from said time;" promising to ratify and approve what they did at Westminster, as fully as if she were present there herself. In 1804 it was so notorious for bribery that the voting was extended to the whole hundred. Before this (in 1702) one Ashby brought an action against White, the returning officer, for refusing his vote. He obtained a verdict, which the Court of Queen's Bench reversed; but, upon appeal, the House of Lords finally decided in his favour. The Commons, in consequence of that, claimed the sole right of judging how members were to be elected, and declared Ashby guilty of a breach of privilege in appealing to any tribunal but theirs, and sent his attorney to Newgate. The case being taken up by the House of Lords, led to some violent proceedings on the part of the Commons, which were terminated only by a prorogation. A similar attempt was made by the Commons, in the case of Stockdale the printer in 1832. At present the supremacy of the regular courts of law is established, and no assertion of privilege would be allowed to contravene public right.

Like most old country towns, it is irregularly built. A small branch of the Thame runs through it to that river, which is 2 miles off. Here are the brick county hall, where the county members are nominated; lodgings for the judges in their circuit, lately built by E. Lamb; a town hall and market house, rebuilt on the site of an ancient pile, in the Grecian style, copied from the Temple of the Winds at Athens, which was of eight sides, facing the principal points of the compass; and a well-endowed grammar school.

The church (in a large churchyard) is a decorated English cross, with a low tower, overlooking the vale, and seen from most parts of it. There is a carved pulpit, and tombs of the Lees of Quarendon, an ancient seat, 2 miles north. The vicarage is on the site of a monastery to St. Osyth, who was born here. She was martyred, and gives name to *Size* Lane, London.

Lace and straw plait are made here; but another *manufacture* peculiar to the town is ducklings, which are forced for the Christmas market. The ducks are kept from laying till about October or November, when they are fed with abundance of stimulating food, and hens employed to sit on the eggs. The young brood being hatched are nursed with great care, opposite a fire, and fetch 15s. or 20s. a couple at Christmas. As many as three quarters of a million ducks are sent to London from this part.

Within a few miles are several seats. *Hartwell*, that of Dr. Lee, was, in the late war, the residence of Louis XVIII. and his family. *Wooton*, belonging to the Duke of Buckingham, has been in that family (the Grenville) since the Conquest. *Weedon* is the Duke of Marlborough's. *Lillies* was the seat of the late Lord Nugent (a Grenville). Further off, on the Banbury Road, is *Wootton Underwood*, consecrated to the memory of Cowper, who lived here with his cousin, Lady Hesketh, near the Throckmorton's old seat. The poet's house is standing. It was while living here, at the close of his life, that he produced his Homer (1791).

L. & N. W. Main Line continued.
Cheddington to Leighton Junction.

The line crosses Aylesbury Vale by an embankment, which is 25 feet in height, and affords an extensive view in every direction. Several pretty villages are scattered over the valley and slopes; and after crossing the Horton Viaduct, we catch a glimpse of the spire of Leighton Buzzard Church, and the country beyond, and shortly after of that town itself. We proceed by alternate embankment and cutting past several beautiful views, and then reach

LEIGHTON JUNCTION.
(Leighton Buzzard).

A telegraph station.
HOTELS.—Swan, Unicorn.

MARKET DAY.—Tuesday.

FAIRS.—Feb. 5th, Whit Tuesday, July 26th, Oct. 24th, and second Tuesday in December.

BANKERS.—Branch of London and County Bank; Bassett, Grant and Co.

This small market town, of 4,465 inhabitants, who make lace, and straw-plat, is situated in Bedfordshire. The branch to Dunstable turns off here; and the Ouzel, a branch of the Ouse, divides the town from Bucks and the chalk hills on the west. These hills are part of the range which, in south Bucks, run through the Chiltern Hundred (see Windsor), giving name to a nominal office, by which a M.P. is enabled to vacate his seat. Leighton *Church* is a good Gothic cross, with stalls (for the priests of one or two priory cells, that were here), and a tall spire, 193 feet high, before about 25 feet was struck down by lightning, 16th July, 1852. Its ancient *Cross* near the market house, also deserves notice, as a genuine relic of early English work, built about 1300, and stands 34 feet high on 5 steps, and set off with pinnacles and niches.

In the neighbourhood are the following places. Stewkley, and its excellent *Norman Church*, on the Chiltern hills, *Liscombe House*, Lady Lovett, the old Elizabethan seat of an ancient family. *Aston Abbot's House*, seat of Sir James Ross, the Polar navigator, *Wing Park*, Lord Overstone the banker. Whaddon, on the hills, once the centre of a large chase or forest. *Great Brickhill*, Hon. P. Duncombe, Esq.

DUNSTABLE BRANCH.

Leighton to Dunstable.

A branch rail, seven miles long, turns off on the right from Leighton Buzzard to Dunstable, in Bedfordshire.

DUNSTABLE.

POPULATION, 3,580.
Telegraph station at Leighton, 6½ miles.
HOTELS.—White Hart, King's Head, Railway.
OMNIBUSES to Luton, twice daily.
MARKET DAY.—Wednesday.
FAIRS.—Ash Wednesday, 22nd May, August 12th, and November 12th.
MAILS.—Two arrivals and departures daily, between London and Dunstable.
BANKERS.—Branch of London and County Bank; Bassett, Grant, and Co.

DUNSTABLE is situated at the foot of the Chiltern hills. The principal attraction of this town was its ancient priory church, and the celebrity of its inns. It is noted for straw-plait manufacture. Many of the houses have an antiquated appearance, and the streets, which are four in number, take the direction of the four cardinal points, intersecting each other at right angles.

The town lies among chalk hills, on the site of a Roman station or Watling Street. It has a large priory church, partly Norman.

The remainder of this route to Luton and Hertford will be found in Section IV.

London and North Western Main Line continued.

Leighton to Bletchley Junction.

Upon leaving Leighton, the line passes over a level country for nearly fifteen miles, but has occasionally to go through a tunnel or cutting in its course. At this distance it makes a curve, and on reaching the open country Linslade Wood is seen on both sides, and Linslade Hall and Church to the right. A short distance beyond is the town of Great Brickhill, standing on one of the hills which lie to the right. In the same direction is Stoke Hammond; and on the left are Stewkley, Soulbury, and Liscombe Park. The church of Stewkley is one of the most enriched and perfect specimens of Norman architecture now existing. From this point the scenery improves, the hills are studded with trees, and the landscape is of a very pleasing character. The train next reaches

BLETCHLEY.

POPULATION, 433.

Distance from station, ¼ mile.

A telegraph station.

MAILS.—One arrival and departure, daily, between London and Bletchley.

MONEY ORDER OFFICE.

From the peculiar position of this station it affords a most extensive prospect of the line of railway, and of the surrounding country, embracing the town of Bletchley, Drayton Parslon on the left, and in the distance may be seen Waddon Chace and Hall, in which Queen Elizabeth was entertained by Arthur Lord Grey.

To the right of the station, and standing on a hill, is the small town of Fenny Stratford. The village of Water Eaton is seen in the foreground in the same direction, and on the wooded hills which rise beyond, the three Brickhills are still discernible.

From the Bletchley station branch rails turn off on the left to Winslow, Oxford, and Banbury, and on the right to Bedford, both of which lines we will here describe.

BEDFORD BRANCH.

Bletchley to Bedford.

The first station on this Branch being partly in the parish of Bletchley is quickly announced.

FENNY STRATFORD.

POPULATION, 1,142.
Distance from the station, ¼ mile
Telegraph station at Bletchley, 1¼ mile.
MARKET DAY.—Monday.
FAIRS.—April 19th, July 18th, October 10th November 28th.

MAILS.—Two arrivals and departures, daily between London and Fenny Stratford.

Fenny Stratford is in a once fenny part of the Ouzel, on the Watling Street, or Roman way, which crosses the Ouse, further on, at *Stony Stratford*, where Richard III. seized his poor little nephew, Edward V. Lace and plait are made at both places. The Ouse, as it sluggishly winds down to Newport Pagnell,

> "Now glitters in the sun, and now retires,
> As bashful yet impatient to be seen."—COWPER'

Much lace and some paper are made at Newport Pagnell; in the church is an epitaph by Cowper. *Gayhurst*, the seat of Lord Carrington, 2 miles to the north-west, is an antique Elizabethan house, and has a portrait of Sir Kenelm Digby, who was born here, "a prodigy of learning, credulity, valour, and romance." *Hanslope*, on a hill, has an old Gothic church, with a spire 190 feet high. Olney, another town of lace-makers, with the house in which *Cowper* lived till 1786.

> "Yon Cottager that weaves at her own door,
> *Pillow and bobbins* all her little store;
> Content though mean, &c."—COWPER'S *Truth*.

Scott the commentator, and John Newton, were curates of Olney, and the latter, in conjunction with Cowper, here wrote his well known Olney hymns.

WOBURN SANDS.

Distance from the station, 2 miles.

Telegraph station at Bletchley, 4¼ miles.

HOTEL.—Bedford Arms.

MARKET DAY.—Friday.

FAIRS.—January 1st, March 23rd, July 13th, September 25th.

WOBURN—situated on a gentle eminence—is surrounded with plantations and evergreens, and consists of four broad streets, which intersect each other at right angles. In the centre of the town is a noble market house, erected by the Duke of Bedford, in the Tudor style of architecture. The church is covered with ivy, and has a remarkably beautiful appearance.

In the immediate vicinity of the town is *Woburn Abbey*, the seat of the Duke of Bedford. It is a modern quadrangular building, handsome, but heavy. The west front has four Ionic columns, and the east four fluted Doric ones. The interior contains a large gallery of portraits, and a collection of Italian and Dutch paintings; and in the pleasure ground is a sculpture gallery formed by the present Duke which contains a group of the Graces, by Canova, which cost £3,000. The park is twelve miles in circuit, and contains a large herd of deer.

Immediately after leaving this station we take our leave of the county of Bucks, and enter that of

BEDFORD.

THE surface, on the north and east, and in he fruitful vale of Bedford, is generally flat; but on the south-west, the chalk hills run to a considerable height, affording many fine prospect—as, at Ampthill, Woburn, and Millbrook, which command an extent of 50 miles. The greatest part is enclosed, and an improved system of agriculture has been adopted. The farms average 200 acres, and let yearly. The stock of cattle is reckoned at 200,000, and the supply of wool, 4,250 packs. The only manufactures peculiar to the county are the pillow lace and straw plait.

RIDGEMONT AND LIDLINGTON stations.

AMPTHILL.

Ampthill Park, Lord Holland's seat, 1½ mile from the station, was the residence of Queen Catherine after her divorce from Henry VIII. The sentence was pronounced by Cranmer in Dunstable Church. There is an inscription to her memory by Horace Walpole, the point of which is—

> "From Catherine's wrongs a nation's bliss was spread,
> And Luther's light from Henry's lawless bed."

BEDFORD.

A telegraph station.

HOTELS.—Swan; George.

OMNIBUSES to and from the station; also to Kimbolton, on Tuesdays, Fridays, and Saturdays.

MARKET DAYS.—Tuesday and Saturday.

FAIRS.—April 21st, July 5th, August 21st, Oct 11th, Dec. 19th, first Tuesday in Lent.

BANKERS.—Branch of London and County Bank; T. Barnard and Son.

The agricultural capital of *Bedfordshire*, 16 miles from Bletchley, at the terminus of a branch from the North Western line. The sedgy Ouse runs through the town, which takes its name from a *ford* guarded by a castle of the Beauchamps, when William the Conqueror gained military possession of the country. A good stone bridge now crosses it. Population, 9,399. Two members returned to parliament. Pillow lace, shoes, and straw plait are made. St. Paul's is the most remarkable of its six Gothic churches, and contains the effigy of a Beauchamp, and a monument to Lord Mayor Harpur, who was born here, and the founder of an extensive charity, to which is attached the celebrated Bedford Schools, open to all inhabitants of the town, well conducted, and amply endowed for boys and girls, and 70 or 80 alms-houses, besides distributing apprentice fees, and marriage portions, and now possessing a revenue of £2,000 per annum from land in Holborn and his native town. Being open to all, it has the effect of drawing many families to the town.

At Mill Lane Chapel *John Bunyan* preached, for which he was cast into gaol (on the site of the county prison), where he wrote his *Pilgrim's Progress* The immortal tinker was born in 1628, at Elstow, 1½ mile south, past the asylum. His cottage and forge are there, while his chair is preserved in the chapel.

One of the oldest houses in Bedford is the George Inn, a remnant of the 15th century.

Within a distance of 5 or 6 miles are—*Kempston House*, seat of R. Newland, Esq.; *Bramham Hall*, Hon. G. Trevor. M.P.; *Newnham Priory* ruins; and *Oakley House*, belonging to the Marquis of Tavistock, a building of Charles II.'s time; *Howbury*, the Polhills' seat.

BLETCHLEY, AND OXFORD BRANCH.

Bletchley to Winslow and Oxford.

SWANBOURNE.

Distance from station, 1 mile.

Telegraph station at Winslow, 2 miles.

MONEY ORDER OFFICE at Winslow.

WINSLOW.

Distance from station, ¼ mile.

A telegraph station.

HOTEL.—The Bell.

MARKET DAY.—Thursday.

FAIRS.—March 20, Holy Thursday, August 21st, September 22nd, Thursday before October 11th.

BANKERS.—Bartlett and Co.

BANBURY BRANCH.

Winslow to Buckingham and Banbury.

A distance of seven miles beyond the junction at Winslow brings us to the town of

BUCKINGHAM.

Distance from station, ¼ mile.

A telegraph station.

HOTEL.—White Hart.

MARKET DAY.—Saturday.

FAIRS.—Monday fortnight after the Epiphany, March 6th, May 6th, July 10th, Sept. 4th, Oct. 2nd, Nov. 8th, Saturday after Old Michaelmas, Whit-Thursday.

BANKERS. — Bartlett, Parrott, and Co.; Branch of London and County Bank.

BUCKINGHAM has a population of 8,069: agriculture and lace making occupy their attention. The church, built in 1781, on the site of a castle, has rather a pretty appearance—the spire is 150 feet. A beautiful painting of Raphael's Transfiguration, the gift of the Duke of Buckingham, decorates the altar.

At a distance of two miles from here is *Stowe*, the late magnificent residence of the Duke of Buckingham. It is a noble structure, in the Grecian style, designed by Lords Camelford and Cobham. Its internal decorations, consisting of works of art in plate, furniture, &c., were of the most costly description, and these, together with a library of 10,000 volumes, a large collection of MSS., portraits and engravings, with the principal family estates, were sold by auction in 1848, to pay off a mortgage debt of one and a half million.

We now pass through a flat country for about seven miles, watered by the river Ouse, over which the rails frequently cross. We then enter the county of Northampton, upon which the arrival of the train is announced at

BRACKLEY.

Distance from station, ¼ mile.

A telegraph station.

HOTEL.—Wheat Sheaf.

MARKET DAY.—Wednesday.

FAIRS.—December 11th, Wednesday after Feb. 25th, Oct. 10th, and 2nd Wednesday in April.

This place has a population of 2,121: staple manufacture, lace and shoes. It is one of the oldest boroughs in the kingdom, and contains some relics of its former state. Brackley gives the title of viscount to the Earl of Ellesmere.

We are now traversing the south western section of the fox-huuting county of Northampton, and, at the distance of 4¾ miles, arrive at the station of

FARTHINGHOE, in the vicinity of which the river Ouse takes its rise. Four miles further brings us to

Banbury, in the county of Oxford.—See Sec. II., page 53.

Winslow to Oxford.

CLAYDON.

Distance from station, ¼ mile.

Telegraph station at Winslow, 4 miles.

MONEY ORDER OFFICE at Winslow, 4 miles.

LAUNTON station.

BICESTER.

POPULATION, 2,763.

Distance from station, ¼ mile.

A telegraph station.

HOTELS.—King's Arms; Crown.

MARKET DAY.—Friday.

FAIRS.—Friday in Easter week, Whit Monday, first Friday in June, August 5th October 10th, and December 11th.

BANKERS.—Henry Michael, and George Tubb.

ISLIP.

Telegraph station at Oxford, 6 miles.

MONEY ORDER OFFICES at Oxford and Bicester, 6 miles.

Oxford.—See Section II., pages 7, 8, 9, and 10.

L. & N. W. Main Line continued.
Bletchley to Blisworth.

Upon leaving Bletchley we pass through a cutting, and cross the London road by an iron bridge, and proceeding onwards we arrive in view of the churches of Loughton and Shewston, the latter of which is a fair specimen of the Norman style of architecture. Near the line on the right is the village of Bradwell, and thence after a short cutting we reach the station at

WOLVERTON.

Distance from station, ¼ mile.

A telegraph station.

HOTELS. — Swan, Cock. Refreshment room at station.

OMNIBUSES to and from Newport Pagnell, and Stoney Stratford, twice daily.

WOLVERTON, near the river Ouse, has an increasing population of 2,070, chiefly dependent on the London and North Western Railway Company, who have a depôt and extensive factories here. It is also a refreshment station. A new church and market house, and hundreds of model cottages, have been built by the Company, whose works cover 12 acres of ground. While Crewe is the nursery, Wolverton is the hospital for locomotives. There are the worn-out, the ricketty, the accidents, and sundry other wards, in all of which locomotives are to be seen undergoing cure. Red hot pieces of iron are being forcibly administered; holes probed and nuts screwed on them; steam lathes are facing down callosities; hundreds of locomotive surgeons—stalwart and iron-fisted—dress and bind up cases in their wards with a tremendous energy. Sickly-looking locomotives are fitted up with bran new outsides; several in the last stages of collapse have strong doses of copper rivets forced into their systems. Metal giants, shaky about the knees, are furnished with new sets of joints. In the most desperate cases a cure is effected. Ninety-nine out of every hundred of these battered patients come out perfectly restored to their bereaved stokers. By the help of a blast furnace and steam hammer, even the most incurable is beaten young again, and reproduced as a new locomotive, called perhaps the "Phœnix."—*(Household Words*, 1853.*)* Nothing is wasted here, for the scraps are welded together in the furnace, for axles or cranks, or any other duty requiring temper and strength. The metal cutting and planing works deserve notice.

Proceeding onwards from Wolverton the train conveys us through a beautifully diversified country. First the lofty spire of Hanslope church is seen, then Bradwell Wharf, Linford, and Mill Mead, appear on the right, and the village of Wolverton on the left, shortly after which we arrive at the far-famed viaduct over the Ouse valley. This remarkable and beautiful structure consists of six arches of sixty feet span, in addition to six smaller ones placed in the abutments. The viaduct presents a noble and magnificent appearance to a person in the valley; and the view from the train in passing over it is exceedingly fine.

After the termination of the Wolverton embankment, we pass through a short cutting, and then proceed along another embankment, through some finely wooded country, interspersed with hill, vale, and picturesque villages. The scenery on the left retains the same characteristic for miles. The country surrounding Stoney Stratford forms a fine rear view; and Stoke Park adds to the beauties of the landscape.

Immediately after coming within sight of these parks we cross the boundary line between Buckinghamshire and

NORTHAMPTON,

AND enter the latter county, which has for centuries been proverbial for its beauty, and the number of its resident gentry. It is distinguished from the neighbouring counties by the extensive forests and private woodlands that are scattered over the face of the county, and add so much to the beauty and picturesque effect of its scenery. The ground on the whole rises towards the north and north west, and presents a sort of inclined plane towards the south eastern extremity of the county, where the river Nene traverses nearly through its whole length, which, generally speaking, rises in the high grounds, and descends in a variety of streams, diffusing their beneficiai influence with singular effect over the whole county. Northamptonshire may justly boast, and we believe exclusively, that in the important article of water it is completely independent; for of the six rivers which flow through or intersect it, every one originates within its boundaries, and not a single brook, however insignificant, runs into it from any other district. The climate of Northamptonshire is mild, and the air exceedingly pure, healthy, and favourable to vegetation. The soil is various, but on the whole fertile and productive. The county is also intersected by several of the most important canals in the kingdom.

The entrance of the line into the county is known by some pretty thatched cottages, which stand on each side of the line, and constitute the village of Ashton. Here the embankment, which has extended nearly a mile, and afforded so many delightful views of the surrounding country comes to a termination. After passing through three moderate cuttings we reach the station at

ROADE.

Telegraph station at Wolverton, 7¾ miles.

MONEY ORDER OFFICE at Northampton.

The village of Roade is situated on the right of the line, but presents no object requiring notice. Shortly after leaving this station we enter an excavation made through the Blisworth ridge, when the open country is again visible. The most interesting scenery lies on the right. Hunsbury Hill, Bury Wood, and Harpole Hills, with Wooton, among the hills, and the prominent village of Milton, or Middleton, and its neat church, form a landscape of no ordinary beauty. Immediately preceding our arrival at Blisworth we perceive the pretty village of Blisworth, situate on the gentle sloping ground on the right.

Blisworth Junction.

NORTHAMPTON AND PETERBOROUGH BRANCH.

Blisworth to Northampton and Peterborough.

The line turns off to the right; and commences in a curve over a bridge across the Grand Junction Canal, where a fine view of the surrounding country is obtained.

NORTHAMPTON.

Distance from station, ½ mile.

A telegraph station.

Hotels.—Angel, George, Peacock,

Market Days.—Wednesday and Saturday.

Fairs.—The 2nd Tuesday in January, Feb. 20th, the 3rd Monday in March, April 5th, May 4th, June 19th, Aug. 5th, Aug. 26th, Sept. 19th, the first Thursday in November, Nov. 28th, and the Friday before Smithfield Great Market.

Bankers.—Northampton Union; Northamptonshire Banking Company.

Races.—Pytchley Hunt, in March.

Cricket Club in June.

Northampton is a borough town, standing on the banks of the river Nene, on the left of the line. It is memorable in the annals of political and local history, for the number of synods and councils held within its walls, its formidable castle and provincial earls, its numerous monastic foundations, military events, and last, not least, for the many important improvements which it has undergone within the last half century.

The capital of Northamptonshire, one of the chief towns in the Midland counties, and a parliamentary borough, returning two members, with an industrious population of 32,000, some thousands of whom are engaged in the boot and shoe manufacture, which has been noted here for centuries. The trade indeed is so flourishing, that there is a saying, "You may know when you are within a mile of Northampton by the sound of the cobler's lapstone." Formerly it was celebrated for its leather bottles, so that St. Crispin has always been its patron saint. The George Inn was given by the Drydens towards the support of their blue-coat school. It was one of two important *hamptons* in Saxon times, which since the Doomsday survey, have been called Northampton and Southampton, and are still prosperous and increasing towns. It is on the river Nene, and the Northampton and Peterborough Railway, 67 miles from London, *via* Blisworth, on the North Western. From 1138, in Henry I.'s reign, to 1380, as many as 20 parliaments were held here, showing its pre-eminence at that period. One of the most important, as regards our constitutional progress, was that called by Henry II., in 1179, when the towns were ordered to send *burgesses* for the first time. One held five years before, confirmed the Constitution of Clarendon, which subjected clergy to the common laws, and led to à Becket's rebellion. On another occasion, when disputes occurred at Oxford, the University was moved hither, but only for a time. A great fire in 1675 destroyed 500 houses. It is a clean, neatly built town, on a gentle slope, with houses of reddish stone. The most bustling quarters are the *Drapery*, and the large open *Market Place* near it, round which All Saints Church, the Corn Exchange, Town Hall, Bank, George and Peacock Hotels, &c., are grouped.

All Saints, close to George Row, is a modern building, except the tower, which was built in the 13th century. Above the Grecian portico is the statue of Charles II., in a Roman toga, and a French wig. It contains a painting by Thornhill, Chantrey's statue of Spencer Perceval, the premier who was assassinated by Bellingham in the House of Commons' lobby, in 1812 (W. S. Jerdan, editor of the Literary Gazette, and still alive, was the first to seize the murderer), a well carved screen and pulpit, one of Hill's large organs (3,000 pipes), and part of the old crypt; an ancient conduit stood at one corner of the churchyard. In the north aisle is the figure of a charity girl, executed by S. Cox, to whom Cowper refers in his letters. When the parish clerk applied for verses to affix to the bills of mortality, the poet told him, "there is a namesake of yours, Cox the statuary, who everybody knows is a first-rate maker of verses; he surely is the man for your purpose." "Ah, Sir," says the clerk, "I have heretofore borrowed his help, but he is a gentleman of so *much reading* that the people of our town cannot understand him." It was from calculations founded on these annual bills that Dr. Price derived his tables, which are in use at some of the Old Life Assurance Offices. They are, however, much less in favour of the assurers than subsequent tables. In St John's Lane, near Bridge, is the old Hospital of St. John, first founded about 1170, by the St. Liz family. The *cotton* mill near this, now occupied by a miller, was first designed for spinning cotton. Close to South Gate is another old hospital, founded in 1450, in honour of à Becket; it is now replaced by a new house in St. Giles Street.

St. Giles Street leads to *St. Giles Church*, formerly a Norman cross, of which the door remains; there are signs of later styles, and of three roofs preceding the one in existence. The old east gate of the town stood near this; and beyond are the Union Workhouse, the new Cemetery (opened in 1846), and the *County Asylum*, a plain but striking building of great size, on a site of 24 acres, built in 1836, of Bath stone. There is a good view from it of Delapre, Abbey, &c., to the South.

The *Town Hall*, at Wood Hill Corner, contains

a portrait of Perceval (who once resided here), by Joseph. At the corner of Market Square, adjoining Newland, is an old house, with shields on the front, in which are the arms borne by the Meredyths and other Welsh families, the motto *Heb dhuw (or dyw) heb dyw, Dhuw a digon, i.e.,* "without God, without everything; God, and enough"—a truly noble sentiment, the essence of Christian philosophy. The *County Gaol*, built by Milne, on the model system, was opened in 1846, for 160 prisoners; it adjoins the Shire Hall (which contains portraits of sovereigns from William III.), and the judges' lodgings, in the Grecian style. There is a good library at the Religious and Useful Knowledge Society's Rooms, in Gold Street, also at the Mechanics' Institute, at the new Corn Exchange.

In the new *Corn Exchange*, built in 1851, by Alexander, is a noble hall, 140 feet long; here the Athenæum and Library are placed, In Sheep Street, opposite the Ram Inn, stood the famous nonconformist academy, carried on by *Doddridge*, which, upon his death at Lisbon, was moved to Daventry, in 1752. There is a monument of this excellent man at Castle Hill Chapel, where he was minister for the last 22 years of his life. The *General Library*, established in 1800, is close to the *Mercury* office, a paper started by the Dicey family, as far back as 1720.

Up Sheep Street, you come to the Royal Terrace, and the *barracks*, built in 1796. The large *Race Ground* (117 acres), is beyond. Here the Pytchley Hunt races are held in March, and the cricket club in summer. In this quarter also is the Roman Catholic chapel of St. Felix, built in 1844, by Pugin, in the Gothic style, with a nunnery and bishop's house attached. But the most noticeable building is the ancient church of *St. Sepulchre*, one of the four remaining churches in England, built by the Knights Templars, on the plan of the Sepulchre at Jerusalem—that is, with a *round* body, which becomes octangular above the massive columns, with early and later English additions in the chancel and aisles, and a good later English spire. One of these Templar churches is at Cambridge (lately restored), another at the Temple Gardens, London, though much altered by repairs; and the fourth at Little Maplestead, Essex, which latter is on the model of the Holy Sepulchre, 70 feet long, with a circular body 30 feet in diameter, and timber-roofed.

The *town gaol* was built in 1846, for 80 prisoners, on the separate system.

Passing up Marefair, is the *Grammar School* (in Free School Lane), founded in 1556, in what was an old chapel, and rebuilt in 1840. Hervey, who wrote Thern and Aspasia, and the Meditations among the Tombs, was educated here. Further on is a cottage (at the bottom of Black Lyon hill), with an arabesque carving in the lintel; and the west bridge, from which the remains of the castle are seen to the north. This was built by Simon de St. Liz, at the Conquest, by the tenure of shoeing the king's horses, and afterwards held by de Montfort and the Barons, against Henry II., who, however, took it by stratagem. It was demolished in 1662, except a round tower, and a house built with the stones, lately occupied by Baker, the county historian. At *St. Peter's* church which was within the precincts, is some Norman work, and a display of grotesque heads and carvings Doddridge's chapel is in this neighbourhood. In College Street, is the Baptist chapel, in which *Dr. Ryland* officiated for 30 years. Bones of an ichthyosaurus have been found in the lias, on the site of St. Andrew's priory, in Francis Street. Here also urns have been discovered.

The *Infirmary* is near the Asylum; a substantial building, founded in 1747. Hereabouts is the new walk, or Victoria Promenade, as it is called, since the Queen passed through in 1844, when a Dispensary was also founded to commemorate that event. The Gothic vault over Becket's well was rebuilt in 1843.

In the neighbourhood are various objects of notice. A series of Saxon and Danish camps on the hills around, as Hunsbury Hill, about $1\frac{1}{2}$ mile from Northampton, in the parish of Hardingstone: in this parish is also *Delapre Abbey*, the seat of E. Bouverie, Esq., where was an old cluniac house. Rothersthorpe, Castledykes, Clifford Hill, and (further off) Borough Hill, Guilsborough. Close to Delapre Abbey is a Gothic relic, in the shape of *Queen Eleanor's Cross*, one of the many built by Edward I. to the affectionate memory of his excellent wife, at every spot where her body rested on its way to Westminster; it is octangular, in three stories, but was repaired for the worse about a century ago. Here poor Henry VI. was defeated and made prisoner by Warwick, 1460, and "ten thousand tall Englishmen" killed. In *Horton Church* (near the seat of Sir R. Gunning, Bart.), is an effigy of Queen Catherine Parr's uncle. *Courteen Hall*, Sir C. Wake, Bart. At *Hartwell* is a new church. All about Salcey to Pottersbury, Stoney Stratford, Whittlebury, &c., is *Crown Forest*, which supplied timber for the navy in the war, but is now to be disafforested, on account of its expense. *Easton Neston*, the Earl of Pomfret's seat, was begun by Wren, and is close to *Towcester* (eight miles), a small town of shoe and lace makers, which was betrayed to Empson, the avaricious tool of Henry VII. The Talbot Inn is ancient. The Roman Watling Street runs through the town and the hills beyond, which are also traversed by two great modern works—the Grand Junction Canal and the North Western Railway—by means of tunnels at Blisworth and Crick. *Fawsley* is the fine Tudor seat of Sir C. Knightley, Bart., a tory and protectionist of the good old school. *Althorp Park* (five miles), the seat of Earl Spencer, contains a gallery of pictures, and a library of rare and valuable books, gathered together by the present peer's father, a member of the Roxburghe Club; the family tombs are at Brington. *Guilsborough*, the seat of W. Ward, Esq., is near a camp on the hills, on the further slope of which, the Avon (Shakspeare's Avon) rises. *Overstone* (4 miles), belongs to Lord Overstone (formerly S. J. Loyd), the banker, is partly Elizabethan, and partly in the renaissance style, by Inigo Jones. *Cottesbrooke*, Sir J. Langham Bart. At *Barton Seagrave* (seat of Mrs Tibbetts), Sanfoin was first grown by the father of Bridges, the county historian.

Northampton to Market Harborough.

A line to Market Harborough here turns off, 18 miles in length. The first station arrived at is Pitsford, then

Brixworth, with its good Norman church. The kennels in connection with the celebrated Pytchley Hunt, formerly kept at Pytchley Hall, near Kettering, have been removed here.

Lamport, the seat of Sir C. Isham, Bart.

Kelmarsh station.

At the distance of 4½ miles further, we arrive at the small town of

MARKET HARBOROUGH.

Population, 2,325.

A telegraph station.

Hotels.—Three Swans; Angel.

Market Day.—Tuesday. Fairs.—Jan. 6th, Feb. 16th, April 29th, July 31st, and Oct. 19th.

This was the place where Charles I. fixed his head quarters immediately before the battle of Naseby. The tower is thought to be of Roman origin, having traces of a Roman Camp in the neighbourhood. Its principal trade is in carpets.

Five miles distant is Kibworth Beauchamp, with its rich living of St. Wilfrid, value £968, patron, Merton College, Oxon; and its well endowed Free Grammar School, Rev. J. B. Hildebrand, Master. Dr. Aiken was a native, and here Doddridge first preached.

Peterborough Line continued.

Northampton to Peterborough.

Billing Road station.

CASTLE ASHBY.

Telegraph station at Wellingbro', 4 miles.

Money Order Office at Wellingbro', 4 miles.

Here is the seat of the Marquis of Northampton, a large quadrangular structure, containing some very rich specimens of oil painting. The dates 1625 and 1635 are seen in the balustrades of the turrets. The castle replaces an old one, having been rebuilt in 1607. *Yardley Chase*, belonging to it, is 27 miles round. Take notice of the stone parapet in the court, which is cut so as to make the words, "*Nisi Dominus aedificaverit domum, in vanum laboraverunt qui aedificant eum.*" (Except the Lord build the house, they labour in vain that build). Many portraits here. In the park is the church, an elegant building, rendered peculiar from its porch and altar tomb. At *Whiston*, a good church. At *Olney* is Cowper's house.

WELLINGBORO'.

Population, 5,061.

Distance from station, 1 mile.

A telegraph station.

Hotel.—Hind.

Market Day.—Wednesday.

Fairs.—Easter and Whit-Wednesday, and Oct. 29th.

In the neighbourhood of this place are a number of medicinal springs, from which, probably, the name of the town has been given. Charles I. and Henrietta, his queen, encamped here a whole season, for the purpose of drinking its waters. It has a very pretty church. Boots, shoes, and lace form its staple trade.

Ditchford station.

HIGHAM FERRERS.

Distance from station, 1 mile.
Telegraph station at Wellingborough, 4½ miles.
Hotel.—Green Dragon.
Market Day.—Saturday.
Fairs.—Thursday before Feb. 5th, March 7th, May 12th, June 28th, August 5th, Thursday after August 15th, October 10th, and December 6th.

Boots and shoes are the staple employment here, with lace making. It has a good church, and was the birth-place of Archbishop Chicheley, founder of All Soul's College, Oxford.

Ringstead, Thrapston, Thorpe, and Barnewell stations.

OUNDLE.

Population, 2,689.
Distance from station, ¾ mile.
A telegraph station.
Hotel.—Talbot.
Market Day.—Saturday.
Fairs.—Feb. 24th, Whit Monday, Aug. 21st, and Oct. 11th.

The town is prettily situated on the banks of the Nene. *Dean Park*, the seat of the "last of the Cardigans," and several others, are in its immediate vicinity. Within a distance of three miles is Fotheringay, celebrated in history for its castle, founded by Simon de St. Liz, at the Conquest. It was the scene of the nativity of Richard III.; and the trial and execution of the ill-fated Mary, Queen of Scots, in 1580. It was demolished by her son. Its situation is indicated by nothing more than a mound of earth.

Elton and Wansford stations.

CASTOR.

Distance from station, ¾ mile.

Telegraph station at Wansford, 1¼ mile.

Money Order Office at Peterborough, 4½ miles.

Overton station.

Peterborough.—See Section IV.

L. & N. W. Main Line continued.

Blisworth to Rugby.

Upon leaving this station the line proceeds along an embankment, which terminates after we have crossed the Grand Junction Canal. We then pass the village of Gayton Wharf on the left; thence through a short cutting, we enter a wide extent of beautiful country, called the Valley of the Nene. Occasionally, but only in very clear weather, the town of Northampton can be discerned, about 5 miles distant to the right, and proceeding on along the western declivity of the valley, we pass several villages too numerous to mention. In crossing the Viaduct over the Harstone Brook, we obtain a view of the aqueduct by which the Grand Junction Canal is carried over the stream. Upon issuing from Stonehill tunnel, a short distance beyond, we are presented with a landscape of unusual beauty, the details of which are frequently shut out from view by the embankment of the canal, but on crossing the Viaduct over the Nene, we obtain a fine prospect of the village of Weedon, and reach the station of that name.

WEEDON.

A telegraph station.

Hotels.—Globe Bull.

Omnibuses to Daventry, at 12 10 p.m. daily.

This village is divided into Upper and Lower Weedon; the latter is bisected by the railway, and the former lies at a short distance on the left. The military depôt is a magnificent establishment, and is capable of containing 240,000 stand of small arms. Four miles west of this station is the ancient town of Daventry.

Daventry, near the Nene's Head, and noted for its shoe manufacture, is situated on a gentle eminence near the source of the rivers Avon and Nene. It formerly possessed a rich priory, which Henry VIII. gave to Wolsey, the ruins of which are still visible. From Borough Hill, in the vicinity, there is a delightful prospect of Naseby, Northampton, Weedon, and Coventry, and this beautiful landscape is rendered peculiarly picturesque by the remains of a Roman encampment and ramparts in the foreground.

From Weedon the line traverses a long cutting, through the occasional openings in which the traveller will catch a glimpse of *Brockhall Park* and mansion, which has a fine appearance. Proceeding alternately along an embankment, or through a cutting, the most conspicuous object in view is Borough Hill, until we perceive on the right the small village of Watford, and shortly after reach

CRICK.

Distance from station, 3 miles.

Telegraph station at Rugby, 6½ miles.

Money Order Office at Weedon, 5½ miles.

The village of Crick lies to the north of the station, and is a place of no importance. The canal passes under a tunnel here 1,524 yards in length, through the hills which stretch before us, and which is the boundary between the counties of Northampton and Warwick. They form also the separating ridge between the valley of the Avon, and that of the Ouse and Nene, and contain the sources of rivers which flow to different sides of the island. In approaching them, we enter a cutting which gradually becomes deeper and deeper, and at length brings us to the Grand Kilsby Tunnel, on emerging from which we perceive a wooded but uninteresting country, the entrance to

WARWICKSHIRE,

The general aspect of which is an agreeable alternation of hill and dale, exceedingly well suited for agricultural purposes. The insulated situation of the county, and its freedom from great inequalities of surface, render the climate mild, and vegetation early. As the train proceeds further into the county, the scenery assumes a more pleasing character. Several villages are spread over the hills on the right, among which is Brownsover, the birth place of Lawrence Sheriff, founder of Rugby School, and shortly after we arrive at

RUGBY.

Population, 6,317.

A telegraph station.

Hotels.—Royal, and Eagle.

Market Day.—Saturday.

Fairs—Feb. 17th, March 31st, May 15th, July 7th, Aug. 21st, Monday before 29th Sept., Nov. 22nd, and Dec. 10th.

Bankers.—National Provincial Bank of England; Butlins and Sons.

From Rugby several lines of railway, as the Trent Valley, Midland, Leamington, &c., branch off, making it a sort of starting point in the centre of England. It was this convenient position which made the late Sir R. Peel, at the opening of the Trent Valley Railway, propose Rugby as a good point to which the general office should be transferred. There is here a Deaf and Dumb College, lately founded, with an old Gothic church, restored by Richman, whose Essay on the subject contributed so much to the revival of this picturesque church style. Rugby stands near the river Avon, on a slight elevation (called *Rocheberie* at the Conquest) above the lias plain, between Watling Street and Dunsmore Heath. This healthy spot was fixed on by Lawrence Sheriff, a London tradesman, but a native of Brownsover, close by, for his school, which was founded in 1567, and endowed with property now worth nearly £7,000 a year. By the exertions of successive masters, especially the late Dr. Arnold, it ranks as one of the best grammar schools in the country. There are about a dozen masters, for whom, by a liberal arrangement, retiring pensions are provided; and 60 foundation scholars; besides 260 who pay, and who really give the tone to the institution. The *School* was rebuilt in the Tudor style in 1808, by Hakewell, with a front of 220 feet long; prize compositions are recited in the great room on Easter Wednesday. In the chapel are monuments to Drs. James and Arnold, the former by Chantrey. One of the prizes was established in honour of Dr. Arnold's memory, by the Queen, after the appearance of *Stanley's* most useful and interesting life of him. He was born at Cowes, and died here almost suddenly on June 12th, 1842. The fagging or monitor system prevails, as at most other large schools, but it was somewhat mitigated by the influence of Dr. Arnold. Parkhurst Cave, Gent., Abercromby Bray, the antiquary, Dr. Butler (the admirable Master of Shrewsbury School), and Sir H. Halford were educated here.

Some old gable houses remain at Rugby. Fossils are occasionally dug in the blue lias. The castle on the east side occupies the site of a Norman castle, which was dismantled by Henry II.

Within a short distance are the following:—*Coton Hall* (4 miles), the Hon. C. L. Butler's seat, has a good prospect; *Newnham Paddox* (5 miles), the ancient seat of the Earl of Denbigh, close to Watling Street, which here runs along the county border. *Ashby St. Ledger's*, Lady Senbourne's seat, was formerly that of the Catesby family, one of whom was Robert Catesby, who shared in the Gunpowder Plot. The church is ancient. To the west of Rugby are, *Holbrook Grange*, seat of J. Caldecott, Esq. *Coombe Abbey* and Coventry are further off. Danes Moor or Dunsmoor Heath was the appointed rendezvous of Catesby and his fellow plotters. At Stretton (where a Roman road or *street* is crossed) was a reformatory school for young criminals, established in 1817, but since given up from want of support.

RUGBY AND STAMFORD BRANCH.

Rugby to Stamford.

With one or two slight exceptions, this railway traverses very nearly the line of boundary dividing the counties of Leicester and Rutland from that of Northampton, taking in the whole breadth of the two former from south-west to north-east. The first station on the line is

Lilbourne, or the ancient *Tripontiam*, where Watling Street crossed the Avon.

STANFORD HALL,

Situated on the Avon, the seat of Baroness Braye, of the Cave family. About 4½ miles to the east is Naseby Hall, near to the place where Cromwell defeated Charles I. and Prince Rupert.

Welford and Theddingworth stations.

Market Harborough.—See page 13.

Medbourne Bridge station.

ROCKINGHAM.

Distance from station, 1 mile.

Telegraph station at Market Harboro', 10 miles.

Fair.—September 25th.

The ancient *Castle*, now the seat of Lord Sondes, about a mile from the station, comprises remains of a fortress built by the Conqueror, which suffered in the civil war, when it was garrisoned for the king. There was a forest here 30 miles long.

Seaton, the station for the town of Uppingham.

SOUTH LUFFENHAM.

Telegraph station at Stamford, 6½ miles.

Money Order Office at Uppingham, 5½ miles.

Stamford. — See Section IV.

Peterborough.—See Section IV.

RUGBY AND LEAMINGTON BRANCH.

Rugby to Leamington and Warwick,

Without stopping at the stations of Birdingbury and Marton, we pass on to

LEAMINGTON.

L. and N. Western Railway, the Avenue station, centrally situated, and Great Western.

A telegraph station.

Hotel.—The Crown—Second-class—Family and Commercial.

Bankers.—Leamington Priors and Warwickshire Banking Company; Warwick and Leamington Banking Company.

Races in March, September, and November.

Leamington Spa, which fifty years since was an obscure and humble village, is now, though still rural and picturesque, become a large and handsome town, containing 15,692 inhabitants, and is proverbial for being better paved, lighted, and regulated, than any other town of its size in the kingdom. The *Hotels* are princely, both as to size and comfort; and the *Shops* equal to those in the metropolis. It abounds also with elegant houses and detached villas, and the lodging houses for visitors are most convenient and well-arranged. Its extraordinary rise and present importance is attributable to its *Celebrated Water and Baths*, the curative properties of which are so fully established as to be annually resorted to by vast numbers of invalids, besides a constant succession of fashionable visitors. Leamington possesses, among its numerous attractions, a splendid *Tennis Court and Racket Ground*, attached to an elegant pile of buildings, forming the Club Rooms of the leading members of the Aristocracy of Warwickshire. It has two Newspapers, the *Advertiser* and the *Courier*, the former published on Thursday, and the latter on Saturday; a Literary and Scientific Institution, Public Libraries and News Rooms, on an unusually spirited scale. Assembly Rooms, Music Hall, Theatre Royal, Pump Rooms and Baths; and for the admirers of the noble game of *Cricket*, a ground kept by the two acknowledged best players in England. Both at Leamington and in the neighbourhood, the fashionable sport of *Archery* is much practised, there being clubs at Leamington and Wellesbourne, in addition to that connected with the renowned *Forest of Arden*. Leamington is remarkable for its salubrity; is situated in the midst of a finely wooded and romantic neighbourhood, is contiguous to *Warwick Castle*, the fine old town of *Warwick*, the magnificent ruins of *Kenilworth Castle*, the beautiful Park of *Stoneleigh Abbey*, *Guy's Cliff*, *Offchurch Bury;* the interesting town of *Stratford-upon-Avon*, renowned as the birth-place of the immortal *Shakspeare;* the City of *Coventry*, full of antiquities: and *Birmingham*, celebrated for its arts and manufactures. *Coombe Abbey*, *Wroxhall Abbey*, *Compton Verney*, *Compton Wynyates; Edgehill*, the scene of the great battle during the reign of Charles I.; *Charlecote*, *Hampton Lucy;* The *Jephson Gardens*, delightfully situate in the centre of Leamington, are easily accessible to visitors, and very attractive. During the summer season a first-rate band performs there daily; and Galas, Archery, and Horticultural Fetes are frequently held in them.

The "*Arboretum and Pinetum*" established by John Hitchman, Esq., comprise upwards of eleven acres, formed for the exclusive cultivation and sale of plants, contains an extensive collection of Deciduous and choice Coniferous Trees and Rare Shrubs, Roses, Rhododendrons, &c. The far-famed *Warwickshire Hounds* hunt within an easy distance of the Spa, rendering the winter season at Leamington particularly gay. The *Hunting Season* commences about the middle of October, and the Warwickshire country is now hunted daily by the *North and South Warwickshire Packs.* A pack of Hounds is kept at the Leamington Kennels; and other arrangements are made particularly advantageous to gentlemen for this enjoyment. The *Leamington College* is established upon the principle of our public foundation schools, for the education of the sons of Noblemen and Gentlemen, and under the superintendence of distinguished masters. The railway communication by the Great Western and North Western Companies, each of which has a station in the town, brings Leamington within reach of visitors from every part of the kingdom; and it will be found on investigation, that whether for a permanent residence or for occasional resort, few places possess so many attractions as this highly favoured town.

Table of average contents, without decimal fractions, of an Imperial Pint of the Leamington Mineral Waters.

Salts in grains.

Sulphate of Soda	Chloride of Sodium	Chloride of Calcium	Chloride of Magnesium
35.	30.	23.	11.

Silica—Peroxide of Iron—Iodine.

Bromide of Sodium—minute proportions.

Gases in cubic inches.

Oxygen, Nitrogen—in minute quantities, Carbonic Acid, 3.

STRATFORD-ON-AVON, see page 55.

KENILWORTH, 18.

DISTANCES OF PLACES FROM THE STATION.

Place	Miles.	Place	Miles.
Alveston	8	Myton	1
Ashorne	4½	Newbold Pacey	5½
Asps	2	Offchurch Bury	3
Aston Cantlow	12	Princethorpe Priory	7
Barford	4	Radford	2
Blacklow Hill	4	Snitterfield	7½
Charlecote Park	9	Stoneleigh Abbey	4
Compton Verney	10	Stratford-on-Avon	10
Clopton House	9	Ufton	4
Cubbington	3	Wasperton	5
Guy's Cliff	3	Wellesbourne	6
Hampton Lucy	9	Whitnash	1½
Lillington	1¾	Wroxhall Abbey	8
Long Bridge	4		

WARWICK.

POPULATION, 10,973.

A telegraph station.

HOTELS.—Warwick Arms, Mrs. Lake, family hotel and posting house. Woolpack, John Court, family and commercial, very good.

MARKET DAY.—Saturday.

FAIRS.—3rd Monday in Jan., 2nd Monday in Feb., Monday before April 5th, 1st Saturday in Lent, 1st Monday in June, 2nd Monday in Aug., Monday before St. Thomas, May 12th, July 5th, Sept. 4th, Oct. 12th, Nov. 8th, and Dec. 21st.

MAILS.—Two arrivals and departures, daily, between London and Warwick.

MONEY ORDER OFFICE.

BANKERS.—Messrs. Greenway and Greaves; Leamington-Priors and Warwickshire Company; Warwick and Leamington Banking Company.

WARWICK is a dull town, in the county of Warwick.

The Castle is one of the finest specimens in the kingdom of the ancient residences of our feudal ancestors. Its appearance, overhanging the Avon, and surrounded by majestic masses of trees, is extremely picturesque, and the views from its lofty turrets are magnificent.

Passing through a road cut through the solid rock, which now presents a plantation of shrubs judiciously arranged, so as to shut out the view of this noble pile till it is suddenly presented to the eye, the visitor finds himself in a spacious area, where he is at once surrounded by ancient fortifications, and Gothic buildings of a later date, now devoted to more peaceful occupations than those of the old chieftains. The keep is no more than a picturesque ruin, but two towers of great antiquity are still entire.

From Guy's Tower the views are exceedingly fine. On the north side lies the town, of which you have a beautiful bird's-eye view. Far stretching in the distance are seen the spires of Coventry churches; the castle of Kenilworth; Guy's Cliff and Blacklow Hill; Grove Park; Shuckburgh and Shropshire Hills; the Saxon Tower on the Broadway Hill; the fashionable Spa of Leamington, which appears almost lying at your feet; while village churches lifting up their venerable heads from amidst embosoming trees, fill up a grand and interesting picture. A fine collection of pictures—splendid state-rooms—fitted up in accordance with the general style of the building, and an extensive armoury, lend a gorgeous air of completeness to this princely and magnificent establishment.

The castellated remains of old England are all of them "beautiful for situation;" but few comprise so many objects of natural and historic interest as Warwick Castle. Standing at the windows of the great hall, the prospect which meets the eye is most delightful.

The spacious and elegant conservatory contains the famous Warwick Vase, which was dug up from the ruins of the Emperor Adrian's Villa at Tivoli. It is considered one of the most entire, and to a certain extent, one of the most beautiful specimens of ancient sculpture which this country possesses. The material of which it is made is white marble. Its form is nearly spherical, with a deep reverted rim. Two interlacing vines, whose stems twine into and constitute the handles, wreath their tendrils with fruit and foliage round the upper part. The centre is composed of antique heads which stand forward in grand relief. A panther's skin, with the thyrsus of Bacchus (a favourite antique ornament), and other embellishments complete the composition. The size of this vase is immense, and it is capable of containing a hundred and sixty-three gallons.

L. & N. W. Main Line continued.

Rugby to Birmingham and Stafford

Upon leaving the station the line proceeds along an embankment which affords a very pleasing prospect of the valley on the right, in which the Swift and several other small rivers unite their waters to form the Avon. Newbold-upon-Avon appears prettily situated on the opposite side of the valley, and across the fields on the left is *Bilton*, where Addison spent the evening of his life.

Five miles from Rugby the line reaches the Brandon embankment which is two miles in length, and affords some beautiful prospects.

It then crosses the Avon by a noble viaduct, and for a time the river gives a highly picturesque character to the scenery on the left.

After passing through a cutting we enter a wide extent of open country, and catch the first glimpse of the magnificent Coventry spires. From the embankment along which we proceed we can also see on the right, Stoke, Ernsford, Grange, Bromley, and the woods surrounding Coombe Abbey. The line crosses the Sowe by a beautiful viaduct of seven arches, and soon after the spires of Coventry rise distinctly above the intervening woods. We pass Whitley Abbey, which stands conspicuously on the left, cross a seven-arched viaduct over the Sherbourne Valley, enter a deep cutting, and shortly after we reach the station at

COVENTRY.

A telegraph station.

Hotel. — King's Head.

Market Day.—Friday.

Fairs.—2nd Friday after Ash Wednesday, May 2nd, Friday in Trinity week, Aug. 26th and 27th, and Nov. 1st.

Bankers.—Warwickshire Banking Co.; Coventry Union Banking Co.; Messrs. Little and Woodcock; Coventry and Warwick Banking Co.

The fine steeples of St. Michael's and Trinity are the first to strike one in this old city, which is the seat of the ribbon trade, and a parliamentary borough, 94 miles from London. It returns two members, and has a population of 36,812. Woollens and blue thread were formerly the staple manufactures; but they are now superseded by ribbons and watches, two branches introduced by the French refugees of the 17th century. About 2,000 hands are employed on the latter, and upwards of 30,000 on silk weaving, throwing, and the weaving and dyeing of ribbons. Alabar and power looms are chiefly used in the manufacture. This trade in late years has greatly increased; many steam factories having been erected: one just completed for Mr. Hart is capable of holding about 300 large looms, and will give employment to 1,000 hands, producing as many ribbons as the whole town could make in 1830. Many women and children are employed. French ribbons are imported by the dealers; but in point of taste as well as cheapness, English productions are now a fair rival to foreign ones (see *Bradshaw's Hand Book to Manufacturing Districts*). Coventry (like Covent Garden in London) takes its name from a monastery, founded in the 11th century, by Leofric, the Saxon, and his wife Godiva, whose memory is honoured by an occasional procession. According to the well known story, she obtained a grant of privileges to the town by consenting to ride naked through the streets. To save her delicacy, the people closed their windows and abstained from looking, except Peeping Tom, whose bust, adorned with a *pigtail*, stands at the corner of Hertford Street. Many old fashioned gable houses are to be seen here in the narrow back streets. The *Guildhall* is a fine middle-age building, with a timbered hall, adorned with escutcheons and stained windows. Another old pile, is the *House of Industry*, near some remains of a priory. Three gates, and fragments of the town walls, the Free Grammar School, Bablake's old hospital (1350), the church, and the Exchange, a handsome building containing a noble hall, recently erected from designs by Mr. James Murray, deserve notice. The beautiful steeple of *St. Michael's* on the Gothic church, is about 300 feet high; it was built by the two Botoners, mayors of the town, between 1373 and '95; near it stands part of a palace belonging to the bishops, when Coventry was a diocese with Lichfield. The Cathedral, dissolved by Henry VIII., stood at Hill Close. Trinity, or the priory church is also Gothic, with a steeple 237 feet high, of later date. Here the Grey Friars acted their miracle plays at the feast of Corpus Christi—a series of Bible dramas, from the Creation to Doomsday. Henry VI. often came to see them. Coventry has an important School of Design.

Within a distance of two miles are *Whitley Park*, an old Elizabethan seat of Viscount Hood. *Kenilworth Castle* (6 miles), the road to which is along an avenue of noble trees, the *Gate House* at which should be visited, on account of the large sculptured mantel piece in it.—Dr. Butler was a native. *Stoneleigh Park*, Lord Leigh, with some Abbey ruins, a portrait of Byron, and Zaffary's famous one, "Garrick telling a Ghost story;" *Packington*, Earl of Aylesford; *Coombe Abbey*, Earl Craven, has Abbey ruins, with a gallery of Vandykes, Lelys, &c., and remains of an Abbey at *Berkswell*, seat of Sir J. Wilmot, Bart., at which is Canaletti's vew of London.

COVENTRY AND NUNEATON BRANCH.

After leaving Coventry, on this branch the unimportant stations of COUNDEN ROAD, FOLESHILL, LONGFORD, and HAWKESBURY LANE, are quickly passed, and we arrive at

BEDWORTH.

POPULATION, 3,012.

Telegraph station at Nuneaton, 3½ miles.

HOTEL.—Haunch of Venison.

MONEY ORDER OFFICE at Nuneaton, 3½ miles.

In the vicinity is *Arbury Hall*, seat of C. N. Newdegate, Esq., M.P.

CHILVERS COTON station.

NUNEATON.

POPULATION, 4,859.

A telegraph station.

HOTELS.—Bull, and Newdegate Arms.

MARKET DAY.—Saturday.

FAIRS.—Feb. 18th, May, 14th, and October, 31st.

BANKERS.—Craddock and Bull.

Here are remains of a nunnery of Stephen's time, old Gothic church, grammar school, and ribbon manufactures.

This station is stone fronted, and in architectural arrangements similar to that at Tamworth, the platform being paved with red, black, and yellow tiles. Indeed, the general character of the stations is much the same, the only difference being that the first class stations are larger and more elaborate in outline than the smaller ones. The piquant Tudor or Elizabethan style is the same in all; and perhaps no style is so well adapted for buildings in which domestic requirements are to be studied. It likewise harmonises thoroughly with English scenery.

COVENTRY & LEAMINGTON BRANCH.

KENILWORTH.

POPULATION, 3,140,

Telegraph station at Leamington.

HOTEL.—King's Arms.

BANKERS.—Branch of the Leamington Priors and Warwick Banking Co.

KENILWORTH, a small town in the county of Warwick. It consists of one main street, nearly a mile in length, and is principally remarkable for the ruins of its once stately and magnificent castle.

During the civil wars between the houses of York and Lancaster it was alternately taken by the partisans of the white and red roses: and very long after their termination, Queen Elizabeth bestowed it upon the Earl of Leicester.

The most memorable incident in the history of Kenilworth Castle, is the Royal entertainment given by the Earl to his Queen. Elizabeth visited him in state, attended by thirty-one barons, besides the ladies of the Court, who, with four hundred servants, were all lodged in the Castle. The festival continued for seventeen days, at an expense estimated at £1,000 per day (a very large sum in those times). Ten oxen were slaughtered every morning; and the consumption of wine is said to have been sixteen hogsheads, and of beer, forty hogsheads daily. An account of this singular and romantic entertainment, published at the time by an eye-witness, presents a curious picture of the luxury, plenty, and gallantry of Elizabeth's reign.

During the civil wars the castle was besieged by Cromwell, and by him given to some of his officers. These matter-of-fact soldiers, who had but little feeling for the beauteous and majestic, soon reduced it to what it now is, a pile of ruins. They drained the lake which once flowed over so many hundred acres, beat down the walls, dismantled the towers, choked up its fair walks, and rooted out its pleasant gardens, destroyed the park, and divided and more usefully applied the lands. The estate and ruins of the castle subsequently passed into the possession of the Earl of Clarendon, in whose family they still remain.

Leamington and Warwick.—See pages 15 and 16.

L. & N. W. Main Line continued.

Coventry to Birmingham.

On leaving Coventry the line passes through several cuttings, in the openings of which a fine view may be obtained of the city, with its lofty spires, rising majestically from the dense mass of houses. The line continues through several cuttings, which exclude nearly all view of the country.

ALLESLEY GATE station.

BERKSWELL.

Distance from station, 1 mile.

Telegraph station at Coventry, 5½ miles,

MONEY ORDER OFFICE at Coventry, 5 miles.

The landscape improves somewhat here, and we have views of several fine seats, comprising *Mercote Hall*, *Packington Park*, and *Berkswell Hall*, Sir J. Wilmot, Bart. After crossing the Blythe, by a viaduct of noble proportions, the traveller will perceive on the left, a very old, and almost ruined bridge, with five arches, which, with a quaint windmill and rich surrounding country, form a pretty picture.

HAMPTON (Junction).

Distance from station, ¾ mile.

Telegraph station at Coventry, 9 miles.

HOTEL.—Railway.

MONEY ORDER OFFICE at Coleshill, 4½ miles.

The village of Hampton lies on the left of the line, and consists of little to interest the traveller. Two miles beyond is *Elmdon Hall.*

MARSTON GREEN.

Distance from station, ¾ mile.

Telegraph station at Birmingham, 6½ miles.

MONEY ORDER OFFICE at Coleshill, 4 miles.

After passing under Marston Hall bridge we traverse some prettily wooded country, having Marston Wood on the right, and *Elmdon Park* on the left. On reaching the Sheldon embankment, a prospect is obtained which is considered equal in beauty to any which the line affords. On the right is *Alcot Park*, the town and church of Coleshill, and *Maxtoke Park* on the left. *Elmdon*, with its fine woodlands, and the pretty village of Sheldon; whilst in advance, the high spire of Yardley church completes the landscape. A short cutting brings us opposite the village of Yardley, near enough to admire the fine tower and spire of the church.

STECHFORD.

Distance from station, ½ mile.

Telegraph station at Birmingham, 3¾ miles.

MONEY ORDER OFFICE at Coleshill, 6 miles.

Shortly after leaving this station, we obtain an imperfect glimpse of Birmingham, which soon extends into a full and splendid view. From the vast and dense mass of confused buildings rise the beautiful spires of its several churches, and the tall chimnies of its still more numerous manufactories; whilst proudly conspicuous in the centre, the Town Hall lifts its noble front.

Barr Beacon is visible on the right, with Aston church, park, and hall. Ashted and Vauxhall soon afterwards appear, and not far distant the Grand Junction railway is seen stretching away in a northerly direction.

BIRMINGHAM.

Telegraph stations—Temple Buildings, New Street, and the railway stations.

HOTELS.—Dee's Royal Hotel, (first class for families and gentlemen), highly recommended for its eligible situation, in the most elevated part of the town, and the excellent accommodation it affords.

The Queen's, North Western Central Railway Station, New-street, first-class hotel, for families and gentlemen.

The Stork; King's Head; Nelson; and Swan.

OMNIBUSES to and from the station.

MARKET DAYS.—Monday, Thursday, and Saturday. FAIRS.—Whit-Thursday, and Thursday nearest September 29th.

BANKERS.—Attwood and Co.; Moilliet and Co.; Taylors and Lloyds; Birmingham Banking Co.; Birmingham and Midland Banking Co.; Branch Bank of England; National Provincial Bank of England; Town and District Banking Co.

This is the great centre of the manufactured metal trades, being situated in North Warwickshire, on the border of the South Staffordshire iron and coal district—112 miles from London by the North Western railway, or 129 miles by the Great Western railway. The town stands upon a series of sandstone hills, of moderate elevation; it is well-drained, and very healthy, although containing a population of 232,841 inhabitants.

Steam power is here used extensively, scarcely a street being without its manufactory and steam-engine; at same time a considerable amount of the labour is of a manual kind, carried on in small workshops attached to the dwelling-houses of the artisans; and, it is worthy of remark, that the houses of the poorer classes here are very superior to those usually met with in large manufacturing or densely inhabited towns.

The public buildings most worthy of note in Birmingham are—first the *Town Hall*, at the top of New Street, a beautiful Grecian Temple, of Mona marble, 166 feet by 100, on a basement 23 feet high, surrounded by rows of Corinthian pillars, 40 feet high; it has a splendid public hall, 145 feet long, at one end of which is the famous organ by Hill, one of the finest in Europe, containing 4,000 pipes, acted upon by four sets of keys. In this hall is held the celebrated Triennial Musical Festival, perhaps the most successful of anything of the kind, drawing together talented artistes from all parts of the world to aid in the performances; here also is a fine bust of Mendelssonn, who presided in this Hall in 1846, at the first performance of his *Elijah.* The *Market Hall* is a fine building of stone, 365 feet long, 108 feet wide, and 60 high, with 600 stalls. It is situated in High Street. King Edward the Sixth's *Grammar School*, in New Street, founded in 1522, and endowed with twenty pounds' worth of land by the monarch whose name it bears, was rebuilt by Barry, in the Gothic style, with a frontage of 174 feet long and 60 feet high. Its income is now about £11,000 a-year, arising principally from the increased value of its lands. The *Queen's College*, in Paradise Street, founded by Mr Sands Cox, in 1843, and built in the Tudor style, has various professorships attached to it, some of them endowed by that liberal contributor, Dr. Warneford. In Summer Lane is the *General Hospital*, a noble institution, founded in 1769, by Dr. Ash. The celebrated musical festivals already mentioned are held for the benefit of this establishment. The Queen's Hospital, in Bath Row, the Deaf and Dumb Asylum, the Blind Asylum, Lying-in-Hospital, Infirmary, Magdalen Asylum, Ragged and Industrial Schools, and a Reformatory, have all more or less handsome and suitable buildings. The *Blue Coat School* is an excellent institution, with an extensive stone building, where are maintained and educated 200 boys and girls; it is situated in St. Philip's churchyard, and is entirely supported by voluntary contributions. *Bingley Hall* is an immense shed, covering nearly two acres of ground, where the Midland Cattle and Poultry Shows are held in December of every year, and which have now become the most extensive and successful in the country. The Gaol, Lunatic Asylum, and the Workhouse. The *Birmingham and Midland Institute*, in course of erection, adjoining the Town Hall, will be a noble pile of building; the foundation stone was laid by H.R.H. Prince Albert, in November, 1855. Opposite the Town Hall is a colossal statue in bronze, of the late Sir Robert Peel, by Peter Hollins; and opposite the Market Hall, another of Nelson, by Westmacott. Edgbaston, the "West End" of Birmingham, where the wealthy manufacturers live, is a beautifully arranged collection of villa residences.

The parish church is *St. Martin's*, in the Bull Ring, originally built in the thirteenth century, and having tombs of the De Berminghams, who founded a castle here in 1155. Some of the oldest houses are in this quarter; in front is Westmacott's statue of Nelson, on a column. *St. George's Church* is a Gothic structure, built in 1822 by Rickman. *St. Paul's* is marked by a good spire. *St. Philip's*, in the upper part of the town, has a large churchyard. Christ Church, St. Mary's, St. Bartholomew's, Trinity, St. Thomas's, St. James's, St. Peter's, All Saints' and about twelve more of recent erection. There is a Roman Catholic cathedral, in brick, by Pugin. The Jews have a splendid Synagogue, lately erected at Singers' Hill.

The principal Establishments worth visiting in Birmingham are:—

Buttons.—Of these goods an endless variety will be found at the manufactory of Messrs. Dain, Watts, and Manton, Regent Works, Regent Street.

Electro-Plate and Silver.—The establishment of Messrs. Elkington, Mason, and Co., in Newhall Street, perhaps without an equal in the world, taking into consideration its range of beautiful show rooms, in connection with its workshops, where may be seen the manufacturing of silver goods, electro-plated wares, and bronzes, in every possible stage.

Glass Manufacture.—In the rich and more elaborate department of the glass trade, the establishment of Messrs. Osler, Broad Street, stands pre-eminent. They manufacture glass chandeliers, candelabras, lustres, and the finer cut glass for the table, in great variety. London House, 44, Oxford Street.

Gun Makers.—For sporting guns, Messrs. Westley Richards and Co., High Street, have an European reputation; and as manufacturers to the army, and for wholesale, we may mention the extensive establishment of Messrs. Tipping and Lawden, Constitution Hill, whose make is highly appreciated by the general trade.

Steel Pen Manufacturer.—We should think the reputation of Messrs. Gillott and Son, Graham-street, has reached all parts of the world.—*See advertisement.*

Tubes, Gas-fittings, Metallic Bedsteads, & General Brassfounders.—The show-rooms of Messrs. R. W. Winfield and Son, of Cambridge Works, Cambridge-street, contain the greatest variety of articles of all kinds, in the above business, of the most ornamental and chaste kind, and are well worthy of inspection.

From Birmingham many interesting *excursions* may be made within a circle of about 20 miles. Among these are—Kenilworth and Warwick Castles; Stratford-on-Avon, the birth-place of *Shakspeare* near Charlecote, the Lucy's seat; Tamworth Castle, near Drayton Manor, the seat of Sir R. Peel; Lichfield Cathedral and town, where Dr. Johnson was born; the iron and coal fields to the north, round Wednesbury, Walsall, Bilston, and other seats of the hardware trade, all honeycombed below, intersected by canals and railways above; Sandwell Park, Earl Dartmouth's seat, and Oscott Roman Catholic College; Dudley Castle and caves; Leasowes (which was Shenstone's seat), and Hagley Park, near Hales Owen; the fine country round Kidderminster and Stourport, on the Severn.

The Central Station.—The progressive extension of the railway system led to the erection of several buildings for its general purposes; and these structures are entitled to rank amongst the most stupendous architectural works of the age.

It was built for the accommodation of their own immense traffic, and that of the Midland, Stour Valley, and South Staffordshire lines.

Situated in New Street, Birmingham, the entrance is at the bottom of Stephenson Place, through an arcade, to the booking offices for the respective railways; passing through these we emerge on a magnificent corridor or gallery, guarded by a light railing, and open to the station (but enclosed by the immense glass and iron roof), from whence broad stone staircases, with bronze rails, afford access to the departure platform. We then stand on a level with a long series of offices, appropriated to the officials of the company, and a superb refreshment room, divided nto three portions by rows of massive pillars, annexed to which is an hotel (the Queen's).

The interior of this station deserves attention from its magnitude. The semicircular roof is 1,100 feet long, 205 feet wide, and 80 feet high, composed of iron and glass, without the slightest support except that afforded by the pillars on either side. If the reader notice the turmoil and bustle created by the excitement of the arrival and departure of trains, the trampling of crowds of passengers, the transport of luggage, the ringing of bells, and the noise of two or three hundred porters and workmen, he will retain a recollection of the extraordinary scene witnessed daily at the Birmingham Central Railway Station.

Birmingham to Wolverhampton, (via Bescot).

Upon issuing from the station at Birmingham the train proceeds on a curve past Duddeston, crosses the embankment over the Fazely Canal and Lichfield road by a viaduct, which affords a fine view of the great manufacturing emporium we are leaving. The line then continues past the suburban station of BLOOMSBURY, to

ASTON,

In the vicinity of which are *Aston Hall* and *Park*. This valuable estate formerly covered an area of 350 acres, 40 of which have been purchased by the subscriptions of the people of Birmingham, at a cost of £35,000, and appropriated as a museum and place of recreation for the inhabitants of that town. The 15th June, 1858, will long be remembered as the day of opening the same by the Queen in person. The park is a beautiful piece of undulating ground, commanding a fine prospect over hill and dale and stream, and the hall itself is a noble specimen of the ancient English manor-house. It was originally erected by Sir Thomas Holte, in 1620, and in which he entertained Charles I. previous to the battle of Edge Hill. Aston Church, which appears at several points of the line, is a beautiful building, having a handsome tower, with a fine lofty spire. The line immediately after crosses the boundary of Warwickshire, and enters

STAFFORDSHIRE.

THIS county is generally of a hilly character. The highest portions are in the north, consisting principally of elevated moorland, some of which rise to the height of 1,100 feet, the valleys being watered by small streams flowing into the Trent. The western districts are traversed by the hills forming a part of the backbone of England, the streams from the west slope of which run into the Severn, which finally loses itself in the Atlantic; those on the east of this ridge fall into the Trent, and this again into the Humber, discharging its waters into the German Ocean. About one-fifth of the county is occupied by roads, wastes, and woods; three-fifths are arable land, and one-fifth pasturage. The soil generally requires careful drainage; and although the fertilising influences arising from the frequency of the floods in the low parts of the county are very great, yet they are not seldom unattended with disastrous consequences to the farmer. The county is rich in minerals, especially coal; the Dudley coal-field occupying the southern portion of the conty, while that of the potteries occupies that of the north. Ironstone is also abundant, and there are several lead and copper mines in the limestone districts of the eastern moorlands. The valley of the Trent is studded by many fine parks and noble mansions.

Passing several gentlemen's seats the line traverses a cutting in a fine open country, and soon reaches

PERRY BAR.

Telegraph station at Birmingham, 3 miles.
MONEY ORDER OFFICE at Birmingham, 2½ miles.

At this station we pass under an arch, and the line then makes a considerable curve in an opposite direction to that hitherto followed, and passes *Perry Hall*, seat of Hon. F. Gough, hidden from view by stately trees. Handsworth Church, in the vicinity, contains a monument of the late James Watt, by Chantrey. This much admired work of art consists of a handsome grey marble pedestal, on which, in a sitting posture, is a figure of Watt, represented in the act of drawing, in pure white marble. The figure seems alive, and is one of the most successful efforts of the sculptor. This statue was erected in honour of Watt's memory, by subscription; and his son built a small chapel for its reception on the north side of the church, at the right of the altar, to the left of which is the bust of Boulton, the partner of Watt.

On leaving Perry Bar and its handsome church, which is worth a visit, we pass through a cutting, and then over an iron bridge, which spans the Tame. This beautiful little river winds through the valley, and gives a very pretty picturesque view to the scenery. Hampstead Valley is a beautiful and luxuriant vale, to the right of which is Hampstead Hall, on the banks of the Tame. The prospect from both sides of the line is particularly fine and exhilarating. Two miles distant is the Roman Catholic College at Oscott. The line then enters a cutting, upon emerging from which we observe *Sandwell Hall* and *Park*, the seat of the Earl of Dartmouth, and shortly after arrive at

NEWTON ROAD.

Telegraph station at Birmingham, 6 miles.
MONEY ORDER OFFICE at West Bromwich, 2 miles.

This station is in the parish of West Bromwich, formerly a small village, but which has risen to considerable importance from the rich iron and coal veins which abound in the vicinity. There are furnaces for smelting the ores in all directions. The gas works here are said to be the largest in the world, and the glass works of Messrs. Chance & Co. are upon a most extensive scale. To the right are *Fairy Hall* and *Red House*.

BESCOT (Junction).

A telegraph station.
MONEY ORDER OFFICE at Darlaston, 1½ mile.

Bescot Hall (from which are fine views) is an old moated edifice. It is the point of junction with the South Stafford line to Walsall and Dudley.

DARLASTON.

POPULATION, 10,590.
Telegraph station at Bescot Junction.
HOTEL.—White Lion.

WILLENHALL.

Telegraph station at Bescot Junction.
HOTEL.—Railway.

WILLENHALL is a large village, population 11,931 the inhabitants of which, like all those in this district are engaged in the manufacture of iron articles but particularly locks, keys, &c. At this place, and at Wednesfield, locks and bolts are manufactured to all parts of England. Here excellent red sand is dug.

After leaving Willenhall the train proceeds over some level ground, and then through a cutting of gravel, where smooth round stones, called boulders, are sometimes found a ton in weight. The line then passes through a cutting where on one side is seen a thick stratum of coal. The change which this abrupt termination of the coal field causes in the aspect of the cutting is very singular.

We now pass in quick succession the stations of PORTOBELLO and WEDNESFIELD HEATH to BUSHBURY, here making a slight detour into the town of

Wolverhampton.—See Section II., page 54.

Birmingham to Wolverhampton, (Via Stour Valley.)

EDGBASTON.

Distance from station, ¼ mile.
Telegraph station at Birmingham, 1 mile.
Here are some fine Botanical Gardens.

SOHO.—See Section II., page 54.

SMETHWICK.

POPULATION, 8,379.
Telegraph station at Birmingham, 3½ miles.
MONEY ORDER OFFICE at Birmingham.
Close at hand is the Summit Iron Bridge, over the canal, of 150 feet span.

SPON LANE.

A telegraph station.
MONEY ORDER OFFICE at Oldbury, 1 mile.
Here, in 1851, the glass for the Great Exhibition was made at the celebrated factory, which employs 1,200 hands.
The next station on our route is that of

OLDBURY.

Telegraph station at Spon Lane, 1 mile.
HOTEL.—Ship.
In the vicinity is an old camp. We are then whirled on past the station of ALBION to

DUDLEY PORT.

A telegraph station.
MONEY ORDER OFFICE at Dudley, 1½ mile.

This is a very busy station, forming as it does the junction of the various lines to Birmingham, Wolverhampton, Dudley, Worcester, Burton, and Derby. From the numerous trains passing and repassing great watchfulness is required, passengers generally having to change carriages when handed over from one Company to another.

TIPTON.

Telegraph station at Dudley Port, 1 mile.
HOTEL.—Albion.

Here are extensive chemical works.

DEEPFIELDS and ETTINGSHALL ROAD are next in succession. They have no particular interest. Leaving these, we soon arrive at

Wolverhampton, for particulars of which see page 54, Section II.

Wolverhampton to Stafford.

BUSHBURY station.

FOUR ASHES.

POPULATION, 2,663.
Telegraph station at Wolverhampton, 6¼ miles.
MONEY ORDER OFFICE at Wolverhampton.

To the left is *Somerford Hall*, and beyond *Brewood*, with its beautiful *Church* and *Grammar School*.

SPREAD EAGLE station.

PENKRIDGE.

Telegraph station at Stafford, 5¼ miles.
HOTEL.—Littleton Arms.
MARKET DAY.—Saturday.
FAIRS.—April 30th, 1st Monday in Sept., and Oct. 10th.
Here is a large church, and two miles north-east, *Teddesley Park*, seat of Lord Hatherton.

Stafford.—See page 30.

Rugby to Stafford via Trent Valley.

From Rugby the line runs on an embankment, and crosses the river Avon on a viaduct, the arches of which are thirty feet span; it then passes over the Oxford canal, and through a very pretty country, crossing the north east section of the county of Warwick.

STRETTON.

Telegraph station at Rugby, 5¼ miles.
HOTEL.—White Horse.
MONEY ORDER OFFICE at Rugby, 4½ miles.
In the vicinity is *Newbold Revel*, seat of Sir G. Skipwith, Bart.

SHILTON.

Telegraph station at Rugby, 8½ miles.
MONEY ORDER OFFICES at Coventry and Nuneaton, 6 miles.
Close at hand is *Anstey Hall*, H. Adams, Esq.

BULKINGTON.

Telegraph station at Rugby, 10¾ miles.
MONEY ORDER OFFICE at Nuneaton, 4 miles.
This station is a red brick erection, with stone dressings.

Nuneaton.—See page 18.

ATHERSTONE.

POPULATION, 3,819.
Telegraph station at Tamworth, 7¾ miles.
HOTEL.—Red Lion.
MARKET DAY.—Tuesday.
FAIRS.—April 7th, July 18th, Sept. 19th, and Dec. 4th.

BANKERS.—Leicester Banking Co.

Here is a fine cruciform church, *Market House*, on pillars, *Devereux's Grammar School*, and the *Three Tuns Inn*, where Richmond remained the night previous to the Battle of Bosworth Field, 1485.

At Atherstone the line crosses the old coach road. *Atherstone Hall* is the seat of C. A. Bracebridge, Esq. The park contains some of the finest old oaks in England. *Merevale*, the fine seat of W. Dugdale, Esq., descendant of the antiquary.

POLESWORTH.

Telegraph station at Tamworth, 3½ miles.

MONEY ORDER OFFICE at Tamworth, 3¾ miles.

On nearing Tamworth the fine old church is a noble object in the view; and the country round being rather pretty the effect is greatly increased. In the vicinity is *Grendon Hall*, Sir T. Chetwynd, Bart. On approaching Tamworth we again enter the county of Stafford.

TAMWORTH.

POPULATION, 8,655.
A telegraph station.
HOTEL.—King's Arms.
MARKET DAY.—Saturday.
FAIRS.—May 4th, July 26th, and Oct. 24th.
BANKERS.—National Provincial Bank of England.

This station is a very handsome and picturesque building. Its gables, bay windows, clustered chimnies, and roofs enriched with tiles of quaint form, are all in excellent taste. The frontage of the building towards the rail extends to one hundred and thirty feet, and the platform to three hundred feet.

TAMWORTH, a market town, population 8,650, who return two members, has an old castle of the Marmions—

> "They hailed him lord of Fontenay,
> Of Tamworth towei and town."

The church is large and ancient, and contains the monument of Peel, whose statue, by Noble, is in the Market-place, with his face turned to Bury (his birth-place). He founded a school here; another was built by Queen Elizabeth, and almshouses by Guy, who founded Guy's Hospital. *Drayton Manor*, Sir R. Peel, Bart. At *Abbots Bromley* lived Mrs. Cooper, who saw her descendants to the sixth generation.

As we approach Lichfield the magnificent and lofty spires of the Cathedral attract attention.

LICHFIELD.

POPULATION, 6,573.
Distance from the Trent Valley station, 1 mile.
A telegraph station.
HOTEL.—George.
MARKET DAY.—Friday.

FAIRS.—Jan. 10th, Shrove Tuesday, Ash Wednesday, May 12, first Tuesday in November.

BANKERS.—National Provincial Bank of England; Stevenson, Salt, and Co., Friday and Monday.

LICHFIELD, a small cathedral town and parliamentary borough (two members), on the Trent Valley line, where the Burton and Dudley intersects it, 116 miles from London. A branch of the Trent (which is 3 miles off) runs through. Population, 6,573. Famous for its ale.

There is a tradition that a a spot called Christian Field, a great number cf martyrs were put to death in the third century by the Romans (who had a station at *Etocetum*, close by); and hence the name of the town is derived, *lich* being Saxon for a dead boy, as we see to this day, in the old Lich-gate, near some churches.

At the corner of Sadler Street is the house in which *Johnson* was born in 1709, then a bookseller's shop, kept by his father, Michael Johnson, who built it on a piece of land belonging to the corporation. It is a high house, resting on two pillars, with pilasters at the corners, and a projecting cornice. When the Doctor became famous the citizens, out of regard to him, renewed the lease at a long term, without payment of a fine. The registry of his baptism is to be seen at St. Mary's opposite. Before he went to Oxford, he had half learnt his father's business, so that books of his binding are said to be still extant.

Nichols, in his *Literary Anecdotes*, says, Johnson always spoke of his birth-place with enthusiasm. "Its inhabitants were more orthodox in their religion, purer in their language, and politer in their manners, than any other town in the kingdom"—a high character, which we hope it still deserves. In the Market-place fronting the house, is his statue, near the old market house. Edward VI.'s *Grammar School*, in which that genius was trained, rebuilt in 1850, in the Tudor style. Here Addison, Garrick, Bishop Newton, who wrote on the Prophecies, Salt, the Egyptian traveller, and other eminent men, were educated. The Doctor used to say that his master, Dr Hunter, never taught a boy in his life; he whipped and they learned. He was a pompous man, always wearing his gown and cassock, with a full dressed wig. He had a remarkably stern look; so that the great Ursa Major himself (the terror of Whigs and small literary fry) would tremble at the sight of Miss Seward, owing to her resemblance to her grandfather Hunter. St. John's Hospital is a very ancient foundation. To the north-west of the city, in that division called the Close, is the *Cathedral*, marked by its three conspicuous tapering spires, and dedicated to St. Chad. It was founded as far back as 665, and afterwards made the seat of an archbishop; but the present building was begun after the Conquest (when Roger de Clinton built a castle and priory here), and finished in 1296. It suffered from the Puritans, who captured the town in 1643, when their leader, Lord Brooke, was shot through the eye, by an accidental shot fired by a deaf and dumb man. At the Restoration, Bishop Hacket collected 20,000*l.* to renovate it. It is 410 feet long, the centre steeple 260 feet high, the other two, over the west front, 190 feet. At this end are the great wheel window, and many large figures of Scripture and other characters. The decorated English porches, and the choir, deserve notice; as well as the effigies of Bishop

Langton (who built the screen and Lady chapel), Bishop Hacket, and one of the Stanleys, the monuments of Johnson, Garrick, Lady Wortley Montague, and the celebrated one ascribed to Chantrey, of Mrs. Robinson's *Sleeping Children*—which is said, on good authority, not to be a work of Chantrey, but of one of his pupils, from a design given by another pupil, who was an Italian. Westmacott's bust of Johnson is in the Dean's Court, on the south side; it was placed there by his friends. Another to Garrick, by his widow, has an inscription ending with Johnson's well known eulogy:—"His death eclipsed the gaiety of nations, and impoverished the public stock of harmless pleasure." Among the curiosities in the *Chapter House* are the Gospels in Saxon, an illuminated copy of Chaucer, and a Koran. The old palace, Vicar's College, and prebendal houses, are within the Close, the bounds of which are marked by a dry moat. Coventry diocese is now merged in that of Lichfield.

Richard II. was confined in the castle, on the site of which are erected Newton's Alms-houses.

There are three other churches, of which St. Chad's is the oldest, and St. Michael's (marked by a tower) contains Johnson's epitaphs on his parents and brother. A Court of Array, one of the most ancient remnants of feudal times, is still held here at Whitsuntide. Queen Victoria, when Princess, paid Lichfield a visit in 1832, with the Duchess of Kent, her mother; and again after she became Queen of England, in 1843.

In the neighbourhood of the city, the following may be visited. *Edial* or Edgehill, an old high-roofed house, where Johnson lived in 1736, when Garrick was his pupil. At *Stow Hill*, he wrote a good part of his "Lives of the Poets," when staying with the Astons, "frequently surrounded by five or six ladies engaged in work or conversation." It was here he scrambled over the great gate one day, having a mind (he said) to try whether he could climb a gate as he used to do when a lad. *Reeford*, seat of General Dyott, an ancient family. *Swinfin*, S. Swinfin, Esq., another old family. Dr. Swinfin was Johnson's godfather. *Elmhurst*, N. J. Lane, Esq.

ARMITAGE.

Distance from station, 1 mile.

Telegraph station at Lichfield, 4½ miles.

Money Order Office at Rugeley, 3¼ miles.

Two miles distant is the Marquis of Anglesea's seat, *Beaudesert Park*, an old house, in Cannock Chase, the best view of which is from the camp on Castle Hill, where the early kings had a hunting seat. At present it is a tract of bare hills, more valuable for the coal and iron below its surface than for what is above. There are several works about *Rugeley* which belong to the Pagets (the Anglesea family).

RUGELEY.

Population, 3,054.

Distance from station, 1 mile.

Telegraph station at Lichfield, 7½ miles.

Hotel.—Talbot.

Market Day.—Thursday.

Fairs.—April 15th, June 1st and 6th, October 21st, and 2nd Tuesday in December.

Races in October.

Bankers.—National Provincial Bank of England.

This station stands in an open place, and faces the town of Rugeley, which will ever be memorable on account of its having been the residence of the sporting doctor, Palmer, who was accused of poisoning his wife, brother, and friend, John Parsons Cook, by strychnine, but at the *post mortem* examinations of the bodies not a particle of that vegetable poison was discovered. An Act of Parliament was passed to enable his trial to take place in London, in lieu of at Stafford, owing to the strong feeling that existed against him in that county.

He was tried at the Old Bailey, in May, 1856, and after the proceedings had lasted ten days, was found guilty of poisoning his friend and confederate on the turf, and was executed on the 14th June, at Stafford, protesting against the justice of his sentence.

The old roadway passes under the line, which is on a lofty embankment. The station is of pleasing design, stone fronted, and has all the variety of outline so essential to the true spirit of the Tudor style of architecture. *Hagley Hall*, seat of Lady de la Zouche.

COLWICH.

Population, 1,828.

Telegraph station at Stafford, 6½ miles.

Hotel.—Railway.

Fair.—Wednesday before Mid-Lent Sunday.

Mails.—One arrival and departure, daily, between London and Colwich.

Money Order Office at Stafford.

Colwich is a pretty village, with a population of about 2,000. The station is situated near the church, and adjoining a beautifully wooded estate belonging to the Earl of Lichfield, at whose seat the celebrated Lord Anson, circumnavigator of the globe, was born. He was also buried here, in close contiguity to the splendid residence of his descendants.

Stafford, see page 30.

For continuation of this route, to Crewe, &c., see page 30.

NORTH STAFFORDSHIRE.

Colwich to Stoke.

From Colwich to Stoke the line passes through a country of singular beauty, having almost the appearance of one continued park, and affording the traveller, amidst varied and lovely scenery, views of *Shugborough Hall* (a seat of the Earl of Lichfield), *Sandon Hall* (the Earl of Harrowby's), *Ingestre* (Earl Talbot's), and many other objects of interest.

Passing Weston and Sandon stations, we arrive at

STONE (Junction).

POPULATION, 3,443.
A telegraph station:
HOTEL —Crown.
MARKET DAY.—Tuesday.
FAIRS.—Tuesday after Mid-Lent, Shrove Tuesday, Whit Tuesday, Aug. 5th, Tuesday before St Michael.
BANKER.—W. Moore; draw on Glyn and Co.

Here are manufactures of shoes. The church contains an altar-piece, by Beechy, and monument to Earl St. Vincent, born at Meaford Hall, in 1734.

Junction of line to NORTON BRIDGE.

From Stone to the Potteries the scenery is scarcely less beautiful, including a view of the woods, &c., of *Trentham* (one of the seats of the Duke of Sutherland); *Meaford Hall* (Viscount St. Vincent's), &c. The line then passes within a near view of the various and very populous series of towns, known as the "Staffordshire Potteries."

Passing BARLASTON station, we arrive at

TRENTHAM.

POPULATION, 2,747.
Telegraph station at Stoke, 3 miles.
HOTEL.—Stafford Arms.
MONEY ORDER OFFICE at Newcastle, 3½ miles.

Trentham Park, the Duke of Sutherland's seat, on the river Trent, is of great extent; the old seat has been rebuilt by Sir J. Barry. It was visited by the Queen, when Princess Victoria, and her mother, the late Duchess of Kent, in 1832. A gallery of pictures, &c. The Trent is made to spread into a fine lake, planted with ornamental timber, the work of Brown, the famous landscape artist, of the last century.

STOKE (Junction).

A telegraph station.
HOTELS.—Railway, Talbot.
BANKERS.—Moore and Co. (Weekly).

This is the busy capital of the *Staffordshire Potteries*, a district 9 miles long, including *Longton Fenton*, *Hanley*, *Burslem*, *Etruria*, *Tunstall*, &c., which, with other places, are incorporated within the new borough, containing a population of 100,000, who return two members, nearly all employed in the manufacture of pottery, or the arts connected with it. Potters' clay (though of a coarse quality) and coal are both abundant; hence the peculiar advantages hitherto possessed by this spot. Stout low kilns, like the martello towers in Kent, are smoking about everywhere; each the centre of a pottery establishment, for which a "Bank" is the local name. Copeland's Bank, for instance, means Copeland's Works. At these, and at Minton's, are produced the most beautiful porcelain, rivalling the best made abroad; also the terra cotta, tesselated tiles, &c., so extensively used in new churches, and the small figures, in imitation of marble statuary.

At Stoke, the principal buildings are, a modern *Town Hall*, vast *Railway Station*, built in the Tudor style, at a cost of £150,000. The approaches are paved with Minton's tiles; new *Church*, in which are the tombs of Wedgwood and Spode, two eminent names in this locality. Wedgwood died in 1795, at Etruria, so called because of his successful imitation of the ancient vases under that name, now the seat of one of his family. At *Stoke*, or *Fenton Manor House*, Fenton, the poet, was born. Dr. Lightfoot, the Hebraist, was a native. Hanley and Longton are both larger than Stoke. Peacock coal is quarried at the former, and at the latter much of the coarser sort of pottery is made.

When the staple manufacture and the people have been thoroughly examined, there is little else attractive in this important quarter, although the scenery is not altogether void of interest. It is well provided with railways and canals. The first sod of the Grand Trunk Canal was cut by Wedgwood himself; and the North and South Staffordshire railways have been opened since 1847, having been amalgamated with the canal.

Hanley, 1½ mile from Stoke, contains a population of 30,000 inhabitants, and is the largest town in the north of Staffordshire. The iron trade is now becoming a most important feature in the commerce of the pottery district. Earl Granville's furnaces, located near Hanley, employ about 3,000 hands.

To the east of Stoke is *Norton-on-the-Moors*. These moors stretch for miles and miles through this end of the county, into Derbyshire and Yorkshire.

Taking Stoke-upon-Trent as the centre, the North Staffordshire lines radiate in almost every direction; the main line from Colwich to Macclesfield going direct through the Potteries; the Derby and Crewe line, commencing at Crewe, falls into the Macclesfield and Colwich line at Harecastle. After traversing the Pottery Valley, it branches eastward from Stoke-upon-Trent, and falls into the Midland (Birmingham and Derby) at Burton-upon-Trent, where it unites with the South Staffordshire, Leicester, and Swannington lines. The Churnet Valley line leaves the Macclesfield and Colwich line at North Rode, about five miles south of the former place, and passing for about 27 miles through one of the loveliest vallies in England, unites with the Derby and Crewe line at Uttoxeter.

Stoke to Burton and Derby.

LONGTON.

POPULATION, 15,249.
Distance from the station, 1 mile.
A telegraph station.
HOTEL.—Eagle.
BANKERS.—Harvey and Son; draw on Glyn and Co.

In the vicinity are *Longton Hall*, seat of H. Wileman, Esq., and *Edensor*, where there is a handsome new church.

Then passing BLYTHE BRIDGE, CRESWELL, LEIGH, and BROMSHALL, stations, we arrive at

UTTOXETER JUNCTION.

Distance from station, 1¾ mile.
A telegraph station.
HOTELS.—White Hart; Lion.

MARKET DAY.—Wednesday.

FAIRS.—Tuesday before Old Candlemas, May 6th, July 31st, Sept. 1st and 19th, Nov. 11th and 27th.

BANKER.—Burton Union Bank.

This is a pleasant market town, with a population of 3,468. Here is a fine church, lately rebuilt, except the old spire, which is 179 feet high; *Free Grammar School*, founded by Allen, the mathematician, in 1570, a native, and a curious six-arched stone bridge. Sir S. Degge, the antiquary, and Lord Gardner, the sailor, were natives. In the vicinity is *Hollingbury House*, the Mynor's old seat.

MARCHINGTON station.

SUDBURY.

Telegraph station at Uttoxeter, 4½ miles.
HOTEL.—Vernon Arms.
MONEY ORDER OFFICE at Uttoxeter, 5 miles.

Here is an old ivy-covered church, containing tombs of the Vernons of *Sudbury Hall*, whose motto is "*Vernon semper viret.*"

Passing SCROPTON station, we reach

TUTBURY.

Distance from station, ¾ mile.
Telegraph station at Burton, 5 miles.
HOTEL.—Dog and Partridge.
FAIRS.—Feb. 14th, August 15th, and Dec. 1st.

Here are ruins of the King of Mercia's Castle, rebuilt by John of Gaunt, in which Mary Queen of Scots was twice confined. A Norman church, with tower, and beautiful door, founded in 1080. In 1831, a great many coins, dated 1321, were found in the river Dove.

Burton.—See Section II., page 61.

EGGINGTON.

Telegraph station at Derby, 8 miles,
MONEY ORDER OFFICE at Burton, 1¼ mile.

In the vicinity is *Eggington Hall*, seat of Sir H. Every, Bart.

Derby.—See Section IV., page 9.

Stoke to Macclesfield.

The northern portion of the county of Stafford, hrough which this line passes, is distinguished from its being the centre of that celebrated district which produces the Staffordshire Pottery, comprised in a large area of about thirty thousand acres, lying a little to the eastward of Newcastle-under-Lyme. If we could survey this industrious region from any elevated position, we should find the whole of the towns and villages of the Potteries resembling one long street, stretching for a distance of nine miles from south-east to north-west, and linked together by intermediate suburbs, and so intimately connected that the eye might travel from one to the other without finding a break in their continuity. There may be seen the surrounding hills, crowned with towering columns and huge pyramids of chimnies, and great rounded furnaces, in which the ware is baked, clustering together like hives. Beneath these are the drying houses, the magnificent warehouses, and the massive walls that enclose the whole of these great establishments, containing the various materials used in the manufactories. Between the great factories or "banks" as they are called, are scattered the houses of the shopkeepers, and cottages of the workmen and artisans associated in these establishments; whilst here and there the intervals are filled up by the churches and chapels, or stately mansions of those who by pottery have become enriched. This district includes an enormous population, so continuously employed in the production of pottery that it seems a matter for wonder where the market could be found. At most of the towns and hamlets the pottery works are kept in incessant action. Very little progress was made in the potteries of Staffordshire until the late Mr. Wedgwood commenced his improvements, to the genius and enterprise of whom may be attributed the present flourishing state of the manufacture of earthenware in this district. But if this celebrated man could have witnessed the evidence of the vast progress made during the last ten years, as displayed by the pottery and porcelain department of the Crystal Palace in 1851, not only in the high specimens exhibited, but in the commonest articles, he would have felt richly rewarded for the genius, enterprise, and perseverance with which he had contributed to establish this branch of our industry on so good a foundation.

NEWCASTLE-UNDER-LYME.

A telegraph station.
HOTEL.—Castle.
MARKET DAYS.—Monday and Saturday.
FAIRS.—Shrove Tuesday, Easter and Whit Mondays, July 14th, Monday after Sept. 13th, first Monday in November.
BANKERS.—National Provincial Bank of England.

NEWCASTLE-UNDER-LYME or under-Lyne, population 10,569, who return two members, is on a little stream called the Lyne, at the head of the river Trent, and had a castle, built by Edmund, Earl of Lancaster, which has long disappeared. General Harrison, the fifth-monarchy leader, was born here. *Keel Hall*, near this, is an old Elizabethan seat of the Sneyds. *Butterton Hall* belongs to Sir W. Pilkington; formerly it was the seat of the Swinnertons, who gave name to *Swinnerton Park*, close by, the seat of T. Fitzherbert, Esq. The beautiful Mrs. Fitzherbert, whom it has lately been proved was *actually* married to George IV., was of this family.

ETRURIA.

Telegraph station at Burslem, 2 miles.
INN.—Etruria.
MONEY ORDER OFFICE at Hanley, 1 mile.

ETRURIA, almost classic ground, is on the east side of the pottery valley. Here the celebrated Wedgwood built his beautiful mansion, and erected the spacious manufactory of earthenware now carried on by one of his grandsons, in conjunction with a partner. Here, too, Flaxman modelled some of his finest forms, to be reproduced in almost pristine beauty by the potter's art. The park, and nearly the whole estate, except the manufactory and the village, a long street of workmen's cottages, have within these few years been sold to the Duchy of Lancaster, whose coal and iron works threaten at no distant period utterly to destroy the waning beauty of the place.

BURSLEM.

POPULATION, 15,954.
Distance from station, ½ mile.
Telegraph station.
HOTEL.—Leopard.
MARKET DAYS.—Monday and Saturday.
FAIRS.—Saturday before Shrove Sunday, Easter Day, Whit Sunday (the only place in England where a fair is held on a Sunday), Midsummer Day, day after Christmas.
BANKERS.—Alcock and Co.

In old times, Burslem was noted for its common yellow ware, so much so that "Butter Pot" was its ordinary name, even on the county map Near here Josiah Wedgwood was born in 1730, and brought his improved wares and porcelain to perfection; but the china clay, felspar or soapstone, and flint, necessary for the finer sorts, are imported from the south, especially Devonshire and Cornwall.

KIDSGROVE JUNC. (Harecastle).

Distance from station, ½ mile.
A telegraph station.
MONEY ORDER OFFICE at Burslem, 3¼ miles.

CREWE BRANCH.

Kidsgrove to Crewe.

This is a short line from Kidsgrove to Crewe, about 9 miles, for the convenience of the salt district of Cheshire, communicating with the line from Crewe to Burton, and so on to the eastern coast. It also opens out a valuable connection with Liverpool and the midland districts. Leaving this ancient seat of the earthenware manufacture—a district now also vieing with the southern part of the county in certain branches of the iron trade—the train enters the Harecastle tunnel, by Telford (1¾ mile), passing through a hill previously perforated by two tunnels of the Trent and Mersey canal, emerging therefrom on the confines of Cheshire. The branch itself affords no extraordinary or interesting feature. The stations are ALSAGER and RADWAY GREEN.

Crewe—See page 31.

From Kidsgrove to Congleton, the main line passes through a fine country, close by the foot of the celebrated Mow Cop.

The various stations on the line are all in the Tudor style of architecture.

MOW COP.

Distance from station, 1¼ mile.
Telegraph station at Kidsgrove, 2¼ miles.
MONEY ORDER OFFICE at Congleton.

MOW COP is a mountain in miniature, precipitous on three sides, bleak, bare, and craggy, except in one part, where there is a fine hanging wood. From the summit of this hill, 1,091 feet high, the finest views imaginable are obtainable in every direction. In certain states of the atmosphere, it is said, that the shipping beyond the port of Liverpool are distinguishable. The Welsh mountains, the Wrekin in Shropshire, Beeston Castle, the Peak of Derbyshire, and the lofty range of hills which form the Staffordshire moorlands, are prominent objects. Nearer, on the south, almost the whole of the Pottery district is seen. Congleton lies nearer still to the north. The whole country northward is studded over with towns and villages, of which a sort of bird's-eye glance is presented. But nothing can be more glorious than the view from it of almost the entire county of Chester. The hill stands on the boundary line between the counties of Stafford and Chester. On the summit there is an artificial ruin, which has a good appearance in every point of view.

In the vicinity are *Lawton Hall*, C. Lawton, Esq.; *Rode Hall*, R. Wilbraham, Esq.; *Moreton Hall*, G. Ackers, Esq. (a fine Elizabethan seat).

CONGLETON.

Distance from station, ¾ mile.
A telegraph station.
HOTEL.—Lion and Swan.
MARKET DAY.—Saturday.
FAIRS.—Thursday before Shrovetide, May 12th, July 12th, and Nov. 22nd.
BANKERS.—Fitz Adams.

A municipal borough and old town, with manufactures of silk and cotton. Population, 10,520. It is on the Dane, in the neighbourhood of the wild moorland country which borders Derbyshire and Staffordshire. Here may be seen several old timbered houses, large silk, cotton, and ribbon factories, town hall, and good grammar school. In the vicinity are *Eaton Hall*, G. Antrobus, Esq., and *Somerford Park*, Sir C. Shakerley, Bart. At *Biddulph* are the picturesque ruins of an Elizabethan house, destroyed in the civil wars. *Knypersley Hall.* Lime quarries are worked under the Mow Cop, a peak 1,091 feet high.

The route from Congleton to Macclesfield is rich in natural beauties, and furnishes various objects worthy attention, amongst which is a stupendous viaduct across the Dane valley.

Cloud-End and Mow Cop are noble features in the landscape to the right, between Macclesfield and the Potteries. Cloud-End is a bold promontory, seen to great advantage near the junction with the Churnet Valley line, at North Rode. It is the termination of the hilly range known as Biddulph Moor, remarkable as the site of the bride-stones, a series of immense blocks supposed to be the remains of a Druidical temple. It also makes a fine background in the view through the arches of the Dane and

Congleton viaducts. Mow Cop, although not really so lofty as Cloud-End, presents a much more striking appearance to a distant observer.

NORTH RODE, the junction of the Churnet Valley railway.

MACCLESFIELD.

A telegraph station.
HOTELS.—Macclesfield Arms, Angel.
MARKET DAYS.—Tuesdays and Saturdays.
FAIRS.—May 6, June 22, July 11, October 4, November 11.
BANKERS.—Brocklehurst and Co.; Branch of the Manchester and Liverpool District Banking Co.

A market town and borough, population, 39,048, who return two members. *St. Michael's Church* restored, with tombs of Archbishop Savage and the Leghs of Lyme, and *Christ Church*, with the tomb of Roe, its founder, are worth visiting. The *Town Hall*, by Godwin, *Free Grammar School*, *School of Design*, and *Public Park*, and the silk and cotton factories should be viewed.

CHURNET VALLEY BRANCH.

North Rode to Uttoxeter and Ashbourne.

BOSLEY and RUSHTON Stations.

RUDYARD.

Distance from station, ¼ mile.
Telegraph station at Leek, 2 miles.
This was the Saxon seat of the Rudyard family.

LEEK.

Distance from station, ¾ mile.
A telegraph station.
HOTEL.—Roebuck.
MARKET DAYS.—Wednesday and Saturday.
FAIRS.—Easter Wednesday, May 18, Whit-Monday, July 3 and 28, October 10, November 13.
BANKERS.—Manchester and Liverpool Banking Company.

A market town, population, 8,877, employed in the silk manufacture. It contains an old early English church, with a broken Danish cross, 10 feet high; *Grammar School*, *Alms Houses*, and factories of silk and cotton. Parker, Lord Chancellor Macclesfield, was a native. In the vicinity is *Westwood Hall*, the seat of J. Davenport, Esq.

Passing CHEDDLETON, FROGHALL, (near which is *Ashcombe Hall*, the residence of W. Sneyd, Esq.), and OAKAMOOR stations, we reach

ALTON.

Telegraph station at Rocester, 3½ miles.
HOTELS.—Swan; Crown.
MONEY ORDER OFFICE at Cheadle, 4 miles.

The ruins of a castle of the De Verdons are situated on a rock 300 feet above the river, commanding a splendid prospect. *Alton Towers*, the princely seat of the Earl of Shrewsbury, built in 1814, contains a magnificent hall, with armoury, 120 feet long, picture gallery, 150 feet, in which are a superb collection of pictures, &c. from Madame Bonaparte's selection; chapel, with stained windows by Pugin; state drawing room, with some of Queen Catherine's ornaments. In the beautiful gardens are the Choragic Temple (after that of Lysicrates), Chinese conservatory, an imitation Stonehenge, Jacob's ladder, Pagoda, 95 feet high, Harper's cottage, Gothic temple, from which the Wrekin can be seen, &c., &c. Near the old castle is *St. John's Hospital*, founded by the Talbots for a Warden and Fellows, with church, school, &c., all worth a visit.

ROCESTER station, and junction of the

ASHBOURNE BRANCH.

After passing NORBURY and CLIFTON stations, we arrive at

ASHBOURNE.

A telegraph station.

HOTEL.—Green Man.

MARKET DAY.—Saturday.

FAIRS.—First Tuesday in January, February 13, second Monday in March, April 3, May 21, July 5.

BANKER.—Burton Union Bank.

This pretty market town, noted for its cattle fairs, of 4,500 inhabitants, is in the beautiful valley of the Henmore, on the western border of Derbyshire, near Dovedale. *Viator*, in Walton's Angler, going down Spittal Hill to the Talbot, with his friendly guide of the angle, says "But what pretty river is this that runs under this stone bridge? Hath it a name?" *Piscator:* "Yes, it is called Henmore, (or Schoo Brook), and has in it both trout and grayling. * * * But we are now come to the Talbot, what will you drink, sir, ale or wine?" *Viator:* "Nay, I am for the country liquor, Derbyshire ale, if you please; for a man should not, methinks, come from London to drink wine in the Peak." *Piscator:* "You are in the right; and yet, let me tell you, you may drink worse French wine in many taverns in London than they have sometimes at this house. What ho! bring us a flagon of your best ale. And now, sir, my service to you: a good health to the gentleman you know of, and you are welcome to the Peak." *Viator:* "I thank you sir."

Though we are in the region of the Lower Peak, there is nothing like Peak scenery at Ashbourne, but its ale is still celebrated. *Ashbourne Hall* is the seat of Captain Holland, R.N. (here Charles Stuart slept in 1745), to one of whose family there is a beautiful monument by Banks, in the fine early English church. The latter is a cross, with triple-lancet windows, built as far back as 1241, and contains a brass of the same age, with other monuments of the Cockaynes, &c.

At Mayfield they show the cottage to which Moore retreated from his gay friends, and in which he wrote "Lalla Rookh."

Piscator says that the foul ways in this part of Derbyshire "seem to justify the fertility of the soil, according to the proverb 'There is good land where there is foul way,' and it is of good use to inform you of the riches of the country, and of its continual traffic to the county town you came from; which is also very observable by the loaden horses you meet everywhere on the road." The roads are better now, and the *pack horses* referred to, for carrying goods, are superseded by rapid locomotives.

Crossing Bentley Brook, full of good trout and grayling, "but so encumbered with weed as is troublesome to an angler," you reach (three miles) Thorp Cloud Hill, 300 feet high, and the Walton Hotel, commanding a view of the bleak craggy ridges near the Dove, the bed of which should be descended here for the peculiar scenery of Dovedale. For two or three miles the swift and sparkling river is strained in its course between limestone rocks into a very narrow stream, 10 to 20 yards wide, which changes its course, motion, and appearance perpetually, and makes a continual noise as it rolls over the loose stones. "The cliffs are heaved into broken and picturesque piles, some naked or perforated into cavities, others adorned with foliage." Dovedale, however, has been much exaggerated, as the scenery is rather romantic than grand. In one part of the defile it is only seven yards across; the broken rocks having such names as the Twelve Apostles. Dovedale Church, Reynard's Cave, &c.

On the Staffordshire side of the Dove, near this, is *Ilam Hall*, the handsome Elizabethan seat of the Russells, where the two rivers Hamps and Manifold rise from under ground, only 15 yards from each other. Here Congreve, who was a Staffordshire man, wrote his first play, the "Old Bachelor;" so clever a thing that Dryden said "he had never seen such a first play." Three miles higher up the river is *Alstonefield* with an embattled church tower. "As I am an honest man," says *Viator*, (who was perhaps apt to be too much astonished), "a very pretty church. I thought myself a stage beyond Christendom." Further up the river is *Okeover Hall*, the old seat of Ward, the author of "Tremaine." After another three miles comes *Beresford Hall*, with its dilapidated fishing house, built by Cotton in 1674, near the Pike Rock, and dedicated to anglers, *sacrum piscatoribus*. His cypher is still seen over the door, but the marble floor and the panel portraits of Cotton, and his worthy father, Izaak Walton (who used to angle here), in full costume, have disappeared. Here the river runs pure and crystalline, but for a mile or two from its head (which is about 12 miles higher in the lofty moorlands round Axe Edge near Buxton) it is a "black water, as all the rest of the Derbyshire rivers of note are, for they all spring from the mosses." On the meadows, in the lower part of its course, the flood of the Dove lays so rich a cake that there is a rhyme which says:—

"In April, Dove's flood
Is worth a king's good."

Ashbourne Green Hall, the Miss Trenbaths, and *Ashbourne Grove*, are in the vicinity.

UTTOXETER JUNCTION.

LONDON AND NORTH WESTERN.

Macclesfield to Cheadle Junction.

PRESTBURY.

Telegraph station at Macclesfield, 2¼ miles.

MONEY ORDER OFFICE at Macclesfield, 2¼ miles.

Here is a curious old church, which has recently undergone considerable improvements and decorations. The curious old Norman chapel, distinct from the church, is appropriated as a National and Sunday school. In 1808, tumuli, urns, and human bones were found here. In the vicinity are *Adlington Hall*, seat of C. Legh, Esq., which was besieged for a fortnight by the parliamentarians; *Butley Hall*, W. Brocklehurst, Esq.; *Mottram Park*, Rev. H. Wright; *Styperson Park*; *Shrigley Hall*, Rev. B. Lowther.

Passing ADLINGTON station, we arrive at

POYNTON.

POPULATION, 7,393.

Telegraph station at Stockport, 5½ miles.

MONEY ORDER OFFICE at Stockport, 5 miles.

In the vicinity is *Poynton Hall*, seat of Lord Vernon, who rebuilt it, together with *St. Mary's Church*, in 1789; and about 1¼ mile to the east, *Lyme Hall*, T. Legh, Esq., is partly ancient, and stands in a vast park, or forest, once abounding in red deer. Sir Perkin à Legh was the favourite follower of the Black Prince, from whom the estate was inherited; their pictures are preserved here (in armour), with the Prince's bed, and other relics. It is a question, however, if the portraits are authentic, though they are undoubtedly ancient.

BRAMHALL.

POPULATION, 1,508.
Distance from station, ½ mile.
Telegraph station at Stockport, 4 miles.

Close at hand is *Bramhall House*, a fine timber residence of the 16th century, partly modernised. It contains portraits of Sir A. Legh, of Adlington, who was at one time said to be Percy's hero, "Will you hear a Spanish lady," in his *Reliques*, but which applied to Sir J. Bolle, of Thorpe, who was present at the siege of Cadiz.

CHEADLE JUNCTION, point of union with the main line from Crewe to Manchester. For continuation of route see page 36.

Colwich to Stafford (L. & N. W.) continued.

On nearing Stafford, the railway passes through a tunnel in *Shugborough Park*, seven hundred and seventy-nine yards in length. The north face of the tunnel is a very striking architectural composition. The lofty trees, clothed with the richest foliage, rising from the elevated ground through which the tunnel is pierced, give a depth of tone and artistic effect to the whole scene, at once peculiarly imposing and beautiful, and form a remarkably fine feature in the scenery of the railway. Emerging from the tunnel the town of Stafford is soon reached. *Wolseley Park* and *Bishton*, Miss Sparrows, are close at hand.

STAFFORD.

A telegraph station.

HOTELS.—Swan; Vine; Grand Junction.

MARKET DAY.—Saturday.

FAIRS.—April, May, June, and October, annually.

BANKERS.—Stevenson, Salt, and Co.; Branch of Manchester and Liverpool District Banking Co.

STAFFORD is the capital, but by no means the largest town, of Staffordshire, at the termination of the Trent Valley Loop, by which it is 132 miles from London. Population, 11,829. Two members are returned. Boots and shoes are the chief articles of manufacture. Near to a ford on the Sow Elfleda, or Ethelfleda, Alfred's daughter, a great virago who reigned over Mercia, built a castle in the year 913. This was improved by the Normans, but reduced in the civil war; some remains of the keep are yet seen at *Stafford Castle*, a seat of Lord Stafford, 1½ mile to the west.

It is a long straggling town, with short streets branching out of the main thoroughfare (which bear curious names), where the best buildings stand, not far from the two parish churches. *St. Mary's* is a venerable early Gothic cross, embattled with an octagonal tower of moderate height. The font is said to be very old. *St. Chad's* contains some Norman work. The Shire Hall, a handsome building in Market Square, consists of the Courts and offices, and a spacious assembly room. The Town or Guildhall, built in 1853, is also in Market Square, and has an excellent covered market behind. Here it was, at the Spring assizes 1854, that the amiable and accomplished Judge Talfourd died on the bench, in the act of addressing the grand jury, and was carried out in his scarlet robes on the shoulders of his friends, before a crowded audience. The Grammar School, in Gaol Square, was endowed by Edward VI. The *County General Infirmary* is a large building in Foregate Street, with no pretensions to beauty, except a handsome portico. To the north, in the suburbs, are the county gaol, built in 1793, recently enlarged, where William Palmer, the sporting doctor, was executed, June 14th, 1856; and the county asylum, on a pleasant site of 30 acres. About a mile to the east of the town has recently been erected a fine building, known as the Coton Hill Institution, for the reception of insane persons of the higher and middle classes. *Izaak Walton*, the father of angling, was born here in 1593. In the neighbourhood are the following seats:—*Rowley*, R. W. Hand, Esq.; *Seighford Hall*, F. Eld, Esq.; and *Ranton* (or Ronton) *Abbey*, a seat of the Earl of Lichfield, now occupied by J. B. Elley, Esq.; some remains of a cell founded by the Fitz-Noels in Henry II.'s time are left. East of Stafford, up and down the Trent, are—*Sandon Hall*, the seat of the Earl of Harrowby; *Tixall*, Sir A. Constable, Bart., a modern seat, near the gateway of an older one, in a large park; *Ingestre*, Earl Talbot; *Shugborough*, another seat of the Lichfield family, having a pillar to Lord Anson, the celebrated navigator (who was born here in 1697), in the grounds, which lie in an elbow made by the Trent and Sow; *Wolseley*, the Hon. W. Warren Vernon; *Teddesley Park*, Lord Hatherton's seat; *Beaudesert*, the Marquis of Anglesea. Between Trent and Dove are *Blithfield*, *Chartley Castle*, and *Bagots Park*.

SHROPSHIRE UNION.

Stafford to Shrewsbury.

HAUGHTON station.

GNOSALL.

Here is a large Church; and close by, *Ranton Abbey*. A distance of four miles further brings the traveller to the verge of the county of Stafford, and the entrance to that of Salop, and another mile to the town of

NEWPORT.

POPULATION, 2,906.

Telegraph station at Wellington, 7½ miles.

HOTELS. — Royal Victoria, Crown.

MARKET DAY.—Saturday. FAIRS.—1st Tuesday in February, Saturday before Palm Sunday, May 28th, July 27th, September 25th, and December 10th.

BANKERS.—National Provincial Bank of England

Here is a fine church of the 15th century, and in the vicinity are *Chetwynd Park* and *Aqualate Hall* and *Mere*, a fine sheet of water covering nearly 200 acres.

DONNINGTON.—In the vicinity are *Lilleshall Abbey* and *House*, Duke of Sutherland's, and *Woodcote Hall*, J. Cotes, Esq.

TRENCH CROSSING station.

HADLEY.

Telegraph station at Wellington, 1¼ mile.

MONEY ORDER OFFICE at Wellington, 1¼ mile.

To the left is *Apley Castle*.

WELLINGTON AND SHREWSBURY.—See Section II., page 62

London and North Western Main Line continued.

Stafford to Crewe.—(Staffordshire.)

Upon leaving Stafford station the Castle appears to the left, and the town to the right of the line, which passes through a somewhat marshy country, and uninteresting portion of the route.

NORTON BRIDGE.

Distance from station, ¾ mile

A telegraph station.

HOTEL.—Railway.

MONEY ORDER OFFICE at Stone, 3 miles.

In the vicinity is *Eccleshall*, the seat of the Bishops of Lichfield since the 13th century. In the church, Margaret of Anjou sought refuge after her flight from Blore Heath, in 1459.

From this station, through STANDON BRIDGE the line proceeds through a similar monotonous part of the country, occasionally diversified by the view of a beautiful park, or well-situated mansion —until we enter a deep cutting leading to

WHITMORE.

HOTEL.—Railway.

Telegraph station at Norton Bridge, 8½ miles.

MONEY ORDER OFFICE at Newcastle-under-Lyne. 5 miles.

This station is situated in a deep cutting of sand stone, in the midst of a wild heath, with hills and woods, and forest scenery. The village of Whitmore, to the east of the line, is a pleasant place, situated in a beautiful valley, and near at hand is *Whitmore Hall*.

Leaving the Whitmore station, the line passes over a considerable bed of peat, and proceeds through a fine open country of pasture land.

MADELEY.

POPULATION, 1,423.

Telegraph station at Crewe, 8 miles.

HOTEL.—Crewe Arms.

MONEY ORDER OFFICE at Newcastle-under-Lyne.

This is a pretty village to the right of the line, consisting of cottages and houses built of stone in the Elizabethan style. The church is a fine old Gothic structure in the form of a cross.

The line proceeds from this station past a deep cutting through undulating hills, between which we obtain beautiful vistas of the country, and thence reach an embankment, whence we have a view of a most romantic dell, bounded by hills, abrupt precipices, and banks of heather. As far as we can see to the right the vale stretches out in variegated beauty. Passing onward the train proceeds along an embankment, beneath which passes the Wrine, which flows through the valley. A lofty embankment and two viaducts carrying the line through the valley of the Wrinehill, the village of that name appearing on the right, and *Wrine Hall* and *Hill*, forming pleasing objects in the prospect on the left Soon after quitting this point the line enters

CHESHIRE,

THE general appearance of which, about fifty miles long and twenty-five broad, is that of an extensive plain, but on the eastern side there is a range of mountainous country connected with the Derby and Yorkshire hills, rather more than 20 miles in length. On the Shropshire side the country is also broken and irregular. This county has been called *the Vale Royal of England;* and when viewed from the high land above Macclesfield, it has the appearance of a beautiful plain, watered by many large rivers. It has long been celebrated for the excellence of its cheese, of which more than 20,000 tons are annually sent to London, besides the various other places at which it finds a market.

We next pass through the cutting of Bunker's Hill, in the occasional openings of which we see *Betley* and *Betley Court*, a fine old English Hall, at the top of a rising lawn, surrounded with woods and fields, and adorned with a large sheet of water or lake in front, forming one of the most pleasant views on the line.

The hills in the vicinity command fine prospects of the country, which is delightfully varied with hills and vallies, woodland and pastures, a cursory view of which we obtain during our passage along the next embankment.

BASFORD.

Telegraph station at Crewe, 2¼ miles.

MONEY ORDER OFFICE at Crewe, 3 miles.

From this station the line curves gently, and then proceeds in a straight direction. After passing through a cutting, and thence along an embankment, we perceive *Crewe Hall*, a very beautiful place, the building being one of those square structures which the nobility and gentry of this country were so partial to in the last century. We again proceed over a somewhat high enbankment, and obtain several fine views of the country between the line of road and Nantwich, over which are scattered hamlets and farm houses, intermingled with rich and luxuriant scenery, until we reach

CREWE.

A telegraph station.

HOTELS.—Refreshment Rooms at station, Crewe Arms.

CREWE is a railway town and first class depôt, standing on the North Western main line, where the Chester, Manchester, and Staffordshire lines fall in. Formerly it was called Oak Farm, which an attorney bought for £35 an acre. The station, and many of the workmen's houses, are imitations of the Elizabethan style. Nearly 2,000 men are employed in the Company's workshops. Here are immense rolling mills for the rails, locomotive factories for the engines, including fitting-up and erecting shops, 300 feet and upwards long. An engine, with its tender, averaging £2,000, is made up of 5,416 separate pieces, and a new one is turned out every Monday morning. Wolverton is the chief hospital for repairs. At the Crewe Grease House, the yellow mixture of tallow, palm oil, and soda, used to grease the wheels is made.

Lord Crewe's seat, near at hand, is the only real remnant of antiquity, being of the age of the renaissance, introduced by Inigo Jones. It is built of brick, and is really a fine specimen of the style of architecture in the reign of James I. At the time of the civil war, it was occupied by both parties. There are some very old portraits.

CREWE TO SHREWSBURY.

This line runs in a south-westerly direction from Crewe. The stations on the line are WILLASTON.

NANTWICH.

POPULATION, 5,426.
Distance from station, 3¼ miles.
Telegraph station at Crewe, 4¼ miles.
HOTEL.—Lamb.

Here is a cruciform church, with pinnacled tower. Lord Byron, who occupied *Dorford Hall*, 1643, was defeated by Fairfax. This place was formerly celebrated for its salt mines, but is now famous for its cheese.

WRENBURY Station.

WHITCHURCH (Salop).

MARKET DAY.—Friday.

This town is prettily situated on a rising ground, at the top of which stands the church, rebuilt in 1722, on the site of one which had fallen down. Amongst the ancient monuments it contains, is one to the celebrated Earl of Shrewsbury. The principal buildings are, a grammar school, house of industry, alms-houses, &c.

PREES Station.

WEM.

This was the birth-place of Jeffries, the infamous chancellor, who was educated at Shrewsbury school. Wem was taken by Sir W. Brereton, and given to Jeffries by James II., who created him Baron Wem.

YORTON and HADNALL stations.

Shrewsbury.—See Section II., page 63.

CHESTER & CREWE BRANCH.

Crewe to Chester.

WORLASTON and CALVELEY stations (Cheshire).

BEESTON.

Telegraph station at Crewe, 10½ miles.

HOTELS.—Tollemache Arms.

MONEY ORDER OFFICE at Tarporley, 1¾ mile.

Here are the ruins of an old castle, built by R. Blundell, Earl of Chester, in 1220. It stands on the ridge of a precipitous rock of sandstone, and covers a space of about five acres. The deep ditch surrounding the keep, cut out of the solid rock, together with the extraordinary thickness of the walls which remain, bear testimony to the once-remarkable strength of the fortress. It is worth a visit.

In the vicinity are *Tarporley Hall*, Lord Alvanley and *Tilstone Lodge*, T. Tollemache, Esq.

TATTENHALL.

Telegraph station at Chester, 7¼ miles.

HOTEL.—Bear.

MONEY ORDER OFFICE at Tarporley, 5 miles.

WAVERTON station.

Chester, full particulars of which will be found at page 69, Section II.

London and North Western Main Line continued.

Crewe to Warrington and Preston.

To the right, soon after leaving Crewe, we perceive Bond Hill and Mow Cop, two large and lofty hills in Staffordshire, to the north of the Potteries. The line of railway here is so completely level that it vanishes in perspective. The church tower of Coppenhall is seen on the left side of the road, and the village on the right. This part of the country abounds with peat, and in many places is extremely boggy, and uninteresting to a railway traveller, from its sombre and cheerless aspect. In the distance to the left, however, the country is well cultivated, and the horizon is bounded by the outline of the Welsh mountains.

MINSHULL VERNON.

Telegraph station at Crewe, 4¾ miles.

MONEY ORDER OFFICE at Winsford, 2¾ miles.

Soon after leaving this station we pass through a cutting of considerable length, and thence the scenery becomes more interesting. We have views of Beeston Castle Hill, the highlands in Cheshire, Wales, and further on, in clear weather, the Derbyshire hills.

Passing onwards we reach the Middlewich embankment, which crosses the canal by a lofty iron bridge, then through a slight excavation, and the train arrives at

WINSFORD.

POPULATION, 1,775.

Telegraph station at Hartford, 4¼ miles.

HOTEL.—Lion.

A mile to the west is the village of Winsford, situated in one of the most important salt districts in the country. There are twenty-eight salt works here, some of them being like small towns in extent. Winsford station lies in a deep excavation, soon after leaving which we approach one of the finest and most remarkable parts of the line. The cuttings conceal it occasionally. There is a beautiful view of *Vale Royal*, the seat of Lord Delamere, situated in one of the most lovely vales in England, on each side of which are tracts of the richest pasture, and east and west the splendid valley, with its wooded hills and glens, spreads out and lengthens as we proceed. The Vale Royal Viaduct is a noble structure of red and variegated sandstone, consisting of five arches, and affords a fine prospect of the river Weaver and its course through this beautiful vale. Passing on through a deep and picturesque ravine we shortly after arrive at

HARTFORD.

A telegraph station.

Money Order Office at Northwich, 2 miles.

This station being in a very deep cutting, much of the romantic scenery in the vicinity is concealed from view, but on issuing beyond we perceive a pretty villa on our left, and further on *Grange Hall* standing on a well wooded eminence near the railway. Near this place is an elegant bridge. Two miles beyond, is *Northwich*, *wich* (sounded witch), being the old name of a salt town.

Northwich is the principal seat of the salt trade. The salt is worked either in the mines, 200 or 300 feet deep, under the gypsum, or produced from the brine springs. One of the largest, the *Marston or Dale's Mine*, should be visited by the curious traveller, descended in three or four minutes by a shaft 250 feet deep, to the excavated chambers below, spread over 35 acres, the sparkling roof being supported by great solid salt columns 60 feet square. When Canning visited the mine, it was lit up with thousands of candles and blue lights, producing a most brilliant effect. The rock salt is variegated and dirty-looking, and was first found in searching for coal; which, according to geological rule, may be reached some hundreds of feet lower. That from the springs is evaporated in immense iron pans; at Droitwich 260,000 tons are annually made in this way. About twice as much more is produced by the rock mines. The Nantwich trade has declined.

ACTON.

Telegraph station at Hartford, 2¾ miles.

Money Order Office at Northwich, 4 miles.

On leaving this station we pass through frequent cuttings, and finally reach a long embankment which leads to the magnificent Dutton Viaduct over the river Weaver, and the Vale of Dutton. This admirable and gigantic bridge is more than a quarter of a mile long, consisting of twenty arches, formed of red sandstone. The imposing grandeur of this fine piece of work is greatly enhanced by the beauty of the scenery, and the almost boundless view from the centre of the viaduct. The prospect from the valley below, including the viaduct, is equally worthy of admiration. Proceeding on the line passes along the Dutton embankment, which is carried over the Dutton Bottoms, where there are many beautiful hills and dells, richly clothed with luxurious plantations, and affording delicious glimpses of scenery. On the left is *Aston Hall*, a noble edifice. Thence we pass through a short tunnel and arrive at

PRESTON BROOK.

Telegraph station at Warrington, 5½ miles.

Money Order Office at Warrington, 5¾ miles.

There is a large and comfortable inn, close to the station, where a good bed may be obtained. Preston Brook, though a small place, is of some importance from being the point of junction of the Bridgewater with the Grand Trunk canal.

From this station we proceed through an excavation and tunnel, and thence pass under an aqueduct for the Bridgewater Canal which runs through *Norton Park*, seat of Sir R. Brooke, Bart. The basement story of the priory still contains some most interesting Norman remains, in a state of good preservation.

The line then proceeds through the Moore Hill excavations, and reaches

MOORE.

Telegraph station at Warrington, 3 miles.

Money Order Office at Warrington, 3¾ miles.

The pretty village of this name is situated to the eastward of the line, but is not in view.

Soon after leaving this station we reach the Arpley embankment, and pass over the Mersey Viaduct. This, though less grand in appearance than the Dutton Viaduct, is a fine work, consisting of twelve arches, through three of which the river Mersey, and the Mersey and Irwell canal pass. The valley of the Mersey is spread before us, and on each side the scenery is very beautiful, consisting principally of rich pasture land, adorned with farm-houses and cottages.

A short distance beyond this the river winds towards the town of Warrington, with its manufactory chimnies, large buildings, and churches, &c.

Continuing along the embankment the train soon arrives at

WARRINGTON.—(Lancashire).

A telegraph station.

Hotels.—Lion, Nag's Head,

Market Days.—Wednesday and Saturday.

Fairs.—Every other Wednesday, July 18th and November 30th; on alternate Wednesdays for cattle.

Bankers.—Parr, Lyon and Co.; Branch of Manchester and Liverpool District Banking Company.

Warrington is an interesting old town on the river Mersey, in Lancashire, 181 miles from London, and about 21 miles from Manchester and Liverpool

The river is free from the sea to this point, above which it belongs to the Mersey and Irwell Navigation Company, represented by the late Earl of Ellesmere. Vessels of 150 tons can get up to Bank Quay in the spring tides.

This town in the oldest documents (*temp.* Henry III.) is called Werinton. It is on the line of the great Roman road from south to north, and considerable remains of this early period have been found at Wilderspool and Stockton Heath, on the left bank of the Mersey, which is supposed to have been the *Condate* of the Itineraries. Here the Royalist army, under General Bailey, after having been defeated at Preston, by Cromwell, in 1648, surrendered prisoners of war. In 1745, the central arches of the bridge (built by the Earl of Derby in the reign of Henry VII.) were broken down, to impede the march of Prince Charles and the Scotch army.

Population, 23,623. One member is returned to parliament. Cotton and fustian goods, pins, glass, and tools of various kinds are manufactured here. It has an old-fashioned look, with several narrow streets, and contained many timbered picturesque houses most of which, however, are pulled down and have given place to ornamented windows and plate glass; one good specimen still remains in the Market Place. The Sessions House and Bridewell were built under an Improvement Act in the year 1840.

The Church is a large building; the chancel and the arches supporting the tower are good; decorated with a crypt at the east end. The Butler Chapel is late perpendicular, and contains a very fine altar tomb of the 15th century; the tower is of the end of the 17th century, the rest of the building is modern. The Butlers, who held this and various other manors from the time of Henry III., became extinct in the reign of Elizabeth; the manor is now the property of J. Ireland Blackburne, Esq., of Hale, and the advowson of the Rectory belongs to Lord Lilford. The Free School was founded under the will of Sir Thomas Boteler in 1526. The *Mote Hill*, probably the original seat of the Lords of Warrington, is now covered with the Diocesan and Orphan Schools.

There was an academy founded here in the last century, described by Mrs. Barbauld as "the nursery of men for future years." Priestly, Enfield, Gilbert Wakefield, Taylor, and Aikin, the father of Mrs. Barbauld, were amongst the professors, and many of their works were printed at Eyres' press in the town. A good substantial building has been erected in Bold Street, containing a Public Museum and Library, and rooms occupied as a School of Art. It has been built by public subscription, and is the property of the corporation.

In the neighbourhood are—*Winwick Hall*, the seat of Rev. F. Hopwood, and a church, in which are effigies, &c., of he Leghs of Lyme, whose ancestor is said to have won his lands in the battle of Agincourt. Sankey gives name to the *Sankey Canal*, which, beginning at St. Helens, bends round to Warrington, and comes out opposite Runcorn, a circuit of 15½ miles, 12 of which were cut between 1755 and 1758, when no other canal existed in England, so that this deserves notice as being the *oldest* of the kind. A direct railway now runs from St. Helens to its outlet. *Bold Hall* is the seat of H. Bold Hoghton, Esq., who represents the old family of Bold, its former residents for many generations. They give name to Bold street, in Liverpool. On the Cheshire side of the Mersey a low range of hills of new red sandstone extends from Runcorn to Dunham, affording many rich and beautiful prospects. *Halton Castle* is a picturesque ruin on one of the higher portions of this range. The famous *Bridgewater Canal* passes this way (near some later cuttings for improving the Mersey navigation). It was cut on a level by Brindley for the Duke of Bridgewater, being 38 miles long from Manchester, through Worsley and Altrincham, and crosses the Bollin by an aqueduct half-a-mile long. The Duke expended all his capital in the construction, but lived to realize a vast fortune by his perseverance. His first efforts were to reduce the carriage of goods and price of coals 50 per cent. It is said that when the Manchester and Liverpool Railway was projected the Bridgewater agent was asked to take shares in the concern; but he had, it seems, such confidence in the superiority of the old canal over the new plan of communication, that he would consent only to take "all or none."

WARRINGTON JUNCTION, NEWTON BRIDGE, and PRESTON JUNCTION stations.

PRESTON AND PARKSIDE.

Preston Junction to Preston.

GOLBORNE.—*Golborne Park*, seat of J. Catterall, Esq.

WIGAN.

Telegraph, at the London and North Western station.

HOTELS.—Clarence, Victoria, Royal.

MARKET DAYS.—Mondays and Fridays.

FAIRS.—Holy Thursday, June 27th, Oct. 28th.

BANKERS. — Manchester and Liverpool District Banking Co.; Woodcock and Sons.

A great cotton town in Lancashire, and a parliamentary borough (two members), near the head of the river Douglas. Population, 31,941. Contains stone and coal in great abundance. The town is well built on the whole, but straggling. Some parts are ancient; the newest houses are on the east side. The large church of All Saints, with its tower, is older than Edward III.'s time. The greater portion of it was rebuilt about 1853. It contains monuments of the Bradshaighs and other lords of the manor. It is a rectory, the value of which exceeds £4,000 a-year, the rector being lord of the manor. The *Town Hall*, near it, was rebuilt in 1720. There are about twenty large factories, employing about 10,000 hands. Bishop Woolton and Dr Leyland were natives.

Much cannel coal is found near Wigan. It is a beautiful jetty black which takes a polish, and is capable of being worked into blocks for building, as well as for ornaments. In digging for coal, some years back, a sulphur spring was discovered near Scholes Bridge, over which a pump-room, &c., were built, and the place styled New Harrogate, but it is now disused.

Wigan, a little while ago, could boast of having the tallest chimney in England. It was exactly 400 ft. high, and took four years to build, being designed for the chemical works; but it fell down. Another, only 3 ft. lower, built for Muspratt's works at Newton, was blown down with gunpowder in 1853. There is a *Grammar School* in Millgate. In Wigan Lane, the northern outlet of the town, there stands a pillar to the memory of Sir T. Tyldesley, who fell in the battle of 25th August, 1651, when the Earl of Derby with 600 horse was defeated by Col. Lilburne. The Earl was beheaded at Bolton six weeks afterwards. He had sustained two defeats in this town in 1643, so that Wigan was unfortunate. Cromwell's Ditch, a cut of the Douglas, on the township border, commemorates a visit paid by him when in pursuit of the Duke of Hamilton in 1648.

Part of a Roman road may be traced towards Standish; it is straight as an arrow for 1½ mile.

STANDISH.

Distance from station, ¼ mile.
Telegraph station at Wigan, 2¼ miles.
HOTEL.—Eagle and Child.
FAIRS—June 29th and Nov. 22nd.
MONEY ORDER OFFICE at Wigan, 3¼ miles.

STANDISH is the seat of the Standishes, a very ancient family. *Haigh Hall*, the seat of the Earl of Crawford and Balcarres, a descendant of the Bradshaighs, who lived here for many centuries. *Ince Hall*, another old seat, belonging to C. Blundell, Esq., near an ancient moat. *Ashton Hall*, a fine seat, is in the district of *Mackerfield.*

COPPULL.

This place derives its name from a copse close to it. Near is *Chisnall Hall*, which was the old seat of the Chisnalls; to the left is *Wrightington Hall*, an old mansion.

EUXTON.—*Euxton Hall*, the seat of W. M. J. Anderton, Esq.

LEYLAND.

Telegraph station at Preston, 4¾ miles.
HOTEL.—Railway
MONEY ORDER OFFICE at Chorley, 4 miles.

Here is an excellent *Free Grammar School*, and old church, with the tombs of the Ffarringtons, of Worden Hall.

FARINGTON.

Cuerden Hall, the seat of R. Townley Parker, Esq., M.P.

PRESTON.

A telegraph station.

HOTELS.—Bull; Victoria; Red Lion; Castle.

MARKET DAYS.—Wednesday, Friday, and Saturday.

FAIRS.—Week before first Sunday after Epiphany, March 27th, August 25th, and November 7th.

BANKERS.—Roskell and Co.; Branch Lancaster Banking Co.; Preston Banking Co.

An ancient borough (two members) and an important cotton manufacturing town in Lancashire, population 69,361, standing some distance without the manufacturing circle, on a hill above the beautiful valley of the Ribble, 210 miles from London. Below the town the river widens considerably. Recent improvements in its navigation have enabled vessels of large tonnage to reach the town. Preston is a place of some historic importance. King John and two of the Edwards, John O'Gaunt, and James the First, visited the town. Cromwell defeated the royalist forces in the suburbs. The first Scottish rebellion in 1715 was quelled here, and the young Pretender passed through in 1745. Henry the First granted it a charter, and successive sovereigns have confirmed and extended its municipal privileges. One of its most peculiar institutions is its ancient guild, held every twenty years, at which the aristocracy of the county have been wont to assemble as participants in the festivities which distinguish it.

In past times Preston was noted for the gentility of its inhabitants. Many Lancashire families made it their occasional residence, and it was, before the introduction of the cotton trade, according to Dr. Whitaker (History of Richmondshire), "an elegant and economical town, the resort of well-born but ill-portioned and ill-endowed old maids and widows." In 1777 the first cotton mill was erected, and since that time the staple trade of Lancashire has so extended within it that Preston has become one of the principal manufacturing towns in the county. There are upwards of 50 cotton mills in the town, the largest establishment being that of Messrs. Horrockses, Miller, and Co., who employ upwards of 3,000 hands. The commercial annals of this town are memorable from two long continued disputes between the employers and employed. The strike or lock-out of 1836-7 lasted fourteen weeks, and caused vast distress in the town; that of 1853 4 was prolonged to a period of thirty-nine weeks, during which 15,000 or 16,000 persons were out of employment, and the greater portion of the factories were entirely closed. The order which was preserved in the town, the good conduct of the operatives, and the support which they received from their class in other towns, were much noticed at the time.

Preston is a well-built town, with some old streets and houses. Its parish church has been recently rebuilt, and all the other churches are modern. The town hall is a structure quite unworthy the town, which is singularly deficient in handsome public buildings, for, excepting the elegant edifice erected as the Mechanics' Institution, and the pile comprising the Grammar School, the Literary and Philosophical Institution, and the Winckley Club, it scarcely possesses any building of architectura importance.

Although Preston was so aristocratic a town in days of yore, it possessed before the passing of the

Reform Act, the only real democratic electoral suffrage in the kingdom; all its inhabitants of six months' residence, and above twenty-one years of age, if free from the taint of pauperism, were entitled to a vote. The Stanleys were long the patrons of the borough, but the democratic suffrage had occasionally democratic suitors. Cobbett was once a candidate for its representation, and Henry Hunt sat in two parliaments for Preston.

Preston is unrivalled for the beauty of its situation, and few towns are so well off for public walks, and these are to be yet further extended. Sir Richard Arkwright, the great improver of the first spinning frame, was a native of Preston; Lady Hamilton, the friend of Nelson, is also said to have been born here.

In the neighbourhood of Preston are *Tulheth Hall*, the seat of the monastic community who afterwards settled at Furness Abbey; *Penwortham Priory*, erected on the site of the ancient priory, that was a cell of the Abbey of Evesham; the Castle Hill; Penwortham, the site of a castle mentioned in Domesday Book; Walton-le-Dale, the recently discouered site of the Roman *Coccium;* Cuerdale, where the immense Danish hoard, comprising above 10,000 Saxon and Danish coins, was discovered; Ribchester, the site of the Roman *Rigodunum; Stonyhurst College*, once the seat of the ancient Lancashire family of Sherburne, now a noted educational establishment of the Jesuits. Preston, which is open to the saline breezes of the west, is also at a very convenient distance from Lytham, Fleetwood, and Blackpool, with all of which bathing places it is directly connected by rail.

For continuation of this route see page 56.

Here we again retrace our journey, and pursue our course from

Crewe to Stockport and Manchester.

SANDBACH.—(Cheshire).

POPULATION, 2,752.

Distance from station, 1¼ mile..

Telegraph station at Crewe, 4¾ miles.

HOTEL.—George.

MARKET DAY.—Thursday.

FAIRS.—Easter Tuesday and Wednesday, and Thursday after Sept. 11th, and Dec. 27th.

This is a town occupying a very pretty situation on the banks of the river Wheelark, and embracing within its prospect a panorama that extends from the Welsh mountains iu the west, to the Derbyshire hills in the east. It has no distinct manufacture of its own, but shares in the silk trade to a small extent, whilst being on the verge of the salt region, it derives some additional traffic from that proximity. Lord Crewe is the owner of the place. Its Grammar School is a well known institution.

There are excellent Brine Springs at Wheelock; St. Mary's perpendicular English Church, and a fine old Cross in the Market Place. *Abbeyfield*, seat of C. Ford, Esq., is in the vicinity.

HOLMES CHAPEL.

Telegraph station at Crewe, 8¼ miles.

HOTEL.—Swan.

OMNIBUSES to Over Winsford and Middlewich, on Mondays, Tuesdays, and Saturdays.

MONEY ORDER OFFICE at Middlewich, 4 miles.

Near Bagmere Pool is *Brereton Hall*, built by Sir W. Brereton, the parliamentary leader.

CHELFORD.

Telegraph station at Stockport, 11¼ miles.

HOTEL.—Dixon's Arms.

MONEY ORDER OFFICE at Knutsford, 4 miles.

Near Chelford are *Tatton Park*, W. Egerton, Esq.; *Tabley Hall*, Lord de Tabley; *Peover Hall*, Sir H. Mainwaring, Bart.

ALDERLEY.

Telegraph station at Stockport, 7 miles.

HOTEL.—Queen's.

MONEY ORDER OFFICE at Knutsford, 4 miles.

Alderley Park is the seat of Lord Stanley of Alderley.

WILMSLOW.

Distance from station, ½ mile.

Telegraph station at Stockport, 6¼ miles.

HOTEL.—Swan.

MONEY ORDER OFFICE at Stockport, 6¼ miles.

HANDFORTH.—*Cheadle Heath*, seat of J. Newton, Esq.

CHEADLE.

Telegraph station at Stockport, 2½ miles.

HOTEL.—White Hart.

MONEY ORDER OFFICE at Stockport, 2½ miles.

This is the point of junction with the line to Macclesfield Congleton, &c. A distance of 2½ miles further brings us to the celebrated Viaduct at Stockport, one of the railway marvels of our time, for it exhibits a roadway actually reared above a populous town, and spanning a valley nearly a third of a mile in length. The height of the parapet above the river Mersey that flows below is 111 feet, and runs on 27 magnificent arches. The cost of the undertaking was upwards of £70,000. It affords the traveller one of the best and most commanding views he can possibly obtain of an English manufacturing town. Thronged streets and narrow lanes stretch out on each side far below; mills and factories rise out of the dense mass of houses, and a forest of chimneys towering upwards, point out the local seats of manufacturing industry. The chief part of the town appears mapped out in bold irregular lines, with the fine church of St. Mary's crowning the summit; and the view altogether is sufficient to invite curiosity to examine the associations of a place presenting such a busy aspect to the eye.

STOCKPORT.—(Lancashire and Cheshire).

A telegraph station.

HOTELS.—Warren Bulkeley Arms.

BANKERS.—Bank of Stockport; Branch of Manchester and Liverpool District Banking Co.

Though greatly improved of late years, Stockport is yet very irregularly built, and the ground on which it stands is remarkable for inequality of surface; from this circumstance, on a winter's night, the numerous and extensive factories elevated above each other, present an appearance when lighted of peculiar and striking grandeur, especially when approached by the high road from the north. It has a population of 53,835, engaged principally in the manufacture of cotton, and returns two members to parliament. The river Mersey divides the town into two unequal parts, the larger portion, that to the south, being situated in Cheshire, and that to the north in Lancashire.

Between 50 and 60 factories are dispersed in and round the town; one of the largest is called Marsland's, a well known name; it is 300 feet long, and has 600 windows in its six storeys. Others are Howard's, Marshall's, Eskrigge's, &c. Here Radcliffe and Johnson invented the machine for dressing the warp about 1803.

There was a castle here (the site of which is an inn) to guard the ford or port between the two county palatines, on the old Roman road. *St. Mary's Church*, of the fourteenth century, is on a hill. It was restored in 1848; and contains several monumental effigies, &c., of ancient families in the neighbourhood. *St. Thomas's*, a large Grecian church, built in 1825. Five bridges cross the Mersey—one of 210 feet span was carried away in the floods of 1798. The *Grammar School*, founded in 1487, has been rebuilt by Hardwicke; it is under the Goldsmith's Company. The *Infirmary* is a large neat building, 100 feet long. One pleasing feature of the wholesale manner in which things are done in this part of the world, is an immense *Sunday School*, built in 1826, 150 or 160 feet wide, and containing 84 class rooms. Between 5,000 and 6,000 children are here gathered together on a Sunday to receive religious instruction from pious and devoted volunteers of various denominations. It is endowed with an income of £560.

The Goyt and Etherow, which join the Mersey a little above Stockport, may be ascended to the moorlands, on the Derbyshire border, where the peculiar scenery of the Peak begins. Glossop, Chapel-en-le-Frith, and Buxton, are not far distant. *Bramall House*, seat of W. Davenport, Esq., is a good specimen of the curious and picturesque timber houses, once so common in Lancashire, and *Poynton Hall*, Lord Vernon's seat, some of whose early ancestors are buried in Stockport Church.

HEATON NORRIS, HEATON CHAPEL, LEVENSHULME, and LONGSIGHT stations.

MANCHESTER.

Telegraph stations—the Electric and International, Ducie Buildings, Exchange; 1, Mosley Street, and at the Railway Stations. The Magnetic and British and Submarine, 11, Ducie Street, Exchange.

HOTELS.—Queen's, Thomas Johnson, first class, for families and gentlemen, recommended.

Albion, Palatine, and Clarence.

MARKET DAYS.—Tuesday, Wednesday (cattle) Thursday, Friday, and Saturday. The Markets are Victoria, Victoria Street; Smithfield, Shudehill Bridge Street; London Road. The Cattle Market i in Cross Lane, Salford.

FAIRS.—Easter Monday and Tuesday, Whit-Monday, Oct. 1st, and Nov. 17th.

RACES.—In Whit-week and September.

MONEY ORDER OFFICES, King Street, Manchester Oldfield Road, Salford.

BANKERS.—Cunliffes, Brooks, and Co.; Sir B. Heywood and Co.; Lloyd and Co.; James Sewell; Bank of Manchester; Edward Whitmore; Branch Bank of England; Manchester and Liverpool District Bank; Manchester and Salford Banking Co.; National Provincial Bank of England; Union Bank of Manchester

MANCHESTER, the metropolis of the cotton manufacture, a cathedral city, and parliamentary borough, in the south-east corner of Lancashire, on the Irwell, 188 miles from London, and 31½ from Liverpool. The last named town is the real port which supplies its staple article in the raw state, but Manchester itself has all the privileges of one, being licensed to bond imported goods as much as if it were by the sea side. It has been the head of a bishop's see since 1848, when a new diocese was taken out of Chester, including the greater part of Lancashire; and the Collegiate Church turned into a cathedral.

Manchester and Salford, though separate boroughs, divided by the Irwell, form one great town, which in 1851 contained a population of 401,321, of which 85,108 belonged to Salford. Manchester returns two members to parliament, and Salford one. With Salford it covers a space of about 3½ miles long, by 2½ broad, and 10 miles in circuit; a line which takes in various suburbs, as Hough, Pendleton, Strangeways, Cheetham, Smedley, Newton, Miles Platting, Mayfield, Beswick, Ardwick, Chorlton-upon-Medlock, Hulme, &c., all of which are continually spreading into the country, and constitute the best built and most modern portion of the town, the most ancient being in the centre, round the Cathedral. Here, in Market-street and the adjacent streets, are the principal buildings of Manchester, which are not numerous; its great features being its vast and busy factories, the industry and spirit of its commercial relations, rather than the display of architectural refinement. But in this respect a great change may be anticipated, as it possesses a government able to give unity of purpose to schemes of improvement, and to carry them into effect, by having acquired the manor, which was bought of the Mosleys a few years ago. Another fund for this object is derived from the surplus profits of the vast *Gas Works*, first established in 1817.

Manchester is seated on a wide plain, with a slight elevation here and there; but not far off are the border lines of the three adjacent counties of Yorkshire, Derbyshire, and Cheshire. Some of the most rugged hills and the finest pass scenery in England, may here be witnessed. Four railways traverse this remarkable district—the Lancashire and Yorkshire, London and North Western, Manchester, Sheffield, and Lincolnshire, and South Junction.

Although it was a Roman station under the name of *Mancunium*, which the Saxons altered to *Mancestre*, yet there are few remains of antiquity, besides some old timber houses and the College. When Leland undertook his topographical survey in the reign of Henry VIII. it was the most populous town in the county, and noted for its woollen goods (even then called cottons), the making of which was introduced by the Flemings of Edward III.'s time. But about 80 years ago calicoes and cotton muslins began to supersede every other manufacture; Watt's steam-engine, Arkwright's power-loom and factory system, and inexhaustible supplies of coal have given a superiority to Manchester, which it has retained to this day. Within that period it has multiplied its population by 7 or 8; and its goods are sent to every corner of the globe. Old people are yet alive who remember the first factory in Miller's Lane, and its great chimney; now there are above 120, a visit to any of which is one of the chief sights of Manchester. Here thread as fine as 460 hanks to the lb. is spun; each hank being 840 yards; and every variety of cotton, silk, and mixed goods, is woven; while, such is the power of production, that cotton may be brought from India, across the sea, made up aud shipped again for India, and there sold cheaper than the native dealer can buy it in his own market: while the whole quantity has increased two hundred per cent., the average price has fallen from 7½d. to 3½d. per yard. It is calculated that, in Lancashire, there are 1,000 factories, with 300,000 hands, and a power of 90,000 horses, moving 1,000,000 power-looms and 20,000,000 spindles. Nine-tenths of them are within thirty miles of Manchester. The annual produce is worth £68,000,000 sterling a-year, or, one-fourth of a million per day. One-half of this is consumed at home. (See *Lancashire Witchcraft*).

A piece of cloth, twenty-eight yards long, may be printed in three or four colours in a minute, or nearly one mile of it in an hour. So rapid are the various processes, that goods sent in the grey state from the mill in the afternoon, are bleached, dressed, starched, finished, and placed in the next day's market. Fustians, hats, machines, and locomotive engines, figure among the subordinate branches of manufacture.

Among the factories, notice Birley's, at Chorlton, and Dewhurst's, in the Adelphi, Salford, with its tall stone chimney, 243 feet high, on a base 21 feet square and 45 feet high. The bleach and dye works are placed up and down the Irwell and its tributaries. Worthington's umbrella factory, in Great Bridgewater Street; Wood and Westhead's smallware manufactory, Brook Street; Whitworth's machine factory in Chorlton Street; Sharp's, Atlas Works, Oxford Street; Fairbairn's, in Ancoats; Nasmyth's, Bridgewater Foundry, at Patricroft, may be visited. Manchester is famed for its magnificent warehouses. For style of architecture and beauty, perhaps Watts's new warehouses in Portland Street excel all others, and ought by all means to be seen.

Public and Commercial Buildings.—After the mills, the chief buildings worth notice are the following:—*Town Hall*, in King Street, built by F. Goodwin; a Grecian colonnade in front, with carved emblems, and a public room under the dome, 130 feet long, ornamented with frescoes. There is a hall for Salford, in Chapel Street: that for Chorlton is in Cavendish Street. *Exchange*, in Market Street, built 1806, by Harrison, of Chester, is a fine building, with a Doric circular front, which renders the exterior imposing. It has been considerably enlarged and beautified, its area 1628 square yards, renders it the largest exchange room in Europe; it is 185 feet long by 82 feet broad. Here may be seen the "Cotton Lords" on a Tuesday, in their legislative assembly. It contains a portrait, by Lawrence, of T. Stanley, Esq., M.P. *Corn Exchange*, in Hanging Ditch; built in 1837. *Chamber of Commerce*, in the Town Hall Buildings, King Street. *Commercial Association*, York Buildings, King Street. *Society of Guardians for the Protection of Trade.* The new large *Market* at Shude Hill (the Manchester Smithfield) should be visited, as its superb glass and iron roof is splendid and unique.

News Rooms, Institutions, Libraries, Places for Recreation, &c.—*Royal Institution*, in Mosley Street, founded in 1823, and built by Barry, a handsome Grecian building, with a six-column Ionic portico, casts of the Elgin marbles, Chantrey's statue of Dalton, the Manchester chemist, and a lecture theatre; a *School of Design* forms part of it. Dalton used to lecture at the *Literary and Philosophical Society*, in George Street, established in 1781. The *Manchester Royal School of Medicine and Surgery* in Pine Street, founded in 1824; average number of pupils, 80 to 100. Lectures are given on practical chemistry, anatomy, surgery, &c. *Athenæum*, in Bond Street, also by Barry; among the pictures is *St. Francis Xavier*, by Murillo; annual literary gatherings are held here, generally presided over by some eminent person. *Mechanics' Institution*, in David Street, a handsome new buiding; opened in September, 1856. *Free Trade Hall.* This fine new edifice, in the pure Italian style of architecture, replaces the large old building in Peter Street, which was without windows, and had no pretensions whatever to architectural display, being principally worthy of notice for the large number of persons it was calculated to hold. It was here, at the first great Anti-Corn Law League Meeting, when the Rev. James William Massie, D.D., had risen to address the assembly, that the lights were entirely extinguished, and the vast assembly left in total darkness until the gas could be again lit. The new building is calculated to hold about 7,000 people: its inaugural opening took place on the 8th October, 1856. *Lyceum*, in Great Ancoats Street; others at Salford and Chorlton. *Portico*, a substantial building, in Mosley Street, designed by Harrison, of Chester. There are upwards of 14,000 vols. in the library. The files of newspapers are the best out of London. Subscription *Concert Hall*, Peter Street. *Old Subscription Library*, Ducie Street, founded in 1765. and has 30,000 volumes; the *New Library*, in the Exchange Buildings, contains 120,000 volumes

Exchange
Cathedral
Watts' Warehouse
Mechanics Institution
Free Library
Royal Infirmary
Free Trade Hall.
Athenæum
Royal Institution.

Free Library, in a handsomely fitted-up building, in Camp Field (which belonged to the Socialists' body), established at a cost of £12,000, and open to all, young and old, properly recommended. Periodicals and newspapers are supplied in profusion, and there is a library of 21,000 volumes, which are *lent out*, without restriction. The losses are few, and the privilege is greatly appreciated. First Shakspeare, then Defoe, Scott, and Macaulay, appear, on inquiry, to be the chief favourites with the steady readers. *Chetham Library*, Chetham's College, contains upwards of 25,000 vols., many of which are rare and valuable. Open to residents and strangers from 10 a.m. to 5 p.m.; during the winter season it closes at 4 p.m. *Newall's Buildings Public Library*, commenced 1830, 20,000 vols. *Foreign Library*, St. Ann's Street, upwards of 7,000 vols.; French, Italian, German, Spanish, &c. *Law Library* in Norfolk Street. At Salford, Lark Hill, formerly the residence of W. Garnett, Esq., has been converted into a handsome *Library and Museum*, with the same object as the Free Library at Manchester, with rooms 60 feet to 75 feet long, for reading, pictures, natural history specimens, &c., the sculpture being placed on the broad staircase. The *Museum of Natural History* in Peter Street contains a good collection. *Theatre Royal*, in Peter Street, built in 1845, in the modern Italian style, with a fine statue of Shakspeare in front. The *Queen's*, or Minor Theatre, in York Street and Spring Gardens.

GARDENS, PARKS, &c.—*Botanical Gardens*, at Old Trafford, a very pretty tract of sixteen acres, with lake, conservatory, &c. *Victoria Park*, between London and Oxford Roads, is a space of 140 acres, covered with villas. The *Queen's Park*, on the Rochdale Road; *Philip's Park*, Bradford Road; and *Peel Park*, Salford, are open to the public, the last having a museum. *Kersal Moor*, where the races were held, is now partly cultivated, and has a good church on one part of it.

COLLEGES, HOSPITALS, &c—*Lancashire Independent College*, established 1840, at Withington. The *Wesleyan Theological Institution*, Didsbury, opened in 1842, accommodates about 40 students for the Wesleyan Ministry. *Chetham College*, or Blue Coat School, close to the Cathedral, was founded in 1651, by Humphrey Chetham, in the old buildings attached to the Collegiate Church, forming an antique dingy quadrangle, one side of which is appropriated to a library of 25,000 volumes (rarely used), with some "curiosities" ranged on the walls; and portraits of John Bradford, the martyr (a native of Manchester); Dean Nowell, who compiled the *Church Catechism*, and others. A statue of the founder, by Theed, was placed in the Cathedral, in 1853. The college is open to the public, and forms an object of attraction. The *Grammar School*, founded by Bishop Oldham in 1524, and since rebuilt, is near this; it has an income of £4,500. *Owen's College*, Quay Street; principal, J. G. Greenwood, B.A., founded by John Owen, who bequeathed upwards of £80,000 for the purpose of endowing it. Certificates are issued to candidates for the degrees of bachelor of arts and bachelor of laws, to be conferred by the University of London. The house was formerly the residence of Richard Cobden, Esq. Chemical laboratory and other conveniences. *Commercial Schools*, Stretford New Road, built in 1848, by the Manchester Church Educational Society. A library, museum, and specimens of natural history, are attached for the use of the pupils. *Ladies' Jubilee School*, established in 1806, nearly opposite the Workhouse. In 1832 Mr. Francis Hall bequeathed £10,000, which increased the number of pupils to 40, and further improved the building. Other educational and literary societies are the Chetham Society, Natural History Society, Geological Society, Statistical Society, and Manchester Law Association. *Royal Infirmary*, in Piccadilly, is a large handsome stone building, to which a new dome and portico have been added. It was founded as far back as 1753. It presents a noble appearance. It has six physicians and surgeons, resident surgeons and apothecaries; an income of £9,000, and annually relieves upwards of 20,000 patients (see *Bradshaw's Hand-book to the Manufacturing Districts*). Bronze statues of the Duke of Wellington, Sir Robert Peel, Watt, and Dalton, adorn the grounds in front of the institution. It is intended to add one of Her Majesty. *School for the Deaf and Dumb*, and *Henshaw's Blind Asylum*, are near the Botanical Gardens, at Old Trafford, with a chapel serving for both, all in a handsome Tudor style, with a front 280 feet long. Lane was the architect, in 1836. *Lunatic Asylum* at Prestwich.

PRISONS, WORKHOUSES, &c.—*The City Gaol*, at Hyde Road, commenced in 1847, completed in 1849, employing 200 workmen, and using ten million bricks, capable of holding about 432 prisoners, carried on upon the solitary system. It is enclosed by a boundary wall 20 feet high, and 2 feet 8 inches thick, and consists of three wings for male prisoners, and one for females, and one (the shortest) contains the chapel, hospital, &c. The *New Bailey Prison*, on the Salford side of the Irwell, was begun in 1787, in Howard's time, who laid the first stone; it is an extensive range, with nearly six hundred cells in it, besides wards, work-rooms, sessions-house, police-court, &c. A high wall, surrounded by an iron *chevaux de frise* encloses the whole; turrets at the angles of the building, with loop holes for firing through, are placed for defence in case of attack. Holds 583 males, and 214 females. *Union Poor-House*, erected in 1792, at a cost of about £30,000, in New Bridge Street, Strangeways, is a little town in itself, capable of accommodating upwards of 1,000 persons. At Swinton, four miles on the Bolton Road, on a site of 34 acres, is a large branch *Industrial School*, in the Elizabethan style, by Tattersall and Dixon, with room for 1,500 pauper children. The *Salford Workhouse* is in Eccles New Road, that for Chorlton-upon-Medlock at Withington.

BARRACKS.—*Cavalry Barracks*, Chester Road, accommodates upwards of 300 men and horses, besides commissioned and non-commissioned officers, &c. *Infantry Barracks*, Regent Road, Salford, will hold above 700 men, besides officers.

RAILWAY STATIONS.—London and North Western, London Road and Victoria; Manchester, Sheffield, and Lincolnshire, London Road; Lancashire and

Yorkshire, Victoria, Hunt's Bank, and New Bailey, Salford; South Junction and Altrincham, Oxford Road and Knott Mill.

BRIDGES.—Several bridges, of short dimensions, cross the Irwell and its two branches, the Irk and Medlock, the best of which is the *Victoria Bridge*, a noble stone arch, 100 feet span, near the Cathedral; rebuilt in 1839, in place of the old Gothic bridge of the time of Edward III. That at Broughton (uniting Broughton with Pendleton) is a very handsome suspension bridge, which had the misfortune to fall in while a detachment of soldiers were passing over it some years ago, but since rebuilt. Other bridges are the *Blackfriars*, at the end or St. Mary's Gate; *Albert Bridge* (late New Bailey), near the prison; *Regent Road; Ducie; Springfield Lane; The Iron Bridge*, New Bridge Street; and *Broughton* (uniting Salford with Broughton); at the latter two tolls are taken, as also at the suspension. In Fairfield Street, on the Birmingham line, is one of the best Skew Bridges in the kingdom, by Buck; it is at an angle of 24° only, built of iron, 128 feet span, six-ribbed, and weighing 540 tons: the width of the street is only 48 feet.

CHURCHES AND CHAPELS.—The *Cathedral*, originally a collegiate church, founded by the Delawarrs, is a handsome perpendicular English cross. A great variety of grotesque carvings are seen without and in the choir; the roof is flat, but adorned with fretwork. There are several chapels, formerly the chantries of the Trafford, Stanley, and other families, of whom it contains some monumental brasses. Theed's statue of Chetham is here. Few of the other churches deserve notice. At *St. Peter's*, is a picture of the *Descent from the Cross*, by G. Caracci. Near this church was the field of "Peterloo," where the celebrated reform meeting, called by Henry Hunt, the blacking maker, was dispersed by the yeomanry, in 1819, with the loss of several lives. *St. Matthew's* large church stands on the site of the Roman station, or Castle Field. There are altogether about 50 churches and chapels. The Roman Catholics possess two or three handsome chapels, the best being their *Cathedral*, at Salford, which is 200 feet long, with a handsome west front, nd spire 240 feet high.

CEMETERIES.—Rusholme Road, Ardwick, Harpurhey, Cheetham Hill (Wesleyan), and the Barnes' (Salford Borough) Cemetery, in the Eccles New Road.*

CLUBS.—Union, Mosley Street; Albion, King Street.

Of two well-known chemists, Henry was a native, and Dalton here developed his great discovery of the Atomic theory, which has done so much to give precision to the science. The first Sir Robert Peel was a "Manchester man;" and among living natives are Ainsworth, the novelist, De Quincey, the English opium-eater, and two poets, C. Swain and T. K. Hervey.

In the neighbourhood is *Heaton Park*, the seat of the Earl of Wilton, modernised by Wyatt.

*The first interment that took place was that of the remains of the late Mr. Joseph Brotherton, the well-known member of parliament for Salford, to whose memory a monument has since been erected by public subscription.

London and North Western continued.

Manchester to Liverpool.

VICTORIA STATION.

ALTHOUGH not strictly speaking the first railway in England, the Liverpool and Manchester line was really the first on which was attempted the practical application of locomotive power for the transit of goods and passengers, and it is, therefore, pre-eminently entitled to rank as the pioneer of those stupendous undertakings which have not only given a new stimulus to the mechanical and architectural genius of the age, but have enabled this country to take the lead of all others in these respects, not less than in manufactures. Important as were the direct objects proposed by the original projectors of this line, of bringing the vast district of our manufacturing industry within an hour's distance of the port where its staple material, and the supplies of food were landed, and whence its fabrics were exported to the ends of the earth, the result is, after all, the lowest in the scale. England has since developed her resources to an extent which, at the time of its trial, would have appeared incredible, and in the space of comparatively a few years, the whole island has been intersected by this new class of roads, as much superior to the old highways, as were those of the Roman conquerors to the tangled forest paths of our Celtic ancestors.

The first and greatest work on this portion was the immense bog of Chat Moss, which comprised an area of twelve square miles, varying in depth from ten to thirty-five feet, consisting of sixty million tons of vegetable matter, of so soft and spongy a texture that cattle could not walk over it. Those who are now whirled over this once trackless waste, the numerous viaducts and embankments, and along the immense excavations of the remainder of the line, can with difficulty appreciate the amount of skill, perseverance, and labour expended in works that are now concealed from general observation. Other lines, too, have been formed under immense difficulties, which have been surmounted by the inventive genius and indomitable energies of our engineers; but it must ever be remembered, that in the accomplishment of this line, every portion of the work was an experiment, and that the engineers and proprietors, virtually, and at their own cost, supplied the civilized world, not only with the initiatory example, but with an invaluable amount of information and experience acquired in the construction, progress, and management of this—the acknowledged model of every succeeding railway.

ORDSAL LANE and WEASTE stations.

ECCLES.

Telegraph station at Manchester, 4 miles.

HOTEL.—Bull's Head.

This little village is prettily situated on the northern banks of the Irwell, and environed by some of the most picturesque rambles; one of which, along the side of the river, about two miles up the stream, leads to a ferry by which the tourist may get ready access to Trafford Park, described Section II.

The place is celebrated for its cakes, also for its old church, which belonged to Whalley Abbey, and gives name (*Ecclesia*) to the parish. It has some monuments of the Booths and Breretons. At the vicarage the Right Honourable William Huskisson expired after his lamentable accident on the opening of the railway. Cotton and silk are woven here.

PATRICROFT.

Telegraph station at Manchester, 5 miles.

Here is Nasmyth's celebrated foundry, the largest in England.

A short walk from this station, along the canal, brings us to *Worsley Hall*, the seat of the Earl of Ellesmere, where Queen Victoria was so nobly entertained on the occasion of her visit to Manchester in 1851. The present splendid mansion was rebuilt by Blore in 1846, in the Elizabethan style of architecture. The late earl inherited the vast estates of the celebrated Duke of Bridgewater, for whom Brindley, the engineer, first made the subterranean canals here. They supply the coal mines below at a depth of 180 feet, and wind in and out for 18 miles. Landseer's well-known *Return from Hawking* may be seen at the house; and in the neighbourhood are a few of the timber and plaster buildings formerly so common in this part of England. One of them, *Peel Hall*, the seat of Lord Kenyon, was built in 1630, and has a great number of old rooms and portraits. From the park you get a view of Leigh and the Cheshire hills.

From Patricroft, a run of about 10 minutes brings us past Barton Moss and Astley.

Bury Lane, the commencement of Chat Moss, and Kenyon, the junction of the line to Bolton, are soon left behind, and we reach

Parkside, a place memorable by the death of W. Huskisson, Esq., the celebrated statesman, on the opening of the line, September 15th, 1830. A tablet is placed here in commemoration of the event.

NEWTON.

Population 3,719.
Hotel.—Legh Arms.

Here the Highlanders where defeated, in 1694. M'Corquodale and Co.'s printing works should be visited. In the vicinity are Castle Hill, with its old oaks, and *Haydock Park*, seat of T. Legh, Esq., used as a private Lunatic Asylum, under the direction of Mr. Sutton.

Warrington Junction, Collins Green, and St. Helens Junction.

ST. HELENS BRANCH.

One portion of this line turns off here to the right. A very few minutes brings us to

ST. HELENS.

Population 14,866.
Hotel.—Raven.
Market Day.—Saturday.
Fairs.—Monday and Tuesday after Easter, Friday and Saturday after September 8th.
Bankers.- Parr, Lyon, and Co.

It is a place celebrated for its manufacture of Plate and Crown Glass, very much of which is certainly got up to great perfection. An hour or two spent in the inspection of some of these works, particularly those of the Union Plate Glass Co. would amply repay the stranger. The streets of the town itself present no definite plan of arrangement, but seem to have been laid out as chance or interest might direct; and the houses are by no means remarkable for their architectural beauty.

The railway has recently been extended in this direction, by which, in connection with the Skelmersdale Branch of the East Lancashire Line from Rainford Junction, a direct communication with Southport had been effected.

The stations passed on leaving St. Helens are Gerard's Bridge, Moss Bank, Crank, Rookery, Rainford, Rainford Junction, Blague Gate, and Ormskirk.

Southport—see page 50.

St. Helens to Warrington, Runcorn, and Liverpool.

From St. Helens Junction the line diverges to the left, passing the stations of Peasley Cross, Sutton, Clock Face, Farnworth, and Appleton, *en route* to Runcorn Gap. By means of a ferry across the river we reach

RUNCORN,

Noted as one of the inland ports of the kingdom, and much resorted to for bathing in the summer season.

From Runcorn Gap the railway again diverges to the right, and after passing the stations of Fidler's Ferry and Sankey Bridges, we arrive at

Warrington, see page 33.

We again return to Runcorn Gap, and in pursuing our journey towards Liverpool, pass the stations of Ditton, Halewood, and Speke, arriving at

GARSTON,

The present terminus of the railway.

In the vicinity are *Allerton Hall*, the old seat of Roscoe, the historian, and *Woolton Hall*, a fine edifice, built by Adam, near which is the site of an old priory and a camp.

The rest of the journey, about six miles, is performed by omnibuses.

Liverpool, see page 51.

London and North Western continued.
St. Helens Junction to Liverpool.

From St. Helens Junction the line passes the stations of Lea Green, Rainhill, Huyton Quarry, Huyton, Roby, and Broad Green, when soon after, the train stops at

EDGEHILL.

Here the traveller sees before him a dark, yawning aperture, which, for the few minutes he is delayed, may excite a temporary imagining as to his probable destination. When informed, however, that this tunnel literally pierces into the very heart of Liverpool, burrowing beneath streets thickly tenanted by the suburban population, and constantly conducting trains freighted with hundreds of travellers like himself, under the surface of a region animated by a mighty multitude, intent upon the pursuits of every-day life, he may feel inclined to pay a just tribute to the engineering skill of those who were enabled to propose and complete a work of such kind in the early days of railway history. This funnel is one mile and a quarter in length; but the one which conveys the merchandise to Wapping, near the King's Dock, is still longer; and a third tunnel, for the conveyance of goods to the North Docks, has also been constructed.

Arrived at the station at Lime-street, the passenger will find it worth his while to bestow a glance at its architecture, its peculiar adaptation to all the requirements of an extensive railway system being best exhibited by the superior accommodation enjoyed by the public, and the regularity with which all the official duties are performed. The building is in the Italian style, presenting a columnar and pilastered front, with four arches for the admission of vehicles, &c.

LIVERPOOL.

Telegraph stations, 35, Castle Street, 9, Exchange Buildings, and at the Lime Street Railway Station.

BANKERS.—Israel Barned and Co.; A. Heywood, Sons, and Co.; Leyland and Bullins; Moss and Co.; Bank of Liverpool; Branch Bank of England; Liverpool Borough Bank; Commercial Banking Company; Branch Manchester and Liverpool District Banking Company; North and South Wales Bank; Royal Bank, Liverpool; Liverpool Union Bank.

HOTELS.—Victoria, and London North and Western Railway Hotel, opposite St. George's Hall, a most comfortable house, and much commended.

Radley's Adelphi; Lynn's Waterloo, Ranelagh Street.

OMNIBUSES to and from the station.

MARKET DAYS.—Daily.

FAIRS.—Every alternate Wednesday, beginning March 12th, July 25th, and Nov. 11th.

RACES.—(At Aintree) in February and July.

The *Lyrpool*, or *Litherpool*, of early times, when it was an insignificant chapelry, sent one little bark with 6 men to the siege of Calais, in 1338, Hastings then sending 21 tall ships, but is now the second port in the United Kingdom, as well as a parliamentary borough, &c., with a population of 375,955, who return two members. It stands fronting the Irish Sea on the north side of the Mersey's mouth, at the south extremity of Lancashire, 210 miles from London, by the North Western Railway, *viâ* Warrington; 230 miles by way of Birkenhead and Chester; and as near as can be in the centre of the British Islands. The site a sloping rock of red sandstone, through which three tunnels are cut from the Edge Hill Station—one to the Lime Street terminus (opposite St. George's Hall), another for goods, of 1¼ mile long, to Wapping, and a third, as long, to Clarence Dock. The Mersey, above the town, widens into a little shallow sea, 2 miles wide in one part; while at the mouth it is choked by large sandbanks, leaving two main entrances—the Victoria Channel, 12 miles long, the most used—and the Rock Channel, 10 miles in length. Besides the Floating Light Ship there is a handsome stone Light House off New Brighton, like the Eddystone, and 90 feet high.

The Docks, which are the grand lions of the town, extend in one magnificent range of 5 miles along the river, from Toxteth Park to Kirkdale; the newer ones being near the latter suburb, to the north, and most of them constructed since 1845. All steamers can enter (except some of the very largest), which are obliged to anchor in the river. The Collingwood, one of the finest docks in this quarter, is 500 yards long and 160 wide, and covers a space of 13¾ acres. Clarence dock to the south of these, near the Fort, is of an older date. Prince's dock is also 500 yards long, and chiefly used by American liners. At George's dock, in front of St. Nicholas' Church, is the new *Floating Pier*, whence steamers run to various points of the river. Canning dock, since it was altered, is 500 yards long, including what was the old dock. Albert dock was opened in 1845, by Prince Albert, with warehouses surrounding it, on the London plan—the usual practice at Liverpool being to build warehouses separate from the docks. Passing the tobacco, timber, salt, and other docks, you come to that called the Herculaneum, at the south end of the chain. Altogether the 21 docks have 15 miles of quay room, will hold 1500 sail, and enclose 200 acres of water. The dock dues in 1849 were £224,000; the tonnage in 1846 belonging to the port was 390,000, while the total tonnage trading inwards and outwards exceeded that of London. Customs, however, were only £3,620.000, while London was 11 millions. In the same year the exports of all kinds were valued at 28½ millions sterling; the imports from Ireland alone were 8 millions. These numbers may serve to give an idea of the extent of its commercial relations. To this we may add that nearly 2 million bales of raw cotton are imported for the staple supply of the factories dispersed through Lancashire—a wonderful quantity compared with the little bag which a private firm sent from America in 1785, as a venture, along with other goods. Liverpool, as might be expected, is a great emigrant port. As many as 206,000, for whose use half a million tons of shipping were required, started in 1851. A large Home has been built near the docks for their accommodation. The ship-building establishments of Messrs. Rennie & Co.—Jordan and Getty—Cato and Miller—Steel and Challoner—and Laird's, Clayton and Kereven, and Glover and Royle's on the Birkenhead side, are particularly worth inspecting.

The town covers a space of 7 to 8 square miles; Castle, Lord, Bold, and other streets near the docks are the most bustling; Rodney, Parliament, and Shaw Streets, the best built. The public buildings are—the *Collegiate Institution*, designed by H. Elmes, in Shaw Street, built in 1843, in the Tudor style, 300 feet long. The *Town Hall*, at one end of Castle Street, is a handsome pile, by J. Foster, on a rustic base, with a portico of four columns, and under an open dome, built in 1795. Lawrence's portrait of George III., and Chantrey's statue of Canning are here. In the *Exchange* quadrangle behind is Westmacott's statue of Nelson. At the other end of Castle Street is the *Custom House*, a very extensive building, also by Foster, with a dome and four Ionic porticoes, in one of which is a statue of Huskisson. It occupies the site of the first dock cut at Liverpool, in 1699. The *Post Office* and other offices are collected under this roof. Close to this is the new *Sailors' Home*, a striking building in the Italian style, built in 1850, 190 feet long, with turrets at the corners, and full of windows.

There are excellent libraries at the Athenæum and Lyceum news rooms, which represent the two great political parties in the town; the former is in Bold Street, and the latter in Church Street. New *Music Hall*, 175 feet long, in Hope Street, built in 1849. *St. John's Market*, in Elliott Street, was built in 1812, by Foster, and is 560 feet long; it covers 2 acres, intersected by five walks, and is a scene of extraordinary bustle on market days. The *Theatre* is in Williamson Square, near the Amphitheatre, both of good size. It was on the stage of the former that the celebrated actor, Palmer, died in 1798, after uttering the words—"there is another and a better world." Large *Poor House*, on Brownlow Hill, near the *Lunatic Asylum*, and the *Infirmary*—the latter built by Foster, with a six column portico.

The best building, and perhaps the finest in all England, is *St. George's Hall*, opposite Lime Street Railway Station. It was originally designed by H. Elmes, a very promising young architect, since dead. Its dimensions are 600 feet by 170, surrounded by Grecian columns of truly magnificent proportions, including assize and other courts. The building was begun in 1841, and was opened by Her Majesty in 1855; it cost about £200,000. Many of its decorations and exterior approaches are still incomplete. The Public Hall is 180 feet long and 84 high, with a marble floor, and a vaulted roof of hollow bricks. The Concert Room will hold 1400 persons. The Nisi Prius and Crown Courts form a half circle, 60 feet by 50, with an arched-panelled ceiling, resting on granite pillars. There are 16 fluted pillars in the east portico, 40 feet high, on a flight of steps 200 feet long. In the south portico are 8 pillars, and Gibson's statue of G. Stephenson. The basement is ventilated by small air-holes along the floor line.

St. James' Cemetery is a really attractive spot, in Upper Duke Street, laid out in an old quarry, with catacombs, and a mausoleum containing Gibson's statue of Huskisson, the statesman, who represented Liverpool when he was killed at the opening of the railway to Manchester, in 1830. The *Necropolis Cemetery* is in the Everton Road. The *Mechanics' Institution*, in Mount Street, is in fact an excellent school, established in 1835, by the liberal party, previous to the Collegiate Institution, which was set up by the conservatives. Lord Brougham laid the foundation stone. In Colquitt Street is the *Royal Institution School*, founded by Roscoe; with a gallery of marbles and casts (among others, the Panhellenium casts, the only ones in England). Romney's cartoons, Gibson's (of his falling angels); and a museum, (Roscoe's portrait is here; he lived when a youth at Mount Pleasant, and published his Lorenzo de Medici at Liverpool). *Blue Coat School* is behind Church Street. *Blind School* (oldest in England) in Hardman Street; Hilton's "Christ giving sight to the blind" is here. The baths and washhouses in Frederick Street, opened June, 1842, were the first of the kind erected in England.

Churches and Chapels.—85 altogether, of which 40 belong to the establishment. Liverpool forms one parish, with two rectors. *St. Nicholas*, the mother church, is near the docks, and has Gibson's monument of Mr. Earle, a tower and lantern, rebuilt in 1810, with the bells of St. Selsher's, Winford, presented by Cromwell; the first church here dates back to 1361, and held a favourite shrine to the patron saint of seamen. *St. Peter's*, the other parish church, is a plain building. *St. Luke's*, at the top of Bold Street, is a very handsome imitation of the Gothic style, finished in 1831, from Foster's designs, at a cost of £44,000. *St. George's*, or the corporation church, in Castle Street, which stands on the site of a castle, begun by Henry II., which came to the Stanleys and Molyneuxs, is also by Foster. *St. Michael's*, in Kent Street, has a steeple 200 feet high. That of *St Martin's*, in Scotland Road, is as high, Gothic, by Foster. *Everton Church*, on a hill, has a conspicuous tower, 340 feet above the river. It was here that Prince Rupert fixed his head-quarters in the siege of 1644. It is a great place for toffy. *St. Paul's*, in Prince's Park, is a fine modern Gothic church, built for *Dr. M'Neile*, in 1850, with a tall spire. The park covers 40 acres, with a lake, villas, &c., round it. Near this is a pretty green spot called the Dingle, opening to the river. Among the *Chapels* are, Dr. Raffles', in George Street; the original one was rather a handsome building, oval within, the seats rising towards the wall, built in 1811, but since burnt, and the present one erected on its site. *Baptist Chapel*, in Myrtle Street. *Roman Catholic Chapels* of *St. Nicholas*, in Blake Street, and *St. Anthony*, in Scotland Road. *Unitarian Chapel*, in Hope Street, with Thorwaldsen's relief. All these are in the Gothic style.

In the vicinity of the town are the *Botanic Gardens*, on a site of 11 acres; the *Cattle Market*, at Stanley; the *Sessions House*, at Kirkdale, near the *Industrial School* for 1,150 children; New Church, in a decorated English style, at *Fairfield*, with a tower of 147 feet; and Mr. Lascelles' *Observatory*, where a satellite of Neptune, and an additional one of Saturn, have been discovered. The *Dock Observatory*, under Mr. Hartnup, is a red granite tower, having a 12-foot equatorial telescope, &c.

Legh Richmond was born in St. Paul's Square, and Mrs. Hemans, in Duke Street. Gibson, one of the greatest living sculptors, though not a native, is best known here by some of his choicest productions. Mr. R. Yates has his *Cupid and Butterfly;* Mrs. Sandbach, his *Greek Hunter and Aurora;* Mr. Elmes, his *Sappho.*

Within a few miles of Liverpool are the following: *Bootle. Waterloo,* and *Southport,* bathing-places on the coast of the Irish Sea. *Ince Hall,* seat of C. Blundell, Esq.; here is a gallery of rare marbles, containing a museum planned like the Pantheon, but one-third smaller. At *Ormskirk* (which is noted for its gingerbread) are the Stanley tombs. *Scarisbrick,* C. Scarisbrick, Esq.; here are pictures by J. Martin, who died in 1854. *Knowsley,* Earl of Derby, in a large park, which till lately contained a valuable museum of natural history, and menagerie (the greater portion of which was collected by that indefatigable, scientific, and learned botanist, Dr. Thomas Whitfield, during a long residence at Sierra Leone, where his gratuitous medical aid to the Western Africans has deeply endeared him to all classes of natives and Europeans); part of which was bequeathed to the people of Liverpool. The Stanley portraits are here, from the first Earl, Henry VII.'s father-in-law. *Croxteth Park,* Earl of Sefton, the seat of the Molyneux family; the house is in part ancient. *Wavertree,* a pretty country village, with part of an ancient well at the pond, dated 1414. At *Childwall,* belonging to the Marquis of Salisbury, are some remains of a priory. *Allerton* was the seat of Roscoe, in his prosperous days, where he lived happy with his books, which he so feelingly laments parting with:—

> "Loved associates, chiefs of elder art!
> Teachers of wisdom, who could once beguile
> My tedious hours, and brighten every toil."

Here Gibson, then a youth, used to visit him. *Hale,* seat of J. Blackburne, Esq., was the birth place of a giant, called the *Child* of Hale, 9¼ feet in height. *Hazles,* Sir T. Birch, Bart. *Prescot* is a thriving town for pottery, watch tools, files, &c., at the west corner of the great coal field. John Kemble was born here in 1757. At *St. Helens* are large and old established plate glass works.

The Cheshire side of the Mersey is now a prosperous suburb of Liverpool, with a softer climate and more attractive scenery. BIRKENHEAD is a growing port, with a *floating dock* formed by Wallasey Pool, of 150 acres. It has two or three handsome churches, a vast square of six acres, market-house, and some fragments of a priory of the 12th century. It has also a public park, certainly not one of the largest, but, as a model, allowed to be one of the finest in England. *Bidston Hill* and lighthouse are behind; and *Stourton Quarry,* in which ripple marks have been discovered by geologists. *Rock Ferry, Bromborough,* and *Eastham,* up the river, are charming spots. *Hooton Hall,* late the seat of Sir T. M. Stanley, a sporting baronet, belongs to J. Naylor, Esq. This part of Cheshire is called the Wirrall.

Hoylake.—This place is approached from Birkenhead by omnibus; it is a quiet watering place at the mouth of the Dee.

New Brighton.—Hotel, Victoria, first class; distance from Liverpool, by steamer, 6 miles; or from Birkenhead, by hired conveyance, 5 miles. It is a very pleasant watering place on the Cheshire side of the Mersey, and derives its chief interest from the beautiful panorama which the shipping on the river constantly affords. Excursions may be made to Leasowe Castle, Birkenhead Park, Eastham, &c.

The facility and cheapness of steam transit, either by rail or boat, gives the tourist an excellent opportunity of making Liverpool the starting point to some delightful spots on the Welsh coast. During the summer months there is steam communication between Menai Bridge, Bangor, Beaumaris, and Liverpool, every Monday, Wednesday, and Friday mornings at 10 o'clock; returning from Liverpool on the alternate days, at 11 morn. The passage is accomplished in about five hours.

Another route for those who like to enjoy the country by occasionally pedestrianising, is to take the packet from Liverpool to Rhyl, or Mostyn, North Wales, and thence continue the journey on foot, or the line of railway from Chester to Holyhead, which affords the same facilities for reaching picturesque stations.

ISLE OF MAN.

THIS island, in the midst of the Irish sea, may be easily reached from the three kingdoms by a few hours' steam—as it is only 70 English miles from Liverpool, 50 from Fleetwood, 42 from Holyhead, 65 from Dublin, and 60 from Belfast. Length 32 miles, average breadth, 10; coast line about 110, with a low sandy shore round Point of Ayre, at the north end; but in other parts, especially near the Calf of Man, at the opposite end, the slaty or sandstone cliffs are 100 to 300 and 400 feet high. It contains above 150,000 acres, of which at least one-fifth is hill and bog. Population 52,400, in 1851. A back-bone of rugged slaty hills runs through the island, the highest being Snafell or Snafield, which is 2,004 feet above the sea. It is easily ascended from Douglas or Ramsey, the rise being gradual all the way, with a broken rock here and there. The north and south Barrule are 1,840 feet and 1,545 feet respectively. Another point between is 1,745 feet; its Gaelic name is Bein-y-phoh, which carries a dignified sound with it, but it is commonly called Penny-pot. Dark masses of slate are patched over with brown heath, like a beggar's tattered coat, resembling the Welsh hills in this respect, as well as in geographical construction. As Justice Shallow says, "it is all barren, barren, barren; marry, good air"—which blows on the hills all day long. These healthy breezes, with the short springy turf, reconcile the pedestrian to the wild desolate character of the scenery, only enlivened by a few small sheep, and occasionally the skulking sheepstealer. A visit to this Island will enable the tourist to fully appreciate the beautiful scenes so powerfully described by Sir Walter Scott in "Peveril of the Peak." The view from the summit of the mountains embraces the island and the sea in which it is set, as far as the shores of England,

Wales, Scotland, and Ireland, if the air is sufficiently clear. The steps in front of the West Portico of St. Paul's Cathedral, London, are of black marble procured from this Island. Strangers before becoming residents should make themselves well acquainted with the Manx laws, they being totally unlike those of England, Ireland, Wales, or Scotland. Arrests for debt can be made *even* for a shilling claim on this Island, and execution follows instanter.

Douglas is the most lively place in the island, and by far the largest, having a population of 10,000, or nearly one-fifth of the whole; living is tolerably cheap here, and lodgings moderate, excellent board and lodging being had for £30 per annum. Ponies and jaunting cars may be hired for 8s. a day. The Island arms consists of *three* legs joined together, booted and spurred, with the motto—*Quocunque jeceris, stabit*, or "However you throw it it stands:" referring probably to its position with regard to the three kingdoms. The roads are good, but there are no roadside inns worth the name; the ale is wretched stuff, and it is the safest plan to take provisions with you on an excursion Supposing Douglas to be your head quarters, a trip round the island, and another across it, to Peel, will embrace almost everything worth seeing. Rare shells, cornelians, fish, and seaweed are picked up along the shore.

DOUGLAS.

HOTELS.—Castle Mona; Fort Anne; Royal.

STEAM PACKETS to and from Liverpool, Whitehaven. and Dublin. See *Bradshaw's Railway Guide.*

A pleasant bathing and fishing port, in front of a fine bay, which it has been proposed to convert into a harbour of refuge. The best view is from the Castle Mona Hotel, (*Mona* is the Latin name for man) which was the seat of the Duke of Atholl, whose rights over the island (through the Stanleys) were finally purchased by government in 1829 for nearly half a million. Prior to this, its chief prosperity arose out of the smuggling business. There is a landing pier 530 feet long, also 4 churches and 6 chapels, in some of which the service is performed in Manx; news rooms, &c. One of the best buildings is the Odd Fellows' Hall. The Duf-glas or Blackwater runs through the town to the bay from the mountains behind.

From Douglas the distances are as follow :—

FIRST ROUTE.

	Miles.		Miles.
Douglas to Kirk Onchan	3	Douglas to Ramsey...	17
,, Laxey......	8	,, Kirk Bride	24
,, Ballaglass.	13	,, Ayre Point	27

SECOND ROUTE.

Ramsey to Sulby......	4	Ramsey to Peel	24
Kirk Ballaugh	8	,, South Barrule	28
Bishop's Court	10	,, Ballasalla.....	32
Kirk Michael.	12	,, Castletown ...	35
Tynwald Hill.	21		

THIRD ROUTE.

Douglas to Nunnery	1	Douglas to Tynwld Hill	9
,, Kirk Marown	6	,, Peel........	13

FOURTH ROUTE.

Douglas to Kirk Stanton	6	Douglas to Port le	
,, Ballasalla...	8	,, Murray	16
,, Castletown.	10	,, Calf of Man..	21

DOUGLAS to POINT OF AYRE.

The road is along the bay, past Castle Mona. At *Kirk Onchan* is a modern parish church, and the seat of Deemster (Judge) Heywood. Here is a very fine Nursery Garden, tastefully laid out, and well worth a visit. All the parishes are styled Kirk in the Isle of Man; there are 17, divided into six "sheadings," to each of which there is a coroner and his "lockman" or deputy. Justice is administered by two magistrates or deemsters (doomsters).

LAXEY.

HOTEL.—Commercial.

Beyond *Kirk Lonan*, is on a stream which passes paper and bleach works, and mines of lead, copper. and slate. Good trout fishing and oysters. *Clover Stones* Druid circle is near. *Snafell*, 6 miles west.

BALLAGLASS.

Balla, as in Irish names, means a Norman town.

Kirk Manghold, 3 miles to the right, has lead mines. various Scandinavian remains, a pillar with runic characters, and a carved cross. From the hill overlooking the church there is a fine view of Ramsey and its bay. Here Prince Albert stood to view it, in 1846, and a small pillar marks the spot.

RAMSEY.

HOTELS.—Mitre, Albert.

A pleasant little port at the mouth of the Sulby, on a wide bay, across which stretches the Bahama sand. One of its churches is in ruins. The Deemster of the north division of the island has a court here. Hence to the Point of Ayre, and round to Kirk Bride and Kirk Andreas is a wide flat.

Ramsey to Peel and Castletown, past *Kirk Clorist Lezavre* (under the north Barrule), and the seat of Deemster Christian, a descendant of the traitor of that name, at *Milntown;* to *Sulby* on that stream which comes down from *Snafell.* It has good trout fishing, and a waterfall, in a pretty glen near the village. At *Kirk Andreas*, to the north, are barrows (burial places of some chief), and a runic cross.

Kirk Ballaugh is in a low marshy spot where the bones of an immense elk (now at Edinburgh) have been found. About 5 miles north-west is *Kirk Jurby*, near Jurby Point, whence there is a vast prospect of the sea and the three kingdoms.

Bishop's Court, under a hill, is the s at of the Bishop of Sodor and Man (Lord Auckland); the oldest part is a tower of the thirteenth century, the rest having been modernised by Bishop Wilson and his successors. Formerly this island was but part of a diocese, which took in also the western islands of Scotland, then called the *Sodoreys* or south islands (as distinguished from the Orkneys, &c.), whence the present designation.

In *Kirk Michael*, which is the bishop's church, is a monument to the excellent Bishop Wilson, with the words, "Let this island speak the rest." He held the diocese 56 years, and among other benefits he procured an act of settlement abolishing vassalage, began the translation of the Bible in Manx, and established parish schools and libraries. Bishop Barrow (uncle of Isaac Hyldersley), who completed the Manx Bible, was a man of the same stamp. Two very old runic pillars with unintelligible characters are to be seen. Passing the old chapel of *Kiels*, near *Kirk German*, you reach

Tynwald Hill, where the roads cross. It is an artificial hillock, a few feet high, ascended by steps, whence the laws passed by the estates are made public every 5th July. The estates of the island consist of an Upper House of 10, including the governor, bishop, deemsters, &c., and a Lower House or House of Keys, composed of 24 freeholders elected for life. They meet at Castletown. Three miles west of this is

PEEL.

HOTEL.—The Castle.

One of the inland towns, at the mouth of a stream near Contrary Head Beacon. There is a *apeel* or castle here on a rock joined to the mainland, formerly a large and strong building, enclosing part of an old church, a moot hill 50 feet high (where the gallows was fixed), and remains of *St. German's* cathedral, built in the thirteenth century. According to some this little rock or island was called *Sodor*, and bearing (it is said) the joint name of *Sodor and Man*. Dame Eleanor, wife of Duke Humphrey, was imprisoned in the castle for life, for conspiring against Richard II. The people (who are excessively superstitious) say that the Moddey Doo or Black Dog, referred to by Scott in *Peveril of the Peak* still haunts this castle. There are grammar and mathematical schools in the town. The inhabitants subsist by fishing. *Kirk Patrick*, a little south of Peel, is on the road to Glenmoij (a pretty spot with a waterfall) and *Dalby Point*, near which are mines of lead and slate.

From Tynwald Hill, the road passes the Peel river, to another fall, and the mines of *South Barrule*, which mountain is 1,545 feet high. Thence before reaching Ballasalla you come to

Rushen Abbey, the seat of Deemster Moore, including some remains of a Cistercian cell, first founded by King Mac Marus, and built by the abbots of Furness in the 12th century. It stands in the hollow of a stream which runs down to Castletown: descending this you pass an old Gothic bridge and *Ballasaila*, a small village, near which is the seat of Sir G. Drinkwater. Leaving *Kirk Arbory*, its Druid circles, and barrows, and *Kirk Malew*, where the celebrated infamous Christian is buried, you come to

CASTLETOWN.

HOTEL.—The George.

This is the little capital of the island, the seat of the Governor and House of Keys, situated on a bay which is divided from Derby Haven by Longness peninsula. Castle Rushen, from which it takes its name, was built as far back as 945 by Guttred the Dane, son of Orry, King of Norway, who took possession of Man, about the time when the Danes founded so many other settlements along the coasts of England and Ireland. It is said to resemble Elsinore Castle (the scene of Hamlet); one tower is 80 feet high. In this castle the "Kings of Man" kept their little court, among whom was the Earl of Derby, who was taken (1651) and beheaded at Bolton, by the parliament party, while his high-minded wife Charlotte de Tremouaille, defended the castle against the forces sent by Fairfax, till she was betrayed by the Lieutenant Governor, Christian; for which he was summarily shot after the restoration (1663). The plot of "Peveril of the Peak" turns upon this catastrophe. In her room in the castle, which is shown to visitors, there is a curious wooden clock in good repair. It is now used as a prison for debtors, convicts, and lunatics, the arrangements of which demand the attention of the Manx legislature. If the various cases of imprisonment of debtors and lunatics who have been confined in this place were publicly known, most curious, romantic, and heart-rending scenes would be brought to light, which would at once render the assimilation of the Manx laws with those of the United Kingdom imperatively necessary. Here are the barracks, deemster's court, prison, &c.; on the parade is a memorial to Governor Smelt, who was the means of founding *King William's College*, in 1830; and so ably presided over for many years by Principal Dr. Phillips, son of the late celebrated bookseller, Sir Richard Phillips. Here the Rev. James Skinner, the Puseyite curate of St. Barnabas, Pimlico, was also a master; and Delamotte and Hablot Browne, the talented artists, Professors of Drawing, in 1839. A handsome Gothic pile, 210 feet long, and at which Manxmen are ordained for the church.

DOUGLAS to PEEL.

By this road, you pass the *Nunnery*, the seat of General Goldie, so called from a ruined priory, founded by St. Bridget in the sixth century, to which Ethelbert's daughter Matilda retired. The grounds are charmingly laid out.

Our road ascending Douglas, past *Kirk Braddan* (one of the prettiest churches in the island) and its runic pillar; and some paper mills. *Kirk Marrown* is under Greeba mountain, 1,480 feet high, on the sides of which are various small "kiels" or chapels, especially the remains of *St. Trinian's*, which Manx tradition asserts was destroyed by the buggane (or bogey!) In *Glendarragh*, there is a druid circle, about 40 feet diameter. Tynwald Hill and Peel are beyond.

DOUGLAS to CALF OF MAN.

Past the Nunnery, &c., to

Kirk Santon, or *Kirk St. Ann*, near a Druid circle. Thence to Ballasalla, Kirk Malew, and Castletown, and round Balvash bay, past Kirk Christ, Rushen, (near Breda copper mine) to

Port-le-Murry, *i. e.*, Maryport, a little fishing place, with lime quarries in the cliffs, which at Spanish Head are 300 feet high, and broken into deep chasms. Here, it is said, one of the ships of the Spanish Armada was wrecked.

VIEWS IN THE ISLE OF MAN.

The south-west extremity of the island is bounded by barren dark slate cliffs sloping to the water, and separated by a narrow but angry channel from the *Calf of Man*, which is a tall green looking rock, 2 miles long, swarming with rabbits and solan geese. Some attempts have been made by the owner (C. Carey, Esq.) to introduce the turnip culture. There are two lights on it, 305 and 396 feet high. At the north corner of it is a little rock called the Kitterland. Boats may be had to cross the channel when the sea is moderate. A passage ship was wrecked near this part in 1853. Cæsar calls this island Mona, a name also applied to Anglesey. The Manx name is *Mannin*, which some explain to mean "Stone Island"—or "Meadhon-in-(Middle Island)."

London and North Western continued.
Manchester to Ashton.

The intermediate stations are MILES PLATTING, PARK (the station for Phillip's Park), CLAYTON BRIDGE, and DROYLSDEN.

ASHTON-UNDER-LYNE.

A telegraph station.
HOTEL.—Commercial.
MARKET DAYS.—Tuesday and Saturday.
FAIRS.—March 23rd, April 29th, July 25th, November 21st.

BANKERS.—Hyde and Glossop Bank; Branch of Saddleworth Banking Co.

This is a busy cotton town and borough, with a population of 29,791, who return one member, in South Lancashire, 6 miles east of Manchester, on the river Tame, which branches out of the Mersey. "Under Line," probably refers to the natural line of division, made by the hills in this quarter. Some of the oldest houses are at Charlestown and Boston,—two places which an American will rightly guess were built during the American war. Here are upwards of ninety cotton mills. Ashton formerly gave name to the Assheton family, now represented by the Earl of Stamford, who is lord of this valuable manor—a bare worthless tract till the cotton trade was introduced in 1769. The parish church is of Henry VI.'s time. Like most feudal lords, they had the power of life and death over their serfs, and asserted it by keeping a gallows, a meadow, adjoining the residence of the ancient lords, where the convicts were buried, being still known as the "gallows meadow." The remembrance of this is kept up by an annual custom of "riding the black lad," on Easter Monday, when the effigy of a knight, in black armour is araded through the streets. to the great diversion of the thousands of persons who come from a distance to witness the ceremony.

Dukinfield, formerly the seat of an old family of that name, is across the Tame, on the Cheshire side. Here also cotton, with all its peaceful advantages, is in the ascendant.

STOCKPORT BRANCH.
Ashton to Stockport.

GUIDE BRIDGE station.

DENTON.

POPULATION 3,146.
Telegraph station at Stockport, 3½ miles.
MONEY ORDER OFFICE, at Hyde, 1½ mile.

Here are several hat manufactories. In the vicinity is *Denton Hall*, the old seat of the Hollands, and *Hyde Hall*, formerly the seat of the Hydes, now both armhouses.

Passing REDDISH and HEATON NORRIS stations, we arrive at

Stockport, see page 37.

London and North Western continued.
STALYBRIDGE (Cheshire).

A telegraph station.
HOTEL.—White Hart.

STALYBRIDGE contains 20,760 inhabitants, and is part in Lancashire, part in Cheshire—the two being joined by an old bridge. Formerly the Staveleighs were seated here. The river, along with the rail and canal, now enter the defile, the rugged limestone ridge, forming the backbone of England, *Wild Hill* being 1,300 feet high; and the scenery becomes still more wild and bold as you ascend towards Saddleworth, in Yorkshire.

MOSSLEY (Lancashire).—This is a telegraph station; and close at hand are the Pillar on Hartshead Pike, from which a beautiful view of the country may be obtained; and Bucton Castle, an old British camp.

GREENFIELD (Yorkshire).—Near at hand is Fairy Hole, a Druidical remain.

There is a short branch hence to Oldham, passing through the unimportant stations of GROTTON and LEES, but forming a valuable connection between the London and North Western and Lancashire and Yorkshire sections. After a run of about fifteen minutes our arrival is announced at

Oldham, described Sec. IV.

DELPH station.

SADDLEWORTH.

Distance from station, ¾ mile.
Telegraph station at Ashton, 8¾ miles.
HOTEL.—Commercial.
MONEY ORDER OFFICE at Ashton-under-Lyne, 5 miles.

This place, situated in the centre of a large woollen district, has a population of 17,799, some of whom are stockingers.

Passing DIGGLE station (where the Marsden tunnel, 3½ miles long, is entered), we then proceed to

MARSDEN.

This is a first-class station, and contains, according to the census of 1851, a population of 2,665, who are principally engaged in woollen mills. At this place are the entrances to the railway and canal tunnels, which run parallel with each other, and are the longest in the world. A large and handsome National School has been erected, which from its position forms a striking object from the railway.

SLAITHWAITE.

Telegraph station at Huddersfield, 4¾ miles.

Here is an excellent mineral spring, similar to that at Harrogate, and a population of 2,852, engaged in the cotton and woollen trades.

GOLCAR.—A town with a population of 4,212, employed in the cloth trade.

LONGWOOD, trade, woollen manufacture. Large reservoirs.

HUDDERSFIELD.

A telegraph station.

HOTELS.—George, Imperial, Rose and Crown, Railway Refreshment Room.

MARKET DAY.—Tuesday.

FAIRS.—March 31st, May 14th, and October 1st.

BANKERS.—Branch of Yorkshire Banking Co.; Halifax and Huddersfield Union Bank; Huddersfield Banking Co.; West Riding Union.

A parliamentary borough, and seat of the woollen trade, among hills, on a hill over the Colne, in the West Riding of Yorkshire, population 30,880; who return one member. Woollens, fancy valentias, shawls, &c., are the staple articles of manufacture, besides corduroys, and cotton, though but little of the last. One short canal, called "The Ramsden," after the name of the lords of the manor who cut it, runs to the river Calder; and another strikes through the moors towards Staleybridge, passing a tunnel 3½ miles long, and being 656 feet above the sea in the highest part. The railway, which follows the same direction, has an equal rise and fall, with a tunnel quite as long. Among the edifices, which are of stone, are *St. Peter's Church*, rebuilt in 1836; *Trinity Church*, *St. John's Church*, built by Sir John Ramsden, at the cost of £12,000, and *St. Paul's Church*, the Arcade and the Railway Station, also a *College*, or proprietary school, chiefly attended by dissenters; large *Wesleyan Chapel*; the Philosophical Hall; a large handsome *Infirmary*, built in 1830, for £10,000; and *Water Works*, supplied rom Longwood, 3 miles distant. There are but a dozen bakers here, the custom being for the inhabitants to bake their own bread.

Within a few miles are *Almondbury Castle*, on the site of the ancient *Campodunum*; *Woodsome Lees*, seat of the Earl of Dartmouth, near Farnley-Tyas, which belongs to the family; *Fixby Hall*, the residence of Captain Edwards; *Kirklees Hall*, Sir G. Armitage, Bart. on the site of the nunnery where that mythical hero Robin Hood was bled to death by the nun, according to the current story. Here may still be seen the grave, with the inscription of his death and burial.

What the rugged character of the moorlands is may be well seen at Saddleworth, a cotton town of 17,799 inhabitants. The town, at the foot of the rocks called *Pots and Pans*, is a little island of stone houses, in the hollow of some hills, which rise in an amphitheatre about them, and consists of two straggling streets of shops and cottages—the ground so abrupt and irregular, that the back door of one house, will be often on a level with the top storey of another. The high road, railway, canal, and river all run side by side, within a few hundred yards of each other, in a deep valley surrounded by a labyrinth of hills; "the ridges forming a combination of perspective, which seem more like clouds than things of solid land." The country is thinly peopled; and every turn of the road shuts out the world here and there. Magnificent cotton mills, with the villas of their proprietors, are seen in all directions, the streams making a splendid water power, and clusters of grey stone cottages for the hands are scattered about, without breaking the loneliness and silence which prevail. (See "The great Saddleworth exhibition" in *Household Words*.) "The hills should be traversed when the heather is in full bloom."

Passing BRADLEY (close to which is *Bradley Park*), HEATON LODGE, and MIRFIELD stations, we arrive at

DEWSBURY.

A telegraph station.

HOTEL.—Royal.

MARKET DAY.—Wednesday.

FAIRS.—Wednesday before old May Day; Michaelmas day, and October 6th.

BANKERS.—Branch of Huddersfield Banking Co.; Branch of the West Riding Union Banking Co.

This place has a population of 5,033, employed in the blanket, carpet, broad cloth, and cotton trades. Here Paulinus, the first Bishop of York, preached in the seventh century, and converted many. At All Saints' Church, there is a cross to his memory.

The next station, BATLEY (which has extensive woollen and carpet manufactures, and a later English church, with some fine monuments), forms the junction of the branch to

BIRSTAL (Branch).

Telegraph station at Dewsbury, 3 miles.

HOTEL.—Coach and Horses.

The people here are principally employed in the woollen and mining trades. Close at hand is *Old Howley Hall*, in ruins.

MORLEY.

Telegraph station at Leeds, 5 miles.

HOTEL.—Royal.

Here are the ruins of *St. Mary's Chapel*, where the Presbyterians congregated during the civil war, in the time of Charles I., and a population of 4,821, engaged as weavers in the woollen trade.

CHURWELL.—In tbe vicinity are *Middleton Lodge*, and *Beeston*, with its old Church and coal mines, which have been used since the time of Charles II.

WORTLEY.

Telegraph station at Leeds, 1½ mile.

HOTELS.—New, and Gun.

Almost the entire population of this place, 7,896 souls, are engaged in the woollen trade.

Leeds, see Section IV.

LANCASHIRE AND YORKSHIRE.

Manchester, Bolton, and Liverpool.

SALFORD (Oldfield Road).

Telegraph station at Manchester.

MARKET DAYS.—Saturday and Wednesday (cattle).
FAIRS.—Whit Monday, and November 17th.

This is a borough town, joining Manchester, with a population of 85,108, who return one member. Its principal buildings are *St. John's* cruciform Roman Cathedral, by Weightman, 200 feet by 130, with a spire 240 feet; the west front is a fac-simile of Howden Church, York. The Town Hall, Market Place, by Goodwin, House of Correction, Barracks, Schools, Trinity Church, built in 1634, Library, Lying-in Hospital, Dorcas Society, print works and factories. In the vicinity is Kersall Moor; here the troops were encamped in 1848. Byrom the poet and stenographer was a native of *Kersall Cell*, the seat of Miss Atherton.

PENDLETON.

This is a populous place, and contains 14,224 inhabitants, employed in the cotton trade.

Passing CLIFTON (the Junction of the Line to Bury, &c.), DIXON FOLD, STONECLOUGH, HALSHAW MOOR, and MOSES GATE, we arrive at

BOLTON-LE-MOORS.

A telegraph station.

HOTEL.—Swan.

MARKET DAYS.—Monday and Saturday.

FAIRS.—Jan. 4th, July 30th and 31st, Oct. 13th and 14th, cattle; and every other Monday.

BANKERS.—Bank of Bolton; Hardcastle, Cross, and Company.

A large manufacturing town, on the moors, where five or six railways meet Population, 61,171, who send two members to parliament Cotton velvets and muslins were first manufactured here about 1760-80, on a large scale, by the new machinery of Arkwright, who resided here when a barber; and Crompton, who lived at *Hall-in-the-Wood*, an old timbered house, (when a weaver, and there invented the mule). It was the Starkies' old seat, and still exists. Long before the cotton trade took root, Bolton was a great place for cloth and fustians, the making of which was introduced by the Flemings in 1337. There are now 60 cotton mills, many of them very large, as are also the bleach and dye-works, the whole employing about 13,000 hands. Muslins, counterpanes, cambrics, dimity, ginghams, &c., are the chief productions. Above 4,000 hands are engaged in the iron foundries and engine works. Much coal is quarried, and a little paper made.

Among the buildings, are the old *Parish Church*, *Town Hall*, Free Library, Public Baths, Infirmary, Church Institute for elementary education, Market Hall, the finest in England. opened in Dec. 1855, cost about £80,000; large *Waterworks* supplied by reservoirs 4 miles distant, Exchange, Theatre, Foundries, Mechanics' Institute, Lever's Grammar School, where the lexicographer Ainsworth was both pupil and master. At Dobson's machine works is an immense brick chimney, 368 feet high. At one time the manor belonged to the Derby family, and it was here that the loyal seventh Earl was brought to be beheaded in 1651, after his defeat at Wigan Lane. His Countess, who defended Lathom House so heroically against the roundheads, a few years before, was the Charlotte de Tremouaille who figures in "Peveril of the Peak." *Smithills Hall* contains a chapel, with stained window and curious old carvings, and is the seat of the Ainsworths, near their bleach-works at Halliwell.

Two miles distant is Eagley, with Messrs. Chadwick's sewing thread and smallware mills, most admirably arranged in every respect; adjacent is a school, with pleasure grounds and excellent library containing the daily papers for the use of the work-people, whose happiness and comfort have been most carefully attended to by those spirited and philanthropic gentlemen.

CLITHEROE BRANCH.

Passing THE OAKS Station (near which is Bradshaw), BROMLEY CROSS, CHAPEL TOWN, ENTWISLE, and SOUGH stations, we reach

OVER DARWEN.

A telegraph station.

MONEY ORDER OFFICE at Blackburn, 2½ miles.

This place contains a population of 7,020, employed in the cotton manufacture; close at hand are the paper mills of Messrs. Potter. Here the Fourdrinier machine is used, and 400 miles of paper (weighing 40 tons) per day produced.

LOWER DARWEN.—This place has a population of 3,521, engaged in the paper factories.

Blackburn, see Section IV.

DAISY FIELD station.

RIBCHESTER.

POPULATION, 1,650.

Distance from station, 2 miles.

A telegraph station.

MONEY ORDER OFFICE at Blackburn, 5 miles.

"This is the Roman *Colcium*, where the 20th legion were stationed, and a bronze helmet, mask, pateræ, inscriptions, coins, anchors, and a vessel's hull, were found in 1796, so that the sea must have come up to this place in ancient times. Near the camp is *St. Wilfred's* Church, which had formerly two chantreys."—Sharp's *British Gazetteer*.

Passing LANGHO station, on the left of which, about 2 miles distant, is the curious old timbered mansion of Henry II.'s time, *Salesbury Hall*, we reach

WHALLEY.

A telegraph station.

HOTEL.—Swan.

This town, the parish of which is one of the largest in the kingdom, contains 108,000 acres, and has a population of 945, engaged in the cotton trade. It contains *All Saints* Church, which the Earl of Derby occupied in 1643. It was built in 1200, and has old carved pews, stalls, and in the churchyard are three pillar crosses. "Here are remains of a Cistercian Abbey, consisting of the moated site, two gables, part of the choir, cloisters, chapter house, dormitory, kitchen (with two great fire-places), oratory and abbot's house, which the Asshetons made their seat."—Sharp's *British Gazetteer.* The last Abbot, Paslew, was hung in 1539, on a charge of rebellion.

CLITHEROE.

A telegraph station.
HOTEL.—Swan.
MARKET DAY.—Tuesday.

FAIRS. — March 5th and 24th, April 4th, Friday and Saturday after Sept. 29th, Dec. 6th and 7th.

BANKERS.—Alcocks, Birbecks, & Company.

This is a market town, with a population of 14,480, engaged in the cotton trade, and who return one member. It contains the ruins of the De Lacy's Castle, built in Henry II.'s time; *Grammar School*, founded in 1554, having a moot hall, with a spire 60 feet high. *St. Michael's* Church, built on the site of an old one, of which Webster, the astrologer, was curate, and where he was buried. Fine views can be obtained of the adjacent country from the castle keep, and cairns on Pendle Hill.

CHATBURN, a small village on the river Ribble.

BOLTON AND KENYON.

Passing DAUBHILL, CHECKERBENT (near which is *Hulton Park*, the seat of W. Hulton, Esq.), and ATHERTON, we arrive at

LEIGH.

Telegraph station at Newton, 5 miles

HOTEL —White Horse.

MARKET DAY.—Saturday.

FAIRS.—April 5th and 24th; Dec 7th and 8th.

A market town, with a population of 5,206, who are employed in the cambric, muslin, and fustian trades. The pasture land is good, and coal and lime-stone abound in the neighbourhood. Cheese is made here. Hight, the *original* inventor of the spinning jenny and water frame, which Ark-wright only improved, was a native.

We then pass BRADSHAW LEACH, and arrive at KENYON, the junction of the lines to Liver-pool (page 41) and Manchester.

Bolton to Wigan and Liverpool.

LOSTOCK JUNCTION.

WESTHOUGHTON.

This place has a population of 4,547, who are employed in the muslin trade. In 1812, a dreadful Luddite riot took place, at which a large quantity of machinery was destroyed by the mob.

HINDLEY.

Distance from station, ½ mile.

A telegraph station.

This place has a mining population of 5,285. "Here is, or was, a burning well of cold water, through which rose an inflammable gas, produced by the decomposition of sulphate of iron."—Sharp's *British Gazetteer.* In the vicinity are *Hindley Hall*, Right Hon. T. Leigh; and *Bradshawe Hall*, T. Bradshawe, Esq.

Wigan.—See page 34.

Wigan to Southport.

Proceeding on our journey we notice the stations of GATHURST, APPLEY BRIDGE, NEWBURGH, and BURSCOUGH BRIDGE, the point of junction with the line from Liverpool to Preston. Passing NEW LANE and BESCAR stations, we presently arrive at

SOUTHPORT.

POPULATION, 4,765.
A telegraph station.
HOTELS.—Bold Arms, Victoria, Royal.
BANKERS.—Robt. Lawe and Co.

SOUTHPORT, some time ago, from its situation and the salubrity of its atmosphere, christened the Montpellier of England, is now a favourite and fashionable watering-place, with accommodation capable of entertaining many thousands of visitors. It is situate on the north-west coast of Lancashire. Its buildings are architecturally elegant, and the broad and beautiful streets (particularly Lord Street, which is more than a mile long) have made it universally admired. It has numerous public buildings, including an elegant Town Hall, the Victoria Baths, and Strangers' Charity. In the last named institution last year 1,100 of our poor fellow-creatures had their sufferings alleviated or removed. Sand hills, resembling small tumuli, surround the town, and the environs are replete with localities for pleasant excursions. A broad expanse of shore affords ample space for equestrian and pedestrian exercise, whilst the bathing is safe and convenient.

Lancashire and Yorkshire continued.

PEMBERTON.—*Winstanley Hall*, M. Bankes, Esq.

ORREL.—In the vicinity are *Orrel Lodge*, seat of J. Horrocks, Esq.; *Upholland*, where are the remains of a priory, of which the church was a part.

Passing PIMBO LANE station, close to which is a tunnel 1,020 yards long, and on the right, Billinge Hill, 633 feet high, with a beacon at top from which views may be obtained of Yorkshire and Cheshire, and Bispham Hill, we reach

RAINFORD (Junction for St. Helens).

POPULATION, 2,333.
Distance from station, 1 mile.
HOTEL.—Railway.

This place is situated in what was once a marshy spot, but now well drained. Its principal manufactures are tobacco pipes and crucibles. Scythe stones abound here.

KIRBY (Walton-on-the-Hill).

Telegraph station at Rainford.

This place is situated close to Kirby Moss. "Kirby" signifies Church Town. In the vicinity is *Knowsley Park*, the seat of the Earl of Derby. There is a fine oval race-course of 1½ mile, with large stands, &c., built in 1698.

FAZAKERLEY, PRESTON ROAD, and BOOTLE LANE stations.

LIVERPOOL.

The entrance to Liverpool may be said to commence at the Walton tunnel. Immediately after leaving the tunnel the line crosses the Leeds and Liverpool Canal by a wooden bowstring bridge of a novel and peculiar construction. A short embankment succeeds, followed by a series of arches and bridges, by which the line is carried into the town.

From Edmund Street to Tithebarn Street, the line is continued by means of arches to the station, the interior of which presents ample accommodation for the traffic of the various lines. Each company has a separate departure station, but the arrival station is for their use in common. The passenger station at Tithebarn Street is covered in by two iron roofs, one of which is of great magnitude, being 136 feet span, without any intermediate supports. The area covered by this single roof alone, is 83,457 square feet. This roof is entirely of iron. It is lighted by four lines of skylights, and is ventilated by galvanised wrought iron courses.

The booking offices and waiting rooms are in a handsome stone building, in the Italian style of architecture, having a frontage to Tithebarn Street, and at right angles to this are two wings, one story high, the one having a frontage to Key Street, and the other to Bixteth Street. In these are contained two distinct sets of waiting and refreshment rooms, one for either company.

The front to Tithebarn Street consists of a two story building, containing a booking office for each company, and over these the committee rooms and other offices.

The station is approached from Tithebarn Street by two large ornamental iron gates, having massive stone piers. From these an incline road brings carriages to the level of the platform, while the approach for foot-passengers is up a flight of stone steps.

One of the immediate effects of the Liverpool and Manchester Railway was to make the latter town a great centre, from which the supply of the manufacturing towns diverged. Many of these places were felt to be of too great importance to rely upon a single and indirect market, and hence it was resolved to connect them with the Liverpool seaport, on which they so much depended.

Amongst the places so circumstanced were Wigan, Bolton, and Bury; to connect which with Liverpool, the Liverpool, Bolton, and Bury Railway Co. was formed. Subsequently events changed and extended the design, and the Lancashire and Yorkshire, and the East Lancashire Railways became jointly interested in the speculation as a great artery for the traffic. The companies found it essential to make Liverpool a grand terminus; and, by their united efforts, the people of Liverpool possess a direct communication with the whole of the important districts of Yorkshire and Lancashire. The Lancashire and Yorkshire carries the traffic of the two Ridings; together with a considerable portion of that for the eastern districts of North and South Lancashire; and the Liverpool and Southport, a part of the same system, opens out the traffic of Bootle and Waterloo.

For description of the town of **Liverpool** see page 42.

Liverpool to Crosby and Southport.

Passing SANDHILLS and MILLER'S BRIDGE stations, we reach

BOOTLE VILLAGE.

POPULATION, 4,106.
Telegraph station at Liverpool, 3 miles.

This is a small village near Liverpool; a watering place, much frequented by the inhabitants of Liverpool. It contains a pretty church, assembly-rooms, and bathing establishments.

MARSH LANE and SEAFORTH, with its pretty church, and Litherland close by.

WATERLOO.

A telegraph station.
Distance from station, ¾ mile.
HOTEL.—Waterloo.
MONEY ORDER OFFICE at Liverpool, 5½ miles.

This is a small but charming watering-place, much visited. It contains a fine church, assembly-rooms, library, and bathing establishment.

CROSBY.

Distance from station, 1¾ miles.
A telegraph station.
HOTELS.—Ship, George.
MONEY ORDER OFFICE at Liverpool, 6½ miles.

This is a much-frequented watering-place, near Crosby Point, at the mouth of the Mersey. It contains 2,600 inhabitants, an excellent free grammar and girls' school. In the vicinity is *Crosby Hall*, the seat of William Blundell, Esq., whose family have held the manor for upwards of seven centuries.

HIGHTOWN.

Telegraph station at Crosby.
MONEY ORDER OFFICE at Ormskirk, 4 miles.

In the vicinity is *Ince Hall*, the seat of C. Blundell, Esq., which contains the *Pantheon*, built after that at Rome, in which are 500 pieces of sculpture, a

Minerva, Diana, Theseus, Canova's Psyche, &c. In the fine collection of paintings may be seen Raphael's Fall of Man, Teniers' Alchymist, and some beautiful landscapes by Wilson.

FORMBY AND ALTCAR.

A telegraph station.
MONEY ORDER OFFICE at Ormskirk, 4 miles.

This bathing-place was once a market-town. It is situated near Formby Point, in the Irish Sea, and outside the bank there is a floating light. It is much frequented by the Lancastrians.

Passing FRESHFIELD, AINSDALE, and BIRKDALE PARK stations, we arrive at

Southport.—See page 50.

Bolton to Preston.

Passing LOSTOCK JUNCTION, LOSTOCK LANE, BLACKROD, with its sulphur spring, and ADLINGTON stations, we arrive at

CHORLEY.

A telegraph station.
HOTEL.—Royal Oak.
MARKET DAY.—Tuesday.
FAIRS.—March 26th, May 5th, August 20th, and September 4th and 6th.

This is a market-town, with a population of 8,907, engaged in the cotton trade, and working the coal, lead, and slate mines. Here is *St Laurence's* Church, with its old monuments, *St George's*, built in the Gothic style in 1825, and an excellent *Grammar School*. In the vicinity are *Astley Hall*, Lady Highten, *Gillibrand Hall*, H. Fazakerley, Esq., and the *Bleaching Works*, which are well worth a visit.

Passing close to *Euxton Hall*, the seat of W. Anderton, Esq., *Shaw Hall*, and *Cuerden Park*, we reach EUXTON, LEYLAND, and FARINGTON stations.

Preston.—See page 35.

Preston to Lytham, Blackpool & Fleetwood.

KIRKHAM.

A telegraph station.
HOTEL.—Railway.
MARKET DAY.—Tuesday.
FAIRS.—Feb. 4th and 5th, April 29th and Oct. 18th.

This is a small market-town, with a population of 2,777, employed in the cotton, linen, sacking, and sail-cloth manufactures. There are remains of an old Norman church. The present edifice was built in 1822. It has a good *Grammar School*. In the vicinity is *Ribby Hall*, the seat of H. Hornby, Esq.

Passing WRAY GREEN and MOSS SIDE stations, we arrive at

LYTHAM (Branch).

A telegraph station.
HOTEL.—Clifton Arms.

This is a small port and watering-place, situated the mouth of the Ribble. It has a population of 2,698, engaged in the fisheries. There is a good *Grammar School*. In the vicinity is *Lytham Hall*, the seat of T. Clifton, Esq., near to which are the ruins of a Benedictine Priory founded by Roger Fitz Roger, in Richard I.'s time.

POULTON-LE-FYLDE.

MARKET DAY.—Monday.
FAIRS.—February 6th, April 13th, and November 3rd.

This town is situated near the Wyre. It contains a fine church, with an old tower, rebuilt in 1751, and a good Grammar School.

BLACKPOOL (Branch).

A telegraph station.
HOTELS.—Rossall's; Clifton Arms; Albion; Lane End; Beach; Royal; Victoria; Brewer's.

This pretty bathing-place is situated on a range of cliffs fronting the Irish Sea. It takes its name from a pool near *Vauxhall*, the old seat of the Tildesleys, and contains a population of 2,180. This place is much frequented by visitors, and possesses an excellent Library, and sea bathing at all times of tide. The sea gains so much here that, on the Penny Stone, 3¼ miles northward, and about a quarter of a mile from the shore, there formerly stood a small inn. Fine views of the Cumberland and Welsh hills, and the Isle of Man, can be obtained from several spots about here. In the vicinity is *Rake's Hall*, the seat of D. Hornby, Esq.

FLEETWOOD.

POPULATION, 3,121.
A telegraph station.
HOTELS.—North Euston; Crown; Fleetwood Arms.
STEAMERS to Belfast, daily (Sundays excepted), at or after 7½ p.m. Fares, 12s. and 3s.
MARKET DAY.—Friday.

FLEETWOOD, at the mouth of the Wyre, built on what was formerly a rabbit warren, is a modern town and port, which had no existence before 1836 but now contains a market, custom house, gas works, quay, 600 ft., a church, four chapels, &c., with a commodious harbour, from which steamers go to Belfast and the Lakes. The Light House is of iron, screwed into the rock below the sand. In the vicinity is *Rossall*, a collegiate school for the sons of clergymen and others, with 250 pupils, and a full staff of masters

A steamer crosses Morecambe Bay, on week days, in summer, from Fleetwood to the Lakes district, at 10¼ a.m., of which the nearest point is Piel.

FURNESS RAILWAY.

Piel and Barrow to Furness Abbey.

PIEL.

STEAMERS.—To Fleetwood, the *Helvellyn*, every afternoon (Sundays excepted) during the season, on arrival of train from Coniston, Ulverston, Furness Abbey, &c.; to Morecambe, occasionally, during the season.

MONEY ORDER OFFICE at Dalton, 6 miles.

It was here that Simnel and his party landed in 1487, to assert his claim against Henry VII. It contains an old castle, which formerly belonged to the abbots of Furness.

BARROW.

A telegraph station.

MONEY ORDER OFFICE at Dalton, 4 miles.

Close by Barrow Island, one mile in length, and beyond Walney Island, eight miles long, which is a mossy, flat sand bank, are the remains of a forest. On Haw Point there is a fixed revolving light, erected in 1790, and which can be seen at a distance of 13 miles.

FURNESS ABBEY.

Telegraph station at Barrow.

MONEY ORDER OFFICE at Dalton, 2 miles.

This abbey, beautifully placed in the wooded glen of Beckunsgill, or Nightshade Vale, was founded by Stephen, in 1127. The remains are part of a Norman church, chapter-house, hall, cloisters, school-gate, lodge, mills, granaries, watch-tower, with a most extensive and superb view of the adjacent country. Iron is now forged in this vicinity, where the stag, wolf, and wild boar were formerly hunted. In the neighbourhood is *Gleaston Castle.*

ULVERSTON BRANCH.

Passing DALTON and LINDAL stations, we arrive at

ULVERSTON.

A telegraph station.

HOTEL.—Sun.

BANKERS.—Branch of Lancaster Banking Co. Petty and Postlewaite.

A telegraph station.

This is a session-town, with a population of 6,433, employed in the cotton, linen, rope, and hat manufactures. It contains St. Mary's Church, rebuilt in 1804, with an old Norman door and stained windows, after Rubens and Reynolds' Holy Trinity, four chapels, theatre, assembly and news-rooms, libraries, custom house, and an iron market, the cross of which was built in 1821. In 1795, Rennie cut a level canal, large enough for ships of 400 tons. On Hoad Hill, 450 feet high, is a beacon of 100 feet, founded by the sons of Sir John Barrow, who, with Richard de Ulverstone, the monk, was a native. G. Fox lived at Swartmoor Hall, and West was a priest here.

ULVERSTON AND LANCASTER.

This important link forms an extension of the Furness line from Ulverston, passing the stations of CARK and CARTMEL, KENT'S BANK, GRANGE, ARNSIDE, and SILVERDALE, and connecting itself with CARNFORTH, a station 6½ miles north of Lancaster, on the Lancaster and Carlisle railway.

Furness continued.

Furness to Broughton.

KIRKBY (Ireleth).

Distance from station, 1¼ mile.

A telegraph station.

This place has a population of 4,000, employed in the blue slate quarries. The church contains some handsome monuments, and stained glass windows. In the vicinity is Kirkby Hall.

FOXFIELD Junction.

BROUGHTON-IN-FURNESS.

HOTELS.—Hare and Hounds; Railway.

MARKET DAY.—Friday.

FAIRS.—April 27th, August 1st, and 1st Friday in October.

This is a small market-town, situated near the top of the estuary of the Dudden, with a population of 1,297, engaged in the slate, iron, and copper mines. It contains a good *Grammar School.* In the vicinity is *Broughton Tower*, the seat of J. Sawrey, Esq., from which there is a most superb view of the adjacent country.

CONISTON BRANCH.

By means of this short line, the Lake District is rendered easy of access to the tourist on the coast of Cumberland. The line commences by a junction with the Furness at Broughton, running a distance of 8½ miles, *viâ* the stations of WOODLAND and TORVER to

CONISTON.

This little village lies about half a mile from the western margin of the lake, and immediately at the foot of the Man Mountain. The lake is six miles long, and about three-quarters of a mile broad; its depth supposed to be about 162 feet. It is fed by streams from Tilberthwaite and Yewdale, as well as those flowing from the tarns on the Man Mountain. Its fish are trout and char, and consequently attractive to the angler. The head of the lake possesses scenery of the most magnificent character, a contrast of which, with that of the lower part of the lake, has a tendency to detract largely from the pretensions of those of the latter. Lady le Fleming, of Rydal Hall, is the proprietress of the largest portion of the lake, as also of some valuable copper mines on the Old Man.

WHITEHAVEN & FURNESS JUNCTION.

Foxfield to Whitehaven.

On leaving Foxfield Junction, and crossing the Dudden by a wooden bridge, we pass GREEN ROAD, UNDER HILL, HOLBORN HILL, and SILECROFT stations, two miles from which is *Millom Park*, a fine seat, and arrive at

BOOTLE.

Distance from station, ¾ mile.

A telegraph station at Kirkby.

MARKET DAY.—Saturday.

FAIRS.—April 5th and 26th, September 24th, and August 5th.

This town, with a population of 811, engaged in the corn and provision trade, is delightfully situated in the midst of beautiful scenery, and commands fine views of Bootle Fell and Black Combe Mountains 1,919 feet high, the latter of which has remains of a nunnery and church at Seton. The old church is a fine edifice, and contains an eight-sided font, and a cross of Sir H. Askew, of Seton Hall.

Passing ESKMEALS station, at which there are remains of a Roman camp, we arrive at

RAVENGLASS.

Distance from station, ¼ mile.

Telegraph station at Whitehaven, 16½ miles.

HOTEL.—King's Arms.

MARKET DAY.—Wednesday.

FAIRS.—May 6th, June 8th, and August 5th.

This market-town and port lies on the Irish Sea, the junction of the Irt, Nile, and Esk rivers. It ontains a population of 400, engaged in the coasting trade and oyster fishery, for which it is celebrated. In the vicinity are Birkly Fell, at which are remains of the "city of Barnscar," with its walls, buildings, roads, &c, near which Roman antiquities have been found. Twelve miles distant is Wast Water, and the Fells, the principal of which, *Scafell*, is 3,160 feet high.—Sharp's *British Gazeteer*.

From Ravenglass, up the Esk, over Hard Knot to Ambleside, is about 20 miles.

Passing DRIGG, and SEASCALE (for Gosforth), we arrive at SELLAFIELD, and *Calder Castle*, in the vicinity of which is *Ponsonby Hall*, the seat of E. Stanley, Esq., delightfully situated in a beautiful spot; and just beyond lie the beautiful unique ruins of Calder Abbey Church, founded in 1134, near the small river Calder, and *Calder Abbey*, the seat of I. Hewison, Esq. We next pass BRAYSTONES and NETHERTOWN stations, and arrive at

ST. BEES.

Telegraph station at Whitehaven, 4 miles.

HOTELS.—Sea Coke, St. Bees.

MARKET DAY.—Saturday.

MONEY ORDER OFFICE.

At St. Bees, so called from St. Bega, an Irish saint who founded a monastery at this place in 650, is the church of an ancient abbey, part of which is used as a college, founded by Bishop Law in 1817, for clerical students, and in which many of the clergy have been educated. The Grammar School was founded by Archbishop Grindall, born at Hensingham. A lighthouse on the cliffs to the west was erected in 1822. An immense quantity of seafowl are in this locality. In the vicinity is St. Bees' Head, the market town of Egremont, with the ruins of a castle of the 12th century, and *Gill Foot*, seat of T. Hartley, Esq.; *Linethwaite*, E. Harrison, Esq.

Passing CORKICKLE station, we reach

WHITEHAVEN.

A telegraph station.

HOTELS.—Golden Lion, Globe.

MARKET DAYS.--Tuesday, Thursday and Saturday.

FAIR.—August 12th.

RACES in August.

WHITEHAVEN.—A prosperous coal port, on the west coast of Cumberland, with a population of 18,000, who are engaged in the coal trade and herring fishery (and return one member), not older than two centuries; and seated under the white rocks at the mouth of the river Poe. Lord Lonsdale is the owner of the land around the town, which is modern, and regularly built of houses covered with slate. There are four churches, of which the oldest dates from 1694; it has a good organ, and the "Last Supper," by Reed. The town contains a theatre, library, baths, race stand, ship yard, battery, good harbour and quays, and a public library and news room, which was established in 1797. At *Whitehaven Castle*, the Earl's seat, there is a picture gallery. The coal measures form a thin strip round the coast past Workington and Mary. port. The mines are worked by deep shafts a quarter of a mile down, close to the edge of *the sea*, under which they run more than *two miles*, the dip of the beds being as much as 1 foot in 10. Some of them are 8 and 10 feet thick with good coal. When raised, th "black diamonds" are turned into the wagons, which descend the tram road by their own weight to the quay, and drag up the empty ones; here they are dropped through the wooden lurries into the vessel's hold. An artificial harbour, by Rennie, has been constructed between two piers, 1,300 and 1,800 feet long. At the proper season the herring fisheries are very productive. In the American war it was attacked by Paul Jones (who was acquainted with the coast, from having been a cabin boy here); he landed, spiked the guns of the little fort, and set fire to two vessels in the harbour, an act which certainly tells much for his daring courage, and the surprising weakness of the authorities.

A railway skirts the best part of the Cumberland coast, and extends into Furness from Workington; a branch strikes into the interior as far as Cockermouth, which may ultimately be carried on to Keswick, which is 10 miles further (see Keswick); or by way of Embleton and Bassenthwaite Water, 14 miles.

Whitehaven to Keswick, on foot, by the road, 28 miles. Passing *Weddicar*, *Arlecdon*, *Lamplugh*, to *Lowes Water*, a small lonely lake, under Blake Fell, 12 miles. Lead and stone are found in this part. Up the side of *Crummock Water*, to *Buttermere*, 7 miles. On the west side of Crummock Lake, which is rather grand, and well wooded at the foot, under Melbreak Fell, is a fine fall of 156 feet, called *Scale Force*. *Grisedale Pike*, to the north, 2,756 feet high. *Buttermere Church* is a curious small old structure. The Lake of *Buttermere* is surrounded by wild and elevated mountains, especially above its head, where Honistar Crag, 1,600 feet high, Red Pike, 2,850 feet, Great Gable, 2,925 feet, the Pillar, 2,893 feet, Glaramara, &c., are seen, backed by the

Borrowdale Fells and Scafell, 3,166 feet, the highest peak of all. From Buttermere through the quiet valley of Newlands, under Hindicar, Cawsey Pike, &c., to Keswick, 9 miles. With a guide you may find your way from Buttermere into Langdale, on the road to Ambleside, about 20 miles, who is necessary, not so much for the difficulty of the path as for safety in case of sudden mists and changes in the weather. Along the coast from Whitehaven, on or near the railway, is *Muncaster Hall*, the seat of Lord Muncaster. Here is Henry VI.'s cup, who took refuge here after the battle of Hexham, in 1464.

WHITEHAVEN, CLEATOR, & EGREMONT.

THIS is a short line of $4\frac{1}{2}$ miles. The first station is MOOR ROW, at which point a branch of two miles diverges to the left, running over

CLEATOR MOOR,

On which iron ore, in very large quantities, and of a very superior quality, is raised. On this moor are three furnaces where Heniatite iron is manufactured.

FRIZINGTON.

In this neighbourhood are a mineral spring and several quarries of ironstone, in which the people are mostly employed.

From Moor Row the line proceeds *viâ* WOODEND, to

EGREMONT.

MARKET DAY.—Saturday.

FAIRS.—February 18; third Friday in May; September 18, horses, cattle, &c.

A neat little town, of about 2,000 inhabitants, belonging to General Wyndham, the son of Lord Egremont. It is situated on the banks of the river Ehen, a small stream, which flows from Ennerdale Lake. At the time when members of parliament were paid for their services, this town enjoyed the privilege of representation, but, the inhabitants deeming it too expensive a luxury, petitioned against it, and were accordingly disfranchised. To the west of the town stand the ruins of Egremont Castle, built by William de Meschines, soon after the Norman conquest.

WHITEHAVEN JUNCTION.

Whitehaven to Maryport.

At PARTON, the first station on this line, is a harbour for small vessels. In the vicinity is *Meresby Hall*, the seat of Miss Tate, built by Inigo Jones. Passing HARRINGTON station, with its harbour and lighthouse at Bella Port, we arrive at

WORKINGTON.

A telegraph station.

HOTEL.—Green Dragon.

MARKET DAYS.—Wednesday and Saturday.

FAIRS.—May 18th and October 18th.

WORKINGTON, to the north of Whitehaven, is a coal port and market town belonging to the Curwens of *Workington Hall*, a fine old seat, in which Mary Queen of Scots took refuge when she fled to England, in 1568, after her defeat at Langside. Her room is shown to visitors. She came from Dundrennan Abbey, on the coast of Kirkcudbright, now a fine old ruin. Here is an old church, built in 1770, with a good tower, and a modern one, erected in 1823; also, five chapels, corn market, assembly rooms, theatre, custom house, grammar school, harbour, three-arched bridge, coal mines, gas works, lighthouse (built in 1825, with two lights, and seen upwards of 11 miles distant), shipbuilding yards, &c. It contains a population of 6,280, principally employed in the coasting and timber trade, salmon fishery (which continues from August to October), and straw plait manufacturing.

COCKERMOUTH BRANCH.

Passing WORKINGTON BRIDGE, CAMERTON, and BROUGHTON CROSS, and BRIGHAM stations, we arrive at

COCKERMOUTH.

Telegraph station at Workington, $8\frac{1}{2}$ miles.

HOTEL.—Globe.

MARKET DAY.—Monday.

FAIRS.—Every other Wednesday from May to Sept., October 10th, Whit and Martinmas Mondays.

A market town, with a population of 7,275, who return two members, situated at the junction of the Cocker and Derwent. It contains manufactories of woollens, ginghams, hats, and stockings, tanwork, collieries, a public walk by the river, market place, three chapels, grammar school (with a good library), hospital, two bridges, St. Mary's Church, rebuilt in 1850, situated on an eminence, with the Wordsworth (a native) memorial window, and ruins of a castle, consisting of walls, west front, drawbridge, tower, &c., which was dismantled in 1648, after having been surprised by Douglas in 1387, and held Mary, Queen of Scots as a prisoner in 1568. In the vicinity are the seat of Major Skelton (at which many Roman antiquities have been found), *St. Helens*, Rev. J. Bensom, and *Woodhall*, J. Fisher, Esq.

Passing FLIMBY station, a small bathing place, we arrive at

MARYPORT.

A telegraph station.

HOTEL.—Golden Lion.

MARKET DAYS.—Tuesday and Friday

BANKERS.—Cumberland Banking Co.

This is a market, seaport, and coal town, in the county of Cumberland. Like most of the towns on the west coast of this county, it derives its origin and importance from that trade. Eighty years ago the beach was occupied only by one house, called Valencia, and about half a score miserable huts that served to shelter a few fishermen; now its population is 5,698. The situation of the town is extremely pleasant, its streets are wide, and the houses neatly built. It stands on the borders of the river Ellen, which divides it into two parts. Strong piers, with quays and lighthouses, have been erected on each side of the river, for the convenience of shipping, which rapidly increases. It contains five chapels shipyards, and grammar schools. In the vicinity are *Nether Hall*, J. Senhouse, Esq., who owns the town, *Ellenborough*, a Roman station, and *Ewanrigg Hall*.

MARYPORT AND CARLISLE.

Passing DEARHAM station (at which place there is a Saxon font and stone cross in the old church), and *Tallentire Hall*, we reach

BULL GILL.

Telegraph station at Maryport, 4¼ miles.

MONEY ORDER OFFICE at Maryport.

ASPATRIA.

This place, which belongs to the Gospatricks of Allerdale, has a population of 2,246, who are principally engaged in the quarries of redstone and coal-pits. It contains a fine old early English church, with chancel, font, and tombs of the Musgraves, and a curious pillar in the churchyard to Oughterside. Close at hand is Beacon Hill barrow, where, in 1790, a male skeleton was found, 7 feet long, with arms, &c. The town is pleasantly situated on the river Ellen.

BRAYTON.

Here is *Brayton Hall*, the beautiful seat of Sir W. Lawson, Bart., with a superb picture gallery. And five miles south-east of Brayton lies the pretty little market town of Ireby, the Caldbeck fells lying in the back ground and beyond High Pike, Saddleback, 2,787 feet high, and Skiddaw, 3,022 feet, towering in the distance, we reach

LEEGATE station.

WIGTON.

A telegraph station.

HOTEL.—King's Arms.

MARKET DAYS.—Thursday and Friday.

FAIRS.—Feb. 20th, April 5th, Whit Sunday, Martinmas, and December 21st.

This town, which was burnt by the Scots in 1322, has a population of 4,568 employed in the cotton trade. The church, rebuilt in 1790, is erected on the site of one founded out of Old Carlisle—the ancient *Olenacum*. Clarke the poet, and Smirke the painter were natives. Here are print and dye works, tanneries, &c. In the vicinity is *Wigton Hall*, seat of Rev. R. Matthews.

CURTHWAITE, on the right of which lies *Crofton Hall*, Sir W. Briscoe, Bart.

DALSTON.—*Rose Castle*, seat of the Bishops of Carlisle, is in the vicinity. Two miles beyond is *Dalston Hall*, formerly the seat of the Dalston family. It is now a farm, and near the church stands a stone cross and some Druidical and Roman remains. In a retired yet beautiful spot, seven miles beyond, under High Pike, 2,011 feet high, is the market town of Hesket Newmarket, which contains a Quaker's chapel, the old hall, and, in the vicinity, molybenda and copper are found.

Carlisle, see page 63.

PRESTON, LANCASTER, AND CARLISLE.

Preston to Oxenholme

Passing BROUGHTON and BROCK stations, at the latter of which is *Claughton Hall*, built in Charles I.'s time, but now a farm, and stone quarries in the neighbourhood, we reach

GARSTANG.

Distance from station, 2 miles.

Telegraph station at Preston, 9¼ miles.

HOTEL.—Royal Oak.

MARKET DAY.—Thursday.

FAIRS.—Holy Thursday, July 10th, and Dec. 22nd.

A market town situated on the Wyre, with a population of 839, employed in the cotton and print trade. It contains town hall, free school, print and cotton factories, four chapels, and a church, rebuilt in 1746. In the river is good trout and chub fishing; close by are the remains of *Greenhalgh Castle*, which was garrisoned by the Earl of Derby for Charles I. in 1643. The Pretender occupied this place in 1715. In the vicinity are *Kirkland Hall*, seat of T. Cole, Esq.; *Bleasdale Tower*, seat of W. J. Garnett, Esq. and *Bleasdale Fell*, 1,709 feet high.

Passing SCORTON station, we arrive at BAY HORSE. In the vicinity are *Ellel Grange*, seat of W. Preston, Esq.; *Thurnham Hall*, the Daltons' seat, and *Ashton Hall*, on the Lune, the finely wooded park and princely seat of Le Gendre N. Starkie, Esq. (formerly of the Duke of Hamilton), which commands an extensive view of the Irish Sea.

Passing GALGATE station, we reach

LANCASTER.

A telegraph station.

HOTELS.—King's Arms and Royal Hotel; Joseph Sly. See *Household Words*, Nos. 395 and 396, October 1857, where this hotel is noticed in the following terms: "The order was promptly executed (truly, all orders were so, in that excellent hotel)." We can certainly endorse this remark of Mr. Dickens.

MARKET DAYS.—Wednesday and Saturday.

FAIRS.—May 1st to 3rd, July 5th to 7th, August 11th to 13th, and Oct. 10th, three days each, first day for cattle, second for cheese, and third for toys.

RACES.—In July.

BANKERS.—Lancaster Banking Co.; Branch of Preston Banking Co.

LANCASTER, capital of Lancashire, a parliamentary borough (two members), and port, with a population of 16,168, engaged in the cotton trade, and a small coasting trade, at the mouth of the Lune, near Glasson Dock. From its Saxon name, *Loncastre*, meaning the camp or fortress on the Lune, it is likely there was a Roman station, but this is an unsettled point. Subsequent to the Conquest, it was the head of a crown manor which, in the person of Edward III.'s son, John of Gaunt, "time-honoured Lancaster," as Shakspeare styles him, was created a duchy, with a separate jurisdiction, which exists to this day, the Chancellorship of the Duchy of Lancaster being a ministerial office, while the dukedom is held by the heir apparent, the Prince of Wales. The Lancashire magistrates are nominated by this duchy officer, and not by the Lord Chancellor. The duchy is not confined to this county, but extends elsewhere, even to several parishes near Westbury-on-Severn, in Gloucestershire; Tutbury, &c. in Staffordshire; and the Savoy, in London, where the Dukes had a large palace.

The castle is the chief object of attraction Standing on a hill, west of the town, on the site of one built after the Conquest, by Roger de Poitou, it includes the shire courts, county gaol, and other buildings, all in the castellated style, by Harrison (the architect of Chester Castle), and cost £140,000. Four or five old towers remain (in a restored condition), of which the dungeon (donjon), 90 feet high, is the oldest; and another, called Adrian's, which may have some Roman work in it. John of Gaunt's round tower, over the gate, is of the 14th century, as is also John of Gaunt's chair, another part of the building, from which, on a clear day may be distinctly seen the Isle of Man. Northcote's portrait of George III. is in the Crown Court.

St. Mary's, the parish church, stands on the same hill, and on the north of the Castle. The exterior walls of the church are of the date of the 15th century. It occupies the site of a Norman edifice built by Roger de Poitou, of which no vestige remains. The church is spacious and lofty, being 140 feet in length, sixty broad, and forty high. It consists of a nave, two side aisles, and a chancel. Eight arches and pillars, of the old Anglo-Gothic, separate the nave from the side aisles, and extend nearly up to the altar. Recent alterations have materially changed the appearance of the church internally; plain glazed windows have given place to beautifully stained ones, the galleries have all been removed, and new ones erected at the west end.

From the churchyard, looking up the vale of the Lune, is seen first a viaduct of wood on the skew plan, which carries you over the branch line of three miles long to Poulton, on Morecambe Bay, a pretty watering-place, now much patronised by strangers.

Further up the Lune is an excellent five-arched bridge, which unites the town to the suburb of Skerton, and forms a bold and handsome entrance into the town from the north; and again further up the Lune is the Aqueduct Bridge, with five semicircular arches, each with a 70 feet span, and 51 feet high. This magnificent undertaking conveys the Lancaster Canal over the Lune, and under one of the above arches the North Western Line passes up to Yorkshire.

The exterior of the church, with its lofty steeple, and the towers of the Castle, are noble objects for the stranger's eye as he passes onward by the Lancaster and Carlisle Line to the Lune Viaduct, which is in the immediate vicinity of the Castle Station. It crosses the Lune on three wide-span wood arches, extending to the north with a stone arch, over the Lancaster and Morecambe railway, and to the south with seven lofty stone arches across the road above the new wood landing-wharf; the buttress between each is perforated with two door-way arches. Owing to its great elevation above the river it forms a prominent object from many points of view in the vicinity of the Lancaster Castle Station, which is situated at the northern terminus of the Lancaster and Preston Railway; the station is a very neat building, erected of fine white freestone.

From the Lune Viaduct the line proceeds towards the shores of Morecambe Bay to

HEST BANK,

A small and pretty village. A few families resort to it in summer for quiet and retirement, and in addition they have every combination of beautiful scenery, with the wide expansive bay, surrounded by the Westmoreland and Cumberland mountains, and when the tide is out, a wide expanse of sands. There is a road across these sands at low water to the Furness side of the bay; a guide is stationed on them by Government, to accompany travellers across the channels, quicksands sometimes rendering crossing dangerous. The lover of scenery will be delighted with the magnificent and bold scenery which presents itself, as the train passes onwards along the shore of Morecambe to the BOLTON-LE-SANDS Station, and thence to Carnforth.

Professor Owen and Professor Whewell both are natives of Lancaster, and received their education at the Grammar School.

CARNFORTH.

A telegraph station.

Two miles distant is a limestone cave, 800 feet deep, called Dunal Mill Hole, out of which a stream issues underground, and falls into the sea near the village. In the vicinity is *Carnforth Lodge*, seat of T. Jackson, Esq.

The line then proceeds along an embankment of great length, and reaches the Burton and Holme station. The former, Burton-in-Kendal, is a market town, with a population of 9,170. It contains an ancient church with side chapels, with monument of Cockin. Six miles beyond is Kirkby Lonsdale, a market town, with a fine old Norman church, which commands a beautiful view of the Valley Lune and Ingleborough; antique old market cross, grammar school, old stone bridge across the river, and an old inn mentioned by "Drunken Barnaby," and the latter is noted for its flax mills under Holme Fell and Tarleton Knot. When opposite Burton we pass from the county of Lancaster into

WESTMORLAND,

THE name of which county is descriptive of its nature, that is the West-moor-land, a region of lofty mountains, naked hills, and bleak barren moors. The vallies through which the rivers flow are tolerably fertile; and in the north-eastern quarter there is a considerable tract of cultivated land. The south-western side is fertile, with a warmer climate. These two sides of the county are divided by lofty fells and extensive moors, intersected with pastoral vales. The climate is exceedingly humid, owing to its contiguity to the western ocean, from which the winds blow at least two-thirds of the year, and with them a quantity of moisture, which afterwards falls in the form of rain. The atmosphere is, however, pure and healthy. Fourteen miles from Lancaster the line crosses the river Bela, and thence passes on the east side of Milnthorpe, by Rowell, Lower Woodhouse, Greenhead, and east of Hincester.

BURTON Station.

MILNTHORPE.

A telegraph station.
HOTEL.—Cross Keys.
MARKET DAY.—Friday.
FAIRS.—May 12th and Oct. 17th.

This place is a market town, with a population of 1,200, who are employed in the coasting trade, flax, flour, and paper mills. It contains a fine Gothic church, school, and chapel. In the vicinity are *Dallam Tower*, seat of George E. Wilson, Esq. *Levens Hall*, Hon. Mrs. Howard. *Sizergh Castle*, the ancient seat of the Stricklands.

The line thence crosses the canal at the tunnel, and pursues its course through a fine and well-wooded country, to the pleasant village of Sedgwick. At this point the magnitude of the Sedgwick embankment is seen to advantage. The course of the line is now by Natland to Oxenholme, previous to which it crosses the Burton turnpike road, about two miles south of Kendal. After passing an embankment, and through some heavy rock cutting, the train reaches the

OXENHOLME station. At this point the line is joined by the Kendal and Windermere railway, which affords an easy and delightful means of access to the lake district from the north and south east.

A fine view of the town of Kendal is enjoyed at this station, the church spires, and blue roofs of the white houses which lie in the vale beneath; whilst far beyond rise the mountains of the west, the giants of the lake district.

Route to Carlisle, see page 61.

KENDAL AND WINDERMERE.

Oxenholme to Windermere.

KENDAL.

POPULATION, 11,829.
A telegraph station.
HOTELS.—King's Arms, Commercial.
MARKET DAY.—Saturday.
FAIRS.—March 22nd, April 29th, Whit Saturday, Nov. 8th and 9th.

This is a market town, on the bank of the river Kent, with a population of 11,829, who return one member, and are principally engaged in the carpet, woollen, linsey, worsted, clog, comb, bobbin, fish-hook, leather, rope, woollen cord, fruit trades, and marble works. The houses are of stone. It contains House of Correction, Gaol, the Town Hall, built in 1825, by Webster, a noble edifice, 148 ft. by 37, which includes Assembly, Lecture, News, and Library Rooms; Mechanics' Institute, Museum, Paper Mills, Market, and Pennington's Grammar School. Shaw, the traveller, was a native, and Dr. Fothergill, and Bishop Law were scholars. A Saxon earthwork obelisk, in commemoration of the Revolution, erected on Castlehowhill; twelve chapels and three churches. That of Holy Trinity had four chantries, and contains tombs and brasses of Bishop Dawson, the Parrs, Stricklands, and Bellinghams. Here are the ruins of three towers of the old castle in which Queen Catherine Parr, who survived Henry VIII., was born, also of old chapels on Chapel Hill and Stranmongate, at which place there is an old house with the motto "Pâx hac domo" inscribed on it. The Dockwras family formerly occupied Dockwray Hall, and Judge Chambré died at Abbot Hall. In 1598 the plague carried off 3,000 of the inhabitants. James I. visited here in 1617, and the rebels halted at this place in 1715 and 1745. Richard of Kendal, Bishop Potter, Dean Potter, Sir G. Wharton, W. Walker, Hudson and Wilson, the botanists (the latter of whom was a stockinger), were natives. The painter Romney died here.

Passing BURNESIDE and STAVELEY stations, beyond which is Orrest Head, from which the most extended and magnificent view of the lake is obtained, we reach

WINDERMERE.

A telegraph station.

HOTEL.—The Windermere Hotel.

STEAMERS on the lake.

From the Windermere station, the *Lake* appears in view, with its beautiful islands, and grassy well-wooded fells round its borders. From north to south it is ten miles long, but at the greatest breadth only two, and fed chiefly by two small streams, the Rothay and Brathay at the top, and discharges itself by the Leven into the sea at Morecambe Bay. It preserves nearly the same level in all weathers. The view from the terminus embraces the village of Bowness, with its white houses, close at hand; the rocky mountains of Rydal, Borrowdale, Langdale, Eskdale, Coniston, and Troutbeck, round its head; while at the bottom, you see Belle Isle and surrounding Islands, the Ferry House, (on the opposite side), the beautiful seat of *Storr's Hall*, near Rawlinson's Nab (on this side), and the Cartmel and Furness fells. In the immediate neighbourhood of the terminus are *Elleray*, the seat of the

Ulleswater

Head of Windermere

Great Langdale

Birker Force

late Professor Wilson, the Editor — "Christopher North"—of *Blackwood's Magazine*, ("Old Ebony);" *Rayrigg* is a charming seat; and *Calgarth*, which in the last century was the constant residence of the late Dr. Watson, Bishop of Llandaff, author of "*Apology for Religion*," and other excellent works.

Windermere is too large to be explored all at once. Bowness and Ferry Inn at the middle, Low Wood near the top, Newby Bridge at the bottom, and Belle Isle, the largest of its thirteen islands, present the most attractive prospects. By the road it is almost 26 miles round, but the views are more varied and magnificent from the higher grounds above it. The lake itself should be seen from the water as well as the shores, to take in all its beauties. Boats may be had at Bowness, Waterhead, and Low Wood Inn; and more than this, steamers now run its whole length, to the delight and convenience of residents and visitors. *Low Wood Inn*, on the north-east side, is on a beautiful bay; Brathay Park, Langdale Pikes, Fairfield, and other fells are visible, and the lake down to Belle Isle. There is a fine walk up the lane to Troutbeck, in which the views are constantly changing. From *High Wray* (opposite) a fine view of the Rydal and Ambleside mountains.

BOWNESS.

HOTEL.—Ullock's Royal.

BOWNESS is the chief port of the lake. Boats and carriages at moderate rates. Bishop Watson, who lived at Calgarth, is buried in the large white church, the east window of which is filled with stained glass brought from Furness Abbey. *Ferry House*, opposite Bowness, where the lake is only half a mile wide, should be visited, for the noble views it commands up and down the lake. Behind it are Esthwaite Water and Hawkshead (three miles), and, further off, Coniston and its fells. *Bell Grange* and *Storr's Hall*, a little below Bowness, are also good points of view, from which Langdale Pikes and the lakes appear to wonderful advantage. The latter is the seat of the Rev. Thomas Staniforth. Here in August, 1825, the late Colonel Bolton entertained Canning, Scott, and Lockhart, on their memorable visit to the Lakes; it was kept as a gala day, with firing of guns and other signs of rejoicing. Wordsworth was the cicerone to all the best points of view, and Professor Wilson acted as captain of the boat. *Fell Foot* and *Newby Bridge* (over the Leven) at the bottom of the lake, are delightfully placed among woods, and possess fine views of its scenery, and the Coniston fells. From the bridge, to Ulverstone and Holker, at the Leven's mouth, it is about eight miles, Cartmel, five miles, Cark Station and Broughton, ten miles. From Holker the sands of Morecambe Bay may be crossed to Lancaster; but *not on any account without a guide.*

AMBLESIDE.

HOTELS.—The Salutation, Commercial, White Lion.

This romantic little town of Westmorland is in the Vale of Brathay, among the mountains at the head of Windermere, from which it is about a mile distant; and is an excellent centre for excursions short and long, in the Lake District. Population 1,592. Within six or seven miles are

Coniston Lake, described at page 53,

Grasmere, *Rydal Water*, *Ulleswater*, &c. Good and cheap lodgings may be obtained. The town itself being on the side of a hill commands views of the beautiful valley beneath, Windermere, Rydal Park, &c. Formerly it was a Roman station, and possesses, therefore, claims to great antiquity; but everything about it has a modern appearance. The church was built in 1852. Population, 1,592. The best way to reach Ambleside, is by rail from Kendal, up the valley of the Kent, to Birthwaite, on the east side of Windermere, where coaches run to Ambleside three times a day, fares one shilling; the distance being four to five miles, amidst fine trees and beautiful scenery. There are also coaches to Grasmere, Keswick, and Cockermouth, from the terminus.

In the immediate vicinity of Ambleside are the following:—*Stockgill Force*, a splendid waterfall, 150 feet down, on the stream which rises in the Kirkstone fells, and runs through Ambleside. *Wansfell Pike* is seen as you look up it. This and Skelgill are easily ascended, but Fairfield, 2,950 feet high, is more fatiguing—the prospect, from which is however magnificent. Another easy point of view is *Loughrigg Fell*, 1,050 feet above the lake. At the foot of Loughrigg is *Fox Howe*, the residence of the late esteemed Dr. Arnold. Following the Brathay, to the right, is Rydal and

GRASMERE.

HOTEL.—Prince of Wales.

You then come to Elterwater, where the two heads of the river come down from Great and Little Langdale. Either dale, or the heights between them, may be followed for prospects. If you ascend Little Langdale, you pass two fine falls of 150 feet, Skelwith Force and Colwith Force (the latter the best), being in four distinct leaps. There is a path by Fell Foot, into Eskdale and Ravenglass, fifteen miles from Ambleside. Great Langdale conducts to Wall End (a noble prospect) and Mill Beck, where the ascent to Langdale Pikes begins. You pass Dungeon Gill, 90 feet down (pronounced *ghill*, which means a thin tumbling stream), and Stickle Tarn. The Pikes, 2,400 feet high, are three pillared rocks, on the top of the mountain, overlooking all this region and the Scottish coast. Bow Fell (2,900 feet), and Sea Fell (3,100 feet), are paths over the stake, through Borrowdale to Keswick (15 miles), or by Wast Water to Ravenglass (18 miles), or by Ennerdale to Egremont (24 miles).

The trip into the Langdales may be made daily during the season by coach, provisions being obtainable at various places on the route. The round from Ambleside and back is thus—

	Miles.		Miles
To Skelwith Bridge ...	3	To Dungeon Gill	$11\frac{1}{2}$
,, Colwith Force	5	,, Langdale Chapel...	$15\frac{1}{2}$
,, Blea Tarn	$7\frac{1}{2}$	By Rydal to Ambleside	19

Ambleside to Keswick and Derwent Water.—The distances are—

	Miles.		Miles.
To Rydal	2	To King's Head Inn	11¼
,, Grasmere	4	,, Castle Rigg	15¼
,, Raise Gap	7	,, Keswick	16¼
,, Wythburn Chapel	8		

This road passes between Helvellyn and the Borrowdale Fells. *Rydal Hall* is the large modernised seat of Lady le Fleming, with a pretty Gothic family chapel. There are two beautiful cascades in the grounds which are shown to visitors, one is 70 feet. Above it rise Fairfield and Rydal Head. On the slope of the latter (which is 3,090 feet high at the top) is the late poet Wordsworth's seat, *Rydal Mount*, looking down on Windermere, &c., and the beautiful secluded lake of Rydal Water, about one mile long, with an island on it. Brown's (Prince of Wales), Lake Hotel, Swan Inn, and Red Lion, as also several respectable lodging-houses, are at Grasmere, which lies in a quiet green valley, overlooked by the mountains—the church and houses being scattered among the trees. Wordsworth, along with the remains of his wife, and Hartley Coleridge are buried in the churchyard. Easedale on the left, is a beautiful yet solitary spot. Near the Lake Hotel was the residence of Mr. and Mrs. Wordsworth, who lived there during the first seven years of their married life, and subsequently became that of De Quincey, author of the "*Confessions of an English Opium-Eater*," a clever description of the alternate bliss and misery of intoxication. The road winds upwards (with Helm, or Lion and Lamb Crag on the left) to the dreary pass, called Raise Gap, or Dunmail Raise, a cairn, or heap of stones, marking the boundary of Westmorland and Cumberland. Here the last King of Cumbria is buried. Helvellyn and Seat Sandal come into view on the right; Borrowdale Fells on the left; Skiddaw in the distance. *Wythburn Chapel*, near Horse or Nag's Head Inn, where a guide may be hired for Helvellyn, and as mists are so sudden and dangerous here, it is the safest plan for a stranger to take one with him.

Wythburn Water is another name for Thirle Mere or Leathe's Water, in which there is good trout and pike fishing. *King's Head Inn* is in Legberthwaite or St. John's Vale, near the pretty Smealthwaite bridge. The scenery around is extremely wild but grand. Past Shoolthwaite Moss to Rongha bridge, beyond which Helvellyn, Skiddaw, and Saddleback, come all into full view. At *Castle Rigg*, you come in sight of Keswick, Crosthwaite Church (where Southey is buried), Bassenthwaite Water, and other objects; and at Brow Top, Derwentwater appears, with Borrowdale mountains at the head of it. See Keswick for further description.

Ambleside to Ulleswater and Penrith.—The distances are as follows—

	Miles.		Miles.
To Kirkstone Top	4	To Pooley Bridge	19
,, Foot of Kirkstone	3	,, Arthur's Round Table	23½
,, Patterdale Inn	10	,, Penrith	24¾
,, Lyulph's Tower	14¼		

Leaving Rydal Head on the left, you ascend the Kirkstone Pass, so called because it looks like a church. Here is a small inn, built for the accommodation of travellers over the dreary pass, and is the highest inhabited house in England. Helvellyn is in view on the left. Down to Cross Keys Inn and Brother Water. At *Patterdale* there is a good inn, and a fine old yew tree in the churchyard. Helvellyn may be ascended here. Harthorpe, Deepdale, and Blowick, all command lovely views of the upper reach of Ulleswater. *Patterdale Hall*, the seat of W. Marshall, Esq. The road winds up the west side of the lake to *Lyulph's Tower*, in Gowbarrow Park, the shooting box of H Howard, Esq.; another excellent point of view. Airey Force, a fall of 80 feet, is at hand. From Pooley Bridge, at the bottom of Ulleswater, a road branches off to *Lowther Castle* and *Brougham Hall* (four miles), Lord Brougham's fine seat, near the old castle; also to Bampton and Hawes Water (eight miles). *Arthur's Round Table* is an amphitheatre, about 30 yards across, not far from a Druid circle, at the centre of which is a stone pillar 11 feet high. *Dalemain Hall*, an old seat; *Dacre Castle*, with the church, and stone bears in the churchyard. *Penrith*, with the Giant's Grave. Giant's Thumb (three stones) in the churchyard, view from the Beacon on the race course, and remains of Richard II.'s castle, close to the station.

KESWICK.

HOTELS.—Royal Oak, Queen's Head, King's Arms.

Good cheap lodgings are abundant at this place, which is the capital of the *Cumberland Lakes*, in the beautiful vale of the Greta, at the bottom of Derwentwater, under Skiddaw. Being as yet inaccessible by rail, the nearest station is Penrith, 14 miles distant, on the Lancaster and Carlisle line. A branch has been projected from Cockermouth, by way of Bassenthwaite Water, about 12 miles. Population, 2,618.

Keswick itself is a neat town of one long street, with a *Town Hall*, the bell of which was brought from the Radcliffe's old seat in the lake, bearing apparently the date of 1001. The Radcliffes were Earls of Derwentwater, but their vast property here was forfeited by their rebellion in 1715, and given to Greenwich Hospital, from which it is leased by the Marshalls. There is a modern Gothic church for the district; and the old parish church of Crosthwaite, in the middle of the valley (near the *Grammar School*), commands an extensive prospect. Specimens of the minerals peculiar to the mountains may be seen at the museum in the town; and at Flintoft's is an excellent coloured model of the whole district, nearly 13 feet long. Guides, boats, ponies, &c., may be hired at the inn at reasonable rates.

Near the bridge on the Greta, is *Greta Hall*, where *Southey* lived, at first with Coleridge for four years, and then by himself in the midst of his own family, "working like a negro" at his books, till he died in 1843, utterly broken down by intellectual labour, but always cheerful and happy, sustained by a feeling of inward worth and the disinterested love of letters for its own intrinsic value. Coleridge (in

1800) describes the prospect from this place. "The room in which I write commands six distinct landscapes—the two lakes, the vale, the river and mountains, and mists, and clouds, and sunshine, making endless combinations, as if heaven and earth were for ever talking to each other. Often, when in a deep study, I have remained there looking, without seeing; all at once, the lake of Keswick and the fantastic mountains of Borrowdale at the head of it, have entered into my mind with a suddenness as if I had been snatched out of Cheapside and placed, for the first time, in the spot where I stood. The river Greta flows behind our house like an untamed son of the hills, and then winds round and glides away in front, so that we live in a peninsula." Southey has also sketched the same view in some of his smoothest hexameters, beginning—

"'Twas at that sober hour when the light of day is receding,
* * * * *
Pensive, though not in thought, I stood at the window beholding mountain, and lake, and vale." * *

The principal attractions to be seen from Keswick are the *Derwentwater Lake*, fed by the river Derwent, which comes from Bow Fell, through Borrowdale, and is, perhaps, the most beautiful in the lake country, from the abundance of foliage on the shores and islands, of which there are four. Friar's Crag and Ashness are good points of view. Others (near Keswick) are Castle Hill, Crow Park, and Cockshot. *Lodore Fell* (best seen, like all falls, in wet weather), is at the upper end; and which Southey has described in some amusing gingle. It flows from a defile in Watendlath. *Skiddaw*, five miles distant, 2,780 feet high, may be reached on foot or ponyback. The view takes in the mountains (Derwentwater excepted), the sea coast, Isle of Man, &c. *Saddleback*, 5 miles off, 2,290 feet high, and Scales Tarn (lake); then take the Penrith road as far as Scales and turn off to the left. The Coldbeck Fells are to the north of Skiddaw; while the Druid Circle at Castle Riggs, is left on the right hand of the road to it. *Borrowdale*, a deep narrow pass through which the Derwent flows, lies six miles from Keswick; here are the great Bowder Rock, 62 feet long, weighing nearly 1,800 tons, and the famous *Black Lead Mines* at Giller Coom, belonging to Mr. Bankes, of Dorsetshire. Further up the dale are Scathwaite, Stye Head, Wast Water, and Scafell Pikes, 3,090 feet high, a road turns round to Buttermere and Crummock Waters. *Helvellyn*, eight miles distant, and 3,060 feet high, a noble granite peak, between Thirle Mere and Ulleswater. The road to Grasmere and Ambleside passes over the shoulder of it at Dunmail Raise gap. The green vale of *Newlands* lies six miles south-west, under Causey and Grisdale Pikes. *Ulleswater*, eight miles distant, and not far from the railway is nine miles long, and surrounded by magnificent mountains. From Watermillock and Gowbarrow Park, you obtain the finest views of it. The latter is the property of H. Howard, Esq., and has a fall in it called Airey Force. There is a mail gig to and from Penrith Station daily, and coaches run during the summer months.

Preston, Lancaster, & Carlisle Main Line continued.

Oxenholme to Carlisle.

From Oxenholme the line proceeds upon embankments and through cuttings, with occasional views of Kendal and its venerable old castle. Soon after passing the Birkland cutting, the line skirts the base of the lofty Benson Knot, one of the highest hills in the neighbourhood, thence through heavy rock cuttings, and across an embankment, we arrive at Docker Gill viaduct, one of the most beautiful structures on the line. It consists of six arches stretching across a valley. Half a mile from this splendid viaduct, the line is carried past *Morsedale Hall*, and half a mile further northward we arrive at Grayrigg Summit, where the line passes through a heavy cutting of hard material called samel.

A mile onward is the Low Gill embankment, one of the *highest* in England.

LOW GILL AND SEDBERGH.

Distance from station, 5 miles.

Telegraph station at Tebay, 4½ miles.

MARKET DAY at Sedbergh, on Wednesday.

FAIRS at Sedbergh, March 20th, Whit-Wednesday, and October 29th.

Five miles distant is the market town of Sedbergh, on the Rothern, a beautiful romantic valley, surrounded by mountains. It has a population of 2,235, who are employed in the cotton mills, and Dr. Lupton's Free Grammar School, founded in 1552, having three fellowships and ten scholarships at St. John's College, Cambridge, attached thereto. In the vicinity is *Ingniere Hall*, on the Lune, seat of Mr. Upton. Under Calf Fell is the beautiful waterfall, Cantley Spout, and near Borrow Bridge village is the Roman Camp, Castlehow.

The railway now skirts the Dillicar hills, and the scenery around increases in picturesque beauty and grandeur. At various points the windings of the silvery Lune are discerned from the line, and soon afterwards the train passes through the great Dillica cut. The line is carried over the Borrow Water, near its junction with the Lune, upon a neat viaduct.

About twenty yards from the line stands the remains of the ancient Roman station of Castle Field, by which the mountain pass was anciently defended. The railway now passes Borrow Bridge, a romantic spot, celebrated for trout fishing, the scenery about which is the most beautiful along the whole line, and the traveller seems to be completely hemmed in on all sides by stupendous hills. The village of Borrow Bridge appears on the right, at a short distance from the line, and near it winds the beautiful stream of the Lune.

Passing through the Borrow Bridge cutting we reach the Lune embankment, 95 feet deep, formed through the old bed of the river, which has been diverted from its course, through a tunnel excavated in the solid rock, 50 feet from the top, and made nearly parallel to the ravine. Proceeding onwards we pass the Lune excavations, Loup's Fell cutting, the Birbeck embankment, and the Birbeck viaduct—thence we arrive at the foot of the great incline—a plain of eight miles, rising 1 in 75, till it reaches the Shap summit.

TEBAY.

Three miles to the north of Tebay station, close to Tebay Fell, lies the market town of *Orton*, under Orton Scar, the neighbourhood of which is rich in mineral treasures. The vicarage of All Saints was held by Burn of Orton Hall, author of the "*Justice of Peace.*" Remains of Castle Folds and other camps, tumuli, &c., are to be seen. Here is a market on Friday, and Fairs, May 3rd, Friday before Whit-Sunday, 2nd Friday after Michaelmas (for cattle). Close at hand is *Langdale*, of which place Bishop Barlow was a native. At *Black Dub*, on the Lyvennet, is an obelisk, in memory of Charles II. having reviewed his troops on that spot on their return from Scotland in 1651. Proceeding from Tebay station we arrive at

SHAP WELLS.

MARKET DAY.—Monday.
FAIR.—May 4th.

Which has a saline spring, a Victoria pillar, close to the inn, an electric telegraph station, and contains remains of an abbey founded in 1119, by Thomas Gospatrick, who belonged to the Hogarth family, and tombs of the Viponts, Cliffords, &c., who were buried here. The railway passes through the fells, over which the Pretender and his army marched in 1745. At *Carl Lofts* are Danish stones, ½ mile long, and at *Gumerkeld* there still remains a Druid circle. Mills the critic was a native of *Hardendale*, distant one mile. Five miles beyond is *Hawes Water*, and eight miles to the east,

Appleby, the county town of Westmorland, with a population of 883. It was the Roman *Galacum*, and taken in 1648 by the parliamentarians, from that celebrated dauntless woman, Ann Dorset Pembroke and Montgomery, who rebuilt St. Lawrence church, which contains her tomb and those of the Cliffords, to whom the old castle on the hill belongs, which was rebuilt in Henry VI.'s time. It has portraits of the Countess Ann, old armour, &c. This town contains Town and Shire Halls, built in 1770, Market Place by Smirke, erected in 1811, on the site of the cloisters. Queen Elizabeth's Grammar School, with six exhibitions at Queen's College, Oxford, at which Bishops Bedell and Langhorne were scholars. Here were formerly some Latin inscriptions placed up by Bainbrig, then the master and friend of Camden, describing the misfortunes of the town, but now removed. *Countess Ann's Hospital*, for poor women, founded in 1563. St. Michael's church contains tombs of the Hiltons of Murton. Bishops Thomas of Appleby, Roger of Appleby, and Thomas de Vipont, were natives. Market Day, Saturday. Fairs, Whitsun Eve, Whit Monday, June 10th, and August 21st. In the vicinity is *Crackenthorpe* (at which Roman antiquities have been discovered), the seat of the Earl of Lonsdale A mile and a half further we reach the Shap Summit,—the highest point of the most stupendous work on the line. We are now 888 feet above the level of the line at Morecambe Bay, and 1,000 feet above the level of the sea. Rising sixty feet overhead, on each side are rugged walls of hard rock, presenting a truly magnificent appearance.

Leaving the Shap summit, we enter a cutting through limestone rock, and before it approaches Shap village, the line runs through a circle of large boulder stones, said to be the inner circle of an ancient Druidical temple.

From Shap the line proceeds on the east side of the town of Shap, along a heavy cutting, and passing thence under a skew bridge, along the flat portion of the route called Shap Mines, and following the valley of the stream, the line again runs under the turnpike road, and thence passes Thrimby, through a thick plantation.

Here the character of the scenery is considerably altered, the bare, rugged, and sterile mountains being succeeded by fertile pastures and picturesque prospects.

The Kendal turnpike road is crossed for the last time, by a skew bridge at Clifton, near the entrance to Lowther Park, 6,000 acres in extent, in which, hidden by a forest of huge trees, stands *Lowther Castle*, the noble Gothic seat of the Earl of Lonsdale, built by Smirke in 1808.

The scenery between Shap and Clifton is very attractive—Cross Fell, Saddleback, Skiddaw, and the other hills in the lake district appearing to great advantage

CLIFTON.

In this neighbourhood, at Clifton Moor, a skirmish was fought in 1745, between the Pretender and the Duke of Cumberland, which is beautifully described by Sir Walter Scott, in "Waverley." Here is a mineral well, and the old turreted ruin close to the farmhouse was the seat of the Wybergs. In the church there is some good stained glass.

From Clifton station we are carried along the Lowther embankment, and about 50 miles from Lancaster, and 20 from Carlisle, we cross the river Lowther on a magnificent viaduct, one of the most beautiful works of art on the line, 100 feet above the stream. Its arches, six in number, are of 60 feet span each. A mile and a half beyond, the line crosses the Eamont, on a viaduct of great beauty, consisting of five semi-circular arches. On the right is *Brougham Hall*, the seat of Lord Brougham, close to the old castle.

Leaving the county of Westmorland at this point we enter

CUMBERLAND,

THE two counties being divided by the stream which we have just crossed.

This county presents the traveller with, perhaps the grandest and most romantic scenery to be met with in England. The south western districts, particularly, form a gigantic combination of rugged, rocky mountains, thrown together with the wildest and rudest sublimity, yet enclosing the softest and most beautiful vallies, fairy streams, lakes, and rich and extensive woodlands, whilst, beside the charms given by nature to this favoured county, it boasts picturesque and interesting addition of many baronial castles, Roman remains, and even Druidical monuments. Its surface is extremely irregular and broken. On the eastern confines of the county, a high range of hills stretches as far as Scotland, and at their feet a broad tract of land extends its whole length, partly cultivated, and partly heathy common. It is watered by the Eden and several other small streams. This tract becomes very extensive before it reaches Carlisle, extending along the country to Wigton.

Proceeding on from the frontier, the line immediately enters a large cutting—and then running nearly level to the town of Penrith, we shortly after reach the station adjoining the ruins of the ancient castle.

PENRITH.

Population, 6,668.

A telegraph station.

Hotel.—New Crown.

Market Days.—Tuesdays and Saturdays.

Fairs.—March 1st, April 5th and 24th, 3rd Tuesday in Oct., Whit and Martinmas Tuesday.

Penrith is a large market town. It contains race stand, assembly, news and library rooms, free grammar school, founded by Bishop Strickland, in 1340, girls' school. St. Andrew's church, rebuilt in 1722, contained a chantry, built by Bishop Strickland, who was the first to have water conveyed to this place. It contains an old tower, and portraits, in stained glass, of Richard Plantagenet and his wife. The grave of Gevain (the giant), 15 feet long, with two pillar crosses, 11½ feet high, and the giant's thumb, with a cross, 5¾ feet high, are in the churchyard. The walls of the castle still remain, and from the Beacon Hill an extensive view of unsurpassable beauty is obtained. In the vicinity are *Ulleswater Lake* and *Eden Hall*, the latter the seat of Sir G. Musgrave, Bart., rebuilt in 1852, "at which is an old drinking glass, called the 'Luck of Eden Hall,' a gift of the fairies, the breaking of which, it is said, will bring misfortune to the house."—*Sharp's British Gazetteer.*

From Penrith the country is flat and uninteresting. The line enters the valley of the Petteril, through which it pursues almost a direct course to Carlisle, past the following stations, viz.:—Plumpton, Calthwaite, Southwaite, and Wreay. In the vicinity are *Hutton Hall*, Sir R. Vane, Bart.; *Barrock Fell, Newbiggin Hall*, H. Aglionby, Esq., M.P.; and *Petterill Bank*, J. Fawcett, Esq.

CARLISLE.

A telegraph station.

Hotels. — County; Bush; Crown and Mitre; White Hart.

Market Days.—Wednesdays and Saturdays.

Fairs.—August 26th, Sept. 19th, every Saturday from Michaelmas to Christmas, on the Sands, Saturday at Whitsuntide and Martinmas.

Races in July.

A cathedral town, parliamentary borough, and port, with a population of about 26,310, who return two members, in a healthy spot on the Eden, in Cumberland, near the Scottish border. Formerly it was the key to Scotland on this side of the island. The Romans made it one of their chief stations on Hadrian's wall, by the name of *Luguvallium;* and here the famous Briton, King Arthur, held his court. Cottons, ginghams, chintzes, checks, and hats are made in considerable quantities. One factory (Dixon's) is marked by an eight-sided brick chimney 305 feet high. A railway, ten miles long, reaches (where the wall ended) to Bowness on the Solway Firth.

It is also celebrated for its manufacture of fancy biscuits, which are produced in a most complete state, all by machinery, and to an extent that would certainly astonish visitors. The leading establishment in this branch of trade is that of Messrs. Carr and Co.; and if curiosity should induce the tourist to make a visit to the manufactory of this noted firm, we do not hesitate to say that it would be found highly interesting. If any prejudice exist against the free use of *fancy biscuits*, it will at once be removed, on an inspection of the works and the process of production, even from the minds of the most fastidious,—the most scrupulous cleanliness being observable throughout the whole works.

The *Cathedral* which has lately been restored and much embellished, under the superintendence of Owen Jones, and rendered more imposing by the removal of a block of buildings, which hid it, to some extent, from the passer by, was originally part of a Norman priory, and is cruciform, though a portion of the nave is gone; the other part is turned into a parish church. Length, 242 feet; tower, 130 feet high. The beautiful east window is 48 feet high. There are two or three fine brasses, and a monument to Paley. Near it are the Deanery, and a refectory, now used as the Chapter-house, the original one having been pulled down in the civil wars. The restored *Castle* includes William Rufus' Keep and the barracks. Henry I. made it a bishop's see.

Some of the oldest houses are in the market place, whence several well built streets diverge. Here stands a cross, built in 1682, and the ancien Moot-hall. The *Court House* and *County Gaol* is an extensive pile by Smirke, at a cost of £100,000, who also built the new bridge over the Eden—an excellent stone way, on five arches of 65 feet span each, which cost £70,000. There are two others across the Caldew. The *Library* and *News Room* is a work of Rickman's. There is a *County Hospital*, with a *Grammar School*, founded by Henry VIII., at which Bishop Thomas and Dean Carlyle, a native, were scholars. At the *Dispensary*, in 1788, "a child was born without any brain, and lived six days." The Pretender's son, Charles Stuart, was here in 1745, on his march to the south. The reader will not forget Fergus Mac Ivor's death in *Waverley*. In 1786 shocks of an earthquake were felt here.

Several interesting spots are in this quarter. The *Roman* (or Picts') *Wall* may be traced at various points, near the railway to Newcastle. *Rickerby*, seat of G. H. Head, Esq. *Corby Castle*, seat of P. H. Howard, Esq., has the claymore of MacIvor (whose real name was Macdonald). Up the Irthing, down the moors, is *Naworth Castle*, belonging to the Earl of Carlisle (a Howard), better known as Lord Morpeth, brother to the Duchess of Sutherland. Formerly it was the seat of Belted Will (Lord Will Howard), when guardian of the marches in Elizabeth's reign. A poor kind of coal is dug here. From the Moot Hill, near Brampton, there is a splendid view of the Cheviots. *Rose Castle*, the Gothic seat of the Bishop of Carlisle, lies situated in a fine well-wooded part of the Caldew. To the north, beyond, is Longtown, a town founded by the Grahams, and their seat, *Netherby*, where farming improvements are being made on a large scale.

CARLISLE AND SILLOTH AND PORT CARLISLE.

We pass KIRK ANDREWS and BURGH stations, at the last of which, the Roman *Akelodunum*, there is an obelisk on the marsh, in memory of Edward I., who died here in 1307. At the old castle (which belonged to De Morville, one of a'Beckett's assassins), there is a Norman door and fortified tower; inscriptions, altars, &c., have been found here.

The next station is DRUMBURGH, from which the line takes a curve to the right for 2¾ miles, *via* GLASSON, to

PORT CARLISLE.

Telegraph station at Carlisle, 10 miles.

HOTELS.—Steam Packet, Ferry, Solway.

MONEY ORDER OFFICE at Carlisle, 11 miles.

From the isthmus between Carlisle and Newcastle, northwards the ground rises gradually, and at last forms a lofty range of mountains, which, beginning at Cheviot on the east, runs across the island to Loch Royan on the west, and forms the boundary between South and North Britain. On the north of these chains of hills the principal part of the lowlands of Scotland are situated, extending quite across the island, from sea to sea, and reaching as far as the Grampian mountains, that stupendous and seemingly impenetrable barrier, which like a mighty wall, stretches along the southern front of the Highlands.

From Drumburgh the line continues through KIRKBRIDE and ABBEY to SILLOTH.

ALLONBY.

This place, a few miles south of Silloth, is remarkable for its sea bathing qualifications, for which it is much frequented in the summer season. It also commands extensive views across the Solway into the counties of Dumfries and Kirkcudbright.

NEWCASTLE AND CARLISLE.

From Carlisle, we pass SCOTBY, to the north of which is *Aglionby* (*by* signifies house, in the Cumberland dialect), the old seat of the ancestors of Walter d'Aquilon; then

WETHERAL,

Pleasantly situated on the Eden, with its old church, in which is Nolleken's beautiful monument of Mrs. Howard, of Corby, and effigies of the Salkelds and Howards. There is a pretty walk to *Wetheral Safeguards*, or *St. Constantine's* three caves, the Hermitage, and Folly summer-house, from which a most magnificent view may be obtained. The gate of the *Priory*, founded by Randulph de Meschines, in 1088, is in a beautiful state of preservation. On the left is *Warwick Hall*, the seat of Mrs. Parker, close to an old church and cotton factory.

HOW MILL station, close to which is *Hayton Church*, and in the distance may be seen the white turrets of *Edmond Castle*, the seat of T. H. Graham, Esq., and *Castle Carrock* church, near which are two forts.

We next pass the ravine of the *Gelt*, over a skew-bridge, on three arches, a little higher than which are the *Written Rocks*, on which inscriptions were cut by the Romans of Agricola's legion. Near Low Gelt Bridge is the *Cupon Oak*, where the judges were met by the sheriffs, and conducted by them, in former times, to Carlisle.

MILTON.

A telegraph station.

HOTEL.—Howard's Arms.

MARKET DAY.—Wednesday.

FAIRS.—April 20th and 23rd, 2nd Monday after Whitsuntide, and 2nd Wednesday in September.

Brampton is a curious old-fashioned place, with 3,304 inhabitants, engaged in the check and gingham factories. Close at hand is *Naworth Castle*, seat of Lord Carlisle. It was occupied by the Pretender in 1745. Here is a *grammar school*, erected on the site of an hospital, founded in 1688. Below, in *Mary's Holme*, are the gate and towers of *Lanercost Abbey*, as old as the 12th century. *Walton House*, seat of W. Johnson, Esq., *Castlesteads*, *Irthingtor Cross*, and *Watchcross*.

Passing LOW ROW and ROSE HILL stations, situated 446 feet above the Tyne, close to the Irthing, the *Roman Wall* is seen, which continues along the road. Near at hand is *Gilsland Spa*,—a good sulphur spring, which issues from a cliff in the glen at the back of Shaw's excellent hotel. Just above, there is a good waterfall at *Wardrew Farm*. At Bewcastle, are ruins of a *Border Fortress*, a *Runic Stone Pillar*, and *Triermain Castle*, so justly celebrated in Sir Walter Scott's "Bridal of Triermain." Then reaching

GREENHEAD, situated in one of the wildest parts of Northumberland, we obtain a sight of *Thirlwall* and *Blenkinsop Castles*, which guarded the rocky pass in the times of the Moss Troopers, and pass through a short tunnel to

HALTWHISTLE.

A telegraph station.
HOTEL.—Crown.
MARKET DAY.—Thursday.
FAIRS.—May 12th and 14th, and Nov. 22nd.

This is a small market town, with a population of 1,420, employed in the mines and quarries. The church contains tombs of the Blenkinsops, of *Bilisten Castle* (opposite the town), and John, Bishop Ridley the martyr's brother. At *Castle Banks*, is a mound, and at *Whitchester*, a Roman camp. *Blenkinsop Hall*, seat of J. Coulson, Esq., and *Unthank Hall*, D. Dixon, Esq., are close at hand.

ALSTON BRANCH.

Passing FEATHERSTONE station, situated on the South Tyne, near which is *Featherstonehaugh Castle*, the seat of the baronets of that name, long before the Conquest, the last of whom died at Up Park, Sussex, we reach *Shaff Hill* and

LAMBLEY, near the church, at which is *Castle Hill Camp*, with its large ash, having ten immense branches. *Nunwick*, the seat of R. L. Allgood, Esq., and large coal and lead mines; and then passing SLAGGYFORD, a small place, situated on the Tyne, we arrive at

ALSTON.

A telegraph station.
HOTELS.—Lowbyer, Golden Lion.
MARKET DAY.—Saturday.
FAIRS.—Last Tuesday in May, Friday before last day in September, and first Thursday in November.

ALSTON or Aldstone.—This market-town, in Cumberland, with a population of 3,409, engaged in the large lead mines, which also produce silver and copper, is situated on a well-wooded hill, in a region of moorland or "hazel grip," as it is called, upon which vast numbers of sheep are pastured. Beneath are the rich lead mines, worked by means of a subterranean canal, which runs through the limestone to the principal shaft at Penthead. They are leased from Greenwich Hospital, to which institution this valuable property was granted by the Crown, upon its forfeiture by the Earl of Derwentwater, who rose for the Pretender, in 1715. The town stands on the south Tyne, under Middle Fell, its appearance being much heightened by the plantations on the hills around. Valuable crystals, spars, and mineral specimens may be procured in the caves. It also contains shot, thread, and woollen manufactories.

Newcastle and Carlisle Main Line continued.

Passing BARDON Mill, on the Tyne, near which is *Ridley Hall*, at the mouth of Allendale, formerly the seat of the Martyr's family, we arrive at

HAYDON BRIDGE.

A telegraph station.
This place belongs to Greenwich Hospital, and originally formed part of the Earl of Derwentwater's property. Martin, the painter, was a native.

Passing FOURSTONES station, near to which are *Chesters*, the seat of N. Clayton, Esq., which is a well-preserved station, in the *Roman Wall*, the history of which has been written by the Rev. J. Bruce, of Newcastle. Simarburn, a large parish belonging to Greenwich Hospital, the revenues of which are appropriated to naval chaplains, and formerly the property of the Radcliffes, who forfeited it in the rebellion, and *Chipchase Castle*, seat of R. Gray, Esq., M.P., we arrive at

HEXHAM.

A telegraph station.
HOTEL.—White Hart.

This is a picturesque old place, containing a population of 4,601, employed chiefly in the leather, shoe, glove, stuff, hat, and woollen manufactories. It was formerly a Bishop's see. Here are a good grammar school, almshouses, town hall, suspension bridge over the Tyne, by Brown, five chapels, St. Andrew's Church, built on the site of St. Wilifrid's, with a tower, 100 feet high. There is a ruined nave, burnt in 1296, by the Scots, with pictures of the founder, St. John of Beverley and Acca, effigies of Umfraville, of Prudhoe, an oratory, three stalls and screen. Part of the gateway, and two cloisters, remain, and a frid-stool, where criminals found sanctuary. King David pillaged the place in 1346. Here Somerset was defeated by Neville; Queen Margaret concealed in a cave by the robber, and in 1761, 48 miners were killed, and 300 wounded, at a militia drawing, and Roman inscriptions have been discovered. John of Hexham, Bate, Hewson, and Richardson, were natives. In the vicinity are *Hexham Priory*, seat of Mrs. Beaumont. *Beaufront*, W. Cuthbert, Esq.

BORDER COUNTIES.

At this junction the Border Counties Railway diverges to the left. It runs through the valley of North Tyne, a district rich with limestone, coal, and iron, and is intended to connect itself with the Hawick Branch of the North British.

WALL, so called no doubt from its situation near to the Cilurnum station of the great Hadrian's wall, which intersected our route at this point. Although this wall was constructed some sixteen centuries ago, some portions, as well as some of its stations are still traceable, particularly in this locality.

WARK, CHOLLERFORD, CHOLLERTON, BARRASFORD, and REEDSMOUTH stations.

BELLINGHAM.

MARKET DAY.—Saturday.

FAIRS.—May, Saturday before the 12th; September, 1st Wednesday after 15th.

A polling town, situated on the North Tyne, with a population of about 800, principally employed in the mines and quarries, the neighbourhood of which abounds in limestone, coal, and iron.

CHARLTON, TARSET, and THORNEYBURN stations, the last of which is the present terminus of the railway, and $21\frac{3}{4}$ miles from Hexham.

Newcastle and Carlisle Main Line continued.

Proceeding through Farnley tunnel, we arrive at

CORBRIDGE.

POPULATION, 1,363.

This place was once a market town, and had a monastery in 771, when it was called Corabridge. It was burnt by the Scots in 1296. The church, which is fortified, was built from the ruins of Corchester, half-a-mile west, where are the Roman *Corstopitum*, and coins, remains of a bridge, altars, two Greek inscriptions, and a silver votive tablet, of 148 oz., have been found, and has a peel tower in the churchyard. In the vicinity is *Dilston*, which was the seat of the unfortunate and misguided Earl of Derwentwater.

Passing RIDING MILL station, near to which is *Styford Park*, we reach

STOCKSFIELD and PRUDHOE stations, in the vicinity of which stands the *keep* of the Bracy's old castle, built by William d'Umfraville, at the Conquest.

WYLAM.

Telegraph station at Blaydon, 4¼ miles.

In the vicinity of Wylam station, are *Wylam House*, C. Blackett, Esq., near which G. Stephenson, the engineer and inventor of the safety lamp (not Davy's), was born. *Close House*, Mrs. Beswicke, and *Dissington*, the seat of the descendant of Admiral Collingwood. Population, 1,091.

Passing RYTON station, near which is *Ryton Hall*, seat of J. Lamb, Esq., we arrive at

BLAYDON.

Close at hand are a large colliery and *Axwell Park*, the handsome seat of Sir T. Clavering, Bart.

SCOTSWOOD.

Telegraph station at Blaydon, 1 mile.

Here are Ramsay's extensive paper mills, well worth a visit. A fine skew bridge crosses the road, and a branch line to Gateshead.

Newcastle-upon-Tyne, see Section IV.

SCOTLAND.

GLASGOW AND SOUTH WESTERN.

Carlisle to Kilmarnock.

GRETNA GREEN—See page 73.

ANNAN.

A telegraph station.

HOTEL.—Queensberry Arms.

MARKET DAY.—Thursday.

FAIRS.—1st Thursday in May and 3rd Thursday in October.

This is a royal and parliamentary burgh, with a population of 4,570, who return one member, jointly with Dumfries, and are engaged in the coasting and shipbuilding trades, salmon fisheries, and gingham factories; contains three chapels, town house, market place, cotton mill, rope houses, three schools, and two churches, the oldest of which has a fine spire, Dr. Blacklock, the blind poet, and the late Edward Irving, were natives.

Next follows the station of CUMMERTREES, which takes its name from "Curmshir-tree" (Long Valley Town), near which lies *Hoddam Castle*, seat of General Sharpe, built by Lord Herries, under a hill on which is placed a Beacon, called the *Tower of Repentance* about 20 feet high; and five miles further on we pass

RUTHWELL station, close to which are *Comlongon Castle*, an old seat of the Earl of Mansfield. The church is ancient, and formerly contained the figured runic pillar, 18 feet high, which was moved to the manse in 1644. *Cockpool*, which belonged to the Murrays and Kirkstyles, which the Knights Templars held.

DUMFRIES.

A telegraph station.

HOTELS.—King's Arms, Commercial.

MARKET DAYS.—Wednesday and Saturday.

FAIRS.—Every Wednesday in January, February, March, and December, last Wednesday in April, Wednesday before the 26th May, Wednesday after June 17th, September 25th, or Wednesday after 2nd Wednesday in October, Wednesday before and after November 22nd.

BANKERS.—British Linen Co.; Commercial Bank of Scotland; Bank of Scotland; National Bank of Scotland; Western Bank of Scotland; Edinburgh and Glasgow Bank.

At the Commercial Inn, Charles Stuart took up his head quarters, in 1745. A Scottish royal and parliamentary burgh (one member), and the capital of Dumfriesshire, on the river Nith, near the Solway Frith. Population 13,166. It has a little shipping trade; shoes and cotton goods are the principal manufactures. The site is flat and mossy, but the soil fertile, with the Nithsdale Hills in the distance, The streets are clean and well built. Pleasant walks line the river's bank. Three slender spires are the first to strike the stranger's eye; one belongs to *St. Michael's*, an old church of the 13th century, containing, it is calculated, in and about it, above 1,800 monuments of all kinds. In the corner of the church yard is the handsome mausoleum to Burns, set up by subscription, in 1815. A beaten path made by those sands of visitors strikes across the other graves Within the church is an emblematic piece of marble, by Turnerelli, to the memory of the poet, who lived here as an exciseman from 1791 to his death in 1796. His widow survived him till 1834 living at a small house in Burns-street.

Here are a Court House, Academy, a Pillar to the excellent Duke of Queensberry, Dr. Crichton's Lunatic Asylum; and an old bridge, built by Baliol's mother, Devergilla, who also founded the Greyfriars, in which Bruce killed the Red Comyn, in 1305. Kean made his first appearance in the Dumfries Theatre. Excellent bacon and hams are cured here and vast numbers of small cattle pass this way to be fattened for market in Norfolk and Essex. Bruce was Lord of Annandale, a district in this neighbourhood, where many events of his early life took place.

On the opposite side of the Nith is *Lincluden Castle*. Further south you come to *Caerlaverock Castle*, the original of "Ellangowan" in Scott's *Guy Mannering*, the scenery of which, and of *Red Gauntlet*, are described from this part of Scotland.

At *Tinwald*, on the hills (near the old Watling-street). Patterson, the founder of the Bank of England, was born.

CASTLE DOUGLAS AND DUMFRIES.

Leaving Dumfries we immediately cross the river Nith, famous for its trout and salmon, pass the stations of MAXWELLTOWN, LOCHANHEAD, and KILLYWHAN, and arrive at

KIRKGUNZEON, a little village in the centre of a hilly grazing district. In the vicinity are the remains of three Roman Camps.

SOUTHWICK station.

DALBEATTIE, a small stone-built town with a population of about 1,500, engaged in shipping.

CASTLE DOUGLAS.

MARKET DAY.—Monday.

This is a town of growing importance with a population of about 2,000, and situated about a mile and a half to the south of Carlingwark Loch, a large sheet of water, abounding with perch, &c. It has also several small well-wooded islands. *Thrieve Castle*, formerly belonging to the Douglasses, is situate a little to the west of the town, on a little island in the Dee. Its remains date from the fourteenth century.

Near *Kirkcudbright*, they profess to show, at Rueberry, Dirk Hatteraick's Cave, and the Gauger's Loup, where poor Frank Kennedy was thrown over by the smugglers.

PORTPATRICK.

CROSSMICHAEL and PARTON stations.

NEW GALLOWAY,

Situate on the river Ken, which at this point widens very considerably, which circumstance, together with the bold and picturesque aspect of the scenery along its banks, render it a place of considerable interest to the tourist.

CREETOWN station.

NEWTON STEWART.

MARKET DAY.—Friday.

FAIRS are held on the second Friday in each month, also on the last Wednesday in April, July, and October.

This town has a population of about 2,600, engaged in the manufacture of leather. It is situated on the river Cree, which here forms the boundary line between the counties of Kircudbright and Wigton. The bridge across the river is a noble structure.

KIRKGOWAN and GLENLUCE stations.

STRANRAER.

MARKET DAY.—Friday. Population 5,738.

Is a seaport town at the top of Loch Ryan, accessible to steamers of heavy tonnage. The town itself has no particular attraction, but the country around is very interesting. Its position however can hardly be over estimated as forming the most expeditious route from Scotland to Ireland, in connection with the Belfast and County Down railway at Donaghadee. The distance will be still further reduced on the completion of the railway to the harbour at Portpatrick which may be shortly expected.

Kennedy Castle, 3½ miles to the east of the town, once the residence of the Earls of Cassilis, was destroyed by fire in 1715. A part of the walls are still remaining, and the grounds are kept in excellent condition.

HOLYWOOD and AULDGIRTH stations.

CLOSEBURN.

Telegraph station at Thornhill.

MONEY ORDER OFFICE at Thornhill, 2¾ miles.

Here are the ruins of an old castle of the Kilpatricks, *Closeburn Hall*, seat of Sir J. S. Menteith, baronet, and at Crichup Linn, a fall of 90 feet, was Balfour of Burley's Cave, the retreat of the persecuted covenanters.

THORNHILL and CARRON BRIDGE stations.

SANQUHAR.

POPULATION, 2,381.

A telegraph station.

HOTELS.—Fergusson's.

MARKET DAY.—Saturday.

FAIRS.—1st Friday in February, 3rd Friday in April, 1st Friday in May, Friday before 17th July, 1st Friday in November.

BANKERS.—British Linen Company; Western Bank of Scotland.

KIRKCONNEL.—The church here has an antique square tower. The "admirable Crichton" was born at Elliock House. In the vicinity are Castle Gilmour, a moot hill, and ruins of a hospital.

AYRSHIRE.

THIS county, which returns one member, is in the shape of two wings, extending to the north-west and south-west, and forming a vast bay at the mouth of the Firth of Clyde, and has abundant mines of coal; also freestone, limestone, iron, lead, and copper; and from the great abundance of sea-weed which is cast ashore, vast quantities of kelp is made. Ayrshire is called the "Land of Burns," who was born near the town of Ayr, and interred in Dumfries, where a monument was erected to his memory. But the most interesting cenotaph of Burns, which so many travellers visit, is that at Alloway, situated in most beautiful and romantic scenery, in the native parish of the poet, near the Auld Brig o' Doon, and "Alloway's auld haunted Kirk," through one of the windows of which Tam O'Shanter saw the witches dancing to the sound of their master's bagpipe. Innumerable pilgrims from all lands visit these scenes, and the place of the poet's residence, to gaze on what has been charmed and sanctified by his genius, or merely to have the satisfaction of standing beneath the roof where Burns first saw the light.

NEW CUMNOCK.

Telegraph station at Auchinleck, 7½ miles.
HOTEL.—Crown.
MARKET DAY.—Saturday.
BANKERS.—Bank of Scotland.

Close by is *Afton Bridgend Castle.* Coal, with graphite and lead, abound in this neighbourhood.

OLD CUMNOCK.

POPULATION, 2,395.
Distance from station, 2 miles.
Telegraph station at Auchinleck, 2 miles.
HOTEL.—Black Bull.
MARKET DAY.—Saturday.
FAIRS.—Weekly in Jan., Feb. and Dec., Thursday after 6th March, Wednesday after 6th June, 13th July, and 27th Oct.

Here is *Terrenzean Castle*, a fine ruin. At *Borland*, the pretty seat of the Hamiltons, are the ruins of a chapel. Plane-tree snuff-boxes are made here.

AUCHINLECK

A telegraph station.
HOTEL.—Dumfries Arms.
MARKET DAY.—Saturday.
FAIRS.—Last Tuesday in August (for lambs).
MONEY ORDER OFFICE at Old Cumnock.

Here are remains of the Boswell's old castle. Dr. Johnson lived here in 1773, and the pious M'Gavin was a native. Close at hand are the ruins of Kyle Castle.

MUIRKIRK BRANCH.

LUGAR station.

MUIRKIRK.

Telegraph station at Auchinleck, 10¼ miles.
HOTEL.—Black Bull.
MARKET DAY.—Saturday.

At *Prieshill* is a memorial to John Brown, whom Claverhouse shot at his own door.

MAUCHLINE.

Distance from station, ¾ mile.
Telegraph station at Auchinleck, 4½ miles.
HOTEL.—Black Bull.
MARKET DAY.—Saturday.

FAIRS.—Second and last Thursday in April, Wednesday after 18th May, 4th Wednesday in June, 1st Wednesday in August, Sept. 26th, Thursday after 4th Nov., and 4th Wednesday in Dec.

On Mauchline Moor is a church lately rebuilt, where Wishart preached in 1544; and here the royalists were defeated in 1647. At the Green is a stone on which is recorded the death of five persons by "Bloody Dumbarton, Douglas, Dundee," &c., in 1685. Burns wrote his "Mauchline Belles," &c., at J. Dow's and Poosie Nansie's Inns. Near at hand is Barskimmey Bridge, erected by Sir T. Miller, of Glenlee, Gavin Hamilton's House, the Lugar, and Ballochmyle.

HURLFORD station.

NEWMILNS BRANCH.

GALSTON.

POPULATION, 2,538.
Distance from station, 2½ miles
Telegraph station at Hurlford, 3½ miles.
HOTEL.—Loudon Arms.
MARKET DAY.—Saturday.
MONEY ORDER OFFICE.
BANKERS.—Union Bank of Scotland.

Close at hand is *Loudon Castle*, seat of the Marquis of Hastings, *Burr Castle*, at which are many cairns, and an elm 24 feet in girth, and *Wallace Hill*, the retreat of that gallant hero, and where he defeated Fenwick.

NEWMILNS.

POPULATION, 2,211.
Telegraph station at Hurlford, 5¼ miles.
HOTEL.—Black Bull.
MARKET DAY.—Saturday.
FAIRS.—1st Thursday in February, 3rd Wednesday in May, 4th Thursday in August, Wednesday after 1st Tuesday in September, 4th Wednesday in October.

MONEY ORDER OFFICE at Mauchline, 2 miles.

In Ramsay's song the scenery near Paties' Mill, on the river, is described.

KILMARNOCK.

POPULATION, 21,443.
A telegraph station.
HOTELS.—George, Black Bull.
MARKET DAYS.—Tuesday and Friday.
FAIRS.—2nd Tuesday in May, last Thursdays in July and October.
BANKERS.—Branch of Bank of Scotland; Branch of Commercial Bank of Scotland; Branch of Union Bank of Scotland; Branch of Western Bank of Scotland.

In the vicinity are the Castle, and Baturre's Castle (in ruins), Catter Hill, at which a court is held, and black mail was levied here in 1744, St. Marnoch, and *Ardoch*, the seat of W. Bontine, Esq.

STEWARTON.

POPULATION, 3,164.
Distance from station, 4 miles.
Telegraph station at Kilmarnock, 4 miles.
HOTEL.—Railway.

Considerable manufactures of woollen tartans, caps, Scotch bonnets, carpets, muslin, damask, &c., are carried on here. *Corsehill*, seat of Sir John Cunninghame, Bart., is close at hand.

DALRY.

POPULATION, 2.706.
A telegraph station.
HOTEL.—Black Bull.

Here the Scottish people rebelled against episcopacy. The church is situated on a hill, which is almost an island. In the vicinity are Auchinskeith, with its cave, and the Temple lands, which belonged to the Knights Templars, with several cairns.

ARDROSSAN, TROON, AND AYR BRANCHES.

KILWINNING JUNCTION.

POPULATION, 3,265.
A telegraph station.
HOTEL.—Eglinton Arms.
MARKET DAY.—Saturday.
FAIRS.—January 21st, and 1st Wednesday November.

Here are the ruins of a Franciscan Abbey, founded by Hugh de Morville, in 1140. The church stands near the old spire of the abbey, the last abbot of which was Gavin Hamilton. An archery club is held here, which was established in 1488, and at which the *popinjay* is held.

STEVENSTON and SALTCOATS stations.

ARDROSSAN.

POPULATION, 2,071.
A telegraph station.
HOTEL.—Eglinton Arms.
MARKET DAY.—Saturday.
FAIRS.—Tuesday before Ayr July fair, and 4th Thursday in November.
BANKERS.—Branch of Bank of Scotland; Branch Western Bank of Scotland.

A modern packet station and bathing place, in Ayrshire, on the Firth of Clyde, on a branch of the Glasgow and South Western, 5 miles from Irvine. This branch joins the main line at Kilwinning.

Steamers to Belfast. Sea passage, 6½ hours

The fine mountain scenery of Arran and Bute fronts this beautiful port, which was founded a few years back by the Eglinton family, and has a fashionable reputation, with baths, terraces, crescents, hotels, &c. The harbour, on which two or three hundred pounds have been expended, lies within a point of land, giving name (*Ard Ross, i. e.*, high head) to the parish, from which a circular pier runs out north-west towards the Horse Rock or island. Another rock, called Grinan, takes its designation from *Grian*, the sun, the worship of which appears to have been common with the Celts in pagan times. For instance, *Grianan* of Aileach, a celebrated sun-altar in Ireland.

Knockgeorgan hill, to the north-west of Ardrossan, is 700 feet high, and offers a striking prospect. *Ardrossan Castle*, now a ruin, was a seat of the Eglinton family, whose present residence here is the *Pavilion*.

IRVINE.

A telegraph station.
INNS.—King's Arms, Wheat Sheaf.
MARKET DAYS.—Monday and Saturday.

FAIRS.—1st Wednesday in January, 1st Tuesday in May, Wednesday before Ayr fair, 3rd Monday in August, and Wednesday after.

A considerable coal and shipping trade is here carried on by a population of 7,534. Here is an old tower belonging to the Eglintons. Galt, and James Montgomery, the poet, were natives. Jack (who was called Mrs. Buchan, who considered herself the woman of the 12th chapter of Revelations), held the living. Burns had a flax shop in Glasgow-Vennel Street, which has been burnt down.

TROON.

POPULATION, 2,404.
Distance from station, 1 mile.
A telegraph station.
HOTELS.—Portland, Commercial.
MARKET DAY.—Saturday.
MONEY ORDER OFFICE.
BANKERS.—Union Bank of Scotland.

Here is a pier 800 feet long, with revolving and fixed lights on it. Plenty of salmon and rabbits are in the vicinity.

MONKTON and PRESTWICK stations.

AYR.

A telegraph station.
HOTELS.—King's Arms, The Ayr Arms, Commercial.
STEAMERS to and from Campbelton, calling off Kildonan, Clauchog Shore, and South End of Arran, Girvan, and Stranraer, calling off Girvan and Ballintrae.
MARKET DAYS.—Tuesday and Friday.

FAIRS.—1st Tuesday in January, last Tuesday in June, September 29th, and 3rd Tuesday in October.

BANKERS.—Clydesdale Banking Company; the Royal Bank of Scotland; Union Bank of Scotland; Western Bank of Scotland; City of Glasgow.

AYR, a port, parliamentary burgh (one member), and capital of *Ayrshire*, on the west coast of Scotland, at the mouth of the Ayr water, a picturesque stream, running between steep banks, from about 30 miles in the interior. Salmon and Water o' Ayr whetstones are produced by it. Population, 17,624. About 5,000 tons of shipping are registered at the port, which has a pier harbour. Shoes, cotton and woollen goods, carpets, and nails, are the chief branches of manufacture.

Its old church of Cromwell's day, is on the site of a friary. About a quarter of a mile from St. John's Church is the Fort. At the latter place Bruce held a parliament to confirm the succession of the crown. Bruce's ancestors were Earls of Carrick.

The southern is the most hilly of the three districts into which this county is divided,

"Where Bruce ance rul'd the martial ranks,
And shook his Carrick spear."—BURNS.

Ayr itself stands in the middle one, called Kyle, after Coyl or Coil,—"Auld King Cole" of the old song.

There was an older church of the 13th century, of which a tower is left at the fort which Cromwell built in his Scottish campaign. It stood close to William the Lion's castle. The county buildings are copied from the Temple of Isis at Rome.

Close by is the new Gothic clock tower, 113 feet high, on the site of Wallace's tower (so called because the Scottish hero was imprisoned here); it supports a statue of Wallace, by Thom.

"We'll sing auld Coila's plains and fells,
Her moors red brown wi' heather bells,
Her banks and braes, her dens and dells,
Where glorious Wallace
Aft bore the gree, as story tells,
Frae Southron billies.

"At Wallace' name, what Scottish blood,
But boils up in a spring-tide flood!
Oft have our fearless father's strode
By Wallace' side,
Still pressing onward, red-wat shod,
Or glorious died."—BURNS.

Thus sings the Ayrshire Bard, whose name is identified with the town, and almost every part of his native county. The oldest of the "twa brigs" is a high, narrow, solid structure, on four arches, built in 1485, by two sisters, near the "Ducat Stream," a ford just above it. About 100 yards off is the new bridge, built by Adam, in 1788, which gave occasion to the *Brigs of Ayr*. In this humorous dialogue, the poet describes the river at the time of the floods. And from Glenbuck down to the Ratton quay, "auld Ayr is just one lengthened tumbling sea." Glenbuck is at its source.

He refers again to the "bonnie banks of Ayr," in what was meant to be his farewell song when leaving for Jamaica, "The gloomy night is gathering fast." About 2¼ miles out of Ayr, on the Maybole road, is Burns' Cottage, "the auld clay biggin'," in which he was born, in 1759. Further on is "Alloway's auld haunted Kirk," where he and his father, William Burness (this was how the family name was spelt), "the saint, father, and husband" of his *Cottar's Saturday Night*, are buried. It is a mere ruin, without a roof or rafters, the wood of which has been converted into snuff boxes, &c.; but the churchyard, which was walled round by Burns' father, is crowded with graves of the poet's admirers, who choose this as their last resting place. Burns put a stone over his father's grave, but this has been gradually carried away, and is replaced by another. Here Tam O'Shanter saw the witches dance—

"A winnock-bunker in the east,
There sat auld Nick in shape o' beast."

This window seat remains, divided by a mullion. About a quarter of a mile north-west, is a solitary tree in the field—

"by the cairn,
Whare hunters fand the murder'd bairn;"

and a little further, on a small branch of the Doon,—

"the ford,
Where in the snaw the chapman smoor'd."

Close to the Doon was a thorn (now gone)—

"abune the well,
Where Mungo's mither hang'd hersel'."

Then comes the "key-stane o' the brig," which Tam, on noble Maggie, made such strenuous efforts to cross, pursued by the hellish legion.

This river is the subject of one of Burns' sweetest songs—"Ye banks and braes o' bonnie Doon." Close to the bridge, on a picturesqe height above the road, commanding a view of these interesting localities, is Burns' *Monument*, a small circular dome, surmounted by a tripod and other ornaments, resting on nine open Corinthian pillars, and a spreading basement in which are deposited Burns' bust, by Park, his portrait, by Nasmyth, the Bible he gave to his Highland Mary, and other relics. The design was by Hamilton, and the first stone was laid by Sir A. Boswell (son of Dr. Johnson's biographer), in 1820, with an eloquent speech. In the grounds of this monument are the two celebrated statues of Tam O'Shanter and Souter Johnnie, by Thom, the self-taught sculptor. These immortal heroes of what Burns justly looked on as his "standard performance in the poetic line," were Douglas Graham, a farmer of Shanter, near Kirkoswald, and John Davidson, a shoemaker (souter), of the same place, where both are buried. The scene is fixed at Jean Kennedy's Inn. Burns wrote "*Tam O'Shanter*" for Grose (who first published it in his *Antiquities of Scotland*), in return for the Captain's sketch of Alloway church.

On the coast in this neighbourhood, is *Colzean*, or *Culzeen Castle*, the noble seat of the Marquis of Ailsa, and, about 3½ miles above Burns' monument, on the banks of the Doon, is *Cassilis Castle*, still more ancient, and a favourite haunt of the fairies, which suggested his *Hallowe'en*.

"Upon that night when fairies light
On Cassilis Downans dance,
* * * *
Or for Colean the route is ta'en, &c."

To the west, are the wild ruins of *Dunure Castle* the fine seat of the same (Kennedy) family, Along the shore to the south stands *Culzeen Castle;* and further still stands *Turnberry Castle*. In a direct line Culzeen Castle will be nine, and Turnberry Castle twelve miles south-west from Burns' monument, at the latter of which Scott, in his *Lord of the Isles*, makes Bruce land from Arran by mistaking a signal, when his country was overrun by the English.

About 10 miles south-west, out in the sea, opposite the mouth of "Girvan's fairy-haunted stream," is *Ailsa Craig*, a huge basalt rock, 1,100 feet high, and two miles round.

"Duncan fleech'd and Duncan pray'd,
Ha, ha, the wooing o't;
Meg was deaf as *Ailsa Craig*,
Ha, ha, the wooing o't.
Duncan sigh'd, baith out and in,
Grat his e'en baith bleart an' blin',
Spak o' lowpin' ower a linn;
Ha, ha the wooing o't."

Christopher North said, he would give all he had written for that line, "Spak o' lowpin' ower a linn."

About 6 miles east of Ayr, is *Coylton Kirk*, and *Mill Mannock*, a quiet spot on the banks of the Coyl, the scene of "The Soldier's Return." He was in an inn, at Brown-hill, when a poor worn-out soldier passed the window, and put this sweet song into his head. At Ochiltree, on the Lugar water, Cumnock Road, Willie Simpson, one of the poet's early friends, and a brother rhymer, was schoolmaster:—

"Auld Coila now may fidge fu' fain,
She's gotten poets o' her ain,
Chiels wha their chanters winna hain,
But tune their lays,
Till echoes a' resound again
Her well-sung praise.
* * * *
Th' Illissus, Tiber, Thames and Seine,
Glide sweet in monie a tunefu' line,
But Willie, set your fit to mine,
And cock your crest;
We'll gar our streams and burnies shine
Up wi' the best."

In ascending the Ayr from the town, you pass *Auchincruive*, a seat of the Oswalds, then *Stair Kirk* and *Barskimmey Bridge*, where was the house of old Kemp, and the *Mill* which suggested his "Man was made to mourn." "*Catrine Lea*," Dugald Stewart's seat, near the Braes of Ballochmyle, where he first met young Lord Daer, and *Sorn Castle*, are higher up. South of this is *Auchinleck House*, the Boswells' seat, with Reynolds' portrait of Johnson's biographer. The Doctor was here in 1773.

"But could I like Montgomerie fight,
Or gab like Boswell,
There's some sark necks I wad draw tight,
And tie some hose well."

Boswell, as might be expected, was fond of shining at public meetings.

A little north of Barskimmey is *Mossgiel Farm*, in Mauchline (or Macklin) parish. His humble farm house remains, with only one window in it. Here, when ploughing in 1785, the little field mouse led him to write his beautiful lines to the "Wee, sleekit, cow'rin' tim'rous beastie."

"I doubt na whyles, but thou may thieve;
What then, poor beastie thou maun live!
A daimen icker in a thrave
's a sma' request:
I'll get a blessin' wi' the lave,
And never miss't!"

Here, too, his equally beautiful *Mountain Daisy*, "Wee, modest crimson-tipped flower," and his noble *Cottar's Saturday Night* were written—the latter for his friend Aikin, a surgeon of Ayr. Another production of this period was his lines to *James Smith*, "Dear Smith, the slee'est, paukiest thief." It was in Smith's company that he dropped in one evening at Poosie Nansie's Inn, in the Cowgate, opposite the church, and witnessed something which suggested the *Jolly Beggars.* The churchyard was the scene of his *Holy Fair;* and W. Fisher, a Mauchline farmer, was the hero of *Holy Willie's Prayer.* Near the Church is *Mauchline Castle*, originally part of a cell to Melrose Abbey, the seat of another friend, Gavin Hamilton, the lawyer, and the poet's landlord. A new church has been built on the Moor; at the Green, is a stone, commemorating the death of five covenanters in 1615, by "Bloody Dumbarton, Douglas, and Dundee." At Morrison's, the carpenters' house, Burns wrote his spirited lines *To a Haggis*—

"Fair fa' your honest sonsie face,
Great Chieftain o' the puddin' race!"

A haggis is a pudding exclusively Scotch, but considered of French origin. Its ingredients are oatmeal, suet, pepper, &c., and it is usually boiled in a sheep's stomach. Although a heavy, yet it is by no means a disagreeable dish.

Going back to Ayr from Mauchline, you pass Tarbolton, whose learned schoolmaster was the hero of *Death and Dr. Hornbook*, and the Mill on the river Faile.

"I was come round about the hill,
And toddlin' down on Willie's Mill
Setting my staff," &c.

Willie, was William Muir, of Tarbolton. "Oh! rough, rude, ready-witted Rankine" had a farm at Adam Hill. Another resident was Anne Ronald, the Annie of *Rigs o' Barley.*

Coilsfield, in this parish (so called because Coilus, the Pictish King was buried here) on the Faile, is the seat of the Montgomeries (Earls of Eglinton), at which Mary Campbell, his immortal "Highland Mary," lived dairy woman; she was to have been married to Burns, but died in early life, and he never forgot her.

"Ye banks and braes and streams around
The Castle o' Montgomerie,
Green be your woods, and fair your flowers
Your waters never drumlie!

"There simmer first unfauld her robes,
And there the langest tarry;
For there I took the last fareweel
O' my sweet Highland Mary."

His exquisite lines to *Mary in Heaven*, "Thou lingering star, with lessening ray," were written at Mossgiel, on the anniversary of her death; and there can be no question that Mary was in his heart when he wrote his *Ae' fond kiss*, which Sir Walter Scott says contains the "essence of a thousand love tales."

Ayr to Maybole and Dalmellington.

By a further opening of the rails the tourist is enabled to continue his route to DALRYMPLE, CASSILLIS, and MAYBOLE to the right; and also to HOLLYBUSH, PATNA, WATERSIDE, and DALMELLINGTON to the left.

Glasgow and South Western Main Line continued.

KILBIRNIE station.

At BEITH is a Market on Friday, and Fairs 1st Friday in January, February, and November, and August 30th, and Witherspoon was minister in 1745.

LOCHWINNOCH, and MILLIKEN PARK stations.

JOHNSTONE.

POPULATION, 5,872.

A telegraph station.

MARKET DAY.—Saturday.

Near at hand are *Johnstone Castle*, seat of L. Houston, Esq., and *Milliken*, Sir W. Napier, Bart.

PAISLEY.

A telegraph station.

HOTEL.—Saracen's Head.

FAIRS.—Third Thursday in February and May, second Thursday in August and November; three days each.

RACES.—Second Thursday in August.

BANKERS.—Branch of British Linen Co.; Branch of Union Bank of Scotland; Branch of Bank of Scotland; Branch of Western Bank of Scotland.

PAISLEY, is a thriving seat of the cotton trade, with a population of 47,952, who return one member, and contains remains of a Norman priory, founded in 1164, by the ancestor of the Stuart line (who emigrated from Shropshire), large *Town Hall*, &c. On the castle site quarries of coal, stone, iron, &c., an alum work at Hurlet, and various old seats, as *Stanley Castle*, with its pillar cross, *Carndonald*, *Cochrane*, and *Elderslie*, which was Wallace's birthplace. The basalt rocks at the braes of Gleniffer are 760 feet high. Professor Wilson, the "Christopher North" of *Blackwood's Magazine*, and Tannahill, the poet, were natives.

The ruins of the palace are worth a visit. In the vicinity are *Hawkhead*, Earl of Glasgow; *Horsehill*, T. Spiers, Esq.; *Railston*, J. Richardson, Esq.; *Crookstone* (where Queen Mary visited Darnley); *Oakshaw Head*, and *Stewart's Raiss*.

Glasgow, page 78.

GLASGOW, PAISLEY, AND GREENOCK.

RENFREW.

THIS county, which returns one member, contains many manufacturing towns and villages. It is bounded by the Firth of Clyde and Clyde River. The waters of this county are of no great magnitude in themselves; but by the industry and enterprise of the inhabitants of the adjacent district, they are rendered of considerable importance to society, by being made instruments of human industry, and made to toil for man. If they descend suddenly from a height, it is not from a picturesque cataract, or to please the eye or ear with the wild and beautiful scenery which nature delights to exhibit, but to turn some vast water-wheel, which gives motion to extensive machinery in immense buildings, where hundreds of human beings are actively engaged in manufactures. In proportion as we approach towards Glasgow, the great theatre and centre of Scottish manufactures and commerce, everything assumes an aspect of activity, enterprise, arts, and industry.

HOUSTON.—In the church here are effigies of the Houston family: the ruins of the castle were used to build the village in 1780, in which is a pillar cross, 11 feet high. Close at hand are cairns, British kistvaens, and urns. A fair is held here on the second Tuesday in May.

BISHOPTON.—The railway here runs through two tunnels of whinstone.

LANG BANK and PORT GLASGOW stations.

GREENOCK.

A telegraph station.

HOTEL.—Tontine, George, White Hart.

STEAMERS to and from Glasgow, and all places on the Clyde, to Gareloch, Helensburgh, Roseneath, Garelochhead, Largs, Millport, Arran, Innerkip, Wemyss Bay, Strone, Kilmun, Kirn, Dunoon, Inellan, Rothesay, Ardrishaig, Crinan, Oban, Inverness, Fort William, Loch Fine, Loch Long, Arrochar, Lochgoilhead, Staffa, Iona, Ballachulish, Glencoe, Skye, Broadford, daily during the season.

MARKET DAY.—Saturday.

BANKERS.—Greenock Bank; Clydesdale Banking Co.; Branch Bank of Scotland; Branch of Royal Bank of Scotland.

GREENOCK, is a large seaport town on the southern bank of the Firth of Clyde (population 36,689, who return one member), and the scenery in its vicinity is remarkable for its picturesque beauty. Greenock is indebted for its present commercial importance to the trade which was opened by the inhabitants of the West of Scotland with the American colonies after the Union. The new *Custom House*, erected on a tongue of land which projects into the harbour, is one of the handsomest buildings in that part of Scotland. The principal street is nearly a mile in length, and there are others which run in a parallel direction along the quays, and are crossed by others at right angles; many modern improvements have recently taken place, which have greatly embellished the town. The harbour has been enlarged from time to time, and is now capable of admitting vessels of great burden. The manner in which this town is supplied with water, the aqueduct through which it is conveyed six or seven miles from the neighbouring hills to a reservoir over the town, are worthy of general admiration. Watt, the architect, was a native.

CALEDONIAN.

Carlisle to Edinburgh and Glasgow.

The railway station in Court Square was built from a design by Mr. Tite, the architect of the London Royal Exchange, and of all the station houses on this line.

Upon starting from the station, the traveller will observe on his right hand the outer wall of the *Castle*, above that the front of the *Deanery*, and further over, the ancient towers of the *Cathedral*. On the left the canal to the Solway, and Dixon's factory. Proceeding onwards, we cross the Calder over a viaduct, and thence over the river Eden by another viaduct, after which the line proceeds through King Moor, and arrives at the ROCKCLIFFE, station. Leaving Rockcliffe, in a few minutes we arrive at the river Esk, which gives its name to Eskdale, one of the most beautiful places in Scotland. On the banks of the river, not visible, however, from the railway, is situated Sir James Graham's elegant mansion of *Netherby*.

Crossing the river on a seven-arched viaduct, we have a fine view to the north-west; thence passing over the Glasgow road, we can perceive the Solway on the right, and Langholm Hills, with Sir John Malcolm's monument on the left. We now proceed along the Guard's embankment, formed through a deep moss, which absorbed thousands of tons of earth before the foundation was sufficiently solid to bear a train. Shortly after this we reach the FLORISTON station. We then cross the Sark, and leaving the county of Cumberland, enter Dumfries-shire, one of the most important of the southern counties of Scotland.

The next station is now in view, and soon recognised as the celebrated

GRETNA.

Telegraph station at Carlisle, 8½ miles.

HOTEL.—Gretna Hall.

POST HORSES, FLYS, &c., at the station and hotel. Tariff—1s. 6d. per mile; post boy, 3d. per mile; one horse vehicle, 1s. per mile or 15s. per day; gig, 12s. per day; riding horse, 6s. to 7s. per day; pony, 5s. to 5s. 6d. per day.

MONEY ORDER OFFICE at Carlisle.

The village of Gretna Green, in Dumfries, Scotland, is built on the banks of the Solway Firth, eight miles north of Carlisle. It is the first stage in Scotland from England, and has for more than eighty years been known as the place for the celebration of the marriages of fugitive lovers from England. According to the Scottish law, it was only necessary for a couple to declare before a justice of the peace that they were *unmarried*, and wished to be married, in order to render the ceremony lawful. An Act of parliament has since come into operation which requires a residence in Scotland of too long a duration to suit the purpose of fugitive lovers, and the blacksmith of Gretna Green, like *Othello*, will now find his "occupation gone." More than three hundred marriages took place annually in this and the neighbouring village of Springfield, and the fees varied from one to forty guineas.

Proceeding onward, the line passes the junction of the Dumfries line and Gretna Hall, through Graham's Hill cutting, and opens into a fine view, which about this point presents a most picturesque, varied, and highly romantic appearance.

Upon leaving KIRKPATRICK station the line soon crosses the "gently winding Kirtle," on a viaduct of nine arches, and then passes the tower of Robert Gill, a noted freebooter, who, with many other reckless "chields" of former times, made this district the scene of their border raids.

Shortly after leaving KIRTLE BRIDGE station we pass through an extensive cutting, and thence over an embankment. We then cross the Mein Water and West Gill Burn, and soon arrive at

ECCLEFECHAN.

Telegraph station at Lockerbie, 6 miles.

HOTEL.—Bush.

MARKET DAY.—Saturday (large pork market).

FAIRS.—Once a month.

The town of Ecclefechan is remarkable for nothing but its frequent and well-attended markets and fairs. From the station may be perceived a strong square keep or tower, the seat of General Matthew Sharpe, and known as *Hoddam Castle*, formerly a place of considerable importance as a border stronghold, and at present distinguished as one of the most delightful residences in Dumfries-shire. Opposite the castle, on a conspicuous mount, stands *Trailtron*, known as the Tower of Repentance, and formerly used as a beacon. It is said that Sir Richard Steele, while residing near this place, saw a shepherd boy reading his Bible, and asked him what he learned from it? "The way to heaven," answered the boy. "And can you show it to me?" said Sir Richard, in banter. "You must go by that tower," replied the shepherd, and he pointed to the Tower of Repentance.

Leaving Ecclefechan, we obtain a grand and extensive view of the surrounding scenery, perhaps the most gorgeous on the whole line. The Solway at the base of its gigantic sentinel; and beyond, the lofty Skiddaw, with its top melting away in the clouds. And before us is Borren's Hill, which from its curious shape is conspicuous long before we come near it. Skirting Brakenhill, we next arrive at the Milk Water, another of the poetical streams of bonnie Scotland, crossed by a viaduct, which commands a prospect of surpassing beauty.

LOCKERBIE.

A telegraph station.

HOTEL.—George.

MARKET DAY.—Thursday.

FAIRS.—Second Thursday in January, February, March, April, May, June, August, September, October, November, and before Christmas and Old Martinmas.

BANKERS.—Branch of Western Bank of Scotland; Branch of Edinburgh and Glasgow Bank.

Lochmaben, in the vicinity, is well worthy of a visit. It is poetically called the "Queen of the Lochs," from its situation amid so many sheets of water. Looking north from this station, there being no curve, we can see down the line a very long way. Here "Old Mortality" died at Brick Hall, in 1801. *Lockerbie Hall*, J. Douglas, Esq., and *Mains Tower*, which belonged to the Johnstones, are close at hand.

From NETHERCLEUGH station to the next there is scarcely an object of interest worth noticing. We pass Dinwoodie, Greens, and Mains, and then arrive at WAMPHRAY. Behind *Raehill*, a fine mansion situated on the banks of the Kinnel, towers the hill of Queensberry, one of the highest mountains in the south of Scotland. Shortly after leaving the Wamphray station, we cross the Annan, on a structure 350 feet in length. Farther on, a long embankment, succeeded by the Logrie cutting. Advancing, we cross once more the Glasgow road, and in a few minutes reach the place where all the visitors to Moffat will alight, at

BEATTOCK (Moffat).

A telegraph station.
HOTEL.—Beattock.
MARKET DAY.—Saturday.
FAIRS.—Third Friday in March, July 29th, Oct. 15th and 20th.
MONEY ORDER OFFICE.
BANKERS.—Branch of Union Bank of Scotland; Branch of Western Bank of Scotland.

About two miles from Beattock, surrounded on every side but one by lofty hills, lies the fashionable village of

MOFFAT, celebrated for its mineral waters. The environs are remarkably beautiful, and the different villas exceedingly pretty. Moffat has long been famed for its mineral waters (the sulphur Spa discovered in 1633, and the iron springs at Hartfell, in 1730), and visitors will find every accommodation, including *Assembly Rooms, Baths, &c.* Among the fine scenery scattered round Moffat, are *Bell Craig*, and the *Grey Mare's Tail* waterfall, the latter being one of the grandest sights it is possible to conceive. The water is precipitated over a rock three hundred feet high. In the vicinity are *Raehills*, Earl Hopetoun; *Drumcrieff*, formerly Dr. Currie's seat. The *Mole Hill*, with its camps, and *Bell Craig*, which commands an extensive view, and where delicious whey milk can be procured.

Resuming our progress from the Beattock station, we proceed onwards through the lovely vale of Annandale, and then passing a deep cutting, we skirt the Greskin Hills, close to which, are the sources of three of Scotland's finest rivers; the Tweed, the Clyde, and the Annan having their rise in the same clump of hills, and each falling into a different sea, in a different part of the kingdom.

The great viaduct over the Elvan is well worth attention. Passing

ELVANFOOT station, where the Clyde and Elvan Water join, we reach

ABINGTON.

Telegraph station at Beattock, 18 miles.
HOTEL.—Hunter's.
MONEY ORDER OFFICE at Biggar, 14 miles.

We now begin to perceive a distinct stream of the Clyde, which shortly after issuing from its source, from the accession of many tributary burns, becomes at this point, a river of considerable size, and keeps gradually increasing—

> "Now sunk in shades, now bright in open day,
> Bright Clyde, in simple beauty, wends his way."

This is the junction of the Clyde and Glengowner water. Some gold was found here in the time of James VI.

Previous to arriving at the next station, we pass, on the right hand, *Lamington Old Tower*, one of the seats of the family, one of whose daughters, it is said, was married to the great Hero of Scotland, Sir William Wallace.

Passing LAMINGTON station, close to which are hilly sheep walks, porphyry, and good trout fishing, Lamington House, Wandell Bower, Windgate House, Arbory Hill (600 feet high), Whitehill (70 yards), Hartside, Woodend, and Braehead, with their Roman and Saxon camps, Druid arches, and Cauldchapel, with its moat of 20 yards, we arrive at

SYMINGTON.

Telegraph station at Carstairs, 7 miles.

A short time previous to reaching the station, we have the famous hill of Tinto appearing in view; towering high above the other giants of nature which surround it. Visitors ascend to the top of Tinto or the "Hill of Fire," in order to enjoy the fine view from its summit.

In the vicinity are *Fatlips Castle*, in ruins, and *Castle Hill*, which is planted all over.

SYMINGTON, BIGGAR, AND BROUGHTON.

This is a line, 19½ miles long, running out of the Caledonian, at Symington, to Peebles, 8¼ miles of which only are yet open. The line passess, *via* the station of COULTER to

BIGGAR—A small town situated in a hilly district, with a population of about 1550. The church, built by the Flemings, is in the form of a cross. Traces of a Roman camp may also be seen.

BROUGHTON.—In the vicinity of which are some border castle ruins. This forms the present terminus of the line.

Caledonian Main Line continued.

THANKERTON and the neighbouring village of Corington Mill are celebrated as having been a favourite haunt of the persecuted Covenanters, and there are many spots pointed out among the surrounding hills as their places of worship. The Clyde, in the vicinity, is remarkable for its many windings.

Leaving Thankerton, and once more crossing the river, we shortly reach the Carstairs Junction, from which point the line forks; the right branch turning off to Edinburgh and the left to Glasgow.

Carstairs to Edinburgh.

CARSTAIRS JUNCTION.

POPULATION, 1,066.

A telegraph station.

MONEY ORDER OFFICE, Lanark, 5 miles.

Here are remains of the Bishops of Glasgow's castle, castle dykes, Roman camp of upwards of five acres, and *Carstairs House*, which is the seat of R. Monteith, Esq.

CARNWATH. — Here are remains of Couthalley Castle, *Carnwath House*, the beautiful seat of the Somervilles, and the church, which contains their effigies and tombs, and the kennel of the Linlithgow hounds.

AUCHENGRAY and HARBURN stations, close to which is *Harburn House*, the seat of J. Young, Esq.

MIDCALDER.

POPULATION, 1,474.

Distance from station, 1 mile.

Telegraph station at Edinburgh, 10 miles.

HOTEL.—Lemon Tree.

BANKERS.—Edinburgh and Glasgow Bank.

Close at hand is *Calder House*, seat of Lord Torphichen, in which is a fine portrait of Knox, who first administered the sacrament here after the Reformation. *Greenbank* was the native plac of Archbishop Spottiswoode, the church historian.

CURRIE.—The scene of Ramsay's *Gentle Shepherd*, and near which is *Currie Hill*, the seat of the Skenes, and close by the ruins of Lennox Tower, the residence of Queen Mary and Darnley; *Buberton*, the hunting seat of James VI., and for some time the abode of Charles X. of France, after the events of 1830.

KINGSKNOWE and SLATEFORD stations, at the latter of which fairs are held on the Wednesday after the 26th August and the Friday before Kirriemuir fair.

Edinburgh, see Section IV.

Carstairs to Glasgow.

Proceeding on to Glasgow the line passes *Carstairs House*, the seat of R. Monteith, Esq.

From Carstairs station we cross the river Mouse, which runs through some wild and romantic scenery, arriving at

CLEGHORN, the junction of the branch to Lanark. Hear are the ruins of an old chapel and a Roman camp.

LANARK BRANCH.

Proceeding onwards, a distance of $2\frac{3}{4}$ miles, the whole of the neighbouring grounds to Lanark are remarkable as having been the hiding place of Sir William Wallace.

"Each rugged rock proclaims great Wallace' fame,
Each cavern wild is honour'd with his name,
Here in repose was stretched his mighty form,
And there he sheltered from the night and storm."

LANARK,

Telegraph station at Carstairs, 5 miles.

HOTEL.—Clydesdale.

MARKET DAYS.—Tuesday and Saturday.

FAIRS.—Last Tuesday in February, second Wednesday in April, last Wednesday in May and July, first Tuesday in July, first Wednesday in November, and last Tuesday in December.

BANKERS.—Commercial Bank of Scotland; City of Glasgow; Western Bank of Scotland; the Royal.

From this point travellers can visit the Falls of Clyde, and the romantic scenery in the neighbourhood. Independent of the more than magnificent grandeur of the various waterfalls themselves, the beauty of the country on every side of the river, and the picturesque succession of views which present themselves to the eye at every turn of the road, are a source of great attraction. A guide to the Falls may be obtained at any of the respectable inns in the town.

The ancient town of Lanark, capital of the county, which returns one member, has a population of 5,305, and although not engaging in outward appearance, possesses many points of interest, and is remarkable as having been the scene of Wallace's first grand military exploit, in which he killed Heslerig, the English sheriff, and drove his soldiers from the town. The burgh consists of a principal street, and a number of smaller ones branching off. The grammar school had General Roy and Judge Macqueen as scholars. The church, built in 1774, contains a figure of Wallace. In the vicinity are Castle Hill Tower, Quair Castle, Cleghorn, with its Roman camp, 600 yards by 420; *Lee House*, seat of Sir N. Lockhart, Bart., at which is the "Lee Penny or Talisman." Judge Lee, and Lithgow, the traveller, were born here.

NEW LANARK village is situated about one mile from Lanark, and contains a population of 1,807. It was established in 1784, by Robert Owen's father-in-law, the late David Dale, and is now the property of Messrs. Walker & Co. There are several cotton mills, at which about 1,100 hands are employed. No stranger ought to omit visiting this far-famed village, which is quite in his way when visiting the Upper Falls of the Clyde.

THE FALLS.—*Bonnington Fall*, although the most inconsiderable, should be first visited, for the remarkable scenery surrounding it.

Corra Linn Fall, 84 feet, considered by some as the finest of the Falls, about half a mile from *Bonnington*, the seat of Sir Charles Ross, at which are Wallace's chair, cup, and portrait, is composed of three slight falls, at an inconsiderable distance from each other, over which the vast body of water rushes with fearful impetuosity into a deep abyss. To describe the beauties of the scene is an almost impossible task, requiring the glowing language of the poet to do justice to them.

Stonebyres. The approach to this (which is 70 feet) fall is by a gently winding road—its *tout ensemble* and the adjacent landscape is sublime. Above we have lofty crags fringed with natural wood. The torrent dashes in one uninterrupted stream into the abyss beneath, raising clouds of stormy spray from the boiling gulph.

Cartland Crags—which extends nearly half a mile on both sides of the river, is a most romantic dell, composed of lofty rocks, beautifully diversified with natural wood. The approach from the north—a level piece of ground, around which the Mouse makes a sweep—conducts to the mouth of this great chasm. As you enter, and through its whole extent, a succession of the most picturesque scenes appear on every hand. In the most sequestered part of the dell is a natural chasm in the rock, called *Wallace's Cave*, which tradition and history concur in informing us was often resorted to by that hero.

Upon emerging from Cartland Crags upon the south, the traveller finds himself surrounded by a beautiful amphitheatre of high grounds, open towards the Clyde, and in the immediate vicinity of the Bridge of Lanark.

Caledonian Main Line continued.

Leaving CLEGHORN and BRAIDWOOD stations (near the latter of which are extensive collieries and lime works), we arrive at

CARLUKE.

POPULATION, 2,845.
Distance from station, ½ mile.
Telegraph station at Motherwell, 7 miles.
HOTEL.—Commercial.
COACH to Lanark and the Falls of the Clyde.
BANKERS.—City of Glasgow Bank.

The line now passes through a district of country rich in mineral wealth—beautiful scenery—celebrated far and near as the Orchard of Scotland, and famous for its fine fruit. The growers clear very large sums by sending the produce of their orchards to Glasgow. On the left side of the railway, shortly after leaving the station, is *Milton*, a handsome building, in the Tudor style of architecture, situated on a fine peninsula, and skirted on three sides by the Clyde. Next appears the stately seat of *Mauldslee Castle*, belonging to the Hyndfords, and St. Oswald's chapel, a hermitage. The next station is

OVERTOWN.

Telegraph station at Motherwell, 3¾ miles.

All the scenery around is so enchanting that the traveller will wish the train to linger over it. Not far from this station is another beautiful spot called *Cambusnethan*, which attracts the notice and admiration of every stranger.

Passing WISHAW station, near which is *Wishaw Castle*, the seat of J. Hamilton, Esq., we reach

MOTHERWELL.

A telegraph station.
MONEY ORDER OFFICE at Wishaw, 2½ miles.
For continuation of route, see page 78.

From this junction we pass the stations of HOLYTOWN and WHIFFLET to

COATBIDGE.—At this place the Dundyvan Iron Works are well worth visiting.

GARTSHERRIE JUNCTION.—Proceeding a few miles beyond this station, we enter

STIRLINGSHIRE,

WHICH returns one member, and occupies the centre of the country between the Firths of Forth and Clyde, and, therefore, descends towards each of these streams, being highest in proportion to its distance from each. The principal mountain in this county is Benlomond, the view from which is grand and interesting beyond conception, and must be seen to be appreciated. At the bottom is seen the beautiful Loch Lomond, stretched out like a mirror; its islands having lost their rugged forms, and appearing as level surfaces, amid the bright expanse. The banks of the lake are seen ornamented with villas and cultivated grounds. Towards the east, the rich plains of Lothian and Stirlingshire are distinctly spread out to the sight. From thence to the south, and pursuing the view towards the west, the high grounds of Lanarkshire, the vales of Renfrewshire, with the Firth of Clyde, with its islands, and the wide Atlantic, are clearly discerned; while the Isle of Man, and the coast of Ireland, blended as it were with the sky, are scarcely discernible. But to one unaccustomed to Highland scenery, the most striking view is undoubtedly on the north side, which may in truth be termed fearfully sublime. The eye, from where it first discovers the Ochil hills, near the east, ranging along the north till it comes near the western ocean, beholds nothing but mountains, elevating their summits in almost every variety and form, and which are covered with snow for a considerable portion of the year.

SCOTTISH CENTRAL.

Greenhill to Stirling.

GREENHILL JUNCTION.—Trains from Glasgow and the south unite here with this line, beyond which circumstance the station possesses no extraordinary attraction.

LARBERT.

Telegraph station at Stirling, 8 miles.
MARKET DAY.—Saturday.
FAIR.—Last Wednesday in April.

Close at hand are some ruins of Danish forts, and *Larbert House*, seat of J. Riddell, Esq.

To facilitate the traffic to and from Edinburgh and the north, a short branch line turns off here, running into the Edinburgh and Glasgow railway at Polmont.

BANNOCKBURN.

POPULATION, 2,000.
Telegraph station at Stirling, 2½ miles.
HOTEL.—Bruce's Head.
MONEY ORDER OFFICE at Stirling, 2½ miles.

The rivulet called "Bannockburn" here runs through a glen, and after a few miles falls into the river Forth. The inhabitants are very industrious, and carry on a considerable trade in carpets, tartan, and woollen cloth in general. It was here that the celebrated battle was fought between Robert Bruce, King of Scotland, and Edward of England, on the 24th of July, 1314. Here James III. was defeated in 1488 by his own subjects. Upon the top of an eminence, called Caldon Hill, and close by the side of the road, is a large earth-fast mountain limestone stone, on which the Scottish King planted his standard at the above battle; and so highly is this stone valued by the Scottish people, that fragments of it are frequently cut off, and set in rings, brooches, &c., and worn as a memorial of one of the proudest days in the annals of Scotland. Randolph's Field, Ingram's Crook, and Gillie's Hill are close at hand.

STIRLING.

A telegraph station.
HOTELS.—Golden Lion (late Gibbs); Royal.

MARKET DAY.—Friday.

FAIRS.—First Friday in February, last ditto in March, first ditto in April, last ditto in May, first ditto in August, third ditto in Sept. and Oct., first ditto in Nov., second ditto in December.

BANKERS.—Branch of Bank of Scotland, Clydesdale; Royal; Branch of Commercial Bank of Scotland; Branch of Edinburgh and Glasgow Bank; Branch of Union Bank of Scotland; Branch of National Bank of Scotland; City of Glasgow; The Western.

STIRLING, a county and garrison town, is built on an eminence in the centre of a fertile plain, which is watered by the river Forth, and above the town rises the Castle of Stirling, so celebrated in Scottish history. The stream which flows by the town is here of considerable depth, and vessels are able to unload their goods on the excellent quay by which it is bordered.

This ancient seat of the Scottish kings, and capital of Stirlingshire, is situated on a beautiful part of the Forth, about half way between Edinburgh and Perth. One member is returned for Stirling and its sister burghs. Population, 12,837. As a key to the Highlands it is an important position, having been frequently contested, and at length became the favourite seat of all the James's, from James I. to James VI. (or first of Great Britain). The best part of the Palace, or *Castle*, was begun by James V., the Knight of Snowdon, a hero of the "Lady of the Lake," known also as the "Gudeman of Ballangeich," an *alias* conferred on him from his taste for disguises and intriguing adventures. The "Gaberlunzie man," and "We'll gae nae mair a roving," are founded on these. Ballangeich is the pass leading to the rock (350 feet high) on which the castle is perched, originally called Snowdon, and overlooking the town—one of the most splendid prospects in Scotland, especially of the Forth and Teith, and the distant Highlands. The oldest portion of the castle is the closet in which James II. stabbed William Earl Douglas. The Parliament Room (120 feet long), with an oak roof, was built by James III., but is now a barrack, as also is the presence chamber in James V.'s palace—this fortress being one of the four which the Articles of Union, in 1762, provides shall be maintained. James VI. added a chapel, which is now the armoury. He was educated here, under the care of the learned Buchanan. The ancient walls, drawbridge, &c., remain. In the park behind is a ring for tournaments. To the north-east of the Castle is the Moat Hill, commonly named Hurley-Hacket; on it executions generally took place. The old portion of the Castle was destroyed by fire 1855. The building is in course of re-erection, strictly in keeping with its former quaint style. The pulpit of the great reformer, Knox, is shewn in the armoury, along with many other relics of the olden time. Argyll's Lodgings, in Castle Wynd, is now the military infirmary. Here the Duke of York and his daughter (afterwards Queen Anne) lodged in 1681.

The Grey Friars' Church was erected in 1494 by James IV. It is a handsome Gothic building, and is now divided into two separate places of worship, in connection with the Church of Scotland, denominated the "Eas and West Churches." The east church is allowed to be a very good, if not the best, specimen of Gothic architecture in Scotland. From the top of the tower a splendid view is obtained Here the Regent Arran publicly renounced Popery in 1543, and James VI. was crowned, while John Knox preached his sermon, in 1567, and his son Henry was baptized with great magnificence. A spire in Broad Street marks the *Town House*, in which a relic of old times, the *Stirling Jug*, or standard pint, similar to our Winchester measure, is kept. For several years it was lost, but was at length discovered by the sagacity of the late Dr. Bryce, in the corner of a garret of a Jacobite brazier. Here also are the keys of the old bridge, which was partly destroyed in 1745, to cut off the retreat of Charles Stuart; likewise the keys of the port gates of the burgh, Stirling being at one time a walled town, much of which still remains. About 1½ mile up the river is the site where Kildean Bridge stood, the place where Wallace defeated the English in 1297. The railway crosses the Forth at Stirling. The old bridge is within a few hundred yards, but the old wooden bridge of the days of Wallace, which stood about 1½ mile up the river at Kildean, has long ago disappeared. The junction of the Forth and Clyde Railway is at Stirling, from whence tourists may reach Loch Lomond in 1½ hour.

Here are various literary and benevolent institutes. The *Athenæum* and *Library*, in King Street, with a clock spire. *Cowan's Hospital*, near the church, founded in 1633, possesses an income of more than £3,000; and the founder's statue. Another hospital exists for the relief of the burgesses. *Drummond's Museum* of agricultural implements, &c., should be visited; it is 160 feet long.

EXCURSIONS from Stirling to *Loch Katrine*, &c. The best companion for this trip is the "Lady of the Lake." The distances are—to Doune, 9 miles; Callander, 8 miles; Coilantogle, Ford, 3 miles; Bridge of Turk, 5 miles; Trosachs, 3 miles; Loch Katrine and Inversnaid, on Loch Lomond, 12 miles; about 40 miles altogether, or 80 round to Glasgow—but this portion includes steam and railway. At Doune, on the Teith, is an old castle of the Stuarts. Callander, where the pass of Leny turns up Strathire and Loch Lubnaig. Ben Ledi in view, 3,000 feet high. From Ben Ledi was seen the cross of fire. Lord John Russell spent the summer of 1853 here, when he was made a freeman of Stirling, and addressed the burgesses on the Duke of Wellington's death. At Coilantogle Ford, on the Teith, Fitz-James defeated Rhoderic Dhu, and began his celebrated ride to Stirling. Loch Vennachar, three miles long, and its banks well wooded. Bridge of Turk, at the bottom of Loch Achray, and the mouth of Glenfinglas. Aberfoyle, on the Forth, is four or five miles to the south (see "Rob Roy"). The naked top of Ben An to the right *Trosachs*, a wild rugged pass of a mile, between Loch Achray and Loch Katrine (*i. e.*, Cateran, a thief), the lake of Scott's poem. "High on the south" is "huge Benvenue," 2,800 feet high, in the district of Menteith. Lochs Ard and Awe are in this direction, but the regular road is on the north side of the lake, to the ferry, the top of which is seven miles. Ponies may be had hence to Loch Lomond, which is descended by steamer. To *Airthrie Wells* and *Bridge of Allan*, a beautiful place of resort on the Allan. *Dunblane*, on the Perth road, was once the bishopric of the excellent Archbishop Leighton; the *Cathedral Church* is of the 12th century. *Sheriff's Muir*, where the Duke of Argyll and Marr fought a drawn battle in 1715, is near. It is said that the Duke was a better Christian than a soldier on this occasion, as he would not let his right hand know what his left hand had done. The river *Devon* rises here; *Allan* may be followed to its crook or bend, and the three *falls* at Caldron Lynn. Ben Cleuch or Ben Buck, in the Ochils, is 2,420 ft. high. Demyatt, near Logie, is 1,345 feet high; a famous view. Up the Forth (10 miles), the seat of Buchanan of old, King of Kippen, *Port of Menteith*, and *Aberfoyle* (20 miles from Stirling). To the south of Stirling the rail traverses a wide plain, on which several battles have been fought, viz.: *Bannockburn* (1314), near St. Ninian's, a great place for nailers, &c.; *Sauchieburn* (1488, James III. killed); *Falkirk* (1298, Wallace defeated). The last is famous for its cattle fair, and is near the Carron Iron Works. *Kilsyth*, where Baillie was beaten by Montrose (1645). This is near Castlecary, and other remnants of the *Antonine Wall*, locally called Graham's Dyke.

For continuation of this route to Perth, Aberdeen, and Inverness, see page 88.

FORTH AND CLYDE JUNCTION.

Stirling to Balloch and Loch Lomond.

This is a short line of thirty miles, connecting the eastern counties with the West Highlands of Scotland. It commences at Stirling, and passes in its route the stations of GARGUNNOCK, KIPPEN, PORT OF MONTEITH, BUCKLIVIE, BALFRON, GARTNESS, DRYMEN, KILMARONOCK, and JAMESTOWN, connecting itself with the Dumbartonshire Railway at

BALLOCH.—See page 82, for continuation of route up Loch Lomond.

Caledonian Main Line continued.

Pursuing our course from the Motherwell station, we pass several places of note. The beautiful village of UDDINGSTON is situated on an elevated spot, commanding an extensive and highly diversified prospect. The Clyde—the city of Glasgow, the Queen of the West—the numerous seats scattered around, the distant hills of Stirling, Dumbarton, and Argyleshires, lie extended before the eye, forming a panorama of great beauty. Then NEWTON station, and crossing the Clyde, we pass near

CAMBUSLANG.—Loudon the naturalist was a native, and in the vicinity are *Kirkburn*, with the remains of a chapel and hospital; *Westburne*, T. Hamilton, Esq., and here "Cambuslang Wark" took place in 1742, at which Whitfield was an eye witness. This station forms the junction of the

HAMILTON BRANCH.

The first and only intermediate station on this branch is four miles from the junction, which requires a very short space of time to annihilate.

BLANTYRE.

In his visit, the stranger must not omit to see *Blantyre Priory*, Bothwell Bridge, where the Covenanters were defeated in 1679, by the Duke of Monmouth, and *Chatelerault*, a summer chateau of the Duke of Hamilton.

HAMILTON.

Telegraph station at Motherwell, 13¾ miles.

HOTELS.—Commercial; Bruce's Arms.

MARKET DAY.—Friday.

FAIRS.—Last Tuesday in Jan., second Tuesday in Feb., Friday after 15th May, last Thursday in June, second Thursday in July and Nov.

BANKERS.—Branch of Commercial Bank of Scotland; Branch of Western Bank of Scotland; Branch of British Linen Co.

Over the whole neighbourhood of this place lie scattered scenes full of historical and poetical interest; and the traveller making it of his head-quarters, might in a short time see a "whole Switzerland of romantic dells and dingles." Many of the places here are classic ground, the interest never flagging, from its being immortalised by the pen of Sir Walter Scott, and other writers of lesser note.

Hamilton Palace, partly as old as 1591, the seat of the Duke of Hamilton, is a noble building. The grounds and picture gallery, in which is Ruben's "Daniel in the Lions' Den," are thrown open to strangers, without any formal application. Cullen was a native of Hamilton. The traveller must of course visit the ruins of *Bothwell Castle*, one of the most picturesque and venerable monuments of the ancient splendour of Scotland. Its stately grandeur excites the admiration of all who have seen it.

Caledonian Main Line continued.

We have scarcely got clear of the junction at Cambuslang than the arrival of the train is announced at the ancient royal burgh of

RUTHERGLEN.

Here fairs are held on the first Friday after March 11th, 25th July, 25th August, May 4th, first Tuesday after June 4th, first Wednesday before first Friday in November, and first Friday after 25th December.

Rutherglen Church is famous on account of two great national transactions; it was here that Edward I. signed the treaty in 1297, and Monteith covenanted to betray Wallace.

GLASGOW.

Telegraph stations at the Exchange, and 147, Queen Street.

HOTELS.—Carrick's Royal Hotel; Walker's George Hotel; Bush's Buck's Head; Mc.Gregor's Queen Hotel.

RESTAURATEURS.—Ferguson and Forrester, 33, Buchanan Street; the Queen's, 81, Queen Street.

NEWS ROOMS.—Royal Exchange, Queen Street, and the Tontine, (free); Athenæum, Ingram Street, and the Telegraphic, 27, Glassford Street, one penny per visit.

COACH OFFICES.—J. Walker, 104, West Nile Street; Wylie and Lockhead, 28, Argyle Street; A. Menzies, 10, Argyle Street.

STEAMERS to and from Ardrishaig, 5½ hours, Helensburgh, in 2½ hours, Roseneath, 2½ hours, Gareloch Head, 4 hours, Gourock and Ashton, 2 hours, Innerkip, 3 hours, Wemyss Bay, 3¼ hours, Largs, 3½ hours, Millport, 3¾ hours, Kilmun, 3 hours, Dunoon, 3 hours, Inellan, 3¼ hours, Rothesay, 3½ hours, Strone, 2¾ hours, Crinan, 7½ hours, Oban, 9¾ hours, Inverary, 7¼ hours, Arroquhar, 4½ hours, Lochgoilhead, 5 hours, &c.

MARKET DAY.—Wednesday.

FAIRS.—May 26, second Monday in July

BANKERS.—Branch Bank of Scotland; Branch of British Linen Co.; Branch Commercial Bank of Scotland; Branch National Bank of Scotland; Branch Royal Bank of Scotland; City of Glasgow Bank; Union Bank of London; Clydesdale Banking Co.; Union Bank of Scotland; North British Bank; Western Bank of Scotland; Branch of Edinburgh and Glasgow Bank.

GLASGOW.—The first port and seat of manufacture in Scotland and a parliamentary burgh, two members, in the lower ward or division of Lanarkshire (which county also returns one member), on the Clyde, 50 miles from the open sea. That which was the ruin of many small places in this part of Great Britain, namely the Union, 1707, was the grand cause of the prosperity of Glasgow, which from its admirable position on a fine navigable river in the heart of a coal-field, and from the spirit of the inhabitants, has risen to be reckoned as the fourth port of the United Kingdom, and a rival to Manchester. When Bailie Nicol Jarvie and his worthy father, the deacon, "praise to his memory," lived in the Salt Market, before the American revolution, it was a great place for the tobacco trade, but since 1792 cotton has been the staple business.

Population 329,097, of which perhaps 50,000 are employed in the spinning, weaving, bleaching, and dyeing of cotton goods, worsted, muslin, silks, &c., while a large number are engaged in the manufacture of iron, brass, steam engines, glass, nails, pottery, umbrellas, hats, chemicals, and other branches of trade, and in wooden and iron ship building, besides numbers engaged in maritime and commercial transactions. These are the distinguishing characteristics of modern Glasgow, and the commercial activity and restlessness of its inhabitants have caused the immense impulse its trade has received within the last fifty years. The site is a level, four or five miles square, chiefly on the north side of the river. On the south side are the suburbs of Tradeston, Laurieston, and Hutchesonton; here are most of the factories. Its port is the open river, fronting the Broomielaw, lined by noble quays above one mile long, and so much deepened that first-class ships, which used to stop at Port Glasgow, 18 miles lower down, can now come up to the city. Formerly people could cross without wet feet, where now there is 20 feet of water. The tonnage owned by the port exceeds 150,000, its income is £90,000, and the customs (which in 1812 were only £3,100) amount to £700,000.

BRIDGES.—Six cross the Clyde, in some parts 400 feet wide. *Jamaica Bridge*, near the Ayr railway and Broomielaw, rebuilt by Telford in 1833, 500 feet long, 60 wide. A wooden bridge rebuilt in 1853. *Victoria Bridge*, rebuilt in 1851-3 by Walker, on five granite arches, the middle one being 80 feet span, and the next two 76 feet. It replaces old *Stockwell Bridge*, which was begun in 1345. *Hutcheson Bridge*, built in 1833, by R. Stevenson, the builder of the wooden bridge, opened 1855. *Rutherglen Bridge* is the highest, near the King's Park, in which stands the Nelson pillar.

CITY AND COMMERCIAL BUILDINGS.—The large new *County Buildings* are in Wilson-street. *Justiciary* or *Law Courts*, in the Salt Market, near Hutcheson Bridge, has a Grecian portico, imitated from the Parthenon. *County Bridewell*, Duke Street, an excellent self-supporting institution, built in 1824, in the Norman style. Large *City Hall*, in the Candleriggs-street, built in 1840. *Old Town Hall* in the Trongate—in front is Flaxman's statue of William IV. *Exchange* in Queen Street, a handsome Grecian building by D. Hamilton, erected in 1840, 200 ft. long by 76 broad; fine Corinthian eight-column portico and tower; news-room, 130 feet long. In front is Baron Marochetti's bronze statue of Wellington. Hamilton is also the architect of the *Theatre Royal*, in Dunlop-street, and the City of Glasgow bank, the latter copied from the temple of Jupiter Stator. *Union Bank* and the handsome *Assembly Room*, now the *Athenæum*, in Ingram-street. *Corn Exchange*, in the Italian style, built in 1842. Trades' Hall, a domed building. *Western Club House*, in Buchanan-street. *Cleland Testimonial*, in Sauchiehall-street, raised to commemorate the services of Dr. Cleland to the city. *Post Office*, in George-square. Campbell's warehouse in Candleriggs and Ingram-streets. The *Vulcan Foundry*, belonging to Mr. Napier, who established the steamers between this, Greenock, and Belfast in 1818, where iron steam-ships and engines for the great mail steamers are built, and the engines for the British Queen, Britannia, and Acadia steamers were made. *St. Rollox's Chemical Works*, north of the town, having an enormous chimney 440 feet high. Monteith's large cotton and bandana factory at Barrowfield.

CHURCHES.—There are above 120 churches and chapels, the most conspicuous of which is *St. Mungo's High Church*, on a hill at the top of High-street. It was part of a monastery planted here by St. Mungo (or Kentigern) in the 6th century, when the town was first founded, and was an Archbishop's Cathedral till episcopacy was abolished by the General Assembly which met here in 1638, in the Mace Church. It is a venerable stone building without transepts, 300 feet long, having a tower 224 feet high, and an ancient crypt of the 12th century, full of monuments, and once used as a church (see Rob Roy). There are about 150 pillars and as many windows. Close to it is the *Barony Church*. A short bridge crosses the ravine (here 250 feet deep) of Molendinar Burn to the *Necropolis*, where a monument to Knox was placed in 1845. *St. John's Church* was Dr. Chalmers's, many of whose labours and writings were commenced here. The *College Church* is as old as 1699. *Tron Church* tower as old as 1484.

St. Andrew's has a good portico; *St. George's*, a spire of 160 feet; *St. Enoch's* was built by Hamilton. Near the Custom House is the Gothic Roman Catholic Chapel. In George's-square are—Sir Walter Scott's monument, Chantrey's statue of Watt, the inventor of the modern steam engine, and Flaxman's of Sir J. Moore, the last of whom was born at Glasgow in 1761.

UNIVERSITY, SCHOOLS, &c.—The *University*, in High Street, visited by Queen Victoria in 1849, one of the oldest buildings in the city, was founded in 1453, by Bishop Turnbull, and consists of two or three brick courts, in the French style, with a good staircase at the entrance; at some distance behind is *Dr. Hunter's Museum*, in the Grecian style, containing objects of anatomy, natural history, books, autographs, illuminations, and Chantrey's bust of *Watt*, who was at first mathematical instrument maker to the University. The most curious thing is a Paisley shirt, woven without a seam or joining. The *College Library* includes about 80,000 volumes. The senior students, called *togati*, dress in scarlet gowns, and the whole number of 1,200 is divided into nations, according to the district they come from. Beyond the Museum is *Macfarlane's Observatory.*

Andersonian University, in the old Grammar School, George Street, is a place for gratuitous lectures, by the professors attached to it, among whom such names have appeared as Birkbeck, Ure, and Combe. It has a museum of models. The *High School* behind it was rebuilt in 1821. The *Normal School*, a handsome Tudor building, is near Garnet Hill, which commands a fine prospect. The *Mechanics' Institution* is in Hanover Street, near the Andersonian University. The *Royal Infirmary*, the *Blind*, and the *Deaf and Dumb Asylums*, are near the Cathedral, and the *Town's Hospital* and *Magdalen Asylum* are not far from these; the former, shaped like a St. George's cross, with a dome in the centre. *Hutcheson's Hospital* or *Asylum*, with a spire, is in Ingram Street, near the Post Office; the new Lunatic Asylum, at the west end of the town, is in the Norman style.

The most bustling parts are in Buchanan Street, Argyle Street, the Broomielaw, &c.; and in the oldest quarters are Trongate, High Street, Stockwell Street, &c., round the cross; in Bridgegate stands the steeple of the old Merchant's Hall; Woodside and Elmbank are two of the finest crescents, not far from the Kelvin. The West End Park is said to be one of the finest in Britain. At Port Dundas, the Firth of Clyde canal terminates; and at Bowling, some miles down the Clyde, near Dumbarton, is a Pillar to the memory of *Henry Bell*, who tried the first steamer on the Clyde, the "Comet," in the year 1812. Though the first cotton factory was Monteith's, in 1795, yet calicoes were woven here in 1742, and the check union kerchiefs of linen as early as 1700, at Flakefield.

Glasgow to Iona.

There is not within the limits of the United Kingdom a succession of more beautiful or varied scenery than in the route from Glasgow to Oban, Oban to Staffa and Iona, round the Island of Mull. Glasgow is an admirable station for the tourist. It is within an easy distance, either by rail or steam-boat, of some of the most celebrated portions of the Western Highlands, and any traveller for pleasure, who finds himself within its smoky and dingy precincts, without having fully decided on the route he intends to take in search of the picturesque, beautiful, and romantic, has only to choose the first conveyance westward, whether it be a Greenock train, a Clyde steam-boat, or Dumbarton coach, to find what he seeks, and to be gratified. Glasgow itself is supposed to offer few attractions to the tourist, but this is a mistake, Old Glasgow, with all its dirt and discomfort, the swarming wretchedness and filth of the celebrated "Salt Market," the "Goose Dubs," the "Gallowgate," and the "Cowcaddens" is well worthy of a visit, if it were only to see how quaint, and even picturesque, in misery, are the haunts of the poor population of one of the richest cities in the world; consequently the traveller should not omit to take a glance at these places and the Wynds, which will be sufficient. Glasgow is in other respects an interesting place. Forty years ago, there were scores of towns within the limits of the kingdom which were superior to it in wealth, extent, and population. It has now no superior or equal except London. It has a larger population than Edinburgh, Dublin, Liverpool, or Manchester; and combines within itself the advantages possessed by the two last mentioned. Like Manchester, it is a city of tall chimnies and daily-increasing manufactures; and like Liverpool, is a commercial port, trading extensively with every part of the known world. Its population amounts to nearly 350,000 souls, of whom 60,000 are Irish. Its prosperity is entirely owing to the industry, perseverance, and intelligence of its inhabitants, The new city of Glasgow, which is rapidly rising to the north-west of the ancient town, is one of the most splendid in Europe, and is not surpassed for beauty of architecture in its public and private buildings, the length, breadth and elegance of its streets, squares, and crescents, even by Edinburgh itself—renowned in all these respects though the latter may be. The motto upon the city arms is "*Let Glasgow flourish.*" It *has* flourished, and bids fair to flourish *more.*

There are several routes from Glasgow to Oban, One is by steam-boat from the Broomielaw, down the magnificent river Clyde as far as Bowling; from Bowling by railway to Balloch, at the foot of Loch Lomond; from Balloch by steam-boat through this renowned lake, up the river Falloch to Inverarnan, at the other extremity; and from Inverarnan by coach to Inverary and Oban. The tourist by this route has the advantage of seeing Loch Awe, and its mighty lord paramount, Ben Cruachan, a loch and mountain not so much spoken of as Loch Lomond and Ben Lomond, but by no means inferior, and, in the estimation of many, far superior to them both. Another route to Oban is by steamer to Ardrishaig at the entrance of the Crinan Canal, through the Crinan in the track-boat to Loch Crinan; and from Loch Crinan in another steam-boat to Oban, the whole distance being performed in less than twelve hours. By this route the tourist passes through the pretty Kyles of Bute, and amid the magnificent coast scenery of the mainland of Scotland and the Island of Mull. The whole of this district is classic ground, and the reader of modern poetry will be reminded at every turn of the paddle-wheel of some incident recorded in poem, song, or drama, by Ossian, Sir Walter Scott, Wordsworth, Joanna Baillie, Thomas Campbell, and others.

The third route, which requires some pedestrianism, is equally attractive. From Glasgow to Greenock by rail, from Greenock to Kilmun, on the Holy Loch, by steam-boat; and from Kilmun along the side of Loch Eck to Strachur, a walk of 18 miles brings the traveller to the shores of Loch Fine, where, if he does not relish another walk of 10 or 12 miles, round the head of the loch, he can take the ferry-boat, and be rowed 5 miles across to Inverary. From Inverary to Dalmally, and from Dalmally to Oban, which will afford the pedestrian two days' delight amid some of the most magnificent scenery in Scotland, including the river Aray and its beautiful falls, Kilchurn Castle, Loch Awe, Ben Cruachan, the Pass of Awe—worthy of its name; Connell Ferry, Loch Etive, and Dunolly and Dunstaffnage Castles, renowned in many a song and legend, and deserving all renown, not only from past history, but for the present grandeur of their ruins, and the splendour of their sites.

At Oban, during the summer season, a steamer plies regularly round the Island of Mull, calling at Staffa and Iona. Mull was pronounced by Dr. Maculloch, in his "*Hebridean Travels*," a "detestable island," but other travellers have not participated in his dislike. On the contrary, Mull is pronounced by all who have sailed round it, or set a foot on it, to be a magnificent island; and though not possessing the advantage of good roads in the interior, and being in other respects in a very primitive state, it possesses manifold attractions for the sportsman, tourist, botanist, geologist, and the man who loves now and then to see human nature as it exists out of the beaten tracks of civilization. But as Iona and Staffa offer attractions of another kind, and enjoy a fame that extends wherever the English tongue is spoken, the great majority of tourists are in too great a hurry to visit them to spend much of their time in Mull. The island, moreover, is not rich in hotel accommodation, except at the one inn of Tobermory, the only town in the island.

Iona, or Icolmkill (the Island of Colm's Church), may be truly called an illustrious spot. It would take a volume to do justice to the claims which Iona has upon the attention of both the scholar and traveller.

DUMBARTONSHIRE RAILWAY.

Glasgow to Dumbarton, Helensburgh, and Loch Lomond.

From Glasgow we pass the stations of MARYHILL, very soon after leaving which we enter

DUMBARTONSHIRE,

Anciently called the Shire of Lennox, and returning one member. The county consists of a mixture of natural pasture, wood, and arable lands. Five miles to the north-west of Dumbarton the traveller from the south obtains the first view of the celebrated Loch Lomond, the most beautiful and picturesque of all the Scottish lakes. The circumstance which renders Loch Lomond more interesting than other great pieces of water, seems to be the woods in its vicinity; the variety of its romantic islands crowned with trees, and the vicinity of the gigantic Grampians, affording a striking contrast to the rich and placid scenery which is exhibited within the immediate neighbourhood. On an eminence to the southern extremity of the lake the whole beauties of this delightful expanse of water appear in full view. The prospect from the summit of Point Firkin, is also very fine, as it includes a view of the towering Ben Lomond, one of the loftiest of all the Grampians.

DALMUIR, and KILPATRICK stations.

BOWLING

Telegraph station at Glasgow, 12¼ miles.
INN.—Frisky Hall.
MONEY ORDER OFFICE at Dumbarton, 4 miles.
Here is a handsome revolving light.

DUMBARTON.

Telegraph station at Glasgow, 15¾ miles.

MARKET DAY.—Tuesday.

INNS.—King's Arms, Elephant.

FAIRS.—Third Tuesday in March and May, Thursday before Easter, first Wednesday in June, second Tuesday in August and November.

BANKERS.—Branch of Commercial Bank of Scotland; Branch of Western Bank of Scotland.

DUMBARTON, is built in a level tract of country, near the confluence of the river Leven with the Clyde. It consists principally of one handsome crescent-formed street, with several smaller ones diverging from it. It has also the advantage of possessing a spacious and convenient harbour. It contains 5,445 inhabitants, chiefly employed in the manufacture of glass, and who return one member.

The ancient *Castle of Dumbarton*, the *Dumbritton* (Britons' Fort) of the Attacote, stands on the summit of a high and precipitous rock, and is a place of great strength and antiquity. From the top of the castle may be seen some of the finest and most extensive views in the whole of Scotland. From the batteries the visitor should ascend to Wallace's Seat, 560 feet high and a mile round. Here the patriot's sword is kept, and Queen Mary sailed from this place to France in 1548. A garrison is kept up here by the Act of Union. Colquhoun, the author of "Police of London" was a native, 1745. Looking towards the north is seen Lochlomond, bounded by rugged mountains, among which Benlomond is conspicuous, rearing its pointed summit far above the rest. Between the Lake and Dumbarton is the rich vale of Leven, enlivened by the widenings of the river. Turning eastward the Clyde is seen forming some fine sweeps. Douglas Castle appears on the left. Beyond the Clyde the distant country is very rich; and on a clear day the city of Glasgow may be discerned, particularly towards the evening. The prospect down the Clyde is no less interesting. The river expands into a large estuary, occupying a great part of the view; beyond are high mountains, whose rugged outlines and surfaces are softened by distance, or what painters call perspective; and under these mountains, on the left, are directly seen the towns of Greenock and Port Glasgow.

CARDROSS station.

HELENSBURGH.

This large and commodious watering place extends a considerable distance along the banks of the Clyde, at the mouth of the Gareloch, with Glenfruin extending behind. It was founded by Sir James Colquhoun, about 80 years ago, and is now become a place of growing inportance.

GARELOCHEAD,

A small village, situate at the head of Gare Loch, and from whence there is a very beautiful drive along the side of Loch Long to Arrochar, a quiet though much frequented retreat durlng the summer months from its delightful situation on the margin of the loch and in the midst of mountain scenery. It is only two miles across the pass from this point to Tarbet on Loch Lomond, and from Garelochhead we retrace our journey to Dumbarton. We then pass the stations of DALREOCH, RENTON and ALEXANDRIA, and arrive at

BALLOCH.

Telegraph station at Glasgow, 20½ miles.

HOTEL.—Railway.

STEAMERS up and down Loch Lomond on Tuesdays and Fridays (daily in summer), calling at Tarbet and Inversnaid, the landing places for Inverary, Loch Katrine, and the Trosachs.

MONEY ORDER OFFICE at Alexandria, 3 miles.

Here are several mills, and an old castle of the Lennoxes.

LOCH LOMOND.

Telegraph station at Glasgow, 20¾ miles.

HOTELS.—Ardlin Inn, at the northern extremity; Tarbet Inn, on the western shore, Rowardennan Inn, on the eastern shore.

MONEY ORDER OFFICE at Alexandria, 4 miles.

LOCH LOMOND is a large lake lying between Dumbarton and Stirlingshires, and may be said to belong to both, as the boundary line which separates the two counties passes through it. Loch Lomond is justly considered one of the finest lakes in Scotland, and we cannot better describe it than in the words of Dr. Maculloch:—

"Loch Lomond is unquestionably the pride of our lakes; incomparable in its beauty as in its dimensions, exceeding all others in variety, as it does in extent and splendour, and uniting in itself every style of scenery which is found in the other lakes of the Highlands. I must even assign to it the palm above Loch Katrine, the only one which is most distinguished from it in character,—the only one to which it does not contain an exact parallel in the style of its landscapes. As to the superiority of Loch Lomond to all other lakes, there can be no question. Everywhere it is, in some way, picturesque; and everywhere, it offers landscapes, not merely to the cursory spectator, but to the painter. From its richness of scenery it presents more pictures than all the lakes of the Highlands united. It possesses, moreover, a style of landscape to which Scotland produces no resemblance whatever. This is found in the varied and numerous islands that cover its noble expanse; forming the feature, which above all others, distinguishes Loch Lomond, and which, even had it no other attractions, would render it what it is in every respect—the paragon of Scottish lakes."

Boats can be hired at Balloch, for visiting the islands and points of interest on the Loch. A steamer is provided for places more remote. The following are a few places of interest, and should not be left unnoticed:—Lennox Castle, Inch Cailliach, near Bealmaha Pass, Banachra Castle, opposite Glen Fruin, where the Macgregors beat the Colquhouns (sounded "Cohoon") of Luss, and Rowardennan, where the ascent to *Ben Lomond* is made—a mountain, 3,240 feet above the sea. At Inversnaid there are ponies ready (make a *bargain* beforehand), to take you to *Loch Katrine*, 5 miles, passing through Rob Roy's country. *Ben Venue*, 2,800 feet, is on the South side of Loch Katrine, which is surrounded by the scenery of the "Lady of the Lake." Then the wild *Trosachs Pass*, under the Ben An, a mile long, to Loch Achray inn; the bridge or "brig" o' Turk, Loch Vennachar, and Callander, at the foot of the Highlands; and down the Teith to Stirling, about 35 miles from Loch Lomond.

From Glen Falloch, at the top of Loch Lomond, you may go to Killin and Loch Tay, in Breadalbane; or to Tindrum, Glencoe (a wild spot), and Fort William, for Inverness or Glenorchy (under Ben Cruachan); Benaw, and Oban (where the steamer stops), for Inverness, or Isle of Mull; or to Arroquhar and Inverary Castle, the Duke of Argyll's seat on Loch Fine, and Kilchurn, on Loch Awe.

GLASGOW AND CROFTHEAD.

This is a line 8¾ miles long. With the exception of Sir J. Maxwell's seat at POLLOCKSHAWS, rebuilt in 1753, where are some old state papers, and amongst them "a Solemn League;" and *Upper Pollock* (the residence of Sir R. C. Pollock, Bart.), the line presents no particular feature of importance.

KIMISHEAD and NITSHILL stations.

BARRHEAD and CROFTHEAD are occupied principally by cotton spinners.

INVERNESS
PERTH
HEAD OF LOCH LOMOND
BALMORAL
ABBOTSFORD

GLASGOW AND AIRDRIE.

From Glasgow, we pass the stations of STEP'S ROAD, and GARNKIRK, near which is the fine seat of J. Dunlop, Esq.

GARTCOSH station.

GARTSHERRIE has very extensive coal and iron works.

AIRDRIE.

POPULATION, 14,435.
Telegraph station at Glasgow, 12 miles.
HOTEL.—Royal.
MARKET DAY.—Thursday.

FAIRS.—Last Tuesday in May, and third Tuesday in November.

BANKERS.—Bank of Scotland.

This town is situated in the centre of the Scottish coal district, which has caused its present prosperity. It was the ancient Arderyth, where in 577 Rydderech defeated Aidan. Bathgate may be reached from this place by rail, 19¾ miles distant. At Monkland Well is a good mineral spa, and *Airdrie House* is the seat of Miss Mitchelson.

EDINBURGH AND GLASGOW.

Glasgow to Edinburgh.

On leaving Glasgow we are immediately plunged into a long tunnel, on emerging from which we soon reach BISHOP BRIGGS, and at a distance of 3¼ miles further, we arrive at CAMPSIE, the junction of the branch to Lennoxtown.

CAMPSIE BRANCH.

Passing KIRKINTILLOCH and MILLTOWN stations we arrive at

LENNOXTOWN.

POPULATION, 3,108.
Telegraph station at Glasgow, 11¾ miles.
Lennox Castle, the seat of J. Lennox, Esq., is in the vicinity.

Edinburgh and Glasgow Main Line continued.

CROY.—Near to this station are *Holme*, the seat of H. Rose, Esq. and *Cantray*, that of J. Davidson, Esq.
CASTLECARY—Here are the ruins of an ancient fort.
GREENHILL station.

FALKIRK.

A telegraph station.
HOTEL.—Red Lion.
MARKET DAYS.—Thursday and Saturday.

FAIRS.—Last Thursday in January and October, (the *largest* in the country), first Thursday in March, April, and November, third Thursday in May and August, second Thursday in June and July.

BANKERS. — Clydesdale Banking Co.; Branch National Bank of Scotland; Branch of Bank of Scotland; Branch of Commercial Bank of Scotland.

MONEY ORDER OFFICE.

This town has a population of 8,752 who return one member, and the county another one, and are employed in the iron, coal, leather and inland trade. It was occupied by the Pretender in 1745, who defeated General Hawley here, and the house at which he took up his quarters is still shown The church, rebuilt in 1810 (in lieu of the old cruciform edifice built in 1105), contains tombs of Sir John the Græme, Stewart, who was killed in 1298, and the Monroes who fell in 1745. In the vicinity are *Callander*, seat of W. Forbes, Esq., M.P., *Carron Hall*, Col. Dundas. Bannockburn is near at hand. The proverb that applies to this place is, "Ye're like the bairns of Falkirk, ye'll end ere ye mend." In the vicinity of Almond inscriptions and urns have been found.

Passing POLMONT Junction, we very soon after enter the county of

LINLITHGOW.

THIS county, which returns one member, does not possess that romantic scenery for which the Scottish mountains are so justly celebrated, but in many parts the estates are laid out with plantations formed in the very best taste, and in such a manner as to improve and shelter all the richer portions of the soil, and exhibit in its most beautiful aspects the face of the country. In the neighbourhood of Queensferry, by the sudden approximation of opposite promontories, the Forth is forced into a narrow strait, which on each side suddenly expands into an extensive bay, with richly ornamented banks. In every quarter, along the shores of the county, the Forth assumes a singular variety of aspects; hills, promontories, winding bays, lofty shores, and cultivated fields, bordering a fine sheet of water, a noble river, or a broad sea, according to the points of view in which it is seen

LINLITHGOW.

Telegraph station at Falkirk, 8 miles.

HOTEL.—Star and Garter.

BANKERS.—Western Bank of Scotland.

This town has a population of 4,213 engaged in the cotton trade and the manufacture of leather. John, Earl of Stair, was a scholar at the Grammar School, where Kirkman was master. The church built by David I., and rebuilt in 1411, contains the tombs of the Livingstones and Dr. Henry's Library and Catherine's Aisle, where James IV., it is stated, was forewarned of the Battle of Flodden Field. Close by it is the Palace on the Loch, of 80 acres, having fish and fowl. It was rebuilt by James IV., V., and VI., and contains some beautiful carvings in the Hall, Banquet Room, a Well, Parliament Hall, and Queen Mary's Room, from which there is a magnificent prospect. James V.'s jester (Rob Gib), was a native. The magistrates, trades, &c., ride the bounds in June.

SLAMANNAN BRANCH.

This branch turns off to the right, taking in the following stations:—Bo'ness, Causewayend, Bowhouse, Avonbridge, Slamannan, Arbuckle, Rawyards, and Airdrie, at which place it unites with the Monkland Railway.

Edinburgh and Glasgow Main Line continued.

Winchburgh.—Here Edward II. stopped after his defeat at the Battle of Bannockburn.

Ratho.—Wilkie, author of "*Epigoniard*," was minister here. In the vicinity are *Ratho Hall*, seat of W. Hill, Esq; *Ratho House*, R. Cadell, Esq.; *Rathobyres*, Danehead, Mrs. Liston; *Kaimes Hill*, 680 feet high, and *South Platt cairns*, from which beautiful views may be obtained of the surrounding country.

BATHGATE BRANCH.

This branch turns off to the right, and runs through Broxburn, (near which is *Broxmouth*, the seat of the Duke of Buccleugh,) Houston (where Cromwell routed Leslie), and Livingston, to

BATHGATE.

Population, 3,341.
Telegragh station at Edinburgh, 19 miles.

Here a corn market is held on Wednesdays, and fairs on the first Wednesday after April, first Wed nesday after the Term, fourth Wednesday in June and October, third Wednesday in July and August, Wednesday after Martinmas. The ruins of Walter Stewart's Castle, given to him by Bruce, may still be seen.

Edinburgh and Glasgow Main Line continued.

Gogar.—Here stone coffins have been found, and in the vicinity are *Gogar House* and *Gogar Bank*, two pretty seats.

Corstorphine.—This place is noted for its cream, and mineral spa. On the hill are several beautiful seats. The cruciform church was built in 1429, and contains effigies and arms of the Foresters, and Lantern to light travellers over the marsh, the expense of which is defrayed from the rent of Lamp Acre, in the possession of the master of the parish school. In the vicinity are *Prestonfield*, seat of Sir W. H. Dick, Bart., *Belmont* and *Beechmont*, two fine residences.

Edinburgh.—For description, see Section IV.

EDINBURGH, PERTH, AND DUNDEE.

Leaving Princes Street, the railway runs on to Scotland Street, after which it divides into two branches, the one to the right running to the Docks at Leith; the other, *via* Trinity station, to

GRANTON.

Telegraph station at Edinburgh, 3 miles.
Hotel.—Granton, Thomas Martin.
Steamers.—See Edinburgh, page 341.

Money Order Office at Edinburgh, 3 miles.

Here is an excellent pier, 1,700 feet, built by Walker, and a floating railway for luggage across to Burntisland, erected by Napier.

FIFESHIRE

Is an extensive maritime county in the eastern part of Scotland, and returns one member. The draining and cultivating of lands and lakes in all parts of this county has had a surprising and beneficial effect on the climate of the district. The fogs, which were constantly exhaling from the lochs and marshes, injured the crops of the better lands and afflicted the people with agues and other diseases. Fifeshire is divided into four districts: St. Andrews, Cupar, Dunfermline, and Kirkaldy. There are many ruins scattered over the surface of this county, consisting chiefly of castles and monastic establishments. The cattle of Fifeshire have long been in high repute, both as fattening and dairy stock.

BURNTISLAND.

A telegraph station.
Hotel.—Forth.
Market Day.—Saturday.
Fair.—July 10th.

This place has a population of 2,724 engaged in the ship building, whaling, and coasting trade, and contains a pier harbour, used by the Romans, chapel, town house, market, distillery, bathing houses, schools, remains of the fortified walls and a fixed light on the pier. Here the General Assembly met in 1601. It was taken by Cromwell, and then by the Earl of Marr, in 1715. Rossend was built by the Druids. At Dunairn Camp there are fossils and volcanic remains.

Leaving Kinghorn we shortly arrive at

KIRKALDY, or Kirkcaldy.

A telegraph station.
Hotel.—Railway.
Fairs.—Third Fridays in February, July, and October.
Market Day.—Saturday.

This town has a population of 10,470, who return one member, and are engaged in the linen trade. It contains six chapels, Town House, erected in 1830, Prison, Custom House, Gas and Water Works, Savings' Bank, Market House, Newsroom, Mechanics' Institution, factories, breweries, rope and linen factories, foundries distilleries. Grammar School, founded by Philip of Edenshead, who bequeathed £70,000 in 1828; *Mason Lodge*, Gilt Box Fund for seamen, a tidal harbour, but narrow, with a fixed light, which can be seen about nine miles distant; *St. Bryce's Church*, with its old Norman portico; and *Port Brae Church*. Adam Smith was a native, in

1724. In the vicinity are *Balwearel Tower*, *Ravenscraig Castle*, *Raith*, seat of Colonel Ferguson, M.P , *Dunniker*, Lady Oswald.

Passing SINCLAIRTOWN, the next station we come to is

DYSART.

Telegraph station at Kirkaldy, 2 miles.
HOTEL.—Railway.
MARKET DAY.—Saturday.
FAIRS.—May 6th, 3rd Tuesday in June, 4th Wednesday in August, and November 8th.

This place contains a population of 8,041, who are employed in the weaving, ship building, and coasting trades, and has a Church, Chapel, Newsroom, Mechanics' Library, School, small tidal harbour, with a new dock, patent slip for repairs, and a forge, on the site of the Black Priory. Wallace, the mathematician, was a native in 1768. In the vicinity is *Dysart House*, seat of the Earl of Rosslyn.

THORNTON station, junction of the

LEVEN BRANCH

Passing CAMERON BRIDGE station, we arrive at

LEVEN.

POPULATION, 2083.
Telegraph station at Kirkaldy, 12 miles.
HOTELS.—Crawford's; Star.
MARKET DAY.—Saturday.
FAIRS.—2nd Wednesday in April, 1st Wednesday in July, and 3rd Wednesday in October.

Here is a suspension bridge, which joins it to *Dubbieside*, a small harbour, library, two chapels, school, and flax factories.

From here the line continues through LUNDIN LINKS, and LARGO to

KILCONQUHAR, a small village situated in the midst of a hilly but fertile district, abounding in coal, limestone, &c. The project of extending the line to Anstruther, a seaport town in the district of St. Andrews, and possessing direct communication with Edinburgh, has been entertained.

DUNFERMLINE BRANCH.

Thornton to Dunfermline.

Passing the intermediate stations of CARDENDEN and LOCHGELLY we come to COWDENBEATH, the point of connection with the

KINROSS-SHIRE RAILWAY.

This short line of 7 miles re-opens a most interesting part of the country, closed, to a certain extent, for a length of time to the general traveller by the development of the railway system around having diverted the traffic from the great north road, which traversed this district.

From Cowdenbeath we pass *en route* the stations of KETTY and BLAIRADAM, arriving at the county town of

KINROSS.

MARKET DAY.—Wednesday.

FAIRS.—March, 3rd Wednesday, *o. s.*, June 12th, July, 3rd Wednesday, *o. s.*, October 18th, *o. s.*

Situated on the west side of Loch Leven. It has a population of about 2,600, engaged in the weaving of linen and cotton.

Loch Leven is about 3½ by 2½ miles and 11 in circumference. It is studded with islands, on one of which—nearest to Kinross—stands the celebrated castle in which was imprisoned the ill-fated Queen Mary in 1567. It was here, too, she was compelled by Lord Lindsay to abdicate her claim to the Scottish crown; soon after which, by the aid of George Douglas, she escaped from the castle. The loch affords fine sport to the angler.

Dunfermline Branch continued.

CROSSGATES and HALBEATH stations, at the latter of which there is good coal.

DUNFERMLINE.

A telegraph station.
HOTELS.—New Inn; Royal.
MARKET DAY.—Tuesday.
FAIRS.—3rd Tuesdays in January, March, April, June, July, September, October, and November.

This is a large burgh town, in the county of Fife, with a population of 13,836, who are engaged in the diaper, damask, and fine linen manufactures, and contains three Churches, seven Chapels, Town House, in which is a shirt without seam, woven by Inglis; Guildry, with a spire 132 feet high; Mechanics' Institute School of Design, libraries, market, mills, breweries, gas works, soap, tobacco, and candle factories. Bridge over a glen, built by Chalmers of Pittencrief. *St. Leonard's Hospital.* The church was rebuilt in 1820, and has a fine view over fourteen counties, from Ben Lomond to Loutra Hill; the nave of the old one still remains, in which lie buried Macolm Canmore and his queen Margaret, whose shrine, in ruins, is shown. The bones of "The Bruce" were reburied under the pulpit in 1818. There are ruins of the Abbey and part of the wall of the palace which James the First's queen built, where Charles I. was born, and at which place he signed the covenant. Her bed is at Broomhall, and her cupboard at Pittencrief. It is built on an eminence, and has an irregular appearance, from its having been erected at various periods of time. The great object of attraction is its Abbey, part of which is now used as a Parish Church; the rest is in ruins, and convey but a faint picture of the former magnificence of the edifice.

Dunfermline has long been celebrated for different branches of weaving, but particularly that of table linen, which is said to be conducted more extensively here than in any other part of the United Kingdom.

In the vicinity are *Broomhall*, seat of Lord Elgin; *Pittencrief*, J. Hunt, Esq.; *Pitfirran*, Sir J. Halket, Bart.; Leggie, Cavil, Pitbier, and *Craiglascar Hill*, with its Pictish Fort.

Edinburgh, Perth, and Dundee Main Line continued.

MARKINCH.

Telegraph station at Thornton, 2½ miles.
HOTEL.—Galloway,
FAIRS.—Second Thursday in January, last Thursday in February, April, and June, first Thursday after August 12th, fourth Thursday in September, and Friday before Edinboro' Hallow Fair.

The church has a later steeple of 104 feet, stands on Markinch Hill, in which are some artificial terraces and the stob cross of stone 7 feet high. In the vicinity are *Balgorice*, Lord Leven; *Balbirnie*, J. Balfour, Esq.; *Balfour*, A. Bethune, Esq. (both old seats). A short branch, 4¼ miles, turns off here to the left to LESLIE, a village prettily situated on the river Leven, and noted for the stone coffins, &c., which have been discovered.

Passing FALKLAND ROAD, near to which is the town of *Falkland*, which contains a palace rebuilt by James V., who died here, on the site of Macduff's Castle, where the Duke of Albany starved his nephew Robert of Rothsay to death (see "*Fair Maid of Perth*"), it has a gate with a double tower, a large carved hall, and was occupied by Charles II., and Rob Roy in 1715. The forest in which James IV. hunted no longer exists. There are camps at Dunshelt and Maiden Castle Hill. We reach KINGSKETTLE, and then proceed on to LADYBANK, the junction of the

FIFE AND KINROSS.

This line branches off from Ladybank Junction, and communicates with the stations of AUCHTERMUCHTY, STRATHMIGLO, GATESIDE, MAWCARSE, and MILNATHORT, finally with that of

Kinross, see page 85.

DUNDEE BRANCH.

Ladybank to Leuchars.

Passing SPRINGFIELD station, near which are Todd's large print works, we arrive at

CUPAR.

Distance from station, ¼ mile.
A telegraph station.
HOTELS.—Tontine, Royal.
MARKET DAY.—Thursday.
FAIRS.—1st Thursday in January, May, June, July, August, and December, 3rd Thursday in February, 3rd Thursday and last Thursday in March, 2nd Thursday in April and October, and November 11th

This place has a population of 5,686 employed in the coarse linen trade, and contains five chapels, town house, assembly rooms, academy erected on the site of the old castle, public library, gas works, almshouses, tanneries, tile, candle, and rope works, breweries, a collegiate church, rebuilt in 1785, retaining the steeple of the old one, which contains effigies of one of the Knights Templars. In the vicinity are *Wemyss*, seat of Capt. Wemyss, M.P., *Carslogie Castle*, R. Clephane, Esq., *Pittencrieff*, J. Huntley, *The Mount*, the old seat of Sir D. Lindsey, whose satires, &c., were acted at Playfield near the castle, and *Garley Bank*, where Argyle treated with the forces of the Queen Regent in 1559. Some cairns are also to be seen. The Scottish proverb for an obstinate man refers to this place:—"He that will to Cupar maun to Cupar."

Passing DAIRSIE we arrive at

LEUCHARS, near which are *Leuchars House*, seat of J. Lindsay, Esq., with ruins of an old castle, *Pitlethie*, the ancient hunting seat of James VI., *Ardet*, *Pitcullo*, and *Drone*, all fine noble seats. Leuchars is the junction of the

ST. ANDREWS BRANCH.

GUARD BRIDGE station.

ST. ANDREWS.

POPULATION, 5,107.
Telegraph station at Cupar, 12 miles.
HOTELS.—Cross Keys, Royal, Star.
MARKET DAY.—Saturday.
FAIRS.—2nd Thursday in April, August 1st, and November 30th.

This old city is a parliamentary burgh with one member and university, and picturesquely seated on the cliffs, near the "East Neuk" of Fife. The first view of its ruined towers and spires, the sea, and the cultivated environs, is very pleasing. Formerly it was the seat of an Archbishopric, an honour which it claimed from possessing the bones of St. Andrew, the patron saint of Scotland. According to Fordun, St. Rule or Regulus, who discovered these precious relics in 345, set sail from Patræ or Patras, in Greece, with the intention of carrying them to Constantinople, but, having no chart on board, was wrecked, after a long and painful voyage, in *St. Andrews Bay!* A church was dedicated to this able navigator, and a larger one was built over the prize he brought with him. This was the first foundation of the Cathedral, but the present structure dates only from the 12th century at the farthest. As usual it was a cross, 350 feet long, of which only the south walls and gable ends are left, the whole having been ruined at the Reformation by the adherents of John Knox, after a powerful sermon from him in 1559. Such had been the bitter persecution they sustained from the Romish party, and their infamous leader, Cardinal Beaton or Bethune, that they might be well pardoned for wishing to destroy every vestige of their power here.

Near this relic of antiquity is the very ancient tower of *St. Rule's Church*, 180 feet high.

It is used as a sea mark, and a light is fixed to the cathedral for the same object at night. Close at hand are fragments of an Augustine priory, founded in 1120, and memorable as the place where Robert Bruce held his first parliament in 1309, when working out the independence of his country. The primate's seat or castle is here, overlooking the sea, from a window of which Beaton watched in triumph while his victim Wishart the martyr was dying at the stake; and here also, by a just retribution, this wicked oppressor was murdered by Norman Lesly in 1546. Patrick Hamilton and three others were also burnt by the dominant party. A bishop of Wishart's family founded a dominican or black friary in the 13th century, of which there are still remains.

St. Andrews is of so much historical celebrity, and so rich in memorials of the past, that no one can say he has seen Scotland who has not paid it a visit. Dr. Johnson was here in 1773, in his tour with Boswell; in its streets, "there is," says he "the silence and solitude of inactive indigence and gloomy depopulation"—a truly Johnsonian burst. Unfortunately it stands out of the beaten track. Something, however, has been done to redeem its neglected air, by a townsman, Major Andrews, who, while provost, exerted himself to stop the progress of decay, and introduced modern improvements. There are three principal streets, most of the houses of which are large and antique-looking; at the end of one, on the west side of the town, is an old gate, a remnant of the walls which surrounded it.

In the parish church is a fine monument to Archbishop Sharpe, "that arch traitor to the Lord and his church," as the Covenanters styled him, whom John Balfour of Burley, Hackstone of Rathillet, and others, barbarously murdered on Magus Muir. They were watching for another person when they met the unfortunate prelate. This muir is 3 miles from the city, and the exact spot where the bloody deed was perpetrated is marked by a stone in the midst of a fir wood, near the village of Boarhills. Its name properly is Mucross, from the boars which used to haunt it in such numbers that a boar is blazoned in the city arms.

Three colleges compose the *University*, which was founded in 1411, by Bishop Wardlaw. *St. Salvador* (or Saviour's) is an unfinished quadrangle, 230 feet long, begun by Bishop Kennedy, whose effigies are in the chapel. *St, Leonard's* was founded by Prior Hepburn in 1552; there is an old ruined Gothic church attached to it, and a modern one by the side. The third is *St. Mary's*, which has been lately restored. About 150 students frequent this University. The library contains upwards of 50,000 volumes.

Close to the old priory of Blackfriars is another valuable institution, the Grammar School, which has been converted into *The Madras College*, at the instance of Dr. Bell, a native, the author of the Bell (or monitor) system of teaching, which prevailed till lately in most of the national schools. He was chaplain to the East India Company, and left £60,000 to his native city for education. Here about 800 children are taught classics, mathematics, &c.

The harbour is rocky, and of little consequence. Formerly it had a good trade. One branch of manufacture still flourishes here that, of making balls for golf—a favourite game, played on the links or flat sands along the esa shore.

Leuchars to Dundee.

Passing Tay Port station we reach

BROUGHTY (Ferry).

Population, 2,272.
Telegraph station at Dundee, 4½ miles
Hotel.—Railway.
Post Horses, Flys, &c., at the station and hotel

Here are the ruins of an old castle, taken by the English after the battle of Prusey. It has a floating bridge to Ferry Port, and *Claypotts Castle* is close at hand.

Dundee, see page 91.

Edinburgh, Perth, and Dundee Main Line continued.

Ladybank to Perth.

From Ladybank Junction we proceed to Collessie station. In the vicinity near a mound are *Maiden Castle*, another camp, and *Newtown*, seat of C Wallace, Esq.

NEWBURGH.

Population, 2,638.
Distance from station ¼ mile.
Telegraph station at Perth, 10¾ miles.
Hotel.—Mrs. Anderson's.
Market Day.—Saturday.
Fairs.—3rd Friday in June and 1st Tuesday in September.

Ships of 500 tons burthen can come up to this place Salmon abounds, and in the vicinity are the ruins of an abbey, Mugdrum and Macduff crosses.

ABERNETHY,

Near Ore, a round tower close to the church, 72 feet high, and 8 in diameter, in a good state of preservation. Pictish remains on Castle Law and Aberinthi, where King Malcolm met the conqueror in 1072.

Bridge of Earn.—This is a pretty watering place near Pitcaithley Spa, on the Earn river.

Perth, see page 89.

DUNFERMLINE BRANCH.

(Edinburgh and Glasgow.)

Stirling to Dunfermline.

Passing Causewayhead and Cambus stations (which latter place signifies *the crooked turn of a river*), we reach

ALLOA.

A telegraph station.
Hotels.—Royal Oak, Crown.
Market Day.—Wednesday and Saturday.
Fairs.—2nd Wednesday in February, May, August, and November.

This place, with a population of 8,125, engaged in the shipping trade, collieries, corn, woollen, glass, tile and brick works, has two churches, one of which is pointed, with a steeple, and at which Fordyce was minister, five chapels, court house, custom house, assembly rooms, libraries, gas and water works, breweries, factories, and schools. The harbour has a good dry dock close to it. In the vicinity are *Alloa House*, the old seat of the Erskines, where James I. was nursed; it has a tower of the thirteenth century, 89 feet high and 11 thick, and was partly burnt in 1800, and *Shaw Park*, Lord Mansfield.

A branch, 3¾ miles long, here diverges to the left for the accommodation of the town of TILLICOULTRY

CLACKMANNAN.

Here is a school, at which M. Bruce the author of "Lochleven" was master. In the vicinity are *Clackmannan House*, near which are Bruce's old tower and church, rebuilt in the pointed style by Gillespie, belonging to the Earl of Zetland, Kennetpans and Kilbaggie distilleries, Devon iron works, and *Brucefield*, the seat of Lord Abercrombie. The county returns one member jointly with Kinross-shire.

KINCARDINE.

Telegraph station at Stirling, 10½ miles.
HOTEL.—Union.
MARKET DAYS.—Wednesday and Saturday.
FAIRS.—Last Friday in July and Monday before Falkirk fair.

Here is a good pier and a cross 18½ feet high. The trade consists of shipbuilding, weaving, and sail making, which employ a population of 2,697. This county returns one member.

Passing the stations of BOGSIDE and EASTGRANGE we soon reach Culross, at which there are remains of an abbey, founded in 1217, on the site of St. Serf's Hermitage, by Malcolm of Fife, and since converted into a church, in which are effigies of the Bruces of Kinross. Close by are the ruins of an old church and St. Mungo's chapel. Dunnemarle, with the ruins of the old castle where Lady Macduff and her sons were murdered by Macbeth; *Gibscroft Camps* where Banquo in the 11th century fought the Danes. *Culross Abbey*, seat of that brave old admiral the Earl of Dundonald, who first made coal tar here; it was built by Sir W. Bruce, and has since been rebuilt—and the salt pans and coal pits which went under the sea, and were visited by James VI., but which are not now worked. Its name signifies "back peninsula." We then proceed to *Torryburn*, which contains a church in which Captain Hill is buried, whose epitaph begins "At anchor now, in death's dark road." Here at Tollzies are some Druid stones, and a companion of Lord Anson's built a house here called Tinian, after the Island at which the Centurion refitted in 1744.

Soon after passing the OAKLEY station we reach

Dunfermline, see page 85.

PERTHSHIRE.

THE highlands occupy about two-thirds of the surface of this county, which returns one member; the lowlands are situated on the eastern and southern extremities, which contain some of the richest tracts in Great Britain; and to the west, where the Grampians first rise, for almost the whole breadth of the country, the high grounds are penetrated by straths and glens of considerable extent, each traversed by its own streams, and diversified by numerous lakes. Several of the mountains in this district are upwards of three thousand feet high, the highest being Ben Lawers, on the west side of Loch Tay, Benmore, on the south-west, and Schehallion, on the north-east. The most considerable lakes are Loch Tay, in the centre of the Highland district, about fifteen miles long and one broad, with a depth varying from fifteen to a hundred fathoms; Loch Ericht on the north-west, extending into Invernessshire, is still longer, but not so broad; Loch Rannoch, south-east of the former, twelve miles long; Loch Earn, south from Loch Tay; and Lochs Vennachar, Achray, and Katrine, on the south-west.

SCOTTISH CENTRAL.

Continued from page 78.

Stirling to Crieff Junction.

BRIDGE OF ALLAN.

A telegraph station.
HOTELS.—Royal; Queen.

BRIDGE OF ALLAN is denominated the Queen of Scottish watering places, and is a place of great resort in summer. It is also much frequented in winter by invalids, on account of the salubrity of its climate. There are several places of worship, and good medical advice. The river Allan runs through the village, in which tolerable trout fishing may be had. The river Teath, a much larger stream, is within an hour's walk. Loch Ard, and other lochs, famous for trout fishing, are easy of access. There are mineral springs close to the village, pronounced by high authority to possess strong purgative qualities. *Kippenross*, the seat of J. Stirling, Esq., famous for its large plane tree, 42 feet in circumference, and 470 years old, is near at hand.

DUNBLANE.

Telegraph station at Bridge of Allan, 2 miles.
HOTEL.—Dewar's.
MARKET DAY.—Thursday

FAIRS.—1st Wednesday in March, Tuesday after May 26th, August 10th, 1st Tuesday in November.

This city, though it has only a village population, is well worth visiting. The Cathedral is much admired, and in good preservation. It has a mineral spring, to which many visitors resort during the summer months. Tannahill's beautiful song of "Jessie, the flower of Dunblane," has given it popularity. The Allan runs through the village. A beautiful foot road by the river side runs between Dunblane and Bridge of Allan.

DUNBLANE, DOUNE, AND CALLANDER.

This line opens out a district full of interest to the tourist, and one which few will overlook who have an opportunity to visit these parts. From Dunblane the line takes a westerly direction, calling at the village of

DOUNE.

HOTEL.—Macintyre's.

This place is remarkable for its Castle, now in ruins, cresting the top of a lofty eminence, overlooking the Jeith. Its noble founder is supposed to be Murdoch, Duke of Albany. It affords a fine opportunity for the rambler.

CALLANDER.

HOTEL.—The Dreadnaught.

This place is perhaps mostly noted as being the centre of a most beautiful and highly picturesque district. It is the station for the Trossachs and Loch Katrine, and of course *viâ* Inversnaid to Loch Lomond and the western Highlands. There are several communications daily during the season by Coach, between this, the Trossachs, and Loch Katrine.

KINBUCK station.

GREENLOANING.

Telegraph station at Stirling, 11 miles.

MONEY ORDER OFFICE at Dunblane, 6 miles.

BLACKFORD and CRIEFF JUNCTION stations.

CRIEFF JUNCTION.

TULLIBARDINE, MUTHILL and HIGHLANDMAN stations.

CRIEFF.

POPULATION, 3,824.
Telegraph station at Bridge of Allan, 23½ miles.
HOTEL.—Drummond Arms
MARKET DAY.—Thursday.
FAIRS.—January 1st, 3rd Tuesday in June, October 1st for cattle.

This town contains a population of 4,333, who are employed in the cotton, linen, and general trade, and has a tolbooth, two churches, four chapels, news and assembly rooms, masonic lodge, corn, flax, and other mills, distilleries, tanneries, dye works, St. Margaret's Ladies' College, obelisk to Sir David Baird, 80½ feet high. The church was rebuilt in 1787, on the site of an old pointed one, and coins bearing Robert I. were found. The west church was built by subscription. In the vicinity is *Drummond Castle*, the seat of Lady Willoughby d'Eresby.

Crieff Junction to Perth.

AUCHTERARDER.

POPULATION, 2,520.
Telegraph station at Perth, 13½ miles.
HOTEL.—Star.
MARKET DAYS.—Friday and Saturday
FAIRS.—Last Tuesday in March, 1st Tuesday in May, December 6th, August, September, and October.

This place is famous for having given rise to the formation of the Free Church in 1843. At Abruthven is the old church, remains of King Malcolm's hunting seat, and St. Mungo's chapel.

DUNNING, FORTEVIOT, and FORGANDENNY stations.

PERTH.

A telegraph station.
HOTELS.—Royal George; Salutation; Star
STEAMERS to and from Dundee, twice daily. Fare 1s. 6d. (2½ hours.)
MARKET DAY.—Friday.
FAIRS.—1st Friday in March, July, and September 3rd Friday in October, 2nd Friday in December, and Tuesday after Inverness fair.
BANKERS.—Perth Banking Company; Branch Bank of Scotland; British Linen Co., Central Bank of Scotland; Commercial and National Banks of Scotland.

The capital of Perthshire, which county returns one member, the middle of Scotland, a parliamentary burgh, and a port, to which steamers and small craft come up from the sea by the Firth of Tay. Population, 23,835, who return one member. Its situation, on the north and south inches, or meadows, of the Tay, is very beautiful. From the Moncrieffs' seat, on a trap hill, to the south, 756 feet high, there are some of the most splendid views in Scotland, embracing the city, and the course of the river, from the Grampians to Dundee. Scott refers to it at the beginning of the "Fair Maid of Perth." When Agricola's Roman legions came in sight of the river, they saluted it with cries of *Ecce Tiber!* but it s hardly a compliment to compare this respectable stream with that now filthy but immortal ditch, the modern Tiber. One of Smeaton's bridges, 900 feet long, crosses the Tay; the greatest width of the Tiber is 200 feet. Both streams, however, are subject to heavy floods. The Romans founded a town here called *Bertha.* Some muslin, cotton, and silk goods are manufactured here, but the trade is not in a prosperous state.

In the present day, Perth is the handsomest town, of its size, in Scotland, and in some respects resembles Edinburgh. It consists principally of two streets, proceeding westward from the Tay, parallel to each other, and these are intersected, from north to south, by cross streets. In the High-street is the *Guild Hall.* At the north-east corner of the town the Tay is crossed by a bridge of ten arches. By far the most pleasing characteristics of Perth, in a popular point of view, are the two large meadows on the north and south sides of the town, which are exclusively appropriated for the recreation of the people.

In 1600 an attempt, or a pretended attempt, the history of which is not accurately settled, was made to seize the person of James I., under the name of the "Gowrie Plot," from the house in which he then resided. The site of this is now occupied by the *County Buildings*, built by Smirke, in the Grecian style; here are the County and Law Courts, with various pictures, one being Raeburn's portrait of Neil Gow,

> "The man that play'd the fiddle weel,
> And dearly lo'ed the whisky O."

St John Baptist's Church, or Kirk, is in fact three churches, and is 270 feet long, with a spire 155 feet high. In the east kirk is the grave of James I. (of Scotland), who was killed in the Blackfriars, in 1437; and a painted window. It was in an older church, on this site, that Knox preached with so much energy, in 1559, that the people sallied out to destroy the Romish monasteries, &c.; but their hearts were on fire from the cruelties of the mother of abominations, and the remembrance of six martyrs hung on the south inch, in front of the Spey Tower of the Greyfriary, in which Cardinal Beaton sat. This spot is now turned into gardens, and a cemetery; a gate only remains.

The *Freemasons' Hall* occupies the place of the old House (pulled down in 1818) and Castle, in which many Parliaments were held, till their meetings were transfered to Edinburgh, upon the death of James I. *Scone Palace* being then the usual residence of the Sovereign. He founded a Carthusian Friary, which James VI. converted into an Hospital. This was rebuilt in 1750, the old one having been battered down along with the city cross by Cromwell in 1651. On this occasion he erected a fort to command the town, on the North Inch. Here is the race course, on which the celebrated combat took place, before Robert II., between Clan Chattan and Clan Kay, thirty on each side, which is so graphically described in Scott's "Fair Maid of Perth."

The *Model Prison*, for 350 prisoners, was used to confine French prisoners, in the revolutionary war. In 1823 a *Public Library* and *Museum* were erected in George-street, in compliment to Provost Marshall. A large *Lunatic Asylum* stands in the north suburbs, near Kinnoul and Dickson's Nursery. Both Inches, beyond the city bounds, are planted with trees, and laid out in beautiful walks.

NEIGHBOURHOOD OF PERTH. — *Kinfauns Castle* (3 miles), Lord Gray's seat, contains the great Charteris sword, nearly 6 feet long—Charteris was the patron of Perth. Behind is Kinnoul Hill, a basalt ridge, at the termination of Siddaw Hills, 630 feet high; the view from it is magnificent. *Errol House* is three miles from this, on that rich and fertile tract of the Tay, called the "Carse of Gowrie," once covered by the river. *Bridge of Earn*, 5 miles south-east of Perth, is a pretty village, near the Pitcaithley sulphur waters. The Earn joins the Tay, a few miles lower down, past Abernethy (and its round tower); it may be ascended here, past *Dupplin Castle*, the Earl of Kinnoul's seat. The road to Crieff crosses Tippermuir, where Montrose routed the Covenanters in 1645. *Huntingtoun*, near it, now a cotton factory, belonged to the Gowries. Following this road you reach Crieff, in Strath-Earn, under a pass of the Grampians, 14 miles from Perth. Thence it is 13 miles to St. Fillans, at the bottom of Loch Earn; which is surrounded by fine mountains, one of which, Ben Voirlich, is 3,050 feet high; then up the Loch and through Glen Dochart, &c., to the top of Loch Lomond, about 30 miles.

ASCENT OF THE TAY.—It is about 20 miles to Dunkeld, and 20 more to Taymouth. *Scone Palace*, the seat of the Earl of Mansfield, is a handsome building, on the site of the royal palace in which Charles II. and the Chevalier were crowned. This was once the seat of the Culdee, and here the famous *Coronation Stone* was kept, which originally came from Tara Hill in Ireland, and which Edward I. carried off to Westminster Abbey, where it is fixed under Edward the Confessor's Chair. The river Almond, from Glen Almond, now joins the Tay. At Luncarty Bleach Works (the spot where the Danes were defeated by Kenneth III. and the Hays), the river turns off to the east up the valley of Strathmore, passing over Campsiefall, near Cargill; and joins the road again near the celebrated Birnam Wood (on a hill, 1,580 feet high), the sight of which, in motion, filled Macbeth with despair.

Siward. What wood is this before us?
Monteith. The wood of Birnam.
Malcolm. Let every soldier hew him down a bough
And bear't before him; thereby shall we shadow
The number of our host, and make discovery
Err in report of us.
MACBETH. Act 5, Scene IV.

It was part of a royal forest. There is a noble view over the valley of the Tay; one of the opposite hills, to the south-east is *Dunsinane*, about 1,100 feet high, with some remains of the usurper's castle.

SCENE V. DUNSINANE.

Within the Castle.—Enter Messenger.

Mess. Gracious, my lord!
I shall report that which I say I saw,
But know not how to do it.
Mac. Well, say, sir.
Mess. As I did stand my watch upon the hill,
I looked towards Birnam, and anon, methought
The wood began to move.
Mac. If thou speakest false,
Upon the next tree shalt thou hang alive,
Till famine cling thee; if thy speech be sooth
I care not if thou do for me as much.
I pall in resolution, and begin
To doubt the equivocation of the fiend
That lies like truth: *Fear not, till Birnam Wood
Do come to Dunsinane.* And now a wood
Comes toward Dunsinane. Arm, arm, and out!

According to some accounts Macbeth escaped from the field of battle and fled up the vale of Strathmore, and was killed at Lumphanan, near Kincardine O'Neil. *Dunkeld*, see page 92. *Logierait*, 8 miles further; here the Tummel, fed by various mountain streams from the Grampians, joins the Tay; most of these feeders unite in the Garry, which comes down the Inverness road, receives the Tilt from Glen-tilt (on the way to Braemar,) and falls into the Tummel by the pass of Killiecrankie, where Claverhouse fell in 1689. From *Logierait* up the Tay, past Grandtully, Murthly, Castle Menzies, &c., to *Taymouth*, the Marquis of Breadalbane's seat. The scenery is truly beautiful. Up Loch Tay (15 miles long) through Glen Dochart, &c., to the head of Loch Lomond, is 45 miles.

PERTH, ALMOND VALLEY, & METHVEN.

Perth to Methven.

This is a line about six miles long, passing through ALMOND BANK, to

METHVEN.

Here is *Methven Castle*, within the grounds of which is the Pepperwell Oak, the trunk of which is eighteen feet in circumference. In this neighbourhood Robert Bruce was defeated, June 19th, 1306, by the English, under the command of the Earl of Pembroke.

DUNDEE, PERTH, AND ABERDEEN.

Perth to Dundee, Arbroath, &c.

Passing KINFAUNS (near which is *Kinfauns Castle*), and GLENCARSE (close to which is the seat of C. Hunter, Esq.), we reach ERROL, INCHTURE, and LONGFORGAN stations. At the latter is a church, rebuilt in the pointed style in 1795, and near which in 1790, 300 coins of Edward I.'s reign were found. In the vicinity are *Drummie*, Lord Kinnaird, and *Myterefield*, T. White, Esq.

Passing INVERGOWRIE station, we arrive at

DUNDEE.

A telegraph station.

HOTELS.—Royal, British, Crown.

MARKET DAYS.—Tuesday and Friday.

FAIRS.—Tuesday after July 11th, August 26th, and September 19th.

BANKERS.—British Linen Co.; Western Bank of Scotland; Dundee Banking Co.; Bank of Scotland; National Bank of Scotland; East Bank of Scotland.

The capital of Forfarshire, seat of the Scottish linen trade, a port and burgh (returning one member), with a population of 78,931, situated on the north side of the Tay. Coming direct from the metropolis, a ferry of two miles must be crossed, from Broughty to Tay Port, in connexion with the railway. A swelling hill behind the town, called Dundee Law, is 525 feet high to the camp on the top. Here Montrose sat while his troops sacked the town, in 1645, after the battle of Tippermuir. Since 1815, Dundee has been greatly improved by the new quays, wet and graving docks, and the deepening of the chief harbour. About 50,000 tons of shipping belong to the port, a small portion being engaged in the whale fisheries. The factories for spinning and weaving flax exceed 100, employing as many as 16,000 hands, three-fourths of whom are women. Coarse linens, osnaburghs, diapers, sail-cloth, rope, canvas, &c., are the chief goods made up.

Near the harbour is the triumphal arch, 82 feet wide, built on the occasion of the Queen's visit in 1844. Among the modern improvements which have taken place in Dundee, may be noticed those in Union Street, which opens a communication with the Craig Pier and the Nethergate; indeed, nearly all the old buildings have been superseded by new ones. In front of the quay, along the margin of the Tay, are the various docks and shipyards, terminated on the west by the Craig Pier, which is exclusively used for the large ferry steam-boats. On the east the piers project into the deep water, on which are placed various coloured lights to guide the seamen after sunset. Opposite the town is a beacon, which is built on a dangerous rock. Nearly the whole of the space now appropriated to the docks, was originally a semicircular sandy beach, but by great exertion the spirited inhabitants have erected a series of quays which are unequalled in Scotland. There are 20 churches and chapels. Three churches stand together on the site of that founded by William the Lion's brother, David (the hero of Scott's "Talisman") in pursuance of a vow made at sea on returning from the Crusades; its square tower, 156 feet high still remains, though damaged by a fierce storm in 1840. David also built a castle, which figures in the war of independence as having been taken by Wallace and Bruce. The former great patriot was educated at the priory in this town, and made himself known, about 1271, by killing Delly, an insolent young Norman knight in the Governor's train. The *Town House* in High Street, was built by Adams, in 1734; other buildings are, the *Exchange*, *Trades Hall*, *Academy*, *St. Andrew's* Church, with a tall spire, &c.

Some of the oldest houses are in Seagate. High Street and Murraygate are the most bustling thoroughfares. When Charles II. was crowned at Scone in 1650, by the Covenanters, he came to reside at *Whitehall*, in the Nethergate, since pulled down. Another house, in the middle of High Street, was occupied by Monk (after taking the town by storm in 1645); and by the Pretender, in 1716; it was also the birthplace of Monmouth's widow, Anne, Duchess of Buccleugh (the Lady of Branxholme Tower, in the "Lay of the Last Minstrel." In the Cowgate is an arch from which Wishart, the martyr, preached during the plague of 1544, the infected part of his congregation being kept by themselves on one side. Towards Dundee Law, at the end of Dunhope Wynd, is *Dunhope Castle* (now a barrack), which belonged to the Scrymgeours, (hereditary standard-bearers of Scotland), and to the famous Graham of Claverhouse, whom James II. created Viscount Dundee, before his death at Killiecrankie. Mackenzie, the great lawyer, and Ivory, one of the first mathematicians of modern days, were natives of Dundee, a name supposed to be derived from *Donum-Dei*, or, God-given, applied to it by David, its founder.

Within a short distance are, *Broughty Castle*; *Gray*, the seat of Lord Gray; *Camperdown*, that of Lord Duncan; and *Mains*, another of Claverhouse's seats.

Passing BROUGHTY FERRY and MONIFIETH (which has an old castle, and in the vicinity *The Grange*, an old seat, and *Fintry*), BARRY (near which is an oval camp 168 yards round, where it is reported that King Arthur's wife Vanora was confined by the Picts), CARNOUSTIE, and EAST HAVEN stations, we arrive at

ARBROATH.

POPULATION, 10,030.

A telegraph station.

HOTELS.—Albion, White Hart, Royal.

MARKET DAY.—Saturday.

FAIRS.—January 31st., 3rd Wednesday in June, and July 18th.

BANKERS.—Branch of British Linen Co., Branch of Western Bank of Scotland, Branch of Commercial Bank of Scotland.

A port and parliamentary burgh, in Forfar. Its proper name is Aberbrothock, signifying that it is situated at the mouth of the Brothock, which here falls into the North Sea. Provisions, paving-stone, linen (which is the staple manufacture) and bone-dust, are its chief exports; and about 8,000 tons of shipping are registered as belonging to the port. Formerly it was noted for a rich mitred abbey, founded in 1178, by King William the Lion, who was buried in it. All that remains of this gorgeous pile is the ruined church, 270 feet long, with its cloisters and fine east window. The latter has a circular light at the top, forming a conspicuous mark for seamen coming into harbour, who call it the "Round O of Arbroath." The three rows of blind arches on the wall produce a fine effect. The chapter house, great gate, and prison, are also left. The portcullis of the abbey figures in the town arms. Close to the site is a modern Parish Church, with a spire 150 feet high. A signal tower here communicates with the famous *Bell Rock Lighthouse*, which is 10 miles, south-east, out at sea, opposite the mouth of the Tay, and is the Inch-Cape Rock of Southey's well-known lines —a dangerous reef of red sandstone, 2,000 feet long, which was under the special care of the abbots:—

> "With neither sign nor sound of shock
> The waves flowed over the Inch-Cape Rock,
> So little they rose, so little they fell,
> They did not move the Inch-Cape bell.
> The pious Abbot of Aberbrothock
> Had placed that bell on the Inch-Cape Rock:
> On the waves of the storm it floated and swung,
> And louder, and louder, its warning rung.
> When the rock was hid by the tempest's swell
> The mariners heard the warning bell,
> And then they knew the perilous rock,
> And blessed the Abbot of Aberbrothock."

There is a bell swung in a wicker frame, something like this, at the corner of a bank at the entrance of Southampton Water, called Jack-in-the-Basket. As to the Inch-Cape bell, the story is, that it was wantonly cut adrift by a pirate, to plague the Abbot, and that his vessel was soon after wrecked on the very rock. In 1807-11, a noble lighthouse was built by Stevenson, on the model of Smeaton's at the Eddystone, which is shaped like the trunk of a tree. It is of solid stone for 30 feet upwards, the total height being 115 feet. The stone blocks are dove-tailed together; there are five stories above. At the base the diameter is 42 feet, which lessens to 15 feet at the top. The light itself is alternately bright and red every two minutes, and can be seen 14 miles off. In foggy weather a bell is tolled. Four men live here, each of whom every six weeks, for a change, takes a fortnight's turn ashore, and there is no want of candidates for this office.

Lighthouses of equal beauty and solidity have been built on this plan upon the Black Rock at Liverpool, and Skerryvore, in the Western Islands.

Passing COLLISTON, LEYSMILL and FRIOCKHEIM, we reach GUTHRIE, where is a Roman camp, and in the vicinity *Guthrie House*, seat of J. Guthrie, Esq., with an old tower 60 feet high and 10 thick, erected by Sir Alexander Guthrie, who was slain at Flodden Field. The church was built by Lord Treasurer Guthrie.

SCOTTISH NORTH EASTERN.

Perth to Forfar and Aberdeen.

Passing LUNCARTY (near which is the largest bleaching field in Scotland, on which Kenneth III., with the aid of the Hays, routed the Danish Pirates in 972), we arrive at

STANLEY (Junction).

A telegraph station.

Here a small spinning trade is carried on by the inhabitants. Population, 1,980

DUNKELD BRANCH.

Passing MURTHLY, near which is the seat of Sir W. D. Stewart, Bart., erected close to the old castle of the Stewarts, we reach

DUNKELD (Birnam).

POPULATION, 1,104.
Distance from station, 7 miles.
A telegraph station.
HOTELS.—Athol, Birnam.
MARKET DAY—Saturday.
FAIRS.—February 12th, April 5th, June 26th, and 2nd Tuesday in November.

Situated at the pass into the Highlands, from which there is a splendid view; also an old Cathedral, and the Duke of Athol's seat, at which are the fine falls of Bran or Braan, and the two first larches brought to England in 1737; there are upwards of 30 millions planted now.

Scottish North Eastern Main Line continued.

Stanley to Cupar.

Passing BALLATHIE we reach CARGILL station, near which is *Shortwood Shaw*, Wallace's hiding place. Close by are ruins of a cell ,Druidical circles, tumuli, Castlehill Roman camp and road, *Stobhall*, an old seat of the Drummond's, where Annabella, wife of Robert III., and ancestress of the Stuarts, was born. Pearl mussels have been found here.

WOODSIDE station.

COUPAR ANGUS, or Cupar.

A telegraph station.
HOTEL.—Strathmore Arms.
MARKET DAY—Thursday.

FAIRS—Tuesday before Old Christmas, 3rd Thursday in March, May 26th, 1st Tuesday in October, and Thursday on or after November 22nd.

This place has a population of 2,004 engaged in the bleach-fields, tanneries, distilleries, and linen factories. It contains three chapels, town hall, schools, public library, meal mills, traces of an old abbey, in which was found an almanac with Arabic figures, dated 1482 and a church, close to which some stone coffins have been discovered.

BLAIRGOWRIE BRANCH.

ROSEMOUNT station.

BLAIRGOWRIE.

POPULATION, 3,914.
A telegraph station.
HOTEL.—Robertson's.
MARKET DAY—Saturday.

FAIRS.—3rd Wednesday in March, May 26th, 2nd Wednesday in August, 1st Wednesday in October and November.

This place is situated on the river Ericht, which abounds with fish. It is celebrated for its pure white marble, highly esteemed by sculptors and architects. In the vicinity are Craighall Rattray, from which some fine views may be obtained, *Ardblair*, and *Newton House*, the seat of the M'Phersons.

Scottish North Eastern Main Line continued.

ARDLER station.

MEIGLE

(Junction with Newtyle and Dundee). In the church yard at this place are some antique sculptured stones to Vanora the wife of King Arthur, who was taken away by his nephew Mordred, and concealed at Burryhill Camp, which is partly vitrified, and 180 feet high by 72. The Belliduff Tumulus has a granite pillar; and in the vicinity are *Belmont*, the seat o Lord Wharncliffe; *Kinloch*, J. Kinloch, Esq.; and *Drumkilbo*. A market is held here on Wednesdays, and there are fairs on the last Wednesday in June and October.

FORFARSHIRE, or ANGUS.

This county, which returns one member, includes the districts of Glenisla, Glenesk, and Glenprassin. Its scenery is extremely beautiful, and presents a variety of picturesque views, not excelled by any other Scottish county. The great level valley of Strathmore runs through the centre of Forfarshire. from east to west; and the lines of hills which border this extensive tract of country, with the Grampians on the north, and some minor ranges on the south, may be said to form the county into a series of continuous ridges, generally pursuing a direction from east to west. The portion of the Grampians in this country contains many fine vallies.

DUNDEE AND NEWTYLE.

NEWTYLE.

POPULATION, 1,141.
Telegraph station at Meigle Junction.
HOTEL.— Stratherch.
MONEY ORDER OFFICE at Meigle, 2 miles.

In the vicinity are *Hatton Castle* in ruins, which was built in 1575, by Lord Oliphant; Castle of *Balcraig* and *Auchtertyre Camp*, both ruins, at the latter of which Montrose rested. From Kilfarnie Beacon a view of ten counties is obtained, as far as St. Abb's Head, on a clear day.

Passing HATTON, near which is the fine seat of General Arbuthnott, M.P., we soon reach AUCHTERHOUSE, the castle near which is the seat of Lady H. Wedderburn, and then proceed to DRONLEY, thence to BALDRAGON, and after reaching BALDOVAN, near which is the handsome seat of Sir J. Ogilvie, Bart., we arrive at

Dundee, see page 89.

Scottish North Eastern Main Line continued.

Meigle to Kirriemuir Junction.

Passing EASSIE, close to which are *Dunkenny*, the seat of J. L'Amy, Esq., and *Nevay*, the Right Hon. Stewart Mackenzie, we proceed to GLAMMISS, where there is a fair held in June, and near which is the Castle in which Malcolm II. was murdered in 1033. It was given to J. Lyon by his father-in-law, Robert II., in 1372, and contains some of the old turrets, walls 15 feet thick, suits of armour, 150 portraits, and some antique sun dials, &c.; close to the Manse is a pillar to King Malcolm, also one at Cossans, and an old fort at Dunoon, all worth a visit. Soon afterwards we reach the station at

KIRRIEMUIR (Branch).

POPULATION, 7,617.
A telegraph station.
HOTEL.—Commercial.
MARKET DAY.—Friday.

FAIRS.—March 13th, Friday after May 26th, 1st Wednesday in June and November, July 24th, and Wednesday after November 18th.

BANKERS.—National Bank of Scotland, G. Brand, Esq., Manager; draw on Glyn and Co.

Scottish North Eastern Main Line continued.

FORFAR.

A telegraph station.
HOTELS.—County Arms, Morrison's.
MARKET DAYS.—Wednesday and Saturday.
FAIRS.—Last Wednesday in February, Second do in April, 1st do. in May, 1st Tuesday and Wednesday in July and August, last Wednesday in September, 2nd do. in October, and 1st do. in November.
BANKERS.—Branch of Bank of Scotland; Branch of British Linen Co; Branch of Commercial Bank of Scotland; Branch of National Bank of Scotland; North of Scotland.

The town of Forfar, with a population of 9,311, engaged in the shoe and weaving trades, is situated in the romantic valley of Strathmore, and is of considerable antiquity. It has lately received many additions to its general appearance. Amongst those edifices which form the most prominent features in the modern improvements are a handsome range of county buildings in Castle Street, an episcopal chapel, excellent subscription room, library, town house, which contains the bridle with which people were harnessed previous to being burnt at "Witches' Howe"; news room, school, academy, and a church lately rebuilt, which has an old bell, the gift of Strange, a native. The Loch should be visited, as it contains the ruins of Queen Margaret's Nunnery. In the vicinity are *Restenet Priory*, and *Finhaven Castle*, at which the Earl of Crawford received James II. Don the botanist was born here in 1800.

Passing CLOCKSBRIGGS we soon reach AULDBAR ROAD station, close to which is the fine seat of P. Chalmers, Esq.

GUTHRIE (Arbroath Junction).

Telegraph station at Forfar, 7 miles.

MONEY ORDER OFFICE at Brechin, 5 miles

Here are a Roman Camp not far from the station, and *Guthrie House*, seat of J. Guthrie, Esq.

Passing FARNELL ROAD, close to which are the ruins of *Airley Castle*, and *Kinnaird*, the seat of the Carnegies (in the vicinity fine trout and salmon may be caught), we proceed to the

BRIDGE OF DUN (which signifies Fort), near which is the fine seat of the Marchioness of Ailsa, *Dun House*, and the salmon fisheries.

BRECHIN (Branch).

A telegraph station.

HOTEL.—Commercial.

MARKET DAY.—Tuesday.

FAIRS.—3rd Tuesday in January, 3rd Wednesday in April, 2nd Wednesday in June and two following days, July 2nd, Monday before last Wednesday in September.

BANKERS.—Branch of British Linen Co.; Branch of Western Bank of Scotland.

This town has a population of 6,637, employed in the making of osnaburghs, sail-cloth, and brown linen; and contains five chapels, town house, academy (the master is also preceptor of Maison Dieu, founded by Wm. de Brechin, in 1205), mechanics' institute, hospital, dispensary, brewery, distilleries, spinning mills, and a Collegiate Church, built in 1808, near the spire of *St. Ninian's Cathedral*, at which there is a leaning round tower, 108 feet high, and at Abernethy is a similar one. In 1572 the battle of Brechin was fought, between James II. and the Crawfords, when the Marquis of Huntly defeated the latter. The Danes burnt the town in 1012, and Montrose destroyed it in 1645. It is the bishop's seat, and near at hand is *Panmure Castle*, the seat of Lord Panmure, which is built on the site of the old one taken by Edward I. in 1303.

DUBTON Junction.

Telegraph station at Montrose, 3 miles.

MONEY ORDER OFFICE at Montrose, 3 miles.

MONTROSE (Branch).

A telegraph station.

HOTELS.—Star, White Horse, Albion.

MARKET DAY.—Friday.

FAIRS.—Friday after Whitsuntide and Martinmas.

BANKERS.—Branch of ank of Scotland; Branch of British Linen Co.; Branch of Western Bank of Scotland; Branch of National Bank of Scotland; Branch of East Bank of Scotland.

MONTROSE, in Forfarshire, was called *Munross*, as it stands on a little headland (*ross* in Gaelic,* *rhos* in Welsh) between the north sea and its harbour, which is a natural lake or basin, a little up the South Esk, inside the town. This basin, though 3 miles in circuit, is very shallow; wet docks have been constructed, and about 15,000 tons of shipping belong to the port. Over a part of the river is one of Sir S. Brown's suspension bridges, built in 1829, 432 feet long, and lying on towers 72 feet high.

As a parliamentary burgh, Montrose returns one member, and has a population of 15,238, many of whom are engaged in the linen manufacture. The late member, the estimable and patriotic Joseph Hume, Esq., was a native of this place, from which he was sent to India, under the patronage of the Panmure family, where he did great service as a Persian scholar. Another native was the late Sir Alexander Burnes, a kinsman of the poet Burns, who was assassinated at Cabool in 1841, on the outbreak of the Affghan war. The great Marquis of Montrose was also born here in 1612, in the house afterwards occupied by the Chevalier on his landing in 1716. Another local event is that related by Froissart of the Douglas, the "good Lord James," who, in 1330, embarked here with the heart of Bruce for the Holy Land. He was killed before he got there, having landed at Seville to fight the Moors; while the casket containing the King's heart was brought home and buried at Melrose.

The site of the town is flat, but there are some moderate hills (Three Horns, &c.), in the environs, from which is a goodly prospect of the town, basin, and the distant Grampians. When the tide is up the basin appears like an animated lake, at the bottom of a cultivated amphitheatre, green to the water's edge, and covered with gardens and country houses.

The basin above alluded to is nearly dry at low water, but is so completely filled up by every tide as to wash the garden walls on the west side of the town, and to afford sufficient depth of water in the channel for allowing small vessels to be navigated three miles above the harbour. At high water, the appearance of Montrose, when first discovered from the public road on the south, is peculiarly striking, and seldom fails to arrest the eye of the stranger. The basin opening towards the left, in all the beauty of a circular lake; the fertile and finely cultivated fields rising gently from its banks; the numerous surrounding country seats which burst at once upon the view; the town, harbour, and bay stretching further on the right; and the lofty summit of the Grampians, nearly in the centre of the landscape, closing the view towards the north-west, altogether present to the eye of the traveller one of the most magnificent and diversified amphitheatres to be found in the United Kingdom. The South Esk is crossed by a very magnificent suspension bridge, which stretches across the river in a noble span, the distance between the points of suspension being 432 feet. The town consists chiefly of one spacious main street, from which numerous lanes run off on each side, as from the High-street of Edinburgh.

None of the buildings are of much account. The *Town Hall* and *Linen Hall* are in High Street. The *Academy* may be known by its dome, and the *Parish Church* by the spire: the *Public Library* is of old date.

* Another derivation makes it *Mons Rosarum*, or Mount of Roses; and, accordingly, on the town seal is a wreath of roses, with a motto signifying that the sea uri he the *Ro e* embellishes

The favourite game of golf is played on the sandy links along the shore; and here (where the races are held) the Queen's Scottish Body Guard of Archers met in 1850 to compete for prizes. Fish, viz., salmon, lobsters, cod, &c., are abundant, the cod being caught at Montrose Pits, in the North Sea—a singular hollow, which is 30 fathoms deeper than the tract around.

All this part of the line passes through the fertile Vale of Strathmore.

Scottish North Eastern Main Line continued.

Dubton to Aberdeen.

CRAIGO station, near which is *Craigo House*, the seat of T. Carnegie, Esq.

KINCARDINESHIRE

Is now almost exclusively of an agricultural character, for though it has a sea-coast of considerable extent, it possesses no harbour of any eminence. The soil is of a very productive kind, and is cultivated in a style nowhere surpassed in Scotland. The county, in its more level parts, is highly embellished with the country seats of its numerous resident proprietors, each amid its own thriving woodland. This county returns one member.

MARYKIRK.

At the old church here are tombs of the Strachans, Thorntons, Barclays of Balmachewan, stone cross and antique font. In the vicinity are *Balmachewan*, seat of Col. Fraser; *Inglismaldie*, Earl of Kintore; *Hatton Castle*, General Arburthnott, M.P.; *Kirktonhill*, R. Taylor, Esq.; the Druid's Stones at Hospital, Balanakillie, &c.; and Inglisburn at which a battle was fought with the English.

LAURENCEKIRK,

Celebrated for the manufacture of wooden snuff boxes. Here Dr. Pitcairn found Ruddiman, the Latin grammar author, master of the school. Beattie, the poet, and opponent of Hume, in his Essay on Truth, was a native. Fairs—3rd Wednesday in January, last Tuesday in April, 26th May, Thursday after 3rd Tuesday in July, November 22nd, Thursday after 2nd Tuesday in August, Monday before last Wednesday in September, 1st Thursday in November. Markets on Monday.

FORDOUN,

Near which Montrose took up his position on the eve of the battle at Kilsyth. The church, which was rebuilt, is near Luther Water, a pretty spot; here are two Roman camps, 249 feet, and a British one close to Drumsleid. The mineral springs are considered good. The learned and eccentric lawyer, Lord Monboddo, was a native. Fordoun, the author of the *Scotichronicon*, was a monk here; and Beattie kept a school until his advancement. Three miles byond is the now insignificent village of Kincardine, which was the capital of that county until James VI.'s time, where are the ruins of Kenneth III.'s Castle, who was killed at Fettercairn.

We then proceed to DRUMLITHIE station, after which we arrive at

STONEHAVEN.

Distance from station, 1½ mile.
A telegraph station.
MARKET DAY.—Thursday.
FAIRS.—Thursday before Candlemas, day before May 26th, 3rd Tuesday in June, 2nd Tuesday in August, 2nd Tuesday in October, day before Nov. 22nd, Thursday before Christmas-day.
BANKERS. — Bank of Scotland; Aberdeen Town and County, and North of Scotland.

Since the reign of James VI. this place has been the county town of Kincardineshire, and contains a population of 3,240, who are principally engaged in the herring fisheries, distilleries, and breweries. It has a market house, town hall, dispensary, bridge over the Cowie which joins the old and new towns, water and gas works, quay, Donaldson's free school, a pier, with two fixed lights, which can be seen at a distance of 13 miles; a harbour, with 16 feet of water; two good churches, and four chapels.

Passing MUCHALLS, NEWTON HILL, PORTLETHEN, and COVE stations, we enter

ABERDEENSHIRE,

WHICH is one of the most extensive counties in Scotland, and returns one member. It forms the north-east corner of the island, being the easternmost point of a large triangle, which juts out far into the German Ocean, and is circumscribed by lines running between Edinburgh, Inverness, and Peterhead. The greater part of it may be denominated a level plain, agreeably diversified by irregular depressions, and gently swelling slopes, forming a congeries of pleasing knolls, with vales between, each intersected by its little rill, so as to exhibit the scenery, the general appearance of which is tolerably uniform, though its particular features are varied at every step.

ABERDEEN.

POPULATION, 71,973.
Telegraph station at the railway station.
HOTELS. — Douglas, near the station; Royal; Aberdeen.
MARKET DAYS.—Thursday and Friday.
FAIRS.—First Wednesday in April, last Wednesday in August, 2nd Friday in May and November, 1st Tuesday in every month at Bridge of Don; last Thursday in April and 1st Wednesday in November at Old Aberdeen; also every Wednesday, for cattle, in King Street.
BANKERS. — Aberdeen (incorporated with the Union), Town and County, and North of Scotland.

ABERDEEN (OLD) is a place of great antiquity. It lies about a mile to the north of the new town, near the mouth of the river Don, over which there is a fine single-arched Gothic bridge, which rests on a rock on each side, and is universally admired. This town consists chiefly of one long street.

ABERDEEN (NEW), the capital of the county, is considered the third city of importance in Scotland.

It lies on a slightly elevated ground on the north bank of the river Dee, near its efflux into the sea, and about a mile and a half from the mouth of the Don. It is a large and handsome city, having many spacious streets, lined on each side by elegant houses, built of granite from the neighbouring quarries.

Aberdeen derives its name from the Dee, on the north bank of which it lies, not far from the *Devana* of Ptolemy, and the river's mouth ("*aber*" in Gaelic), which makes an excellent port, whence cotton, linen, woollen goods, combs, and writing papers, in large quantities, granite, cattle, and agricultural produce from the interior, salmon, &c., are exported in great quantities. The salmon is sent to Billingsgate Market packed in ice, an ingenious plan for preserving it, which was first adopted here. The fisheries on the Dee, worth £10,000 a-year to the city, were originally granted by Bruce, on account of the gallant behaviour of the people in driving out the English garrison planted here by Edward I. Their watchword was "Bon-Accord," which is the motto of Aberdeen to this day. A history of the town has been written under this title. Its harbour, improved by Telford at a great cost, contains 34 acres, the pier i 1,200 feet long. Recently a large wet dock has been constructed, for the shipping of which there are registered at the port 230, nearly 70,000 tonnage.

Most of the houses are built of white granite, which gives it a handsome and durable appearance. The almost inexhaustible supplies of this stone are close at hand. Leaving the old "Brig o' Dee," or Dee Bridge, above the suspension bridge, where Montrose, in one of his descents, fought a battle with the Covenanters and walking about a mile, we find ourselves in a fine street of high stone houses, called Union Street, a mile long, which leads over the Denburn (a ravine crossed by a dry bridge) to Castle Square, in the centre of the town, where it meets Castle Street, in a square surrounded by high houses. The principal buildings stand in these two thoroughfares. Near the site of the old castle, which Edward I. besieged in 1298, is an octagonal building (the market cross), in the Gothic style, with medallion heads of Scottish Kings, and coats of arms upon it, first built in 1686, and restored in 1842. Close to this is a statue of the Duke of Gordon, a branch of which family (Earl of Aberdeen), lately Prime Minister, takes his title from this city.

Not far off, a spire, 120 feet high, marks the *Town House*, built in 1730; it has portraits by Jameson, a native of Aberdeen, with an armoury. The new *Assize Court* and *Prison* stand on the site of the old Tolbooth, or "Mids o' Mar," *i.e.*, Middle of Mar, as the district round Aberdeen is called. The Earl of Mar, it will be remembered, was one of the most devoted partisans of the Stuarts; but the citizens, as a commercial body, were too "Aberdeen awa'," as they say, to mix themselves up with his projects. Some of the handsomest buildings in this city are the *County Rooms* in Union Street (with portraits by Lawrence and Pickersgill), *Athenæum News Room*, and *Aberdeen* and *North of Scotland Banks*, mostly in the Grecian style, for which the granite is best suited. Some idea of the prosperity and importance of Aberdeen may be derived from the fact that the deposits in the local banks amount to three millions sterling. The new *markets* are 315 feet long.

The *East* and *West churches*, though in the Gothic style, are both modern, and close to the site of *St. Nicholas's* old church, the tower of which is seen in the East Church. Beattie, the poet of the "Minstrel," is buried in the latter. The *North* Church has a fine spire of 159 feet. Altogether there are between 20 and 30 churches and chapels, including four for the Episcopalians, whose bishop (Skinner, is uncle to the celebrated curate of St. Barnabas' Church, Pimlico) or primus is seated here.

There are many educational and benevolent establishments, among which, the *Grammar School* (built in 1757, but founded as far back as 1418), *Dr. Bell's Schools*, *Gordon of Straloch's Hospital* (lately enlarged), *Deaf and Dumb School*, the *Infirmary*, &c., may be noticed. Barbour, Jameson, Gregory, Abercrombie, Gibbs, Anderson, Bishop Elphinstone, Dunbar, Patrick Forbes, Burnet, T. Reid, and R. Hamilton, were natives. One of the first printed Scottish books was the "Breviary of Aberdeen." In Broad Street *Byron* lived in his youth. His mother was a Gordon.

MARISCHAL COLLEGE, founded in 1393 by the Keiths, Earls Marischal (or Marshal) of Scotland, but rebuilt of granite, in the Gothic style, by Simpson, in 1837. It is an imposing pile, with a tower 100 feet high; the museum is 74 feet long, and contains portraits by Jameson, the "Scottish Vandyck," who was an excellent painter. His daughter, too, was an artist; some of her embroidery used to adorn St. Nicholas's Church. Above 20 professors are attached to this college, which numbers 600 students designed chiefly for the church and parochial schools. One of the Gregorys connected with this university invented the reflecting telescope.

At OLD ABERDEEN, is *King's College*, with 360 students, founded in 1494; like its fellow it is in the Gothic style, and has a very elegant tower, a lantern on springers, an ancient chapel, and a library of 35,000 vols., with portraits by Jameson; Hector Boece, the first principal, is buried in it. Here also is the old *Cathedral*, the seat of a bishop in episcopal times; it contains many tombs, blazoned arms in the oak ceiling, and a beautiful west window. This old part of the town is on the Don, which falls into the sea about half a mile beyond Balgownie Bridge, a curious Gothic arch, 67 feet span, built by Bruce between two dark rocks. Byron refers to it, and the legend connected with it, in *Don Juan*. There is a new bridge, remarkable from the fact that it was built from a bequest of £2 5s. in the time of James VI., which, with care and economy, amounted to £20,000, a remarkable instance of how money accumulates at compound interest.

Besides cotton and woollen mills, ironworks, and ship-yards, Aberdeen possesses granite polishing works, all of which deserve notice. Its fine steamers and clippers, with the "Aberdeen bow," are well known.

DEESIDE.

Aberdeen to Banchory.

Leaving GUILD station at Aberdeen, we proceed to RUTHRIESTON, thence to CULTS, so named from "Quilques," a corner, which has a fine church, the living of which was held by Wilkie's father, who with his son were natives. Close at hand is *Walter Hill*, with a Roman camp, and *Cranford Priory*, the seat of Lady M. Cranford—and quickly reach MURTLE; from thence the train proceeds to MILLTIMBER, and then arrives at

CULTER.

Telegraph station at Aberdeen, 7¾ miles.

Here are paper and saw mills, and close at hand is *Culter House*, the seat of J. Duff, Esq.

Passing DRUM, close to which is Drumoak, the seat of A. Irvine, Esq., which has an old tower with walls 12 feet thick, we arrive at PARK station, and thence forward to MILLS OF DRUM; leaving which, we soon reach

BANCHORY TERNAN.

A telegraph station.

HOTEL.—Douglas' Arms.

Banchory Ternan, or Upper Banchory, is a small village on the banks of the Dee, at the confluence of that river with the Feugh. In the vicinity are *Banchory Cottage* and *Inchmarlo*, the seat of D. Davidson, Esq.

GLASSEL and TORPHINS stations.

LUMPHANAN.—Here is shown Macbeth's cairn, a heap 120 feet high.

DESS station.

ABOYNE.

The terminus of the railway, and beautifully situated at the confluence of the Tanar with the Dee, and surrounded with hills thickly covered with wood on every side. *Aboyne Castle*, a seat of the Marquis of Huntly, is close at hand. It offers an excellent starting point for the tourist to visit the picturesque scenery extending between Ballater, Braemar, and Balmoral.

BALLATER.

This watering place, which is close to the Pannanich Springs, is the Tunbridge Wells and Keswick of Aberdeenshire, where people go to drink the waters and enjoy the walks and excursions among the neighbouring hills, from some of which (Craigendarroch in particular) there are extensive and beautiful views. The objects of interest in the district are—the *Burn of the Vat*, a natural wall of perpendicular rock; *Lochnagar*, which commands a splendid prospect; the *Linn and Loch of Muich*, and the *Dhu Loch*; and lastly, *Mont Keen*.

Ballater to Balmoral and Braemar.

Following the course of the Dee, the coach proceeds long the south bank (past *Abergeldie Castle*), formerly the seat of M. F. Gordon, Esq., which has an ol. tower among the birches, and belonged to H. R. H. te late Duchess of Kent, to *Crathie*, the castle of which, an old Flemish house) is the seat of Sir R. Burnett, Bart., a small village on the north side of the river, in the vicinity of which are *Invercauld*, J. Farquharson, Esq., Malcolm Canmore's hunting seat, *Monaltrie*, *Marr Lodge*, Duke of Leeds, and the salmon fisheries. About a quarter of a mile beyond is the summer residence of Her Majesty, *Balmoral Castle*, situated in a picturesque vale or dell, surrounded by beautiful mountain scenery; and close by is *Birkhill*, which belongs to the Prince Consort.

CASTLETON OF BRAEMAR.

HOTELS.—Invercauld Arms, Fife Arms.

This is only an old Highland village, surrounded by mountains, and situated in the centre of a region of forests; but it is the best place for the tourist to select to start from on a visit to the different excursions and places of interest in the neighbourhood. *Braemar Castle*, and view from Invercauld Bridge; the Falls of the Garrawalt, and Corriemulzie, the Linns of Quirch and Dee, are the nearest excursions. The more distant are Lochnagar, and other peaks in Glen Tilt, and beyond Ben Macdhui, in the heart of the magnificent scenery of the Grampians. The latter, to the south of Braemar, is 4,390 feet high, or second only to Ben Nevis, the highest mountain of Great Britain.

GREAT NORTH OF SCOTLAND.

Aberdeen to Huntly and Keith.

Passing the intermediate stations—KITTYBREWSTER, WOODSIDE, BUXBURN, and DYCE, where are a Druid circle of 10 stones on Tirebeggar Hill, *Dyce House*, seat of Gordon Skene, Esq., a fine church with an old font, and KINALDIE, we arrive at

KINTORE.

POPULATION, 1,342.

Telegraph station at Aberdeen, 15½ miles.

This was formerly a forest, and had a hunting seat given by Bruce to the Keiths. In the vicinity are *Thainston*, seat of D. Mitchell, Esq., Castle-hill Law, Bruce's Howe, some Cairns, and the remains of four Druid circles.

ALFORD VALLEY.

This is a railway 16½ miles long, having on its route the stations of KEMNAY, MONYMUSK, TILLIFOWRIE, and WHITEHOUSE, and terminating at

ALFORD,

A place remarkable for the defeat of the Covenanters by Montrose in 1645. It is situated on the Don, in which are salmon fisheries, and has a fair once a month for cattle

Great North of Scotland continued.

INVERURY.

POPULATION, 2,649.

A telegraph station.

HOTEL.—Kintore Arms.

MARKET DAY.—Saturday.

FAIRS.—Every month or fortnight.

MONEY ORDER OFFICE at Kintore, 3 miles.

BANKERS.—Aberdeen Town and County Bank; Branch of North of Scotland; Branch of Aberdeen Banking Company.

Here Bruce defeated the Comyn. In the vicinity are *Keith Hall*, Earl of Kintore.

From this point a branch turns off to the right, through LETHENTY to OLD MELDRUM, a distance of 5¾ miles.

INVERAMSAY station.

BANFF, MACDUFF, AND TURRIFF JUNCTION.

WARTLE, ROTHIE, and FYVIE stations.

AUCHTERLESS, on the river Ythan, in which pearls have been known to be found, and in which there are salmon fisheries.

TURRIFF.

Population about 1,650, engaged in the manufacture of thread and linen. Situated on the river Doveran, in which are salmon and trout.

PLAIDY and KING EDWARD stations.

BANFF.

MARKET DAY.—Friday.

FAIRS.—January 7th; February 1st, Tuesday, *o. s.*; May, Tuesday, on or after the 26th; August 1st, Friday, *o. s.*; November, Friday before the 22nd.

A parliamentary borough and Coast Guard station, at the mouth of the river Doveran. It has a population of 6,000 engaged in the fisheries, and to a limited extent in the manufacture of leather, linen, &c. The extensive park and mansion of the Earl of Fife is in the vicinity. Its situation commands a series of beautiful views, and possesses a good gallery of pictures.

Great North of Scotland Main Line continued.

Passing PITCAPLE, the seat of M. Lumsden, Esq., we proceed to OYNE, near which are *Pittodrie*, seat of R. Erskine, Esq. and *Tillyfour*, R. Grant, Esq., and reach BUCHANSTONE; thence to

INSCH, close to which is *Craigievar*, the seat of Sir W. Forbes, Bart.; here fairs are held, on Friday before 18th May and November, 3rd Wednesday in May, and 3rd Tuesday in October, after which the train arrives at WARDHOUSE, and then proceeds on to the

KENNETHMONT and GARTLEY stations, near which are excellent trout streams, and the fine old ruin, *Gartley Place*, the ancient seat of the Gordons, now belonging to the Duke of Richmond. Soon afterwards we stop at

HUNTLY.

POPULATION, 4,061.

HOTEL.—Gordon Arms, W. Beattie.

A telegraph station.

MARKET DAY.—Thursday.

FAIRS.—Last Wednesday in January, last Tuesday in February and March, Wednesday before May 26th, last Tuesday in May, 2nd Tuesday in June, 3rd Tuesday in June, Wednesday after 1st Tuesday in July, Wednesday after 2nd Tuesday in August and September, 4th Tuesday in September, Thursday before November 22nd, 1st Tuesday in November and December.

BANKERS.—Branch of Aberdeen Town and County Bank; Branch of Aberdeen Banking Company; Branch of North of Scotland.

Huntly is a picturesque village, standing on a point of land formed by the confluence of the Bogie with the Deveron, where there is excellent garnet, trout, and salmon fishing. It contains the ruins of Huntly Castle, the two halls and gate of which still remain. *Huntly Lodge*, the Duke of Richmond's seat, is close at hand, and also the splendid modern mansion of the present Marquis of Huntly.

From hence the line continues through ROTHIEMAY to GRANGE, the point of junction with the

BANFF, PORTSOY, AND STRATHISLA.

This is a line 16¼ miles long, passing through KNOCK and CORNHILL to TILLYNAUGHT, where the line turns to the left, a distance of 2¾ miles, to the harbour at Portsoy, a seaport of growing importance. The continuation of the line from Tillynaught is *via* LADY'S WELL to the harbour at BANFF, see above.

Great North of Scotland Main Line continued.

KEITH,

A small town of about 1,800 inhabitants, consisting only of one long street. The church stands on the site of a very old one, and was rebuilt, in a pointed style, in 1819. The tower is 104 feet high. Ferguson, the astronomer, was born here.

MORAYSHIRE

Is now divided into three several shires, viz., Banff, Moray, and Nairn. In describing this beautiful district of country, known by the name of Morayshire, it is usual to include the small county of Nairn with which it is intimately connected. Some parts of this district partake of the wild, rocky, and mountainous character of the Highlands. The low country is a large plain extending from the Spey westward, between the shore and a range of mountains for nearly forty miles. This plain, however, is diversified over its whole extent by short ridges of lower hills, in general nearly parallel to the shore. There are many plains in the course of the Spey, and some of the tract of the Findhorn, of great fertility and beauty. It returns one member in conjunction with Nairn.

INVERNESS & ABERDEEN JUNCTION.

Keith to Inverness.

By means of this line there is now an unbroken connection between Aberdeen and Inverness. Continuing our journey from Keith, we pass the station of MULBEN, and arrive at

ORTON,

The junction of a short branch line to ROTHES an CRAIGELLACHIE, six miles to the left.

Leaving Orton, onward, we pass FOCHABERS and LHANBRYDE, and arrive at

ELGIN.

A telegraph station.

HOTEL.—Gordon Arms; Star Inn (called Devies' Hotel.)

MARKET DAYS.—Tuesday and Friday.

FAIRS.—3rd Friday in February, March, and April, 2nd Friday in May, 1st Tuesday in June, 3rd Tuesday in July, August, September, and October, 3rd Wednesday in December.

BANKERS.—British Linen Company; Caledonian; North of Scotland; Commercial Bank of Scotland; Aberdeen Banking Company.

This town has a population of 7,277, who return one member—the county another, and was founded by Helgy, a Norwegian. It is situated 5 miles from the sea, on the river Lossie, and contains 5 chapels, prison, library, news and assembly rooms, literary and horticultural societies, breweries, gas and water-works, woollen factory, grammar school, free school, hospital school of industry, founded by General Anderson (a native who was a poor boy of this town), and the site of Bishop Andrew's *Domus Dei*, erected in 1227; hospital founded by Dr. Gray, a native, and built by Gillespie; pauper lunatic asylum, church in the Grecian style, the walls, towers, chapter house, and palace of the cathedral. It was rebuilt in 1397, after that of Lichfield, and had a tower 178 feet high, which fell in 1711; some of the tombs remain. In the vicinity is *Pluscarden*, with the ruins of a priory.

From Elgin a short branch of six miles turns off to the right to

LOSSIEMOUTH (Branch).

Telegraph station at Elgin, 6 miles.

HOTEL.—Railway

STEAMERS to and from Aberdeen, Edinburgh, Inverness, &c.

Here lead with silver is found to the west in the quartz.

Retracing our steps to Elgin and again proceeding onward, we pass the stations of ALVES, KINLOSS (the junction of a line, three miles long, to the town of Findhorn), FORRES, and BRODIE, and arrive at

NAIRN.

A telegraph station.

HOTEL.—Anderson's

MARKET DAYS.—Tuesday, Thursday, and Friday.

FAIRS.—April 2nd, June 19th, August 13th, September 4th, October 3rd, and November 1st.

This is the county town of Nairnshire, and has a population of 2,977, about three-fourths of whom speak Gaelic, and contains 2 chapels, court house, jail, Richardson's inn, where "the Nairnshire Harvest Home" is held annually; schools, gas and waterworks, bridge built in 1632, but considerably damaged by the floods in 1829, Smith's monument, baths. In the vicinity are *Kilhavock Castle*, seat of Colonel Rose (to Mrs. M'Kenzie of which family Lord Forbes's song refers—"Ah, Chloris could I now but sit," &c.), and *Castle Finlay*, which is vitrified. It gives the title of Baroness to Lady Keith. Excellent salmon and trout fisheries are close at hand.

CAWDOR,

Telegraph station at Keith.

At which is *Cawdor Castle*, Lord Cawdor, an ancient moated edifice built in 1400, on the site of that which belonged to Macbeth, "The Thane of Cawdor." It contains some old tapestry, secret passages, a vault under the tower, in which is an ancient tree, where success to the hawthorn (house of Cawdor) is drunk by the peasantry; and some old timber. A fair is held here on the 2nd Tuesday in March. Then proceed to

FORT GEORGE.

This fort, erected in 1746, covers 10 acres, holds a small garrison, and of which Colonel Findlay (18 years on the Western coast of Africa, and late Governor of Sierra Leone) is the Governor.

Further on we reach DALCROSS, the castle at which has an old tower of the Clan Chattan, and just beyond is

CULLODEN,

Not far from which is Culloden Moor, where Charles Stuart was defeated by the Duke of Cumberland, in May, 1746 (who laid out Virginia water, near Windsor), and *Culloden House*, seat of G. Forbes, Esq., at which Prince Charles lodged the night before the battle, and left his stick, which, with pieces of armour, &c., are shown to visitors. Where the Duke stood, a cairn 100 feet high has been erected.

INVERNESS-SHIRE.

THIS is one of the largest counties of Scotland, and returns one member. Its surface is in general extremely ragged and uneven, consisting of vast ranges of mountains, separated from each other by narrow and deep vallies. These mountains stretch across he whole country, from one end of the island to another, and lie parallel to every valley, rising like immense walls on both sides. while the intersected country sinks deep between them, with a lake, or rapid river, or an arm of the sea, following in the centre. No sooner is one defile passed over than a second range of hills comes into view, which contains another, and a strath of uninhabited country. The great Caledonian Glen, which runs in a straight line nearly north-east and south-west, divides the county into two almost equal parts. This valley, in the greater part of its length, is naturally filled with water, and forms a long chain of lakes succeeding each other—a circumstance which suggested the idea transferring the whole into the Caledonian Canal.

INVERNESS.

A telegraph station.

HOTELS. — Caledonian, Church Street; Union, High Street.

BANKERS.—Branch of British Linen Co.; Branch of Bank of Scotland; Caledonian Banking Co.; Branch of Commercial Bank of Scotland; Branch of National Bank of Scotland; Branch of North of Scotland.

Inverness, with a population of 12,793, who return one member, at the foot of the Northern Highlands, on the Moray Firth, where the Caledonian Canal terminates, 106 miles from Aberdeen. The mouth of the Firth is guarded by Fort George and Fortrose, where Sir J. Mackintosh went to school. A small river, called the *Ness*, opening into a little estuary, or *Inver*, in Gaelic, gives name to the town, which is situated among plantations, and moderate hills, fertile and cultivated. Small ships are able to unload at Kessock Ferry, which divides the Firth from Loch Beauly. Inverness lies as it were at the back of Scotland, in a part formerly little visited or accessible. About the year 1770, it had no banks, lamps, or tiled houses, and one cargo of coals (called "black stones") a year was enough to supply the demand; but smuggled tea, brandy, fish, and game were plentiful. It was not too far north for Cromwell, who paid it a visit in 1651, and built a fort; and it was occupied about a century later by Charles Stuart and the Duke of Cumberland, both of whom had their quarters at the Drummuirs' house in Church Street, then the best one in the town. At present it contains severa well built streets and houses, among which are the *Court House*, on the site of a castle, built by the Thanes of Cawdor; *Tolbooth* or *prison*, with a spire, and a stone called Clach-na-Cudden in front of it; twelve *churches* and *chapels;* six banks, besides *Assembly Rooms*, an *Athenæum*, and a well-endowed *Academy*. There is a pleasant walk by the river, which rose so high in the great floods of 1849 as to break down the old stone bridge.

In the neighbourhood are various cairns and Druid's stones; Craig Phadic (or Patrick's Stone) Mountain, 1,150 feet high, with a vitrified fort on the top, cemented together by melting the surface of the stone; *Dochfour*, seat of E. Baillie, Esq., near Dochfour Loch, and the Roman station of *Bonatrie*, not far from Loch Ness. At the top of Loch Beauly is the seat of Lord Lovat (the head of the Frasers), and remains of a priory where the Frasers and Chisholms are buried. *Eilan-agash* in *Strath-Glass*, is a pretty sheltered spot, which Sir Robert Peel bought for a Highland seat a little before his death.

The road to Perth leads up Strath-Spey (which gives name to the Highland Dance), and through a pass of the Grampians. To the left of the road, three miles from Inverness, is the *Culloden Cairn*, a pile 100 feet high, in the midst of the desolate moor, where the Duke of Cumberland defeated Charles Stuart, 16th May, 1746. It is traversed by the Nairn river; descending which you pass *Cawdor Castle*, a remarkable pile of the 15th century, belonging to the Earl of Cawdor, and Rait Castle. Dunsinane and Birnam Wood are near Perth. About twenty miles from Inverness, through Nairn, is *Forres Castle*, on the heath where Macbeth met the weird sisters, and murdered Banquo; there is also Sweno's Pillar, an ancient carved stone, 20 feet high, commemorating a treaty with the Danes.

Good roads made by the Government and the landholders strike through the Highlands in various directions, in the counties of Inverness, Ross, and Sutherland; fir timber, deer, game, and sheep are the chief products. Vast tracts are preserved for deer-stalking, while (in Sutherland especially) thousands of clansmen have been transplanted to Canada, to make room for sheep-farms. The narrow passages between the mountains are called *Glens*, the wider valleys are *Straths*, each beihg watered by its own stream, and the character of the scenery resembles that of Wales, with a more piercing mist, keener air, more lakes, and a more broken coast. Some of the highest peaks are 3,000 to 4,000 feet high. The coach road to the north runs near the coast past Dingwall; Bonar Bridge, Laing to Tongue, 88 miles; or to Tain, Dornoch, and Wick, 123 miles.

From Inverness to Fort William is 61 miles by coach, the road running close to the Caledonian Canal, which is traversed by steamers on the return trip to Glasgow, through Loch Ness, Lochar, &c. On the west side of Loch Ness are Glens Urquhart and Moriston, two of the finest in the Highlands, with Mealfourvonie between them, a mountain 2,730 feet high, opposite the magnificent *Falls of Foyers*. From Fort Augustus (about half-way) you may turn up Glengarry to Glenelg and Kyle, where there is a ferry over the Sound of Sleat to Skye; or you may visit the heads of the Spey, and the *Parallel Roads* of Glenroy, in Lochaber. At Fort William there are *Ben Nevis*, *Lochiel*, and *Prince Charles's Monument* (the spot where he hoisted his standard in 1745), and the fine views at Cam-na-Gaul Bay, near Corran Ferry. The county returns one member.

LONDON AND NORTH WESTERN RAILWAY.

SUMMER ARRANGEMENTS, COMMENCING JULY, 1861.

TOURISTS' TICKETS,

AVAILABLE FOR ONE CALENDAR MONTH,

ARE ISSUED TO

North Wales, Killarney Lakes, Ireland,

FURNESS ABBEY, CONISTON, &c.,

WINDERMERE AND PENRITH,

For Cumberland and Westmoreland Lakes.

STATIONS. FROM	Lakes of Killarney, Cork, &c.		TO NORTH WALES. Rhyl or Abergele		Conway.		Llandudno.		Bangor.		Carnarvn or Holyhead		Dublin by CargoSteamer f.m Holyhead to North Wall		Grange, in Cartmel over Sands.		Windermere, Furness Abbey, or Ulverstone.		Coniston Lake, or Penrith for Ullswater.	
	1 cl.	2 cl	1 cl.	2 cl	1 cl.	2 cl	1 cl.	2 cl	1 cl	2 cl.	1 cl.	2 cl.	1 cl.	2 cl	1 cl.	2 cl.	1 cl.	2 cl.	1 cl.	1 cl.
	s.	s	s.	s.	s.	s.	s.	s.	s.	s	s.	s.	s.	s.	s.	s.	s.	s.	s.	s.
Euston	115	95	54	40	56	42	57	44	59	49	60	50	61	51	68	47	70	50	73	52
Watford	110	90	49	38	51	40	52	42	54	47	55	48	56	49	58	40	65	48	68	50
Oxford, Bedford, Bletchley	110	90	44	29	45	31	47	32	49	34	50	35	51	36	53	37	60	45	63	47
Northampton, Wellingboro' Market Harboro'	105	85	39	27	41	29	42	30	44	32	45	33	46	34	48	32	50	35	53	37
Peterborough, Stamford	105	85	44	29	46	31	47	32	49	34	50	35	51	36	53	37	55	40	58	42
Rugby, Coventry, Leamington	100	80	30	21	32	26	33	27	35	29	37	31	38	32	45	34	47	37	50	39
Birmingham, Tamworth	90	75	26	17	25	22	29	23	31	25	33	27	34	28	41	32	43	35	46	37
Dudley Port, Great Bridge, Wednesbury, Walsall	90	75	25	16	27	20	28	21	30	24	32	25	33	26	39	30	41	33	44	35
Wolverhampton	90	75	24	15	26	18	27	19	29	23	31	24	32	25	38	29	40	32	43	34
Stafford, Shrewsbury, Wellington, Newport	90	75	22	15	24	18	25	19	27	21	28	23	29	24	35	27	37	30	43	34
Stockport	75	63	18	13	20	15	21	16	22	18	22	18	23	19	20	14	23	17	28	22
Manchester (Lon. Rd., Vic. St.)	75	63	18	13	20	15	21	16	22	18	22	18	23	19	20	14	22	16	27	21
Manchester (Oxford Rd. Sta.)	75	63	18	13	20	15	21	16	22	18	22	18	23	19	..	..	..	..	..	..
Huddersfield, Dewsbury, Halifax, Wakefield, Bradford, Leeds	80	67	18	13	20	15	21	16	22	18	22	18	23	19	22	16	24	18	28	22
Chester	75	63	10	8	12	10	13	11	15	13	17	15	18	16	22	16	26	21	29	23
Birkenhead	75	63	10	8	12	10	13	11	15	13	17	15	18	16	..	..	..	..	..	..
Crewe	84	70	14	11	16	13	17	14	19	16	21	18	22	19	24	18	28	23	31	25
Warrington	75	63	14	11	16	13	17	14	19	16	21	16	22	17	20	14	22	16	27	21
Liverpool (Lime St. & Edge H.)	..	..	..	..	..	..		..	..	..	..	..	..	..	20	14	22	16	27	21
Wigan	75	63	15	12	17	14	18	15	20	17	22	19	23	20	16	10	20	15	23	17
Preston	75	63	15	12	17	14	18	15	20	17	22	19	23	20	14	8	18	13	22	16
Lancaster	..	..	18	14	20	16	21	17	23	19	25	21	26	22	..	..	..	..	..	..
Kendal	..	..	21	16	23	18	24	19	26	21	28	23	29	24	..	..	..	..	..	..
Penrith	..	..	25	20	27	22	28	23	30	25	32	27	33	28	..	..	..	..	..	..
Carlisle	..	..	30	24	32	25	33	27	35	29	37	31	38	32	..	..	..	..	..	..
Bolton or Atherton	75	63	15	12	17	14	18	15	20	17	22	19	23	20	18	12	20	14	25	19
Macclesfield, Congleton	80	70	21	16	23	18	24	19	26	21	28	23	29	24	23	17	25	20	28	22
Stoke, Burslem, Longton, or Newcastle	80	70	18	15	20	17	21	18	23	19	25	21	26	22	..	..	30	24	33	26
Uttoxeter and Leek	85	75	22	16	24	18	25	19	27	21	28	23	29	24	..	..	38	28	41	30
Derby or Burton	90	77	26	18	28	22	29	23	31	25	33	27	34	28	..	..	40	30	43	32
Nottingham, Leicester, Lincoln	90	77	30	21	32	26	33	27	35	29	37	31	38	32	..	..	..	..	..	..
Craven Arms, Ludlow	90	77	27	20	29	22	30	23	32	25	33	26	34	27	..	..	45	35	48	37
Leominster, Kington, Hereford	90	77	30	22	30	22	31	23	32	25	34	26	35	27	..	..	45	35	48	37
Worcester	90	77	30	22	30	22	31	23	33	25	34	26	35	27	..	..	45	35	48	37
Cheltenham, Gloucester	90	77	35	25	35	25	36	26	38	28	39	29	40	30	..	..	50	40	53	42
Bristol	100	85	40	30	41	31	42	32	43	33	44	34	45	35	..	..	52	42	55	44
Abergavenny, Pontypool	100	77	39	29	40	30	41	31	43	33	44	34	45	35	..	..	50	40	53	42
Newport (Monmouth)	95	80	40	30	40	30	41	31	43	3	44	34	45	35	..	..	52	42	55	44
Cardiff	112	80	42	32	42	32	43	33	45	35	46	36	47	37	..	..	55	45	58	47

LONDON AND NORTH WESTERN—*Continued.*

NORTH WALES RESIDENTIAL TICKETS.

Any one Member of a Family who are holders of not less than Three Tourists' Tickets to North Wales can obtain a Monthly Ticket, entitling the Holder to travel daily by all Trains calling at the following Stations on the Chester and Holyhead Line. These Tickets can be had on application to Mr J. O. BINGER, Chester Station, but they will not be extended for more than 14 days beyond the first Month.

STATIONS. FROM	Rhyl or Abergele.		Conway or Llandudno.		Bangor, Carnarvon, or Holyhead.	
	1st Class.	2nd Class.	1st Class.	2nd Class.	1st Class.	2nd Class.
	s.	s.	s.	s.	s.	s.
Chester	60	45	70	55	80	60
Birkenhead	84	63	90	70	100	75
Warrington, Manchester, Stockport	80	60	100	75	120	90
Huddersfield	120	90	140	110	140	110
Leeds	140	110	160	130	160	130
Shrewsbury	100	75	120	90	140	110
Stafford, Wolverhampton, Dudley Port, Birmingham	120	90	140	110	140	110

LYTHAM, FLEETWOOD, BLACKPOOL, SOUTHPORT, GIANT'S CAUSEWAY, &c.

STATIONS, FROM	To Lytham, Fleetwood, Blackpool, & Southport.		Giant's Causeway, Lakes Erne &c.	
	1st cl.	2d cl.	1st cl.	2d cl.
	s.	s.	s.	s.
Euston, Watford	60	45	96	76
Oxford, Bedford, Bletchley	45	35	85	70
Northampton, Wellingbro', Market Harbro'	40	32	..	..
Peterborough	45	35	..	..
Rugby, Tamworth	41	30	..	..
Coventry, Leamington	41	30	73	60
Birmingham	33	25	69	53
Dudley Port, Great Bridge Wednesbury, Walsall	30	23	..	..
Wolverhampton	29	22	66	56

STATIONS. FROM	To Lytham, Fleetwood, and Blackpool.		Southport.		Giant's Causeway, Lakes Erne, &c.	
	1st cl.	2d cl.	1st cl.	2d cl.	1st cl.	2d cl.
	s.	s. d.	s. d.	s.	s.	s.
Stafford, Shrewsbury, Wellington, Newport (Salop)	26	19 0	26 0	19	66	56
Warrington	9	7 0	9 0	7	..	..
Liverpool (LimeSt.&EdgeH)	10	8 0	10 0	8	51	44
Wigan	8	6 0	8 0	6	..	..
Atherstone or Leigh	8	6 6	6 6	5	..	..
Craven Arms, Ludlow	33	26 0	33 0	26	..	..
Leominster, Kington, Hereford	40	30 0	40 0	30	..	..
Worcester	40	30 0	40 0	30	..	..
Abergavenny, Pontypool	45	35 0	45 0	35	..	..
Newport (Monmouth)	47	37 0	47 0	37	..	..
Cardiff	50	40 0	50 0	40	..	..

Passengers to Southport change at Wigan into the Lancashire and Yorkshire Company's Trains.

SCARBRO', WHITBY, FILEY, BRIDLINGTON, HARROGATE, AND REDCAR.

STATIONS. FROM	To Harrogate.		Scarborough, Whitby, Filey, Bridlington, or Redcar.	
	1st Class.	2nd Class.	1st Class.	2nd Class.
	s. d.	s. d.	s. d.	s. d.
EUSTON, Oxford	43 0	32 6	51 0	35 0
Watford, Leighton	36 0	29 0	42 6	31 6
Northampton	35 0	27 0	45 0	33 0
Liverpool	21 6	16 0	35 0	25 6
Manchester, Oldham, Stockport, Ashton, Staleybridge	15 6	11 6	28 0	21 6
Huddersfield	10 0	7 0	23 6	17 0
Macclesfield	16 6	12 0	29 0	22 0
Crewe, St. Helens Junction, Warrington	17 6	13 6	30 0	23 0
Stafford, Shrewsbury	20 0	15 0	32 6	24 0
Wolverhampton	22 6	16 0	35 0	25 0
Dudley, Dudley Port, Great Bridge, Wednesbury, Walsall, Lichfield	22 6	16 0	35 0	25 0

BUXTON.

STATIONS. FROM	Seven Days' Ticket.		Monthly Ticket.		Tickets for One Member of a Family (having taken Two Tickets) for any number of Journeys during the Month.	
	1 class	2 class	1 class	2 class	1st class	2nd class.
	s. d.	s. d.	s. d.	s. d.	s. d.	s. d.
Euston, Watford	..	..	35 0	26 0	..	..
Oxford	24 0	18 0	28 0	20 0	100	80 0
Bedford	20 0	16 0	22 0	17 0	74 0	57 0
Northampton	17 0	14 0	20 0	15 0	70 0	50 0
Peterborough	26 0	19 0	28 0	20 0	65 0	50 0
Leamington, Rugby, Coventry	14 0	10 0	15 0	11 0	50 0	39 0
Birmingham, Walsall, W'hampton.	11 0	8 0	2 0	9 0	40 0	30 0

STATIONS. FROM	Seven Days' Ticket.		Monthly Ticket.		Tickets for One Member of a Family (having taken Two Tickets) for any number of Journeys during the Month.	
	1 class	2 class	1 class	2 class	1st class	2nd class.
	s. d.	s. d.	s. d.	s. d.	s. d.	s. d.
Stafford, Shrewsbury, Liverpool	11 0	8 0	12 0	9 0	40 0	30 0
Manchester (Lon. Rd)	8 0	5 0	9 0	6 0	40 0	30 0
Wigan, Preston	10 0	7 0	11 0	8 0	40 0	30 0
Bolton or Atherton.	9 0	6 0	10 0	7 0	40 0	30 0
Huddersfield	10 0	8 0	12 0	10 0	40 0	30 0
Leeds	12 0	10 0	14 0	12 0	40 0	30 0
Dublin (Kngstwn P / Wstnd R)	25 0	20 0	30 0	25 0	75 0	55 0

LONDON AND NORTH WESTERN—*Continued.*

ISLE OF MAN.

STATIONS.	1st class and Cabin.	2nd clss and Cabin.
FROM	s. d.	s. d.
Euston Station	70 0	50 0
Oxford, Bedford	50 0	40 0
Leighton, Dunstable	55 0	48 0
Northampton and Peterboro'	50 0	40 0
Rugby	45 0	35 0
Coventry	35 0	30 0
Leamington	40 0	30 0
Birmingham	35 0	25 0
Dudley Port, Walsall, W'hampton	30 0	21 0
Stafford, Shrewsbury, Wellington, Newport (Salop)	25 0	20 0
Crewe	20 0	15 0
Cheltenham and Gloucester	45 0	34 0
Bristol	47 0	35 0

STATIONS.	1st class and Cabin.	2nd clss and Cabin.	2nd clss and Deck.	3rd cls and Deck.
FROM	s. d.	s. d.	s. d	s. d.
Wigan	12 6	11 6	8 0	7 0
Bolton, Leigh, or Atherton	15 0	12 6	9 0	7 6
Macclesfield	18 0	15 0	12 0	10 0
Stockport and Heaton Norris	16 0	14 0	10 0	8 6
Leeds	21 0	18 0	..	10 0
Dewsbury, Mirfield	20 0	17 0	..	10 0
Wakefield and Bradford	20 0	16 0	..	10 0
Huddersfield and Halifax	18 6	15 0	..	9 6
Oldham	16 0	14 0	10 0	8 6
Staleybridge	16 0	14 0	10 0	8 6
Manchester (Vic. & Ord. Lane Stas.)	16 0	13 0	9 0	8 0
Patricroft	15 6	13 0	9 0	7 6
Longsight and Levenshulme	16 0	13 0	9 0	8 0
Warrington	15 0	13 0	10 0	8 0

MALVERN.

STATIONS	FARES. 1st class.	FARES. 2nd class.
FROM	s. d.	s. d.
Liverpool or Birkenhead	32 0	24 0
Manchester (London Road)	31 0	23 0
Preston	35 0	26 0
Bolton or Atherton	33 0	22 0
Wigan	33 0	22 0
Warrington	29 0	21 0

STATIONS.	FARES. 1st class.	FARES. 2nd class.
FROM	s. d.	s. d.
Huddersfield	38 6	28 0
Dewsbury	38 6	28 0
Stockport	31 0	23 0
Chester	29 0	21 0
Crewe	24 0	18 0
Stafford	19 0	14 0

MATLOCK.

STATIONS.	Seven Days' Ticket.		Monthly Ticket.		Tickets for One Member of Family (having taken Tickets for Two Persons) available for any number of Journeys during the Month.	
	1st Class.	2nd Class	1st Class.	2nd Class.	1st Class.	2nd Class.
FROM	s. d.	s. d.	s. d.	s. d.	s. d.	s. d.
London (Euston Square)	31 0	23 0	33 6	25 0	112 0	84 6
Oxford	27 0	19 0	30 0	22 0	100 0	80 0
Dudley, Dudley Port, Great Bridge, Wednesbury, Walsall	..	..	12 6	9 6	..	..

SCOTLAND.

From London to Edinburgh, Glasgow, the Scotch Lakes, &c.

FARES FOR THE DOUBLE JOURNEY.

EUSTON STATION,	1st class. s. d.	2nd class. s. d.	3rd class. s. d.
To Edinburgh	110 6	79 6	40 0
,, Glasgow	113 0	82 0	42 0
,, Stirling	118 6	87 0	44 0
,, Dunkeld	120 0	90 0	44 0
,, Perth	120 0	90 0	44 0

	1st class. s. d.	2nd class. s. d.	3rd class. s. d.
To Dundee, ,, Forfar, ,, Brechin, ,, Montrose, ,, Arbroath, ,, Aberdeen	120 9	90 0	46 0

EXPLANATION.

LAKES OF KILLARNEY, CORK, &c., via Holyhead.—The Tickets enable the Holders to proceed to **Chester**, thence to **Bangor**, **Holyhead**, and **Dublin**; from **Dublin** to **Cork**, situated on the picturesque River Lee, and within Ten Miles of the celebrated Harbour, Dockyard, and Naval Station of **Queenstown (Cove)**. From Cork back to Mallow, and thence by the Killarney Junction Railway to the far-famed **Lakes of Killarney.** The Tourist can remain as long as convenient to himself at Chester, Bangor *(for the inspection of the Britannia Tubular Bridge)*, Holyhead *(the new Refuge and Ocean Steam Harbour)*, Dublin, Cork, and Killarney, provided he returns to the Station in England at which he took his Ticket, not later than One Month from the date of his departure therefrom. Supplemental Tickets for CONNEMARA, GLENGARIFFE, The GIANT'S CAUSEWAY, and other places of interest, are issued at Reduced Fares to Visitors holding "Irish Tourist Tickets."

NORTH WALES.—The Tourist Tickets enable the holder to break the Down Journey at any Station between Chester (inclusive) and the Station for which the Ticket is available. Coaches, at moderate fares, run daily (Sundays) excepted) both from Conway and Bangor to Ogwen Lake, Capel Curig, Bettws-y-Coed, Llanrwst, &c. *Passengers from England* by Cargo Boat to North Wall, to ensure being in time for steamer, should arrive in Holyhead not later than 8 50 p.m. The latest train for this Boat leaves Chester at 5 25 p m; for morning sailings (1 a m. or after). Passengers may leave Chester by 10 15 p.m. train, and proceeed direct to Dublin, or by steamer the following night, Passengers by Cargo Boat, from North Wall, Dublin, if steamer arrives at Holyhead in time, may go forwardly 2 0 a.m train; or first and second class passengers may proceed by 7 45 a.m. train; third class by 8 a.m. train: only subsequent trains during the day, according to class of ticket.

GREAT WESTERN RAILWAY—Season 1861.

Summer Arrangements for the Season, for Seaside, Family, and Tourists' Tickets,

TO BRIDPORT (FOR LYME REGIS), DORCHESTER, WEYMOUTH, JERSEY, GUERNSEY, WESTON-SUPER-MARE,

Exeter, Dawlish, Teignmouth, Torquay, Paignton, Brixham Road (for Dartmouth), Plymouth, Truro (for Falmouth & Newquay), Penzance, and Barnstaple, Instow, or Bideford, for ILFRACOMBE and the NORTH COAST of DEVON, ISLE OF MAN, NORTH WALES, Bangor, Beaumaris, Aberystwith, Llandudno, Bala, Dolgelly, Capel Curig, Carnarvon, Llanberis, Llangollen Road, CHESTER, MALVERN, Ross, Hereford, Chepstow, Swansea, Neath, Carmarthen, Narberth Road, and New Milford, for TENBY, LIMERICK, and KILLARNEY.

EXCURSIONS TO THE SEASIDE.

Family Tickets To Weston-Super-Mare, Exeter, Dawlish, Teignmouth, Torquay, Paignton, Brixham Road (for Dartmouth), Plymouth, Truro (for Falmouth and Newquay), Penzance, Bideford, Instow or Barnstaple (for Ilfracombe), will be issued by any Train until OCTOBER 31st, to parties of not less than Three Persons, available for ONE CALENDAR MONTH.

FARES THERE AND BACK (EACH PASSENGER):—

	Weston-super-Mare 1 cl. s. d.	Weston-super-Mare 2 cl. s. d.	Exeter 1 cl s. d	Exeter 2 cl. s. d	Barnstaple 1 cl. s. d.	Barnstaple 2 cl. s. d.	Instow and Bideford 1 cl. s. d.	Instow and Bideford 2 cl. s. d.	Dawlish 1 cl. s. d.	Dawlish 2 cl s. d.	Teignmouth 1 cl s. d.	Teignmouth 2 cl s. d.	Torquay, Paignton, Brixham Road 1 cl. s. d.	Torquay, Paignton, Brixham Road 2 cl. s. d.	Plymouth 1 cl. s. d.	Plymouth 2 cl. s. d.	Truro 1 cl s. d.	Truro 2 cl. s. d.	Penzance 1 cl. s. d.	Penzance 2 cl. s. d.
London	40 0	29 0	50 0	35 0	50 0	35 0	50 0	35 0	50 0	35 0	50 0	35 0	50 0	35 0	55 0	37 6	60 0	40 0	65 0	45 0
Windsor / Slough	38 0	28 0	48 0	34 0	48 0	34 0	48 0	34 0	48 0	34 0	48 0	34 0	48 0	34 0	53 0	36 6	58 0	39 0	63 0	44 0
Reading / Basingstoke	36 0	27 0	46 0	33 0	46 0	33 0	46 0	33 0	46 0	33 0	46 0	33 0	46 0	33 0	51 0	35 6	56 0	38 0	61 0	43 0
Oxford	35 0	26 0	45 0	32 0	45 0	32 0	45 0	32 0	45 0	32 0	45 0	32 0	45 0	32 0	50 0	34 6	55 0	37 0	60 0	42 0

Passengers for places beyond Exeter may break the Journey for one day, at Exeter or Plymouth, either going or returning. If parties are desirous of extending their time beyond the above period, the following additional payments must be made prior to their commencing the Return Journey, and before the expiration of the Ticket. 10 per cent. upon the fare for the first 15 days after the expiration of the Ticket, and 5 per cent. additional for every week, or portion of a week, beyond the first fortnight; but no Tickets will be extended to be available after the 31st December, 1861. Applications for extension of time must be made at the station from which the Return Ticket is available.

Family Tickets to Weymouth, Dorchester, and Bridport (for Lyme Regis), are now issued by any Train at the following REDUCED FARES each Passenger, to parties taking not less than Three Tickets:—

	Available for 2 Weeks. 1st Class. s. d.	2 Weeks. 2nd Class. s. d.	Available for 1 Month. 1st Class. s. d.	1 Month. 2nd Class. s. d.	Available for 2 Months. 1st Class. s. d.	2 Months. 2nd Class. s. d.	Available for 3 Months. 1st Class. s. d.	3 Months. 2nd Class. s. d.
Paddington	30 0	20 0	35 0	25 0	40 0	30 0	45 0	35 0
Reading	23 4	17 6	27 0	21 0	31 0	25 0	35 0	29 0
Oxford	22 1	16 7	26 0	20 0	30 0	24 0	34 0	28 0
Leamington	29 7	22 2	35 0	25 0	40 0	30 0	45 0	35 0
Stratford-on-Avon	33 8	25 3	38 0	30 0	43 0	35 0	48 0	40 0
Birmingham	33 8	25 3	38 0	30 0	43 0	35 0	48 0	40 0
Wolverhampton	36 0	27 0	42 0	32 0	48 0	38 0	56 0	46 0
Shrewsbury	41 0	30 9	45 0	35 0	55 0	45 0	62 0	52 0
Chester	46 8	35 3	47 6	36 0	62 0	52 0	70 0	60 0
Birkenhead or Warrington	49 2	37 3	50 0	33 0	65 0	53 0	73 0	61 0
Liverpool or Manchester	49 6	37 7	50 4	38 4	65 4	53 4	73 4	61 4
Gloucester	22 7	17 0	25 0	20 0	29 0	24 0	33 0	27 0
Cheltenham	23 9	17 10	25 0	20 0	29 0	24 0	33 0	27 0
Hereford	28 0	21 0	33 0	26 0	38 0	31 0	43 0	36 0
Bath	13 6	9 8	16 0	12 0	18 6	14 6	21 0	17 0
Bristol	15 6	11 0	18 0	14 0	21 0	17 0	24 0	20 0

Passengers holding Family Tickets to Weymouth will have the privilege of proceeding to Jersey or Guernsey and back, by the Weymouth and Channel Islands Company's Boats, at Single Fares for the Double Journey.

Tourists' Tickets from **Paddington** and other principal Stations, available for ONE CALENDAR MONTH, are issued to **Narberth Road and New Milford (for Tenby and Milford Haven),** as under:—

FARES:—	1st class.	2nd class.		1st class.	2nd class.		1st class.	2nd class.
From London	£3 10 0	£2 10 0	Windsor or Slough	£3 5 0	£2 5 0	Reading	£3 0 0	£2 0 0

The above Tickets will be issued until the 31st OCTOBER, *via* Gloucester, with liberty to proceed to Ross and Hereford (for the River Wye), and to stop at Gloucester, Chepstow, Neath, Swansea, and Carmarthen, either going or returning.

GREAT WESTERN RAILWAY—*Continued.*

Tourists' Tickets are available by any Train, but are not transferable, and they do not entitle the holder to travel twice in the same direction over any portion of the Lines of Railway.

Seaside Family Tickets to Narberth Road and New Milford (for Tenby and Milford Haven), will be issued until the 31st OCTOBER, by any Train, to parties of not less than Three Persons, available for ONE CALENDAR MONTH.

Fares each Passenger—	1st class.	2nd class.		1st class.	2nd class.		1st class.	2nd class
From London........	£3 3 0	£2 5 0	Windsor or Slough..	£2 18 6	£2 0 6	Reading..	£2 14 0	£1 16 0

Children under three years of age, free ; above three and under twelve, half-price.

NOTE.—The holders of Tourists' or Sea Side Family Tickets can go from New Milford to Tenby on payment of 5s. 6d. extra. Family Tickets do not entitle the holders to stop at any intermediate station except Gloucester.

Tourists' Tickets to Limerick and Killarney, via Waterford, offering facilities for visiting the **South of Ireland.**—Tourists' Tickets will be issued at the undermentioned Stations for Limerick and Killarney, *via* Milford Haven and the Waterford and Limerick Railway, as under:—

	1 cl. & Saloon by Steamer.	2 cl. & Saloon by Steamer.
Paddington to Limerick or Killarney and back, *via* Waterford...........	£5 5 0	£4 0 0
Cheltenham or Gloucester to Limerick or Killarney and back, *via* Waterford	4 10 0	3 10 0

These Tickets will be available for One Month from the date of issue ; but the Waterford and Killarney portion of the route must be performed within Thirteen days from the date of departure from Waterford.

Passengers will be allowed to stop at Gloucester, Chepstow, Swansea, Narberth Road, New Milford, Waterford, Tipperary, or Mallow, either going or returning.

The Waterford and Milford Haven Company's Steamers, by which these Tickets are available, sail between the Ports of New Milford, Milford Haven, and Waterford daily, in connection with the Express Trains on the Great Western and South Wales Railways.

Tourists' Tickets, available for ONE CALENDAR MONTH, by any Train, to the **Isle of Man ;** also to **Bangor and Beaumaris. via Liverpool,** calling at **Llandudno** (weather permitting), *via* the Great Western and Shrewsbury Railways to Birkenhead and Liverpool; thence by the Isle of Man Steam-Packet Company's Steamers, *Douglas, Mona's Queen,* and *Tynwald,* every morning (Sunday excepted), at half past Eleven ; or to Bangor and Beaumaris, calling at Llandudno (weather permitting), daily (Sunday excepted), by the *Prince of Wales* or *Druid* Steamers, from the New Landing-Stage, Liverpool, at 11-0 a.m. Also to **Aberystwith, via Oswestry, Newtown, and Llanidloes Railway, and Carnarvon, through Capel Curig and Llanberis, or Bala and Dolgelly, via Llangollen Road; thence by Coach.**

FARES THERE AND BACK.

STATIONS.	To Aberystwith.		To Carnarvon or Bala and Dolgelly		To Isle of Man *via* the Isle of Man Co.'s Boats, *Douglas, Mona's Queen,* or *Tynwald.*		To Bangor and B'maris from L'pool, weather permitting.		To Llandudno, from Liverpool, weather permitting.		*Via* Chester and Holyhead Railway. To Rhyl or Abergle.		To Conway		To Llandudno.		To Bangor.		To Carnarvon or Holyhead.	
	1st class and Inside or Outside Coach.	2nd class and Outside Coach	1 cl. & Inside or Outside Coah.	2nd class and Outside Coach	1st class and Best Cabin.	2nd class and Best Cabin.	1st class and Best Cabin.	2nd class and Best Cabin.	1st class.	2nd class.	1st class.	2nd class.	1st class.	2nd class.	1st class.	2nd class.	1st class.	2nd class.	1st class.	2nd class.
	£ s. d.	£ s.	£ s	£ s.	£ s. d	£ s. d.	£ s.	£ s.	s. d.	s. d.	s. d.	s. d.	s. d.	s. d.	s. d.	s. d.	s. d.	s. d.	s. d.	s. d.
London	3 10 0	2 15	3 0	2 10	3 10 0	2 10 0	2 19	2 9	57 0	44 0	..	..	..	..	..	..	..	..	..	..
Windsor or Basingstoke	3 10 0	2 15	3 0	2 10	3 0 0	2 10 0	2 19	2 9	57 0	44 0	54 0	40 0	56 0	42 0	57 0	44 0	59 0	49 0	60 0	50 0
Reading	3 5 0	2 10	2 15	2 5	2 15 0	2 5 0	2 15	2 5	52 0	40 0	49 0	36 0	51 0	38 0	52 0	40 0	54 0	45 0	55 0	46 0
Oxford	2 15 0	2 5	2 10	1 15	2 10 0	2 0 0	2 9	1 14	47 0	32 0	44 0	29 0	46 0	31 0	47 0	32 0	49 0	34 0	50 0	35 0
Warwick or Leamingtn	2 10 0	2 0	1 17	1 11	2 0 0	1 10 0	1 15	1 9	33 0	27 0	..	..	..	..	..	..	..	..	..	..
Birmingham..........	2 7 6	1 17	1 13	1 7	1 15 0	1 5 0	1 11	1 5	29 0	23 0	..	..	..	..	..	..	..	..	..	..

The holders of the above Tickets will be allowed to break the journey at any Station between Shrewsbury and Chester, both inclusive, either going or returning, except passengers to Aberystwith, who can break the journey at any Station between Shrewsbury and Llanidloes.

Passengers return from the Isle of Man by Royal Mail-Packet Company's Boats only.

These Tickets are available by any Train, but are not transferable, and they do not entitle the holder to travel twice in the same direction over any portion of the Railway. Passengers, in taking Coach Tickets, must state whether they go to Carnarvon, or to Bala and Dolgelly, as they cannot alter their route after the Tickets are taken, the Coaches belonging to different proprietors.

The Aberystwith Coach runs daily in connection with the Trains on the Oswestry, Newtown, and Llanidloes Railway.

The "Carnarvon," Tourist Coach, leaves the Llangollen Road Station every morning at 11 45 a.m., but will not run after the 28th of September, and all Tickets issued available by this Coach will then expire—although they may have been issued within a period of one month from the time the Coach ceases to run.

The "Cambria," through Corwen to Bala and Dolgelly, leaves the Llangollen Road Station at 1 20 p.m., and will run daily up to the 28th September, after which it will run three days a week only.

Passengers from London, Windsor, Reading, or Oxford (except those with Tickets issued from Oxford by Chester and Holyhead Railway), may return by Shrewsbury, Hereford, Ross, and Gloucester, and thence, *via* Swindon and Didcot, without extra payment.

Further information may be obtained on application at any of the Stations of the Great Western Railway, or at the Company's Office, James Street, Liverpool ; the Monk's Ferry Station, Birkenhead ; and at the Great Western Offices at the General Railway Station, Chester ; and at their Office in Eastgate Street, Chester.

Return Tickets to the **Channel Islands,** available for ONE MONTH, are issued by any Train. Fares from Paddington or Reading to Guernsey or Jersey and back, 1st class, 45s ; 2nd class, 35s. Steward's fee, Saloon, 2s.; Fore Cabin, 1s. Passengers may break the journey at Chippenham, Dorchester, Weymouth, or Guernsey, either going to or returning from Jersey.

[13-Lo.

LANCASHIRE & YORKSHIRE RAILWAY.

TOURISTS' TICKETS,

1st and 2nd Class,

Available for One Calendar Month, from 1st June to the 31st October, 1861, to

SOUTHPORT, FLEETWOOD, BLACKPOOL, LYTHAM,

GRANGE, ULVERSTON, CONISTON,

WINDERMERE, THE ISLE OF MAN, FURNESS ABBEY,

AND DISTRICT;

HARROGATE, SCARBRO', WHITBY, BRIDLINGTON,

AND THE NORTH OF IRELAND:

Belfast, for Lough Neagh, the Giant's Causeway, Lakes Erne, Londonderry, Enniskillen, Armagh, &c., &c.,

FROM THE FOLLOWING AND OTHER PRINCIPAL STATIONS ON THE LINE:

FROM	Fleetwood, Lytham, or Blackpool.		Southport.		Isle of Man.				Ulvrstne, Furness Abbey, Wndrmre, &Lks of Cumbrlnd and Westmorland		Coniston Lake, &c.		Grange, in Cartmel, over Sands.		Harrogate.		Scarbro, Whitby, and Bridlington.		Lough Neagh, Giant's Causeway, and Lakes Erne, available for 1 month.	
	1st clss	2nd clss	1st clss	2nd clss	1st class & Saloon.	2nd class & Saloon.	2nd clas & Deck.	3rd class & Deck.	1st clss	2nd clss	1st clss	2nd clss	1st clss	2nd clss	1st clss	2nd clss	1st clss	2nd clss	1st clss	2nd clss
[Victoria Station	s. d.	s. d.	s. d.	s. d.	s. d.	s. d.	s. d.	s. d.	s. d.	s. d.	s. d.	s. d.	s. d.	s. d.	s. d.	s. d.	s. d.	s. d.	s. d.	s. d.
Manchester	10 0	7 6	8 0	6 6	16 0	13 0	9 0	8 0	22 0	16 0	27 0	21 0	20 0	14 0	15 6	11 6	28 0	21 6	51 0	43 6
Oldfield Road, Salford	10 0	7 6	8 0	6 6	16 0	13 0	9 0	8 0	22 0	16 0	27 0	21 0	20 0	14 0	..	..	..	..	..	..
Pendleton	10 0	7 6	8 0	6 6	16 0	13 0	9 0	8 0	22 0	16 0	27 0	21 0	20 0	14 0	..	..	..	..	51 0	43 6
Clifton Junction	10 0	7 6	8 0	6 6	15 6	12 6	9 0	7 6	..	..	..	..	..	..	..	..	..	..	..	..
Miles Platting	10 0	7 6	8 0	6 6	16 0	13 0	9 0	8 0	..	..	..	..	..	..	15 6	11 6	28 0	21 6	..	..
Black Lane	9 6	7 0	8 0	6 6	16 0	13 0	9 0	8 0	..	..	..	..	..	..	..	..	..	..	..	..
Bolton	8 0	6 6	6 6	5 0	14 6	12 0	8 6	7 6	20 0	14 0	25 0	19 0	18 0	12 0	17 0	12 6	29 6	22 6	49 0	42 6
Blackburn	7 6	6 6	7 0	6 0	..	..	..	..	22 0	16 0	27 0	21 0	20 0	14 0	15 6	11 6	28 0	21 6	48 6	42 6
Preston	..	..	..	..	..	..	..	..	..	..	..	..	..	..	15 6	11 6	28 0	21 6	..	..
Wigan	..	..	5 0	4 0	12 6	11 6	8 0	7 0	..	..	..	..	..	..	19 0	14 0	31 0	23 6	51 0	43 6
Liverpool	10 0	8 0	3 0	2 0	..	..	..	..	..	..	..	..	..	..	21 6	16 0	35 0	25 6	51 0	44 0
Southport	8 0	6 0	..	..	..	..	..	..	..	..	..	..	..	..	21 6	16 0	35 0	25 6	49 0	42 0
Bury	10 0	7 6	8 0	6 6	16 0	13 0	10 0	8 0	22 0	16 0	27 0	21 0	20 0	14 0	16 0	12 0	28 6	22 0	51 0	43 6
Heywood	10 0	7 6	8 0	6 6	16 0	13 0	10 0	8 0	22 0	16 0	27 0	21 0	20 0	14 0	15 6	11 6	28 0	21 6	51 0	43 6
Ashton	10 0	7 6	9 0	7 0	16 0	14 0	10 0	8 6	22 0	16 0	27 0	21 0	20 0	14 0	15 6	11 6	28 0	21 6	51 0	43 6
Staley Bridge	10 0	7 6	9 0	7 0	16 0	14 0	10 0	8 6	22 0	16 0	27 0	21 0	20 0	14 0	15 6	11 6	28 0	21 6	51 0	43 6
Middleton	10 0	7 6	9 0	7 0	16 0	13 6	10 0	8 6	22 0	16 0	27 0	21 0	20 0	14 0	15 6	11 6	28 0	21 6	51 0	43 6
Werneth	10 0	7 6	9 0	7 0	16 0	14 0	10 0	8 6	22 0	16 0	27 0	21 0	20 0	14 0	15 6	11 6	28 0	21 6	51 0	43 6
Oldham	10 0	7 6	9 0	7 0	16 0	14 0	10 0	8 6	22 0	16 0	27 0	21 0	20 0	14 0	15 6	11 6	28 0	21 6	51 0	43 6
Rochdale	10 0	7 6	9 0	7 0	16 0	13 6	10 6	8 0	22 0	16 0	27 0	21 0	20 0	14 0	15 6	11 6	28 0	21 6	51 0	43 6
Todmorden	12 0	9 0	10 6	7 6	17 6	14 6	11 0	8 6	24 0	18 0	28 0	22 0	22 0	16 0	13 0	9 6	26 6	19 0	53 0	45 0
Sowerby Bridge	14 0	11 0	14 0	10 6	18 6	15 6	11 6	9 0	24 0	18 0	28 0	22 0	22 0	16 0	11 0	8 0	24 6	18 0	..	..
Burnley	11 0	9 0	10 0	7 6	..	..	..	..	22 0	16 0	27 0	21 0	20 0	14 0	15 0	11 0	28 0	21 6	52 0	45 0
Hebden Bridge	13 0	10 0	13 0	9 0	..	..	..	..	..	..	..	..	..	..	13 0	9 6	26 0	18 6	54 0	46 0
Halifax	14 0	11 0	14 0	10 6	18 6	15 0	..	9 6	24 0	18 0	28 0	22 0	22 0	16 0	10 6	7 9	24 0	17 6	55 0	47 0
Bradford	15 0	12 0	15 0	12 0	20 0	16 0	..	10 0	24 0	18 0	28 0	22 0	22 0	16 0	9 6	7 0	24 0	17 6	56 0	48 0
Brighouse	15 0	12 0	15 0	12 0	..	..	..	..	24 0	18 0	28 0	22 0	22 0	16 0	9 0	6 6	22 6	16 6	56 0	48 0
Mirfield	15 0	12 0	15 0	12 0	20 0	17 0	..	10 0	24 0	18 0	28 0	22 0	22 0	16 0	9 0	6 6	22 6	16 6	56 [illegible]	[illegible]8 0
Huddersfield	15 0	12 0	15 0	12 0	18 6	15 0	..	9 6	24 0	18 0	28 0	22 0	22 0	16 0	10 0	7 0	23 6	17 0	56 0	48 0
Dewsbury (Thornhill)	15 0	12 0	15 0	12 0	20 0	17 0	..	10 0	24 0	18 0	28 0	22 0	22 0	16 0	8 6	6 3	22 6	16 6	..	..
Wakefield	15 0	12 0	15 0	12 0	20 0	16 0	..	10 0	24 0	18 0	28 0	22 0	22 0	16 0	7 0	5 0	22 6	16 6	56 0	48 0
Leeds	15 0	12 0	15 0	12 0	21 0	18 0	..	10 0	24 0	18 0	28 0	22 0	22 0	16 0	..	..	..	..	56 0	[illegible]
Normanton	15 0	12 0	15 0	12 0	..	..	..	..	..	..	..	..	..	..	..	..	..	..	56 [illegible]	[illegible] 0

Tourists' Tickets for Cork and Killarney, and other Stations in Ireland, may be obtained at the Railway Stations for Ireland. Forty-Eight Hours' Notice required for Tickets for the North of Ireland. Application to be made to Mr. Scott, Clerk in Charge, Victoria Station, Manchester.

Superintendent's Office, Victoria Station, Manchester, July, 1861.

BY ORDER.

GREAT NORTHERN RAILWAY.

GENERAL TOURIST ARRANGEMENTS FOR 1861.

TICKETS, AVAILABLE FOR ONE CALENDAR MONTH, TO

SCOTLAND,

COMMENCING 1st JUNE, AND ENDING 31st OCTOBER,

Will be issued from LONDON, King's Cross Station,

To the undermentioned places at the following reduced fares, with the option of returning so as to arrive at King's Cross Station on any day not exceeding one calendar month from the day of issue :—

From King's Cross Station.	FARES. 1st class s.	d.	2nd class s.	d.	3rd class s.	d.
To Edinburgh and Back	110	6	79	6	40	0
,, Glasgow ,,	113	0	82	0	42	0
,, Stirling ,,	118	6	87	0	44	0
,, Dunkeld ,,	120	0	90	0	44	0
,, Perth ,,	120	0	90	0	44	0

From King's Cross Station.	FARES. 1st class s.	d.	2nd class s.	d.	3rd class s.	d.
To Dundee and Back	120	0	90	0	46	0
,, Forfar ,,	120	0	90	0	46	0
,, Brechin ,,	120	0	90	0	45	0
,, Montrose ,,	120	0	90	0	46	0
,, Arbroath ,,	120	0	90	0	46	0
,, Aberdeen ,,	120	0	90	0	46	0

First and Second Class Tourist Tickets are only issued by the Down Trains leaving King's Cross at 9 0 a.m. and 9 15 p.m., and Third Class Tourist Tickets only by the Train leaving at 9 15 p.m. Tourists cannot be conveyed beyond Edinburgh by the Train leaving King's Cross at 9 15 on Saturday Evenings.

First and Second Class Tourist Tickets are only available for return by the Up Trains leaving Edinburgh at 10 0 a.m., 2 0 and 9 30 p.m., and Third Class Tourist Tickets only by the Trains leaving at 2 0 p.m. or 9 30 p.m.

Passengers to points beyond Edinburgh may break their journey at Edinburgh, Glasgow, or Perth. They are, however, not at liberty to break their journey both at Edinburgh and Glasgow, but only at one of these places, which must be the same on the Return as on the Down Journey.

No extension of the time beyond the one calendar month can in any case be granted.

Tickets are issued daily at Edinburgh and Glasgow Stations for Excursions through Scotland, including every charge for conveyance throughout the journey.

To Scarborough, Filey, Bridlington, Whitby, Withernsea, Redcar, or Harrogate,

By any Through Train from the 1st June to the 31st October, at the following **Reduced Fares,** with the option of returning, so as to arrive at the Station at which the Tickets were issued, on any day not exceeding One Calendar Month from date of issue.

To Scarbro', Whitby, Redcar, Filey, Bridlington, or Withernsea, and back. 1st class. s. d.	2nd class. s. d.	STATION.	To Harrogate and back. 1st class. s. d.	2nd class. s. d.
51 0	35 0	FROM LONDON (King's Cross Station).	43 0	32 6

Tickets can also be obtained from other principal stations on the Great Northern Line, at proportionate fares, to the above Yorkshire Watering Places.

Tickets for Filey and Bridlington are available either *via* York or Milford Junction and Hull.

Holders of these Tickets, going to or returning from Scarboro', Whithy, or Redcar, are at liberty to break their journey by remaining One Night at York; going to or returning from Filey or Bridlington, by remaining One Night either at York or Hull; and going to or returning from Withernsea, by remaining One Night at Hull; but they are required, in every case, to resume their journey not later than by the Second Train to their destination the following morning.

Extension of Tickets.—Passengers wishing to stay at any of these places for a longer period than the One Calendar Month, can do so by paying 10 per cent. on the price of the Ticket for the first fortnight, or portion of a fortnight, additional, and 5 per cent. more on the price of the Ticket for each week, or portion of a week, after the first fortnight; but the time will in no case be extended beyond the 31st December, 1861. Applications for extensions of time are to be made to the Station from which the Return Ticket is available, in all cases not later than on the day on which the term of the Ticket expires.

GREAT NORTHERN RAILWAY—*Continued.*

Tickets, available for one Calendar Month, will be issued

FROM THE 1st JUNE TO THE 31st OCTOBER, TO

WINDERMERE AND PENRITH,

FOR THE LAKES OF CUMBERLAND AND WESTMORELAND.

THE FURNESS ABBEY DISTRICT, and to

SOUTHPORT, BLACKPOOL, FLEETWOOD, OR LYTHAM,

From the undermentioned Stations, at the following Reduced Fares, with the option of returning so as to arrive at the Station at which the Tickets were issued on any day not exceeding One Calendar Month from the date of issue.

STATIONS.	To Windermere, Furness Abbey, or Ulverston, and Back.		To Coniston Lake or Penrith, for Ulleswater, and Back.		To Southport, Blackpool, Fleetwood, or Lytham, and back.	
	1st Class.	2nd Class.	1st Class.	2nd Class.	1st Class.	2nd Class.
	s. d.	s. d.	s. d.	s. d.	s. d.	s. d.
Hatfield, Hertford, Hitchin	65 0	48 0	68 0	50 0	50 0	40 0
Biggleswade	60 0	45 0	63 0	47 0	47 0	37 0
St. Neots	55 0	40 0	60 0	43 0	45 0	35 0
Huntingdon	55 0	40 0	60 0	43 0	45 0	35 0
Peterboro'	55 0	40 0	58 0	42 0	45 0	35 0
Stamford	55 0	40 0	58 0	42 0	40 0	30 0
Nottingham	42 0	32 0	45 0	34 0	35 0	25 0
Grantham	42 0	32 0	45 0	34 0	35 0	25 0
Newark	42 0	32 0	45 0	34 0	30 0	20 0
Boston	45 0	35 0	48 0	37 0	35 0	25 0

Extension of Tickets.—Passengers wishing to stay at any of the above places for a longer period than One Calendar Month, can do so by paying 10 per cent. on the price of the Ticket for the first fortnight, or portion of a fortnight, additional, and 5 per cent. more on the price of the Ticket for each week, or portion of a week, after the first fortnight; but the time will in no case be extended beyond the 31st December, 1861. Applications for extension of time are to be made to the Station from which the Return Ticket is available, in all cases not later than on the day on which the term of the Ticket expires.

Windermere District.—Passengers travel by the London and North Western Railway from Manchester. Coaches run daily from Windermere to Ambleside, Grasmere, and Keswick, and back. Return Tickets may be obtained of the Proprietor, Mr. Rigg, Windermere Hotel, available for 16 days, at moderate fares.

Coniston District.—Passengers travel by the London and North Western Railway from Manchester, and may break the journey at any of the Stations between Carnforth and Coniston Lake, to enable Passengers to visit Furness Abbey, Calder Abbey, and Wast Water. Coaches also run daily from Coniston to Ambleside, Grasmere, Keswick, and Windermere, and back, at moderate fares.

Southport, Blackpool, Fleetwood, and Lytham.—Passengers travel by the Lancashire and Yorkshire Railway, from the Victoria Station, Manchester.

Passengers holding any of these Tickets must travel *via* Manchester, where they may break their journey by remaining one night.

The above **Reduced Fares** do not include the cost of any conveyance that may be required between the **Stations at Manchester.**

TO THE ISLE OF MAN,

From the 1st June to the 30th September, at the following REDUCED FARES, with the option of returning so as to arrive at the Station at which the Tickets were issued on any day not exceeding One Calendar Month from the date of issue.

STATION.	Fares to Douglas, Isle of Man, and back.	
	First Class and Saloon Cabin.	Second Class and Fore Cabin.
	s. d.	s. d.
LONDON (King's Cross Station)	70 0	50 0

Passengers holding these Tickets arrive at Lime Street Station, Liverpool, and thence proceed to Douglas by the Isle of Man Company's Royal Steam Packets, "Mona's Isle," "Douglas," "Mona's Queen," or "Tynwald," which leave Prince's Pier Head, Liverpool, at 11 30 a.m. every week-day. The above Reduced Fares do not include the cost of any conveyance that may be required between Lime Street Station and the Packet at Liverpool.

On returning, Passengers must leave Douglas by one of the above-named Steamers, which sail for Liverpool every week-day at 9 a.m. (Greenwich Time), and thence by Train from Lime Street Station.

Passengers holding these Tickets may break their Journey at Liverpool.

The Tickets are not Transferable, neither will they be recognised for the Return Journey unless they have been presented and stamped at the Booking Office of the Station on the day of return.

[41-Lo.

MANCHESTER, SHEFFIELD, & LINCOLNSHIRE RAILWAY.

EXCURSION ARRANGEMENTS FOR SEASON 1861.

CHEAP PLEASURE EXCURSIONS

TO THE LINCOLNSHIRE SEA SIDE.

TO GRIMSBY, FOR CLEETHORPES, &c.

EXCURSIONS TO GRIMSBY FOR ONE WEEK.

On Friday and Saturday, the 3rd and 4th May, and every Friday and Saturday until the 26th of October,

FIRST & SECOND CLASS RETURN TICKETS AT ONE FARE,

Will be issued by any of the Through Trains from the undermentioned Stations to Grimsby and Back, which will be available for Return on any day within SEVEN DAYS from the date of issue.

Manchester, Guide Bridge, Newton, Glossop, | Barnsley, Penistone, Sheffield, Woodhouse, | Kiveton Park, Worksop, Retford, Gainsborough, | Kirton Lindsey, Scawby, Brigg | Lincoln, Market Rasen, Barnetby.

Commencing the 1st May, and until the 31st October,

EXCURSION TICKETS,

AVAILABLE FOR ONE CALENDAR MONTH,

Will be issued at the undermentioned Stations, by any of the Through Trains, to

GRIMSBY AND BACK,

At the following REDUCED FARES, available for return on any day within ONE CALENDAR MONTH from the date of issue.

FARES TO GRIMSBY AND BACK.

STATIONS.	1st Class.	2nd Class.	STATIONS.	1st Class.	2nd Class.	STATIONS.	1st Class.	2nd Class.
	s. d.	s. d.		s. d.	s. d.		s. d.	s. d.
Manchester	20 0	15 6	Kiveton Park	14 0	10 0	Scawby	5 6	4 0
Barnsley	20 0	15 0	Worksop	13 0	9 0	Brigg	5 0	3 6
Penistone	19 0	14 0	Retford	11 0	8 0	Lincoln	11 0	8 6
Sheffield	16 6	11 6	Gainsborough	9 0	6 6	Market Rasen	7 6	5 0
Woodhouse	15 0	10 6	Kirton Lindsey	6 6	4 6	Barnetby	4 0	3 0

At Grimsby the Trains are met by Conveyances to CLEETHORPES, which is within two miles of Grimsby, and deservedly celebrated as the most attractive Sea Bathing Place on the coast of Lincolnshire.

[over

MANCHESTER, SHEFFIELD, AND LINCOLNSHIRE—*Continued.*

Commencing 1st June, and ending 31st October.

EXCURSION TICKETS FOR ONE CALENDAR MONTH

WILL BE ISSUED AT THE UNDERMENTIONED STATIONS TO

SCARBRO', WHITBY, REDCAR, BRIDLINGTON,

FILEY, or WITHERNSEA, and Back,

At the following Reduced Fares, which will be available for Return so as to arrive at the Stations at which the Tickets were taken, on any day not exceeding One Calendar Month from the date of issue:—

STATIONS.	To Scarbro', Filey, or Redcar & Back.		To Whitby and Back		To Bridlington or Withernsea & Back.	
	1st class	2nd class	1st class.	2nd class.	1st class.	2nd class.
	s. d.	s. d.	s. d.	s. d.	s. d.	s. d.
Ashton or Staleybridge	28 0	21 0	23 0	21 0	28 0	21 0
Worksop, Retford, or Lincoln	24 0	17 0	24 0	17 0	24 0	17 0
Gainsborough, Kirton Lindsey, or Market Rasen	21 6	16 6	21 6	16 6	18 0	15 0
Brigg or Grimsby	18 6	14 6	20 0	15 0	16 0	12 6

☞ The above Reduced Fares do not include the cost of conveyance required between the Corporation Pier and Paragon Street Station, in Hull.

Passengers with the above Tickets will have to proceed *via* Hull, and thence forward by the North Eastern Railway.

☞ The Tickets are not transferable, and will not be recognised for the journey back unless they have been presented and stamped on the day of return, at the Railway Booking Office, at either Scarboro', Filey, Redcar, Whitby, Bridlington, or Withernsea, as the case may be.

Arrangements can be made for an extension of the time beyond one Calendar Month, on payment of 10 per cent. on the price of the Ticket for the first fortnight, or portion of a fortnight, additional, and 5 per cent. on the price of the Ticket for each week, or portion of a week, after the first fortnight; but no extension will be made beyond the 31st December.

CHEAP EXCURSIONS

TO THE

ISLE OF MAN.

Commencing the 18th May, and until 30th Sept., 1861,

(SUNDAYS EXCEPTED),

RETURN TICKETS,

At the following Fares, will be issued from the undermentioned Stations to

DOUGLAS, ISLE OF MAN,

Which will be available for Return by any Train of same class, arriving at the Stations at which they were taken, on any day not exceeding ONE CALENDAR MONTH from the date of issue.

STATIONS.	FARES to DOUGLAS, Isle of Man, and Back. First Class & Saloon Cabin.	Second Class & Fore Cabin.
	s. d.	s. d.
Grimsby or Barton	33 6	23 6
Ulceby or Barnetby	32 6	22 6
Lincoln	30 0	21 0
Gainsborough	27 0	19 0
Retford	25 0	18 0
Worksop	24 0	17 6
Kiveton Park	23 6	17 0
Sheffield	23 6	17 0
Wortley	22 0	16 0
Barnsley	21 0	15 6
Penistone	21 0	15 6

The above Reduced Fares do not include the cost of any conveyance that may be required between Lime Street Station and the Packet at Liverpool.

Passengers will have to proceed from the above Stations to Liverpool, "*via* Manchester," and from thence to Douglas by the Isle of Man Company's Royal Mail Steam Packet, "Mona's Isle," "Douglas," "Mona's Queen," or "Tynwald," which leave the Prince's Pier Head, Liverpool, at 11 30 a.m. every Week Day.

On returning, Passengers must leave Douglas by one of the above Steamers, which sail for Liverpool every Week Day, at 9 a.m., and thence by Train from Lime Street Station.

Two Tickets will be provided, one for the Railway and the other for the Packet, and the latter Ticket will have to be given up at Liverpool, on returning from the Isle of Man.

The Tickets are not transferable, are for one journey each way only, and are not available at any intermediate Station except Liverpool.

MANCHESTER, SHEFFIELD, AND LINCOLNSHIRE—*Continued.*

COMMENCING THE 1st JUNE, AND UNTIL 31st OCTOBER, 1861,

Tourists' Tickets, available for One Calendar Month,

WILL BE ISSUED TO

NORTH WALES, THE LAKES OF KILLARNEY, &c.,

AT THE UNDERMENTIONED STATIONS, VIZ. :—

STATIONS.	NORTH WALES.										To the Lakes of Killarney, Cork, &c., and Back.	
	To Rhyl or Abergele and Back.		To Conway and Back.		To Llandudno and Back.		To Carnarvon or Holyhead and Back.		To Bangor and Back.			
	1 cls.	2 cls.	1 cls.	2 cls	1 cls.	2 cls.	1 cls.	2 cls.	1 cls.	2 cls.	1 cls.	2 cls
From	s. d.	s. d.	s. d.	s. d.	s. d.	s. d.	s. d.	s. d.	s. d.	s. d.	s. d.	s. d.
Hull, Grimsby, Barnetby	41 0	30 0	43 0	32 0	44 0	33 0	47 0	37 0	..	..	107 6	88 6
Lincoln	30 0	21 0	32 0	26 0	33 0	27 0	37 0	31 0	35 0	29 0	90 0	77 0
Gainsboro', Retford, Worksop	30 0	21 0	32 0	26 0	33 0	27 0	37 0	31 0	..	..	90 0	77 0
Sheffield	26 0	21 0	2[illegible] 0	23 0	29 0	24 0	33 0	28 0	31 0	26 0	90 0	77 0

The Tickets will be available for One Journey *only*, and for return by any Train of corresponding class arriving at the Stations at which they were taken, on any day not exceeding One Calendar Month from the date of issue

Excursionists will have to proceed to Manchester, thence by London and North Western Railway.

LAKES OF KILLARNEY, CORK, &c., via Holyhead.—The Tickets enable the holders to proceed to **Chester**, thence to **Bangor**, **Holyhead**, and **Dublin**; from **Dublin** to **Cork**, situated on the picturesque River Lee, and within 10 miles of the celebrated Harbour, Dockyard, and Naval Station of **Queenstown, (Cove)**. From Cork back to Mallow, and thence by the Killarney Junction Railway to the far-famed **Lakes of Killarney.** The Tourist can remain as long as convenient to himself at Chester, Bangor (for the inspection of the Britannia Tubular Bridge), Holyhead (the new Refuge and Ocean Steam Harbour), Dublin, Cork, and Killarney, provided he returns to the Station in England at which he took his Ticket not later than One Month from the date of his departure therefrom. Supplemental Tickets for **Connemara, Glengariffe**, the **Giant's Causeway**, and other places of interest, are issued at Reduced Fares to Visitors holding "Irish Tourist Tickets."

NORTH WALES.—The Tourist Tickets enable the holders to break the journey at any Station between Chester (inclusive) and the Station for which the Ticket is available. Coaches, at moderate Fares, run daily (Sundays excepted) both from Conway and Bangor to Ogwen Lake, Capel Curig, Bettws-y-Coed, Llanrwst, &c.

The Tickets are not transferable, neither will they be recognised for the Return Journey, unless they have been presented and stamped at the Booking Office of the Station on the day of return.

The usual weight of Luggage will be allowed to each Passenger, and care should be taken to have it properly addressed.

Extension of Tickets.—Passengers wishing to stay at any of the above places for a longer period than that for which the Monthly Ticket is issued, can do so by paying 10 per cent. on the price of the Ticket for the first fortnight, or portion of a fortnight, additional, and 5 per cent. more on the price of the Ticket for each week, or portion of a week, after the first fortnight; but the time will in no case be extended beyond the 31st December, 1861. Applications for extension of time are to be made at the Station from which the Return Ticket is available, in all cases not later than on the day on which the term of the Ticket expires.

EXCURSIONS TO THE LAKES DISTRICT.

Commencing 1st June, and until 31st October, 1861.

THROUGH TICKETS for the above will be issued as understated (available for one calendar month).

STATIONS.	To Windermere, Ulverstone, or Furness Abbey, and Back.				To Coniston Lake and Back.			
	1st class.		2nd class.		1st class.		2nd class.	
	s.	d.	s.	d.	s.	d.	s.	d.
Grimsby, Barton, New Holland, Ulceby	45	0	35	0	48	0	37	0
Barnetby, Brigg, Kirton	43	0	33	6	46	6	35	6
Gainsborough, Lincoln, Retford	42	0	32	0	45	0	34	0
Worksop, Kiveton Park	38	0	29	0	42	0	31	0
Sheffield	35	0	26	0	39	0	28	6
Penistone	33	0	25	0	37	0	27	6

The Tickets will be available for one journey ONLY, and for return by any Train of corresponding class, arriving at the Stations at which they were taken, on any day not exceeding One Calendar Month from the date of issue.

The Tickets are not Transferable, and will not be recognised for the journey back unless they are presented and stamped on the day of return at the Railway Booking Offices either at Windermere, Ulverstone, Furness Abbey, or Coniston.—Excursionists will have to proceed to Manchester, thence by the London and North Western Railway.

GENERAL CONDITIONS.

The Tickets are not transferable.

The Tickets are available by the Trains specified, but the Company do not undertake that the Trains shall start or arrive at the times named in the Bills, nor will they be accountable for any loss, inconvenience, or injury, which may arise from delays or detention.

Unless when otherwise stated, these Tickets are not available for any but the Stations named upon them, nor can they be used more than once in the same direction.

In cases where tickets are stated to be available for a calender month, it is intended that Passengers holding tickets taken (for example) on the 15th of one month may return on the 15th of the following month.

Attention must be paid by the Holders of these Tickets, on the Outward Journey, to see that the right half of the Ticket for the Return Journey is retained by them.

The Company does not hold itself liable to make any return to Passengers who, by neglect, or from any other cause, fail to produce their Tickets.

The usual weight of Luggage will be allowed to each Passenger and care should be taken to have it properly addressed.

Children under Three years of age, Free; above Three and under Twelve, Half-fares. [25-z.

EDINBURGH AND GLASGOW
TO THE
TROSSACHS AND LOCH-LOMOND,
Via DUNBLANE, DOUNE, and CALLANDER RAILWAY.

				1	2	3	4	5	6
				mrn	mrn	mrn	mrn	aft	aft
RAILWAY.	Edinburgh	Train	leaves	..	6 25	9 0	12 45	4 0	6 0
	Glasgow	"	"	..	6 40	9 30	1 0	4 15	6 15
	Stirling	"	"	..	8 25	10 45	2 30	5 40	7 50
	Callander	"	arrives	..	9 15	11 25	3 20	6 20	8 50
COACH ...	Do.	Coach	leaves	..	9 20	11 30	3 25	6 25	..
	Trossachs	"	arrives	..	11 0	1 45	4 50	8 0	..
LOCH-KATRINE..	Do.	Steamer	leaves	8 0	11 20	2 15	5 30	..	..
	Stronaclacher	"	arrives	8 45	12 5	3 0	6 15	..	..
COACH	Do.	Coach	leaves	9 0	12 15	3 20	..	..	..
LOCH-LOMOND..	Inversnaid	Steamer	"	..	1 45	4 45	..	..	..
	Balloch Pier	"	arrives	..	3 40	6 40	..	..	..
	Balloch	Train	leaves	..	4 0	7 0	..	..	..
RAILWAY.	Glasgow	"	arrives	..	5 10	8 15	..	..	..
	Edinburgh	"	"	..	7 20	11 5	..	..	..

*** Edinburgh Passengers change carriages at Cowlairs.

Via DUMBARTONSHIRE RAILWAYS.

				1	2	3	4	5	6
				mrn	aft	mrn	mrn	mrn	mrn
RAILWAY.	Edinburgh	Train	leaves	..	..	..	..	..	9 0
	Glasgow	"	"	..	..	..	..	7 20	10 45
	Balloch	"	arrives	..	..	..	..	8 35	12 0
LOCH-LOMOND..	Inversnaid	Steamer	"	..	..	..	..	10 40	2 5
	Do.	Coach	leaves	..	4 45	..	..	10 50	2 10
LOCH-KATRINE..	Stronaclachar	"	arrives	..	6 15	..	..	11 50	3 20
	Do.	Steamer	leaves	..	6 30	10 0	..	12 30	3 35
	Trossachs	"	arrives	..	7 15	10 40	..	1 15	4 10
COACH....	Do.	Coach	leaves	..	8 0a	..	..	1 30	5 0
	Callander	"	arrives	..	9 15	..	..	3 0	6 20
RAILWAY.	Do.	Train	leaves	7 0	9 35	..	11 37	4 20	6 30
	Stirling	"	"	8 10	10 35	..	12 30	5 48	7 36
	Glasgow	"	arrives	9 30	11 45	..	1 40	7 10	8 55
	Edinburgh	"	"	9 50	12 0	..	2 0	7 40	9 0

FARES FOR THE ABOVE TOUR ROUND EITHER WAY:—

	1st class, Cabin, and Outside of Coach.	3rd class, Cabin, and Outside of Coach.
From Glasgow	17s. 6d.	13s. 6d.
From Edinburgh	23s. 0d.	16s. 6d.

To the TROSSACHS, via STIRLING and CALLANDER.

	SINGLE JOURNEY. 1st class.	2nd clss.	3rd clss.	RETURN TICKETS. 1st class.	2nd clss.
From Edinburgh	10s. 0d.	8s. 6d.	6s. 0d.	15s. 0d.	12s. 7d.
From Glasgow	9s. 0d.	7s. 6d.	5s. 6d.	14s. 0d.	11s. 1d.

TO CRIEFF,
For Drummond Castle and Gardens, Grounds of Ochtertyre, &c.

RETURN TICKETS TO CRIEFF.

From Edinburgh..............1st class, 12s. 0d.
From Glasgow .... " 10s. 0d.

Friday and Saturday Tickets available to return upon the following Monday.

TO DUNKELD.
On FRIDAYS and SATURDAYS,

RETURN TICKETS TO DUNKELD are issued.

From Edinburgh..1 cl., 14s. 0d. 2 cl., 10s. 6d.
From Glasgow .. " 14s. 0d. " 10s. 6d.

Tickets available to return up to the following Monday.

GLASGOW, LOCH-LONG, and LOCH-LOMOND.

Passengers booked at Queen Street Station by 10 45 a.m. Train to Tarbet, where they cross over to Arroquhar, Loch-Long, where they join the "Chancellor" Steamer, which leaves at 2 45 for Greenock, thence to Glasgow by Railway.

FARES FOR THE ROUND:—

1st class and Cabin .... 6s. 6d. | Third class and Cabin .... 5s. 0d.

138-J,R.

MAPPIN & COMPANY,

Opposite the Pantheon, Oxford Street.

"THE ONLY LONDON ADDRESS."

MAPPIN & CO.'s ELECTRO SILVER PLATE,

Guaranteed to have a strong deposit of the purest silver according to prices charged.

MAPPIN & CO.'s ELECTRO SILVER PLATED SPOONS & FORKS.

CAUTION.

Correspondents should direct in full,

MAPPIN & COMPANY,

Opposite the Pantheon,

OXFORD STREET.

Full Size	Fiddle.	Double Thread.	King's.	Lily.
	£ s. d.	£ s. d.	£ s. d.	£ s. d.
12 Table Forks ..	1 16 0	2 14 0	2 16 0	2 14 0
12 Table Spoons..	1 16 0	2 14 0	2 16 0	2 14 0
12 Dessert Forks	1 7 0	2 0 0	2 0 0	2 0 0
12 Dessert Spoons.	1 7 0	2 0 0	2 0 0	2 0 0
12 Tea Spoons .	0 16 0	1 4 0	1 4 0	1 8 0

The largest and most beautiful stock in London.
Every description of Plated Goods, "Quality warranted"

CAUTION.

Correspondents should direct in full,

MAPPIN & COMPANY,

Opposite the Pantheon,

OXFORD STREET.

MAPPIN & CO.'s UNRIVALLED TABLE KNIVES

Of their own manufacture.

	Good.	Medium.	Superior.
	£ s. d	£ s. d.	£ s. d.
1 doz. Table Knives, Ivory Handles	0 13 0	1 0 0	1 15 0
1 doz. Cheese Knives	0 10 0	0 15 0	1 5 0
1 pr. Regular Meat Carvers	0 4 6	0 7 0	0 12 0
1 pr. Extra size ditto	0 5 6	0 8 0	0 13 6
1 pr. Poultry Carvers	0 4 6	0 7 0	0 12 0
1 Steel for sharpening.............	0 2 6	0 3 6	0 4 6
Complete Service	2 0 0	3 0 6	5 2 0

The Table Knives are guaranteed the best sold in London, at the prices charged. They are made from the very best steel, and the handles are so secured that they cannot become loose in hot water. It is in consequence of MESSRS. MAPPIN & COMPANY being manufacturers, that they are enabled to offer their Table Knives at such unprecedentedly low prices.

MAPPIN & COMPANY'S

CELEBRATED

RAZORS, PEN AND SPORTSMEN'S KNIVES, AND SCISSORS.

Razors in Handsome Cases, for 7 days or otherwise. Scissors, in very elegant Cases, well adapted for Presents.

DRESSING BAGS AND CASES:

Gentleman's Travelling Bag and Dressing Case combined, fitted complete, £2 2s.

Lady's Travelling Bag and Dressing Case combined, fitted complete £1 10s.

MAPPIN AND COMPANY,

London Show Rooms—77 and 78, Oxford Street (W.), opposite the Pantheon.

SHEFFIELD MANUFACTORY—ROYAL CUTLERY WORKS.

"Costly Catalogues, post free."

(20)-10.

SECTION IV.

BRADSHAW'S TOURS

THROUGH THE COUNTIES OF

ESSEX, SUFFOLK, NORFOLK, HERTFORD, CAMBRIDGE, HUNTINGDON, RUTLAND, LEICESTER, NOTTINGHAM, LINCOLN, LANCASTER (SOUTH EAST), YORK, DURHAM, NORTHUMBERLAND, BERWICK,

AND

THE SOUTH-EASTERN COUNTIES OF SCOTLAND.

CHINA AND GLASS ROOMS,

Nos. 49 and 50, OXFORD STREET, LONDON.

PARIAN CHINA ORNAMENTS

AMAZON.

IN STATUARY, GROUPS, AND FIGURES.

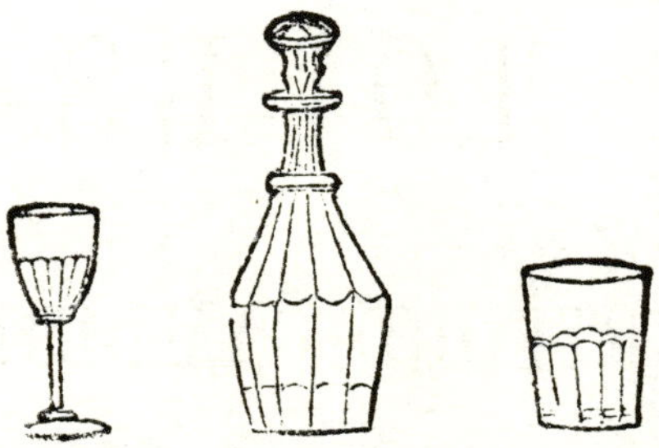

5s. 6d. Dozen. **12s. 6d.** Pair. **4s. 6d.** Dozen.

Small Breakfast Set (White China, Gold edge) – 6 cups and saucers, 2 plates, 1 slop, 1 sugar, and 1 milk jug, 12s. 6d.

2s. Pair. Parian Violet Vase, **1s. 6d.** White & Gold China, **4s. 6d.** Half-dozen.

JOHN W. SHARPUS

Begs respectfully to call the attention of the Public to his IMMENSE STOCK, which is now replete with all the most MODERN AND CLASSIC DESIGNS IN

CHINA, GLASS, EARTHENWARE,

PARIAN STATUARY, AND BOHEMIAN GLASS.

DINNER SERVICES.

	£	s.	d.
Dinner Services, to dine 12 persons ....from	2	2	0
Ditto, richly gilt ....from	3	13	6
Handsome painted and gilt ....from	5	15	6
Rich coloured Bands, handsomely gilt ....from	7	7	0
Porcelain Services, rich coloured bands, handsomely gilt........................from 25 guineas.			

A variety of patterns, expressly for India and the Colonies, at the same moderate prices.

DESSERT SERVICES.

	£	s.	d.
For twelve persons, in neat coloured borders ..from	1	1	0
Ditto, antique borders and coloured wreaths ..from	1	8	0
A variety, coloured borders, with gold and flowers, on the finest Porcelain..................from	3	15	0
Ditto, ditto, from 5 to 10 guineas and upwards.			
China Breakfast Set, gold edge, viz., 6 breakfast cups and saucers, 2 plates, 1 slop, 1 sugar basin, 1 milk jug ....from	0	12	6

A LARGE ASSORTMENT OF PATTERNS AT THE SAME MODERATE PRICES.

TEA SERVICES.

	£	s.	d.
White china, gold edge ....from	0	17	0
Neat painted band and flowers...............from	1	8	0
Elegant pattern, handsomely painted and gilt from	2	2	0
Splendid Services, of the most elaborate workmanship and design, rich painted and gilt, £8 8s. to	14	14	0

GLASS DEPARTMENT.

	£	s.	d.	
Particularly neat cut Wine Glasses	0	5	6	per dozen.
Handsome cut ditto ....from 12s. 6d. to	1	1	0	per dozen.
Neat good strong Tumblers	0	4	6	per dozen.
A large variety of patterns ...10s. 6d. to	1	4	0	per dozen.
Pale Ale Tumblers, for India..12s. 6d. to	2	2	0	per dozen.
Modern shape Decanters..................	0	8	6	per pair.
Cut glass and engraved ....21s. to	2	2	2	per pair.
Custard and Jelly Glasses......4s. 6d. to	0	10	6	per dozen.
Cut glass Water Jugs ....5s to	1	1	0	each.
Best glass Salts (modern shaped) ..9d. to	0	2	9	each.

A Price Catalogue may be had on application, containing full description of Kitchen Requisites, Toilet Ware, Papier Trays, Cutlery, Plated Cruet Frames, Hot Water Plates and Dishes, and every requisite required for furnishing, at extremely reduced Cash Prices.

A China Dinner Service, to Dine 12 persons, Torquoise and Gold, 15 Guineas.

All orders from the Country must be accompanied with a reference or remittance. [29-Lo.

CONTENTS TO SECTION IV.

PAGE

BLYTH AND TYNE 88

EASTERN COUNTIES—

Broxbourne to Hertford 21
Cambridge to Bury and Haughley........ 24
Cambridge to Wisbeach and Lynn........ 25
Ely to March and Peterborough 26
Ely to Lynn Regis 27
London to Cambridge, Ely, & Yarmouth 19 to 31
London to Chelmsford and Colchester ... 32
Loughton Branch 20
Lynn to Dereham 29
Reedham to Lowestoft 31
Water Lane to Enfield 20
Witham to Braintree and Maldon 33
Wymondham to Fakenham and Wells ... 30

EASTERN UNION—

Bentley to Hadleigh 35
Colchester to Ipswich and Norwich 34
Colne Valley........ 33
Manningtree to Harwich 34
Marks Tey to Sudbury 33
Tivetshall to Harleston and Bungay...... 37

EAST SUFFOLK—

Woodbridge to Lowestoft and Yarmouth 36
Framlingham Branch 36
Lowestoft Branch 36

GREAT NORTHERN—

Boston to Great Grimsby 46
Bourne and Essendine 47
Grantham to Nottingham........ 48
Grantham to Sleaford........ 48
Hertford, Luton, and Dunstable 22
Hitchin to Royston and Cambridge 41
Holbeach Branch 45
Kirkstead to Horncastle 46
Lincoln to Gainsborough 46
London to Peterborough .... 39 to 44
Peterborough to Boston, Lincoln, & Retford 44
Peterborough to Grantham, Newark, Doncaster, Leeds, and York 47
Potton and Sandy 42

HULL AND HOLDERNESS 66

IPSWICH AND WOODBRIDGE AND EAST SUFFOLK 36

LANCASHIRE AND YORKSHIRE—

Accrington to Blackburn, Ormskirk, and Liverpool 58
Manchester to Bury. Accrington, Colne, and Skipton 57
Burscough to Southport 59
Manchester to Rochdale, Todmorden, Halifax, Bradford, and Leeds 59
Middleton Junction to Oldham and Middleton........ 59 to 60
Mirfield to Bradford 62
Ramsbottom to Bacup 57
Sowerby Bridge to Wakefield and Normanton 62
Todmorden to Burnley 61
Wakefield to Pontefract and Goole........ 63

PAGE.

MANCHESTER, SHEFFIELD, AND LINCOLNSHIRE—

Barton and New Holland 56
Lincoln to Barnetby 54
Manchester to Sheffield, Retford, Gainsborough, Grimsby, and Hull........ 51 to 56
Penistone to Barnsley 52
Penistone to Holmfirth and Huddersfield 52
Retford to Lincoln 54

MIDLAND—

Ambergate to Matlock and Buxton 11
Ambergate to Sheffield, Swinton, Normanton, and Leeds........ 14
Birmingham to Bristol 10
Bradford, to Skipton, Lancaster, and Morecambe 18
Derby to Ambergate 11
Derby to Birmingham 10
Gildersome Branch........ 18
Leeds to Bradford 17
Leicester to Burton........ 2
Leicester to Hitchin 4
Long Eaton to Derby........ 9
Long Eaton Junction to Nottingham and Lincoln 5
Masborough to Sheffield 15
Mexborough to Doncaster 16
Nottingham to Mansfield (direct) 7
Nottingham to Mansfield, *via* Erewash Vly 7
Ripley Branch 10
Rugby to Leicester........ 1
Sheffield and Rotherham 15
Syston to Peterborough 3

NORTH BRITISH:—

Berwick to Dunbar, Leith, and Edinbro' 94
Dunse Branch 94
Eskbank to Peebles 93
Galashiels to Selkirk 92
Hawick Branch 91
Jedburgh Branch 91
Longniddry to Haddington 95
North Berwick Branch 95

NORTH EASTERN:—

Berwick to Kelso and Roxburgh........ 90
Bilton to Alnwick 88
Church Fenton to Harrogate 68
Dalton to Richmond 80
Darlington to Barnard Castle 81
Driffield to Malton and Thirsk........ 67
Ferryhill to Hartlepool 82
Hull to Bridlington and Scarborough...... 66
Leamside to Durham........ 83
Leeds to Harrogate, Ripon & Northallerton 77
Melmerby Junction to Thirsk 78
Milford to Church Fenton and York 68
Milford to Leeds 77
Newcastle to Berwick 88
Normanton to Selby and Hull........ 64
Northallerton to Bedale and Leyburn ... 78
Northallerton to Newcastle 80
Northallerton to Stockton........ 79

NORTH EASTERN *Continued:*— PAGE.
Pensher to Sunderland 84
Pilmoor Junction to Boroughbridge 77
Rillington to Pickering and Whitby 73
Selby to Market Weighton 64
Witton Junction to Stanhope 82
South Shields Branch.......................... 84
York to Knaresborough and Harrogate... 72
York to Market Weighton 72
York to Northallerton 76
York to Scarborough 73

NORTH SHIELDS AND TYNEMOUTH ... 87

SOUTH YORKSHIRE—
Sheffield to Doncaster and Thorne........ 15

STOCKTON AND DARLINGTON—
Darlington to Stanhope and Carrhouse... 82
Middlesbrough and Guisborough............ 79
Stockton to Darlington 79
Stockton to Middlesbrough and Redcar... 79

ILLUSTRATIONS.

PLANS:— PAGE.

Edinburgh.. 98
Hull 66
Leeds 16
Sheffield.. 54

VIEWS:—

Chatsworth 14
Dove Holes 14
Dove Dale.. 14

EDINBURGH:—

Burns' Monument 96
Commercial Bank 96
Donaldson's Hospital.................... 96
Edinburgh, View of 96
Holyrood Palace 96
Physician's Hall 96
Scott's Monument 96

VIEWS:—*Edinburgh*, continued. PAGE.

Tron Church.............................. 98
Victoria Hall.............................. 96
Waterloo Place 96

Haddon Hall.................................... 14
Matlock Bath 14

ABBEYS:—

Bolton 18
Fountains 18
Furness 18
Kirkstall 18
Llanercost.................................. 18
Netley 18
Newstead 18
Rivaulx 18
Tintern 18

INDEX.

Abbotsford, 92
Accrington, 58
Acklam Hall, 79
Acklington, 88
Ackworth Park, 63
Addle Church, 77
Adwalton, 18
Agecroft Bridge, 57
Ainderby, 78
Aintree, 59
Aintree Race Course, 59
Airy Hill, 74
Aislaby, 74
Albury Hatch, 32, 35
Alcester, 10
Aldam, 15
Aldborough, 37
Aldby, 72
Aldeby, 37
Alderwasley, 11
Aldham Common, 36
Aldoborough, 77
Aldwark Hall, 15
Alford, 47
Alfreton, 15
Algarkirk, 45
Algarkirk House, 45
Allanbank, 94
Allan Ramsay's House, 99
Allan Water, 92
Allerton, 72
Allerton Mauleverer, 70
Alne, 77
Alne House, 77
Alnwick, 88
Alnwick Castle, 89
Alum Cliff, 78
Alvechurch, 11
Ambergate, 12
Ampthill, 42
Amotherby, 67
Ampleforth, 67
Amwell, 21
Ancaster, 49
Ancrum Moor, 91
Annesley Park, 7
Authorpe, 47
Apperley, 18
Ardleigh, 35
Ardsley, 18
Ardwick, 51
Arksey, 51
Arlesey, 42
Arlsey House, 42
Armley, 17, 62
Armley Park, 17
Arms Factory, Government, 20
Arnold, 5
Arno's Grove, 41
Arram, 67
Arthington, 77
Arthington Hall, 78
Arthur's Seat, 98
Ashbury's, 51
Ashby-de-la-Zouch, 3
Ashchurch, 11
Ashestiel, 92
Ashford, 14
Ashfordby, 3
Ashford Hall, 15
Ashridge, 22
Ashwell, 3, 42
Askerne, 51
Aske Hall, 80
Askrigg, 81
Aslockton, 49
Attercliffe, 53
Attercliffe Hall, 54
Attleborough, 30
Auburn, 67
Audley End, 23
Aunsfield, 96
Austhorpe, 77
Axe Edge, 14
Aycliffe, 82
Aylestone, 2
Aysgarth, 81
Ayton, 74, 94

Bacup, 58
Backenham House, 30
Bagworth, 3
Bailey Hill, 54
Bakewell, 13
Baldersby, 78
Baldock, 42
Balls, 21
Bamber Bridge, 59
Bamborough Castle, 89
Bamford Hall, 60
Bamford Moor, 54
Bankton House, 96
Barden Fell, 19
Bardney, 46
Bardon Hill, 3
Barking, 32
Barkley Hall, 3
Barlborough, Hall, 15
Barmston, 67
Barnard Castle, 81, 82
Barnby Dun, 16
Barnet, 41
Barnetby, 55
Barnsley, 15, 52
Barnt Green, 11
Barrow, 4
Barton Hall, 26
Barton Hill, 73
Barton and Walton, 10
Barton-le-Street, 67
Barton-on-Humber, 56
Barton-under-Needwood, 10
Basford, 5, 7
Bawtry, 50
Bawtry Hall, 50
Baxenden, 58
Bayon's Manor, 55
Bayfordbury, 21
Beacon, 19
Beal, 89
Bealings, 36
Beccles, 37
Bedale, 78
Bedale Grange, 78
Bedavale Abbey, 7
Bedford, 5
Bedlington, 88
Bedwell Park, 21
Beechburn, 82
Beech Hill, 21
Beeston, 5
Belford, 89
Belgrave Hall, 2
Bell Busk, 19
Belmont, 83
Belper, 12
Belton, 18, 37, 95
Belton Hall, 48
Belvey, 29
Belvoir Castle, 49
Bemerside, 91
Bempton, 68
Benningboro' Hall, 77
Bentley, 36
Berkeley, 11
Berkeley Castle, 11
Berry Brow. 52
Berwick, 89
Berwickshire, 89
Bescar Lane, 59
Beverley, 66
Biggleswade, 42
Billinge Hill, 59
Billingham, 79
Bilney Hall, 31
Bilten, 88
Binchester, 82
Bingham, 6, 49
Bingley, 18
Binham, 29
Birkenshaw, 18
Birdwell, 16
Birmingham, 10
Bishop Auckland, 82
Bishop's Stortford, 23
Bishopton, 79
Bixley Church, 38
Blackadder House, 94
Black Bank, 27
Blackburn, 15, 59
Black Castle Camp, 95
Black Hambleden, 79
Black Lane, 60
Blackstone Edge, 60
Blackwell, 11, 81
Blanchley Abbey, 54
Blatherwycke, 44
Blankney, 9
Blickling, 40
Blickling Hall, 40
Blue Pits Junction, 60
Blyborough Hall, 55
Blyton 55
Blyth,, 55 88
Blyth Hall, 50
Blythe Hall, 59
Boinsley, 7
Bolane, 81
Bolingbroke Castle, 46
Bolsterstone Hill, 54
Bolton, 60
Bolton Abbey, 19, 70, 78
Bolton Hall, 81
Bolton Park, 19
Bolton Percy, 70
Boltom Head, 73
Bonnyrigg, 93
Bootle, 59
Border Bridge, Royal, 90
Boreham House, 33
Boroughbridge, 77
Borrowash, 9
Borthwick Castle, 93
Borves Manor, 40
Bosmere Hall, 37
Bossall, 73
Boston, 46, 48
Boston Spa, 68
Bosworth Field, 2
Bosworth Hall Church, 3
Bottesford, 49
Bottisham, 25
Boughton House, 5
Boulsworth Hill, 58
Bourn, 48
Bourne, 48
Bowes Manor, 41
Bowling, 62
Bowling Hall, 18, 62
Bowland Bridge, 93
Boynton Hall, 67
Braceborough Spa, 48
Bradley Fold, 60
Bradbury, 82
Bradfield, 35, 53
Bradford, 62
Bradford (York), 18
Bradgate Park, 2
Bradley, 19
Brafferton, 77
Braintree, 33
Bramcote, 7
Bramford, 37
Bramford Park, 37
Bramley, 62
Brampton, 37

Brampton Park, 43
Bramwith, 16
Brancepeth Castle, 83
Brancepeth Park, 82
Brandon, 30
Brandon Hill, 83
Brandon Park, 29, 30
Branston Hall, 9
Braunston Hall, 2
Breadsall Priory, 10
Brear Yard, 92
Bredon, 11
Brentwood, 33
Brickendenbury, 21
Bridlington, 67
Bridlington Quay, 68
Brierfield, 58
Brigg, 55
Brighouse, 62
Brightside, 15
Brimham Rocks, 70
Broadgate or Bradgate, 2
Brocket Hall, 22
Brockholes, 52
Brocklesby, 55
Brompton, 79
Brompton Hall, 74
Bromsgrove, 11
Bromwich Hall, 11
Brookman's Park, 41
Brooksby, 3
Brooksby Park, 3
Broom Close, 31
Brough, 64
Broughton, 19
Broughton Astley, 1
Broughton Hall, 19
Broxbourne, 21
Broxbourne Bury, 21
Brundall, 31
Brundall House, 31
Bruntsfield Links, 99
Brunstone, 93
Bubwith, 64
Buckden, 43
Buckenham, 31
Bucknal, 46
Bulwell, 7
Bungay, 38
Bunny Park, 7
Burdale, 67
Burdenscales Tower, 19
Bures, 34
Burgh, 47
Burgh Castle, 32
Burleigh House, 4, 48
Burley House, 4
Burngrar, 92
Burnham Thorpe, 31
Burn Hill, 82
Burnley, 58, 61
Burnmouth, 94
Burnt Mill, 23
Burscough Bridge, 59
Burscough Junction, 59
Burston, 38
Burstwick, 86
Burton, 10
Burton Agnes, 67
Burton Agnes Hall, 67
Burton Constable, 66, 78, 81
Burton Joyce, 8
Burton Park, 9
Burton Salmon, 64
Burwell Park, 47
Bury, 57
Bury Hall, 21
Bury St. Edmunds, 25, 37
Bushell Hill, 81
Bush Hill Park, 21
Butterley Iron Works, 15
Buxton, 13
Byland Abbey, 67
Byfrons, 32
Byron Hall, 51

Caister, 38, 40
Caister Castle, 32
Caister Cliff Camp, 58
Caistor, 55
Caldron Snout, 81
Call Green, 22
Calverley, 18
Cam, 10
Cambridge, 23, 41
  Fitzwilliam Museum, 24
  New Library, 24
  Observatory, 25
  Public Schools, 24
  Senate House, 24
  University Library, 24
  University, or Pitt Press, 24
  Colleges.—
  Catharine's Hall, 24
  Christ's College, 24
  Clare Hall, 24
  Corpus Christi College, 24
  Downing College, 24
  Emmanuel College, 24
  Gonville and Caius or Key's College, 24
  Jesus College, 24
  King's College, 24
  Magdalene College, 24
  Pembroke College, 24
  Peterholme or St. Peter's College, 25
  Queen's College, 25
  St. John's College, 25
  Sidney College, 25
  Trinity College, 25
  Trinity Hall, 25
Cam Fell, 19
Camlet Moats, 21
Camp Hill, 11
Cankey, 31
Cantley, 31
Cantley (York), 51
Canwick Hall, 9, 46
Capel, 36
Carberry Hut, 16
Cardington, 4
Carham, 90
Carham Castle, 90
Carnaby, 67
Carlton, 5, 8, 19, 50, 80
Carlton Colville, 37
Carlton Hall, 64
Carrington, 5
Carwood, 68
Castle Acre, 30
Castle Bromwich, 11
Castle Carlton, 47
Castle Eden, 83
Castle Eden Dean, 83
Castle Hill, 54, 55, 74
Castle Howard, 73
Castle Howard Station, 73
Castle Rising, 28
Castleford, 64
Casewick, 48
Cavers, 92
Caton, 20
Cattal, 72
Catterick Bridge, 80
Catton Hall, 10
Cat Tor, 13
Caudlesby, 46
Cawton, 80
Cayton, 68
Chaddesdon Hall, 10
Chadwell, 21
Chamber Hall, 57
Chapeltown, 16
Chappel, 34
Charnwood Forest, 3
Chathill, 89
Chatsworth, 13
Chatteris, 26
Chatteris House, 26
Chauntry, 36, 37
Chee Tor, 14
Chelker, 19
Chelmsford, 33
Cheltenham, 11
Cherry Tree, 59
Cheshunt, 21
Cheshunt House, 21
Chesterfield, 15
Chesterford, 23
Chesterton, 44
Chevet Hall, 16
Chevy Chase, 90
Chipping Sodbury, 12
Chirnside, 94
Chisholm, 92
Chittisham, 27
Choppington, 88
Christon Bank, 89
Church, 58
Church Fenton, 68
Clapham, 20
Clapham Caves, 78
Claybrooke Hall, 1
Clay Cross, 14
Claydon, 37
Claypole, 49
Claythorpe, 47
Claythorpe Hall, 47
Cleckheaton, 62
Cleckington, 96
Cleethorpes, 56
Cleeve, 11
Cleveland Port, 79
Cliff Common Gate, 64
Clifton, 7
Clifton Junction, 57
Clitheroe, 19
Clumber, 50, 54
Coalville, 3
Coby Castle, 79
Cocker Bar, 59
Cockburnspath, 95
Cockerington House, 47
Cockthorpe, 29
Codnor Park, 7
Coggeshall, 34
Colchester, 34
Cold Coniston, 19
Cold Rowley, 82
Coldstream, 90
Coleshill, 10
Cole Green, 41
Collingham, 8
Coleorton Hall, 3
Coleshill House, 11
Coleshill Park, 11
Colne, 58
Colne Valley, 34
Colney Hatch, 41
Colney Hatch Lunatic Asylum, 41
Colstoun, 96
Colville, 36
Colwick, 6
Compsall, 51
Cononley, 19
Conisborough, 16
Conisborough Castle, 16
Connington, 44
Connington Round Hill, 43
Constable Burton, 78
Cornhill, 90
Copford, 33
Copford Church, 34
Copgrove, 78
Copley, 61
Copmanthorpe, 70
Copper Hall, 21
Corby, 48
Costessey or Cossey Park, 40
Cottam, 54
Cottenham, 26
Cottingham, 66
Cottingham Castle, 66
Countesthorpe, 1
Cowdenknowes, 92
Cowpen Lane, 88
Coxbench, 10
Coxhoe, 80, 82
Coxhoe House, 80
Coxwold, 67

Cracow Hill, 19
Craike Castle, 67, 77
Crake Hall, 78
Cramlington, 88
Cressbrook, 14
Crichton Castle, 93
Cringletie, 93
Croft, 81
Crofton, 63
Cromer, 40
Cromer Hall, 40
Cromford, 12
Cromwell's Fort, 96
Crook, 82
Croome Park, 11
Cross Gates, 77
Croston, 59
Crowfield, 37
Crowland or Croyland, 44
Crowle, 16
Croxton, 55
Cudworth, 16
Culford Hall, 26
Culland's Grove, 21, 41
Cusworth, 51
Cusworth Park, 16

Dalhousie, 93
Dalhousie Castle, 93
Dalkeith, 93, 94
Dalkeith Palace, 93, 94
Dalton, 80
Danbury Church, 33
Darcey Lever, 60
Darfield, 16
Darley, 13
Darlington, 79, 81
Darnall, 54
Darsham, 37
Darwen, 58
Dean Bridge, 99
Dean's House, 94
Debden, 23
Deddington House, 42, 43
Deep Car, 53
Defford, 11
Denber, 11
Denby Dale, 52
Denton, 78
Denver, 28
Derby, 9
Derby Arboretum, 10
Dereham, 31
Derpham, 30
Desborough, 4
Desford, 2
Devil's Arrows, The, 70,
Diamond Hill, 14
Diddington, 43
Diddington House, 43
Dinsdale Spa, 79
Dinting, 51
Dirleton, 95
Diss, 37
Doddington, 27
Doddington Park, 12
Dodworth, 52
Dogdyke, 46
Dognam Park, 33
Doncaster, 15, 50
Donnington Park, 5
Dovecliffe, 16
Dover Court, 35
Downham, 28
Doynham Park, 32
Dragon's Den, 53
Draughton, 19
Draycott, 9
Draycott House, 9
Drayton Manor, 10
Dreghlington, 17
Drem, 95
Driffield, 67
Druid Hemlock Stone, 7
Druid's Hill, 93
Dryburgh Abbey, 91
Dudley Hill, 18
Duffield, 12
Dullingham, 25
Dunbar, 95
Dunbar Castle, 95
Dunbar House, 95
Duncombe House, 67
Dunford Bridge, 52
Dunglas, 95
Dunham, 30
Dnnham Lodge, 30
Dunkenhalgh Park, 58
Dunmow, 23
Dunse, 94
Dunse Castle, 94
Dunse Law, 94
Dunse Spa, 94
Dunster Pillar, 8
Durham, 83
Dursley, 11
Dyrham, 41

Earby, 58
Earlham, 39
Easingwold, 77
East Bilney, 31
Eastby, 19
East Dereham, 39
East Fortune, 95
East Halton, 19
East Lodge, 21
East Thorndon, 33
East Winch, 29
Easton, 48
Eastrea, 27
Eastrington, 64
Eastville, 47
Eastwood, 61
Eastwood Hall, 7
Eaton Soken, 43
Ebbing Well, 14
Eccles Road, 30
Eckington, 11, 15, 49
Eddlestone, 93
Edensor, 15
Edinburgh, 94, 97
Edinburgh Castle, 97
Edinken's Bridge, 95
Edmonstone, 96
Edmonton, 21
Ednam Manse, 90
Edrom, 94
Egton Bridge, 74
Eildon Hills, 91
Elland, 62
Ellshaw Barrow, 78
Elmham, 31
Elmham Hall, 31
Elmswell, 26, 37
Elphinstone Tower, 96
Elslack, 58
Elslob, 80
Elsenham, 23
Elsynge Hall, 21
Elton, 49
Elton Hall, 44
Elvaston Castle, 9
Ely, 27
Embsay, 19
Embsay Crag, 19
Emneth, 27
Enderby Hall, 2
Enfield, 21
Enfield Wash, 21
Epping Forest, 21, 32
Eshton, 19
Eshton Hall, 19
Eskbank, 93
Eskdale, 73
Essendine, 48
Eston, 79
Eston Nap Camp, 79
Etherly, 82
Eustby, 19
Eustby Fell, 19
Euston, 23
Euston Park, 26, 30
Evenwood, 82
Ewood Bridge, 57
Exam, 14
Exton Park, 4
Eye, 37

Fairfield, 51
Fakenham, 31
Falkingham,, 48
Falside Castle, 97
Fangfoss, 72
Farnham, 78
Farnley Park, 17
Farnley Tyas, 78
Fast Castle, 90, 95
Faulkborne Hall, 33
Fazakerley Hall, 59
Featherstone, 63
Felbrig Church, 40
Felbrig Hall, 40
Felix Hall, 34
Fence Houses, 84
Feniby, 64
Feniscowles, 59
Fenwick Tower, 51
Fern Islands, 89
Ferry Hill, 82, 83
Filey, 68
Fimber, 67
Finchale Priory, 83, 84
Finedon, 5
Finghall Lane, 79
Finningham, 37
Finningley, 50
Firsby, 47
Fishwive's Causeway, 96
Fiskerton, 8
Fiskerton Old Church, 46
Fixby Hall, 62
Fixton, 41, 59
Flamborough Head, 68
Flaxton, 74
Flaxton Lodge, 73
Fleurs Castle, 90, 91
Flodden Field, 90
Florden, 38
Florden Hall, 38
Foggathorpe Gate, 64
Ford Castle, 89
Foremarks, 7
Forge Mills, 11
Forest Gate, 32
Forncett, 38
Forty Hall, 21
Foulridge, 58
Fountainhall, 93
Fountain's Abbey, 7
Foxhill Bank, 58
Foxholes, 60
Foxton, 42
Framlingham, 36
Fransham, 30
Frisby, 3
Friskney, 46
Frocester, 11
Frosterley, 82
Frystone Hall, 51
Fulbourn, 25
Fulwell, 84
Furness Abbey, 19
Fushie Bridge, 93

Gainford, 81
Gainsborough, 46, 55
Gala Water, 92
Galashiels, 92
Galtreas Forest, 77
Ganton, 74
Ganton Hall, 74
Garforth, 77
Gargrave, 19
Garrowby, 72
Garton, 67
Gate Burton, 47
Gateshead, 84
Gawthorpe, 58
Giggleswick, 19
Gidea Hall, 33
Gildersome, 18
Gilling, 67
Gilling Park, 67, 77

Gimby Hall, 47
Gisburn Park, 10
Gisburne Park, 58
Glen, 4
Glenesk, 94
Glossop, 51
Glossop Hall, 52
Gloucester, 10
Goathland, 73
Godnow Bridges, 16
Gogmagog Hills, 24
Goldsborough, 72
Goldsborough Hall, 72
Goodmanham, 72
Goole, 64
Gore Water, 93
Gorebridge, 93
Gorleston, 31
Gorton, 51
Gotham, 7
Goxhill, 56
Grange Lane, 16
Grange Lea, 17
Grantchester, 25
Grantham, 48
Grant's House, 90, 95
Greasley, 7
Great Coates, 56
Great Grimsby, 56
Great Ponton, 48
Great Whernside, 19, 78
Greatham, 81
Grendon Park, 5
Gresley, 3
Grimsthorpe, 48
Gristhorpe, 68
Gristhorpe Lodge, 68
Grosmont, 73, 74
Grove Hall, 54
Grueldyke's Farm, 94
Guide Bridge, 51
Guisborough, 79
Gunton, 40

Habrough, 55
Haddington, 95
Haddingtonshire, 95
Haddiscoe, 31
Haddon Hall, 10, 12, 14
Hadfield, 52
Hadfield Chase, 50
Hadleigh, 36
Hag Tor, 13
Haggerleases, 82
Haileybury, 21
Halesworth, 37
Halidon Hill, 90
Halifax, 62
Hallam Moor, 54
Halnaby, 81
Halstead, 34
Halton, 20
Hambleton, 64
Hambleton House, 64
Hammerton, 72
Hampton, 10
Hams Hall, 10
Hansley Beacon, 72
Harden Grange, 18
Hardingham, 30
Hardingham Hall, 31
Hardwick, 80
Hardwick Hall, 15
Hare Park, 25
Haresfield, 11
Harewood, 17
Harewood Hall, 70, 78
Harlanton Church, 49
Harleston, 38
Harling Road, 30
Harlow, 23
Harlow Carr, 69
Harlow Hill, 69
Harpenden, 22
Harperley Park, 82
Harpham, 67
Harringay House, 41
Harrogate, 69, 73, 78
Harston, 42
Harswell Gate, 64
Hartlepool, 80
Hartley Pit, 88
Harwich, 35
Haselour, 10
Hasland House, 15
Haslingden, 58
Hassendean, 91
Hassendean Burn, 91
Hatfield, 41
Hatfield House, 21, 41
Hatfield Priory, 33
Hatton Height, 19
Haughley, 26, 37
Hawden, 87
Hawes, 81
Hawick, 91
Hawskel, 74
Hawsker Hall, 74
Hawthornden, 93
Haxby, 73
Hay of Dunse, 94
Hazlehead Bridge, 52
Headingley, 77
Heanor, 7
Heath Hall, 16
Heaton, 88
Heaton Hall, 57
Hebden Bridge, 62
Heckington, 48
Heckmondwike, 62
Heigham Church, 39
Heighington, 82 [12
Heights of Abraham, 11,
Hellifield, 19
Helmingham, 37
Helmshore, 58
Helmsley, 67
Helpstone, 4
Hemingbrough, 64
Hemingford Abbots, 26
Henlow, 4
Hensall, 64
Hepscott, 88
Heriot, 93
Hermitage Castle, 91
Hertford, 21
Hertingfordbury, 22
Heslerton, 74
Hessay, 72
Hessle, 64
Heston, 25
Hethersett, 31
Hewell Grange, 11
Heywood, 60
Higham, 25
High Bentham, 20
Highbury College, 41
Highfield House, 5
High Force, 81
High Kettle Springs, 81
High Park, 7
High Tor, 13
Hildenley, 73
Hilgay Fen, 28
Hinchin Brook House, 43
Hipperholme, 62
Histon, 26
Hitchin, 5, 42
Hitchin Priory, 42
Hoddesden, 21
Hoghton, 59
Hoghton Tower, 59
Holbeach, 45
Holbeck, 62, 77
Holcombe Hill, 57
Holderness, 66
Holkham, 31
Hollingworth, 60
Holloway, 41
Holme, 28, 40, 44
Holme Bridge, 19
Holmes, The, 15
Holmfirth, 52
Holton, 55
Holton-le-Clay, 47
Holyrood Palace, 98
Holywell, 88
Homersfield, 38
Honcot, 92
Honington, 49
Honley, 52
Hoo Park, 22
Hooseholme Priory, 16
Hopewell Hall, 9
Hoppiland, 12
Horbury, 62
Hornby, 20
Hornby Castle, 20, 80
Horncastle, 45, 46
Hornsey, 41
Hornsea, 66
Hornsea Mere, 66
Hornsey Wood House, 41
Horsforth, 77
Horsforth Hall, 77
Horton House, 18
Horton, 19
Hougham, 49
Houghton, 31
Houghton Hall, 72
Houghton-le-dale, 29
Hovingham, 67
Howden, 64
Howen's Gill, 82
Howick Grove, 55
Howsham, 55, 73
Hubbart's Bridge, 49
Hucknall Torkard, 6, 7
Huddersfield, 52
Huncoat, 58
Hunmanby, 68
Hunmanby Hall, 68
Huntcliffe, 74
Huntingdon, 43
Huntingdonshire, 43
Huntington, 72
Hunslet, 16
Hunstanton, 28
Humberstone, 48
Humberstone Grange, 48
Hull, 64
Hurley's Cave, 93
Hutton, 73, 79
Hutton's Ambo, 73
Hutton Cranswick, 67
Hyde, The, 33
Hykeham, 8
Hylton, 84
Hylton Castle, 84

Ilford, 32
Ilkeston, 7
Ilkeston Park, 7
Ilkley, 77
Impington, 26
Impington House, 26
Ingatestone, 33
Ingatestone Hall, 33
Ingleborough, 20
Ingleton, 20
Innerwick, 95
Inveresk, 96
Ipswich, 36
Irby, 47
Irchester, 5
Irnham Park, 48
Isham, 4
Islington, 94
Ixworth, 25

Jack Hill Fewston, 78
Jarrow, 84
Jedburgh, 91
Jedfoot Bridge, 91
Jervaulx Abbey, 78, 81
John of Gaunt's Palace, 55
Joppa, 94

Keadby, 16
Kedlestone Hall, 10
Kegworth, 5
Keighley, 19
Kelham Hall, 50
Kelloe, 94

Kelso, 90
Kelvedon, 34
Kelvedon Hall, 34
Kempson, 30
Kennet, 25
Keso, 79
Kettering, 4
Kettleness, 74
Kettlethorpe, 47
Kettlewell, 19
Ketton, 4
Keyingham, 66
Kibworth, 4
Kilburn, 10
Kildwick, 19
Kilham, 67
Killingworth, 88
Kilnhurst, 16
Kilnwick Percy, 72
Kimberley, 30, 40
Kimbolton, 43
Kimmeryhawe, 94
Kingsbury, 10
King's Norton, 11
Kippax Hall, 77
Kippax Park, 16, 17
Kirby, 73
Kirby Muxloe, 2
Kirby Park, 3
Kirkby, 7
Kirkby Castle, 2
Kirkby Mallory, 2
Kirkby Moorside, 67
Kirkham, 73
Kirkham House, 73
Kirk Leatham, 79
Kirklees Hall, 62
Kirk Sandall Church, 50
Kirkstall, 18
Kirkstall Abbey, 18, 77
Kirkstall Grange, 77
Kirkstead, 46
Kirton, 46
Kirton Lindsey, 55
Kiveton Park, 54
Knaith, 47
Knaith Hall, 47
Knapton, 74
Knapton Lodge, 74
Knaresbro', 72
Knaresbro' Castle, 70, 73
Knaresborough Dropping Well, 72
Knaresborough Forest, 78
Knavesmire, 72
Knebworth Hall, 42
Knebworth Park, 22
Kneesworth, 42
Knottingley, 51, 64

Laceby, 48
Laird of Cockpen's House, 93
Laister Dyke, 18, 62
Lakenheath, 30
Lakenheath Hall, 30
Lake House, 32
Lambton Castle, 83, 84
Lamb Close, 7
Lancaster, 20
Lancashire, 57
Lands, 82
Langley Mill, 7
Langrick, 46
Langton Hall, 67, 73
Langworth, 54
Larport Hall, 74
Lathom House, 59
Lauder, 91
Layer Marney, 34
Lazenby, 79
Lea, 47
Lea Bridge, 20
Leadburn, 93
Lead Hall, 55
Lea Hall, 47
Lea Hurst, 11
Leamside, 84
Leathley Cayley, 78
Ledstone Hall, 16, 17
Leeds, 16, 62, 77
Leeming Lane, 78
Lees, 90
Legbourne, 47
Leicester, 1
Leicestershire, 1
Leidborough, 47
Leiston, 37
Leith, 94, 96
Lenton, 5, 7
Leverton, 54
Lewisham, 73
Lexham Hall, 30
Leyburn, 79
Lightcliffe, 62
Lilliard's Edge, 91
Linby, 7
Lincoln, 8, 46, 54
Lincolnshire, 44
Lindean, 93
Lindisfarne Abbey and Castle, 89
Linton, 95
Litcham, 30
Littleborough Ferry, 47
Little Bytham, 48
Little Casterton, 48
Little Eaton, 10
Littleport, 28
Little Sodbury House, 12
Little Steeping, 47
Little Warley, 33
Littleworth, 45
Livermore Hall, 26
Liverpool, 59, 60
Liversedge, 62
Lochend, 95
Lockington, 67
Lockwood, 52
Loddon, 38
Londesborough, 72
Long Eaton Junction, 5
Longhoughton, 89
Longhurst, 88
Longniddry, 95
Long Preston, 19
Long Stanton, 26
Long Sutton, 28
Lostock Hall, 59
Loughborough, 5
Louth, 47
Lowdham, 8
Lowestoft, 31, 37
Low Moor, 62
Low Stakesby, 74
Lowthorpe, 67
Lowthorpe Hall, 67
Loxley Chase, 54
Lucker, 89
Luddendenfoot, 61
Luflenham, 4
Lumley Castle, 83
Luton, 22
Luton Hoo, 22
Lutterworth, 1
Lydiate, 59
Lynn Regis, 28

Madingley, 25
Magdalen Gate, 27
Maghull, 59
Makerstown, 91
Maldon, 33
Malham Tarn, 19
Malham Cove, 19
Malton, 67, 73
Malvern Hills, 10
Mandon Hill, 82
Manea, 27
Mangotsfield, 12
Manningham House, 18
Manningtree, 35
Manston, 77
Mapperley Plain, 6
March, 27
March Bun, 93
Marfleet, 66
Marishes Road, 73
Markeaton Hall, 10
Market Bosworth, 2
Market Deeping, 48
Market Harborough, 4
Market Rasen, 55
Market Weighton, 72
Marks Tey, 34
Marlesford, 36
Marske Hall, 79
Marston, 72
Marston Moor, 72
Marton, 47, 68
Masborough, 15
Masham Swinton, 78
Masson, 13
Matlock Baths, 13
Maud, 16
Maxton, 91
Medge Hall, 16
Melandra Castle, 52
Melbourne Bury, 42
Meldreth, 42
Mellis, 37
Melmerby, 78
Melrose, 92
Melrose Abbey, 92
Melton, 36, 40
Melton Castle, 31
Melton Mowbray, 3
Merchiestoun Castle. 99
Meresbrook House, 54
Merton, 30
Methley, 16
Methley Park, 17
Mexborough, 16
Micklefield, 77
Middle Drove, 27
Middleham, 81
Middleham Castle, 78
Middle Rasen Drak, 55
Middlesborough, 79, 80
Middlesex County Asylum, 41
Middleton, 29, 60, 79
Middleton Junction, 59
Midshields, 92
Mildenhall House, 30
Mildenhall Road, 30
Mileham, 31
Miles Platting, 59
Milford, 77
Milford House, 12
Milford Junction, 64, 77
Miller Hill, 94
Miller's Dale, 14
Millfield, 84
Millington, 72
Milnrow, 60
Milton Abbey 44
Minsal Dale, 13
Mirfield, 62
Mission Carr, 50
Misterton Hall, 1
Mistley, 35
Mistley Hall, 35
Mitford, 88
Moira, 3
Molineux Brow, 57
Monk Bretton, 52
Monkwearmouth, 84
Monsal Dale, 14
Montague Cave, 70, 72
Moortown, 55
Morecambe, 20
Morecambe Bay, 20
Morpeth, 88
Moseley, 11
Moulton, 45, 80
Mountgrace Priory, 79
Mount Sorrel, 5
Mount Surrey House, 39
Mount Teviot, 91
Mousehold Heath, 39
Mowbray Lodge, 3
Mugget Hill, 92
Muker, 81

Mulgrave Castle, 74
Musbury Heights, 58
Muskham Grange, 50
Musselburgh, 94
Muswell Hill, 41
Mutford, 31
Mytholmroyd, 61
Myton Hall, 77

Nafferton, 67
Narborough, 29
Necton, 30
Needham, 37
Nelson, 58
Netherton, 88
Neville's Cross, 83
Newark, 8, 49
New Belses, 91
Newbiggin, 88
Newbottle Abbey, 93
Newburgh, 67
Newby Hall, 70, 78
Newby Park, 77, 78
Newby Wiske, 78
Newcastle-upon-Tyne, 85
Newchurch 58
New Hailes, 94
New Hall Nunnery, 33
Newham, 89
New Holland, 56
Newlay, 18
Newmarket, 25
New Mill End, 22
Newnham Paddox, 1
Newport, 23, 79
Newsham, 88
Newstead Abbey, 6, 7
Newton Bank, 19
Newton Bewley, 80
Newton Cap Bridge, 82
Newton Don, 90
Newton Grange, 19
Newton Heath, 59
Newton Kyme, 68
Newton-le-Willows, 78
Newtown, 91
New Whitby, 74
Nidd, 78
Niddrie, 94
Niddrie Maréchal, 94
Ninevah, 94
Ninewar, 95
Nisbit, 91, 94
Norham, 90
Normanton, 4, 16, 63
Northallerton, 77, 78
Nuthall Temple, 7
North Berwick, 95
Northborough, 45
North Grimstone, 67
North Kelsey, 55
North Leda, 62
North Mims, 41
Northorpe, 55
North Shields, 87
North Thoresby, 47
North Thoresby House, 47
Northumberland, 85
Norton, 51, 54
Norton Conyers, 78
Norton Junction, 77
Norwich, 38
Norwood Hall, 49
Nottingham, 5, 49
Notton, 16
Nunthorpe, 79
Nunthorpe Hall, 79

Oakenshaw, 16
Oakham, 3
Oak Hill, 41
Oakington, 26
Oakley, 5
Oakley Park, 37
Offord Cluny, 43
Offord Darcy, 43
Ogston Hall, 15
Oldham, 59
Old Junction, 77
Old Leake, 47
Old Melrose, 92
Old Ormiston, 91
Old Warden House, 42
Ormerod Hall, 58
Ormesby, 47, 79
Ormesby Hall, 79
Ormskirk, 59
Osmaston Hall 9
Osmotherly, 79
Ossington, 50
Otes, 23
Otley, 70, 78
Otterington, 77
Ottringham, 66
Ottringham Hall, 66
Oughty Bridge, 53
Ouse Bridge, 28
Overton Longeville, 44
Oxen Hall, 81
Oxwell Park, 87

Palgrave, 37
Pallion, 84
Pallion House, 84
Pannal, 78
Panshanger, 21, 41
Parham, 36
Park Lane, 21
Pattrington, 66
Peakirk, 45
Peas Bridge, 90
Peebles, 94
Peebles-shire, 93
Pelaw Junction, 84
Pendle Hills, 58
Pendleton, 57
Penicuick, 93
Penistone and Thurlstone, 52
Pensher, 84
Penygant, 19
Percy Main, 88
Pershore Abbey Church, 10
Peterborough, 27, 44
Phicksand Priory, 42
Pickenham Hall, 30
Pickering, 73
Pickering Beck, 73
Pickering Hall, 73
Pickering Park, 73
Pickle Bridge, 62
Picton, 79
Piel, 19
Piercebridge, 81
Pilmoor Junc., 67, 77
Pinchbeck, 45
Pinkie House, 94
Pinnacle Hill, 98
Pinxton, 7
Pleasington, 59
Pleasington Hall, 59
Pleshy Castle, 33
Pocklington, 72
Ponder's End, 21
Pontefract, 63
Pool's Hole, 14
Poppleton, 72
Port Clarence, 80
Portholm Mead, 43
Portmore, 93
Portobello, 94, 96
Portsmouth, 61
Potter's Bar, 41
Potton, 43
Poulton-le-Sands, 19
Powder Mills Govmnt., 21
Preston, 59
Preston Junction, 59, 79
Prestonpans, 96
Prestwold Hall, 5
Prospect Hill, 88
Pulham Market, 38
Pulham, St. Mary, 38
Pye Bridge, 7
Pymmes, 21

Quebec Castle, 31
Quenby, 2
Quendon Hall, 23
Quernmoor Park, 20
Quorndon Hall, 2, 5
Quorndon House, 5

Raby Castle, 81
Rackheath, 39
Radcliffe Bridge, 57
Radding Park, 69
Radford, 5, 7
Radford Priory, Gate of 54
Rainham, 31
Ralph's Cross, 67, 73
Ramsbottom, 57
Ramsey Abbey, 43
Ranskill, 50
Raskelf, 77
Ratcliffe, 49
Ravenfield, 16
Ravensworth Castle, 87
Rawcliffe, 64, 74
Rawmarsh, 15
Rawtenstall, 58
Raydon, 36
Ravensnook Ruins, 93
Rearsby, 3
Redbourn Hall, 55
Redcar, 79
Redditch, 11
Redgrave Hall, 37
Redmarshall, 80
Reedham, 31
Reepham, 54
Reeth, 80
Reneshaw Park, 15
Repton, 9
Reston, 94
Retford, 46, 50, 54
Richard's Well, 2
Ribston Hall, 72
Richmond, 80
Rievaulx Abbey, 67, 77
Ringley Road, 57
Rillington, 73
Rilston, 19
Rilston Fell, 19
Ripley, 10, 78
Ripley Castle, 70
Ripley Park Castle, 78
Ripon, 78
Ripon Cathedral, 70
Rishton, 58
Risley Hill, 7
Robin Hood's Bay, 74
Robin Hood's Butts, 74
Robin Hood's Well, 54
Roby Hall, 48
Rochdale, 60
Rock House, 11
Rockingham Castle, 4
Rockingham Mausoleum, 16, 54
Rokeby, 81
Rolleston, 8
Roman Cross, 19
Romford, 33
Roseberry Topping, 79
Rosegrove, 58
Roslin, 93
Rossington, 50
Rotherham, 15, 54
Rothley Temple, 2, 3, 5
Rougham Hall, 26
Routh, 66
Rowsley, 13
Roxburgh, 91
Roxburghshire, 90
Roydon, 23
Royston, 16, 42
Royston and Notton, 15
Royton, 60
Rudding Park, 78
Rudstone, 67
Rufford, 59
Rufford House, 50
Rumbold's Moor, 18
Runswick, 74

Rushbrooke Hall, 26
Rushton, 4
Ruswarp, 73
Rutherford, 91
Ryburgh, 31
Rye House, 21
Ryhall, 48
Ryston Hall, 28

Sadberge, 79
Saffron Walden, 22
Salisbury Crags, 98
Saltaire, 18
Saltfleet, 47
Saltley, 11
Sandal Castle, 63
Sand Hutton, 72, 73
Sandiacre, 7
Sandsend, 74
Sandy, 42
Sandy Park, 42
Sawbridgeworth, 23
Saweley Abbey, 44
Sawley, 9
Saxby, 3
Saxham, 25
Saxilby, 47
Saxmundham, 37
Scampton, 47
Scarborough, 68, 74
Scarborough Castle, 76
Scarisbrick Hall, 59
Scar Reefs, 79
Scarthingwell Hall, 68
Scawby & Hibaldstow 55
Scawby Hall, 55
Scorton, 80
Scremerston, 89
Scrivelsby, 46
Scrooby, 50
Scruton, 78
Seamer Junction, 68, 74
Seaton, 80
Seaton Delaval, 84
Seaton House, 96
Seaton Snook, 80
Sebsey, 46
Sedgebrook, 49
Sedgefield, 80
Seghill, 84
Selby, 64
Selkirkshire, 93
Selkirk, 93
Serlby, 50
Sessay, 77
Sessay Hall, 77
Settle, 19
Settrington, 67
Sharnbrook, 5
Shaw Hall, 60
Sheffield, 15, 53
Shefford, 4
Shefford Road, 42
Shelford, 6
Shelford, 22, 49
Shepley, 52
Shepreth, 42
Shepreth Hall, 42
Sherburn, 83
Sherburn, 68, 74
Sherburn Hospital, 83
Sherburn House, 74
Sheriff Hutton Park, 73
Sherwood Forest, 7
Shilton, 82
Shimpling, 37
Shincliffe, 83
Shincliffe Hall, 83
Shipley, 18, 18
Shipley Gate, 7
Shipley Hall, 7
Shipton 72, 76
Shireoaks, 54
Shrubland Hall, 37
Shunor Hoe, 73
Sibsey, 47
Sileby, 5
Silkstone, 15, 52
Silsden, 19
Sinderby, 78
Sinton, 92
Sixhill or Segshill. 2
Six Mile Bottom, 25
Skeyness, 47
Skelton Castle, 79
Skendleby, 47
Skibden, 19
Skipton, 19, 58
Skipton Castle, 19
Skipton Lodge, 19
Skipton Priory, 19
Sleaford, 45, 49
Sleights, 73, 74
Slingsby, 67
Smallholm Tower, 91
Smeeth Road, 27
Smithley, 15
Snaith, 64
Snape, 37
Sneaton, 74
Sneaton Castle, 74
Sneinton, 5
Spelland, 54
Somerby Hall, 55
Somerleyton, 31
Somerleyton Hall, 31
Somersham, 26
South Cave, 66
South Dalton Hall, 72
Southend, 81
Southgate, 41
Southill, 4
Southhill Park, 42
South Kelsey, 55
South Lodge, 21, 41
South Mims, 41
Southport, 59
Southrey, 46
South Shields, 84
South Skerlaw, 66
South Town, 31
Southwell, 8, 49
Southwick, 84
Sowerby, 47
Sowerby Bridge, 61
Spalding, 45
Spaldington Grange, 64
Speeton, 68
Spennymoor, 80
Spilsby, 47
Spofforth, 69, 78
Spondon, 9
Spondon Hall, 9
Springwell. 84
Springwood, 91
Sprotborough, 16, 51
Sprotborough Hall, 16
Sprouston, 90
Spurn Head, 66
Spurn Head Light, 56
St. Abb's Head, 90
St. Albans, 41
St. Andrew's Hall, 30
St. Bennett's Abbey, 40
St. Bernard's Mineral Well, 99
St. Boswell, 91
St. Germains, 96
St. Helens, 82
St. Ives, 18, 26, 44
St. James Deeping,
St. John's Weardale, 82
St. Margaret's, 21
St. Neot's, 43
St. Olaves, 37
St. Robert's Chapel, and Cave, 70, 72
Stacksteads, 58
Staddlethorpe, 64
Stainacre, 74
Staindrop, 81
Stainforth, 16
Staithes, 74
Stallingborough, 56
Stamford, 4, 48
Stamford Bridge, 72
Standard Hill, 80
Stanfield Hall, 30
Stanhope, 82
Stanhope Cave, 82
Stanhope Hall, 82
Stanhope Park, 82
Stanstead Mountfichet, 23
Stanton Gate, 7
Stapleford Park, 3
Stapleton Park, 51
Starbeck, 73, 78
Starston, 37
Steeton, 19
Stellington, 80
Steill's Hospital, 96
Stepe Priory, 26
Stevenage, 42
Stevenson, 96
Stichell, 90
Stilton, 43
Stirtloe, 43
Stixwould, 46
Stobbs, 92
Stocks Moor, 52
Stockton-on-the-Forest 72
Stockton-on-Tees, 79
Stoke Rochford, 48
Stokesley, 79
Stoke Works, 11
Stonehouse, 11
Stonele Abbey, 43
Stonnis, 13
Stonyhurst, 59
Stow, 28, 93
Stow Hall, 28
Stowe, 47
Stowmarket, 37
Stradsett, 28
Stratford, 20, 32
Stratton House, 38
Stratton Park, 42
Streeton, 19
Strensall, 73
Strensham, 11
Streton, 18
Stretton, 2, 15
Strid, The, 19, 73
Strumpshaw Hill, 31
Stubbins, 57
Studley, 10
Studley Royal, 70, 78
Sturton, 19, 55
Stutton, 68
Sudbury, 34
Suffolk, 36
Summerseat Hall, 57
Sunderland, 84
Sunken Island, 66
Surfleet, 45
Sutterton, 45
Sutton, 7, 43
Sutton-in-the-Forest, 77
Sutton Hall, 77
Sutton (York), 50
Swaffham, 29
Swainsthorpe, 38
Swannington, 3
Swavesey, 26
Swillington House, 16, 17
Swinderby, 8
Swinehope, 47
Swineshead, 49
Swinnow Hall, 69
Swinton, 16
Swithland Hall, 5
Syston Junction, 3
Syston Park, 49

Tadcaster, 68, 70
Tallington, 48
Tamworth, 10
Tattershall, 46
Tattershall Castle, 54
Temple Newsam, 17, 77
Templenewsam House, 16
Tewin House, 22
Tewkesbury, 11
Tewkesbury Park, 11

Theobalds, 21, 22
Theobald's Park, 21
Thetford, 30
Thewles, 80
Thimblethorpe Hall, 19
Thirsk, 67, 77
Thirkleby, 67, 77
Thoresby, 50, 54
Thorltby, 19
Thorndon Hall, 33
Thorne, 16
Thornhill Lees, 62
Thorn Island, 27
Thorney, 44, 47
Thorney Abbey, 27
Thornton, 19, 78
Thornton Abbey, 56
Thornton Curtis, 55
Thornton Force, 20
Thornton-le-Craven, 58
Thornton Park, 77
Thornton Scar, 20
Thorpe, 8, 39, 80
Thorpe Arch, 69
Thorpe Hall, 44
Thorpe Perrow, 78
Thornbury Castle, 12
Thrumpton Hall, 56
Thrybergh Hall, 15
Thundercliffe Grange, 54
Thurgarton, 8
Thurlstone, 52
Thurston, 26, 37
Thuxton, 31
Tickhill Castle, 51
Tilbridge Lane, 47
Tinsley Park Collieries, 54
Tiptree Heath, 33
Tivetshall, 38
Todmorden, 61
Todrig, 92
Tollerton, 7
Tong Hall, 18
Topcliffe, 78
Torksey, 54
Tortworth Court, 12
Toten, 7
Tottenham, 21
Tottenham Church, 41
Towneley, 61
Towneley Park, 58
Town Green, 59
Tow Law, 82
Towton, 68
Tranent 96
Trent Park, 41
Trent Place, 21
Trimdon, 82
Trowse, 31
Tunnel Junction, 82
Tupholme, 46
Tupton Grove, 15
Tupton Hall, 15
Turn, 19
Tuxford, 50
Tweedmouth, 90
Twizel Chapel, 90
Tyne Head, 93
Tynemouth. 86, 87
Tynemouth Priory, 87

Uffington, 4
Ugglebarnby, 74
Ulceby, 55
Ulleskelf, 70
Ullesthorpe, 1
Uppingham, 4
Undercliff Hall, 18
Underwood, 7
Uphaltham Hall, 79
Ushaw College, 83
Usselby, 55
Velvet Hall, 90

Wadborough, 11
Wadsley Bridge, 53
Wainfleet, 46
Wakefield, 63
Walderslow, 54
Walker, 87
Walliford, 96
Wallingwells, 54
Wallsend, 87
Walnstone, 79
Walsden, 61
Walsingham, 31
Walsingham Abbey, 31
Waltham, 21
Waltham Abbey, 21
Waltham Cross, 21
Waltham (Lincoln), 48
Walton, 4
Walton Hall, 10, 59
Walton House, 5
Walton-le-Soken, or
Walton-on-the-Naze, 35
Walton-on-the-Hill, 59
Walton Park, 16, 63
Wanlip Hall, 3
Wanstead Park, 32
Ware, 22
Ware Hill House, 22
Ware Park, 22
Ware Priory, 22
Wark or Werk, 90
Warkworth, 88
Warterwith, 72
Washingborough, 46
Washington, 84
Waterbeach, 27
Water Lane, 21
Water Orton, 11
Wath, 16
Watlington, 27, 28
Weald Hall, 33
Weeton, 78
Welbeck Abbey, 54
Welbury, 79
Wellersley Castle, 11
Wellingborough, 5
Wells, 31
Well Vale, 47
Welwyn, 22, 41
Welwyn Viaduct, 41
Weltham, 33
Weltham Lodge, 33
Wendling, 30
Wennington, 20
Wennington Hall, 20
Wensleydale, 81
Wentworth House, 16, 54
Werneth, 59
West Dereham, 28
Westerfield, 36
West Heslerton Hall, 74
West Lodge, 21
Weston, 45, 78
Westwood, 16
Wetherby, 69
Wetherby Grange, 69
Wetwany, 67
Whaplode, 45
Wharran, 67
Wharncliffe Crags, 53, 54
Wharncliffe Lodge, 53
Whatstandwell Bridge, 12
Wheathampstead, 22
Wheatley Hall, 51
Whernside, 19
Whisendine, 3
Whitacre Junction, 10
Whitburn Bay, 84
Whitburn House, 84
Whitby, 73
Whitby Abbey, 74
Whitehall, 94
White Webbs House, 21
Whitewell Hall, 73
Whitley Bridge, 64
Whittlesford, 22
Whittlesea, 27
Whitton House, 80
Whitworth, 80
Whorlton, 79
Wichnor Park, 10
Wickenby, 54
Wickham Market, 36
Widdrington, 88
Widdrington Castle, 88
Wigganthorpe, 67
Wigston, 1, 4
Wigston Hall, 1
Wilberfoss, 72
Willesley Park, 3
Willingdon, 9
Willingham House, 55
Willow Green, 41
Willoughby, 46, 47
Wilnecote, 10
Wilton Beacon, 72
Wimblington, 27
Wimpole, 42
Winchmore Hill, 41
Winestead Castle, 66
Wingate, 82
Wingerworth Hall, 15
Wingfield, 15
Winston, 81
Wisbeach, 27
Wistow Hall, 2
Witham, 33
Witham Lodge, 33
Withernsea, 66
Wittle Hill, 60
Witton-le-Wear, 82
Witton Park, 59, 82
Witton Park Station, 82
Wiverton, 6, 49
Woll, 92
Wollaton Hall, 5, 6
Wolsingham, 82
Wombwell, 16
Womersley, 51
Womersley Park, 51
Woodbridge, 36
Woodchester Park Nunnery, 11
Woodend, 77
Woodford Park, 52
Wood Green, 41
Woodhall Park, 22
Woodhall Spa, 46
Woodhead, 52 [17
Woodhouse Grove School,
Woodhouse Mill, 15
Woodhouse Junction, 54
Woodlands, 82
Woodlesford, 16
Wood Walton, 44
Woolaton, 7
Woolsthorpe, 48
Wooton-under-Edge, 11
Worcester, 10
Worksop, 54
Worksop Manor, 54
Wormald Green, 78
Wormley, 21
Worsbro' 15
Worsted, 40
Wortley, 52
Wortley Hall, 53, 54
Wrabness, 35
Wressel, 64
Wressel Castle, 64
Wrest Park, 42
Writtle, 33
Wydale, 74
Wyham, 47
Wykeham Abbey, 74
Wylam, 86
Wymondham, 30, 39 [81
Wynch Suspension Bridge,
Wynyard, 79

Yarborough, 47
Yarm, 79
Yarmouth, 32, 36
Yate, 12
Yaxham, 31
Yaxley, 43
Yeddingham, 74
York, 5, 70
York Race Course, 72
Yorkshire, 61

BRADSHAW'S DESCRIPTIVE RAILWAY HAND-BOOK

OF

GREAT BRITAIN AND IRELAND.

SECTION IV.

NOTE.—Shunts, or Marks thus ⌐—⌐ *, or thus* ⌐—⌐ *, introduced into the following pages, are intended to show the point at which a Branch deviates from the Main Line. Its position to the right or left hand of the Column indicates the right or left hand of the Railway on which the deviation takes place. The termination of the Branch is known by the Shunt being reversed.*

MIDLAND.

RUGBY TO LEICESTER.

PROCEEDING due north, by the river Swift, we pass the foot of the mound of *Cester-over*, supposed to have been a Roman station; then we have *Newnham Paddox* on our left, and passing over the Old Watling Street, which here divides the counties of Warwick and Leicester, we enter the latter and stop at

ULLESTHORPE.

Near three miles to the right is the old town of *Lutterworth*, chiefly interesting for its church, in which the great Reformer, Wickliffe, preached against the "Man of Sin," and spread the Word of God in a language that could be understood by the people. Here he died and was buried (1384), but he only lay in peace 50 years—his body was then taken out of the quiet grave, in which he lay entombed, burnt to ashes, and cast into the river. They still show his old oaken pulpit, and the high-backed wooden chair in which he died; also his portrait, said to have been done by one of the Fieldings, some of whose monuments may be seen in the church. Near it is *Misterton Hall*. *Claybrooke Hall* to the left of the station, and beyond some Roman remains.

BROUGHTON ASTLEY, and COUNTESTHORPE Stations are then passed, when we cross the Union Canal, and a tributary of the Soar, by a viaduct of eleven arches, and arrive at

WIGSTON.

Wigston Hall, Captain Baddenley. Near it is an old moated manorial seat of the Davenports.

Shortly after leaving Wigston, we see the Ashby line, bearing away to the westward, and, passing through the Knighton Tunnel, 100 yards long, we arrive at

LEICESTER.

A telegraph station.

HOTELS.—Bell; Three Crowns.

MARKET DAYS.—Wednesday, Friday, and Saturday.

FAIRS.—January 14th, March 2nd, May 12th, June 1st, July 5th, August 1st, September 13th, October 10th, November 2nd, December 8th, Palm Saturday, and Saturday in Easter Week.

RACES in September.

BANKERS. — Leicestershire Banking Company; Branch Bank of England; Paget and Kirby; Pares's Leicestershire Banking Company; National Provincial Bank of England.

LEICESTER, the capital of Leicestershire, a parliamentary borough, and seat of the hosiery trade, on the river Soar, and Midland Railway, 103 miles from London, *via* Rugby. Population 60,584. Two members. Here was a castle, rebuilt by John of Gaunt after its destruction by Henry II., but finally destroyed by Charles I. in 1645, and of which nothing now remains but the mound. It stood on a site of 26 acres, at Castle View or Newark (New work), a mound above the river, and was first built before the Conquest, by the Earls of Mercia. There are some remains of a collegiate foundation close by, of a later date, where John of Gaunt's wife, Constance of Castile, Mary de Bohun, first wife of Henry IV., and others of the princely line of Lancaster, were interred.

There was a station here in Roman times, when it was called *Ratæ*, which guarded the Fossway and Via Devana, the proofs of which exist in medals, urns, and pavements from time to time discovered, as well as a piece of an arched *Roman wall*, in the Jewry (where the Jews used to live), 70 feet long, and above 20 high; but especially in an almost unique *Roman milestone* of Hadrian's time, nearly 3 feet high, now deposited in the town Museum.

Another interesting relic is the wall of the terrace of *St. Mary's Augustine Abbey*, built by Robert le Bossu, or Hunch-Back, one of the first Earls of Leicester, in the meadows (by the river), and therefore called *St. Mary de Pratis*, the site of which is a large florist's nursery. Here Wolsey died.

In the Castle View the *Assize Hall*, deserves notice; it was the grea hall of the castle, and is 78 feet long by 50 broad, supported by oak pillars. It still retains many interesting architectural details of the Norman period. Two of the gateways of the Castle remain, one in ruins. The Guildhall is 80 feet long. At the Assembly Rooms is a painted ceiling, by Reinagle, the subjects being Aurora, Night, &c. The *Collegiate School* is in the Tudor style. Some of the hospitals for the poor are ancient; that called Trinity was founded in 1331. *Wigston's Hospital* was founded in 1513, and possesses very large revenues. Pleasant views from the new walk on the south side of the town.

Leicester was of so much consequence in Saxon days that it was made the seat of a bishop for a time, with a palace close to *St. Margaret's Church*, an early Gothic building. *St. Martin's*, near Southgate Street, and *St. Mary's*, near the castle, are both half Norman—the former being a cross, and the latter (distinguished by its tall spire) having stalls in it, with a fine timber roof. Robinson, author of the work on "Scripture Characters," was vicar of *St. Mary's*. *St. Nicholas*, in that street, near the castle, has a Norman tower.

Another *bossu*, the famous crook-backed Richard III., was brought here after the battle of Bosworth Field, and buried at the Grey Priory. He slept before the battle at a timbered house called the Blue Boar Inn (which was his crest), using the upper part overhanging the lower. The stone coffin, in which his body was interred, was used to form the horse trough at the Inn, "*Sic transit gloria mundi.*" Leicester stands as near as possible in the centre of England.

"This foul swine
Lies here low in the centre of the isle
Near to the town of Leicester, as we learn."
RICHARD III.

Stocking-making, the staple manufacture here, employs many wholesale dealers, and 4,000 or 5,000 hands, and many more in the neighbourhood, in worsted, wool, and cotton spinning, wool stapling, the weaving and sewing of the hose, and the making of needles, frames, &c. The large mills of Messrs. Harris, Brewin and Whetstone, Ellis, &c., rival those of Lancashire. Berlin gloves and lace are also made. Upwards of 20,000 stockingers altogether are engaged in the manufacture in this town, and at Loughborough, Hinckley, Lutterworth, &c.

Within a few miles of Leicester the following may be noticed: *Belgrave Hall*, J. Ellis, Esq.; *Aylestone*, with the ivy patch on its church spire, the ancient seat of the Vernons and of the Earls of Rutland, is now occupied by N. C. Stone, Esq., the Duke of Rutland's agen.t *Enderby Hall*, in a hilly spot near the Soar, belonged to the Nevills; *Kirkby Mallory*, Lady de Clifford, where the Noels are buried; *Rothley Temple*, once the seat of a preceptory of the Templars. *Quorndon Hall*, Sir R. Sutton, Bart. Here the famous Quorn hounds are kennelled. *Nimrod* says, "of all the countries in the world, the Quorn certainly bears the bell." This superiority arises from the peculiar nature of the soil, which, being for the most part good, is highly favourable to the scent; the immense proportion of the grazing land, in comparison with that which is ploughed, and the great size of the enclosures, many of which run from 60 to 100 acres each. Trueman, a black and white hound, which belonged to the Duke of Rutland, is "perhaps as perfect a hound as ever was littered, both as to shape and work." In one of the courts is a polished statuette of another called Tarquin. At *Sixhill* or *Segshill*, to north-east, the *Fosse Way*, high and paved, is plainly distinguishable. *Quenby*, W. Ashby, Esq., a large old Elizabethan seat. *Wistow Hall*, Sir H. Halford, Bart., was the seat of George the Fourth's favourite physician. Here Charles I. staid on his way to Naseby in 1645. *Stretton*, *i.e.*, Street Town, because of a Roman way or street, is the seat of the Rev. Sir G. Robinson, Bart.

LEICESTER & BURTON BRANCH.

KIRBY MUXLOE.

Telegraph station at Leicester, 5½ miles.

In the vicinity is *Bradgate Park*, in which are the remains of the mansion, where Lady Jane Grey was born in 1537. Here her old tutor, Roger Ascham paid her a visit, and found her reading Plato, while the family were hunting in Charnwood Forest, then a desolate moor. *Kirby Castle*, and *Braunston Hall*, C. Winstanley, Esq.

DESFORD.

Telegraph station at Leicester, 8 miles.

HOTELS.—Red Lion, and Roe Buck.

Near this, Bosworth Hall church, with its spire and tombs, is worth a visit; also the famous *Bosworth Field*, where Richard III. was defeated, August 22, 1485, by the Earl of Richmond,

"Here pitch our tents, even here in Bosworth Field."
RICHARD III., Act 5. sc. 3.

who succeeded as Henry VII., thus terminating the long and bloody contest between the rival houses of York and Lancaster. At *Richard's Well* is an inscription by Dr. Parr. There are other localities around commemorating the battle, but all actual traces have now disappeared. Johnson was usher at the Grammar School, at the town of Market Bosworth.

BAGWORTH station.

BARDON HILL.

Telegraph station at Leicester, 14½ miles.
Distance from station, 1 mile.
HOTEL.—Birch Tree.

Bardon Hill, a peak of the Charnwood Forest group, 853 ft. high, should be ascended, for the remarkable panorama it commands of the centre of England; where, being little elevated, the prospect from this point takes in a vast circle of 60 or 80 miles radius; and if the weather be favourable you may see the *Peak Hills*, the *Wrekin* in Shropshire, *Lincoln Cathedral*, *Malvern Hills*, the *Dunstable*, in Derbyshire, the *Sugar Loaf*, in Monmouthshire, &c. Some one has calculated that as much as one fourth of England is brought within this range of view. A monastery of St. Bernard was built near this in 1845.

Hard basalt (like lava) stone for edge tools; slate and coal are quarried in Charnwood Forest, now a wild, naked tract, belonging to the Marquis of Hastings.

COALVILLE.—Here is an immense coal district.

SWANNINGTON station.

ASHBY-DE-LA-ZOUCH.

Telegraph station at Burton, 9¾ miles.
HOTELS.—Royal; Queen's Head.
MARKET DAY.—Saturday.
FAIRS.—Easter and Whit-Tuesdays, September 4th, and November 8th.
BANKERS.—Leicestershire Banking Co.

ASHBY-DE-LA-ZOUCH, in Leicestershire, a thriving manufacturing town of 3,762 population, where stockings, hats, and fire bricks are made, and iron smelted, is situated in the middle of a coal field of 100 square miles. The coal is a shining hard sort. A bath-house has been built over some valuable springs which rise from the pits, and are very beneficial in cases of scrofula and similar complaints. Bishop Hall, one of the most famous divines of the English church, was born here in 1574, and brought up at the Grammar School, of which he became master. Formerly the town belonged to the Zouches, and was named after them—now it is the property of the Hastings family. Their castle here was built in 1480 in the Tudor style, by Sir William Hastings, who had the misfortune to be beheaded in the Tower by Richard III. As master of the mint to Edward IV. he was the first to coin nobles, worth 8s. 4d. each. This castle was one of the prisons of poor Mary, Queen of Scots; and being dismantled in the civil war, only the chapel, tower, &c., of the original pile remains. A front of later date has been added. In the old church, among the family tombs, is that of the excellent Countess of Huntingdon, one of Wesley's earliest and most steadfast adherents, from whom the present Marquis is descended.

Near Ashby is *Coleorton Hall*, seat of Sir G. Beaumont, Bart. *Willesley Park*, to the west, belongs to Sir C. Hastings, Bart.

MOIRA and GRESLEY stations.

Burton, see page 61.

LEICESTER AND PETERBOROUGH BRANCH.

SYSTON JUNCTION.

A telegraph station.
In the vicinity are *Wanlip Hall*, Sir G. Palmer, Bart.; *Barkley Hall*, W. Pochin, Esq.; *Rothley Temple*, seat of the Babingtons.

REARSBY station.

BROOKSBY.

Telegraph station at Syston, 4½ miles.
In the vicinity is *Brooksby Park*, the seat of the Dowager Lady Listowel, at which the Duke of Buckingham, James I.'s favourite, was born.

FRISBY and ASHFORDBY stations follow next in succession, in the vicinity of the latter of which is *Kirby Park*, formerly the seat of Sir Francis Burdett. Here he wrote his celebrated Reform Letter, which caused his committal to the Tower of London.

MELTON MOWBRAY.

A telegraph station. Population, 4,391
HOTEL.—George.
MARKET DAY.—Tuesday.
FAIRS.—Tuesday after Jan. 17th, Holy Thursday, Whit Tuesday, and August 21st.
MONEY ORDER OFFICE.

MELTON MOWBRAY is the centre of a famous hunting country. Horses are bred here; its pork pies and Stilton cheese are also valuable productions. All about this quarter is excellent pasture for superior breeds of stock, well known as Leicestershire, especially the old or short-horned cattle and the new Leicestershire sheep, a large long-woolled breed. The cheeses are flat, weighing 30 to 50lbs. each. *Mowbray Lodge*, seat of General Wyndham.

Saxby.—In the vicinity is *Stapleford Park*, the old seat of the Earl of Harborough.

WHISENDINE, the entrance to the county of Rutland, and ASHWELL stations.

OAKHAM.

A telegraph station.
HOTEL.—Crown.
MARKET DAY.—Saturday.
FAIRS.—March 15th, April 8th, May 6th, September 9th, November 19th, December 15th, Saturday after October 10th, and Saturday after Whitsuntide.

BANKERS.—Eaton, Cayley, and Co.; Branch of the Stamford, Spalding, and Boston Banking Company.

This little capital of the least of English shires (Rutland) contains an agricultural population of 2,800.

Besides the county courts, there is a well-endowed *Grammar School* and *Hospital* for 100 boys, founded by Archdeacon Johnson just after the Reformation, the income of which amounts to the handsome sum of £3,000. There are 40 university exhibitions attached to it, and on this account it is much sought after. The *Shire Hall* stands within the ruined walls of the old *Castle*, founded by the Ferrers family soon after the Conquest. Over the gate are several gilded *horse-shoes*, with the names of noblemen by whom they have been given, it being quite an immemorial custom to ask every peer who visits the town for one, or else to pay a fine. Three horse shoes figure in the arms of the Ferrers, and one from George IV. when Regent.

There are some large seats in the neighbourhood. *Burley House*, Earl of Winchelsea, is a large Grecian building, from which you may obtain a prospect of the whole county. The former seat (destroyed in the civil war) belonged to the Duke of Buckingham, or "Steenie," who here entertained his "dad and gossip," James I., with a masque got up by Ben Jonson, and afterwards received "babie Charles," on which occasion Geoffrey Hudson, the Oakham dwarf, was served up in a great pasty. The little fellow was then seven years old, and only 18 inches high; but he lived to be 3½ feet high, and to kill his man in a duel, on horseback, as Sir Walter Scott makes him relate with so much emphasis in "Peveril of the Peak." His opponent came out armed with a large squirt. The Finches of Burley divide the manor of Oakham with the Dean of Westminster; the two shares being called the Lord's and the Dean's. *Exton Park*, the Elizabethan seat of the Earl of Gainsborough, was once the property of David of Huntingdon (who succeeded to the Scottish throne), and Robert Bruce, till he forfeited it by asserting the independence of his country. There are many monuments, banners, and other memorials of the Noel and Harrington families. *Normanton*, seat of Sir G. Heathcote, Bart. *Belvoir Castle*, the Duke of Rutland's seat, described elsewhere.

MANTON station, for *Uppingham*, at which place there is one of Archdeacon Johnson's schools, and a church of which Jeremy Taylor was once rector.

LUFFENHAM station.

KETTON.

Telegraph station at Stamford, 3½ miles.

The Old Church here has a fine Norman r, 1t0 feet high. It was the custom in ancient times for the lord of the manor to hold it by the tenure of providing the Queen with boots.

STAMFORD (Lincolnshire).

Distance from station, ¼ mile.

A telegraph station.

HOTELS.—Stamford Arms, Crown.

MARKET DAYS.—Monday and Friday.

FAIRS.—Tuesday before Feb. 13th, Mondays before Mid Lent and May 12th, Mid Lent Monday, Monday after Corpus Christi, August 3rd and Nov. 8th.

RACES at Wittering in July.

BANKERS.—Eaton, Cayley and Co.: Northamptonshire Banking Co.; Stamford, Spalding, and Boston Banking Co.

STAMFORD is an ancient borough town, in the county of Lincoln, with a population of 8,933, who return two members. It is pleasantly situated on the banks of the Welland river, and bordering the counties of Rutland and Northampton. It is a town of great antiquity, being a place of considerable importance in the time of the Danes and the Saxons. The appearance of the town, when seen from a distance, is remarkably picturesque, many of the old buildings being grouped together with the towers and steeples of the neighbouring churches, the principal of which are *St. Mary's*, *St. Martin's*, *St. George's*, *All Saints'*, and *St. John's*. They are handsome edifices, and the latter one contains the ashes of Richard Cecil and his wife, the immediate progenitors of Lord Burleigh. There is also a splendid monument to the memory of William Cecil, Baron Burleigh, one to Daniel Lambert, the fat man, who was 9½ feet in girth, and several others, well worthy of attention. The charitable institutions in this town are both numerous and well endowed; there are also many handsome public edifices, among which we may mention the *Theatre*, *Assembly Rooms*, the *Town Hall*, &c. Here Hengist routed the Picts, and Alfred allowed the Danes to live. In the vicinity is *Burleigh House*, the Marquis of Exeter's.

Passing UFFINGTON, HELPSTONE, and WALTON stations, we arrive at the Crescent Station,

Peterborough, described at page 44.

LEICESTER AND HITCHIN BRANCH.

This line was opened on the 8th of May, 1857, taking a direct route from Leicester to Hitchin. The stations on the route are—WIGSTON, GLEN, KIBWORTH, MARKET HARBOROUGH, DESBOROUGH, RUSHTON.

KETTERING.

HOTELS.—The Royal; George.

A small old town in Northamptonshire, slightly elevated. It has a population of about 5,000, engaged principally in the working of wool. The commentator, Dr. Gill, was born here. Here is the chapel in which Andrew Fuller, a rough but clever

Baptist divine, officiated till his death, in 1815. He was walking with Jay, of Bath, one day, when an owl flew by. "Is that a Jay?" said Fuller. "What a naturalist you are, brother," said the other; "it can't be a jay. It is fuller in the head, fuller in the eye, fuller in the body, fuller all over." *Boughton House*, the seat of the Buccleuch family, about two miles away, contains a valuable collection of paintings. We then pass through ISHAM, FINEDON, WELLINGBOROUGH, IRCHESTER, SHARNBROOK, and OAKLEY, arriving at

Bedford, for description of which see Section III., page 8. Then the stations of CARDINGTON, SOUTHILL, SHEFFORD, and HENLOW; immediately after which the arrival of the train is announced at

Hitchin, the junction of the line with that of the Great Northern, particulars of which will be found on page 42.

Midland Main Line continued.

SYSTON Junction, see page 3.

SILEBY.

Telegraph station at Syston, 2¾ miles.
MONEY ORDER OFFICE at Loughborough, 4¾ miles.

In the vicinity is *Mount Sorrel*, a lovely spot; *Swithland Hall*, Lord Lanesborough; and *Rothley Temple*, J. Parker, Esq.

BARROW.—Here Bishop Beveridge was born. *Quorndon Hall*, Sir R. Sutton, Bart.; and *Quorndon House*, close at hand.

LOUGHBOROUGH.

A telegraph station.
HOTELS.—King's Head, Bull, and Archer.
MARKET DAY.—Thursday.
FAIRS.—March 28th, April 25th, August 12th, and November 13th.

This town, with a population of 10,900, is a seat of the lace and stocking trades. In 1557 it was depopulated by the sweating sickness. In the vicinity are *Prestwold Hall*, with its fine collection of pictures, seat of C. Packe, Esq., M P.; *Garendon Park*, C. Philips, Esq.; and *Walton House*, E. Dawson, Esq.

KEGWORTH.

POPULATION, 1,782.
Distance from station, 1 mile.
A telegraph station.

In the vicinity is *Donnington Park*, seat of the Marquis of Hastings, at which Moore passed his boyish days.

LONG EATON JUNC. (Derbyshire).

A telegraph station.
MONEY ORDER OFFICE at Nottingham, 5½ miles.

In the vicinity is *Thrumpton Hall*, the old Elizabethan seat of the Pigots, now belonging to Captain Byron.

NOTTINGHAM AND LINCOLN BRANCH.

BEESTON (Nottinghamshire).

Telegraph station at Nottingham, 3¼ miles.

In the vicinity are *Wollaton Hall*, Lord Middleton, a descendant of the celebrated Sir Hugh Willoughby.

NOTTINGHAM.

A telegraph station.

HOTELS.—George IV., Lion, Flying Horse, Black Boy, Maypole.

MARKET DAYS.—Wednesday and Saturday.

FAIRS.—March 7th and 8th, October 2nd, 3rd, and 4th, Thursday before Easter, and Friday after June 13th. RACES in July.

BANKERS.—Messrs. J. and J. C. Wright and Co.; Messrs. Smith and Co.; Messrs. Robinson and Moore; Messrs. Hart, Fellowes, and Co.

NOTTINGHAM, the Saxon *Snatinghaham*, and capital of the county of Notts, near the beautiful river Trent, well known to the angler, is situated on a rocky eminence of red sandstone, and is allowed by competent judges to be not only one of the healthiest, but one of the most picturesque inland towns in England. At a height of 300 feet above the level of the town towers Castle Hill, from which a noble prospect of the town, and a vast extent of country may be obtained. Up to a recent date Nottingham, though well built, paved, and so forth, has been excessively crowded, from the circumstance that the town limits were strained to the utmost, so that persons connected with its trade were obliged to resort to the neighbouring parishes, where populous villages have sprung up, as at Radford, Lenton, Basford, Carrington, Arnold, Sneinton, Carlton, &c., at the latter of which is to be found the largest quantity of the purest red clay in the world, so that a very extensive trade is carried on in the making of bricks, &c. The town is now rapidly increasing, and bids fair to rank amongst the first manufacturing towns in England, some warehouses of great architectural beauty having already made their appearance. Within the last six or seven years, a beautiful Arboretum has been opened, which, together with the delightful walks off the Mansfield Road, and others adjoining the Queen's Road, and that leading to the banks of the Trent, crossed by means of a ferry boat to the Clifton side (whose beautiful grove is frequented by all the admirers of nature) and the subject of Kirke White's muse, form pleasant sources of recreation and enjoyment. The total population of the borough is upwards of 75,000, but the industrial population in and around Nottingham, and dependent upon its trade, is nearly three times that number. Silk, cotton stockings, and bobbin-net lace are the staple manufactures. Until recently the stockings were usually worked upon frames, rented from the employers; but this, to a great extent, has been altered since the introduction of the round frames, which are now generally confined to factories. Hand and power machines are used for the net, which, succeeding Lindley's point net (used first in 1780), was invented by Heathcote in 1809. Arkwright set up here (before 1771) one of his earliest spinning machines; it was moved by horse-power. It was on the occasion of the distress among the frame-work knitters and twist hands here that Lord Byron delivered his two speeches in Parliament, in 1812 which are usually to be found in his works. This was just after the publication of his "English Bards and Scotch Reviewers." One of the wards of Nottingham is named Byron ward, and another Sherwood ward, that forest being only a few miles distant. In 1817 the frame-work knitters and twist hands broke out again, under the name of Luddites, and went about destroying machinery, &c. The Market Place is one of the finest in England, and stands on an area of upwards of five acres of land, well paved, &c., at one end of which stands the *Exchange*. Here will be found most of the principal shops in the town. The second floors of these houses hang over the pavement, supported by large pillars, and form an elegant piazza. The *Corn Exchange*, in Thurland Street, 77 feet long by 50 broad, has a glass roof, and was built in 1850. The *Mechanics' Institution*, in Milton Street, at the bottom of Mansfield Road, is a fine building of modern date. The *Assembly Rooms*, in the Low Pavement, the exterior of which lays claim to no great pretensions, as to its interior may be found worthy of notice. The *County Hall*, on a rock near the High Pavement, was built in 1770, by J. Gandon (the architect of the Custom House, and other first class buildings in Dublin): behind it is the *County Prison*. The *Town Hall*, in the Middle Pavement, where the sessions and assizes are held for the town. The town *House of Correction* is at the bottom of Lower Parliament Street, and stands on the site of an ancient Preceptory of the order of Knights Hospitallers.

St. Mary's church is an ancient building, on a rock, shaped like a cross, and having a pinnacled tower of later date. There is a chapel (formerly a chantry) in it to the memory of J. Plumtre, who in 1392, founded an hospital here, lately rebuilt. *St. Peter's* church has a crochetted spire, and is partly Norman. *Trinity* is modern Gothic, with a spire. Pugin's Romish *Cathedral* is also in the Gothic style, 180 feet long, with a tall spire. The painted windows were the gift of the late Earl of Shrewsbury. The *General Hospital* was founded in 1781. The *County Asylum* occupies a site of 8 acres. The new *Blind Asylum*, for the Midland counties, by Messrs. Aickin and Capes, is in the Elizabethan style. The *Forest Cemetery* is in the outskirts. The Lene is converted into an unhealthy marsh on the south side of the town, and after dividing into several branches, joins the Trent at the long straggling bridge or causeway of 19 arches, which replaces one made by Edward the elder, who first fortified Nottingham. The *Castle* was built by the Conqueror's nephew, William Peverell, to command the Trent, and after various events, dismantled by Cromwell, in common with other feudal places in England. A mansion, erected on the site, by the Duke of Newcastle, in 1680, was burnt down in the riots of 1831, on account of the part taken by the late Duke against the Reform Bill, for which he obtained £21,000 damages from the hundred. After Richard II.'s death, his worthless queen, Isabella, came here to live with her favourite, Roger Mortimer, where they were betrayed by Sir Wm. Eland, the Governor, to Edward III., who found an entrance from below by a secret passage from the rock, still called *Mortimer's Hole;* Mortimer was executed, and Isabella banished. In 1642, Charles I. occupied it, and first hoisted his flag against the parliament, on a hill in the Park, since called Standard Hill, close to the former cavalry barracks. But the royalist party only kept possession of it till the next year, when Colonel Hutchinson was appointed Governor of the Castle on behalf of parliament. Mrs. Hutchinson, in her delightful Memoirs, describes the Castle and the stirring events in which her husband took a leading part; among others of the temporary surprise of the town by the Newark cavaliers, through the treachery of Alderman Toplady, a great malignant, and how they were hindered from pursuing them, when driven out, by the obstinacy of an "old dull-headed Dutchman." On this occasion, the former church of *St. Nicholas*, was pulled down, because its steeple commanded the platform of the Castle. Colonel Hutchinson was born here in 1616, his father being obliged to remove from Owlthorpe to winter here just at that time; his mother was a Byron of Newstead. Another native was Henry Kirke White, born in 1785, a butcher's son. He was first brought up at Mr. Blanchard's School, and after a year's application at a stocking loom, was apprenticed to Messrs. Coldham and Enfield, solicitors here, and studied so hard that he was chosen Professor of Literature in the Literary Society, by acclamation, when only 15 years old. The hopes excited by his earliest poems (published three years after), were nipped by a sharp notice in a review, but they led to his acquaintance with Southey, the publication of his "Remains," and his posthumous celebrity. Southey says that Coleridge was present when he opened White's papers after his death, and both were astonished at the industry and ability they displayed. Besides papers on literature, science, poems, tragedies, and political articles, he had planned a history of Nottingham. "I have inspected (says the generous biographer) all the existing MSS. of Chatterton, and they excited less wonder than these." On *Mapperley Plain*, an elevated spot to the north, there is a prospect of Belvoir Castle and Lincoln Cathedral. Here it is intended to erect the Midland Observatory, founded in 1853, chiefly by the liberality of Mr. Lawson, of Bath, who gave instruments to the institution, together with £10,000. At Mr. Lowe's Observatory, *Highfield House*, a temperature of 6° below zero (38 below freezing point) was noted on the 3rd January, 1854, being lower than anything that had happened for 85 years past.

In the neighbourhood are caves in the Park and in the cliffs at Sneinton; those in the town are used as wine vaults, &c. *Colwick* (2 miles), was the seat of the late J. Musters, Esq., who married Miss Chaworth, Byron's first love when he was a young boy, and she two years older. He appears, however, never to have forgotten her. "Our union would have healed feuds in which blood had been shed by our fathers," alluding to the unfortunate duel in which his uncle, the former peer, killed a Mr. Chaworth in a drunken squabble, for which he was tried and acquitted. *Woolaton* (3 miles), among coal mines, is the seat of Lord Middleton, a remarkably handsome specimen of an Elizabethan mansion, built in 1508. Among the family portraits is Sir Hugh Willoughby, the navigator, who was frozen to death in the White Sea. At *Clifton* (3 miles), the ancient seat of Sir J. Clifton, Bart., and his family for many generations, are the Groves, described in K. White's longest poem; the old church and the churchyard were his favourite haunts. *Bunny Park*, Lord Rancliffe, belonged to Sir T. Parkyns, who was so fond of wrestling that, besides writing an erudite treatise on the "Cornish Hug," he left an annual bequest of a guinea for its encouragement. *Foremarks*, on the Derbyshire side, was the seat of that weak but amiable politican, Sir F. Burdett. His youngest daughter, Miss Burdett Coutts, so fruitful in good works, is the well known heiress of the late Duchess of St. Albans, *nee* Miss Mellon, the actress, the second wife of the *millionaire*, the late Mr. Coutts, the banker. *Tollerton* (4 miles), P. Barry, Esq. *Gotham* (8 miles), an old place famous for its wise men, rivals even to the men of Coggeshall, in Essex. The men of Gotham are, however, said to have been the first to find a mare's nest.

MANSFIELD BRANCH,

Nottingham to Mansfield, Via Erewash Valley.

The first two stations on this line are Toton and Sandiacre, in the vicinity of the latter of which are *Stapleford Hall; Bramcote*, I. Sherwin, Esq. Close at hand is the Druid Hemlock Stone, 50 feet high, on a bare knoll; and *Risley Hall*, Captain Hall.

Stanton Gate station.

ILKESTON.

Telegraph station at Long Eaton, 6¼ miles.

Market Day.—Thursday.

Fairs.—March 6th, Whit-Thursday, and Thursday after Christmas.

This place is celebrated for its mineral springs, and is much frequented. *Ilkeston Park*, seat of S. Potter, Esq., is in the immediate neighbourhood.

Shipley Gate, in the vicinity are *Shipley Hall, Nuthall Temple, High Park, Beauvale Abbey*, and *Lamb Close.*

LANGLEY MILL (Heanor).

Distance from station, 1 mile.

Telegraph station at Long Eaton, 9¾ miles.

In the vicinity is *Greasley*, the old seat of the Cantilupes, who founded Beauvale Priory, some parts of which are left standing; also *Eastwood Hall*, *Heanor*, *Brinsley*, and *Underwood*, all beautiful seats.

CODNOR PARK.

Distance from station, 2 miles.

Telegraph station at Belper, 5½ miles.

Money Order Office at Belper, 5½ miles.

On the hill are the ruins of the Zouches' and Greys' old seat.

Passing Pye Bridge, Pinxton and Sutton stations, we reach

Mansfield.—Described further on.

NOTTINGHAM AND MANSFIELD BRANCH.

Nottingham to Mansfield.

This is another but shorter route between Nottingham and Mansfield. The stations passed are Lenton, at which are the ruins of a Priory and old Court House; Radford, noted for its lace and stocking trade: Basford; Bulwell, in the vicinity of which is *Nuthall Temple*, seat of R. Holden, Esq.

HUCKNALL TORKARD.

At this place, a village of stockingers, is the church (having a low square tower) in which Byron is buried, with many of his ancestors. Among them are Admiral Byron, or "Foulweather Jack," who sailed round the world.

LINBY.

In the vicinity of this place is *Newstead Abbey*, formerly Byron's seat, to which he succeeded when only 10 years old, and was sold by him to Colonel Wildman. Mr. Rogers of Nottingham was his tutor before he entered the army. Part of the abbey church (founded in the 12th century) is the mansion, round which are grouped the great hall, cloisters, and other remains of the original Gothic pile. His favourite Newfoundland dog, Boatswain, is buried in a garden, under the well-known cynical epitaph. In clearing the lake on one occasion, a brass eagle was found, whose hollow breast contained the Abbey papers, sealed up; the eagle is now in Southwell church. *Annesley Park* was a seat of the Chaworths, from whom it came to the late J. Musters, Esq., of Colwick. The church contains some old monuments.

Kirkby and Sutton stations.

MANSFIELD.

Population, 10,012.

Hotel.—Swan.

Market Day.—Thursday.

Fairs.—First Thursday in April, July 10th, and Second Thursday in October.

Bankers.—Robinson and Co.; draw on Glyn and Co. Wylde and Co.; draw on Lubbock and Co. Branch of Nottingham and Notts Banking Co.; draw on London and Westminster Bank.

Mansfield is a market town in the county of Nottingham, agreeably situated on the banks of the river Man. It consists of two principal streets, with several smaller ones branching from them, which contain a great number of handsome buildings. The church (Gothic building), contains over each aisle a handsome gallery. The trade of the town consists principally of corn, malt, cotton goods, hosiery, lace, and also in the valuable stone which abounds in the neighbourhood. The circumstance related in the tale of the "Miller of Mansfield," occurred about the reign of Henry II. Near the Town Hall in the Market Place is a florid Gothic cross, to the memory of the late Lord G. Bentinck, the protectionist leader, and upright member of the turf. *Sherwood Forest*, of which this is the centre, extended from Nottingham to Worksop, and included all the parks and seats which lie between those places. Most of it is cleared, and some parts excavated for coal and iron; but picturesque tracts of woodland still bring back to mind the unsettled times when Robin Hood, Hugh Little John, and Friar Tuck hunted the king's venison, without license under the great seal. Whoever Robin Hood really was, whether a bold outlaw, or a patriotic descendant of the Saxon Earls of Huntingdon, as Stukeley affirms, none for the future will take him but as he is described in the pages of *Ivanhoe*, by the inimitable Scott.

Lincoln Branch continued.

Pursuing our course on the Lincoln branch, the train brings us to CARLTON, a small village; BURTON JOYCE, in the church at which are monuments to the Jaez family, to whom this place formerly belonged; LOWDHAM; THURGARTON, near to which is the *Priory*, R. Milward, Esq., founded by Ralph d'Ayncourt in 1130; and FISKERTON.

ROLLESTON, the junction of the Branch to

SOUTHWELL.

MARKET DAY.—Saturday.

Population, 3,516, is a place where a Christian church was founded as far back as 627, by Paulinus, archbishop of York, and has a large and ancient Collegiate Church or Minster, 306 feet long. The nave is Norman, with great massive pillars, and the rest is early English. The west towers, choir, beautiful screen, monuments of archbishop Sandys and other York primates, Schmidt's *old* organ, as well as the brass reading desk, with an eagle brought from Newstead lake, from which it was fished up, with the abbey papers hid inside, deserve notice. Over the belfry door is a very ancient piece of sculpture, supposed to refer to Christ. The chapter house, some parts of the archbishop's palace, and college, yet remain; the bounds of the Prebendage are marked by an old auclury, with an empty niche on the crown. One of the mineral springs in the neighbourhood gave the town its modern name; Bede calls it *Tisfulfingaceaster*—where the termination seems to point to the Roman state of *ad Pontem*, which was near. The *Saracen's Head*, here, is memorable in English history, as being the house where Charles I. surrendered himself in 1646 to his Scottish adherents, to be afterwards sold by them to Cromwell; his room is on the south side of the gate. It was then called the King's Arms. There are some remains of *Wolsey's Palace*, which Cromwell's troopers destroyed. A public walk is near *Norwood Hall*, the seat of Sir John Sutton, Bart. For Sherwood Forest, Newstead, &c., see Nottingham, page 5.

NEWARK.—The particulars of this town will be found on page 49.

Then passing COLLINGHAM, SWINDERBY, THORPE, and HYKEHAM stations, we arrive at

LINCOLN.

A telegraph station.

HOTEL.—Great Northern Railway Station. Saracen's.

MARKET DAY.—Friday.

FAIRS.—Friday in Easter Week, last whole week in April, Tuesday after April 11th, July 5th, October 6th, and November 28th.

RACES in September and February.

BANKERS.—Smith, Ellison and Co.; Lincoln and Lindsey Banking Co.

LINCOLN, a city and parliamentary borough, population 17,536 (two members), cathedral town, and the capital of Lincolnshire, on a hill near the Witham. Lincoln was the Roman *Lindum* or *Lindum Colonia*, from which the present name is derived. The great North Road, identical with the Roman Ermine Street, runs through it from south to north for a length of two miles, passing in the true Roman style straight over the hill, on which the noble cathedral stands. Part of it is still called Herman Street. Another Roman road came to Lincoln, the Fosseway, which gives name to the Fosse Dyke Canal, first cut in the reign of Henry I.

In High Street, "below hill," are the principal shops and inns, and the old Guildhall bow gate of Richard II.'s time, but the best houses are in the upper part of the town, "above hill," to which you ascend by a steep hill and a long flight of steps. Here, on the site of the Roman station, the cathedral, castle, and other buildings are placed.

The *Cathedral* or Minster is a splendid object, seen at 30, 40, and even in clear weather 50 miles round, rising over everything, as if to the clouds. It is a double cross, that is, it has two transepts, like Salisbury, and is 475 feet long internally. One transept is 220 feet, the other 170 feet; the great tower, 240 feet high; two west towers, 180 feet. Formerly, the latter had spires which made them 100 feet more. In one is the new bell, Great Tom, cast by Mears, in 1835, which is seven feet across, and weighs 12,000lbs. The church is mostly early English, having been built between 1186 and 1324. The west front, 175 feet broad, has a noble window and doorway, with various pinnacles and niched figures, besides a Galilean or porch. The timber roof is 80 feet from the pavement, and in one sense the highest pitched in the kingdom. Among the monuments are those to Bishop Cantelupe and Dean Welbourne, of Edward III.'s time, a chapel to the memory of Edward I.'s Queen, Eleanor, and another with the Burghersh tombs. There is an ancient *brass* of Lady Swinford, the mother of the Beauforts, by John of Gaunt. It contained a rich gold and silver shrine of great value, removed at the Reformation, by Henry VIII.'s vicegerent Cromwell, whose reforms were so ill received that the people rose in rebellion under Mackerel, or "Captain Cobler," Prior. The *Chapter House* is a ten-sided building, by bishop Hugh, 60 feet across, and 42 feet high to the vaulted roof, which rests on one pillar. Cloisters 116 feet long. The library contains a very early charter, such as the Norman kings were used to grant, to please their Saxon subjects. The Deanery and Vicars' College are of the 13th century. An old palace was ruined in the civil war; parts of the great hall are standing. The *Exchequer* gate is one of three or four old gates worth notice, especially the *Newport* (or north) gate, which is Roman, as well as the piece of wall adjoining, which corresponds with the *Mint Wall* near the castle. The Newport gate was erected 40 years after Christ, and is consequently upwards of 1,816 years old.

Opposite the cathedral is the castle, within the walls of which are contained the County Hall and the Prisons, built by Smirke at a cost of £40,000. Just within the gateway is a very beautiful Oriel window, recently removed from a house standing opposite to John of Gaunt's stables. This spot of eight acres still belongs to the Duchy of Lancaster, the possessions of which merged in the crown, on the accession of John of Gaunt's Son, as Henry IV. Parts of the Norman keep and walls of the castle which the Conqueror built here still remain. At that time Lincoln had upwards of 1,000 houses, of which 166 were pulled down to make room for the castle.

The *Guildhall* is very ancient; the *Corn Exchange*, a modern building; the *Asylum*, on the slope of Castle Hill, has a front of 260 feet, and a good prospect. The *County Asylum* is at Bracebridge, about a mile from the city, and is a most extensive establishment. An old Grey Friary of the 13th century, turned into a *Mechanics' Institute* and school, is timber roofed. The *Blue Coat School* is well endowed. The *Grammar School* was founded in 1567.

Lincoln at one time possessed so many churches and religious houses that it gave rise to a proverb, "He looks like the devil over Lincoln," because it was supposed to be the object of his peculiar envy. Many of those edifices may be still recognised by the remains of Gothic windows and doors. Of the 50 churches, 15 remain, mostly of little consequence. Those of *St. Benedict*, *St. Mary-le-Wigford*, and *St. Peter-at-Gowts*, (*gout*, a short cut for water), offer some Norman and early English work. *St. Paul's* in the Bail, is on the site of the first Christian church planted here. *St. Nicholas*, on the Brigg Road, is a handsome new church. On Steep Hill is an ancient carved house, which they say belonged to a Jew of Edward I.'s time, who was executed for clipping coin; about this period many of that persecuted race were hung (for their money) on the less tenable charge of having crucified a child. Their wealth and commercial habits contributed to make Lincoln one of the most prosperous towns in the kingdom. At a later period the Flemings introduced the manufacture of woollen and camlet stuffs, which went under the name of "Lincoln Green." It now brews good ale. An old proverb says—

> "Ankham (*i. e.*, Ancholme) eel, and *Witham Pike*,
> In all England is none like."

On the Horncastle Road is the Monk's House, on a good point of view.

In the neighbourhood of Lincoln are the following—*Canwick Hall*, the seat of Major G. T. W. Sibthorpe, M.P. for Lincoln; *Burton Park*, the seat of Lord Monson; *Branston Hall*, the seat of the Hon. A. L. Melville. *Blankney*, C. Chaplin, Esq. Near this is also Dunston Pillar, placed there in the last century to guide travellers over the waste which stretched around, now reclaimed, and made good turnip land at 20s. an acre. Bardney and Tupholme Abbey ruins are down the Witham. Within a short distance, on the Great Northern line, are also the picturesque ruins of Tattershall Castle. Bailing Priory, on the Wragby Road. Kirton-in-Lindsey, on the old Ermine Street road, has a large old early English church (kirk). This road runs along the top of the heath and warren hills just spoken of, which, north and south of Lincoln, formed, till cultivated, a useless and desolate tract, ten miles long; so much for guano, oil-cake, draining, and Lincolnshire enterprise. Lindsey, in the north division of the county, takes its name from *Lindum*.

Midland Main Line continued.

Long Eaton to Derby.

From LONG EATON we pass SAWLEY and DRAYCOTT stations, in the vicinity of which are *Draycott House*, and *Hopewell Hall*, T. Pares, Esq. Near to BORROWASH is *Elvaston Castle*, seat of the Earl of Harrington.

SPONDON.

Telegraph station at Derby, 2¾ miles.

In the vicinity are *Spondon Hall*, W. J, Cox, Esq.; *Chaddesden Hall*, Sir H. Wilmot, Bart.: and *Osmaston Hall*, Sir Robert Wilmot, Bart.

DERBY.

A telegraph station.

HOTEL.—The Midland, Family and Commercial. It is gratifying to be able to refer to an establishment like this, which deservedly enjoys the highest reputation. It possesses all the comforts of a home, and there is no lack of the spirit necessary to provide to the fullest extent every thing which can recommend it to its patrons. It is conducted in the most able manner by Mrs. Chatfield, and it may claim to rank amongst the first Hotels in England. If further commendation were needed, we may add that the utmost politeness and economy may be anticipated. It is also very convenient to travellers wishing to view this interesting portion of the country, for from it Elvaston Castle, the seat of Lord Harrington, Kedleston Park, the seat of Lord Scarsdale, and Alton Towers, with their beautiful grounds, may be visited. The latter claim especial notice, and will amply repay the time and trouble of visiting them.

MARKET DAYS.—Tuesday and Friday.

FAIRS.—Monday after January 6th, March 3rd and 21st, Easter Friday, Friday after May 1st, Whit-Friday, July 25th, Sept. 19th and 27th, and Oct. 4th.

BANKERS.—Derby and Derbyshire Bank; W. and S. Evans; Sam. Smith and Co.; Crompton and Co.

DERBY takes its name from Derwent-by, the town of the Derwent, the capital of *Derbyshire*, and a borough with a population of 40,609, represented by two members. There was a Roman station called *Derventio* not far off, at Little Chester. The Conqueror gave it, with nearly the whole county, to William Peveril, "Peveril of the Peak;" and in modern times it was the point at which Charles Stuart and his Highlanders, in their famous march towards London, despairing of help from the English Jacobites, turned back to the north. The neighbourhood is fertile and somewhat hilly. Derby is the chief depôt of the Midland Company, having, besides its splendid station 1,050 feet long, large engine and carriage sheds, workshops, &c., some nearly 200 feet in length. The Engine House is a 16-sided polygon, 134 feet across, with a conical roof. In the large Market Place on the south-side is the *Town Hall*, a handsome building, restored in 1842, with a rustic base, carvings in relief, and clock tower. One of the most conspicuous objects is the beautiful tower of *All Saints*, built in Henry VII.'s reign, in a rich florid Gothic style, with buttresses and pinnacles; the low square body is a miserable addition of Gibb's in the last century. Within are the Cavendish tombs and a fine screen. The Gothic spire of *St. Alkmund's*. New Church is 205 feet high; and the tower of *St. Mary's* Roman Catholic Church, by Pugin, deserves notice. *St. Peter's* is the oldest here. The new *Athenæum* and *Post Office* are in the Corn Market. An excellent *Infirmary* was founded in 1806. The *County Asylum*, by Duesbury, is in the Elizabethan style. A large *County Prison*. A Lecture Hall at the *Mechanics' Institute*, where an industrial exhibition was held, in 1839; and a well stocked *Museum*, open from ten to four, at the Philosophical Society, first established by Dr. Darwin.

Various manufactures are carried on here, the most flourishing being silk, stockings, ribbons, tape, cotton, and porcelain.

Derby was the place where the *first Silk Mill* in England was built in 1718, by Lombe; it is now occupied by Mr. Taylor. Both it and the Strutts' cotton mill, by the river side, are on a large scale. There are about twenty-five silk mills at present. At Handyside's foundry, castings of all kinds, vases, tripods, columns, &c., are seen, besides slotting and rolling mills. Hall's fluor spar, and black marble works, are open from eight to six. The porcelain factory; Holme's carriage factory, and Cox & Co.'s shot tower may be noticed.

Not far from the station is the new *Arboretum* of 16 acres, laid out in 1840, by Loudon, given to the town by Joseph Strutt, Esq.—a noble gift, estimated at £10,000. It contains two Elizabethan lodges and arbours, a great variety of shrubs and trees; and is open gratis on Wednesday and Saturday, other days 6d.

Wright, "of Derby," the painter, and Richardson, the novelist, were natives, 1734.

From the central situation of Derby, it is often selected by Tourists as their head quarters, whence they branch off in excursions to Chatsworth, Haddon Hall (to be seen every Friday), Hardwick, Dovedale, Matlock Baths, Alton Tower Garden; all very beautiful places.

In the neighbourhood are *Chaddes-den*, seat of Sir H. Wilmot, Bart.; *Kedlestone Hall*, the noble seat of Lord Scarsdale, with fine picture gallery, grounds, spa, &c. *Breadsall Priory*, where Dr. Darwin lived and died; *Markeaton Hall*, W. Mundy, Esq., and other seats.

DERBY, LITTLE EATON, AND RIPLEY.

Three quarters of a mile beyond the station at Derby the line passes under the Nottingham Road, and onward to the station at LITTLE EATON, from whence it diverges to the right, a distance of 6¼ miles, passing *en route* the stations of COXBENCH, KILBURN, and DENBER, to the small town of

RIPLEY, the inhabitants of which are mainly employed in the iron and coal mines around.

BIRMINGHAM & DERBY BRANCH.

Derby to Birmingham.

WILLINGTON AND REPTON.

Telegraph station at Burton, 4½ miles.

The village of Repton is one of the most ancient places in the county, and supposed to have been a Roman station.

MONEY ORDER OFFICE at Burton, 4½ miles.

BURTON—described Sec. II., page 61.

BARTON AND WALTON

(Barton-under-Needwood).

POPULATION of Barton, 1,561.

Telegraph station at Burton, 4 miles.

In the vicinity are *Wichnor Park*, J. Levett, Esq., and *Walton Hall*, Mrs. M. Gisborne.

CROXALL and HASELOUR stations.

TAMWORTH—See Section III., page 23.

In the vicinity of WILNECOTE is *Drayton Manor*, seat of the late and present Sir Robert Peel.

KINGSBURY.—This manor has been held by the Bracebridge family ever since 851.

WHITACRE JUNCTION.—In the vicinity is *Hams Hall*, seat of C. Adderley, Esq., M.P.

HAMPTON BRANCH.

COLESHILL.

POPULATION, 1,980.

Telegraph station at Whitacre Junction, 2 miles.

HOTEL.—The Swan.

MARKET DAY.—Wednesday.

FAIRS.—Shrove Monday, May 6th, Wednesday after New Michaelmas.

The church has a fine crocketted spire, and tombs of the Clintons and Digbys. *Coleshill Park*, the seat of Earl Digby, and *Coleshill House*, the seat of Captain A. Adderley, are close at hand.

Hampton station.

Birmingham and Derby continued.

FORGE MILLS, station.

The stations of WATER ORTON, CASTLE BROMWICH (*Bromwich Hall*, seat of the Earl of Bradford), and SALTLEY, are next passed, and we arrive at

Birmingham.—See Section III., page 19.

BRISTOL AND BIRMINGHAM BRANCH.

Birmingham to Bristol.

On our departure from Birmingham we pass the stations of CAMP HILL, MOSELEY, and KING'S NORTON, to

BARNT GREEN station, for *Studley* and *Alcester;* also the junction of a line 4¾ miles long, and running, *via* the station of ALVECHURCH,, to

REDDITCH, a place remarkable for its extensive needle manufactories. It has a population of 4,800. Fairs in August, 1st Monday; September, 3rd Monday.

BLACKWELL STATION.

BROMSGROVE

Distance from station, 1½ mile.

A telegraph station.

HOTELS.—Golden Cross, and Crown.

MARKET DAY.—Tuesday.

FAIRS.—June 24th and Oct. 10th.

This place has a population of 4,,426 chiefly nailers. The church, with its tall spire, and tombs of the Talbots, the Town Hall, and Grammar School should be visited. *Hewell Grange*, seat of the Hon. R. Clive, is close at hand.

STOKE WORKS.

Distance from station, 1 mile.

A telegraph station.

MONEY ORDER OFFICE at Bromsgrove, 2 miles.

The large chemical works here should be visited.

WADBOROUGH station.

DEFFORD.—The Abbey Church at *Pershore*, and *Croome Park*, the Earl of Coventry's fine seat, are well worth a visit.

ECKINGTON.—The *Malvern hills* are distant six miles. In the vicinity is *Strensham*, the birth-place of Butler.

BREDON. — Here are remains of a Roman camp on the hill, 800 feet high, which commands an extensive view.

ASHCHURCH station.

TEWKESBURY (Branch.)

POPULATION, 5,898.

A telegraph station.

HOTEL.—Swan.

MARKET DAYS.—Wednesday and Saturday.

FAIRS.—Second Monday in March, first Wednesday in April, May 14th, June 22nd, Sept. 4th, and Oct. 10th.

BANKERS. — Branch of Glo'ster Banking Co. Lechmere and Co. Cheltenham and Glo'ster Bank.

This place is famous for the great defeat by Edward IV., in 1417, at Bloody Meadow, of the Lancastrians under Queen Margaret. The heroic queen was taken prisoner by the Yorkists, and her son was killed. Its Abbey Church is Norman, and contains wall paintings and effigies of the De Spencers, Warwick, Abbot Alaunus (the friend of Thomas à Becket), Lord Clare, and Lady Clarke, by Flaxman, An arch of the cloister, with beautiful tracery, still remains. *Tewkesbury Park*, seat of Rev. J. Shapland, is famous for its salmon fishery. Here cloth and mustard were made in Shakspere's time, hence the proverb, "As thick as Tewkesbury mustard."

CLEEVE station.

CHELTENHAM and GLOUCESTER.—See Section II., pages 13 and 14.

HARESFIELD and STONEHOUSE stations.

FROCESTER.—In the vicinity is *Woodchester Park Nunnery*.

DURSLEY JUNCTION.

DURSLEY BRANCH.

CAM station.

DURSLEY,

A small town containing a population of 2,617, engaged principally in the manufacture of woollen cloths. The church is of the style of the later English, with arms of the Berkeley family, to whom the town originally belonged.

Birmingham and Bristol Line continued.

BERLELEY station, about 2½ miles to the right of which he town of

BERKELEY.

MARKET DAY.—Wednesday. FAIR.—May 14th.

This is a small country town in Gloucestershire, in the vale of Berkeley, a fat loamy tract, between the Cotswold Hills and the Severn, noted for its rich pasture and Double Gloucester cheese. Each cow yields on an average, nearly 1lb. per day. Dr. Jenner, the discoverer of vaccination, was born here. An early English church, with a detached tower, contains his tomb, that of Dicky Pearce, with Swift's epitaph, and those of the Berkeleys, who came here in Henry II.'s time, and are represented by Earl Fitzhardinge, of *Berkeley Castle*. This is an ancient moated pile, with a Norman gateway and keep. Here the unfortunate Edward II. was murdered in 1327, by a red-hot iron being driven through his body, at the instigation of his Queen Isabella, and her paramour, Mortimer.

> "Mark the year, and mark the night,
> When Severn shall re-echo with affright,
> The shrieks of death through Berkeley's roof shall ring;
> Shrieks of an agonizing king."—GRAY.

A pretended cast of his face, some very old family portraits, and the cabin furniture of Drake, the navigator, are seen in the apartments.

Tortworth Court, 5 miles south of Berkeley, was the seat of the late Earl Ducie, a great agriculturist, whose breeding stock was sold off in 1853, at extraordinary prices. One cow, called the Duchess, fetched as much as 800 guineas! Further south is *Thornbury Castle*, a fine Gothic ruin, begun by Stafford, Duke of Buckingham, but stopped by his execution in Henry VIII.'s time. On the other side of the railway, up the hills, are the picturesque clothing towns of Wotton-under-Edge and Dursley, the latter having been the first seat of the Berkeleys, and has some hot springs near the churchyard. The former has a good church (with some of their monuments), and a chapel and house, built by Rowland Hill, whose favourite retreat it was, and in which his wife is buried.

CHARFIELD.—In the vicinity is *Tortworth Court*, seat of Earl Ducie.

YATE.—In the vicinity are *Doddington Park*, C. Codrington, Esq.; *Little Sodbury House*, W. Hartley, Esq.; and *Chipping Sodbury*, celebrated for its large cheese market.

MANGOTSFIELD station.

Bristol.—See Section II., page 19.

Midland Main Line continued.

Derby to Ambergate.

The next station after leaving Derby is DUFFIELD. In the neighbourhood is *Milford House*, seat of G. H. Strutt, Esq.

BELPER.

Distance from station, 1 mile.
A telegraph station.
HOTEL.—Lion.
MARKET DAY.—Saturday.
FAIRS.—May 12th and October 31st.
BANKERS.— Derby Banking Co.

BELPER, 7 miles up the Derwent, is a thriving town, containing Strutt's cotton mills, nail factories, potteries, &c.; visited by Her Majesty in 1832.

AMBERGATE.

A telegraph station.
MONEY ORDER OFFICE at Belper, 3¼ miles.

MATLOCK BRANCH.

Ambergate to Rowsley.

This portion of the line, from Ambergate to Rowsley, goes through one of the most enchanting districts in the world, unsurpassable in boldness, grandeur, and magnificence of character.

On starting from Ambergate there is nothing particularly worthy of notice, if we except the noble woods of Alderwasley, in which is situated the beautiful seat of F. Hurt, Esq. On approaching Whatstandwell Bridge, the rails, canal, turnpike-road, and river being all in juxtaposition, is certainly rather extraordinary, and a circumstance seldom or never occurring.

WHATSTANDWELL BRIDGE.

Telegraph station at Ambergate, 2¼ miles.
MONEY ORDER OFFICE at Matlock Baths, 3¾ miles.

With the appearance of a dwelling-house planted on the top of a masoned tunnel, the great and increased beauty of the scenery may be said to commence. The valley narrows, and as you pass over the chaste metal bridge which crosses the Derwent, and approach the south entrance to the Lea Wood tunnel, the view around and in front is exquisitely grand. Nearly on the top of the hill you see nestled the picturesque spot of Lea Hurst, the residence of Miss Florence Nightingale. A metal aqueduct for the canal here crosses the rail. On emerging from the Lea Wood tunnel, at the north end, the country appears to open out a little more, and you pass Lea Valley and manufactories to the right, and the highly cultivated rich pastures (belonging to P. Arkwright, Esq.) to the left. There, also, is the terminus of the High Peak Railway, an object of great curiosity, from its numerous inclined planes, and the manner in which it is worked by stationary engines and endless chains.

Further on, as you approach Willersley Tunnel, you see Willersley Castle, Rock House, Cromford Church, and the Heights of Abraham. Willersley Tunnel is long and dreary, but you emerge from it to the Matlock Bath station, where a majestic amphitheatre of scenery opens to the view. To the left, on the opposite side of the river, is the celebrated Matlock Bath.

You next pass through the High Tor Tunnel, dry and comfortable, and the gloom is dissipated by an opening in the centre, wherein you enjoy the daylight for a second or two, and a pretty view of the road and river. On emerging from the High Tor Tunnel, another picturesque amphitheatre strikes the eye. The river, new bridge, neighbouring woods and rocks, the residence of John Greaves, Esq., and Boat House Inn, all tend to render this, perhaps, as interesting a scene as any of the foregoing.

The High Tor is one of the most remarkable rocks in England, in consequence of the immense mass of bare perpendicular rock exhibited at such an altitude. The limestones of the Jura, in Southern Germany, do not show so bold a face. The granite of the Alps have perpendicular faces or chasms to the depth of 2,000 feet, but then no living being has ever been able to descend and look up to their gigantic forms; on the contrary, in Derbyshire, you can walk in amongst these masses, admire, and somewhat estimate their proportions. In Wales, Scotland, and on the Alps, the scale of altitude and breadth is vast and profound, requiring time to consider and estimate their vast proportions; but in Derbyshire the exquisitely beautiful prevails. The lofty rocks and bold crags, richly wooded; the magnificent uplands and rounded knolls; the sweet vallies, intersected with silver streams, such as the Derwent, the Wye, and the Dove, are comprised in one beautiful picture; whilst the attractions of either of these rivers, the lovers of the rod and line can well attest. They are, perhaps, the best for trout and grayling in the kingdom.

CROMFORD.

POPULATION, 1190.
Distance from station, 1 mile.
Telegraph station at Matlock Baths, 1 mile.
HOTEL.—Greyhound.

Money Order Office at Matlock, 1 mile.

Here Arkwright set up his first mill in 1771. In the vicinity is *Willersley Castle*, the Arkwrights' seat.

MATLOCK BATHS.

A telegraph station.

Hotels.—Greave's Old Bath Hotel.—First-class accommodation for families and gentlemen.

The New Bath Hotel—first-class for families and gentlemen.

Walker's Hotel and Boarding House.

The Devonshire Hotel.

Market Day.—Saturday.

Matlock Baths.—Unquestionably the sweetest and most charming of the Derbyshire spas (with a population of 4,010). It is at the bottom of Matlock Dale, a narrow defile, the rocky limestone sides of which are piled up in the manner of the Undercliff, in the Isle of Wight, but covered with a profusion of pine, fir, yew, box, and other hardy trees. The scenes through Matlock Bath are exquisitely beautiful, and may be compared to a Switzerland in a nut shell. The High Tor, the Hag Tor, the Cat Tor, on the left, with Stonnis or the Black Rocks in the distance, form a semi-amphitheatre of most imposing objects, while on the right is Masson Low, or the Heights of Abraham (from the likeness it bears to the scene of Wolfe's Victory at Quebec), 1,600 feet above the river—with the tower on the lower height—and the range of hills which slope upwards from the valley, present a most perfect and enchanting *coup d'œil.* Many of the lodging houses are perched on these slopes, looking down on the river and the rail, which run close to the road beneath. These Tors and hills shelter the valley in winter, and in summer offer the most tempting and invigorating walks on their summits. The waters at the old and new Bath Hotels are warm (only 68°) and slightly tonic, and delightful to bathe in during the hot weather. Being charged with limestone-tufa the springs soon cover anything placed in them with a crust, or convert it into a stony substance.

Baths.—The prices are, tepid swimming or shower bath, 1s.; hot bath, 2s. 6d. The waters are recommended in nervous disorders, and the first stage of consumption. As they contain much free carbonic acid, they may be drunk as a common beverage. Their sources are 2,000 or 3,000 feet down.

Objects worth Seeing.—Walker's and other geological museums, the petrifying wells, the Cumberland, Rutland, and Devonshire caves, the "romantic rocks," &c., &c., the guides to which are exceedingly civil, unassuming, and reasonable.

There are numerous fine views in and about Matlock, but the most beautiful of all, and the crown and glory of all the magnificent scenery in Derbyshire, is the view from Stonnis. We stand on a large upheaved mass of sandstone rock having a perpendicular descent of 50 feet, beneath runs the Cromford and High Peak Railway, one of the oldest in the kingdom; from this point, such a prospect lies before us as can never properly be described; on the right are the hills of Crich, the woods of Lea and Holloway, the valley of the Derwent, threaded by rail, canal, road, and river, the sides of Riber sweeping over against Matlock. *Willersley Castle*, the seat of the Arkwrights, and Matlock Baths, with its white houses, craggy steeps, masses of intermingled rock and foliage, its spired church, and sparkling river, with Masson raising its proud head above them all. It is from Stonnis, and Stonnis alone, that Masson can be seen. while a little to the left beyond stands the High Tor, with its Titanic front. Still further beyond are the purple moors of Tansley, standing in relief, completing a picture of such beauty and grandeur as cannot be surpassed in England. The following are the principal Drives and Walks, with the prices of conveyance. Drives: 1. The Black Rocks, round by Middleton and via Gellia s. 2. Wingfield Manor, and return by Old Matlock, 13s. 3. Router Rocks, Druidical remains, and Rocking Stone, 16s. 6d. 4. Haddon Hall, 13s.; Haddon Hall and Chatsworth, 21s.; Dove-Dale, 23s.; ditto pair of horses, 30s.; Lea Hurst, 6s. 6d. These charges include the driver. Walks: Willersley Grounds, Monday and Thursday. Lovers' walk, every day; Ferry, 3d. Heights of Abraham, entrance, 6d. Walker's boat for a sail or row, 6d. each passenger.

Darley—At Darley is a very old church (Norman) and yew coeval with it. Paper and cotton factories, the river being here turned to good account as a motive power.

ROWSLEY.

A telegraph station.

Hotel.—Peacock.

Omnibuses to and from Bakewell and Chatsworth, to meet all trains. Fare, 6d.

Money Order Office at Bakewell, 3 miles.

Greaves' Posting Establishment; Post Horses in readiness on arrival of every train.

Haddon Hall.—A romantic old hall, of the Elizabethan period, once the residence of Sir George Vernon, the "King of the Peak," but now uninhabited. The fine old state bed; tapestry or Arras; pictures; carvings in wood; the Eagle tower gate; great Hall (the Martindale Hall, described in "Peveril of the Peak"); chapel; long gallery; kitchen gardens; Dorothy Vernon's walk, terraces, &c., remain all kept in good condition.

BAKEWELL.

Hotel.—Greaves' Rutland Arms.

Here are a fine old Church, where the Vernons and Rutland family are buried; an old cross, and excellent trout fishing in the Wye, which runs up through Monsal Dale; baths, chalybeate springs, marble works, &c.

From Bakewell the road ascends to Buxton, through one of the most stupendous valleys in Derbyshire, which contains a succession of some of the most remarkable Tors and wild picturesque views imaginable. It is, in fact, a magnificent ride, sublimely grand at all seasons.

BUXTON.

A telegraph station.

HOTELS.—St. Ann's.

Old Hall; Wood's Eagle; Shakspeare; Grove.

BUXTON is situated in the midst of one of the most picturesque parts of Derbyshire. The crescent is the principal building at Buxton. It was erected by the late Duke of Devonshire, and has three stories, the lowest of which forms a colonnade. The crescent, extending 257 feet, is chiefly occupied by the St. Ann's Hotel and family boarding-houses, in one of which is the public ball-room. Immediately opposite the hotel, and at the western angle of the hill, is St. Ann's Well. The spring has been in use for centuries. The water is clear and tasteless, and possesses a stimulating property. There is a public bath for each sex, and two private plunge baths for gentlemen. and two for ladies. The temperature of the water at the spring is 82 degrees Fahrenheit. The slight sensation of chilliness experienced on first entering the bath is soon succeeded by an agreeable feeling of warmth, and on coming out, most persons find themselves refreshed and invigorated. Chronic gout and rheumatism are the principal disorders for which the course is usually taken. The bracing nature of the climate is, however, not the least efficacious of the remedial agents. The church, situated not far from the crescent, is neat and commodious. Opposite are the large stables of the Duke of Devonshire, built at a cost of £120,000. About a mile from Buxton is the cavern called *Pool's Hole*, a magnet sufficiently potent of itself to attract crowds of tourists. The various singular forms in the cave have each their peculiar names; large stalactites are everywhere hanging from the roof, and the water is continually rushing past beside the feet of the spectators. Queen Mary's pillar, so called from a visit that unfortunate queen made to the cavern during her sojourn at Buxton, is a lofty column formed by nature to support the roof, and is scratched with names innumerable. On account of the rapid transitions of temperature, and the bleakness of position, Buxton is more frequented during the summer months than at later periods of the year. Two miles from Buxton is the *Diamond Hill*, where the Buxton diamonds are found, and close by is a tower built by the Duke of Devonshire. There are various places in the vicinity that deserve a visit, such as *Chee Tor*, a huge mass of limestone rising above 300 feet perpendicular; *Miller's Dale; Cressbrook; Monsal Dale; Ashford*; *Axe Edge;* from which, in clear weather, the mountains of North Wales may be seen; and the *Ebbing Well;* situated five miles from Buxton, on the Castleton Road. Buxton is 160 miles from London, 10 from Macclesfield, 12 from Leek, 16 from Congleton, and 23 from Manchester.

CHATSWORTH.

Chatsworth, ten miles from Matlock or Chesterfield stations, near the *Peak of Derbyshire*, on the crystal Wye. Omnibuses from the Rowsley station (6d.) meet the train. This splendid seat of the Duke of Devonshire (who has the lease of the mines here from the crown), is called the Palace of the Peak, and may be seen daily from 11 to 5. Parties are let in by turns. Apply early if you want to save time.

A belt of moorland cliffs, richly wooded with pines, chesnut, beech, limes, sycamore, and other trees, and about 11 miles in circuit, surrounds the park and grounds, which are stocked with 2,000 head of deer. The best view of the house is from a point near the bridge, and Queen Mary's Bower, where the old hunting tower is seen on the hills behind. A seat was begun by the founder of the family, Sir W. Cavendish (who was gentleman-usher to Wolsey, and wrote his life), about 1570, when he had the custody of Mary of Scotland here; and finished by his widow, a rich and clever woman, who married the Earl of Shrewsbury, her fourth husband. This was rebuilt in 1688-1706 by the first Duke, from designs by Wren, and now forms the principal building—a noble Grecian, or Italianised-Grecian pile, about 180 feet square, much in the style of the Governor's house at Greenwich Hospital (another of Wren's works), with a rustic base, Ionic columns, pilasters, frieze, and balustrade, ornamented by urns and statues. To the north is Wyatville's new wing in the Grecian style, built of the variegated stone from Beely quarry. The terraces in front are 1,200 feet long. The Sub Hall at entering contains busts, &c., and leads through a corridor (closed with velvet hangings) to the Great Hall, with its marble floor. Here are paintings by Verrio and Laguerre (French artists, whose works figure at Hampton Court and elsewhere), a Turkish caique, a marble slab, 11 feet long, and an inscription stating that "These paternal halls were begun *anno libertatis Anglicæ* (year of the great Revolution, which the first Duke helped materially to bring about) and finished *anno mœreus* 1840" (when the Duke's niece died). The *State Rooms*, 190 feet long, are full of cabinets, paintings, tapestries, &c., with alabaster doors, carved wainscot, mosaic oak floor. Some of the best of G. Gibbon's wood carvings are seen here, especially a pen and a net of game in he Ante-Room. Vansomers's portrait of the first Duke is in the Dining Room. The South galleries contain above 1,000 original drawings, by foreign masters, and cabinet pictures. Granet's Monks at Prayer, is on the west stairs. In the Billiard Room—Landseer's well-known "Bolton Abbey in the Olden Time," and Eastlake's Spartan Isadas. The Chapel is ornamented with paintings, Cibber's Faith and Hope, in alabaster, &c.; the Communion table is a beautiful piece of malachite, from Russia. Music Room—Rembrandt's "Jewish Rabbi," Giardano's "Neptune" and Murillo's "Belisarius." Grand Drawing Room, 45 feet long—portraits of Mary, Queen of Scots, HenryVIII., Charles I., Philip II. (by Titian); marble tables, Bartolini's Venus de Medicis, &c. North Staircase—portraits of George IV. by Lawrence, and the late Emperor Nicholas (who was here when archduke; in 1816, the duke was sent ambassador to him n his accession to the throne in 1826). Library, 90 feet long—carved mahogany doors and bookcases, marble mantel-piece. In the Dining Room are family portraits, marble slabs and chimney pieces. The *Sculpture Gallery* is extremely rich in original works, as well as casts, busts, marble tables, &c. Among others are Napoleon's Mother—Madame Mère, as she was called—by Canova; Canova's large bust of Napoleon; Pozzi's Latina and her Children. Schadon's Filatrice or Spinning Girl; Hebe, by

Dove Holes.

Dove Dale.

Matlock Bath.

Haddon Hall.

Chatsworth.

Canova; Petrarch's Laura, by the same; bronze copy of his Kneeling Magdalene; Gibson's "Man Cupid" (his first work from Rome), and "Hero and Leander;" Finelli's "Cupid and the Butterfly" (*i. e.*, Psyche, or the soul); Chantrey's bust of Canning; Canteen's granite vase, 20 feet round, &c. In the Orangery, further on, 108 feet long, are Thorwaldsen's "Priam and Achilles," and trees which belonged to the Empress Josephine. In one room is a very large enamel of Lady Southampton, 10 inches by 6, by Pettet. Over the Ball Room is a temple with a fine view of the park. All these rooms form a suite nearly 560 feet long, when the doors are thrown open.

Descending to the Green House, you pass two figures of Isis and Osiris, brought from the Great Temple at Carnac, by Mr. Bankes. The Water Works (by Grillet) are in the style of those at Versailles; one is shaped like a coffee tree; another throws a jet of 90 feet; and the great one, a jet of 200 feet. The *Grand Conservatory* is the chief ornament here; it is 300 feet long and 65 feet high, of metal and glass, from the designs of Sir Joseph Paxton, M.P., the late Duke's celebrated gardener. His success here led him to offer a similar plan for the Great Exhibition, which being accepted, has been still further carried out in the Crystal Palace, and the Dublin and New York Exhibitions. A carriage drive and a railway run round it. Besides palms and other tropical plants, there is the large Victoria Regia, an immense piece of Blue John, or fluor spar, and Queen Victoria's Oak, planted by Her Majesty when on a visit, in 1852. Also, Chesnuts, planted by the late Emperor of Russia, and the Duke of Kent. Marshal Tallard was on parole, Hobbs lived, and Christian VII. visited here in 1768.

Edensor Church is an old building, and has a fine monument of the first Earl of Devonshire. The cottages are in the Tudor, Swiss and other styles.

Within a few miles are—*Ashford Hall*, seat of Hon. — Cavendish, M. P., where black and grey marble are quarried. Eyam, its lead mines, and a rock called Cucklett Church, where its ancient rector, Mompesson, preached during the plague of 1666.

Midland Main Line continued.

Ambergate to Masborough and Sheffield.

WINGFIELD (Alfreton.)

Distance from station, 1½ mile.
A telegraph station.
HOTEL.—George.
MARKET DAYS.—Monday and Friday.
FAIRS.—Oct. 8th, Nov. 29th.

Here is the old *Manor House*, built by Lord Cromwell, in which the Queen of Scots was confined. In the vicinity are Crich Stand, Alfreton Hall, and Butterley Iron Works.

STRETTON.—In the vicinity is *Ogston Hall*, seat of G. Turbut, Esq.

CLAYCROSS. — *Tupton Hall* (where the great engineer, George Stephenson, died), *Tupton Grove; Castle Hill*, *Wingerworth Hall*, and *Hasland House* are close at hand. Clay Cross tunnel, near Chesterfield, is about 1,738 yards long, and the Milford tunnel, near Belper, is half a mile long.

CHESTERFIELD.

POPULATION, 7,101.
A telegraph station.
HOTELS.—Angel, and Commercial.
MARKET DAY.—Saturday.
FAIRS.—Jan. 27th, Feb. 28th, 1st Saturday in April, May 4th, July 4th, Sept. 25th, and Nov. 25th.
RACES in April and September.

BANKERS.—Chesterfield and North Derby Banking Co. Crompton, and Co.; Robinson and Co.

CHESTERFIELD has greatly increased with the prosperity of the coal mines round it, and the improvement in its various manufactures. Here battles were fought in 1261 and 1643. The handsome early Gothic Church is surmounted by a spire 230 feet high. To the south-east of it (6 miles) is *Hardwick Hall*, a noble Elizabethan seat, belonging to the Duke of Devonshire, finished in 1584, by the famous Countess Elizabeth. The picture gallery (full of historical portraits) is a magnificent apartment, lit by vast bay windows; and one room contains the bed worked by Queen Mary of Scotland, who was kept prisoner here.

STAVELEY station.

ECKINGTON.—In the vicinity are *Renishaw Park* and *Barlborough Hall*. Then passing WOODHOUSE MILL station we reach

MASBOROUGH.

A telegraph station.
HOTEL.—Crown.

SHEFFIELD & ROTHERHAM BRANCH.

ROTHERHAM.

POPULATION, 6,325.
Telegraph station at Masbro'
HOTEL.—Crown.
MARKET DAY.—Monday.
FAIRS.—Every other Monday, Whit-Monday, and 1st December.

BANKERS.—Sheffield Banking Co.

Here is a large old church, and the *Independent's College*. Sandstone is quarried here for the cutlers.

In the vicinity are *Aldwark Hall*, *Thrybergh Hall*, and *Ravenfield*.

The HOLMES and BRIGHTSIDE stations.

Sheffield.—See page 53.

DONCASTER BRANCH.

Sheffield to Doncaster.

This line forms the direct route to Doncaster. Retracing our steps by the Sheffield and Rotherham Branch, and passing MASBOROUGH station. The next in our course is

RAWMARSH.

Near to this station is Earl Fitzwilliam's seat, *Wentworth House*, a noble pile, 600 feet long. Among other pictures is contained Vandyke's Lord Strafford, one of his most striking portraits—the famous but ill-requited statesman, of Charles I.'s time. In the ground stands the *Rockingham Mausoleum*, 90 feet high, with busts of Burke, Fox, and other leading Whigs of the last century. Coal is abundant all around here; and is sent by rail to London, &c.

KILNHURST station.

SWINTON.

POPULATION, 1,817.

Distance from station, ½ mile.

Telegraph station at Masborough, 5 miles.

HOTEL.—Railway.

Here is a large earthenware factory, and old church, with a Norman porch.

MEXBOROUGH JUNCTION.

CONISBOROUGH.—Here is a castle belonging to the Duke of Leeds, built at the time of the Conquest, with a keep 78 feet high, in a good state of preservation.

SPROTBOROUGH.—In the vicinity is the *Hall*, seat of Sir J. Copley, Bart., built in the 17th century, and *Cusworth Park*, a beautiful place, is near at hand.

Doncaster.—See page 50.

SOUTH YORKSHIRE.

Sheffield to Doncaster and Keadby.

This line forms a communication from Sheffield with Barnsley, Doncaster, and Keadby. The first three miles of this is also over the Sheffield and Rotherham line, turning to the left at a place called Blackburn, we pass the stations of GRANGE LANE, CHAPELTOWN, WESTWOOD, BIRDWELL, DOVECLIFFE, and WOMBWELL, none of which need occupy much of the tourist's attention. At this point, a short branch runs in a westerly direction through ARDSLEY to

BARNSLEY, of which particulars will be found on page 52. There is also another branch from the same point running nearly parallel with that to Barnsley, through WORSBRO', uniting the South Yorkshire with the Barnsley and Penistone branch at Silkstone.

Proceeding from Barnsley we pass the unimportant stations of WOMBWELL, WATH, MEXBOROUGH, and CONISBOROUGH, and arrive at

Doncaster.—See page 50.

From Doncaster, we proceed through the stations of BARNBY DUN, BRAMWITH, and STAINFORTH, at the latter of which is a canal excavated in 1793, fifteen miles in length, and having only two locks. The line then goes on to

THORNE.

Telegraph station at Doncaster, 11 miles.

HOTEL—White Hart.

MARKET DAY.—Wednesday.

FAIRS.—Monday and Tuesday after June 11 and October 11.

This place contains a population of 3,507 engaged in the rope making, barge building, and carrying trades. The church of St. Nicholas is later English, at which De la Prime, the antiquary, was curate.

MAUD, MEDGE HALL, GODNOW BRIDGES, and CROWLE stations.

Keadby, a small town on the river Trent.

Midland Main Line Continued.

Swinton to Leeds.

The next three stations, WATH, DARFIELD, and CUDWORTH, have no particular interest.

ROYSTON AND NOTTON.—In the vicinity are *Chevet Hall*, Lady Pilkington; and *Walton Park*, with its menagerie and collection, the seat of C. Waterton, Esq., the South American traveller.

OAKENSHAW.—In the vicinity is *Heath Hall*, seat of J. Smythe, Esq.

NORMANTON.

A telegraph station.

HOTELS.—Normanton Station, Commercial.

MONEY ORDER OFFICE at Wakefield, 3 miles.

This is a station of growing importance, as being the junction of three extensive railway companies—the Midland, Lancashire and Yorkshire, and North Eastern. Many of the trains change carriages here.

METHLEY.—Here is an ancient church, with the Savile's tombs. In the vicinity are *Kippax Hall*, seat of T. Bland, Esq., a noble range, partly Elizabethan; *Ledstone Hall*, H. Ramsden, Esq.; and *Methley Park*, Lord Mexborough's.

WOODLESFORD.—In the vicinity are *Templenewsam House*, seat of the Marquis of Hertford, with fine collections of paintings and gems of *vertu*. Here Darnley, Mary Queen of Scots' husband, was born. *Swillington House*, Sir S. Lowther, Bart. Population, 1,771.

HUNSLET station.

LEEDS.

Telegraph station at Park Row and Railway Station, and 6, Bond Street.

HOTELS.—Scarborough, F. B. Fleischmann; White Horse, C. Wilks.

MARKET DAYS.—Tuesday and Saturday.

FAIRS.—July 10th and 11th, November 8th and 9th, and quarterly for leather.

BANKERS.—Becket and Co. W. W. Brown and Co. Branch Bank of England. Leeds Banking Co. Yorkshire Banking Co.

LEEDS.—This great seat of the cloth trade, and actual capital of *Yorkshire*, a parliamentary borough in the West Riding, with a population of 172,270, returning two members, stands on a hill-side by the river Aire. The parish, about six or seven miles square, with its 18 or 20 townships, was formerly a moorland tract of little value, like the rest of Yorkshire, till the discovery of coal and iron enriched it by giving such a wonderful stimulus to the progress of manufactures. Several large factories and partnership mills are established in the borough, (so distinguished from the town, where there are but few); however, most of the cloth is made at home, by the hand-loom weavers, a respectable and industrious class, who carry on the business of dairy farming in addition to the loom. There may be 16,000 looms thus employed in the neighbourhood, of which only one-third are in the borough. Leeds is at the extremity of the great Yorkshire manufacturing district, which ends here so suddenly that few looms are found in the north half of the borough, which is purely agricultural. The wool having been prepared by the various processes of scouring, carding, and so forth, is handed over to the weaver, who works it on his loom, and then brings it in a rough state to the market to be sold to the finisher, in the form of mixed (or coloured) cloth, and white (or undyed) cloth. Saturday is the day for sale, which lasts under strict regulations one hour only, in which short space business to a vast extent is done with expedition and quietness. The *Mixed Cloth Hall*, in Wellington Street, is a quadrangular pile, 380 feet long, by 200 broad, and contains 1,780 freehold stalls, arranged in six streets. Before this hall was built, in 1758, cloth was sold in Briggate Street, and in the 17th century it was even exposed on the parapet of the old bridge (built, 1376). The *White Cloth Hall*, in Calls, built in 1775, is a similar structure, 300 feet long, with five streets, and about 1,200 stands.

Though stone is abundant, yet most of the houses are brick-built, the best of the kind being the Red House, which Charles I. had made his head quarters, when Fairfax, the parliamentary general, captured the town, in 1643. Leeds was then of so much importance that it returned members to the long parliament, a privilege which it was again deprived of till the Reform Bill. The modern public buildings are of stone. On Mill Hill, where the Lacys (who, after the Conquest, held a wide manor in Yorkshire) built their feudal castle, are the *Commercial Buildings*, including an Exchange and News Room, in the Grecian style, built in 1829. In front of the *Court House*, built in 1813, to replace the ancient *Moot Hall*, is Behnes's statue of Peel, placed there in 1852, and standing 8½ feet high, on a pedestal of 20 feet. A marble statue of Queen Anne in the *Corn Exchange;* it formerly stood in the *Moot Hall*, at the head of Briggate. A splendid Corinthian building, to include *Assize Courts* and *Public Hall* (to hold 8,000 persons) was commenced in 1853, by C. Brodrick, on a base of 250 feet by 200, which will be approached by a flight of steps, and have a lofty spire, pedestals for statues, a portico of 10 columns, besides others round the sides, 65 feet high.

The large parish church of *St. Peter*, in Kirkgate, is a modern Gothic cross, rebuilt in 1840, 160 feet long, and contains sittings for nearly 4,000, with a picture of the Last Supper, and one of Greenwood's organs. Dr. Hook is the present vicar. *St. John's*, built in 1634, is now the oldest church. *St. George's* was built in 1837, for £11,000. At Holbeck is a new church, built by Messrs. Marshall, near their great flax spinning factory, which is a peculiar construction in the Egyptian style, only one story high, but 400 feet long, resting throughout on many pillars. A new Puseyite church, with a tall spire, was opened in 1843. The Roman Catholic chapel of *St. Anne* has a pointed tower 150 feet high, and the Unitarian chapel near the Commercial Buildings is a handsome specimen of the same style; the two Wesleyan chapels here will hold 3,000 persons each. The *Central Market* in Duncan Street, cost £35,000. There are the *Circular Leather* and *Free Market* (a vast open space), besides many flax mills (which spin for the Irish market), dyehouses, and Messrs. Fairbairn's manufactories.

Leeds has *Public Baths*, a Society for the encouragement of the Fine Arts, *Music Hall*, a *Mechanics' Institute*, to which is attached an excellent library (in union with others in the riding), *Philosophical Societies, Museums, Libraries, &c.;* also a *General Infirmary*, with a picture of "Jairus's Daughter," a *Lying-in* and other *Hospitals*, and an excellent *Industrial School* at Birmantofts, in the Elizabethan style, built in 1848. The *Cavalry Barracks* cover 10 acres; a *Cemetery* at Woodhouse Moor, 10 acres; *Botanical Gardens*, 20 acres. At Headingley, there is the old Shire Oak, which gives name to Skyrack Wapentake. There are six bridges, of which the Briggate is much the oldest, though altered by necessary restorations, Monk Bridge was the first suspended on the bow and string plan. The former, which is near the water works, the large Aire and Calder warehouses, leads over to Hunslet, and the latter to Holbeck. Several short ones cross the deep hollow of the Timble Beck, a stream from the north, which, after being joined by the Sheepscar Beck, falls into the Aire at the Lower Wear, near East Street, and is lined with dye-houses.

The *Grammar School*, founded as long ago as 1552, had Archbishop Pullen for its first master; he was one of the seven Yorkshiremen who about the same time rose to be archbishops. Here Dean Milner and his brother Isaac, sons of a weaver, were educated. The Saxons called the town *Loidis*, from which the modern name is formed. Penda, the savage King of Mercia, was defeated near this by the Northumbrians, in 655.

The *Leeds Mercury*, one of the best papers in the north of England, was first published in 1720.

In the neighbourhood are the following: *Temple Newsam*, (3 miles), seat of H. Ingram, Esq., was formerly a preceptory of the Knights Templars. Queen Mary's husband and James I.'s father was born here, when it belonged to the Lennoxes. The battlements round the roof make this inscription—"All glory and praise be given to God the Father, Son, and Holy Ghost, on high. Peace on earth, good-will to man. Honor and true allegiance to our gracious King; loving affection among his subjects; health and plenty within this house." *Swillington*, Sir J. Lowther, Bart., near the old Gothic church. *Harewood*, Earl of Harewood. *Fa nley Park*, W. Armitage, Esq.

Leeds to Bradford.

ARMLEY station, near which is the Leeds Borough Gaol, and *Armley Park*, seat of Mrs. Gott. Population, 6,190.

KIRKSTALL.

POPULATION, 2,934.
A telegraph station.
HOTEL.—Star.
MONEY ORDER OFFICE at Leeds, 3¼ mile

In the neighbourhood is *Kirkstall Abbey*, founded by the Lacys in the 12th century, beautifully situated by the river. The lofty tower, doorway, and other remains of the church, half Norman in its style, with the Chapter-house, &c., are covered with ivy. *The Grange*, seat of W. Beckett, Esq., M.P.

NEWLAY and CALVERLEY stations.

APPERLEY.

Distance from station, ¼ mile.
A telegraph station.
HOTEL.--George and Dragon.
MONEY ORDER OFFICE at Shipley, 3¾ miles.

Here is a noble edifice for the education of the children of Wesleyan Ministers—Woodhouse Grove School.

SHIPLEY: Population, 3,272.

BRADFORD.

Telegraph station at 9, Leeds Road, and Piccadilly.
HOTELS. — Bowling Green, George, Sun, and Talbot.
CABS from the station and stands, 8d. per mile for two passengers, 1s. for more than two.
MARKET DAYS.—Monday and Thursday.

FAIRS.—March 3, June 9 and 11, December 9 and 11.

BANKERS.—Harris and Co.; Bradford Banking Co. Commercial Banking Co.; Branch of Yorkshire Banking Co.

This great seat of the worsted trade, 11 miles from Leeds, is finely placed among the Yorkshire hills, where three valleys and three branch rails meet, the Lancashire and Yorkshire, the Great Northern, and the Midland main line, traversing the valley down to the Aire. A parliamentary borough, returning two members. Population 103,778. One of the most beautiful spots in the picturesque scenery round Bradford is Shipley Valley on the Leeds line. Coal and iron are abundant; and the ironworks at Low Moor, Bowling, &c., are on a large scale; but the spinning and weaving of worsted form the staple branches of manufacture. Three centuries ago when Leland made his tour through England, as historiographer to Henry VIII., it "stood much by clothing," like its Wiltshire namesake, and for this it is still noted. About 12,000 hands are employed in 180 mills. St. Blaize, the patron saint of woolcombers, whose effigy is still preserved at Blayzey Church in Cornwall, is here duly honoured by a festival in February every seven years. Many of his successful votaries in Bradford started at first as journeymen weavers. By suggesting improvements in the machines under their charge, they have brought themselves into notice, and are now at the head of large concerns. Alpaca cloth from the wool of the South American Llama was firs manufactured here. Woven stuffs are sold on Thursday and Monday, much of it is sold to Leeds and other buyers to be dyed. Most of the houses are of stone, roofed with brown slate. The Parish Church of *St. Peter* is a large later English building, with a monument by Flaxman. A new *Court House* has been lately erected, but the most striking building is *St. George's Music Hall*, by Lockwood and Mawson, opened in 1853. It is in the Italian style, supported by Corinthian columns and pilasters, 75 ft. high, and contains a fine hall 152 ft. by 76, calculated to hold 3,350 persons. The cost was £21,000.

There are 54 places of worship here, of which 12 are Churches, and 24 Chapels. The Calvinistic Baptists have a *College* at Horton, and at Airedale is one for Independents. Newsrooms in the *Exchange* and *Mechanics' Institution*. A Grammar School of Edward VI.'s time.

Bowling Hall, the seat of W. Walker, Esq., is an old Elizabethan seat. *Tong Hall*, near Cutlar Height, seat of Col. Tempest. *Manningham House*, S. C. Lister Kay, Esq. *Horton House*, Mr. Thorpe. *Undercliffe Hall*, W. Garnett, Esq. Abraham Sharpe, the mathematician, was a native of Little Horton.

GILDERSOME BRANCH.

This is a short line from Bradford to Gildersome and Ardsley. It passes through the stations of LAISTER DYKE, DUDLEY HILL, BIRKENSHAW, DRIGHLINGTON.

ADWALTON.

FAIRS.—January 26, February 26, Easter Thursday, and every other Thursday until Michaelmas (horse and cattle).

Close at hand is Adwalton Moor, where the Earl of Newcastle routed Fairfax in 1642.

The line passes through a district rich in mineral products, through GILDERSOME, MORLEY, and TINGLEY, to ARDSLEY, the junction of the Bradford, Wakefield, and Leeds line.

Bradford to Skipton and Morecambe.

SHIPLEY station.

SALTAIRE.

This place owes its origin to the erection of an immense mill on the banks of the river Aire, by Titus Salt, Esq. The scale on which the various buildings have been erected are as complete as they are extensive, including as they do, houses for the work-people, chapel, &c., &c. Lockwood and Mawson were the architects.

BINGLEY.

POPULATION, 5,019.
A telegraph station.
HOTELS. — Elm Tree, Fleece
MARKET DAY.—Tuesday.
FAIRS.—January 25 to 27, August 2nd.
MONEY ORDER OFFICE at Shipley, 3¼ miles.
In the vicinity are *St. Ives* and *Harden Grange*, the old seats of the Ferrands, and *Rumbolds Moor* 1,808 feet high.

ABBEYS OF ENGLAND.

KEIGHLEY.

Population, 18,259.
Distance from station, 1 mile. A telegraph station.
Hotel.—Devonshire Arms.
Market Day.—Wednesday.
Fairs.—May 8th and November 7th.
In the church is an antique tombstone, and a curious clock.
Steeton, Kildwick, and Cononley stations.

SKIPTON.

Population, 4,962.
A telegraph station.
Hotel.—Devonshire Arms.
Market Day.—Saturday.
Fairs.—Every other Monday, March 25, Saturday before Palm and Easter Sundays, 1st and 3rd Tuesday after Easter, Whitsun Eve, August 5th, September 23rd, November 23rd.
Bankers.—Branch of Yorkshire Banking Co.; Alcocks, Birkbeck & Co.

Distances of Places from the Station.

	Miles.		Miles.
Barden Fell	5½	Gargrave	3½
Beacon	4	Hatton Height	4½
Bolton Park	7	Holme Bridge	3½
Bradley	1¾	Newton Bank	5
Broughton	3	Newton Grange	4½
Broughton Hall	2	Rilston	5½
Burdenscales Tower	7	Rilston Fell	6
Carlton	1	Roman Cross	4½
Chelker	5	Silsden	4½
Cold Coniston	6	Skibden	1½
Cracow Hill	6	Skipton Castle	1¼
Draughton	3½	Skipton Lodge	1¾
Embsay	3	Skipton Priory	1½
Embsay Crag	4	Strid, The	6½
Eshton	5	Sturton	1½
Eshton Hall	5½	Thimblethorpe Hall	2
Eastby	3½	Thornton Station	5
Eastby Fell	6	Thorltby	1¾
East Halton	4½	Turn	2¾

The old church and tombs of the Cliffords, and the castle built at the Conquest, and rebuilt by the celebrated Countess of Pembroke (in which the "Shepherd Lord," Henry Clifford, was concealed after the Battle of Towton), should be visited. It has a *Grammar School*, founded as far back as 1568.

BOLTON ABBEY

Lies about six miles to the north-east of Skipton, most charmingly situated on the banks of the river Wharfe Indeed, the picturesque character of this and the surrounding districts is peculiarly striking and impressive. The priory was originally founded in 1121, at Embsay, by William de Meschines, but afterwards removed to its present situation by his daughter Adeliza, in memory of the loss of her son, who, in attempting to cross the "Strid," a chasm in the rock through which the Wharfe rushes, about a mile from the abbey, was fearfully precipitated and drowned. The Duke of Devonshire has a hunting seat formed out of one of the entrances to the abbey.

Passing Gargrave, Bell Busk, Hellifield (near which is *Hellifield Peel*, the seat of J. Hammerton, Esq., the descendant of Helge, the Saxon), and Long Preston stations, we arrive at

SETTLE.

Distance from station, 1¼ mile.
Telegraph station at Skipton, 15½ miles.
Hotel.—Golden Lion.
Market Day.—Tuesday.
Fairs.—April 26, Whit Tuesday, August 18 and 20, Tuesday after October 27, every Tuesday from Easter to Whit Sunday, and every alternate Monday.
Bankers. — Branch of Yorkshire Banking Co.; Alcocks, Birkbeck and Co.

A small market town in the Vale of the Ribble, at the top of the West Riding of Yorkshire, among the mountains at the back-bone of England. From Leeds it is 42 miles, and 24 from Lancaster, the two being united by a line held by the North Western and Midland Companies.

It contains cotton and paper works, but no remarkable building. Formerly there was a fort on a cliff above the town, called Castleberg, whence you have a view of Ingleborough, Pennigant, and other mountains. Here Dr. Birkbeck, the philosopher, was born in 1776; after whom schools have been established in which a general education is given, without regard to religious dogmas. He was the founder of the London Mechanics' Institution. There are distinct market days for fat and lean cattle, the pasture being excellent. At *Giggleswick*, across the river, is the mother church; a *Grammar school*, in which Paley was educated, and an intermitten spring.

Various Excursions may be made. Over the moors to *Malham Cove* (5 miles), a limestone ridge, nearly 300 feet high, over which there is a good waterfall in rainy weather. A little further is *Malham Tarn*, a small lake at the river Aire's head. only 4 miles round, yet the largest in Yorkshire, *Kettlewell*, 7 miles further, is a mountain village, at the head of the Wharfe. Great Whernside, above it, is a mountain, 2,225 feet high. Down the Ribble are *Gisburn Park*, the seat of Lord Ribblesdale, where there is a rare breed of hornless wild cattle, all white, except the tips of their noses. At *Bolton* are the boots and gloves of Henry VI., who found a hiding place here after the battle of Hexham. This corner of Yorkshire was part ot Bolland, or Bowland Forest, of which the Parkers of Browsholme, are hereditary keepers. *Clitheroe* is a parliamentary borough (1 member), having a castle, belonging with the *honour* to the Buccleugh family. Fine view from Pendle Hill. The railway descends the *Aire* through the fertile vale of Skipton, an old seat of the Cliffords; past Keighley to Bingley, both industrious cotton towns, and of ancient date. Up the Ribble, above Settle, are *Horton* (4 miles), in the neighbourhood of *Penygant*, a mountain, 2,270 feet high; and further up the head of Castleberg, between Ingleborough (2,360 feet high), Whernside (2,885 feet), Cam Fell (1,925 feet), and other elevated peaks. Hence there are roads to Hawes (over Newby Head pass), and to Sedbergh (up Dent Dale). The railway to Lancaster down the Lune, passes Clapham, a large moorland parish, of which, among other plants, the poisonous Hub Christopher *(actæa spicata)* is indigenous, and is occasionally given in nervous complaints. Then *Ingleton*, under Ingleton Fell, and Ingleborough. Here are the *Yordas* and other caves, in limestone, of the moors; and at *Thornton Scar*, which is 300 feet high, there is a *waterfall*, 90 feet down. *Ingleborough*, which is best ascended on this side, is green to its summit, which is usually clouded in mist, but when the weather is clear, there is a splendid view over Lancashire and Cumberland and the sea beyond.

CLAPHAM station, near to which is *Thornton Force*, a fall of 90 feet, and *Thornton Scar*, 300 feet high.

HIGH BENTHAM and WENNINGTON stations, near he latter of which is *Wennington Hall*, a fine old seat.

HORNBY.

Telegraph station at Lancaster, 8½ miles.

FAIRS.—Every other Tuesday, and July 30th.

MONEY ORDER OFFICE at Bentham, 5½ miles.

Here is *Hornby Castle*, the old seat of Lord Monteagle, to whom the letter about the Gunpowder Plot was sent; now the property of P. Dawson, Esq.

CATON STATION.—The view of the Lune here is exceedingly pretty. Population, 1,434.

HALTON station, in the neighbourhood of which *Quernmoor Park*, W. Garnett, Esq.

LANCASTER.—See Section III., page 56.

MORECAMBE.

Telegraph station at Lancaster, 3¼ miles.

HOTEL.—North Western.

Morecambe station and harbour, from whence steamers sail, occasionally, during the season, to Piel.

Morecambe Bay is a fine sheet of water, 8 or 10 miles wide, when the tide is up; but at low tide its quicksands are extremely treacherous, and must on no account be crossed without the guide, who is paid by Government, and carries you over in a cart from Poulton-le-Sands, to the opposite coast of Furness—a region of fells, vallies, lakes, &c., in the north, but flat and broken by the sea, in the south or Lower Furness, where the beautiful remains of the *Abbey* may be visited. Near Dalton, Walney island light-house, and the old peel or tower of Foudray, built by the Abbots for a watch tower, are in view.

Having now completed our tour through the midland districts, we retrace our steps to the Metropolis of the British Empire and continue our course through the

EASTERN COUNTIES.

THE terminus of the Eastern Counties Railway is situated at the end of Bishopsgate-street, from which it is separated by a lofty iron railing and gates. Passing through the "Way In" we enter an interior court, extending round each side of the terminus, the road up the ascent to the left leading to the booking offices, and that to the right to the platform of the arrival trains. The terminus is built on an elevation, and is one of the handsomest (externally) in London.

Threading our course through the labyrinth of streets which present themselves in this part of London, the train, after clearing the station at MILE END, soon emerges from the gloom consequent thereon, upon a purer and more congenial atmosphere. Leaving Victoria Park a little to our left, we pass the North London station at Bow, about half a mile beyond which we cross the river Lea, and enter the county of

ESSEX.

A maritime county, bounded on the north by Suffolk and Cambridgeshire, on the west by the counties of Hertford and Middlesex, on the south by the river Thames, and on the east by the sea. Essex composes part of that tract of country on the eastern side of England, which forms the largest connected space of level ground in the whole island; not one lofty eminence or rocky ridge being found in several contiguous counties. The surface of Essex is not, however, totally flat, having many gentle hills and dales; and towards the north-west, from which nearly all the rivers proceed, the country rises, and presents a continued inequality. The coast is broken into a series of islets and peninsulas, deeply cut in by arms of the sea. Extensive salt marshes border most of it, the greater part of which is protected by embankment.

STRATFORD.

POPULATION, 10,586.

A telegraph station.

HOTEL.—The Swan.

OMNIBUSES to and from London every five minutes.

This station forms an important junction of the lines to Cambridge, Ipswich, Tilbury, and places on the North London Railway. Here a collier dock of 600 acres is being constructed. At West Ham are distilleries, Gutta Percha factories, and the gate of an abbey.

WOODFORD AND LOUGHTON BRANCH.

This is a line 7¾ miles long, skirting the borders of Epping Forest, in which Queen Elizabeth was accustomed to engage in the stag hunt. Modern times, however, have greatly changed its aspect; still it has its attractions for the lover of picnics.

LOW LEYTON station.

LEYTONSTONE, near to which Roman, &c., remains have been discovered. The church is very old; it has the tomb of Strype, the antiquary.

SNARESBROOK AND GEORGE LANE stations.

WOODFORD, a place affording a quiet retreat to the citizens of London, after the toils of business. In the churchyard is a yew tree of immense circumference.

BUCKHURST HILL station.

Loughton, a small town near the river Roding. Loughton Hall, remarkable as being once the residence of Queen Anne, is in the vicinity.

Stratford to Water Lane.

The next station on leaving STRATFORD is

LEA BRIDGE.

Distance from station, ½ mile.

Telegraph station at Stratford, 2½ miles.
HOTELS.—Horse and Groom, and Greyhound.
MONEY ORDER OFFICE at Stratford, 2¼ miles.
A favourite resort of the London anglers.

TOTTENHAM.

POPULATION, 9,120.
Distance from station, 1 mile.
A telegraph station.
HOTEL.—White Hart.

The collection of Turner's drawings, &c., belonging to the late F. Windus, Esq., can be viewed on Mondays. The Hermitage, near the old wooden cross, was Izaak Walton's delight. Bruce Castle (a school kept by the Messrs. Hill), stands on the site of a house which belonged to King Robert Bruce's father.

PARK LANE station.

WATER LANE follows immediately after, important only as being the junction of the

ENFIELD BRANCH.

This railway was, at first, projected by a few spirited inhabitants at Enfield, but after the bill was obtained arrangements were made with the Eastern Counties Railway Company, who became proprietors of the line, and by whom it was constructed. It is about three miles in length, nearly on a level, and the curves are favourable and unfrequent.

EDMONTON

Telegraph station at Water Lane Junction, 1 mile.
HOTELS—Bell (Johnny Gilpin's famous Inn); Angel.
FAIRS.—St. Giles' and Ascension Days, at Beggar's Bush.

Lord Burleigh, President Bradshaw, Drs. Fothergill and Taylor (a native), resided here. In the vicinity are *Culland's Grove*, Sir W. Curtis, Bart., *Pymmes*, *Theobalds*, *Bury Hall*, and *Bush Hill Park* (here are some of Gibbon's carvings).

ENFIELD.

A telegraph station.
HOTEL.—Enfield Arms.
MONEY ORDER OFFICE.

ENFIELD is a market town in the county of Middlesex. It contains part of an ancient royal palace, in which Edward IV. held his court before he removed to London. Enfield was formerly celebrated on account of its Chase, which comprised a large tract of woodland well stocked with deer, but during the civil wars it was stripped of both game and timber. It was disforested in 1779. The environs of Enfield are exceedingly pretty, and the scenery quite picturesque. The church is a fine building which has undergone many repairs. It contains brasses of the 14th centuary, of the Smith's, Earl Tiptoft's wife, Lord Roos, Raynton, and Stringers. Charles Lamb is buried here. At Enfield House (a school), are remains of Queen Elizabeth's Palace. In the vicinity are *Forty Hall*, built by Inigo Jones, *Trent Place*, R. Bevan, Esq., *Beech Hill*, A. Paris, Esq., *South Lodge* (willed to the great Lord Chatham), *East Lodge*, *West Lodge*. Gough, the antiquary, lived and died here. Jeffreys lived at Durant. *White Webbs House* was frequented by the Gunpowder Plotters. At *Camlet Moats* Dick Turpin lived. At *Enfield Wash* lived the notorious perjurer, Eliza Canning, tried in 1753. A visit should be made to the Government Arms Factory, an order for which must be previously obtained from the Ordnance Office, London. *Elsynge Hall*, where Edward IV. held his court, which was visited by Queen Elizabeth, and given by her to the Cecils, was near Forty Hall.

Eastern Counties Main Line continued.

PONDER'S END.—In the vicinity is the old seat of the Earls of Lincoln.
ORDNANCE FACTORY.

WALTHAM.

Distance from station, 1 mile.
A telegraph station.
HOTEL.—Four Swans.
MONEY ORDER OFFICE at Waltham Cross, 1 mile.

WALTHAM ABBEY is a market town in the county of Essex, standing on the banks of the river Lea, surrounded on several sides by fruitful gardens and meadow land. The town is irregularly built, but of great antiquity. It derives its name from its once stately abbey, erected by Harold, sonof Earl Godwin. This edifice has almost entirely passed away, but enough remains to show the magnificence of design and elaborate finish of the buildings. In the vicinity is *Waltham Cross*, one of the fifteen erected by Edward I., to Queen Eleanor's memory; *Theobald's Park*, Sir H. Meux, Bart., where James I., Charles I., and Lord Burleigh resided; the *Government Powder Mills;* the remains of a monastery founded by Canute, in which Harold, the last Saxon King, was buried. Cranmer resided here. *Copper Hall*, H. Conyers, Esq., and *Epping Forest*.

CHESHUNT station, near which is *Cheshunt House* (Wolsey's seat), Sir G. Prescott, Bart., and Lady Huntingdon's College. Here Richard Cromwell died (under the name of Clark), in 1712.

BROXBOURNE.

Distance from station, ¼ mile.
A telegraph station.
HOTELS.—New, Gun.
MONEY ORDER OFFICE at Hoddesdon, 1 mile.

Here is a good flint church, with pillared font, and brasses of the Sayes, Borrels, Cocks and Monsons. At *Broxbourne Bury*, the seat of the Bosanquets, Sir H Cock entertained James I. In the vicinity is *Wormley*, the seat of the Earl of Brownlow, with its old church. At *Hoddesden*, is a college for farmers (here Izaak Walton ruralised), and the old gate of Rawdon house.

HERTFORD BRANCH.

Broxbourne to Hertford.

RYEHOUSE (the scene of the Ryehouse plot in 1683), and ST. MARGARET'S stations.

WARE.

Population, 4,884. A telegraph station.

Hotel.—Saracen's Head (here is shown the "Bed of Ware," of carved oak, 12 feet quare, dated, 1460).

Coaches to and from Buntingford, daily.

Market Days.—Tuesdays and Mondays.

Fairs.—Last Tuesday in April, and Tuesday before September 21st.

Bankers.—London and County Bank; Unity Bank, Head Offices, London.

This is a market town in the county of Hertford, built on the banks of the river Lea. It originally contained two ecclesiastical edifices, of which, however, but few traces remain. The old church, with a timbered roof, has an old font and brasses, one to Ellen Cock, dated 1450 (the oldest *Arabic* date in England); and effigies of D. Amory, Clure, Bouchier, and Fanshaw, the poet, and Dr. Mead, who died in 1652, aged 148 years. Here a tournament was held in 1242, at which the Earl of Pembroke was killed. It contains about 75 malt houses, and is the largest malting district in England. In the vicinity are *Ware Priory*, Mrs. Hadeley. *Ware Park*, W. Parker, Esq.; and *Ware Hill House*, Major Ware. At Amwell, is a small island, with a monument to Sir Hugh Myddleton, who finished the New River in 1613. In the church are buried, Reed, the editor of Shakspeare. Scott, the Quaker poet, lived at Amwell Place. Izaak Walton and Hoole lived here.

HERTFORD.

A telegraph station.

Hotel.—Salisbury Arms.

Market Day.—Saturday.

Fairs.—May 12th, July 5th, and November 8th.

Bankers.—London and County Bank; Unity Bank, Head Offices, London.

Hertford, capital of *Hertfordshire*, close to an old ford on the river Lea, where Ermine Street crossed it. Population 6,605. It is a small, irregularly-built country town, with some trade in grain and malt, and remains of a royal *castle* or palace, which having been modernised, is now turned into a school. A tower or two of the original structure may be noticed. Here John of Gaunt had the custody of two captive monarchs. One was his father's (Edward III.) prisoner, the king of France, taken at the battle of Poictiers, in 1356; and the other was David of Scotland, who was captured in 1346, at the battle of Nevill's Cross, by Queen Philippa, while her husband was in France. Afterwards it became the seat of several queens-consort, one of whom was Henry VI.'s wife, Queen Margaret; and the retreat of Elizabeth, when a plague drove the court and judges out of London. A branch of *Christ's Hospital*, or the blue-coat school, consisting of 500 or 600 of the younger children, is stationed here in a large quadrangular pile The *Sessions House* and *Town Hall* are united in one building. The *County Gaol* is a fine large edifice. There is an old cross-shaped church, with a low spire, a fine corn market and prison, but nothing else remarkable.

A great number of seats are situated about this part of the country. *Balls*, the Marquis of Townshend. *Brickendonbury*, W. Dent, Esq. *Bayfordbury*, W. Baker, Esq., has a famous gallery of the *Kit-Cat-Club* portraits, all by Kneller; among them are those of Marlborough, Sir R. Walpole, Addison, Steele, &c. *Ware Park*, W. Parker, Esq., near Ware Priory. *Chadwell*, at Amwell, is at the head of the *New River*, which was cut between 1607 and 1613, by Sir Hugh Myddleton, and runs by a serpentine course, 36 miles, to Clerkenwell. *Haileybury*, is the East India Company's College for civil cadets, about to be given up under the Rev. Mr. Melville. *Theobalds*, seat of Sir J. Prescott, is on the site of Lord Burleigh's seat, to which Elizabeth came frequently to hunt. Here James I. died, in 1625. *Panshanger*, seat of Earl Cowper, in a charming park; a Madonna by Raphael is here. *Bedwell Park*, seat of Sir C. Eardley, Bart. *Hatfield*, one of the most splendid seats hereabouts, belongs to the Marquis of Salisbury—a quadrangle in the Tudor style, some part being as old as 1480, but most of it not earlier than 1605. Many curious portraits on panel, and a large and beautiful park. Edward VI., and Elizabeth were here when proclaimed. Cromwell's chair is shown. In 1835, part was burnt, and the Dowager Marchioness perished. *Brocket Hall*, the seat of Viscount Melbourne, where the late premier died, *Tewin House* belongs to Earl Cowper. In the churchyard is the tomb of Lady Grimstone, which the ash trees growing from beneath have displaced in a most singular manner. There is a silly story connected with it. *Knebworth Park*, Sir B. Lytton, Bart., the distinguished novelist. *Hoo Park*, Lord Dacre's seat. *Woodhall Park*, J. Abel Smith, Esq., the banker. *Welwyn* or "Wellin," was the rectory of Young, who wrote his "Night Thoughts" here, and died in 1765, leaving a bowling green for the use of his parishioners. The great viaduct of the Great Northern, on the Waran, 90 feet high in the middle, is near Welwyn.

HERTFORD, LUTON, & DUNSTABLE.—
(Great Northern.)

By means of this cross line from Hertford to Dunstable, the Midland and Eastern Counties districts are rendered much easier of access. The line takes a north-westerly direction, passing the stations of Hertingfordbury and Cale Green, calling at

Hatfield, to take up or set down passengers to or from the north or south. Described page 41.

Wheathamstead.—This was the place of meeting of the barons, to oppose Edward II.

Harpenden.—Church cruciform; has monuments to the family of the Cresseys, to whom the place formerly belonged.

New Mill End station.

LUTON.

Another town of straw plaiters. The Gothic church, built of chalk and flints, deserves notice. *Luton Hoo*, the fine seat of the Leighs. *Hoo* or *Hoe* means hill, and Luton *Lea Town*, probably from being at the source of the Lea; *Ivinghoe* lies among the hills. *Ashridge*, seat of Earl Ellesmere.

Dunstable, see Sec. III., page 7.

Eastern Counties Main Line continued.

Broxbourne to Cambridge.

Leaving Broxbourne, a distance of 7 miles brings the tourist beyond the stations of Roydon and Burnt Mill to

HARLOW.

Distance from station, ¾ mile
A telegraph station.
Hotels.—George, New (at the Railway Station).
Fair.—September 9th, for horses, called Harlow Bush Fair.
Money Order Office.
In the vicinity is *Otes*, the seat of the celebrated Mrs. Masham (Queen Anne's favourite). Here died Locke, in 1784; and *Laver* church.
Sawbridgeworth station.

BISHOP'S STORTFORD.

Population, 5,280.
A telegraph station.
Hotels.—Railway, George.
Market Day.—Thursday. Fairs.—October 11th, Holy Thursday, and Thursday after Trinity Sunday.
Mails.—Three arrivals and departures, daily, between London and Bishop's Stortford.

A small market town in Hertfordshire,* placed on the side of a hill, near the western borders of Essex. The streets are disposed in the form of a cross, with two long streets intersecting each other at right angles Though no particular manufacture is carried on here, yet the town is respectable and populous. Seated in the midst of a corn country, it is remarkable for the number of its malthouses, and for the quantity of malt annually made here. The church, dedicated to St. Michael, is a large lofty structure, standing on the highest ground in the neighbourhood, and contains many monuments. Here Bonner roasted a martyr, on Goose Green. In the vicinity are *Euston*, seat of Viscount Maynard, and *Dunmow*, famous for the gammon of bacon gifts to married people, who have lived in peace 366 days

Stanstead Mountfichet.—In the vicinity are *Quendon Hall*, the seat of Mrs. Cranmer, descendant of the Archbishop's family, and Ugley Church, with its steeple.
Elsenham station.
Newport.—In the vicinity is *Debden*, Sir F. Vincent, Bart

AUDLEY END, for Saffron Walden.

Population of Saffron Walden, 5,911.
A telegraph station.
Hotels.—Cross Keys, Rose and Crown.
Market Day.—Saturday.
Fairs.—Saturday before Midlent Sunday, the following Monday, August 3rd, Nov. 1st and 2nd.
Bankers.—London and County Bank, J. Viall, Esq., Manager.

Close to the station is the magnificent seat of Lord Braybrooke, *Audley End*, which cost upwards of £200,000, built on the site of Saffron Walden Priory, full of portraits, &c.; the bridge by Adams, in the grounds, is beautifully built. Here is the Hon. R. Nevill's Museum.

Chesterford.—Antiquities abound in this vicinity, the most remarkable of which is a villa uncovered in 1848, by The Hon. R. Nevill.

CAMBRIDGESHIRE.

The whole of this extensive county is penetrated by artificial drains, and every exertion is made by the landed proprietors to redeem as much ground as possible from its former swampy condition. Cambridgeshire is remarkably flat, the great Bedford level alone containing 400,000 acres of land. The climate varies considerably. Cambridgeshire is an agricultural county; grain, hemp, flax, mustard seed, osiers, &c., are grown in great abundance.

Whittlesford.—The ancient chapel near the bridge was founded before the time of Edward I. In the vicinity is Thriplow Heath, where, after Charles I.'s capture, Cromwell and Fairfax held a council. Large oil mills are established here, for crushing seed, and making oilcake for cattle.

Shelford, at which traces of Roman remains have been discovered. Close at hand are the *Gogmagog Hills*, seat of Lord Godolphin, with a camp.

CAMBRIDGE.

A telegraph station.
Hotels.—Bull, family and commercial, and posting house; Red Lion, commercial and family, and posting house; Eagle, family and commercial.
Market Day.—Saturday.
Fairs.—June 24th; Sept. 25th.
Boat Races from Ditton Church to Chesterton, every term.

Bankers.—Thos. Fisher and Sons; J. Mortlock and Sons; C. F. and G. E. Foster; Branch of the London and County Bank.

The capital of *Cambridgeshire*, and seat of one of the two ancient English Universities. The University of Cambridge is second to no other in Europe in any single department of literature; but in one (mathematics) she has no rivals. The Cam, a branch of the Nene, runs through it, hence the name, which is not unlike the Roman name *Cambricum.* The houses are brick, the ground flat (a part of the great Fen Level). On approaching the town, whether by rail or otherwise, the first object that meets the eye is the magnificent Chapel of King's College, its lofty turrets being seen at the distance of some miles. Population, 27,815, including above 7,000 persons attached to the University, which is represented by two members in parliament, two more being sent by the town. The buildings are of three classes, those belonging to the *Town*, the *University*, and the 17 *Colleges and Halls* comprising the University, the last being merely a name for the body corporate, and serving to indicate the universality of the provision made for teaching any branch of learning. Most of the colleges, &c., are in Trumpington and the neighbouring streets, on or not far from the river.

There are fourteen parish churches, and about the same number of places of worship belonging to various dissenting bodies. Among the town buildings are 16 churches (out of 25 places of worship); the *Town Hall* in the Market Place, near the conduit, built by old Hobson the carrier and horse-letter, from whom originated the saying of "Hobson's choice, this or none." The market-place has lately been repaved with granite cubes; and by the restoration of Hobson's Conduit, which is now placed in the centre, presents an object of uniformity and elegance. The *Shire Hall* and prison, on Castle Hill (a good view here), where the Conqueror built a fortress to overawe the stubborn defenders of the Isle of Ely. Addenbrooke's *General Hospital* and the *New Cemetery.* The church of *St. Andrew the Great*, of stone, has a monument to Cook the navigator, whose widow died here in 1835. *St. Andrew the Less* is near Barnwell Priory, a foundation as old as the 11th century. The *Abbey Church*, in Barnwell Priory, a very ancient foundation, has recently been restored and appropriated for worship as a chapel of ease to St. Andrew the Less, rendered necessary through the greatly increased population of the parish. *St. Benedict's*, *St. Clement's*, and *St. Peter's*, are in part very ancient. *St. Sepulchre's* is a curious round church, originally built by the Templars, and lately restored. At *St. Mary the Great*, a perpendicular English church, the University Sermons are preached. Some of the oldest houses are in Petty Cury.

The *University*, according to some accounts, was founded as far back as the year 630, but if so, it made no figure till the Abbots of Croy sent monks to give lectures here in 1209. The oldest college *(Peter House)* dates from 1257. The *University Buildings*, as distinct from the colleges, are as follows. *Senate House*, with a hall 101 feet long, where degrees are conferred, and Prince Albert, the present Chancellor, was installed in July 1849, in presence of the Queen. The narrow oak galleries are for the graduates. *Public Schools*, forming a quadrangle, with the *University Library* overhead, in which are many rare books and MSS. A copy of every printed book is given to it. *New Library*, 167 feet long, with a collection of minerals on the basement floor. *University* or *Pitt Press*, a modern building, by Blore, with a tower like a church. Further on in Trumpington Street, is the *Fitzwilliam Museum*, with its lions and beautiful portico, 75 feet high; a collection of paintings, casts, &c., was left with a bequest of £100,000, by Lord Fitzwilliam to rebuild it.

The Colleges, with a few exceptions, were founded and built before the 16th century; but additions have been made of later date. Each includes a chapel, common hall for meals, generally adorned with portraits, library, apartments for the masters (or Dons) fellows, &c. Their total income is about £150,000. There are 430 fellows, *i.e.*, seniors, with a settled income, and mostly residents. One walk should be along the river at the back of St. John's, Trinity, King's, &c.

The colleges in alphabetical order are the following:—

CATHERINE HALL, in Trumpington Street, founded in 1475. A quadrangle or quad, rebuilt in 1700. Bradford the martyr, and Archbishop Sandys, were of this college.

CHRIST'S COLLEGE, in St. Andrew's Street, founded in 1442, and refounded in 1506, by Henry VI.'s half-sister, the lady Margaret. Two courts, one rebuilt by Inigo Jones. Beautiful gardens, and Milton's mulberry tree. Milton was called the "lady" of Christ's College.

CLARE HALL, near King's College, in Trumpington Street, founded in 1326, and refounded by one of the Clare family. Court, rebuilt in 1638, in the Italian style, with good chapel. Old bridge over the Cam.

CORPUS CHRISTI COLLEGE, in Trumpington Street, founded in 1351, street front, 222 feet long. Two courts, one rebuilt in 1823, by Wilkins; library and good chapel. Portraits of Erasmus, Wolsey, Sir T. More, John Foxe, &c. Old Father Latimer was of this college.

DOWNING COLLEGE, near the station, founded as late as 1807, by Sir J. Downing. One part of a court is finished. Gardens and extensive grounds.

EMMANUEL COLLEGE, in St. Andrew's Street, founded in 1584. Two courts, good hall, and pleasant gardens. Archbishop Sancroft's books in the library He was of this college; and Gulliver graduated here, according to Swift's account.

GONVILLE AND CAIUS, called *Key's College*, in Trumpington Street, founded partly by Edward Gonville, in 1348, and partly by Queen Mary's physician, Dr. Caius, in 1557. Three courts in the Italian style, with three gates in succession leading into them, named Humility, Virtue, and Honour, *Jeremy Taylor*, who was born at Cambridge in 1605, Harvey, the physician, and Lord Thurlow were gradates.

JESUS COLLEGE, in Jesus Lane, founded in 1496, on the site of a nunnery, the chapel of which, lately restored by Mr. Sutton, remains. *Old Hall*, three courts, behind a front of 180 feet, gardens, &c. Cranmer, Sterne, Coleridge, &c., were of this college.

KING'S COLLEGE, founded in 1441, by Henry VI., consists of a provost and seventy fellows and scholars, the latter supplied by a regular succession from Eton. Two modern courts, hall, and the beautiful later English chapel, built 1441. This is 316 feet long by 84 wide, with small octagonal owers at the corners, 146 feet high to the little domes. The interior contains work at which Sir C. Wren was never tired of looking. Bishop Cloos or Close was the designer. The exquisite fan-tracery roof is in twelve parts, all of carved stone, unsupported by a single column; and twenty-four richly stained windows run down the sides between the buttresses, each about 50 feet high.

MAGDALENE COLLEGE, in Bridge Street, founded by the Duke of Buckingham and Lord Audley in 1502-42. Two courts, many old books and ballads in the library.

PEMBROKE COLLEGE, in Trumpington Street, founded in 1343, by the Countess of Pembroke. Two small ancient courts; water works in the gardens; and a tin globe 18 feet diameter; chapel built by Sir Christopher Wren. Bishop Ridley, Spencer, Gray, and Pitt, were of this college.

QUEEN'S COLLEGE.—Founded by the two queens, Margaret of Anjou, consort of Henry VI., in 1448, and Elizabeth Woodville, consort of Edward IV., 1465. Three old courts, with cloisters, lately restored. Erasmus, the Greek Professor, was of this college. His portrait and walk in the gardens are shown.

ST. JOHN'S COLLEGE, in St. John's Street, founded in 1508, by Henry VII.'s mother, the Lady Margaret, (who also founded Christ's College). Three old Tudor brick courts on one side of the Cam, and a modern Gothic pile on the other side, by Rickman, in 1830. They are joined by a covered bridge of one arch, called the Bridge of Sighs, and various other comical names. Chapel and library, both 150 feet long; old hall; fine gardens. Lord Burleigh, Prior, Ben Jonson, Wordsworth, Bishop Beveridge, Kirke White, Wilberforce, &c., were of this college, which is the great rival to Trinity, and turns out most senior wranglers.

PETERHOLME OR ST. PETER'S COLLEGE, in Trumpington Street, is the oldest of all, dating from 1257, and founded by Bishop de Balsham. Two old courts, and a modern one built in 1826; the old chapel is curious.

SIDNEY SUSSEX COLLEGE, called Sidney, in Sidney Street, was founded in 1598, by Frances Sydney, Countess of Sussex. Two modernized courts. A portrait and bust of Cromwell, who graduated here. He was a gambler then, and a "fast" man, though a hard reader at times. In 1642, when he sat for the town, and the civil war broke out, he seized the University plate to pay expenses.

TRINITY COLLEGE, in Trumpington Street, was founded by Henry VIII. in 1540, in place of two earlier halls, and ranks the first in consideration. It is customary for the Master of Trinity (now Dr. Whewell) to entertain the Sovereign on the occasion of a visit to Cambridge. Three courts, one being nearly a quarter of a mile round, with a conduit, worth notice; ancient Tudor hall, timber roof, 102 feet long, with numerous portraits; large and beautiful gardens, with an avenue of tall elms. Famous *library*, 190 feet long, in which are Roubiliac's busts of Newton, Bacon, &c.; wood carvings of Gibbons, Thorwaldsen's statue of Byron, Newton's telescope, Milton's MS. of Sampson Agonistes, &c. Newton, Bacon, Raleigh, Dryden, Barrow, Porson, Bentley, and Byron, were of Trinity. Here Byron kept his pet bear, "training him," as he said, "for a fellowship at St. John's," the rival college.

TRINITY HALL, founded in 1350, for lawyers, is near Trinity College. Bishop Horsley, Lord Chesterfield, and Bilney the Martyr were graduates. The front of this college has been recently burnt down and rebuilt.

The *Observatory* is outside the town, on the Madingley Road. *Parker's Piece*, the graduates' cricket ground, is in Regent Street. All students go about the town in costume, *i.e.*, a cap and gown—the latter being differently cut for each college. Grave proctors, attended by "bull-dogs," are appointed to look after delinquents, while taxors see to the markets. Butter is sold by the yard in Cambridge, that is, a pound is rolled out into a stick of that length, for the convenience of cutting off "butters" for the students.

Within a few miles are *Madingley*, the Cottons' seat; *Trumpington Church*, with a fine brass, almost the oldest in England; *Grantchester*, on the old Roman way; *Bottisham* (near which are remains of Anglesea and Swaffham priories), was the seat of Soame, Jenyns, &c.

NEWMARKET AND BURY ST. EDMUNDS BRANCH.

Cambridge to Bury St. Edmunds and Haughley Junction.

After passing in succession the stations of FULBOURN, SIX MILE BOTTOM, (near which is *Hare Park*, seat of W. Portman, Esq.), and DULLINGHAM, we arrive at

NEWMARKET.

A telegraph station.
HOTELS.—Rutland Arms; Stars.
MARKET DAY.—Tuesday.
FAIRS.—Whit Tuesday and November 8th.

RACES.—Easter Monday (Craven); 2nd and 4th Mondays after (first and second spring); July; Monday before 1st Thursday in October; 1st October, 2nd October, 3rd October, or Houghton.

BANKERS.—Eaton, Hammond, and Son; Forster and Co.

A market town in the county of Cambridge, with a population of 3,356, long celebrated in the annals of horsemanship for its extensive heath, in the immediate vicinity of which has been formed one of the finest race-courses in the kingdom. The principal part of Newmarket is situated in Suffolk; but the whole of the race course, on whose attractive charms its support mainly depends, is in Cambridgeshire. Most of the houses are modern and well built; and many of them, which have been erected as residences for the nobility and private gentlemen who attend the races, are extremely handsome. The church contains a tomb to Frampton, trainer to Queen Anne and George I. and II. Bishop Merks, and Harewood the physician, were natives.

KENNET, HIGHAM, and SAXHAM stations.

BURY ST. EDMUNDS.

POPULATION.—13,900.
Distance from station, ½ mile.
A telegraph station.
HOTELS.—Angel; Bell.
MARKET DAYS.—Wednesday and Saturday.
FAIRS.—October 2nd and December 1st.
MONEY ORDER OFFICE.

BANKERS.—Oakes, Bevan, and Co.; John Worlledge and Co.; National Provincial Bank of England; Harvey and Hudsons.

An old Saxon town and parliamentary borough, situated in so healthy a spot that it has been called the Montpelier of England, in a beautiful part of West Suffolk, founded by Canute along with an abbey, to commemorate the martyrdom of Edmund, a King of East Anglia, by the Danes, in the year 870. This became one of the largest and most richly endowed monasteries in the kingdom, being "505 feet long and 212 wide, with twelve chapels and churches, cloisters, offices, &c., attached, forming a little town in itself. The abbot was mitred, and reigned over an establishment of monks, chaplains, and servants, amounting to 200. He had a mint and a *gallows* in the town, of which he was chief magistrate, with a jurisdiction over the entire liberty (*i.e.*, six hundreds and a half in this shire), the royalties of which together with 53 knights' fees, and other possessions, made a revenue equivalent to £50,000 in the present day" *(Sharp's British Gazetteer).* Of this luxurious house, which our early sovereigns frequently visited, all that now remains are part of a tower, a beautiful Norman gate, 80 feet high, the abbey church, and gate.

Bury stands on the slope of a gentle and well cultivated sand-hill, the best prospect of it being from the Vinefield. *St. Mary's* old parish church contains the effigies of Henry VIII.'s sister, Mary, who married Charles Brandon, Duke of Suffolk, and of Reeve, the last Abbot of Bury. At one time it possessed 40 churches and religious foundations. The *Shire Hall* occupies the place of St. Margaret's church. The *Guildhall* has an ancient porch. There is a large *County Prison*, and a *Bridewell* in the Norman style; a handsome *County Hospital.* The *Grammar School* has produced many eminent men, such as Archbishop Sancroft, Dr. Blomfield (late Bishop of London), a native, Lord Keeper North, Sir Samuel Romilly, Cumberland, the dramatist, &c. Bloomfield the poet was born at Honington. The famous Bishop Gardiner of Mary's time, was also a native.

Some ancient houses, as well as many remnants of antiquity will be noticed. The *Cock Inn* was a chapel, and the old workhouse part of a college. There still remains a gate of *St. Saviour's Hospital*, founded as far back as 1184, by Abbot Sampson. Here good Duke Humphrey was captured by Henry VI., and (it is stated) smothered in 1446, between the bolsters of his bed; and Dudley unsuccessfully tried to get up a rising on behalf of Lady Jane Grey.

Several fine seats are in the neighbourhood, built on the property which once belonged to the abbey, and was granted away at the dissolution. *Rougham Hall*, P. Bennet, Esq. *Rushbrooke Hall*, Colonel Rushbrooke; a moated Elizabethan seat. *Barton Hall*, Sir H. Bunbury, Bart. *Livermore Hall*, Colonel Peel. *Culford Hall*, R. Benyon, Esq. *Euston Park*, Duke of Grafton.

THURSTON.—In the vicinity are the Pakenham's old seat; *Ixworth*, R. Cartwright, Esq., with remains of a priory.

ELMSWELL station.

HAUGHLEY.—See page 37.

ST. IVES BRANCH.

Cambridge to St. Ives, Wisbeach, and Lynn.

HISTON.

Distance from station, ¾ mile.
Telegraph station at Cambridge, 4¾ miles.
MONEY ORDER OFFICE at Cambridge, 4¾ miles.

In the vicinity are *Impington*, (birth place of Pepys, secretary to the navy in Charles II.'s time, and author of Pepys' Diary, to which family the late lord Chancellor Cottenham belonged). *Impington House* seat of Mrs. Knight; near this spot, "a woman was in 1799 buried under the snow for eight days and dug out again."

OAKINGTON. In the vicinity is *Cottenham*, birth place of Archbishop Tennyson, and the spot on which the Abbots of Crowland elected lecturers prior to the founding of the University of Cambridge.

LONG STANTON station.

SWAVESEY.—The Church founded by the Zouche family is worth a visit.

ST. IVES.

POPULATION, 3,522.
Distance from station, ¼ mile.
A telegraph station.
HOTELS.—Golden Lion, Unicorn.
MARKET DAY.—Monday.
FAIRS.—Whit Monday and October 10th.
BANKERS. — E. and C., F. and G. E. Forster; Rust and Veaseys; Branch of London and County Bank.

Here is a Gothic bridge, which crosses the Ouse, and supports an old Chapel, a Spire, Church, and Priory, called Stépé founded in 1017. In the vicinity is Hemingford Abbots, the birth place of the "Three Graces," the Miss Gunnings, who married respectively the Duke of Argyle, Earl of Coventry, and an Irish gentleman.

A continuation of this line extends to the Great Northern Railway, connecting itself with it at the town of Huntingdon.

SOMERSHAM.

Distance from station, ½ mile.
Telegraph station at St. Ives, 6 miles.
MARKET DAY.—Friday.
FAIRS.—June 22nd, and Friday before Nov. 12th.

The church is a spacious and noble edifice, containing several ancient brasses and monuments. The chancel is supposed to be of the time of Henry III.

CHATTERIS.

Telegraph station at March, 8 miles.
HOTEL.—George.

On the site of *Chatteris House* (T. Fryer, Esq.), stood a nunnery, founded in the time of King Edgar.—

The living is worth £1,370.—Vermuyden, the Dutch engineer, cut Forty Foot Drains in 1670.

WIMBLINGTON station.

MARCH.

Distance from station, ½ mile.
POPULATION, 4,171.
A telegraph station.
HOTEL.—Griffin.
MARKET DAY.—Wednesday.
FAIRS.—Whit Monday and Monday before it, and October 27th.
MAILS.—Two arrivals and departures, daily, between London and March.
MONEY ORDER OFFICE.
BANKERS. — Gurneys and Co.; Sub Branch National Provincial Bank of England; Harvey and Hudsons.

This is a village in the parish of Doddington, having a spacious and elegant church. Numerous Roman coins and other antiquities have been discovered in this neighbourhood.

WISBEACH.

A telegraph station.
HOTEL.—Rose and Crown.
MARKET DAY.—Saturday.
FAIRS.—Saturday and Monday before Palm Sunday, Monday before Whit Sunday, July 25th, Aug. 1st and 2nd.
BANKERS.—Gurneys and Co.; National Provincial Bank of England.

WISBEACH is half a port, with a population of 10,594, though some distance inland up the Ouse, and possesses an old *church*, half Norman, as well as the *Rose Inn*, which under the sign of the Horn, existed in 1475. Archbishop Herring, and Clarkson, the coadjutor of Wilberforce, against the slave trade, were educated at the Grammar School. The benefice is worth nearly £1,800. Godwin, the author of "Political Justice," was a native.

After passing in succession the stations of EMNETH, SMEETH ROAD, MIDDLE DROVE, MAGDALEN GATE, and WATLINGTON, we arrive at

Lynn, see page 28.

Eastern Counties Main Line continued.

Cambridge to Ely.

Pursuing our onward course we pass WATERBEACH, and arrive at

ELY.

A telegraph station.
HOTELS.—Lamb, Bell.
MARKET DAY.—Thursday.
FAIRS.—Ascension Day, and October 29th.
BANKERS.—John Mortlock and Sons; E. and C., F. and G. E. Forster; Harvey and Hudsons.

A city and Bishop's see, in the county of Cambridge. It is built on the banks of the Ouse, in the Isle of Ely, with a population of 6,176, and consists of one principal street, and several others which diverge from it. But the principal object of interest is its venerable *Cathedral*, founded in 1070. It is 510 feet long, and the Norman Nave 270 feet high. Bishop Alcock's perpendicular Chapel, Nortwold's tomb, Scot's screen, the Lady Chapel, and the Lantern Tower, should be noticed. In the vicinity is Cromwell's residence at Stuutney, and a Norman church. "Ribbons" were formerly blessed here at St. Audry's shrine, hence the word "tawdry."

MARCH AND PETERBOROUGH BRANCH.

After our departure from Ely, and passing in succession the stations of CHITTISHAM and BLACK BANK, we arrive at

MANEA.—At this place Roman medals, &c., have been found, and things have been discovered which lead to the supposition that some sudden irruption of the sea has formerly happened here.

EASTREA station.

WHITTLESEA.

POPULATION, 5,472.
Distance from station, ¼ mile.
Telegraph station at Peterbro, 5¼ miles.
HOTEL.—Falcon.
BANKERS. — Gurney and Co.

General Sir Harry Smith, the hero of Aliwal, was a native. In the vicinity are *Thorn Island*, and the ruins of a Saxon Abbey, founded in 602, and *Thorney Abbey*, seat of T. Wing, Esq.

Peterborough.—See page 44.

EAST ANGLIAN.

Ely to Lynn.

The line between Ely and Lynn is the most important section of the East Anglian line, as it brings a very valuable district of the eastern part of the country into railway communication, not only with the metropolis, but with the northern and western parts of the kingdom, while it adds materially to that of the low land traversed by the various companies.

Although this line runs through a perfectly level country, it possesses a peculiar interest from its passing through a vast and fertile district, less than a century ago covered with water—many vain, because unscientific, attempts having been made, dating even from the Roman occupation of this Island, to reclaim and adapt the land to cultivation. The productive and remunerative farming of the Fens of Norfolk, is one of the greatest triumphs of *steam*, for that was the effective agent employed to give value to, or rather to *create*, this extensive territory. Even within a recent period, lands estimated at £3 or £4 an acre, have been enhanced in value, not only one hundred per cent., but even one hundred fold.

With the exception of a few viaducts, from the line passing through a level, easy, as well as fertile country, it exhibits few specimens of ambitious or costly engineering; all is simple, strong, substantial, as well as economical.

On the first section from Lynn to Downham there is a rather expensive iron bridge raised over the turnpike road, not far from the town; beyond this, for ten or eleven miles continuously, there is neither embankment nor excavation. There are three viaducts over the Ouse. In the mode of crossing the bog leading to the main viaduct, and in forming a foundation upon beds of quicksand for the piers of an iron girder bridge, crossing the canal at Wisbeach, great skill is exhibited. In the former case, foundation after foundation was swallowed up in the swamps, piles sunk, trenches dug, thorns, brushwood, and timber spread over the surface; and the difficulty was only surmounted by topping a dry sandy soil till it settled firmly in the bed as the moisture was pressed out from beneath. A different contrivance was resorted to in the case of the Wisbeach quicksands. A platform of timber was actually laid under the bed of the canal, extending all along the adjacent ground; and upon this were firmly sunk the piers for an iron bridge of 35 feet span, consisting of six girders of four tons each.

LITTLEPORT station.

NORFOLK.

THIS county, from its numerous objects of antiquity, geographical situation on the German Ocean, as well as its seaport towns, seats, agricultural and manufacturing products, is particularly deserving of notice. In the fenny part of the country the air is not only cold, but exceedingly damp; but the county to the north and north-west of Thetford, forming the greater part of Norfolk, consisting of a sandy or gravelly soil, is peculiarly salubrious and pleasant. The manufactures of Norfolk, which consist almost exclusively of woollen goods, are nearly all centred in the city of Norwich and its vicinity. Yarmouth and Lynn are the two principal ports, from which nearly all the manufactured goods are exported.

HILGAY FEN.—*Hilgay Church* was the rectory of Phineas Fletcher, the poet.

Then passing on to OUSE BRIDGE station, we arrive at

DENVER.—The Church here has a thatched roof. In the vicinity is *Ryston Hall*, seat of E. Pratt, Esq., and *West Dereham*, with its abbey gate and ruined towers, founded by Archbishop Hubert in 1188.

DOWNHAM.

POPULATION, 2,867.

Telegraph station at Lynn, 11 miles.

HOTEL.—Castle.

MARKET DAY.—Saturday.

FAIRS.—February 3rd, May 8th, and November 13th.

BANKERS.—Gurneys and Co.

This place is famous for its butter and wild fowl, and has an ancient church and bridge.

Then passing in succession the stations of STOW, (near which are *Stow Hall*, Sir T. Hare, Bart.; *Stradsett*, W. Bagge, Esq., M.P.; and *Watlington*, General Peel, M.P.); and *Holme*, within sight of which is the very ancient *Church of Runckton*, we arrive at

WATLINGTON (Junction).

Telegraph station at Lynn, 6 miles.

MONEY ORDER OFFICE at Downham, 5½ miles.

This station forms a junction of the railway to Wisbeach and Peterborough; but our present course lies northward, to Lynn, at which place we arrive about fifteen minutes after leaving the junction.

LYNN REGIS.

A telegraph station.

HOTELS.—Globe, Crown.

OMNIBUSES to South and North Wootton, Castle Rising, Dersingham, Sanderingham, Ingoldsthorpe, Heacham, Clench Warton, and Tarrington St. Clements.

MARKET DAYS.— Tuesdays and Saturdays.

FAIRS.—February 13th, and October 6th.

BANKERS.—East of England Bank; Everards and Co.; Lynn and Norfolk Bank; Gurneys and Co.

A borough town, in the county of Norfolk, which stands on the banks of the Ouse. It was formerly called Lynn Episcopi, having been granted at the Conquest to the bishops of Norwich, who had a palace at *Gaywood*. It consists of two principal streets, with a number of smaller ones branching from them.

Four rivulets run through the town and divide it into separate parts, over which are thrown several bridges. The streets are on the whole well paved, and the modern houses handsome, but still a number of old irregular buildings remain. The Exchange or Custom House is a fine stone building. The Market Cross was built in 1710, and is ornamented with Ionic columns. Population—19,355, who return one member. The port is formed by the mouth of the Ouse, but it is choked with shifting sands, and the harbour reached only by an intricate channel between them, 15 miles long. A new channel has been made for the river, called the Gan Brink Cut. When the siege of Calais was undertaken by Edward III., Lynn supplied 19 ships—a proof of the activity of its trade. *St. Margaret's Church*, near the Saturday market and St. James' Street, is as old as the 12th century, being a cross, with two *odd* west pinnacled towers, and a large window between. Within are two Flemish brasses deserving notice. That of St. Nicholas, was built in Edward III.'s reign, and is 200 feet long, with a steeple of 170 feet; the porch is elegant. *All Saints'*, in South Lynn, is also an old building, having one of Snetzler's organs, with 30 stops. This parish forms a narrow strip of 4¼ miles along the Ouse. The town is clean and well built, and intersected by the river Narr and several little streams or "fleets," one of which, the Purfleet fleet, divides it into two equal parts, north and south, and has long been a recognised boundary. There are pretty public walks on the east side, of some extent. Three or four roads unite at the Long Bridge or Old South Gate, over the Narr, near the gas works, in South Lynn. North Lynn and West Lynn are on the opposite side of the Ouse.

At the old *Guildhall*, are portraits of the late Lord George Bentinck and Sir R. Walpole, both representatives of the borough; also King John's silver cup, given to the "mayor and good men of Lenn;" and a sword ascribed to him, but actually the gift of Henry VIII. The principal, or Tuesday market, is a space of three acres, with a stone cross in one corner, 70 feet high, but not older than 1710. A statue of Charles II. in the Exchange, built in 1683. In College Lane is the *Grammar School*, of which Bulwer's sentimental hero, Eugene Aram, was usher, when apprehended for the murder of Clarke, in 1759. This is an old foundation, as are various almshouses, which exist under modern names.

Among the remains of antiquity are the *Lady's Mount*, east of the town, so called from the small Lady Chapel there; it is a cross only 17 feet long, with a beautiful fan-tracery roof, but enclosed by an octangular brick wall. The beautiful *Grey Friar's Lantern* is a tower of six sides, supported by buttresses, pierced by elegantly shaped windows, and resting on open groined arches, making the total height 90 feet. It was erected about 1260. There are also remains of the Austin Friar's Gate, and of the old town wall, which had a ditch outside.

About 18,000 tons of shipping belong to the port amount of custom dues, £50,000. Oil-cake, timber, and other Baltic produce, are among the chief imports; the silt brought down the river is used by the glass-makers. Since 1850, works on a large scale have been carried out for reclaiming part of the Wash, but its practicability is doubtful. Here, as in the Trent, the Solway, &c., the tide comes in sometimes with a sudden rush, carrying everything before it. It was while crossing it under such circumstances that King John was nearly drowned a little before his death at Newark. Dr. Burney was organist here for nine years, and at that period wrote his great work the "History of Music," and married his second wife. Two of his children, Madame D'Arblay, authoress of Cecilia, and Charles Burney, the scholar, were natives, as also were Bishop Keene and "Miss Breeze, who kept a pack of hounds, and was a dead shot."

At *Castle Rising*, which, according to a local saying "was a sea-port when Lynn was a marsh, now Lynn is a sea-port town, and *Rising* fares the worst," are the keep and other remains of a Norman fortress, built by the ancestors of the Howard family, on the site of the one in which Edward III. confined his mother; also an old Norman church. This place was one of the rotten boroughs extinguished by the Reform Bill, at the date of which it had exactly two voters, namely, the rector and an alderman of the corporation, while the surviving alderman acted as mayor and returning officer.

Lower down the Nene is *Sutton*, or *Long Sutton*. *Houghton*, the fine seat of the Marquis of Cholmondeley. It belonged to Sir Robert Walpole, who built it (he being a native), and formed a gallery of pictures, which were bought by the Empress Catherine of Russia; about 200 of the best were engraved by Boydell. The hall is a cube of 40 feet; and all the apartments are sumptuously fitted up. *Rainham*, the old seat of the Townshend's, contains Salvator Rosa's "Belisarius," a most remarkable picture. One of this family, a friend of Walpole's, was the great patron of the turnip culture. At *Hunstanton*, Sir Roger Lestrange, who edited the first "London Gazette," was born; there are remains of the old seat, and a lighthouse on the low cliffs which border this side of the Wash. *Burnham Thorpe*, one of several Burnhams, near the north coast of Norfolk, was the birthplace of *Horatio Nelson*, who was born at the parsonage (his father being rector), in 1758. When sent to sea he was so delicate looking that his uncle, Capt. Suckling, predicted he would be carried off by the first puff of wind; and he retained a thin battered appearance to the last. His name, for which the world was not too wide, is an anagram on one of his great battles,—*Honor a te Nilos*, literally "Honour to thee by the Nile." Norfolk has produced several great seamen; at *Cockthorpe*, in particular, were born,—Sir Christopher Mengs, of Charles II.'s time, a rough but hearty seaman, killed in battle with the Dutch, to the bitter grief of his sailors, who, as Pepys tells, "came him and Sir W. Coventry, after the funeral, begging a fire-ship that they might show their regard for their dead Commander, and their revenge, by the sacrifice of their own lives." He calls it one of the "most romantique cases that ever I heard in my life." Sir Jno. Narborough, another Admiral, was at first cabin boy to Mengs, and Sir Cloudesley Shovell was Narborough's—all three were natives of Cockthorpe. Lord Hawke was born at Docking. *Holkham*, the Earl of Leicester's seat, was built by the famous "Coke of Holkham," a descendant of the lawyer, and a distinguished agriculturist. Lord Burlington, who designed Burlington House, in Piccadilly, was the architect of this beautiful structure, which contains a rich collection of pictures (especially Claudes), marbles, books, busts, &c. Before Mr. Coke's time (1770), not a grain of wheat was sown all the way to Lynn.

Lynn to Dereham.

After passing, in succession, Middleton, East Winch, Bilney, and Narborough stations, we arrive at

SWAFFHAM.

Population, 3,858.
Distance from station, ¼ mile.
Telegraph station at Dereham, 12¼ miles.
Hotel. — Crown.
Market Day.—Saturday.
Fairs.—May 12th, July 21st, and November 3rd.

This town, noted for its butter market, has a population of 3,858, is situated on an eminence, and consists of four principal streets. The parish church, which is the finest in the neighbourhood, is a large edifice in the form of a cross, and consists of a nave with two aisles, a chancel, and two transept chapels. It contains several monuments, a roof of finely carved oak, and a library. Here are also several meeting houses, an assembly room, theatre, house of correction, &c. Races are held annually on an extensive heath, to the south of the town; and coursing matches are not unfrequent on the same ground.

In the vicinity are the following seats, *Pickenham Hall*, Wm. Chute, Esq.; and *Necton*, Col. Mason.

DUNHAM.

Distance from station, ¼ mile.
Telegraph station at Dereham, 8¾ miles.
MONEY ORDER OFFICE at Swaffham, 4 miles.

In the vicinity are *Dunham Lodge*, seat of Sir — Clarke; *Castle Acre*, remains of a Priory; *Kempson*, Gen. Fitzroy; *Lexham Hall*, E. Keppel, Esq.; and *Litcham*, with its ancient church.

Then passing the FRANSHAM and WENDLING stations we arrive at

Dereham.—See page 31.

Eastern Counties Main Line continued.

Ely to Wymondham.

MILDENHALL ROAD.

Distance from station, 8½ miles.
Telegraph station at Ely, 7 miles.
HOTELS.—Bell, White Hart.
MARKET DAY.—Friday. FAIR.—October 10th.

In the vicinity is *Mildenhall House*, sea of Sir H. Bunbury, Bart., and which belonged to Speaker Hammer. The Church is timber-roofed, with tombs of the Norths, whose old seat is here.

LAKENHEATH.

Distance from station, 2 miles.
Telegraph station at Brandon, 3¾ miles
MONEY ORDER OFFICE at Brandon, 3¾ miles

Here we leave the fen country and enter upon a wooded and picturesque district. *Lakenheath Hall*, the seat of R. Eagle, Esq.

BRANDON.

POPULATION, 2,022.
Distance from station, ½ mile.
A telegraph station.
HOTEL.—Chequers.
MARKET DAY.—Friday.
FAIRS.—February 11th, Monday before Easter, July 5th, and November 16th.

This place formerly supplied Government with gun flints. Lord Mayor Eyre, who built Leadenhall Market, was a native.

In the vicinity are *Brandon Park*, seat of E. Bliss, Esq.; *Backenham House*, Lord Petre's; *Merton*, Lord Walsingham's, in the Elizabethan style, &c.

THETFORD.

A telegraph station.
HOTEL.—Bell.
MARKET DAY.—Saturday.
FAIRS.—May 14th, August 2nd, December 9th and 25th, and Holy Thursday.

A market town, the ancient capital of East Anglia with a population of 4,075, who return two members situated at the junction of the Ouse and the Thet. The principal part of Thetford is in Norfolk, but a small part is in Suffolk. The part which is situated in the latter county is now very small but on the Norfolk side there are several good streets, and of late years the town has much improved in its general appearance. Remains of its former splendour are noticeable. King's or John of Gaunt's Palace, remains of Bigod's Priory, where several noble families were interred, St. Sepulchre's Gate, Chapel of Canute's Nunnery, St. Peter's dark flint Church, the Guildhall, and Castle Hall, 100 feet high, should be visited. In the vicinity is *Euston Park*, the seat of the Duke of Grafton. The celebrated Tom Paine was a native.

After passing the HARLING and ECCLES ROAD stations we arrive at

ATTLEBOROUGH.

A telegraph station.
HOTEL.—New.

The Church is a half Norman Cross. This was the seat of the Anglian Monarchs. In the vicinity are the seat of Sir W. B. Smyth, Bart., *St. Andrew's Hall;* Sir F. Baring, Bart. *Derpham*, at which was a lime 90 feet high and 48 in girth, &c.

WYMONDHAM.

POPULATION, 2,970.
A telegraph station.
HOTEL.—King's Head.
MARKET DAY.—Friday.
FAIRS.—February 13th, May 17th, and September 7th.

WYMONDHAM is a town of crape weavers, with an old *Abbey Church* (in which are the D'Albine monuments, the founders of it), and the Norman front of the abbey itself, belonging to the Ladies Alfred Paget and Macdonald, the co-heiresses of the late George Wyndham, Esq., of Cromer Hall, descendant of the celebrated Secretary of State Wyndham. Kett, the tanner, a native, was hanged from the steeple here in 1549, for heading the Norwich insurrection, Bentham was vicar, and Peacham master of the school. It gives name to the Wyndhams of Felbrige Hall. In the vicinity is *Stanfield Hall*, the seat of the Prestons, where Jeremy Preston, Esq., was murdered by Rush in 1849. Potash Farm, where the assassin lived, has been pulled down.

DEREHAM AND FAKENHAM BRANCH.

Wymondham to Fakenham and Wells.

KIMBERLEY station.

HARDINGHAM.

A telegraph station.
MONEY ORDER OFFICE at Wymondham, 5¾ miles.

This is the birthplace of Sir Thomas Gresham, the celebrated London Merchant: he founded a Grammar School at Holt, and the townsmen of that place claim him also as a native. In the vicinity is *Hardingham Hall*, seat of Mrs. Edwards.

Passing on we reach the THUXTON and YAXHAM stations, and then arrive at

DEREHAM.

POPULATION, 3,372.
Distance from station, 1 mile.
A telegraph station
HOTEL.—King's Arms.
MARKET DAY.—Friday.
FAIRS.—Thursday and Friday before Old Midsummer, Thursday and Friday before New Michaelmas.
BANKERS.—Branch of East of England Bank.

The Church of St. Nicholas, which was founded by Withburga, the daughter of an Anglian monarch, should be visited; its font, with carved figures, and chest in Edward's Chapel will be appreciated. Here lie buried the poet Cowper, who died at his cousin's in 1800, and Mrs. Unwin; there is an epitaph on his tomb by Hayley. In the vicinity is *Quebec Castle*, seat of W. Warner, Esq.

ELMHAM.—Here are traces of a castle, erected by the fighting Bishop Spencer. In the vicinity are *Elmham Hall*, the seat of Lord Sondes; and *Broom Close*, where Roman antiquites have been found; *Bilney Hall*, J. Culison, Esq.; *East Bilney*, where the Martyr Bilney was born; *Mileham*, of which Coke the lawyer was a native.

RYBURGH station.

FAKENHAM LANCASTER.

A telegraph station.
HOTELS.—Red Lion and Crown.
FAIRS.—Whit Tuesday, November 22nd for cattle.
MARKET DAY. Thursday.
BANKERS.—Gurneys and Co.; Branch of East of England Bank.

In the Church, which is later English, there is a fine doorway, brass, and font. In the neighbourhood are *Rainham*, Lord Townshend's seat, at which may be seen Salvator Rosa's "*Belisarius begging;*" *Houghton*, the Marquis of Cholmondeley; *Holkham*, Lord Leicester's, the finest seat in the county; *Melton Castle*, Lord Hastings'; and *Burnham Thorpe*, the birthplace of the gallant Nelson.

WALSINGHAM.

At *Walsingham Abbey*, seat of H. L. Warren, Esq., are remains of an abbey of the 11th century, where used to be shown a model of the Holy Sepulchre. The beautiful east window of the chancel is 60 feet high. In the *Parish Church*, the father of Sir Philip Sidney is buried. *Walsingham* was a great place for pilgrimages to the Virgin, whose image was burnt at Chelsea, by order of Henry VIII., though he had walked bare-footed in his youth from Basham, to give her a handsome necklace. At Binham and Houghton-le-Dale are some old ecclesiastical ruins.

WELLS.

A small seaport town, having a spacious harbour, but not easy of access. Here is an oyster fishery. Corn and malt are shipped. Coals, timber, deals, bark, &c., &c., imported.

Eastern Counties Main Line continued.

Wymondham to Reedham.

We again proceed on our journey, calling at HETHERSETT and TROWSE, and very quickly reach

Norwich, for particulars of which see page 38.

BRUNDALL.—Near to this station is *Brundall House*, seat of the Rev. L. B. Foster, and several ruined churches.

BUCKENHAM.—From *Strumpshaw Hill*, in the vicinity, is an extensive view of the flattish country between Norwich and the sea.

CANTLEY station.

REEDHAM (Junction).

POPULATION, 771.
A telegraph station, and junction of the branch line to Lowestoft.

At this place, "Lothbrock the Dane was murdered."

LOWESTOFT BRANCH.

HADDISCOE.

Distance from station, $1\frac{1}{4}$ mile.
A telegraph station.

The Church has a fine Norman door and round tower.

SOMERLEYTON.

A telegraph station.
MONEY ORDER OFFICE at Lowestoft, $4\frac{1}{2}$ miles.

In the vicinity is *Somerleyton Hall*, the old Elizabethan seat of the Jerninghams, but now the residence of Sir S. M. Peto, Bart., who has greatly enlarged the building.

MUTFORD station.

LOWESTOFT.

Distance from station, $\frac{1}{2}$ mile.
A telegraph station.
HOTEL.—Queen's Head.
MARKET DAY.—Wednesday.
FAIRS.—May 12th, and October 10th.
BANKERS.—Gurneys and Co.; Lacon and Co., Sub Branch of National Provincial Bank of England.

A market and seaport town (the most eastern point in the kingdom), with a population of 4,647. It stands on a considerable eminence, commanding extensive views of the German Ocean and surrounding country. Its appearance from the sea is extremely picturesque. The town is neat, clean, and well lighted; contains Theatre, Assembly Rooms, Baths, and a fine church, dedicated to St. Margaret, which should be visited, and its Porch, "Maid's

Chamber" over it, brasses, steeple 120 feet high, and font should be noticed. In it are monuments to Bishop Scroope (brother to Bishop Tanner), Whiston, Potter, and Hudson, with the quaint epitaph "Here lie your painful ministers, &c.," all of whom held that living. A chapel of ease, dedicated to St. Peter was erected a few years since by subscription. Admirals Usher, Ashby, Mighell, (all natives), and Chief Justice Holt. Here, in 1665, the Duke of York defeated the Dutch Admiral Offdam. George II. landed at this place in 1737, and Adams, the first American Ambassador in 1784. Admirals, Sir T. Allen and Sir Thomas Leake, Nash, the author, and Gillingwater, the historian, were natives. Harbour of Refuge, Tram Way, Promenade, Pier, Light Houses, Warehouses, and Sea Wall were erected in 1848, by Sir S. M. Peto, Bart.

Main Line Reedham to Yarmouth.

YARMOUTH.

A telegraph station.

HOTEL.—Angel.

STEAM VESSELS to Hull every Tuesday. Fares, 11s. and 6s.; to London, twice weekly. Fares, 8s. and 5s.; to Newcastle every Wednesday. Fares, 15s. and 8s.

MARKET DAY.—Wednesday and Saturday.

FAIRS.—Easter Friday and Saturday.

RACES in August. Marine Regatta in July or August.

BANKERS.—Gurneys and Co.; Lacon and Co. Branch of East of England Banking Co.; National Provincial Bank of England.

GREAT YARMOUTH is a seaport at the eastern extremity of the county of Norfolk, situate on the east bank of the Yare; the parliamentary borough extending on the west side with the county of Suffolk, comprising the hamlet of South Town and parish of Gorleston. Population, 30,879. It returns two members. The town stands on a tongue of land, having the sea on the east, and the river on the south and west, and joined to the mainland at Caister on the north. It is connected with South Town, by a very handsome lifting bridge (finished in 1854), constructed by Grissel and Co. The borough was incorporated by King John. In 1260 the town was surrounded (except on the river side) by a wall, having ten gates and sixteen towers, the remains of which are still to be seen. The town has, however, greatly extended itself beyond the walls. The Church, dedicated to St. Nicholas, is one of the largest parish churches in the kingdom. It was founded in 1123, and has lately been restored. It contains a celebrated organ. Near it is the hall of the Benedictine Priory, restored and used as a school-room. The chief attraction of Yarmouth has always been its noble quay, extending upwards of a mile in length, and having for the most part admirable rows of trees, forming an agreeable promenade; adjoining to which are several Elizabethan houses, exhibiting rare specimens of carved work. The Town Hall and the Police Court are on the Quay. The Market Place is very spacious. There is a Theatre and a Public Library. On the beach a newly-erected Marine Drive extends (with the Victoria Terrace and Esplanade) for nearly a mile. At the south end, the Wellington (promenade landing) Pier, extends 700 feet from the terrace into the sea. At the northern extremity another pier is contemplated, and between them there is a free jetty, near to which are the Bath Rooms Bathing machines are placed both on the north and south beach.

The old town contains about 150 narrow streets or passages, locally called "Rows," extending from east to west, in which many remains of antiquity may still be traced. On the south Denes there is a column, 140 feet high, to the memory of Nelson. The inhabitants are chiefly engaged in the mackerel, herring, and deep-sea fisheries, which are here prosecuted to a very great extent with much success.

The Health of Towns Act has been introduced, and the town is well drained, and supplied with an abundance of pure water from Ormesby Broad.

In the immediate neighbourhood may be seen *Burgh Castle*, one of the most perfect *Roman Camps* in the kingdom; and the remains of *Caister Castle*, which was erected by Sir John Fastolfe, K.G., *temp.* Henry VII.

The town is defended seaward by three *Batteries;* and it contains a *Naval Hospital*, and *Barracks* for the East Norfolk regiment of Militia, and the Norfolk Artillery Militia.

EASTERN COUNTIES AND UNION.

London to Witham.

STRATFORD.—See page 20.

FOREST GATE.

Telegraph station at Stratford, 1¼ mile.

MONEY ORDER OFFICE at Stratford, 1¼ mile.

In the vicinity are *Epping Forest*, *Wanstead Park* (the deserted seat of the Tylney Poles), the *Infant Orphan Asylum*, *Lake House* (where Hood wrote his "Tylney Hall," in 1834), and the *Whitechapel School of Industry*.

ILFORD (Barking).

POPULATION, 3,745.

Telegraph station at Stratford, 3½ miles.

HOTEL.—Angel.

MARKET DAY.—(At Barking) Saturday, for North country cattle.

FAIR.—October 22nd.

The *Town Hall* is an old-fashioned timber-roofed building, *St. Margaret's Church* contains brasses and effigies of Sir C. Montague, and monument of Day, who founded Fairlop fair; near it are the remains of the Abbey gate, and Holyrood chapel over it. In the vicinity are *Byfrons*, the seat of the Sterry family; and *Albury Hatch*, in Hainault Forest, in which stood the famous Fairlop Oak, 36 feet in girth. It is stated that Hainault may be spelt 2,304 different ways by as many different Frenchmen.—*Sharp's British Gazetteer*. The Grampus, of 54 guns, was wrecked on Barking Shelf in 1799; the shoal is ⅝ mile long.

ROMFORD.

A telegraph station.
HOTELS.—White Hart, Dolphin.
MARKET DAYS.—Wednesday (corn).
FAIRS.—Midsummer Day, June 24th.

The town, which was the Roman *Durolitum*, contains a population of 3,790; the church, built in 1407, contained a stained figure of the Confessor, with effigies of Hervey and Sir Anthony Cooke (who entertained Queen Elizabeth at his seat, *Gidea Hall*, now occupied by Mrs. Blake), which was pulled down and a new one erected on its site in 1850, with a spire 150 feet high; Quarles, the poet, and his son, the royalist, were natives. In the vicinity are *Little Warley*, the East India Company's *Cavalry Barracks*, *Dognam Park*, and *Weald Hall*, C. Tower, Esq.

BRENTWOOD.

A telegraph station.
HOTEL.—White Hart.
MARKET DAY.—Saturday.
FAIRS.—July 18th, and October 15th.

This town, which contains the *Shoreditch Industrial School*, *County Asylum*, *Rich Grammar School*, and a population of 2,205, was formerly a large market and assize town, and is 281 feet above the level of the sea. The Old Town Hall is now occupied by a coachmaker. The *New Church*, built in 1835, has a handsome square tower, the old one erected in 1221 being converted into a National School. The *Crown* is a very ancient inn. In the vicinity are *Thorndon Hall* (built by Payne) the seat of Lord Petre, having a noble front 300 feet long, with a splendid collection of portraits, &c. *East Thorndon*, at which place is the gate of the Tyrell's old seat, and *Weald Hall*, C. T. Tower, Esq.

INGATESTONE.

Telegraph station at Brentwood, 5½ miles.
HOTEL.—Peter's Arms.
MARKET DAY.—Saturday. FAIRS.—1st & 2nd Dec.

This town, which contains a population of 860, derives its name from Ing (a meadow) and alte (the Roman mill-stone). The church contains monuments and effigies of the Petre family, who formerly lived at their old seat, *Ingatestone Hall*. In the vicinity is *The Hyde*, seat of the Disneys, one of whom discovered at Blunt's Walls, near Billericay, the *Disney Antiquities*, placed in the Fitzwilliam Museum.

CHELMSFORD.

A telegraph station.

HOTELS.—Bell, Greyhound, White Hart, Saracen's Head.

MARKET DAY.—Friday.
RACES.—In August.
FAIRS.—May 12th and November 12th.
BANKERS. — Sparrow and Co.; Branch of the London and County Bank.

CHELMSFORD.—A market, assize, and sessions town in Essex, of which it is the capital, with a population of 6,033. It is built in a beautiful valley between the rivers Chelmer and Can. The town contains shire hall, county room, with basement for corn exchange (in which it carries on a large trade), county gaol, house of correction, theatre, and Edward VI.'s Grammar School (at which Holland, a native, who translated Camden with one pen, Dr Dee the astrologer, Sir W. Mildmay, and Plume were scholars), several handsome buildings, and has been greatly improved of late years. In St. Mary's are monuments of the Mildmays, who possess the manor from Queen Elizabeth.

In an open space adjoining the *Town Hall* stands an ancient conduit, of a quadrangular form, and about fifteen feet high, which is built of stone and brick, with a pipe from each of the four bridges, opposite to which is Lord Chief Justice Tindal's (a native) monument. There is a considerable thoroughfare through this town, as the great east London road passes through it.

In the vicinity are *Writtle*, seat of the Conyers; *Pleshy Castle*, that of the ancient High Constables of England; *Danbury Church*, near a camp; the new palace of the Bishop of Rochester; *Boreham House*; *New Hall Nunnery*, with its Gothic chapel; *Hatfield Priory*, seat of P. Wright, Esq., &c.

WITHAM (Junction).

POPULATION, 3,303.
A telegraph station.
HOTEL.—White Hart.
MARKET DAY.—Tuesday.
FAIRS.—Friday and Saturday in Whit-Week.

In the church are Roman bricks, and effigies of Judge Heathcote, and the spire is fine later English. In the vicinity are *Witham Lodge*, W. Luard, Esq., at which George II. and Queen Charlotte visited on their tour to Hanover. *Faulkborne Hall*, J. Bullock, Esq. *Tiptree Heath*, on which is Mr. Mechi's celebrated model farming establishment.

MALDON (Branch).

A telegraph station.
HOTEL.—King's Head.
MARKET DAY.—Thursday.

FAIRS.—First Thursday in May, Whit-Tuesday, and September 13th.

MALDON, or Malden Water, an ancient borough and market town in the county of Essex, population 5,888, situated on the estuary of the Blackwater. It consists of one principal street, extending nearly a mile from east to west, along Cross Street, and several back streets and lanes. The whole town has been much improved of late years. It contains an old Town Hall, built by Henry VI., Custom House, Barracks, Library (founded by Plume, a native, in 1680), Grammar School; and handsome baths have been erected, which attract numerous visitors during the bathing season. The principal church of *All Saints* is a large and ancient building, with an equilateral triangle tower. Maldon carries on a great coasting, and considerable foreign trade. The channel of Blackwater river forms a convenient haven for vessels of a moderate burden. Here Bright, the fat man of Maldon, lived and died, aged only 28 years, but weighing 44 stone, and it is stated that seven men could be buttoned into his waistcoat.

BRAINTREE (Branch).

POPULATION, 2,836.
A telegraph station.
HOTEL.—White Hart.
COACHES to Halstead and Gosfield, twice daily.
MARKET DAY.—Wednesday.
FAIRS.—May 8th, and October 2nd.

Here is Coker's *Free Grammar School*, in which Kay, the naturalist, (son of a blacksmith at Black-Notley) was a scholar. *St. Michael's Church* was enlarged previous to the Reformation "with the proceeds of three plays acted in it;" it has a fine tall spire, and contains the tomb of Dr. Collins, physician to Peter the Great. Tusser, the clever agricultural poet, was born at Rivenhall in 1515.

Eastern Union Main Line continued.

Witham to Marks Tey.

KELVEDON.

Distance from station, 2 miles.
A telegraph station.
HOTEL.—Star and Fleece.
FAIR.—Easter Monday.

In the vicinity are *Kelvedon Hall*, seat of W. Wright, Esq., with a magnificent prospect: *Felix Hall*, T. B. Western, Esq.; *Coggeshall*, with its ruins of a priory; *Layer Marney* (with the old brick gate,) Q. Dick, Esq., M.P.

MARKS TEY.

Distance from station, ½ mile.

A telegraph station.

In the vicinity is *Copford Church*, with a Norman circular apse.

SUDBURY BRANCH.

CHAPPEL (or Pontisbright).

Distance from station, ⅓ mile.

Telegraph station at Marks Tey, 3½ miles.

MONEY ORDER OFFICE at Halstead, 6 miles.

COLNE VALLEY.

This short line of 6¼ miles, runs along the northern banks of the river Colne, passing through the little village of COLNE, once the property of the Wakes' family, to

HALSTEAD.

MARKET DAY,—Friday.
FAIRS.—May 6th, and October 29th.
It has a population of 5,658, employed mainly in the manufacture of silk velvet, and straw plait. It has several churches, and other places of worship; also, a market house, collegiate Institution, &c., &

Sudbury Branch continued.

BURES station.

SUDBURY.

POPULATION, 6,043.
A telegraph station.
HOTEL.—Rose and Crown.
COACHES to and from Melford, daily.
MARKET DAY.—Saturday.
FAIRS.—March 12th, July 10th, and Dec. 12th earthenware.
BANKERS.—Alexander and Co.; draw on Barnett and Co. Oakes, Bevan, and Co.; draw on Barclay and Co.

SUDBURY is a market town and borough, in the county of Suffolk, situated on the north-eastern side of the river Stour, over which there is a bridge. Formerly it was a place of much greater importance than at present. It was one of the first places at which Edward III. settled the Flemings, whom he invited to England to instruct his subjects in the woollen manufacture. This business accordingly flourished here for some centuries, but the trade has long since declined. *St. Gregory's Church* was built by Archbishop Simon de Sudbury (a native), who was murdered here by Wat Tyler's mob, and buried near the college, the gate of which remains. Gainsborough, the painter, and Enfield, author of the "Speaker," &c., were natives.

Eastern Union Main Line continued.

Marks Tey to Manningtree.

COLCHESTER.

A telegraph station.
HOTELS.—Three Cups, Red Lion, George.
OMNIBUSES to Clacton, Frating, Bentley, St. Osyth, Halstead, Walton-on-the-Naze, Kirby, Thorpe, Weeley, Elmstead.
MARKET DAYS.—Wednesday and Saturday.
FAIRS.—July 5th, Oct. 20th, 21st, 22nd, and 23rd, July 23rd.
BANKERS.—Mills and Co., Round, Green, and Co.; London and County Joint Stock.

COLCHESTER, formerly an important town (*Colonia*) of the Romans, now a parliamentary borough, returning two members, in the north-east corner of Essex, on the river Colne, and the Eastern Counties Railway, 51 miles from London. Population, 19,443. Here the famous British King, Cunobiline, (or Cymbeline), and his sons Guiderius and Arvisagus (or Caractacus) reigned, till dispossessed by Claudius

Cæsar. A few years after it fell into the hands of Boadicea, but was retaken; and in the third century became the seat of Constantius Chlorus, whose wife Helena, daughter of King Coel (according to the monkish accounts), gave birth to Constantine the Great here. But the real birth-place of this emperor was Naissus, in European Turkey. His mother founded the Holy Sepulchre at Jerusalem; there was a church called after her in this town, where the Friend's Meeting House now stands. Among the objects of notice are the gate of an Abbey, founded by William the Conqueror's Steward (Endo Dapifer), who also built a Castle, of which the keep, gate, and other parts remain; and a *Moot Hall*, since rebuilt. There are fragments of the ancient town walls. Many of the houses are old; one dates from 1490 *St. Botolph's* Norman church (part of the Abbey), was all battered down in the siege of 1648, except the west front. *St. Martin's* was ruined from the same cause. *All Saints*, *St. Leonard's*, and *Trinity*, are of the 14th century. At *St. James's* there is a picture of the Adoration of the Shepherds, and many old tombs. Other buildings are the *Theatre*, a *Custom House*, *County Hospital*, and a *Grammar School*, of which Dr. Parr was master; also a spacious Public Hall, erected in 1851. Small vessels come up to the Hythe; oilcake, timber, corn, malt, &c., are traded in. Silk for umbrellas is made here; some of the most costly velvet is also manufactured here. Excellent oysters at Pyfleet. There is a commodious quay on the river, which has been rendered navigable for vessels of 150 tons burden. Colchester is an important military station, a camp for 5,000 men having been formed during the Russian war; Middlewich Farm was bought by the Government, in 1856, for a drilling and exercise ground. In 1857 Lord Panmure, the Secretary-at-War, presented to the town two Russian guns, iron 30-pounders, trophies of the Russian war. Near this place is

WALTON-LE-SOKEN,

Or *Walton-on-the-Naze*, a rapidly-improving watering-place. Its peculiar appellation of "Soken" was derived from some exclusive privileges formerly granted to certain refugees from the Netherlands, who here established themselves, and introduced several manufactures, particularly that of cloth. Adjoining the old hall is a square tower, built by the Corporation of the Trinity House, as a mark to guide ships passing or entering the port of Harwich, and on other parts of the coast are two martello towers and a signal station. The church of All Saints was erected and consecrated by Bishop Porteus about forty years ago, the ancient structure having a few years before been entirely swept away by the tides, as well as the churchyard, and every house but one of the old village. In the clay base of the Walton cliffs fossils and elephant tusks, with antediluvian remains of gigantic animals long since extinct, are frequently found embedded. The beach presents a gradual declivity, affording excellent facilities for bathing, and as the ebb tide leaves a fine firm sand several miles in extent, it is also peculiarly available as a promenade.

We pass Ardleigh station, and then arrive at

MANNINGTREE (Junction).

Distance from station, ½ mile.
A telegraph station.
Hotel.—Packet.
Market Day.—Thursday.
Fairs.—Whit-Thursday.

This place is mentioned by the immortal bard, Shakspeare, in his play of Henry IV., 2nd part, act 2, scene 4th, "A roasted Manningtree ox with a pudding in his belly." In the vicinity is *Mistley Hall*, E. Rigby, Esq.

HARWICH BRANCH.

The stations we pass are Mistley, Bradfield, Wrabness, and Dover Court, arriving at

HARWICH.

A telegraph station.
Hotels.—Three Cups, White Hart.
Market Days.—Tuesday and Friday.
Fairs.—May 1st and October 18th.

A sea-port, packet station, and borough town in the county of Essex, with a population of 4,451, who return two members. It is built on a peninsular point of land, close to where the rivers Stour and Orwell join the German Ocean; and from the number of maritime advantages which Harwich possesses, it has become a place of fashionable resort, especially as the scenery in its neighbourhood has considerable beauty. The Stour and Orwell are both navigable for large vessels twelve miles above the town, the one to Ipswich, the other to Manningtree. In uniting at Harwich, these rivers form a large bay on the north and west of the town. Their joint waters then proceed southward, and fall into the sea about a mile below it, in a channel from two to three miles wide, according to the state of the tide, and in which the harbour is situated. The western bank of it is formed by the tongue of land which projects towards the north, and on which the town itself stands; the eastern bank is formed by a similar projection towards the south of the opposite coast of Suffolk, and between these two promontories the harbour is completely sheltered. It is of great extent, and forms, united to the bay, a roadstead for the largest ships. Harwich derives considerable profit from its shipping trade, fisheries, and annual visitors. It has hot, cold, and vapour baths, every accommodation for sea bathing, and a number of other sources of amusement. From this place Queen Isabella (1326), Edward III. (1338 and 1340), William III., George I. and II., sailed on their visits to France, Holland, and Hanover. Queen Charlotte and Louis XVIII. first landed here; and from hence was embarked, in 1821, the body of that much abused princess, Queen Caroline, consort of George IV. In the vicinity is *Dover Court*, in the church of which is a tomb to Secretary Clarke, killed in 1666 in action against De Ruyter. Here was a miraculous crucifix (at least so it was stated to be), for burning which three men were hung in 1532. Captain Hewitt sailed in H.M. surveying brig Fairy, from this port, and was lost, with his crew, on the 13th Nov. 1840, in a storm.

Eastern Union Main Line continued.

Immediately on leaving Manningtree we cross the river Stour, and enter the county of

SUFFOLK.

THIS county is level, compared with many of the other English ones. The highest land is in the west, where the great chalk ridge of this part of the kingdom extends from Haverhill by Bury, to Thetford in Norfolk. The climate is considered the driest in the kingdom. Suffolk is one of the best cultivated districts in England; besides its arable lands, it contains heaths, which are employed as extensive sheepwalks. Indeed, it may be called almost exclusively a farming county, agriculture being conducted on the most improved principles.

BENTLEY.

Distance from station, ¾ mile.

A telegraph station.

MONEY ORDER OFFICE at Ipswich, 5¼ miles.

HADLEIGH BRANCH.

Passing CAPEL and RAYDON stations, we reach

HADLEIGH.

POPULATION, 3,338.
A telegraph station.
HOTEL.—White Lion.
MARKET DAYS.—Monday and Saturday.
FAIRS.—Whit-Monday, and October 10.

A market town in the county of Suffolk, built on the banks of the river Breton. It was celebrated some years back for the manufacture of cloth, but the inhabitants are now principally employed in the spinning of yarn for the Norwich weavers. It is of great antiquity, and is believed to have been the burial place of the kings of East Anglia. On *Aldham Common* Rowland Taylor was burnt, in 1555.

Eastern Union Main Line continued.

IPSWICH.

A telegraph station.
HOTELS.—White Horse, Crown and Anchor.
MARKET DAYS.—Tuesday and Saturday.
FAIRS.—First Tuesday in May, July 25, August 22, and September 25. RACES in July.
BANKERS.—Bacon, Cobbold, and Co.; Alexander and Co.; National Provincial Bank of England.

IPSWICH, a port, borough town, and capital of the county of Suffolk, has a population of 32,914, who return two members. It is built on the northern bank of the river Orwell, and when viewed in ascending the river has somewhat the appearance of a crescent. The streets are rather narrow and irregular, like those of most ancient towns, but they are all well paved and lighted. The houses are many of them handsome modern buildings; and the rest, though old, are substantial, commodious, and many have gardens attached to them. At the corners of several streets are yet to be seen the remains of curious carved images, and several of the ancient houses are covered in profusion with this description of ornament.

It contains Town Hall, Corn Exchange, New Market, Custom House (with an old ducking-stool), Barracks, Baths, Theatre (here Garrick made his début, in 1741, as Aboan, in Oronooko), Lunatic Asylum, Hospital, Public Library, Assembly Rooms, Mechanics' Institute, Race Stand, Old Malt Kiln (once Lord Curzon's residence), Grammar School (of which Jeremy Collier was master), thirteen churches; Wolsey's House, where he was born, in 1471, stands near St. Nicholas. Sparrow's House, Christ's Hospital, Ransome and Sim's Machine and Agricultural Implement Works, which cover 14 acres; Public Park, Arboretum, the old churches of St. Lawrence, St. Margaret, &c. Wolsey, Butler (physician to James I.), Bishops Brownrigg and Laney, Dick, Mrs. Reeve. In 1848 a two storied house was removed 70 feet without injury, and in 1850 a large apricot tree was carried a mile off—Sharp's *British Gazetteer*. In the vicinity is the *Chauntry*, the seat of Sir Fitzroy Kelly, M.P.

Ipswich is favourably situated for commerce Vessels of any burden can navigate the Orwell to the town itself, where a wet dock of considerable magnitude has been constructed. Vessels are constantly passing from Ipswich to Harwich. They are fitted up for the accommodation of passengers, like the Gravesend boats at London. This excursion forms one of the amusements of the place, for the beauty of the scenery along the banks of the river, bordered on either side, almost the whole way, with gently rising hills, villas, and woods, renders the sail delightful.

IPSWICH AND WOODBRIDGE AND EAST SUFFOLK.

These railways, now open throughout, form much the nearest route between London and Yarmouth. From Ipswich we pass the stations of WESTERFIELD and BEALINGS, and shortly after stop at that of

WOODBRIDGE.

This is a little town of some commercial importance, having a considerable coasting trade, besides exporting large quantities of grain. It lies on the banks of the river Deben, about 8 miles from the sea, but which is here navigable for vessels of about 120 tons. The church is a fine spacious building and has several monuments.

MELTON and WICKHAM MARKET Junction.

FRAMLINGHAM BRANCH.

MARLESFORD and PARHAM stations.

FRAMLINGHAM.

This ancient little town occupies an elevated situation, near the source of the river Ore. The church is a fine building, with a tower of 90 feet, fine carved roof, and eight-sided pillars. Amongst the monuments it contains are those of the second Duke of Norfolk, and the Earl of Surrey, his son, beheaded by order of Henry VIII. Here are the ruins of a fine castle, built by Hugh Bigod, and held successively by the Mowbrays and Howards, but now in the possession of Pembroke Hall, Cambridge.

East Suffolk continued.

SNAPE and SAXMUNDHAM stations, from the latter of which is a short branch to LEISTON, and the little watering-place of ALDBOROUGH, rendered important as being the birth-place of the poet Crabbe.

DARSHAM station.

HALESWORTH.

POPULATION, 2,665.
A telegraph station.
HOTEL.—Angel.
MARKET DAY—Tuesday.
FAIRS. — October 29th, Easter, and Whitsun-weeks.

The Church, which is built of flint, is a fine edifice. The principal manufactures are sail-cloth and yarn, and general iron foundries. The most extensive malting and corn trade in the conuty is carried on here.

BRAMPTON station.

BECCLES.

This town stands on the banks of the river Waveney, from which it is navigable, in the midst of a very pleasant country. The porch of the Church affords a beautiful specimen of the florid Gothic, and the church yard, a series of many interesting views of the country around. At Endgate are the ruins of another parish church, destroyed in the reign of Queen Elizabeth.

A short branch here turns off to the right passing through CARLTON COLVILLE, to LOWESTOFT, described page 31.

ALDEBY, ST. OLAVES, on the river Waveney, and near to which are the ruins of a Priory; and BELTON stations.

Yarmouth, described page 32.

Eastern Union Main Line continued.

Ipswich to Norwich.

BRAMFORD.—In the vicinity is *Bramford Park*, seat of Sir G. Broke, Bart.; the *Chauntry*, the seat of Sir Fitzroy Kelly, Knight.

Passing CLAYDON station, we arrive at

NEEDHAM.

A telegraph station.
HOTEL.—Swan.
FAIR.—October 28.

The railway station is an Elizabethan building, substantially constructed of red and white Suffolk bricks, the string-courses and cornices being of Caen stone, and the roof covered with fancy tiles in patterns, and ornamental ridge crests. The centre portion contains the booking office, which communicates on either side with a passengers' waiting room, forming the ground story of the wings. The gateways at the ends are for the egress of the passengers from the up and down trains. The platforms, which are roofed in the whole length, are connected by a passage way below the line, thereby avoiding the danger of crossing on the level. The chapel of ease has a curious wooden bell turret. In the vicinity are *Crowfield*, *Helmingham*, seat of the Tollemache (Earl of Dysart) family; *Shrubland Hall*, Sir W. F. F. Middleton, and *Bosmere Hall*.

STOWMARKET.

A telegraph station.
HOTEL.—King's Head.
MARKET DAY.—Thursday.
FAIRS.—July 10, aud August 12.
BANKERS.—Oakes and Co.; draw on Barclay and Co.

The Stowmarket station is of brick, in the Elizabethan style. The distance from Stowmarket to Ipswich is about 12 miles, and Bury St. Edmunds, 14½.

Stowmarket is situated at the confluence of two branches of the river Gipping, on the road from Ipswich to Bury St. Edmunds. The church is Gothic, and at the parsonage is Milton's tree, planted by him when studying with his tutor, Dr. Young, the Puritan. Here are tombs of the Tyrrels. A large quantity of malt is made here, and there is only one place in the kingdom where a larger amount is paid to Government.

HAUGHLEY (Junction).

The line here turns off to the left, passing Emswell and Thurston stations, to BURY ST. EDMUNDS, a description of which will be found at page 25.

FINNINGHAM, close to the borough of Eye, population 2,590, who return one member. In the vicinity are *Oakley Park*, seat of Sir E. Kerrison, Bart.; Edmund the Martyr's oak stood here till 1848. *Redgrave Hall*, E. Wilson, Esq. (the old seat of Lord Bacon's father and Chief Justice Holt, both of whom, as well as Lord Bacon, lie buried in Redgrave Church); *Palgrave*, where the late Lord Denman was educated under Mrs. Barbauld.

MELLIS station.

DISS (Norfolk).

POPULATION 2,419.

Distance from station, ½ mile.

A telegraph station.

HOTEL.—King's Head.

MARKET DAY.—Friday. FAIR.—November 8.

BANKERS.—Oakes and Co.; Harvey and Hudsons.

The church was built by the Fitzwalters. Skelton (the witty poet laureate to Harry the Bluff) was rector. In the vicinity is *Shimpling*, the Duke of Grafton's seat.

Passing Burston station, we arrive at Tivetshall Junction.

WAVENEY VALLEY.

Pulhams station.

HARLESTON.

Market Day.—Wednesday.

Fairs.—July 5th and 6th, and September 9th and 10th, for stock and pedlary. Races in August.

Situated on the river Waveney, population about 1,500, engaged in the bombazine trade.

Homersfield station.

BUNGAY.

Market Day.—Thursday.

Fairs.—May 14th and September 25th, for cattle.

On the borders of Suffolk, watered by the Waveney, which is here navigable, there are ruins of a castle and nunnery of the Bigod's, with a parish church having one of the round towers so frequent in Norfolk and Norwich. *Loddon* was another possession of the Bigods.

Eastern Union—continued.

Forncett station.

FLORDEN.

In the vicinity are *Florden Hall*, seat of the Rev. Sir W. Kemp, Bart., and *Stratton House*, the Rev. E. Burroughes.

SWAINSTHORPE.

At this place there is a church with a round tower and six-sided lantern. In the vicinity is *Caistor*, the site of a large Roman city, and *Bixley Church*.

NORWICH.

A telegraph station.

Hotels.—Royal, Norfolk, Castle.

Market Days.—Wednesday and Saturday.

Fairs.—Day before Good Friday, Saturday before and after Whit-Sunday.

Bankers. — Gurneys and Co.; Harvey and Hudsons; Robert Balls; Branch of Bank of England; Branch of East of England Bank.

An old cathedral town, parliamentary borough (two members), and the capital of Norfolk. Population, 68,195. Norwich is agreeably situated on the banks of the Wensum, at a short distance from its junction with the Yare. The Wensum flows through the town, the principal part of which, however, is on the south side of the river, occupying the summit and sides of a hill, which rises by a gentle ascent from the south and west, but is much more steep on the other two sides, which are terminated by the valley of the river. The prospect of the city from a little distance is both imposing and beautiful. The massive walls of the old castle, crowning the summit of the hill, form the central object in the view, the lofty spire of the cathedral, and those of the numerous parish churches rising in all directions, give it an air of great magnificence, and mixed with this architectural grandeur is much more than the usual share of rural scenery to be found in populous cities, arising from the many large spaces of ground that are laid out as gardens, or planted with fruit trees. The introduction of the woollen manufacture first established the wealth and eminence of Norwich. A short distance south of it is Caistor, once an important Roman station *(Venta Icenorum)*, upon whose decline Norwich grew apace, so that at the Conquest it had 25 churches of wood, and in 1300 had 60. Thirty-six of these remain, one to each parish, built of flint, all destitute of spires to the towers, (many of which are round), and none later than the 15th century. The noble *Cathedral*, on the east side of the town, was begun in 1096 (when the see was moved hither from Thetford), by Bishop Herbert de Lozinga, and after various events was finished in 1510. It is shaped as usual like a cross, 398 feet long internally, to the choir, which is rounded off at the east end; 15 flying buttresses support the sides, and the whole is surmounted by a Norman tower (rebuilt in 1361), and crochetted spire, 315 feet high. The west front is partly Norman. The stone roof of the nave rests on massive pillars with spiral flutings. It has a fine commemorative window of stained glass, to Bishop Stanley, late of that see, which is very beautiful. There are various chapels and monuments, among which are those of Roger Bigod, Anne Boleyn's grandfather, and Chantrey's statue of Bishop Bathurst, one of his latest works. The fine Gothic cloister, 185 ft. square, is of the 15th century. Close by is the *Bishop's Palace*, begun in 1318; its old hall, 110 feet long, was utterly ruined by the Puritans, who destroyed the Chapter House, all the brasses and painted windows of the Cathedral, and suspended Bishop Hall, who describes their ravages in his "Hard Measure." "What work was here, (says the Bishop); what beating down of walls; what tearing up of monuments, what pulling down of seats; what wresting out of irons and brass from the windows and graves; what defacing of arms; what demolishing of curious stonework, that had not any representation in the world but only of the cost of the founder and skill of the mason; and what a hideous triumph on the market-day before all the country; when organ-pipes, vestments, surplices, and service books were burnt near the cross (now gone)." Here Master Bilney, the martyr was burnt in bloody Mary's disastrous reign, in 1531. The Ethelbert and Erpingham gates leading to the close, and the gates of the Bishop's Palace, also deserve notice. On the hill to the south is the castle built by Bigod at the Conquest; the great Norman keep, 70 feet high (with a tomb in it, both by W. Wilkins, a native architect, and called after him). The barbican bridge, and two other towers are incorporated with the *County Gaol*, built in 1818, for 200 prisoners, and the *Shire Hall*, built in 1822, in the Tudor style. The bridge just mentioned is said to be a complete circle, as much being below the ground as above it. A double railing runs round the castle precincts; the hill on which it stands is artificial. The *Cattle Market*, one of the largest out of London, is held on a piece of ground to the south.

A little west of the Castle is the *Town Market*, a large open space, with some old fashioned gable-fronted houses, above which rises the solid tower of *Mancroft Church.* The *Guildhall* is in one corner, an old flint Gothic edifice, built in 1453; besides portraits of William III. (with his serious face and hooked nose), it contains an interesting relic, namely, a letter of Nelson's sent with the sword of one of the Spanish admirals, taken at St. Vincent. A short distance from here stands St. Andrew's Hall, built by the Erpinghams, in 1415, and afterwards given, in the reign of Elizabeth, to the banished Walloons, who introduced the bombasin manufacture, now turned into a room for festivals and public meetings. It is, along with the Friars' Kitchen, incorporated with the buildings of the Home of Industry. As modernized in 1774, it is 124 ft. long by 70 broad, resting on pillars, lit by upwards of 48 windows, and ornamented with many portraits by Opie, Gainsborough, and other artists. One of the best is Beechey's portrait of Nelson, said to be an excellent likeness; Queen Anne and her husband, ("*Est-il possible?*") by whom she had nineteen children, and Horace Walpole, are in the list. At a grand dinner given to the Duke of Norfolk in this hall, three centuries ago, the Mayor's share of the cost was £1 12s. 6d., but flour was then only 6d. per bushel. He died at the residence of Sir Thomas Browne. There is a *Museum* in St. Andrew's-street.

St. Peter Mancroft Church is the largest in the city (after the cathedral), 212 feet long, and later English in the style; tower, 100 feet high. One tomb is that of Sir Thomas Browne the physician, and author of the "Religio Medici:" his portrait is in the vestry. The oldest church in Norwich is that of *St. Julian* near the river and Southgate; part is Norman, but the church was founded before the Conquest. *St. Ethelred's* near it is almost as old. A little beyond St. Stephen's Gates is the *Norfolk and Norwich Hospital. St. Giles'*, is the highest church, and is marked by a tower of 120 feet; an old town gate stood here, and the site of the fortified walls and ditch may be traced; beyond it is the *City Gaol and House of Correction*, built in 1827, by P. Barnes. The tower of *St. Lawrence* is 112 feet high; the saint and his gridiron are carved over the gate. In Saxon times the tide came up to the church, which had a quay for fish in front.

About ten short bridges cross the Yare and Wensum, the most ancient being *Bishop's Bridge*, built in 1295, near *St. Helen's Church.* Close at hand is the *Dungeon Tower*, 52 feet high, built in the 14th century. *Cavalry Barracks* at Porkthorpe.

The *Grammar School* is a very old institution, dating from 1325, when it was founded by Bishop Salmon; it was held in what was the Charnel House, at the west end of the Cathedral. Here Archbishop Parker, a native of Norwich, (born in 1504); Dr. Kaye or Caius, another native, founder of Caius' College Cambridge; the great lawyer Coke; Nelson; Maltby, the late Bishop of Durham; Dr. Samuel Clarke, also a native, were educated. The last became chaplain to Bishop More. He was so full of logic and so precise in its employment that Voltaire styled him a *moulin à rasionnement* "a reasoning machine." The *Boy's Hospital* is near St. Edmund's, Fishergate; and the *Girl's* in Golden Dog Lane, St. Saviour's parish. An *Hospital* for old men and women, near the cathedral; also *Doughty's Hospital*, in Calvert Street. The *Blind Asylum*, in Magdalen Street; the *Infirmary* for pauper lunatics, in the outskirts, just out of St. Augustine's Gates.

On Bank Plain is Gurney's Bank, established by an old Norfolk family, equally known for their good works and philanthropy. The Norwich Union Insurance Office, in Surrey Street founded in 1808, which insures three-sevenths of the whole farming stock insured by the country offices. Dr. Enfield, the well known author of the "Speaker," died here in 1797, minister of the *Octagon Chapel* (for Unitarians); here Taylor the German scholar was buried. He corresponded much with Southey, and edited the *Norwich Iris* for the two years it lasted. One of the earliest country papers was the *Norwich Gazette*, which Cave (of the *Gentleman's Magazine*) published in 1706.

Norwich covers a tract of about $1\frac{1}{2}$ by 1 mile. In Fuller's time most of the houses were thatched. "Norwich," he says, "is like a great volume with a bad cover, having at best but parchment walls about it." Silk and worsted stuffs are the chief manufactures of Norwich, with shoes, &c., and various articles incidental to a large agricultural town. The staple branches of trade are in a flourishing state. There are factories for mohair, silk, and worsted. Opposite St. James's Church is Fastalff's House or Palace, once the seat of Sir John Fastalft of Caistor, a valiant knight of (Henry VI.'s. time) Erpingham, who built the gate near the Cathedral, on which his effigy is carved, and distinguished himself at Agincourt in the next reign.

Excursions.—Many interesting objects are within a short distance of the city. A little west is *Heigham Church*, in which Bishop Hall was buried, our English Seneca, as he has been aptly called by Fuller, though he was indeed something better, for he practised that philosophy and resignation which the other only wrote about, and did not practise so well. Never were the proportions of a Christian divine, a sweet gravity, useful learning, manly piety, clear common sense, and a genuine English style more truly hit than in the character and writings of this wise and excellent prelate. The house in which he died in 1656, aged 82 (nine years after the sequestration of his diocese) is now an inn. *Mousehold Heath*, which overlooks the city, was the head quarters of Kett the tanner, in his rising in 1549. What is called Kett's Castle is part of a priory which was given to the Dukes of Norfolk, and made a seat by them, bearing the name of Mount Surrey House. They had another, a very magnificent one, near Newgate, in the city. Three miles this side also is *Thorpe*, a fine open spot, covered with villas, and the seat of Colonel Harvey. *Rackheath*, (4 miles), Sir E. Stracey, Bart., formerly a priory cell. *Earlham*, (2 miles), the Gurneys' seat, where the pious and inestimable Elizabeth Fry was born, of a Quaker family of four generations. She married and came to London, and began that life of usefulness which has made her name honoured throughout the land. Though a preacher at the meeting, and placed in the midst of scenes calculated to harden her manners, she always retained her own natural soft low voice, womanly tenderness, and retiring modesty, "touching you with the gentlest hand in the world." One of her works, besides her labours at Newgate, was to induce the Government to establish libraries for the Coast Guard service. *Costessey* or *Cossey Park*, the Jerningham's seat (Lord Stafford), has been rebuilt in the Elizabethan style. *Kimberley*, the ancient seat of Lord Wodehouse, the descendant of a very ancient family. *Melton*, belongs to E. Lombe, Esq. *Blickling* was the seat of the Boleyn family, and here Anne Boleyn was born, and afterwards married to Henry VIII. There is a brass of her in the church. The seat, *Blickling Hall*, Dowager Lady Suffield, was rebuilt 1628, in the Elizabethan style. *Gunton*, the seat of Lord Suffield. *Cromer*, a pleasant bathing place on the cliffs of the North Sea, is suffering from its encroachments, by which the land is fast swallowed up, and converted into dangerous shoals for the coasters. Crabs, lobsters, amber, and shells are got. *Cromer Hall*, the late seat of the Wyndhams, but now of the Buxton Family. *Felbrig Church* contains good brasses of the *Felbrigs*, and is near *Felbrig Hâll*, the Lucan's seat, who took the name of Wyndham. *Worsted* is worth notice as having given an English name to the manufacture of worsted. first introduced by the Flemings in Henry I.'s reign. The soil about here and along the coast is sand and gravel; several shallow lakes and ruined churches are seen, the parishes being frequently overrun with sand, or half engulphed by the sea. At *Holme*, near Horning, are the remains of *St. Bennett's Abbey*, which, though visited by Henry VIII.'s commissioners, was not destroyed, but given by act of parliament to the Bishop of the diocese, who sits, or may claim to sit, as titular Abbot of Holme. *Caistor* (3 miles), so called from *Castram*, a camp, was the ancient *Garionum*, an important Roman position, where several military ways met. In Henry V.'s time it was the seat of Sir John Fastalff, a famous soldier, who greatly contributed to the victory of Agincourt; and no way related to the immortal Jack Falstaff, whose best exploits were those of robbing tapsters and serving-men, misusing the king's press, easing fat citizens of their purses in the dark on Gad's Hill, and routing men in buckram, or fighting with Harry Hotspur (after he was down) a long hour by Shrewsbury clock.

GREAT NORTHERN.

The terminus for the passenger and goods traffic of this railway at King's Cross presents a most imposing appearance. In the *façade*, the two main arches mark the end of the arrival and departure platforms, and have each a span of no less than 71 feet.

Three large doorways admit passengers, on their arrival with their luggage, into the booking office. Convenient and spacious apartments, right and left of it, accommodate passengers until the trains are about to start, when they pass on to the platforms. Near the first-class waiting room, and to the platform where it communicates, is an excellent refreshment and coffee room.

On reaching the platform the traveller cannot fail to admire the size and character of the station, the semi-spherical roof, the immense area covered in, and the general arrangement to afford accommodation for several distinct lines of railway.

The goods station of this terminus covers a surface of ground of about 45 acres, laid out for the receiving, sorting and despatching of minerals, merchandise, and produce of every kind from every place, and to any destination, communicating with the railway, and is situated in Maiden Lane, Battle Bridge, north of the Regent's Canal, by which it is bounded on two sides, and from which water-communications are made to the docks constructed in the station. In the whole of the buildings Mr. Lewis, the architect, sought to combine with the greatest strength and cheapness of construction the utmost facilities for the transit and stowage of goods.

The Granary, which fronts the canal dock is 70 feet high, has six stories, 180 by 100 feet, and will hold 60,000 sacks of corn.

The goods-shed, the largest of its kind in the kingdom, is of brick, 600 feet in length, 80 feet wide, and 25 feet high. It is a model warehouse, complete with platforms. railway trucks, wagons, cranes, canal. and the ease and rapidity with which goods can be laden or unladen, lifted from the canal or shipped in barges, is extraordinary.

Nearly half the tonnage of the line is in grain, consisting of corn, chiefly from Lincolnshire. Until the opening of the Great Northern line, it was almost exclusively conveyed coastwise, at great delay and risk of loss and damage; but now it reaches the metropolis within 24 hours from the most distant markets, with the most perfect punctuality and safety by rail; and for the accommodation of this traffic the company keep a stock of 100,000 sacks. The carriage of potatoes has reached 300 tons per week; hay, from 30 to 40 tons; carrots, as much as 20 tons per week; and on a single market day from the neighbourhood of Biggleswade and Sandy, no less than 30 tons of cucumbers have arrived at the London station. Vegetables can now be brought by rail from 50 to a 100 miles off in as short a time, and in as fresh condition as by market cart from any place within 10 miles of London. The rails, in short, give a radius of full fifty miles for metropolitan market gardens, and however great may be the present consumption of fruit and vegetables, there can be no doubt that it is infinitely below the wishes of the population.

The conveyance of coal by the Great Northern Railway from the north has become a source of large revenue to the Company, and proves of invaluable advantage in supplying the wants of the metropolis.

Upon leaving the platform the train enters and passes through a tunnel which runs under the Regent's Canal, and emerging near the goods station, we pass under the North London Railway, thence through a shorter tunnel under Copenhagen-fields, the site of the new Cattle Market. Emerging from this tunnel the train proceeds along an embankment from which the traveller obtains a fine view of the northern suburbs of London, studded with churches, mansions, villas, and gardens of the wealthy citizens, who have abandoned their houses in the city for the more salubrious residences in this elevated suburb.

HOLLOWAY station.

The edifice on the right is *Highbury College*, the white building further on is *Hornsey Wood House*, where Queen Victoria stopped, Oct. 25th, 1843. *Muswell Hill* is on the left.

HORNSEY.

Distance from station, ¼ mile.
Telegraph station at London (King's Cross), 4 miles.
MONEY ORDER OFFICE at Islington, 3½ miles.

The village is very beautifully situated, and the parish of Hornsey includes a great part of Highgate and Finchley Common, now studded over with pretty villas and mansions. The salubrity of this neighbourhood is proverbial proving the truth of the theory that elevated regions are the most healthy. The neighbourhood of Highgate and Finchley were celebrated as the scenes of many of the exploits of Turpin and other highwaymen of notoriety. Pursuing our route we pass on the right *Tottenham Church*, and the *Middlesex County Asylum*. Near the church is the tomb of Moore's two children, who died at Muswell Hill. Here Lightfoot, the Hebraist, resided. In the vicinity is *Harringay House*, seat of J. Chapman, Esq.

WOOD GREEN station. We then reach

SOUTHGATE & COLNEY HATCH.

Distance from station, ½ mile.
Telegraph station at Barnet, 2¾ miles.
MONEY ORDER OFFICE at Barnet, 2¾ miles.

SOUTHGATE, situated on the skirts of Enfield Chase, a large tract of woodland, formerly stocked with deer. There are numerous beautiful mansions in the vicinity of Colney Hatch, close to which is the *Lunatic Asylum*, on a site of 118 acres. *South Lodge*, the seat of the illustrious Chatham, is in a charming spot. The neighbourhood affords some very fine views; and a visit to Colney Hatch, during the summer season, is esteemed a great treat by the lovers of fine sylvan scenery. In the vicinity are *Arno's Grove*, seat of the Welds; *Culland's Grove*, Sir W. Curtis, Bart.; *Bowes Manor*, Lord Truro; and *Winchmore Hill*, a pretty rural spot.

BARNET (Hertfordshire).

Distance from station, 1½ miles.
A telegraph station.
HOTELS.—Green Man, Red Lion.
MARKET DAY.—Wednesday.
FAIRS.—April 8th, 9th, and 10th, and Sept. 4th, 5th, and 6th.

BARNET is a considerable market town in Hertfordshire, situated on the top of a hill. The church is of great antiquity. At the twelfth mile stone beyond the town, is erected a pillar to commemorate a battle fought on that spot, April 14th, 1471, between the House of York, headed by Edward IV., and that of Lancaster, commanded by the Earl of Warwick, who, with many of the nobility, and nearly 10,000 men, were slain. Here is an ancient *Grammar School*. In the vicinity are *Oak Hill*, seat of Sir S. Clark, Bart., *Trent Park*, R. Bevan, Esq., and *Dyrham*, Capt. Trotter.

POTTER'S BAR (South Mims).

Distance from station, ¾ mile.
Telegraph station at Barnet, 3½ miles.
HOTELS.—Railway, Green Man.
MONEY ORDER OFFICE at Barnet, 3½ miles.

South Mims is in the county of Middlesex so called to distinguish it from North Mims, Herts. The tower of the church forms a highly picturesque object, being entirely mantled with ivy.

Proceeding onwards we enter the county of Hertford, passing *Willow Green* on the right, and *North Mims* on the left, the seat of F. Greville, Esq. In the same direction, a little to the right, stands *Hatfield House*, with its extensive grounds. In the vicinity is *Brookman's Park*, where the great Lord Somers lived.

HATFIELD (for St. Albans).

A telegraph station.
HOTEL.— Salisbury Arms.
OMNIBUSES to St. Albans, six times daily; to Luton and Westhampstead, twice daily; to Hertford, once daily.
MARKET DAY.—Thursday.
FAIRS.—April 23rd, and October 18th

HATFIELD is a market town, in the county of Herts, built on the banks of the river Lea. It is well known on account of the royal palace, which was for some time the residence of Queen Elizabeth, previous to the death of her sister Mary. Here is also the magnificent palace erected by Cecil, first Earl of Salisbury, which retains, to this day, nearly all its original splendour. Passengers are set down here for St. Albans; for a description of which see page 25. Continuing our route, we pass through a very pretty country of hill and dale, and reach the Welwyn Viaduct, a noble structure, which crosses a beautiful valley.

WELWYN.

Distance from station, 1¼ mile.
Telegraph station at Hatfield, 6 miles.
HOTEL.—White Hart.

WELWYN is remarkable as having been the residence of Dr. Young, the author of "Night Thoughts," and rector, who gave a Bowling Green and Assembly Rooms to the parish, and lies buried in the church. A short distance farther on s *Panshanger Park*, which is extremely beautiful. It belongs to the Earl Cowper, who permits the most free access to the park and grounds, and also to his picture gallery. In the private garden stands the famous oak, "Sylva Britannica," remarkable for its size, symmetry, and grandeur of appearance. From this point so many tunnels obscure the view that there is little to be seen after passing the Welwyn Viaduct.

It is also the junction with the HERTFORD, LUTON and DUNSTABLE.—See page 21.

STEVENAGE.

Telegraph station at Hitchin, 3½ miles.

STEVENAGE stands to the right, and in the vicinity is *Knebworth Hall*, the fine seat of Sir E. Bulwer Lytton, the novelist.

HITCHIN (Junction).

POPULATION, 5,258.
Distance from station, ½ mile.
A telegraph station.
HOTELS.—Refreshment Room at the station; Sun.
MARKET DAY.—Tuesday.
FAIRS.—Easter and Whit Tuesdays and Wednesdays.
BANKERS.—Sharples, Exon and Co.; draw on Barclay. Wells, Hogge and Co.; draw on Barnett and Co.

HITCHIN is a market town in the county of Hertford, situated in a pleasant valley. The church is a handsome edifice, containing several fine monuments, and the whole town has a clean and prepossessing appearance. In the neighbourhood of Hitchin is *Hitchin Priory*, the seat of F. Radcliffe, Esq., and several fine old mansions. Between this and Luton are numerous barrows, supposed to contain the bones of those slain in the battle fought by the Saxons and Danes, at the village of Hexton, in 914.

Hitchin is also the junction of a new line in connection with the Midland Company, running direct, through Bedford, &c., to Leicester; see page 4.

ROYSTON AND CAMBRIDGE BRANCH.

Passing BALDOCK and ASHWELL stations we arrive at

ROYSTON.

Distance from station, ¾ mile.
Telegraph station at Hitchin, 12¾ miles.
HOTEL.—Bull.
MARKET DAY.—Wednesday.
FAIRS.—Ash Wednesday, Easter Wednesday, Whit Wednesday, first Wednesday in July, and first Wednesday after October 10th.

BANKERS.—J. G. Fordham and Sons; E., C. F. and G. E. Forster

This market town, in the county of Hertford, is pleasantly situated in a valley, among the chalk downs of Hertford, on the borders of Cambridgeshire, and crossed in the lower part by the celebrated Roman road called the Icknield Way. Royston is chiefly supported by its corn trade. The old *Priory Church*, and remains of King James I.'s hunting box, where his favourite, Carr, was arrested for killing Sir T. Overbury, are worth notice. In the vicinity are *Kneezworth*, Sir C. Nightingale's, Bart., and *Wimpole*, Lord Hardwicke's, at which are Titian's portraits of Loyola and Raphael.

Passing MELDRETH station we arrive at

SHEPRETH.

Telegraph station at Cambridge, 8¼ miles.

In the vicinity are *Melborne Bury*, seat of J. Fordham, Esq., and *Shepreth Hall*, W. Woodham, Esq.

Passing FOXTON and HARSTON stations, we reach

Cambridge.—See Page 23.

Great Northern Main Line continued.

Hitchin to Peterborough.

ARLESEY & SHEFFORD ROAD.

Distance from station, ½ mile.
Telegraph station at Biggleswade, 4 miles.

ARLESEY is a parish in Bedfordshire, four miles from Baldock. *Arlsey House*, seat of J. Edwards, Esq. Shefford is a chapelry, in the vicinity of which are *Phicksand Priory*, Sir G. Osborne, Bart.; *Southill Cark*, W. Whitbread, Esq., and several mansions and gentlemen's seats. *Ampthill*, the seat of Lord Holland, is a noble edifice; and the park, noted for its ancient oaks, affords some agreeable views. The adjacent town of Ampthill is a market town. Four miles south of Shefford is *Wrest Park*, the seat of Earl de Grey.

BIGGLESWADE.

A telegraph station.

HOTEL.—Swan.

MARKET DAY.—Wednesday.

FAIRS.—Feb. 13th, August 2nd, Nov. 8th, Whit Monday, and Saturday in Easter Week.

A market town in Bedfordshire, with a population of 3,976, pleasantly situated in a fertile valley, on the eastern bank of the river Ivel, which is navigable as far as its junction with the river Ouse. The town consists of an early English Church, with brasses of Holstede, and angels, with St. John's Head; neat and modern houses, and was formerly one of the most extensive corn markets in England. Some of the finest vegetables are produced here, in large quantities, for the London market. In the vicinity are *Stratton Park*, C. Barnet, Esq. Here the *Coton Library* figured during the civil wars. Old *Warden House*, near the ruins of Warden Abbey, Lord Ongley.

SANDY.

Telegraph station at Biggleswade, 3 miles.

HOTEL.—Greyhound.
MONEY ORDER OFFICE at Biggleswade, 3 miles.

Passengers are set down here for Bedford and Potton, to the latter of which the line is now open.

SANDY, the ancient Salina, was formerly a military station, surrounded with ramparts, and to the north-east is an immense hill called Cæsar's Camp, supposed to have been the spot where the Conqueror encamped, after sailing up the river Ivel, from Lyne. On the top of this hill is a beautiful walk. The gardeners in this neighbourhood send large supplies of vegetables, especially cucumbers, to the London market. The railway now runs in the direction of the river Ouse, leaving the town of Eaton Soken on the left. About three miles distant is the town of POTTON (now accessible by the railway), and *Sutton Park*, the seat of Sir J. Burgoyne, Bart.; and *Sandy Park*, Hon. Mrs. Ongley, where coins have been found of an ancient date.

Potton and Sandy.—A short line diverges to the right from Sandy to the market town of POTTON, at which fairs are held in January, 3rd Tuesday *o. s.*; April, last Tuesday; July, 1st Tuesday; October, Tuesday before the 29th.

HUNTINGDONSHIRE.

HUNTINGDON is a large county which borders on the fenny districts of Lincolnshire and Cambridgeshire. It was formerly covered with woods, but has been disforested. Along the course of the river Ouse extends a tract of beautiful and fertile meadows, including the well-known Portholm Mead, near Huntingdon, nearly the whole of which are now abundantly productive, the extensive system of drainage adopted having in the course of a quarter of a century rendered them comparatively free from floods; and, where the clay bed is not too deep, the process of mixing it with the top soil has been of great service to its productive powers. The fen lands are estimated at 44,000 acres. The most celebrated article produced by the dairies of Huntingdonshire is the cheese termed "Stilton," which is chiefly made at a village of that name. Though a great portion of this much-approved article is from the luxuriant pastures of Leicestershire, it received its name rather from having been at first brought into notice at Stilton during the time that this place was of much greater importance than it is now. The extensive barracks, in which thousands of French prisoners were confined during the long war terminating in 1814, have been entirely removed, and its military character altogether lost.

ST. NEOTS.

POPULATION, 2,951.
Distance from station, ¾ mile.
A telegraph station.
HOTEL.—Cross Keys.
MARKET DAY.—Thursday.
FAIRS.—Saturday before third Tuesday in January, Ascension Day, Corpus Christi, and Dec. 17th.
BANKERS.—Rust and Veaseys; Wells, Hogge & Co.

The town is situated on the eastern bank of the river Ouse, which is here crossed by a handsome stone bridge, with three low towers on it. It contains many streets of well-built houses, a spacious market place; large decorated English church; Towgood's paper factory. Hugh, of St. Neots, Bishop White, and the Lord Mayors, Drope and Gedney, were natives. After leaving St. Neots, we pass several places of great historical interest, among which are the picturesque ruins of *Stoneley Abbey*, *Kimbolton*, and its venerable Castle, and *Buckden*, formerly the episcopal mansion of the Bishops of Lincoln.

OFFORD.—This forms two parishes called Offord Darcy, and Offord Cluny, pleasantly situated on the eastern bank of the Ouse. In the vicinity are *Diddington House*, G. Thornhill, Esq.; and *Stirtloe*, J. Linton, Esq. After crossing the river by a splendid iron bridge we arrive at

HUNTINGDON.

A telegraph station.
HOTELS.—Crown, Fountain.
MARKET DAY.—Saturday. FAIR.—Tuesday before Easter.
BANKERS.—Rust, Veasey, and Co.; Branch of the London and County Bank.

A borough town, and the capital of the county, with a population of 3,880, who return two members, in conjunction with the adjoining borough of Godmanchester. It stands on a gently rising ground on the northern bank of the Ouse, and is surrounded by a number of beautiful meadows, and principally consists of one handsome street, with a number of minor ones branching from it; and is connected by a causeway and several bridges with the town of Godmanchester, which lies opposite. The houses are, generally speaking, handsome. The principal edifices are the church of *St Mary's*, with tombs of the Sayers; and that of *All Saints*, with tombs of the Levitts, Fullwoods, and Cromwell's ancestors; and the *Town Hall*. There are also several chapels. Huntingdon is remarkable in history for being the birthplace of Oliver Cromwell; himself and children were born in the house now the seat of G. Rust, Esq., and his baptism is entered in the register for the year 1599.

On the left of the station is *Hinchinbrook House*, the seat of the Earl of Sandwich, formerly the residence of Sir Oliver Cromwell, uncle to the Protector. The view from the house and grounds is, perhaps, one of the most beautiful and picturesque in the county. The new *Hospital* is a most conspicuous object from the railway. Murry, of Huntingdon (a chronicler), and Prior Gregory (Hebrew scholar), were natives. Cowper, the poet, was a resident here in 1765, with the Unwin family.

Within a few miles are, *Brampton Park*, the seat of Lady Olivia B. Sparrow. and *Kimbolton Castle*, an old stone pile, seat of the Duke of Manchester. Catherine of Arragon, Henry VIII.'s wife, died here *Diddington*, G. Thornhill, Esq.; St. Neots has a good decorated English church, which belonged to an Abbey, founded in the twelfth century, in honour of St. Neot, a Cornish saint, whose relics were stolen from their original resting place, St. Neot, near Liskeard.. *Ramsey Abbey* (built by Cromwell), E. Fellowes, Esq.; here are a large church, and a gate of the Saxon Abbey, which Henry VIII. gave, with many other possessions in the county, to the Cromwells. Ramsey and Whittlesea meres, though they continue to figure in the maps as lakes, are now perfectly drained, and produce heavy crops of wheat. A range of low hills runs in from Huntingdon, past Alconbury and Little Gidding, where the pious Nicholas Ferrar, in Charles I.'s. reign, established his little ascetic community, called the Protestant Nunnery, to the edification of the Puseyites of that age, and the great scandal of the friends of Scriptural and undefiled religion.

St. Ives, described in Section II.

Proceeding on our journey we pass the *Union Workhouse*, after crossing the great north road by a viaduct, and a little farther on, in the same direction, the *County Gaol*, thence through some deep cuttings we reach the level country. On the right is the spire of *Wood-walton*. On the left the remains of *Sawely Abbey*, then the castle and tower of *Connington*, the seat of John Moger Heathcote, Esq.

HOLME.

Distance from station, ½ mile.

Telegraph station at Peterborough, 7 miles.

This parish was formerly famed for the immense quantity of fish caught in the fens. Whittleseamere is now drained by means of the centrifugal pump, and its 3,000 acres of land brought into cultivation. Connington round hill is one of the wonders of Huntingdonshire. Two miles distant is Stilton, famous for its cheese, the greatest portion of which is made at Melton Mowbray, in Leicestershire, and beyond is Yaxley, with its handsome Gothic church and crocketed spire, where S. Olinthus Gregory, the mathematician, was born in 1774.

PETERBOROUGH.

A telegraph station.

Hotel.—Crown, family and commercial.

Market Days.—Wednesday and Saturday.

Fairs.—July 10th and October 2nd.

Bankers.—National Provincial Bank of England; Branch of the Stamford, Spalding, and Boston Banking Company; D. Yorke and Co.

A borough and cathedral town, with a population of 8,672, who return two members, in Northamptonshire, on the river Nene, and on the Great Northern Railway, where three or four other lines strike off. The country is flat and uninteresting in winter, and when the floods are up, the roads are almost impassable. *Town Hall*, in the Market Place, was built in 1671. It has but one church, besides the *Cathedral*, which is the only object worth notice. Till the Reformation it was the church of an abbey, founded by the Mercian Kings, about 660, by the name of *Medes Ham Stede*, but rebuilt after the Conquest, when the town was styled *Petersburgh*, after St. Peter, to whom the Cathedral was dedicated. Length 464 feet, including the porch; the tower is 150 feet high. It is chiefly a Norman cross, the choir, transept, nave, abbey gate, &c., having been all built before 1200. The noble west front, 160 feet broad, is, however, of a later date, being comprised of three lofty early English recessed arches; and the east, or *Lady Chapel*, was not built till 1518. *Becket's Chapel* is in the middle of the front, which looks towards the Market-place. The churchyard is prettily laid out and planted. There are several monuments of the Abbots and others, all much defaced during the civil wars. One is ascribed to King Peada, the first founder. Henry VIII.'s divorced queen, Catherine (who died at Kimbolton Castle), was buried here. The body of Mary Queen of Scots was also brought hither, after her execution at Fotheringay, but her son James I. removed it to Westminster. Both of them were buried by Old Scarlet the Sexton, who died at the age of 95, of whom there is an effigy, "You see Old Scarlet's picture stand on high." There was a shrine here, a pilgrimage to which, by a convenient reckoning, was considered equal to one at Rome. The cloisters cover a space of 130 to 140 feet square; in the stained windows are the portraits of abbots, &c. Formerly, Peterborough was the poorest and smallest diocese, but both the income and duty are now equalised with others.

Dr. Paley was born here in 1743. Abbot Benedict, Bishop Chambers, and Gunton were natives. The counties of Hunts and Cambridge are immediately adjacent to this corner of Northamptonshire. Near the city are the following:—*Milton Abbey*, the seat of Earl Fitzwilliam, originally a country seat of the Abbots of Peterborough, but rebuilt in the reign of Elizabeth. There is here a portrait of Mary of Scotland given by her to Sir W. Fitzwilliam the day she was beheaded at *Fotheringay Castle*, which was built in the shape of a fetter lock by Edmund Langley Duke of York, 10 miles up the Nene, in 1580, of which there are scarcely any traces, as it was pulled down by her son James I. There are remains of a nunnery, where Richard III. was born. *Blatherwycke*, the seat of Right Hon. A. Stafford. *Elton Hall*, Earl Carysfort. *Thorpe Hall*, the Rev. W. Strong. At *Chesterton*, where Ermine Street crosses the Nene, was a Roman villa and station. *Overton-Longeville*, the Marquis of Huntley's seat, is near an old church. At *Thorney* there was a mitred abbey, of which part only of the Norman church is left. It belonged to the Bedford family. *Crowland* or *Croyland*, among the former fens of Lincolnshire, has the church and part of the gate, &c., of a third abbey, also a curious antique triangular bridge, of three arches, with a common centre, which parts off three streams at once—the Nene, Welland, and another. The wide enny country between Peterborough and the sea was many centuries ago a fertile tract, remarkable for its richness and prosperity, of which the accounts of old writers, remains of religious houses, and existing churches, afford undoubted proofs; but it was gradually overwhelmed by the ravages of the sea, and the silt brought down by the rivers, in feudal times, especially in the dismal contest of the Roses,—the Thirty Years' War of English history. Within the last twenty or thirty years, it has, however, been brought back to something like that state which made William of Walmesly describe it as a paradise of cultivation.

Peterborough to Boston, &c.

The entire line from Peterborough to Boston, lies on a dead level; the only difficulty in constructing which was in securing a firm foundation in some parts of the fens. It passes through the artificially drained district known as the Fens, being principally below the level of the high water at sea, and probably the richest and most productive land in the kingdom. The works of the line present few striking features to the eye of the traveller, though possessing considerable interest to the engineer. The principal of them are the bridges, which carry the line across the various rivers, both natural and artificial, which serve as outlets for the drainage upon which the district depends; the chief are those over the rivers Welland and Witham, and the artificial rivers, known as the Forty Foot, Red Stone Goit, Vernatts, South Drone, &c.; the largest and most remarkable of them being that over the Witham, at Horsley Deeps, near Bardney, which consists of one span of one hundred feet, and three smaller ones, of thirty feet each, and is in connection with, and forms the middle portion of, a viaduct, about three quarters of a mile in length. The material of all these bridges is timber; but in one or two cases, as in the bridge over the river Witham, at Boston, and Vernatts, near Spalding, the line is carried by cast-iron girders on timber piers.

The stations are plain and inexpensive; they are, however, suitable, and picturesque in appearance, although rather diminutive.

Great excellence was aimed at in the construction of what is technically called the permanent way; which consists of the rails, chairs, and sleepers, and the ballast in which the last are imbedded; this point, on which the comfort and safety of the passenger, and economy of the stock of engines and carriages, materially depend, has been most sedulously attended to.

Before making further progress along the main line, an opportunity is here afforded to explore the districts above alluded to, by means of the Boston and East Lincolnshire Junctions of the Great Northern Railway, which from Peterborough diverges to the east.

PEAKIRK (Market Deeping).

Distance from station, 3 miles.
Telegraph station at Peterborough, 5½ miles.
MARKET DAY.—Thursday.
FAIRS.—Second Wednesday after May 11th, August 1st, Wednesday before Lammas, Oct. 10th, and Nov. 22nd.
BANKERS.—Boston Banking Company.

In the vicinity of Peakirk is *Northborough*, where Mrs. Claypole (the Protector's favourite daughter) lies buried. Her old seat is now a farmhouse. The old church of Market Deeping is worth a visit. We now enter

LINCOLNSHIRE.

LINCOLNSHIRE lies between the estuaries of the Humber and Wash; and next to Yorkshire, is the largest county in the kingdom. The ecclesiastical architecture of Lincolnshire has long been justly celebrated for its magnificence, and the numerous churches in the county are objects of continued admiration. It is not unworthy of remark that the most splendid edifices which adorn this district, were erected chiefly in its lowest and most fenny situations, and we are at a loss to assign a reason why our ancestors should have preferred such a tract of country to the higher districts. Though the beauties of nature are scattered with a very sparing hand over Lincolnshire, the fruitfulness and richness of its soil make ample recompense for this deficiency. It has no manufactures of any consequence. Its trade consists almost entirely in the exchange of its produce for manufactured grocery, and other consumable commodities. There are several great fairs held in the county: that of Horncastle is especially celebrated for the number and quality of its horses.

Passing ST. JAMES (Deeping) and LITTLEWORTH stations, we arrive at

SPALDING.

A telegraph station.
HOTEL.—White Hart.
MARKET DAY.—Tuesday.
FAIRS.—April 27th, June 29th, August 26th, Sept. 25th, Wednesday before Dec. 6th.
BANKERS.—Garfet, Claypons and Company; Sub Branch National Provincial Bank of England; Branch of the Stamford, Spalding and Boston Banking Company; Boston Banking Company.

This is a market town, with a population of 7,627, and capital of the district termed Hollands. It contains five Chapels, Town Hall (by Hobson, a native), Theatre, Literary Club, Assembly Rooms, Market House, &c. Its church is of the 15th century, and has a good porch and a crocketed spire. Roman cisterns have been found here. Bentley was master of the grammar school. Johnson, the antiquarian, was a native. In the vicinity is a curious old moated seat at Pinchbeck.

HOLBEACH BRANCH.

Leaving the station at Spalding, we quickly pass those of WESTON, MOULTON, and WHAPLODE, and stop at

HOLBEACH.

This is a town of great antiquity; Roman ruins, coins, and foundations of buildings have been discovered. The style of the church is Gothic, and contains several monuments. Bishop Holbeach, compiler of the Liturgy, and Stukeley, the antiquarian, were natives.

Then passing SURFLEET station, we reach

ALGARKIRK (Sutterton).

Distance from station, ¾ mile.
Telegraph station at Spalding, 7½ miles.
MONEY ORDER OFFICE at Boston, 6 miles.

This place derives its name from the Mercian chief, Algar, who lies buried here. The church is good, and contains tombs of the Berridges of *Algarkirk*

Kouse, an old seat of that family. In the vicinity are Sutterton and Swineshead churches, at the latter of which it is reported that a monk poisoned King John, after his escape, when crossing the Wash.

Passing KIRTON station, we arrive at

BOSTON.

A telegraph station.
HOTELS.—Peacock, White Hart, Refreshment Room at the station.
MARKET DAYS.—Wednesday and Saturday.
FAIRS.—May 4th and 5th, August 11th, Nov. 30th, and Dec. 11th.
BANKERS.—Boston Banking Company.

BOSTON is a borough and port in Lincolnshire, on the Witham, near the Wash, with a population of 17,578, who return two members. About 8,500 tons of shipping belong to this port, which has declined from its ancient standing, through the silting of the river. Wheat is exported, and hemp, timber, and other Baltic produce, besides oilcake from Holland, imported. Old John Foxe, the martyrologist, and Dimond, a blind calculator, were born here. Its namesake, one of the most polished towns in the United States, was founded by a company of settlers from this place, who fled thither for conscience sake about 1630 (to turn persecutors themselves). One of the beautiful churches so common in Lincolnshire is to be seen here, close to the river; it is a noble Gothic pile of the 13th century, lately restored, 245 feet long by 100 broad, with a splendid tower 300 feet high, ascended by 365 steps, and surmounted by an eight-sided lantern, rising far above everything for many miles round. In some respects this is copied from Antwerp cathedral, and there is also here a copy of Rubens's famous picture, the "Descent from the Cross," which adorns that building. The church is dedicated to *St. Botolph*, the patron of seamen (from which the name of the town, meaning Botolph's Town was derived); it has been beautifully restored within these few years, and stained glass put in some of its 52 windows. The *Wesleyan Centenary Chapel* contains an immense organ, by Gray, with 2,490 pipes, and 49 stops. There are two old brick towers, called *Hussey* and *Kyme*, remaining; the latter stands 2 miles north of Boston. An iron bridge, 86 feet span, crosses the river. At the free grammar school, founded in 1554, Stukeley the antiquarian was educated. Within a few miles are *Tattershall Castle*, an old brick tower, 100 feet high, *Bolingbroke Castle* (5 miles beyond Langrick Ferry), where Henry IV., son of John of Gaunt, was born; and *Wainfleet* on the coast, giving name to William of Waynfleet (Bishop Patten), founder of Magdalen College, Oxford

Boston to Lincoln and Retford.

Passing LANGRICK and DOGDYKE stations, we reach

TATTERSHALL.

Telegraph station at Kirkstead, $2\frac{1}{2}$ miles.
MARKET DAY.—Tuesday.
FAIRS.—Friday after May 4, and 14, Sept. 25.
MONEY ORDER OFFICE at Coningsby, $5\frac{1}{2}$ miles.

In its ruined yet beautiful church is a brass to Sir R. Cromwell, the ruins of whose castle (built in 1440) is close at hand, with its well preserved keep, 100 feet high. In the vicinity are *Scrivelsby*, seat of the hereditary champion of England, Sir H. Dymoke, whose family tomb is at Horncastle, so famous for its August horse fair; *Hooseholme Priory*, Earl of Winchelsea, and Sleaford, with its spire church and handsome cross.

KIRKSTEAD.

Distance from station, $\frac{3}{4}$ mile.

A telegraph station.

MONEY ORDER OFFICE at Coningsby, 2 miles.

Nonconformist divines have generally been inducted to this living. The learned Hebraist, Dr. Taylor, held it. That "treble refined Christian," Hugh Kirkstead, was a native.

HORNCASTLE BRANCH.

Kirkstead is the station at which this branch turns off. A distance of $1\frac{3}{4}$ mile brings the tourist to the station of WOODHALL SPA, at which there is no need for more than a temporary stoppage; $5\frac{3}{4}$ miles more brings him to the terminus of the branch at

HORNCASTLE.

POPULATION, 25,088.
Telegraph station at Kirkstead, $7\frac{1}{2}$ miles.
HOTELS.—Bull, Red Lion.
FAIRS.—March, for cattle; 5th Thursday in Lent; June 21 and 22; August 10 to 21 (for horses); October 28 and 29.

MARKET DAY.—Saturday.

HORNCASTLE.—A market town, in the county of Lincoln, built on the banks of the Bane, and almost surrounded with small streams of water, celebrated for its large horse fair. The Bane has been rendered navigable to the river Witham; the town was formerly noted for the tanning of hides, but this trade has of late years gradually declined, and at this time there is not a tanner in the place. It is well built, amply supplied with excellent water, and, notwithstanding its low situation, the air is considered very wholesome. The church contains tombs of the Dymokes.

STIXWOULD.

In the vicinity is *Tupholme*, at which are the ruins of an abbey built by the Nevilles.

SOUTHREY Bucknal) station.

BARDNEY.—Here is a cross to the memory of Ethelred of Mercia, who founded the monastery built here in the 7th century, and of which he died abbot.

WASHINGBOROUGH.—In the vicinity are *Canwick*, seat of the late Colonel Sibthorpe, M.P., and Fiskerton Old Church.

Lincoln, described on page 8.

Lincoln to Gainsborough.

SAXILBY.

Distance from station, 1 mile. Population, 1,137.
Telegraph station at Lincoln, 6¼ miles.
MONEY ORDER OFFICE at Lincoln, 6¼ miles.

In the vicinity are *Thorney*, seat of the Nevilles; *Kettlethorpe*, Sir W. Ingilby, Bart; *Scampton*, and its Roman way; and *Tilbridge Lane*, old seat of the Bolles.

Retford.—See page 54.

MARTON.

Distance from station, 2 miles.
Telegraph station at Gainsborough, 6¼ miles.
MONEY ORDER OFFICE at Gainsboro', 5¾ miles.

In the vicinity are *Stowe*, with its Norman church and park, near *Trent*, seat of J. Landell, Esq. *Gate Burton*, the seat of W. Hutton, Esq. *Littleborough Ferry* (the old Roman station called *Legele-cum.)*

LEA.

Telegraph station at Gainsboro', 3½ miles.
MONEY ORDER OFFICE at Gainsboro', 2¼ miles.

In the vicinity is *Lea Hall*, seat of Sir H. Anderson, Bart; *Knaith*, where Sutton, the founder of the Charter House, was born: *Knaith Hall*, a seat of the Wyndhams of Cromer; and *Sowerby*, seat of Sir T. Becket, Bart.

Gainsborough.— See page 55

EAST LINCOLNSHIRE.

Boston to Grimsby.

Passing SIBSAY end OLD LEAKE stations, we reach

EASTVILLE (Friskney).

Distance from station, 3¼ miles.
Telegraph station at Firsby, 5½ miles.
MONEY ORDER OFFICE at Wainfleet, 5 miles.

The grammar school of Wainfleet was built by the founder of Magdalen College, Oxford, Bishop Wayn-Gate, in 1433, a native of this place.

Passing LITTLE STEEPING station, we arrive at

FIRSBY.

Distance from station, ¾ mile. A telegraph station
MONEY ORDER OFFICE at Spilsby, 4 miles.

At *Spilsby* there is an old church, with tombs of the Willoughbys, and a curious eight-sided market cross. The adventurous yet unfortunate Sir John Franklin, the Arctic Polar Navigator, was a native. The Irby family had a seat at *Irby*.

BURGH.

MARKET DAY.—Thursday.
FAIRS.—May 12 and October 2.

The tower of the church is curious. On the coast is the little watering-place *Skeyness.* In the vicinity are *Gimby Hall* and *Candlesby*, both seats of the Massingherds, an ancient family.

Passing the WILLOUGHBY station, we arrive at

ALFORD.

Distance from station, 1 mile.

A telegraph station.

HOTELS.—Red Lion; White Horse.

MARKET DAY.—Tuesday.

FAIRS.—Whit Tuesday and November 8.

BANKERS.—Bourne and Son; Branch Lincoln and Lindsey Banking Co.

This is a market town, with a good free grammar school, an old church with thatched chancel and ancient tombs, salt springs, and is the head quarters of a Wesleyan Circuit. In the vicinity are *Ormesby*, the seat of Mr. Massingherd; *Willoughby*, the seat of the brave Lord Willoughby; *Well Vale*, R. Dashwood, Esq.; and *Skendleby*, Sir E. Brackenbury, Bart.

CLAYTHORPE.

Telegraph station at Alford, 3 miles.
MONEY ORDER OFFICE at Alford, 3 miles.

In the vicinity is the seat of C. Packe, Esq., where Sir Harry Vane, of Cromwell's time, lived.

Passing AUTHORPE and LEGBOURNE stations, in the vicinity of which are *Burwell Park*, seat of M. Lisler, Esq., at which the celebrated Duchess of Marlborough, Sally Jennings, the Whig, Beauty, and Queen-Ruler was born; and *Castle Carlton*, seat of the Bardolphs, we reach

LOUTH.

A telegraph station.
HOTELS.—Fleece, King's Head.
MARKET DAYS.—Wednesday and Saturday.
FAIRS.—April 30, August 5 and 17, November 22, 3rd Monday after Easter.

BANKERS.—Branch Lincoln and Lindsay Banking Co.; Garfitt, Claypons, and Co.

A large municipal town, with a population of 10,467. It contains a beautiful Gothic church, with a spire 288 feet high. In the cemetery formerly stood St. Mary's Church, the vicarage of which was converted into a hermitage. The Corn Exchange is a fine edifice. Edward VI. founded the grammar school; its income amounts to £1,463, and the seal is "a boy birched by his master," with the pithy motto, "Qui parcit verge," &c., ("Whoso spareth the rod hateth the child.")—Sharp's *British Gazetteer*. In the vicinity are *Yarborough*, the old seat of the Yarburgh family, *Cockerington House*, W. Scrope, Esq., descendant of the ancient family of that name in Richard II.'s time; and the decayed port of Saltfleet.

We pass LUDBOROUGH, a telegraph station, in the vicinity of which are *Wyham*, J. Heneage, Esq., and *Swinehope*, seat of G. Alington, Esq, and then reach

NORTH THORESBY.—In the vicinity is *North Thoresby House*, C. Wood, Esq.

Then passing HOLTON-LE-CLAY station we arrive at

WALTHAM.

Distance from station, 2 miles.
Telegraph station at Great Grimsby, 2¾ miles.
MONEY ORDER OFFICE at Great Grimsby, 2¾ miles.
In the vicinity are *Roby Hall*, W. Tomline, Esq.; *Laceby*, J. Fardell, Esq.; *Humberstone Grange* (here was an abbey in Henry III.'s time); *Humberstone*, with its grammar school, founded and richly endowed by a foundling of that name, a native who realised a large fortune in trade.

Great Grimsby and stations between that and Hull, will be found on page 56, as belonging more especially to the Manchester, Sheffield, and Lincolnshire Company.

Great Northern Main Line continued.

Peterborough to Grantham.

TALLINGTON.

A telegraph station.
MONEY ORDER OFFICE at Market Deeping, 3½ miles.
Stamford, four miles distant. In the vicinity are *Burleigh House*, the beautiful seat of the Marquis of Exeter, built by the celebrated Lord Burleigh; *Casewick*, Sir J. Trollope, Bart., M.P.; *Market Deeping* (the church is ancient); *Bourn*, with an old church. The Lord Treasurer was a native. Roman pavements have been discovered here.

ESSENDINE.

A telegraph station.
MONEY ORDER OFFICE at Stamford, 4¼ miles.
The Stamford and Essendine branch here leaves the main line from Peterborough to York, and after passing RYHALL reaches STAMFORD, see page 4.

BOURNE & ESSENDINE

This short line of 6¼ miles diverges to the right, passing the stations of BRACEBOROUGH SPA and THURLBY, to the small but important town of

BOURNE.

MARKET DAY.—Saturday.
FAIRS.—April 7, May 7, Sept, 30, Oct. 29.
Situated in a fenny district; has a population of 2,789, engaged to some extent in the woollen and leather trades. It has a medicinal spring; there are also traces of a Priory, built in 1138.

Great Northern Main Line continued.

The cutting between Essendine and the next station is known by the name of Dane Hill, in allusion to a wood on the right, where the vestiges of a Danish encampment can still be traced.

LITTLE BYTHAM.—The country in this neighbourhood is exceedingly pretty, and abounds with woodlands, hill and dale, and picturesque scenery. The church of *Little Casterton* has been lately restored. In the vicinity are *Grimsthorpe*, Lord Willoughby d'Eresby, with a deer park 15 miles in circuit. It contains ruins of *Odo's* (the Conqueror's relative) *Abbey of Vallis Dee*, the house was built by the Duke of Suffolk (in Henry VIII.'s time) and Vanburgh.

CORBY.

Distance from station, 1½ miles.
Telegraph station at Grantham, 8 miles.
HOTELS.—Railway; White Hart.
MARKET DAY.—Thursday.
FAIRS.—August 26 and Monday before October 10.

CORBY is a market town pleasantly situated on the river Glen. In the vicinity are *Irnham Park*, seat of Lord Arundel of Wardour; *Falkingham*, at which is the ditch of the Beaumont's old castle. At *Stoke Rochford* to the left of the line there is an obelisk in memory of Sir Isaac Newton, who was born at *Woolsthorpe* in 1642, at which manor house are preserved his oak study, sun-dials, and a chair made of the apple-tree (which fell in 1835) which led him to discover the theory of gravitation.

GREAT PONTON.

Distance from station, 1 mile.
Telegraph station at Grantham, 3 miles.
MONEY ORDER OFFICE at Colsterworth, 4 miles.

GREAT PONTON is so called to distinguish it from Little Ponton, another parish betwixt this and Grantham. The Church of *Holy Cross* is a fine building, and the lofty tower, containing fine bells, forms a conspicuous feature in the landscape. In the vicinity is *Easton*, seat of Sir M. Cholmondeley, Bart.

GRANTHAM.

A telegraph station.
HOTEL.—Angel, family and commercial.
MARKET DAY.—Saturday.
FAIRS.—July 10th, October 26th, December 17th, Monday before Palm Sunday, Holy Thursday.
BANKERS.—Hardy and Co.; Branch of Stamford, Spalding, and Spilsby Banking Company.

A parliamentary borough of 10,873 inhabitants, who return two members, in the Soke of Grantham (as this part of *South Lincolnshire* is called), near the river Witham, among some long wolds. It is noted not only for its trade in malt, but for the manufacture of Grantham cakes, a very superior sweetmeat, sold in boxes at 1s. Bishop Still, and More the platonist, were natives. At the *Free School* founded by Bishop Fox (servant of Henry VII., and founder of Corpus Christi College, Oxford), Newton was educated. There is an iron spring; but the beautiful crocketed church spire of eight sides, with pinnacles at the base, is the chief object; it is 250 feet high. The church itself, 116 feet long, is of the 13th century, including an older crypt. The "Angel" is on the site of a preceptory of the Knights Templars. "Here it was (states De Foe, in his *Memoirs of a Cavalier*) that we began to hear of Oliver Cromwell who, like a little cloud, rose out of the east, and spread first into the north, till it shed down a flood that overwhelmed the three kingdoms." It was at Grantham, with only his own regiment, that he defeated 24 troops of the King's horse, in 1643. Here formerly stood one of Queen Eleanor's Crosses.

Within a short distance are the following:—*Belton Hall*, seat of Earl Brownlow, a large pile, shaped like an H, and built by Wren, or from his designs.

Harlanton Church, and the Tudor seat of the Gregorys, *Syston Park*, Sir J. Thorold, Bart.

Belvoir Castle, on the Leicestershire borders, seat of the Duke of Rutland, stands on the wolds above the vale of Belvoir (or "Beevor" as it is sounded), from which you ascend by steps, and has been partly rebuilt since the disastrous fire of 1816. Some good pictures and the old Quixote tapestry are seen; also remains of a priory founded by Ralph de Todeni, standard-bearer to William the Conqueror, and ancestor to the present (Manners) family. The late duke, who was a "mighty hunter," had a fine pack of sixty couple of hounds kennelled here; "very level, and well adapted to the Melton country which they hunt," says an enthusiastic authority, and under the care of William Godall, "who though but 31 years of age, has actually passed 20 in company with hounds," his entry at 11 years of age having been "unexceptionable." Besides the gentlemen riders "good men and true," "there are also some fox-hunting farmers who go well, and look upon a litter of foxes as the most valuable stock their farms can produce. If this book (Fore's *Guide to the Hounds)* were printed in golden type, such men would deserve to have their names recorded in it."

NOTTINGHAM BRANCH.

Grantham to Nottingham.

SEDGEBROOK.

Telegraph station at Grantham, 4½ miles.

About three miles S.W. is *Belvoir Castle*, the seat of the Duke of Rutland. Its collection of pictures will vie with any in the kingdom.

Bottesford, Elton, and Aslockton Stations.

BINGHAM.

Situated near the Fosseway, is a small market town in the vale of Belvoir, with a good early Gothic church; close to which are *Shelford*, a seat of the Stanhopes, and *Wiverton*, an old deserted house of the Chaworths, both of which were on the royalist side in the civil war, and made work for Hutchinson in an occasional skirmish.

Ratcliffe station.

Nottingham, described page 5.

SLEAFORD AND BOSTON BRANCH.

Grantham to Sleaford and Boston.

Turning to the right, from Grantham, the Line runs *via* Honington and Ancaster to

SLEAFORD.

This little town contains 4,000 inhabitants. The streets and houses have a remarkably clean appearance. The construction of the houses is of red brick, covered with slates and red tiles, which impart to it rather a novel aspect.

Heckington, Swineshead and Hubbart's Bridge stations.

Boston, see page 46.

Great Northern Main Line continued.

Grantham to Newark, Doncaster, and York.

We then pass Hougham and Claypole stations and enter the county of

NOTTINGHAM,

Which, from its inland situation, and lying between the mountainous district of Derbyshire on the one hand, and the level districts of Lincolnshire on the other, may be said to be one of the most healthy, fertile, and agreeable in the kingdom. Except the level tract through which the Trent flows, the surface of the county may be considered lofty, though none of the little hills rise to any considerable degree of elevation. The climate is mild, salubrious, and remarkable for its dryness, a circumstance which has been thought to bring it nearly on a par with the most southerly districts with regard to seed time and harvest.

NEWARK.

A telegraph station.

Hotel.—Clinton Arms, family and commercial, and posting house.

Market Day.—Wednesday.

Fairs.—May 14th, Whit Tuesday, Aug. 2nd, Wednesday before Oct. 2nd, Nov. 1st. and Monday before Dec. 12th.

Bankers.—Godfrey and Riddell; Handley, Peacock, and Handley; Nottinghamshire Banking Co.

A fine old town of *Nottinghamshire*, with a population of 11,330, who return two members. The Roman Fosseway and a bend of the Trent run through it, the latter being partly formed by the Devon. It was called *New-wark*, or new work, before the Conquest. In behalf of Charles I. it made a stout and successful resistance to the parliament forces, who besieged it three times, and battered a church down. The chief strength of the town lay in the *Castle*, the picturesque ruins of which still hang over the river. They consist only of the broken walls, having on the river or north front, between two towers, a noble bay window, which lit the hall. The crypt beneath the interior (now a bowling green) was mounted with cannon in the civil war, when embrasures were cut in the wall. Alexander, bishop of Lincoln in Stephen's time, built the castle, and most of it is of that early date. Here King John died, in 1216, after losing his baggage, &c., in the Wash. The breath had hardly left his body before the servants about him made off with what they could carry, not leaving as much as would cover his dead carcase. Close to the castle is the brick bridge, built by the Newcastle family about a hundred years back. There is another bridge or causeway outside the town, for raising the road above the marshes.

The fine parish Church of *St, Mary*, near the Market Place, is a noble cross, rebuilt in the later Gothic style in place of an earlier one, of which the Norman base of the tall spire is a remnant. The apostles stand in niches round the spire, and they are also carved on the shaft of the font. Most of the spouts, &c., end in grotesque heads. The tower is light, and the tracery of the windows elegant and good; several of which are stained. A carved screen fronts the choir, at the end of which is the "Raising of Lazarus" by Hilton. Besides the arms of neighbouring families there is a curious brass, under a three-arched canopy in the south transept of Alan Flemynge, the supposed founder of the church; he has curly hair, coat, mantle, sleeves buttoned at the wristbands, and pointed boots; the date, 1361. The interior has been recently restored, under the superintendence of Mr. Scott, and is now one of the finest parish churches in the kingdom.

A *Grammar School* founded in Henry VIII.'s reign with a "song" (choral) school attached, is near the church; Here Bishop Warburton, who was born at Newark, in 1698, and Stechelly the antiquary were educated. There are many old houses in the large *Market Place* which had the later Gothic cross in the middle which now stands in the *Town Hall*, built in 1805, on a rustic basement; and a handsome *Corn Exchange*, built in 1849, by Duesbury, in the Italian style; it is 84 feet long, with a clock tower, and a glass roof. Newark is a great place for corn, and malting. for which kilns are seen everywhere. One large brewery is in *Northgate Street*, so called from; he old town gate, which remains here. There is another in Appletongate, near the site of an old friary, now the Sykes's seat.

A little lace is made here; and at Beacon Hill gypsum is quarried, which makes excellent stucco. Arderno the surgeon, Lightfoot the Hebrew scholar, and Hartley the metaphysician, Drs. White and Bishop Magnus were natives.

In the neighbourhood are *Kelham Hall*, seat of J. Manners Sutton, Esq. *Muskham Grange*, J Handley, Esq., an old building of the 17th century. *Ossington*, J. Denison, Esq. At *Rufford House*, near Ollerton, the seat of Mr. Lumley, is some Elizabethan work, with family portraits &c. It was the site of a priory.

CARLTON station.

TUXFORD.

Telegraph station at Retford, 6¾ miles.

HOTEL.—Newcastle Arms.

MARKET DAY.—Monday.

FAIRS.—May 12th, September 28th.

This place is celebrated for the wheat grown in the neighbourhood; it has a large old church with stained windows, and effigy of a Knight and Lady. In the vicinity are *Thoresby*, seat of Lord Manvers, and *Clumber*, the Duke of Newcastle.

RETFORD.—See page 54.

Then passing SUTTON station we arrive at

RANSKILL.

Distance from station, ½ mile.
Telegraph station at Retford, 5¾ miles.
MONEY ORDER OFFICE at Bawtry, 3½ miles.

In the vicinity are Blyth, the old church at which was founded by Roger de Busli at the Conquest. *Blyth Hall* the seat of H. H. Walker, Esq., the ruins of a priory at Mattersey, an old seat of the Neviles.

Then passing SCROOBY station, in the vicinity of which at a farm house are ruins of the York primates' hunting seat — Wolsey (whose mulberry tree is shown), and Archbishop Sandys were residents—and *Serlby*, seat of Viscount Galway, M.P., we reach

BAWTRY.

POPULATION 1,170.
Telegraph station at Doncaster, 8¼ miles.
HOTEL.—Crown.
MARKET DAY.—Thursday.
FAIRS.—Whitsun Thursday, and Nov. 22nd.

BANKERS. — The Yorkshire Banking Co., W. Cooper, Esq., Manager; draw on Williams, Deacon, and Co.

This is a small market town, and contains a Gothic church, built of Roche Abbey limestone, much esteemed by sculptors. In the vicinity are *Bawtry Hall*, seat of Dowager Lady Galway, Mission Carr, which is so level "that a base line for the grand survey, was measured on it," the ruined castle and priory of Tickhill, which was built by Roger de Busli, but demolished by the parliamentarians. In the fine old church are some beautiful monuments.

Passing ROSSINGTON station, in the vicinity of which are *Cantley*, the seat of J. W. Childers, Esq., M.P. *Finningley*, J Harvey, Esq.; *Hatfield Chase*, a barren level, on which Cadwallo the English King, and his ally Penda, defeated Edwin of Northumbria, in 633; Edward III., son of William de Hatfield, was a native. We arrive at

DONCASTER.

A telegraph station.
HOTEL.—Royal.
MARKET DAY.—Saturday.
FAIRS.—Feb. 2nd, April 5th, August 5th, and Nov. 16th.
RACES.—Third week in September and March.
BANKERS.—Sir W. B. Cooke and Co.; Branch of the Yorkshire Banking Co.,

Doncaster.—The Roman *Danam*, and Saxon *Donacastre*, in the *West Riding of Yorkshire*, on the river Don, and the North Midland Railway, best known for its *Races*, established in 1703, in March and September. Population, 15,000. The most important race is the St. Leger, in September, for 3-year old horses, so called from a sporting man who established it in the last century. The course for the St. Leger is 1¾ miles round, and was run by Mr. Peirse's "*Reveller*," in 1818, in 3 minutes 15 seconds; in 1846, "*Sir Tatton Sykes*" ran it in 3 minutes 16 seconds Everything relating to the ground and the *Race Stands*, is carefully kept up by the Corporation, to whom they produce a valuable yearly income of

£2,000. Another feature of the town is the beautiful *Church*, now in the course of erection, by J. G. Scott, at a cost of £60,000, in place of the one destroyed by fire Feb. 28th 1853. *Christ Church* was built and endowed by the Jarratt family.

Doncaster is clean and well built. Among the principal buildings are the new *Town Hall* and *Mansion House*, and *Markets*. Lacy, the dramatist, was a native; and Miller, the historian, a resident; and the Yorkshire *Deaf and Dumb School*, founded in 1829. It was here, in 1536, that Aske, the leader of the Pilgrimage of Grace (a rising of 40,000, in favour of the old religion), met the herald of Henry VIII., who took him to court, and afterwards hung him at York.

The scenery is rather tame, but the flat carrs (*carse* land in Scotland), to the east, having been well drained, are very fertile—much clover and woad are raised, and hunters, of course, are bred. Vast quantities of potatoes also are grown on the warp land, near the Trent and Humber.

Near Doncaster are the following:—*Cusworth*, the residence of W. B Wrightson, Esq., M.P., situate on a hill, with a view of Lincoln and York Cathedrals. *Wheatley Hall*, Sir W. Cooke, Bart., was built about 1680. *Cantley*, J. W. Childers, Esq. Here the famous horse, "*Flying Childers*," was bred. *Sprotborough*, Sir J. W. Copley, Bart. *Tickhill Castle*, at present the seat of the Earl of Scarborough, is near to Sandbeck, and has in its immediate neighbourhood the picturesque ruins of Roche Abbey.

Passing ARKSEY station, to the right of which is Kirk Sandall old church, in which is a chantry, built in 1481, by Archbishop Rokeby, with his coat of arms, stained glass and carved work thereon, an antique specimen of that age, we arrive at

ASKERNE.

Telegraph station at Doncaster, 6¼ miles.
HOTEL.—Swan.
MONEY ORDER OFFICE, Doncaster, 6¼ miles.

This place is celebrated for a sulphur spa, and as having been the spot where Ambrosius killed Hengist, the Saxon, in 489. In the vicinity at Compsall is the seat of B. Franks, Esq.

Passing NORTON station, near which is *Fenwick Tower*, we reach

WOMERSLEY.—In the vicinity are *Womersley Park*, Lord Hawke's; and *Stapleton Park*, the handsome seat of J. Barton, Esq.

KNOTTINGLEY Junction.

A telegraph station.
HOTEL.—Railway.
MONEY ORDER OFFICE at Ferry Bridge, ¾ mile.

The line here branches off to Goole, Leeds, and Wakefield, and forms rather an important junction.

In the vicinity are *Byrom Hall*, seat of Sir J. Ramsden, Bart.; and *Frystone Hall*, R. M. Milnes, Esq., M.P.

Leeds.—See page 16.
York.—See page 70.

For continuation of this route northward, see pages 64, 68, 70 and 76.

MANCHESTER, SHEFFIELD, AND LINCOLNSHIRE.

Manchester to Penistone.

ARDWICK and ASHBURY'S stations.

GORTON.—In the vicinity are the *Great Manchester Reservoirs* of about 42 acres, with a well of 210 feet, sunk in a fine sandstone rock.

FAIRFIELD.—This place is celebrated for its extensive *Moravian Settlement*, and has a population of 900, chiefly cotton spinners.

GUIDE BRIDGE station.

NEWTON (Hyde).

Distance from station, ½ mile.

A telegraph station.

HOTEL.—Railway.

MONEY ORDER OFFICE at Mottram, 2½ miles.

This place has a population, conjointly with Hyde, of 11,569, principally engaged in cotton spinning.

MOTTRAM.

Distance from station, 1¼ mile.
A telegraph station.
HOTEL.—Junction Inn.

This place is beautifully situated in the moorlands. It possesses Garside's Free Grammar School, and a later English church, built of pebbly stone, on a hill. In the church are the tombs of Serjeant Bretland, "Old Roe and his wife," and Earnshaw. Car Tor commands extensive views of the Cheshire, Derbyshire, and Yorkshire hills.

DINTING (Junction).

Telegraph station at Glossop, 1 mile.

HOTEL.—Railway.

This station is remarkable not only as the junction of the branch to Glossop, but for the splendid viaduct of three arches over the river Etherow, formed of stone and timber. The arches are composed of three timber ribs each, formed of three-inch planks, put together on the laminating principle, with tar and brown paper between each layer The extreme length of the viaduct is 506 feet. Its length, however, is inconsiderable, compared with other similar undertakings, and is not so remarkable a feature as the extraordinary height at which the trains are safely carried across the valley below. The extreme height from the foundation to the top of the viaduct is 136 feet, more than 10 feet higher than the one at Stockport, and about 14 feet higher than the celebrated chain bridge over the Menai Straits.

GLOSSOP.—(Branch.)

POPULATION, 5,467.
A telegraph station.
HOTEL.—Railway.
FAIR.—May 6, for cattle.

It contains an ancient church, with tomb of Hague, of Park Hall; several mills, foundries, bleach and print works. In the vicinity are *Glossop Hall*, seat of Lord Edward Howard, and *Melandra Castle*, an ancient Roman camp.

HADFIELD station.

WOODHEAD.

Distance from station, 1 mile.
Telegraph station at Hadfield, 5¾ miles.
MONEY ORDER OFFICE at Glossop, 7 miles.

Here are large *Reservoirs* for Manchester, occupying 150 acres; close by is the famous tunnel 943 feet above the sea, 5,192 yards long, the extremity of which is in Yorkshire; to construct which it occupied 1,500 men two years, and took 157 tons of gunpowder in blasting the rock.

Then passing DUNFORD BRIDGE and HAZLEHEAD BRIDGE stations, we arrive at

PENISTONE AND THURLSTONE

(Junction).

Distance from station, ½ mile.
A telegraph station.
HOTEL.—Railway.
MARKET DAY.—Thursday.
FAIRS.—Last Thursday in February and March; first Thursday in May; and Thursday after Old Michaelmas.

This is a small market town, situated on the banks of the Don, in the midst of a wild and dreary district. It contains several large cotton and woollen factories, and a free *Grammar School*. Sanderson, the blind professor, was a native. Distant one mile lies *Thurlstone*, in which are fulling mills, and woollen and hair cloth manufactories.

HUDDERSFIELD BRANCH.

Penistone to Huddersfield.

From Penistone nothing particularly striking arrests the tourist's attention for some miles. The stations passed are DENBY DALE, SHEPLEY, STOCKS MOOR, and BROCKHOLES, the junction of the branch line to

HOLMFIRTH BRANCH.

THONG'S BRIDGE Station.

HOLMFIRTH.

A telegraph station.
HOTEL.—Victoria.
MARKET DAY.—Saturday.
FAIRS.—Saturday after 27th March, Saturday before Old May Day, and Saturday after May 28th.

HOLMFIRTH (6 miles) on the line to Sheffield, in a fine hollow of the mountains, where the Ribble and Diglee brooks join, was dreadfully avaged in 1852, by the bursting of Bilberry Dam, a r servoir above the town, nearly 200 yards long, and 70 feet deep in one part, fed by springs from the hills, and used to turn the cotton mills below. The valley is about 6 miles long, and only 100 yards broad at the widest; and the immense volume of water set free in this narrow gutter carried away 100 lives, with houses, mills, and other property, worth £600,000. The bridge was entirely destroyed; and only the bare walls of the church left. Upwards of £120,000 was collected through the country for the poorer sufferers, — so abundant, indeed, were the subscriptions that a good proportion was returned to the donors.

HONLEY.

Telegraph station at Huddersfield, 3¼ miles.
HOTEL.—Coach and Horses.

This place is the centre of the Woollen trade, and has a population of 5.595.

BERRY BROW and LOCKWOOD stations.

Huddersfield. — See Section III., page 48.

BARNSLEY BRANCH.

Penistone to Barnsley.

SILKSTONE, remarkable for its extensive coal mines.
DODWORTH station.

BARNSLEY.

A telegraph station.
HOTELS.—Royal, King's Head.
MARKET DAYS.—Wednesday and Saturday.
FAIRS.—Last Wednesday in Feb., May 13, Oct. 11.
BANKERS.—Barnsley Banking Company; Branch of the Wakefield and Barnsley Union Bank, draw on Barnett, and Co.

A town in the West Riding of Yorkshire, on a cultivated part of the Dearne, 21 miles from Leeds, belonging to the Duke of Leeds; formerly noted for wire works, but now a seat of the linen trade, especially diapers, drills, ducks, ticks, &c. Pop. 13,437. Here are several good Churches, Market-Place, and free Grammar School. Most of the weavers work at home, with yarn spun at Leeds. Here Unions, a mixture of cotton and linen, are made. There are many dyeworks, ironworks, and collieries. At Oaks colliery 72 lives were lost in 1847.

Monk Bretton, where there are the ruins of a priory of the 12th century, belongs to Rt. Hon. Sir C. Wood, Bart.

Manchester and Sheffield Main Line continued.

Penistone to Sheffield and Retford.

WORTLEY.

POPULATION 1,095.
A telegraph station.
Distance from station, ½ mile.
HOTEL.—Wortley Arms.
MONEY ORDER OFFICE at Penistone, 4½ miles.

In the vicinity is *Wortley Hall*, the beautiful old seat of Lord Wharncliffe, *Wharncliffe Lodge*, *Wharncliffe Crags*, and the *Dragon's Den*, from all of which may be obtained most beautiful views, most especially so from the summit of the ancient lodge of Wharncliffe (built in 1510), on the summit over the chase, (in which the Dragon of Wantley was captured), and the adjacent country. At *Wharncliffe Lodge*, Lady Mary Wortley Montague resided, and here her eccentric son was born.

Then passing Deep Car, Oughty Bridge, and Wadsley Bridge stations, we arrive at

SHEFFIELD.

A telegraph station.
Hotels.—King's Head, Royal.
Market Day.—Tuesday and Saturday.
Fairs.—Trinity Tuesday, and November 28th.
Bankers.—Sheffield Banking Co.; Sheffield and Hallamshire Banking Co.; Sheffield and Rotherham Banking Co.; Sheffield Union Bank.

This great seat of the Cutlery trade is beautifully placed on the river Sheaf, where it joins the Don, among some of the most picturesque hills in the West Riding of Yorkshire, in the district of Hallamshire, and 162½ miles from London, by the Great Northern Railway. Its suburbs spreading mile after mile in all directions, hill and dale, and every accessible point on the slopes between being occupied by houses and villas, in endless variety, offer to the stranger new objects of pleasure at each turn, and to residents, prospects of great extent and beauty. To one fond of the country, rambling along river, over hills and through forests to obtain some distant point of view, no matter which, Sheffield possesses almost inexhaustible attractions. Two members returned. Population in 1851, 135,310, but it has now upwards of 155,000 inhabitants, of whom about 145,000 live in the town and its immediate suburbs, which embrace more than seven-eighths of the buildings and population of the townships of Ecclesall, Bierlaw, and Brightside-Bierlaw, and about two-thirds of those of Nether Hallam. Knives, forks, razors, saws, scissors, printing type, optical instruments, Britannia metal, Sheffield plate, scythes, garden implements, files, screws, other tools, stoves, fenders, as well as engines, railway springs, buffers, &c., are among the articles manufactured here—steel being the basis of nearly all; the best of which is made from iron imported from Sweden. Sheffield plate, or silver laid on copper, was discovered here by a Sheffield man, T. Bolsover, and taken up by Mr. Handcock, about 1758. The Britannia metal and German silver are both compositions imitating this plate, the manufacture of which is much promoted by the discovery of electro-plating. Rodgers' cutlery and Wilkinson's plate warehouses are among the largest; while metal foundries, vast grinding and polishing works, are dispersed in the town, and along the Porter and other streams; coal and stone are abundant.

Sheffield has 40 churches and chapels. The Parish Church of *St. Peter* is a large rectangular structure in the perpendicular style of architecture, and has a tower in the centre, surmounted by a lofty crocketed spire. It contains the graves of the Talbots, who formerly held the Manor, and Chantrey's bust of the Rev. J. Wilkinson. This was the first performance of the great sculptor, who was originally a Sheffield milkboy. Another of his busts is in *St. Paul's Church*. The seat of the Talbots was on a hill to the south-east, now occupied by an old timbered building near the *Cholera Mount*, where many victims of that disease were buried in 1832, now marked by a stone cross. George, the 6th Earl of Shrewsbury (of the Talbot family), had the custody of Mary, Queen of Scots, for 14 years at the *Manor House* here, and elsewhere. Her Secretary, Rolet, and Walker the executor of Charles I., are buried in the Church with Lady Arabella Stuart's mother, &c. At the *Literary Society's Hall*, in Surrey Street, is a large music room, 100 feet long, with a museum, &c., and a portrait of James Montgomery, not a native (he was born at Irvine), but a long time resident at Sheffield, and died at his house on the Mount, in May, 1854, and lies buried in the Cemetery.

> "Grave, the guardian of his dust;
> Grave, the treasury of the skies!
> Every atom of thy dust,
> Rests in hope again to rise.
>
> "Hark! the judgment trumpet calls—
> 'Soul, rebuild thy house of clay:
> Immortality thy walls,
> And Eternity thy day.'"

These are some of his own forcible lines. The *Town Hall* was built in 1808; there is also a handsome *Cutler's Hall*, in Church Street, rebuilt in 1832—an important corporation, chartered in 1621. This was many centuries, however, after Sheffield became noted for its staple article; for even Chaucer, who wrote his Canterbury Tales about 1490, speaks of its "thaytles" (whittles) or knives, as being generally known, and his miller is made to carry one in his hose Here the annual Cutlers' Feast is held. The *Theatre* is a large edifice of brick. An *Assay Office* for marking plate was established in 1773. An *Athenæum*, opened in 1849. The *General Infirmary* was founded in 1793, on the south side of the town, on an open tract of 31 acres; with the *Queen's Tower* and the *Park* beyond. A well-endowed *Hospital* was founded in the 17th century, by the Talbot and Howard families (the latter—the Duke of Norfolk's—has the Manor); and there is another amply supported by the cutlers. The *Grammar School* was incorporated by James I. A good stone bridge, besides several others, crosses the river. Dr. Balguy Cawthorne, and Bishop Saunderson were natives.

Wesley College, pleasantly situated, near Glossop Road, is one of the largest and handsomest scholastic institutions in the kingdom. It was finished in 1838, at the cost of more than £10,000, exclusive of more than £4,500 paid for six acres of land, tastefully laid out in pleasure grounds. It is a long and lofty building, with an elegant Corinthian portico in the centre, and has accommodation for 250 boarders.

Evelyn in his "Sylva" speaks of an oak felled in the Park, "so high when lying on the ground, that two men on horse-back could not see each other's heads; and of another which produced 10,000 feet of timber." There is still much woodland.

Excursions from Sheffield. — Only a few of these can be indicated. Up the Sheaf are *Meresbrook House*, in Derbyshire, whence a fine view; *Blanchiey Abbey*, founded by Fitz Ranulph, to atone for his share in Becket's murder, in the twelfth century. Little remains besides part of the church. Near this is *Norton*, the seat of S. Shore. Esq., with the church in which Chantrey is buried (who was born here in 1782), and has an endowed school. Roads hence to Chesterfield and to Chatsworth, 18 miles from Sheffield. The rivers Porter and Rivelin may be followed to Oxten Stones, Lord Seats, and Stanedge Rocks, 1,483 feet high, on the Derbyshire borders, on *Hallam Moor*, in the outer region of the High Peak, a scene of the most rugged wildness. The Oxten Stones are 1387 feet high; and on *Bamford Moor* beyond Stanedge are the Rocking Stone and other Druid remains. Ascending the Don, you come to *Loxley Chase* and *Robin Hood's Well*; here it is stated that famous outlaw was born. To the west of this are Castle and Bailey hills near Bradfield, near the stream of that name, which descends from the plantation by which the moors are enlivened. Further up, the scenery of the Don becomes more bold and striking, especially about Wharncliffe Crags, Walderslow, and the ruins on Bolsterstone Hill, (976 feet high), and *Wortley Hall*, the seat of Lord Wharncliffe. *Attercliffe*, 2 miles below Sheffield, deserves notice, as the place where cast steel was first made. The *Hall*, is the seat of J. Milner, Esq. Archbishop Secker was educated at the dissenting academy here. *Thundercliffe Grange*, Earl of Effingham.

Passing Darnall station, on the left of which is *Tinsley Park Collieries*, we arrive at

Woodhouse —This station forms the junction of branch 5 miles long, running *via* Beighton to Eckington, a station on the Midland Railway, by which the Midland districts became much easier of access. Proceeding onward the next station we ome to is that of

Kiveton Park.

Passing Shireoaks station, and *Wallingwells*, the seat of Sir T. White, Bart., we arrive at

WORKSOP.

A telegraph station.
Hotel.—Lion.
Market Day.—Wednesday.
Fairs.—March 3, and October 14.
Bankers.—Sir W. B. Cooke and Co.; Branch of Nottingham and Notts Banking Company.

This is a market town, with a population of 6,058. The manor, which is held by the presentation of a pair of gloves at the coronation, belonged till recently to the Norfolk family, who sold it to the Duke of Newcastle, in whose possession it now remains by the same tenure. The old cruciform church contains towers, carved pulpit, effigies of William de Furnival, Neville, and Lovetot. Near it are the *Gate of Radford Priory* (Henry I.'s time), and St. Mary's Chapel. It is situated in the "Dukery," which comprises four ducal seats. *Worksop Manor*, Duke of Newcastle: In the house are a painted staircase, great hall, chapel, drawing and dining rooms. The old mansion and some of the Arundel marbles were destroyed by fire in 1761. *Welbeck Abbey*, Duke of Portland, which contains portraits of the Cavendishes, Queen Elizabeth, Prior Stratford, Archbishop Laud (by Vandyke), Sir W. Myddleton, &c. *Riding House and Stables*, 130 feet long. The Park is 8 miles long, and contains the Greendale Oak, 700 years old, 35 feet in girth, and a road through it; the Duke's Walking Stick, 111 feet high; two Porters, 98 and 88 feet high, 38 and 34 feet in girth, and the Seven Sisters all on one root, 88 feet high and 30 feet in girth. Here Lord George Bentinck died in 1840. *Clumber* (Duke of Newcastle), in a park 11 miles in compass. The *House*, with a lake in the front, contains a fine collection of sculpture, pictures, and family portraits of the Clintons, Pelhams, Lincolns, &c. Here are several pictures by Correggio, Rubens, Sneyders and Poussin. *Thoresby Park* (Lord Manvers), the ancient seat of the Duke of Kingston, rebuilt after the fire in 1745 in a park 13 miles round, contains an Ionic portico, with a fine collection of portraits of P. Paoli, Howe, &c. The celebrated Lady M. W. Montague, was born here. The Spread Oak, in the park, extends 180 feet and would, it is asserted, shelter 1,000 horsemen.—Sharp's *British Gazetteer*. Here Liquorice was grown in ancient days, about Camden's time.

RETFORD.

Distance from station, ¼ mile.

A telegraph station.

Hotel.—White Hart.

Bankers.—Sir W. B. Cooke and Co.; Nottingham and Notts Banking Company.

Retford, a borough town in the county of Nottingham, population 46,504 (two members returned), is pleasantly situated on the banks of the river Idle. Properly speaking, Retford consists of two towns, east and west Retford, so called from their situation on each side the river, but as they are united by a substantial bridge they constitute for all local purposes but one town. The principal edifices are the Corporation Church, Town Hall, St. Michael's Church, a Free Grammar School, just erected, and Dorrell's Hospital. The trade carried on by the inhabitants is very small, but they manufacture hats, sail-cloth, and paper, in considerable quantities. The Chesterfield canal from the Trent has been of great advantage to the trade of the town. In the vicinity is *Grove Hall*, the Herby's old seat.

Retford to Lincoln.

Passing Leverton, Cottam, and Torksey stations, we reach

Lincoln.—See page 8.

Lincoln to Barnetby.

Continuing our journey northward from Lincoln, we come to the stations of Reepham, Langworth, Snelland, and Wickenby, and stop at

MARKET RASEN.

A telegraph station.
HOTEL.—White Hart.
BANKERS.—Lincoln and Lindsay Banking Company; Smith, Ellison and Co.

Here is an old hospital, and curious embattled towered church, whose vicar takes tithe of ale. Close at hand is *Middle Rasen Drak*, bestowed upon Sir J. Burlingthorpe, "for reclaiming the land." In the vicinity are *Willingham House*, A. Beucherett, Esq., *Bayons Manor*, Right hon. C. D'Eyncourt, with its ancient moat and drawbridge.

Then passing USSELBY and HOLTON stations, we arrive at

MOORTOWN (South Kelsey).

Distance from station, 2¼ miles.
Telegraph station at Barnetby, 7 miles.

Caistor, so called *Thong*, (because Hengist, after destroying the Picts, obtained from Vortigern as much land as an ox hide would cover, and imitating the founder of Carthage, he cut it into thongs) should be visited, as the curious old Norman Church stands on the site of Hengist's Castle.

NORTH KELSEY, and HOWSHAM stations.

Barnetby.—The junction with the main line to Hull.

Manchester, Sheffield, and Lincolnshire Main Line continued.

Retford to Ulceby.

STURTON station.

GAINSBOROUGH.

A telegraph station.
HOTEL.—White Hart.

MARKET DAY.—Tuesday.
FAIRS.—October 20, and Easter Tuesday.
BANKERS.—Smith, Ellison, and Co.; Branch of Lincoln and Lindsey Banking Company.

GAINSBOROUGH a market town, population 7,506 (who are chiefly employed in the carrying trade), in the county of Lincoln. It is agreeably situated on the eastern bank of the river Trent, which joins the Humber about 20 miles below the town. Gainsborough is celebrated in history as being the anchoring place of the Danish ships, when Sweyne laid waste the surrounding country.

The town consists almost entirely of one long street, parallel with the river, and is clean, well lighted, and paved. The most conspicuous public edifice is the *Church*, with an ancient tower, the rest of which is of modern erection. Over the Trent (which here forms the natural boundary of the counties of Lincoln and Nottingham), an elegant stone bridge, of three elliptical arches, was erected in 1791, and forms a great ornament to the town. Alfred the Great married Egelswitha at this place. The *Town Hall* is of brick, with shops beneath it; it is situated in the *Market Place*, and is occasionally used as an assembly room. It also contains a *Theatre*, which is a very neat modern edifice. Here is the old timbered hall called *John of Gaunt's Palace*, with tower, chapel, &c.; it belongs to the Hickmans of *Howick Grove*, who have restored it lately. In the vicinity are *Somerby Hall*, Sir T. Becket, *Lea Hall*, Sir C. Anderson, Bart., and *Castle Hill*, which Cromwell occupied in 1643.

Passing BLYTON and NORTHORPE stations, we arrive at

KIRTON LINDSEY.

Distance from station, ½ mile.

A telegraph station.

Here is a curious old church. In the vicinity are *Blyborough Hall*, C. Luard, Esq.; and *Redbourne Hall*, Duke of St. Albans.

SCAWBY AND HIBALDSTOW.

Distance from station, 1 mile.

Telegraph station at Brigg, 2¾ miles.

Scawby Hall, seat of Sir J. Nelthorpe, Bart., is close at hand.

BRIGG (Glandford Brigg).

Distance from station, 2 miles.
A telegraph station.
HOTEL.—Angel.
MARKET DAY.—Thursday.
FAIR.—August 5.

BANKERS.—Smith, Ellison, and Co.; Branch of Lincoln and Lindsey Banking Company.

A large trade is carried on here in corn, coal, and timber. The grammar school is well endowed. In the vicinity is *Elsham Hall*, T. Corbet, Esq.

BARNETBY station.

BROCKLESBY.

(Croxton nearest town.)

Distance from station, 1½ mile.

Telegraph station at Ulceby, 1 mile.

MONEY ORDER OFFICE at Ulceby, 2¾ miles.

The seat of the Earl of Yarborough, marked by the Pelham pillar, is on the Wolds, and is one of the finest places in the country. At Thornton-Curtis, close to the railway, are the venerable remains of the *Church*, the *gate*, &c., of an Abbey of the 12th century.

ULCEBY station.

GREAT GRIMSBY BRANCH.

HABROUGH (Brocklesby).

Distance from station, ½ mile.
Telegraph station at Ulceby, 1¾ mile.
MONEY ORDER OFFICE at Ulceby, 1¾ mile.
Lord Yarborough's seat is on the right.

STALLINGBOROUGH.

Distance from station, ½ mile.
Telegraph station at Great Grimsby, 4¼ miles.
MONEY ORDER OFFICE at Great Grimsby, 4¼ miles.

Then passing GREAT COATES station, we reach

GREAT GRIMSBY.

A telegraph station.
HOTEL.—Yarborough Arms.
MARKET DAY.—Wednesday.
FAIRS.—June 15, September 15.
BANKERS.—Branch of Hull Banking Company; Smith, Ellison, and Co.

This town is built on the south bank of the river Humber, population 8,863. The borough includes villages within four miles, and returns one member. It was formerly a place of considerable importance, but, on the harbour becoming choked up, the trade gradually declined, and its commerce was transferred to the neighbouring city of Hull. Of late, however, the affairs of the town have taken a favourable turn, and many improvements have been made.

GREAT GRIMSBY DOCKS. — About fifteen years have now elapsed since a far-seeing mercantile company fastened upon this spot which the sagacity of the old roving sea-kings chose to give them the command of the Humber; and there they commenced planting, in defiance of all natural obstacles, a new commercial city, to become the great *entrepôt* of the trade between western, northern, and eastern Europe.

The company invaded the domain of the rolling waters, and, upon the treacherous mud, they have raised massive superstructures, and thus added nearly 140 acres of solid land to the occupation of man; and by the happy union of science, capital, and labour, have founded the finest harbour on the eastern coast of England. The first stone was laid by Prince Albert in 1849. The New Docks present a striking example of the advantage to be derived from a union of railways, docks, and warehouses, executed under one complete plan, and worked under one management Grimsby, at the mouth of the Humber, five miles from its confluence with the sea, has in front a deep roadstead, with excellent anchorage in blue clay, protected from the ocean by the promontory of Spurn Point. Great Grimsby Roads affords the only refuge between the Thames and the Firth of Forth. The Old Dock was purchased by the Manchester, Sheffield, and Lincolnshire Company, when they decided on their "Water Terminus." It has an entrance-lock of 150 feet in length, and 37 feet in width, with 18 feet on its sill at high tide.

The new tidal basin has an area of 15 acres: its depth at low spring tide is nine feet; low neaps, 12½; high springs, 27⅝; high neaps, 24¼; at the landing slip within the tidal basin the largest steamers can lie-to safely, at any time of tide. The dock is entered from its tidal basin by two locks of massive masonry, with double gates for ebb and flood tides. The hydraulic tower is 300 feet high. It has a water area of upwards of 25 acres.

In constructing these works, 135 acres have been reclaimed; wharves or quays extend 3,600 feet in length—quays traversed by railways from the main lines into sheds and warehouses. Sheds are close to the quays, 750 feet in length, and 50 feet in breadth, affording a covered area of 4,000 feet, and a vaulted warehouse 150 feet square, for free and bonded goods. All the machinery and accessories are on the newest and most perfect principles, and the arrangements for passenger traffic and light or perishable merchandise are on an equally complete scale. The railway extends to the edge of a low-water landing stage in the outer tidal basin, where a station is built provided with accommodation for passengers, who, within the cover of the station, may be carried by trains in attendance, as goods also may, to any part of England or Scotland.

A communication is open to London through Louth, Boston, and Peterborough, through Market Rasen to Lincoln, and, by the Midland Railway, with Nottingham and Derby, and the Great Northern Railway to Boston, through Gainsborough to Retford. Thence it communicates by the Great Northern with Doncaster and York, from Retford to Worksop into Sheffield, where the Midland and Lancashire and Yorkshire Railway affords intercourse with Leeds, and all the Yorkshire districts. The parent line completes a communication between Sheffield, Manchester, Liverpool, the hardware, iron, pottery, and cotton districts.

The church of the town is a very large and handsome structure, built in the form of a cross. Archbishop Whitgift and Bishop Fotherby were natives. The Blow Wells in the vicinity were long considered as natural curiosities; the appearances which they present, however, have been observed in various places, and are now as familiar to naturalists as they are well understood. In the vicinity are *Cleethorpes*, a watering-place on the flat sands; and *Spurn Head Light*.

Manchester, Sheffield, and Lincolnshire Main Line continued.

Ulceby to Hull.

THORNTON ABBEY.

Telegraph station at Ulceby, 2½ miles.

Here are the remains of a priory, founded by William le Gros, Earl of Albemarle, in the 12th century, and converted into a college by Henry VIII. The Abbott's Lodge is now a farm house.

Passing GOXHILL station, we reach

NEW HOLLAND.

A telegraph station.
HOTEL.—Yarborough.
Steamers to Hull several times, daily.
HULL, described at page 64.

BARTON-ON-HUMBER (Branch).

POPULATION, 3,866.
Telegraph station at New Holland.

BOATS to Kingston-upon-Hull.
MARKET DAY.—Monday.
FAIR.—Trinity Thursday.
BANKERS.—Hull Banking Co.

LANCASHIRE.

A MARITIME county, situated on the north-western coast of England. This county includes part of the great coal fields of the north of England, and this circumstance, combined with its natural advantages for trade and manufactures, has gradually raised it to the rank of the greatest manufacturing county in the kingdom, containing Manchester, the centre of the cotton manufacture, and Liverpool, the great emporium of commerce for that side of our island. The soil and surface of the county are various; and its features in some parts, particularly towards the north, and all along its eastern border, are strongly marked. Here the hills are in general bold and lofty, and the valleys narrow and picturesque. On the sea-coast, and nearly the whole of the southern side of the county, following the course of the river Mersey, the land is low and flat. Moorlands are much more extensive than might have been expected in so populous a district, and where land is consequently very valuable. The manufactures of Lancashire are the most extensive in the kingdom, chiefly those of cotton, in all its branches; also of silk, woollen, linen, hats, stockings, pins, needles, nails, watch tools and movements (nearly the whole of which that are used in the United Kingdom being made in this county), tobacco, snuff, glass, earthenware, porcelain, paper, &c.

The cotton trade, of which Lancashire engrosses by far the greatest share, has risen to an extent, and with a rapidity beyond example. Manchester is the principal seat of this vast manufacture, From thence it spreads on all sides, to the south and east into Cheshire and Yorkshire, over the greater part of Lancashire, extending from Furness to Derby on the one hand, and from Liverpool to Halifax on the other. The raw material being principally collected in Manchester, it is thence distributed to all parts of the surrounding districts, where thousands are employed in preparing it, from that depôt to be sent to all parts of the world. Around Manchester, various of the principal towns and villages form subordinate stations of this extensive traffic, each being the centre of its own little sphere. Of these secondary towns, the principal are Bolton, Blackburn, Wigan, and Preston, on the west and north; Stockport on the south, and Ashton on the east. A variety of other employments, as those of bleachers, dyers, printers, tool-makers, engine and machine makers, &c., entirely depend for their existence on this manufacture. The commerce of Lancashire consists principally in the exchange of its manufactured goods; Liverpool engrosses nearly the whole of the export trade, and has risen accordingly, within less than two centuries, from a small village to its present importance.

LANCASHIRE AND YORKSHIRE.

Manchester to Ramsbottom.

Leaving New Bailey Street, Salford, we pass the stations of PENDLETON, CLIFTON JUNCTION, MOLINEUX BROW and RINGLEY ROAD, and arrive at

RADCLIFFE BRIDGE.

Telegraph station at Bury, 2¾ miles.
RACES in August.
MONEY ORDER OFFICE

This place contains a population of 5,002, chiefly employed in the cotton mills and collieries. Bishop Kilbye, a translator of the Bible, was a native.

BURY.

A telegraph station.
HOTEL.—Derby.
MARKET DAY.—Saturday.
FAIRS.—March 5th, May 3rd, and Sept. 18th.
BANKERS.—Branch of Manchester and Liverpool District Banking Co.,; Bury Banking Co.

A cotton town and parliamentary borough, population, 31,262 (one member), on the Irwell, formerly noted for its cloth manufacture, which is still carried on. Coal and stone are quarried. The manor belongs to the Earl of Derby, and half the township to the rector; the living is therefore a very good one, above £2,000 a year. The late Sir Robert Peel was born in 1778, at *Chamber Hall*, now the seat of Thomas Price, Esq. The first Sir Robert was a great benefactor to the town, by promoting its manufactures. A bronze statue to the great statesman, 10 feet high, on a pedestal, stands in the market place. Two other natives were the Kays, father and son, who invented the fly-shuttle (hitherto thrown by the hand), and the drop-box (for three shuttles, for coloured fabrics). There is a *Grammar School* founded by the Rev. Roger Kay, sometime Rector of Fittleton, Wilts. A new *Town Hall*, built by Smirke, in the Italian style, at the cost of Lord Derby, contains a hall 75 feet long. *Athenæum*, erected by public subscription, adjoining the Town Hall. Walker and Lomax's, Openshaw's, and Grundy's are the largest mills here. There are print and dyeworks, foundries, paper mills, &c. In 1841, a beautiful Roman Catholic chapel was built by J. Harper. *Heaton Hall*, the seat of the Earl of Wilton, is in a large park, 4 miles south-west.

SUMMERSEAT. — *Summerseat Hall*, seat of Mrs. Leigh.

RAMSBOTTOM JUNCTION.

A telegraph station.
MONEY ORDER OFFICE.

The line here follows the course of the river Irwell, which it crosses and re-crosses by several bridges, until it enters Newchurch, in the beautiful picturesque country of Rossendale.

Near is the tower built by Messrs. Grant, Dickens' "Cheeryble Brothers," and Holcombe Hill, on which there is a tower erected to the memory of Sir R. Peel.

BACUP BRANCH.

STUBBINS and EWOOD BRIDGE stations.

RAWTENSTALL.

A telegraph station.
HOTEL.—Queen's Arms.
This place contains a population of 5,643.

NEWCHURCH, in Rossendale.

POPULATION, 16,915.
Distance from station, ½ mile.
Telegraph station at Rawtenstall, 2 miles.
HOTEL.—Watson's Arms.

MONEY ORDER OFFICE at Rawtenstall, 1½ miles.
This place contains a population of 16,910, chiefly engaged in the cotton and woollen trades, of which it is the centre.

Passing STACKSTEAD station, we arrive next at

BACUP.

A telegraph station.
HOTELS.—Queen's.
BANKERS.—Alcocks, Birkbecks, and Co.; (on Thursdays only.)

This place contains a population of about 12,000, who are chiefly employed in the cotton and baize manufactures.

Lancashire and Yorkshire Main Line continued.

Ramsbottom, Burnley, Colne, and Skipton.

Passing HELMSHORE station (to the right of which are *Musbury Heights*) we reach.

HASLINGDEN.

A telegraph station.
HOTEL.—Commercial Inn.
MARKET DAY.—Saturday.
FAIRS.—Feb. 2nd, Easter Tuesday, May 8th, July 4th, and Oct. 2nd.

This market town, with a population of 6,150, engaged in the cotton trade, lies on the borders of Rossendale Forest, on an elevated spot. Its church has some old tombs and a font of Henry VIII.'s time.

Passing BAXENDEN station, we arrive at

ACCRINGTON.

POPULATION, 10,374.
A telegraph station.
HOTEL.—Hargreaves' Arms.

Here are the print-works of Messrs. Graftou aud Co., Mr. Grimshaw, and Messrs. J. Losh and Co., and a number of cotton mills. In the neighbourhood are also Messrs. Steiner and Co.'s large turkey-red dye and print works, the largest in the trade, and several large chemical works.

HUNCOAT, ROSEGROVE, and BURNLEY BARRACKS stations.

BURNLEY.

Distance from station, ½ mile.
A telegraph station.
HOTEL.—Bull.
MARKET DAYS. Monday and Saturday.
FAIRS.—March 6th, Easter Eve, May 9th and 13th, July 10th, and October 11th.
BANKERS.—Birkbecks and Co.

BURNLEY—A large market town, on a pretty part of the Calder, 24 miles from Manchester. Here are many extensive cotton and some worsted mills, with several foundries. Population, 20,828. It is a modern place, though near the site of a Roman station. Coal, slate, freestone, and flagstone are abundant. The houses are of stone. Here is a Grammar School, founded by Edward VI., in which Dr. Whittaker was educated. A large old Gothic church contains the tombs of the Towneleys, of *Towneley Park*. This is an ancient seat, in a beautifully wooded spot, with portraits of the family for many ages back. The late Charles Towneley collected here the marbles which were sold at his death to the British Museum. *Ormerod Hall*, General Scarlett, is another ancient seat of the 16th century; also *Gawthorpe*, the seat of Sir J. P. Kay Shuttleworth, Bart. On the west side of the Calder valley are the Pendle Hills, 1,800 feet high, overlooking Clitheroe and its old castle, taking in a view of the Isle of Man, &c., from the cairns on the top; the limestone strata are violently thrown up. A range of hills runs along the Yorkshire border on the east side of the valley; one of which is Boulsworth Hill, 1,689 feet high.

BRIERFIELD and NELSON stations.

COLNE.

A telegraph station.
HOTEL.—Red Lion.
MARKET DAYS.—Wednesday and Saturday.
FAIRS.—March 7, May 13, Oct. 11, and Dec. 21.
BANKERS.—Birkbecks and Co.

This was the Roman *Colonio*. Population, 6,644, of cotton and woollen spinners. Here is a fine church, in which is a handsome screen. At the grammar school, Archbishop Tillotson was educated. The poor house was the Lacy's seat, and Barnside that of the Towneley's. Caistor Cliff camp is double ditched, and 360 feet by 330.

FOULRIDGE and EARBY stations. Near the latter is *Gisburne Park*e, the seat of Lord Ribblesdale, with its fine collection of pictures, and race of wild cattle.

THORNTON-LE-CRAVEN and ELSLACK stations.

Skipton.—See page 19.

Accrington to Southport and Liverpool.

CHURCH (Kirk).

POPULATION, 2,035.
Telegraph station at Accrington, 1 mile.

Here are extensive calico, print, dye, and chemical works. In the vicinity is *Dunkenhalgh Park*, seat of E. Petre, Esq., and *Foxhill Bank*, the seat of James Simpson, Esq.

Passing RISHTON station, we arrive a

BLACKBURN.

A telegraph station.
HOTEL.—Bull.
MARKET DAYS.—Wednesday and Saturday.
FAIRS.—Easter Week, from the 1st to 12th May, October 17th.
BANKERS.—Cunliffes, Brooks and Co.; Branch of Manchester and Liverpool District Bank

A borough town in Lancashire (returning two members), on the river Darwen, with a population of 46,536, employed in the cotton trade, Here is a gymnasium, erected by Messrs. Hornby and Kenworthy, for their workpeople. In the 17th century it was noted for its checks (a mixture of linen and cotton), and unbleached "greys;" but cottons, calicoes, and muslins are now the staple articles. The invention of the spinning jenny, by Hargreaves, who was a carpenter here, and the introduction of cotton printing, by the Peels, have mainly contributed to its improvement. A little cloth is woven. The scenery is flat and uninteresting. *St. Mary's* large parish church was built in 1826, close to the tower of the old building. Queen Elizabeth's Grammar School, at which Bolton, a native, and compiler of the *Liturgy*, was a scholar. *Witton Park*, the seat of J. Fielden, Esq., is near Billinge Hill, 633 feet high, at the end of the Yorkshire hills, whence you get a view of the Cumberland and Welsh mountains, *Stonyhurst*, is a Tudor built College for Roman Catholics, at which 180 students are received.

Passing CHERRY TREE and PLEASINGTON stations, (near which are *Pleasington Hall*, J. Bowdon, Esq., *Woodfold Park* and *Fennis Cowles*, Sir W. Fielden, Bart.), we reach

HOGHTON.

POPULATION, 1,373.
Telegraph station at Preston, 3¾ miles.
MAILS.—One arrival and departure, daily, between London and Hoghton.
MONEY ORDER OFFICE at Preston, 5 miles.

Close at hand is *Hoghton Tower*, the old seat of the Hoghton's, now of *Bold Hall*. Here James I. knighted the sirloin of beef, and authorised games to be played after church service on Sundays.

BAMBER BRIDGE and PRESTON JUNCTION stations.

Preston.—See Section III.

LOSTOCK HALL, MIDGE HALL, CROSTON, and RUFFORD stations.

BURSCOUGH JUNCTION.

POPULATION, 2,480.

A telegraph station.

MONEY ORDER OFFICE at Ormskirk, 2½ miles.

Here are remains of a priory, founded in the time of Richard I., by the Lathams, and was the burial place of the Stanleys' until the tombs were removed to Ormskirk. In the vicinity is *Blythe Hall*, seat of the Wilbrahams.

The line here branches off to SOUTHPORT, the route for which will be found in section III.

ORMSKIRK.

Distance from station, 3 miles.
A telegraph station.
HOTEL.—Wheat Sheaf.
MARKET DAY.—Thursday.
FAIRS.—Whit Monday, June 21st, Sept 1st & 10th.
BANKERS.—Robert Lawe & Co.

A market town, with a population of 5,548, noted for its gingerbread. The church contains tombs of the Derby family, removed from Burscough, and a separate bell tower. About two miles distant is *Scarisbrick Hall*, seat of the Scarisbrick's, which contains a splendid collection of paintings. Near at hand is Martin Mere, drained effectually in 1799, and *Lathom House*, Lord Skelmersdale's seat, rebuilt on the site of the Stanley's old seat, which was defended by Charlotte de la Tremouille, the celebrated Countess of Derby, against the parliamentarians, for three months, given up and dismantled in 1645.

The Skelmersdale Branch now turns off to the left, thereby giving a direct communication with Southport and St. Helens, *via* Rainford Junction.

Passing TOWN GREEN station (close to which is *Lydiate*, where there is an abbey begun at the time of the Reformation), we reach MAGHULL and

AINTREE.

The Liverpool races are held here in February and July. The Grand Stand was built in 1830, and the course is 1½ mile round.

WALTON-ON-THE-HILL (Junction).

POPULATION, 2,469.
Telegraph station at Aintree, 1½ mile.
MAILS.—One arrival and departure, daily, between London and Walton Junction.
MONEY ORDER OFFICE at Liverpool, 3½ miles.
The church here is prettily situated on a slight declivity, and was the mother church to Liverpool till 1698. *Walton Hall*, seat of T. Leyland, Esq., and *Fazakerley Hall*, H. Fazakerley, Esq., are close at hand.
BOOTLE station.
Liverpool.—See Section III.

Manchester to Bradford and Leeds.

Leaving Victoria station we pass the stations of MILES PLATTING (near which is the Mechanics' Institute), and NEWTON HEATH, of no particular note, and arrive at MIDDLETON, the Junction of the branches to Oldham and Middleton.

OLDHAM BRANCH.

A run of ten minutes takes us past WERNETH, and brings us to

OLDHAM.

A telegraph station.
HOTEL.—Angel.
MARKET DAY.—Saturday
FAIRS.—First Thursday after Feb. 14th, May 2nd, July 8th, and first Wednesday after Oct. 11th; for Cattle, on the second Monday in each month.

BANKERS.—Branch of Manchester and Liverpool District Banking Company; Branch of Saddleworth Banking Company.

This large and populous borough of Lancashire has no antiquity to boast of, but is a noted manufacturing town,—cotton, fustians, corduroy, hats, and coal being its staple products. Returns two members. Population 72,357; a rough, but hearty, industrious class. Above 2,000 looms a week are made.

"Oudham," which is the common name of the town, stands on a slightly elevated coal field, between the Irk and Medlock, near the Yorkshire border, seven miles from Manchester.

There are about eighty factories, and more than forty Sunday and other schools. A *Free Grammar School* was founded by the Asshetons, who are lords of this manor as well as that of Ashton-under-Lyne. Next to the large and ancient church, and the *Town Hall*, built in 1840, with a Grecian portico, the most striking building is *Henshaw's Blue Coat School*, at Oldham Edge, built in 1834, by Lane, with a munificent bequest from the founder, a successful hatter, who left nearly £100,000 for this purpose, and for the blind school at Manchester. He was a native, and died here in 1810; as also were Bishop Hugh Oldham and S. Ogden. This borough was represented for many years by the late celebrated William Cobbett, Esq. Coal and stone are quarried in abundance round the town; sometimes with alumina or alum-rock. *Royton* was a seat of the Lancashire Byrons. *Shaw Hall*, the seat of W. Farington, Esq., contains a valuable picture gallery and museum of antiquities.

MIDDLETON.—(Branch.)

This town, accessible by a short branch from Middleton Junction, like most others in Lancashire where the Cotton Manufacture is carried on, is now a place of some importance. It has also some extensive works for printing and bleaching,—but beyond these there are no particular attractions for the general tourist.

On again returning to the Junction at Middleton, a few minutes more brings us to

BLUE PITS JUNCTION.

At this place the line branches off to the left for Liverpool; but passengers from Yorkshire taking this route change carriages at Rochdale, about three miles further on the main line.

HEYWOOD.

POPULATION, 19,194.
A telegraph station.
HOTEL.—Queen Anne.
MONEY ORDER OFFICE.

Here are large cotton and woollen mills. In the vicinity is *Bamford Hall*, a fine old seat of J. Fenton, Esq.

BURY, see page, 57.

The line beyond Bury passes the stations of BLACK LANE, BRADLEY FOLD, and DARCY LEVER, to BOLTON, and thence to LIVERPOOL, for which route see Section III.

ROCHDALE.

A telegraph station.
HOTEL.—Wellington.
MARKET DAYS.—Monday and Saturday
FAIRS.—May 14th, Whit-Tuesday, and Nov. 7th.
BANKERS.—Clement Royds and Co.; Messrs. J. & J. Fenton; Branch of Manchester and Liverpool District Banking Company.

A modern borough (one member) in the southern division of the county of Lancaster, and the principal centre of the flannel trade, 12¼ miles from Manchester, is situated in the valley or dale of the Roche, a branch of the Irwell. Population, 29,195. The borough bounds are an exact circle of ¾ mile radius from the bridge; but the parish stretches into the West Riding of Yorkshire, its extent being about 10 miles square. Stone, coal, and slate are quarried in great plenty in the neighbouring moorlands; and cotton, woollen, and flannel are the staple articles of manufacture.

The mother church of *St. Chad* is a large Gothic building, on a hill; the vicarage is worth above £2,000. Besides the *Town Hall*, *Assembly Rooms*, Archbishop Parker's *Grammar School*, and other public edifices, there are about 150 mills in and around the town, employing 20,000 hands. At Castleton, on the south side of the river, are traces of a fortress, as old, if not older, than the Conquest. It belonged, with the manor, to the Byrons (ancestors of the poet) the first peer of whom, with his five sons, fought so gallantly for Charles I. They have been styled Barons Byron "of Rochdale."

Foxholes, near Rochdale, is the seat of the Entwistles. At *Milnrow* or Milrow, lived the well-known Tim Bobbin, an eccentric schoolmaster, whose real name was Collier; he published various specimens of the Lancashire dialect, which attains a peculiar vigour and raciness about this part. The moorland becomes more wild and imposing to the north of Rochdale, on the Haslingden road. *Wittle Hill* is about 1,600 feet high, while *Blackstone Edge* and other points in the Yorkshire border are proportionably high. The canal, railway, and road run side by side up the valley of the Roche, past Littleborough, where there was a Roman post guarding the road to York; the tunnel here is nearly 1¾ mile long

LITTLEBOROUGH.

A telegraph station.
MONEY ORDER OFFICE.

This place is situated close to the great tunnel, which is 1⅝ mile long, 541 feet above the sea, and 400 feet below the surface. It was constructed with 23,000,000 of bricks, and cost £110,000. In the vicinity are *Blackstone Edge*, from which there is a fine prospect, and *Hollingworth*, with its large Reservoir, upon which a small steamer plys, and pleasure boats may be had.

YORKSHIRE,

WHICH is a most important county, both as respects its topographical position and commercial advantages, returns six members. It extends 130 miles in length from east to west, and is 90 miles in breadth from north to south; being not less than 460 miles in circumference. It is divided into three ridings, called the north, east, and west. The East forms the least of the three grand divisions of the county. Many parts of the wolds or hills in it afford magnificent prospects. From their northern edge the Vale of Derwent is seen extended like a map below, and beyond it the black moors towards Whitby rise in sublime grandeur. The western hills command an extensive view of the Vale of York, reaching far beyond that city into the West Riding. But the southern edge of the wolds is the most distinguished for the beauty and diversity of its prospects. The eastern portion of this elevated district skirting the Humber commands a most magnificent view of that vast estuary, extending to the south east till it is lost in the horizon. It presents to the eye an interesting spectacle of numerous vessels floating to and from the port of Hull; while that opulent and commercial town, in its low situation, close to the banks, and surrounded by the masts of the shipping in the docks, seems to rise, like Venice, from amidst the sea; the whole composing a scene which, for beauty and grandeur, can scarcely be exceeded. The district of the North is bounded on the north by the river Tees, which separates it from the county of Durham. The length of this riding from east to west is 83 miles, and its breadth from north to south 38 miles. The climate is exceedingly various. In the Vale of York the air is mild and temperate, except on the moors, where the influence of the winds from those mountainous regions is sometimes severely felt.

The West Riding is about 95 miles in its greatest length from east to west, and 48 miles in breadth from north to south. Amidst the hilly and mountainous tracts of this riding are many romantic vallies, presenting the most beautiful scenery. The most extensive of these are Netherdale, or Niddersdale, watered by the Nid; Wharfdale, by the Aire, which in many places affords views the most delightful that can be imagined. The important rank which the manufactures of this county have long maintained in the estimation of the world, their manifest utility in furnishing employment and support for a great part of our population, and in supplying the comforts and conveniences of life, has often been the subject of just and well-merited commendation. The amount of patient thought, of repeated experiment, and happy exertion of genius, by which our various manufactures have been created and carried to their present excellence, is scarcely to be imagined. The establishment of manufactures in the West Riding has been the principal cause of its present wealth. The county is admirably adapted for carrying on manufactures. The raw materials are abundant on every hand; and coals plentiful and cheap. The staple commodities of the county are wool and cotton; the former is particularly deserving of notice, from the extent of the manufactures connected with it.

Passing WALSDEN station we arrive at

TODMORDEN.

POPULATION, 4,532.
A telegraph station.
HOTEL.—Queen's.
MARKET DAY.--Saturday.
FAIRS.—1st Thursday in every month, Thursday before Easter, September 9th and 27th.

BANKERS.—Manchester and Liverpool District Banking Co.

Here are very large cotton factories and coal mines, and the town is beautifully situated in the fertile valley of the Calder.

BURNLEY BRANCH.

The intermediate stations passed on this branch are PORTSMOUTH, HOLME, and TOWNELEY; and in the course of about half an hour the usual signals announce our arrival at

Burnley, particulars of which will be found at page 58.

Lancashire and Yorkshire Main Line continued.

EASTWOOD station.

HEBDEN BRIDGE.

POPULATION, 3,763.
A telegraph station.
MONEY ORDER OFFICE at Sowerby Bridge, 4½ miles.

The vale of Todmorden in this locality is rich in picturesque grandeur. In close proximity, along the valley of the Lee, is a splendid prospect; from an eminence, to the north-east of Wood End in the bottom of a deep dale, is seen the little village of Hebden Bridge, surrounded by lofty ridges of moorland heights, partly clothed with wood, and partly spotted with groups of cottages and farm houses, several of them embowered in groves of trees, whilst through the dark recesses is heard the roar of the Calder, and its various tributaries, rushing occasionally in sheets of spray over the precipitous heights, and rendered subservient to the purposes of the various cotton and woollen manufactories with which the valley is nearly every where studded.

Passing MYTHOLMROYD and LUDDENDEN FOOT stations, we reach

SOWERBY BRIDGE JUNCTION.

POPULATION, 7,908.
Distance from the station, 1 mile to the town of Sowerby.
A telegraph station.
In St. Peter's church is a statue of Archbishop Tillotson, a native of Haughead. In 1678 some Roman coins were found here.
COPLEY station.

HALIFAX.

A telegraph station.
HOTEL.—Swan.

MARKET DAY.—Saturday.

FAIRS.—June 24th, and 1st Saturday in November.

BANKERS.—Halifax Joint Stock Bank; Halifax Commercial Bank; Halifax and Huddersfield Union Bank.

HALIFAX, a seat of cloth manufacture, and a parliamentary borough, near the Calder, in the West Riding of Yorkshire, is built of stone, on a hill. The parish is a vast stretch (76,000 acres) of moor land, once part of Hardwick Forest, and nearly as large as the whole county of Rutland, containing a population of 150,000, dispersed in upwards of thirty townships; the borough population is 33,580, who return two members. The spirit of commercial enterprise has recently manifested itself in Halifax by the rapid growth of the town, as well as the great increase of its population. Carpets and stuffs form the staple manufacture of the town. Perhaps there is no town in England, in proportion to its size, that can boast of so large an outlay of capital in promoting sanitary and architectural improvements as that of Halifax within the last few years. Coal, iron, and stone are found, which employ a large number of hands; while many more are weavers of woollen and other stuffs, as well as shalloons, baizes, serges, and worsted cloth, such as broad cloths; they are sold at the *Piece Hall*, which was built in 1779, and contains nearly 320 small rooms or stalls for the dealers.

In connection with the town there is a splendid park, the result of the munificence of Frank Crossley, Esq., who, when completed, according to the designs of Sir Joseph Paxton, handed it over to the corporation for the benefit of the pnblic. The grounds are most tastefully laid out, and decorated with beautiful statuary. The fountain in the centre is a jet of water surrounded with a representation of wicker work, which has a very pleasing effect.

St. John's Parish Church, the parent church of this wide district, is a large later English building of the 15th century (finished, in 1470); 192 feet long, with a low tower, and ornamented with the coats of arms of its successive rectors, as far back as 1274. Sir W. Herschell was organist here, before he turned his attention to astronomy.

Four centuries ago, just before the cloth trade began to flourish, Halifax had but thirteen houses; but it was long noted for a gallows or guillotine, on Gibbet Hill, under the management, at first, of its feudal Lords, and afterwards of the town authorities, where thieves and poachers were disposed of, till 1650. The Duke of Leeds is now Lord of the Manor. Briggs, who first made a logarithm table, was a native.

Within the parish are Ealand or Elland, the scene of the "Ballad of Sir Jno. Ealand," and the feud between him and the Beaumonts of Crossland. Here is a training college for Church Missionary Students. At Haughead, in Sowerby township, Archbishop Tillotson was born, 1630, the son of a Calvinist. Sir H. Savile the Greek scholar and provost of Eton, was born at Bradley, in Stainland; he shared in translating the Gospels and the Book of Revelations, in the current version of the Holy Scriptures. Hartley, the metaphysician, was a native of Illingworth. Though this part of the West Riding is very naked, yet the wild ruggedness of the hills and vallies, and the prospects to be obtained from the highest points, are wonderfully striking, especially towards the back bone of England, in the Lancashire and Derbyshire borders, where some points (edges they are called) are upwards of 1,800 feet high.

Passing HIPPERHOLME, LIGHTCLIFFE, PICKLE BRIDGE, and LOW MOOR stations, we arrive at

BRADFORD, see page 18.

BOWLING.

Telegraph station at Laister Dyke, 1 mile.
HOTEL.—Railway.
MONEY ORDER OFFICE at Bradford, 2 miles.

Close at hand is *Bowling Hall*, the seat of J Sturge, Esq., which was the Earl of Newcastle's quarters when he routed Fairfax, in 1642, on Odwalton Moor.

Next in succession follow the stations of LAISTER DYKE, STANNINGLEY, BRAMLEY, ARMLEY, HOLBECK, and

Leeds. For description of which see page 16.

Sowerby Bridge to Wakefield.

We now return to the station at Sowerby Bridge, and pursue our course beyond NORTH DEAN (the junction of the easterly branch line to Halifax), and ELLAND, and arrive at

BRIGHOUSE.

POPULATION 6,995.
A telegraph station.

Close at hand is *Fixby Hall*, the seat of the Thornhills.

COOPER BRIDGE station, near which is *Kirklees Hall*, the seat of Sir G. Armitage, Bart., at which seat Robin Hood died.

MIRFIELD.

POPULATION 6,966.
A telegraph station.
HOTEL.—Black Bull.

CLECKHEATON BRANCH.

Mirfield to Bradford.

This little branch is important, as reducing very materially the distance between Bradford, Huddersfield, and the Midland Districts. The stations on the line are HECKMONDWIKE, LIVERSEDGE, CLECKHEATON, and LOW MOOR. Heckmondwike is noted for its large blanket sales on Mondays and Thursdays, at the large Hall. Liversedge has a population of 6,974, engaged principally in the coal trade. Low Moor is justly celebrated for its very extensive iron works. Its locality can be clearly distinguished on a dark night for many miles round, from the illuminated atmosphere, produced by the smelting department.

Bradford.—See page 18.

On again returning to the main line we pass THORNHILL LEES, for Dewsbury, and HORBURY stations, and quickly arrive at

WAKEFIELD.

Distance from station, ½ mile.
A telegraph station.
HOTEL.—Strafford Arms.

MARKET DAYS.—Friday, and every second Wednesday.

FAIRS.—July 4th, 5th, and 11th, and Nov. 2nd.

BANKERS.—Leatham, Tew and Co.; Wakefield and Barnsley Union Bank; Branch of West Riding Union Banking Co.

WAKEFIELD.—This is the county town of the West Riding of Yorkshire, a modern parliamentary borough (one member), and centre of the corn trade, prettily situated od the banks of the river Calder. Population, 22,060. By means of the Calder, vessels of 100 tons ascend from the Humber, laden with corn, &c. Ship yards, rope factories, as well as malt houses, are established here.

The town contains several important public buildings, the property of the West Riding, viz:—the Pauper Lunatic Asylum, on the York Road, originally intended for 400, but now capable of accommodating 800 patients; the House of Correction, Westgate, capable of holding above 1,000 prisoners; the Court House, Wood Street, in which the Petty and Quarter Sessions are held; the Register Office for deeds relating to the West Riding; and the office of the clerk of the peace for the West Riding. The office of the chief constable of the West Riding constabulary is in Bond Street.

The other public buildings in the town are, the Moot Hall and Rolls Office, belonging to the extensive manor of Wakefield; the Corn Exchange Buildings; the Mechanics' Institution, under which is the Public Subscription Library and News Room; and the Grammar School, near St. John's, which has been removed from the original building, erected in the time of Queen Elizabeth. The new School is a remarkably fine building in the collegiate style. Attached to the Grammar School are several scholarships and exhibitions to college. Drs. Ratcliffe, Potter, and Bentley, were educated at the Wakefield Grammar School.

There are five churches—the parish church of All Saints, with which is established a lectureship of £100 a year, by Lady Camden; St. John's; Holy Trinity; St. Andrew's, and St. Mary's; besides the Chantry Chapel on Wakefield Bridge, a choice relic of antiquity, which has lately been restored at considerable cost, and is used as a place of worship in connection with St. Mary's Church. The Catholic Chapel, in Wentworth Terrace, has lately been enlarged and beautified. The Independents, Baptists, Wesleyan and Primitive Methodists, &c., have each chapels in the town.

The fortnightly Cattle Market is one of the largest and best frequented in the kingdom. The Corn Market is second to none except Mark Lane.

The town has a considerable trade in Wool and the manufacture of Worsted Yarn, and a large business is done in dyeing. There are numerous and extensive collieries in the town and neighbourhood.

In addition to the public buildings enumerated there is the Clayton Hospital and Dispensary, and the House of Refuge, both supported by donations and subscriptions.

There are several charitable and educational establishments, belonging to the church and other religious denominations.

The Market, lately removed to the New Borough Market, bottom of Northgate, was established by a private company, by virtue of an Act of Parliament.

The charities of the town are administered by a body of gentlemen called the Governors of the Wakefield Grammar School and Charities: they have a considerable estate.

At Sandal, near Wakefield, are the remains of Sandal Castle, the baronial residence of the Earls of Warren, lords of the manor of Wakefield, until the time of Edward III., when, in consequence of the death of the last Earl of Warren without legitimate issue, it reverted to the crown; and Sandal Castle was the occasional residence of the stewards of the manor. It was demolished during the civil war between Charles I. and his parliament. The manor has been vested for several generations in the families of the Dukes of Leeds, and is now the property of S. L. Fox, Esq., son-in-law to the late duke.

The Soke, which extended over several townships, the inhabitants of which were compelled to grind corn at the Lord's or Soke Mills, was, some time ago, purchased for £18,000, under an Act of Parliament, the money being borrowed on the credit of a rate, payable by the householders and owners of property.

Walton Hall, near Wakefield, is the seat of Charles Waterton, Esq., the great naturalist and South American traveller.

NORMANTON, connection of the Midland Railway to Leeds, and the North Eastern to York, &c.

WAKEFIELD, PONTEFRACT, AND GOOLE

Passing CROFTON and FEATHERSTONE stations, (close to which is the beautiful seat of J. Gully, Esq., formerly M.P. for Pontefract, *Ackworth Park*), we arrive at

PONTEFRACT.

POPULATION 11,515.
A telegraph station.
HOTELS.—Red Lion, Dragon.
MARKET DAY.—Saturday.
FAIRS.—Every other Saturday after York Fair, 20 days' Fair, beginning 20th day after Christmas, Saturday after February 13th, April 8th, May 4th, Saturday before Palm, Low, aud Whit Sundays, Saturday after September 12th, and 1st Saturday in December.
RACES.—First week in August.
BANKERS.—Leatham, Tew and Co.; Branch of Yorkshire Banking Co.

PONTEFRACT, so called because of a broken bridge, near which is the keep of the Lacys' Castle, in which Richard II. was starved to death in 1399. Archbishop Scrope, executed by Henry IV.; Earls Rivers and Grey, by Richard III.; and the Duke of

Orleans and other French prisoners were confined here after the battle of Agincourt. Here is a large old Gothic church, with a fine picture of the crucifixion. Archbishop Bramhall, and Lund, the barber poet, were natives. Liquorice cakes are made here, the root being grown in the fields around Ackworth. Here the Quakers have an excellent school, in a healthy spot. Edward Sixth's *Grammar School* and Waterloo Pillar.

KNOTTINGLEY, WHITLEY BRIDGE, HENSALL, and SNAITH stations near the latter of which is the effigy of Lord Downe, of Cowick, in the antique church; and the seat of Lord Beaumont, *Carlton Hall*, is close at hand.

RAWCLIFFE station.

GOOLE.

A telegraph station.

HOTELS.—Lowther, Crown.

STEAMERS to Hull daily (Sunday excepted) on arrival of early trains leaving Leeds and Wakefield. Fares, 1s. 6d. and 1s.

MARKET DAY.—Wednesday.

BANKERS.—York City and County Banking Company.

This market town has much increased in importance. It has excellent dry docks and a good harbour, with a population of 4,722, who are chiefly engaged in the coal and coasting trades.

NORTH EASTERN.

Normanton to Hull.

Resuming our seats at Normanton, we pursue our course beyond CASTLEFORD and BURTON SALMON, and arrive at

MILFORD, the junction of the lines to Leeds and Hull.

Milford to Selby.

The next station to Milford is HAMBLETON, near which is *Hambleton House*, the seat of J. Smith, Esq.

SELBY.

POPULATION, 5,109.
A telegraph station.
HOTEL.—George.
MARKET DAY.—Monday.

FAIRS.—Easter Tuesday, Monday after 22nd June, and October 11th.

BANKERS.—Branch of York City and County Banking Co.; Branch of Yorkshire Banking Co.

This was the ancient *Salebia.* Here is an old timber swing bridge, and half ruined cruciform church, which was built in 1069; the tower fell down in 1690; it contains an old font, chapter house, and Norman porch. The Custom House, Town Hall, Shipyard, and the old Gothic Market Cross are worthy of notice. Henry I. was a native.

Selby to Market Weighton.

This branch turns out of the Hull and Selby line to the left, and passes the unimportant stations of CLIFF COMMON, DUFFIELD and MENTHORPE GATES, BUBWITH, FOGGATHORPE GATE, HOLME, and HARSWELL GATE.

Market Weighton, see page 72.

Hull and Selby Line continued.

Selby to Hull.

In returning to the main line we pass CLIFF (near which is *Hemingbrough*, with its old cruciform church and spire) and WRESSEL, close to which are the ruins of *Wressel Castle*, erected by the Percys, who lived here in regal state in 1390; and now the property of the Wyndham family. Here the Derwent is crossed by an iron swing bridge.

We then arrive at

HOWDEN.

POPULATION, 2,235.
Distance from station, 1¼ mile.
A telegraph station.
HOTELS.—Half Moon, Bowman's Commercial.
MARKET DAY.—Saturday.
FAIRS.—Second Tuesday in Jan., April 15th, 2nd Tuesday after July 13th, and every 4th Tuesday, for cattle, Sept. 25th, and six following days (great horse fair for supplying the army, and hunters).
BANKERS.—York City and County Banking Co.

HOWDEN has a fine decorated church, with the beautiful east window and chapter house of a college of the 13th century, belonging to the Bishops of Durham, and founded in 1266; it contains a fine tower 140 feet high, east window, and handsome octagon chapel house. The Bishop's Palace is now a farmhouse. Close by is *Spaldington Grange*, the seat of Lord Howden. Roger de Howden, a monkish chronicler, was a native. A great horse fair is held here for hunters, cavalry horses, &c.

Passing EASTRINGTON, STADDLETHORPE, BROUGH, FERRIBY, and HESSLE stations we arrive at

HULL (Kingston-upon-Hull).

Telegraph stations at Nos. 36 and 53, Lowgate, and Railway stations.

HOTELS.—Royal Station Hotel, first class for families, private or commercial gentlemen; Dodsworth's Commercialand Family Hotel; The George; Glover's Commercial Hotel; Victoria Hotel on the Quay.

POST HORSES, FLYS, &c., at the hotels. Tariff—1s. 6d. per mile. 1s. from any railway station the town.

MARKET DAYS—Tuesday and Friday.

RACES in the Autumn.

BANKERS.—Pease and Liddells' (Old Bank) Trinity House Lane; Smith, Brothers and Co.'s Bank, 5, Whitefriar Gate; Harrison, Watson, and Co.'s Bank, 53, Whitefriar Gate; Branch Bank of England,

Salthouse Lane; Hull Banking Company, 32, Silver Street; Yorkshire District Bank, 56, Lowgate. Attendance at all the Banks from 10 a.m. to 3 p.m.

PLACES OF RESORT, &c., IN HULL.

The ZOOLOGICAL GARDENS, situate on the Spring Bank. In addition to the splendid menagerie and aviaries, there is the panoramic painting (fresh subject annually), the cameræ obscuræ, the music hall, the model of the Crystal Palace, and a host of other attractions, calculated to gratify the old and instruct the young. Galas, concluding with fireworks, are held, weather permitting, every Monday during the season. The gardens occupy about seven acres of land.

The BOTANICAL GARDENS are on the Anlaby Road. An agreeable resort to the pleasure-seeker and practical botanist. Admission by order from subscribers.

The CITADEL, with its antiquated buildings and grim-looking guns, commanding the Humber, is a place of great attraction.

The THEATRE ROYAL, Humber Street; QUEEN'S THEATRE, Paragon Street.

The LITERARY and PHILOSOPHICAL SOCIETY'S MUSEUM—ROYAL INSTITUTION, Jarratt Street. Admission by orders from any of the directors or subscribers.

The MUSEUM of the MECHANICS' INSTITUTE may be viewed on application to the Librarian at the Institute, George Street.

Mr. SEAMEN'S MUSUEM is at that gentleman's residence, immediately opposite the Zoological Gardens, and contains many valuable natural curiosities.

MISCELLANEOUS SOCIETIES.–Amongst the societies designed to improve the social condition of the people, may be noticed the Hull Temperance League; the Hull Auxiliary Peace Society. W. Morley, Esq., President; the Harmonic Society; the Subscription Musical Society—Conductor, Mr. H. Deval, R.A. Mus.; and the Vocal Society—Conductor, Mr Skelton.

This parliamentary borough and old town, founded by Edward I., as a King's Town, or Kingston-upon-Hull (which is still its official name), stands on the *Yorkshire* side of the Humber, in a very flat and uninviting spot, but admirably fitted for trade, which has much augmented in the last few years. Population, 84,690, who send two members. The river Humber, the main estuary into which the Ouse and the Yorkshire streams, with the Trent, all four flow, is here 2 miles broad, and widens to 5 or 6 before it joins the sea at Spurn Head, which is 20 miles below. All this coast of the East Riding is in progress of change—the sea gaining on the shores of the north sea, where Ravenspur, Potterfleet, and other ports, once in existence, have been swallowed up, while it is retiring, if anything, on the Hull shore, where Sunk Island (towards Spurn Head), which first appeared above water in 1630, is now a fertile cultivated tract of 4,500 acres in extent. So flat is the county that the railway to Selby westward, though 31 miles long, runs for the most part on a made embankment, and has neither tunnel nor viaduct. The loss of the ancient sea ports of the Riding led to the foundation of Hull, but its unhealthy site, and the dirt inherent to a flourishing trade, make it the certain victim of cholera whenever it appears.

Brick clay is abundant, and Hull has several specimens of *very old* brick buildings. The *Citadel* with its old moated fortress contains the barracks and magazines, and stood two sieges in the civil war; the first being in 1642, when the refusal of Sir J. Hotham, the Governor, to deliver the town to Charles I., who appeared in person before it, was the first act of hostility between the King and Parliament. Hotham in the next year proving treacherous, was executed at Tower Hill. A bridge of three arches crosses the Hull in the middle of the town, near the upper entrance of the *Docks*, which form a loop with it and the Humber, and contain 30 acres, besides two basins of 3 acres more. *Old Dock*, cut in 1778, contains 13 acres, and is 1,700 feet by 254 feet; the others are the *Humber Junction*, *Railway*, and *Victoria Docks*, and all surrounded by large warehouses. and timber yards. Upwards of 100,000 tons of shipping are owned by the port; and the custom duties amount to nearly half a million. Pottery, bricks, white lead, soap, oil-cake, rope, sails, grain, timber, iron—figure among the articles of trade. Many seamen are engaged in the Greenland whale fisheries and Baltic trade. Fox, who attempted the north-west passage up Fox's Channel, and perished in 1586, Johnson the botanist, Spence the entomologist, and B. Thompson, and his brother were natives.

Among the buildings are the *Public Rooms*, built in 1830, having a hall 90 feet long. Large parish *Church of Trinity*, in the Market Place, built in 1312, one of the largest in the kingdom, in the shape of a Gothic cross, 270 feet long and 170 feet through the *early brick transept;* steeple, 150 feet high; and a fine organ, by Foster and Andrews, *Wilberforce Column*, near the Junction Bridge, founded in his honour, on the 1st August, 1834 (the day of negro emancipation), 80 feet high. Wilberforce was born at Hull, in 1759, and died in 1853, but not till he had the happiness of knowing that the bill was safe, and that the great work of his useful life was achieved. "Thank God (he said), that I have lived to see the day when an English parliament is willing to give 20 millions to abolish slavery," A gilt statue of William III., by Schermaker, in the Market Place. The large *House of Correction*, on the site of the Hotham's friary, founded in 1331. *Baths* and *Wash-houses*, built in 1850. *Trinity Hospital* and *School*, for the merchant service, founded in 1369, is a brick quadrangle, with a Museum attached, in which there are portraits of Andrew Marvel (a native), the poet, and secretary to Cromwell, who represented Hull in the civil war, and George III., a picture of Hawke's victory, all by Sevres, and a curious Greenland boat. Marvel was educated at the *Grammar School*, founded by Bishop Alcock, of which Cathin and J. Milner were masters. Mason, the poet (another native), as well as Wilberforce and Dean Milner, were also educated here. The *Charter House* asylum is nearly as old a foundation as Trinity Hospital, and was established by the De la Poles, a family of rich merchants, when they left the decayed port of Ravenspur to settle here. Cardinal Pole was of this family; they became Dukes of Suffolk, and built a palace, which stood here till 1771. The *Infirmary*, built in 1782, has bas-reliefs by Westmacott. At the *Mechanics' Institute* is a large picture by Briggs, the "Britons instructed by the Romans." There are also the *Hull Club*, in Charlotte Street; the *Conservative* and *Exchange News Rooms*, in Lowgate; the new *Corn Exchange*, in High Street, built in 1856; the *Royal Institution*, opened in 1854; a large *Lunatic Asylum* for the Riding, &c., and a *Botanic Garden*, in a piece of ground covering 5 acres. Edward III. visited here in 1322, Henry VI. in 1448, Henry VIII. in 1541, Charles I. in 1639, and Queen Victoria and the Prince Consort in October, 1854.

South Cave may be visited from Hull. It is situated in a wooded hollow of the wolds, and was a seat of Washington's ancestors, whence they emigrated in the 17th century to the United States; there is a portrait of him at Cave Castle.

HULL AND HOLDERNESS.

This flat corner of the Riding, called Holderness, naturally marshy, like the fens of Lincolnshire, has been well drained, by means of levels, &c.; the soil is light, sandy, and fertile. A breed of short-horns, called Holderness, is reared here; they fatten well, and are good milkers.

Hornsea is a bathing place on the North Sea, at a part where the sea has sensibly gained a footing. Hornsea Mere, near it, is the only lake in Yorkshire, except one, and offers some sport after field fowl. *Spurn Head* is a low sandy point at the Humber's mouth, which Ptolemy called *Ocellum Promontorium*, from *ocellus*, an eye, which is its shape now. Near this place, in 1682, James II. (then Duke of York) was wrecked on his way to Scotland, when himself, his priests, dogs, and the Great Duke of Marlborough, were fortunately saved. The lights upon it were built by Smeaton.

Taking train at the Holderness station we pass through MARFLEET, HEDON, BURSTWICK, and KEYINGHAM, arriving at

OTTRINGHAM,

Near which is Sunken Island—reclaimed land —first inhabited in 1801. The *Hall* is the fine old seat of A. Maister, Esq.

WINESTEAD station.

PATTRINGTON.

Here is a cruciform church with a fine spire, and from which a most magnificent view is obtained of the Humber—and a model farm of 1,000 acres, the property of Mr. Marshall, of Leeds. At Welwich is a pretty church.

WITHERNSEA.

Telegraph station at Hull, 18 miles.

Recently converted into a watering place, is making rapid advances to a very good one. It has an excellent Hotel, and commands one of the best possible views of the German Ocean. Situate about 18 miles from Hull.

The site of the church of St. Nicholas is now one-third of a mile out in the sea. About the fourteenth century, *Ravenspur Haven* stood here, but was washed away by the sea, and the De la Poles then settled at Hull.

SCARBOROUGH, BRIDLINGTON, AND HULL.

Hull to Driffield.

COTTINGHAM.

In the neighbourhood are *Cottingham Castle*, the seat of J. B. Barkworth, Esq., the site of Barnard Castle, the old seat of the Wake family before the fourteenth century; and in the middle of Holderness, *Burton Constable*, the fine ancient seat of Sir T. C. Constable, Bart. In the church are the tombs of Stuteville, who built it and the tower in 1272, the Burtons of Hull-Bank House, with two brasses of a monk and priest. Once in every three years an intermitting spring flows here. The Castle is the seat of T. Thomson, Esq.

BEVERLEY.

A telegraph station.

HOTEL.—Beverley Arms.

MARKET DAY.—Saturday, and every alternate Wednesday.

FAIRS.—Tuesday before Feb. 25th, Holy Thursday July 5th, Wednesday before Sept. 25th, and Nov. 6th

RACES in June.

BANKERS.—Bower & Co.; Machell & Co.; Branch of Hull Banking Co.; Branch of Yorkshire Banking Company.

BEVERLEY, 10 miles up the Hull, with its noble *Minster*, 333 feet long, built on the spot where St. John of Beverley was buried, whose standard was carried about by Edward I., in his invasion of Scotland, to encourage his soldiers. It contains the beautiful Percy screen, old sanctuary, quaint portraits of the founders, St. John of Beverley and King Athelstane, tombs of the patron saint and the "freed stool" for criminals to fly to. There is a good grammar school, at which the three bishops, Fisher (executed by Henry VIII.), Alcock (who founded Jesus College, Cambridge), and Green were scholars, who together with Alfred of Beverley and Mary Woolstonecroft were natives. Ruins of Meaux Abbey. It has a population of 10.058, who return two members. At *Routh* is a Norman church; *South Skerlaw* has a church built by Bishop Skerlaw; close at hand is *Dalton Hall*, Lord

Hotham. Beverley means "beaver lake." Its horse fair is important. Formerly this part was a complete forest, but cleared for fuel. Passing ARRAM, LOCKINGTON, and HUTTON CRANSWICK stations we arrive at

DRIFFIELD.

POPULATION, 3,792.

A telegraph station.

HOTEL.—Blue Bell.

MARKET DAY.—Thursday, for grain.

BANKERS.—Bower & Co.; Branch of York Union Bank; Harding, Smith & Co.

DRIFFIELD is a market town, in the East Riding of Yorkshire. It is built on the banks of a canal, which communicates with the river Humber. Its principal manufactures are the weaving of cotton and silk.

MALTON AND THIRSK BRANCH.

Driffield to Malton and Thirsk.

From Driffield we pass the stations of GARTON, WETWANG, FIMBER, BURDALE, WHARRAM, NORTH GRIMSTONE, near to which are *Langton Hall*, the seat of N. Norcliffe, Esq., and SETTRINGTON, where there is an elm 24 feet round, the seat of Sir T. Sykes, the benefice of which is valued at £1,000 per annum.

MALTON.

POPULATION, 7,661.

A telegraph station.

HOTELS.—Talbot, White Horse.

MARKET DAYS.—Tuesday and Saturday.

FAIRS.—Saturdays before Palm and Whit Sunday, Oct. 1st and 10th.

RACES in April.

BANKERS.—Bower & Co.; Branch of York City and County Banking Company; Branch of York Union Bank.

A borough town, which returns two members, in the North Riding of Yorkshire, beautifully situated on the banks of the Derwent. *St. Michael's Church*, in the Market Place, is a large building of Anglo-Norman architecture, much mutilated; at the best end is a good tower. A handsome stone bridge connects this place with Norton, the river forming a boundary between the East and North Ridings.

The Derwent is navigable up to this place; and corn, the produce of the surrounding country, is conveyed in large quantities from hence to Hull, Leeds, Wakefield, and London; while from Hull are returned salt, sugar, and groceries of different kinds; coals, and all sorts of woollens, are brought here from Leeds and other parts of the West Riding in considerable quantities. This place was founded in the twelth century, by Colebrand the Dane; it contains the ruins of a castle, seat of the Vescisshires, and a church with a truncated spire.

AMOTHERBY and BARTON-LE-STREET, situated under the Cleveland Moors, Ralph's Cross, the highest point, being 1,864 feet above the level of the sea. Close at hand is

SLINGSBY, with its old castle and Gothic church. We now arrive at

HOVINGHAM.

Telegraph station at Malton, 9½ miles.

Close at hand are *Wigganthorpe*, the seat of W. Garthorpe, Esq. *Kirkby Moorside*, in the market-place of which is shown the house where Charles II.'s favourite Villiers died neglected—the town was part of his property. After passing the station of GILLING, close to which is *Gilling Park*, the seat of C. Fairfax, Esq.; *Helmsley*, with the ruins of the Villiers' Castle; *Duncombe House*, the seat of Lord Feversham, built by Vanburgh, with its magnificent galleries of pictures and marbles, and the fine picturesque ruins of *Rievaulx Abbey*, erected in the twelfth century—we then proceed to AMPLEFORTH, near which are *Newburgh*, the seat of Sir G. Wombwell, erected on the site of the Abbey, built by William of Newburgh, a native; and *Craike Castle*, the old Royal palace of the Northumbrian monarchs, and quickly pass on to

COXWOLD, close to which are *Byland Abbey*, founded in the 12th century, by the Mowbray family; and the Frankland's seat, *Thirkleby*, after which we reach PILMOOR Junction for

Thirsk. For continuation of line from which, see page 77.

Driffield to Scarborough.

From Driffield we pass in succession the stations of NAFFERTON where are considerable linen and rope manufactures, also at *Danedales* and *Danesgraves*; in the vicinity are tumuli.

LOWTHORPE.—Here are *Lowthorpe Hall*, seat of — St. Quintin, Esq., and *Harpham*, of which place St. John of Beverley, Archbishop of York, was a native.

BURTON AGNES.—*Burton Agnes Hall*, the princely seat of Sir H. Boynton, Bart., which was built by Inigo Jones on a pretty slope of the Wolds, forming a striking object from the railway, about midway between Driffield and Bridlington; Kilham (with its Norman church); Auburn (which has been partly washed away by the sea); and Barmston (the old seat of the Boynton family).

CARNABY.—Near at hand are *Boynton Hall*, the seat of Sir G. Strickland, Bart., M. P., from which most beautiful views may be obtained, and *Rudstone*, so named from a pillar of grit, 24 feet high, close to the church, (which is called Roodstone). We next arrive at

BRIDLINGTON.

POPULATION, 2,432.

A telegraph station.

HOTEL.—Black Lion.

MARKET DAY.—Saturday.

FAIRS.—Monday before Whitsuntide, Oct. 21st for cattle and cloth.

RACES in October.

BANKERS.—Harding, Smith, and Co.; York Union Bank.

This attractive resort lies on the Yorkshire coast, but at that point where the line turns westward from Flamborough Head, and then sweeping round to the south, forms a capacious bay, called Bridlington Bay. Here Charles I.'s Queen, Henrietta, landed in 1643, and Paul Jones was defeated by two vessels of war in 1779. In this sheltered harbour, about a mile southward of the old town, lies Bridlington Quay. It is a modern built place, and is distinctively known as Bridlington Quay; the principal street running direct to the harbour, and being very wide. The north pier commands a view of Flamborough Head, and forms a broad and splendid promenade. The bathing accommodation is excellent; and the beach has a fine hard sand, which affords a good walk at low water. An ebbing and flowing spring furnishes an abundant supply of water of remarkable purity; in addition to which there is also a chalybeate spring, situate about a quarter of a mile to the north-east of the quay, the medicinal properties of which resemble the chalybeate springs of Scarborough and Cheltenham, though the water seems less purgative..

The *Esplanade* is a spacious level green, commanding a beautiful view of the Holderness coast, which stretches in a curve as far as the eye can trace. The *Victoria Promenade* and *Polytechnic Rooms* adjoin the north pier. It contains an upper and lower promenade room, news, billiard, and exhibition rooms, with promenade on roof, and prospect tower. The old part or Bridlington is situated in the Gipsey Race, a beautiful valley, and contains a church which was part of the old priory, with fine front. John of Bridlington, Robert the Scribe, Ripley the Alchemist, and Kent the landscape gardener, were natives.

The neighourhood abounds with walks and rides, affording extensive prospects of Bessonby, Carnaby, Boynton, Thorpe, Rudston, &c., on the west; Sowerby, Marton, Flambro', &c., on the north; and Hiderthorpe, Barmston, &c., on the south. The face of the country (generally undulating) is rich in woodland scenery.

We then pass the stations of MARTON (the point of deviation for Flambro' Head, a place of great celebrity for its fisheries; the light on the cliffs is 400 feet high.) The Thornwick Hotel, at Flambro', is of recent erection, and offers good accommodation to visitors. BEMPTON, SPEETON, and HUNMANBY, near which is the *Hall*, Admiral Mitford's seat, formerly that of the Osbaldistons.

FILEY.

POPULATION, 1,511.
Telegraph station at Scarborough, 9¼ miles.
HOTEL.—Taylor's.

This is a modern watering place, and contains the usual accommodation to be obtained at such. The church is an old half Norman structure. Here is a good mineral spring. Owing to a great number of the men having been drowned in 1851, the population of women is considerably greater than that of the men.

Passing GRISTHORPE station close to which is *Gristhorpe Lodge*, the seat of W. Beswick, Esq., we then reach CAYTON, near which is *Flixton*, where there was an Asylum for Pilgrims ("Carman's Spittle"), founded by King Athelstane's courtier, Acchern, and passing on to SEAMER JUNCTION soon reach

Scarborough.—See page 74.

From hence we return to Milford, and pursue our course northwards.

North-Eastern Main Line continued.

Milford to Church Fenton.

The first station on leaving Milford is

SHERBURN.

POPULATION 1,440.
Distance from station, 1 mile.
Telegraph station at Milford Junction, 2 miles.
HOTEL.—Red Bear.
MARKET DAY.—Friday.
FAIR.—September 25th.
MONEY ORDER OFFICE at Milford Junction, 2 miles.

Here the Archbishops of York had a palace and Athelstane a seat. From the church a fine view may be obtained. Teazel is grown in the neighbourhood, and it is celebrated for its wine and sour plums.

At a distance of 2¼ miles further we come to

CHURCH FENTON.

Distance from station, 1 mile.
A telegraph station.

Close at hand are *Cawood*, with the ruins of the Archbishop of York's palace, at which Wolsey was arrested. *Scarthingwell Hall*, Lord Hawke's, and *Towton*, where the Yorkists gained the celebrated victory in 1461.

HARROGATE BRANCH.

Church Fenton to Harrogate.

Passing STUTTON station, we arrive at

TADCASTER.

POPULATION, 2,527.
Telegraph station at Church Fenton, 4½ miles.
HOTELS.—Angel, Railway.
MARKET DAY.—Wednesday.
FAIRS.—Last Wednesdays in May, October, and November.

The Roman name of this place was *Calcaria* (Calx). It is a market town, and has a long stone bridge having little water under it, whence the epigram, "magnificè structum sine flumine pontem." Bishop Oglethorpe's Grammar School and Hospital, and a later English Church. Limestone abounds in the vicinity, and of which York Minster is built.

NEWTON KYME station.

THORP ARCH, and *Boston Spa*. The former is so called from the bridge which crosses the river Wharfe at that spot, and the latter has been frequented for its mineral spring since 1744.

WETHERBY.

Population, 1,494.
Telegraph station at Harrogate, 8 miles.
Hotel.—Angel.
Market Day.—Thursday.
Fairs.—Holy Thursday, August 5th, October 10th 1st Thursday after 22nd November, and every two weeks for cattle.

This town is situated on the Wharfe. Near St. Helen's Ford is a noble bridge. It was forfeited by the Knights Templars in 1312, and twice garrisoned by Fairfax in 1642. There is excellent salmon fishery in the Weir. Close at hand are Wetherby Grange, with its fine heronry, and *Swinnow Hall.*

SPOFFORTH, for Knaresborough.

Telegraph station at Harrogate, 5 miles.
Money Order Office at Wetherby, 3 miles.
This place contains the ruins of the Percy's seat (the hall of which is still seen), demolished by the Yorkists after the battle of Towton. Close at hand is *Rudding Park*, the seat of Sir J. Radcliffe, Bart., of Milnes Bridge.

HARROGATE.

A telegraph station.
Hotels.—The White Hart, Low Harrogate, for families and gentlemen; The Granby, High Harrogate, for families and gentlemen; Gascoigne's Commercial Hotel, High Harrogate.
Races in July.
Bankers.—Knaresborough and Clare Banking Co.

Harrogate has a resident population of about five thousand, but during the season which continues from the beginning of June to the end of October, the visitors alone are more than double that amount. High and Low Harrogate are half-a-mile distant from each other, and as far as matters parochial are concerned, form two distinct villages, whose line of division, two brooks, is not obvious to the eye. The former is in the parish of Knaresborough, the latter of Pannal; but a more singular distinction was made until Ripon was formed into a Bishopric, for then the villages were under the jurisdiction of two different episcopacies, the See of Chester, and the See of York. Dr. Hunter divides the Harrogate springs into four classes, such as springs impregnated with sulphuretted hydrogen gas and saline matter; saline chalybeate springs; pure chalybeate; and springs containing earthy salts with little iron and no sulphuretted hydrogen. The "*Tewit well*" is on the common, to the east side of the Brunswick Hotel, and near the road to Leeds. The "*Sweet Spa*" was discovered in 1631, some years after, and occupies a more commanding position. It is now the chief chalybeate. In 1766, Lord Loughborough erected a stone canopy over the spring, which was removed in 1842, when the present neat building was substituted. The "*Old Sulphur Wells*" drew attention to the spot in the first part of the seventeenth century. In 1842 the commissioners enclosed the springs and erected an octagonal pump-room of ample dimensions and appropriate decoration. That this, however, might not interfere with the claims of those who could not afford a trifling gratuity to the attendant, a pump is placed without the walls available to the public, with only such restrictions as are necessary for the preservation of the water. The "*Montpellier Sulphur Well*" is private property, and an appurtenance to the Crown Hotel. It was found in 1822, and is enclosed, together with the saline chalybeate pump connected with the spring at a short distance, in an octagonal apartment decorated after the Chinese style. A trifling subscription gives the public the benefit of the springs, and entitles them besides to admission in the pleasure-grounds adjoining. The "*Knaresborough or Starbeck Spa*" is situated midway between Harrogate and Knaresborough, and is about 200 yards from the roadside. Though known as a sulphur spring at an early period, it was not until 1822 that the inhabitants of Knaresborough erected a neat and appropriate building over it with a suite of baths, and a residence for the attendant. To delicate constitutions it has often afforded relief when stronger remedies have failed. The "*Saline Chalybeate or Royal Cheltenham Pump-room,*" contains the properties of a tonic, aperient, and alterative spring. It was found by Mr. Oddy, in 1819, whilst searching for sulphur water to supply the baths. In 1835, the original little pump-room was superseded by the present splendid building, which affords a pleasant promenade and a library for the literary lounger. Balls and concerts are frequently given here throughout the season. "*Harlow Carr*" *springs* are situated in Harlow Carr, a small but picturesque valley about a mile from the Brunswick Hotel, and beyond the tower on the road from Harrogate to Otley. There are several springs both of sulphur and chalybeate water in the grounds, but three only of the former, and one of the latter quality are at present used. There is a comfortable inn adjoining, built in the Elizabethan style, which commands an agreeable prospect. A suite of ten baths, either for hot or cold water, have also been provided in a detached building, with every requisite convenience for the accommodation of visitors. There are a few other springs of minor importance in Low Harrogate, and numerous bathing establishments for those who are advised to try their remedial effects.

Amusements are not wanting; there is a race-course, laid out in 1793, and libraries and collections in natural history to beguile the leisure of the studiously disposed. Those delighting in fine prospects should not omit visiting the lofty tower erected on Harlow hill, in 1829, by Mr. Thompson, of High Harrogate. It occupies a lofty acclivity about a mile from Low Harrogate, and though placed at an altitude of 596 feet above the level of the sea, is not difficult of ascent. The tower is 100 feet high, and presents a magnificent panorama of the surrounding country on a clear day. To assist the vision there are seven mounted telescopes, of great optical power, placed at the summit. To give some idea of the amazing extent of the view afforded, it may be mentioned that when the atmosphere is favourable, the Peak, in Derbyshire, is distinctly visible, and the tower of a church in Hull may be seen, though the latter is distant sixty miles.

Within a short distance the following excursions may be made. *Ripley Castle*, on the Nidd, the Ingilby's seat. *Brimham Rocks*, a group of immense rocking and other stones, a fine point of view. *Allerton Mauleverer*, seat of Lord Stourton. *Ripon Cathedral*, a small cross, 270 feet long, with two towers, and St. Winifrid's needle in the crypt; the diocese was founded in 1836, and the learned Dr. Longley, Head Master of Harrow, was installed Bishop. *Studley Royal*, the seat of Earl de Grey, with the ruins of the church, &c., of *Fountain's Abbey* in the beautiful grounds. *Newby Hall* is another seat of the Earl's, having a very fine collection of marbles. The *Devil's Arrows* (three stones), near Boroughbridge, the Roman *Isurium*. *Harewood Hall*, a large building in the Grecian style, seat of the Earl of Harewood. *Otley*, near Weeton, an old Elizabethan seat of the Vavasours. *Tadcaster*, and its long bridge on the Wharfe, near Towton, where the Lancastrians were finally beaten by Edward IV., on Palm Sunday, 1461. The Wharfe and Nidd should be ascended for the fine mountain scenery round Skipton and Settle, where Ingleborough rises 2,361 feet high. Passing the Nidd you come to *Bolton Abbey*, near a cleft called the Strid, a Norman ruin, belonging to the Duke of Devonshire, who has the original of Landseer's "Bolton Abbey in the olden time." Here Mary Queen of Scots was confined two years, in charge of the Scropes.

North Eastern Main Line continued.

Church Fenton to York,

Ulleskelf, Bolton Percy, and Copmanthorpe, are passed in succession, and we stop at

YORK.

Population 50,000.

A telegraph station.

Hotels.—Harker's Family and Commercial; Railway Station, for families, private and commercial gentlemen; Braithwaith's Family; Old George; Commercial.

Market Day.—Saturday.

Fairs.—Every fortnight, stock; every two months, flax; every three months, leather; every Thursday from Lady Day to Michaelmas, wool; week before Christmas, horses.

Races.—August.

Bankers.—Swann, Clough, and Co.; Branch of Yorkshire Banking Co.; York City and County Banking Co.; York Union Bank.

The ancient capital of York and seat of the Primate of England, situated at the juncture of its three Ridings (tri-things, or *thirds)*, on the Ouse. The neighbourhood is flat and agricultural, Leeds being the nearest important seat of the manufactures by which the county is distinguished. Boots shoes, combs, and confectionery are the chief articles made here. Having been an imperial city, by the name of *Eboracum* (which the Saxons softened down to *Yurewicke*, &c.), all the time the Romans kept possession of Britain, from A.D. 70, when Agricola made it his head quarters, down to 427, there are, of course, many vestiges of antiquities, and historical incidents connected with them. The Emperor Severus died here (and his body was burnt on Siver's Hill, Acomb), as did also Constantius Chlorus, the father of Constantine, the first Christian Emperor. Here Paulinus built the first Christian church in the north of England, after converting Edwin of Northumber and (though it appears that a bishop of Eboracum presided at the Council of Arles, in 314), and there is scarcely any important event subsequent to this in which it did not make a figure. From 1536 to the beginning of the civil war, through the unsettled interval which succeeded the Reformation, a Lord President of the North kept court here, to awe the disaffected. His seat was at the old Manor House, near St. Mary's Abbey. The Castle is on the south side of the city, in a corner between the Ouse and Foss. The seat of the Roman governors, or *Palatium*, occupied a space between Parliament-street (in the middle of the city) and the Cathedral, towards Beddern and Aldwark.

Old Wall.—Most part of the ancient *Wall* remains, though altered by frequent patching. Having been paved with brick in 1831, it forms an agreeable promenade round the city, about 2½ miles long. Six gates, bars, 20 towers and posterns are left; formerly there were 40. *Micklegate* crosses the London road; upon its battlements the heads of Richard, Duke of York, his son Rutland (a mere boy of 19), &c., were placed after the battle of Wakefield in 1460.

> "Off with his head, and set it on York gates,
> So York may overlook the town of York."
> *Queen Margaret, in Henry VI.*

Richard's head was crowned with a paper crown, in derision of his claims to the throne (Edward IV. was his son). Near this gate a wide Tudor arch has been cut in the Walls to admit the Great Northern, North of England, and other railways, which have a general station in Tanner Row. At North Street postern, close to the river (where a ferry must be crossed), is an excellent view of the Cathedral and St. Mary's Abbey (to the left). Bootham bar, on the Edinburgh road, has some Roman inscriptions in it. Monk bar, on the New Malton road, is very ancient; so is Walmgate on the Hull road. Fishergate postern is near the Castle.

Cathedral.—This noble Minster is the chief glory of the city, and one of the most triumphant specimens of the pointed style; but, unfortunately, shut in, by houses and narrow streets. It is a regular cross, 480 feet long and 110 feet broad along the nave. The oldest part is the south transept and its marigold window, built in 1246 by Archbishop De Grey, in the early English style. Two elegant towers, surmounted by pinnacles, and each 196 feet high, with a rich window between, and a rich display of carved work, adorn the fine *West Front*, at which one never tires of looking. In one of these towers (rebuilt since 1840) is Dr. Beckwith's peal, in the other a new Great Tom of 12 tons. The

Centre Tower, begun at the end of the 14th century by Archbishop Thoresby, is only 213 feet high, the spire being wanting. In the north transept is a window 50 feet high. The timber roof of the nave, 99 feet high, has been renewed since an accidental fire took place here in 1840. In 1829 the choir also suffered from fire, but this was the wilful act of Martin, a lunatic, the brother of Martin the painter. The restorations, by Smirke, cost £50,000. On the decorated English screen are carved 15 figures, life-size, of Kings from the Conquest to Henry VI., during whose reign it was constructed. The new organ is 70 feet high; it contains 56 stops and 4,200 pipes, the largest of which is 32 feet high. At the east end is the splendid great window, 75 feet long by 32 feet broad, full of painted figures of Scripture characters, each about 2 feet high. This is a work of the 15th century. One of the best tombs is that of Archbishop De Grey, who died in 1216; his effigies are under a canopy. Another is Edward III.'s son, William of Hatfield (where he was born). Many Saxon prelates and chiefs were buried here in the former Cathedral, but their graves are without any mark. There is a monument to Mrs. Matthew, who must have lived and died in the full splendour of episcopacy, as her father was Bishop of Chichester, her two husbands were archbishops (Canterbury and York), and her four sisters each married a bishop.

The *Chapter House*, adjoining the north transept, built about 1340, is eight sided, 63 feet across, and 68 feet high to the keystone of the roof, which stands without any support beneath; the stained windows are 50 feet long. Among other relics are the horn of Ulphus, by which lands were held, and the cup of Archbishop Scrope, who headed the rebellion of Hotspur, &c., against Henry IV., and was beheaded for it. The *Library* contains Queen Elizabeth's copy of Wickliffe's MS. Testament, the Testament of Erasmus, and some of Caxton's printed books. It is open to the public. There are the Gothic gate and other remains of Priests' College in Vicar's Lane.

CHURCHES AND CHAPELS.—There are 24 churches and 15 chapels. Most of the churches are of stone, in the later Gothic style, and deserving of notice. *All Saints*, North Street, has a spire and some Roman stones in its walls. *Christ Church* is said to be on the site of the Roman Emperor's palace, some remnants of which are preserved in the King's Court and Conyng-garth, or King's Ditch. The church in the highest part of the city is All Saints, at one end of the Pavement, where some of the chief Roman buildings stood. Formerly there was a light in its beautiful tower for the guidance of travellers. The church of *St. Crux* (or Cross) is in the Shambles, near the other end of the Pavement; it contains a monument to the Percy who headed the rising in the north in Queen Elizabeth's reign. The Temple of Diana stood, it is said, where *St. Helen's*, in the Stonegate, is placed. Near this is Coney Street, which was originally Conyng (or King) Street; at *St. Martin's* is a monument of Bishop Porteus, a native. *St. John's*, at the top of Micklegate, is very old. At *St. Martin's*, in the same street, "R. T.," that is, Richard Turpin, the highwayman, is buried. His ride to York to escape detection is beautifully described in one of Ainsworth's novels. *Holy Trinity*, at the bottom of the street, is close to the gate of a priory and Trinity Gardens; many Roman relics have been found in this quarter. *St. Lawrence's* and *St. Margaret's*, in Walmgate, on the Hull road, are both ancient, and have pendant porches; the latter full of carved figures. *St. Mary's*, in Castlegate, is marked by a tall spire. The *Independent Chapel* is in Lendal, near the Manor Shore. The *Wesleyan Centenary Chapel*, built in 1840, is in St. Saviourgate. The *Friends' Meeting House*, in Far Water Lane near Castlegate. the *Roman Catholic Chapel*, in Little Blake Street, and the titular bishop of the district resides near York.

PUBLIC BUILDINGS.—Between Lendal and the river is the *Guildhall*, an ancient Gothic pile, built in 1446, 96 feet long, on oak pillars. The roof is pannelled, and the sides adorned with portraits and escutcheons. Here the Lord Presidents of the North kept their state; and Prince Albert, at his visit in 1850, explained the objects of the Great Exhibition. It stands behind the *Mansion House*, or official seat of the Mayor (who by courtesy is styled Lord Mayor), which is a Grecian edifice, containing various portraits. The *Post Office* is in Lendal. In Blake Street, not far from these, are the handsome *Assembly Rooms*, designed by the Earl of Burlington in 1736, with a portico, &c. The Great Hall is in the Composite style, 112 feet long, by 40 feet broad, and 40 feet high. A *Music Hall*, for the triennial festivals, in Lendal, near this, was built in 1825, having a concert-room 90 feet long, the frieze of which was ornamented by Rossi. In the grounds of St. Mary's Abbey, or the Mint Yard, is the *Museum* of the Philosophical Society, a solid Doric building, 200 feet long, built in 1830, by Wilkins, the architect of the National Gallery, who was generally successful in his porticoes. Various Roman marbles, inscriptions, Saxon remains, and geological specimens have been collected here. Close to it is the Manor, a large pile, built in Henry VIII.'s reign, on the suppression of the abbey, and now occupied as a *School for the Blind*, founded in honour of Wilberforce, in the Negro Emancipation year, 1833. The *Abbey of St. Mary* was founded by William Rufus, on the site of a temple; parts of the church, with its picturesque ruined towers, cloisters, crypt, &c., are still visible. An old Roman tower is also here; it figures in the city arms. An old hall of the Merchants' Company is in Fossgate, behind the Pavement; that of the Merchant Tailors is now used as an *Eye Hospital*. York was once noted for its coverlets. The *Theatre* is in Blake Street, on the site of the ancient hospital of St. Leonard. The *Baths* are on the Esplanade at Lendal, and the New Walk above and below the bridge. This bridge at the Staiths (*i. e.*, landings for goods) at the bottom of Lower Ousegate, is 40 feet broad, on three arches, the middle being 75 feet span; it was built in 1820. Formerly there was a Gothic structure of the 13th century here. Near Skeldergate postern is the *House of Correction*, built in 1807; adjoining which, close to the City Wall, is the *Vetus Ballicum*, or Old Bailey mound, once covered by a fort.

York Castle, which includes the Courts of Law, as

well as the Prison, is an imposing mass of buildings, with little of the ancient Castle about it, except the Round Keep, or *Clifford's Tower*, and a fine machicolated gate, 76 feet wide, the whole having been rebuilt between 1826 and 1836, and adapted to modern uses at a cost of very nearly a quarter of a million of money. An embattled wall surrounds the site two-thirds of a mile long. The *County Hall* is 150 feet long, with two domes and a portico. Here public meetings are held, or adjourned to the Castle Yard in front, where 40,000 people can assemble. *Clifford's Tower* is a picturesque ruin, overgrown with trees and ivy. It was dismantled after the siege of 1644.

There are various schools and institutions. St. Peter's *Grammar School* was built or rebuilt in 1833, in Minster Yard. It is simply a free school, in the Tudor style. A large and handsome *Diocesan School* is in the Elizabethan style; it cost £12,000. The County *Infirmary* was founded in 1749. At Heslington, near the Yarboroughs' old seat, is the *Friends' Retreat*, or Lunatic Asylum for the Quakers. That for the city, outside Bootham Bar, was built in 1777, and is a large and convenient pile, with extensive grounds behind. There are large *Barracks* at Fulford. Among the natives of York are—Alcuin, a famous scholar in the reign of Charlemagne; Flaxman, the sculptor; Etty, the painter; Earl Waltheof; Flower the Hermit; Archbishop le Romaine; Waldby Ergham, Admiral Holmes, Swinbourne, Stoke, Bishops Morton and Porteus, Sir T. Herbert, Cartwright, Fothergill, Wintringham, Eliza Montague, G Wallis, and Archdeacon Narnes. Hugo Goes, from Antwerp, first set up printing here in 1536.

On the Leeds road, at Knavesmire, is the *Race Course*, occupying a level about 1¾ mile in circumference, with a Grand Stand on the east side. Camden says that the best horse had a golden bell hung over his head; hence the phrase "to bear away the bell." Beyond this stretches the Ainstey, a wide tract, once covered by Galtres Forest, and, till 1837, annexed to the city, but now forming a separate Wapentake.

The Chapter House.—On the door is an old Latin rhyme:—

> "Ut *rosa* phlos phlorum (*ph* for *f*)
> Sic est domus ista domorum."

Or, "What the rose is among flowers this house is to other houses."

YORK & MARKET WEIGHTON BRANCH.

York to Market Weighton.

The stations on this branch in succession are:—

HUNTINGTON.

STOCKTON (on the Forest).

GATE HELMSLEY.—*Sand Hutton*, the seat of J. Walker, Esq., and *Aldby*, that of Henry Darley, Esq., are at hand.

STAMFORD BRIDGE.—In the neighbourhood is the ford of Derwent, the Roman *Derventro*, where Harold in 1066 routed Harfager; and cakes are made by the inhabitants of this district at the present time on that day, in commemoration of the achievement.

FANGFOSS.—Close at hand are *Wilberfoss* where the Wilberforce family formerly lived, and *Garrowby*, the seat of Sir C. Wood, Bart.

POCKLINGTON.

POPULATION, 2,546.
Telegraph station at York, 16½ miles.
HOTEL.—Feathers.
MARKET DAY.—Saturday.
FAIRS.—March 7th, May 6th, August 5th, Nov. 8th and 9th.

In the Grammar School at this place which has a population of 2,559, the celebrated Wilberforce was educated. In 1848 upwards of 500 coins from Henry VIII. to Charles II.'s reigns were found here. In the vicinity are *Kilnwick Percy*, the seat of R. Denison, Esq. *Millington* with its Roman antiquities, and *Wilton Beacon*, 809 feet high, the most celebrated spot of the Wolds.

BURNBY, close to which are *Nunburnhome* and *Warterwith*, the site of an old priory, near Lord Muncaster's seat.

SHIPTON.—Close at hand is *Londesborough* (built on the site of the ancient *Delgovitier*), the seat of the celebrated archæologist, Lord Londesborough.

MARKET WEIGHTON.

POPULATION, 2,001.
Telegraph station at Beverley, 8 miles.
HOTEL.—Londesborough Arms.
MARKET DAY.—Wednesday.
FAIRS.—May 14th, September 25th, for horses.

Here is a large old church. In the vicinity are *Hunsley Beacon*, 530 feet high; *Houghton Hall*, the seat of the Hon. C. Langdale; *Goodmanham*, with its Norman church, built on the site of a Pagan Grove, which was burnt by Crifin in the 7th century, on his conversion by Paulinus, and Lord Hotham's seat, *South Dalton Hall*, where bones of the elephant and rhinoceros have been found.

EAST AND WEST YORKSHIRE.

York to Knaresborough and Harrogate.

POPPLETON and HESSAY stations,

MARSTON.—Close at hand is *Marston Moor*, where Fairfax and Cromwell defeated Prince Rupert in 1644.

HAMMERTON station.

CATTAL.—Telegraph stations at Harrogate and York, 10¼ miles.

ALLERTON, near which is Lord Stourton's seat.

GOLDSBRO'.

Close to which is *Goldsborough Hall*, the seat of the Earl of Harewood; *Ribston Hall*, the old residence of the Goodrickes, at which the Ribston Pippin was first cultivated, and the Knights Templars had a preceptory. The Roman inscription found at York in the 17th century is carefully preserved here.

KNARESBOROUGH.

Telegraph station at Harrogate, $1\frac{3}{4}$ mile.

HOTELS.—Crown, Commercial.

MARKET DAY.—Wednesday (for corn).

FAIRS.—First Wednesday after January 13th, March 12th, May 5th, August 12th, October 11th, Wednesday before November 23rd, and Dec. 10th.

BANKERS.—Harrison and Co.; Knaresborough and Clare Banking Company.

A borough and parliamentary town in the West Riding of Yorkshire, with a population of 5,536, who return two members, pleasantly situated on the north eastern bank of the river Nid, which is here of considerable breadth, and the opposite bank is covered with thick foliage down to the water's edge. There are many beautiful and extensive prospects from this town, as it overlooks the greater part of the Vale of York. Towards the west the country has a gradual ascent, and the views are less extensive; but they are agreeably variegated by vales, eminences, woods, groves, country seats, and farms.

Knaresborough Castle, in which Richard II. was confined, dismantled by Fairfax in 1644, once the ornament and security of the town, has mouldered to decay, but the remains of its former magnificence show how great must have been its original strength and importance.

There is a large ancient church in which are monuments of the Slingsbys of Scriven Hall; here Becket's murderers took refuge,

Close by the river is the celebrated *Dropping Well*, a petrifying spring which falls over a limestone rock 45 feet broad, near to which are *Montague Cave*, *St. Robert's Chapel* and *Cave* (the scene of Eugene Aram's murder of Clarke), and close at hand is the birthplace of Mother Shipton.

STARBECK, for **Harrogate,** see page 69.

York to Rillington.

On leaving York we pass the stations of

HAXBY AND STRENSALL.—Close at hand is *Sutton Hall*, at Sutton-in-the-Forest, the seat of W. Harland, Esq. near Galtres Forest and Pen Moor.

FLAXTON, near which are *Flaxton Lodge*, the seat of B. Dobsworth, Esq., *Sheriff Hutton Park*, L. Thompson, Esq., and the towers of an old castle in which Richard III. confined Henry VII.'s wife, Elizabeth of York; and *Sand Hutton*, J. Walker, Esq.

BARTON HILL.—This place is the boundary of the North and East Riding, close to which are *Bossall* with its old church, cross, and spire, and *Howsham*, Col Cholmeley's seat, built in the Elizabethan style, of the stones of Kirkham Abbey, which is near the station.

KIRKHAM.—*Kirkham House*, E. Taylor, Esq.; and *White well Hall*, Mrs. Haigh.

CASTLE HOWARD.

Distance from station, $2\frac{1}{2}$ miles.
A telegraph station.
HOTEL —Crow.
MONEY ORDER OFFICE at Malton, $5\frac{1}{4}$ miles.
Close to which is *Castle Howard*, Lord Carlisle's seat, which was built by Vanburgh, and contains, amoug other pictures, Carracci's "Dead Saviour," and some marbles, the gift of the gallant Nelson. An obelisk 100 feet high, with a Doric colonnade, a round chapel, and a tree planted by Queen Victoria, who visited it in 1850.

HUTTON station, close to which are *Hutton's Ambo*; *Hildenley*, the seat of Sir G. Strickland, Bart., M.P.; *Langton Hall*, N. Norcliffe, Esq.

Passing MALTON station, (see page 67), we reach RILLINGTON, the junction of the

WHITBY BRANCH.

Passing MARISHES ROAD station, we reach

PICKERING.

A telegraph station.
HOTEL.—Black Swan.
MARKET DAY.—Monday.
FAIRS.—Monday before February 14th, May 13th, September 25th, Monday before November 23rd.
BANKERS.—Bower and Co.; Sub Branch of York Union Bank.
Passes through the most picturesque scenery. Pickering Park and Eskdale abound in rich woodlands; while the vales of Newton and Goathland present a wild country, with bold ranges of rock on either side. These glens add much to the interest of the trip along the railway.
LEVISHAM station.

GROSMONT.

Where the moorland commences. This town, which has a population of 3,112, contains an old church and the ruins of a castle founded by the Saxon Morcar, where Richard II. was kept a prisoner until his removal to Pontefract. Two towers still remain bearing the names of Queen Elizabeth and Rosamond's. In the vici y are *Pickering Hall*, seat of Mrs. Dowker; *Pickering Beck*; *Shunor Hoc*, 1,404 feet high; *Ralph's Cross*, 1,485 feet and *Boltom Head* 1,485 feet.
SLEIGHTS and RUSWARP stations.

WHITBY.

A telegraph station.
HOTELS.—Royal, on the West Cliff, for families and gentlemen; the Angel, family and commercial; Ward's Magnet, Commercial.
MARKET DAY.—Saturday.
FAIRS.—August 25th, Martinmas Day.
RACES.—In September, on the sands.
BANKERS.—Branch of York City and County Banking Co.; Simpson and Co.
There are, among the watering places of England, few that have been more greatly benefited than Whitby from railway communication, or that have become better adapted for the reception of visitors. The

town stands at the north east angle of the county of York, where the romantic river Esk pours its stream into the German Ocean. Enclosed between precipitous cliffs, the old town is scarcely to be seen, until nearly approached, though its locality is well pointed out by the ruins of its once stately abbey, which is still a beautiful object, adorning the east cliff; while on the west cliff, *New Whitby*, a magnificent pile of buildings, including a splendid hotel recently built, containing warm baths, and every convenience for the accommodation of visitors, is admirably situated at an elevation of 100 feet above the level of the sea, commanding varied prospects, and at the same time accessible from the sands and the piers. Whitby has long been admired for the peculiarity of its position and the grandeur of its coast scenery. To the eastward the cliffs rise abruptly, nearly 200 feet above the sea, and towards the south present a succession of bold headlands. To the north the views along the coast are not less imposing. The headlands at Sandsend, Kettleness, Runswick, Staithes, Huntcliffe, and Rawcliffe, abrupt in outline, and varying in elevation from 200 to 600 feet, present a succession of coast scenery scarcely to be exceeded for beauty in England; whilst the vallies, opening up the country from the sea, are replete with picturesque beauty. The old church of *St. Mary* stands close to the abbey, from which extensive prospects present themselves on every side. The ocean washing the beach, enlivened with passing vessels; the woods and castle of *Mulgrave* (the domain of the Marquis of Normanby); the piers, unequalled in this country for boldness of design; the town, harbour, shipping, and swing bridge across the river, all immediately beneath the eye; the fertile valley of the Esk, the hills intersecting one another, villas, hamlets, plantations, and the high moors beyond, covered with heath, altogether form a picture rarely surpassed. The west pier, extending 1,030 feet into the sea, with an elegant columnar lighthouse at its extremity, forms a favourite promenade; and the road cut through the solid rock and extending from the battery to the west cliff, is found to be highly advantageous to visitors.

There is probably no spot in England possessed of more varied rides and walks than the Whitby district. In every direction excursions may be formed: Robin Hood's Bay, Mulgrave Castle and woods, and the villages of Hawsker, Stainacre, Sneaton, Ugglebarnby, Aislaby, Sleights, Egton Bridge, Grosmont &c., are most accessible. Steamers are constantly plying to Scarborough, Redcar, Hartlepool, Stockton, Newcastle, &c., whilst sailing craft can be obtained at any hour to take trips in the offing, There is the usual accommodation provided for sea bathing. The beach extends three miles. Chambers the marine painter was a native. In the vicinity are *Whitby Abbey*, the seat of G. Cholmley, Esq., Lord of the Manor; *Airy Hill*, James Walker, Esq.; *Low Stukesby*, John Chapman, Esq.; *Sneaton Castle*, the Rev. W. Giles; *Larport Hall*, late E. Turton, Esq.; *Hawsker Hall*, B. Gatliff, Esq.; and *Robin Hood's Butts*, distant six miles, "the mark where Robin Hood's arrow flew when he shot before the Abbot of Whitby."

Rillington to Scarborough.

From RILLINGTON we pass the station of KNAPTON, near which is *Knapton Lodge*, the seat of I. Tindall, Esq.

HESLERTON, near to which are *West Heslerton Hall*, seat of M. Foulis, Esq., and *Yeddingham*, at which are the ruins of a priory, founded by Roger de Clerc, in the 12th century.

SHERBURN, close to which are *Ganton Hall*, seat of Sir T. Legard, Bart.; *Wykeham Abbey*, with a ruined nunnery, founded in 1153; *Sherburn House*, M. Langley; *Brompton Hall*, Sir G. Cayley (or Cailli) Bart.; *Wydale*, E. Cayley, Esq., M.P.; and *Castle Hill*, near which the kings of Northumberland had a strong fortress.

GANTON, and SEAMER, close to which is *Ayton*, the seat of the Cliffords of Brampton, and celebrated as having been the place where the parish clerk, Dale, in 1548, broke forth into rebellion for the restoration of the old religion.

SCARBOROUGH.

Distance from station, 1 mile.

Telegraph station.

HOTELS.—The Royal Hotel, for families and gentlemen; Winn's Crown, for families and gentlemen; Millhouses' Commercial and Family; Bull Inn, family and commercial.

MARKET DAYS.—Thursday and Saturday.

FAIRS.—Holy Thursday, and Nov. 22.

RACES.—In September.

BANKERS.—Woodall and Co.; Branch of York City and County Banking Co.

SCARBOROUGH is undoubtedly the most interesting marine spa in England. With the advantages of mineral springs it combines those of a convenient sea-bathing shore, and on the land side it is surrounded by numerous objects of attraction, to which either roads, or footpaths over moors and dales, offer a ready access to visitors. Of its origin we have no satisfactory information, but its name has been most probably derived from the Saxon *Scear*, a rock, and *Burgh*, a fortified place. No mention of it occurs in the Norman survey, but in the reign of Stephen we hear of the castle being erected, and doubtless that fortress soon became the nucleus of the town. Its situation is extremely beautiful and romantic, being in the recess of a fine open bay, on the coast of the North Sea, and the town consists of several spacious streets of handsome well-built houses, rising in successive tiers from the shore, in the form of an amphitheatre; the beach, of firm and smooth sand, slopes down gradually to the sea, and affords at all times that commodious open sea-bathing for which the place is so deservedly celebrated. From Robin Hood's Bay, northward, to Flamborough Head, southward, there are thirty-three miles of coast, which may be inspected at low water, over a course of the finest sands in England, and which, with their caverns and promontories, rugged fissures and pre cipitous elevations, form a geological panorama of the greatest interest. Flamborough Head, with its lofty cliffs of nearly five hundred feet elevation, teeming in the spring and summer months with thousands of birds of every hue and species, and exhibiting yawning caverns of stupendous size—that called "Robin Lyth Hole," being peculiarly noticeable—is of itself a promontory of unusual grandeur, and would be alone worth a pilgrimage from town. Not far distant either is Rievaulx Abbey, the beautiful ruins of which are presumed to indicate the first Cistercian monastery founded in Yorkshire, and which, in their magnificence of decay, are only surpassed by the famous Fountain's Abbey, that may be also brought within the compass of a summer day's ramble. In short, let the sojourn be ever so brief, the visitor will hence carry away with him a store of many memories of beauty, to which remembrance will afterwards recur with delight. To begin with one of these celebrities:—

A fine terrace, one hundred feet above the level of the sands, forms a delightful marine promenade. The dissevered cliffs are connected by a handsome iron bridge of four arches, on stone pillars, in the chasm between which runs the stream called Millbeck. This bold undertaking, to afford facility of access to the spas, was completed in 1827, and its opening day was signalised by a bold charioteer, who, with four well-trained steeds in hand, drove a coach across the yet untested structure, amidst the acclamations of myriads, who covered the adjoining buildings and surrounding hills, all swarming with eager faces, intent on the hazardous performance of what appeared so perilous a feat. This bridge, which is one of the principal ornaments of the town, is 414 feet in length and 75 feet in height, whilst the floor of the bridge is 14 wide, formed of transverse planks, and protected by an iron railing along each side. This airy fabric affords a view remarkably bold and striking, and far away beneath are the fine broad sands of the shore, where the Scarborough races are held, and where, says Dr. Granville, in his happiest graphic vein, "what at one hour was the estuary of living waters, murmuring in successive bow-like waves towards the foot of the cliffs, becomes in the next hour, upon that occasion, the course-ground and the theatre of the equestrian as well as pedestrian display of man's skill and animal's agility." The view of the horse-races from a place suspended in the air, and at such an immense altitude as this, is a sight only enjoyed, perhaps, by the people of Scarborough and the visitors to the Spa; for the cliff-bridge may be well described, on such an occasion, as the grandest stand of any in the world. Adjoining is the Museum, an elegant circular building, for the display chiefly of British geological specimens, though possessing a fine collection besides of other rare and interesting objects, among which the skeleton of an ancient Briton and his oak-tree coffin, supposed to be 2,000 years old, will be found particularly attractive: the teeth are all perfect, and the skeleton would appear to have been preserved by the *tannin*, found dissolved by the water which had penetrated into the coffin. A very moderate monthly subscription will entitle the visitor to admission to the Museum, and as a pleasant lounge, fraught with interest and instruction. it may be considered a valuable addition to the general attractions of the town.

The mineral springs of Scarborough have been, for more than two centuries, held in the very highest repute. These springs are saline chalybeates, varying in the proportions of their several ingredients, and were for some time lost by the sinking, in 1737, of a large mass of the cliff; but, after a diligent search, they were recovered. The principal are the West and South Wells, situated at the base of the cliff south of the town, near the sea-shore, where a convenient building has been erected for the accommodation of visitors. The water of the south well contains 98 ounces, and that of the north well 100 ounces of carbonic acid gas in a gallon; the former is purgative, and the latter tonic. An elegant saloon in the building affords an opportunity for exercise in rainy weather; and being lighted by several windows facing the sea, the visitor has an opportunity of enjoying various picturesque views of the sea and coast. In a small sunken court, paved with flagstones, and surrounded by stone walls, are the lion-mouthed spouts from which the water is continually pouring—the excess passing away through a small stone basin; and the substitution of this plan for the pumping-up process usually adopted, imparts a zest and a freshness to the draught that invalids can thoroughly appreciate.

Fronting the sea are some neat houses, let as lodgings, and called the "Marine Houses;" they have a small adjoining building for cold and warm baths—the sea, at spring tides, reaching to nearly the threshold of its garden front. A lofty and sloping bank, from 150 to 200 feet high, thickly covered with shrubs and trees, rises hence, and goes to join the cliff bridge, in a southern direction, like a crescent bower. On the brow of this green embankment stand many of the best houses, with a south or south-western aspect; and, on the sands below, a file of thirty or forty bathing machines, ranged on their broad wheels, stand ready for use. The gradual declivity of the shore, the softness of the sand, and the peculiar transparency and purity of the returning tide upon these open bays, render sea-bathing here not only perfectly safe, but absolutely luxurious. The town is supplied with fresh water by means of a reservoir holding 4,000 hogsheads, and being derived from land-springs is somewhat hard, but clear and wholesome to the eye and palate—an advantage few watering-places possess.

The harbour, easy of access, and safe and commodious within, is protected by two piers; one of them having been found insufficient to prevent the accumulation of sand, a new one was constructed, designed by Smeaton, the celebrated engineer. The breadth of its foundation is sixty feet; and at the curvature, where it is most subject to the action of the waves, sixty-three feet; it is forty feet high, and 1,200 feet in length.

The church, dedicated to St. Mary, was anciently the conventual church of the Cistercian Monastery, and was formerly a spacious and magnificent cruciform building, with three noble towers; it sustained considerable damage in the siege of the castle in the time of the Parliamentary war, and retains but few portions of its ancient character: the present steeple stands at the eastern end. Christ Church, a handsome edifice in the later style of English architecture, was erected in 1828, at a cost of £8,000. Other places of worship, and numerous hospitals and infirmaries, are scattered through the town. To the north of St. Sepulchre's Street are the remains of a Franciscan convent, supposed to have been founded about the 29th of Henry III., and now used as a workshop.

The season may be reckoned to begin on the first of July, and terminate about the middle of October. During this period, houses and apartments can only be had at high prices; but, after the latter date, a residence may be obtained at half the amount. The railway, as in other instances, has materially increased the influx of visitors, and now new streets are being rapidly formed, to provide additional houses for their reception.

By a walk to the summit of Mount Olive, or Olive's Mount, from a tradition connected with Oliver Cromwell, a most superb panorama of land and water is to be enjoyed from a terrace 600 feet above the ocean, and these, together with excursions to the environs, which include much picturesque scenery, form the especial attractions of the strangers.

The climate of Scarborough is considered by Dr. Granville to be extremely favourable, and the longevity of the inhabitants over those of other parts of Yorkshire is fully established. From its exposure on the east coast a mistaken notion is entertained by many that winds in an easterly direction must be of longer continuance at Scarborough than elsewhere; but this experience has shown to be an unnecessary fear. The mean average temperature in the month of January was found to be higher by six degrees than at York, four degrees than in London, and only two degrees less than at Torquay. In respect of climate, therefore, this "Queen of Watering Places" affords immense advantages to invalids in the northern counties, who are unable to endure the fatigue of long journeys; and it is seldom that the sanitary effects of the sojourn, and the potent curative agency of the spas, are without their due influence in promoting and perfecting a return to health.

We now advert to the first object that strikes the eye of the visitor as he enters the town, but which we have reserved to the last, in order to give it that fulness of detail which its venerable ruins warrant.

Scarborough Castle crowns a precipitous rock, whose eastern termination, which advances into the sea, rises about 300 feet above the waters. The principal part of the ancient castle now remaining stands at a considerable distance back from this bold and inaccessible front, but on ground which is nearly as elevated. It is a huge square tower, still nearly 100 feet high, but the walls of which show, by their ragged summit and other indications, that its original height must have been considerably greater. Each side is between fifty and sixty feet in length; but the walls being about twelve feet thick contract the space in the interior to only thirty feet square. This tower was probably the keep of the ancient castle; and, as usual, has been preserved from destruction by its extraordinary solidity and strength. As this old feudal stronghold looks down upon the sea on one side, it has the town of Scarborough stretched below it, and around it on the other, and imparts a bold and romantic aspect to the eastern extremity of the town.

The castle was built about the year 1136, by William, Earl of Albermarle, one of the most powerful of the old Norman nobility, and who was thus permitted by King Stephen to ensconce himself in the fortress, as a defence against the turbulent and but half-subdued inhabitants of the district. No situation could possibly have been chosen better adapted for defence; and, in the infancy of the art of warfare. it must have been absolutely impregnable. Within the boundary of its walls was once comprised an area of twenty acres; and what was of the greatest importance to the besieged, a spring of excellent water, that never failed its supplies even in the driest summer.

When Henry II. ascended the throne, the first act of his reign was the promulgation of an order that all the castles built in the reign of King Stephen should be dismantled and destroyed. The earl was therefore compelled to resign his fortress; but when Henry, from a personal visit, became acquainted with its wondrous powers of defence, he acted on the proverbial superiority of second thoughts, and, taking possession of the structure, was so far from demolishing its walls that he increased its strength by adding new ones, and appointed as governors men of the highest rank, who were taught to regard the office as a reward and privilege, rather than mere employment.

In 1666, George Fox, the founder of the "Society of Friends," was imprisoned in the castle, and in his Memoirs he speaks of three different rooms that he successively occupied. One of them faced the sea, and "laying much open, the wind drove in the rain forcibly, so that water came over his bed, and ran about the room, so that he was fain to skim it up with a platter." In enumerating the suffering and persecution that he unjustly endured, he states that a threepenny loaf lasted him three weeks, and that most of his drink was water with wormword steeped in it. In the rebellion of 1774, the castle was, for political purposes, put into temporary repair; and three batteries have since been erected for the protection of the town and harbour. None can view this relic of the olden time without a feeling of intense interest and delight; and the views of the sea through some of the old crumbling arches, afford fine subjects for the painter.

North Eastern Main Line continued.

York to Pilmoor Junction.

SHIPTON.

Telegraph station at York, 5¾ miles.

HOTELS.—Ship, Black Swan.

Close at hand are *Benningboro' Hall*, the fine seat of the Hon. P. Dawnay.

Sutton Hall, W. Harland, Esq., *Sutton-in-the-Forest*, and *Galtreas Forest*, where the celebrated Sterne was vicar for many years; and near which is *Alne House*, the seat of E. Strangewayes, Esq.

TOLLERTON, ALNE AND RASKELF. — Near the latter of these stations is *Myton Hall*, the seat of S. Stapleton, Esq.: *Easingwold*, with its mineral springs; *Ruins of Crake Castle*, the Northumbrian king's seat, erected on the spot where St. Cuthbert rested on his tour to Durham, and *Gilling Castle*, seat of C. Fairfax, Esq.

PILLMOOR JUNCTION.

BOROUGHBRIDGE BRANCH.

Pilmoor Junction to Boroughbridge

This branch turns off to the left at Pilmoor Junction, and after passing BRAFFERTON, we arrive at

BOROUGHBRIDGE.

POPULATION, 1095.

Telegraph station at Pillmoor Junction, 5¾ miles.

HOTEL.—Crown.

MARKET DAY.—Saturday.

FAIRS.—April 8th and 27th, Oct. 9 and 23, June 22nd.

MONEY ORDER OFFICE.

This place was the scene of a battle in 1321, when he Earl of Lancaster was routed by Edward II. The *Crown Inn* here was once the seat of the Tancreds. Close to the stone bridge are three Druidical Stones, named the *Devil's Arrows.* Close at hand is *Aldoborough*, the ancient *Isurium*, where old walls, coins, and pavements have been found.

North Eastern Main Line continued.

Pilmoor to Northallerton.

SESSAY STATION.—In the neighbourhood are *Sessay Hall*, the seat of Lord Viscount Downe, whose family, the Downays, settled here at the Conquest; *Thirkleby*, the seat of the Frankland family; *Newby Park*, near Topcliffe, an ancient seat of the Percy's, where the fourth Earl was murdered in Henry VII.'s time; and the River Colbeck.

THIRSK (Junction).

Distance from the station to Thirsk, 1¼ mile.
Telegraph station at Thirsk, 1¼ mile.
HOTELS.—Three Tuns, Golden Fleece.
MARKET DAY.—Monday.

FAIRS.—Shrove Tuesday, April 4th and 5th, Aug. 4th and 5th, Oct. 28th and 29th, first Tuesday after Dec 11th Easter and Whit-Monday.

BANKERS.—J, Backhouse and Co.; Branch of Yorkshire Banking Co., Branch of York Union Bank.

This borough has a population of 5,319, chiefly engaged in the sacking and leather trade. The *Old Church*, which contains three sedilia and old tombs, was built with the stones of the Castle, erected by the Mowbray's, and razed by Henry II. In the old town is an *Elm Tree*, close to which it is stated that Henry Percy was slain by the rabble, in the time of Henry VII.; although some chroniclers state that he was murdered at Topcliffe. In the vicinity are *Thornton Park*, the seat of R. Hutton, Esq., R. Kilvington, Esq., T. Meynell, Esq.; *Woodend*, the seat of Lord Greenock; and at some little distance, *Rievaulx Abbey*, near which the Cleveland Moors are 1,800 feet high.

Passing OTTERINGTON station, we arrive at

Northallerton.—For continuation of this route to the north, see page 80.

Before proceeding further northward, it is necessary to return again to MILFORD, in order to take in the Leeds and Thirsk line, which has a connection with the main line at Northallerton.

Milford to Leeds.

Turning to the left we pass the stations of the OLD JUNCTION, MILFORD, and MICKLEFIELD, and reach the station at GARFORTH, near to which is *Kippax Hall.*

We next pass MANSTON and CROSS GATES stations, close to which are *Temple Newsom*, seat of the Marquis of Hertford, and Austhorpe, of which Smeaton, the engineer, who built Eddystone Lighthouse, was a native.

Leeds, See page 16.

Leeds to Melmerby Junction.

HOLBECK station.

HEADINGLEY. — The Leeds Botanical Gardens, the Old Shire Oak, *Kirkstall Grange*, the seat of W. Becket, Esq., M.P.; and the ivy clad ruins of *Kirkstall Abbey*, founded in the twelfth century, by the Lacys, are close at hand.

HORSFORTH.—Near which are *Horsforth Hall*, the seat of the Rev. J. Rhodes; *Addle Church*, close to the ancient *Burgodunum*, of Rumbold's Moor, 1,808 feet high.

ARTHINGTON.—About 9 miles from this place is situated the beautiful village of

Ilkley, in Wharfdale, so celebrated for having been the first in England where Hydropathy was practised, owing to the purity of its water, and much resorted to by invalids from all parts, on account of the romantic beauty or its situation, and bracing mountain air. Here is a magnificent *Hydropathic Establishment*, opened on the 28th May, 1856, built of stone in the Italian style, which contains billiard room, library, dining room for 100 guests, 2 large drawing rooms, coffee room, 12 sitting rooms on the ground floor; in the upper one are, 2 drawing rooms, 87 bed rooms, and 6 bath rooms. It is under the direction of Dr. Smith, Hydropathic and Homœopathic Physician, formerly of Sheffield, and is delightfully situated in beautiful grounds on an elevation, which commands extensive and picturesque views of the adjacent country. In the immediate vicinity, the traveller can visit the trout streams about Ilkley, the wooded heights of the Wharfe, *Bolton Abbey*, with its fine woods; the rich scenery of Malham, Goodale, and Brimham; together with those singular phenomena, the Caves of Clapham, Yordas, and Weathercote, which can easily be reached by railway or road. Close at hand, are *Arthington Hall*, seat of E. Wilson, Esq.; *Leathley Cayley*, *Farnley Tyas*, seats of the Fawkes' family; *Ottley*, with its Church and the interesting monuments of that amily; *Weston*, the Elizabethan seat of V. Carter, Esq.; *Dentin*, the birth-place of Lord Fairfax; *Harewood Park*, the princely residence of the Earl of Harewood; and *Alum Cliff*.

Passing WEETON and PANNAL stations (beyond which is *Jack Hill Fewston* celebrated for its flax dressers; Knaresborough Forest, *Rudding Park*, the beautiful seat of Sir J. Radcliffe; and *Spofforth*, the Percys' old seat), we arrive at

STARBECK, for **Harrogate,** see page 69.

Close to RIPLEY Station, are *Ripley Castle*, built in 1550, the seat of Sir W. Ingilby, Bart.; Nidd, Farnham, and Great Whernside, the moors near which are 2,265 feet high.

WORMALD GREEN—Close at hand are *Copgrove*, the seat of T. Dimcombe, Esq.; *Newby Hall*, the seat of Earl de Grey, which was built by Wren; and contains a fine Sculpture Gallery, in which is Barberini's Venus, &c., a room of Gobelin tapestry, and inlaid marble.

RIPON.

A telegraph station.

HOTELS. — Unicorn, Black Bull, Crown and Anchor.

MARKET DAY.—Thursday.

FAIRS.—Last Thursday in January; May 13th and 14th; first Thursday and Friday in June; first Thursday in October, for sheep; first Thursday in November, and November 23rd; also wool fairs, commencing first Thursday in June, and every alternate Thursday during the season.

RACES in August.

BANKERS.—York City and County Banking Co.; Terry and Harrison; Knaresbro' and Clare Banking Company; Yorkshire Banking Co.

This is a parliamentary borough, with a population of about 6,080, employed chiefly in agriculture, and returns two members, and a bishop's see, since 1836, whose seat is near the city. The principal objects of attraction are the Cathedral, with its low towers, high stained window, and an underground Saxon Chapel, called St. Wilfrid's Needle, after the founder of the original Minster, in the seventh century. There are some antique royal portraits in the Deanery. The new Trinity Church; Aislabie pillar, 90 feet high; Edward VI.'s Grammar School; two old Hospitals (one dated 1140); and a Bridge of seventeen arches. In the vicinity are *Ellshaw Barrow*, 900 feet, and 216 slanting to the top—near which bones and Saxon coins have been found. *Fountain's Abbey* at Studley Royal, the seat of Lord de Grey, founded in 1132 and lately excavated to its original level by the noble owner. Burton, the antiquary, was a native.

MELMERBY JUNCTION.

A telegraph station.

In the vicinity are *Norton Conyers*, seat of Sir B. Graham, Bart.; and *Newby Park*, the beautiful residence of the late "Railway King," G. Hudson, Esq. M.P.

The line turns off to the right to Thirsk, passing BALDERSBY and TOPCLIFFE stations.

In continuation of the same line to Stockton we pass

SINDERBY, close to which are *Masham Swinton*, seat of Admiral G. Harcourt; *Thornton*, Sir E. Dodsworth, Bart.; *Thorpe Perrow*, M. Milbank, Esq.; *Middleham Castle*, *Jervaulx Abbey*, the Marquis of Ailesbury; *Burton Constable*, M. Wyvill, Esq.

NEWBY WISKE.—Here is the beautiful seat of the Mitford family.

NORTHALLERTON.

A telegraph station.

HOTEL.—Golden Lion.

MARKET DAY.—Wednesday.

FAIRS.—February 14th, September 5th and 6th, October 3rd and 4th, and 2nd Wednesday in October.

RACES in October.

BANKERS.—J. Backhouse and Co.; Branch of Darlington District Banking Co.; Branch of Yorkshire Banking Co.

This is a small borough, with a population of 4,995 (who return one member), employed in the linen trade. Here are remains of Friaries founded in 1341 and 1354. It has an old Church; Grammar School, in which Archbishop Palliser, Rymer, Kettlewell, Dean, Hickes, Burnet, and Dr. Radcliffe were educated.

BEDALE AND LEYBURN BRANCH.

Passing AINDERBY, SCRUTON, and LEEMING LANE stations (so called from the old ways being paved) we then reach

BEDALE.

Telegraph station at Northallerton, 8 miles.

HOTEL.—Black Swan.

MARKET DAY.—Tuesday.

FAIRS.—Easter and Whit-Tuesday, July 5th, October 10th, and last Monday but one before Christmas.

BANKERS.—Swalesdale and Wensleydale Banking Company.

This place has a population of 2,892, chiefly employed in horse breeding, and contains an early English church, formerly a retreat for the borderers. In the vicinity are *Bedale Grange*, seat of the Rev. J. Monson (which is built on the site of a castle erected by the Fitzalan's), and *Thorpe Perrow*, M. Milbanke, Esq.

The line continues past CRAKEHALL, NEWTON-LE-WILLOWS, FINGHALL LANE, and CONSTABLE BURTON, to

LEYBURN.

Telegraph station at Northallerton, 18 miles.
HOTEL.—Bolton Arms.
FAIRS.—2nd Friday in February, May, October, and December.
MONEY ORDER OFFICE at Bedale, 10 miles.

A fine view is obtained from the terrace of rocks above this place, which extends a mile.

Northallerton to Stockton.

BROMPTON.

Distance from station, ½ mile. A telegraph station.

Near at hand is *Osmotherly* with the priory of *Mountgrace* in ruins, and *Black Hambleden* 1,400 feet high, which commands a magnificent view.

Passing WELBURY, close to which are *Whorlton*, the old castle of the D'Arcy family, *Walnstone*, 1,300 feet high, and *Stokesley*, with that curious peak called *Roseberry Topping*, we reach PICTON, the junction of the *North Yorkshire* Railway, a line running, *via* STOKESLEY, to CASTLETON, and which it is ultimately intended to connect with the Whitby branch, between the stations of Grosmont and Sleights.

From Picton proceed on to YARM, crossing an ancient Gothic bridge, near which is the *Friarage*, seat of F. Meynell, Esq.: we next proceed to PRESTON Junction, and thence to

STOCKTON-ON-TEES.

A telegraph station.
HOTELS.—Black Lion, Vane Arms.
MARKET DAYS.—Wednesdays and Saturdays.
RACES in August.
FAIRS.—Wednesday before 13th March, 23rd November, last Wednesday in every month (for cattle)

BANKERS.—J. Backhouse and Co. National Provincial Bank of England. Branch of Darlington District Banking Co.

A market town in the county of Durham, with a population of 10,000, employed in the coal and shipping trade. It is situated on the Tees, and celebrated for the manufacture of cloth and rope. The church of St. Thomas, Stone Bridge, and Town Hall are very fine buildings. Josiah Reed, Lord Mayor Crosby (whose obelisk is at Southwark), Ritson, and Alison were natives. The first bar of the line to Darlington was laid here in 1825, by F. Meynell, Esq.

STOCKTON AND DARLINGTON.

Stockton to Middlesborough and Redcar.

Passing NEWPORT station we reach

MIDDLESBOROUGH.

Distance from station, ¾ mile.
A telegraph station.
MONEY ORDER OFFICE at Stockton, 2¼ miles.

This town, which was only founded in 1831, has a population of 7,431, employed in the coal trade. It contains some excellent docks. *Acklam Hall*, the seat of T. Hulster, Esq., is in the neighbourhood.

GUISBOROUGH BRANCH.

Middlesborough to Guisborough.

ORMESBY.—*Ormesby Hall*, the seat of Sir W. Pennyman, Bart.

NUNTHORPE.—*Nunthorpe Hall*, the seat of J. Simpson, Esq.

PINCHINTHORPE.—*Pinchinthorpe House*, the seat of J. Lea, Esq.

HUTTON station.

GUISBOROUGH.

A telegraph station.
HOTEL.—Cock.
MARKET DAY.—Tuesday.
FAIRS.—Last Tuesday in April, March, June, July, Tuesday before Whit Sunday, third Tuesday in August, second Tuesday in November.
BANKERS.—National Bank of England.

This town, with a population of 2,308, engaged in the alum works, contains the ruins of a priory, which was given by Queen Elizabeth to Sir T. Challiner, the traveller, who first opened alum works here; a fine pure mineral spring.

In the vicinity are *Eston Nap Camp*, from which an extensive view may be obtained of the country. *Upbaltham Hall*, Hon. T. Dundas, *Kirkleatham*, H. Vansittart, Esq., *Skelton Castle*, (which formerly belonged to the Bruces), J. Wharton, Esq.

Stockton and Darlington continued.

Passing CLEVELAND PORT, and ESTON, we reach LAZENBY, at which place the sands are three miles across, and fine marine views may be obtained. Close at hand are *Kirk Leatham*, the seat of H. Vansittart, Esq.

REDCAR.

POPULATION, 1,032.
A telegraph station.

This is a small bathing place near the Scar Reefs, on the north sea. Close at hand is *Martke*, the seat of the Earl of Zetland.

Stockton to Darlington.

PRESTON JUNCTION and YARM stations.

MIDDLETON.—Near this is Keso, close to Dinsdale Spa, which has a good sulphur spring and bathing house. Sadberge, Bishopton and Coby Castle are at hand.

Darlington.—See page 81.

WEST HARTLEPOOL.

Stockton to West Hartlepool.

NORTON JUNCTION the church of which is ancient, and had Bernard Silpia for its vicar. *Wynyard*, the seat of the Marquis of Londonderry, is at hand.

BILLINGHAM JUNCTION (a telegraph station). Here the line turns off to the right to

PORT CLARENCE.

Telegraph station at Billingham, 3½ miles.
MONEY ORDER OFFICE at Stockton, 6 miles.

This is a port for the shipping of coal, and is gradually becoming of importance.

Middlesborough is easy of access from this place by a ferry across the River Tees.

GREATHAM.—Here is an excellently well-endowed institution, formed in 1272 by Bishop Stichell, called the Hospital of God, close to which is Newton Bewley, where the Durham Priors resided, about which are several good granaries.

SEATON.—A small bathing place, much frequented during the summer season. At Seaton Snook beautiful views of the coast are obtained.

HARTLEPOOL.

A telegraph station.
HOTEL.—Railway, King's Head.
MARKET DAY.—Saturday.
FAIRS.—May 14, August 21, October 9, and November 27.
BANKERS.—Sub Branch of National Provincial Bank of England; J. Backhouse and Co.

HARTLEPOOL is situated at a short distance from the mouth of the river Tees, has a population of 9,503, employed in the coal trade. It contains a Guildhall, Custom House, the ruins of a priory founded by Robert de Brus in 1275, an excellent pier, 462 feet long, with fixed light and harbour, within a lake or pool in the parish of Hart—hence the name—and Black Hall Caverns, from which fine views may be obtained of the coast. It was formerly strongly fortified, and a place of great strength. It is built on a promontory, and is surrounded on all sides by the sea, with the exception of the north-west, where it communicates with the main land by a narrow neck, and where the water, advancing into the interior, has of itself scooped out a bay of considerable size. Sometimes a submarine forest is visible here. The two Hartlepools now have a population upwards of 20,000, and carry on a large shipping trade with Hamburg and other parts of the world. The entrance of the harbour has an average depth of available water of upwards of 20 feet at spring, and of 16 feet at neap tides. Besides its harbour it has three capacious wet docks, with large graving docks (350 and 320 feet long), and ship-building yards, extensive timber and bond yards, wharfage, &c., covering an area of upwards of 175 acres. Vessels of 2,000 tons are most conveniently loaded and discharged, lying afloat. Romaine was a native in 1715. In July, 1856, one of the most terrific storms ever known in England visited this place. The electric fluid appeared in the heavens darting about like clusters of magnificent rockets, and the rain deluged the place for some time.

Stockton to Spennymoor and Coxhoe.

Passing CARLTON (close to which is Redmarshall with its ancient church, Thorpe, Thewles, and *Whitton House*, G. Hutchinson, Esq.), we reach Stillington (near which is Elslob) and then proceed on to SEDGEFIELD (close to which is *Hardwich*, the beautiful seat of the Russells), and passing FERRY HILL (near which is *Whitworth*, the seat of R. E. Shaftoe, Esq., M.P.) we arrive at

SPENNYMOOR station.

COXHOE.

POPULATION, 4,101.
A telegraph station.
MONEY ORDER OFFICE at Ferryhill, 4 miles.

Close at hand is *Coxhoe House*, seat of A. Wilkinson, Esq.

North Eastern Main Line continued.

Northallerton to Newcastle.

COWTON.—On the moor to the left is Standard Hill, where the celebrated "*battle of the standard*" was fought, in 1138, at which King David was made prisoner, and 10,000 Scots slain.

DALTON JUNCTION.

Distance from station, 1 mile.
Telegraph station at Darlington, 5¾ miles.

Close to Dalton is *Sockburn Hall*, the seat of H. Blackett, Esq., at which place every new Bishop of Durham is presented with a faulchion.

RICHMOND BRANCH.

Passing MOULTON and SCORTON stations, we arrive at CATTERICK BRIDGE near to which is the site of Cataractorium and *Hornby Castle*, the beautiful seat of the Duke of Leeds.

RICHMOND.

A telegraph station.
HOTEL.—King's Head.
MARKET DAY.—Saturday.

FAIRS.—Saturday before Palm Sunday, Saturday before Thomas a'Becket's day, and Holyrood day.

RACES.—In October.

BANKERS.—Roper and Priestman; Swaledale and Wensleydale Banking Company.

This new borough and ancient town has a population of 4,969, returns two members, is situated among the moorlands, in a fine part of the Swale, in the North Riding. Close to the river, on a tall cliff, are the great pinnacled keep, 100 feet high, and other remains of its Norman *Castle*, built at the Conquest by Alan of Brittany, and made an earldom to which 200 broad manors were annexed. Through John of Gaunt it descended to the Earl of Richmond, who succeeded to the Crown as Henry VII. On the other side of the river are vestiges of a priory, coeval with the castle. St. Mary's Church is an old building. Queen Elizabeth's *Free Grammar School*, for which the cantins of the Rev. J. Tate, editor of *Horace*, &c., have established so decisive a character, was lately rebuilt in the Tudor style, as a standing memorial to his honour.

Aske Hall, the Earl of Zetland's seat, commands a fine prospect of the scenery up and down the Swale This and other mountain streams may be ascended. Up the Swale is *Reeth* at the junction of its principal heads, which take their rise in Shunner and its neighbouring fells, 2,100 to 2,300 feet high, on the Westmoreland border. All this part was once thickly covered with forest; at present it yields much lead, but the waterfalls or forces are as numerous and picturesque as ever, especially round Muker. Excellent pasture and grouse shooting. About 5 miles south of Richmond is *Burton Constable*, near the fine natural terrace or scar at Leyburn, which overlooks *Wensleydale* the old castle and collegiate church at Middleham, with the ruins of *Jervaulx Abbey*, 3 miles lower down. This, like many other parts of Yorkshire, is a great place for horse-training. *Winsleydale*, gives title to Judge Parke about the assuming of whose seat in the House of Lords there has been so much discussion, owing to that peerage having been conferred only on himself and not on his descendants, which renders it a life and not an hereditary peerage, and which has ended in it being made an hereditary dignity. The valley of the upper Eure, is famous for its rich pasture and stocking knitters. In making the ascent you pass *Bolton Hall*, the seat of Lord Bolton, near the old castle in which Mary of Scotland was for a time confined. At *Aysgarth* is the old mother church of a vast moorland parish of 80,000 acres. Here is also a striking fall which Powche the traveller thought equal to the Nile cataracts. From the bridge, which has a span of 70 feet, a fine view can be obtained of it. *Askrigg* has a small chapel and is in the neighbourhood of several falls, forces, or gills—large and small, according to the height and weather. Occasionally the outer rim of a fall has been known to freeze into a transparent tube, through which the water continued to run. Lead is got at Hawes; where the limestone cliffs on each side of the river are seen to rise in regular gigantic steps. Hence it is 10 miles to Sedburgh and 14 to Ingleton, in the heart of the highest part of the West Riding. To the north of Richmond are *Halnaby*, the seat of Sir J. Milbanke, Bart. (Lady Byron was a Milbanke of this family). *Rokeby*, on the Tees, the seat of J. Morritt, Esq., gave name to Scott's last ballad poem. Many Roman antiquities have been found here. About 12 or 14 miles up the Tees is the *Wynch Suspension Bridge*, 63 feet long from cliff to cliff; it was built in the 17th century, and is said by Mr. Stephenson to be the first suspension bridge ever constructed. Above this is the *fall* of *High Force*, where the water dashes down 70 feet between dark cliffs; and 5 miles further is *Caldron Snout*, another remarkable fall.

DURHAM.

THIS county, which returns four members, is bounded on the north by Northumberland, the east by the German ocean, the south by Yorkshire, from which it is divided by the river Tees, and on the west by the counties of Cumberland and Westmoreland. A very large portion of it is bleak and barren, having not less than 144,000 square acres of heath land. Its general aspect is hilly and mountainous. The eastern and central parts of Durham include some beautiful and fertile valleys, and are pleasantly varied with hill and dale, alternately appropriated to the growth of corn and pasture. The western part, where the blue or mountain limestone prevails, is rich in lead ore and iron-stone, which are extensively worked. The east and north-east parts of the county are celebrated for their extensive coal mines. The seams (or *strata*) extend horizontally for many miles, and are from 10 to 250 fathoms beneath the surface; each stratum is from 3 to 8 feet thick.

North Eastern Main Line continued.

CROFT, near which is an old church, is much frequented by invalids, on account of its mineral waters; it is also a very fashionable place during the summer months.

DARLINGTON.

A telegraph station.

HOTELS.—King's Head, family and commercial; Omnibuses to and from every train.

BANKERS. — Darlington District Banking Co.; Backhouse and Co.; National Provincial Bank of England.

DARLINGTON, a market town in Durham, situated at the foot and side of a hill on the banks of the river Skern, over which there is a handsome bridge, has a population of 11,228 engaged in the cotton, flax, and worsted mills, foundries, and glass works. The principal ornament of this town is its church, which is built in the form of a cross, with a tower and spire rising from the centre to the height of nearly 200 feet and was founded in 1160 by Bishop Pudsey, in whose palace Princess Margaret stopped in 1504 on her way to Scotland. Many improvements have been made in this town, and considerable manufactures are carried on in linen, wool, and cotton. There are also several mills in its immediate neighbourhood. In 1805 a mineral spring was discovered near Darlington, which has gained much celebrity for its efficacy in scorbutic complaints.

The celebrated bull "Comes" was sold here for £1,050. In the vicinity are Oxen Hall with the High Kettle salt springs. Bushell Hill, from whence York cathedral can be seen, *Blackwell*, the seat of R. H. Allan, Esq., and of his late brother the antiquarian, and *Southend*, J. Pease, Esq.

BARNARD CASTLE BRANCH.

Passing PIERCEBRIDGE we arrive at

GAINFORD, the church at which was first built bp Bishop Egfred, and at Bolane in the vicinity of which the poet Garth was born.

WINSTON.—At the Rectory here Bishop Burgess lived, and close at hand is Staindrop, where there were formerly three Chantries and a College, no remains of which are extant. In the church are effigies of the Nevilles of Raby. *Raby Castle*, the seat of the Duke of Cleveland, one mile from Winston, a magnificent edifice begun in the 14th century by the Nevilles, is near at hand. The much-celebrated gate and baron's hall, 90 feet in length, of that period, still remain. From the terrace, nearly half a mile in length, most beautiful views are obtained.

Markets held on Saturdays, and Fairs on St. Thomas à Becket's eve.

BARNARD CASTLE.

A telegraph station.
HOTEL.—King's Head.
BANKERS.—J. Backhouse and Co.; Sub Branch of the National Provincial Bank of England; Branch of the Darlington District Banking Co.
MARKET DAY.—Wednesday.
FAIRS.—Easter and Whit-Wednesday.

This town derives its name from Bernard Balliol, who was the ancestor of the Scottish monarchs, and founded a castle here in 1120, soon after his arrival from Normandy with the Conqueror, the ruins of the walls and towers of which still remain, and belong to the Duke of Cleveland. It has a mineral spring, cruciform church, hospital founded in 1180, by the Balliols, and well endowed with 180 acres of land. The population amounts to 4,357, who are engaged in the manufacture of carpets, plaids, stockings, hats, and shoe tapes. Hutchinson, the county historian, was a native.

Darlington to Stanhope and Carrhouse.

Passing AYCLIFFE, near which is Heighington church, we reach SHILDON, at which place the Stockton and Darlington Company have their locomotive works. It is also the junction of the line to Haggerleases. The stations *en route*, are the TUNNEL JUNCTION, ST. HELENS, EVENWOOD, and LANDS.

BISHOP AUCKLAND.

A telegraph station.
HOTEL.—Talbot.
MARKET DAY—Thursday.
FAIRS.—March and October.
MONEY ORDER OFFICE.
BANKERS.—J. Backhouse and Co.

BISHOP AUCKLAND has a population of 4,400, and contains the Bishop of Durham's palace, part of which is of a date prior to the Reformation, especially the beautiful chapel built by Bishop Bell. It covers five acres, and was restored by Wyatt. Here is a fine collection of pictures, among which are Reynolds' Resurrection, Titian's Comara Family, Spagnoletto's Patriarchs, and a portrait of Tycho Brahe. The park, which contains 800 acres, commands fine prospects. In the church is the tomb of Bishop Cosin its restorer. Sherwood the comedian was a native. In the vicinity are Newton Cap Bridge over the Wear, built 1390, and Binchester the ancient Vinovium.

ETHERLEY, a telegraph station, near to which s *Witton Park*, the seat of Sir W. Chaytor, Bart., with its old castle. 12 miles distant are *Hoppiland*, R. G. L. Blenkinsopp, Esq.; *Harperley Park*, G. H. Wilkinson, Esq.,; and WITTON PARK JUNCTION.

STANHOPE BRANCH.

Passing WITTON-LE-WEAR and HARPERLEY stations we reach

WOLSINGHAM.

A telegraph station.
MARKET DAY.—Tuesday.

FAIRS.—May 12th, and Nov. 2nd.

Here are remains of the Bishop's seat, which was moated.

FROSTERLEY.

A telegraph station.
MAILS.—One arrival and departure, daily, between London and Frosterley.

MONEY ORDER OFFICE at Wolsingham.

STANHOPE.

Telegraph station at Frosterley.

FAIRS.—Wednesday before Easter, second Friday in September, and December 21.

This place is celebrated for its lead works which employ upwards of 8,000 hands; close by is Heatherhouse cave half a mile long, an old church, *Stanhope Hall*, the old seat of the Featherstonehaughs the race of which is now extinct. *Stanhope Park* (12 miles round) and *Cave*, in which the ancient Bishops of Durham hunted, and Douglas retreated from Edward III. in 1327.

From this to *St. John's Weardale* by coach.

We next pass BEECHBURN near to which are *Brancepeth Park* and *Mandon Hill*, 845 feet high.

CROOK.

POPULATION, 2,764.

A telegraph station.

Surrounded by collieries, and famous or its manufactory of coke. It has been estimated there are upwards of 2,000 coke ovens in this district.
TOW LAW and BURN HILL stations.

COLD ROWLEY.

Telegraph station at Tow Law, 9 miles.
Close to this station are the *Woodlands*, seat of — Richardson, Esq.

Carrhouse station.

North Eastern Main Line continued.

Darlington to Ferryhill.

AYCLIFFE.

Telegraph station at Darlington, 5½ miles.

Passing BRADBURY and FERRYHILL, junction of the

HARTLEPOOL BRANCH,

We arrive at COXHOE, TRIMDON, and WINGATE, and pass on to

CASTLE EDEN.

Telegraph station at Hartlepool, 7 miles.

Here is *Castle Eden* the seat of R. Burdon, Esq., a large castellated edifice, crowning the top of a wooded precipice. It forms the southern boundary of the romantic defile called Castle Eden Dean. There are several collieries in the neighbourhood.

Hartlepool, see page 80.

North Eastern Main Line continued.

SHINCLIFFE.

POPULATION, 1,175.

Telegraph station at Ferryhill, 4¾ miles.

Shincliffe Hall, seat of J. Prince, Esq., is in the vicinity.

At SHERBURN, the next station, is a well-endowed hospital founded in 1180 by Bishop Pudsey, in which are a master and thirty brethren; the learned Faber held the mastership.

LEAMSIDE JUNCTION.

A telegraph station.

At a farm-house to the left, are the remains of Finchale Abbey. From this point we are conducted, by means of a short branch to the left, to

DURHAM—(Branch).

A telegraph station.

HOTELS. — Waterloo, family and commercial; Ward's Family.

MARKET DAYS.—Wednesday and Saturday; for cattle, each alternate Monday.

FAIRS — March 29th and 31st, Whit Tuesday, Saturday before May 13th, Sept. 15th, and Saturday before Nov. 23rd.

RACES in Aprll.

BANKERS.—J. Backhouse and Co.; Branch of the North Durham District Banking Company; Northumberland and Durham District Banking Co.

DURHAM is situated on a rocky eminence, rising near the central part of the county, and almost surrounded by the river Wear. From all the neighbouring points of view its appearance is unique and striking, and the public edifices exhibit a great degree of magnificence. The centre of the eminence is occupied by the Cathedral and Castle, which, with the streets called the Baileys, are included within the remains of the ancient city walls. Below the walls, on one side, the slope is ornamented with hanging gardens and plantations, descending to the river; on the other the acclivity is high, rocky, and steep. The rich meadows, cultivated sides of the adjacent hills, and various seats in the vicinity, add greatly to the beauty of the prospect.

This ancient cathedral city and borough (two members), is the capital of Durham County. Population, 13,188. When St. Cuthbert's bones were raised by Eardalph the last Bishop of Lindisfarne (or Holy Island) in the Danish invasion of 876, they were carried in succession to Craik, Chester-le-street, Ripon, and at last to Dunholme as the Saxons called it, where they found a final resting place under the *Cathedral.* This venerable building is a cross, 420 feet long, built between 1093 and 1220, chiefly Norman, with many interesting examples of the early pointed style, and the gradual change to it, especially in Bishop Pudsey's Galilee at the west end. The bishop's towers at this end are 138 feet high; and Prior Melsonby's great tower, with its tracery, &c., is 214 feet. At the east end, where once stood the richly decorated shrine of St. Cuthbert, is *Nine-Altars' Chapel*, 130 feet long; and the eight-sided turret tower, on which are figures of a woman, cow, &c., in allusion to the story of the first foundation of the Cathedral. The Norman work may be noticed. Bishop Hatfield's throne and monument (he founded Durham College, Oxford), the monuments of Cardinal Langley and Venerable Bede, the Neville screen and monument; the Gothic cloisters, 147 feet square, &c. In the old Refectory of the Convent is now contained the library of the Dean and Chapter. Among its other treasures is a valuable collection of M.SS. Of these we may name, the four Gospels, and "Cassiodorus on the Psalms," both said to be in the handwriting of the venerable Bede. A noble copy of the Bible, in four vols., in the original stamped leather binding, given to the monastery by Bishop Pudsey. From the Square called the Palace Green, by which the Cathedral is generally approached, the whole of the noble front is at once seen. On one side of the square is *Durham Castle*, once the bishop's residence, but now occupied by the University. It was first built by the Conqueror, as a military defence for this part of England, and rebuilt in the 12th century by Bishop Pudsey. It consists of a conspicuous solid eight-sided keep, about 60 feet across, Norman gate, and a great Hall, 180 feet long, containing portraits of prelates. *Durham University* was founded in 1832, and endowed by the liberality of the Dean and Chapter, whose revenues have vastly increased from the opening of coal mines. In 1856, an Act of Parliament was obtained to enable the Bishops of London and Durham to retire from their sees, with handsome pensions. The *Guildhall* was rebuilt in 1850 on the site of one erected by Bishop Tunstal (Bernard Gilpin's uncle). *St. Nicholas* and *St. Oswald* churches are Norman, in part. From the small ancient church of *St. Giles* there is an excellent prospect. The river, as it winds round the cliffs below the city, is lined with public walks outside the old walls, and crossed by three bridges,—one of which was rebuilt on three arches in 1777, and commands a fine prospect of the Cathedral; another at Framwellgate is as old as 1120.

In the neighbourhood are—*Neville's Cross*, where David Bruce was defeated, in 1346; *Sherburn Hospital*, a rich endowment in the bishop's gift, worth more than £3,000 a year; *Finchale Priory*, in ruins; *Ushaw College* for Roman Catholics, near Brandon Hill, which is 875 feet high, &c. Up the Wear are *Brancepeth Castle*, the seat of Lord Boyne. Below *Finchale Priory*, in the descent of the river, you pass *Lumley Castle*, the Earl of Scarborough's seat; and *Lambton Castle*, the Earl of Durham's. Sunderland is at the mouth of the river.

North Eastern Main Line continued.

From Leamside we pass FENCEHOUSES (a telegraph station), and reach

PENSHER JUNCTION, or Painshaw.

Telegraph station at Fencehouses, 2 miles.

In the vicinity is *Lambton Castle*, the beautiful seat of the Earl of Durham.

PENSHER BRANCH.
Pensher to Sunderland.

In a very few minutes after leaving the junction and passing COXGREEN, HYLTON presents itself to our notice. Here is *Hylton Castle*, seat of J. Bowes, Esq., with ruins of the Hiltons' old seat, who settled here in King Athelstane's time, and tombs of their ancestors in the church.

PALLION.—Near to this station are *Pallion House*, seat of A. Fenwick, Esq., and *Whitburn House*, seat of Sir H. Williamson, which overlooks Whitburn Bay.

MILLFIELD station.

SUNDERLAND.

A telegraph station.
HOTELS.—Brook's Palatine, Commercial Hotel, near the Railway Station; Bridge; George.
MARKET DAY.—Saturday.
FAIRS.—May 4th and 13th, October 3rd and 12th.

BANKERS.—W. H. Lambton and Co.; Newcastle and Shields Union Bank; Branch of Newcastle Union Bank; Branch of Northumberland and Durham District Bank.

A borough town and sea port, with a population of 67,394, who return two members, in the county of Durham, situated near the mouth of the Wear. The High Street is spacious, and tolerably handsome, especially the central part, which rises with considerable ascent. Some of the other streets are narrow and dirty; but of late years the general appearance of the town has improved. The harbour is formed by two piers, on the south and north sides of the river. The iron bridge consists of an arch of iron frame-work, thrown over the river, 237 feet span, and rising 100 feet above the level of the water, so that ships of 400 tons can sail under it, by striking the top-gallant masts. The manufactures are chiefly of flint and bottle glass, earthenware and copperas. Coal is the staple article, one million tons being exported annually, and ship building is carried on to a great extent.

The harbour is formed by a north pier, 1,890 feet, and south pier, 1,850 feet long, with fixed lights, put up in 1780 and 1802. "In 1841 the north lighthouse, of stone, was moved bodily 500 feet from its old place by that skilful engineer, Murray." The new docks were opened in 1850. They contain 18 acres, and will hold 300 vessels. There is a self-registering tide gauge, by Meek and Watson, which shews the height by day or night.

North Eastern Main Line continued.

WASHINGTON.

POPULATION, 1,224.

A telegraph station.

MONEY ORDER OFFICE at Gateshead, 7 miles.

PELAW JUNCTION.

SOUTH SHIELDS BRANCH.

A short line, which takes the name of the Brandling Junction, turns off here to the right, which shortly after passing the station of Felling, divides into two, the one taking a north easterly direction to SOUTH SHIELDS (see North Shields, page 87), and the other a south easterly one to

MONKWEARMOUTH.

POPULATION, 16,911.

Distance from station, ¼ mile.

Telegraph station at Sunderland, 1¼ mile.

MARKET DAY.—Thursday.

MONEY ORDER OFFICE at Sunderland, 1¼ mile.

Near this place is *Fulwell*, where a skeleton 9½ feet long was found in 1759. At *Southwick* are remains of a monastery, founded by St. Bega, and refounded in 674, by Biscopias (who first brought glass into use in this country). It was burnt by the Danes in 793, and by the Scots in 1083. At *Monkwearmouth Pit* is the largest shaft in England, being 292 fathoms deep. The *Church* contains effigies of the Hiltons, and remains of the monastery at which the venerable Bede was a monk. Here Paley was some time rector.

North Eastern Main Line continued.

GATESHEAD.

Telegraph station at Newcastle, 3¾ miles.

HOTEL.—Half Moon.

MARKET DAY.—Saturday.

FAIRS.—Second Monday in April and first Monday in November.

GATESHEAD, is a borough town (population, 24,805, who return one member), connected with Newcastle by a stone bridge over the Tyne river, and is a place of considerable antiquity. It has an old cross church, and excellent stone for grindstones at Gateshead Fell, where the cliffs rise to a great height above the river. The town originally consisted of one long street, which was built on the declivity of a steep hill that leads down to the bridge. Several modern improvements, however, have taken place, one of the most prominent of which is the erection of a handsome street in a curved line, to avoid the danger of the descent. The inhabitants are employed in manufacturing cast and wrought iron,

&c. but from its proximity to Newcastle, the trade is less extensive than might be expected from the advantages of its situation.

NORTHUMBERLAND.

This large county in the north of England was originally a distinct kingdom. It returns four members, and is bounded on the north and west by the river Tweed, which divides it from Scotland, the Cheviot Hills, and part of Cumberland. The face of it, especially towards the west, is roughened with huge mountains, the most remarkable of which are the Cheviot Hills and the high ridge called Ridesdale; but the lands are level towards the sea-side and the borders of Durham. It is particularly distinguished for agriculture, which has reached a very high degree of perfection.

NEWCASTLE-UPON-TYNE.

Population, 87,784.

Hotels.—Turk's Head Hotel, family and commercial; Central Exchange, family and commercial; both in Grey Street.

A telegraph station.

Races in April and June.

Market Days.—Tuesday and Saturday.

Fairs.—1st and 8th of August, October 22nd and 30th, and 7th and 22nd of November.

Money Order Office.

Bankers.—W. H. Lambton, and Co.; Branch of Bank of England; Newcastle, Shields, and Sunderland Union Banking Company; Northumberland and Durhaum District Banking Company.

One of the largest borough towns in the county of Northumberland. It stands on the northern bank of the river Tyne, and is a place of great antiquity. Newcastle has rapidly increased in its dimensions since the commencement of the present century; the town, if we include at least the adjoining suburbs, extends for nearly two miles along the river, and about one mile from the river towards the north and north west, rising along the hill, and crowning its summit. Its situation on the banks of a navigable river, and in the greatest coal district in the world, are the chief causes which have tended to raise it to wealth and importance.

There was a Roman station here, called *Pons Ælii*, on Hadrian's Wall, which began or ended at Segedunum or Coresin's House, and gives name to the Wall's End Coal. Before the conquest it was called Monkchester, which was altered when William built a new castle here, in place of one occupied by the Northumbrian king. This town, in 1354, when the port was made a staple for wool, &c., was styled, in the legal French of that day, *Neuf-Chastile-sur-Tyne*, and hence the modern name.

Though the channel of the Tyne is wide, deep, and sheltered, the larger collier ships remain at Shields, to which the coal is carried in barges or keels, by the keelmen, a rough and hardy set of people. Close to the river side, which rises abruptly from the long and excellent quay (⅓ mile long), the houses are in narrow alleys or chares, the seat of filth and disease, especially the cholera, which made great ravages here in 1853. This is old Newcastle, where all the business is carried on; but the new town, in St. Andrew's parish, in the higher parts, 200 feet or more above the river, is handsome and well laid out, having been planned by Grainger, an architect to whom the town is indebted for the Exchange (a half circle, about 150 feet long, with a glass dome, &c., and three Corinthian porticoes), Post Office (in the Arcade), Market, Music Hall, Hall of Incorporated Trades, Theatre Royal, and other buildings, many of which are built of solid, durable granite, at a cost of nearly two millions. The *County Courts*, on the site of the castle, in Carliol Square, built in 1810, by Stokoe, has a front 144 feet long, and Doric porticoes. Many Roman remains were uncovered in digging the foundation. Here are the gate, fine keep, 80 feet high (now a prison), and the beautiful Norman chapel, 46 feet long, of the old castle; the chapel being occupied by the Newcastle Antiquarian Society and their excellent museum. John Balliol did homage for his kingdom of Scotland to Edward I. in this castle, in 1292. The *Guildhall* was built in 1658, and is marked by a steeple, where a pair of crows built a nest in 1783. It contains the chamber of commerce, in which a fine oak mantelpiece, a statue of Charles II., and various portraits of sovereigns and natives, among whom are the two brothers, Lords Eldon and Stowell, who were born in Love Lane, near Forster Street, their father being a coal fitter, and Lord Collingwood. One piece of furniture in the mayor's room is the "branks or gag for scolds." The mayor is allowed £2,000 a year, a coach, barge, &c. The *Post Office* is a handsome building, by Grianger, with a front 100 feet long; the stamp, excise, and other offices are also under this roof. The *Market House* is 240 feet long, and covers two acres of ground. At the elegant *Assembly Rooms* is Downman's picture of Falstaff and Mrs. Ford. There is also a coffee room and library. A *Philosophical Society* was founded in 1793; it has a good library, museum, &c., with busts of Dr. Hutton, the mathematician (a native, who died at Woolwich), and Bewick, the engraver – the latter by Bailey, the former by Chantrey. Another native mathematician was Edward Riddle, who died in 1854, after a brief retirement from the Nautical School of Greenwich Hospital, entirely worn out by his indefatigable zeal to promote the character of that institution, which now occupies the first place in the kingdom as an institution of nautical science. To this many hundreds of officers in the naval and merchant services, trained under Mr. Riddle's eye, are alive to bear witness. In his early days he was Master of the Navigation School attached to the Trinity House here, founded in the 15th century.

The *Grammar School* was founded in 1525, by Horsley, a mayor of Newcastle. Here Bishop Ridley, and Akenside, the poet (who was born in Butcher Bank), Collingwood, Eldon, &c., were educated. There is a *Cemetery* at Jesmond, or Jesus Mount Hill, over Ouse burn. The *General Infirmary* was commenced in 1751; there is also a separate hospital for the keelmen.

What is termed the *High Level Bridge*, is a splendid iron viaduct, 1,400 feet long, for the railway, across he river, above which it rises 112½ feet; and having, 32 feet below it, a common roadway, on six wide arches of 125 feet span. It crosses Dean Street by an arch 80 feet span and 80 feet high; and was built by R. Stephenson, the engineer of the line, whose great locomotive works, established by his father in 1824, are here, at which the Rocket, which gained the prize in 1829 on the Liverpool and Manchester line, was built. The old stone bridge, near Sand Hill, is on 9 arches, and formerly had houses along it, like London Bridge. Here stood the *Pons Ælii* of Hadrian, who belonged to the Ælian family. It was immensely strong, but without springs for arches. Pandon Dean Bridge crosses a ravine on the east side of the town.

On a spot which the Roman wall passed over stands the old parish church of *St. Nicholas*, a Gothic cross, 240 feet long, built in 1359. It has a handsome pinnacled tower, above which is a flying steeple or lantern, supported by arches springing from the corners of the tower, making the whole 194 feet high. Wren built the tower of St. Dunstan-in-the-East near Thames Street, London, in this style, and was rather proud of the work. Within are a choir, stalls, various monuments, the old font, large Flemish canopied brass of R. Thornton (dated 1429), tombs of the Percies and Moises (the latter by Flaxman, and the epitaph by Lord Stowell). Cousins and Tomlinson's libraries, an illuminated Bible, 600 years old, and other books, are worthy of attention. On Shrove Tuesday the bell rings punctually at noon as a signal to the towns-people to fry pancakes. *St. Andrew's* and *St. John's* churches are both ancient, the former being Norman in its character; and there is an old crypt under *All Saints*, which was rebuilt in 1783, on a circular plan, with a steeple 200 feet high. At the top of Grey Street is Bailey's statue of the first Earl Grey, on a column 136 feet high.

"The strength and magnificens of the waulling of this towne far passeth all the walles of the cities of England." According to Leland's account, it had 7 strong gates, and 17 towers in them for defence, one of which, New Gate, remains. Newcastle being an important frontier town great pains were taken to strengthen it. Many of the neighbouring barons had mansions here, such as the Percys, Nevilles, Scropes, and others; and there was a house provided for the Scottish kings over the Nungate. It is recorded of one of the Anderson family that, having dropped his ring over Newcastle Bridge, his servant bought a salmon a little while after, in which the ring was found. It is still in the possession of the family.

Coal, the true riches of Newcastle, was first worked here in 1260, but the produce was scanty till steam power was used in 1714. Within a circle of 8 or 10 miles, more than 50 important collieries are open, among which are the Hetton, Hartley, Wallsend, and other familiar names, employing 10,000 to 15,000 hands, High-main coal is got from a rich bed 6 feet thick, nearly 200 fathoms beneath the surface. The great northern field, of which this is the centre, covers about 500 square miles in Northumberland and Durham, and may be 1,800 feet deep. Many and various calculations have been made by practical men and geologists as to the extent of supply, but all agree that it will take some hundreds, if not thousands, of years to exhaust it. At Painshaw and Monkwearmouth, near Sunderland, are mines 300 fathoms, or 1,800 feet, or ⅓ mile, deep, the deepest in England. The coal being brought to the water side, by truck or railway, is shot through staithes into the holds of vessels, or it is carried down the river in barges or keels, and then shovelled on board. The old collier ships are clumsy, "built by the mile," as sailors say, enough being cut off for a ship each time one is wanted; but they form a nursery of first-rate seamen. Of the three million tons sent to London, one million and upwards come from Newcastle. Latterly screw steamers have been put on to expedite the delivery in the metropolitan market, and a proposal for a coal railway has been favourably entertained.

The North Tyne rises in the Cheviots, and is joined by the South Tyne at Hexham. There is nothing very striking in the scenery up or down it. Below Newcastle its banks are lined with collieries, foundries, glass and chemical works, and such like, all the way to North and South Shields and Tynemouth. At South Shields may be seen, in the church, a model of Greathead's first life boat, invented and used in 1790. Tynemouth has the fine remains of an important priory, and a monument to Lord Collingwood. Above Newcastle, and to the west of the rail to Carlisle, are several traces of the famous Picts' Wall, also called Hadrian's, and by other names, and nearly 700 miles long from sea to sea. There were, in fact, two or three walls or lines, in the military sense, built between the first and third centuries by the Roman conquerors of Britain to secure themselves from the troublesome savages beyond; the first two, by Agricola and Hadrian, were earthworks and the third only, by Severus, was of stone; they were 10 to 12 feet high, and proportionately thick, with ditches, towers, &c., and 18 principal stations along the whole, of which 10 were in Northumberland. Two of these, Walwick Chestus and Housestead, still yield much information to the "painful" antiquary.

Other objects near Newcastle are the following.—*Wylam*, the birthplace of George Stephenson (father of Robert), in 1780. From this he went to Killingworth mines, belonging to Lord Ravensworth, and there showed his great mechanical genius, among other things by inventing a locomotive engine for the tram way in 1814, and a safety lamp jn 1815, independent of Davy's, with which it was tried, and found to do as well. Here also he made his improvements on railways, which he carried out in 1821-5, on the Stockton and Darlington line, 22 miles long, and memorable as the first locomotive rail in England. The second was the more important, Liverpool and Manchester, opened in September, 1830.

Ravensworth Castle (5 miles) the large modern seat of Lord Ravensworth, rebuilt in 1803; some parts of the old house are preserved. *Oxwell Park* (4 miles), Sir T. Clavering, Bart., on the Derwent, which joins the Tyne at Derwent Haugh, lower down. The country is hilly towards its source in the Allendale Hills.

NORTH SHIELDS AND BLYTH AND TYNE.

Passing WALKER, WALLSEND, and HAWDEN stations, we reach

NORTH SHIELDS.

A telegraph station.
HOTELS.—Albion, and Commercial.
MARKET DAY.—Every Friday.
FAIR.—First Friday in November.
BANKERS.—Newcastle, Shields, and Sunderland Union Banking Company; Branch of Northumberland, and Durham District Banking Company; National Provincial Bank of England.

The inhabitants are principally employed in the sail-cloth, rope, anchor, glove, and hat trades. Here is a market-place, theatre, eleven chapels, gas and water works. Clifford Fort, built in 1672, has a fixed light, 77 feet high. The Mutual Ship Insurance Clubs here are excellently conducted. The docks will hold 300 sail.

TYNEMOUTH,

which is to Newcastle-on-Tyne what Brighton is to London, is situated nine miles from that busy and much-improving town. In the time of the ancient Britons the village was denominated Pendal Crag, or the "Head of the Rampart on the Rock," and this pretty clearly indicates its situation. Coal in abundance, some ironstone, and the only limestone strata in the county, are its chief geological features; and though it is little better than a village, the influx of visitors for bathing during the season raise it to almost the dignity of a town. There is one long street, possessing the necessary adjuncts of a "marine hotel," a library, and commodious baths, which were erected in 1807. The parish church was originally in North Shields, but a new one has been lately erected; and a large school, for which a Mr. Kettlewell bequeathed £7,000 in 1825, has been built and endowed in a manner which would have afforded the liberal donor the highest gratification to have beheld. In 1758, some barracks were erected in the village, for the accommodation of 1,000 men, but they were sold at the general peace, and now form Percy Square, never, we hope, to be metamorphosed back again. A mineral spring in some local repute at Collercoats Sands—a place of ominous name to solitary bathers who leave their garments on the beach—gives a pretext for a pleasant walk in that direction; and, as Tynemouth is only one mile from North Shields, those who like bustle and activity have not far to go to behold both. But the chief attraction is unquestionably its Priory, which lies to the east of the town, and is of such very remote antiquity that no authentic record exists of its original foundation, but there is some reason to conjecture the seventh century saw its first elevation. Whether Tynemouth was or was not of Roman origin, it was at a very early date selected as an ecclesiastical site, and for this, by the beauty and peculiarity of its situation, it was well adapted. "The exalted height," says Grose, "on which the monastery stood, rendered it visible at sea a long way off in every direction, where it presented itself as it reminding and exhorting seamen in danger to make their vows and promise masses and presents to the Virgin Mary and St. Oswin." Thus, though the situation in stormy weather was perhaps not very enviable, the advantages it afforded in those credulous and unsettled times of presenting to the eye of the sailor in distress an object towards which he could direct his prayers and bend his course, were also increased by its being an outpost from which a hostile armament might be descried, and an alarm inland easily communicated. Neither its sanctity or utility were, however, sufficient to preserve it long, for the Danish pirates thrice plundered the priory and once burned the church. From 625 to 1110, its history seems to be that of alternate destruction and renovation, continually repeated. In 1090, Robert de Mowbray fled hither, and defended himself within its walls against William Rufus, whom he had conspired to dethrone, but after a time, finding that he could hold out no longer, he sought sanctuary at the altar of the church, from which he was taken by force, carried to Windsor, and, after suffering a long imprisonment, was put to death. During the reign of Elizabeth it was occupied as a fortress, and in the civil wars of the seventeenth century it was frequently besieged. In 1644 it was taken by the Scots, when thirty-eight pieces of ordnance, and a large store of arms, ammunition, and provisions, fell into their hands. The garrison were permitted to march out with their baggage, but bound themselves to submit to the instructions of the Parliament. Soon after this, £5,000 was voted to repair the damages it had sustained, and Colonel Henry Lilburne was made its deputy governor; but having declared for the king, Sir Arthur Hazelrig immediately marched from Newcastle against him, and stormed the fortress at the very cannon's mouth. During the assault Lilburne was slain.

When the reputation of Tynemouth Priory was at its greatest height, the dead were brought from all parts of the neighbourhood to be interred therein, great sanctity being attribnted to the place in consequence of the number of illustrious persons who performed divine service in the oratory of the Virgin. Among those thus buried were the royal martyr, Oswald, King Eldred, Henry the Hermit of Coquet Island, Malcolm King of Scotland, and other illustrious persons.

After the period when all danger might be supposed to have passed away, its extensive and exquisitely beautiful ruins were demolished for the sake of their materials. It is probable that much of the priory at Tynemouth was built with the materials of the hewn stone from the Roman station at the *Law*, South Shields, and a great part of the town of North Shields, in return, is said to be built from the ruins of the monastery. Dockwray-square, in particular, is popularly spoken of as having been constructed from this source. Nor did the work of destruction here stop. Being used as a barrack and military store, the work of demolition and alteration has been going on down to a very recent period, until the most conspicuous part of the ruin now standing is that which contains the three very beautiful eastern windows of the chapel. The castle, about a hundred yards west of the monastic ruins, is now merely a plain and picturesque building, fitted up as barracks for the accommodation of a corps of infantry, which, with some artillery, are always stationed there. The broken arches and the picturesque foreground of fishermen's cottages, mouldering ruins, and lichen-festooned turrets, creates a most pictorial contrast to the extensive range of sea and sky beyond.

The lighthouse stands in the Castle yard, and is built of stone in the shape of a tower; the lantern is sixty-two feet above the groud on which it stands, and one hundred and forty-eight feet above the level of the sea. There are two other light-houses near the town of North Shields, the one being forty-nine and the other seventy-six feet in height, the lesser one having a compensation in its more exalted position.

Passing Percy Main, Prospect Hill, Backworth, Seghill, Seaton Delaval (which was built by Vanburgh, having an old castle and church), Hartley, and Newsham, we arrive at

BLYTH.

Telegraph station at North Shields, 10 miles.

This place is the property of the Ridley family. It has a very considerable coal trade.

From Newsham the line continues through Bebside to Bedlington, the junction of a short line to Newbiggin, a watering place on the sea coast, Choppington, and Hepscott, to Morpeth, for which see below.

Newcastle to Berwick.

Passing Heaton, Benton, Killingworth (at this place G. Stephenson, began to show his turn for mechanics, and invented a safety lamp), Dudley, Cramlington, Plessy, and Netherton stations, we arrive at

MORPETH.

A telegraph station.
Hotel.—Queen's Head.
Market Day.—Wednesday.
Fairs.—Wednesday before Whitsuntide, June, Wednesday before Martinmas.
Races at Cottingwood in April and September.
Bankers.—W. H. Lambton and Company.

This borough has a population of 4,100, who return one member, and are employed in the woollen trade. The town was built by Vanburgh It has a fine suspension bridge, by Telford. The gate of the old castle is worth a visit. Turner, the botanist, Gibbon, the herbalist, and Morrison, the Chinese scholar, born in 1782, were natives; and here Horsley, the learned author of *Britannia Romana*, was a minister. In the vicinity is *Mitford*, seat of Mrs. Mitford.

Passing Longhirst we reach Widdrington, close to which is *Widdrington Castle*, seat of Lord Vernon, (the descendant of that daring knight "who fought upon his stumps" at Chevy Chase), distant 20 miles, and then proceed to Acklington, and soon reach the station of

WARKWORTH,

A village of considerable extent and of much beauty. On one side the sea approaches close to it, and the Coquet, which, of all British rivers, best deserves the epithet, *silvery*, winds so nearly round it from the other half as to form it into a peninsula. Here are fine ruins of a Norman Church. The castle was formerly of great note, being the residence of the Lords Percy when wardens of the marches, and from it many an order was issued which let havoc loose on the Scottish border. Nor were the wardens themselves allowed to remain here unmolested: one of the Earls of Northumberland wrote to the King and Council that he had dressed himself at midnight by the blaze of the neighbouring villages burnt by the Scottish marauders. Its remains are considerable, and the walls of many of the apartments, especially those of the banquet-room, are still perfect. At the hermitage hewn out of the cliff, which is about a mile from the castle, in a deep romantic valley, Dr. Percy (no relation to the Northumberland family), laid the scene of his popular poem, the "Hermit of Warkworth."

We next arrive at Bilton, the junction of the

ALNWICK (Branch).

Distance from station, ¼ mile.

A telegraph station.

Hotels.—White Swan, Black Swan, Star, and Queen's Head.

Market Day.—Saturday.

Fairs.—Palm Sunday, May 12th, last Monday in July, 1st Tuesday in October, October 28th, Saturday before Christmas.

Alnwick, *i. e.*, *Alnewick*, the town on the Alne, is a borough by prescription, having grown up under the protection of the Dukes of Northumberland, whose noble baronial castle covers a height over the river. Population, 5,779. The houses are of stone, and a handsome bridge of the same material crosses the stream. Formerly the town was surrounded by battlements, but these have disappeared, only the Bondgate, now used as a prison, remaining to show what its character was in feudal times. This gate was built by the famous Hotspur. Beside the old clock tower at Pottingate, and the Percy column, there is a *Town Hall*, built in 1731, where the town freemen are entered after a curious ceremony. On St. Mark's day (25th April), candidates assemble in the Market place, girt with swords and on horseback; from hence they are conducted by the castle bailiff to the town moor, where they alight, and being dressed in white, they rush through a muddy pool called the Freeman's Well. King James, it seems, was bogged here on one occasion, and thereupon condemned them in the terms of his charter to undergo this delightful purification. All new members submit to it to this day, the pool being kept up to an efficient standard of filth for neophytes by the anxious zeal of those who had already passed through it. The Gothic *Parish Church* deserves notice. In *St. Paul's* is Carew's monument of the late Duke of Northumberland.

Alnwick Castle was first built by the De Vescis at the Conquest, but coming to the Bishop of Durham, was granted in 1309 to the Percys, with the wardenship of the East Marshes. It was in this capacity that Hotspur met Douglas at the battle of Chevy Chase, in 1338, where the latter was killed, and they have held the lordship ever since. As restored in the Gothic style, the castle walls enclose five acres, three courts, &c., and are surmounted by 16 towers and a pinnacle. The family chapel has a beautiful fan-tracery roof and five east windows; and among the sculpture is Gibson's *Piping Shepherd*, besides several of Zobel's marmotinto (or sand) paintings. In the large grounds are two pillars that mark where Malcolm of Scotland was killed in 1093, when besieging the castle, and William the Lion was taken prisoner, in 1172, upon a similar attempt. Here are remains of the De Vescis' Abbey, and Hulme Abbey, which was founded by a crusader, because the site reminded him of Mount Carmel. Bale, the historian, was a brother in this abbey. There is also the figure of a hermit. Brisley's pillar, 90 feet high, commands a fine view of the whole. Martin of Alnwick, and Bishop William of Alnwick were natives.

Algernon is a favourite name in this ancient family, the founder of it, who came from Percy in Normandy, having been surnamed *Algernon*, or whiskered. Their pedigree is at Sion House, and is also on the walls of the chapel here. Richard de Percy was one of the barons who extorted the Magna Charta from King John. Henry, the first earl, and father of Hotspur, is the same who figures in Shakspeare's Henry IV. The ninth earl was grandfather to Algernon Sidney, the patriot. Upon the death of the eleventh Earl, without male issue (his daughter married the proud Duke of Somerset), the honours were claimed by one John Percy, a trunk-maker, whom the House of Lords were obliged to pillory in Westminster Hall, as "a false and impudent pretender to the title." The present peer is a Smithson by the father's side. The dowager duchess was governess to Queen Victoria.

Passing in quick succession the stations of LONGHOUGHTON, LITTLE MILL, CHRISTON BANK, CHATHILL, NEWHAM, we come to

LUCKER, near to which lies *Bamborough Castle*, a Saxon fortress, built in the seventh century, on a rock, 150 feet high. It has been lately restored, and serves as a beacon for seamen. There is a well, 145 feet deep, close to the chapel. Not far off are the *Ferne Islands*, where that courageous heroine, Grace Darling, saved the crew of the Forfarshire steamer. Herself and father had charge of the Longstone light; in the churchyard is her tomb. We soon reach the snug little market town of BELFORD, close to the sea, and then arrive at BEAL, to the right of which lies *Lindisfarne Abbey* and *Castle*, so beautifully described in Scott's *Marmion;* and a short distance to the west is *Ford Castle*, the beautiful seat of the Marquis of Waterford, on the borders of Flodden Field, where James IV. was defeated by Lord Surrey in September, 1513.

Passing SCREMERSTON and TWEEDMOUTH, we enter the county of

BERWICK,

A maritime county in Scotland, which returns one member. Its extreme length from east to west is 31 miles; many hill forts erected by its former possessors, the Romans, are still to be seen on the numerous eminences, interspersed with several Roman camps. Indeed the whole county is rich in local antiquities. This county is now divided into Merse, Lammermuir, and Lauderdale. Merse, the southern district, bordering on the Tweed, is very fertile, and when seen from an eminence resembles a vast garden, watered by two tributary streams of the Tweed, called Black and White Waters. Lammermuir, situated to the north of Merse, is a pastoral district, mountainous, hilly, and abounds in game. Lauderdale is situated to the west of the other divisions, and is a mixture of hill and dale. The lower part is very fertile, and like the rest of the county of Berwick.

BERWICK.

A telegraph station.

HOTELS.—Red Lion, King's Arms, Salmon.

MARKET DAY.—Saturday.

FAIRS.—Trinity Friday, second Wednesday in May, Wednesday before 25th August, and first Wednesday in November.

BANKERS.—Branch of Northumberland and Durham District.

BERWICK, or BERWICK-ON-TWEED, at the Tweed's mouth, is a port, and parliamentary borough, sends two members, and has a population of 22,000 on the Scottish side of the river, 58 miles from Edinburgh. Before the Union it was an important frontier post, as it commanded the east road, between the two countries. It is still a garrison town, having a military governor, barracks, and fortified walls in the old style; but there are few remains of the castle, that scene of so many contests. Here Edward I. crowned his humble servant Balliol, the competitor of Bruce, and barbarously exposed the limbs of the patriot Wallace after his execution. Here, too, he shut up the Countess of Buchan in the infamous wicker cage, for six years. On one occasion, seven Scots took it by surprise, and on another, it was recovered by Henry IV. from the Percys (then in rebellion), by the firing of a single shot, which was an entirely new thing to the garrison.

Close to the site of it, is Stephenson's Royal Border Bridge or viaduct, for the railway, 216 ft. long, on twenty-eight brick arches, 61 feet span. There is an old one to the Tabart of Tweedmouth, besides the Union Suspension Bridge, some miles up the river, built by Brown, and one of the earliest on this principle. The *Town Hall*, built in the last century, by Dodd, has a clock tower, 150 feet high. Much of the produce from the interior is shipped here, in the Berwick schooners and clipper ships, but the harbour is full of reefs. About 80 vessels belong to the port—annual customs £15,000. The salmon fisheries in the Tweed, once worth £15,000 a-year, have declined to £4,000. About Christmas, the people here eat kippered salmon and plum-pudding. Salmon is sent to London, packed in ice. Much whisky is exported. It is an exciseable article on the *town* side of the turnpike gate. Berwick, which is naturally part of Berwickshire, in Scotland, was made independent of both countries, by Henry VIII.; latterly it went with Islandshire, an isolated part of Durham; but since the Act of Union, which transferred such portions of counties to that in which they actually stand, it belongs to Northumberland.

KELSO, TWEEDMOUTH, AND HAWICK BRANCHES.

Berwick to Kelso and Roxburgh.

This line runs along the south bank of the Tweed. Passing *Halidon Hill*, where the Scotch were defeated by Edward III., we very soon arrive at the station of

NORHAM.

Here is a very old church and a border castle, the ruins of which are approached by means of a suspension bridge across the river. It is thus referred to by Sir Walter Scott, in his *Marmion* :—

"Day sets on Norham's castled steep,
And Tweed's fair river, broad and deep,
And Cheviot's mountains lone."

The tide flows to this point; *Twizel Castle*, seat of Sir F. Blake, Bart., on the "sullen Till," which falls in here, near the old Gothic bridge, which Surrey crossed on the way to Flodden Field.

"High sight it is and haughty, while
They dive into the deep defile
Beneath the castle's airy wall."

The present castle is modern.

CORNHILL (for Coldstream).

Telegraph station at Tweedmouth, 12¼ miles.

Hotel.—Railway.

Fair.—December 6th.

Money Order Office at Kelso, 10 miles.

Close at hand is Flodden Field, noted for the battle fought between James IV. of Scotland and the Earl of Surrey, in 1513, in which the former was defeated and slain. Near the church is a mineral spring, and traces of a castle taken by the Scots in 1549.

Coldstream stands opposite an old ford of the river, and being on Scottish ground, it has become, like Gretna Green, a place for runaway matches—Lord Brougham's, for instance. Here Monk waited his time to declare for Charles II., with some veterans who formed the earliest regiment of the Coldstream Guards. *Lees*, seat of Sir J. Marjoribanks, Bart.

Wark station.

ROXBURGHSHIRE, or TEVIOTDALE.

The western portion of this county is very mountainous, and in the greatest part of its length its southern boundary is also mountainous, adjoining the great ridge called the Cheviot Hills, which, in the upper or western part of Roxburghshire, stretch northward into Scotland. Its external appearance is, upon the whole, extremely beautiful, containing a succession of hills and dales, through which a great number of small rivers take their course along deep and winding vallies. The county is divided into four districts, and returns one member. The most westerly and mountainous part of it is called Hawick; the second or middle district, which is farther down the county towards the east, Jedburgh; the third and lowest district, occupying the eastern part of the county on both sides of the Tweed, Kelso; the fourth and last, Melrose, and is formed of that portion of the county which is situated to the northward of the rest.

CARHAM.

Close at hand are the lone green round-headed Cheviot Mountains, and *Carham Castle*—another celebrated border fortress. There is good fishing in the river, and fine views from Skiddaw, one of the Cheviot Hills, to the south, where the highest peak rises 2,660 feet high. The famous border fight of *Chevy Chase*, or *Otterburn*, took place in one of its passes, in 1338. After leaving Carham, we now cross the March Burn, and enter Scotland, soon after which we arrive at

Sprouston, near which is a fall of 40 feet, at *Newton Don*, on the Eden, the seat of R. Balfour, Esq. At *Ednam Manse*, the poet Thomson was born in 1700; *Stichell*, the old seat of the Homes, on a hill, 900 feet high.

KELSO.

A telegraph station.
Hotels.—Cross Keys, and Queen's Head.
Market Day.—Friday.
Races in spring and autumn.
Fairs.—Monthly, and second Friday in May, 6th July, August, and 2nd November.

Kelso is a market town (population 4,783) in Scotland, which stands on the north side of the Tweed, opposite the junction of that river with the Teviot. It may be considered as the provincial capital of the surrounding fertile country, and noted for its manufacture of woollen tweeds, &c. Its inhabitants are polished, well-informed, and live in a style of considerable elegance, or rather luxury. The situation of the town is uncommonly beautiful. It stands on the bank of a noble river, at the foot of that fertile tract of country which descends gradually from the heights of Lammermuir, and terminates on the borders of the Tweed. Here Scott's *Border Minstrelsy* was first published by Ballantyne, and in 1800 Rennie erected a noble five-arched bridge.

Nothing can be more beautiful than the scenery in this neighbourhood, when viewed from an eminence called Pinnacle Hill, on the southern bank of the river, from whence the country is seen to great advantage. The town lies in front, in a low valley. Immediately round it the country rises as if formed into terraces; cultivated fields, woods, and country seats, gradually ascend above each other, to the distance northwards of twelve or fourteen miles, forming an extensive landscape, which in richness and variety is scarcely to be equalled in Scotland.

The principal ornament of Kelso is its ancient abbey, founded by David I., and public library, the former of which suffered considerable damage during the Reformation, but was subsequently converted into a Protestant church. Close at hand are *Fleurs Castle*, the fine modern Gothic seat of the Duke of Roxburgh, and *Springwood*, Sir W. Douglas, Bart.

NORTH BRITISH.

ROXBURGH.

Population, 1,141.

A telegraph station.

Money Order Office at Kelso, 3 miles.

This place was formerly the capital of the county. The moat of the castle still remains. Kings Alexander II. and III. were married here in great pomp. Close to a holly in the river, James II. was killed by the bursting of a cannon, in 1460. Good purple trout abound in the streams. In the vicinity are *Makerstoun*, the fine country seat of Sir T. Brisbane, Bart., and *Smailholm Tower*, "the scene of one of Scott's ballads, and the frequent resort of his grandfather."

JEDBURGH BRANCH.

From Roxburgh Junction we turn to the left, and pass the stations of Old Ormiston, Nisbet, and Jedfoot Bridge, and soon arrive at

JEDBURGH.

A telegraph station.

Hotels.—Spread Eagle, The Commercial, and The Harrow.

Market Days.—Thursday and Saturday.

Fairs.—Monthly.

This place contains the ruins of an abbey older than 1000, rebuilt by David I. Here Alexander III. was married, at which ceremony it is reported that a masque dressed as Death appeared, and Mary Queen of Scots fell ill after her visit to *Hermitage Castle* to meet Bothwell. The Church is part of that which belonged to the old abbey, having the ancient tower (100 feet), Norman door, nave, &c. Grey Friars was built in 1513. There Bell wrote his "Rota Temporum," and the Relief Synod began here in 1755. The tower where Queen Mary staid, is in an ancient street. Caves are to be seen at Hunderlee and Linthaughlee Camp. Thomson and Rutherford were educated at the Grammar School. Sir David Brewster and Mrs. Somerville were natives. St. Boswell and Dryburgh Abbey are easily accessible from this place.

North British Main Line continued.

Passing Rutherford, we soon arrive at

MAXTON,

to the left of which are Lilliard's Edge, *Ancram Moor*, where Archibald "Bell the Cat" defeated the English in 1544; *Mount Teviot*, seat of the Marquis of Lothian, close to the Waterloo pillar, from which can be seen Teviotdale and Jedburgh, now reached by a rail, seven miles long, with its antique abbey church.' Not far distant is *St. Boswell*, celebrated for its large July cattle fair, and *Dryburgh Abbey* (in St. Mary's Aisle lies Sir Walter Scott and his family), which was founded by De Marville in 1157, and round the Witch's Wheel Window the ivy clings most beautifully. A most magnificent view can be obtained in clear weather from Wallace's statue on the hill. At

Newtown, we behold on the left the Three Eildon Hills, having Trimontium, a Roman camp, on the highest, which is 1,630 feet, and keeping *Bemerside*, the fine old seat of the Haig family, in view, we arrive at the

HAWICK BRANCH.

Passing New Belses and Hassendean stations near the latter of which is *Hassendean Burn*, the seat of Miss Dickson, we arrive at

HAWICK.

A telegraph station.

Hotels.—Tower; Crown.

Market Day.—Thursday

Fairs.—May 17th, first Thursday after St. Boswell's, 1st and 20th September, 3rd Tuesday in October, and November 8th.

This town stands near the confluence of the rivers Teviot and Sletterich, on the great road from Edinburgh to London. It has of late years undergone considerable improvements. Population, 6,683, chiefly engaged in the woollen, lambswool, and cotton hose trade. It contains an excellent library (4,000 vols.), established in 1762, and Trades' Library, (1,500 vols.), School of Arts, Mechanics' Institute, Farmers' Club (the oldest in Scotland), established in 1770, Nursery, Grammar, and Sunday School (the latter of which was one of the first established in Scotland). The church, which is a fine edifice, is built on the site of that from which Sheriff Ramsay was carried off in 1342, by William Douglas, and contains the books of Orrocks, secretary to the Queen of James VI. In 1500, the rector was Gavin Douglas. Here are remains of Roman and British camps, from which are beautiful prospects. Somerville, the historian of Queen Anne's reign, was a native. In the vicinity are *Cavers* seat of J. Douglas, Esq. (here Dr. Leyden was born), *Stobbs*, Sir W. Elliott (birthplace of General Lord Heathfield), *Briaryard*, T. Turnbull, Esq., *Burngrar*, W. Watson, Esq., *Midshields*, A. Douglas, Esq., *Todrig*, G. Pott, Esq., *Sinton*, J. Scott, Esq., *Woll*, Colonel Scott, *Honcot*, J. Stuart, Esq., *Chisholm*, W. Chisholm, Esq.

Newtown to Galashiels.

MELROSE.

Population, 7,365.

A telegraph station.

Hotels.—The George, Family and Commercial; Thompson's, King's Head, Family and Commercial.

Coaches to and from New Belses, (*via* Jedburgh rail, fares, 3s., 2s. 3d., and 1s. 6d.), Drygrange, Cowdenknowes, Earlston, and Carrolside, daily.

Flys to and from Abbotsford (3 miles), one-horse fly, 5s., post-boy, 1s. 6d., toll, 6d.; two-horse fly, 6s., post-boy, 1s. 6d., toll, 1s.: to and from Dryburgh, *via* Bemerside Hill, (6 miles), returning *via* Newton St. Boswells, one-horse fly, 7s.; post-boy, 3s., toll, 6d.; two-horse fly, 10s. 6d., post-boy, 3s.; toll, 1s.; to Selkirk and Newark, returning *via* Bowhill and south side of the Yarrow, (13 miles), one-horse four-wheel carriage, 13s., post-boy, 2s. 6d., toll, 1s. 6d.; two-horse carriage, 20s., post-boy, 3s. 6d., toll, 3s.; gig, 10s., toll, 1s. 6d.: to Kelso, *via* Mertoun, returning by the opposite side of the Tweed, (15 miles); one-horse four-wheel carriage, 15s., post-boy, 2s. 6d. toll, 1s. 6d.; two-horse carriage, 22s. 6d., post-boy, 4s., toll, 3s.

Market Day.—Saturday.

Bankers.—Edinburgh and Glasgow Bank, M. Dunn, Esq., Manager; draw on Williams and Co.

Melrose is situated in a fertile vale, at the foot of Eildon Hills, through which flows the Tweed. Outside the town stands *Melrose Abbey*, founded by David I., one of the most celebrated and magnificent ecclesiastical edifices in Scotland. Even in its present state of decay the pile remains a monument of architectural taste and skill of almost unrivalled beauty. "The stone," says Scott, "though it has resisted the weather for so many ages, retains perfect sharpness, so that even the most minute ornaments seem as entire as when newly wrought. In some of the cloisters there are representations of flowers, vegetables, &c,. carved in stone with accuracy and precision so delicate, that we almost distrust our senses." In the "Lay of the Last Minstrel" we have the following graphic description of this splendid ruin:

> "Spreading herbs and flow'rets bright
> Glistened with the dew of night;
> Nor herb nor flow'ret glistened there,
> But was carved in the cloister arches fair.
>
> The darkened roof rose high aloof
> On pillars lofty, light and small;
> The key-stone that locked each ribbed aisle,
> Was a fleur-de-lys. or a quatre feuille;
> The corbels were carved grotesque and grim,
> And the pillars with clustered shafts so trim,
> With base and with capital flourished around,
> Seemed bundles of lances which garlands had bound."

There is no other remnant of antiquity in Scotland which has of late years been so much visited by strangers as Melrose. Since the publication of the poem in which the above lines occur the fame of the place has been carried wherever our language is known. This general admiration has caused a good deal to be done for the preservation of the ruin. In the market place stands an old cross. Near at hand is *Old Melrose*, the seat of W. Lockhart, Esq.

SELKIRKSHIRE,

Which county returns one member.

GALASHIELS.

A telegraph station.

Hotels.—Bridge Inn, Commercial, Victoria, Railway.

Market Day.—Tuesday.

Fairs.—Third Wednesday in March, July 8th, and October 10th.

This town contains a population of 5,918 engaged in making tartan and tweed cloths. A fine church, three chapels, ten woollen mills, brewery, large tan yards, library, grammar school; close to which was the Hunting Tower of the Scottish Kings. Close at hand are Mugget Hill, Gala Water, Allan Water (*the Glendeary of the Monastery*), Lauder, Cowdenknowes, with its vitrified fort, and Ashestiel, where Scott wrote his *Marmion*.

SELKIRK BRANCH.

Galashiels to Selkirk.

ABBOTSFORD.

Telegraph station at Galashiels, 2½ miles.

Hotel.—The Abbotsford.

Money Order Office at Galashiels, 2½ miles.

Abbotsford, 2 miles from Galashiels station, was the country seat of the great novelist and poet, Sir Walter Scott. This "romance in stone" is an irregular, though picturesque, Gothic pile, begun by Scott in 1816, and completed as fancy or convenience dictated in the course of years. It overlooks the rippling Tweed, and the beautiful haughs of Ettrick on the opposite banks. The front is about 150 feet long. A fine entrance hall is ornamented with oak panelling, and blazoned coats of arms, by D. Hay. In the drawing-room is a collection of antique furniture, and portraits, among others, one of "glorious John" Dryden—the "great high priest of all the nine." The armoury contains a great two-handed Swiss sword, the very counterpart of Rudolph Donnerhügel's, as described in Anne of Gierstein, and presented to Scott by his Swiss admirers; also King James's bottle, the great Marquis of Montrose's sword, Andrew Hofer's gun, Bonaparte's pistols, &c. Among the portraits in the dining-room are Cromwell, Graham of Claverhouse, Scott of Harden, and a curious one of Mary Queen of Scots' head on a charger. One room is full of drawings by Turner another is the library, 50 feet long, containing the Byron urn, the identical study where most of his delightful works were written, with his desk and clothes, which are preserved as memorials.

The visitor is also shown the various antiquarian relics, such as the pulpit of Erskine, the preacher, and the real iron-bound gate of the "Heart of Mid-Lothian," or Edinburgh Tolbooth, which the mob attempted to burn in the Porteus riot. Scott died here in 1832, utterly broken down by the wonderful exertions he made to pay off the immense incumbrances in which his connection with the Ballantynes had involved him. As they brought him in, helpless with palsy, on his return from Italy, he murmured, "Now I know I am at Abbotsford." See Washington Irving s *Abbotsford and Newstead Abbey*, for an interesting account of his pilgrimage to this spot. It is an heirloom in the poet's family; but all his direct descendants are extinct.

From a hill near it about thirty places, celebrated in Scottish song, may be counted, a few of which are—Yarrow Braes, Ettrick Forest, Gala Water, the banks of Allan Water, the Bush aboon Traquair, Cowdenknowes, Melrose Abbey ruins, Selkirk, &c.

LINDEAN and SELKIRK stations.

North British Main Line continued.

Soon after leaving BOWLAND BRIDGE we enter the county of Edinburgh, and continue our course to **STOW**, a place of no importance.

We next pass FOUNTAINHALL and HERIOT stations, which are part of the Lammermuir range, and end at Muirfoot Hills. On the latter hill there is a Druidical circle, 70 feet in diameter.

We then proceed to TYNE HEAD, near which is the high keep of Borthwick Castle, built near a Roman station in 1430, and *Crichton Castle*, the seat of the Bothwells. Then passing FUSHIEBRIDGE and GOREBRIDGE, situated near South Esk, on the Gore Water, to the left of which, in a romantic glen, are situated the Reshire strawberry beds, the half Roman Chapel and Castle of St. Clairs, built in 1440, we soon arrive at DALHOUSIE, near which is the *Castle*, the handsome seat of the Marquis of Dalhousie, the late distinguished Governor General of India, on whom the H. E. I. Company in 1856 settled a pension of £5,000 per annum as a reward for the ability with which he governed their immense territories. Close at hand is the *Laird of Cockpen's House*, *Newbottle Abbey*, the Marquis of Lothian's, and a large camp on the adjacent eminence, from which beautiful and extensive views of the country may be obtained.

ESKBANK (for Dalkeith).

A telegraph station.

MONEY ORDER OFFICE at Dalkeith, ¾ mile.

Three quarters of a mile distant is *Dalkeith Palace*, the magnificent seat of the Duke of Buccleugh.

PEEBLES BRANCH.

Eskbank to Peebles.

On this branch the intermediate stations are BONNYRIGG, near which is an extensive colliery.

HAWTHORNDEN, close to which is the seat of Sir J. Drummond (the old residence of Drummond the poet, whom Ben Johnson came to see). It contains the dress which Charles Stuart wore in 1745, the Cypress Grove, celebrated by the poet, caves from which Ramsay of Bruce came out to assault the English, and was visited by Queen Victoria in 1848.

ROSLIN, at which are remains of a castle and chapel, beautifully situated in a fine glen. The grounds are turned into strawberry beds.

PENICUIK, a large burgh, with a population of 2,580, employed in weaving, and at the powder, paper, and saw mills. The church and house were built by Sir J. Clerk, Bart., both of which have noble porticoes; in the latter are a good library, fine gallery of paintings, Roman antiquities, Dundee's buff coat, which he wore at Killiecrankie, and in the grounds a pillar to Allan Ramsay, Arthur's Oven, Roman Temple, Fish Pond, Hurley's Cave, 150 feet long: and in the vicinity are the ruins of *Ravensnook*, the St. Clair's seat, *Brunstane*, the Crichtons', &c.

LEADBURN and EDDLESTONE, at which are the Druid's Hill, 2,100 feet high, traces of two camps, and the following seats: *Cringletie*, Lord Murray, and *Portmore*, W. Mackenzie, Esq., M.P.

PEEBLESSHIRE, OR TWEEDDALE.

WHEN this county, which returns one member, is viewed from a distance, it appears to be one continued chain of hills, but on internal investigation, there are found along the sides of its rivers, many rich and fertile vallies of arable land. The county on the whole, however, is extremely mountainous, particularly along the southern side of the river Tweed. There is perhaps no river in Scotland on the banks of which there have been erected so many places for private defence against the hostile depredations of the borderers. Amid the many handsome country seats which now adorn its banks there are still to be seen the ruins of castles and towers, which exhibit the predatory spirit that prevailed formerly; yet, so great is the change, that there is probably no county in Scotland in which a more zealous and active spirit of agricultural improvement now prevails than in Peebles.

PEEBLES.

A telegraph station.

HOTEL.—Tontine.

MARKET DAY.—Tuesday.

FAIRS.—2nd Tuesday in Jan. and Oct., 1st Tuesday in March, 2nd Wednesday in May, Tuesday after July 18th, Tuesdays before August 24th, and Dec. 12th.

PEEBLES is an important Scottish burgh, and the capital of the county of that name, with a population of 2,673, employed in the stocking and leather trade. Here James I. composed "Peblis to the Play," at Beltane Festival. The church, with a fine steeple, is built on the site of an old chapel and castle. Here is St. Mungo's well, ruined chapels, camp at Cademuir Hill, Hill Forts, *Dean's House*, the seat of the late Lord March, and the scene of Scott's "Maid of Neidpath," and Campbell's "Earl March gazed on his dying child." It is situated on the north bank of the Tweed, and is usually divided into the "old" and "new" towns. It is a place of great antiquity. The old town consists of little more than a single street, and has little of architectural uniformity to recommend it, but the new town is a very handsome suburb.

North British Main Line continued.

DALKEITH.

A telegraph station.

HOTEL.—Cross Keys.

MARKET DAYS.—Monday and Thursday.

FAIRS—1st Thursday after Rutherglen May Fair, and 3rd Tuesday in October.

This burgh, with a population of 5,086, is beautifully situated on the Esk river. *Dalkeith Palace*, the seat of the Duke of Buccleugh, was built by Ann, Duchess of Monmouth, on the site of the old castle, visited by Froissart, James VI., Charles I., who was a prisoner here, General Monk, who took it, George IV. in 1822, and Queen Victoria in 1848.

Passing GLENESK and MILLER HILL stations we arrive at

MUSSELBURGH.

A telegraph station.

HOTEL.—Musselburgh Arms.

MARKET DAY.—Friday.

FAIR.– 2nd Tuesday in October.

This burgh and bathing place contains 7,092 inhabitants, a fine church, five chapels, library, bathing establishments, masonic lodge, on the site of which Randolph died in 1322, Grammar School, Lunatic Asylum, Sailors' Society, founded in 1669. An old bridge with a drawbridge in the middle, and Rennie's five-arched bridge. In the vicinity are *Pinkie House*, Sir J. Hope, Bart., Fisherow, a Roman station, Sheriff Hall, with its remains of a camp, the Links, on which in 1774, a golf club played for a silver cup, Huntley met the Covenanters in 1638, Cromwell encamped in 1650, and where the Edinburgh races are held. J. Burnet, the engraver, and Ritchie, the sculptor, are natives.

Passing NEW HAILES and NIDDRIE, near which is *Niddrie Marechal*, seat of A. Wauchope, Esq., whose ancestors in 1389 founded a small chapel here, we proceed to JOPPA, at which are a mineral spring, quarry, and saltworks, and arrive at PORTOBELLO, page 96 thence proceed to Leith, page 96 and soon reach

Edinburgh, see page 97

NORTH BRITISH MAIN LINE.

Berwick to Edinburgh.

Passing BURNMOUTH station, a place formerly celebrated for smugglers, and near which are some large stone quarries, we reach

AYTON.

POPULATION, 1,959.

Distance from station, ½ mile.

Telegraph station at Reston Junction, 4 miles

HOTEL.—Red Lion.

Passing RESTON station, the junction of the

DUNSE BRANCH,

We arrive at CHIRNSIDE, at which there are paper and flax mills, and in the vicinity *Whitehall*, seat of Sir J. Hall, Bart., *Nineveh*, A. Home, Esq., Islington, and Hay of Dunse, where Roman millstones and urns have been found. Fairs at Chirnside, last Thursday in November, for linen and sacking.

EDROM.—Here is good trout fishing. In the vicinity are *Nisbet*, seat of Lord Sinclair, Dunse Spa, *Kelloe*, G. Buchan, Esq., *Kimmeryhawe*, R. Bonar, Esq., Allanbank and Blackadder House.

DUNSE.

A telegraph station.

HOTEL.—Houram's.

MARKET DAY.—Saturday.

FAIRS.—1st Thursday in June, August, and Nov.

This place, with a population of 3,162, employed as weavers, contains two chapels, Town Hall, by Gillespie, in the pointed style, in which is a portrait of Duns Scotus, born at Grueldykes Farm in 1274. At Dunse Law, 630 feet high, Leslie resisted the episcopacy of Charles I., in 1639. Dunse Castle. rebuilt on the site of Lord Randolph's seat, has portraits of the Setons, and commands fine views. Boston and Dr. M'Crie were natives. In September, 1790, a Hoopoe was killed here. It is a meet for the Berwick Hunt.

North British Main Line continued.

GRANT'S HOUSE.

On the Eye Water, on the wild hilly slope of the Lammermuir hills, which terminate at the coast on the right in St. Abb's Head and Fast Castle—the latter on a point usually identified as the Wolf's Crag of the Master of Ravenswood, in the *Bride of Lammermuir.* The slate cliffs here are 300 feet high, and pass after a time into the primitive basalt formation. A little beyond Grant's House, is the deep pass of Peas Bridge.

COCKBURNSPATH.

So called after a resident named Coldbrandspath. Close at hand is *Dunglas*, the seat of Sir J. Hall, Bart., the old seat of the Homes and Douglases, which was visited by James VI. in 1603 and 1617. Over the Peath there is a bridge built in 1786, about 123 feet high and 300 long, near to which is *Fast Castle* and the remains of camps, the original of Sir W. Scott's "Master of Ravenswood."

INNERWICK.—This place contains ruins of the Hamiltons' castle, destroyed by Protector Somerset in 1547, and close at hand lies Edinken's Bridge, with the tumuli, on the spot where King Edwin of Northumbria was killed, *Black Castle Camp*, and an old chapel.

HADDINGTONSHIRE, OR EAST LOTHIAN,

WHICH is situated on the east coast of Scotland. at the mouth of the Firth of Forth, returns one member. The southern part of this county consists of a range of lofty mountains, which formed in ancient times a barrier for the defence of the county, and of the Scottish capital, against the invasions of the English. This elevated district overlooks towards the north and north-east a fertile peninsula, descending gradually to the sea on the north and west, and which in every part exhibits marks of the most successful industry These mountains are called the Lammermuir Hills, and form part or branch of a great range which crosses the whole island. A great portion of this county, or at least of the western part of it from the borders of Lammermuir to the sea, rests upon a bed of the most valuable mineral strata; lime, coal, ironstone, and freestone, everywhere abound.

No county is, perhaps, embellished with a greater number of gentlemen's seats, all of them elegant and well situated, and some built in a style of great magnificence.

DUNBAR.

POPULATION, 3,038.
A telegraph station.
HOTEL.—Cossar's.
MARKET DAY.—Tuesday.
FAIRS.—Tuesday after May 26th and Nov. 22nd.

A royal burgh and seaport town. It is situated at the mouth of the Firth of Forth, on a gentle eminence. The appearance of the country around, in every direction, presents a variety of striking and picturesque objects. To the east is seen St. Abb's Head, with its bold and rocky coast; to the south are the hills which border upon Lammermuir; westward Dumpenderlaw and North Berwick, and on the north the Firth of Forth, Bass Rock, and the coast of Fife.

Many vestiges of *Dunbar Castle* yet remain, which give a wild and picturesque effect to the rocks on which they stand. Here a celebrated battle was fought in 1276, in which Lord Warren defeated the Scots, and Cromwell routed Leslie in 1650. Mary Queen of Scots resided in the castle after Rizzio's death. The town contains baths, library, assembly rooms, foundries, grammar school, mathematical school, at which navigation is taught. The church, which is cruciform, was rebuilt in 1819 on the site of the old one founded in 1176 by the Earl of March. Here are tombs as old as 1480, and a fine one of the Lord Treasurer Home. The Rocky Pier has a dry dock, quay, and batteries, it was repaired by Cromwell, and has latterly been improved at a cost of £15,000. It commands views of the Bass, May Island, Forfar, &c. Here General Cope landed in 1745, and Paul Jones anchored. The late Emperor Nicholas of Russia visited it in 1814. Close at hand are *Dunbar House*, seat of the Earl of Lauderdale—*Lochend*, Sir G. Warrender, Bart., *Ninewar*, J. Hamilton, Esq., and *Belton*, Captain Hay, R. N.

Passing LINTON, EAST FORTUNE, and DREM stations—junction of the

NORTH BERWICK BRANCH,

we reach DIRLETON station, near which is the castle taken by Edward I., and now the seat of Mrs. Ferguson.

NORTH BERWICK.

Telegraph station at Drem, 4¾ miles.
HOTEL.—Dalrymple Arms
BANKERS.—Western Bank of Scotland.

This place contains ruins of a nunnery, founded in 1154 by the Earl of Fife. The port is a very bad rocky tidal harbour, and has a small pier. The rocks of Craigleith and Bass can be seen. In the vicinity is *North Berwick House*, seat of Sir H. Dalrymple, Bart.

North British Main Line continued.

LONGNIDDRY (Junction).

Telegraph station at Prestonpans, 3¾ miles.

Near at hand, is the old ruined seat at which John Knox was tutor.

HADDINGTON (Branch).

POPULATION, 3,883.
A telegraph station.
HOTELS.—George, Star.
MARKET DAY.—Friday.
FAIRS.—Friday after Rutherglen, 2nd Tuesday in July, July 15th, Friday before Edinbro' Hallow fair.
BANKERS.—Branch of British Linen Co.; Branch of Bank of Scotland.

HADDINGTON is the capital of the county bearing the same name. It stands on the left bank of the Tyne, and consists of four principal streets, with several smaller ones branching from it. Within the last twenty years this town has been greatly improved. One of its most elegant buildings is the church, formerly a Franciscan monastery. The suburb of Nungate is connected by a bridge of three arches across the Tyne. Being situated in the heart of a rich agricultural district, Haddington is an important place for the sale and purchase of grain in the open market. It contains a population of 3.883, who return one member; two churches, the oldest of which dateing as far back as Edward I., has a ruined choir, with tombs of Rev. John Brown, Maitlands, and Blantyres; five chapels; county-hall, with spire 150 feet high; town-hall, by Adams; School of Art, founded in 1820; museum, Gray's Public Library, brewery, tanneries, corn mill, four-arched bridge, grammar school, and dispensary. Here the Earl of Athol was murdered, in 1242. Knox was born, in 1505, in Gifford-street. Andrew Maitland, who married in 1657, had nine children, whose ages counted 738 years. Here prevails the custom of the bellman going round every night, singing the following:—

> "A' guid men's servants, whoe'er ye be,
> Keep coal and can'el for charitie," &c.

In the vicinity are *Colstoun*, the seat of the Marquis of Dalhousie; *Annsfield*, Earl Wemyss (on the site of which stood a woollen factory in Cromwell's time); *Cleckington*, Sir R. Houston, Bart.; and *Stevenson*, Sir J. Sinclair, Bart.

EDINBURGHSHIRE, OR MID-LOTHIAN.

THE principal part of this county, which returns one member, is mountainous. To the eastward of Edinburgh the country is agreeably variegated, by being formed, at the distance of every two or three miles, into ridges, in a direction from south to north, the whole of which are well cultivated. Each ridge, proceeding to the east, is more lofty than the former, till it terminates in the hills of Lammermoor. Towards the north, that is, upon the coast, the face of the country is rich and beautiful; but on receding from the sea, it gradually loses that aspect, and the mountains are bleak, naked, and barren on the south and south-west. The rivers belonging to this county are of no importance from their magnitude, but they are rendered interesting by the beautiful scenery exhibited almost everywhere upon their steep woody banks. The North and South Esk have beautiful wooded banks, adorned with splendid villas of the nobility or gentry. It rises on the southern side of the Pentland Hills, above Newhall, about 14 miles from Edinburgh, and its banks are not only uncommonly romantic and beautiful, but they form a species of classic ground. The eastern division of this county contains one of the most extensive and rich fields of coal that is anywhere to be found; but notwithstanding the abundance of the coal, the seams being of great thickness, the mines have generally proved unprofitable, in consequence of the enormous expense of working them, from the seams running to great depths. The maritime traffic of the county, which is very considerable, is concentrated in Leith, which possesses the best port in the county. The navigable canal and various lines of railway proceeding from Edinburgh to the rest of Scotland, makes the capital of this county the entrepôt of import as well as of export goods.

North British Main Line continued.

PRESTONPANS.

This place was celebrated for the battle of that name, between Prince Charles Stuart and the Royalists under Sir John Cope, in which the latter was defeated, Sept. 21st, 1745. In its neighbourhood is *Tranent*, with its Church, rebuilt in 1838, containing the tomb of Col. Gardiner, who fell at the battle of Prestonpans. In the vicinity is *Seton House*, rebuilt by Adam in 1790, on the old site close to the Collegiate Church, and *Falside Castle*, the Seton's seat, which was captured by Somerset on the day of Pinkie Battle.

We then reach INVERESK, beautifully situated in a healthy spot above the Firth of Forth, close to Pinkey, where the Scots were defeated in 1547, and Carberry Hill, 540 feet high; Fullerton's seat, where Mary surrendered to Kirkaldy of Grange, and which was occupied by Cromwell, and by the Highlanders in 1745. In the Church, lately rebuilt, was found, in 1565, an altar to Apollo, coins, bust, &c. Close at hand is *Cromwell's Fort*, remains of Loretto Chapel, *New Hailes*, Sir J. Ferguson, Bart.; *Edmonstone*, J. Wauchope, Esq.; and *Walliford*, A. Finlay, Esq.

PORTOBELLO.

Population, 3,497.
Telegraph station at Edinburgh, 3 miles.
HOTELS.—Commercial; Crown.

This place has gradually increased since a sailor who was at the capture of Porto Bello in 1739, built a residence here; it now contains six chapels, bank, baths, Union Hall, glass, soap, brick, and pottery works, paper mill, and various schools. It is one of the principal watering places on the east coast of Scotland. In 1822 George the Fourth held a review on the sands, which extend about a mile in length. Fishwives' Causeway, leading to Edinburgh, an old Roman road.

LEITH.

A telegraph station.
HOTELS.—Old Ship, 28, Shore; New Ship, 20 Shore; Globe, 23, Sandfort Street.

VIEWS IN EDINBURGH

OMNIBUSES to and from Edinburgh every five minutes, from 9 a.m. until 10 p.m.

STEAMERS—See Edinburgh.

RACES in July.

BANKERS.—Branch of Bank of Scotland; Branch of British Linen Co.; Branch of Commercial Bank of Scotland; Branch of National Bank of Scotland; Branch of Royal Bank of Scotland.

This port to the city of Edinburgh has a population of 30,919, who return one member along with the burghs of Portobello and Musselburgh. It was formerly called Inverleith, and is built on the river Leith, from which it derives its name; it was frequently plundered, the shipping burned, and the pier destroyed by the English, from 1313 to 1544. About four years after, during the minority of Qneen Mary, it was fortified by a French General, who came over to suppress the Reformation. Queen Mary landed here from France in 1541. In 1650 Cromwell occupied the town, and exacted an assessment from the inhabitants; after his return to England the citadel was built, which was taken in 1715 by some of the Stuart family, and held for a short time; in 1822 George IV. landed. There are about 20 churches, among which may be mentioned the parish church of South Leith, a Gothic edifice supposed to have been built in the 15th century. John Home, author of "Douglas," is interred here. It contains Court House, Town Hall, Police Office, Post Office, Exchange Buildings, Chamber of Commerce, Assembly Rooms, Reading Rooms, Libraries, Schools, Hospital, Infirmary, Trinity House, rebuilt in 1817 on the site of the old one built by Queen Mary (whose portrait, by Mytens, it contained). Custom House, built in 1812, at a cost of £12,000. Docks, Bonded Warehouses, Harbour, and two beautiful piers extending on each side of the harbour to about a mile in length, making a delightful promenade.

EDINBURGH.

Telegraph station at 68, Princes Street, and at the Parliament House.

HOTELS.—Mc.Gregor's Royal, first-class, for families and gentlemen, in Princes Street; Murray's London, family and commercial, St. Andrew's Square; Mackay's, for families and gentlemen; Barry's British, for families and gentlemen; Douglas's, for families and gentlemen; Rampling's Waterloo.

NEWS ROOMS.—Harthill's, 23, Waterloo Place; Robertson and Scott, 76, George Street. Tariff—1d. per visit.

OMNIBUSES to and from the stations and Leith every five minutes.

STEAMERS from Granton Pier and Leith Harbour; Edinburgh offices for Aberdeen and Inverness at 6, South St. Andrew Street; General Steam Navigation Co., for London, 21, Waterloo Place; Leith and Edinburgh Co., for London, 9, Waterloo Place; Stirling, 10, Princes Street.

MARKET DAYS.—Wednesday, vegetable and fruit market; Tuesday, Thursday, and Saturday.

POST OFFICE at Waterloo Place.

BANKERS.—Alexander Allan and Co., Union Bank of Scotland; Bank of Scotland; Edinburgh and Glasgow Bank; Branch City of Glasgow Bank; British Linen Co.; Clydesdale Banking Co.; Commercial Bank of Scotland; National Bank of Scotland; Royal Bank of Scotland.

This city, which has not nnaptly been termed the "modern Athens," is one of the most ancient in this country. Its schools for the acquirement of useful knowledge have long held a high rank amongst the universities of Europe, and have supplied some of the most distinguished statesmen, warriors, poets, and divines, who have graced our annals.

It contains beauties and peculiarities which give it a high claim to attention amongst the capitals of Europe, and is the capital of Scotland in a superb situation on the north slope of the Pentland Hills, fronting the Firth of Forth, two miles from it. Two members returned. Population 160,302.

EDINBURGH, so called from Edwin, king of Northumbria, who built a castle here in the seventh century, while others claim the origin from the two Gaelic words, "*Dun Edin*," which signifies "*the face of a hill*." It covers a space of from two to two and a half miles square, and contains the old town on the east between the Castle, Holyrood Palace, and the Abbey; the south town, round Heriot's Hospital, Newington, and Morningside; and the new town on the north and north-west. Both the south and new towns have been erected within the last hundred years; the latter especially, comprises many noble streets and squares, built of the beautiful stone from Craigleith quarry (two miles distant from the city). In the old town, along the High Street, Canongate, Grassmarket, &c., many houses are of Queen Mary's time, divided by narrow dark closes (or alleys), and from six to ten stories (or flats) high. Between it and the new town are east and west Princes Street Gardens, beautifully laid out, and through which the Edinburgh and Glasgow, and North British railways pass; this was formerly called the North or Nor' Loch, a sheet of stagnant water; there are the North and Waverley bridges, and Mound, forming a connection with the old and new town. Of the numerous fine structures which adorn the "Modern Athens," as it has been styled from a similarity in its general appearance, the

Castle on a hill, 383 feet above the level of the sea, is surmounted by modern batteries, the state prison and arsenal, Queen Mary's room (where she gave birth to James VI.), the regalia room (*admittance free by order from City Chambers*); among the regalia are Bruce's Crown and Sceptre. Mons Meg, a large cannon, said to be cast at Mons, in Brittany, in 1486, is mounted on a carriage on the Bomb Battery. The Queen and Prince Albert ascended it for the view in 1842. The castle ought to be visited an account of the magnificent prospect it affords; on the north side of the castle esplanade is a statue to the *Duke of York*. *College of Justice*, in Parliament Square, where the 13 judges sit, where are statues of President Forbes, Blair, Lord Melville, Duudas, and the late Lord Jeffrey; adjoining is the *Advocates' Library*, containing nearly 200,000 printed volumes, and 1,700 manuscripts. Among the MSS.

is a Bible of the 11th century, and the original Solemn League and Covenant. *Signet Library* is peculiarly rich in the department of History, especially British and Irish. In the centre of the square is a *Statue of Charles II.*, on horseback. *General Post Office*, in Waterloo Place, a Grecian building. *Stamp and Excise Offices*, in Waterloo Place. *General Register House*, Princes Street (foot of North Bridge), a handsome Grecian pile, with a tower 200 feet high; immediately in front is the *Equestrian Statue of the Duke of Wellington*, by Steel. *Nelson's Monument*, on Calton Hill, 102 feet in height—on the top is a *Time Ball*, which is lowered at one o'clock, Greenwich time. *National Monumeut*, on Calton Hill, *unfinished*, consists of 12 great pillars, and erected at a cost of £13,000; it is a model of the Parthenon of Athens. Close by are monuments to Dugald Stewart and Professor Playfair, and the *Royal Observatory*, shaped like a St. George's Cross, 62 feet long. *Scott's Monument*, in East Princes Street Gardens, one of the finest ornaments of Edinburgh, is shaped like a pyramid, 200 feet high, from the designs of G. Kemp (a self-taught architect), with niches for statues illustrative of characters in the works of Scott. Only five have been filled. *A Statue of Scott*, by Steel, is placed underneath. *Royal Institution*, on the Mound, founded in 1819, a handsome Grecian portico, with Steel's statue of Queen Victoria in front, contains a gallery of casts (open every day, except Saturday), and a fine gallery of paintings (open Wednesday and Saturday, *free*); here are held the meetings of the Society of Arts, Royal Society, and Society of Antiquarians, offices of the Board of Trade for Manufactures, and Board of Fisheries in Scotland. *National Gallery*, behind the Royal Institution, lately completed, was built for the annual exhibitions of the Royal Scottish Academy, the School of Design, and the institution of a Scottish National Gallery of paintings and sculpture. *University*, on South Bridge, founded in 1582, by a charter from James VI., the present building was begun in 1789, by Robert Adams; there are 32 professorships, divided into four faculties, viz.:—Medicine, Law, Theology, and Arts; a *Museum* open daily, 6d. (Saturday *free*), and *Library*, 198 feet in length, containing about 100,000 volumes. *Royal College of Surgeons' Museum*, in Neilson Street, admittance by member's order. *John Knox's Honse*, foot of High Street, open on Tuesdays, Fridays, and Saturdays (6d.), consists of three rooms, the principal object being the chair which belonged to the Reformer. The *Canongate*, containing many houses of note, extends from the foot of High Street to Holyrood Palace. In this street is situated the *White Horse Inn*, at which Dr. Samuel Johnson arrived on his way to the Hebrides in 1773; *Moray House*, on the south of the street, was erected in 1618 or 1628. Here Oliver Cromwell took up his residence on his first visit to Edinburgh, 1618.

Holyrood Palace (open daily, 6d., Saturday, *free*) and *Abbey*, the latter being founded for Augustine Canons, by David I., in 1128; the *present palace* is for the most part a building about 200 years old, here Queen Mary was married to Darnley, in 1565; the Gothic tower, doorways, and Chapel Royal, still remain. The palace, which has been partially restored for the Queen, contains a quadrangle in the style of Hampton Court. *Queen Mary's* bedroom and cabinet, with the mark (?) of David Rizzio's blood; in the picture gallery there are about 110 manufactured likenesses of Scottish sovereigns, principally executed by De Witt, a Flemish painter. *Queen Mary's Dial* is in the gardens. *Arthur's Seat*, in the park behind, 822 feet above the level of the sea, is surrounded by a fine carriage-way called the "Queen's Drive;" on the north side is the ruins of a chapel dedicated to *St. Anthony* the Eremite. *Salisbury Crags* (forming part of Arthur's Seat), is a range of precipitous rocks, and from the road winding round the foot may be seen the cottage of "Davie Deans," rendered famous by Scott's celebrated novel, the "Heart of Mid-Lothian;" in this work is to be had the best description of old Edinburgh.

City and Commercial Buildings.—Edinburgh is governed by a Lord Provost, six Magistrates or Bailies, and Councillors. *Bailie Court* and *Council Chambers* are in the Old Exchange Buildings, High Street; nearly opposite is the *Police Office*, in front of which is the spot where formerly stood the City Cross, removed in 1756. *County Hall*, Parliament Square, occupied as offices for the Sheriff and Procurator Fiscal; the Small Debt Courts are held here; between it and St. Giles' Church formerly stood the famous "Old Tolbooth Prison," or heart of Mid-Lothian, the scene of the Porteus riots. Its gate is now at Abbotsford. *Corn Exchange*, in the Grassmarket, a handsome Italian building, 156 feet long. *Commercial Bank* (George Street) and *British Linen Company's Bank* (St. Andrew's Square); the interior of which are well worth a visit. *County Jail*, in Waterloo Place, was completed in 1847, and has accommodation for criminal and debtor prisoners. *Water Works*, on the Castle Hill, capable of containing 1,800,000 gallons of water, and filled by pipes about 8 miles long, from the vale of Glencarse, in the Pentland Hills.

Places of Amusement, &c.—*Horticultural Society Gardens*, Inverleith Row, admitted by a member's order; close to are the *Royal Botanic Gardens*, open daily, *free*. *Zoological Gardens*, at Claremont Crescent, open daily, 1s. *Antiquarian Museum*, 24, George Street (Wednesday and Saturday, by member's order). Here are preserved many interesting relics of antiquity. *Highland and Agricultural Society Museum*, George IV. Bridge, every day, except Monday, *free*; *Royal* and *Queen's Theatres*, *Waterloo Rooms*, *Music Hall*, *Hopetown Rooms*, *St. Cecilia Hall*, and *Queen Street Hall*, used principally for lectures and concerts. *Short's Observatory*, on Castle Hill, containing many fine astronomical instruments.

Public Cemeteries and Churchyards,—*Greyfriars*—here Mackenzie, "the Man of Feeling," is buried, &c. *Warresten*, near Inverleith Row; *Western* or *Dean*, where Francis Jeffrey, and Wilson, "The Christopher North," of *Blackwood's Magazine*, are buried; *Southern Grange*, Dr. Chalmers is buried here.

Churches and Chapels.—There are about 10[?] places of worship, about thirty of which belong to the Established Church. Three churches are comprised under the roof of *St. Giles'*, in the form of cross, 206 feet long, of the 14th century, with a spire 160 feet high, and musical bells; John Knox, the Regent Murray, and Montrose, are buried here. *Victoria* or *Assembly Hall*, with a spire 240 feet high. Here the General Assembly of the Church of Scotland meets in May. *Old Greyfriars Church*, built in 1612, destroyed by fire in 1845, and now in course of requilding. Uniform with it is the *New Greyfriars*, with which it is contiguous. *Tron Church*, High Street, marked by a *new* spire of 140 feet. The church was built in 1663; here Chalmers preached. Opposite the church is a cellar where the Treaty of Union is said to have been signed. *St. Andrew's*, in George Street, with spire 168 feet. In St. Andrew's Square, at the east end of this fine street, is the *Melville Pillar*, copied from Trajan's; in the square Lord Brougham was born. In a line with Melville in George Street, are statues of Pitt and George IV. *St. George's*, at the west end of this street, in Charlotte Square, with fine portico and dome, 15 feet high, after the model of St. Paul's. *St. Stephen's* St. Vincent Street, a fine building, with a tower, 162 feet high. *St. Cuthbert's* or *West Church*, Princes Street, is a large church, the mother church to a number of chapels of ease. *Canongate*, in the form of a cross, finished in 1688, with figures of the deer and cross on it, which is said to have appeared to David I., and led him to found Holyrood. Smith, author of the "Wealth of Nations," and Ferguson, the poet, are buried here. *St. John's* Episcopal Chapel, Princes Street, is in the Gothic style, built in 1818. *St. Paul's* Episcopal Chapel (the Bishop officiates here), in York Place, a Gothic building. *St. Mary's* Roman Catholic Chapel, in Broughton Place, built 1813, is the principal place of worship of that body in Edinburgh, has a fine organ, and a painting, by Vandyke, of the Entombment. *Trinity Episcopal Church*, at the Dean Bridge; *St. Mary's*, belonging to the Established Church, in Belle Vue Crescent, with a spire 180 feet high, and opened in 1824; *John Knox Church*, close to the Reformer's house. *Free Church College*, a modern building, erected shortly after the disruption.

Schools, Hospitals, and Benevolent Institutions.—The public and private schools exceed 200, and the benevolent and religious societies are very numerous. The *High School*, Calton Hill, dates as far back as 1517, was rebuilt on its present site in 1829. *Edinburgh Academy*, Henderson Row, built in 1824; *Naval and Military Academy*, in Lothian Road; *Normal School*, for the training of pupil teachers, is at the back of the Castle. *Heriot's Hospital*, in Laurieston, is an Elizabethan quadrangle, by Inigo Jones, 160 feet square; Heriot is "Jingling Geordie," in the Fortunes of Nigel, by Scott. *George Watson's Hospital*, in Laurieston; *John Watson's Hospital*, at the Dean, in the Grecian style of building; *Gardner's Orphan Hospital*, at the Dean, opposite Watson's; *Stewart's Hospital*, close to the two last mentioned, is built in the Elizabethan style; *Merchant Maiden's Institution*, to the west of George Watson's; *Trade's Maiden Hospital*, in the Meadows. These hospitals are all for the training and education of children of both sexes. *Gillespie's Hospital*, Bruntsfield Links, for the aged and infirm. This is the only hospital of the kind in Edinburgh. *Lunatic Hospital*, Morningside; *Royal Infirmary*, is a large building close to the University, and supported by subscriptions. There are many other excellent charitable institutions, maintained by private subscriptions—among them may be mentioned the *House of Refuge*, *Blind Asylum*, *Night Asylum for the Houseless*, *Deaf and Dumb Institution*, *Destitute Sick Society*, two *Ragged Schools*, *Public Dispensaries*, *&c.*

In George Square, near the Meadows, Sir Walter Scott was born, in 1771. *Allan Ramsag's House*, on Castlehill. A small stream, called the "*Water of Leith*," runs through the new town to the sea at Leith, passing the *Dean* and two other *bridges*. The Dean bridge is a very fine one, by Telford, in four arches, spanning a deep ravine, 106 feet high from the bed of the stream, and commanding an extensive view. Three or four unhappy creatures have leaped over. A short distance to the east of Dean Bridge, on the right side of the stream, is *St. Bernard's Mineral Well*, and much frequented by invalids and others. *Bruntsfield Links*, a famous place for the game of golf; near to it is *Merchieston Castle*, the birth place of Napier, the inventor of Logarithms. It is now used as an educational institution.

MAP SECTION

BRADSHAW'S TOURS

PLANS OF

CHANNEL IS. & ISLE OF MAN, ISLE OF WIGHT, LONDON,

ENVIRONS OF LONDON 25 MILES ROUND, NORTH WALES,

BRISTOL, DUBLIN, OXFORD, LAKE DISTRICT, SCOTLAND,

BIRMINGHAM, GLASGOW, LIVERPOOL, MANCHESTER,

EDINBURGH, HULL, LEEDS, SHEFFIELD

The contents pages at the start of the four sections refer to the maps and plans as originally included. These have been left as first printed in 1861.
The list above shows the maps and plans in the order they appeared in the four sections.

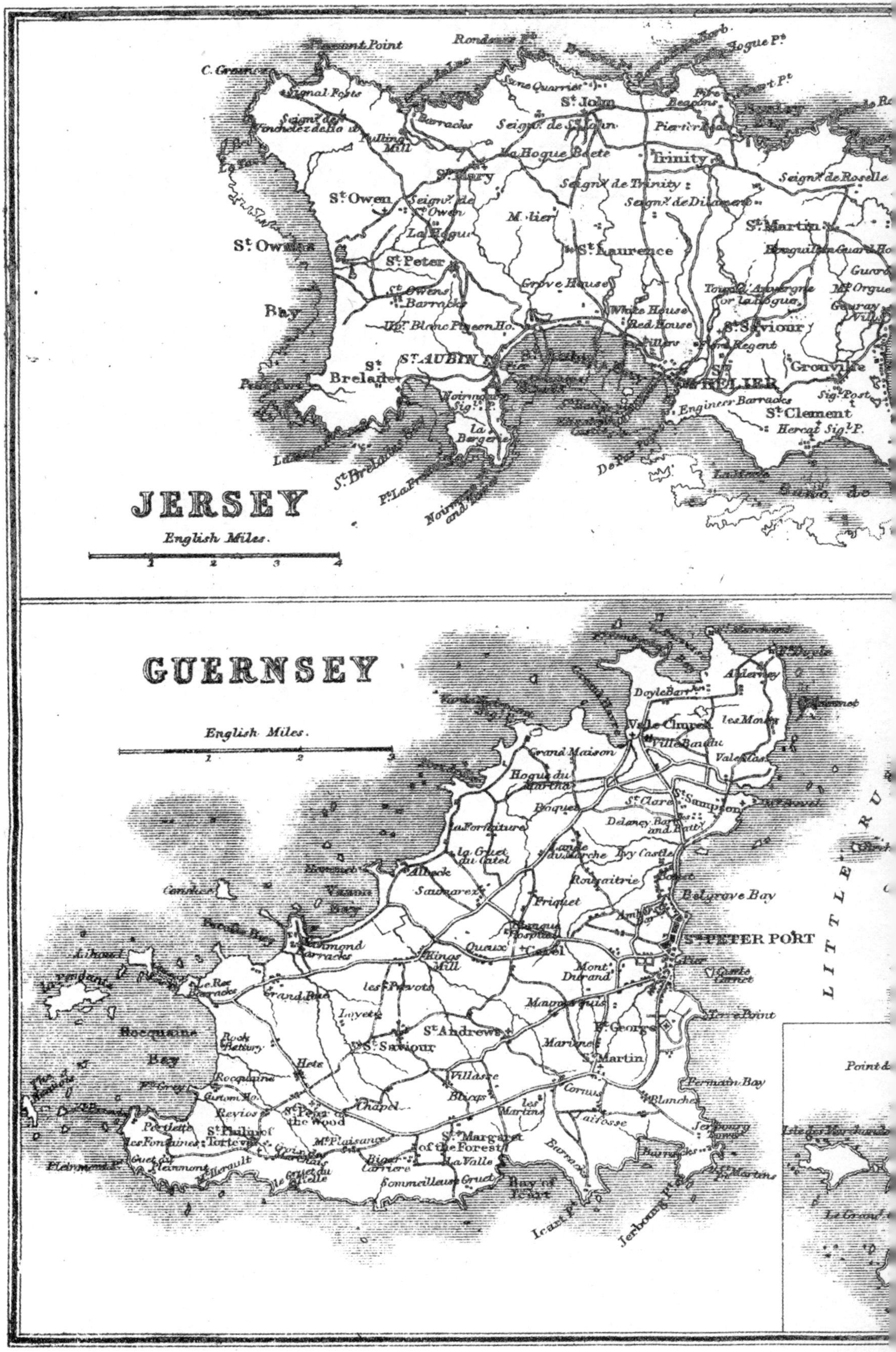
JERSEY
English Miles
1
2
3
4
Plemont Point
C. Grosnez
Signal Posts
St. John
Barracks
Trinity
St. Mary
St. Owen
St. Owens
Bay
St. Peter
St. Laurence
Grove House
White House
Red House
St. Saviour
St. Martin
St. AUBIN
St. Brelade
Grouville
St. Clement
Engineers Barracks
La Hogue Boete
Seignr. de Trinity
Seignr. de Roselle
Upr. Blanc Pigeon Ho.
St. Owens Barracks
La Bergerie
GUERNSEY
English Miles
1
2
3
Grand Maison
Vale Church
Ville Baudu
les Moies
Doyle Bar.
Hogue du Martha
St. Clare
St. Sampson
Delancy Barks. and Batty.
Ivy Castle
Belgrove Bay
St. PETER PORT
Pier
Castle Cornet
Mont Durand
Castel
Quaux
Kings Mill
Saumarez
Priquet
Rousaitrie
les Prevots
Grand Rue
Lovette
St. Andrews
St. Saviour
Marine
Martin
Villasse
Blicqs
Chapel
Cornu
Blanche
Jerbourg
Permain Bay
Rocquaine
Bay
St. Peter in the Wood
St. Philip of Torteval
Portlette
les Fontaines
Pleinmont
Mt. Plaisance
St. Margaret of the Forest
La Valle
Sommeillaux
Bay of Icart
Icart Pt.
Jerbourg Pt.
Barracks
Richmond Barracks
Le Ree Barracks
Rock Battery
Hets
Custom Ho.
La Forteiture
La Gruet du Catel
Mt. Plaisance
LITTLE RU

ALDERNEY
Singe
Passage
Town
English Miles.
ISLE OF MAN
Kirk Bride
K. Andreas
Kirk Jurby
Ramsey Bay
RAMSEY
Sulby
Ballaugh
K. Christ Lizayre
Kk. Michael
Barnugh
Largy Kenny
Snaefield
Garrahill
Ulliam
Glen Roy
Laxey
Kirk Lonan
Peel
K. St. Germain
Contrary Pt.
K. Patrick
Kirk Marown
K. Braddan
Onchan
Douglas Hd.
DOUGLAS
Dalby Pt.
Kirk Arbory
Ballasalla
K. Malew
CASTLETOWN
Scarlet Pt.
Spanish Hd.
Calf of Man
Light Ho.
Langness Pt.
Derby Haven
Kk. Santon
English Miles.
1 2 3 4 5 6 7 8

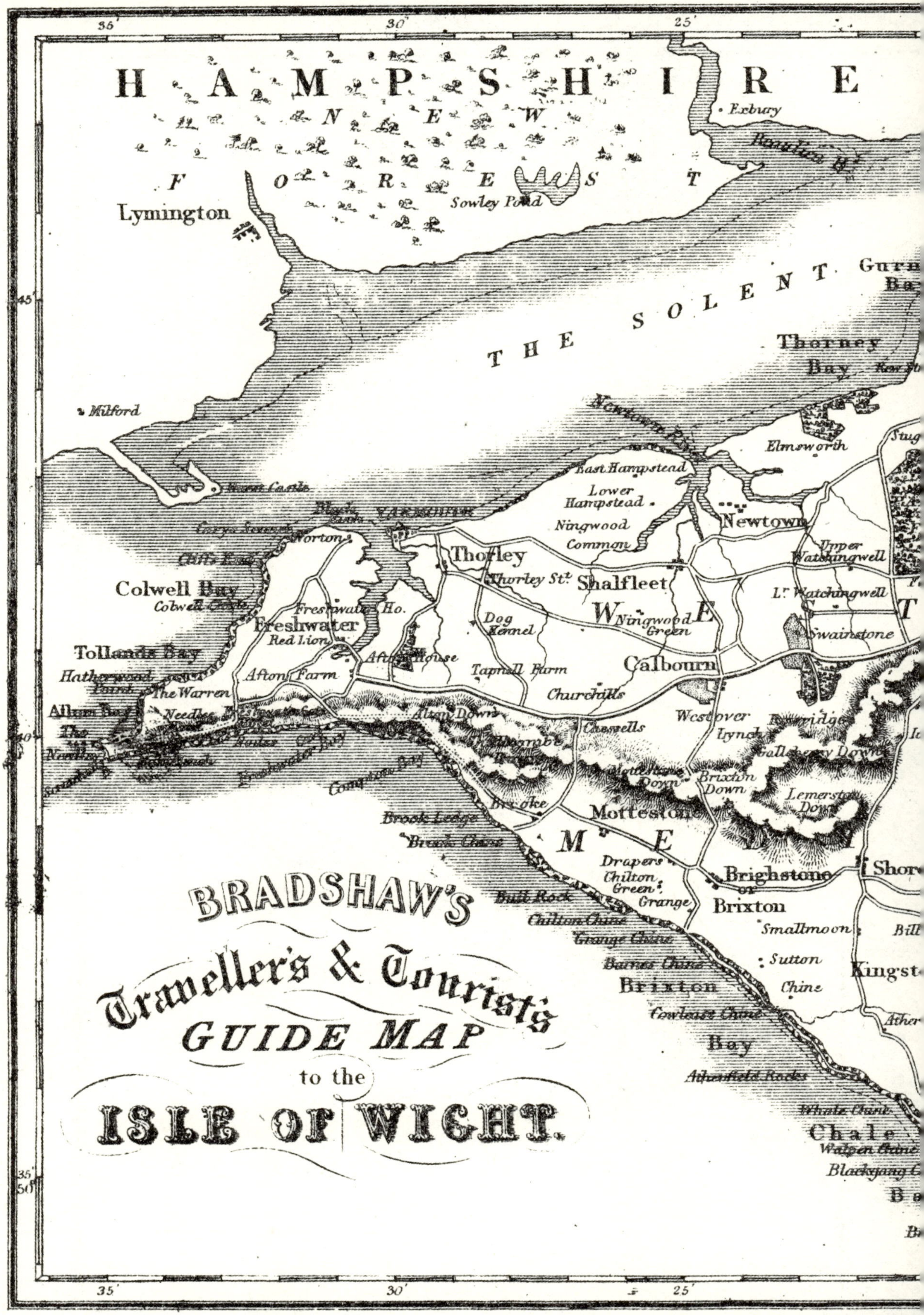
BRADSHAW'S
Traveller's & Tourist's
GUIDE MAP
to the
ISLE OF WIGHT.
HAMPSHIRE
NEW FOREST
Lymington
Sowley Pond
Exbury
THE SOLENT
Thorney Bay
Milford
East Hampstead
Lower Hampstead
Ningwood Common
Newtown
Elmsworth
YARMOUTH
Norton
Thorley
Thorley St.
Shalfleet
Upper Watchingwell
Lr. Watchingwell
Swainstone
Colwell Bay
Freshwater Ho.
Freshwater
Red Lion
Tollands Bay
Dog Kennel
Ningwood Green
Calbourn
Tapnell Farm
Afton Farm
The Warren
Alum Bay
Churchills
Westover
Chessells
Lynch
Afton Down
Compton Bay
Brixton Down
Lemerston Down
Brooke
Mottestone
Brook Ledge
Brook Chine
Drapers
Chilton Green
Grange
Brighstone or Brixton
Bull Rock
Chilton Chine
Grange Chine
Barnes Chine
Brixton Bay
Cowleaze Chine
Smallmoon
Sutton
Chine
Kingst
Atherfield Rocks
Whale Chine
Chale
Walpen Chine
Blackgang
35'
30'
25'
45'
40'
35'
50'

BRADSHAW & BL

LITHrs 47 BROWN St. MANCHESTER

BRADSHAW'S

WEST END
KENTISH TOWN
LOWER HOLLOWAY
HAVERSTOCK HILL
CAMDEN NEW TOWN
PRIMROSE HILL PARK
REGENT'S PARK
HYDE PARK
ROTTEN ROW
GREEN PARK
ST JAMES PARK
EARLS COURT
NEW BROMPTON
CHELSEA REACH
BATTERSEA PARK
SOUTH LAMBETH

OF LONDON

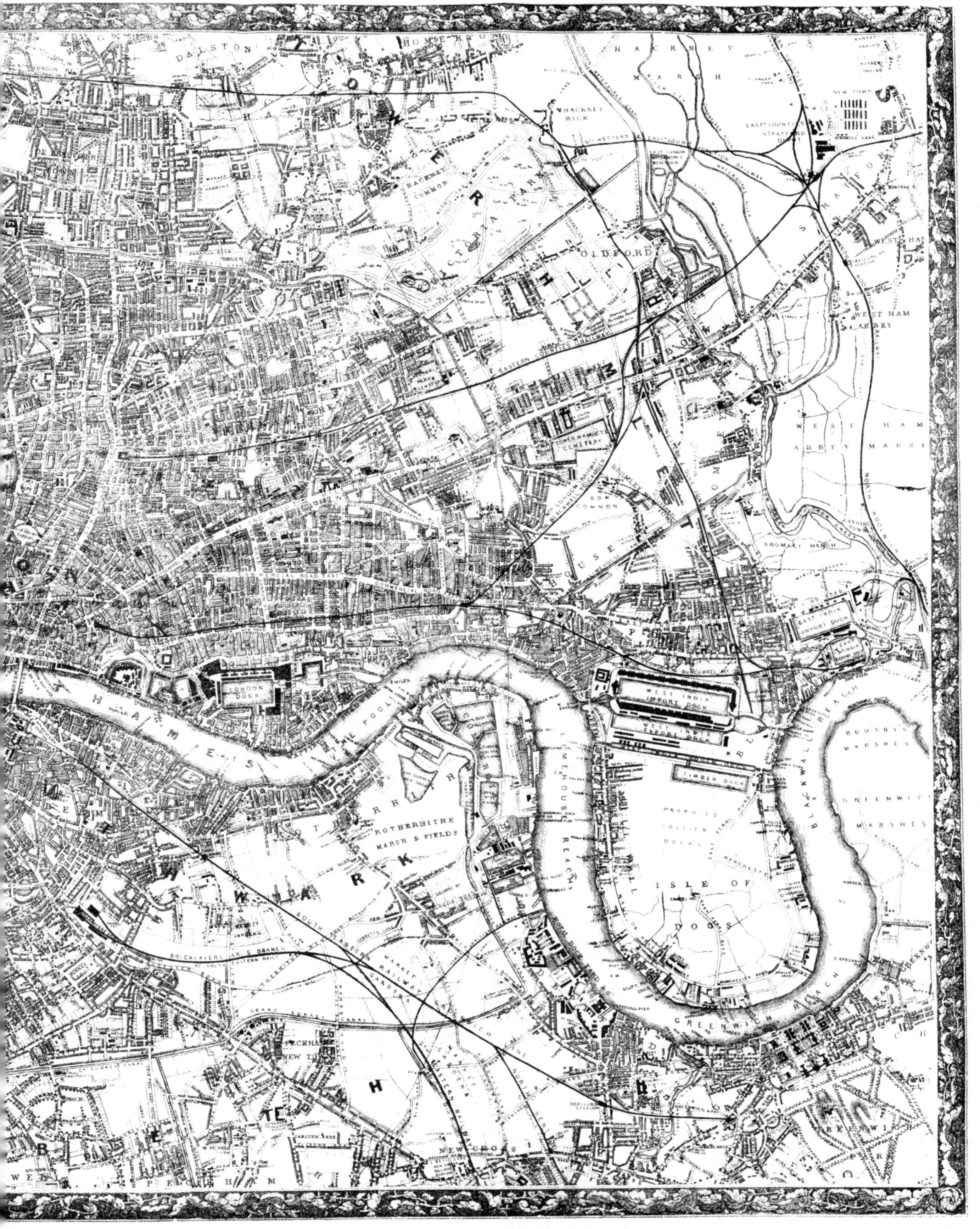

DALSTON
HOMERTON
HACKNEY
MARSH
HACKNEY WICK
HACKNEY COMMON
VICTORIA PARK
OLD FORD
NEW TOWN
STRATFORD
WEST HAM
WEST HAM ABBEY
WEST HAM
ABBEY MARSH
EASTERN COUNTIES RAILWAY
TOWER HAMLETS CEMETERY
BOW COMMON
BROMLEY MARSH
COMMERCIAL ROAD EAST
LONDON DOCK
EAST INDIA IMPORT DOCK
WEST INDIA IMPORT DOCK
WEST INDIA EXPORT DOCK
TIMBER DOCK
PROPOSED COLLIER DOCKS
ISLE OF DOGS
LIMEHOUSE REACH
BLACKWALL REACH
GREENWICH REACH
BUGSBYS MARSHES
GREENWICH MARSHES
THE POOL
ROTHERHITHE MARSH & FIELDS
BRICKLAYERS ARMS BRANCH
GRAND SURREY CANAL
PECKHAM NEW TOWN
NEW CROSS
PECKHAM

BRADSHAW'S GUIDE MAP TO THE EN

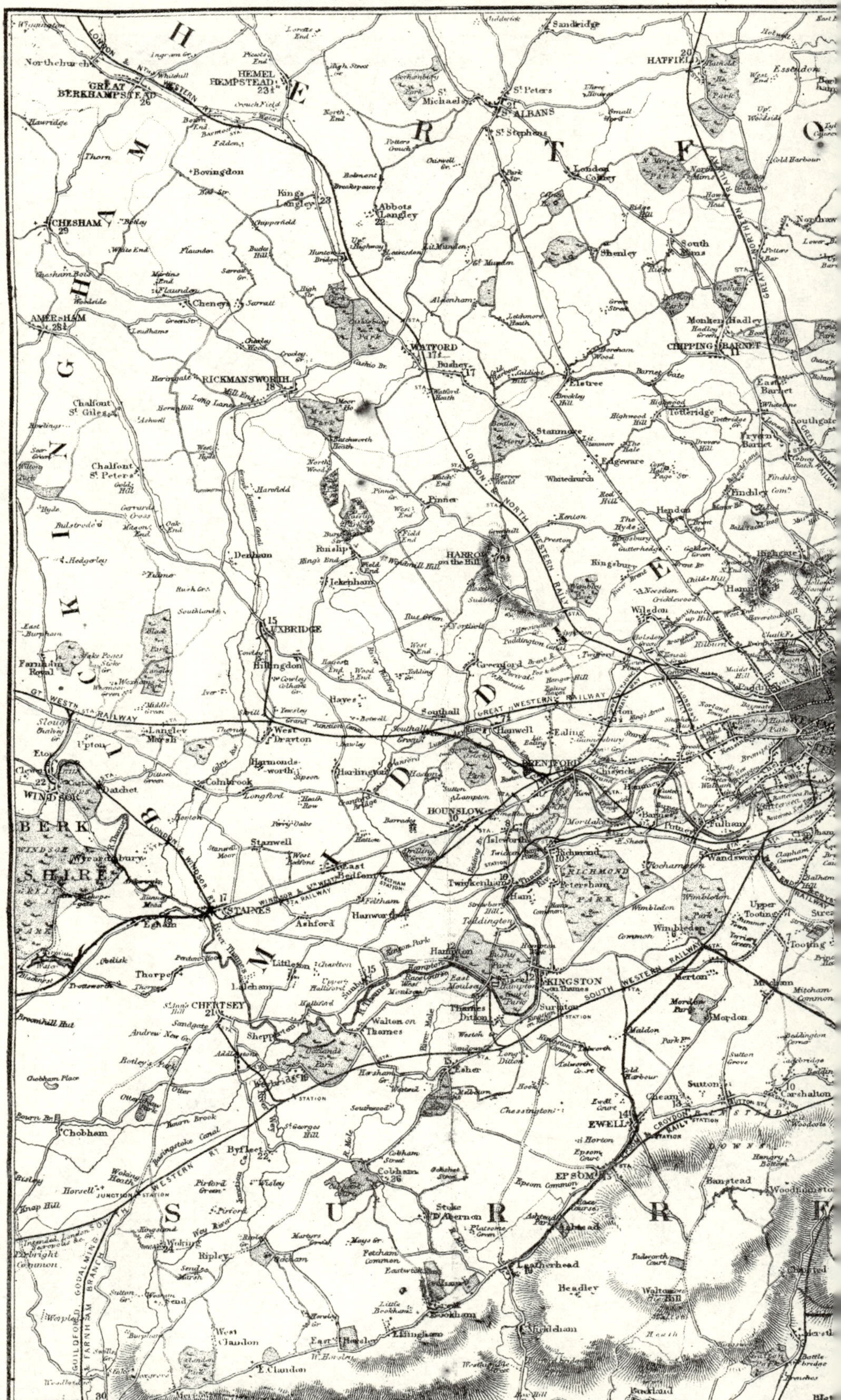

The figures to the Towns &c. denote the distance in miles from London.

SCALE OF MILES.

0 1 2 3 4 5 6 7 8

OF LONDON 25 MILES ROUND.

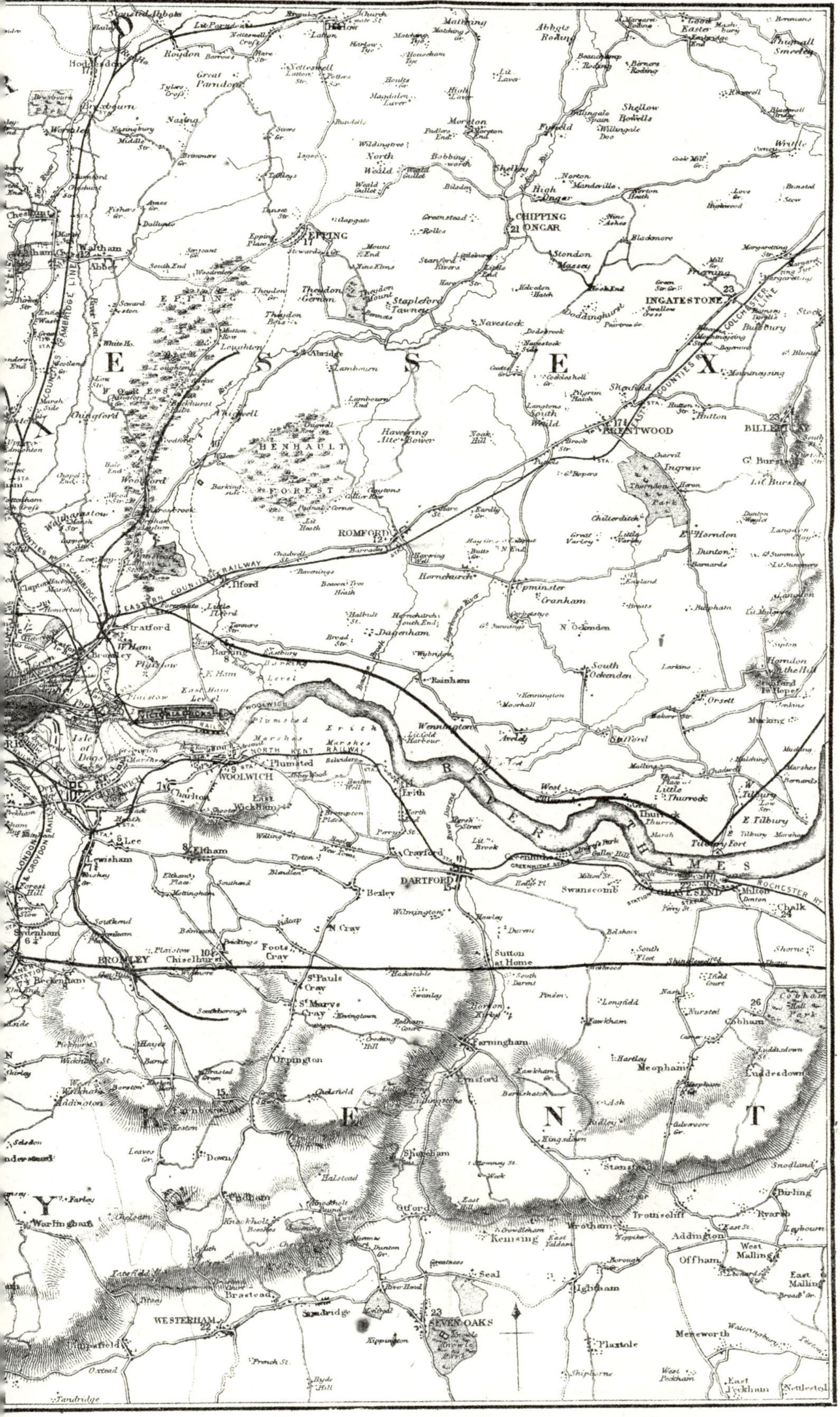

BRADSHAW'S
TOURIST'S MAP
OF
NORTH WALES.
SCALE OF MILES.
0 5 10 15
CARDIGAN
BAY
CAERNARVON BAY
HOLYHEAD
LLANERCHYMEDD
LLANGEFNI
CAERNARVON
LLANBERIS
SNOWDON
BEDDGELERT
TREMADOG
NEVIN
BARMOUTH
ABERDOVEY
ABERYSTWITH
BARDSEY I.
Light House
GREAT ORMES HEAD
CARNEDD LLEWELLYN
CARNEDD DAVID
Cader Idris
Llyn Ogwen
Llanelltyd
Dolgelley
Towyn
Borth
R. Rheidol
Llangelynin
Llanfihangel Geneu'rglyn

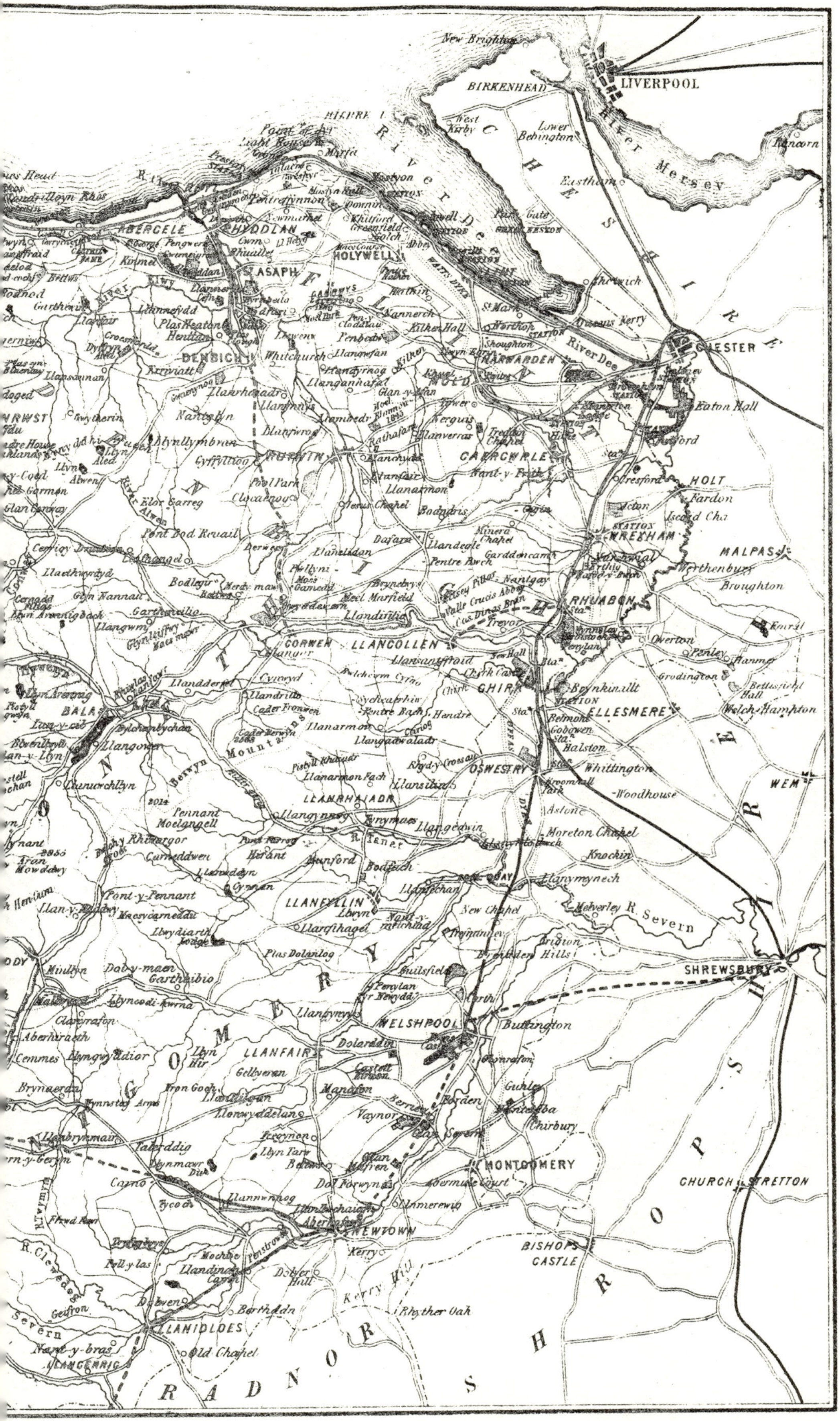

New Brighton
BIRKENHEAD
LIVERPOOL
River Mersey
Runcorn
West Kirby
Lower Bebington
Eastham
HILBRE I.
Point of Air Light House
CHESHIRE
River Dee
Mostyn
Holywell
HOLYWELL
RHUDDLAN
ABERGELE
ST ASAPH
DENBIGH
Whitchurch
FLINT
Shotwick
Queens Ferry
CHESTER
HAWARDEN
MOLD
Eaton Hall
Pulford
CAERGWRLE
Nant-y-Frith
Gresford
HOLT
Farndon
Acton
WREXHAM
MALPAS
Worthenbury
Broughton
RHUABON
Overton
Penley
Hanmer
Bettisfield Hall
Welch Hampton
ELLESMERE
Brynkinallt
Belmont
Gobowen
Halston
Whittington
OSWESTRY
WEM
Woodhouse
Aston
Moreton Chapel
Knockin
Llanymynech
R. Severn
Melverley
Breidden Hills
SHREWSBURY
Guilsfield
WELSHPOOL
Buttington
Chirbury
MONTGOMERY
CHURCH STRETTON
BISHOPS CASTLE
NEWTOWN
Kerry
Kerry Hill
Rhyther Oak
LLANIDLOES
Old Chapel
Nant-y-bras
Severn
R. Clewedog
Llandinam
Carno
Llanbrynmair
Talerddig
Llanfair
LLANFAIR
Manafon
Llangynyw
Dolarddyn
LLANFYLLIN
LLANRHAIADR
Llangedwin
Llansilin
Berwyn Mountains
Llanarmon
Pennant Moelangell
Garthbibio
Dolymaen
Llangower
BALA
Llandderfel
Llandrillo
CORWEN
LLANGOLLEN
CHIRK
Llansantffraid
Trevor
Llandegla
Clocaenog
RUTHIN
Llanrhaiadr
Nantglyn
Henllan
Llannefydd
Kinmel
R. Elwy
R. Alwen
Pont y Pennant
Llan-y-mawddwy
Aran Mowddwy
Cemmes
Pennal
Trefeglwys
RADNOR
SHROPSHIRE
MONTGOMERY
DENBIGH

BRI
Nursery
Nursery
Nursery
COTHAM
Pembroke Ho
Zoological Gardens
Oakfield Ho
County Boundary
Harley Pl
Somerset Build^s
Conservative Rooms
Park Gate
Clifton Rd
Horticultural Rooms
Suspension Bridge
Clifton Ch
Clifton Hill
Royal York Cres
Lower Crescent
Foot Path to Clifton
Hotwell Road
The Dock Act of 1803 extends the boundaries of the City for certain objects to Rownham Ferry & includes the Locks & meadow with the paths & roads on each side back to the houses or Walls.
Ship Yard
Sand Rocks
Coronation
Nursery

TOL.
51
MONTPELLIER
St. Matthews Ch
Turnpikes
Stokes Croft
Portland Sq.
Horse St.
Broad Mead
Castle Street
Old Market Street
West Street
Red Cross St.
COALPITHEATH RAILY.
RAILWAY
Temple Ch
Temple Meads
Gt. WESTERN
Cattle Market
Queen Square
Princes Street
The Grove
The Quay
The Back
St. Augustine
Bath St.
Temple Street
Redcliff Street
Thomas Street
Portwall Lane
Bath Parade
Redcliff Hill
WAPPING
New Gaol
Road to Bath
Road from
Coronation
St. Pauls Ch
BRISTOL & EXETER

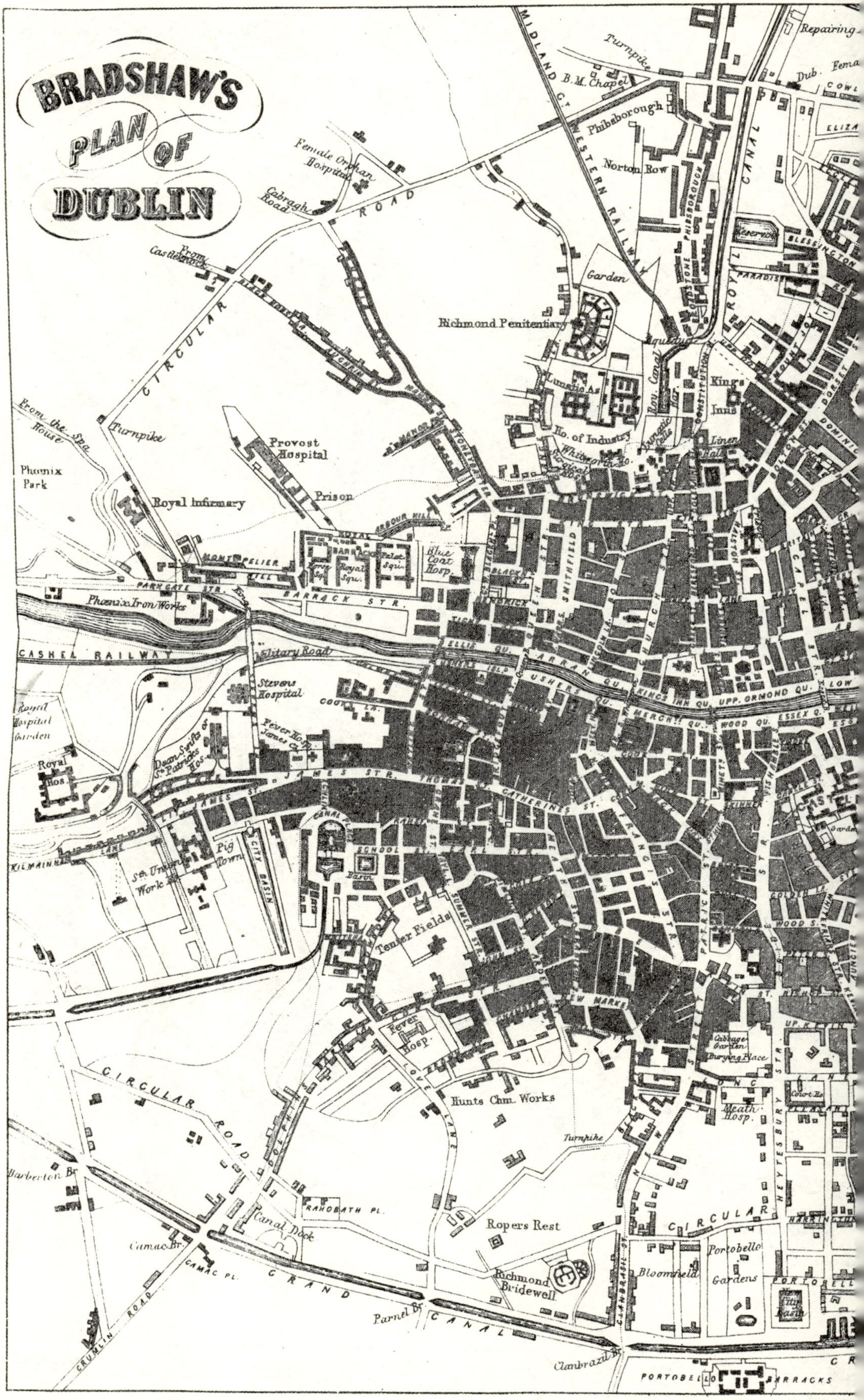
BRADSHAW'S
PLAN OF
DUBLIN
Phibsborough
Norton Row
Female Orphan Hospital
Richmond Penitentiary
Garden
Lunatic As.
Ho. of Industry
Kings Inns
Provost Hospital
Prison
Royal Infirmary
Phœnix Park
Turnpike
Phœnix Iron Works
Military Road
CASHEL RAILWAY
Stevens Hospital
Royal Hospital Garden
Royal Hos.
Tenter Fields
Fever Hosp.
Hunts Chm. Works
Ropers Rest
Richmond Bridewell
Bloomfield
Portobello Gardens
Canal Dock
Meath Hosp.
CIRCULAR ROAD
GRAND CANAL
PORTOBELLO BARRACKS
Camac Br.
Harberton Br.
Parnel Br.
Clanbrazil Br.
CRUMLIN ROAD
JAMES STR.
THOMAS ST.
USHERS QU.
ARRAN QU.
UPP. ORMOND QU.
WOOD QU.
ESSEX Q.
SMITHFIELD
BARRACK STR.
PATRICK STR.
FRANCIS STR.
Pig Town
CITY BASIN
RAHOBATH PL.
CAMAC PL.
MIDLAND GT. WESTERN RAILWAY
ROYAL CANAL
B.M. Chapel
Cabbage Garden Burying Place

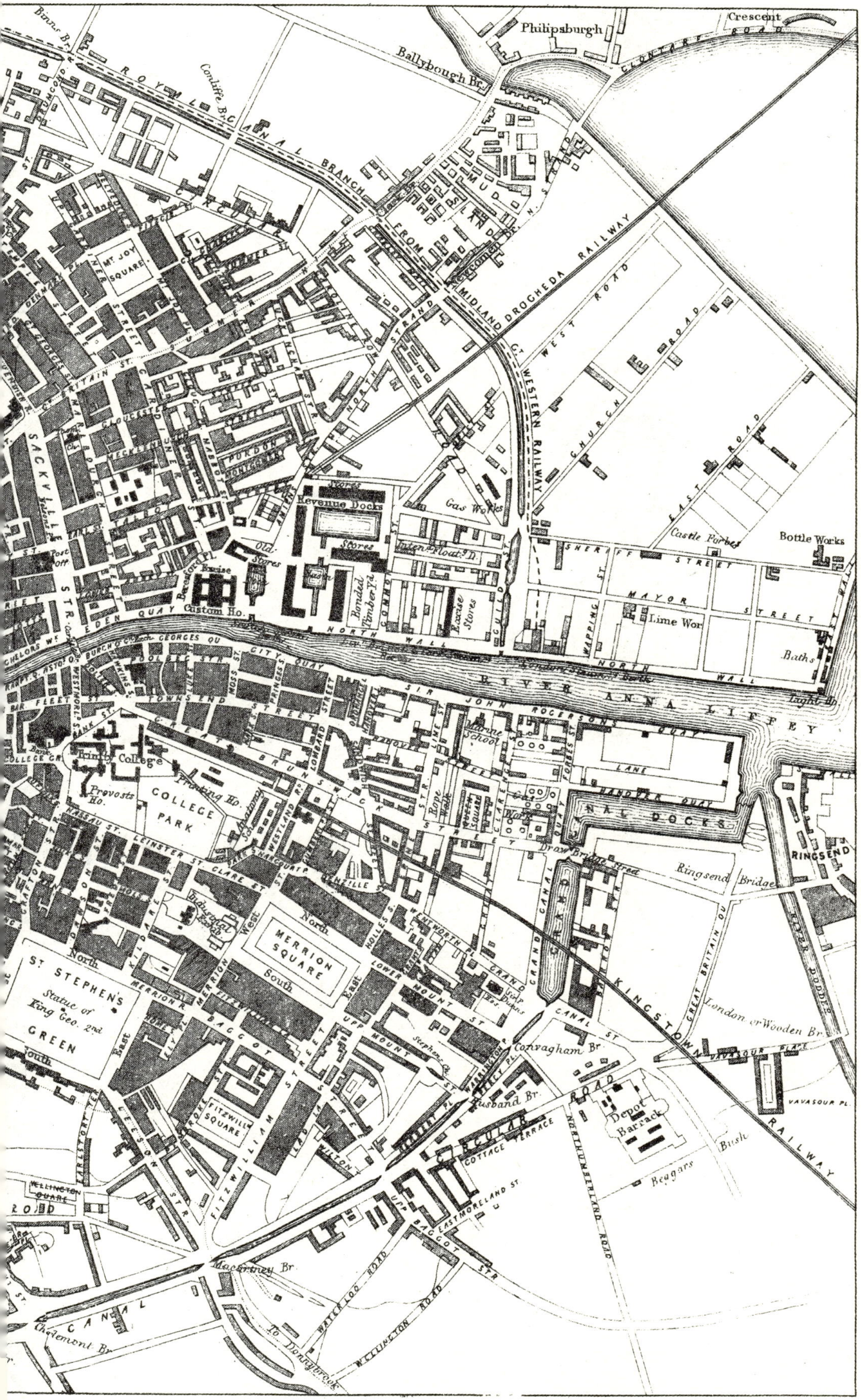
Philipsburgh
Crescent
Clontarf Road
Ballybough Br.
Royal Canal Branch
Circular
Mud Island
Mt. Joy Square
Midland Drogheda Railway
Gt. Western Railway
West Road
Church Road
East Road
North Strand
Sackville Street
Revenue Docks
Stores
Gas Works
Custom Ho.
Excise
Old Stores
Bonded Timber Yd.
Excise Stores
Castle Forbes
Bottle Works
Sheriff Street
Mayor Street
Lime Wor
Baths
Wapping St.
Eden Quay
North Wall
River Anna Liffey
Light Ho.
Sir John Rogerson's Quay
City Quay
Townsend St.
Great Brunswick Street
Trinity College
Provosts Ho.
College Park
Printing Ho.
Marine School
Rope Walk
Hanover Quay
Grand Canal Docks
Draw Bridge Street
Ringsend
Ringsend Bridge
Great Britain Qu.
Grand Canal
Nassau St.
Leinster St.
Clare St.
Merrion Square
North
South
East
West
St. Stephen's Green
Statue of King Geo. 2nd
Fitzwilliam Square
Fitzwilliam Street
Baggot St.
Upp. Mount St.
Lower Mount St.
Kingstown Railway
London or Wooden Br.
Vavasour Place
Vavasour Pl.
Conyagham Br.
Husband Br.
Depot Barrack
Cottage Terrace
Circular Road
Northumberland Road
Beggars Bush
Eastmoreland St.
Wellington Road
Waterloo Road
Macartney Br.
To Donnybrook
Canal
Charlemont Br.
Wellington Square

OX
COLLEGES, HALLS, and CHURCHES.
A Jesus Coll
B Exeter Coll
C Lincoln Coll
D University Coll
E All Souls Coll
F New Coll
G Queens Coll
H Brazennose Coll
I Oriel Coll
J Pembroke Coll
K Corpus Coll
L St Marys Hall
M Magdalen Hall
N Edmund Hall
O Alban Hall
P New Inn Hall
Q St Magdalens Ch
R St Peters Ch in the Baylie
S Merton Ch
T St Aldates Ch
New University Printing Office
Observatory
Infirmary
St Giles Ch
Bicester Road
House of Industry
Alfred St
St Giles's Street
Worcester Coll
Beaumont Street
High Bridge
Cheltenham Road
New Road
George Lane
Broad
St Thomas Ch
County Jail
Queen St
Corn Market
Market
Christ Church Coll
Gas Works
River Isis
Railway Station
Folly Bridge
Chr

RD
50
PUBLIC BUILDINGS, HOTELS STREETS &c
1 Post Office
2 Town Hall
3 Police Office
4 Star Hotel
5 Martys Memormail
6 Taylor Building
7 Mitre Hotel
8 Oriel Str.t
9 Angel Hotel
10 Kings Arms Hotel
11 Theatre
12 Museum
13 The Schools
THE PARKS
Part of the Old Fortifications
CHARWELL RIVER
Way to the Parks
Wadham Coll
Holywell Ch
New Coll
Holywell Mill
St Peters Ch
STREET
Magdalen Coll
Water Walk
Water Walk
KING STREET
BRIDGE STREET
Merton Coll
ROSE LANE
Physic Garden
The City Wall
Magdalen Br.
Baths
Walks
LONDON ROAD
Roman Catholic Chapel
CHARWELL RIVER
Cowley Road
Henley Road

ALLONBY
MARYPORT
WORKINGTON
WHITEHAVEN
St. BEES
EGREMONT
GOSFORTH
COCKERMOUTH
PLUMBLAND
GILCRUX
BRIDE KIRK
BOLTON
IREBY
TORPENHOW
HESKET
DEAN
DISSINGTON
ARLECDON
LORTON
KESWICK
Derwent
THRELKELD
MATTERDALE
NEWCHURCH
DACRE
BARTON
ASKHAM
BAMPTON
SHAP
GREYSTOKE
GREYSTOKE PARK
PENRITH
KIRK OSWALD
ORTON
AMBLESIDE
LANGDALE
GRASMERE
R. Eden
R. Petteril
R. Eamont
R. Greta
Sebergham
Caldbeck
Clea Hall
Salkeld Gate
Lazonby
Addingham
Longwathby
Ousby
Brougham Hall
Clifton
Morland
Reagill
Greyhound
Crosby
Ravensworth
Shap Wall
Skelton
Blencow
Lamonby
Sowerby
Newbiggin
Penruddoch
Dalemain
Mungrisdale
Berrier
Springfield
Helton
Butterswich
Thornthwaite Hall
Greenholm
Halfway House
Kirkstone
Hartsop
Deepdale
Fairfield
Helvellyn
High Pike
Carrock
Mosdale
Dash
Braefell
Sandal
Uldale
Cock Bridge
Brayton
Aspatria
Melay
Canonby
Ellenborough
Flimby
Seaton
Camerton
Harrington
Parton
Moresby
Cleator
Eskdale
Wasdale
Calder Bridge
Ponsonby
Beckermont
Bassenthwaite
Embleton
Wythop
Setmurthey
Whinlatter
Braithwaite
Portinscale
Grisedale Pike
Whiteside
Grassmoor
Causey Pike
Lamplugh
Cross
Kirkland
Croasdale
Floutern
Taylor Gill
Red Pike
Gatesgarth
Scawfell
Burnmoor
Hardknot
Wrynose
Bowfell
Langdale
Rydal
Low Wood Inn
Brothers Water
Raise Gap
Swindale
Marsdale
Wet Sleddale
Shap Fells
Branstree
COPELAND

BRADSHAW'S
TOURIST'S MAP
OF THE
LAKE DISTRICTS.
Turnpike Roads are marked thus.
Cross Roads.
Mountain Roads.
Foot Roads.
Waterfalls.
Chapels.
SCALE OF MILES
1 2 3 4 5 6 7 8 9 10
BAY OF
CARTMELL
WHARFS.
MORECAMBE
ISLE OF WALNEY
Walney Island
KENDAL
LANCASTER
ULVERSTON
DALTON
CARTMEL
BOOTLE
BROUGHTON
BLAWITH
LOWICK
KIRKBY IRELETH
FINSTHWAITE
CROSTHWAITE
MILNTHORPE
BURTON
ARNSIDE
HORNBY
KIRKBY LONSDALE
OLD HUTTON
TORVER
Broad Oak
Stoneshead
Whitbeck
Whicham
Millom
Haverigg
Pennington
Conishead
Bardsea
Stainton
Aldingham
Leece
Barrow
Grange
Newton
Witherslack
Levens
Sizergh
Heversham
Warton
Yealand
Whittington
Melling
Kellet
Bolton
Slyne
Halton
Claughton
Caton Green
Poulton
Heysham
FLEETWOOD
Docker
Braithwaite
Oxen Holme
Natland
Preston
Richard
Hollins
Casterton
Gatehouse
Grizedale
Satterthwaite
Graythwaite
Rusland
Dale Park
Penny Br.
Greenod Beck
Broughton
Woodland
Oxen House
Beckside
Winster
Crook
Plumgartas
Lyth
Underbarrow
Meduh
Dalham Tower
Beetham
Winder
Flookborough
Holker
Frith
Heaves Lodge
Sedgwick
Marsh Grange
Ireleth
Lindal
Urswick
Gawthwaite
Cark

Applecross
Lochcarron
Glenshiel
Kintail
Scalpa
Rum
Ardnamurchan
Coll
Isle of Mull
Ross of Mull
Colonsay
Oronsay
Jura
Islay
Port Askaig
Bowmore
Kildalton
Kilchoman
Mull of Oe
Kilmore
Kilninver
Kilmelford
Craignish
Scarba
Lochgilphead
Inverary
Strachur
Kilfinan
Helensburgh
Greenock
Port Glasgow
Dunoon
Paisley
Lochwinnoch
Dalry
Kilmarnock
Isle of Arran
Kilbrannan Sound
Kintyre
Gigha Isle
Loch Leven
Fort William
Caledonian Canal
Bonaw
Appin
Aberarder
Stewarton
Galston
Dunlop

BRADSHAW'S
TOURIST'S MAP
OF THE
LAKE DISTRICTS
OF
SCOTLAND.
ABERDEEN
FIRTH OF TAY
FIRTH OF FORTH
PERTH
St. Andrews
Montrose
Brechin
Dunbar
St. Abbs Head
Eyemouth
Berwick
Kelso
Coldstream
Peebles
Selkirk
Stonehaven
Inverbervie
Haddington
Dalkeith
Falkirk
Stirling
Dunblane
Crieff
Aberfeldy
Kinross
Kirkcaldy
Lanark
Carnwath
Biggar
Lauder
Duns
Greenlaw
Kirkcaldy
Aberdour
Methven
Comrie
Coupar Angus
Kirriemuir
Forfar
Kincardine
Arbroath
North Berwick
Ellon
Old Meldrum
Inverurie
Banchory
Ballater
Braemar
Clova
Glenshee
Blair Atholl
Dunkeld
Blairgowrie
Inverness

Hockley Abbey
Birmingham Heath
Grosvenor Place
Church
from Wolverhampton
from Dudley
Wolverhampton and Birmingham Canal
Stour Valley Railway
Turnpike Road
Winstone Lane
Soho Hill
Summer Hill Terrace
Parade
Crescent
Cambridge Str
Broad Str
Sheepcote Lane
Crown Street
Small Gardens
Monument Lane
Reservoir Road
Russel Row
Grosvenor Street
Glass Works
Islington
Gardens
Stone Wharf
Coal Wharf
Timber Wharf
Brick Kilns
Birmingham Coal Company Wharf
Wharf Street
from Halesowen
Halesowen Rd
Hagley Row
Long Lane
Harborne Road
Calthorpe St.
Bath Row
Holloway Head
New Road to Smi
Worcester Canal
Wheeleys Lane
Botanic Gardens
St. Georges Chapel
Deaf and Dumb Asylum
Church Road
Blind Asylum
Wellington Road

BRADSHAW'S
PLAN
OF
BIRMINGHAM
Asylum
SUMMER LANE
WALMER LANE
JOHN STREET
NEW JOHN
TOWER
NEW SUMMER STREET
Birmingham and Fazeley Canal
RICHARD ST
LISTER ST
ASTBURY ROW
GREAT BROOKE STREET
Bloomsbury Lane
Vauxhall Gardens
VAUXHALL
GRAND JUNCTION RAILWAY
LONDON & BIRMINGHAM RAILWAY
BIRM & DERBY RAILY
Goods Depôt
DUDDESTON ST
Curzon St
COLESHILL ST
Prospect Row
Belmont Row
Aston St
Steelhouse
GREAT WESTERN
SNOW HILL
COLMORE ROW
Masshouse La
FAZELEY ST
BORDESLEY
Coal Wharfs
MOOR STREET
NEW STREET
NORTH WESTERN CENTRAL
New Market Place
Edgbaston St
Jamaica Row
Smithfield Market
DIGBETH
BRADFORD STREET
HIGH STREET
Small Gardens
Dartmouth Street
Burial Ground
Trinity Street
To Coventry and London
BROMSGROVE
Sherlock Street
TURNPIKE ROAD
Warwick Canal
Great Western

BRADSHAWS
PLAN OF
GLASGOW
ROYAL BOTANIC GARDEN
NORTH PARK
GREAT WESTERN ROAD
Hillhead
GREAT GEORGE STR.
GIBSON STR.
Saughfield
Gilmourhill
WOODLANDS
KELVIN GROVE
Quarry
WOODSIDE STREET
Claylap Mills
Bunnhouse Mills
Kelvinbank
Overnewton
VILLAGE OF PARTICK
Road from Dumbarton
ROAD FROM DUMBARTON TO GLASGOW
SAUCHIEHALL ROAD
SAUCHIEHALL STREET
WEST BATH STREET
KENT ROAD
ROYAL CRESCENT
FINNIESTON
ANDERSTON
MAIN STREET
ARGYLE
Yorkhill
Thornhill
THE RIVER CLYDE
Salters Croft
Haughhead
Bankton
Mavis Bank
Greenbank
Greenlaw
Park-slm
RAILWAY DEPOT
ROAD TO RENFREW AND GREENOCK
PLANTATION HOUSE
ROAD TO PAISLEY
APSLEY PLACE
STAFFORD ST
BROOKE ST
CARICHANK
TRACK OF THE CALEDONIAN AND DUMBARTONSHIRE
GLASGOW GREENOCK

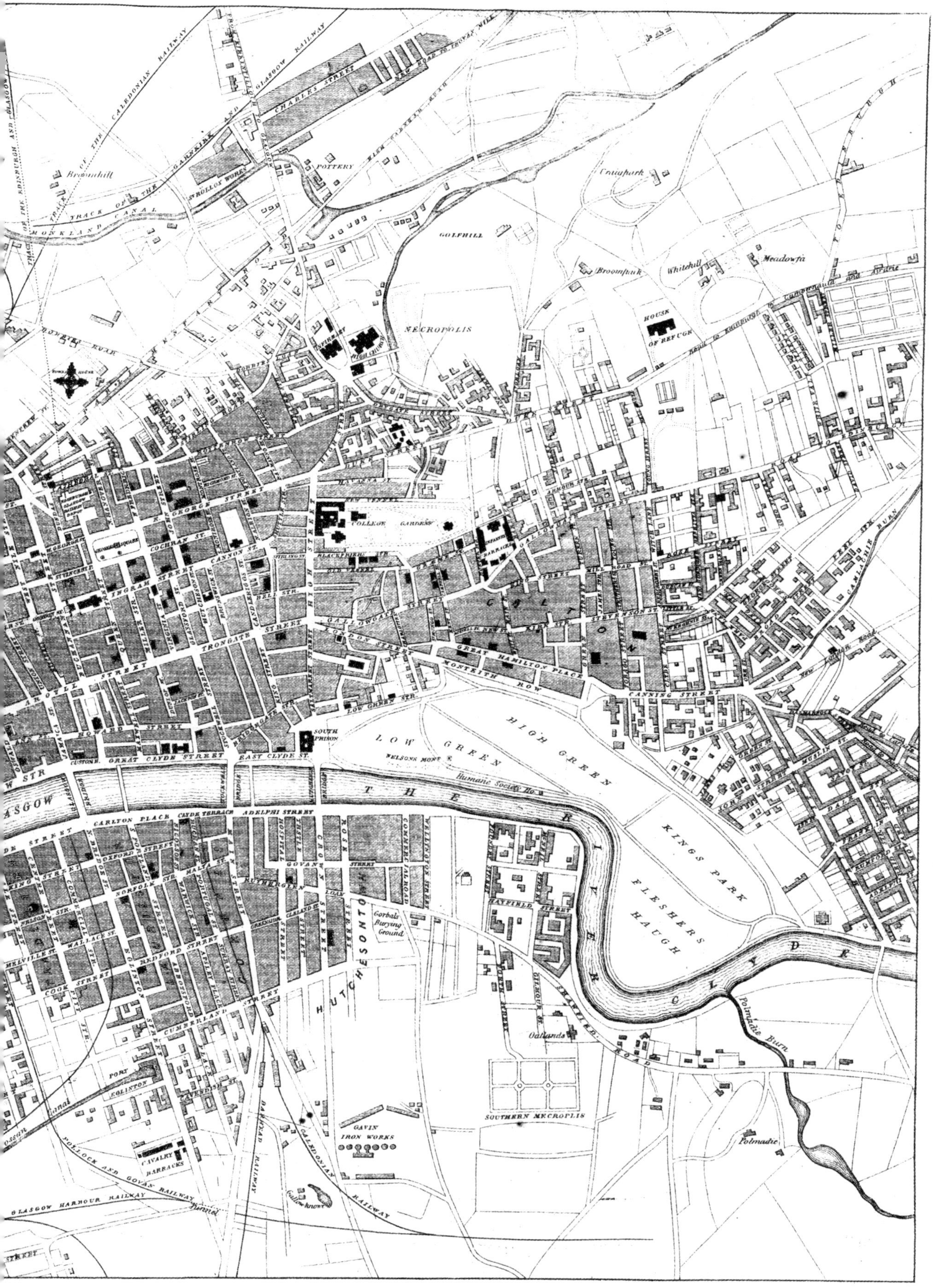

MONKLAND CANAL
TRACK OF THE GARNKIRK AND GLASGOW RAILWAY
Broomhill
ST ROLLOX WORKS
CHARLES STREET
POTTERY
GOLFHILL
Craigpark
Broompark
Whitehill
Meadowpark
NECROPOLIS
HOUSE OF REFUGE
HIGH CHURCH
GEORGE STREET
COCHRAN ST.
CANNON ST.
INGRAM STREET
HIGH STREET
COLLEGE GARDENS
GALLOWGATE
CALTON
TRONGATE STREET
ARGYLE STREET
LONDON STREET
GREAT HAMILTON PLACE
MONTEITH ROW
CANNING STREET
HOWARD STREET
SOUTH PRISON
GREAT CLYDE STREET
EAST CLYDE ST.
LOW GREEN
HIGH GREEN
NELSONS MONT
Humane Society Ho
THE RIVER CLYDE
KINGS PARK
FLESHERS HAUGH
CARLTON PLACE
CLYDE TERRACE
ADELPHI STREET
OXFORD STREET
NORFOLK STR.
RUTHERGLEN LOAN
HAYFIELD STREET
Gorbals Burying Ground
HUTCHESONTOWN
CUMBERLAND STREET
Oatlands
Polmadie Burn
SOUTHERN MECROPLIS
GAVIN IRON WORKS
CAVALRY BARRACKS
POLLOCK AND GOVAN RAILWAY
CALEDONIAN RAILWAY
Gallow knowe
GLASGOW HARBOUR RAILWAY
Polmadie

BOUNDARY OF THE BOROUGH OF LIVERP
MUNICIPAL AND PARLIAMENTARY
TOWNSHIP OF KIRKDALE
LEEDS AND LIVERPOOL CANAL
LANCASHIRE and YORKSHIRE
SOUTHPORT and BOOTLE
CROSBY ROAD
VICTORIA ROAD
VAUXHALL ROAD
NEW SCOTLAND ROAD
GREAT HOWARD
WATERLOO ROAD
BATH STREET
PRINCES DOCK
HUSKISSON DOCK
FORT
GRAVING DOCKS
CHURCH STREET
PLANTATION
SCALE
1/4
1/2
3/4
1
Mile
R I V E R
New Brighton Ferry
Egremont Ferry
Seacombe Ferry
EGREMONT
POULTON CUM SEACOMBE
NEW BRIGHTON
LISCARD
Magazines
Halfway Ho
Zigzag Hall
Old Manor Ho
Liscard Hall Farm
Sea View Cottage
St Albans Catholic Ch
St Johns Ch
Moor Hall
Hotel
Copper Mills
Foundry
Varnish Manufactory
STONE
PROPO

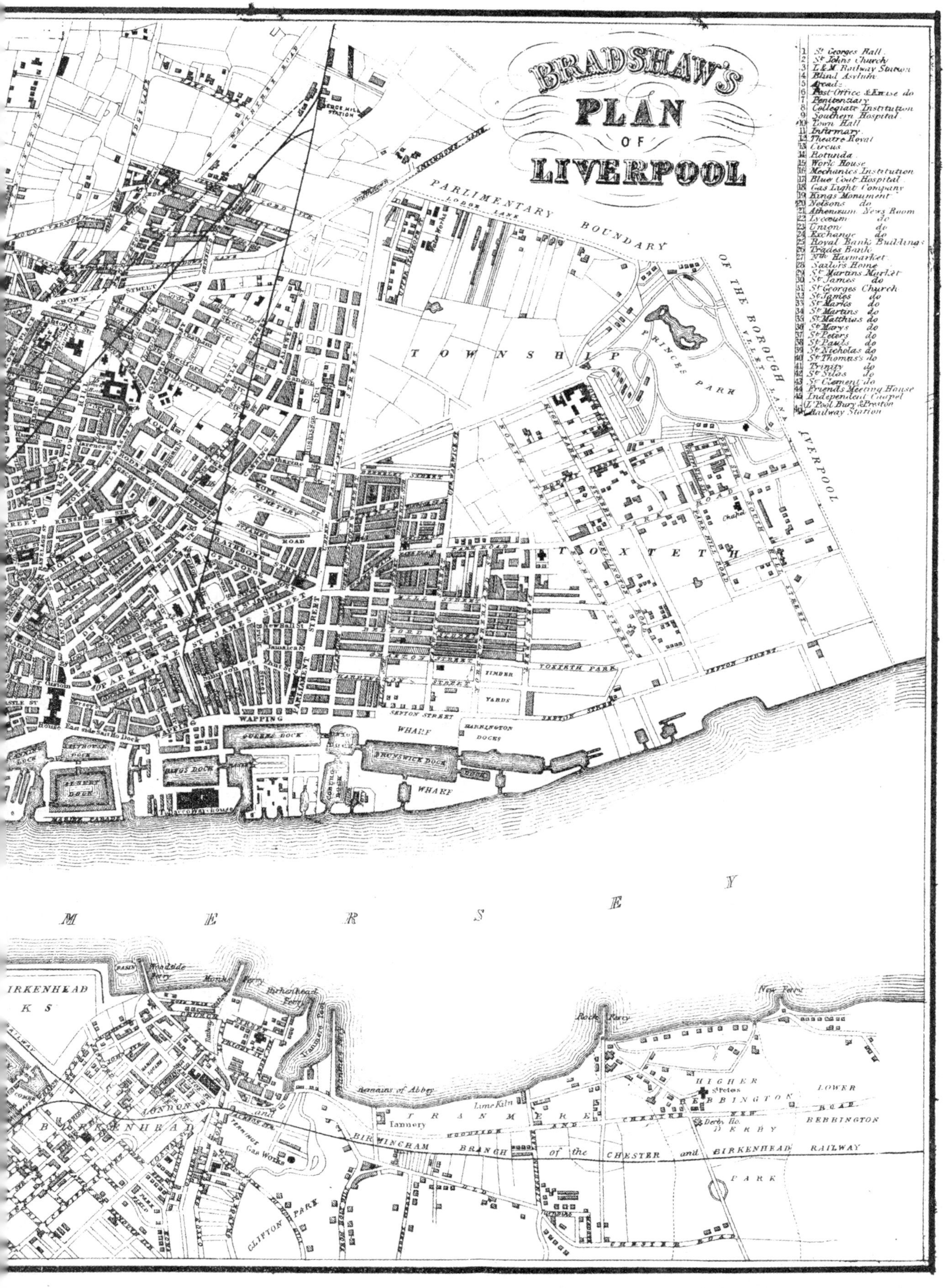
BRADSHAW'S
PLAN
OF
LIVERPOOL
1 St Georges Hall
2 St Johns Church
3 L&M Railway Station
4 Blind Asylum
5 Arcade
6 Post Office & Excise do
7 Penitentiary
8 Collegiate Institution
9 Southern Hospital
10 Town Hall
11 Infirmary
12 Theatre Royal
13 Circus
14 Rotunda
15 Work House
16 Mechanics Institution
17 Blue Coat Hospital
18 Gas Light Company
19 Kings Monument
20 Nelsons do
21 Athenæum News Room
22 Lyceum do
23 Union do
24 Exchange do
25 Royal Bank Buildings
26 Trades Bank
27 Nth Haymarket
28 Sailors Home
29 St Martins Market
30 St James do
31 St Georges Church
32 St James do
33 St Marks do
34 St Martins do
35 St Matthias do
36 St Marys do
37 St Peters do
38 St Pauls do
39 St Nicholas do
40 St Thomas's do
41 Trinity do
42 St Silas do
43 St Clement do
44 Friends Meeting House
45 Independent Chapel
46 L'Pool Bury & Preston Railway Station
PARLIMENTARY BOUNDARY OF THE BOROUGH OF LIVERPOOL
LODGE LANE
TOWNSHIP
PRINCES PARK
TOXTETH
TOXTETH PARK
CROWN STREET
PARK LANE
ST JAMES STREET
WAPPING
WHARF
HARRINGTON DOCKS
BRUNSWICK DOCK
KINGS DOCK
QUEENS DOCK
TIMBER YARDS
SEFTON STREET
MARINE PARADE
M E R S E Y
Woodside Ferry
Monks Ferry
Birkenhead Ferry
Rock Ferry
New Ferry
Remains of Abbey
Lime Kiln
Tannery
Gas Works
T R A N M E R E
HIGHER BEBBINGTON
LOWER BEBBINGTON
Derby Ho.
DERBY PARK
BIRKENHEAD
CLIFTON PARK
CHESTER ROAD
BIRMINGHAM BRANCH of the CHESTER and BIRKENHEAD RAILWAY

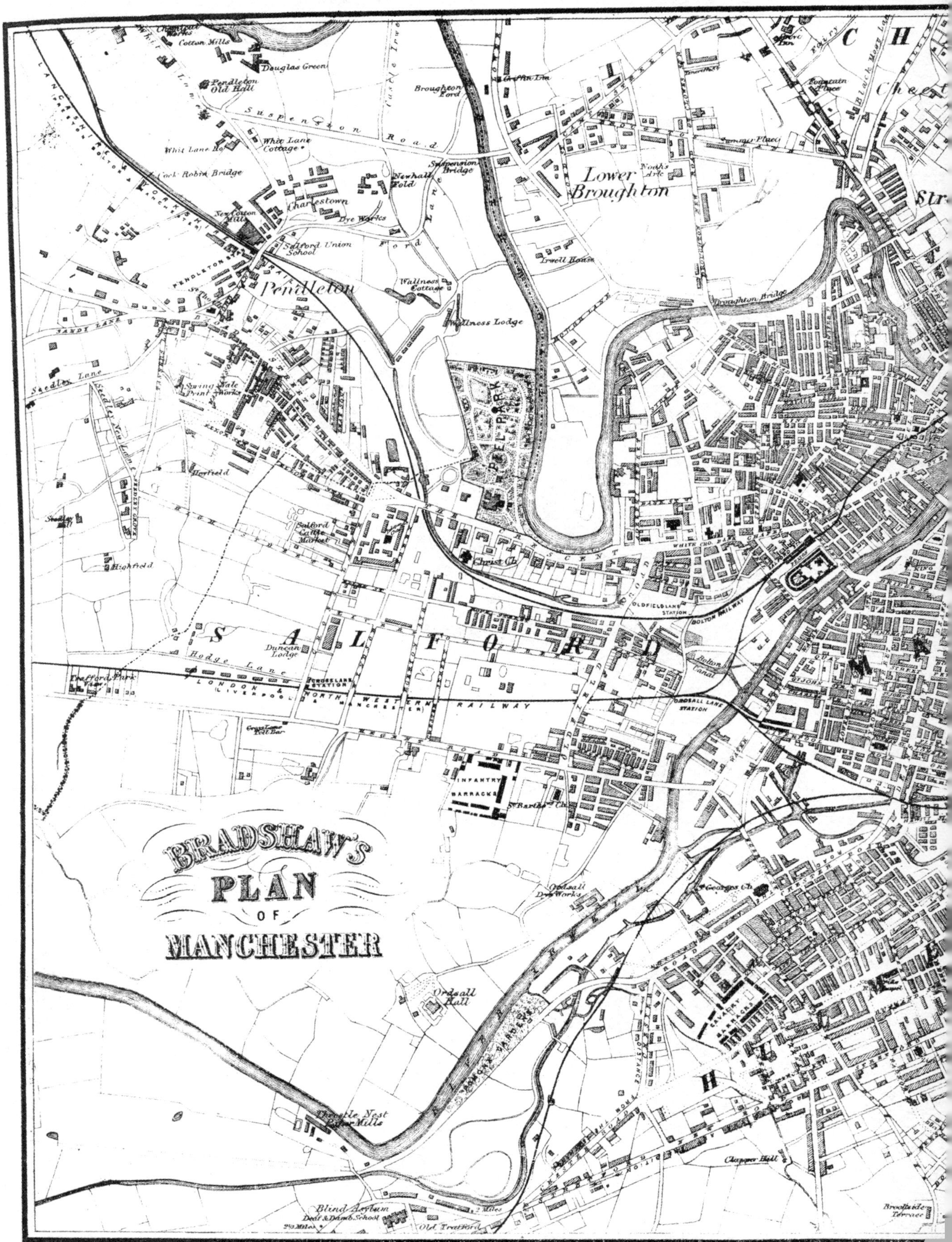
BRADSHAW'S
PLAN
OF
MANCHESTER
SALFORD
Pendleton
Lower Broughton
Pendleton Old Hall
Douglas Green
Cotton Mills
Suspension Road
Broughton Ford
Griffin Inn
Whit Lane Cottage
Whit Lane Bo.
Cock Robin Bridge
Charlestown
Newhall Fold
Suspension Bridge
Dye Works
Salford Union School
Irwell House
Wallness Cottage
Wallness Lodge
Broughton Bridge
Sandy Lane
Seedley Lane
Spring Vale Print Works
PEEL PARK
Christ Ch.
CRESCENT
Salford Cattle Market
Highfield
Duncan Lodge
Hodge Lane
Trafford Park
OLDFIELD LANE STATION
BOLTON RAILWAY
Bolton Canal
ORDSALL LANE STATION
LONDON & NORTH WESTERN RAILWAY
LIVERPOOL & MANCHESTER
INFANTRY BARRACKS
St. Bartho. Ch.
Ordsall Dye Works
Ordsall Hall
POMONA GARDENS
CAVALRY BARRACKS
St. Georges Ch.
Throstle Nest Paper Mills
Blind Asylum
Deaf & Dumb School
Old Trafford
2 Miles
Clopper Hall
Brookside Terrace
Fountain Place
Strangeways
Cheetham

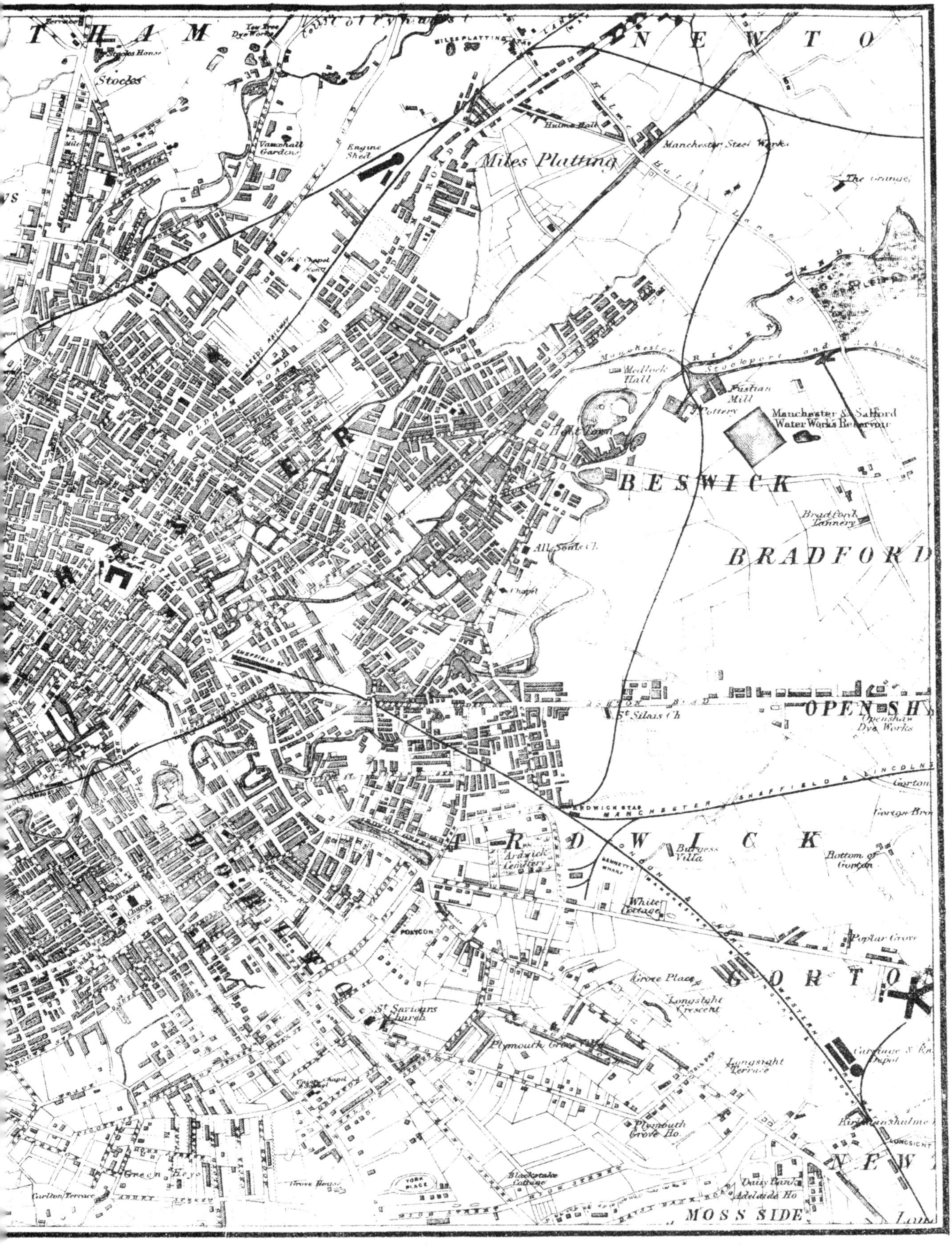

Stockes
Vauxhall Gardens
Engine Shed
Miles Platting
Hulme Hall
Manchester Steel Works
The Grange
Mellock Hall
Fustian Mill
Pottery
Manchester & Salford Water Works Reservoir
BESWICK
Bradford Tannery
BRADFORD
All Souls Ch
Chapel
SHEFFIELD ST.
St Silas Ch
Openshaw Dye Works
Gorton
Bottom of Gorton
Burgess Villa
Ardwick Cemetery
White Cottage
Poplar Grove
POLYGON
Grove Place
Longsight Crescent
St Saviours Church
Longsight Terrace
Plymouth Grove Ho
Kirkmanshulme
Green Heys
Carlton Terrace
Grove House
York Place
Blackstake Cottage
Daisy Bank
Adelaide Ho
MOSS SIDE

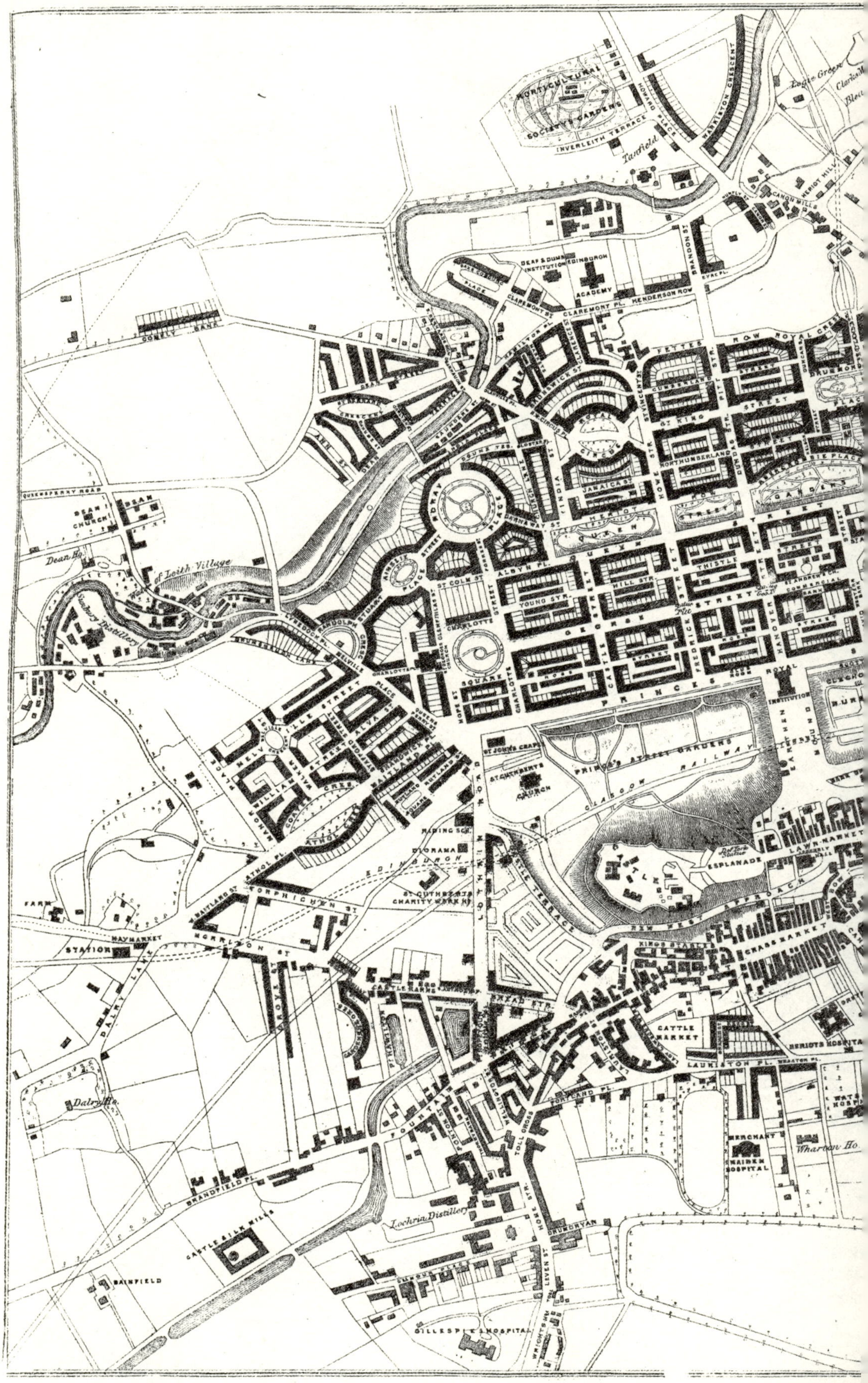

HORTICULTURAL SOCIETY'S GARDENS
INVERLEITH TERRACE
Tanfield
WARRISTON CRESCENT
CANON MILLS
Logie Green
DEAF & DUMB INSTITUTION
EDINBURGH ACADEMY
HENDERSON ROW
CLAREMONT PL.
BRANDON ST
COMELY BANK
QUEENSFERRY ROAD
DEAN CHURCH
Dean Ho.
Water of Leith Village
Distillery
FETTES ROW
ROYAL CRESCENT
ROYAL CIRCUS
GT KING STREET
NORTHUMBERLAND
JAMAICA ST
HERIOT ROW
QUEEN STREET
MORAY PLACE
AINSLIE PLACE
ALBYN PL.
ST COLM ST
YOUNG STR.
HILL STR.
THISTLE
GEORGE STREET
CHARLOTTE SQUARE
FREDERICK STREET
HANOVER
PRINCES STREET
ROYAL INSTITUTION
MELVILLE STREET
ST JOHN'S CHAPEL
ST CUTHBERT'S CHURCH
PRINCE'S STREET GARDENS
GLASGOW RAILWAY
RIDING SCH.
DIORAMA
EDINBURGH
ST CUTHBERT'S CHARITY WORK HO.
CASTLE
ESPLANADE
LAWN-MARKET
KINGS STABLES
GRASS MARKET
CASTLE TERRACE
LOTHIAN ROAD
TORPHICHEN ST
ATHOL PL.
MAITLAND ST
MORRISON ST
HAYMARKET STATION
DALRY LANE
Dalry Ho.
FARM
CATTLE MARKET
HERIOTS HOSPITAL
LAURISTON PL.
PORTLAND PL.
TOLL CROSS
MERCHANT MAIDEN HOSPITAL
Wharton Ho.
BRANDFIELD PL.
Lochrin Distillery
CASTLE SILK MILLS
BAINFIELD
GILLESPIE'S HOSPITAL
HOME STR.
LEVEN ST
DRUMDRYAN

Bradshaw & Blacklock Engravers Manchester & Lon[illegible]

BRADSHAW'S PLAN OF HULL.
Zoological Gardens
Spring Bank
Lunatic Asylum
Burlington Br.
Selby D°
Hull and Selby Railway
Fair Field
St. Stephens Church
Anlaby Road
Passengers Station
Ocean Place
Carr Lane
Osborne Street
Botanic Garden
Walker Street
Hessle Road
Lister Street
English Street
Bellevue Ter.
Humber Bank
Railway
River
Cogan Street
Kingston Street
Wellington Street
Railway Dock
Humber Dock
Junction Dock
H. Trinity Burial Ground
Castle St
Myton Pl.
Nile St.
William Str.
Waverley St.
Edward Pl.
Bath Pl.
Wellington Lane
Wellington Pl.
Beverley Road
Kingston Ter.
Kingston College
Cottingham Drain
Providence Row
Liddell Street
Spring Row
Marlbro Ter.
Cottingham Pl.
Pryme Street
Francis
Prospect Street
Portland Pl.
Wright Street
Baker Street
Albion Street
Fanning St.
North St.
Colliers St.
West Street
South St.
Paragon St.
Waterworks St.
Storey St.
Short St.
Caroline St.
Jackson St.
Humber St.
Adelaide St.
Thornton St.
Porter St.
Great Thornton St.
St. James St.
Manor St.
Castle Row
Walker St.
Waterhouse Lane
Railway

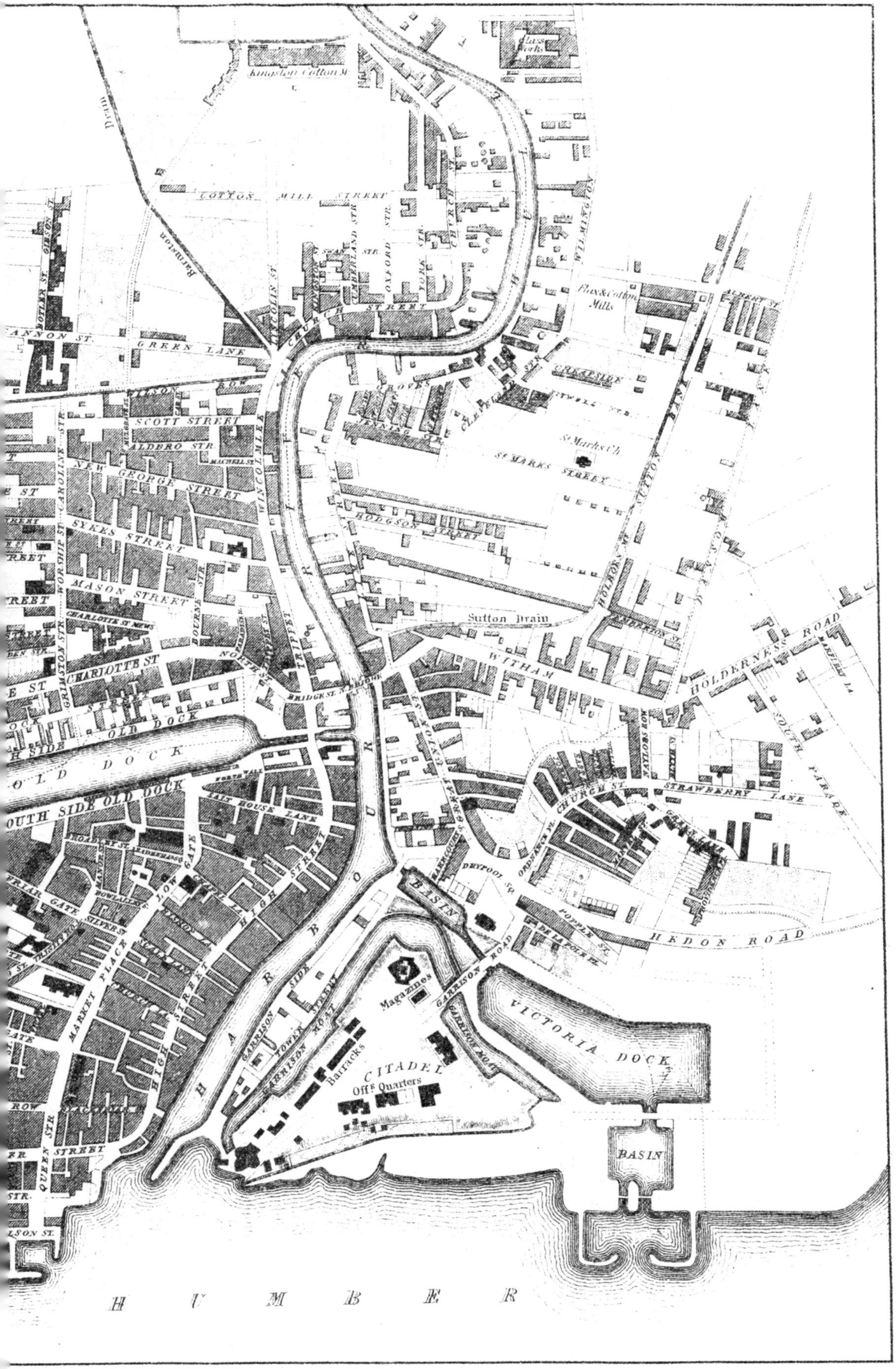

Glass Works
Kingston Cotton M.
Drain
COTTON MILL STREET
Barmston
WILMINGTON
Flax & Cotton Mills
ALBERT ST
CHURCH STREET
GREEN LANE
CHEAPSIDE
St Marks Ch.
ST MARKS STREET
HODGSON STREET
SCOTT STREET
ALDBRO STR.
NEW GEORGE STREET
SYKES STREET
MASON STREET
WINCOLMLEE
TRIPPET
CHARLOTTE ST
WORSHIP ST
CAROLINE STR.
GRIMSTON STR.
Sutton Drain
HOLDERNESS ROAD
WITHAM
SOUTH PARADE
OLD DOCK
SOUTH SIDE OLD DOCK
SALT HOUSE LANE
HIGH STREET
LOW GATE
MARKET PLACE
QUEEN STR.
STRAWBERRY LANE
CHURCH ST.
DRYPOOL SQ.
BASIN
HEDON ROAD
GARRISON ROAD
Magazines
VICTORIA DOCK
Barracks
CITADEL
Offs Quarters
HARBOUR
BASIN
HUMBER

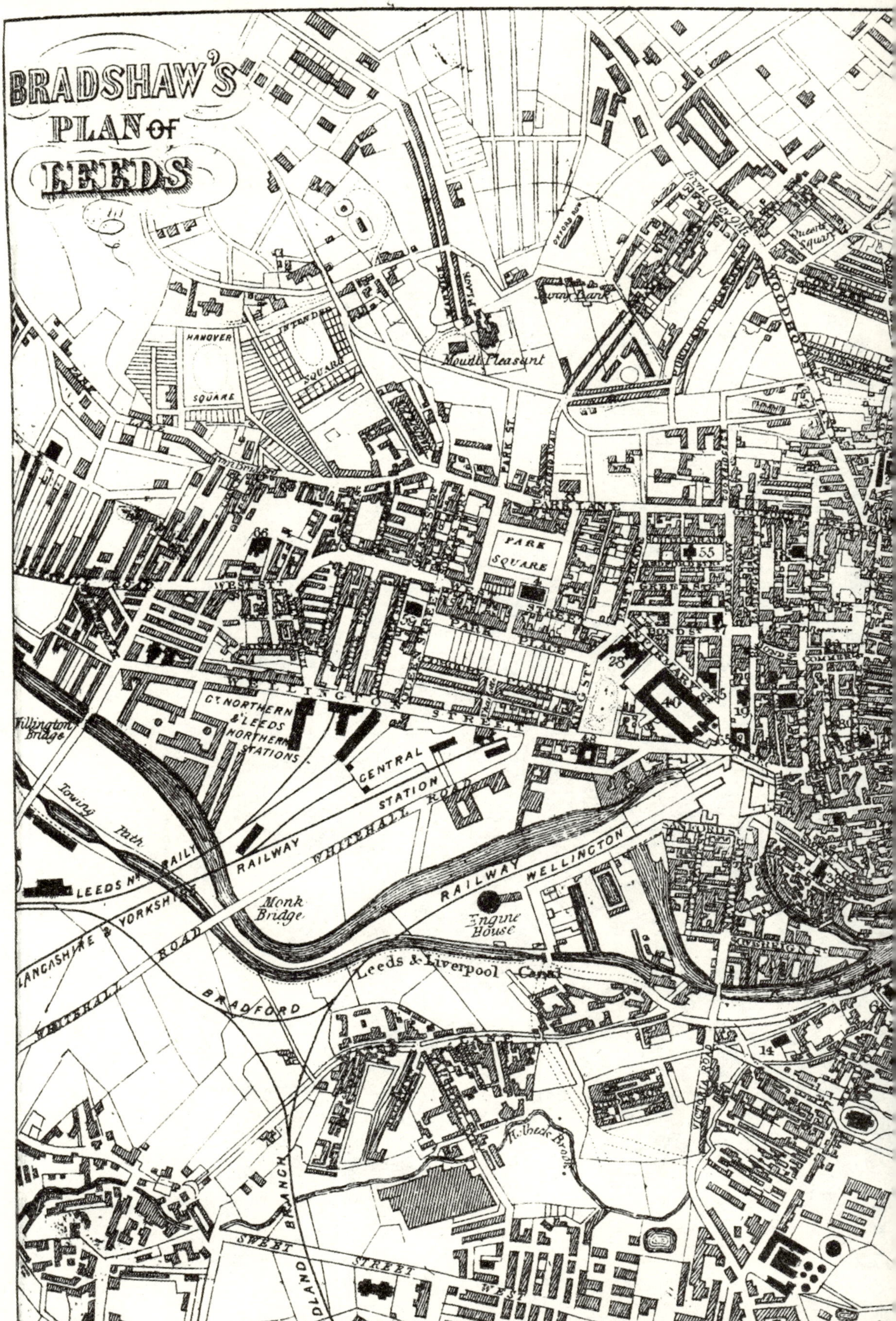
BRADSHAW'S
PLAN OF
LEEDS
HANOVER SQUARE
Mount Pleasant
PARK ST.
PARK SQUARE
PARK PLACE
WEST ST.
WELLINGTON STREET
GT. NORTHERN & LEEDS NORTHERN STATIONS
CENTRAL STATION
WHITEHALL ROAD
Wellington Bridge
Towing Path
LEEDS NR. RAILY
LANCASHIRE & YORKSHIRE RAILWAY
WELLINGTON RAILWAY
Monk Bridge
Engine House
Leeds & Liverpool Canal
BRADFORD
Holbeck Brook
BRANCH
MIDLAND
SWEET STREET WEST
Queen Square
WOODHOUSE
VICTORIA RD

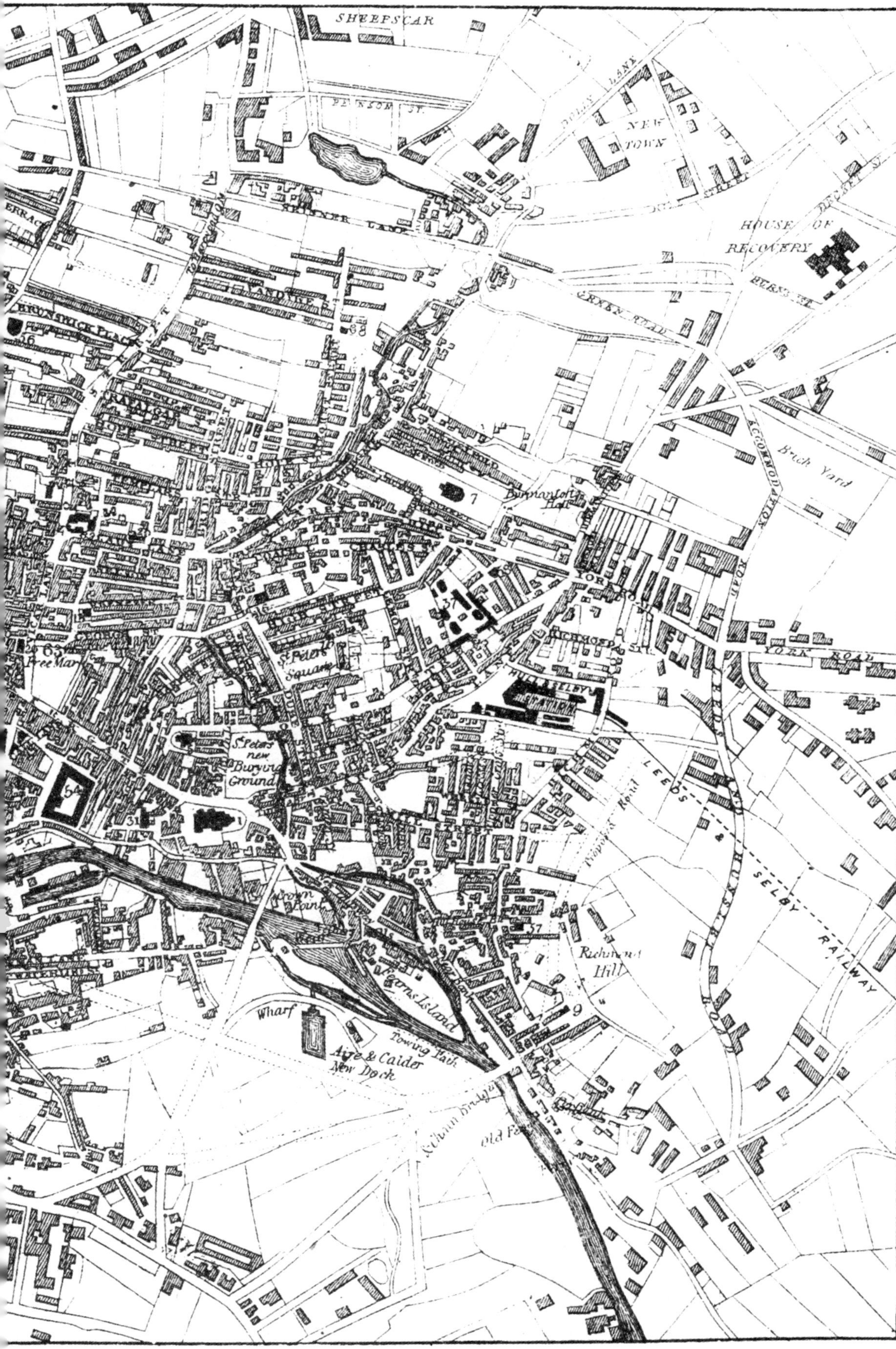

SHEEPSCAR
NEW TOWN
HOUSE OF RECOVERY
BRUNSWICK PLACE
TRAFALGAR
Birch Yard
Burmantofts Hall
YORK ROAD
St. Peter's Square
St. Peter's new Burying Ground
Crown Point
Wharf
Aire & Calder New Dock
Towing Path
Richmond Hill
LEEDS & SELBY RAILWAY

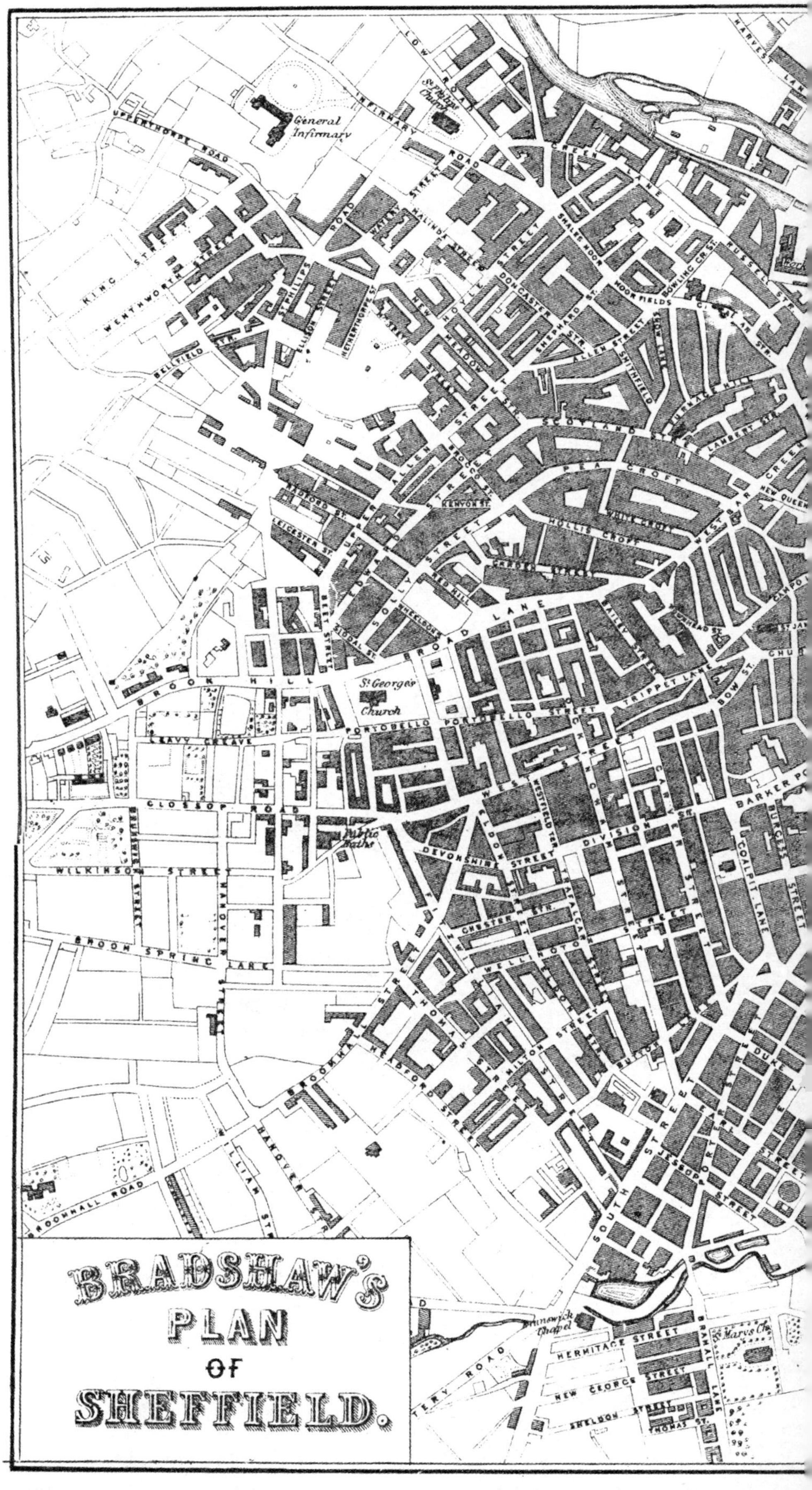
BRADSHAW'S
PLAN
OF
SHEFFIELD.
General Infirmary
St. Philips Church
St. George's Church
Public Baths
Brunswick Chapel
St. Mary's Ch.
INFIRMARY ROAD
UPPERTHORPE ROAD
KING STREET
WENTWORTH STREET
BELLFIELD STR.
ST. PHILIPS ROAD
ELLISON STREET
HETHERINGTON ST.
MEADOW STREET
DONCASTER ST.
SHEPHARD ST.
ALLEN STREET
SMITHFIELD
SCOTLAND ST.
PEA CROFT
HOLLIS CROFT
WHITE CROFT
LAMBERT STR.
WEST BAR
NEW QUEEN
KENYON ST.
RED HILL
BROAD LANE
BROOK HILL
PORTOBELLO STREET
GLOSSOP ROAD
LEAVY GREAVE
WILKINSON STREET
BROOM SPRING LANE
DEVONSHIRE STREET
DIVISION STR.
CHESTER STR.
WELLINGTON ST.
TRAFALGAR ST.
THOMAS ST.
MILTON STR.
BROOMHALL STREET
HANOVER STREET
WILLIAM STR.
BROOMHALL ROAD
SOUTH STREET
JESSOP STREET
COALPIT LANE
BARKER POOL
TRIPPET LANE
BOW ST.
HERMITAGE STREET
NEW GEORGE STREET
SHELDON STREET
THOMAS ST.
BRAMALL LANE
GREEN LANE
RUSSELL STR.
BOWLING GR.
MOOR FIELDS
LOW ROAD
MALINDA STREET
HARVEST LANE

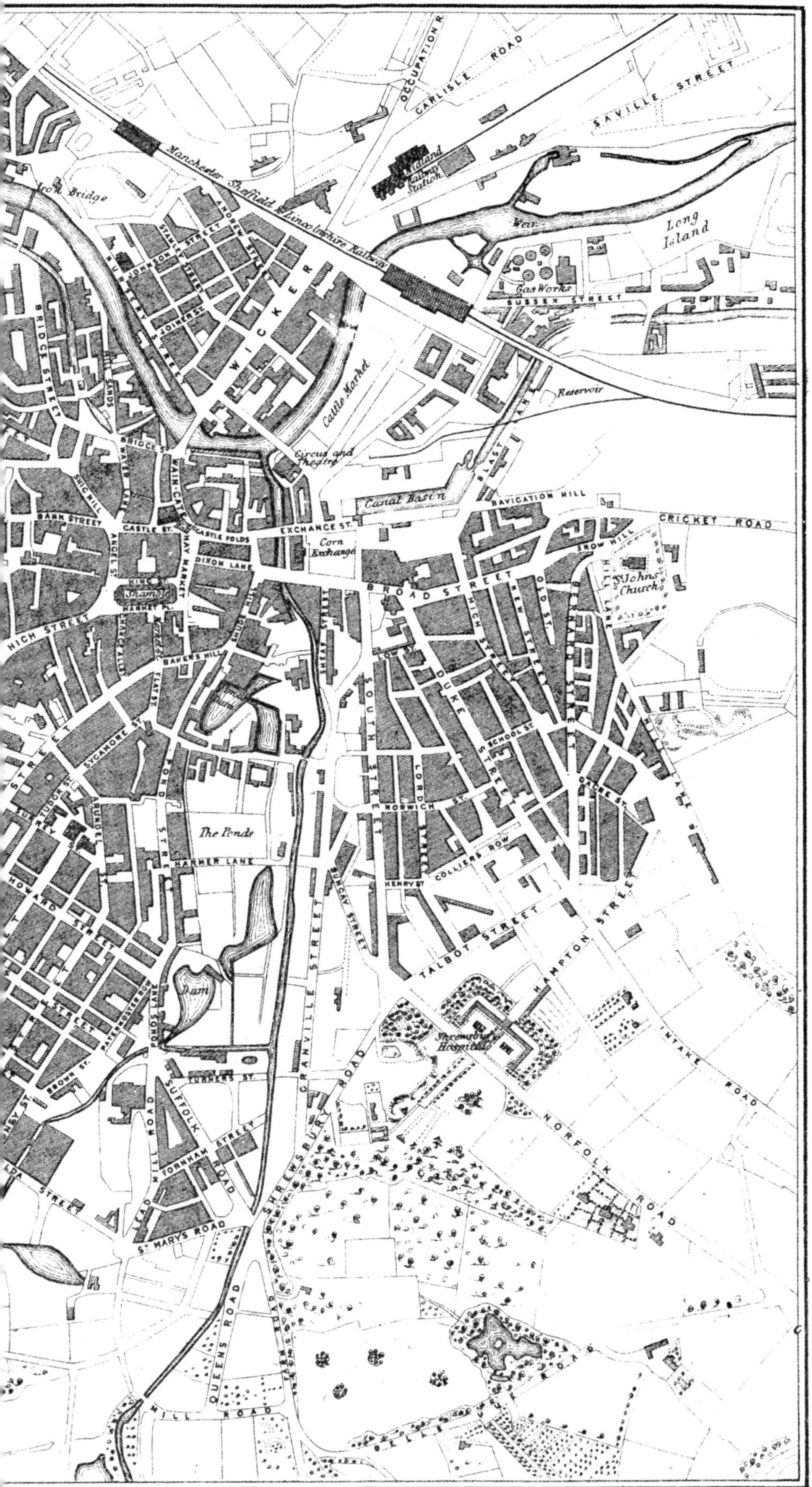
Manchester Sheffield & Lincolnshire Railway
Iron Bridge
Occupation R.
Carlisle Road
Saville Street
Midland Railway Station
Weir
Long Island
Gas Works
Sussex Street
Reservoir
Wicker
Bridge Street
Nursery Street
Cattle Market
Circus and Theatre
Canal Basin
Navigation Hill
Cricket Road
Exchange St.
Corn Exchange
Bridge St.
Bank Street
Castle St.
Castle Folds
Angel St.
Hay Market
Dixon Lane
Snow Hill
St. Johns Church
Broad Street
High Street
Sycamore St.
Pond Street
Duke Street
South Street
Lord St.
Norwich St.
School St.
The Ponds
Harmer Lane
Howard Street
Henry St.
Colliers Row
Talbot Street
Hampton Street
Shrewsbury Hospital
Intake Road
Granville Street
Shrewsbury Road
Norfolk Road
Dam
Paternoster Row
Ponds Lane
Brown St.
Turners St.
Suffolk Road
Fornham Street
St. Marys Road
Queens Road
Hill Road